Lecture Notes in Computer Science 13412

Founding Editors

Gerhard Goos
Juris Hartmanis

Editorial Board Members

The series Lecture Notes in Computer Science (LNCS), including its subseries Lecture Notes in Artificial Intelligence (LNAI) and Lecture Notes in Bioinformatics (LNBI), has established itself as a medium for the publication of new developments in computer science and information technology research, teaching, and education.

LNCS enjoys close cooperation with the computer science R & D community, the series counts many renowned academics among its volume editors and paper authors, and collaborates with prestigious societies. Its mission is to serve this international community by providing an invaluable service, mainly focused on the publication of conference and workshop proceedings and postproceedings. LNCS commenced publication in 1973.

Shin'ichiro Matsuo · Lewis Gudgeon ·
Ariah Klages-Mundt · Daniel Perez Hernandez ·
Sam Werner · Thomas Haines ·
Aleksander Essex · Andrea Bracciali ·
Massimiliano Sala
Editors

Financial Cryptography and Data Security

FC 2022 International Workshops

CoDecFin, DeFi, Voting, WTSC
Grenada, May 6, 2022
Revised Selected Papers

 Springer

Editors
Shin'ichiro Matsuo (iD)
Georgetown University
Washington, DC, USA

Ariah Klages-Mundt (iD)
Cornell University
Ithaca, NY, USA

Sam Werner
Imperial College London
London, UK

Aleksander Essex (iD)
Western University
London, ON, Canada

Massimiliano Sala (iD)
University of Trento
Trento, Trento, Italy

Lewis Gudgeon (iD)
Imperial College London
London, UK

Daniel Perez Hernandez
Imperial College London
London, UK

Thomas Haines
The Australian National University
Canberra, ACT, Australia

Andrea Bracciali (iD)
University of Stirling
Stirling, UK

ISSN 0302-9743   ISSN 1611-3349 (electronic)
Lecture Notes in Computer Science
ISBN 978-3-031-32414-7   ISBN 978-3-031-32415-4 (eBook)
https://doi.org/10.1007/978-3-031-32415-4

This Springer imprint is published by the registered company Springer Nature Switzerland AG
The registered company address is: Gewerbestrasse 11, 6330 Cham, Switzerland

CoDecFin 2022
3rd Workshop on Coordination of Decentralized Finance

These proceedings collect the papers accepted at the *Third Workshop on Coordination of Decentralized Finance (CoDecFin* - http://fc22.ifca.ai/codecfin/*)* associated to the Financial Cryptography and Data Security 2022 international conference (FC22). This year we went back to an in-person event, and it was brilliant to have the opportunity to meet colleagues in person and exchange ideas with them during the conference and the workshop. Nonetheless, we were able to offer technical support to a number of speakers that could not yet travel to Grenada and allow them to present their contributions on-line.

The main purpose of the series of Workshops on Coordination of Decentralized Finance (CoDecFin) is to discuss multi-disciplinary issues regarding technologies and operations of decentralized finance based on permissionless blockchain.

From an academic point of view, security and privacy protection are some of the leading research streams. The Financial Cryptography conference discusses these research challenges. On the other hand, other stakeholders than cryptographers and blockchain engineers have different interests in these characteristics of blockchain technology. For example, regulators face difficulty to trace transactions in terms of anti-money laundering (AML) against privacy-enhancing crypto-assets. Another example is consumer protection in the case of cyberattacks on crypto-asset custodians. Blockchain business entities sometimes start their business before the technology has matured, but the technology and operations are not transparent to regulators and consumers. The main problem is a lack of communication among stakeholders of the decentralized finance ecosystem. G20 discussed the issue of insufficient communication among stakeholders in 2019. It concluded that there is an essential need to have a multi-stakeholder discussion among engineers, regulators, business entities, and operators based on the neutrality of academia.

The CoDecFin workshop was initiated in 2020 to facilitate such multi-stakeholder discussion in a neutral academic environment. The goals of CoDecFin were to have a common understanding of technology and regulatory goals and to discuss essential issues of blockchain technology with all stakeholders mentioned above. It was especially a historic workshop because we could involve regulators and engineers in the discussion at the Financial Cryptography Conference.

The workshop consists of four sessions; Keynote, (1) Energy Consumption and Sustainability, (2) Soundness, Trust and Economic Stability, (3) Governance, Failure and Abuse, and (4) Privacy.

This year's edition of CoDecFin received eighteen submissions by about thirty-eight authors. Given the high quality of the submissions, fourteen papers were accepted after double-blind peer review. Thanks to the generous efforts of the PC, each paper received at least 3 reviews, providing constructive feedback to authors, followed by PC discussion where appropriate. Revised papers after the discussion at the workshop are collected in the present volume.

CoDecFin also hosted, jointly with the 6th Workshop on Trusted Smart Contract (WTSC 2022), an interesting panel on *Current and future trends,* an open title like the lively discussion which followed between panellists and audience on the interesting problems and trends in the area. A brief summary has been included in these proceedings.

The presentations made a full day of interesting talks and discussion. Video presentations are made available on-line on a dedicated YouTube channel, which can be reached from the workshop's web page.

CoDecFin22's chair and program committee members would like to thank everyone for their usual effort and valuable contributions: authors, reviewers and participants, as well as the support by the IFCA, the FC22 committees, the workshop coordinator Carla Mascia from the University of Trento for her valuable support, and Ray Hirschfeld for the usual exceptional organisation of the event.

Shin'ichiro Matsuo
CoDecFin22 Chair

CoDecFin 2022 Organization

Program Committee Members

Julien Bringer	Kallistech, France
Joaquin Garcia-Alfaro	Télécom SudParis, France
Arthur Gervais	Imperial College London, UK
Byron Gibson	Stanford University, USA
Feng Chen	University of British Columbia, Canada
Shin'ichiro Matsuo (Chair)	Georgetown University, and BSafe.network, USA
Steven Nam	Stanford Journal of Blockchain Law & Policy, USA
Michele Benedetto Neitz	Golden Gate University, USA
Roman Danziger Pavlov	SafeStead Inc., USA
Robert Schwentker	DLT Education, BGIN and Bluesky Community, USA
Yonatan Sompolinsky	Harvard University and DAGlabs, USA
Shigeya Suzuki	Keio University, Japan
Ryosuke Ushida	JFSA, Japan
Robert Wardrop	University of Cambridge Judge Business School, UK
Pindar Wong	BSafe.network, USA
Aaron Wright	Cardozo Law School, USA
Anton Yemelyanov	ASPECTRON, Inc., Canada
Aviv Zohar	The Hebrew University of Jerusalem, Israel

DeFi 2022 Preface

These proceedings collect the papers accepted at the Second Workshop on Decentralized Finance (DeFi 2022 - http://fc22.ifca.ai/defi/), held in association with the Financial Cryptography and Data Security 2022 conference (FC 2022) on May 6, 2022.

The focus of the DeFi workshop series is decentralized finance, a blockchain-powered peer-to-peer financial system. This second version of the workshop again sought to solicit contributions from both academia and industry which focussed on addressing fundamental, timely, and important questions at the centre of DeFi.

The workshop received 32 submissions, of which 14 were accepted either as a short paper (8) or as a talk (6). All of the short papers and a subset of the talks, as précis, appear in these proceedings. Overall, the organizers were extremely impressed by the quality of submissions received and were delighted by the strong attendance and lively discussion during the workshop. While the COVID-19 pandemic meant that the first version of this workshop was conducted online, for this second version we were fortunate to be able to conduct it in person in Grenada.

In addition to talks pertaining to submissions we had a guest speaker, Philip Daian, from IC3 and Flashbots, and we would like to thank him for his talk. The workshop closed with a panel, hosted by Daniel Perez and featuring Philip Daian (IC3, Flashbots), Patrick McCorry (Infura), and Alexei Zamyatin (Interlay), which covered a wide range of topics. We would like to sincerely thank the panelists for taking part and for the lively discussion.

The Organizing Committee would like to extend sincere thanks to all those who submitted their work, the Program Committee for their careful work, and all those who participated in the workshop. In addition, we would like to extend our thanks to Rafael Hirschfeld for his flawless support, organization, and encouragement of this second version of the workshop.

Lewis Gudgeon
Ariah Klages-Mundt
Daniel Perez
Sam Werner

DeFi 2022 Organization

DeFi 2022 Organizing Committee

Lewis Gudgeon   Imperial College London, UK
Ariah Klages-Mundt   Cornell University, USA
Daniel Perez   Imperial College London, UK
Sam Werner   Imperial College London, UK

DeFi 2022 Program Committee

Cuneyt Akcora   University of Manitoba, Canada
Raphael Auer   Bank for International Settlements, Switzerland
James Hsin-yu Chiang   Technical University of Denmark, Denmark
Tarun Chitra   Gauntlet Networks, USA
Jeremy Clark   Concordia University, Canada
Martin Florian   Humboldt-Universität zu Berlin, Germany
Dominik Harz   Imperial College London, UK
William Knottenbelt   Imperial College London, UK
Jiasun Li   George Mason University, USA
Jun-You Liu   Cornell University, USA
Patrick McCorry   Infura, UK
Andrew Miller   University of Illinois, Urbana-Champaign, USA
Daniel Moroz   Harvard University, USA
Mahsa Moosavi   Concordia University, Canada
Andreas Park   University of Toronto, Canada
David Parkes   Harvard University, USA
Julien Prat   Polytechnic Institute of Paris, France
Tim Roughgarden   Columbia University, USA
Palina Tolmach   Nanyang Technological University, Singapore
Alexei Zamyatin   Imperial College London, UK
Ariel Zetlin-Jones   Carnegie Mellon University, USA
Fan Zhang   Duke University, USA

VOTING 2022 Preface

VOTING 2022 marks the 7th Workshop on Advances in Secure Electronic Voting (Voting), associated with the Financial Cryptography and Data Security 2022 conference (FC 2022) held on May 2–6, 2022. The workshop was held on May 6, 2022, and was delivered in a hybrid format due to the ongoing COVID-19 pandemic.

This year's workshop received 16 submissions, of which 7 were accepted for publication. We are grateful to our Program Committee for their time and effort. In addition, we thank the authors of all submitted papers, presenters of accepted papers, and attendees for accommodating us during the ongoing COVID-19 crisis.

We are grateful to Ray Hirschfeld, Sergi Delgado Segura, and IFCA for organizing the event logistics and to the FC workshop chairs for their continued support of VOTING. Special thanks to Braden Crimmins for session chairing. The tradition of staggered chairs will continue next year, with Aleks Essex and Oksana Kulyk serving as program chairs. We look forward to an in-person program again for 2023.

January 2023

Thomas Haines
Aleksander Essex

VOTING 2022 Organization

Program Chairs

Thomas Haines   Australian National University, Australia
Aleksander Essex   Western University, Canada

Program Committee

Roberto Araujo   Universidade Federal do Pará (UFPA), Brazil
Josh Benaloh   Microsoft Research, USA
Matthew Bernhard   University of Michigan, USA
Constantin Catalin Dragan   University of Surrey, UK
Jeremy Clark   Concordia University, Canada
Chris Culnane   University of Melbourne, Australia
Jeremy Epstein   SRI International, USA
Kristian Gjøsteen   Norwegian University of Science and Technology, Norway
Rajeev Gore   Australian National University, Australia
Rolf Haenni   Bern University of Applied Sciences, Switzerland
Oksana Kulyk   IT University of Copenhagen, Denmark
Johannes Mueller   University of Luxembourg, Luxembourg
Olivier Pereira   UCLouvain, Belgium
Daniel Rausch   University of Stuttgart, Germany
Peter Roenne   Polish Academy of Sciences, Poland
Peter Y. A. Ryan   University of Luxembourg, Luxembourg
Steve Schneider   University of Surrey, UK
Carsten Schürmann   IT University of Copenhagen, Denmark
Philip Stark   University of California, Berkeley, USA
Vanessa Teague   Thinking Cybersecurity, Australia

WTSC 2022
6th Workshop on Trusted Smart Contracts

These proceedings collect the papers accepted at the *Sixth Workshop on Trusted Smart Contracts (WTSC22* - http://fc22.ifca.ai/wtsc/*)* associated to the Financial Cryptography and Data Security 2022 international conference (FC22). This year we went back to an in-person event, and it was brilliant to have the opportunity to meet colleagues in person and exchange ideas with them during the conference and the workshop. Nonetheless, we were able to offer technical support to a number of speakers that could not yet travel to Grenada and allow them to present their contributions on-line.

The WTSC series' main focus is on *smart contracts*, i.e. self-enforcing agreements in the form of executable programs, and other *decentralised applications* that are deployed to and run on top of (specialised) blockchains. These technologies introduce a novel programming framework and execution environment, which, together with the supporting blockchain technologies, carry unanswered and challenging research questions. Multidisciplinary and multifactorial aspects affect correctness, safety, privacy, authentication, efficiency, sustainability, resilience and trust in smart contracts and decentralised applications.

WTSC aims to address the scientific foundations of Trusted Smart Contract engineering, i.e. the development of contracts that enjoy some verifiable "correctness" properties, and to discuss open problems, proposed solutions and the vision on future developments amongst a research community that is growing around these themes and brings together users, practitioners, industry, institutions and academia. Over the years, the number of theoretical problems and applications has increased and this is shown by the wide set of topics that are discussed at WTSC. The multidisciplinary Programme Committee of this sixth edition of WTSC comprised members from companies, universities, and research institutions from several countries worldwide. The association to FC22 provided, once again, an ideal context for our workshop to be run in.

This year's edition of WTSC received eighteen submissions by about forty-five authors. Given the high quality of submissions, twelve papers were accepted after double-blind peer review. Thanks to the generous efforts of the PC, each paper received from 3 to 5 reviews, providing constructive feedback to authors, followed by PC discussion where appropriate. Revised papers after the discussion at the workshop are collected in the present volume. These analyse the current state of the art of smart contracts and their development. Important aspects that were discussed included: verifiable blockchains, smart contract coding, decentralized finance and e-payments.

WTSC also hosted, jointly with the 3rd Workshop on Coordination of Decentralized Finance (CoDecFin22), an interesting panel on *Current and future trends*, an open title like the lively discussion which followed between panellists and audience on the interesting problems and trends in the area. A brief summary has been included in these proceedings.

The presentations made a full day of interesting talks and discussion. Video presentations are made available on-line on a dedicated YouTube channel, which can be reached from the workshop's web page.

WTSC 2022's chairs would like to thank everyone for their usual effort and valuable contributions: authors, program committee members and reviewers, and participants, as well as the support by the IFCA, the FC22 committees, the workshop coordinator Carla Mascia from the University of Trento for her valuable support, and Ray Hirschfeld for the usual exceptional organisation of the event.

Andrea Bracciali
Massimiliano Sala
WTSC 2022 Chairs

WTSC 2022 Organization

The WTSC 2022 Program Committee

Monika di Angelo	Vienna University of Technology, Austria
Igor Artamonov	Emerald, USA
Daniel Augot	Inria, France
Fadi Barbara	University of Turin, Italy
Massimo Bartoletti	University of Cagliari, Italy
Stefano Bistarelli	University of Perugia, Italy
Christina Boura	University of Versailles Saint-Quentin-en-Yvelines, France
Andrea Bracciali	University of Stirling, UK
Daniel Broby	Strathclyde University, UK
Martin Chapman	King's College London, UK
Nicola Dimitri	University of Siena, Italy
Josselin Feist	Trail of Bits, USA
Murdoch Gabbay	Heriot-Watt University, UK
Oliver Giudice	Banca d'Italia, Italy
Davide Grossi	University of Groningen, The Netherlands
Yoichi Hirai	BedRock Systems GmbH, Germany
Ioannis Kounelis	Joint Research Centre, European Commission, Italy
Pascal Lafourcade	University of Clermont Auvergne, France
Andrew Lewis-Pye	London School of Economics, UK
Carsten Maple	Warwick University, UK
Akaki Mamageishvili	ETH Zürich, Switzerland
Carla Mascia	University of Trento, Italy
Patrick McCorry	Pisa Research, UK
Sihem Mesnager	University of Paris VIII, France
Bud Mishra	NYU, USA
Carlos Molina-Jimenez	University of Cambridge, UK
Alex Norta	Tallin University of Technology, Estonia
Akira Otsuka	Institute of Information Security, Japan
Federico Pintore	University of Bari, Italy
Massimiliano Sala	University of Trento, Italy
Darren Tapp	Arizona State University, USA
Jason Teutsch	Truebit, USA
Philip Wadler	University of Edinburgh, UK

Yilei Wang   Hong Kong Polytechnic University, China
Tim Weingärtner   Lucerne University, Switzerland
Santiago Zanella-Beguelin   Microsoft, UK
Dionysis Zindros   Stanford University, USA

Contents

DeFi22

Voting22

WTSC 2022 Short Summary: WTSC22 - Current and Future Trends

CoDecFin22

Stakechain: A Bitcoin-Backed Proof-of-Stake

Robin Linus[✉]

Saarbrücken, Germany
robin@capira.de

Abstract. We propose an energy-efficient solution to the double-spending problem using a bitcoin-backed proof-of-stake. Stakers vote on sidechain blocks forming a record that cannot be changed without destroying their collateral. Every user can become a staker by locking Bitcoins in the bitcoin blockchain. One-time signatures guarantee that stakers lose their bitcoin stake for publishing conflicting histories. As long as 34% of the stakers are honest the sidechain provides safety, and with a 67%-majority it provides liveness. Overwriting a finalized block costs at least 34% of the total stake. Checkpoints in Bitcoin's blockchain mitigate classical attacks against conventional proof-of-stake algorithms. A stakechain's footprint within the mainchain is minimal. The protocol is a generic consensus mechanism allowing for arbitrary sidechain architectures. Spawning multiple, independent instances scales horizontally to a free market of sidechains which can potentially serve billions of users.

1 Introduction

Bitcoin is a revolutionary alternative to the traditional, government-approved banking system [1]. However when Satoshi Nakamoto introduced it in 2008 the world's first response was: *"We very, very much need such a system, but the way I understand your proposal, it does not seem to scale to the required size"* [2]. Ever since numerous scalability solutions have been proposed. Still, as of today, the Bitcoin network processes less than seven transactions per second because growing the chain faster reduces decentralization significantly. In contrast, centralized payment services such as PayPal or Visa serve billions of users at up to 50,000 TX/s.

Currently, off-chain payments via the Lightning Network are the most promising approach to scale Bitcoin [3]. They allow a much higher throughput, yet they hardly scale to billions of users. They still require too many on-chain transactions to open and close payment channels because the required block space grows linearly with the number of users. Adoption is even further constrained by the inbound-capacity of payment channels and the need to lock funds for every new user to receive a payment. These constraints lead to many layers of complexity and a tendency towards centralized and custodial solutions which contrast Bitcoin's purpose of being permissionless, trustless and censorship-resistant.

R. Linus—Independent Researcher.

© International Financial Cryptography Association 2023
S. Matsuo et al. (Eds.): FC 2022 Workshops, LNCS 13412, pp. 3–14, 2023.
https://doi.org/10.1007/978-3-031-32415-4_1

Sidechains have been proposed as an alternative solution for scalability [4]. They introduce parallel blockchains enabling payments within a simplistic system similar to Bitcoin. Yet, their consensus mechanisms depend on trusted federations or Bitcoin miners validating sidechain blocks, which limits social scalability, and thus, security. We introduce a novel sidechain consensus mechanism with a permissionless, bitcoin-backed proof-of-stake. This results in a fast, flexible and scalable consensus mechanism, that enables a free market of trustless sidechains.

2 Bitcoin Stake

It is impossible to produce distributed consensus except by consuming an external resource. This is because if block production has no ongoing costs, neither does attacking the chain [5,6]. The security of a consensus mechanism is proportional to the amount of external resources consumed. We anchor our proof-of-stake mechanism into Bitcoin's proof-of-work consensus which is computationally, and therefore thermodynamically, very expensive to change. We leverage the value of bitcoins as an external resource to produce sidechain consensus. One-time signatures ensure stakers lose their bitcoin stake when voting on conflicting sidechain histories. This forms a linear record, which is costly to change without burning significant amounts of resources.

2.1 One-Time Signatures

A characteristic of Bitcoin's digital signature algorithm is that it needs to produce, for each signature generation, a fresh random value (hereafter designated as *nonce*). Reusing the nonce value on two signatures of different messages allows attackers to recover the private key algebraically.

This *nonce reuse vulnerability* can be used to discourage stakers from participating in double-spending attacks [7,8]. Each staker pre-commits to his sequence of nonces, such that the system can constrain a vote for the n-th block to be valid only if a staker signed it using their n-th nonce. This guarantees stakers can not create valid signatures for conflicting blocks without leaking their private key and losing their collateral (Fig. 1).

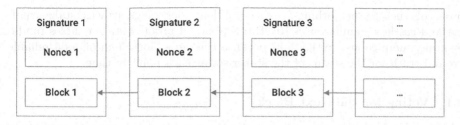

Fig. 1. A staker votes for blocks using one-time signatures. A vote for the n-th block is valid only if it is signed with their n-th nonce. Voting twice with the same nonce leaks the staker's private key.

2.2   Staking Contracts

For stakers' one-time signatures to be scarce, each of them has to lock a collateral such that the bitcoin network can penalize malicious actors for signing conflicting histories. In the following we discuss a *staking contract* which serves as an adaptor to produce a sidechain consensus from Bitcoin's consensus.

Our contract expresses: *If Alice leaks her key she loses her bitcoins.* So, for Alice to become a staker she locks bitcoins in an output such that:

- Option A: One year later she gets her money back.
- Option B: She can destroy her money right now.

This simple contract is sufficient to make her one-time signatures scarce. If Bob sees two signatures of her with a reused nonce, Alice leaks her key and loses her stake. In Appendix A.1 we summarize different implementations of this staking contract in bitcoin script. We describe the ideal, trustless solution using a *Bitcoin Covenant* [8]. This is possible with one of various future bitcoin features such as either SIGHASH_NOINPUT or OP_CHECKTEMPLATEVERIFY. Furthermore, we discuss two trust-minimized workarounds that are possible with Bitcoin's current consensus rules. In Appendix A.2 we describe a scheme for stakers to commit to a unique sequence of nonces. The key idea is that each staker forms a chain of nonces by signing their next nonce with their previous signature.

3   Consensus Mechanism

The sidechain's consensus is anchored into Bitcoin's proof-of-work consensus. Stakers are defined by staking contracts included in Bitcoin's UTXO set. Assuming all sidechain nodes are running a Bitcoin full node, they implicitly are in consensus about the exact staker set without exchanging any messages. All randomness is determined by Bitcoin's proof-of-work, which is studied well [9].

The staker set is determined only by Bitcoin's blockchain. There are three operations on the staker set: *stake, redeem,* and *burn*. All three are executed in the bitcoin blockchain. This prevents many classical problems of pure proof-of-stake protocols such as the nothing-at-stake problem, long-range attacks, stake grinding and costless simulation [5,10]. Bitcoin-backed proof-of-stake enables fundamentally more robust mitigations because Bitcoin's blockchain offers a reliable ground truth for the status of the staker set at each point in time.

3.1 Voting for the Next Block

The set of stakers is known and so is the number of possible votes per sidechain block. An election is economically final as soon as there is a majority of votes such that stakers would have to burn stake to attack it.

The leader is determined from randomness derived from bitcoin's most recent block. The leader proposes a signed sidechain block and all other stakers confirm that block by signing it, too. Once 34% of stakers voted for a block it cannot be reverted without burning stake. A block is considered *final* once a supermajority of 67% signed it. Changing finality costs at least 34% of all stake. As soon as the next leader receives a final block, it starts waiting one minute until it proposes a next block.[1]

If a leader does not propose a block within a given time then all other stakers start broadcasting skip messages for that block. Once 67% of stakers signed a skip message that block is skipped and the next round begins with a block proposed by the next staker.

3.2 Safety and Liveness

By definition, a decentralized system must be susceptible to malicious majority attacks whether by hashrate, stake, or other permissionlessly-acquirable resources (Fig. 2).

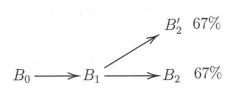

B_2' 67%

$B_0 \longrightarrow B_1 \longrightarrow B_2$ 67%

Fig. 2. Finalizing a block requires a supermajority of 67%. Therefore, the chain can fork only if an attacker controls at least 67% of all stake and at least 34% of all stake is slashed.

In our mechanism, forks require burning 34% of all stake. Forks are impossible if 34% of all stakers are honest or offline. Violations of the 34% assumption can be mitigated to some degree by selecting the chain that requires the most

---

[1] A staker is incentivized not to wait for too long before broadcasting their block because otherwise the other stakers will skip it. Also they cannot speed up the block time much, as we will see in the next chapter.

capital to burn to attack its finality. That means a block with more votes wins over a block with fewer votes. E.g., in the ideal case a block has 100% of all votes; then 100% of the total stack has to get burned to overwrite that block. Such a supermajority block finalizes all previous blocks, because overwriting any previous block requires to also overwrite that supermajority block when the fork reaches the same height. Waiting for a supermajority block to confirm a transaction has a similar effect as waiting for confirmations in a proof-of-work mechanism, because it increases the cost to attack the chain (Figs. 3 and 4).

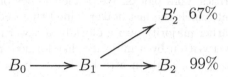

Fig. 3. The fork with the most votes wins because reverting it requires the most stake to burn.

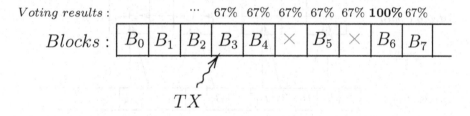

Fig. 4. Finality of a transaction depends on the best voting result that comes after it. In this example, the votes for block B_6 guarantee that 100% of all stakes have to get burned to reverse the transaction in block B_3.

To harden voting results, the next leader commits in their block to all votes received for the previous block. At least 67% of all votes are required for a successor block to be valid. Honest stakers try to collect as many votes for the preceding block as possible while waiting to broadcast their current block. Majorities larger than 67% make finality proportionally more costly to attack.

Liveness requires a honest majority of 67%. Thus, an attacker can halt the network as long as 34% are offline or malicious. They can halt the chain until honest stakers stake enough bitcoins such that they can form again a 67% majority to fill up the missing votes to finalize and unstall the current block. In the worst case 100% of all stakers are offline. Then new stakers have to stake two times the total stake to form a new 67% majority (Fig. 5).

However, introducing this recovery mechanism for stalled chains introduces a new attack vector. Now we have to mitigate the case that newer majorities

$$34\%$$

$$B_0 \longrightarrow B_1 \longrightarrow B_2 \quad 66\%$$

Fig. 5. Liveness requires a majority of 67%. So, 34% malicous or offline stakers can halt the chain.

overwrite older majorities' final blocks. We define the *age* of a staker set as the bitcoin block height at which the last staker joined that set. Honest full nodes select a block by an earlier majority over a block by a newer majority. Therefore, a block cannot get overwritten by a majority that formed after that block was finalized. This ensures again that an attacker has to burn at least 34% of all stake to create a fork.

For more strict finality, we enforce sideblocks to commit to the most recent bitcoin block hash (Fig. 6).

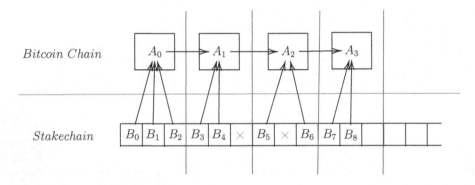

Fig. 6. Sidechain blocks have to commit to bitcoin block hashes. The height of the bitcoin block must be at least the same height as in the preceding sideblock. In this example there are at most 3 sideblocks per mainblock. This ensures basic synchronicity.

We allow new stakers to change previous majorities only up to a certain number of bitcoin blocks in the past. E.g. Stakers can vote at most one week (1008 bitcoin blocks) back in the past. This implies, if the chain ever stalls for a week it will stall indefinitely until the current stakers finalize the current block. New stakers cannot overwrite a one week old chain. However, if that happens and there's a malicious 67% majority, then the sidechain's incentive model must be already fundamentally broken in some other way (Fig. 7).

An even stricter model is to enforce stakers to periodically publish signatures in the bitcoin blockchain to remain within the staker set. However, this costs block space and fees, so we want to minimize the on-chain footprint. The most simple anchor is to let new stakers commit to sidechain blocks within their

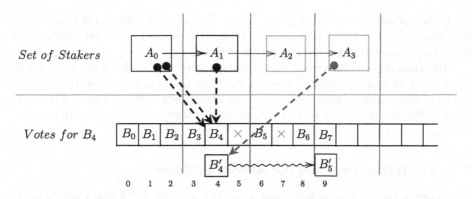

Fig. 7. In this example the older stakers voted for B_4 but a newer majority votes for B'_4. This chain split will get resolved at the latest in slot number 9, because then the set of stakers is unambiguous again. Honest nodes don't accept a rewrite by a newer majority, if they already know a block finalized by an older majority. Additionally, the newer majority can vote at most 1 week back in the past to recover a stalled chain.

funding transaction for the staking contract within the bitcoin blockchain. Incentives are aligned if we enforce that new stakers can only vote on the same chain they committed to. Other stakers implicitly sign the on-chain commitment by accepting the new staker's votes and signing it in subsequent blocks.

3.3   Ongoing Cost to Attack the Chain

One might argue that time value of locked bitcoins is too cheap to derive a secure consensus. That is a misunderstanding of the fundamental underlying market mechanism.

In Bitcoin, the proof of work security is not determined by the price of electricity, but by the Dollar value of the block revenue. Miners have an incentive to spend about

$$1 \text{ revenue} = 1 \text{ reward} + \text{fees} \approx 7.25 \text{ BTC} \approx \$250000$$

to produce a block (as of June 2021). The mining difficulty adjustment stabilizes this price of block production. The cost of block production equals the cost of attacking the chain. So, more demand for Bitcoin leads to a higher bitcoin price and thus, a higher value of the block revenue and subsequently, to more security. The exact same market forces align the incentives for our proof of stake. In a free market the total time value of all staked bitcoins converges against 1 sidechain revenue per block. Whenever there is less time value locked, someone will stake their bitcoins to earn the cheap sidechain revenue.

Therefore, the ongoing cost for an attacker to stall the chain is about 1 sidechain revenue per block time. This is independent of the consumed resource. Security depends only on the value of the sidechain's revenue. The sidechain asset price is mostly driven by usage and resulting network effects. Thus, a sidechain provides security proportional to the network effect of its user base. The seemingly low investment of time value of bitcoins is automatically priced in by the competition for the stakechain rewards.

Additionally, it is important to notice that overwriting the chain costs slashing 34% of all stake, which is orders of magnitudes more expensive than a year worth of time value of that stake. For that reason, stakechains have a quick settlement finality because a reorg is significantly more expensive than the cost of block production.

3.4 Limitation: Pegs and the Altcoin Problem

This system requires an independent asset per stakechain. A stakechain's security is limited by its asset's value. Only if a sidechain's revenue is sufficiently valuable, it can motivate many Bitcoin holders to protect it. Therefore, only large sidechains with lots of users and valuable assets can provide security. Small sidechains are insecure.

We do not want to introduce another speculative asset because that creates unnecessary friction to users. Trustless two-way pegs between bitcoin and sidechains are an ongoing research topic. As of today there are at least two workarounds to peg sidechain assets to BTC. For example, the peg of the Liquid Sidechain is a federated 2-way-peg. A trustless alternative is a perpetual one-way peg [11]. It dampens the price fluctuation of a sidechain's asset. Additionally, it is possible to demand from stakers to burn a certain amount of BTC to become a staker. Those burned BTC can be issued in the sidechain as block subsidy. Existing research [12] and future research on *trustless* two-way pegs e.g., based on zero-knowledge proofs [13] can be developed and deployed on top of a stakechain consensus.

4   Conclusion

We have proposed a consensus-mechanism that potentially scales to a global payment system. We started with the usual framework of a sidechain, which provides strong control of ownership, but is incomplete without a trust-minimized way to prevent double-spending. To solve this, we proposed a bitcoin-backed proof-of-stake consensus mechanism that quickly becomes economically impractical for an attacker to change if honest nodes control a majority of stakes. Stakers and leaders are elected via Bitcoin's consensus with little coordination. Nodes can leave and rejoin the network at will, accepting checkpoints in the bitcoin blockchain as proof of what happened while they were gone. Stakers can not create conflicting histories without losing their Bitcoin collateral. They vote with their signatures, expressing their acceptance of valid blocks by signing them and rejecting invalid blocks by refusing to sign them. Any needed rules and incentives can be enforced with this consensus mechanism. Spawning multiple stakechains scales horizontally to potentially billions of users.

A   Appendix

A.1   Staking Contracts in Bitcoin Script

Currently, burning funds is not supported in Bitcoin script. Committing to a certain spending transaction requires a construct called *Covenants*[2]. Yet, upcoming Bitcoin features such as SIGHASH_NOINPUT[3] or OP_CHECKTEMPLATEVERIFY[4] or OP_CAT allow trustless covenants. For now, we need a workaround to implement the staking contract. In the following we discuss solutions. All of these trust-minimizing workarounds are highly undesirable additional complexity. Fortunately, in the long term, we will certainly have some clean solution for covenants.

A.1.1   Trust-Minimized Workaround 1
A simple solution is to introduce a trusted party, say, Bob:

- Alice creates a funding transaction with the following output:
    - Alice can spend her money in one year.
    - Alice and Bob can always spend her money collaboratively.
- Bob pre-signs and publishes a punishment transaction:
    - burn her collateral now to address 0x000...000 (if Alice agrees).
- Bob immediately deletes his secret key (in case his machine gets compromised).

There is no counter-party risk here for Alice, because she executes her funding transaction only after she received Bob's signature for the punishment transaction and completed her setup.

For the system to minimize trust in Bob, multiple parties can participate and if only one is honest and deletes their key, then this scheme is secure. Bitcoin script currently supports more than 60 participants per multi-signature transaction [14].

Containing more than 60 signatures, the punishment transaction becomes large and expensive, but as long as the staker is honest, the transaction doesn't need to be included in Bitcoin's blockchain. To incentivize Bitcoin miners to execute the punishment transaction quickly in case of misbehavior, it pays a high miners fee.

It is possible to further minimize trust in single parties by using ECDSA signature aggregation to allow for thousands of Bobs participating in a single combined signature [15]. When Schnorr signatures become available in Bitcoin, such aggregated signatures will become more simple because of the linearity of Schnorr's scheme [16].

The Bobs could be a trusted federation or a percentage of the current stakers. With aggregated signatures they could also be a significant percentage of current coin holders. The trusted parties sign blindly to reduce the risk of censorship.

---

[2] https://medium.com/blockstream/cat-and-schnorr-tricks-i-faf1b59bd298.
[3] https://github.com/bitcoin/bips/blob/master/bip-0118.mediawiki.
[4] https://github.com/bitcoin/bips/blob/master/bip-0119.mediawiki.

A simple scheme exploits that Bitcoin transactions use double SHA256. Thus, Alice can ask Bob to sign the single-round SHA256 hash of her transaction. The second round is Bob's hashing function for his signature algorithm. This way Bob doesn't learn what he signs until Alice publishes her contract.

A.1.2   Trust-Minimized Workaround 2

The bitcoin mailing list member, *ZmnSCPxj*, came up with the following trust-minimized covenant construction based on replace-by-fee, which requires no soft-fork.

We can implement the staking contract with a simple

```
<one year> OP_CHECKSEQUENCEVERIFY OP_DROP <A> OP_CHECKSIG
```

OP_CHECKSEQUENCEVERIFY ensures, as a side effect, that the spending transaction opts in to replace-by-fee. Thus, if the pubkey <A> is used in a single-sign signature scheme (which reveals the privkey if double-signed), then at the end of the period, anyone who saw the double-signing can claim that fund and thus act as "Bob". Indeed, many "Bob"s will act and claim this fund, increasing the fee each time to try to get their version onchain. Eventually, some "Bob" will just put the entire fund as fee and put a measly OP_RETURN as single output. This "burns" the funds by donating it to miners.

From the point of view of Alice this is hardly distinguishable from losing the fund right now, since Alice will have a vanishingly low chance of spending it after the collateral period ends, and Alice still cannot touch the funds now anyway. Alice also cannot plausibly bribe a miner, since the miner could always get more funds by replacing the transaction internally with a spend-everything-on-fees OP_RETURN output transaction, and can only persuade the miner not to engage in this behavior by offering more than the collateral is worth (which is always worse than just losing the collateral).

A OP_CHECKTEMPLATEVERIFY would work better for this use-case, but even without it you do not need a trusted party to implement the staking contract.

Drawback of this solution is that cheating stakers are not immediately removed from Bitcoin's UTXO set. Yet, this might be a decent tradeoff because we have a succinct proof to exclude a cheating staker: knowledge of his private key.

Another drawback is that it requires trust in miners. If Alice cooperates with a significant share of Bitcoin's hash power, she has proportional chances of mining the transaction herself. Then she would not have any cost of attacking the chain.

A.2   Staker Signatures

In this chapter we discuss details of the stakers signatures. We explain how to pre-commit to a particular nonce per block efficiently. Finally, we explain a scheme for better hot key security.

A.2.1 Compact Nonce Commitments

Constructed naively, stakers would have to pre-commit to millions of nonces within their funding transaction. A more efficient construction is to let stakers subsequently commit to their next nonce by signing it within their previous signature. This amortizes the inclusion proof size to basically zero. Furthermore, each staker has to store only one nonce at each point in time.

Jeremy Rubin contributed this scheme for constant-sized commitments to sequences of nonces. Furthermore, he implemented a staking contract in Sapio[5].

A.2.2 Hot Key Security

Hardware wallets are usually stateless and therefore they're incompatible with nonce commitments. Thus, to protect the stakers' nodes, they can use a *staking key* to sign sidechain blocks and a separate *redeem key* to spend the bitcoin deposit once it is unlocked. Until then, the redeem key remains in a cold wallet. Nodes having access only to the staking key are a much less attractive target for attackers.

References

1. Nakamoto, S., et al.: Bitcoin: a peer-to-peer electronic cash system (2008)
2. Donald, J.A.: The cryptography mailing list - bitcoin P2P e-cash paper. Bitcoin Stack Exchange
3. Poon, J., Dryja, T.: The bitcoin lightning network: scalable off-chain instant payments (2016)
4. Back, A., et al.: Enabling blockchain innovations with pegged sidechains, p. 72 (2014). www.opensciencereview.com/papers/123/enablingblockchain-innovations-with-pegged-sidechains
5. Poelstra, A., et al.: Distributed consensus from proof of stake is impossible (2014)
6. Pérez-Solà, C., Delgado-Segura, S., Navarro-Arribas, G., Herrera-Joancomartí, J.: Double-spending prevention for bitcoin zero-confirmation transactions. Int. J. Inf. Secur. **18**(4), 451–463 (2019)
7. Ruffing, T., Kate, A., Schröder, D.: Liar, liar, coins on fire!: penalizing equivocation by loss of bitcoins. In: Proceedings of the 22nd ACM SIGSAC Conference on Computer and Communications Security, pp. 219–230. ACM (2015)
8. Möser, M., Eyal, I., Gün Sirer, E.: Bitcoin covenants. In: Clark, J., Meiklejohn, S., Ryan, P.Y.A., Wallach, D., Brenner, M., Rohloff, K. (eds.) FC 2016. LNCS, vol. 9604, pp. 126–141. Springer, Heidelberg (2016). https://doi.org/10.1007/978-3-662-53357-4_9
9. Bonneau, J., Clark, J., Goldfeder, S.: On bitcoin as a public randomness source. IACR Cryptology ePrint Archive 2015:1015 (2015)
10. Brown-Cohen, J., Narayanan, A., Psomas, A., Matthew Weinberg, S.: Formal barriers to longest-chain proof-of-stake protocols. In: Proceedings of the 2019 ACM Conference on Economics and Computation, pp. 459–473. ACM (2019)
11. Somsen, R.: 21 million bitcoins to rule all sidechains: the perpetual one-way peg. Medium (2020)

---

[5] https://github.com/sapio-lang/sapio/blob/master/sapio-contrib/src/contracts/staked_signer.rs.

12. Teutsch, J., Straka, M., Boneh, D.: Retrofitting a two-way peg between blockchains. arXiv preprint arXiv:1908.03999 (2019)
13. Garoffolo, A., Kaidalov, D., Oliynykov, R.: Zendoo: a zk-SNARK verifiable cross-chain transfer protocol enabling decoupled and decentralized sidechains. CoRR, abs/2002.01847 (2020)
14. Wuille, P.: Will SegWit allow for m of n multisig with very large n and m? Bitcoin Stack Exchange
15. Gennaro, R., Goldfeder, S.: Fast multiparty threshold ECDSA with fast trustless setup. In: Proceedings of the 2018 ACM SIGSAC Conference on Computer and Communications Security, pp. 1179–1194. ACM (2018)
16. Maxwell, G., Poelstra, A., Seurin, Y., Wuille, P.: Simple Schnorr multi-signatures with applications to bitcoin. Des. Codes Crypt. **87**(9), 2139–2164 (2019)

Drivers of Bitcoin Energy Use and Emissions

Hass McCook[1,2(✉)]

[1] Bitcoin Mining Council, Tyson's Corner, VA, USA
h.mccook@chch.oxon.org
[2] Monochrome Asset, Brisbane City, QLD 4000, Australia

Abstract. The global Bitcoin mining industry has grown to a size where its overall energy consumption is frequently compared to that of entire countries. Indeed, as of 30 April 2022, following the successful migration of the entire Chinese mining industry after its expulsion from China in mid-2021, Bitcoin uses approximately 247.0 TWh of primary energy per year, slightly less than the entire nation of New Zealand, the 63rd ranked nation by total energy consumption. To understand what drives Bitcoin's energy use and emissions however, one must understand four key concepts: how Bitcoin works and incentivises its miners, the nature of competition in the mining industry, the nature of mining hardware and innovation, and importantly, international energy and electricity markets and the differences between them. This paper will provide a thorough explanation of these concepts, as well as provide commentary on Bitcoin's current state, and what the Bitcoin Mining Industry may potentially look like towards the end of the decade.

Keywords: Bitcoin · Energy · Emissions · Perfect Competition

1 How Bitcoin Works and Incentivises Its Miners

Bitcoin's creators hypothesised that *"a purely peer-to-peer version of electronic cash would allow online payments to be sent directly from one party to another without going through a financial institution."* [1] To achieve this, a peer-to-peer network with a timestamped, append-only, distributed ledger, commonly known as The Blockchain, was proposed. To keep all actors honest, miners are required to expend computational energy to earn the right to add the next block of transactions to The Blockchain, and the associated economic rewards that come with it.

To oversimplify an extremely technical process, Bitcoin mining is effectively guessing a number, "hashing" it with a universally agreed upon algorithm, and hoping that you are the first to guess correctly. You can think of performing a single hash as scratching a single lottery ticket. You can perform a hash by hand, however, modern mining rigs undertake several trillion hashes per second (TH/s), or, to continue the analogy, scratch trillions of lottery tickets per second.

© International Financial Cryptography Association 2023
S. Matsuo et al. (Eds.): FC 2022 Workshops, LNCS 13412, pp. 15–33, 2023.
https://doi.org/10.1007/978-3-031-32415-4_2

All tickets are identical, save their unique serial number. The more tickets you scratch, the higher the chance of winning the lottery. If you control 10% of the network hash power, you could expect that, on average, you will earn 10% of block rewards. It takes energy to scratch the ticket. If you have the right number, but a bad ticket (i.e. you are trying to behave dishonestly), all your effort scratching tickets goes to waste. At any moment in time, on average, the network is only ten minutes away from the next correct guess. Every two weeks, or more precisely 2016 blocks, the Bitcoin network checks to see if a ten minute average cadence was achieved. If the correct guesses occur too frequently, the set of numbers to guess from, or, "the difficulty" increases to bring the frequency back to ten minutes. If the correct guesses are too infrequent, the difficulty is reduced, and the pool of numbers to guess from decreases. This defining feature of Bitcoin, known as "The Difficulty Adjustment" guarantees the stability of the predetermined issuance schedule [2].

People invest energy into Bitcoin because they are incentivised to do so. As long as the cost to mine is lower than the market price of bitcoin, the incentive exists. When it comes to energy expended by miners, the incentives can be broken into two broad categories; endogenous incentives, i.e., the economic incentives built into the Bitcoin Protocol, and exogenous incentives, i.e., the entrepreneurial instinct to remain alive amid extreme competitive pressures.

1.1 Endogenous Incentives

Bitcoin primarily incentivises its miners with the block reward, which consists of the predetermined supply issuance for the successful mining of a block (or, "block subsidy"), plus, all transaction fees associated with that block [3]. During Bitcoin's bootstrapping, miner income was heavily skewed towards the block subsidy, with the initial subsidy being 50 bitcoin per block. With the block subsidy halving every 210,000 blocks, or, roughly 4 years, miners will eventually be compensated strictly by transaction fees [4]. The block subsidy is currently 6.25 bitcoin per block, with transaction fees now becoming a larger percentage of miner income. Importantly, bitcoin mining uses application-specific hardware which can only be used for mining bitcoin (alongside a few other SHA256-based micro-cap altcoins and Bitcoin forks) [5], so any attacker who amasses the necessary hardware and energy to control more than 51% of the network should rationally be more incentivised to earn 51% of the block reward, rather *"than to undermine the system and the validity of his own wealth."* [1]

1.2 Exogenous Incentives

As mentioned previously, the specificity of the infrastructure required by miners incentivises them to make sure Bitcoin prospers, otherwise, the billions of dollars spent on Bitcoin mining rigs and energy infrastructure will be near worthless. That said, the more that Bitcoin prospers, the more incentives miners have to capture profit, which typically means more competition and pressure to stay alive. Miners are thus incentivised to continue expanding and improving their operations to maintain their share of the network computing power, or "Hashrate." [6] The circularity of the incentives make them robust and self-reinforcing.

2 The Nature of Competition in the Bitcoin Mining Industry

2.1 Perfect Competition

The example of "the hypothetical firm in a perfectly competitive market" is taught in most introductory economics classes. A literature review of primary academic texts identifies eight conditions that define a perfectly competitive market, as shown in the table below [7–12]. The following subsections will provide a point-by-point demonstration of how Bitcoin mining is a near-perfectly competitive market, and what this typically means for industry competitors (Table 1).

Table 1. Conditions of a Perfectly-Competitive Market

Homogeneous Products	Perfect Factor Mobility	Zero Transaction Costs
Non-increasing Returns to Scale	Guaranteed Property Rights	Perfect Information
No Barriers to Entry or Exit	Many Buyers and Sellers	

Homogeneous Products, Guaranteed Property Rights and Zero Transaction Costs. Bitcoin's digital signature algorithm, combined with proof-of-work mining, guarantee ownership rights. Bitcoins are simply entries in a global ledger, and are entirely homogeneous and fungible. Whilst Bitcoin transaction costs are not zero and never will be, transactions on Bitcoin's second (and higher) layers, such as the Lightning Network [14], will eventually approach zero for most end-users. It is possible to store bitcoins indefinitely at zero cost, i.e., one could simply remember a seed phrase, a list of words that contains all the information you need to access and spend your funds [13]. All three criteria are currently met by Bitcoin.

Perfect Information and Many Buyers and Sellers. In research from July 2021, leading cryptocurrency exchange Crypto.com estimated that there were 176 million Bitcoin users globally in January 2022, up from 113 million in June 2021 [15]. Whilst this is a large number, there is no explicit definition of "many" laid out in the literature, and compared to the user-bases of tech giants such as Facebook, Netflix and YouTube, an argument could be made that 176 million users are not that many. Further, the high volatility still experienced in Bitcoin indicates imperfections in the proliferation, or even creation of, market information. That said, if the user-base grows into the billions over the coming decades in a similar way to the tech giants' user-bases, both of these criteria will be met.

Non-increasing Returns to Scale. When one dishonest entity controls more than 51% of the network hashrate, they can potentially double-spend their own funds, and prevent others from transacting on the network, effectively destroying the value proposition of Bitcoin [34]. Bitcoin has never been openly 51%-attacked, and likely never will be due to both cost and physical semiconductor industry limitations. That said, in 2014, a popular cloud mining platform, GHash.io managed to attract over 51% of the hashrate to their pool, in what was described by the media as a "doomsday scenario" [16]. What quickly ensued was mass user panic and migration away, and within a few months, GHash.io ceased to exist. Not only can returns stop scaling, but excessive growth can put you out of business.

Bitcoin: Mean Hash Rate (14d Moving Average)

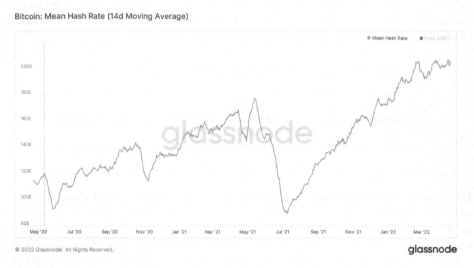

Fig. 1. Bitcoin Mean Hash Rate (14-day Moving Average), April 2020 - April 2022. Dotted vertical line indicates Block Reward Halving in May 2020 [19].

No Barriers to Entry or Exit and Perfect Factor Mobility. The mobility of Bitcoin's factors of production has thus far been best publicly demonstrated by the Chinese mining industry. This can be observed in Fig. 1, where throughout 2020, prior to being expelled from the country in mid-2021, *"miners within China were staying mostly in the more stable coal-fired regions like Xinjiang in late autumn, winter and spring ('dry season'), and migrated to regions with significant temporary overcapacities in low-cost hydropower, like Sichuan, between May and October during the 'wet season'."* [17] Here, we see between 20 to 25% of the network hashrate successfully relocate within a matter of weeks. The more obvious and extreme example in Fig. 1 is the expulsion of miners from China in late-May 2021, resulting in a 50% reduction in the 14-day average hashrate from an all-time-high 177.5 exahashes per second (EH/s) on 13 May 2021 to 89.0

EH/s on 9 July 2021. After one month however, over 25% of the hashrate was back online, after 3 months, the majority, almost two-thirds, had returned, and just under 6 months later, on 2 January 2022, an all-time high 14-day average hashrate of 177.5 EH/s was reached. To be sure, deployment of brand new equipment accounts for some of this hashrate increase, however, due to the ongoing global semiconductor shortage and broader COVID-related supply chain issues, it is not a major contributor [18]. Although truly "perfect" factor mobility would require teleportation, the speed and relative ease at which the bitcoin network recovers from major shocks demonstrates very high factor mobility and limited barriers to entry or exit.

2.2   Characteristics of a Perfectly Competitive Market

Economic profit tends to zero in long-term equilibrium in a perfectly competitive market, and the marginal cost of producing and the market price oscillate around an equilibrium point [7]. Therefore, so long as the price of bitcoin is greater than the cost to mine it, competition will enter the market to close the gap, and vice versa. In such competitive markets, there is also a natural tendency for the market to be dominated by three or four players [20,22]. The Pareto Principle, also known as the 80/20 rule, states 20% of the market participants will tend to control 80% of the market [23]. In terms of Bitcoin's mining pools, the top six collectively control 77.2% of the total hashrate, with the biggest pool, Foundry Digital, controlling 19.2% of hashrate, and ViaBTC, the sixth biggest, controlling 9.7% [24]. As will be discussed in the next sections, the only way to stay in business in such an environment is through cost and/or innovation leadership [25].

Cost Leadership. There are two main routes to cost leadership; having the lowest capital expenditure (CAPEX) per unit of hashing and/or having the lowest operating expenditure (OPEX) per unit of hashing. For the former, this may involve a miner fabricating their own ASIC hardware to save on the fabricator's margin, or developing favourable relationships with ASIC manufacturers, infrastructure providers and other partners throughout the capital expenditure supply chain. In terms of OPEX, cost leadership could mean finding cheaper power and hosting facilities than your competitors, or tailoring your energy inputs and datacenter model to the type of hardware you deploy [40]. Miners are not necessarily environmentalists, however, the cheapest power in the world is increasingly becoming renewable [59].

Innovation Leadership. Innovation leadership relates to doing things better than your competitors rather than cheaper. The two broad areas that Bitcoin miners can innovate within are their technological capabilities and managerial approach.

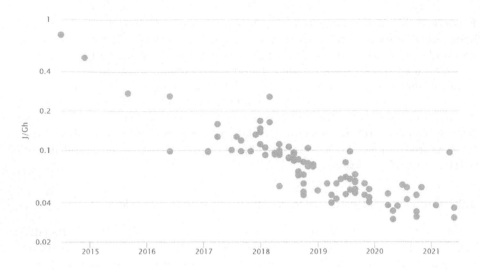

Fig. 2. Evolution of Bitcoin Mining Equipment Efficiency (2014–2021) [27].

Technological Innovation. Ever since Application-Specific Integrated Circuits (ASICs) became the dominant computing force behind Bitcoin Mining in late 2013, improvements in hashing power per unit of energy have improved at a steady, yet dramatic pace [26]. Figure 2 shows the evolution of Bitcoin mining equipment efficiency, measured in joules or Watts per gigahash (W/GH). Efficiency has improved from 0.77 W/GH in July 2014 (Bitmain Antminer S3) to 0.04 W/GH in June 2021 (Bitmain Antminer S19j), a reduction of almost 95%. As of this writing, the currently sold Bitmain Antminer S19 Pro has improved a further 26% to 0.0295 W/GH, with Bitmain's next model to be shipped in July 2022, the S19XP, boasting an additional improvement of 27% to 0.0215 W/GH [29]. This consistent improvement, coupled with the profit motive, has driven exponential growth in network hash rate over the past 8 years, as shown in Fig. 3. Although the ramifications of the global semiconductor shortage will impact procurement of new hardware in the short-to-medium term, it will not slow the pace of innovation.

Those miners not fabricating their own hardware can still innovate in areas such as datacentre cooling and configuration. Publicly listed Bitcoin miners, such as Riot Blockchain, are now investing in liquid immersion cooling to increase reliability, equipment lifetime, and reduce energy needed for cooling [43]. Importantly, immersion allows miners to reduce capital expenditure per unit of hashing due to the ability to dramatically overclock the mining equipment safely [43]. In terms of datacentre layout innovation, there are also publicly listed Bitcoin mining companies, such as Mawson Infrastructure Group, who deploy modularised or shipping-container-based solutions, which allows them to take their operations anywhere on Earth, land or sea, with a reliable power source and internet connection [44]. This modularity is already having a real-world impact, which will be discussed further in Sect. 3.

Bitcoin: Mean Hash Rate (14d Moving Average)

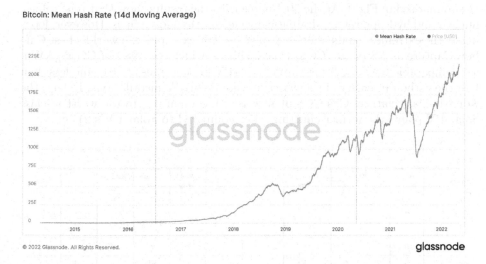

Fig. 3. Bitcoin Mean Hash Rate (14-day Moving Average), April 2014–April 2022. Dotted vertical lines indicate Block Reward Halvings [19]

Managerial Innovation. Whilst not as easy to measure as improvements in cost or energy per hashing unit, innovation in management and entrepreneurial techniques can make or break a business. For example, large Chinese miners who had robust risk management and business continuity plans in place in the face of increasingly hostile legislation, were able to relocate their operations with speed and minimal disruption and financial loss. Financially innovative and publicly listed miners also have the benefit of access to capital markets for funding to take advantage of or damp market shocks. Finally, innovation in procurement through industry partnerships can also provide a competitive edge.

3 International Energy and Electricity Markets

3.1 Energy and Emissions

Although energy and emissions are closely related, the terms are frequently conflated. Using more energy does not necessarily mean more emissions. The use of energy has allowed our civilisation to prosper, and future prosperity will depend on our ability to produce more energy at a lower environmental cost. The amount of greenhouse gas emissions (GHGs) per unit of energy, sometimes referred to as carbon or emissions intensity, differs dramatically across different energy sources and geographical locations, as will be discussed in detail in the next section.

Carbon Intensity. The International Panel on Climate Change (IPCC) published figures on the carbon, or emissions, intensity of different electricity generation technologies, based on a literature review of almost 300 Life-cycle analyses, as summarised in Fig. 4. At the 50th-percentile, the results show that renewables, nuclear and hydropower are dramatically cleaner than fossil fuels. However, looking at the extremes paints a different picture. For example, the world's best Carbon Capture and Storage (CCS) Coal facilities, which emit 98 g of CO_2eq/kWh, are comparable to the 75th-percentile Solar-PV installations at 80 g, and less than half the carbon intensity of the worst-in-class Solar-PV installations. In fact, the worst-in-class Natural Gas CCS plant was still comparable to the worst-in-class Solar-PV plant, the former emitting 245 g compared to Solar-PV's 217 g.

Table A.II.4 | Aggregated results of literature review of LCAs of GHG emissions from electricity generation technologies as displayed in Figure 9.8 (g CO_2eq/kWh).

Values	Bio-power	Solar		Geothermal Energy	Hydropower	Ocean Energy	Wind Energy	Nuclear Energy	Natural Gas	Oil	Coal
		PV	CSP								
Minimum	-633	5	7	6	0	2	2	1	290	510	675
25th percentile	360	29	14	20	3	6	8	8	422	722	877
50th percentile	18	46	22	45	4	8	12	16	469	840	1001
75th percentile	37	80	32	57	7	9	20	45	548	907	1130
Maximum	75	217	89	79	43	23	81	220	930	1170	1689
CCS min	-1368								65		98
CCS max	-594								245		396

Note: CCS = Carbon capture and storage, PV = Photovoltaic, CSP = Concentrating solar power.

Fig. 4. Aggregated results of literature review of LCAs of GHG emissions from electricity generation technologies (g CO_2eq/kWh) [30].

The recent Chinese ban on mining has helped shift bitcoin mining away from worst-in-class non-CCS Chinese coal plants towards best-in-class Natural Gas in the USA and other cleaner sources of energy around the world, helping Bitcoin dramatically reduce its carbon intensity. This migration and Bitcoin's carbon intensity will be discussed in more detail in Sect. 4.

For context, based on the 50th-percentile figures shown in Fig. 4, the carbon intensity of the world's energy production in 2020 was 622.7 g CO_2eq/kWh [53], and 487.12 g for the world's electricity production [54]. Data from the International Energy Agency (IEA) in 2018 showed an electrical grid intensity of 476 g CO_2eq/kWh as a global average, 709 g in India, 613 g in China, 571 g in Southeast Asia, 405 g in The USA, and 269 g in The EU [55].

Greenhouse Gases (GHGs) and Carbon Dioxide. While not as dangerous a conflation as energy, electricity and emissions, we again arrive at a similar position: whilst carbon dioxide is a GHG, not all GHGs are carbon dioxide. In fact, only 65% of GHGs come from CO_2 from fossil fuel and industrial processes, 11% from CO_2 from forestry and land use, 16% from methane, 6% from nitrous oxide, and 2% from F-gases [31]. In terms of warming potential, over a 20 year period, methane is 56-times more potent than CO_2, nitrous oxide is 280-times more potent, and F-gases are hundreds to thousands of times more potent, with sulfur hexafluoride, for example, having 16,300-times more global warming potential than CO_2 over 20 years [33]. This is why carbon intensity metrics are measured in "CO_2 and CO_2-equivalents". For example if a certain activity emitted 1 g of methane, it will have emitted 56 g of CO_2-equivalents. In total, 49,360 megatonnes (MT) of GHGs were emitted globally in 2016 [52], of which CO_2 made up only 35,200 MT [51].

In 2019, 150 billion cubic metres of methane were flared around the world as part of routine oil and gas industry operations, equivalent to around 1,500 terrawatt-hours (TWh) of energy, or, enough to power Bitcoin almost 15 times over [32]. Bitcoin miners will play a practical, profitable and pivotal role in methane flare mitigation, which is discussed further in the next section.

3.2   Energy and Electricity

Energy and electricity are often conflated but are strictly distinct. Whilst all electricity is energy, not all energy is electrical. Based on data by The University of Oxford's Our World in Data (OWID) project, of the approximately 173,000 TWh of primary energy produced in 2020 [35], less than 15%, or roughly 26,000 TWh was electrical energy [36]. Further, similar to the hundreds of millions of people around the world surviving without an electrical grid [37], Bitcoin does not need an electrical grid, only an energy source. The next sections provide a summary of how Bitcoin is currently capturing and using both energy and electricity in innovative, profitable, and importantly, sustainable ways [40].

Converting Energy into Electricity. All electricity starts off as raw, primary energy, be it oil, gas, wind or sunlight, and a proportion of this can be converted to electrical energy. Natural Gas has a conversion factor of 44%, meaning that 0.44 kWh of electricity is generated for every 1 kWh of raw energy input [41]. Conversion factors for coal and nuclear are similar at 32% and 33% respectively, with non-combustible renewables providing 39% conversion [41]. Hydroelectric is the most efficient, boasting 90% conversion efficiency [42].

Flared Methane and Stranded Energy. As mentioned earlier, methane has a far higher warming impact than CO_2 if left unchecked. Whilst flaring, or burning, of vented methane from oil and gas operations can reduce the impact substantially, the flaring process is negatively impacted by strong wind. Venting of methane is a necessary part of the drilling process, and although all vented methane is useful as fuel, distributing it can be cost prohibitive, and thus, it is simply burned to reduce environmental impact. Since 2017, when Upstream Data pioneered the concept, Bitcoin miners have been going directly to the oil and gas fields with a containerised mining and generator solution, plumbing directly into the site's flared gas line, and allowing oil and gas providers to ensure a maximum reduction in environmental impact from methane, as well as earn a profit from this source of waste [45]. Empirical research from the field has shown a reduction of 63% of emissions is achieved from using methane as an energy source for mining when compared to flaring alone [64]. In 2021, Upstream was joined by other well-funded private companies Giga Energy, Crusoe Energy, Great American Mining, Nakamotor Partners, and Jai Energy [40]. making enough of an impact on the West Texas Energy Grid to draw the attention and praise of Texas Senator Ted Cruz at the 2021 Texas Blockchain Summit [40]. In 2022, two of the largest Oil and Gas companies in the world, Exxon-Mobil and ConocoPhillips confirmed that they had also entered the flared Bitcoin mining game [66]. This comes to no surprise for industry experts, as mining using flared gas has been described by veteran industry investor and analyst that "Flared gas mitigation is as close to a free lunch as you can get," [40] and it would be rational to expected that every single oil and gas producer will attempt to eat this free lunch as the years progress.

Flared methane is only one example of a remote, isolated, or stranded source of energy. Due to the modularity possible with Bitcoin mining, there is almost nowhere on Earth that Bitcoin miners cannot or will not move their operation to for the right incentive.

Curtailed Energy and Load Balancing. Energy curtailment is when produced, but unsold, energy is allowed to go to waste by the producer, typically when cost of sale exceeds cost of production. In China in 2016 and 2017 alone, 100 TWh of solar, hydroelectric and wind power, enough to power the entire Bitcoin network for almost a year, was curtailed [46]. In 2018, this figure improved due to Bitcoin miners ramping up operations in Yunnan province to capture the cheap energy [47]. In the USA, specifically, the Texas ERCOT grid, 100 MW of Bitcoin mining power is being used as a Controllable Load Resource (CLR) [48]. Due to the ability of Bitcoin miners to effectively switch their operations on or off at a whim, software solutions providers such as Lancium are allowing miners in Texas to dial directly into the utility provider's data feeds, and level energy demand automatically [49]. Indeed, this system was put in play in March 2022 when Bitcoin miners shut down their operations to help the ERCOT grid brace for a freak winter storm [66].

Non-rival. The characteristic that waste, stranded and curtailed energy sources mentioned above share, is that they would all remain wasted, stranded and curtailed if there were no electrical loads as dynamic and flexible as Bitcoin. These are non-rival energy sources, meaning that Bitcoin miners are not competing with other customers to obtain this power.

4   Bitcoin's Current Energy Use and Emissions

Electricity Use. The Cambridge Bitcoin Electricity Consumption Index (CBECI) estimated that the Bitcoin network demanded 17.30 gigawatts (GW) of power as of 30 April 2022, which is equivalent to 151.65 TWh per year [50]. Based on a network hashrate of 213.4 EH/s on that day, this equates to an assumed average network efficiency of 0.081 W/GH, substantially less efficient than the current state of the art S19 Pro (0.0295 W/GH) mentioned earlier, but more efficient than the Antminer S9 (0.098 W/GH). Whilst the S9 was still powering 30% of the network in October 2021 due to huge energy arbitrage opportunities based on Bitcoin's all-time-high price at the time, the current proportion is substantially less [40]. Therefore, a more appropriate, and still highly conservative average network efficiency of 0.07 W/GH is assumed for all energy and efficiency related figures in this paper, resulting in an electricity demand of 130.9 TWh per year. This can be backed up by looking at Fig. 2, where over the past 4 years, there has rarely been an ASIC produced that is less efficient than 0.05 W/GH. Cambridge concedes that knowing the exact composition of mining equipment on the network is difficult, if not impossible, without voluntary industry participant disclosure. Principles of competitive economics leads to the conclusion that miners will necessarily have to upgrade their equipment to remain competitive, and therefore, power demand may be as low as 6.61 GW, or, 58 TWh per year, if it is optimistically assumed that most operating mining rigs are state of the art [50].

Energy Use. Based on the sustainable electricity mix shown in Fig. 6, heavily dominated by Natural Gas (30%) and Hydroelectric Use (30%) [21], the Bitcoin network has an estimated conversion efficiency of 53%. Therefore, the 130.9 TWh of electrical energy used by Bitcoin requires 247.0 TWh of primary energy to produce. Using the 247.0 and 130.9 TWh figures respectively calculated earlier as a baseline means that Bitcoin consumes 0.14% of the world's 173,000 TWh of energy production, or 0.5% of the world's 26,000 TWh of electricity production. In terms of "energy rankings" among countries, based on 2019 figures from OWID representing only 79 countries, Bitcoin would be the 63rd ranked country in the world, between Ecuador (206.5 TWh) and New Zealand (254.5 TWh) [36]. In terms of electricity, 2020 OWID data from 70 countries places Bitcoin at rank 28, in between Ukraine (133.5 TWh) and The Netherlands (122.7 TWh) [35]. Emissions-wise, Bitcoin would rank 80th out of 2019 countries, in between The Domincan Republic (38.2 MT CO_2e) and Denmark (36.0 MT CO_2e) [38] (Fig. 5).

Country	Rank	Energy Used (TWh) (2020)		Country	Rank	Electricity Used (TWh) (2019)		Country	Rank	Emissions (MT CO$_2$e) (2020)
Portugal	59	289.7		Poland	23	157.6		Syria	76	42.0
Hungary	60	275.9		Norway	24	142.9		North Korea	77	40.3
Morocco	61	263.6		Pakistan	25	132.7		Tunisia	78	38.7
New Zealand	62	254.6		Argentina	26	132.0		Dominican Republic	79	38.2
Bitcoin		**246.9**		**Bitcoin**		**130.9**		**Bitcoin**		**36.6**
Ecuador	63	207.5		Netherlands	27	122.7		Denmark	80	36.0
Bulgaria	64	206.7		Kazakhstan	28	103.6		Lebanon	81	35.7
Trinidad and Tobago	65	198.3		Philippines	29	98.3		Jordan	82	35.0
Denmark	66	193.6		Belgium	30	87.5		Angola	83	30.5

Fig. 5. Bitcoin energy and electricity use compared to other nations [35, 36].

Emissions and Intensity. Whilst miners, especially privately held ones, may be reluctant to disclose specific details about their commercial agreements or composition of their mining rig fleet for commercial reasons, many miners have elected to voluntarily self-report their energy mixes. Formed in 2021, the Bitcoin Mining Council represents 33% of the network hashrate, and provides quarterly updates on sustainable power mix [56].

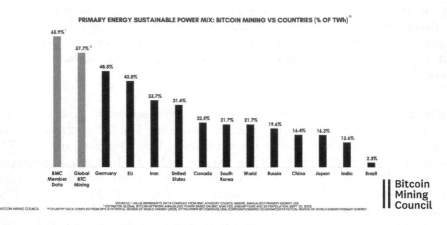

Fig. 6. Bitcoin Sustainable Energy Mix 2021. Sustainable sources include Renewables, Hydroelectric and Nuclear Energy [57].

Based on data collected post-China migration in 2021, and shown in Fig. 6, the membership of the Bitcoin Mining Council drew its power from 65.9% sustainable, low-emissions sources, with an estimate that 57.7% of the entire network is powered by low-carbon, sustainable sources (i.e. renewables + nuclear and hydroelectric). In contrast, the world average energy mix is only 21.7% sustainable, The USA at 31.4%, and The EU at 43.5%. In research by The Cambridge University Centre for Alternative Finance (CCAF) in late 2020, prior to the China ban, it was estimated that up to 49% of Bitcoin was powered by sustainable sources (10% Nuclear, 28% Hydroelectric, 11% Wind, Solar and other renewables) [58]. That same report found that 65% of Chinese miners used coal as their energy source. Therefore, a jump from 49% sustainable to 57.7% post-migration is to be expected.

In terms of emissions, the 49%-sustainable CCAF scenario resulted in 418.5 g CO_2eq/kWh, skewed quite dramatically by coal use in China. Post-migration, in the 57.7%-sustainable BMC scenario, the carbon intensity dropped by almost a third to 280 g CO_2eq/kWh [21]. Whilst quite dramatic, the China migration meant that 65% of 50% of the network was no longer powered by high-percentile emitting coal, but to far cleaner natural gas and renewable sources. As shown in Fig. 4, worst-in-class coal plants emit 6 times more than best-in-class non-CCS Natural Gas plants, and almost 26 times more than best-in-class CCS Natural Gas plants. Even 75th-percentile Natural Gas plants emit far less than best-in-class coal plants. The Chinese migration has reduced the use of coal on the network dramatically, having an overall effect of increasing the sustainable energy mix of the network by almost 15%.

Using our figure of 130.9 TWh per year for electricity consumption, and an assumed carbon intensity of 280 g CO_2eq/kWh, or 0.28 MTeq/TWh, we arrive at 36.6 MT CO_2eq emitted. This is roughly 0.07% of the world's 49360 MT of GHG emissions cited earlier.

5   The Next Decade in Bitcoin Mining

Whilst it is impossible to tell the future, knowing that the nature of competition in Bitcoin mining is near-perfect, and becoming increasingly perfect with time, logical conclusions can be made. Many topics have been discussed in this paper except for the speculative subject of Bitcoin's price. Effectively, Bitcoin miners mine bitcoin when the cost to mine is cheaper than market price, or when mining is the only means available to acquire bitcoin. When the gap between cost and price is large, fierce competition and innovation closes the gap. When cost and price are similar, as in extended bear markets, only the most efficient miners survive to see better days. One thing is for certain, as Bitcoin's price climbs, more energy will be spent in the pursuit of its acquisition. For example, if a speculative bubble sent the bitcoin price to, say, $1 million, with a cost to mine of, say, only $50,000 (i.e. $950,000 profit per mined bitcoin), competition for securing scarce hardware to mine may drive hardware prices so high, that traditional firms like Intel may opt to profit by providing hardware to Bitcoin miners to capture the high premium. Indeed, as of April 2022, Intel is now a player in the ASIC manufacturing game, partnering up with soon to be public miner GRIID, who will purchase 25% of Intel's manufacturing output [67]. Whilst ASIC manufacture may not be as "free" a lunch as flared methane mining, should Intel see commercial success with their foray into the industry, their competitors are sure to follow.

Mining Industry Outlook. In line with the principles discussed in Sect. 2, we should expect strong competition, and importantly, horizontal and vertical integration to the point where there are three to four players dominating 80% of the Bitcoin mining space [20, 22, 23]. A fully integrated Bitcoin mining company would provide their own power and hosting sites, as well as design, fabricate, mine with, and sell their own mining hardware. With 20-year-long agreements currently being formed between large US-based miners and utilities [62], tighter integration is the natural next step. Finally, in addition to the handful of public miners today, many more miners will likely go public in order to scale and gain access to capital markets.

Carbon Intensity and Emissions. The International Energy Agency (IEA) have a Sustainable Design Scenario (SDS) which sets out energy and emissions goals from 2020 to 2050 [60]. The United Nations also has 17 Sustainable Development Goals (SDGs) calling for dramatic decarbonisation of world grids. As Bitcoin generally relies upon "the grid", general decarbonisation efforts will positively improve Bitcoin's carbon intensity profile. However, due to the economic incentives on offer for mining with wasted and stranded energy and acting as a controllable load resource, Bitcoin should improve at a far faster pace than the world grid. Due to continual improvement in mining equipment efficiency and the Chinese migration, it is likely that Bitcoin's emissions have already peaked, considering the mass migration away from worst-in-class Chinese coal, to best-in-class (or at least 50th-percentile) Natural Gas, an emissions drop in emissions of between 70 to 80% per unit of energy, despite energy use trending upwards [39]. In other words, for emissions to return to pre-China migration levels, energy expenditure would need to grow three-fold, and the demonstrably false assumption that there will never be any further efficiency gains in mining hardware.

Energy Use. So long as mining a coin is cheaper than buying one, energy will be dedicated to mining bitcoin. Theoretically, there is no bound to how much energy the Bitcoin network could use. Practically however, there is a physical limit to how many hashes can be performed per second, i.e., there are only so many application-specific Bitcoin mining chips that can be manufactured. Depending on the price of bitcoin and the amount of profit on offer, a future where power plants are built by investors for the single purpose of mining bitcoin could be imagined.

Technological Innovation and Constraints. Although physical production can be hampered by chip shortages and supply chain difficulties, it is difficult to hamper the human mind and entrepreneurial spirit. Thus, even though chips aren't being shipped as frequently, or in as large a quantity, improvement and innovation is not slowing down. The Antminer S9, released in 2018 had 16 nm (nm) architecture, the S17 and S19 in 2017 and 2019, respectively, had 7 nm architecture, and the upcoming S19XP will be 5 nm [29]. The world's largest semiconductor company, TSMC, will be releasing 3 nm and 2 nm processes in 2023 and 2025 respectively [63]. It can be expected that the efficiency gains of

25–30% between architecture generations will continue for the majority of the next decade, especially with commodification of mining equipment to happen near decade's end (Fig. 7).

	Energy Produced (TWh)	Electricity Generated (TWh)	Total Emissions (MT CO2e)	Grid Intensity (g CO_2e/kWh)
World	173000	26000	49360	487
USA	26291	4049	5833	405
EU	16896	2760	3162	269
China	39361	7623	11577	613

	Energy Consumed (TWh)	Electricity Consumed (TWh)	Total Emissions (MT CO2e)	Grid Intensity (g CO_2e/kWh)
Bitcoin	247.0	130.9	36.7	280
% of World	0.14%	0.50%	0.07%	57.49%

Fig. 7. Summary of Key Data. *Bitcoin data as at 9 December 2021* [50,56]. *Emissions data as at 2016* [52]. *Energy data as at 2019* [35]. *Grid intensity data as at 2020* [55].

6   Conclusion

This paper has discussed the drivers of energy use, and thus, emissions, of Bitcoin mining. Whilst the fundamental driver is profit, the drive to survive amidst near-perfect competition makes Bitcoin mining a unique landscape. Whilst Bitcoin does use a large amount of energy, it was shown that the use is negligible on a global scale, and far cleaner than the world or US average on a per unit of energy basis. Most importantly, Bitcoin's current role as a buyer-of-last-resort for stranded or wasted assets, and being a driver of innovation in energy markets as a buyer-of-first-resort, will play a pivotal part in greening the world's grids and achieving the IEA and UN's sustainability goals.

References

1. Nakamoto, S.: Bitcoin: A Peer-to-Peer Electronic Cash System (2008). https://www.bitcoin.org/bitcoin.pdf. Accessed 8 Dec 2021
2. Bitcoin Wiki: Difficulty (2021). https://en.bitcoin.it/wiki/Difficulty. Accessed 8 Dec 2021
3. River Financial: Block Subsidy. https://river.com/learn/terms/b/block-subsidy/. Accessed 8 Dec 2021

4. River Financial: What Is a Bitcoin Halving?. https://river.com/learn/what-is-a-bitcoin-halving/. Accessed 8 Dec 2021

5. Lutz, G.: Application specific integrated circuits. In: XXIV International Conference on High Energy Physics, pp. 1249–1255 (1989). https://doi.org/10.1007/978-3-642-74136-4_147

6. Bitcoin Wiki: Hashrate. https://en.bitcoinwiki.org/wiki/Hashrate. Accessed 8 Dec 2021

7. Parkin, M.: Microeconomics, 11th edn., pp. 272–296. Pearson, New York (2014)

8. Mankiw, N.: Principles of Economics, 6th edn., pp. 291–314. South-Western Cengage, Mason (2001)

9. Makowski, L., Ostroy, J.: Perfect competition and the creativity of the market. J. Econ. Lit. **XXXIX**, 479–535 (2001)

10. Stiglitz, J., Walsh, C.: Economics, 4th edn., pp. 205–222. W.W. Norton & Company, New York (2006)

11. Dean, J.: Managerial Economics. Prentice Hall, New York (1951)

12. Semulson, W., Marks, J.: Managerial Economics, 7th edn., pp. 283–318. Wiley, New York (2012)

13. Bitcoin Wiki: Seed Phrase. https://en.bitcoin.it/wiki/Seed_phrase. Accessed 8 Dec 2021

14. Lightning Network: Lightning Network Homepage (2021). https://lightning.network/. Accessed 8 Dec 2021

15. Crypto.com: 2021 Crypto Market Sizing Report & 2022 Forecast (2022). https://crypto.com/research/2021-crypto-market-sizing-report-2022-forecast/

16. Wile, R.: Today, Bitcoin's Doomsday Scenario Arrived. BusinessInsider.com.au (2014). https://www.businessinsider.com.au/today-bitcoins-doomsday-scenario-arrived-2014-6?r=US&IR=T. Accessed 8 Dec 2021

17. Cambridge Centre for Alternative Finance: Bitcoin Mining Map. University of Cambridge (2021). https://ccaf.io/cbeci/mining_map. Accessed 20 Mar 2022

18. Attinasi, M., et al.: The semiconductor shortage and its implication for euro area trade, production and prices, Econ. Bull. Boxes **4** (2021)

19. Glassnode Studios: Bitcoin Hash Rate. Glassnode Studios (2022). https://studio.glassnode.com/metrics?a=BTC&category=Miners&m=mining.HashRateMean. Accessed 30 Apr 2022

20. Henderson, B.: The Rule of Three and Four. Boston Consulting Group (1976)

21. McCook, H.: Bitcoin's energy use compared to other industries. Bitcoin Magazine (2021). https://bitcoinmagazine.com/business/bitcoin-energy-use-compare-industry. Accessed 8 Dec 2021

22. Sheth, J., Sisodia, R.: Competitive Markets and the Rule of Three. Ivey School of Business, London (2002)

23. Pareto, V.: Manual of Political Economy. Oxford University Press, Oxford (2014)

24. MiningPoolStats: Bitcoin Hashrate Distribution (2021). https://miningpoolstats.stream/bitcoin. Accessed 20 Mar 2022

25. Afuah, A.: Innovation Management: Strategies, Implementation and Profits, 1st edn., pp. 13–46. Oxford University Press, Oxford (1998)

26. Cambridge Centre for Alternative Finance: CBECI SHA-256 Mining Equipment List (2021). https://sha256.cbeci.org. Accessed 8 Dec 2021

27. Cambridge Centre for Alternative Finance: CBECI Methodology (2021). https://ccaf.io/cbeci/index/methodology. Accessed 8 Dec 2021

28. International Energy Agency: Key World Energy Statistics (2021). https://iea.blob.core.windows.net/assets/52f66a88-0b63-4ad2-94a5-29d36e864b82/KeyWorldEnergyStatistics2021.pdf. Accessed 8 Dec 2021

29. Compass Mining: The Antminer S19XP: What is it? (2021). https://compassmining.io/education/bitmain-antminer-s19xp/. Accessed 8 Dec 2021

30. International Panel on Climate Change: Special Report on Renewable Energy Sources and Climate Change Mitigation (2012). https://archive.ipcc.ch/pdf/special-reports/srren/SRREN_FD_SPM_final.pdf. Accessed 8 Dec 2021

31. United States Environmental Protection Agency: Global Greenhouse Gas Emissions Data (2019). https://www.epa.gov/ghgemissions/global-greenhouse-gas-emissions-data. Accessed 8 Dec 2021

32. The World Bank: Global Gas Flaring Tracker Report - July 2020, p. 5 (2020). https://pubdocs.worldbank.org/en/503141595343850009/WB-GGFR-Report-July2020.pdf. Accessed 8 Dec 2021

33. United Nations Framework Convention on Climate Change: Global Warming Potentials (IPCC Second Assessment Report). https://unfccc.int/process/transparency-and-reporting/greenhouse-gas-data/greenhouse-gas-data-unfccc/global-warming-potentials. Accessed 8 Dec 2021

34. MIT Digital Currency Initiative: 51% attacks (2020). https://dci.mit.edu/51-attacks. Accessed 8 Dec 2021

35. OurWorldInData.org: Global primary energy consumption by source. University of Oxford (2021). https://ourworldindata.org/energy-production-consumption. Accessed 8 Dec 2021

36. OurWorldInData.org: Electricity Mix. University of Oxford (2021). https://ourworldindata.org/electricity-mix. Accessed 8 Dec 2021

37. OurWorldInData.org: Access to Energy. University of Oxford (2019). https://ourworldindata.org/energy-access. Accessed 8 Dec 2021

38. OurWorldInData.org: Data on CO2 and Greenhouse Gas Emissions by Our World in Data. https://github.com/owid/co2-data. Accessed 30 Apr 2022

39. McCook, H.: Projecting Bitcoin's Future Energy Use. Bitcoin Magazine (2021). https://bitcoinmagazine.com/business/projecting-bitcoins-future-energy-use. Accessed 8 Dec 2021

40. Carter, N.: Bitcoin Mining Is Reshaping the Energy Sector and No One Is Talking About It. Coindesk.com (2021). https://www.coindesk.com/policy/2021/10/11/bitcoin-mining-is-reshaping-the-energy-sector-and-no-one-is-talking-about-it/. Accessed 8 Dec 2021

41. U.S Energy Information Administration: Table A6 Approximate Heat Rates for Electricity, and Heat Content of Electricity. U.S. Energy Information Administration (2021). https://www.eia.gov/totalenergy/data/browser/index.php?tbl=TA6#/?f=A. Accessed 8 Dec 2021

42. Killingtveit, A.: 15 - Hydroelectric Power. Future Energy, 3rd edn., pp. 315–330. Elsevier (2020). https://doi.org/10.1016/B978-0-08-102886-5.00015-3

43. Riot Blockchain Inc: Riot announces first industrial-scale immersion-cooled Bitcoin mining operation (2021). https://www.riotblockchain.com/investors/news-events/press-releases/detail/117/riot-announces-first-industrial-scale-immersion-cooled. Accessed 8 Dec 2021

44. Mawson Infrastructure Group Inc.: Infrastructure and Hosting (2021). https://mawsoninc.com/infrastructure-hosting/. Accessed 8 Dec 2021

45. Upstream Data: Homepage (2021). https://www.upstreamdata.ca/. Accessed 8 Dec 2021

46. Dong, W., Qi, Y.: Utility of renewable energy in China's low-carbon transition. Brookings (2018). https://www.brookings.edu/2018/05/18/utility-of-renewable-energy-in-chinas-low-carbon-transition/. Accessed 8 Dec 2021

47. Carter, N.: Noahbjectivity on Bitcoin Mining (2021). https://medium.com/@nic_carter/noahbjectivity-on-bitcoin-mining-2052226310cb. Accessed 8 Dec 2021
48. Potomac Economics: 2020 State of the Market Report for the ERCOT electricity markets (2021). https://www.potomaceconomics.com/wp-content/uploads/2021/06/2020-ERCOT-State-of-the-Market-Report.pdf. Accessed 8 Dec 2021
49. Lancium: Homepage (2021). https://lancium.com/. Accessed 8 Dec 2021
50. Cambridge Centre for Alternative Finance: Cambridge Bitcoin Energy Consumption Index. University of Cambridge, Judge Business School (2021). https://ccaf.io/cbeci/index. Accessed 8 Dec 2021
51. OurWorldInData.org: CO_2 emissions. University of Oxford (2019). https://ourworldindata.org/co2-emissions. Accessed 8 Dec 2021
52. OurWorldInData.org: Greenhouse Gas Emissions. University of Oxford (2019). https://ourworldindata.org/greenhouse-gas-emissions. Accessed 8 Dec 2021
53. OurWorldInData.org: Energy Production and Consumption. University of Oxford (2019). https://ourworldindata.org/energy-production-consumption. Accessed 8 Dec 2021
54. OurWorldInData.org: Electricity Production by Source, World. University of Oxford (2019). https://ourworldindata.org/grapher/electricity-prod-source-stacked. Accessed 8 Dec 2021
55. International Energy Agency: Carbon intensity of electricity generation in selected regions in the Sustainable Development Scenario, 2000–2040 (2020). https://www.iea.org/data-and-statistics/charts/carbon-intensity-of-electricity-generation-in-selected-regions-in-the-sustainable-development-scenario-2000-2040. Accessed 8 Dec 2021
56. Bitcoin Mining Council: Homepage (2021). https://bitcoinminingcouncil.com/. Accessed 8 Dec 2021
57. Bitcoin Mining Council: Global Bitcoin Mining Data Review - Q3 2021 (2021). https://bitcoinminingcouncil.com/wp-content/uploads/2021/10/2021.10.19-Q3-BMC-Presentation-Materials-Final.pdf. Accessed 8 Dec 2021
58. Cambridge Centre for Alternative Finance: 3rd Global Cryptoasset Benchmarking Study. University of Cambridge (2020). https://www.jbs.cam.ac.uk/wp-content/uploads/2021/01/2021-ccaf-3rd-global-cryptoasset-benchmarking-study.pdf. Accessed 8 Dec 2021
59. Lazard: Levelized Cost of Energy, Levelized Cost of Storage, and Levelized Cost of Hydrogen 2020 (2020). https://www.lazard.com/perspective/lcoe2020. Accessed 8 Dec 2021
60. International Energy Agency: The Sustainable Development Scenario (2019). https://iea.blob.core.windows.net/assets/ebf178cc-b1c9-4de9-a3aa-51a080c0f8c3/SDS-webinar-2019-draft06.pdf. Accessed 8 Dec 2021
61. United Nations Department of Economic and Social Affairs - Sustainable Development: The 17 Goals (2021). https://sdgs.un.org/goals. Accessed 8 Dec 2021
62. DiCamillo, N.: Bitcoin Mining Firm Compass Inks Deal With Nuclear Microreactor Company Oklo. Coindesk (2021). https://www.coindesk.com/business/2021/07/14/bitcoin-mining-firm-compass-inks-deal-with-nuclear-microreactor-company-oklo/. Accessed 8 Dec 2021
63. Shilov, A.: TSMC Roadmap Update: 3 nm in Q1 2023, 3 nm Enhanced in 2024, 2 nm in 2025. Anandtech (2021). https://www.anandtech.com/show/17013/tsmc-update-3nm-in-q1-2023-3nm-enhanced-in-2024-2nm-in-2025. Accessed 20 Mar 2022

64. Crusoe Energy: Understanding The Problem Crusoe Solves (2021). https://www.crusoeenergy.com/blog/3MyNTKiT6wqsEWKhP0BeY/understanding-the-problem-crusoe-solves. Accessed 20 Mar 2022

65. Sigalos, M.: These 23-year-old Texans made $4 million last year mining bitcoin off flare gas from oil drilling (2022). https://www.cnbc.com/2022/02/12/23-year-old-texans-made-4-million-mining-bitcoin-off-flared-natural-gas.html. Accessed 20 Mar 2022

66. Sigalos, M.: Bitcoin miners are helping the Texas grid brace for winter storm impact (2022). https://www.cnbc.com/2022/02/03/winter-storm-descends-on-texas-bitcoin-miners-shut-off-to-protect-ercot.html. Accessed 20 Mar 2022. CNBC, https://www.cnbc.com/2022/03/26/exxon-mining-bitcoin-with-crusoe-energy-in-north-dakota-bakken-region.html

67. Alcorn, P.: Intel's Second-Gen Bitcoin Miner's Performance and Pricing Listed, Leads the Market (2022). https://www.tomshardware.com/news/intels-second-gen-bitcoin-miners-performance-and-pricing-listed. Accessed 20 Mar 2022

Integrated Power Plant and Bitcoin Mining Economics

Cal Abel[✉][iD]

Signal Power and Light, Inc., Cordova, AL 35550, USA
crabel@signalpowerandlight.com
https://signalpowerandlight.com

Abstract. Bitcoin mining can be a difficult process to understand much less model. It is confounded by currency exchange rates and jurisdictional taxes along with rapid historical technological development. We present a framework for simplifying the economic modeling process for bitcoin. To account for historical and potential future technological changes, we model trends in bitcoin miner performance showing that further gains in efficiency have plateaued. Then, we derive the marginal value of bitcoin treating the process of the block reward in a quantum mechanical framework and show that the measure of bitcoin's value is the energy used to mine it. Finally, we use the energy value of bitcoin to model the dollar price of bitcoin with a power law relationship over bitcoin's entire price history.

Keywords: bitcoin mining · quantum mechanics · statistical economics · EROI · Moore's Law

1 Introduction

Bitcoin mining has been something where it historically was relatively difficult to quantify the returns. The primary objective of this paper is to arrive at a methodology that is firmly rooted in first principles and is simple and intuitive in application.

Two of the chief problems that bitcoin valuation has are managing the exchange rates and price fluctuations. This has existed because the primary unit of account has not been fundamental and was tied to directly fiat currency. The primary objective of this paper is to establish a universal and absolute measure of bitcoin's value.[1]

This is far easier said than done. We need to understand how mining computational technology has evolved over time. We will also discuss how to look at bitcoin mining in a more wholistic manner. To do this, we need to first understand how bitcoin mining works at its deepest and most fundamental level. Once we have these two components, we can derive the marginal value of bitcoin.

---

[1] For the code and data used to analyze the models see https://github.com/crabel99/BTC-Mining-Economics.

The author thanks Roman Pavlov for inviting him to write this paper.

S. Matsuo et al. (Eds.): FC 2022 Workshops, LNCS 13412, pp. 34–54, 2023.
https://doi.org/10.1007/978-3-031-32415-4_3

From bitcoin's measure of value, we will develop the economic model. We need to understand first how bitcoin mining can be integrated into the electric grid, as this understanding is what informs how we construct and think about the overall economic model. By considering bitcoin mining as a part of the grid, we create the overall constraints with in which we have to work. This model establishes a cost basis using the universal metric of value, energy, and simplifies how we can account for the long term performance of the miners.

2 Trends in Mining Performance

Moore's Law is commonly thought of as being an axiom of computational power increases. There are some very real physical limits to this trend that effect how well our silicone based chips perform. To understand the trends in mining performance we need to first understand what these physical limitations are. Once we have this understanding, we will look at trends in microprocessor performance over the last 48-years along with trends in computer hashing performance. While transistor density is an important metric, it is not germane to the economics of bitcoin mining. The single most important parameter is the energy utilization of the chip per operation conducted.

2.1 The Classical Limit

When we start talking about *nanometer* level scales we are talking about the something on the order of the size of several atoms. So to put some perspective on the scale, we will consider the classical limit of an electron as being its DeBroglie wavelength,

$$\lambda = \frac{h}{p}. \tag{1}$$

where, h is Plank's constant and p is the electron's momentum.

We will look at the ionization energy of a valence electron from silicon in its *3p* orbital. There are two electrons in the shell with an binding energy of 7.81 eV [17]. Because the energy level is low, the electron's velocity is low and far away from the speed of light, and we can use the classical formula for energy and momentum,

$$E = \frac{1}{2}mv^2 \text{ and} \tag{2}$$

$$p = mv. \tag{3}$$

This results in an ionized electron wave length of 0.44 nm. Keep in mind this is for the free electron. If the electron remains in the shell, the actual Van der Waals radius of silicon is smaller and is on the order of 0.21 nm [19]. The Van der Waals radius is also a function of the thermal energy of the atom. As the temperature increases, so too does the internal energy of the atom. As a result the electron energy increases as the electrons occupy higher quantum states.

This forms a complex relationship with the temperature of the silicon and the electric field applied with relation to transistor cascade (electron ionization) [15].

For the sake of simplicity, we will place the classical limit at 0.44 nm. Because a transistor width consists of a minimum of three layers of atoms (NPN or PNP), the classical limit to transistor width is 1.32 nm. With current transistors at 5 nm. We are already on the same order of magnitude as the classical limit. Thus, further increases in transistor density are fundamentally limited as each transistor layer is now only about *4 atoms wide*. There may be problems with doping the boron and phosphorous atoms into the transistors that will limit any further decrease in transistor size.

Trends in processor development are towards changing the transistor geometry. This will make the processors physically more dense, but because our scale is already at the atomic level, increases in power efficiency and clock speed are not likely.

2.2   Trends in Processor Performance

When we take a step back from the atomic scale and look at the overall trends in processor performance, we can see the impacts of approaching the classical limit. Rupp presents the data from 1971–2019 in Fig. 1 [16].

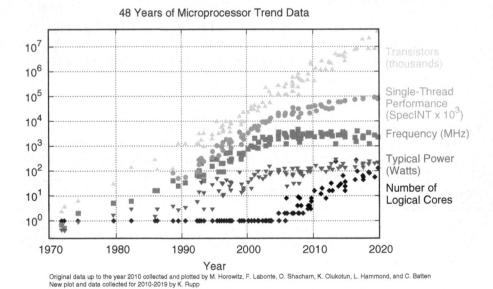

Fig. 1. Trends in microprocessor development [16].

Beginning with the physical limitations, we can see that the clock speed has plateaued. This is likely due to several factors: the capacitance of the transistors and the time needed to charge/discharge them and the limitations on transistor dielectric breakdown combined with chip design temperatures. If we can keep the chips cooler, well below their design temperature we can increase the clock speed. We will revisit the concept of chip thermal dissipation later. What is interesting is that transistor density is continuing Moore's Law of exponential growth and will likely continue [3].

Using the data from Rupp [16], we can estimate future performance in general computation (See Fig. 2).

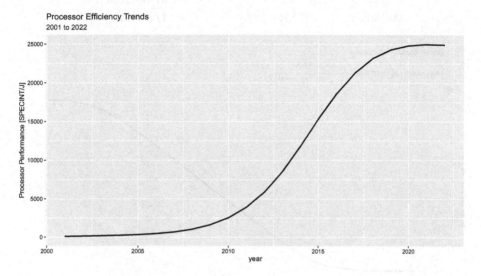

Fig. 2. Fitted model of computations per unit energy consumed. This is based upon [16].

2.3   Trends in Mining Efficiency

We can see similar fundamental limitations in mining performance as we can see in general computation. Using the data collected by Kufoglu and Ozkuran [14], we can create a similar plot as to Fig. 2 (See Fig. 3). Their original dataset was updated with a selection of more recent miners, Table 1.

The fitted curve in Fig. 3 is given by,

$$\eta(t) = A + \frac{K - A}{1 + e^{-B(t-M)}} \tag{4}$$

where the parameters are $A = 0.01\,\mathrm{Mh/J}$, $K = 4.27 \times 10^4\,\mathrm{Mh/J}$, $B = 1.26\,\mathrm{a}^{-1}$, and $M = 2019.2\,\mathrm{a}$.

Table 1. Selection of more recent bitcoin miners and their efficiency.

Manufacturer	Model	Efficiency [J/Th]	Release Date
AntMiner	S15	57	11/11/2018
AntMiner	S17	39.5	19/04/2019
AntMiner	S19	34.5	01/05/2020
AntMiner	S19j	36.11	01/06/2021
AntMiner	S19 Pro	29.55	01/05/2020
AntMiner	S19j Pro	30.5	01/06/2021
AntMiner	S19 XP	21.5	1/2/2022 (est)

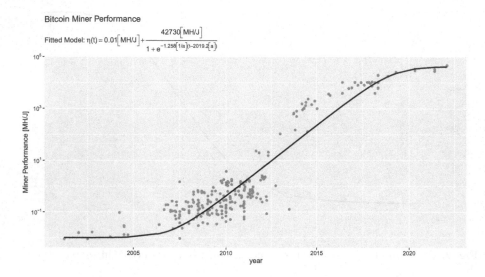

Fig. 3. Fitted model of computations per unit energy consumed. This is based upon [14].

Miner Tuning and Overclocking. We can see with Fig. 3 that mining performance is clearly plateauing. As a result of this there is an ever increasing trend for miner optimization. For example Braiins OS for the older and programable Antminer S9 series, has implemented features such as chip specific autotunning to optimize hashrate efficiency for each chip individually [7]. Other open source miner firmware options exist, e.g. Hive OS, but they tend to be limited to older models due to firmware protection installed on newer miners by their manufacturers [11].

It seems that the miner manufactures are attempting to limit the performance of rigs that they sell to the public. Bitmain for example builds a number of miners for themselves and could very easily write better firmware so that their miners are more productive than the ones they sell. While this might be an effective short term strategy to maximize returns, in the long run and especially with miner performance plateauing, the manufacturers will face increased competition.

Furthermore, there is a tremendous lack of standardization with the different boards even with the same model from the same manufacturer. These small dimensional fluctuations, make it very difficult to retrofit the miners with more efficient and dense cooling mechanisms. The author developed a containerized liquid cooled system, but had to abandon the project because the miners kept on changing their dimensions.

Heat Removal. While the energy efficiency of bitcoin miners has plateaued, the increasing trend in smaller and smaller processors is going to impose a thermodynamic limit on the current designs. Air as a heat transfer fluid is absolutely terrible. It is characterized by a low density and a low Prandtl number, 0.7. The Prandtl characterizes the preference of the fluid for thermal diffusivity $Pr < 1$ and momentum diffusivity $Pr \gg 1$. Because liquids tend to be much more dense having a large momentum diffusivity greatly enhances heat transfer from the surface, with a much thinner thermal boundary layer. This translates to needing much less surface area to remove an equivalent amount of heat.

In addition to the author's own work with immersion cooling, there has been a significant trend in the growth of this in bitcoin mining. There are some drawbacks associated with using an oil dielectric for cooling.

- Generally, they are flammable.
- They can have adverse reactions with board components shortening board life.
- They are expensive.

While recent immersion cooling operations have been relatively simple, they have done little optimization to increase performance. For this next step, hash board standardization is absolutely critical. What we will need is to separate the cooling liquid from the board circuitry. This can readily be achieved using aluminum brazed plates sandwiched between the circuit board layers and using a coolant like either pure water or an ethylene glycol water mixture. These are inexpensive and common coolants that are non combustible. These coolants support a wide temperature operating range from $-45\,°C$–$100\,°C$. If the objective is to limit chip temperature to $<90\,°C$, then the coolant needs to be at most $<35-40\,°C$ to support effective heat transfer at low enough temperatures to support safely overclocking the chips.

As chip transistor density continues to increase, air cooling will no longer be adequate to remove the heat generated during operation. This will only exacerbate the drive toward more compact heat exchange surfaces with densities of plate side $>200\,\text{m}^2 \cdot \text{m}^{-3}$. Because of the tight dimensional tolerances needed in compact heat exchangers, boards will have to have consistent dimensions.

Power Usage Effectiveness. The current method of air cooling has a very low Power Usage Effectiveness, PUE, $\approx$1.044.[2] PUE is the ratio of the total power of the system to the power sent to the miners. Keep in mind this is using outside ambient air which is blown, filtered, through the miners. If air cooled system is moved to warm climates, the miners have to be under clocked to keep the chip temperatures in specification. If air conditioning is used then the PUE significantly increases.

The use of liquid cooling, including immersion, where the coolant is directly cooled in a cooling tower, reduces the PUE to 1.016. This is because the pumping of a liquid requires much less energy for an equivalent mass flow rate. Even the use of the cooling tower fan to drive air for the ultimate heat sink is more efficient because the cooling tower is simply better engineered than the small computer fans on the miners. If the miner coolant can be cooled directly with water, e.g. the ocean, the PUE is 1.01. This is the limit of how efficient a mining system can be.

The PUE is important in the economic analysis because it is the energy overhead on top of the energy used for mining. While it is a small quantity in bitcoin mining applications, a 2.5–4% improvement in a process's energy efficiency is non trivial.

3   Bitcoin's Marginal Value

Now that we have covered some of the more granular details necessary for the foundations of the overall economic model, we have one more foundation to set. That foundation is to establish a consistent and stable metric for which to evaluate the value of the bitcoin mined. We will first look at estimating the marginal value as being derived from on chain metrics. Then we will look at establishing a more absolute measure.

3.1   On Chain Metrics

Before we delve too far into developing the on chain metrics for marginal value, we need to look at the process of how a block is discovered/mined. To be awarded a block a miner has to generate a random number called a nonce, number used once, and combine that into a specific structured 80 byte packet of data, the block header. The header is then hashed generating a unique 32 byte (256 bit) number for that data. The hashed number has to have a value less than target number, $Target$. If the hashed value is less than the target that miner is awarded the block reward, called the coinbase.

The target is computed by:

$$Target = \frac{MaxTarget}{Difficulty} = \frac{2^{224} \text{ bits}}{Difficulty}. \tag{5}$$

---

[2] This is based on private communication from Upstream Data, "2x 0.5 HP (0.745 kW) fans every 180 kW of PDU" (17 Nov 2021) and for an Antminer S19XP which has 4 fans (assuming 2.7A @ 12V) 130 W for 3.25 kW of 29.5 J/Th.

The max target was set in the genesis block with a byte string of "1d00ffff" and the initial difficulty for the first 2016 blocks was 1.[3]

After the first 2016 blocks were mined, the target number was adjusted in the first difficulty adjustment. The difficulty is adjusted every 2016 blocks so that the next 2016 blocks will take an anticipated 14-days,

$$Difficulty_{new} = Difficulty_{prev} \frac{\Delta t_{nom}}{\Delta t_{prev}}, \tag{6}$$

$$\Delta t_{nom} = 2016 \, \text{blocks} \cdot 600 \, \text{s} \cdot \text{block}^{-1}. \tag{7}$$

The new difficulty is $Difficulty_{new}$. The previous blocks difficulty is $Difficulty_{prev}$. The nominal times between blocks is Δt_{nom}. And Δt_{prev} is the difference in time between the first block and the last block of that difficulty period.

We can now define the probability, p_i, of finding the next block with a hash less than $Target$ as being,

Definition 1.

$$p_i = \frac{Target}{2^{256} \, \text{bits}}. \tag{8}$$

We can express Definition 1 in terms of $Difficulty$ through Eq. 5 as,

$$p_i = \frac{1}{2^{32} Difficulty_i}. \tag{9}$$

Transmission Probability. There are a number of similarities between radioactive decay and bitcoin mining. From a quantum prospective the occurrence of decay occurs when the wave function has a small portion that exists outside of energy well of the nucleus. These probabilities are incredibly small and are independent from similar processes in other nuclei.

This very is similar to how the hash for the next block reward is found. We could think of a hash being generated as a wave function propagating from the CPU to the network. This hash has a certain potential p and must tunnel past an infinitely thin barrier of a potential $c_0 \delta(x)$. Where $\delta(x)$ is the Dirac δ function and c_0 represents the finite potential of the barrier. We will use a wave equation of the form:

$$-\frac{1}{2}\psi''(x) + c_0 \delta(x)\psi(x) = 0 \tag{10}$$

Equation 10 has the following solution:

$$\psi(x) = \begin{cases} e^{ipx} + re^{-ipx} & x < 0 \\ te^{ipx} & x > 0 \end{cases} \tag{11}$$

We define $p = 1$ amd the transmission probability, $T = t^*t$ is:

$$T = \frac{1}{1 + c_0^2}. \tag{12}$$

---

[3] There is an off-by-one bug in the source code where the target computation uses 2015 blocks instead of the 2016 blocks of a difficulty epoch.

where t^* is the complex conjugate of t. Which if $c_0 \gg 1$ Eq. 12 becomes:

$$T = \frac{1}{c_0^2}. \tag{13}$$

With Eq. 13, we have recovered Definition 1, with the real quantum barrier potential being $c_0 = 2^{-16}\sqrt{Difficulty}$. We will revisit the quantum formulation once we have laid out the foundations for the statistics of how bitcoin measures value and time in the next section.

Block Discovery as a Poisson Process. Mathematically we characterize the process of radioactive decay as a Poisson Point Process as it satisfies the four conditions defining a Poisson process.

1. Independent increments: the numbers of arrivals occurring in the disjoint intervals of time are independent.
2. Stationary increments: the number of arrivals occurring in a given time interval depends only on the length of the interval.
3. The probability of one arrival occurring in a time interval of length δt is $H\delta t + O(\delta t^2)$ for $\delta t \to 0$.
4. The probability of two or more arrivals occurring in a time interval of length δt is $O(\delta t)$ for $\delta t \to 0$ [18].

We note that the quantum state transitions occur at infinitesimally small probabilities with each isotope being independent of all of the other isotopes.[4]

For bitcoin we observe that the transmission probabilities are fixed by Definition 1 or equivalently Eq. 9. We note that the discovery of a suitable block header follows the exact same statistical process as radioactive decay, because block discovery equivalently satisfies the four conditions of a Poisson process.

We note that the transmission probability of a winning block is defined by Eq. 9 and is uniform for all processors generating all hashes within a given difficulty epoch with a difficulty of $Difficulty$. Because the transmission probability is uniformly distributed expected time to discover a block for k hashes is,

$$\mathbb{E}\left[(S_k - S_{k-1}|\mathcal{H}(t) = H\right] = \frac{t}{H+1}. \; [18] \tag{14}$$

where S_k is the random variable of the inverse hash rate for $1 < k < H$ attempts.

Given that the number of hashes to discover a block, H, is defined as $H \equiv 1/p_i$ and t is the observed time between blocks. Because the hash rate, $\dot{H}$, is defined based upon the arrival of new blocks, we will assume that it is constant for a given block. Thus it will be a piecewise step function for each block in the blockchain. We can describe the mean of this function as being,

$$\frac{1}{t_N - t_0} \int_{t_0}^{t_N} dt \dot{H}(t) = \frac{1}{N} \sum_i^N \dot{H}_i = \langle \dot{H} \rangle. \tag{15}$$

---

[4] For processes with infinitesimally small transition rates, $1 - e^{-h} = h - \frac{h^2}{2!} + \frac{h^3}{3!} + \ldots = h + O(h^2)$ as $h \to 0$ [18].

where the first block's beginning time is t_0 and the Nth block's discovery (end) time is t_N.

From Theorem 1.3.1 of [18], we can describe the stepwise non stationary Poisson process for $t, \Delta t > 0$ as,

$$P\{\mathcal{H}(t + \Delta t) - \mathcal{H}(t) = H\} = \frac{(\langle \dot{H} \rangle \Delta t)^H}{H!} e^{-\langle \dot{H} \rangle \Delta t} \qquad (16)$$

where $\mathcal{H}$ is the random variable of the number of hashes and Δt is some positive time step.

By Theorem 1.1.1 of [18], the expected block hashes for each block in the kth epoch is,[5]

$$\langle H_k \rangle = \frac{1}{N} \Delta t \langle \dot{H} \rangle$$

$$\langle H_k \rangle = \frac{1}{N} \Delta t \frac{2^{32} Difficulty_k}{N} \sum_{i \in N} \Delta t_i^{-1}$$

$$\langle H_k \rangle = \frac{1}{N} \sum_{j \in N} \Delta t_j 2^{32} Difficulty_k \frac{1}{N} \sum_{i \in N} \Delta t_i^{-1} \qquad (17)$$

Each epoch is defined by a block potential corresponding to the inverse probability of finding a block and is the expected hashes per block,

$$V_{B,k} = 2^{32} Difficulty_k \qquad (18)$$

and has units of hashes/block. We can think of the term $I_{B,k} = \frac{1}{N} \sum_{i \in N} \Delta t_i^{-1}$ as the average block current within an epoch.

Just like electrical current is the transmission of fundamental units of charge, Coulombs, the block current is the transmission of a similarly conserved object, a block. Bitcoin was designed to have a fixed block current of 1 block every 600 s.

The hash is thus analogous to energy as the block potential, and gives us Ohm's Law in a bitcoin context,

$$P_{B_k} = V_{B,k} I_{B,k}, \qquad (19)$$

and represents the average hash power per block in the kth epoch.

The miner potential, the inverse of Eq. 4, represents the potential between the thermodynamic system of the bitcoin network, brought into equilibrium with the surrounding economy through the miners. We can thus express the average power of the bitcoin network for a given epoch as

$$P_k = \frac{1}{\eta_k} P_{B_k}. \qquad (20)$$

---

[5] We use the convention of geological time to define periods of time associated with the bitcoin network. *Era* like the Cenozoic, Mesozoic are equivalent concepts to currency eras: metallic era, fiat era, bitcoin era. *Period* like Quaternary or Tertiary within the bitcoin era are defined by the coin issuance or as they are colloquially known as "halvenings" and are 210 000 blocks long. *Epoch* like the Holocene or Pleistocene are equivalent to the difficulty adjustments done every 2 016 blocks.

Measuring Time. Bitcoin presents us with an interesting consequence of how the blocks are created, there is a time stamp for each block. This timestamp can have a significant amount of error in it, approximately an hour behind to two hours ahead of network consensus time. So it is entirely possible and, in fact, not uncommon to have a negative time difference between timestamps. This does not work with the derivation of the Poisson process for block discovery as time and time steps are defined only on the positive half-line.

Fortunately, Bitcoin has a hard stop defining the allowed zero time for each block, the Median Time Past, MTP, rule [6]. This rule requires that the timestamp of a new block be greater than the median timestamp of the previous 11 blocks. When we measure the time step for a block it is always with reference to this number.

We express the time step for a particular block as,

Definition 2.

$$\Delta t_i = \frac{nTime_i - Mdn_{i,11}}{6}. \tag{21}$$

where Δt_i is the ith time step, $nTime_i$ is the ith block's timestamp, and $Mdn_{i,11}$ is the median of the previous 11 blocks to the ith block.

We observe that by Definition 2 it is impossible to have a negative time step because the MTP rule invalidates any blocks which would have a negative time step. Additionally, when we look at the data contained in the blockchain, we find that $\Delta t_i \sim \Gamma(\alpha, \beta)$, ($\alpha = 5.55, \beta = 1.01 \times 10^{-2}\,\text{s}^{-1}$ for blocks 717696–719185 See Fig. 4) and that the hashrate is $H_i \sim \text{Inv-Gamma}(\alpha_H, \beta_H)$.

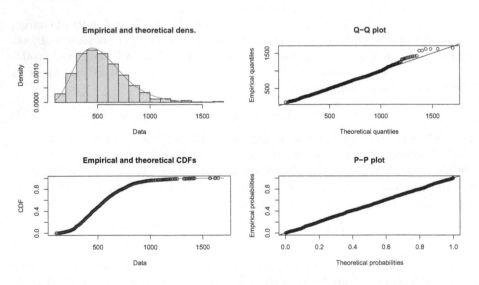

Fig. 4. Estimating the empirical distribution of the MTP block time for blocks 717696–719185. Fitted model is $\Gamma(\alpha, \beta)$ where $\alpha = 5.55$ and $\beta = 1.01 \times 10^{-2}\,\text{s}^{-1}$.

3.2   Computing Marginal Value

To establish what the marginal value is, we need to have a solid metric for measuring value that is absolute in its measure and is a conserved quantity. During our quantum mechanical discussion we showed that hashes, through the conservation of their current, are conserved. This is an absolute measure and we could use it to establish value, however, this is only valid on chain. We need a metric that is referenced to an absolute off chain.

In Proof–of–Work coins, the hashes represent the proof–of–work. Because of the incredibly low transmission probability of a hash, there is a significant amount of computational effort that has to be expended to find the winning hash. This computational effort requires two things: capital investment in the equipment and energy to power the equipment. Energy is by far the single most important consideration in bitcoin mining. We previously related energy to hashes using historical data of bitcoin miner performance. So, we will adopt that function to estimate the value of bitcoin in the real world.

We now have everything that we need to define the per block marginal value of bitcoin,

Definition 3.

$$\lambda_{\mathcal{B},i} \equiv \frac{\langle \dot{H}_i \rangle 600\,[\text{s}]}{Coinbase_i \eta(t_i)}. \tag{22}$$

where for the ith block, λ_i is the marginal value [MJ/BTC], $\langle \dot{H}_i \rangle$ is the block's average hashrate [Th/s], 600 is the number of seconds between nominal blocks, $\eta(t_i)$ is the miner efficiency [Mh/J], and $Coinbase$ is the sum of the utxos [satoshi] in the block's first transaction, nTxOut=0. The term utxo stands for unspent transaction output. The $Coinbase_i$ needs to be divided by 10^8 to convert from satoshi to BTC.

We can see the results of Definition 3 in Fig. 5. The presented histogram shows the per block variation of the marginal value around the 14-day moving average of the marginal value. We can project the growth in marginal value from January 2014, block 278000, using an exponential model,

$$\lambda_{\mathcal{B}}(t) = 1.400 \cdot 10^4\,\text{MJ/BTC} \cdot e^{0.4319\,[\text{a}^{-1}](t - 2014\,[\text{a}])} \tag{23}$$

The evaluation of the test data set residuals of the marginal value projection, Eq. 23 can be seen in Fig. 6. The model clearly represents a 8-year trend in the exponential growth of bitcoin's value. 80% of the time series data was used for developing the model. The remaining 20% was used to evaluate the model which had an $R^2 = 0.780$, $p < 2.2 \cdot 10^{-6}$, and normal residuals. This model predicts bitcoin's marginal value will double every 1.44 years and has been doubling at such a rate for the past 8-years. This trend will likely give way to the latter part of the sigmoid curve as this level of growth is fundamentally constrained by humanity's access to energy.

We can explore the relationship of bitcoin's marginal value to price as well. For this we take the data from [10] and evaluate it against the marginal value

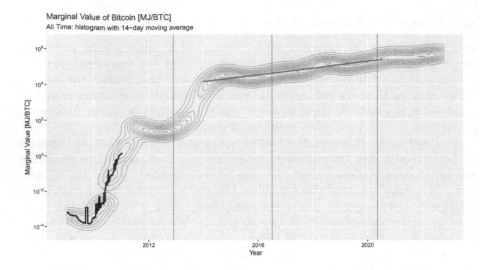

Fig. 5. Histogram of the per block marginal value plotted with the 14-day moving average. The vertical red lines represent halvenings. (Color figure online)

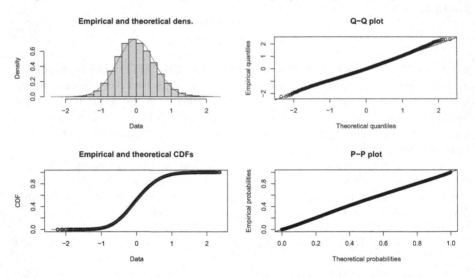

Fig. 6. Evaluation of the test dataset for the model predicting current growth in bitcoin's value. The model is given in Eq. 23.

daily average for each day.[6] Following the same convention as before, we use 80% of the data for the training dataset and reserve 20% for testing. Figure 7 shows the bitcoin price as a function of its marginal value. The graph is log − log and the fitted model is to a power law relationship,

---

[6] The additional 12-h is so that the daily moving average represents the daily average.

$$price = 0.49\,\text{USD/BTC} \cdot \lambda_{\text{B}}^{0.78}. \tag{24}$$

This left 855–days for evaluation. The resulting dataset had an $R^2 = 0.909$, $p < 2.2 \cdot 10^{-6}$, and normal residuals. The graphical evaluation of the residuals is presented in Fig. 8.

3.3 Simultaneous Measurement of Value and Time

Because the measurement of value depends upon the measurement of time and time depends on the measurement of value, we need to consider the consequences of their simultaneous measurement. From quantum game theory, we can show that value's observable is the Hamiltonian operator [1]. Because of this definition, value and time are complementary measurements and are governed by the uncertainty principle,

$$\sigma_t \sigma_H \geq \frac{c}{2}. \tag{25}$$

We need to consider the unadjusted hash rate to provide a common basis of comparison, because the network adjusts difficulty every epoch. If we did not do this, we would loose any meaningful comparison between epochs because each mining epoch is effectively measuring a different system due to the different potential, c_0, of the quantum barrier. We adjust Eq. 17 to represent this comparable hash rate as,

$$\langle H_{\text{comp}} \rangle = \frac{1}{N} \sum_j \Delta t_j \frac{1}{N} \sum_i \Delta t_i^{-1} \tag{26}$$

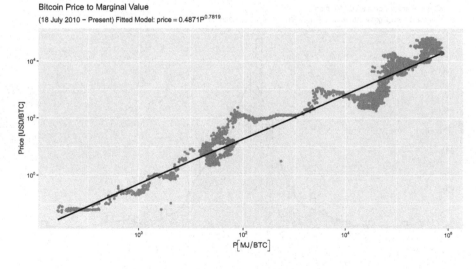

Bitcoin Price to Marginal Value
(18 July 2010 – Present) Fitted Model: price = 0.4871P^{0.7819}

Fig. 7. Comparison of Bitcoin's price and marginal value from 18 July 2010 – 31 October 2022. The red dot is the most recent data. The model is given in Eq. 24 (Color figure online).

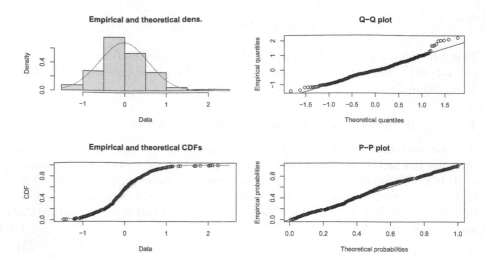

Fig. 8. Evaluation of the test dataset for the model predicting the present trend in the relationship between bitcoin's price and marginal value. The model is given in Eq. 24.

Examining the variance of comparable hashes and block time for each of difficulty epochs shows the network stabilizing after the first 40 difficulty adjustments with $\sigma_t \approx 240$ s, $\sigma_H \approx 0.001\ s^{-1}$, and $c = \frac{1}{2}$. The observed distribution for the mining Plank's constant, c, is given in Fig. 9. It is unclear if $c = \frac{1}{2}$ represents a fundamental limit or if the actual limit is lower.

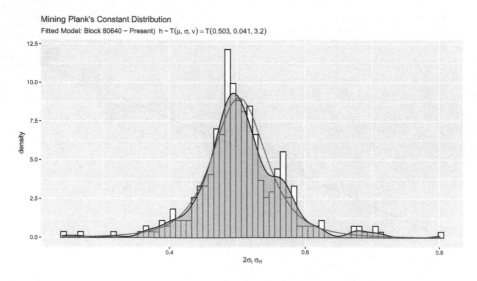

Fig. 9. Evaluation of the estimated fit of the mining Plank's constant, c. The model is given in Eq. 26.

4   Mining Economics

To begin an economic analysis we need to first define what it is that we are modeling. A bitcoin mining operation will have to convert bitcoin into fiat currency in order to be able to repay loans, pay for electricity, and pay employees. An alternative to converting accumulated bitcoin to fiat is to use the mined bitcoin as collateral for a loan to pay for operations. For the sake of simplicity we will look at a conventional mining operation that is funded through debt and equity with the fraction of equity being α and the fraction of debt being $1 - \alpha$.

With the development in Sect. 3.2 of a relationship between bitcoin's marginal value and price, one could use those relationships to do conventional economic forecasting for project evaluation. While this presents a known path for comparison moving forward it will miss out on the benefits of the methods developed in this section.

4.1   Cost of Energy

Energy is the single largest cost for bitcoin mining operations. It's cost is also not a constant value and can be relatively inelastic. The use of power in grid connected applications can be a significant friction point for miners and their host countries. In off grid applications such as flare gas operations, the flaring of excess natural gas from oil wells imposes a non trivial cost on the oil rig operators. Each of these two scenarios have very different considerations in how the miners are operated and how capital is recovered and costs realized.

Grid Integration. Grids, especially in well developed markets, are very complex and have even more complex markets. However, this complexity does open up some options where there is no discovery mechanism for the price of power. A Purchase Power Agreement (PPA) is typically negotiated with an agreed upon price of power and can contain an option for demand response. Demand response is when a consumer voluntarily shuts down or restricts their operations in response to price signals [12].

Because mining can have highly granular control over the clock frequency of the individual processors on the hash boards, a mining operation can have incredibly precise control over their power usage. This control can be tied in real time to the economic value of mining bitcoin (using market price API data from an exchange), and with the realtime price of power. For simplicity let us assume that the operator manages to negotiate a base power rate of $65/MW h [8]. They then negotiate to begin demand response when the price of power reaches the realtime breakeven price using an agreed upon calculation. For example using an S19XP, as of 13 Dec 2021, this would be around $470/MW h, but floats based on the network difficulty and market price.

The miners would then regulate their hashrate to maintain that price. They would first reduce their clock to the most efficient clock. Then, they would continue throttling back to the minimum clock on the board. For an initially overclocked miner, this could be on the order of 20–30% power reduction and would be agreed upon in the PPA. Meanwhile they would be paid for the power averted based on the power that they did not consume at the market price.

The next stage is to start shutting down miners after reaching certain price levels. This option places thermal stresses on the chips and could shorten chip life. Actually determining the lost economic use value is a very involved calculation. This would require careful negotiation.

Power Plant Integration. In new power plant construction actually integrating the mining operation with the power plant can eliminate transmission losses and transmission costs. In the United States transmission costs amount to approximately $11/MW h [13], while transmission losses are 6% [5]. This translates to an onsite cost of power of $50/MW h.

In this situation the power plant is the primary source of power and the grid is the backup. The mining operation would also benefit from directly accessing the power plant's water cooling system. This would result in significantly less capital expenditure for the mining operation's heat rejection system. Depending on the ultimate heat sink and using liquid cooling, this could provide an additional 2.4–4% savings in electricity use.

There is another synergy with collocating mining with a power plant. If the mining operation is large enough compared to the power plant, it could prevent a plant trip on a loss of offsite power by providing the minimum required load to keep the plant running. This would simplify grid restoration in large scale blackouts because the power plant would not have to be black started, it would already be running.

In areas where grid capacity is limited, such as the developing world, integrating mining with the power plant would enable the power plant to be sized larger (lower capital cost [$/kW]). In some cases having a minimum guaranteed power offtake improves the ability to finance the project if there is not a sovereign PPA. This minimizes the possibility of transmission interruption.

The author was present at a power plant in Central America where the main output breaker opened due to an under voltage protection causing a plant trip. The power plant (coal) had very specific actions that had to be executed rapidly to prevent steam pressure and tube wall temperature excursions. The impact of these actions, only mitigate the damage to the boiler. They do not prevent it. They said that this happened at least once a week and would take them 12–24 h to recover, if they didn't have significant tube damage. Meanwhile, the already strained grid went down in the surrounding region because of the loss of 60 MW of generation from (2) units.

4.2   Common Cost Basis

This is a very complex problem to tackle. We are dealing with local currency, local currency inflation, changes in network hashing power, using bitcoin as a currency, tax implications of purchases using bitcoin, taking loans against bitcoin to prevent taxable events, volatile exchange rates, etc. The reason why we spent so much time formally developing the marginal value of bitcoin in terms of $[MJ/\text{\textbeta}]$ was to alleviate as much of the complexity as we could by providing a common measurable reference indicator.

While $[MJ]$ and $[kW\ h]$ are both units of energy, we need to keep these concepts separate in terms of how and where they fit into the model. When referring to economic value, the unit will always be $[MJ]$ it could also be written as $[MJ_E]$ to make the distinction more explicit. Measurements of electrical energy will always follow the SI convention with base units of $[W\ h]$, appended with the appropriate prefix denoting the order of magnitude.

We will look at converting things priced in local currency units to an energy basis, instead of traditional deflators such as the Consumer Price Index, CPI. Then will develop a model for the net return on mining over the economic life of a miner. We will develop a method to minimize the tax liability in jurisdictions where bitcoin is treated as a commodity instead of a currency.

Energy Price Index. Energy is central to the level of economic activity in which we engage in. From a first law of thermodynamics perspective, this is intuitive as *ALL* action is constrained by the available energy. The impact and roll of energy can be measured using traditional econometrics. In fact, 80% of all economic activity is derived from the useful work input into the economy [4]. And, the price of energy is the single most important factor affecting economic growth [4].

For these reasons and also for the derivation of bitcoins value in terms of energy it is not unreasonable to consider using the cost of all useful work $[\$/MJ]$ into an economy as the basis of the marginal value of a currency. In this case, exergy, useful work, is the unit of economic value, just as it is for Bitcoin. The problem that we have is that this econometric measure is not published anywhere and to develop it would take a considerable amount of effort. Instead, we will use as a proxy the average price of electricity, as electricity is effectively pure exergy. For the purposes of this paper we will use the average price of electricity for all sectors as the value of the dollar [9]. To convert this into units of value we will apply the following formula,

$$\lambda_\$(t) = \frac{3.6[\frac{MJ_U}{kW\ h}]}{Price(t)[\$/kW\ h]}. \tag{27}$$

In all analysis multiply any dollar priced item (including debt) by $\lambda_\$(t)$. One will have to make a projection of $\lambda_\$(t)$, using a seasonally adjusted value.

Mining Revenue. The projection of mining revenue especially when considering it in terms of fiat currency is a very difficult thing to model. For a given miner hash rate, $\dot{h}_i$, the average miner reward can be expressed as,

$$\langle Reward_i \rangle = \frac{\dot{h}_i}{\langle \dot{H}_i \rangle} Coinbase_i \tag{28}$$

$$\langle Reward_i \rangle = \frac{Difficulty_0}{Difficulty_i} \langle Reward_0 \rangle \tag{29}$$

If we combine this with Definition 3, we can express the value $\langle E_i \rangle$ generated in the ith period as being,

$$\langle E_i \rangle \equiv \lambda_{\cancel{B},i} \langle Reward_i \rangle \tag{30}$$

$$\langle E_i \rangle = \frac{\eta_{\text{miner}}}{\eta(t_i)} \frac{\dot{h}_i}{\dot{h}_0} \langle E_0 \rangle \tag{31}$$

where η_{miner} is the miner efficiency. It is interesting to note that the average value produced by each block is only a function of the efficiency of the miner relative to the current state of the art. Barring any drastic technological changes, miner performance has plateaued. Thus the value returned by a miner is constant with time and only subject to its continued rated performance.

Equation 31 can be appropriately discounted over the lifetime of the facility to provide and equivalent value today. The selection of the discount rate is very important and should not be done using conventional values, especially if any bitcoin is used in making capital purchases. The reason why is that bitcoin is a long time preference currency [2]. If a facility is purchased using bitcoin, the value of the purchase less its costs has to be greater than the bitcoin used to make the purchase. Because if one is investing any capital the alternative is to buy and hodl bitcoin. The investment has to beat that. For this reason and because value is a conserved quantity, we express the total value, E_{total}, as being,

$$E_{total} = \sum_i \langle E_{in,i} \rangle - E_{expenses,i} \tag{32}$$

where $E_{in,i}$ is the value defined in Eq. 31 and $E_{expenses,i}$ is sum of all of the expenses incurred in that period of time.

5   Conclusion

It is clear that increasing processor chip density has plateaued due to reaching the physical limits of transistor construction. While there are other ways of constructing transistors at the atomic scale, it is unclear if these will result in increased processor efficiency. We can say that for now bitcoin miner efficiency has clearly plateaued due to reaching the atomic limits of the silicone transistor.

If we are going to predict future gains in bitcoin mining performance we need to approach chip cooling from a more rigorous thermohydraulic perspective. Air cooling, while effective for when chip designs were rapidly changing, is not adequate moving forward. We showed at a high level the need to shift to liquid cooling and suggest that miner construction be similar to that of a plate-frame heat exchanger to reduce material costs and improve the system's overall thermodynamic efficiency.

We developed an analogy of bitcoin mining to that of radioactive decay including the use of the wave equation to describe the transmission probabilities of a hashed value less than the target value. This analogy allowed us to use the Poisson Point Process to derive an expression for the marginal value of bitcoin.

While the expression of marginal value is ultimately quite profound, it allows us to express the economic considerations of miners across time very simply. It removes the complexity of the difficulty adjustments, miner subsidy, and currency exchange rates into a simple and powerful tool.

It was always clear from the early days of bitcoin mining, how important the price of power is in mining. This paper hopefully shows how to approach bitcoin mining and its relationship to the electric grid as being symbiotic rather than parasitic. Grid integration is an incredibly complex subject as the markets can be complex, but we can select the guiding principle of being a good neighbor to provide a constructive approach to resolving the complexity. If we seek to understand the needs of electricity consumers, producers, and distributors, there are opportunities that allow bitcoin mining to limit power price fluctuations, while providing additional sources of revenue for the miner operator. The relationship of the parties on the grid is not zero-sum especially when we consider contracts that include demand response provisions.

References

1. Abel, C.: The quantum foundations of utility and value. Phil. Trans. R. Soc. A, **381**, 20220286 (2023). https://doi.org/10.1098/rsta.2022.0286
2. Ammous, S.: The Bitcoin Standard: The Decentralized Alternative to Central Banking. Wiley, Hoboken (2018)
3. Anthony, S.: Transistors will stop shrinking in 2021, but Moore's law will live on. Ars Technica (2016). https://arstechnica.com/gadgets/2016/07/itrs-roadmap-2021-moores-law/. Accessed 9 Dec 2021
4. Ayers, R.U., Warr, B.: The Economic Growth Engine: How Energy and Work Drive Material Prosperity. International Institute for Applied Systems Analysis, Northampton (2009)
5. Bank, W.: Electric power transmission and distribution losses. https://data.worldbank.org/indicator/EG.ELC.LOSS.ZS. Accessed 13 Dec 2021
6. BitcoinCore: Bitcoin core: Median time past validation (2021). https://github.com/bitcoin/bitcoin/blob/master/src/validation.cpp#L3155. Accessed 9 Dec 2021
7. Braiins: Autotuning vs. overclocking for bitcoin miners (SHA-256 ASICs) Bitcoin Mining Insights (2021). https://braiins.com/blog/autotuning-vs-overclocking-for-bitcoin-miners-sha-256-asics. Accessed 9 Dec 2021
8. EIA: Electric power monthly (2021). https://www.eia.gov/electricity/monthly/epm_table_grapher.php?t=epmt_5_6_a. Accessed 9 Dec 2021
9. EIA: Electricity data browser (2021). https://www.eia.gov/electricity/data/browser/#/topic/7. Accessed 13 Dec 2021
10. CMD Encyclopedia: Asset metrics - bitcoin - price USD API (2022). https://community-api.coinmetrics.io/v4/timeseries/asset-metrics. Accessed 30 Mar 2022

11. HiveOS: Going to update your official bitmain firmware? Don't hurry up! Medium (2020). https://medium.com/hiveon/going-to-update-your-official-bitmain-firmware-dont-hurry-up-7cd2899d5a6e. Accessed 9 Dec 2021

12. IEA: Demand response (2021). https://www.iea.org/reports/demand-response. Accessed 13 Dec 2021

13. IER: Electricity transmission (2021). https://www.instituteforenergyresearch.org/electricity-transmission/. Accessed 13 Dec 2021

14. Kufoglu, S., Ozkuran, M.: Bitcoin mining: a global review of energy and power demand. Energy Res. Soc. Sci. **58**, 1–12 (2019). https://doi.org/10.1016/j.erss.2019.101273

15. Maes, W., De Meyer, K., Van Overstraeten, R.: Impact ionization in silicon: a review and update. Solid-State Electron. **33**(6), 705–718 (1990). https://doi.org/10.1016/0038-1101(90)90183-F

16. Rupp, K.: Microprocessor trend data (2020). https://github.com/karlrupp/microprocessor-trend-data. Accessed 9 Dec 2021

17. Shattuck, T.: Atomic orbital ionization energies (2017). https://www.colby.edu/chemistry/PChem/notes/AOIE.pdf. Accessed 9 Dec 2021

18. Tijms, H.C.: A First Course in Stochastic Models. Wiley, Hoboken (2003)

19. WolframAlpha: Van der waals radius silicon From WolframAlpha–A Wolfram Web Resource. https://www.wolframalpha.com/. Accessed 9 Dec 2021

Carbon-Neutral Bitcoin for Nation States

Troy Cross[1,2](✉) and Andrew M. Bailey[2,3]

[1] Reed College, Portland, OR, USA
troy.cross@reed.edu
[2] The Bitcoin Policy Institute, Washington, D.C., USA
[3] Yale-NUS College, Singapore, Singapore

Abstract. Sovereign adoption of bitcoin, whether as legal tender or in treasury reserves, increases the profitability of energy-intensive bitcoin mining, creating significant carbon emissions. This paper explores methods for adopting bitcoin while mitigating or eliminating associated carbon emissions. We survey three solutions: regulation/taxation, carbon offsetting, and finally, state-directed or state-supported carbon-neutral mining, arguing for the advantages of the latter. We then compare two ways of executing this last approach: (1) the state must mine all its bitcoin holdings; (2) the state must mine the same percentage of mining as its percentage of all bitcoin holdings. We show that (2) is a superior method, and that a nation state can adopt bitcoin in a carbon-neutral manner with a relatively small investment in carbon-neutral mining. At present levels of bitcoin mining and bitcoin pricing, an annual allocation of around 1% of the state's bitcoin holdings towards mining will suffice, and may generate a positive return. El Salvador is used throughout as a case study, and we make specific suggestions for how much El Salvador should mine to achieve carbon neutrality with respect to their bitcoin holdings.

Keywords: Bitcoin · environment · carbon · carbon-neutral · ESG · mining · cryptocurrency

1 Introduction

In 2021, El Salvador adopted bitcoin as legal tender alongside the U.S. Dollar, setting aside $150 million for a trust to facilitate dollar/bitcoin exchanges [1]. The bitcoin network is known to be energy-intensive—consuming a quantity of electricity somewhere between that of the Netherlands and Argentina—and El Salvador's actions would arguably, in the absence of countervailing initiatives, increase their nation's CO_2 emissions [2]. But how much emissions does such adoption involve? And what countervailing initiatives are at El Salvador's disposal? Is it possible to adopt bitcoin with no addition to carbon emissions, or even in a carbon-negative way, achieving emissions targets or commitments? If so, what would that require, and how much would it cost?

The present paper answers these questions, not just for El Salvador, but for any state exploring bitcoin adoption. We first review the energy consumption and emissions associated with bitcoin adoption and show how bitcoin holdings and transactions incentivize

© International Financial Cryptography Association 2023
S. Matsuo et al. (Eds.): FC 2022 Workshops, LNCS 13412, pp. 55–65, 2023.
https://doi.org/10.1007/978-3-031-32415-4_4

mining and its externalities. We then critically examine the options for mitigating those externalities through regulation or taxation. We next entertain carbon offsets, calculating the cost of such measures and evaluating their effectiveness. Finally, we propose an alternative, which is state-sponsored or state-incentivized carbon-neutral mining. We argue that due to the unique properties of bitcoin—its limited supply, fungibility, and fast, nearly-free transportability—such mining can fully offset the emissions from adoption.

We then compare two systems of calculating how much carbon-neutral bitcoin mining the state must either manage itself, or else incentivize through subsidy: (1) the state must mine all its bitcoin holdings; (2) the state must mine the same percentage of mining as its percentage of all bitcoin holdings. Our conclusion is that (2) is the superior method, and that a nation state can adopt bitcoin in a carbon-neutral manner with a relatively small investment in carbon-neutral mining, allotting, at present rates of mining and bitcoin pricing, only 2% of the state's bitcoin holdings annually towards mining, which should itself have a positive expected return. In the case of El Salvador, the nation is, in fact, already engaged in the sort of carbon-neutral mining that we prescribe, using geothermal energy [3]. We conclude by showing exactly how much hashrate El Salvador's pro-bitcoin policy decisions require them to generate if they wish their bitcoin adoption to be carbon neutral.

2 Externalities of Bitcoin Adoption

In the rest of this paper, "sovereign adoption of bitcoin" means any combination of the following: legal tender laws, treatment as currency (not property) under tax law, direct acquisitions in the treasury, and/or state-owned or state-guided bitcoin wallet services, bitcoin ATMS, or "airdrops" to citizens. Bitcoin stands apart from other cryptocurrencies on account of its founding, culture, and product-market fit [4]. A standard suite of reasons for individuals to use bitcoin include its censorship resistance and independence from legacy monetary institutions [5–7]. Sovereigns may or may not endorse that suite of reasons. But they have their own distinctive reasons to adopt, including enhancing financial inclusion, seeking protection from inflation, attracting foreign investment, lowering the cost of remittances, and escaping the colonial effects of dollarization [1]. These reasons are all, unsurprisingly, contested by organizations from the IMF to the Bank of England, who warn against bitcoin adoption on the grounds of volatility and regulatory risk [8].

We will not here adjudicate these disputes. Instead, we simply ask how states that have already decided to adopt bitcoin can best do so, especially with respect to emissions. The thought here is not complicated. States are positioned, perhaps uniquely, to coordinate behavior towards climate goals. Many have made explicit emissions commitments, and so are morally or legally obligated to pursue carbon-neutral or carbon-reducing strategies across the board. Bitcoin's poor environmental reputation at present offers states an additional reason to adopt bitcoin only in a way that minimizes emissions. Cleaning up bitcoin can only advance the other goals of bitcoin adoption, say, financial inclusion or monetary independence from the dollar.

We mark bitcoin adoption along two dimensions: (a) additional holdings of bitcoin due to government measures, whether by the government itself or by private entities as a result of favorable legal measures; (b) additional on-chain bitcoin transactions, again due either to the government itself engaging in bitcoin transactions or an increase in private transactions due to favorable policy. The process of calculating any particular instance of adoption in these terms lies, again, beyond the scope of this paper, which simply takes adoption as a two-fold input: additional transactions and additional holdings of bitcoin. From these two inputs, we can roughly estimate how much additional CO_2 is emitted into the atmosphere. Since this paper is a proof of concept only, we will use a rough estimate, to be refined in later work.

3 Economics of Bitcoin Mining

Mining is the process by which new transactions are published to the blockchain. Miners assemble candidate transactions from the mempool into blocks and search for a number, a nonce, which when appended to the block header and fed into double SHA-256, yields an output number. If that output number begins with a certain number of zeros, the miner's block will be accepted as valid by the network of full nodes, provided there are no competing chains of blocks that are longer.

The winning miner publishes a block and receives a block subsidy for their efforts, as well as any fees associated with candidate transactions. What matters for our purposes is that the block subsidy and transaction fees exhaust the sources of miner income, and both are denominated in bitcoin. Currently, the block subsidy is 6.25 bitcoin per block, and transaction fees are less than 2% of mining rewards.

Note three points. First, the miners' search is essentially random, and involves checking vast quantities of numbers to see if they solve the puzzle. That search, in turn, requires both energy and specialized hardware. Second, the difficulty of the search adjusts to ensure that on average, new blocks are created every ten minutes. If blocks are mined faster, the search becomes more difficult—more zeros must appear in front of the output of the nonce-appended-to-block-header input. If blocks are being mined at intervals of greater than ten minutes, the difficulty will decrease—fewer preceding zeros required—until, once again, block times return to ten minutes. Third, the issuance of bitcoin is scheduled to halve every four years. In the first epoch, miners were rewarded with 50 bitcoin for publishing one block, then 25, then 12.5, and now 6.25, and soon 3.1255, and so on. This schedule creates a capped supply approaching 21 million bitcoin prior to the year 2140, at which time mining will be incentivized entirely by fees.

Bitcoin mining, then, is a world-wide search for the next block, to be rewarded in bitcoin, and the issuance of new bitcoin is entirely predictable over a long time scale. More mining, crucially, does not, except in the very short-term, lead to more bitcoin being found. Rather, more mining simply means more computing power chasing after exactly the same amount of bitcoin, which right now is 6.25 bitcoin per block, or 900 per day.

The value of that reward, while entirely predictable in bitcoin terms, is itself a function of bitcoin's market price. A 6.25 bitcoin block reward when bitcoin trades at $60,000, is significantly more enticing than a 6.25 bitcoin block reward when bitcoin trades at $6,000. Miners make capital investments in specialized mining hardware, substations, copper wire, and so on. They also carry operating expenses including labor, but most of all, electricity itself. These investments are made, broadly, by estimating bitcoin's future price, the chance of winning block rewards, and the costs of power, infrastructure, and labor required to win those rewards. Predictions of a higher future price inspires miners to invest, while increasing hashrate, and therefore, increasing competition for the fixed issuance of new bitcoin, depresses miners' investment. A predicted drop or stagnation in prices depresses mining investment, and a drop in hashrate promotes mining investment, since with less competition the same block reward requires less work—computing cycles, and hence, less infrastructure and electricity, to win.

4   The Adoption-to-Mining Emissions Relationship

We have marked adoption in two ways: sustained or increased holding of bitcoin over time, and adding to the quantity of transactions. And we have seen how mining is incentivized: price of bitcoin and lack of competition from other miners over a fixed reward. We are now in a position to say how sovereign adoption of bitcoin creates bitcoin-mining-related emissions.

Begin with transactions. Each transaction carries a bitcoin-denominated fee, paid to miners for inclusion in a block. If adoption were to increase demand for scarce blockspace—on-chain transactions are limited to a maximum of about seven transactions per second—that would increase the rewards for mining, which would lead to more mining, which would lead to more emissions. Estimating the on-chain transaction increase *due to* adoption is difficult, because the state only knows its own transactions are "due to" its actions; other increases will be indirect. But again, that estimate is outside of the scope of our paper, which simply takes the increase as an input. Once given the increase in transactions over a give time period, one need only multiply the additional transactions by the average on-chain fee during the time period in question, and multiply that by the average price of bitcoin at that time to estimate the additional incentive offered to miners by the transaction-fee-related adoption of bitcoin in that time period.

$$\text{Adoption from fee incentives to miners} = \text{additional txs} \times \text{avg tx fee} \times \text{avg BTC price} \tag{1}$$

As stated earlier, transaction fees constitute only 2% of miner revenue. States will likely adopt bitcoin using more efficient second-layer solutions like the Lightning Network or other custodial payment systems, which minimize blockspace demand and thus fees, by settling on-chain infrequently. Despite dire warnings that the bitcoin network would be unable to handle the volume of transactions caused by Salvadoran adoption, blockspace has actually become cheaper and more available than before the bitcoin laws were passed, proving that second-layer solutions can support a high volume of transactions without burdening the base layer. Because transactions are such a small percentage of mining rewards and because sovereign adoption does not appear to put pressure on block space, we will hereafter ignore the channel of influence that adoption has on emissions via transaction fees. In terms of the formula above, the additional transactions are negligible, and the average transaction fees are negligible as well.

What we must focus on, instead, is the other channel of influence: sovereign adoption increasing the price of bitcoin. El Salvador, for instance, has acquired 1,400 bitcoin [9].

Doubtless, more bitcoin are also held by citizens because of the state's decision, and one may or may not want to include this increase in bitcoin holdings as well as the government's responsibility. Again, such an estimate is difficult, and again, it is beyond the scope of this paper. For the purpose of this exercise, we will limit ourselves to calculating the emissions due to the government's own holdings, leaving the additional private holdings as the responsibility of those private entities.

Here is how the state's holding, say, 1,400 bitcoin, causes carbon emissions. By buying and holding that quantity of bitcoin, the government removed that same quantity from order books, driving up price to the next-most-reluctant seller. That increase in price makes the fixed block reward more valuable. 6.25 bitcoin is worth more than it otherwise would be. That leads to more mining, which in turn leads to more emissions. This influence on price from holding, crucially, *is not a one-time event.* Purchasing bitcoin removes it from the marketplace, leaving the same dollars (bids) chasing fewer available bitcoin (asks). Additionally, every day the bitcoin holdings are not sold is a day when price is higher than it otherwise would be. This stable and high price (as opposed to a mere momentary spike) is what induces miners to make long-term investments in the aforementioned specialized mining hardware, substations, copper wire, and so on.

When it comes to determining exactly how much price impact a given purchase, and subsequent period of holding bitcoin, causes, there are two distinct methods. The first is our preferred method, and that is to begin with the recognition that price is a function of the entirety of buyers-and-holders of bitcoin. That is, the price being as high as it is reflects the collective decisions of all holders of bitcoin, any of whom could sell at any moment, but doesn't. Every non-seller is like every other non-seller, who is not selling an equal amount of bitcoin, in other words. And it is the aggregate non-selling of all bitcoin holders that keeps the price from dropping. Thinking in this way, an individual holder's responsibility for price is strictly proportionate to their holdings. So, if one owns 1% of bitcoin, one is 1% responsible for price.

Extending this thought to the incentivization of mining, an individual holder can be thought to incentivize a certain percentage of all mining. For instance, if someone holds 1% of all bitcoin, one is incentivizing 1% of all bitcoin mining by bearing 1% of all responsibility for price. This formula distributes the responsibility for incentivizing mining evenly across all holders. It leaves no mining unaccounted for, and it does not double-count incentives by concluding that the total incentives created by holders is greater than the total amount of incentives.

The formula here is that at a given time:

$$\text{One's holdings as a \% of market cap} = \% \text{ of all mining one incentivizes} \quad (2)$$

For El Salvador, this method would first calculate the government's share of all bitcoin. Since nearly 3 million bitcoin have been lost, the total number of bitcoin is close to 16 million, of which El Salvador's 1,400 bitcoin is 0.00875%. So, according to this method of accounting, El Salvador's adoption of bitcoin is responsible for incentivizing roughly .00875% of all bitcoin mining over the period during which they have owned that bitcoin. To determine the emissions caused by adoption, we need two further steps, which is to calculate the total energy required by the network, and then calculate the carbon emissions required to produce that amount of energy, given the mix of energy sources of the bitcoin mining network. Then we can attribute .00875% of those emissions to El Salvador's bitcoin adoption.

On the question of how much energy the bitcoin network consumes, there is little disagreement. We know the difficulty of the math problems miners are solving, and the block times, which hover around 10 min, and we know roughly the hardware mix being used by miners, and how fast that hardware solves the math problems, and, as well, how much electricity those machines must consume in order to solve the problems at the rate they are being solved. Currently, the estimates are that the bitcoin network is calculating at a rate of 165 exahash/second: 165 quintillion total guesses by miners, per second [10].

The bitcoin network's mix of power sources is more contested, with estimates ranging from 39% to 73% renewable energy [11]. The Bitcoin Mining Council is composed of large commercial miners and surveys its constituents—65.9% renewable powered—as well as estimating the power mix of non-members, arriving at a total estimate of 57.7% renewable-powered [12]. Uncertainty is multiplied because carbon-intensive forms of electricity production vary in the quantity of carbon emitted per unit of power produced. And further, miners vary in efficiency, and the exact distribution of miners in operation is unknown. Alex de Vries, a well-known critic of bitcoin mining estimates that the total emissions from the network is currently 97 megatons of CO_2 annually, or roughly equivalent to the carbon footprint of Kuwait [13]. Taking de Vries' estimate, together with one's percentage of the network, one can derive one's share of all emissions incentivized by adoption. For El Salvador, that is .00875% of 97 megatons, or roughly 8.5Kt of CO_2.

In sum, adoption incentivizes mining in two ways: by creating new block demand, driving up transaction fees, and by elevating the price of bitcoin. We suggest that transaction fees are, at this time, such a small percentage of miner's income, and so unaffected by sovereign adoption due to layer-2 payment systems built atop bitcoin's main chain, as to be safely ignored at this time. We also propose that the right way to calculate the percentage of all mining due to bitcoin price increases resulting from adoption is to treat the entirety of bitcoin investment as the entirety of price-based incentive for mining, and then to determine how particular holdings incentivize mining, calculate the same percentage of all mining as the percentage of all holdings: if a state's adoption is x% of all bitcoin holdings, the state has incentivized x% of all mining. Finally, to calculate the emissions caused by adoption, find x% of all bitcoin-mining-related emissions during the period of adoption. This total number is difficult to estimate, depending as it does, on a number of factors including the energy mix and the efficiency of mining hardware. There are further complications to any simple calculation due to the substitution of bitcoin mining for existing electric heating, and mining's role in stabilizing the electrical grid. Those are important, but will be ignored in this paper for the sake of simplicity.

5   Three Emissions Mitigation Strategies

In this section, we examine three strategies for reducing the carbon footprint associated with sovereign adoption of bitcoin: regulation, carbon offsets, and carbon-neutral bitcoin mining, arguing for the advantages of the latter. We then present two strategies for calibrating carbon-neutral bitcoin mining: purchasing only renewably-mined bitcoin and creating or subsidizing renewably-powered hashrate in ongoing fashion, in proportion to state holdings.

5.1 Coase and Pigou

The policymaker's toolkit for managing externalities derives from work by Ronald Coase and Arthur Cecil Pigou [14, 15]. The former argues that with sufficiently clear property rights, information about externalities, and bargaining power, externalities will be properly priced in and efficiency achieved by free exchange. The latter argues that externalities are best managed by a tax that adds the social cost to the price of a good. Coase's observations are inapplicable to bitcoin mining because the externalities of bitcoin mining are diffuse, spanning the entire global population and following generations, who lack the standing or the ability to sue for ill-defined damages and thereby prompt bargaining before creation of the externality. Pigouvian taxes, on the other hand, are feasible, and might be implemented as a tax on miners using carbon-intensive methods of power generation so as to discourage the activity and prompt miners to shift to using renewable sources of energy.

The problem with taxing carbon-intensive mining operations, or for that matter, banning them entirely, is the global, frictionless, nature of the mining market, as well as the difficulty of enforcement. When China banned bitcoin mining, global hashrate dropped by 50%, but recovered within a few months, with a significant proportion still happening in China itself [16]. The mining incentives outlined above do not recognize national borders, and with a ban in one country, mining will simply move elsewhere. Because bitcoin's payment network is expensive to censor and pseudonymous, there is also no viable way to tax bitcoin that has been mined using carbon-intensive energy sources, as one could, for instance, with manufactured goods, by interdicting them at ports and other borders.

Indeed, bitcoin mining represents the limit case of carbon arbitrage. A carbon tax or a ban moves production elsewhere while affecting total mining not in the least. Bitcoin's issuance is an inelastic 900 bitcoin per day, and that remains the same regardless of who is banning mining. So a ban in one location drops global hashrate and makes profitability per unit of computing power rise, thereby spurring additional mining elsewhere.

5.2 Carbon Offsets

A second mitigation strategy is the purchase of carbon offsets. We have already calculated, very roughly, the carbon footprint of El Salvador's adoption, for instance, at 8.5 Kt annually. Carbon offsets are devices that either remove carbon from the atmosphere, e.g., by planting trees, or prevent other greenhouse gas emissions, e.g., burning landfill methane to generate power, or not harvesting a forest that otherwise would have been harvested. Thus, the emissions that result from mining are offset by emissions removals or reductions elsewhere.

Carbon offsets currently range widely in price, and are projected to rise dramatically in value over the next decade, as it is a common means of meeting pledges to achieve "net zero emissions" for firms and organizations, and there simply are not enough offsets available to meet all of those pledges via offsetting. At a price of $10 per ton of CO_2, for quality offsets, El Salvador's annual cost for offsetting its holdings would be $80,500 on their $150,000,000 holding or .054%.

Carbon offsetting may work as intended. But it has two major drawbacks. The first is cost: while .054% annually is minor at present, these prices are expected to rise ten-fold, and potentially more, as the technique becomes more widespread. Second, and more worryingly, it is unclear that carbon offsets actually work as intended. For instance, the Massachusetts Audubon Society pledged not to log 10,000 acres of forest land, and in turn was awarded and then sold ½ million carbon credits, which were then sold to oil and gas companies for $6 million [17]. The oil and gas companies could then claim to have offset the emissions associated with their product, while arguably no actual offsetting was achieved. Had the credits not been sold, the Audubon Society would still not have logged their forest, destroying bird habitat and angering their donors. So while money exchanged hands, no additional carbon was removed from, or prevented from entering, the atmosphere by the purchase of those carbon credits.

This example is by no means unique. Some estimates suggest that over half of offsets induce no net change in carbon emissions [18]. And other analysts estimate that more than 90% of offsets deployed by large corporations are pointless and may even exasperate global climate change [19]. Of course, such abuses may be tamed, but they remain a concern, and if an option is available that simply prevents carbon emissions associated with mining, that would seem more certain a reduction, other things equal, than an option that first emits carbon, then attempts to find carbon savings elsewhere.

5.3   State-Sponsored Carbon-Neutral Bitcoin Mining

The final approach to mitigating mining's externalities is for the state either to engage in mining itself, or to incentivize private companies to mine bitcoin, but on the condition that such production is accomplished with carbon-neutral sources of energy. We will consider two such methods.

First, the state could simply buy bitcoin directly and only from "green" miners, i.e., mining operations that have used renewable energy sources to mine their bitcoin. At scale, this would create a price premium for "green" bitcoin. Equivalently, firms could issue one token for each "greenly-mined" bitcoin, and sell the tokens to nation states and other actors wishing to hold "green bitcoin."

The problems with simply buying "green" bitcoin are many. Some stem from the nature of mining incentives from holding bitcoin reviewed above. Miners are incentivized to make capital investments not by a single purchase, but by the sustenance or increase in bitcoin price due to holdings over time. A long holding period of a given amount of bitcoin incentivizes mining over that entire period, whereas a short holding period of the same amount of bitcoin provides less incentive. To illustrate, some of the earliest coins were mined with a negligible amount of energy, as the network was very small, difficulty was low, and there was almost no competition from other miners. Those coins were "green", if any are. But despite that unimpeachable provenance (they have been held since 2009), those coins have incentivized a great deal of mining. For the non-selling of those coins has been equivalent to the non-selling of any other coins in the period. Simply buying "green" coins ignores this temporal variable entirely: once green always green, regardless of holding period, which is a mistake. Green provenance is not enough.

Along these same lines, more than 90% of all bitcoin have already been mined. Since the "greening" designation is a recent introduction, at most around 10% of coins can be deemed green. To see the absurdity of this limitation, consider that if the entire bitcoin network were to operate on renewable energy in perpetuity, and the network as a whole produced zero carbon, only 10% of bitcoin would be considered green under the provenance accounting. This would be another serious mistake.

Finally, the designation of some bitcoin as green and other bitcoin as non-green threatens the fungibility of bitcoin itself. Since fungibility is a key property of money, and bitcoin's promise and value is tied to its monetary functions, the sacrifice of fungibility threatens the value and identity of bitcoin itself. Essentially, designating some coins as "green," one is creating a new token--green bitcoin--which is a bitcoin fork and only has, at most, 2 million coins. This is a non-started for any parties interested in bitcoin as an emerging asset and monetary network.

There is a better way.

5.4   Our Proposal: Proportional Green Bitcoin Mining

What we propose, rather than the state buying "green" bitcoin, is that the state itself mines with renewable energy, or incentivizes a certain amount of such mining with subsidies or tax breaks, in proportion to their holdings. To review our explanation of miner incentives, recall that sovereign adoption of bitcoin incentivizes the same proportion of all mining as the proportion of all bitcoin that adoption entails. Our proposal is that the state should mine, or sponsor, this very same amount. In other words, our proposal is that, in order to claim their bitcoin adoption is carbon neutral, the state should, in a carbon-neutral way, mine the amount of all mining that their adoption incentivizes, which is—recall Eq. 2—the same percentage of all mining as their percentage of all bitcoin.

$$\% \text{ of all mining one incentivizes} \times \text{all mining for the duration of holding} \\ = \text{amount of mining required} \tag{3}$$

To illustrate, El Salvador's $150m in bitcoin holdings represent 0.00875% of all bitcoin. The total rate of mining is 165 exahash/second. That same percentage of all mining is 14.4375 petahash/s. Our recommendation is that, right now, El Salvador use its geothermal facility to achieve this same hashrate: 14.44 petahash/s. If they do, they will have done the very same amount of mining that their holdings incentivize. They will have done their part to make their portion of bitcoin carbon-neutral: no more, no less.

What would such a mining facility look like? An Antminer S19 Pro operates at 100 TH/s; to achieve 14.44 PH/s would require 144 machines. Each machine draws 3,050W of power, so the whole mining operation would only require 440 KW.

How much would that cost? We might attempt to model an entire facility and its costs. But there is an easier way. First, assume that mining operates on at least a break-even basis. Find the ratio of bitcoin's market cap to miner revenue for a given period. Total annual mining revenue is approximately $16b, of which El Salvador is incentivizing $1.4m. If mining is break-even for El Salvador, then, they should spend $1.4m on mining annually--approximately 1% of their total bitcoin reserve--or $350,000 quarterly, in order to achieve carbon-neutral bitcoin adoption.

Note that mining is, in truth, profitable–those $350,000 quarterly investments in mining will inject new bitcoin into the country's reserves–so they may, on net, actually spend less than our estimate. They will also have to readjust their investment over time, as hashrate and price both fluctuate, and the percentage of all holdings El Salvador holds will also drop slowly with new issuance, in order to make sure they continue to mine all of the bitcoin mining they incentivize.

6 Conclusion

We have surveyed three strategies for ensuring that bitcoin adoption by states is carbon neutral. The first strategy--taxation and regulation--while familiar to policymakers, is uniquely ill-suited to managing bitcoin's externalities. Because bitcoin is fungible, easily-transported, uncensorable, and not easily located, and because its issuance is fixed by the protocol, any attempt to heavily tax or ban carbon-intensive bitcoin mining will simply displace mining to friendlier locales with no effect on the bitcoin network's total emissions.

The second strategy, carbon offsets, fares better, but has at least two drawbacks: a rising cost and difficulty proving "additionality," i.e., that one's offsets are actually reducing carbon emissions.

Finally, the third strategy of the state mining itself, or incentivizing such mining with tax breaks, in a carbon-neutral way, can take two forms. The first is for the state to mine all of its own coins with renewable power, or to purchase its coins from a green miner. We criticized this solution on a number of fronts: it both recommends too much green mining, since if the entire network were green mined in perpetuity, this system would wrongly deem 90% of all bitcoin non-green, and it also recommends too little green mining, since it ignores the temporal variable, the length of one's bitcoin holding period, in calculating mining incentives.

We offer a different formula. We suggest that a state should mine, using carbon-neutral sources of energy, the same percentage of all mining as the percentage of all bitcoin that it owns during the entirety of its interval of ownership. In this way the state will mine all of the incentive that it provides to bitcoin miners by virtue of its holdings. The state will, therefore, be responsible for no additional mining except its own. What this means in practice is that the ratio of a state's holdings to its mining budget for a period is equal to the ratio of bitcoin's market capitalization to bitcoin's entire mining budget for a given period. As of this writing, that ratio is close to 99-to-1 on an annual basis, and higher if we choose a shorter time period. What we conclude, then, is that a relatively small amount of bitcoin mining is sufficient to "green" a large bitcoin holding. Sovereign adoption of bitcoin can, therefore, very easily be made carbon neutral, and consistent with any emissions commitments. All of this is possible without the aid of either carbon offsets or more drastic regulatory measures.

References

1. Raskin, M.: A Global First: Bitcoin as National Currency. Wall Street Journal, 15 June 2021
2. Cambridge Bitcoin Electricity Consumption Index (CBECI). https://ccaf.io/cbeci/index. Accessed 30 Dec 2021
3. Ostroff, C.: El Salvador to issue 'Bitcoin Bond' in 2022. Wall Street Journal, 22 November 2021
4. Bailey, A.M., Warmke, C.: Bitcoin is king. In: Liebowitz, J. (ed.) Cryptocurrency: Concepts, Technology, and Issues, pp. 175–197. Taylor & Francis, London (2023)
5. Bailey, A.M., Rettler, B., Warmke, C.: Resistance Money. Routledge, London (forthcoming)
6. Bailey, A.M., Rettler, B., Warmke, C.: Money without state. Philos. Compass **16**(11), 1–15 (2021)
7. Bailey, A.M., Rettler, B., Warmke, C.: The moral landscape of monetary design. Philos. Compass **16**(11), 1–15 (2021)
8. Russell-Jones, L.: BoE Chief Concerned over El Salvador Use of Bitcoin as Legal Tender. CityAM, 27 November 2021
9. El Salvador Turns into a Major Bitcoin Whale, Ending at 1,400 BTC in 2021 - CoinCu News. https://news.coincu.com/49644-el-salvador-turns-into-a-major-bitcoin-whale-ending-at-1400-btc-in-2021/. Accessed 27 12 2021
10. BitInfoCharts. "Bitcoin Hashrate Chart". https://bitinfocharts.com/comparison/bitcoin-has hrate.html. Accessed 30 Dec 2021
11. CoinShares Bitcoin Mining Network Report December 2019 | Research. https://coinshares. com/research/bitcoin-mining-network-december-2019. Accessed 31 Dec 2021
12. Welcome to the Bitcoin Mining Council. https://bitcoinminingcouncil.com/. Accessed 31 Dec 2021
13. Energy Consumption by Country Chart. https://api.everviz.com/share/yjazijo. Accessed 31 Dec 2021
14. Coase, R.H.: The problem of social cost. J. Law Econ. **3**, 1–44 (1960)
15. Pigou, A.C.: The Economics of Welfare. Macmillan, London (1920)
16. China Is Mining Bitcoin Underground: Report | Nasdaq. https://www.nasdaq.com/articles/china-is-mining-bitcoin-underground%3A-report. Accessed 31 Dec 2021
17. Song, L., Temple, J.: A nonprofit promised to preserve wildlife. In: Then it Made Millions Claiming it Could Cut Down Trees. MIT Technology Review, 10 May 2021
18. Calel, R., Colmer, J., Dechezleprêtre, A., Glachant, M.: Do Carbon Offsets Offset Carbon? CESifo Working Papers (2021)
19. Greenfield, P.: Revealed: More Than 90% of Rainforest Carbon Offsets by Biggest Certifier are Worthless, Analysis Shows. The Guardian, 18 January 2023

Soundness of Stablecoins

Yusuke Ikeno[✉], James Angel, and Sankalp Panigrahi

Georgetown University, Washington, D.C., USA
{yi106,angelj,sp1300}@georgetown.edu

Abstract. Stablecoin regulation is an important topic in crypto assets. As some assumed there were no regulations for crypto assets before, it can be painful for the crypto industry to be compliant with financial regulations. Traditional finance (tradfi) has experienced numerous crises over the centuries, and thus is strictly regulated. Regulators, having seen the impact of new financial technologies in the recent financial crisis, should not and cannot neglect the impact of new financial products, whether they are tradfi or defi. We can learn from history to find appropriate regulatory standards. In particular, we discuss monitoring items which can show the soundness of stablecoins. Regulators should require regular disclosure of assets backing stablecoins, sufficient overcollateralization, appropriate asset quality requirements to assure safety and liquidity, auditing for operational risk, AML/KYC compliance, and a dispute resolution process.

Keywords: Stablecoins · soundness · regulatory monitoring · smart contracts

1 Introduction

Stablecoins are those digital assets whose values are intended to peg to some assets. Many stablecoins are pegged to a sovereign, or "fiat" currency, such as the US dollar. They are usually issued on a public blockchain such as Ethereum and serve as substitutes for fiat currencies on crypto assets markets.

As the size of crypto markets has exploded in recent years, there are many concerns over their contribution to financial instability. Since there appeared to be no explicit regulations in this area, "buyer beware" is implicitly understood in the crypto assets market. However, the growing size of stablecoins make regulators worry about the economic impact of potential failures of stablecoins. While regulation is anathema to some in the crypto sphere, it is inevitable that a mature crypto industry must be regulated. It is time to consider appropriate rules for the industry.

The epicenter of the 2008++ global financial crisis involved complicated innovations including securitized products and derivatives. The crisis highlighted many problems and stricter regulations were imposed to deal with them. It is important to understand there are good reasons for financial regulations, which are found in every country on the planet. People want to make sure that their money is safe, that money won't be stolen from their wallets, that they won't be sold fraudulent assets, that the economy won't collapse, and that the economy has the funds needed to grow.

© International Financial Cryptography Association 2023
S. Matsuo et al. (Eds.): FC 2022 Workshops, LNCS 13412, pp. 66–73, 2023.
https://doi.org/10.1007/978-3-031-32415-4_5

Since there are many types of crypto assets and services, it is helpful to concentrate on some specific cases. Stablecoins pegged to a fiat currency are of interest to regulators for several reasons. First, as the entry point to crypto markets for many users, they may provide a natural place to apply anti-money laundering (AML) and know-your-customer (KYC) rules. Second, their resemblance to bank deposit accounts and money market mutual funds (MMMFs) arouses regulator interest in their soundness and contribution to systemic risk. Finally, their link to fiat currencies brings up concerns about monetary policy and foreign exchange rates. The situation is further complicated by the rapid evolution of crypto markets, making it difficult for regulators to keep up. In this short paper, we discuss how to demonstrate the soundness of a stablecoin and investigate how technology could potentially contribute to it.

2 Monitoring

2.1 Background

There are many methodologies for stabilization and stablecoins are often classified by their stabilization [3, 10]. Some are backed by traditional assets and others are backed by crypto assets. There are also those stablecoins stabilized algorithmically.

Some stablecoins like USDT(Tether) and USDC(USD Coin) offer redemption into US dollars. Other stablecoins (e.g. DAI) do not provide a direct redemption-to-fiat method, but users use the coins for trading or buying items on some markets. It is reasonable to assume that a stablecoin can offer redemption with cash or some methods if the stablecoin is successfully pegged to a fiat currency. For this point, users should know whether they can redeem their coins and regulators would like to examine their solvency.

Redeemable-to-fiat stablecoins are similar to bank deposits. Customers deposit money into banks, and banks promise to pay cash to their customers upon demand, hence the name "demand deposits." These deposits are debt liabilities in which banks owe money to depositors. Banks construct assets through lending and investment. From this perspective, it would seem reasonable to force stablecoins to comply with at least some banking-style regulations [11].

MMMFs, or money market mutual funds, are mutual funds that seek to maintain a stable net asset value (NAV) just like stablecoins. Users can redeem their shares at the NAV upon demand, and thus MMMFs resemble banks. However, they are technically investment companies and thus are regulated very differently from banks in the United States. Regulators are considering changes to MMMF regulation since they faced liquidity issues during the pandemic. We can learn many things from this experience [8].

One regulatory method for demonstrating soundness is to require regulated entities to report detailed information relevant to soundness to regulators and the public. This information includes information about the quantity and quality of both assets and liabilities. For example, MMMFs in the US are required to publicly disclose detailed lists of all their assets on a monthly basis[1]. Furthermore, regulators are keenly interested in

---

[1] https://www.law.cornell.edu/cfr/text/17/270.2a-7.

whether regulated entities have policies and procedures in place to assure regulatory compliance with soundness and other regulations including customer protection.

Regulators also find innovation is useful to apply technology to their business. The Bank for International Settlements (BIS) published a report which discussed "embedded supervision" [4]. It is usually a burden for financial institutions to prepare for regulatory reports. Since stablecoins or DLT based financial services operate on smart contracts, it would be helpful to include some modules to report their soundness automatically.

Our analysis is based on typical stablecoins pegged to a fiat currency and redeemable into that fiat currency.

2.2   Risk Based Perspectives

Financial institutions are exposed to credit risk, market risk and operational risk[2]. It is reasonable to evaluate these risks for stablecoins as they also serve a financial service. The primary risk is that the market value of the assets will be insufficient to redeem all of the stablecoins. There may be some credit risk as well, in assets such as commercial paper, but for the moment we assume this is small, and the issuer is not making commercial loans in which credit risk is the major factor. As for operational risk, it is widely discussed with respect to AML/KYC process. We do have to pay attention to operational resilience since ordinary users herd into and out of crypto assets in a panic. The following sections discuss these in more detail.

3   Proof of Redeemability

3.1   Basic Idea

Issuers have to prove they have enough assets to cover their liabilities. Since stablecoins peg their value to a fiat currency, the total value of liability is fixed. However, assets can and do fluctuate in value. The assets usually include some financial products like Treasury bills which are stable but exposed to market fluctuations. If issuers pay holders in cash, they have to monetize the assets to create cash.

The frequency of proof is up to stakeholders and regulators. Some may request real time reporting but others may do only on a daily basis. There exist pros and cons for each frequency.

- Real-time: As market conditions can change abruptly, real-time proof can reassure stakeholders as to the soundness of a particular stablecoin. This can also prevent runs on the stablecoin in which many holders demand redemption simultaneously. However, real-time can be difficult to implement as it requires real-time valuation of assets whose values may not be transparent. Third party auditing or validation may be impossible or expensive to obtain.
- Daily basis (as MMMFs do): Most market instruments have a closing or end-of-day price, which is easily observed or calculated. It is reasonable to evaluate assets based on these prices.

---

[2] https://www.bankofengland.co.uk/knowledgebank/what-risks-do-banks-take.

- Monthly or fiscal basis: it takes some time to create exact reporting and there could be relatively illiquid assets so that scrutiny might be required.

Practically speaking, issuers use both data about their inventory of assets and market data on values to determine total asset value. After that, they can publish their solvency report, which should convince stakeholders, assuming the stakeholders believe in the credibility of the report. Credibility can be enhanced by having independent auditing firms periodically verify the existence and value of assets.

Redeemability of a stablecoin relies on the underlying balance of assets held in the stablecoin's reserve. Confidence in the stablecoin requires not only a belief that the assets at the moment are greater than liabilities, but also a belief that they will continue to do so in the future, even in the case of foreseeable adverse events. In this regard, the underlying assets serve as collateral for their respective token's value. In an ideal scenario, a particular token would be at least 100% collateralized. In the event of a run on the digital currency, the stablecoin issuer would be able to redeem each holders' token for its respective value in the underlying asset. However, it is not clear that all stablecoins are 100% collateralized, suggesting that some holders may not be able to redeem their tokens at face value.

The underlying value of a token relies on the belief that it can be redeemed for some monetary value, whether that be a fiat currency, commodity, or some other monetary asset. If a stablecoin holder loses faith in the redeemability of a token, the token no longer holds value in that users' mind and the token's value may fall.

3.2 Valuation

We should estimate asset values conservatively because it is sometimes difficult to sell assets at their estimated values in the market, especially during times of market stress when a run is most likely. In other words, an asset whose valuation is one US dollar in a market cannot always be turned into one US dollar in cash. It is reasonable to apply a haircut to valuations as below:

$$\text{Valuation of asset per unit} = (1 - \text{haircut}) * \text{market price per unit}$$

The haircut of each asset is based on its risk. "Expected shortfall" or "Value at Risk" are calculations that can inform the size of the haircut.

It is also difficult to estimate how much we should set for the haircut. Fortunately, there are tables for eligible assets by central banks[3], which repo market or banks refer to. Under the assumption of backed assets, we can refer to those tables as a standard.

Even though we assume highly liquid assets, there remain concerns as to how liquid they are [2]. Information vendors supply quoted prices, but it is not always possible to trade at those prices. Obtaining actionable quotes from potential trade counterparties might be preferable, but there will always be concerns as to the quality of the quotes. If we extend our discussions to more general assets such as securities, commodities and crypto assets, we need to construct more resilient risk evaluation.

---

[3] https://www.frbdiscountwindow.org/Home/Pages/Collateral/Discount%20Window%20Marg
ins%20and%20Collateral%20Guidelines.

3.3 Assuring Ability to Deliver

Users generally assume conservative situations in which the assets are properly invested, and that the assets are more than enough to redeem all of the issued tokens. However, reality can be more tragic. The history of banking is one of crises and runs on banks. Depending on the nature of a particular stablecoin, we can expect crises and runs if and when users lose confidence in that stablecoin. The history of tradfi is that a run on one financial institution often leads to contagion and runs on other financial institutions.

Tradfi regulation seeks to reduce the likelihood of a bank run and the associated contagion through a variety of means. These include capital requirements stringent enough that a bank can withstand all reasonably foreseeable losses without jeopardizing its ability to honor customer withdrawals. In the defi space, what can restore user confidence when there are sudden market movements? Or, who can absorb those losses which are more than expected?

Several credit enhancements are possible. Capital requirements are only one option. With stablecoins, this effectively means an overcollateralization of the tokens that are issued. Alternatively, the parent company of the issuer could issue its own guarantees and thus support confidence in the stablecoin. MMMF issuers have frequently stepped in to purchase impaired assets from their funds in order to maintain a stable NAV. Letters of credit or other guarantees from third parties are another possibility. In tradfi, banks enjoy explicit deposit insurance, along with central bank credit facilities designed to reduce liquidity pressures on banks facing large withdrawals. However, any type of support, whether from a government, central bank, or other guarantor, will come with a regulatory price. The backed entity must now submit to demands for information as well as documented and enforced policies and procedures designed to produce safe and sound operations.

Bank regulators tend to rely upon capital requirements. On the other hand, MMMF regulators tend to rely upon asset quality requirements designed to ensure that MMMFs only hold very high quality liquid assets that will mature into cash in a matter of days. In this way, MMMFs are highly unlikely to suffer serious credit losses or to lack the cash needed for redemptions.

Another big issue is the issue of resolution of the failure of an institution. Who pays? Again, a variety of methods are available. One approach is to rely on a guarantee from other players who agreed to do so (e.g. creditors who have agreed to "bail in" provisions in their debt instruments that turn their debt into equity under certain conditions). Another is to assess the loss to the depositors/token holders, as occurs with mutual funds.

4   Anti-Money Laundering (AML) and Know Your Customer (KYC)

4.1   Basic Idea

One of the primary goals of financial regulators is to prevent bad actors from using the financial system and to enlist financial services entities in law enforcement. Entities that facilitate illegal players can easily become corrupt and prone to failure, both from fraud by illegal customers as well as embezzlement by employees. The Financial Action Task

Force (FATF) is a global body that leads these regulations and has published several reports [6]. Since many view anonymity as one of the key merits of cryptos, there is a conflict between regulators and users who view any cooperation with governments as a betrayal of the spirit of crypto freedom.

Traceability is one of the features of digital assets. We can trace the address on a blockchain for trades. However, blockchains generally don't include the legal identity of the parties to a trade. It is necessary to link addresses in the crypto spaces with legal identity in order to comply with regulatory requirements.

Fortunately, most users of cryptos access them through software wallets and/or service providers. Regulators can exert pressure on service providers and wallet services to bring them into compliance with appropriate regulations. Users of those services will have to comply with wallet and service provider requests for AML/KYC information.

4.2 Listing Approach

One approach to AML/KYC compliance uses lists of customers. Customers with confirmed identities can be placed on "positive lists", which means the customers on the list are eligible to engage in transactions. Such information is useful not only for regulatory enforcement, but also for good business purposes. Knowing the customer allows merchants to make better credit decisions, and to reach out for resolution in case of any disputes. If they do not know their customers, they have no options to reach out.

It is much more difficult to create "negative lists" of people with whom service providers should not trade. Bad guys generally don't label themselves as bad guys. In traditional finance, regulators sometimes provide lists of prohibited individuals, while additional negative lists may be strictly confidential[4].

The use of lists is burdensome. It creates problems accessing and maintaining such lists, as well as operational problems when good people are incorrectly placed on such lists. Alternatively, being listed in the positive lists can be a benefit for those cooperative users. On the other hand, there is a need to protect personal privacy at the appropriate level.

5 Operational Resilience

5.1 Basic Idea

All financial applications, both traditional and crypto, are vulnerable to operational risks including hacking, fraud, and operational mistakes. If a bug in a defi app sends assets to the wrong address, there is generally no recourse. The crypto world is one of buyer beware. In order for the crypto world to mature, it has to evolve mechanisms for assuring users that operational risks are addressed as well as mechanisms for resolving disputes. The tradfi world relies upon clear assignments of risk to traditional players, regulations requiring risk to be addressed at the board level, and rigorous inspections by regulators, along with well established dispute resolution mechanisms. Defi, on the other hand, often pretends there are no intermediaries other than the code itself.

---

[4] For example, see https://www.treasury.gov/ofac/downloads/sdnlist.txt.

5.2 Auditing and Dispute Resolution

Theoretically, the transparency of the open source code used in crypto guarantees that any problems will be quickly highlighted and fixed. However, the well known hacks of the DAO and other apps show that this does not always happen quickly enough to prevent serious problems. Who really is checking the code? There is a free rider problem in which everyone assumes that somebody else has determined that there are no problems. Such reliance on others to find problems was one of the factors that contributed to the 2008++ financial crisis.

One approach would be for stablecoin operators to hire auditors to check the code and operational processes, both at the development stage and regularly in operation. The operational auditors could give standardized certificates to support the issuers' confidence. These would be in addition to the usual accounting auditors who would verify the existence and valuation of assets.

In order to establish and maintain consumer confidence, there needs to be a fair and efficient dispute resolution process to deal with the inevitable bugs and operational glitches. While some claim there are no intermediaries in defi, in practice there are business "owners", developers, and administrators who have some power to intervene if required.

6 Conclusion

We can learn from the experience of traditional finance what many of the potential problems are with stablecoins, along with their solutions. A loss of confidence in the ability of a stablecoin to redeem its liabilities can cause a run on the stablecoin. Contagion can also cause a run on other financial institutions, both tradfi and defi. Regulators can assure the soundness of stablecoins by requiring regular disclosure of the assets backing stablecoins, sufficient overcollateralization, appropriate asset quality requirements, auditing for operational risk as well as asset verification, AML/KYC compliance, and a dispute resolution process.

References

1. Angel, J.J. Re: Docket # FSOC-2012-0003 (2013). https://www.sec.gov/comments/mms-response/mmsresponse-27.pdf
2. Angel, J.J. Re: money market fund reform; Amendments to Form PF (2013). https://www.sec.gov/comments/s7-03-13/s70313-228.pdf
3. Ayten, K., et al.: Reducing the volatility of cryptocurrencies – a survey of stablecoins. eprint arXiv:2103.01340 (2021)
4. BIS, Embedded supervision: how to build regulation into blockchain finance (2019). https://www.bis.org/publ/work811.pdf
5. BIS and IOSCO, Application of the Principles for Financial Market Infrastructures to stablecoin arrangements (2021). https://www.bis.org/cpmi/publ/d198.pdf
6. FATF, Updated Guidance for a Risk-Based Approach to Virtual Assets and Virtual Asset Service Providers (2021). https://www.fatf-gafi.org/publications/fatfrecommendations/documents/guidance-rba-virtual-assets-2021.html

7. FSB, Regulation, Supervision and Oversight of "Global Stablecoin" Arrangements (2021). https://www.fsb.org/wp-content/uploads/P071021.pdf
8. FSB, Policy Proposals to Enhance Money Market Fund Resilience (2021). https://www.fsb.org/wp-content/uploads/P111021-2.pdf
9. IMF, Global Financial Stability Report (2021). https://www.imf.org/en/Publications/GFSR/Issues/2021/10/12/global-financial-stability-report-october-2021
10. Klages-Mundt, A., et al.: Stablecoins 2.0: economic foundations and risk-based models. In: Proceedings of the 2nd ACM Conference on Advances in Financial Technologies, pp. 59–79 (2020). https://doi.org/10.1145/3419614.3423261
11. The President's Working Group on Financial Markets, et al.: Reports on Stablecoin (2021). https://home.treasury.gov/system/files/136/StableCoinReport_Nov1_508.pdf

Estimating (Miner) Extractable Value is Hard, Let's Go Shopping!

Aljosha Judmayer[2]([✉]), Nicholas Stifter[1], Philipp Schindler[1],
and Edgar Weippl[2]

[1] SBA Research, Vienna, Austria
{nstifter,pschindler}@sba-research.org
[2] University of Vienna, Vienna, Austria
{aljosha.judmayer,edgar.weippl}@univie.ac.at

Abstract. The term *miner extractable value* (MEV) has been coined to describe the value which can be extracted by a miner, e.g., from manipulating the order of transactions within a given timeframe. MEV has been deemed an important factor to assess the overall economic stability of a cryptocurrency. This stability also influences the economically rational choice of the security parameter k, by which a merchant defines the number of required confirmation blocks in cryptocurrencies based on Nakamoto consensus. Unfortunately, although being actively discussed within the cryptocurrency community, no exact definition of MEV was given when the term was originally introduced. In this paper, we outline the difficulties in defining different forms of extractable value, informally used throughout the community. We show that there is no globally unique MEV/EV which can readily be determined, and that a narrow definition of MEV fails to capture the extractable value of other actors like *users*, or the probabilistic nature of permissionless cryptocurrencies. We describe an approach to estimate the *minimum* extractable value that would incentivize actors to act maliciously and thus can potentially lead to consensus instability. We further highlight why it is hard, or even impossible, to precisely determine the extractable value of other participants, considering the uncertainties in real world systems. Finally, we outline a peculiar yet straightforward technique for choosing the individual security parameter k, which can act as a workaround to transfer the risk of an insufficiently chosen k to another merchant.

Keywords: Miner Extractable Value · Extractable Value · Expected Extractable Value · Cryptocurrencies · Game Theory

1 Introduction

The term *miner extractable value* was first introduced by Daian et al. [8] to refer to the value which can be extracted by a miner from manipulating the order of transactions within the blocks the respective miner creates. This ability

© International Financial Cryptography Association 2023
S. Matsuo et al. (Eds.): FC 2022 Workshops, LNCS 13412, pp. 74–92, 2023.
https://doi.org/10.1007/978-3-031-32415-4_6

can be used for *front running* attacks [9], which can lead to guaranteed profits through token arbitrage, or other related types of attacks like *back-running* and combinations thereof [28]. Such attacks, which exploit the ability of miners to arbitrarily order transactions within their blocks, are feasible and currently observed in practice [33,35–37]. Thus, order fairness evidently poses an issue for prevalent permissionless PoW cryptocurrencies [21]. When the stakes are sufficiently high, MEV can even incentivize blockchain forks and thereby also have consequences not only on transactions in future blocks, but also for the underlying *consensus-layer security*, as also noted by Daian et al. [8] and Zhou et al. [35]. Related attacks aimed in this direction are *undercutting attacks* [7], *time-bandit attacks* [8], or more broadly: Attacks involving economic incentives in general, such as any form of *bribing attack* [4,5,23,24], which have been summarized under the term *algorithmic incentive manipulation* [19].

Given all these attacks and their far-reaching consequences, MEV undoubtedly is an essential concept when reasoning about economic stability aspects and cryptocurrency security under economical considerations. Recently, a related term called *blockchain extractable value* [28] (BEV) was introduced. BEV refers to the value extractable by different forms of front running attacks which are not necessarily performed by miners, but *users*. Unfortunately, in the case of MEV as well as in the case of BEV, no exact definition was given by the authors when the term was originally introduced[1].

As the concept of MEV/BEV is tied to the economic incentives of whether or not to fork a certain block/chain [35], this question also relates to economic considerations regarding the choice of the personal security parameter k of merchants. An accurate estimation of the overall MEV/BEV value, would allow to adapt and increase k accordingly in periods of high overall MEV/BEV. The choice of the security parameter k, which determines the number of required confirmation blocks until a payment can safely be considered confirmed, has been studied in a variety of works. Rosenfeld [29] showed that, although waiting for more confirmations exponentially decreases the probability of successful attacks, no amount of confirmations will reduce the success rate of attacks to 0 in the probabilistic security model of PoW, and that there is nothing special about the often-cited figure of $k = 6$ confirmations. Sompolinsky and Zohar [31] defined different acceptance policies with different error probabilities and use-cases. According to [31] an acceptance policy that is resilient to a double spend anywhere in the chain cannot rely on a static parameter k, but has to be logarithmic in the chain's current length. Garay, Kiayias and Leonardos [13] defined the security parameter k, after which a transaction can be considered part of the *common prefix*, as a function of the security parameter of the hash function (κ), the typical number of consecutive rounds for which a statement would hold, and the probability of at least one honest party finding a valid PoW in a round. In spite of these well-founded theoretical results under honest majority assumptions, in practice there is no global and agreed-upon security parameter

---

[1] Concurrent work [2,26], also attempts to initially define different forms of *extractable value*. For a comparision we refer to the extended version of this paper on eprint.

k for prevalent PoW cryptocurrencies. Instead merchants choose their individual k on a best-practice basis, taking their individual economical risk into account. Since the likelihood of potential forks increases when sufficiently large extraction opportunities for miners arise, the question on how to define and estimate the extractable value of a block (or a chain) also relates to the choice of the personal security parameter k. This has also been studied in the context of bribing, especially in the *whale attack* [23], where large fees are offered on competing chains, as well as in context of incentives for miners to fork high value blocks when the majority for the block reward comes in form of transaction fees [7,34].

Contribution: In this paper we *describe different forms of extractable value* and how they relate to each other. Furthermore, we outline a series of observations which highlight the *difficulties in defining these different forms of extractable value* and why a generic and thorough definition of it (and thus its precise calculation) is *impossible for permissionless cryptocurrencies* without assuming bounds regarding all available resources (e.g., other cryptocurrencies) that are, or could be of relevance for economically rational players. We also describe a way to estimate the minimum extractable value, measured in multiples of normalized block rewards of a reference resource, to incentivize adversarial behaviour of participants which can lead to consensus instability[2]. In the end, we propose a peculiar yet straightforward technique for choosing the personal security parameters k regardless of extractable value opportunities.

2   Economic Rationality and Extractable Value

Rationality depends on the criteria which should be optimized. This could be reward in terms of cryptocurrency units in some PoW cryptocurrency, or a more abstract criteria such as the overall robustness of the cryptocurrency ecosystem. We start out with a simplified definition of *economic rationality* to model the preferences of *actors*, or *parties*[3] within the system. Hereby, actors are divided into two disjoint sets: *miners* ($\mathcal{M}$) and *users* ($\mathcal{U}$), where $\mathcal{M} \cup \mathcal{U} = \mathcal{P}$. Compared to miners, users do not having any direct voting power in the system (e.g., hashrate). Whenever, we refer to rational within this work, we refer to the definition of *economically rational in $\mathcal{R}$*:

Definition 1 (Economically rational in $\mathcal{R}$). *An actor (i) is **economically rational**, with respect to a finite non-empty set of resources $\mathcal{R}_i := \{R_0, R_1, \dots\}$, when it is his single aim to maximize his profits measured in these resources. To also map the individual preferences of an actor regarding this set of resources, the quantities of all resources from that actor are converted into **value units**. Therefore, from the perspective of an actor i each resource R is a tuple $\langle r, e \rangle$ consisting of: The quantity r the actor i holds in the respective resource; and*

---

[2] All source code and artefacts can be found on GitHub https://github.com/kernoelpanic/estimatingMEVishard_artefacts.

[3] Also the term *players* is commonly used to refer to the involved parties.

the individual exchange rate e for the conversion in value units which reflect the individual preference of that actor.

A quantity of a certain resource $\langle r, e \rangle$, which is optimized by a rational actor (indexed by i), is denoted as $f_i(r, e)$. This function returns the *value units*, also referred to as *funds*, actor i has in r, calculated using his individual exchange rate e for r. If the exchange rates are the same for every party, or clear from the context, they can also be omitted. For practical purposes and to aid comparability, we will use *normalized block rewards* of a reference resource (e.g., Bitcoin block rewards including average fees) as *value unit* in which all funds are denoted. Therefore, all exchange rates of other resources convert their respective quantities into normalized block rewards of the reference resource.

In other words, value units can also be thought of as fiat currency, which in turn can be received in exchange for cryptocurrency units. In this paper, value units are measured in multiples of the block reward of a reference cryptocurrency, which is the first resource in $\mathcal{R}_i$ (i.e., R_0). A resource can be anything of value to an actor e.g., a cryptocurrency, a token within a cryptocurrency, or a fiat currency. If not stated differently, all parties care about the same set of resources and the exchange rate for each resource is globally defined (e.g., by an exchange service) and thus the same for every actor. This means, for the simplest case where all parties only care about one resource and have the same global exchange rate (e_{global}), we have: $\forall i \in \mathcal{P} (|\mathcal{R}_i| = 1 \wedge e \in R_0 \wedge e = e_{global})$, where the valuation of an actor i is given by $f_i(r, e_{global})$, or abbreviated just $f_i(r)$. We start our evaluation with such a scenario.

Summing up: By our definition of economic rationality actors want to maximize their overall funds (valuation) from all their resources, which are measured in value units, i.e., $f_i(\mathcal{R}_i) = \sum_{\langle r_j, e_j \rangle \in \mathcal{R}} f_i(r_j, e_j)$.

2.1 Miner Extractable Value

To calculate the gain or profit an actor has made within a chain of blocks c, with their sequence of transactions τ, it is essential to estimate the costs as well as the extractable value for the respective actor. This has been done in previous works [8,28] mostly by analyzing past Ethereum blocks with their associated transactions, while looking for profitable trades on the blockchain in retrospect. The gathered data was then also used when analyzing how to automatically detect and exploit such trading situations [35,37]. In this context, the term *miner extractable value* (first introduced by Daian et al. [8]) was informally used to describe the value which can be extracted by a miner by including a certain transaction in terms of fees, or guaranteed profits through token arbitrage. We now provide a definition within the context of our model and in accordance to the literature. Therefore, we first focus on a scenario where we assume that there is only one resource, as well as one exchange rate, which is the same for every actor.

Definition 2 (Miner Extractable Value MEV$_i(c)$). *The miner-extractable value* MEV$_i(c)$, *describes the total value (denominated in value units), transferred to a **miner** i from a sequence of transactions τ, included and thus mined in the respective chain of blocks c, which is part of the main chain.*

This definition focuses on identifying the extractable value in retrospect and is thus suited for empirically analyzing the MEV of historic blocks. We extend this to a more forward looking definition later in Sect. 2.3, where we also take the probabilistic nature of most cryptocurrencies into account.

Regardless of the time when the MEV is determined, there are couple of characteristics all types of MEV have in common. First, the total extractable value depends on the type of optimization the miner i is performing. If transactions are only ordered by fee, the miner extractable value can be expressed as the "usual" mining reward from fees and block rewards i.e., MEV$_i(c)$:= FEE(c) + BLOCKREWARD(c). If there is a value gain from received transactions, or rewards from performed token arbitrage and order optimizations, then the respective income opportunities, e.g., income from received transactions and attacks, have to be taken into account as well. In other words, a general definition of MEV describes the value (i.e., the reward) which can be extracted by a miner, extended by additional revenue opportunities originating from the capabilities to interact with the system the miner is tasked to validate. This leads to the question: What *possibilities* to extract value are available to miners?

This question already outlines why the concrete amount of MEV is difficult to generalize for all miners, as it can be different for every individual miner. The MEV of a given miner i depends on the type of value extraction optimization the respective miner is capable and willing to perform. Hereby, the possibilities reach from simple fee optimization techniques, like selecting the transactions which provide the highest fees, over order optimization (for example, attempting to maximize gas consumption in smart contracts[4]), to participating in sophisticated front running attacks. Moreover the MEV is affected by the information available to the miner (e.g., her view of the transaction pool). Therefore, we can make the following observation:

Observeration 1. The miner extractable value (MEV) is different for every miner depending on the optimization techniques the miner is capable and willing to perform, as well as other transactions which directly affect her individual revenue during the respective period (e.g., received funds).

In other words, there may exist a miner m_1 that has a higher MEV than a miner m_2 because he has received a large incoming payment transaction in the same sequence of transactions $\tau \in c$, i.e., MEV$_{m_1}(c) >$ MEV$_{m_2}(c)$. Therefore, miner m_2 may be more willing to participate in an attack which changes the past blocks c than the miner m_1.

---

[4] Note that, a naive algorithm for finding the optimal ordering of all transactions is factorial in the number of transactions, which is computationally infeasible even for most current Ethereum blocks which have more than 200 transactions.

2.2   Extractable Value

Since not all attacks (or more generally, ways to maximize profit) necessarily require the capabilities of a miner, the given definition of MEV does not capture these. Front running attacks for example, can be performed by actors which do not necessarily have to be miners themselves, but can be *users* instead. From their perspective the definition of MEV does not apply, as they are not capable of mining a block on their own (as they have zero hashrate).

Observeration 2. The definition of MEV is focused on *miners* and does not capture opportunities for *users* to gain (more) value units from a certain sequence of transactions τ than from another sequence of transactions τ'.

In contrast to MEV, *blockchain extractable value* (BEV) [28], was previously described in a broader context and thus also refers to the value extractable by different forms of front running attacks which are not necessarily performed by miners. As recent analysis [8, 28, 33, 35, 37] show, front running is performed by bots, which bid for an early slot in a block by raising the miner extractable transaction fee[5]. However, these earlier discussions regarding BEV [28] omit a precise definition, which we provide in the general form of *extractable value* (EV_i), for the amount that is transferred to any actor i from a given blockchain c, or sequence of transactions τ.

Definition 3 (Extractable Value $EV_i(\cdot)$). *The extractable value $EV_i(\cdot)$, describes the total value, which is transferred to actor i from a transaction, or sequence of transactions τ, if it is included and thus mined in the respective chain of blocks c, which is part of the main chain.*

Using this definition of extractable value, the miner extractable value can also be defined as $EV_i(c)$ of any miner $i \in \mathcal{M}$. As with miner extractable value, the extractable value of different actors i and j for the same chain of blocks c can also be different. Again $EV_i(c)$ and $EV_j(c)$ depend on whether they have received, or sent, transactions within this chain or not.

   In other words, Observation 2 shows that MEV is just a way to extract value which can be executed by a subset of actors i.e., miners. Since we also know from Observation 1 that there is no globally unique MEV, which is the same for all miners, the same argument can also be extended to EV. So there also cannot be a globally unique EV, that is the same for all actors. The question is if the EV can be meaningfully estimated, or bounded? Assume we have two parties i and j, where j wants to estimate the extractable value of i for a certain chain c. If j wants to estimate $EV_i(c)$, then this means j has to attribute all transactions generating value for i in c correctly. If the respective actor i pseudonymously performs and receives transactions under various different addresses (or in other privacy preserving ways like shielded transactions in Zcash [15, 20]), this hampers the correct estimation of $EV_i(c)$ for any third party j which does not know which transactions belong to a certain actor.

---

[5] In Ethereum the extractable fee is a combination of `gasPrice` multiplied by `gasUsed`.

Observeration 3. If there are transactions in c that are not uniquely attributable to other parties from the perspective of actor j, then the upper bound of the $\mathrm{EV}_i(c)$ for a certain actor i is the total value transferred by those non-attributable transactions.

This means, for known finite chains of blocks in certain cryptocurrencies where the overall value that has been transferred is observable, the extractable value can be upper-bounded in retrospect as soon as the respective chain is known.

Note that, even if all transactions can be correctly attributed to an actor, the exact effect of an outgoing transaction on the EV in a smart contract capable cryptocurrency is still difficult to measure. Generally, all outgoing transactions reduce the EV, as the miner loses funds. Although, if the outgoing transaction is a guaranteed profit token arbitrage, or other profitable type of front running, the EV might very well increase. We omit the details of analyzing the EV of a particular transaction in a smart contract capable cryptocurrency and refer to a strain of research dealing with this topic [8,33,35–37].

2.3 Expected Extractable Value

So far we have only considered the extractable value of past blocks in retrospect ($\mathrm{MEV}_i(c)$), or blocks and transactions under the assumption that they eventually will make it into the main chain ($\mathrm{EV}_i(c)$, or $\mathrm{EV}_i(\tau)$). Hereby, we did not account for the probability with which the estimated value can be realized. As mining in prevalent cryptocurrencies is a stochastic process, getting a certain chain accepted into the common-prefix depends on several factors - one of which being the hashrate that supports a given chain[6]. Therefore, it is more appropriate to refer to the *expected extractable value* (EEV) when comparing potential/future rewards of mining strategies, pending blocks, or forks.

Definition 4 (Expected Extractable Value $\mathrm{EEV}_i(\cdot)$). *The expected extractable value $\mathrm{EEV}_i(\cdot)$, describes the total value in value units, which is transferred to actor i on expectation using a certain strategy which produces a transaction, sequence of transactions (τ), or blocks (c) that later become part of the main chain with some probability.*

To maximize the EEV, actors will pick an according strategy. Hereby, the probability space depends on the concrete model under which a given strategy is analyzed.

Observation 4. In permissionless PoW cryptocurrencies, the number of participants $|\mathcal{P}|$ is theoretically unbounded, as miners can join and leave at any time. Thus sample space of possible events is theoretically unbounded as well.

Therefore, certain assumptions e.g., regarding the available resources of (potential) players are required, to bound their influence (i.e., action space) on a given cryptocurrency.

---

[6] Another one being propagation times, but we will ignore that for now.

We now describe a simple idealized system model and strategy and use it as a reference to compare deviating strategies and changes in the model against this setting. We therefore, assume that there is only one resource of interest and no further actors join the cryptocurrency.

Definition 5 (The strategy Honest). *We define the strategy* HONEST *for miners in a cryptocurrency R, as the process of always extending the currently known longest (heaviest) chain and immediately publishing and forwarding every found block and transaction.*

If every miner plays HONEST and has a constant hashrate, then this results in an infinitely repeated game, in which every miner receives exactly the reward that is proportional to his hashrate. Therefore, HONEST satisfies *ideal chain quality* [12], as the percentage of blocks in the blockchain of every actor is exactly proportional to their individual hashing power[7]. We assume that this is the desired ideal state in which the system should be and thus the goal of the mechanism design. Moreover, it is more-or-less the empirically observed behavior of miners as serious deviations are rarely observed in mainstream cryptocurrencies[8].

Assume a miner i that does not receive or send any transactions (apart from collecting rewards from mined blocks), and that the extractable value is given in normalized block rewards (including fees) as a value unit. Then if everybody plays HONEST, the strategy HONEST for a sequence of n blocks, would have the EEV depicted in Eq. 1. The strategy would be profitable if the mining costs ($costs_{mining}$) for mining the respective number of blocks is lower than the EEV. This also assumes that the hashrate (p_i) of actor i is common knowledge and static for the duration of the evaluation.

$$\mathrm{EEV}_i\left(R, \mathrm{HONEST}, n\right) := n \cdot p_i \tag{1}$$

$$\rho_i := \mathrm{EEV}_i\left(R, \mathrm{HONEST}\right) - costs_{mining} \cdot n \tag{2}$$

If the respective actor i also performs and receives transactions, and all of them are uniquely attributable to i, then expected extractable value has to be extended by the extractable value from those transactions. As we are in a scenario where all actors act HONEST, no malicious forks[9] will happen.

Apart from such simple toy examples, estimating the expected extractable value becomes more involved, as soon as different attacks and their probabilities and consequences should be captured. As there are plenty of possible attacks, we

---

[7] Note that, in a model with constant hashrate and difficulty, deviations like selfish mining [10], only increase the relative reward of an actor compared to others and not the absolute reward over time [25,30]. So in a constant difficulty model, selfish mining would not be more profitable over time than ordinary mining. This observation also holds in a model with variable difficulty until the difficulty is adjusted. In Bitcoin for example, this happens roughly every two weeks (2016 blocks).

[8] As an analysis of Bitcoin shows [16], miners more-or-less stick to the rules despite preferring transactions with higher fees and smaller blocks for faster propagation.

[9] With the simplifying assumption that no blocks are found concurrently.

cannot cover them all in this paper and refer to the related research on estimating the success probability in such cases [14,23,29,31,37]. For the rest of the paper we focus on the potential economic consequences of large scale attacks and their relation to the minimum EEV (given in normalized block rewards) required to incentivize deviating strategies that could lead to consensus instability while accounting for *all* future rewards.

3   Estimation of the Min. EEV in the Context of Attacks

We now look at the question how much EEV for a participant can lead to consensus instability. Thus we have to investigate the EEV in presence of attacks and especially their economic consequences. Therefore, we view the cryptocurrency R from a game theoretic standpoint and model it as an infinitely repeated game. But first we describe how the EEV can be used to compare different strategies against each other. The question whether any attack strategy is profitable for some actor i, can be summarized by comparing the EEV as well as the costs of the attack against the behavior intended by the protocol designer, i.e., the strategy HONEST, for that actor.

$$\text{EEV}_i\left(R, \text{ATTACK}\right) - costs_{\text{ATTACK}} > \text{EEV}_i\left(R, \text{HONEST}\right) - costs_{\text{HONEST}} \qquad (3)$$

In other words, if a deviation form the HONEST strategy is more profitable, then this strategy is economically rational. Here the costs can also incorporate potential losses of value of already accumulated resources due to negative consequences of the attack on the exchange rate of those resources. The security and incentive compatibility of a cryptocurrency, against an attack strategy ATTACK, can thus be ensured if the following condition in Formula 3 holds at any time for all actors. Formula 3 can also be described as a version of the formula provided by Böhme in a presentation [1].

Observeration 5. The expected extractable value, as well as the utility of an actor, describe the achievable gain from a certain strategy. Thus the utility of an actor as well as the EEV are equivalent and can be used as synonyms.

In our model a side-payment, or "bribe", can be expressed as part of the EEV e.g., as an incoming payment that is only valid on the chain desired by the attacker (hence conditional). This illustrates that (side-)payments can influence the incentives of actors. If the EEV of an attack is large enough to overcompensate for the induced costs, an attacker can use a portion of his profit to bribe other miners to convince them to mine on the attack chain. Using side-payments any economically rational actor can be incentivized to support an attack. The question directly related to EEV is: How large does such a side-payment have to be to incentivize illicit activity of other actors. To address this question we also have to take into account potential future EEV (or payoffs/rewards in terms of game theory) and the reduction of such, in case of an event that reduces the exchange rate for the attacked resource, i.e., a value loss.

3.1   Single Resource (R)

We now compare potential future EEV and thus the overall payoff for different strategies. From a game-theoretic point of view, we model a cryptocurrency as an infinitely repeated game with discounting[10]. Therefore, we have to define a *discount factor* $\delta \in (0,1)$, which specifies the preference of either immediate or future rewards. If δ is close to 0 immediate rewards are preferred. If δ is close to 1 future rewards are almost as good as immediate rewards. If $\delta = 0$ we would have a single-shot game as there would not be any future reward. To account for mining shares and δ, we have to extend our definition of a resource:

Definition 6 (A resource R). *From the perspective of an actor i each resource R is a quadruple $\langle r, e, p, \delta \rangle$ consisting of: The quantity r the actor i holds in the respective resource. The exchange rate e for the conversion in value units which reflect the individual preference of that actor. A parameter p which represents the power (e.g., hashrate) of that actor in this resource, which is used together with a discount factor δ to denote expected future rewards in that resource.*

As the payoffs in an infinite game create a geometric series ($p + p \cdot \delta + p \cdot \delta^2 + p \cdot \delta^3 \dots$), the payoff for the first n rounds can be written as:

$$r_n := \frac{p_i \cdot (1 - \delta^n)}{1 - \delta} \tag{4}$$

This can be rewritten as a closed form formula for the infinite case since δ^n goes to 0 as n goes to infinity. Thus the EEV for a single actor i with hashrate $p_i \leq 1$ in our infinite game, where every actor plays HONEST, can be approximated by:

$$\text{EEV}_i(R, \text{HONEST}, \infty) := \frac{p_i}{1 - \delta} \tag{5}$$

This estimation again denotes the EEV in normalized block rewards as a value unit (with $e = 1$) and assumes that the hashrate of actor i remains static in relation to the hashrates of all other actors.

We now compare this payoff to another strategy which requires a different (attack) action once and then falls back to the original honest behavior, but with a potential negative consequence on future rewards as the exchange rate has dropped. This is comparable to a *grim trigger* strategy in infinitely repeated games, although in our case the environment executes the grim trigger strategy by devaluing the global exchange rate ($e < 1$).

In our scenario, ε is the one-time side-payment to motivate the deviation and e is the value loss in terms of a drop in exchange rate, which of course also has the same negative impact on future EEV and thus must also be accounted for in all potential future mining rewards if the loss is (in the worst case) permanent.

$$\text{EEV}_i(R, \text{ATTACK}, \infty) := \varepsilon + \frac{\delta \cdot p_i \cdot e}{1 - \delta} \tag{6}$$

---

[10] Pass et al. [27] pointed out that PoW blockchains cannot stop without becoming insecure, so they have to run infinitely long.

As we are only interested in an approximation, we abstract the particular success probability calculations to evaluate the likelihood of a single attack being successful. Furthermore, we omit the loss of blocks a miner potentially faces if the chain he contributed to becomes stale. If known, this value can be included by adding it to the required bribe ε.

We now estimate how high this one-time side-payment ε has to be to incentivize a one-time deviation form the HONEST strategy with permanent consequence on e for a mainstream cryptocurrency. Therefore, we first have to define some plausible range for the discount factor δ miners might have in practice. Figure 1 shows the normalized block reward after a certain number of passed blocks for different values of δ and a hashrate of $p = 0.1$. It can be observed that a relatively high value $\delta = 0.99995$ is needed already to approximate (within a 5% margin) the average income in normalized block rewards after one Bitcoin difficulty period (2016 blocks). For a far sighted miner that has a one to two year interest in Bitcoin a $\delta = 0.999999$ would suffice to be within a margin of 5% of the average number of normalized block rewards after two years.

Now that we have picked some plausible values for δ, we can approximate the required total side-payment ε that would be required to change the incentives of participating miners with different hashrates. Therefore, we compare the EEV of honest behavior with the EEV of the attack. Assuming the costs of mining in both cases are identical, the EEV of the attack has to be more profitable than the honest behavior, for the attack to be realistic.

So far we have not taken into account that miners could also hold funds ($f_i(r)$), which are distinct from hashrate (which describes future gains given out as currency units). Since a successful attack will lead to a potential drop in the exchange rate, we have to consider this for all future rewards, as well as all funds the miner is currently holding. Equation 9 compares the two strategies under the assumption that there is only one resource (r) the respective miner cares about. Hereby, the hashrate is viewed as some share in the protocol which provides future rewards in the respective cryptocurrency (in r) proportional to the size of the share.

$$\text{EEV}_i(R, \text{HONEST}, \infty) := \frac{p}{1 - \delta} + f_i(r) \tag{7}$$

$$\text{EEV}_i(R, \text{ATTACK}, \infty) := \varepsilon + \frac{\delta \cdot p \cdot e}{1 - \delta} + f_i(r, e) \tag{8}$$

$$\text{EEV}_i(R, \text{HONEST}, \infty) < \text{EEV}_i(R, \text{ATTACK}, \infty) \tag{9}$$

Solving Eq. 9 for ε, we can calculate the required side-payment for the following example: To compensate a five percent value drop ($e = 0.95$) for a miner with zero funds ($f_i(r) = 0$) and 10% hashrate ($p = 0.1$), a side-payment in approximately the size of 500 times the normalized block reward is needed (if $\delta = 0.99999$). If the side-payment itself is performed in r, and thus subject to the same value drop of 5% as well, then ≈ 527 times the normalized block reward is required as a side-payment.

Although theoretically possible, such high bribes in the size of hundreds of normalized block rewards appear unlikely in practice from a current stand point. Moreover, for an attack to be economically viable for an attacker, he would have to perform a double-spend of a transaction which is much larger than the required overall side-payments. Ideally the attacker himself (as well as the victim) does not possess any hashrate in the targeted cryptocurrency, such that his personal future income will not be negatively affected by the consequences of the attack, i.e., drop in exchange rate. Moreover, the attacker is advised to use all his funds in r in the double-spend transaction to further minimize the negative effects on the exchange rate. The leftovers from the double-spend, after subtracting the required side-payments to incentivize a sufficient portion of the hashrate to support the attack chain, could be viewed as profit for the attacker. So for such an attack to work, funds would have to be unevenly distributed amongst actors and an individual payment must only be limited by the available overall supply of the respective resource. Then the amount of a double-spend can theoretically be high enough that the excess profit of the attacker can be used to bribe a majority of miners to support an attack chain.

Observeration 6. In a scenario where there is only one cryptocurrency particⁱⁱpants care about, the side-payment necessary to incentivize a deviation has to account for all current and future losses.

3.2   Multiple Resources ($\mathcal{R}$)

The analysis so far assumed that all actors only care about the same single resource, i.e., cryptocurrency, and express their extractable value in normalized block rewards of this resource. The resulting question is, what if there are multiple resources and not all actors necessarily care about the same set of resources to a comparable degree?

To approach this question, we modify Eq. 9 to estimate the EEV for the honest strategy, as well as for the attack strategy, by accounting for all resources (e.g., cryptocurrencies) a player i cares about. Hereby, we model the individual hashrates (p) as a part of each resource which defines the share of future rewards an actor will receive in the respective resource. Additionally there is a set of δ values for each resource. Moreover, in this scenario a bribe does not necessarily have to be paid in the resource where the attack action should happen, thus several bribes are possible $\{\varepsilon_0, \varepsilon_1, \varepsilon_2, \dots\}$.

$$\text{EEV}_i(\mathcal{R}, \text{HONEST}, \infty) := \sum_{j=0}^{|\mathcal{R}|} \left(\frac{p_j}{1-\delta_j} \right) + \sum_{j=0}^{|\mathcal{R}|} f_i(r_j) \tag{10}$$

$$\text{EEV}_i(\mathcal{R}, \text{ATTACK}, \infty) := f_i(r_0 + \varepsilon_0, e_0) + \frac{\delta_0 \cdot p_0 \cdot e_0}{1-\delta_0} \tag{11}$$

$$+ \sum_{j=1}^{|\mathcal{R}|} \left(\frac{p_j \cdot e_j}{1-\delta_j} \right) + \sum_{j=1}^{|\mathcal{R}|} f_i(r_j + \varepsilon_j, e_j) \tag{12}$$

Compared to the single resource case in Sect. 3.1 the multi-resource case now allows actors to escape certain negative consequences on the exchange rate e_0, e.g., by moving their hashrate to another permissionless PoW cryptocurrency (like for example R_1). This of course only works if the miner's hardware can also be efficiently used in the other cryptocurrency and e_1 is not affected to the same degree, or generally much higher to begin with ($e_1 \geq e_0$ and $\delta_1 \geq \delta_0$). If also current holdings in resources can be transferred to other resources through exchange services, then in the worst case it may be possible to evade all negative consequences from attacks on a certain target resource R_0. To which degree such negative consequences can be evaded depends on several factors: The availability of adequate alternatives, the type of the attack, as well as how fast resources can be moved and exchange rates adopt (cf. [3]).

If such evasion techniques are possible, this raises an interesting question from a game theoretic point of view. The previously infinitely repeated game, now becomes a finite game, as actors can leave the system at will. Therefore, the option to defect in the (personally) last round of the (now) finite game suddenly becomes an economically rational strategy.

Observeration 7. If appropriate alternative resources exist, parties can evade negative attack consequences on their overall EEV, by moving their assets to another less, or even positively affected resource. Thereby, the once infinite game becomes finite from their perspective.

We provide some visual examples for this multi-resource model in Appendix B, by comparing the EEV before a certain event with the EEV after the event. These examples further illustrate, that miners who are tied to a cryptocurrency due to their specific mining hardware, have a higher incentive not to risk negative consequences on the exchange rate of that cryptocurrency. If switching to another equally, or more profitable alternative is possible though, attacks become more attractive. This highlights, that in an environment in which multiple cryptocurrencies co-exist and represent alternative resources to each other, the EEV cannot be estimated by looking at a single resource/cryptocurrency alone. Especially since cryptocurrencies can be created at any point in time, for example through forks, which change the overall cryptocurrency landscape and potentially affect the exchange rates of existing cryptocurrencies in one, or the other way.

Observation 8. In the multi-cryptocurrency environment where new resources can be created, the EEV can be influenced by these new resources, since the set of available resources for actors changes. Thereby, providing new alternatives, or modifying existing exchange rates and discount factors.

This problem of considering out-of-band income streams in economic security models of permissionless PoW cryptocurrencies, is also nicely illustrated by various bribing, or algorithmic incentive manipulation attacks which utilize out-of-band payments [4,18,19,24,32] as well as other economic arguments regarding the incentive structure of such systems [6,11].

4   Discussion

The presented observations highlight that accurately estimating the EEV of a particular miner is impossible, even when knowing all transactions belonging to this miner, as well as all current preferences regarding cryptocurrencies and resources the respective miner cares about and to which degree. There are two major reasons for this: First, it is not possible to predict the actions taken by other actors interacting with the system by issuing transactions which either directly, or indirectly affect the respective miner i, or the exchange rate of a resource. Second, if miner i is open for accepting payments or new resources (e.g., validator roles which provide future incomes), then the fact that new cryptocurrencies can be forked, or created at any point in time (with a free choice of rules and distribution of funds) provides new possibilities of income to i. As even the sheer existence of new cryptocurrencies can have a negative affect on the valuation of existing cryptocurrencies, this can also influence the EEV of i. Even more so, if the rules of the newly created cryptocurrencies are designed in a way that actively harm existing ones, as outlined in [17].

In other words, precisely calculating the EEV of a miner i is impossible even with perfect information on the current global state. Nevertheless, it may still be possible to approximate the EEV, if the number of possibly available resources $\mathcal{R}$, the computational capabilities of actors, as well as their overall number, can be meaningfully bounded. As cryptocurrencies provide the possibility to virtually create new resources at any point in time, this can technically not be prevented in practice. It is therefore questionable, if economic security models of permissionless cryptocurrencies that take the interplay between multiple resources into account, will be able to produce satisfactory security guarantees, compared to the high standards regarding security proofs that we are used to, for our cryptographic primitives, formally verified smart contracts, or classical Byzantine fault tolerant consensus systems.

This leaves us with the open question on how to best include economic considerations into the choice of the security parameter k determining the number of required confirmation blocks. In Sect. 4.1 we show a simple workaround that relieves us from the burden of correctly determining the right value for k.

4.1   The Let's Go Shopping Defense

We now describe a simple defensive strategy a merchant M can use to transfer the risk of choosing an insufficient security parameter k_M, to another merchant W. In our scenario we, assume that merchant M offers some quantity v of resource r for sale to a customer C. For this technique to work, we need to assume that there exists a merchant W with an already defined security parameter k_W. Furthermore, merchant W offers some easily tradable good/resource r' that is purchasable in arbitrary quantity and also stable in price. Then merchant M can now choose his k_M such that $k_M > k_W$, and immediately use all received funds directly to acquire r'. Therefore, M has to create a transaction tx_M that immediately uses all funds that were used by the customer to purchase r. In other words the transaction of M builds up on the transaction of C, i.e., $tx_C \rightarrow tx_M$. In an UTXO model cryptocurrency this can be achieved by using the respective UTXO as input, whereas in an account based model a dedicated account can be created to handle the purchase Technically, in most prevalent cryptocurrencies tx_C and tx_M can even be part of the same block if included in the right order and if M broadcasts tx_M immediately after observing tx_C in the P2P network.

Using this technique, merchant M can be sure to receive $v_{r'}$ before he has to hand out v_r. If now transaction tx_C is double-spent, or otherwise is invalidated so will be tx_M, but at that point either M has not yet handed out v_r, or already received $v_{r'}$. In both cases M does not face any direct damage from an attack.

5   Conclusion

We have shown that MEV is a special form of value extractable by miners, and that there is a difference between the *extractable value* that is computed in retrospect and *expected extractable value* (EEV) that is also forward looking and takes the probability of events influencing it into account. Further we have shown that estimating the EEV of any actor i is hard or even impossible in practice as we have to deal with imperfect information and possibly multiple cryptographically interlinked cryptocurrencies. The EEV depends on several factors: Transactions affecting i, which reach from incoming and outgoing regular payments, over bribes, to front running and arbitrage opportunities, as well as all consequences of actions affecting the valuation of assets in different resources actor i cares about. The difficulty to accurately estimate the EEV is further amplified by the fact that new cryptocurrencies might pop up, increasing the set of resources actors care about, or putting pressure on existing cryptocurrencies. Although, theoretically workable, a rather unsatisfactory workaround is described to transfer the risk of choosing an insufficiently large security parameter k to another merchant. In the wake of more and more attacks that exploit aspects of the economic rationally of actors (like for example front running), a better understanding of the economic interplay between such actors, as well as cryptocurrency systems as a whole, is desperately required to more accurately model the security guarantees of prevalent permissionless cryptocurrencies under such economical considerations and attacks. If the lack of descriptive models (which take practical economic considerations into account) persists, we have to ask ourselves if economic incentives in permissionless cryptocurrencies can ever produce satisfactory security guarantees, our just occasionally worked "better in practice, than in theory" for a while.

Acknowledgements. This material is based upon work partially supported by (1) the Christian-Doppler-Laboratory for Security and Quality Improvement in the Production System Lifecycle; The financial support by the Austrian Federal Ministry for Digital and Economic Affairs, the Nation Foundation for Research, Technology and Development and University of Vienna, Faculty of Computer Science, Security & Privacy Group is gratefully acknowledged; (2) SBA Research; the competence center SBA Research (SBA-K1) funded within the framework of COMET Competence Centers for

Excellent Technologies by BMVIT, BMDW, and the federal state of Vienna, managed by the FFG; (3) the FFG Industrial PhD projects 878835 and 878736. (4) the FFG ICT of the Future project 874019 dIdentity & dApps. (5) the European Union's Horizon 2020 research and innovation programme under grant agreement No 826078 (FeatureCloud). We would also like to thank our anonymous reviewers for their valuable feedback and suggestions.

A   Figure to Approximate δ

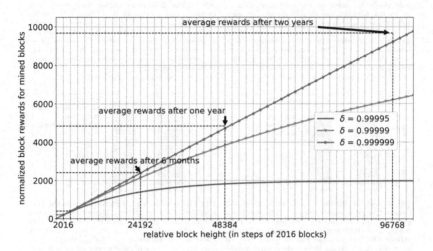

Fig. 1. Figure to approximate δ by comparing the average block rewards received by a miner with $p = 0.1$, to the expected infinite game rewards for the same miner with different discount factors δ. All rewards are given in normalized block rewards.

B   Illustration of Different Events and Their Consequences

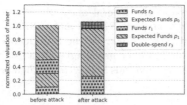

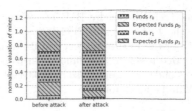

(a) A double-spend attack on a cryptocurrency R_0 from the perspective of a miner. *Before*: The total expected future income from mining is $p_0 = 0.2$ and $p_1 = 0.5$, in relation to the currently held funds in $r_0 = 0.1$ and $r_1 = 0.2$. *After*: A double-spend of all available funds r_0, leads to an additional gain of $r_3 = 0.1$ through the double-spend, but also to negative consequences on the exchange rate $e'_0 = 0.65$. This drop is evaded by moving all hashrate to R_1, where the exchange rate remains constant $e'_1 = 1$. This leads to a gain of exactly the exchange rate in R_0 as the double-spend funds cannot be moved without losses: $r_0 \cdot e'_0 + (p_0 + p_1 + r_1) \cdot e'_1 + r_3 = 1.065$

(b) A Goldfinger attack [22,24,5] on a cryptocurrency R_0 from the perspective of a miner. *Before*: The total expected future income from mining is $p_0 = 0.2$ and $p_1 = 0.3$, in relation to the currently held funds in $r_0 = 0.05$ and $r_1 = 0.45$. *After*: The Goldfinger attack leads to a drop in the exchnage rate in R_0 of 50% ($e'_0 = 0.5$), while the exchange rate in R_1 increases by 30% ($e'_1 = 1.3$). Due to the distribution of his current holdings and expeceted future income in those two resources R_1 and R_2, at the end of the day m profits more from the increase than he loses from the decrease: $(p_0 + r_0) \cdot e'_0 + (p_1 + r_1) \cdot e'_1 = 1.1$

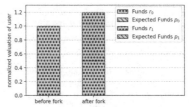

(c) A fork of R_0 into R_0 and R_1 from the perspective of a miner. *Before*: The total expected future mining rewards are $p_0 = 0.85$ while $r_0 = 0.15$ come from current holdings. *After*: The fork changes the exchange rate to $e'_0 = 0.5$, thus cutting the previous total valuation in half and at the same time adds the funds from the new resource $r_1 = r_0 = 0.15$ with an exchange rate $e'_1 = 0.7$. This leads to an overall loss for the miner: $(p_0 + r_0) \cdot e'_0 + r_1 \cdot e'_1 = 0.605$

(d) The same fork as in Figure 2c from the perspective of a user. *Before*: There is no expected future income $p_0 = 0$, thus 100% come from current holdings in R_0 ($r_0 = 1$). *After*: The forks changes the exchange rate to $e'_0 = 0.5$, thus cutting the previous total valuation in half, but at the same time adds the funds from the new resource $r_1 = r_0 = 1$ with an exchange rate $e_1 = 0.7$. This leads to a surplus of 0.2 for the user in this case: $(p_0 + r_0) \cdot e'_0 + r_1 \cdot e'_1 = 1.2$

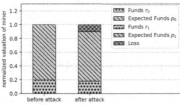

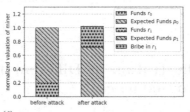

(e) An attack on a R_0 from the perspective of a miner. *Before*: The total expected future income from mining is $p_0 = 0.8$, while $r_0 = 0.2$ come from current holdings. *After*: An attack with negative consequences on the exchange rate $e'_0 = 0.9$ is depicted leading to a loss for the miner: $(p_0 + r_0) \cdot e'_0 = 0.9$

(f) The same attack as Figure 2e, but in this case the funds $r_0 = 0.2$ can be transferred to an alternative cryptocurrency R_1 in which no value loss occures ($e'_1 = 1$). Furthermore, a bribe $\varepsilon = 0.1$ is payed in r_1 to the miner to accommodate for the induced losses. In this case the miner would have surplus, although his hashrate p_0 is non-transferable. $(p_0 + r_0) \cdot e'_0 + (r_1 + \varepsilon) \cdot e'_1 = 1.02$

Fig. 2. Visual illustration of different events and their consequences on a participant with $\mathcal{R} := \{R_0, R_1\}$. The total valuation of a participant *before* the respective event is normalized to 1. This means that the values for the initial exchange rates are $e_{0,1} = 1$ (s.t. $f(r_{0,1}, 1) = r_{0,1}$), and that δ is static and thus ignored ($\delta_{0,1} = 0$). In other words expected future rewards where already accounted for in the relation between $p_{0,1}$ and $r_{0,1}$, s.t. $p_0 + r_0 + p_1 + r_1 = 1$.

References

1. Talk: A primer on economics for cryptocurrencies. School of Blocks, Blockchain summer school at TU Wien (2019). Accessed 15 Sept 2020
2. Babel, K., Daian, P., Kelkar, M., Juels, A.: Clockwork finance: automated analysis of economic security in smart contracts. CoRR, abs/2109.04347 (2021)
3. Bissias, G., Böhme, R., Thibodeau, D., Levine, B.N.: Pricing security in proof-of-work systems. arXiv preprint arXiv:2012.03706 (2020)
4. Bonneau, J.: Why buy when you can rent? Bribery attacks on bitcoin-style consensus. In: Clark, J., Meiklejohn, S., Ryan, P.Y.A., Wallach, D., Brenner, M., Rohloff, K. (eds.) FC 2016. LNCS, vol. 9604, pp. 19–26. Springer, Heidelberg (2016). https://doi.org/10.1007/978-3-662-53357-4_2
5. Bonneau, J.: Hostile blockchain takeovers (short paper). In: Zohar, A., et al. (eds.) FC 2018. LNCS, vol. 10958, pp. 92–100. Springer, Heidelberg (2019). https://doi.org/10.1007/978-3-662-58820-8_7
6. Budish, E.: The economic limits of bitcoin and the blockchain. Technical report, National Bureau of Economic Research (2018)
7. Carlsten, M., Kalodner, H., Weinberg, S.M., Narayanan, A.: On the instability of bitcoin without the block reward. In: Proceedings of the 2016 ACM SIGSAC Conference on Computer and Communications Security, pp. 154–167. ACM (2016)
8. Daian, P., et al.: Flash boys 2.0: frontrunning in decentralized exchanges, miner extractable value, and consensus instability. In: 2020 IEEE Symposium on Security and Privacy (SP), pp. 910–927. IEEE (2020)
9. Eskandari, S., Moosavi, S., Clark, J.: SoK: transparent dishonesty: front-running attacks on blockchain. arXiv preprint arXiv:1902.05164 (2019)
10. Eyal, I., Sirer, E.G.: Majority is not enough: bitcoin mining is vulnerable. In: Christin, N., Safavi-Naini, R. (eds.) FC 2014. LNCS, vol. 8437, pp. 436–454. Springer, Heidelberg (2014). https://doi.org/10.1007/978-3-662-45472-5_28
11. Ford, B., Böhme, R.: Rationality is self-defeating in permissionless systems (2019). ePrint arXiv:1910.08820
12. Garay, J., Kiayias, A., Leonardos, N.: The bitcoin backbone protocol: analysis and applications (2014). Published: Cryptology ePrint Archive, Report 2014/765
13. Garay, J.A., Kiayias, A., Leonardos, N.: The bitcoin backbone protocol: analysis and applications (2020). Publication Title: IACR Cryptology ePrint Archive, Report 2014/765
14. Gervais, A., Karame, G.O., Wüst, K., Glykantzis, V., Ritzdorf, H., Capkun, S.: On the security and performance of proof of work blockchains. In: Proceedings of the 2016 ACM SIGSAC, pp. 3–16. ACM (2016)
15. Hopwood, D., Bowe, S., Hornby, T., Wilcox, N.: Zcash protocol specification (2021). Accessed 06 Sept 2021
16. Hou, B., Chen, F.: A study on nine years of bitcoin transactions: understanding real-world behaviors of bitcoin miners and users (2021)
17. Judmayer, A., Stifter, N., Schindler, P., Weippl, E.: Pitchforks in cryptocurrencies: enforcing rule changes through offensive forking- and consensus techniques (short paper). In: Garcia-Alfaro, J., Herrera-Joancomartí, J., Livraga, G., Rios, R. (eds.) DPM/CBT 2018. LNCS, vol. 11025, pp. 197–206. Springer, Cham (2018). https://doi.org/10.1007/978-3-030-00305-0_15
18. Judmayer, A., et al.: Pay-to-win: cheap, crowdfundable, cross-chain algorithmic incentive manipulation attacks on pow cryptocurrencies. Cryptology ePrint Archive, Report 2019/775 (2019)

19. Judmayer, A., et al.: SoK: algorithmic incentive manipulation attacks on permissionless pow cryptocurrencies. Cryptology ePrint Archive, Report 2019/775 (2020)
20. Kappos, G., Yousaf, H., Maller, M., Meiklejohn, S.: An empirical analysis of anonymity in Zcash. In: 27th USENIX Security Symposium (USENIX Security 2018), pp. 463–477 (2018)
21. Kelkar, M., Zhang, F., Goldfeder, S., Juels, A.: Order-fairness for Byzantine consensus. In: Micciancio, D., Ristenpart, T. (eds.) CRYPTO 2020. LNCS, vol. 12172, pp. 451–480. Springer, Cham (2020). https://doi.org/10.1007/978-3-030-56877-1_16
22. Kroll, J.A., Davey, I.C., Felten, E.W.: The economics of Bitcoin mining, or Bitcoin in the presence of adversaries. In: Proceedings of WEIS, vol. 2013, p. 11 (2013)
23. Liao, K., Katz, J.: Incentivizing blockchain forks via whale transactions. In: Brenner, M., et al. (eds.) FC 2017. LNCS, vol. 10323, pp. 264–279. Springer, Cham (2017). https://doi.org/10.1007/978-3-319-70278-0_17
24. McCorry, P., Hicks, A., Meiklejohn, S.: Smart contracts for bribing miners. In: Zohar, A., et al. (eds.) FC 2018. LNCS, vol. 10958, pp. 3–18. Springer, Heidelberg (2019). https://doi.org/10.1007/978-3-662-58820-8_1
25. Nayak, K., Kumar, S., Miller, A., Shi, E.: Stubborn mining: generalizing selfish mining and combining with an eclipse attack. In: 1st IEEE European Symposium on Security and Privacy. IEEE (2016)
26. Obadia, A., Salles, A., Sankar, L., Chitra, T., Chellani, V., Daian, P.: Unity is strength: a formalization of cross-domain maximal extractable value (2021)
27. Pass, R., Shi, E.: Hybrid consensus: scalable permissionless consensus (2016)
28. Qin, K., Zhou, L., Gervais, A.: Quantifying blockchain extractable value: how dark is the forest? arXiv preprint arXiv:2101.05511 (2021)
29. Rosenfeld, M.: Analysis of Hashrate-based double spending, vol. abs/1402.2009 (2014). Publication Title: CoRR
30. Sapirshtein, A., Sompolinsky, Y., Zohar, A.: Optimal selfish mining strategies in Bitcoin (2015). Publication Title: arXiv preprint arXiv:1507.06183
31. Sompolinsky, Y., Zohar, A.: Bitcoin's security model revisited. arXiv preprint arXiv:1605.09193 (2016)
32. Teutsch, J., Jain, S., Saxena, P.: When cryptocurrencies mine their own business. In: Grossklags, J., Preneel, B. (eds.) FC 2016. LNCS, vol. 9603, pp. 499–514. Springer, Heidelberg (2017). https://doi.org/10.1007/978-3-662-54970-4_29
33. Torres, C.F., Iannillo, A.K., Gervais, A., State, R.: The eye of horus: spotting and analyzing attacks on Ethereum smart contracts (2021). ePrint 2101.06204
34. Tsabary, I., Eyal, I.: The gap game. In: Proceedings of the 2018 ACM SIGSAC Conference on Computer and Communications Security, pp. 713–728. ACM (2018)
35. Zhou, L., Qin, K., Cully, A., Livshits, B., Gervais, A.: On the just-in-time discovery of profit-generating transactions in DeFi protocols (2021). ePrint: 2103.02228
36. Zhou, L., Qin, K., Gervais, A.: A2MM: mitigating frontrunning, transaction reordering and consensus instability in decentralized exchanges. arXiv:2106.07371 [cs] (2021)
37. Zhou, L., Qin, K., Torres, C.F., Le, D.V., Gervais, A.: High-frequency trading on decentralized on-chain exchanges. arXiv preprint arXiv:2009.14021 (2020)

Teaching PoW Algorithm to a Classroom Environment

Yaacov Kopeliovich[✉]

Department of Finance, University of Connecticut,
2100 Hillside Road, Storrs, CT 06269, USA
yaacov.kopeliovich@uconn.edu

Abstract. In this note we explain our method to teach various consensus algorithms in the classroom. We accomplish that by creating slightly modifying PoS algorithm to create a version which is equivalent to PoW consensus algorithms.

1 Introduction

Since the invention of Nakamoto consensus there is an explosion of consensus algorithms that are divided into two main categories. The first one is PoW (Proof of Work) implemented in the first decentralized asset and the other one is PoS (Proof of Stake). While PoS is relatively easy to explain and simulate in a classroom the explanation of the first consensus algorithm i.e. PoW presents challenges for students in particularly if they don't have a background in computer science. In this note we explain that one can replace PoW consensus with an equivalent version of PoS which is way easier to implement and thus provide the students a better grasp and a better understanding of PoW algorithms. This note has two sections. In the first section we briefly explain a simplified version of PoS and PoW algorithms and in the second section we will explain how one can replace a PoW consensus algorithm with a proof of stake version.

Importantly this note isn't trying to invent any new consensus algorithms (there is a huge body of work done in this direction by [ZoSo,R,N] and the numerous inventors and launchers of cryptoassets but to attempt and clarify the differences and similarities between the different methods employed by digital assets.

2 PoS and PoW - A Survey

2.1 PoS - Proof of Stake

The fundamental problem of any consensus algorithm is to arrange transactions into a linear list (called block-chain) in a trust-less (decentralized) way. The most natural solution for this problem is to have more than one entity (we refer to these entities as miners) who has the privilege to arrange transactions. Then

© International Financial Cryptography Association 2023
S. Matsuo et al. (Eds.): FC 2022 Workshops, LNCS 13412, pp. 93–96, 2023.
https://doi.org/10.1007/978-3-031-32415-4_7

each round of arranging transaction is selected randomly where the probability is weighted by the amount of digital assets any of these miners pledged towards the selection process in the current round. Once the leader is selected he arranges the new transactions in a block and then adds the block in a cryptographically secured way (by using a cryptographic function to serialize the data.) Any user can verify the correctness of this block and the entire block-chain by applying the same cryptographic function. If the block is confirmed the miner will benefit by earning fees on the block that was just created. For example if we have two miners one that has 60% of the digital assets and the other has 40% of the total pool of the digital assets the probability of the selection will be 60% for the first user and 40% for the second user. As noted in the introduction the current PoS algorithms employ more sophisticated versions of selecting the leader who will arrange the transactions in the current round. However the basic scheme is what was described above and thus it's quiet easy to simulate and explain this kind of consensus algorithm in a classroom environment.

2.2   PoW - Proof of Work

PoW was the first consensus algorithm based on a competition between miners that arrange transactions by performing a work solving a hash puzzle. More specifically the algorithm for transaction sequencing into a block is performed:

1. Miners get a pool of transactions from the Web
2. Miners arrange those transactions in a cryptographic way
3. after arranging the transactions Miners solve a cryptographic puzzle that has a fixed average time for its solution.
4. The miner who solves this cryptographic puzzle published it's suggested new block together with a cryptographic solution that can be validated by any user that runs the block-chain software (it is called PoW client). If the puzzle is verified the new chain is accepted by the PoW clients. (usually after 6 confirmations)
5. The first miner that created the puzzle wins a reward by collecting the fees and digital asset that are awarded to him.
6. As the miners can see different pool of transactions coming from different users of the system it may be that we have conflicting chains of blocks. The chain of blocks (or a linked list) that has the most electric energy (while solving the puzzle) spent on it is the one that is chosen by the PoW clients if they see two conflicting chain on the Web.

Remarkably this sequence of steps results in convergence and a stable chain emerges. However as we see from the algorithm it's challenging to discuss and simulate this algorithm in a classroom environment. For starters a usual classroom doesn't have equipment to solve massive cryptographic puzzles. It's also challenging to discuss with students the amount of energy spent on different chains. In the next section we propose a simplified PoW algorithm which replaces the cryptographic puzzle solution with upfront payments that can programmed easily within the context of a classroom.

3 PoW Adjusted Algorithm

In this section we produce a modified PoW algorithm which implies that it's basically a subclass of PoS algorithms with certain twists. We start from the observation that we can estimate how long it will take each miner to produce the solution to the cryptographic puzzle based on the average performance time it can take to solve the cryptographic puzzle which is going to be essentially the miner who is going to arrange the transactions in a block. Indeed assuming that the amount of bit-wise operations it takes to solve the cryptographic puzzle is n steps and assuming q we have k miners that can do m_k operations per unit of time that the miner is able to do m_1 operations per second will solve the puzzle with a probability of approximately: $\frac{m_i}{\sum_{i=1}^{k} m_k}$. Further it's clear that the i-th miner will take the time of $\frac{n}{m_i}$ and therefore we can estimate what how much he will pay to solve the puzzle (if he solves it first) based on the current price of electricity available in the market. These two observations immediately lead to the following modified PoW algorithm that one can relatively easy implement in a class:

1. In the beginning there are k miners each one who is assigned the following:
   (a) p_i the probability of winning the selection lottery to arrange transactions. In reality this will be based on the miners ability to perform m_i operations per second i.e. it's hashing power.
   (b) initial payment h_i that the miner will pay regardless whether he wins the selection lottery or not. This is the initial price miners have to pay to enter into a competition
2. A randomly selected miner based on probability p_i will arrange the transactions and will send them cryptographically secured to PoW clients. (**He will not solve the puzzle**, will just arrange them apply the cryptographic function and will send them to the PoW clients)
3. PoW clients will perform the confirmation and once it's confirmed it will be added to the block-chain
4. The total price of the chain (total payments of the fees paid by the winners) is recorded and maintained to the block-chain.
5. The fees of the transactions and any rewards minted by the system will go to the miner that arranges the transaction.

3.1 Local Selection

The PoW algorithm described above is equivalent to Satoshi PoW and is relatively easy to simulate in a classroom environment. It also allows for local competition i.e. we don't need to know all the miners in the world to organize a lottery. We can do a local list of miners as if we have conflicting chains the most expensive chain (i.e. those who paid the most money) will be selected to be the unique Block-chain available to all the participants of the system.

4   Summary

In this note I explain a methodology to implement a PoW algorithm in a class-room environment so that students can see how the PoW algorithm works. From my experience students respond positively to this modification and grasp the various algorithms and its nuances in a much more pronounced way. This also contributes to their understanding of the differences and the problems that each of this class of algorithms has.

References

[N]   Nakamoto, S.: Bitcoin: a peer to peer electronic cash system. https://web. archive.org/web/20140320135003/https://bitcoin.org/bitcoin.pdf

[ZoSo] Sompolinsky, Y., Zohar, A.: Secure high-rate transaction processing in bitcoin. In: Böhme, R., Okamoto, T. (eds.) FC 2015. LNCS, vol. 8975, pp. 507–527. Springer, Heidelberg (2015). https://doi.org/10.1007/978-3-662-47854-7_32. https://www.semanticscholar.org/paper/Secure-High-Rate-Transaction-Proce ssing-in-Bitcoin-Sompolinsky-Zohar/728b60c04afb5b87853b59265e49f430dbf6 31db

[R]   Russell, A.: Private communication

The Compatibility of CBDCs with "DeFi" Protocols: A Governance Rather Than a Technological Issue to Comply with Financial Crime Regulations

Stéphane Blemus[1,2](✉)

[1] Faculty of Law, Copenhagen University, Copenhagen, Denmark
[2] Secretary General, Societe Generale-Forge, Paris, France

Abstract. Decentralized finance ("DeFi") has become a cornerstone of crypto-asset markets since 2020. While most academic studies focus primarily on technological impacts, this paper is rather based on the factual observation that corporations are struggling to use decentralized protocols at a larger scale mainly for governance, compliance and operational reasons. It provides insights about greater interactions between centralized finance and decentralized finance in the near future and about the governance and operational tools that could be developed to foster the use of DLTs for more efficient digital markets.

Keywords: CBDC · Decentralized finance · financial crime · KYC-AML

1 Defining Decentralized Finance ("DeFi")

Decentralized finance has been in 2021 a key trend of innovation and digitized markets, and the focus of several studies by global regulators[1], companies[2] and academics[3]. In 2021, the value of assets used in DeFi has risen from $15 billion to more than $100 billion[4], including more than $50 billion used in decentralized lending arrangements[5],

---

[1] International Monetary Fund, "Global Financial Stability Report I COVID-19, Crypto, and Climate: Navigating Challenging Transitions", October 2021; S. Aramonte, W. Huang, A. Schrimpf, "DeFi risks and the decentralization illusion", BIS Quarterly Review, December 2021.

[2] Chainalysis, "Introducing the Chainalysis Global DeFi Adoption Index", 2021: https://blog.chainalysis.com/reports/2021-global-defi-adoption-index.

[3] F. Schär, "Decentralized Finance: On Blockchain- and Smart Contract-based Financial Markets", Federal Reserve Bank of St. Louis, vol. 103(2), April 2021, pp. 153–174.; C.R. Harvey, A. Ramachandran, J. Santoro, "DeFi and the Future of Finance", August 2021.

[4] IMF, "Global Financial Stability Report", October 2021, p. 42–43.

[5] G. Keyes, "DeFi Tops $100 Billion for First Time as Cryptocurrencies Surge", Bloomberg.com, 20 October 2021.

© International Financial Cryptography Association 2023
S. Matsuo et al. (Eds.): FC 2022 Workshops, LNCS 13412, pp. 97–105, 2023.
https://doi.org/10.1007/978-3-031-32415-4_8

raising the interest of both the general public and financial experts in these technological evolutions[6].

1.1 Absence of a "DeFi" Legal Definition Approved at International Level

Given the recent emergence of "DeFi" use cases, an iterative assessment of its impacts and consequences by public actors is only in its infancy. There is not yet a legal definition approved at global level of this terminology. There is neither a universally accepted definition by OECD countries nor even a legal definition at national level in these countries.

Within the European Union, so far, the EU member states' regulations related to distributed ledger technology and crypto-assets have not included rules specific to "DeFi" protocols and activities[7]. At the EU level, there is an ongoing debate about the inclusion of "DeFi" provisions within the major crypto-asset regulation proposal currently discussed by European institutions (the "Markets in Crypto-Assets" ("MiCA")). There has not yet been an approval at this time to provide a legal definition of "DeFi" or "decentralized assets" (such as algorithmic stablecoins[8]) in the "MiCA" regulation, even though this EU regulation will provide a clear taxonomy of crypto-assets and define some types of "stablecoins" (i.e. "e-money tokens" and "asset-referenced tokens"[9]).

1.2 Discussion on the FATF-GAFI Definition Proposal

With the exception of the US State of Wyoming[10], the first definition of "DeFi" proposed at international level has been drafted by the FATF-GAFI in its updated guidance on virtual assets and virtual asset service providers ("VASP") of October 2021[11].

---

[6] The Economist, "Down the rabbit hole – The beguiling promise of decentralised finance", 18 September 2021; G. Keyes, "DeFi Tops $100 Billion for First Time as Cryptocurrencies Surge", Bloomberg.com, 20 October 2021.

[7] E.g. French "Blockchain" Ordinance of 2017 and "PACTE" law of 2019, German cryptocustody regulation of 2019, Luxemburg "Bill 7363" of 2019 and "Bill 7367" of 2021, Swiss "DLT" law of 2021.

[8] EU Proposal for a Regulation on Markets in Crypto-Assets ("MiCA"), Recital 26: "*So-called algorithmic 'stablecoins' that aim at maintaining a stable value, via protocols, that provide for the increase or decrease of the supply of such crypto-assets in response to changes in demand should not be considered as asset-referenced tokens, provided that they do not aim at stabilising their value by referencing one or several other assets*".

[9] "E-money tokens" and "asset-referenced tokens" are crypto-assets whose function is to maintain a stable value, for e-money tokens by referring to the value of a single fiat currency, and for asset-referenced tokens by referring to the value of several fiat currencies, one or several commodities or one or several crypto-assets.

[10] Wyoming Senate Bill 38, April 2021.

[11] FATF-GAFI, «Updated Guidance for a Risk-Based Approach for Virtual Assets and Virtual Asset Service Providers», octobre 2021; FATF-GAFI, "Public consultation on FATF draft guidance on a risk-based approach to virtual assets and virtual asset service providers", VA Guidance update, 6th draft, March 2021.

Two key definitions have been proposed by the intergovernmental organization FATF-GAFI which is dedicated to set and promote anti-money laundering ("AML") standards:

- "DApp" as "a term that refers to a software program that operates on a P2P network of computers running a blockchain protocol – a type of distributed public ledger that allows the development of other applications"[12], and
- "DeFi": "Where these DApps offer financial services, such as those offered by VASPs, the term 'decentralised finance' (DeFi) is commonly used"[13]. According to the international institution, "A DeFi application (i.e. the software program) is not a VASP under the FATF standards, as the Standards do not apply to underlying software or technology"[14].

The approach of the FATF-GAFI has been to include "DeFi" arrangements within the scope of its guidance on the application of AML rules for crypto-assets markets. The FATF-GAFI has notably started to analyze the identification of the people "who maintain control or sufficient influence in the DeFi arrangements, even if those arrangements seem decentralized, may fall under the FATF definition"[15].

The difficulty with regard to the FATF-GAFI's definition proposal is that "DeFi" use cases are extremely broad and diverse (lending, brokerage, exchange trading, 'staking', etc.), and can neither be summarized narrowly as only a "software program" nor be analyzed as a whole as a unique services category. Decentralized finance could refer to the implementation of a minimal set of computer code through "smart contracts", but it can also refer to decentralized processes, institutions (distributed autonomous organizations) and even potentially market participants/infrastructures (decentralized trading exchanges or market makers). Besides, "DeFi" cannot be assumed by principle as a classical financial service as decentralized transfers are—at least partly— automated. The differences with traditional financial services are important, because several "DeFi" projects allow end-users to provide financial services, which highlights the need to study whether "DeFi" projects are financial services *per se* or whether they are 'only' building blocks enabling regulated entities to provide financial services.

1.3 Proposal for a "DeFi" Definition and Regulatory Assessment

As indicated by the FATF-GAFI, the so-called "Decentralized finance" (or "DeFi") is a technology, and as such "the European Union follows the principle of technological neutrality"[16]. Technological neutrality is a central pillar for entrepreneurship creativity.

In order to foster innovation while promoting investor protection and protecting market integrity, the effective regulation of decentralized finance projects could be to

---

[12] *Ibid.*, page 23, §56.

[13] *FATF-GAFI*, "Updated Guidance for a Risk-Based Approach for Virtual Assets and Virtual Asset Service Providers", octobre 2021, page 27, §66.

[14] *Ibid.*, page 27, §67.

[15] *Ibid.*

[16] "*Proposal for a Regulation of the European Parliament and of the Council on a pilot regime for market infrastructures based on distributed ledger* technology", published by the European Commission on 24th September 2020, pp. 3–4.

regulate the users of the technology, notably when they use "DeFi" protocols to provide financial services to clients, and not the technology *per se*. The fundamental promise of "DeFi" protocols is to allow economic exchanges in a more efficient way than traditional services, and it should be analyzed with this perspective in mind. The "decentralization" of services should not be interpreted as a lack or weakening of responsibility. "DeFi" could lead instead to a different set and sharing of responsibilities, by making certain existing services obsolete and instead strengthening other kinds of financial services. For instance, trading venues and market makers are deeply involved in "DeFi" markets, their role and functions are the same as on traditional capital markets, but their operating models and digital processes strongly differ. For regulated entities and corporations, "DeFi" is an important opportunity to digitalize, intermediate and automatize in a natively digital way the cash leg and the asset leg of any asset-based transaction, through the use of distributed ledgers and "smart contracts".

In our view, and on the basis of the FATF-GAFI studies, 'decentralized finance' refers to the programs, processes, institutions and/or infrastructures that operate on a peer-to-peer network of computers running a distributed ledger protocol to facilitate the realization of banking and/or financial services.

2 The Potential Interoperability of "DeFi" Protocols with CBDCs

The issuance of central bank money in a digital form, notably on distributed ledger technology (referred to thereafter as "CBDC"), has been a key topic of crypto-asset markets in 2021[17]. Various study reports and experiments have been realized by central banks and public institutions, notably about the design choices and from a macroeconomic perspective. The issue about the interoperability between CBDCs and decentralized protocols has been less discussed for the moment while it is one of the most disruptive potentialities at stake.

2.1 No Fundamental Incompatibility of CBDCs with "DeFi" Existing Use Cases

There is an apparent opposition between "DeFi" current use cases and the creation of CBDC (wholesale/retail). CBDC experiments have been accelerated due in part to concerns related to the development of privately-issued stablecoins (project "Libra"/"Diem" by a consortium led by the company Facebook, etc.), while "DeFi" protocols are frequently linked to stablecoins. It is undeniable that CBDCs have nowadays two main advantages on stablecoins: (i) legal certainty, and (ii) sovereign capacities (e.g. collection and distribution of taxes). Besides, as duly noted by a McKinsey study on "CBDC and stablecoins"[18]: "although a solid case can be made for the coexistence of stablecoins

---

[17] European Central Bank, "Eurosystem report on the public consultation on a digital euro", public report, April 2021; Sveriges Riksbank, "E-krona pilot – Phase 1", public report, April 2021; Banque de France, "Wholesale Central Bank Digital Currency Experiments with the Banque de France | Results & key findings", November 2021.

[18] McKinsey, "CBDC and stablecoins: Early coexistence on an uncertain road", article, 11 October 2021 .

and CBDCs (providing separate services such as DeFi services and liquidity provisioning, and direct access to central bank money, respectively), plausible scenarios could also lead to the long-term preeminence of either instrument. Some regulatory bodies have already expressed concern over substantial value flows settling via private stablecoins, implying potential actions to manage or curtail their use".

Nevertheless, the current trend is the development of a two-tiered system of fiat currencies and stablecoins in DLT-based protocols. Notably given the rapidly growing role of stablecoins in crypto-asset markets, where they play the role of safe-haven 'virtual currencies'. "DeFi" projects are not anymore theoretical problems, due to the substantial activities processes on "DeFi" protocols. As a significant example, the value locked in the "DeFi" protocol MakerDAO as collateral for crypto-assets-based loans has been estimated at 17 billion dollars in November 2021[19]. The coexistence between CBDCs and stablecoins will require interoperability, regulation and mutual flows. The role of CBDCs would be greatly impacted if they are structured without any capacity to interact with digital ecosystems such as crypto-asset trading platforms, NFTs, metaverse, etc. The interaction between CBDCs and various crypto-assets/decentralized ecosystems could be twofold: either (i) direct via the structuring of CBDCs with adapted features and architecture, and/or (ii) indirect through technological and operational interoperability between CBDCs and stablecoins (based on a similar set-up than the traditional two-tier model between central banks and commercial banks).

Besides, the use cases based on "DeFi" protocols could have economic advantages for the private sector beyond the sole role of stablecoins. As "DeFi" projects have benefited from a massive inflow of liquidity since the summer of 2020, many corporations are now expanding their exposures to crypto-assets' pools of liquidity (to diversify their treasury management, respond to their clients' requests, etc.). Given the flexibility and automation possibilities of "smart contracts", conditions related to key financial notions such as 'interest rates' and 'margin calls' could be substantially improved, with potential impacts on securities loans, repurchase agreements, tripartite repo activity, etc. These opportunities should be analyzed in conjunction with the risks related to "DeFi projects" such as financial crime/compliance risk, counterparty risk, market risk, technological risk (which includes both the "smart contract risk" and the "DLT risk") and regulatory risk. This is the reason why regulated entities are slowly studying "DeFi" experiments, as described below.

---

[19] TheBlockCrypto.com, "Value Locked by DeFi Project (Gross)", and "Value Locked in Lending", infography updated as of 2 November 2021.

2.2 "DeFi" for Regulated Financial Institutions: A Growing Evolution in 2022–2023

To date, the main examples that highlight the deepening connections between centralized finance and decentralized finance are the following:

- The common experimental projects directly developed between "DeFi" ecosystems and market participants, e.g.: Nivaura/Pairwyse Foundation, Societe Generale-Forge[20];
- The development of targeted "DeFi" offers designed for financial institutions by "DeFi" protocols, e.g. Aave whitelisting project, which aim to balance the advantages of "DeFi" technology and "whitelisting" KYC-AML processes.

Nivaura/Pairwyse project:
The Nivaura/Pairwyse project consists in creating a "fixed-rate marketplace for borrowers and lenders" in order to facilitate the possibility for MakerDAO lending activities to offer fixed-rate instruments. The aim of this project would be to foster the financing of traditional assets using crypto-assets, through the conclusion of fixed-rate peer-to-peer lending between investors via a smart contract system.

Societe Generale-Forge/MakerDAO project (2021–2022) (Fig. 1):
The project proposed by Societe Generale-Forge, a fully-owned subsidiary of Societe Generale Group, is related to the acceptance by the MakerDAO ecosystem of bond securities issued by a Societe Generale subsidiary on a public blockchain (the "OFH Tokens") as collateralized asset to generate the stablecoin DAI. This transaction would allow the refinancing of tokenized bonds through MakerDAO protocol. This real world transaction would be the first of its kind realized by a systemic financial institution.

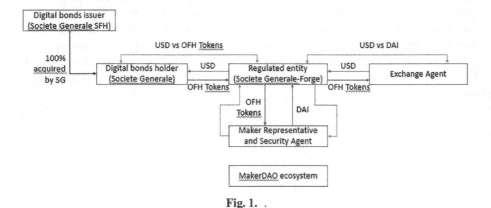

Fig. 1. .

---

[20] Société Générale-Forge, "[Security Tokens Refinancing] MIP6 Application for OFH Tokens", MIP6 proposal submittedto the vote and published on the MakerDAO forum website, 30 September 2021; Pairwyse Foundation, "Adding Pairwyse Fixed-Rate Core Unit", proposal published on MakerDAO forum website, 22 October 2021.

This transaction illustrates the possibility to link traditional assets (securities) with new types of crypto-assets (stablecoins) through the tokenization of assets. In this first ground-breaking experiment, an initial loan of US dollars by a regulated entity (here, Societe Generale-Forge) would be granted to a digital bonds holder (Societe Generale) and would be collateralized by digital bonds issued on a distributed ledger. The regulated entity will thereafter borrow DAI 'stablecoins' from the Maker Representative and pledge the digital bonds to the benefit of the Security Agent for that purpose. Technically speaking the digital bonds will be 'locked' within the Maker protocol and such locking will allow the creation and transfer of newly minted 'stablecoins' to the regulated entity. Once having obtained the 'stablecoins', the regulated entity will enter into a legal agreement with the Exchange Agent to receive US dollars in exchange of the DAI 'stablecoins'. The US dollars obtained pursuant to this agreement would allow the regulated entity to make the initial loan to the digital bonds holder.

This first experiment is a perfect example of the potentialities based on "DeFi" protocols to facilitate the coordination of capital market projects by financial actors. Various types of assets, including CBDCs, could be subject to a locking into a distributed ledger and allow the creation of 'stablecoins', fostering the links between traditional assets (securities, CBDCs, etc.) and new types of assets ('stablecoins', 'utility tokens', etc.).

3   The Potential Interoperability of "DeFi" Protocols with CBDCs

"DeFi" protocols offer the possibility to obtain peer-to-peer services similar to traditional banking services, such as high-yield deposits, collateralized lending, 'staking' and payments services. The role of CBDCs, notably wholesale CBDCs, could be important to add legal certainty to various use cases.

3.1   CBDC Use for DeFi-Based Deposits, Lending and Repurchase Agreements

The first use of CBDC for "DeFi" purposes would be related to deposits and lending activities. Currently the collateralized assets used on "DeFi" protocols are mainly crypto-currencies such as bitcoin (BTC) or ether (ETH). With the CBDC creation it could gravitate towards the use of CBDCs as the main collateral type backing stablecoins. It would have regulatory and financial strong repercussions, and maybe deepen the coexisting link between CBDCs and stablecoins.

The rationale for CBDC use instead of crypto-currencies as collateral of stablecoins would have to be assessed on a case-by-case basis. When the issuer of a stablecoin is a renowned corporation or financial institution, it could be interesting to mitigate the financial risks related to the asset by pegging this asset to a digital fiat currency instead of commodities or crypto-assets.

3.2   The Payment of Transactions on Decentralized Exchanges

Being issued by a central bank, a CBDC could be used as a settlement tool for the delivery versus settlement of various kinds of crypto-assets (and security tokens) transactions.

The EU regulation would provide the possibility to use CBDC for the payments of such transactions, even on MiFID financial instruments based on distributed ledger technology, as provided in the EU "Pilot Regime" regulation for market infrastructures based on distributed ledger technology[21].

The importance of using wholesale CBDC could be a game changer for decentralized exchanges willing to gain regulatory approvals and/or market credibility in their potential future competition with traditional exchanges, and vice versa. Due to various kinds of limitations, stablecoins could have difficulty to gain traction at a systemic scale from a regulatory and business perspective, notably due to the lack of regulatory certainty and the capacity sub-optimal limitations of current existing DLTs with regard to the amount of transactions validated per second.

4 The Assessment of Financial Crime Checks Through "DeFi" Protocols

In all the experiments on which the author has participated on CBDCs and DeFi, the main blocking points have been to foster solutions to respond to compliance requirements, notably on financial crime regulations (know-your-customer/know-your-transaction, anti-money laundering, assets freezing and sanctions-embargoes processes and checks).

4.1 The Permissioned Use of Permissionless Distributed Ledgers

There are many ways to facilitate a permissioned use of permissionless DLTs. On permissionless DLTs, to the opposite of permissioned DLTs, anyone can participate and access to the technological validation of the transactions. Whatever the technology used, there are common possibilities to permission the use of DLTs by intermediaries, notably through the use of an adequate operating model including the action of agents such as the registrar and the settlement agent.

4.2 The "Whitelisting" Possibilities

The first possibility would be to whitelist all the actors of the concerned ecosystem, notably the investors that will be the counterparties of transactions on "DeFi" protocols. In such way, these closed-door sessions of tokenized securities' and other types of crypto-assets' transfers could be monitored at all times. Such possibility has been developed by "DeFi" projects such as, among others, the partnership between Fireblocks and Aave.

---

[21] "The settlement of payments shall be carried out through central bank money, including in tokenised form, where practicable and available [. . .]." Cf.: Proposal for a Regulation of the European Parliament and of the Council on a pilot regime for market infrastructures based on distributed ledger technology, 2020/0267 (COD), 16 December 2021.

4.3   The Need for Standardized Governance and Operational Model

More broadly, the permissioned process for a DLT via an effective operating model should foster the protection of privacy and AML-KYC checks, based on some key elements: (i) the lack of direct identification of the crypto-asset holders on the DLT, (ii) the off-chain identification of the pseudonym identity of the holders, (iii) the KYC-AML checks provided either off-chain or on-chain through innovative KYC processes and pre-trade machine learning checks.

The following chart (Fig. 2) represents this process of settlement intermediate on through a balanced on-chain/off-chain process for native crypto-assets settlement[22]:

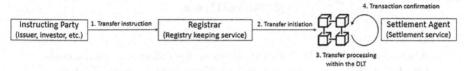

Fig. 2. .

5   Conclusion

This paper presents several opportunities and examples for a potential interoperability between CBDCs and "DeFi" protocols. "DeFi" is a clear opportunity to rethink the conditions to transfer value on internet in a more peer-to-peer and digital way, and for financial services providers (existing and new ones) to intermediate digitally the cash leg and the asset leg of a transaction on a distributed ledger, whatever a public or a private one.

Under which conditions would such interoperability be feasible?

From a legal standpoint, it is already feasible nowadays to conclude legal transactions related to existing assets on "DeFi" protocols (e.g. Societe Generale's current experiment with "MakerDAO"), though questions remain as to the industrialization of the use of these technologies by financial institutions.

From an operational and regulatory standpoint, there are strong conditions required to the gradual use of "DeFi" protocols by corporations, notably: (i) the compliance with financial crime checks through existing and new tools; and (ii) the urgent need to develop standardized operational and governance model for crypto-asset and security tokens handling by regulated entities (e.g. CAST Framework, etc.). Beyond legal certainty, creating effective operating models which responds to concrete questions for back-offices and middle-offices constitute the second step of crypto-assets markets normalization. This paper has indicated some clear opportunities and possibilities in this direction.

---

[22] Compliant Architecture for Security Tokens (CAST), «CAST I Compliant Architecture for Security Tokens – White Paper - 'Call to Action'», white paper, version 1.0, May 2021.

Broken Proofs of Solvency in Blockchain Custodial Wallets and Exchanges

Konstantinos Chalkias[1], Panagiotis Chatzigiannis[2(✉)], and Yan Ji[3]

[1] Mysten Labs, Palo Alto, USA
kostas@mystenlabs.com
[2] Visa Research, Palo Alto, USA
pchatzig@visa.com
[3] Cornell University, Ithaca, USA
yj348@cornell.edu

Abstract. Since the Mt. Gox Bitcoin exchange collapse in 2014, a number of custodial cryptocurrency wallets offer a form of financial solvency proofs to bolster their users' confidence. We identified that despite recent academic works that highlight potential security and privacy vulnerabilities in popular auditability protocols, a number of high-profile exchanges implement these proofs incorrectly, thus defeating their initial purpose. In this paper we provide an overview of *broken* liability proof systems used in production today and suggest fixes, in the hope of closing the gap between theory and practice. Surprisingly, many of these exploitable attacks are due to a) weak cryptographic operations, for instance SHA1 hashing or hash-output truncation to 8 bytes, b) lack of data binding, such as wrong Merkle tree inputs and misuse of public bulletin boards, and c) lack of user-ID uniqueness guarantees.

Keywords: blockchain · custodial wallets · solvency proofs · light clients · Merkle trees · public bulletin board · cryptographic attacks · data binding · hash-truncation · dispute resolution

1 Introduction

It is considered a good practice for organizations that accept and manage customer funds (ranging from banks to blockchain custodial wallets) to be periodically audited for their financial solvency, i.e., showing that they have enough assets to pay back their customers. These solvency audits imply that the amount of total assets owned by the organization at least matches[1] its total liabilities, which are effectively its customers' deposits.

---

[1] In certain cases, partial solvency might be sufficient, however for the purposes of our paper these cases are equivalent.

Kostantinos Chalkias did part of this work while at Meta.
Panagiotis Chatzigiannis did part of this work during his PhD studies at George Mason University.

S. Matsuo et al. (Eds.): FC 2022 Workshops, LNCS 13412, pp. 106–117, 2023.
https://doi.org/10.1007/978-3-031-32415-4_9

With many cryptocurrencies emerging during the last decade, several centralized organizations appeared offering various types of services such as exchanges, online wallets and interest accounts [29]. With blockchain technology at its infancy, these unregulated services remained opaque to their internal operations. Unsurprisingly, given the absence of a universal legal framework and centralized protection against fraudulent or malicious acts, combined with the delicacy of handling private keys required to spend cryptocurrency assets, a number of exchanges have lost their deposits and declared bankruptcy. In the most infamous case, the collapse of Mt. Gox (one of the oldest exchanges in Bitcoin's history), over $450M in customer assets were lost [34,35]. Other bad practices on behalf of those organizations include investing users' funds without their consent [19].

Towards implementing methods for preventing such fraudulent behavior against the cryptocurrency users, decentralized solutions [24,26–28,30,33,36] requiring customers to jointly participate on the auditing process were proposed as an alternative or complementary method to conventional auditing; therefore placing less trust on centralized auditors and empowering customers to verify that their own account and balance is indeed part of a Proof of Liabilities (which in turn is part of a Proof of Solvency), which cannot be achieved by centralized auditing. Ultimately, the goal exchanges proving their solvency is to earn users' trust in a distributed fashion while minimizing disclosure of additional information that could potentially expose clients' data, therefore preserving the "decentralization" and "(pseudo)-anonymity" characteristics. Naturally, we are now observing a rising demand in standardizing proof of solvency in the digital assets industry [23,28].

However, these new technologies, especially those in the blockchain space, are still being studied in terms of their security guarantees, and special considerations around potential weaknesses must be made during implementation. Proof of liabilities is no exception to this rule. All liability proving systems should serve the same goals: prove liabilities without understating obligations, while preserving privacy. However, recent works showed that these goals are not always met [28,29,32].

Our contributions. This work is the product of recent academic research on auditability and solvency, combined with extensive discussions with blockchain researchers in academia and auditing firms and stakeholders in blockchain associations and organizations. We show that improvements are still needed towards earning user trust, as we observe several cases of "broken" proof of liabilities implementations, therefore making these proofs disputable. After pinpointing to exploitable real world solvency processes, we provide the relevant discussion and context for addressing these issues towards closing the gap between theory and practice. Unfortunately, every analyzed solvency tool in this paper suffers from one or more exploitable security issues.

Paper Organization. The rest of the paper is organized as follows: In Sect. 2 we provide informal definitions for the related auditability proofs, and discuss different types of wallets to highlight the setting where these proofs are applicable.

In Sect. 3 we provide a high-level overview of existing Proof of Liabilities schemes in the literature, and their potential security or privacy issues. In Sect. 4 we show the weaknesses of existing practical PoL implementations in the blockchain space and suggestions for fixing them. In this Section we also highlight subtle differences which exist in some of those implementations, which do not make them necessarily insecure, but implicitly operate under a different trust model. We provide our final remarks and conclusions in Sect. 5.

2   Background

2.1   Definitions

We first informally present the basic properties required for the auditability proofs we are exploring based on the formal definitions in [33]. The participating parties in a Proof of Liabilities (PoL) protocol are the following: a) The exchange $\mathcal{P}$ which is in the prover role and b) The exchange customers $\mathcal{U} = \{u_1, \cdots, u_n\}$ in a verifier role. In our setting, $\mathcal{P}$ publishes a commitment to a liabilities dataset L on a public bulletin board such as a blockchain. Then on a user's query, $\mathcal{P}$ proves that the user's balance with the exchange is indeed part of L. A PoL scheme should ensure:

- *Security*: $\mathcal{P}$ will not be able to "hide"/"understate" its liabilities (note that $\mathcal{P}$ has no incentive to increase the total liabilities).
- *Privacy*: Any user u_i should not learn from the proof any information besides that its account balance is indeed included in L (e.g. total number of clients, other users' balances etc.)

2.2   Types of Cryptocurrency Wallets/Exchanges

The key management process is an important component of digital asset custody that clients should evaluate when choosing a wallet. This work focuses on custodial wallets, but as we realized many misconceptions around terminology even among experts, we provide a wallet-type categorization depending on who controls the on-chain private keys. Interestingly, blockchain wallets exist in different flavours regarding the offered capabilities and processes. There are also cases of hybrid types, where both the users and some custodian(s) mutually control the private keys [10]. Based on the above, we enlist four of the most popular wallet-types in the blockchain industry.

Pure Non-Custodial (PNC). In PNC wallets [11, 14] (often mentioned as self-custody), users control their on-chain assets by having full control over an actual blockchain address. Most of these will expect a recovery key or passphrase that lets users load the wallet on other devices and wallet software. These keys must be kept safe because once compromised anyone can access and control funds contained in the wallet. There exist many kinds of PNC wallets, such as mobile, desktop, hardware, paper, secure-enclave based, browser plugins and more.

Remark 1. *PNC wallets poses account recoverability risks, especially for non-experts, given many recent examples of people losing their keys [25], but indeed there is no dependency on custodians and solvency proofs are irrelevant.*

Assisted Non-Custodial (ANC). To circumvent the key-loss issue, ANC wallets (e.g. ZenGo and Conio [8,22]) remove the burden of the single atomic private key and split the responsibility between multiple parties. Typically, these wallets use a 2-out-of-3 key share policy, where one part of the key is known to the user (i.e., a passphrase), the other part is stored encrypted in some user-controlled encrypted storage (i.e., iCloud) and the third share is controlled by a custodian. In practice, two of the shares should participate in transaction signing, which implies that the custodian is a minority and cannot spend without the user's permission. If users forget their passphrase, they can still sign a transaction using their iCloud plus custodian's shares.

Remark 2. *There are variants of the above 2-out-of-3 approach, where instead of cloud storage, the user's bank has a share (i.e., see Conio.com wallet). In the above approach, the two "custodians" need to collude in order to cheat, so although no entity controls more than 33.3% of the key material, it would be interesting to explore if legislation will enforce requiring a custodial operation license. However, it is clear that ANC wallets don't require the custodian to prove solvency either.*

Omnibus Custodial (OC). An OC wallet (e.g., Coinbase[2] [7] and Binance [3] exchanges) holds user funds in pools of funds on-chain while balances are managed on a private ledger. The bulk of user funds is usually stored in one or more on-chain addresses even though the exchange might have millions of users. This means that there is not a 1-1 matching between a user account and an on-chain address. In fact, users do not interact with the blockchain at all and typically they are not even aware of what addresses their wallet provider controls. Due to user-experience benefits, reports from Chainalysis [13] show that custodial services are very popular among current cryptocurrency owners. Clearly, this is the major wallet type where proofs of solvency should apply.

Remark 3. *In case a user loses his/her password to an OC wallet, in most cases funds can be restored by KYC (know your customer) or "forgot my password" 2FA methods. Another benefit is protection of user's privacy against outsiders (only the custodian can see who owns what).*

Segregated Custodial (SC). In SC wallets, each user is assigned with one (or more) blockchain addresses, but the custodian controls all of the private keys on behalf of the users, as in Dapper wallet [9]. It is highlighted that if wallet users

---

[2] Note that Coinbase.com exchange is different from Coinbase wallet: Coinbase.com is an OC exchange, while Coinbase wallet is a PNC wallet, similar to Metamask. This subtle distinction [6] has caused confusion in the past with people losing their keys in the Wallet (and therefore their funds as well).

cannot track which on-chain addresses correspond to their accounts, a proof of solvency solution is also recommended.

Remark 4. *In SC wallets there is no mixing of cryptocurrencies from different users under the same address. This allows for public observability of "which account owns what" and this is usually considered as more transparent, but less privacy preserving, compared to OC.*

2.3 Proof of Liabilities in Wallets and Exchanges

Having discussed the above flavors of wallets and exchanges, we now need to emphasise that PoL is applicable to *custodial* wallets only, as in any non-custodial wallet type, users are directly involved in their assets management. Intuitively, a PoL protocol is easier to implement in a SC approach, and is more challenging in an OC approach, as the absence of a 1-1 match between user and on-chain address makes implementing a secure PoL (that prevents an exchange from hiding liabilities) more complex. In addition, as custodial wallets are popular among cryptocurrency owners [13], implementing secure proof of reserves for custodial wallets has already been proposed as an essential tool for the blockchain industry [23].

3   Proof of Liabilities Schemes

We now provide a brief overview of PoL schemes proposed in the blockchain setting [26–28, 30, 36]. All schemes follow the same paradigm we discussed in the previous section: the prover publishes a commitment and each user checks if his/her balance is properly included accordingly.

Provisions [30] proposes a PoL scheme in which $\mathcal{P}$ commits to each user's balance on a public bulletin board (PBB) so users can check if their balances are properly included. In particular, the balances are in homomorphic Pedersen commitments and proven positive in a zero-knowledge manner so that the values of users' balances are concealed. However, the commitment size on a PBB is linear in the number of users so it doesn't meet the efficiency requirement in [33]. Additionally, the number of users is public and dummy accounts need to be added to mitigate this privacy issue.

Maxwell-Todd scheme [36] initiated the line of works using a "summation" Merkle tree to prove total liabilities while minimizing the cost on PBB. In this Merkle tree variant, apart from the hash field h in each tree node, there's an additional value field v which is the sum of the values of the child nodes as shown in Fig. 1. In this approach, $\mathcal{P}$ generates the summation tree and publishes the Merkle root, with the value of the root representing the amount of $\mathcal{P}$'s total liabilities. Then any u can query $\mathcal{P}$ for a Merkle proof to make sure the amount is included in the tree. For example, in Fig. 1, on query by User 1, say Alice, $\mathcal{P}$ would reply with the Merkle path $(h_2, v_2), (h_6, v_6)$, which would enable Alice to verify the proof for the total liabilities in the root v_{root}.

This approach however is problematic, as it enables P to claim less liabilities [32] by computing each tree node value as $v = \max(v_l, v_r)$ while still being able to generate inclusion proofs and successfully pass any user queries. In addition, the value of the total liabilities is public (which is not ideal), and anyone can infer the population and/or individual liabilities though a series of inclusion proofs. Unfortunately, this scheme is still being used in existing cryptocurrency exchanges; we explain the security issues by an easy to follow example in Sect. 4.1.

Maxwell+ [32] fixes the vulnerability in the previous protocol by simply modifying each node field to include both values and hashes of child nodes, i.e., $h = \mathcal{H}(v_l||v_r||h_l||h_r)$. This modification effectively binds the value of each node in the parent, and prevents the manipulation of the tree we discussed previously. However this scheme still does not address the privacy issues we mentioned.

Maxwell++ [27] further extends Maxwell+ to conceal the population and individual liabilities by breaking and shuffling values into small units, but still without concealing P's total liabilities.

Camacho [26] provides privacy of liabilities by replacing the values in Maxwell-Todd by Pedersen commitments associated with zero-knowledge range proofs. The hiding and binding properties of Pedersen commitments provide privacy while preventing liability manipulation, and their homomorphic properties allows summation in commitments. The total liabilities can only be disclosed by voluntarily opening the commitment, or alternatively, P can prove the range of the total liabilities by utilizing zero-knowledge proofs. While Camacho hides liabilities, it leaks the number of users, and is also susceptible to the flaw we discussed in Maxwell-Todd's scheme.

DAPOL [28] and *DAPOL+* [33] improve Camacho by adopting the proposed fix in [32], and use sparse Merkle trees (SMT) to more efficiently hide the number of users.

4   Vulnerabilities in PoLs in Practice and Mitigations

Despite extensive theoretical research around PoL, as discussed in the previous section, we still observe a significant gap between these works and the implementations in practice. Among the hundreds of blockchain exchanges, only a handful of them support PoL [15]. Some rely on a trusted auditor to prove their liabilities, such as Kraken [1]. However, this trust model is not desired due to the possibility of collusion between the auditor and the exchange. Such auditing might fail when the auditor is deceived such as in the infamous Enron scandal [12]. On the other hand, while other exchanges assume a decentralized and trustless model (in line with the blockchain space), their implementation suffers from exploitable attacks that could result in understated liabilities.

In this section we present our survey of the existing landscape for performing PoL by highlighting these "problematic" implementations and our suggested fixes. We highlight, that although cryptocurrency exchanges could potentially take advantage of these incorrect implementations by under-reporting liabilities,

Table 1. Vulnerabilities in existing PoL implementations in practice.

Issues identified	Affected VASPs/auditors	Mitigation
Vulnerable summation tree	BHEX, Deloitte's audits	Bind left/right values vs. sum
Short hash collisions	BHEX	Avoid hash truncation
Shared user ID	Coinfloor, Kraken, BitMEX, Armanino's audits	Ensure unique user IDs
Inconsistent root commitment	Coinfloor, BitMEX	Commit on PBB
Leak of individual liabilities	BHEX, Deloitte's audits, Coinfloor	Use Pedersen commitments
Leak of number of users	BHEX, Deloitte's audits, Coinfloor, Kraken	Use sparse Merkle tree

our observations by no means imply that exchanges acted through malicious intent. In fact, it is highly possible that lack of a) proper code/protocol auditing and/or b) cryptography expertise are the major factors of the observed insecure implementations.

We do believe however that our results can be taken into account by the respective exchanges, blockchain associations and auditors to further increase customer confidence and potentially result in a healthier cryptocurrency ecosystem.

4.1 Vulnerable Summation Tree

We first observe exchanges or auditors using the vulnerable Maxwell's summation tree [36] in practice for proof of liabilities, such as [18] or [16] used by BlueHelix Exchange (BHEX/HBTC) and [2] by Deloitte's audit for ICONOMI. In these implementations, the hash field of each node in the tree is defined as $h(v_l + v_r || h(l) || h(r))$, as shown in Fig. 1, where l and r denote the child nodes. However, as we discussed in Sect. 3, this opens up the possibility for the exchange to claim less liabilities, as shown in Fig. 2, namely computing each parent as $h(max(v_l + v_r) || h(l) || h(r))$ therefore computing a different "version" of the liabilities tree on the fly, without the clients ever realizing this. For instance, User 1 will receive a proof with a valid Merkle path $(h_2, v_2' = 5), (h_6, v_6' = 0)$ without detecting any misbehavior (Fig. 3). In the worst case, a malicious VASP could only report the highest user balance as being its full liabilities (and not the sum of every balance). To mitigate this vulnerability, we can apply the technique in [32] by defining the tree as $h(v_l || v_r || h(l) || h(r))$. This construction includes both the left and right child value separately (instead of just the sum), so the trick of reduced liabilities is no longer feasible.

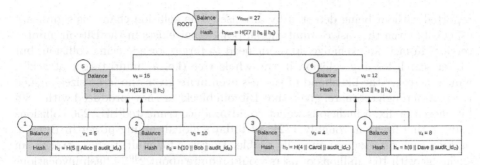

Fig. 1. Exploitable summation tree

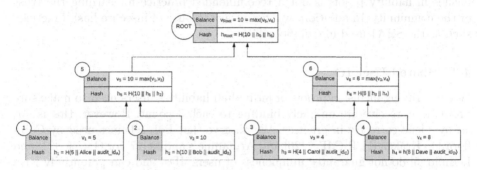

Fig. 2. Claiming reduced liabilities

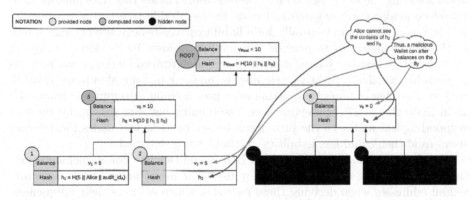

Fig. 3. Proof of reduced liabilities

4.2 Short Hash Collisions

In BHEX's PoL implementation [18], we also observe that a 64-bit truncated SHA256 hash is used for all nodes in the tree. However, this level of truncation is insecure due to increased possibility of hash collisions. Once an adversary finds a collision in hash for two users, she can assign them to the same leaf node and return the same Merkle path to them. The total liabilities can then be under-reported without being detected by any user. The collision chance is significant especially given the vast computational power that exists in the Bitcoin mining setting. In fact, an exchange does not need to target for a specific collision, but rather search for *any* collision in the whole tree (i.e. a "multi-target attack"), which increases the likelihood of success even more given the large sizes of such trees. As a rough estimate, given that Bitcoin blocks are now produced with a 80-bit chosen prefix, a malicious wallet could produce truncated SHA256 collisions using a tiny fraction, roughly $1/2^{16}$ of today's global mining power in Bitcoin, making such attacks economically viable. However for multi-target attacks, an exchange with 16+ millions of users would require about 2^{40} of hash invocations to find a match, making this attack practically feasible. In short, truncating hashes in liability proofs is not a recommended practice for earning the trust of the community. In addition, we discourage the use of insecure hash functions such as the SHA1 used in Coinfloor [4].

4.3 Shared User ID

When verifying inclusion proofs of individual liabilities, users need to make sure proofs they receive are uniquely binding to each account. However, this is not always done correctly in practice. We observe that PoL schemes used by Coinfloor [4], Kraken [1], BitMEX [20] and Armanino's audits [17] for Gate.io [21] and Ledn.io [5] do not guarantee uniqueness of users' IDs, and can potentially let a malicious prover to reuse the same user ID for different users. This in turn would allow selecting the same user ID for different users having the same balance (and therefore mapped to the same leaf node in the Merkle tree or the same entry in the report file) and eventually hide liabilities. We believe the original intent of those exchanges was to provide privacy for the user by randomly assigning them user IDs, however having user IDs purely determined by the prover remains exploitable. Similarly, BitMEX attempts to preserve privacy of individual liabilities and number of users by splitting each user account into multiple leaf nodes as in Maxwell++ [27]. However, there's no binding between a user and the corresponding leaf nodes, so the prover can reuse the same leaf nodes for different users (and then claim less liabilities) without being detected.

On the other hand, we observe that BHEX and Deloitte PoL implementations do not suffer from such issues, as they use their users' unique usernames and e-mail addresses when deriving these user IDs, which enforces their uniqueness. In practice, to comply with EU's GDPR regulation, exchanges could ask from the users to provide a long unique-ID and avoid hashing private information, such as email addresses. All in all, we encourage binding unique user credentials with user IDs and all corresponding leaf nodes in Maxwell++ style constructions or better DAPOL+.

4.4 Multiple Root Commitments

In a secure PoL scheme, the prover needs to publish the commitment on a public bulletin board (PBB) to guarantee users have consistent views of the public commitment. Otherwise, a malicious prover can supply different commitments to different users so that the proofs received are all valid but are not binded to the same commitment. In this way, the prover can effectively omit some balances in each commitment without being detected. Although most PoL implementations we looked into, such as in BHEX, Deloitte and Kraken, mentioned that the commitment should be "published", the operation of *publishing on PBB* are sometimes done inappropriately. For example, Coinfloor publishes a hash of the report file on blockchain and then the transaction ID on its website [4]. Since blockchains are considered as a practical implementation of a PBB [31], the former operation guarantees non-equivocation of the commitment. However, when the prover serves the transaction ID on its own website, the whole liability proof becomes problematic. If users only access this particular website, the prover who controls that website might present different versions of the commitment to different users, thus opening the possibility of hiding liabilities. Similarly, BitMEX publishes the commitment on an AWS server, which however remains exploitable.

To avoid equivocation, we encourage exchanges to publish these commitments on a PBB such as a blockchain, and users verifying their commitments would be confident that proof manipulation would be practically infeasible because of the blockchain's immutability properties. Users should also ensure that no more than one commitment for the same solvency round is published in the PBB. As an alternative approach, the commitment could be digitally signed by a trusted auditor.

4.5   Privacy Concerns

As discussed in Sect. 2.1, there are also privacy concerns on PoLs in addition to the potential attacks to claim less liabilities. While DAPOL+ includes a formal general definition of privacy [33], here we particularly focus on the privacy of individual liabilities and number of users, and demonstrate how much sensitive data is leaked in each scheme.

First, the PoL implementations by BHEX, Deloitte's audits and Coinfloor leak individual user liabilities. In particular, PoL proofs received by users consists of the balance of one or multiple other users. We recommend using Pedersen commitments like in DAPOL+ to hide individual liabilities. Alternatively, the prover can split each account into multiple entries as in BitMEX, but this results in an efficiency degradation proportionally to the number of entries each account is split into.

Additionally, the schemes of BHEX, Deloitte's audits, Coinfloor and Kraken leak the total number of users. Using sparse Merkle tree as suggested in DAPOL+ could mitigate such problem. As above, the exchanges could simply split each account into multiple entries and therefore also hide the number of users, but again this approach comes at a cost of efficiency.

4.6 Dispute Resolution and Private Verification Pattern

Apart from the fundamental security and privacy requirements for PoL, there are a few additional problems that may be of concern in practice but not carried out right now. One is dispute resolution, which is still an open research problem [29]. For instance, a user might fail to verify a liability proof, however there is no mechanism or protocol in place to resolve a dispute between an exchange and a user against a third party judge, when the former claims that the user's account balance is indeed included in the liabilities proof and the latter claims the opposite.

Private verification pattern as discussed in [33] is another subtle problem to be concerned. For each audit, not all users actually query for PoL proofs and perform verification. If a malicious prover learns that some users never verifies the proofs, she can safely omit their balances in the next solvency round. Therefore it would be nice to hide users' verification pattern from the prover. Outsourcing proofs to a trusted auditor like in Kraken helps mitigate this issue but there is privacy leak to the auditor and Kraken's implementation doesn't provide verifiability of the sum but only individual inclusions. It remains an open problem to efficiently hide verification pattern without a trusted third party, although private information retrieval techniques have been proposed [28].

5 Conclusion

Having provided an extensive survey of the cryptocurrency exchange landscape in terms of their liability proofs, by pinpointing problematic implementations and their mitigations, we observe that few exchanges implement a Proof of Solvency protocol, and even fewer implement it correctly. We highlight 4 different attack types in these proofs, as well as trust models inconsistent with blockchain decentralization and privacy concepts. We believe that lack of user education combined with these few, exploitable implementations are responsible for the slow adoption of those proofs. We hope our work, being practical in nature, will directly serve as a standard towards improving cryptocurrency exchange auditability and improve user trust in the blockchain ecosystem.

References

1. Audit: learn about kraken's audit process. https://www.kraken.com/proof-of-reserves-audit
2. Bhex 100% proof of reserve. https://medium.com/iconominet/proof-of-solvency-technical-overview-d1d0e8a8a0b8
3. Binance exchange. https://www.binance.com/
4. Bitcoin audits. https://web.archive.org/web/20210706073111/. https://coinfloor.co.uk/hodl/proof/#reports
5. Check your proof of reserves in 5 simple steps. https://blog.ledn.io/en/blog/proof-of-reserves/step-by-step

6. Coinbase blog. https://blog.coinbase.com/goodbye-toshi-hello-coinbase-wallet-the-easiest-and-most-secure-crypto-wallet-and-browser-4ba6e52e4913
7. Coinbase exchange. https://www.coinbase.com/
8. Conio wallet. https://www.conio.com/en/
9. Dapper account manager. https://www.meetdapper.com/
10. Digital wallets - variations and features. https://cryptoapis.io/blog/41-digital-wallets-variations-and-features
11. Electrum bitcoin wallet. https://electrum.org
12. Enron scandal. https://en.wikipedia.org/wiki/Enron_scandal
13. Mapping the universe of 460 million bitcoin addresses. https://blog.chainalysis.com/reports/bitcoin-addresses
14. Metamask - a crypto wallet & gateway to blockchain apps. https://metamask.io/
15. Nic's PoR wall of fame. https://niccarter.info/proof-of-reserves/
16. Proof of liabilities implementation. https://github.com/olalonde/proof-of-liabilities
17. Proof of reserves. https://www.armaninollp.com/software/trustexplorer/proof-of-reserves/
18. Proof of solvency: technical overview. https://support.hbtc.co/hc/en-us/articles/360046287754-BHEX-100-Proof-of-Reserve
19. Tether's bank says it invests customer funds in bitcoin. https://www.coindesk.com/tethers-bank-says-it-invests-customer-funds-in-bitcoin
20. Tool suite for generating and validating proofs of reserves (PoR) and liabilities (PoL). https://github.com/BitMEX/proof-of-reserves-liabilities
21. Your gateway to cryptocurrency. https://www.gate.io/
22. Zengo wallet. https://zengo.com/
23. Chamber of digital commerce: proof of reserves - establishing best practices to build trust in the digital assets industry (2021)
24. Bitfury: on blockchain auditability (2016)
25. Blackshear, S., et al.: Reactive key-loss protection in blockchains. Cryptology ePrint Archive, Report 2021/289 (2021). https://ia.cr/2021/289
26. Camacho, P.: Secure protocols for provable security. https://www.slideshare.net/philippecamacho/protocols-for-provable-solvency-38501620 (2014)
27. Chalkias, K., Lewi, K., Mohassel, P., Nikolaenko, V.: Practical privacy preserving proofs of solvency. Amsterdam ZKProof Community Event (2019)
28. Chalkias, K., Lewi, K., Mohassel, P., Nikolaenko, V.: Distributed auditing proofs of liabilities. Cryptology ePrint Archive, Report 2020/468 (2020). https://eprint.iacr.org/2020/468
29. Chatzigiannis, P., Baldimtsi, F., Chalkias, K.: Sok: Auditability and accountability in distributed payment systems. In: ACNS (2021)
30. Dagher, G.G., Bünz, B., Bonneau, J., Clark, J., Boneh, D.: Provisions: privacy-preserving proofs of solvency for bitcoin exchanges. In: CCS (2015)
31. Garman, C., Green, M., Miers, I.: Decentralized anonymous credentials. In: NDSS. Citeseer (2014)
32. Hu, K., Zhang, Z., Guo, K.: Breaking the binding: attacks on the Merkle approach to prove liabilities and its applications. Comput. Secur. 87, 10585 (2019)
33. Ji, Y., Chalkias, K.: Generalized proof of liabilities. In: CCS (2021)
34. McMillan, R.: The inside story of Mt. Gox, bitcoin's $460 million disaster (2014). https://www.wired.com/2014/03/bitcoin-exchange/
35. Moore, T., Christin, N.: Beware the middleman: empirical analysis of bitcoin-exchange risk. In: FC (2013)
36. Wilcox, Z.: Proving your bitcoin reserves. https://bitcointalk.org/index.php?topic=595180.0

Privacy-Preserving Post-quantum Credentials for Digital Payments

Raza Ali Kazmi[✉], Duc-Phong Le, and Cyrus Minwalla

FinTech Research, Bank of Canada, 234 Wellington Street, Ottawa, Canada
{rkazmi,dle,cminwalla}@bankofcanada.ca

Abstract. Digital payments and decentralized systems enable new financial products and services for users. A core challenge stems from the need to protect users from fraud and abuse while retaining privacy in individual transactions. Proposed herein is a pseudonymous credential scheme for use in payment systems. The scheme is privacy-preserving, efficient for practical applications, and hardened against quantum-compute attacks. A constant-round, interactive, zero-knowledge proof of knowledge (ZK-POK), relying on a one-way function and an asymmetric encryption primitive, both of which need to support at most one homomorphic addition, is presented. The scheme is instantiated with SWIFFT as a post-quantum one-way function and Ring Learning With Errors (RLWE) as a post-quantum asymmetric encryption primitive, with the protocol deriving its quantum-hardness from the properties of the underlying primitives. Performance of the ZK-POK instantiated with the chosen primitive was evaluated to reveal a memory footprint of 85 kB to achieve 200 bits of security. Comparison reveals that our scheme is more efficient than equivalent, state-of-the-art post-quantum schemes. A practical, interactive, credential mechanism was constructed from the proposed building blocks, in which users are issued pseudonymous credentials against their personally identifiable information (PII) that can be used to register with financial service providers without revealing personal information. The protocol is shown to be secure and free of information leakage, preserving the user's privacy regardless of the number of registrations.

Keywords: zero-knowledge proof · pseudonymous credentials · post-quantum · digital payments · digital finance

1 Introduction

The impact of digitization on the financial industry cannot be understated. From open banking to smart contracts to decentralized finance, the increasing sophistication of financial instruments in the marketplace will empower individuals in previously unforeseen ways and usher in a new economic era. Participating in the new economy can be challenging for individuals, as institutions need

© International Financial Cryptography Association 2023
S. Matsuo et al. (Eds.): FC 2022 Workshops, LNCS 13412, pp. 118–137, 2023.
https://doi.org/10.1007/978-3-031-32415-4_10

to balance access and privacy of users yet remain compliant with legal frameworks to prevent money-laundering and anti-terrorism financing. Registration can often be an awkward and painful process for users if the service is internet based and the provider is unable to make physical touch-points available to verify traditional forms of government-issued identification. Furthermore, users are required to share their personally identifiable information (PII) to multiple service providers, increasing the risk of a confidentiality breach in the event of a data breach at any one service provider.

On the other hand, intermediaries offering financial services are compelled by a strict legal and regulatory framework to know their customers. Traditionally, this necessitates that the organizational record the PII data of each user at the time of registration. However, in doing so, it places a strong burden on the organization to protect this 'treasure trove' of user data against breaches and cyber-attacks. Therefore, a mechanism is desired where individuals can register against their PII data in a zero-knowledge fashion. As such, a pseudonymous credential scheme is proposed with the following properties: (1) users can prove ownership of PII in a zero-knowledge fashion (2) the organization can work with the credential issuing authority to uncover the identity of a user suspected of illicit or illegal activity. The first property enables users to access services without revealing their personal information, while the second allows organizations to satisfy their legal and regulatory compliance burden while offering services to said users.

1.1 Related Work

Pseudonymous credentials and privacy-preserving authentication schemes have a long history in cryptography and computer science. Early work by Chaum [1] in 1985 introduced blind signatures to generate pseudonymous credentials. Similarly seminal work by Damgård [2] in 1988 developed anonymous credentials in the form of a commitment scheme, negotiating a set of pseudonymous signatures with participating organizations for transactions. Both schemes are privacy-preserving, such that pseudonymous credentials could not be linked back to the user. However, Chaum's scheme requires a trusted authority to sign and validate credentials, thereby linking credentials and identifying the user. Damgård's variant is more private, where even the trusted authority has no mechanism to link two pseudonymous credentials for the same user. Unfortunately, both the Chaum and Damgard schemes are not efficient for practical applications.

Chen [3] refined Chaum's scheme by eliminating the cut-and-choose protocol. His scheme was relied on discrete-logarithm-based blind signatures and retained the reliance on a trusted authority to sign each pseudonymous credential issued by the user. Lysanskaya et al. [4] extended Chaum's scheme by associating each user with a master key pair signed and validated by a central authority, and subsequent credentials are issued as one-time pseudonymous pairs that are cryptographically linked to the master secret key. This allowed the issuer to confirm keys as valid pairs without revealing the user's identity. Similarly, Brands [5] proposed a scheme to produce one-time signatures by controlling the attributes of the pseudonym. Camenisch et al. [6] propose a private pseudonymous credential scheme where a user enrolls at a specific organization via pseudonymous credentials, which are issued by a central authority once the user presents their real credentials. Key features of the scheme include protection against forgeability and the use of circular encryption primitives as an alternative to blind signatures to reveal any reuse of credentials. The work was refined further in [7], culminating in CL-Signatures [8] that create verifiable yet anonymous zero-knowledge proofs of knowledge from the strong RSA assumption. In all of the aforementioned schemes, reliance on an honest central authority is crucial to ensure the security of the protocol. Blomer et al. [9,10] construct practical credentials that are delegatable and upgradable. Relying on Pointcheval-Sanders blind signatures [11] as a fundamental building block, the credentials are parameterized as a vector of attributes, where verification of one or more attributes can be zero-knowledge.

In the schemes discussed so far, the primitives are not secure against quantum computing attacks, or in the case of Damgård, a purely theoretical scheme. Pseudonymous credential schemes that are quantum-hard include work by Ben-Sasson et al. [12], who presented an anonymous credential system built on ZK-STARKs and an interactive oracle proof construct that relies on probabilistic verification. The work was further refined as a practical, lightweight implementation called Aurora [13]. Malleable signatures, introduced by Chase et al. [14], allow approved transformations to be performed on digitally signed messages while maintaining unforgeability of the original signature. The authors proposing the scheme as a natural fit for anonymous credentials, however the construction relies on the availability of a succinct non-interactive argument (SNARG) and fully homomorphic encryption, and the scheme is neither efficient nor practical. Later work by Chase et al. [15] introduced upgrades to the ZKBoo protocol [16], with ZKB++ as a post-quantum non-interactive zero knowledge proof, and Fish and Picnic as two options for a lightweight post-quantum signature scheme based on symmetric encryption. Ligero [17] introduced by Ames et al. improves upon Chase's work by reducing the complexity requirement for ZKB++. Both Aurora and Ligero are provably secure from a post-quantum perspective, and as such, are suitable candidates for a performance comparison with the proposed protocol.

1.2 Contributions

This paper proposes a credential scheme that satisfies all five of the aforementioned qualities. The credential mechanism can be instantiated by any one-way function and encryption scheme that supports at least one homomorphic addition. The scheme is secure against polynomial-time quantum adversary provided the underlying cryptographic primitives are secure against a quantum adversary. The scheme satisfies the following properties:

1. An honest user can convince a verifier in polynomial-time that credentials C corresponds to their **PII**.
2. No polynomial-time verifier can learn personal identifiable information (**PII**) from a credential.

3. Any two credentials (even corresponding to the same **PII**) are computationally indistinguishable.
4. No polynomial-time malicious user can convince a verifier that a credentials belongs to them except with negligible probability.
5. The issuer can revoke and learn the identity of a user from their credentials.

At the heart of our scheme is a new constant round computational zero-knowledge interactive proof for the language

$$L_f = \{y \mid y = f(s) \text{ for } s \in \{0,1\}^*\},$$

where f is a one-way function that supports at least one homomorphic addition. The scheme is instantiated with SWIFFT, a provably secure post-quantum hash function [18] and RLWE public-key crypto-system [19], which is a provably secure post-quantum asymmetric encryption algorithm.

2 Building Blocks

2.1 Notations

Let $\mathbb{N}$ be the set of positive integers. For $k \in \mathbb{N}$, we set $[k] = \{1, \cdots, k\}$. We denote the set of all binary strings of length n by $\{0,1\}^n$. An element $s \in \{0,1\}^n$ is called a bitstring, and $|s| = n$ denotes its length. Given two bit strings x and y of equal length, we denote their bitwise XOR by $x \oplus y$. For a finite set X, the notation $x \xleftarrow{\$} X$ indicates that x is selected uniformly at random from X.

A function $\texttt{negl} : \mathbb{N} \to \mathbb{R}^+ \cup \{0\}$ is *negligible* if for every positive polynomial $poly(n)$, there exists a positive integer n_0 such that for all $n > n_0$, $negl(n) < 1/poly(n)$. A typical use of negligible functions is to indicate that the probability of success of some algorithm is too small to be amplified to a constant by a feasible (*i.e.*, polynomial) number of repetitions.

2.2 Computational Assumptions

Let $\Pi = (\texttt{KeyGen}, \texttt{Enc}, \texttt{Dec})$ be a CPA-secure public-key encryption scheme that supports at least one-homomorphic addition. Where $\texttt{Keygen}$ and $\texttt{Enc}$ are probabilistic polynomial-time algorithms and $\texttt{Dec}$ is a deterministic polynomial-time algorithm. The $\texttt{Keygen}$ takes a security parameter 1^λ and outputs a pair of public/private keys (pk, sk). $\texttt{Enc}$ takes a public key and a message m from underlying plaintext space and outputs a ciphertext $c \leftarrow \texttt{Enc}_{pk}(m)$. And $\texttt{Dec}$ takes a private key sk and a ciphertext c, and outputs a message m or a symbol $\bot$ denoting failure. We define a language L_f for f as follows,

$$L_f = \{y \mid y = f(x) \text{ for } x \in \{0,1\}^*\},$$

where f is a one-way function that supports at least one homomorphic addition.

3   Constant Round Zero-Knowledge Proof of Knowledge

In this section we provide a constant-round computational zero-Knowledge interactive proof of Knowledge for the language L_f (Sect. 2.2) from any CPA-secure public-key encryption scheme Π that supports at least one homomorphic addition.

Theorem 1. *The Algorithm 1 is a (constant-round) computational zero-knowledge interactive proof of knowledge for L_f with an efficient (polynomial-time) prover.*

Proof. The protocol must be shown to satisfy the following four properties.

(a) **Completeness:** Suppose the statement is true i.e., $y \in L_f$. Then there exist an x such that $y = f(x)$. Note that ciphertexts received by the prover is of form:

$$c_i = \begin{cases} Enc_{pk}(s_i), & \text{if } b_i = 0 \\ Enc_{pk}(x + s_i), & \text{otherwise.} \end{cases}$$

An honest prover can recover plaintexts from each ciphertexts c_i and from the plaintexts can compute the quantity $f(x + s_i)$ or $f(s_i)$. Verifier knows

---

Common Input: $y \in L_f$.

1. Prover generate a public/private key-pair $(pk, sk) \leftarrow$ Keygen(1^λ).
2. Prover sends $(pk, Enc_{pk}(x))$ to the Verifier. Note x is the secret such that $y = f(x)$.
3. Verifier computes for each $i \in [k]$, where $k \in O(poly(|y|))$.
   - $b_i \overset{\$}{\leftarrow} \{0, 1\}$
   - $s_i \overset{\$}{\leftarrow} \{0, 1\}^{|y|}$
   - Verifier computes ciphertexts

   $$c_i = \begin{cases} Enc_{pk}(s_i), & \text{if } b_i = 0 \\ Enc_{pk}(x) + Enc_{pk}(s_i), & \text{otherwise.} \end{cases}$$

   - Verifier sends $(c_1, \ldots, c_k)$ to the prover.
4. Prover:
   - Using the private-key sk computes $m_i = Dec_{sk}(c_i)$ for each $i \in [k]$.
   - Prover computes $f(m_1), \ldots, f(m_k)$.
   - Prover sends $(f(m_1), \ldots, f(m_k))$ to the verifier.
5. Verifier accepts the proof if and only if for all $i \in [k]$.

$$\Big(\big(b_i = 0 \wedge f(m_i) = f(s_i) \big) \vee \big(b_i = 1 \wedge y = f(m_i) \oplus f(s_i) \big) \Big) = 1.$$

Algorithm 1: Computational Zero-Knowledge Proof for the language L_f

b_i, s_i and $f(x)$ can check using the homomorphic property of f if y is in the language. Therefore an honest verifier will be convinced that the input y is in the language.

(b) **Soundness:** Suppose $y \notin L_f$, i.e., there does not exists a binary string x such that $y = f(x)$. Then the only way a prover can deceive a verifier is to guess bits b_i for all $i \in [k]$ and sends $f(s_i)$ if $b_i = 0$ and $y + f(s_i)$ otherwise. The probability of verifier correctly guessing all randomly and independent chosen bits is 2^{-k}. Therefore, the protocol is sound.

(c) **Complexity** Clearly both prover and verifier runs in expected polynomial-time.

(d) **Zero-Knowledge:** Let V^* denote a verifier (possibly malicious). What V^* learns by participating in the proof can be describe by the following transcript

$$(y, pk, Enc_{pk}(x), (c_1, \ldots, c_k), (f(m_1), \ldots, f(m_k))).$$

For any $y \in L_f$, we denote the set of all possible transcripts that could be produced as a result of prover and verifier carried out the interactive proof as

$$\mathcal{T}(V^*, y).$$

We introduce a simulator $\mathcal{S}$ that can forge transcripts as per Algorithm 2. Let $P_{\mathcal{T}(V^*,y)}(T)$ denote the probability that a transcript $T \in \mathcal{T}(V^*, y)$ is produced by V^* taking part in the proof. Let $\mathcal{T}(\mathcal{S}(V^*), y)$ be the set of transcripts generated by the simulator $\mathcal{S}(V^*)$ on input y and given the oracle access to V^*. And let $P_{\mathcal{T}(\mathcal{S}(V^*),y)}(T)$ denote the probability that a transcript $T \in \mathcal{T}(V^*, y)$ is produced by $\mathcal{S}(V^*)$.

To prove computational zero-knowledge, we need to illustrate that the probability distribution $P_{\mathcal{T}(V^*,y)}(T)$ and $P_{\mathcal{T}(\mathcal{S}(V^*),y)}(T)$ are computationally indistinguishable,

$$P_{\mathcal{T}(V^*,y)}(T) \approx_c P_{\mathcal{T}(\mathcal{S}(V^*),y)}(T).$$

Common Input: $y \in L_f$

(a) Generate a public-private key-pair $(pk', sk') \leftarrow \mathsf{Keygen}(1^\lambda)$.
(b) Compute $Enc_{pk'}(x')$ for any plaintext x' in the message space.
(c) Concatenate y, pk' and $Enc_{pk'}$ onto the end of transcript $T_\mathcal{S}(y)$.
(d) Call V^* with input y, pk', and $Enc_{pk'}(x')$ and obtain ciphertext $c'_1, \ldots, c'_k$.
(e) Compute $m'_i = Dec_{sk}(c'_i)$ for $i \in [k]$.
(f) Compute $f(m'_1), \ldots, f(m'_k)$.
(g) Concatenate $(c'_1, \ldots, c'_k)$ and $(f(m'_1), \ldots, f(m'_k))$ onto the end of $T_\mathcal{S}(y)$.

Algorithm 2: Simulator $\mathcal{S}$ for forging transcripts

The transcript generated in the interactive proof is

$$(y, pk, Enc_{pk}(x), (c_1, \ldots, c_k), (f(m_1), \ldots, f(m_k))),$$

and the transcript generated by the simulator is

$$(y, pk', Enc_{pk'}(x'), (c'_1, \ldots, c'_k), (f(m'_1), \ldots, f(m'_k))).$$

Note that both have the same common inputs y, the keys pk, and pk' are generated using the same key generation algorithm KeyGen with the same security parameter as an input. Moreover, from semantic security of the encryption scheme it follows that both encryptions $Enc_{pk'}(x')$ and $Enc_{pk}(x')$ are computationally indistinguishable. Therefore,

$$(y, pk, Enc_{pk}(x)) \approx_c (y, pk', Enc_{pk'}(x')),$$

For each $i \in [k]$ ciphertexts c_i and C'_i are produced by V^* (on inputs $y, pk', Enc_{pk'}(x')$), but since $(y, pk, Enc_{pk}(x)) \approx_c (y, pk', Enc_{pk'}(x'))$, therefore

$$(c_1, \ldots, c_k) \approx_c (c_1', \ldots, c_k')$$

are also computationally indistinguishable.

Finally, $f(m_i)$'s and $f(m'_i)$'s are completely determined by c_i, c_i' and f we have

$$(f(m_1), \ldots, f(m_k)) \approx_c (f(m'_1), \ldots, f(m'_k))$$

Therefore, the two probability distributions are computationally indistinguishable, i.e.

$$P_{T(V^*,y)}(T) \approx_c P_{T(S(V^*),y)}(T).$$

$\square$

(e) **Proof of Knowledge:** To prove that Algorithm 1 is also a proof of knowledge, we first slightly modify this algorithm to Algorithm 6 (see Appendix A). The modified protocol is information theoretically equivalent and has the same time complexity (up to a polynomial factor) as the original protocol. The reason for this modification is that it is much simpler to construct an extractor (Algorithm 3) for the modified version[1]. Let P^* be a (possibly malicious) prover that convinces the honest verifier with probability 1.

Note the extractor fails if for all $i \in [k]$, $b_i = b'_i$, which happens with probability 2^{-k}. Therefore, the knowledge error here is 2^{-k}.

---

[1] The main difference is in the step 4, the prover also sends n uniformly random strings to the verifier (see Appendix A).

1. Initialize P^*: Copy fresh random bits to the prover's random tape and fill up the Auxiliary-Input tape with a witness x.
2. Run P^* to obtain $Enc_{pk}(x)$. The prover now in state Q
3. Computes for each $i \in [k]$,
   - $b_i \xleftarrow{\$} \{0,1\}$
   - $s_i \xleftarrow{\$} \{0,1\}^{|y|}$
   - $c_i = b_i \cdot Enc_{pk}(x) + Enc_{pk}(s_i)$
   - Sends $(c_1, \dots, c_k)$ to P^* and obtain

$$(b_1 x + s_1 + t_1, f(b_1 x + s_1)), \dots, (b_1 x + s_1 + t_1, f(b_k x + s_k))$$

4. Rewind P^* to state Q.
5. Compute for each $i \in [k]$,
   - $b_i \xleftarrow{\$} \{0,1\}$
   - $c_i' = b_i' \cdot Enc_{pk}(x) + Enc_{pk}(s_i)$
   - Send $(c_1', \dots, c_k')$ to P^* and get

$$(b_1' x + s_1 + t_1, f(b_1' x + s_1)), \dots, (b_k' x + s_k + t_k, f(b_k' x + s_k)))$$

6. Pick any $i \in [k]$ such that $b_i \neq b_i'$
7. Output

$$x = \begin{cases} b_i' x + s_i + t_i - (b_i x + s_i + t_i), & \text{if } b_i = 0 \\ b_i x + s_i + t_i - (b_i' x + s_i + t_i), & \text{otherwise.} \end{cases}$$

Algorithm 3: Knowledge Extractor $\mathcal{E}$

3.1 Instantiation of Constant-Round ZKIP

In this section the protocol is instantiated with cryptographic primitives that are provably secure against polynomial-time quantum adversaries and are efficient enough for practical application. Our protocol requires a one-way function and a semantically secure encryption that supports at least one homomorphic addition.

Lattice-based cryptography offers provable security against quantum attacks. Several works [20] showed that lattice-based PKE can have performance competitive with those based on classical mechanisms like RSA or Discret Logarithm. Among lattice-based PKEs, schemes based on Learning with Errors (LWE) [21] or its variants such as RLWE [19] are more efficient. The LWE problem was introduced by Regev in [21] proven to be as secure as certain lattice problems under a quantum reduction. This problem can be seen as a generalization of the learning parity with noise (LPN) problem [22]. In the original Regev PKE scheme, which is based on LWE, the public and secret keys are very large (megabytes). A more efficient LWE-based PKE is Frodo [23,24], an alternate in NIST PQC competition. [2] Frodo's public key and ciphertext sizes are both approximately 11KB each. Using structured lattices in the LWE problem can lead to more efficient schemes in terms of space. Both ring learning with errors (RLWE) public-key

---

[2] https://csrc.nist.gov/projects/post-quantum-cryptography.

cryptosystems [19,25–27] and Module Learning with Errors (MLWE) [28,29][3] offer small public key and ciphertexts approximately 10× smaller than plain LWE-based cryptosystems.

SWIFFT for One-Way Function. SWIFFT [18] is a family of hash functions that are efficient, highly parallelizable and provably secure against quantum-safe adversaries. The throughput of SWIFFT is comparable to that of SHA2 and even exceeding on modern computers [18]. This is considering that the parallelization of SWIFFT is not fully exploited [18].

The SWIFFT takes a binary string of length $m'n'$ as an input and outputs a binary string of length $n' \log_2 p$ (for appropriate parameters n', m' and p). One recommended choice for $m'n'$ is (see [18] for details):

$$n = 2^6, \quad m = 2^4, \quad p = 257$$

For these concrete values the hash function takes an input of length 1024 bits and outputS a message digest of 528 bits, with throughput of 40 MB/s and 106 bits of security.[4] For parameters $n' = 2^7, m' = 2^4, p = 257$ SWIFFT maps 2048 bits to 1024 bits and provides a 206 bits of security [18].

RLWE Cryptosystem for Encryption. In [21], Regev introduced the Learning with Errors (LWE) problem that was proven secure under quantum attacks. It was demonstrated that solving a random LWE instance is as hard as solving certain worst-case instances of certain lattice problems. Ring Learning with Errors (RLWE) problem is a variant of LWE that is defined over the ring of integers or polynomial rings [19,25]. Due to its efficient public key and ciphertext in terms of space, a ring learning with errors (RLWE) public-key cryptosystem is a viable option. The encryption scheme is additively homomorphic and is provably semantically secure against quantum adversaries under worst-case lattice assumptions. In addition, the schemes has much smaller key sizes compared to most other post-quantum public key encryption schemes. For instance, NewHope [26,30] offers both public key and ciphertext sizes are approximately 1KB each for a 100+ bit security level.

3.2 Cost of the Zero-Knowledge Proof of Knowledge

The communication cost of the protocol is the total number of bits exchange between prover and verifier.

$$|pk| + |Enc(x)| + \sum_{i=1}^{k} |c_i| + \sum_{i=1}^{k} |f(m_i)|,$$

---

[3] Kyber and Saber are two finalists in NIST PQC competition.

[4] The implementation was tested on 3.2GHz Intel Pentium 4, written in C and and compiled using gcc version 4.1.2 (compiler flags -O3) on a PC running under Linux kernel 2.6.18. The implementation can be found https://github.com/micciancio/SWIFFT.

Where k is the number of messages send by the verifier to the prover (see Algorithm 1). If we implement our protocol with SWIFFT and RLWE, then the size $Enc(x)$ is $n(1 + \log(q))$ [20]

$$|pk| + (k + 1) \cdot n(1 + \log(q)) + k|\text{SWIFFT}(m_i)|$$

The ring-LWE encryption provide at least 233 bits of security against quantum attacks for parameters $n = 1024, q = 12289$, and $|pk| = 1824$ bytes respectively [30,31]. Recall that for 106 and 206 bits of security SWIFFT generate a message digest of 528 bits and 1024 bits respectively. Therefore, to provide at least 206 bits of security against quantum attacks with soundness error 2^{-40}, the communication cost of our protocol is

$$\frac{1824 \cdot 8 + 41 \cdot (1024(1 + \log(12289))) + 40 \cdot 1024}{8000} \approx 85 \text{ kB}$$

A similar analysis shows that to achieve 101 bits of security against quantum attacks we can set $n = 512, q = 12289$, and $|pk| = 928$ bytes []. This cost in communication

$$\frac{928 \cdot 8 + 41 \cdot (512(1 + \log(12289))) + 40 \cdot 528}{8000} \approx 42 \text{ kB}$$

The Table 1 provides a comparison between our proposed scheme and existing Zero-Knowledge Proof protocols. All considered protocols are plausibly post-quantum secure.

3.3   Comparison to Other Schemes

Table 1 shows a comparison between communication cost of our and various zero-knowledge proof systems that are plausibly secure against quantum attacks. However, the security and parameters of our scheme is based on primitives that are rigorously evaluated against known quantum attacks [30,31]. Whereas other schemes in the Table 1 have only analysed security against classical adversaries. It may be that the communication cost for these proof systems may increase when their security is analysed against quantum attacks.

Table 1. Communication Complexity of the ZKPOK.

Name	Round(s)	Security	Soundness	Communication Cost
Ligero [17]	2	128 bit	unbounded adversaries	4000 kB
zk-STARK [12]	1	128 bit	polynomial-time adversaries	3200 kB
Aurora	1	128 bit	polynomial-time adversaries	130 kB
this work	3	206 bit	unbounded adversaries	85 kB
this work	3	101 bit	unbounded adversaries	42 kB

A straightforward run-time comparison of schemes with those identified in Table 1 is not possible, as our scheme is procedural whereas others are circuit-based. Nevertheless, in Table 1 we have provided an asymptotic comparison between our proof system and these proof systems.

Table 2. Computation Time Complexity of the ZKPOK. Here, N is the number of gates in the circuit and the cost is the number of field operations. Whereas lowercase n is the degree of the cyclotomic polynomial $\phi(x)$ and the cost is the number of operations in quotient ring $\mathbf{F}_q[x]/\phi(x)$.

Name	Prover Time	Verifier Time	Operation Type
Ligero [17]	$O(N\log(N))$	$O(N)$	finite field
zk-STARK [12]	$O(N\log(N))$	$O(N\log(N)^2)$	finite field
Aurora	$O(N\log(N))$	$O(N)$	finite field
this work	$O(n\log(n))$	$O(n\log(n))$	finite quotient ring

All schemes are transparent in that a trusted setup is not required. While the security of our protocol is based on the hardness of the learning with error (LWE) problem, and can be proven in the standard model, the security of other protocols is reduced to the collision-resistance of hash functions in the random oracle model (Table 2).

While our ZKPOK is interactive, requiring three rounds, other schemes are non-interactive. Although non-interactive protocol, requiring no synchronization between the prover and the verifier, is useful when we need to broadcast a proof to more than one verifiers, an interactive scheme is applicable in authentication/authorization scenarios controlling access to services. Furthermore, Pass [32] showed that non-interactive zero-knowledge schemes do not preserve *deniability* that may be required in authentication systems.

4   Pseudonymous Credentials

4.1   Overview

We now take the underlying building blocks to develop a pseudonymous credential issuance and verification scheme. Figure 1 illustrates the enrollment and authentication workflow for the credential management scheme. Issuers are organizations authorized to issue credentials against government-issued identification or equivalent by conducting an approved Know Your Customer (KYC) process. Although the most typical form of identification is likely to be federal and provincial government-issued ID such as a driver's license, the space is evolving as third-party providers and digital identity providers, including self-sovereign identity, are gaining market-share in this space. Note that an ID provider can also act as a credential issuer, potentially simplifying the KYC process. A credential data store with limited read access and privileged write access is deployed and operated by an arms length organization. A smaller pool of issuers are allowed to create, append, update or revoke credentials on the store, whereas a larger pool of service providers can read and query credentials. Service providers may be established organizations offering financial products, emerging Fin-Techs, payment service providers or other entities as appropriate. Practical implementation for the store can take the form of a distributed database, a distributed ledger, or some other form of redundant, highly available service. Note that the credential data store is a platform owned and operated by an entity distinct from the pool of issuers and the pool of service providers to prevent collusion and information leakage. More broadly, the proposed scheme may be paired with a digital identity service to provide a holistic solution for all cases where government-issued identification is required for registration.

4.2 High-Level Description

A high-level description of a credential enrollment and verification mechanism capturing the entities and relationships is depicted in Fig. 1. The user enrolls into the service by providing a government issued identification document and associated personally identifiable information (PII) to a credential issuer. The issuer verifies the user through an established verification process such as a Know Your Customer (KYC) check, with appropriate steps taken to prevent identity theft and fraud. Once satisfied, the issuer generates a signed credential against the supplied PII data and updates the credential store. Upon success, the issuer transmits the credentials to the user.

The user may now use the credential to pseudonymously register with financial services providers. To do so, the user provides a handle to the pseudonymous credential and a corresponding zero-knowledge proof attesting to ownership of the credential to the service provider. Note that the attestation of a specific statement must already exist on the credential store prior to verification. The service provider can verify the pseudonymous credentials as being issued by a trusted issuer and the corresponding proof to validate the user.

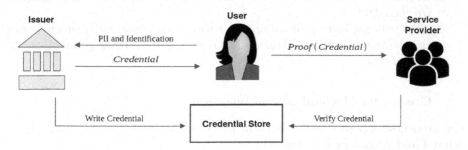

Fig. 1. A high-level workflow capturing credential enrollment and verification to register a customer for a service with a service provider against a credential issued by an issuer.

Once credentials are verified, registration is complete and the user is success-fully on-boarded into the system. In case of malfeasance, the service provider can approach the issuer with the supplied pseudonymous credentials, who has suf-ficient information to link the pseudonymous credentials to PII data, revealing the user's identity.

4.3   Formal Definition

A credential mechanism is a procedure that takes a personal identification infor-mation as input and outputs a credential. We can assume without loss of gen-erality that any **PII** can be converted to a binary string of length $|\textbf{PII}|$. This operation is agnostic of the specific details of the PII, provided that the creden-tial issuing organization is confident that the supplied documents belong to that individual user and claims made are truthful and valid i.e. the user has under-gone a Know Your Customer (KYC) process. The credentials are constructed with a property that users can prove to an organization some statement about their relationship with another institution anonymously. The mechanism will take as input the **PII** and a publicly known hash function H that supports at least one homomorphic addition.

Definition 1 (Credential Mechanism).
*A credential mechanism is a pair of probabilistic polynomial-time algorithms (*CredentialIssue, CredentialVerification*) such that:*

○ CredentialIssue *takes a personal identification information* **PII** *as an input and outputs a credential* C. *It satisfies the following properties:*
1. *No polynomial-time malicious verifier can learn* **PII** *from* C.
2. *Any two credentials, even if linked to the same* **PII**, *are computationally indistinguishable.*
3. *There exists an efficient mechanism for the issuer to learn or revoke* C *from* **PII**.

○ CredentialVerification *satisfies the following properties:*
1. *Honest users can convince a verifier in polynomial-time that* C *is linked to their* **PII**.
2. *It is with negligible probability that a polynomial-time, malicious user can impersonate or forge a credential to convince the verifier of unauthorized ownership.*

4.4   Credential Mechanism Instantiation

The credential issuance and validation processes are instantiated as per Algo-rithm 4 and Algorithm 5 as follows:

Common Input: PII

1. User sends **PII** to Issuer
2. Issuer conducts a KYC process to verify that User's **PII** is legitimate
3. Issuer picks a binary string $x \xleftarrow{\$} \{0,1\}^l$. In practice $1024 \le l \le 2048$.
4. Issuer computes the credential $\mathcal{C} \leftarrow H(x)^a$
5. Issuer stores (**PII**, x, $\mathcal{C}$) in its private database.
6. Issuer uploads the tuple $(pk_I, Sign_{sk_I}(\mathcal{C}), \mathcal{C})$ to the permissioned credential store or blockchain. Where sk_I is a issuers secret signature key.
7. Issuer sends $(x, \mathcal{C}, Sign_{pk_I}(\mathcal{C})$ along with location metadata to User[b]

---

[a] $H()$ is a publicly known hash function.
[b] May use any efficient quantum-safe KEM to create a secure channel between Issuer and User.

Algorithm 4: `CredentialIssuance`

Common Input: (Credential $\mathcal{C}$, $Sign(\mathcal{C})$)

1. The User supplies the block ID to the Service Provider to locate the credential.
2. The service provider accesses the permissioned store and extracts the credential $\mathcal{C}$ associated with the block ID. If the credential is valid, the protocol proceeds to the next step. If not, the request is rejected.
3. Using the zero-knowledge interactive proof (Algorithm 1) the service provider satisfies the constraint that the user is the rightful owner of the credential.

Algorithm 5: `CredentialVerification`

Proof of Protocol Correctness

Theorem 2. *Algorithm 4 and Algorithm 5 jointly define a credential mechanism.*

Proof.

– Algorithm 4 constructs a credential $\mathcal{C}$ by applying a hash function H to a uniformly random string. Therefore Algorithm 4 satisfies the first two properties of `CredentialIssuance` (Definition 1). Clearly, given a block ID an issuer can recover the identity of the corresponding user efficiently.
– Algorithm 5 is essentially the zero-knowledge proof system (Algorithm 1) defined in Sect. 3. Therefore, by completeness property of the interactive proof the first property of `CredentialVerification` is satisfied (Definition 1). The soundness property ensures that a malicious user can successfully impersonate only with negligible probability. The only other way a malicious user can forge a credential is to find an x' such that $H(x') = H(x)$ or to recover x from the encryption of x, both of which are infeasible for any polynomial-time malicious user, except with negligible probability.

Cost of Implementation. Table 3 illustrates the communication cost of Algorithm 4 (`CredentialIssue`). The post-quantum cryptographic schemes of KHYBER [33], DILITHIUM [34] and FALCON [35] were chosen from the NIST Round 3 finalists [36]. Note that this cost does not include the size of **PII** or any associated metadata. In addition, the cost of Algorithm 5 (`CredentialVerification`) is essentially the cost of the zero-knowledge proof (Algorithm 1). If we instantiate Algorithm 1 with RLWE and SWIFFT (Sects. 3 and 3.2), then the communication cost of `CredentialVerification` is computed to be 85 kB and 42 kB for 206 bits and 101 bits of security respectively.

Table 3. Communication complexity of the credential issuance process (Algorithm 4).

KEM	Signature Scheme	Hash	Security	Cost
KHYBER-512	DILITHIUM-512	SWIFFT-1024	101-bit	72 kB
KHYBER-1024	DILITHIUM-1024	SWIFFT-2048	206-bit	139 kB
KHYBER-512	FALCON-512	SWIFFT-1024	101-bit	37 kB
KHYBER-512	FALCON-1024	SWIFFT-2048	206-bit	68 kB

4.5 Practical Verification Protocol

A practical instantiation of the credential verification protocol with defined primitives is illustrated in Fig. 2. The protocol is interactive and constructed using the primitives formally defined in Algorithm 1 and Algorithm 5.

The symbol $\oplus$ denotes a homomorphic addition, while x is the secret information that the prover demonstrates knowledge of via a zero-knowledge proof-of-knowledge to convince the verifier. The credential and the associated cryptographic material are stored in a unique block on a permissioned blockchain that can only be accessed by issuers and verifiers. As such, the prover supplies an identifier (ID_{Block}) such that the verifier can find the appropriate block in the chain and extract its contents. The remaining steps in the protocol executes the zero-knowledge proof of knowledge as originally described in Algorithm 1. Note that the verifier must generate the nonces b and s in a uniformly random fashion and keep them secret from the prover, otherwise the prover can cheat.

The described protocol implements single proof of knowledge against a single issued credential. It is straightforward to expand this scheme such that multiple, independent statements of knowledge linked to the same credentials are stored on the block. For instance, the block may store assertions that were validated during the KYC process, such as the age of majority (above 18), or residence in a particular locality, and each statement may be proven independently by the prover as per the requirements of the verifier's registration process, as verifiers may only care about a subset of those statements. In all cases, however, the statement must be committed to the blockchain prior to attempting a proof for the verification to succeed.

Privacy guarantees of this protocol are strong. Due to the zero-knowledge proof of knowledge, the service provider (verifier) learns nothing about the user during the execution of the protocol. Furthermore, the credential issuance and validation processes are asynchronous, and the verification protocol does not require a live connection to the issuer. This ensures that the issuer remains unaware when the credential store is accessed by one or more service providers. Depending on the construction of the block, the verifier may learn details about the issuer, including the organization name, the date of issuance and any other associated attributes stored in the block metadata.

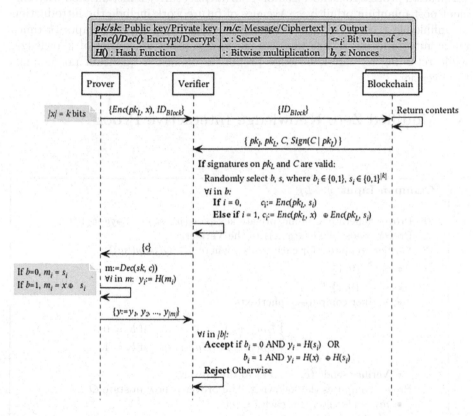

Fig. 2. Practical instantiation of a three-round interactive verification protocol, where the Prover is the User and the Verifier is the Service Provider.

5 Conclusion

In this paper, we presented a credential issuance and verification scheme for use in payment systems that can be generalized to any system where registration is required. The building blocks are a constant-time, interactive, zero knowledge proof relying on a one-way function and asymmetric encryption, both of which only need to support a single homomorphic addition. An instantiation of the ZKPOK based on SWIFFT and RLWE was analyzed and the protocol was formally demonstrated to be secure from post-quantum assumptions. Performance evaluation of the instantiated version indicates that the scheme has an ZKPOK memory footprint of 85 kB and a computational cost bounded by the RLWE encryption operation. A credential issuance and verification mechanism is constructed based on the proposed ZKPOK and a permissioned blockchain. The credential mechanism is shown to be private and secure against adversaries and incurs a communication cost of 68 kB for the issuance process and 85 kB for the verification process to achieve 206-bit equivalent security if instantiated with efficient post-quantum primitives. Avenues of future work include the introduction of unlinkable credentials, a fixed number of authentication attempts (k-times anonymity) and proof that the zero-knowledge proof is a proof of knowledge, while retaining its zero-knowledge properties against a quantum polynomial-time verifier.

A Modified Zero-Knowledge Interactive Proof

Common Input: $y \in L_f$.

1. Prover generate a public/private key-pair $(pk, sk) \leftarrow \texttt{Keygen}(1^\lambda)$
2. Prover sends $(pk, Enc_{pk}(x))$ to the Verifier.
3. Verifier computes for each $i \in [k]$, where $n \in O(poly(|y|))$.

   - $b_i \xleftarrow{\$} \{0, 1\}$
   - $s_i \xleftarrow{\$} \{0, 1\}^{|y|}$
   - Verifier computes ciphertexts

$$
c_i = \begin{cases} Enc_{pk}(s_i) & \text{if } b_i = 0 \\ Enc_{pk}(x) + Enc_{pk}(s_i) & \text{if } b_i = 1 \end{cases}
$$

   - Verifier sends $(c_1, \ldots, c_k)$ to the prover.
4. Prover computes the following. The prover is now in state Q.
   - $m_i = Dec_{sk}(c_i)$ for each $i \in [k]$.
   - $f(m_1), \ldots, f(m_k)$.
   - Prover sends $((m_1 + t_1, f(m_1)), \ldots, (m_k + t_k, f(m_k)))$ to the verifier.
5. Verifier accepts the proof if and only if for all $i \in [k]$.

$$
\left(\big(b_i = 0 \wedge f(m_i) = f(s_i)\big) \vee \big(b_i = 1 \wedge y = f(m_i) \oplus f(s_i)\big) \right) = 1.
$$

Algorithm 6: Modified Computational ZKIP for the language L_f

Remark

Note strings $m_1 + t_1, \ldots, m_k + t_k$ are distributed uniformly therefore do not provide any information to a verifier. Therefore, this proof system is equivalent to the proof system described in Algorithm 1.

References

1. Chaum, D.: Security without identification: transaction systems to make big brother obsolete. Commun. ACM **28**(10), 1030–1044 (1985)
2. Damgård, I.B.: Payment systems and credential mechanisms with provable security against abuse by individuals. In: Goldwasser, S. (ed.) CRYPTO 1988. LNCS, vol. 403, pp. 328–335. Springer, New York (1990). https://doi.org/10.1007/0-387-34799-2_26
3. Chen, L.: Access with pseudonyms. In: Dawson, E., Golić, J. (eds.) CPA 1995. LNCS, vol. 1029, pp. 232–243. Springer, Heidelberg (1996). https://doi.org/10.1007/BFb0032362
4. Lysyanskaya, A., Rivest, R.L., Sahai, A., Wolf, S.: Pseudonym systems. In: Heys, H., Adams, C. (eds.) SAC 1999. LNCS, vol. 1758, pp. 184–199. Springer, Heidelberg (2000). https://doi.org/10.1007/3-540-46513-8_14
5. Brands, S.: Rethinking Public Key Infrastructures and Digital Certificates: Building in Privacy. MIT Press, Cambridge (2000)
6. Camenisch, J., Lysyanskaya, A.: An efficient system for non-transferable anonymous credentials with optional anonymity revocation. In: Pfitzmann, B. (ed.) EUROCRYPT 2001. LNCS, vol. 2045, pp. 93–118. Springer, Heidelberg (2001). https://doi.org/10.1007/3-540-44987-6_7
7. Camenisch, J., Lysyanskaya, A.: A signature scheme with efficient protocols. In: Cimato, S., Persiano, G., Galdi, C. (eds.) SCN 2002. LNCS, vol. 2576, pp. 268–289. Springer, Heidelberg (2003). https://doi.org/10.1007/3-540-36413-7_20
8. Camenisch, J., Lysyanskaya, A.: Signature schemes and anonymous credentials from bilinear maps. In: Franklin, M. (ed.) CRYPTO 2004. LNCS, vol. 3152, pp. 56–72. Springer, Heidelberg (2004). https://doi.org/10.1007/978-3-540-28628-8_4
9. Blömer, J., Bobolz, J.: Delegatable attribute-based anonymous credentials from dynamically malleable signatures. In: Preneel, B., Vercauteren, F. (eds.) ACNS 2018. LNCS, vol. 10892, pp. 221–239. Springer, Cham (2018). https://doi.org/10.1007/978-3-319-93387-0_12
10. Blömer, J., Bobolz, J., Diemert, D., Eidens, F.: Updatable anonymous credentials and applications to incentive systems. In: Proceedings of the 2019 ACM SIGSAC Conference on Computer and Communications Security, pp. 1671–1685 (2019)
11. Pointcheval, D., Sanders, O.: Short randomizable signatures. In: Sako, K. (ed.) CT-RSA 2016. LNCS, vol. 9610, pp. 111–126. Springer, Cham (2016). https://doi.org/10.1007/978-3-319-29485-8_7
12. Ben-Sasson, E., Bentov, I., Horesh, Y., Riabzev, M.: Scalable, transparent, and post-quantum secure computational integrity. Cryptology ePrint Archive, Report 2018/046 (2018). https://ia.cr/2018/046
13. Ben-Sasson, E., Chiesa, A., Riabzev, M., Spooner, N., Virza, M., Ward, N.P.: Aurora: transparent succinct arguments for R1CS. In: Ishai, Y., Rijmen, V. (eds.) EUROCRYPT 2019. LNCS, vol. 11476, pp. 103–128. Springer, Cham (2019). https://doi.org/10.1007/978-3-030-17653-2_4

14. Chase, M., Kohlweiss, M., Lysyanskaya, A., Meiklejohn, S.: Malleable signatures: complex unary transformations and delegatable anonymous credentials. Cryptology ePrint Archive, Report 2013/179 (2013). https://eprint.iacr.org/2013/179
15. Chase, M., et al.: Post-quantum zero-knowledge and signatures from symmetric-key primitives. In: Proceedings of the 2017 ACM SIGSAC Conference on Computer and Communications Security, pp. 1825–1842 (2017)
16. Giacomelli, I., Madsen, J., Orlandi, C.: ZKBoo: faster zero-knowledge for Boolean circuits. In: 25th {Usenix} Security Symposium ({Usenix} Security 16), pp. 1069–1083 (2016)
17. Ames, S., Hazay, C., Ishai, Y., Venkitasubramaniam, M.: Ligero: lightweight sublinear arguments without a trusted setup. In: Proceedings of the 2017 ACM SIGSAC Conference on Computer and Communications Security, pp. 2087–2104 (2017)
18. Lyubashevsky, V., Micciancio, D., Peikert, C., Rosen, A.: SWIFFT: a modest proposal for FFT hashing. In: Nyberg, K. (ed.) FSE 2008. LNCS, vol. 5086, pp. 54–72. Springer, Heidelberg (2008). https://doi.org/10.1007/978-3-540-71039-4_4
19. Lyubashevsky, V., Peikert, C., Regev, O.: On ideal lattices and learning with errors over rings. J. ACM **60**, 1–35 (2013)
20. Peikert, C.: Lattice cryptography for the internet. In: Mosca, M. (ed.) PQCrypto 2014. LNCS, vol. 8772, pp. 197–219. Springer, Cham (2014). https://doi.org/10.1007/978-3-319-11659-4_12
21. Regev, O.: On lattices, learning with errors, random linear codes, and cryptography. J. ACM **56**(6), 1–40 (2009)
22. Blum, A., Furst, M., Kearns, M., Lipton, R.J.: Cryptographic primitives based on hard learning problems. In: Stinson, D.R. (ed.) CRYPTO 1993. LNCS, vol. 773, pp. 278–291. Springer, Heidelberg (1994). https://doi.org/10.1007/3-540-48329-2_24
23. Lindner, R., Peikert, C.: Better key sizes (and attacks) for LWE-based encryption. In: Kiayias, A. (ed.) CT-RSA 2011. LNCS, vol. 6558, pp. 319–339. Springer, Heidelberg (2011). https://doi.org/10.1007/978-3-642-19074-2_21
24. Bos, J., et al.: Frodo: take off the ring! practical, quantum-secure key exchange from LWE. In: Proceedings of the 2016 ACM SIGSAC Conference on Computer and Communications Security, pp. 1006–1018 (2016)
25. Stehlé, D., Steinfeld, R., Tanaka, K., Xagawa, K.: Efficient public key encryption based on ideal lattices. In: Matsui, M. (ed.) ASIACRYPT 2009. LNCS, vol. 5912, pp. 617–635. Springer, Heidelberg (2009). https://doi.org/10.1007/978-3-642-10366-7_36
26. Bos, J.W., Costello, C., Naehrig, M., Stebila, D.: Post-quantum key exchange for the TLS protocol from the ring learning with errors problem. In: 2015 IEEE Symposium on Security and Privacy, pp. 553–570. IEEE (2015)
27. Reparaz, O., de Clercq, R., Roy, S.S., Vercauteren, F., Verbauwhede, I.: Additively homomorphic ring-LWE masking. In: Takagi, T. (ed.) PQCrypto 2016. LNCS, vol. 9606, pp. 233–244. Springer, Cham (2016). https://doi.org/10.1007/978-3-319-29360-8_15
28. Bos, J., et al.: Crystals-Kyber: a CCA-secure module-lattice-based KEM. In: 2018 IEEE European Symposium on Security and Privacy (EuroS&P), pp. 353–367. IEEE (2018)
29. D'Anvers, J.-P., Karmakar, A., Sinha Roy, S., Vercauteren, F.: Saber: module-LWR based key exchange, CPA-secure encryption and CCA-secure KEM. In: Joux, A., Nitaj, A., Rachidi, T. (eds.) AFRICACRYPT 2018. LNCS, vol. 10831, pp. 282–305. Springer, Cham (2018). https://doi.org/10.1007/978-3-319-89339-6_16
30. Newhope. https://newhopecrypto.org/index.shtml. Accessed 16 Dec 2021

31. Alkim, E., Ducas, L., Pöppelmann, T., Schwabe, P.: Post-quantum key exchange: a new hope. In: Proceedings of the 25th USENIX Conference on Security Symposium, SEC 2016, pp. 327–343. USENIX Association, USA (2016)
32. Pass, R.: On deniability in the common reference string and random oracle model. In: Boneh, D. (ed.) CRYPTO 2003. LNCS, vol. 2729, pp. 316–337. Springer, Heidelberg (2003). https://doi.org/10.1007/978-3-540-45146-4_19
33. Kyber. https://pq-crystals.org/kyber/index.shtml
34. Dilithium. https://pq-crystals.org/dilithium/index.shtml
35. Falcon. https://falcon-sign.info/
36. Nistpqcsubmission. https://csrc.nist.gov/Projects/post-quantum-cryptography/round-3-submissions

ZKFlow: Private Transactions in Corda with ZKP

Matthijs van den Bos, Victor Ermolaev, Scott King, Alexey Koren,
and Gamze Tillem[✉]

ING Bank, Amsterdam, The Netherlands
blockchain@ing.nl

Abstract. Corda is a permissioned distributed ledger platform that
enables enterprises to manage their business deals and obligations in
a decentralized manner. Its unique ledger structure, which requires sharing the content of a transaction only to participating parties, contributes
to the protection of privacy-sensitive transaction data. Despite improved
privacy guarantees, the platform cannot assure complete data protection
due to two main issues: the leakage of transaction data to the validating
notaries and the leakage of historical transaction data in the backchain
to future participants. These issues can be handled using cryptographic
techniques whose adoption in Corda requires a dedicated protocol design.

In this paper, we present a protocol that overcomes the problem of
data leakage in the notarization and transaction backchain validation of
Corda transactions using zero-knowledge proofs (ZKPs). Our protocol
enables the platform participants to validate their transactions without
revealing their content to the non-trusted parties. We provide the technical details of our protocol and show how ZKPs can be efficiently adopted
into the Corda ecosystem.

Keywords: Blockchain Applications · Data Privacy · Applied
Cryptography

1 Introduction

Corda is a permissioned DLT that enables enterprises to manage their business
deals and obligations in a decentralized manner. The efficient and scalable structure of the platform made it suitable for different use cases in several industries
such as healthcare, telecommunications, and capital markets [4,13]. The platform's requirement to share the content of a transaction only with the parties
involved in it, boosts its performance and also contributes to data privacy since
access to transaction content is restricted to a permitted group of users [4].

However, Corda platform does not guarantee complete privacy protection. In
the current design, there are mainly two privacy concerns:

Privacy of Notarisation: The consensus mechanism in Corda comprises
notary services, who provide uniqueness consensus and contribute to validity consensus as a required signer. The platform provides two types of notary services:

validating and non-validating notaries [6]. Validating notaries approve and sign a transaction after validating its content. They have full visibility of the transaction content and the entire transaction history back to the state issuance [8]. Granting full visibility of their data to a possible untrustworthy party is not desirable for the participants due to privacy concerns associated with compliance and operational risks. In practice, this means the validating notary is seldom used in production. Currently, the Corda Network notary is a non-validating notary [11].

Non-validating notaries overcome the privacy problem of Corda by restricting access for notaries to only certain public information. They do not validate the full transaction content, nor its history. Instead, they verify whether the state identifiers of the transaction have not been spent by checking their list of spent states. While restricting access to transaction eliminates the privacy problem, it might lead to a denial-of-state attack (DoSt), which enables attackers to spend existing states that do not belong to them. We refer readers to [8] for details.

Privacy of Transaction Backchain: Before sending a new transaction to the notary for validation, each participant of the transaction validates the current transaction contents and the contents of all historical transaction leading up to it. To do so, the participants resolve the transaction backchain for each input and reference state in the current transaction, up until their issuance. The participants of the current transaction have access to the content of the transaction. However, granting participants access to its backchain content is not desirable for the ones that were involved in the past transactions due to the leakage of their potentially sensitive data to future participants in the chain.

Trivial solutions to overcome the privacy problems in Corda exist such as re-issuance of assets, keeping data off-ledger, or using non-validating notaries. These workarounds do not necessarily achieve full privacy protection and might be still vulnerable [8]. Two techniques stand out as promising solutions for the privacy concerns in Corda: trusted hardware and zero-knowledge proofs (ZKPs).

Trusted hardware is a specialized hardware design that resists adversarial access with the usage of some cryptographic techniques [14]. Intel's Software Guard Extensions (SGX) is a well-known example of trusted hardware design which assures confidentiality and integrity against any malicious actor, including the owner of the hardware [10]. Despite its computational efficiency, the frequent vulnerabilities reported on the SGX remains a drawback in its adoption by DLT systems [5,6,8]. Furthermore, requiring the vendor, i.e., Intel, as the trust anchor weakens the trust proposition of SGX [9].

ZKPs provide an alternative solution to the privacy problems in Corda by eliminating the issues around the vendor dependency and hardware vulnerabilities. ZKPs are cryptographic tools that enable a party to prove their knowledge of certain information without leaking anything about that information. ZKPs have some shortcomings compared to SGX regarding their performance, flexibility, and dependency on non-standard cryptography. However, they are still practical to use in current systems, as in the example of Zcash [7]. Their provable security makes ZKPs a viable alternative to overcome privacy issues in Corda.

In this paper, we present a zero-knowledge transaction validation protocol for Corda, ZKFlow, that overcomes the privacy problem in Corda's transaction validation mechanism. Our protocol uses ZKPs to achieve data protection. With ZKFlow, transaction participants can validate the backchain of a transaction without having access to the historical sensitive state content. Similary, a notary can validate the contents of a transaction and its backchain without seeing transaction contents. We explain how a Corda transaction can be converted to a zero-knowledge transaction while adhering to the original Corda communication flow. Our protocol provides practical proving and verifying time for Corda transaction validation such that validation time can be even shorter than the original one due to the constant verification time of ZKPs. As an example, for a transaction of size 12KB, ZKFlow can perform ZKP setup in 4 min, generate the proof in 2 min, verify it in 20 ms on a standard MacBook Pro.

ZKFlow builds on top of Corda's original transaction protocol and extends it with privacy-preserving features. In the explanation of the protocol, we use the terms and concepts defined in the Corda technical paper and documentations [6]. We refer the readers who are not familiar with these concepts to Corda resources.

2 Protocol Overview

In Corda, transaction validation involves three types of parties: *an initiator*, who creates a new transaction, *a counterparty*, who is the recipient of the new transaction, *a notary*, who notarizes the transaction. Once an initiator builds a transaction, they should validate it via a counterparty that validates 1. the content of the transaction by recomputing its transaction id (tx id) from its content that is **fully visible** to the counterparty, 2. the backchain of the transaction by resolving the past transactions up until the issuance transaction, which is **fully visible** to the counterparty, 3. the smart contract rules of the current transaction; and a notary, where a validating notary validates 1. the transaction by recomputing tx id from its **fully visible** content, 2. the transaction backchain, that is **fully visible** to the validating notary, 3. and the smart contract rules [6].

In ZKFlow, we change this validation procedure by restricting access of the counterparties and notaries to privacy-sensitive data. The validation of private data is only possible with ZKPs. The initiator, a.k.a., *prover*, should prove to the counterparty and the notary, a.k.a., *verifiers*, that a transaction is valid while preserving its confidentiality. For the counterparty, confidential information is the state data stored in the transaction backchain. For the notary, the content of the current transaction and the transaction backchain is confidential information.

Figure 1 illustrates the subprotocols of ZKFlow during transaction validation. The setup phase, where the cryptographic parameters for the ZKP are generated, is performed beforehand as a one time operation. When there is a change in the transaction structure or validation, the setup phase might be repeated if the ZKP scheme does not support universal or updateable setup.

Once an initiator builds a valid transaction, it should perform three subprotocols:

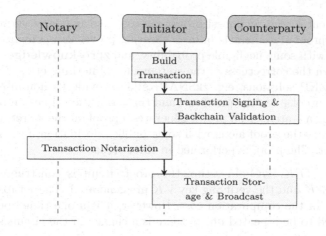

Fig. 1. ZKFlow main protocol.

- a **transaction signing and backchain validation protocol** with a counterparty, where a counterparty validates
  - the content of the transaction by recomputing its tx id from its content that is **fully visible** to the counterparty,
  - the backchain of the transaction by resolving the historical transactions up until the issuance transaction, where the counterparty has **limited visibility** for each historical transaction that consists of a certain public information accompanied with a zero-knowledge proof of its private content,
  - the smart contract rules of the current transaction.
- a **transaction notarization protocol** with a notary that validates
  - the content of the transaction by recomputing its tx id with **limited visibility** of the transaction content,
  - the historical transactions by validating the transaction backchain based on a certain public information and the accompanying ZKPs,
  - and the smart contract rules.
- and a **transaction storage and broadcasting protocol**, where the initiator stores the transaction along with its signatures and broadcasts the notary signature to the counterparty(s) for storage.

In the following sections, we explain the transaction structure used in ZKFlow, how a party can validate the transaction backchain, and what is proven with a ZKP. We also provide a brief summary on the cryptographic primitives used.

3   Cryptographic Preliminaries

Zero-Knowledge Proofs. ZKPs enable a prover to prove to a verifier that they possess the knowledge of information that satisfies certain criteria without revealing the information itself. A ZKP scheme must satisfy: **Completeness**, if the proof statement is true, an honest prover can convince an honest verifier, **soundness**, if the proof statement is false, a cheating prover can convince an honest verifier only with some negligible probability, and **zero-knowledge**, the verifier can only learn the correctness of the statement and nothing else.

Today's ZKP solutions, e.g. zkSNARKs [3], provide us non-interactiveness and succinct proofs, i.e., the proof size and the verification time can be constant. When proving a statement, a prover generates a proof on the secret, i.e., *witness* w, and provides the proof along with some public information, i.e., **instance x**, to the verifier. The proof is performed in three steps:

SETUP$(1^\lambda) \to (PK, VK)$: In setup, the proof circuit is constructed, and the proving key PK and the verifying key VK are generated. The setup constitutes the majority of the computation cost. However, it is a one time operation and does not need to be repeated unless there is a change in the circuit structure.

PROVE$(PK, \mathbf{x}, w) \to \pi$: A prover can generate a proof π on their private witness using the proving key PK. Proving requires considerably shorter computation time than the setup. Some ZKP schemes enable proofs of fixed size.

VERIFY$(VK, \mathbf{x}, \pi) \to bool$: Once receiving a proof, any verifier that has access to the verification keys can verify a ZKP. In succinct ZKPs, verification can be performed efficiently in short time (or in constant time).

Hash Functions. The transaction validation in Corda requires to compute certain hash functions on the transaction data. In ZKFlow, we need to perform these operations within the ZKP circuit since the input data might be privacy-sensitive. The hash functions in Corda, such as SHA256, cannot perform efficiently with ZKPs. In ZKFlow, we use two other hash functions that are efficient in ZKPs.

Blake2 is an improvement of Blake hash [1]. In ZKFlow, we use Blake2s variant which has 64 bytes input size and 32 bytes digest size. An important property of Blake2 is its resistance to length extension attacks, which eliminates the need of double hashing operations different than the original Corda. Despite its efficiency compared to SHA256, Blake2 is still expensive in ZKPs. In our design, we limit its usage as much as possible and use Blake2s to compute nonces. In the rest, we use $\mathbf{BH}(x) = \mathbf{Blake2s}(x)$, where $\mathbf{Blake2s}(x)$ represents the hash computation on the preimage x and $\mathbf{BH}(x)$ is the hash digest.

Pedersen is a secure hash function based on elliptic curve cryptography [2]. The advantage of the Pedersen hash is its efficiency in arithmetic circuits. It is known to be collision resistant for fixed length messages. In ZKFlow, we use Pedersen hash in the Merkle tree computations by prefixing the preimage with the message length for variable length messages. In Appendix B, we provide a detailed security analysis for the usage of Pedersen hash in ZKFlow. In the rest, we use the notation $\mathbf{PH}(x) = \mathbf{Pedersen}(x)$, where $\mathbf{Pedersen}(x)$ represents the hash computation on the preimage x and $\mathbf{PH}(x)$ is the hash digest.

4   Transaction Structure

In ZKFlow, the computation of tx id is same as the original Corda. However, transaction structure is moderately limited compared to original Corda considering the privacy protection and efficiency of computations. We use two transaction types to prevent leakage of sensitive data, which are 1. a private *WireTransaction (WireTx)* that contains the transaction content and only accessed by the owners of transaction, i.e., the initiator and the counterparty, 2. a public *ZKVerifierTransaction (ZKVerifierTx)* that contains a filtered transaction[1] and the ZKP that is computed on the witness WireTransaction, and is accessible by the notary and the future counterparties. In this section, we explain the structure of both transaction types.

The structure of a Corda WireTransaction. In order to make it easier to understand the structure of a ZKVerifierTx, we first describe the structure of a standard Corda WireTx. On a high level, a transaction in Corda consists of several components such as inputs, outputs, references, commands, etc. A transaction should contain at least one command, one signer that is associated with the transaction, and an input or output. The other components are not necessarily included.

In the case of ZKFlow, the cardinality of each component and the content of components are crucial since their size affect the computations in the ZKP circuit. More explicitly, the number of items in each component group should be fixed to a predetermined number. Changing the number of components results in a new ZKP circuit which indicates that the setup phase should be repeated, which is not desirable and practical. Also, the size of each component element should be fixed. Thus, arbitrary size elements are not allowed since they require a new setup and also larger input sizes degrade the performance significantly.

The following are the components that are included in a WireTx:

- **inputs**, `StateRef` objects that points to a UTXO meant to be consumed,
- **references**, `StateRef` objects that points to a UTXO meant to be referenced and not consumed,
- **outputs**, that are `TransactionState` objects,
- **commandData**, the command associated with the transaction, such as Issue, Move, Redeem, etc.,
- **commandSigners**, the public keys of the parties that sign the transaction,
- **notary**, the service that signs the transaction,
- **attachments**, the SHA256 hashes (AttachmentId) of any file or document that is related to the transaction,
- **timeWindow**, the period that the transaction should be validated within,
- **networkParametersHash**, the hash of the set of parameters that are used for correct interoperation among participant nodes in a network.

---

[1] https://docs.corda.net/docs/corda-os/4.7/tutorial-tear-offs.html#introduction.

Calculation of Transaction id. The tx id is deterministically calculated from the contents of WireTx. If any part of the transaction changes, the id will change. This can be used to prove the integrity of the transaction. For a valid tx id, it should be possible to 1. calculate the tx id efficiently from an arithmetic circuit, given a WireTx, 2. calculate the tx id, given a ZKVerifierTx, 3. efficiently prove the membership of a component in a transaction.

Corda uses a Merkle tree to represent the transaction structure and calculate the tx id based on its contents. In Fig. 2, we provide an illustration of WireTx represented with a Merkle tree. Elements of component groups are stored in the leaf nodes of the tree. We use different colors to differentiate the representation of inputs, outputs, and references from other component groups.

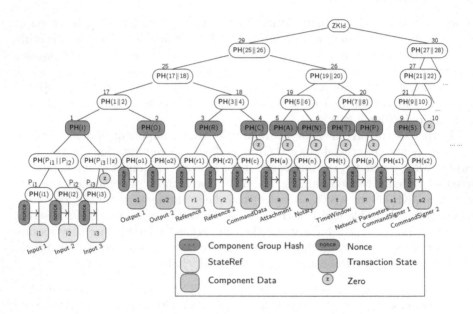

Fig. 2. Merkle Tree representation of a transaction. (Color figure online)

In ZKFlow, the nonces for each leaf node are computed using Blake2s while the component leaf hashes and the internal nodes are computed using Pedersen hash. This is different from Corda, which uses double SHA-256. Our choice of hash function does not affect the structure of the transaction and Merkle tree. The computations on the Merkle tree start from the leaf nodes. Each component group corresponds to a Merkle subtree, where the root gives the component group hash (purple nodes). The Merkle root of main tree, i.e. tx id, is calculated from component group hashes. In Corda, when there is a single element in a component group, an auxiliary input (green nodes) is added to the group to make its size a positive integer power of two. Then, the hash of these two elements become the component group hash. When the number of leaves of a Merkle tree is greater than one and not an integer power of two, then the auxiliary elements are added to the tree until the number of leaves is an integer power of two.

Calculating the Hash of a Transaction Component. In the computation of leaf hashes, to avoid collisions and pre-image attacks, each leaf node is prefixed with a nonce that is unique for each element. Given a 256-bits privacy salt $s \in_R \{0,1\}^{256}$ and a transaction $Tx = (C_1, \ldots, C_n)$ consisting of an ordered list of n component groups C, such that each group $C_i = (c_{i,1}, \ldots, c_{i,m})$ consists of an ordered list of m components $c_{i,j}$, the nonce $n_{i,j}$ for a component $c_{i,j}$ in the group C_i is $n_{i,j} = \mathbf{Blake2s}(s \parallel i \parallel j)$, s.t. $i \in \{1, n\}$ and $j \in \{1, m\}$. Using this deterministic nonce, the leaf hash of transaction component $c_{i,j}$ in component group C_i is computed as $h_{i,j}^0 = \mathbf{Pedersen}(n_{i,j} \parallel c_{i,j})$, where the superscript 0 in $h_{i,j}^0$ represents the corresponding level for the hash in the subtree.

Computing the Root of the Merkle Tree. To compute the Merkle root, the first step is to compute the component hashes. If the number of elements in C_i is m, then the depth of the subtree becomes $\Delta = \lceil \log_2 m \rceil$. The list of the hash values in the leaf level of a subtree is represented as $H_i^0 = (h_{i,1}^0, \ldots, h_{i,m}^0)$. To compute the hashes on a level d of the subtree, the child nodes are concatenated and hashed with Pedersen hash for each $h_{i,j}^d = \mathbf{Pedersen}(h_{i,2j}^{d-1} \parallel h_{i,2j+1}^{d-1})$ in the list $H_i^d = \left(h_{i,1}^d, \ldots, h_{i,\lfloor \frac{m}{2^d} \rfloor}^d \right)$. Once the group hashes are computed, the computations in the main tree are the same as the subtrees.

The Structure of a ZKVerifierTransaction. Different from the WireTx, a ZKVerifierTx contains much less information regarding the transaction content to prevent leakage of sensitive data, most importantly the output contents. It is a filtered transaction with a ZKP that validates the WireTx. The tx id of the ZKVerifierTx is identical to the WireTx. Sharing less information does not threaten the validity of a transaction since the ZKP and the available public information is sufficient for validation. The components of a ZKVerifierTx are:

Fully visible:

- **inputs**, `StateRef` objects that points to a UTXO meant to be consumed,
- **references**, `StateRef` objects that points to a UTXO meant to be referenced and not consumed,
- **commandData**, the command associated with the transaction,
- **notary**, the service that signs the transaction,
- **timeWindow**, the period that the transaction should be validated within,
- **networkParametersHash**, the hash of the set of parameters that are used for correct interoperation among participant nodes in a network.
- **commandSigners**, the public keys of the parties that sign the transaction.

Not present, only leaf hashes visible:

- **outputs**, the leaf hashes of the output states of the WireTx that are digests of Pedersen hash function,

Not present, represented by their group hash:

- **attachments** group hash, the component group hash of attachments.

We illustrate the structure of the ZKVerifierTx in Fig. 7 in Appendix C. The data shared with the verifier is required for the validation of the transaction and does not leak information. The information leaked to the verifier is the command, the number of outputs, and the public keys of the signers.

The command is leaked to identify the circuit type used for the proof. Since each command has different input-output structure and contract rules, using a circuit that covers all possibilities might result in a significant performance bottleneck. To optimize the cost of computations, we create a separate circuit type for each command. The number of outputs is also leaked intentionally for the validation of the backchain. The leaf hashes of output states are used in subsequent transactions for backchain validation.

Additionally, the number of signers and their public keys are leaked due to performance/privacy trade-off. Including the signature validation within the ZKP circuit increases the cost of computations in the setup and proving times. Furthermore, the signature schemes and their underlying elliptic curves that are efficient in arithmetic circuits are not supported in the current Corda design. Thus, we move the validation of signatures outside of the circuit.

Calculation of Transaction Id. In ZKVerifierTx, a component group is represented as $A_i \subset (\{c_{i,1}, \ldots, c_{i,m}\} \cup \{h_{i,1}^0, \ldots, h_{i,m}^0\})$, s.t. if $c_{i,j} \in A_i$ then $h_{i,j}^0 \notin A_i$ and if $h_{i,j}^0 \in A_i$ then $c_{i,j} \notin A_i$. The ordered list K_i^0 of transaction component for each subtree is calculated as $K_i^0 = (k_{i,1}^0, \ldots, k_{i,m}^0)$ s.t.

$$\forall k_{i,j}^0 = \begin{cases} h_{i,j}^0 & \text{if } h_{i,j}^0 \in A_i, \\ \mathbf{Pedersen}(n_{i,j} \| c_{i,j}) & \text{otherwise.} \end{cases}$$

Once K_i^0 is computed for a component group, the computations on the upper levels of the subtree and the main tree is the same as the unfiltered transaction. The only difference is that, in level $d = 1$, the Pedersen hash values computed on the values $k_{i,j}^0$ instead of $h_{i,j}^0$ as $h_{i,j}^1 = \mathbf{Pedersen}(k_{i,2j}^0 \| k_{i,2j+1}^0)$, such that the ordered list of $h_{i,j}^1$s is $H_i^1 = (h_{i,1}^1, \ldots, h_{i,\lceil \frac{m}{2} \rceil}^1)$.

5   Transaction Backchain Validation

In Corda, the input states to a transaction are identified by a `StateRef` which is a combination of the tx id of the transaction that created that state and its index in the output list. It enables a verifier to resolve the chain of previous transactions to verify them. So that the verifier can confirm that the contents of each `TransactionState` pointed to by current input or reference states are valid. These `TransactionStates` are called the unspent transaction outputs (UTXOs) and they are used as the inputs of the subsequent transaction verification.

Revealing the content of `TransactionState`s in the transaction backchain to other parties is an important privacy concern in Corda. For a participant of the current transaction, it is legitimate to have access to the content of relevant `TransactionState`s of the current transaction. Similarly, these participants should also have access to the UTXO contents of the current transaction to validate it. However, granting them visibility of the full transaction backchain is not desirable for the participants that were involved in the historical transactions due to the leakage of their potentially sensitive data to future participants in the chain. In ZKFlow, we overcome this privacy problem by including the validation of the backchain in the ZKP along with the validation of tx id.

Zero-Knowledge Backchain Validation. The output states of a WireTx are `TransactionState`s. Its input and reference states are `StateRef` objects, each of which points to a `Transaction State` of a previous transaction. To prove the validity of a transaction's history, the prover must prove that the `Transaction State` from the respective `StateRef` is valid by computing the leaf hash of the `Transaction State` in the corresponding transaction.

In the validation of the transaction backchain in ZKFlow, the initiator, counterparty, and the notary have the same view of the transaction backchain. We illustrate the view of the initiator and the counterparty in Fig. 3. It shows the resolution of the backchain based on a single input state for simplicity. However, in the original protocol, the chain resolution is performed for each input and reference state of every transaction in the backchain.

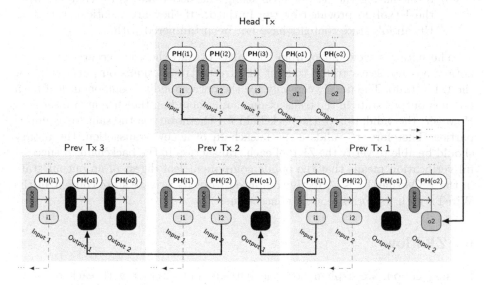

Fig. 3. Initiator and counterparty's view of backchain.

As the participants, the initiator and the counterparty can view the content of the output states of the current transaction. They also have access to the content of UTXOs and to their nonces. The UTXOInfo used by the initiator and the counterparty are stored in $\mathcal{I}$ and $\mathcal{R}$ for inputs and references, respectively. For each state, the UTXOInfo contains a `StateRef`, a `TransactionState`, and the nonce. The state information in the UTXOInfo is used for the validation of the head transaction, and it has no relation to the backchain.

The initiator has gathered all related UTXOInfo before transaction creation from their local storage or requested it from the counterparty. The counterparty receives the UTXOs, $\mathcal{I}$ and $\mathcal{R}$, along with the proposed transaction. Both initiator and counterparty do not have access to the content of all other historical output states in the transaction backchain, unless they were involved in it. Instead, they have access to the leaf hash digest of each output state, whose validity can be checked by validating their corresponding ZKP.

After receiving the UTXO information from the initiator, the counterparty first validates the state contents in $\mathcal{I}, \mathcal{R}$ since the proposed transaction's validity is dependent on the contents of these states. To do so, the counterparty

1. resolves and validates the backchain of each UtxoInfo's StateRef in $\mathcal{I}, \mathcal{R}$ by verifying the corresponding ZKP that validates the UTXO hash by recomputing them for each output state pointed by inputs or references of the corresponding transaction using their corresponding nonces.
2. verifies the integrity of each UTXOInfo's `TransactionState` by:
   (a) fetching the output hash pointed to by the UTXOInfo's `StateRef` from the ZKVerifierTx,
   (b) recalculating the output hash using the nonce and state contents from the UtxoInfo provided by the Initiator. If they are identical, the state UtxoInfo's state contents have not been tampered with.

The notary's view differs from the initiator and the counterparty since the notary has no access to the content of current transaction's output states nor the UTXOInfo. The notary can only see the corresponding component leaf hash for each output state in the transaction chain, including the current transaction. However, the validation of the backchain for the notary is the same as counterparties. Therefore, to validate the backchain of a new transaction, the notary should be able to verify the ZKP of each transaction in the backchain. A successful verification means that the public component leaf digest of an output state in the ZKVerifierTx is correctly computed from its private state content in the WireTx with its corresponding nonce value.

6   ZKFlow

In this section, we explain how the participants interact with each other to validate a Corda transaction confidentially using these building blocks. As shown in Fig. 1, the ZKFlow protocol consists of three main subprotocols, which are 1. transaction signing and backchain validation, 2. transaction notarization, 3. transaction storage and broadcast subprotocols. In the following, we explain how each subprotocol works.

Transaction Signing and Backchain Validation. The first phase of ZKFlow is the validation and signing of a newly built transaction by counterparty(s) (see Fig. 4). The counterparty validates both the new transaction and its backchain. If the validation succeeds then the counterparty signs the transaction.

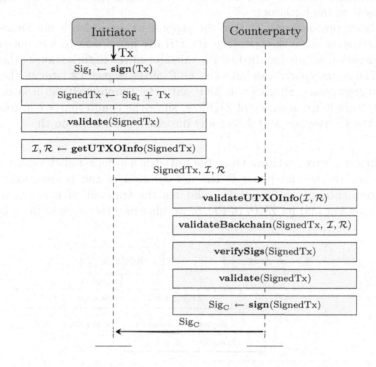

Fig. 4. ZKFlow transaction signing and backchain validation subprotocol.

The subprotocol starts after the initiator creates a WireTx. To do so, the initiator should have already obtained all the states included in the transaction from their storage or request them from the counterparties. The initiator should validate the backchain of each state by checking whether they have already validated its backchain and, if not, then by resolving the backchain of the state and validating it as explained in Sect. 5.

Once an initiator builds the WireTx, they sign its tx id and append the signature to the WireTx, which forms a SignedTransaction (SignedTx). Subsequently, the initiator performs standard Corda checks on the SignedTx for the transaction validity. Counterparties should have access to the contents of the input and reference states of the current transaction to validate it. Therefore, the initiator collects the UTXOInfo (the tuple of `TransactionState`, `StateRef`, and the nonce) for each state that is pointed by the input and reference states of the head transaction in two separate arrays as $\mathcal{I}, \mathcal{R}$. After that, the initiator sends the SignedTx and the UTXOInfo $\mathcal{I}, \mathcal{R}$ to the counterparty.

Upon receiving the proposed SignedTx and the UTXOInfo, the counterparty first validates the state contents in $\mathcal{I}, \mathcal{R}$, and resolves and validates the backchain of each state as explained in Sect. 5. As the next step, the counterparty validates the content and smart contract of SignedTx and verifies the initiator's signature. If all validations succeed, then the counterparty signs the tx id of the SignedTx and sends it to the initiator.

In this subprotocol, the ZKP of the proposed transaction is not shared with the counterparty since the counterparty already has access to its content. The proof generation is only handled by the initiator in the notarization of the transaction. The counterparty validates the ZKP of the SignedTx later in the transaction storage phase. Sharing the ZKP with the counterparty in a later stage, does not degrade the security of ZKFlow, since the counterparty can relate the proof to the transaction and detect any inconsistencies between them.

Transaction Notarization. Once the initiator has collected the counterparty signature(s), the second phase is the notarization of the transaction. In the notarization subprotocol, a notary validates the transaction from its publicly available content and its ZKP. In Fig. 5, we illustrate the steps of notarization.

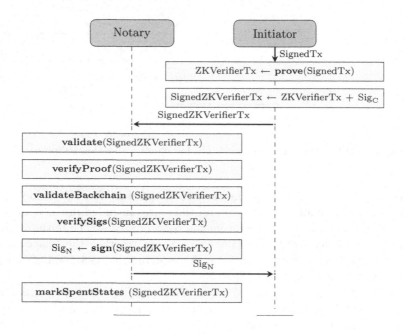

Fig. 5. ZKFlow transaction notarization subprotocol.

Notarization starts with the generation of ZKVerifierTx by the initiator. A ZKVerifierTx is a public transaction structure that contains a filtered transaction of the private SignedTx and a ZKP of the SignedTx. The initiator appends the signatures collected from the counterparties to the ZKVerifierTx and sends it to the notary as a SignedZKVerifierTransaction (SignedZKVerifierTx).

After receiving the notarization request from the initiator, the notary first validates the SignedZKVerifierTx by performing standard Corda checks. Then, the notary verifies the ZKP in the SignedZKVerifierTx. The notary should perform the verification of the ZKPs in the transaction backchain with other necessary validity checks as well. Once all validations passed successfully, the notary verifies the signatures of parties involved in the transaction and signs the tx id of SignedZKVerifierTx. The notary sends their signature to the initiator for the finalization of the transaction. Finally, the notary marks the input and reference state identifiers of the notarized transaction as **spent** in its state identifiers list to prevent future double-spent attempts.

Transaction Storage and Broadcast. The last phase of the ZKFlow is transaction storage and broadcast. If the proposed SignedTx is validated, it means that

- the ZKP of the transaction verifies that the Merkle root computation of the private SignedTx corresponds to the public tx id of the SignedZKVerifierTx,
- the transaction has a valid backchain for each of its input and reference states that both the counterparty and the notary can confirm by validating the transaction backchain in a zero-knowledge way,
- the transaction satisfies the contract rules required for that transaction (Fig. 6).

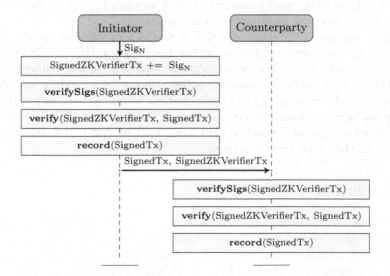

Fig. 6. ZKFlow transaction storage and broadcast subprotocol.

When the initiator receives the notarization approval from the notary, the initiator appends the notary signature Sig_N and verifies the signature. Furthermore, the initiator performs several verification operations on the SignedTx and SignedZKVerifierTx to validate that they truly belong to the same transaction structure. If the validation succeeds the initiator records the transaction into their local storage and sends the SignedTx and SignedZKVerifierTx to the counterparty. The counterparty performs the same validation checks on the them and finally stores the transaction in their local storage.

7   Discussion

Zero-knowledge proofs provide strong security guarantees to protect sensitive data. Despite their strong security guarantees, adopting ZKPs to an existing platform is not trivial. Rather it requires careful consideration regarding performance, flexibility, and compliance.

One concern in the adoption of ZKPs is their performance, which is related to the circuit size. The circuit size is affected by both the number of component elements and the size of each element. ZKPs cannot provide efficient setup and proving time for transactions with hundreds of input or output states. Similarly, we recommend not to include large documents as attachments within the circuit.

Another concern related to ZKPs is their flexibility when the ZKP scheme does not support universal or updateable setup. Not only does any change in the smart contract require to setup the zero-knowledge circuit anew, but also to re-distribute the new proving and verifying keys to the respective parties. Besides that, technically, this step is the most time-consuming part of ZKPs. In our protocol, updating smart contracts is still an open issue. Contract updates and key management is a subject to future work.

A final concern in the usage of ZKPs is the lack of standardization. So far, there is no international standard regarding the usage of ZKPs or ZKP-friendly cryptographic primitives. However, the extensive research and development effort around the adoption of ZKPs eliminates this concern by providing an independent review of the existing schemes from multiple resources with respect to their security and performance. Furthermore, the standardization effort for ZKPs by the ZKProof community, which is also supported by NIST [12], enhances the reliability of the cryptographic scheme.

8   Conclusion

In this paper, we presented the ZKFlow protocol that addresses the privacy problems in the Corda ledger during transaction validation. Our protocol uses ZKPs to achieve data protection in a verifiable setting due to their provable security guarantees. We explained how new transactions are introduced to enable the usage of ZKPs in Corda. We showed that our protocol aims to adhere to the original Corda design and adds new structures only if necessary.

A   Zero-Knowledge Proof Statement

In this section, we explain the content of the ZKP statement that is used in the validation of a transaction in ZKFlow. We use **bold** text style to represent **public** information, and *italic* text style to represent *private* information. On a high level, the initiator aims to prove the following statement: For the **tx id**, **Input UTXO digests**, and **Reference UTXO digests**; I know valid *WireTx*, *Input UTXO states*, *Input UTXO nonces*, *Reference UTXO states*, and *Reference UTXO nonces*; such that

- the Merkle root calculated from the *WireTx* is identical to **tx id**,
- the UTXO digests computed from the (*Input UTXO states*, *Input UTXO nonces*) and (*Reference UTXO states*, *Reference UTXO nonces*), which input and reference states of the *WireTx* point to, are identical to **Input UTXO digests** and **Reference UTXO digests**,
- *WireTx* satisfies the contract rules.

To generate the proof, the initiator first

- gathers UTXOInfo for the inputs and references it want to use: *Input and Reference UTXO states* (`TransactionStates`) and *Input and Reference UTXO nonces*, **Input and Reference UTXO digests**,
- generates a *WireTx* between the initiator and the counterparty which is represented as a Merkle Tree,
- calculates the **tx id** of the *WireTx* that is the root of the Merkle Tree that represents the transaction.
- computes a **ZKVerifierTx** which includes the public information about *WireTx* and its ZKP. This transaction has the same id as the *WireTx*, since its Merkle tree is a filtered version of the original,

    The prover sends the following proof statement to the verifier(s):

$\pi = ZKPoK\{($ *Witness* : {WireTx, Input_UTXO_States, Reference_UTXO_States,

Input_UTXO_Nonces, Reference_UTXO_Nonces}, *Instance* :

{ZKId, Input_UTXO_Digests, Reference_UTXO_Digests}) :

Predicate :

- `CalculateMerkleRoot`(WireTx) is identical to ZKId
- `ComputeUTXODigests`(Input_UTXO, Reference_UTXO, Input_Nonces,

Reference_Nonces) identical to Input_UTXO_Digests & Reference_UTXO_Digests,

- `ValidateContractRules`(WireTx) returns true.}

B   Pedersen Hash Security Analysis

Pedersen is a secure and efficient hash function based on elliptic curve cryptography. Its efficiency in arithmetic circuits makes them a favourable option to use in ZKP schemes compared to other standard hashing algorithms. The hash function guarantees collision resistance for fixed length messages for a chosen personalization input [7]. Therefore, for variable-length inputs with the same personaliztion value, it is not collision resistant. Furthermore, it is not suitable as a PRF due to its visible structure. Its security guarantees makes it suitable for Merkle tree constructions, where existence of collision resistance is adequate to construct the Merkle tree.

In the initial design of ZKFlow, we used Blake2s to compute the component leaf hashes since they have variable length preimages. We computed the rest of the tree using Pedersen hash on fixed length input with the same personalization value. Blake2s was chosen due to its efficiency compared to other standard hash algorithms and its resistance against length extension attacks. Despite its efficiency compared to other standard hash algorithms, the computation cost of Blake2s was still significantly higher than Pedersen hash (21K constraints vs 1.3K constraints), which impacts the performance of ZKFlow significantly.

In this section, we first investigate security guarantees of Pedersen hash with respect to its collision-resistance, preimage resistance and second preimage resistance. We discuss how desired security guarantees can be achieved in ZKFlow with prefixing techniques and sufficiently large input sizes.

In the second part, we analyze the risk and impact of using Pedersen hash in the computation of component leaf hashes in the existence of collisions. Our main objective is to analyze how likely collisions can impact the security in practice. We discuss whether using fixed length input per component group reduces the collision probability. We also look at if Corda provides mechanisms to prevent such attacks. We analyze each level of the tree to understand what a failure means in the corresponding level. For each level, we answer the following questions:

- What is the impact of an attack by collision for the corresponding input structure?
- Does Corda protocol provide a mechanism that prevents the attack?

B.1   Pedersen Hash

Pedersen hash is an algebraic hash function whose security is based on the hardness of the discrete logarithm problem. In our protocol, we use the Zcash variant of the hash function that is optimized for efficient instantiation [7].

Pedersen hash processes a message in message blocks, where each message block is split into small sized chunks for injective mapping. In Zcash, the chunk size is 3. Therefore, prior to hashing, a message M is padded to a multiple of 3 bits, M', by appending 0 bits. For message blocks $M' = M_1||\cdots||M_n$, the hash digest is computed as

$$PH(D, M) = \sum_{i=1}^{n} \langle M_i \rangle I_i^D.$$

In the computation, the value D is the personalization parameter that is used in the generation of the generators I_i^D. The length of each message block M_i is $3c$ bits. The last block M_n might be shorter. c is the largest integer that assures the range of function $\langle M_i \rangle$ is in $\left[-\frac{r-1}{2}, \frac{r-1}{2} \right] - \{0\}$, where r is the group order. The function $\langle \cdot \rangle$ is computed on each chunk $m_j = [s_0^j, s_1^j, s_2^j]$ as

$$\langle M_i \rangle = \sum_{j=1}^{k_i} enc(m_j) 2^{4(j-1)}, \quad enc(m_j) = (1 - 2s_2^j)(1 + s_0^j + 2s_1^j)$$

In the following, we analyze the collision resistance and preimage resistance of the Pedersen hash for the message format used in the ZKFlow protocol.

Collision Resistance

Collision Due to Padding. Pedersen hash requires each message to be a multiple of 3. Therefore, the messages are padded with zero bits if they do not satisfy this requirement. Unfortunately, this padding causes collisions for the messages in the same window. Explicitly, given message $|M| \equiv 1 \mod 3$, the hash digests for messages $PH(M)$, $PH(M||0)$, and $PH(M||0||0)$ are equal since they are all padded to $M||0||0$. This security issue can be avoided by prefixing each message with its message length as $PH(\ell_M || M)^2$.

Collision in Prefixed Messages. We discussed that adding the message length as a prefix to the preimage prevents collision risks due to padding. However, we might still observe collisions, if the outputs of $\langle M_1 \rangle$ and $\langle M_2 \rangle$ are the same for the different messages M_1 and M_2, i.e.

$$\sum \langle M_i^1 \rangle I_i^D = \sum \langle M_i^2 \rangle I_i^D .$$

As proved in [7], the function $\langle \cdot \rangle$ is injective, therefore the output is distinct for each distinct message. Furthermore, the message blocks constructed in a certain format that the output cannot exceed the group order r. Under these conditions, finding messages with the same hash digests is equivalent to finding a discrete logarithm relation between the generators, which is not feasible with the chosen security parameters.

Exploiting Homomorphism.

Pedersen hash is a homomorphic hash function. Therefore, it is possible to compute a hash digest from two different hash digest as

$$PH^{I_1}(M_1) + PH^{I_2}(M_2) = PH^{I_1||I_2}(M_1||M_2).$$

A malicious adversary can exploit this property, if there are some unused generators for shorter messages to compute valid hash digests. We can prevent such an

---

[2] https://forum.zcashcommunity.com/t/pedersen-hash-collision-resistance/33586/2.

attack using message size prefixing. Thus, an adversary that wants to compute the concatenation of two messages will get the digest

$$PH^{I_1}(\ell_{M_1}||M_1) + PH^{I_2}(\ell_{M_2}||M_2) = PH^{I_1||I_2}(\ell_{M_1}||M_1||\ell_{M_2}||M_2),$$

instead of

$$PH^{I_1||I_2}(\ell_{M_1||M_2}||M_1||M_2).$$

Alternatively, an active adversary can alter hash computation by removing the prefix message length to perform the following homomorphic computation as

$$PH^{I_1}(\ell_{M_1}||M_1) + PH^{I_2}(M_2) = PH^{I_1||I_2}(\ell_{M_1}||M_1||M_2).$$

An attacker might attempt to use the aforementioned homomorphic computations to attack ZKFlow in following scenarios:

– **To replace a component leaf hash with a malicious hash value:** An attacker might alter the leaf hash of a component $PH(M)$ with a malicious digest $PH(M||M^*)$. To be able to succeed the attacker should find a collision such that $PH(M) = PH(M||M^*)$ due to Merkle tree validation.

$$PH(M) = \sum \langle M_i \rangle I_i^D$$
$$PH(M||M^*) = \sum \langle M_i \rangle I_i^D + \sum \langle M_j^* \rangle I_j^D.$$

However, this is not a trivial computation. The output of function $\langle \cdot \rangle$ is non-zero. Thus, the attacker should find a message whose homomorphic addition along with a specific generator results in the same hash value. This is equivalent to finding discrete logarithm.

– **To create a new component group hash from the old one:** If an attacker knows the structure of preimage, they can alter certain parts of the message or append new values by using homomorphic property of the Pedersen hash. For example, given the hash of a component leaf hash in a simple form as

$$PH(M) = \ell \cdot I_1 + \text{nonce} \cdot I_2 + M \cdot I_3,$$

an attacker can alter the hash to a message of same size as

$$PH(M + M') = \ell \cdot I_1 + \text{nonce} \cdot I_2 + M \cdot I_3 + M' \cdot I_3.$$

The attacker cannot use this new value in the current transaction since the Merkle root validation is going to fail.

The attacker might attempt to use this value to create a new transaction. Thus, by keeping the structure $\ell \cdot I_1 + \text{nonce} \cdot I_2$ fixed, attacker can alter the computation $M \cdot I_3 + M' \cdot I_3$ for each component value. Despite the attacker might create a valid Merkle tree structure with this attack, they cannot convince an honest verifier for the validity of structure since the corresponding ZKP for the transaction cannot be validated without knowing the privacy salt. The ZKP requires to validate the computation of nonce values from the privacy salt. Without having access to the privacy salt, an attacker cannot replay the computation of nonce as a Blake2s digest from the privacy salt.

Alternatively, an attacker might try to remove the nonce from the hash digest using the homomorphic property of the Pedersen hash to apply a preimage attack on the message. If the message length is small, then attacker might be able to find the preimage. For the public components of the transaction this do not pose an extra risk since preimage is already publicly available. For instance, for the input component group both nonce and input `StateRef` values are already available. It might pose a risk for output states but, to succeed, the attacker should first find the right nonce value for the output states which is a private value in ZKFlow. Knowing the nonce values of other component group elements does not give an advantage to the attacker since each nonce value is computed randomly using Blake2s hash function. Therefore, the preimage attack cannot succeed.

Preimage Resistance. The preimage search cost of Pedersen Hash is $2^{\frac{\ell}{2}}$, where ℓ is the length of the message in bits. In ZKFlow, the preimage of component leaf hashes have the following structure

$$PH(\ell||\text{nonce}||M),$$

where ℓ is a 32-bit integer for the message length, nonce is a 256-bit hash digest. Depending on the component group, the message size might vary. In our computation, we take the shortest message size in ZKFlow which is a byte. Then, the total message length is at least 296 bits. The preimage search cost will be at least

$$2^{\frac{296}{2}} = 2^{148},$$

which is secure with the current computational limits (112 bits or 128 bits for long term[3]).

Multi Target Preimage Resistance. The multi target preimage search cost of Pedersen Hash is $2^{\frac{\ell}{2}-\frac{k}{2}}$ for 2^k pre-images with ℓ-bit message size. In ZKFlow, given the 296-bit message length for shortest message, achieving this attack requires at least

$$2^{\frac{296}{2}-\frac{k}{2}} > 2^{128},$$

$$148 - \frac{k}{2} > 128,$$

$$40 > k,$$

---

[3] https://www.keylength.com/en/4/.

2^{40} preimages, which makes the attack possible for the chosen message size. In Table 1, we look at the multi target preimage search cost of different component element types in ZKFlow.

Table 1. The multi target preimage search cost for several component element types in ZKFlow.

	element bits	preimage bits	min #preimages for 112-bit	min #preimages for 128-bit
boolean	8	296	2^{72}	2^{40}
integer	32	320	2^{96}	2^{64}
hash digest	256	544	2^{320}	2^{288}
public key	352	640	2^{416}	2^{384}

The numbers in Table 1 show that for the commonly used types in ZKFlow, i.e., hash digest and public key, the search cost for multi target preimaga attacks are not feasible. For the types that have lower search cost, an attack can be mitigated by padding the messages with random values to a minimum length, where an attack is infeasible.

B.2   Analysis on Each Component Group Element

In this section, we look at the impact of a failure in the security of Pedersen hash for each component group individually. When the size of the element is fixed, as in the current design, an adversary cannot attack the ZKFlow protocol. Since Pedersen hash is collision-resistant for fixed size messages, it is not feasible to find other messages with the same length that have the same hash value as the original message. An attacker might be able to generate the same hash value from a different length message. However, due to fixed size constraint in the protocol, this message value will not be accepted by the protocol. Therefore, in the rest, we only look at risks in the existence of arbitrary element sizes.

Input and Reference Component Groups. Element type: `StateRef` = Merkle root + index = HashDigest + Integer

Arbitrary Element Size

– **What is the impact?** The attacker might attempt to replace the valid `StateRef` value with the arbitrary message that has the same hash digest as the valid input. Thus, the attacker is able to break the transaction backchain of the attacked input element.

– **Does Corda prevent it?** The validation of the transaction requires validation of the backchain. If the backchain validation does not succeed, then the transaction will not be validated and discarded. Therefore, the attack does not succeed. Furthermore, `StateRef` values are hash digests of an expected fixed length, and the protocol expects to operate on the predetermined length input size. Therefore, in practice, the attacker cannot change the size of `StateRef` to an arbitrary value.

Output Component Group. Element type: `TransactionState` = Variable content/length based on the application.

– **What is the impact?** The attacker can replace the valid `TransactionState` value with an arbitrary message that has the same hash digest as the valid input. The attacker can implement a different contract state that gives the same hash digest.
– **Does Corda prevent it?** Despite the attacker's ability to find a collision, this attempt will fail due to Corda's validation mechanism. In the Corda protocol, one of the attachments to every transaction is the contract code jar. The hash of this attachment, is a SHA256 digest, i.e. `AttachmentId`. This is added to the Merkle tree as an attachment. When a transaction is verified, the verifier loads the contract code for the contract's `AttachmentId` and verifies the transaction contents using that contract code's logic.
  It is not trivial to provide malicious contract code to a verifier, since its `AttachmentId` is SHA256, which is collision resistant for arbitrary length messages. The contract code will expect TransactionState contents to be of a certain type for the command component found in the transaction. If the TransactionState is of a different type, contract verification will fail. This leaves the attacker with one option: to find a collision for a TransactionState of the same type, but with changed values.

Command Component Group. Element type: `CommandData` = Variable content based on application

– **What is the impact?** The attacker can replace the valid `CommandData` value with the arbitrary message or another valid command value that has the same hash digest as the valid command.
– **Does Corda prevent it?** Corda provides two mechanisms to prevent this attack. The first one is during the validation of transaction structure. In the validation of `LedgerTransaction`, each command is matched with its signer keys. Therefore, when an arbitrary value is assigned as the `CommandData`, the check on the signers and `CommandData` value is going to fail and attack cannot succeed.
  On the other hand, the `CommandData` value used by the attacker can be a valid one and it might have the same signers list as the original one. In that case, the contract rules validation can help to prevent the attack. If the

transaction structure does not meet the contract rules of the chosen malicious `CommandData` value, then contract rules validation will fail and attack cannot succeed.

Attachment Component Group. Element type: `AttachmentId` = SHA256(Attachment)

– **What is the impact?** In the case of attachments, the arbitrary message length does not affect the security. Because the challenge for the attacker is to find a collision in SHA256 which is not possible currently. This attack is not feasible due to the collision-resistance guarantee of the SHA256 hash.
– **Does Corda prevent it?** A possible attack is prevented thanks to Corda's design of including attachment ids to the transaction instead of attachment content.

Notary Component Group. Element type: `Party` = CordaX500Name ‖ Pub-Key

– **What is the impact?** An attacker can modify the content of CordaX500Name and find a fake value that has the same has digest as the original value. Similarly, the attacker might also find arbitrary length values for PubKey. The attacker might attempt to introduce a fake notary to the network. Alternatively, the attacker might destroy the PubKey of the notary by changing its content to an arbitrary value.
– **Does Corda prevent it?** Corda maintains a list of `legalIdentities`, where each party's validity is checked during transaction validation. Therefore, an arbitrary CordaX500Name cannot be validated. An arbitrary PubKey value cannot be used in validation since there would not be a corresponding private key for it.
– If the two Party elements have the same hash digest, is there a way to validate the identities?

TimeWindow Component Group. Element type: `TimeWindow` = Instant (12-byte date value)

– **Is there a feasible attack?**
– **What is the impact?** An attacker might alter the value of `TimeWindow` value.
– **Does Corda prevent it?** A fake `TimeWindow` value will fail in transaction validation. Therefore, the attack does not succeed.

Network Parameters Hash Component Group. Element type: `NetworkParam` = SHA256(NetworkParameters)

- **What is the impact?** Similar to the `AttachmentId`, the preimage of the network parameters hash component elements is SHA256 digest. Therefore, finding a collision is only possible if collision in SHA256 is feasible. There is no known vulnerability around collision-resistance of SHA256. Therefore, an attack would not be successful.
- **Does Corda prevent it?** A possible attack is prevented thanks to Corda's design of including network parameters hash digest to the transaction instead of its full content.

Signers Component Group. Element type: `Signer` = PubKey

- **What is the impact?** An attacker might block the usage of PubKey.
- **Does Corda prevent it?** The fake value cannot be used in the validation of signatures since there is no corresponding valid private key value for it. Therefore, the validation will fail and transaction proposal will not be accepted.

Cross Component Group Collision. Apart from within component group collisions, it is also possible to observe collisions cross component groups. For instance, the component leaf hash of an Input component group element might have the same Pedersen digest value with the component leaf hash of the Notary group element. However, the probability of this collision is very low since in the computation of leaf hashes unique random nonce values are used.

If anyhow a collision is found, in the existence of fixed length message sizes, an attacker cannot swap the preimages of two colliding hashes since the protocol will fail. Even in the existence of arbitrary length messages, the validation mechanisms of Corda will abort transaction validation as explained above.

Analysis on Component Group Hashes. On the level of component group hashes, the following possibilities for collision do not threaten the correctness of the protocol:

1. Two component group hashes might have the same hash value
2. A component group hash might have the same hash value with another component group leaf hash.

Fixed or variable length message size in component groups does not affect the collision likelihood since in both cases it is possible to have collisions. Both cases do not threaten the protocol since we do not perform validation on component group hash level.

Analysis on the Upper Levels of Merkle Tree. On the upper levels of the tree, a collision among one of the internal nodes of the tree and one of component leaf hashes can be observed. However, similar to the previous case, this does not have an impact on the correctness of the protocol.

C Additional Figures

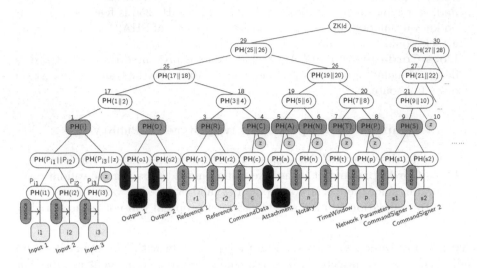

Fig. 7. Merkle Tree representation of a ZKVerifierTransaction. The data stored in the black nodes is **not** shared with the verifier due to their private content.

References

1. Aumasson, J., Neves, S., Wilcox-O'Hearn, Z., Winnerlein, C.: BLAKE2: simpler, smaller, fast as MD5. IACR Cryptol. ePrint Arch. **2013**, 322 (2013)
2. Baylina, J., Belles, M.: 4-bit window pedersen hash on the baby jubjub elliptic curve. iden3 (na)
3. Ben-Sasson, E., Chiesa, A., Tromer, E., Virza, M.: Succinct non-interactive zero knowledge for a von neumann architecture. In: USENIX Security Symposium, pp. 781–796. USENIX Association (2014)
4. Corda: Corda v hyperledger v quorum v ethereum v bitcoin (2019). https://www.corda.net/blog/corda-v-hyperledger-v-quorum-v-ethereum-v-bitcoin/
5. Grad, P.: Reports: intel chips have new security flaws (2020). https://techxplore.com/news/2020-06-intel-chips-flaws.html
6. Hearn, M., Brown, R.G.: Corda: a distributed ledger. Corda Technical White Paper 2019 (2016)
7. Hopwood, D., Bowe, S., Hornby, T., Wilcox, N.: Zcash protocol specification version 2020.1.11 [overwinter+sapling+blossom+heartwood] (2020). https://github.com/zcash/zips/blob/master/protocol/protocol.pdf
8. Koens, T., King, S., van den Bos, M., van Wijk, C., Koren, A.: Solutions for the corda security and privacy trade-off: having your cake and eating it. White Paper (2019)
9. Lindell, Y.: The security of intel SGX for key protection and data privacy applications. Unbound Tech (2018)
10. McKeen, F., et al.: Innovative instructions and software model for isolated execution. In: HASP@ISCA, p. 10. ACM (2013)

11. Network, C.: Understanding corda network services (na). https://corda.network/faq/frequently-asked-questions/#1-network-choice
12. Peralta, R., Brandao, L.T., Robinson, A.: Privacy-enhancing cryptography (na). https://csrc.nist.gov/Projects/pec/zkproof
13. R3: Enterprise blockchain success stories for every business in every industry (na). https://www.r3.com/customers/insurance/
14. Sion, R.: Trusted Hardware. In: Liu, L., Özsu, M.T. (eds.) Encyclopedia of Database Systems, pp. 3191–3192. Springer, Boston (2009). https://doi.org/10.1007/978-0-387-39940-9_1491

User-Perceived Privacy in Blockchain

Simin Ghesmati[1,3]([✉]), Walid Fdhila[3], and Edgar Weippl[2]

[1] Vienna University of Technology, Vienna, Austria
[2] University of Vienna, Vienna, Austria
[3] SBA Research, Vienna, Austria
{sghesmati,wfdhila,eweippl}@sba-research.org

Abstract. This paper studies users' privacy perceptions of UTXO-based blockchains such as Bitcoin. It elaborates – based on interviews and questionnaires – on a mental model of employing privacy-preserving techniques for blockchain transactions. Furthermore, it evaluates users' awareness of blockchain privacy issues and examines their preferences towards existing privacy-enhancing solutions, i.e., add-on techniques to Bitcoin versus built-in techniques in privacy coins. Using Bitcoin as an example, we shed light on existing discrepancies between users' privacy perceptions and preferences as well as current implementations.

Keywords: blockchain · privacy · anonymity · Bitcoin · mixing · wallets

1 Introduction

Blockchain is a disruptive technology that offers innovative solutions for distributed and secure transactions. By relying on a P2P network, blockchain technology offers the compelling properties necessary to develop new forms of distributed applications. However, despite the significant amount of research to address the challenges posed by such a new technology, several privacy and security issues remained partially unresolved. In particular, in a public blockchain where details about transactions are publicly available (e.g., senders' and receivers' addresses and transaction amounts), it becomes possible for an adversary to use such data in combination with heuristics and auxiliary information (e.g., address tags) to cluster and identify users and their transactions, and eventually, linking Bitcoin addresses to real identities [1,4,18,24]. For example, common input ownership, change addresses detection, address reuse, side-channel attacks, tagging addressee by auxiliary information from the Internet, transaction graph are some of the most prominent techniques [2,16] used for de-anonymization in the Bitcoin blockchain. We refer to [7] for privacy attacks and to [8,9] for privacy-preserving techniques. Related works are also discussed in Appendix B. To overcome such privacy challenges, several solutions have been proposed, which provide users with mechanisms and techniques to hide their transactional data and preserve their anonymity. This includes i) add-on

ⓒ International Financial Cryptography Association 2023
S. Matsuo et al. (Eds.): FC 2022 Workshops, LNCS 13412, pp. 164–194, 2023.
https://doi.org/10.1007/978-3-031-32415-4_12

techniques that can be used on top of existing blockchain solutions such as Bitcoin (e.g. CoinJoin), or ii) blockchain solutions with built-in privacy features such as privacy coins (e.g., Zcash or Monero). Our research seeks to unravel the difference between users' expectations and the current implementation of such privacy solutions, raising intriguing questions regarding the effectiveness of proposed techniques when adopted in practice.

RQ 1: To what extent are users aware of privacy issues and privacy-enhancing technologies?

RQ 2: What preferences do the users have for privacy-enhancing technologies? i. Do they prefer using add-on privacy techniques on top of Bitcoin or built-in features in privacy coins (e.g., Monero)? ii. Are they willing to use privacy-preserving techniques despite the higher fees and longer transaction time? iii. Do they trust third-party privacy-preserving services? iv. Which privacy features interest users the most (e.g., hiding the source, hiding the destination, hiding the amount)?

The paper is structured as follows: In Sect. 2, we describe our quantitative and qualitative study, while in Sect. 3, we present the results and discussion. Finally Sect. 4 concludes the paper.

2   Study Design

We present both a qualitative and a quantitative evaluation of users' perception of privacy in UTXO-based blockchains such as Bitcoin.

2.1   Qualitative Research

Methodology. In this subsection, we explain designing the questionnaire and the interview procedure. Recruitment, the coding methodology, limitation, and sampling are provided in Appendix C.1.

For the questions, we conducted multiple rounds of pilot interviews and -discussions, including collecting the answers to the questionnaire in a Blockchain workshop with eleven participants, a think-aloud study with four blockchain experts, and consulting security- and privacy usability experts, a legal expert, and an English proofreader. We revised the questions to ensure that the technical terms and questions were clear. The procedure for designing the questionnaire is illustrated in Fig. 1.

Interview Procedure. Before the interview, participants were briefly informed about the research context and signed a consent form. Each interview lasted about 30 min. We conducted semi-structured interviews both in-person and via online meetings. The researchers used an interview guide with open-ended questions (Appendix A) to ensure consistency. The questions were revised and validated in two pilot rounds. All interviews were recorded and anonymized, and fully transcribed.

2.2   Quantitative Research

Methodology. We conducted quantitative research to get a larger and geographically more distributed set of participants for the study. We hosted a survey on SurveyMonkey. The follow-up questions in the questionnaire were shown according to the logic set to the answers. The overall logic is illustrated in Fig. 2. For the reliability of the answers, in the quantitative part, we did not show the questions regarding Bitcoin privacy attacks and privacy-enhancing solutions if the respondents selected Bitcoin is fully anonymous. Those respondents were redirected to questions specific to privacy-unaware users. Additionally, those unaware respondents were informed about privacy issues and privacy-enhancing tools in Bitcoin and were asked if they value having better privacy despite the extra fees or longer transaction times. Sampling and ethical considerations are provided in Appendix C.2 and C.3.

2.3   Validity and Reliability

In total, 101 participants took part in our survey in the quantitative part. After applying our exclusion criteria, we reached a final sample of n = 58 for our analysis. Interviews with non-users with absolute no knowledge about cryptocurrencies were omitted from the study. Our final dataset includes responses from 12 participants (cryptocurrency users) in the qualitative part and 58 participants in the quantitative part. We asked the respondents to specify if they studied or worked in an IT-related field in the demographic part. This was the case for 58.33% of the participants in the qualitative part and 65.52% of the respondents in the quantitative part. The questionnaire was distributed in English. Adding the "other" option allowed us to have unassisted answers. Re-submission was prevented by restricting one submission per device and IP. The respondents were not allowed to change their responses to the previous questions. We followed [17], to ensure the dataset reliability, five exclusion criteria were considered:

- No knowledge of cryptocurrencies. 8 respondents who selected "not at all familiar" with cryptocurrencies were eliminated.
- Who partially replied to the questionnaire. 27 respondents were eliminated.
- Who wrongly answered the quality control question with shuffled options (they should select "Homophonic substitution cipher in one of the questions"). 7 respondents were eliminated.
- Who selected invalid answers (if they chose fake options in two questions, Dram, a fiat currency as a privacy coin, and MyMaps, a map application as a Bitcoin wallet), 1 participant, who selected invalid answers to two questions was eliminated.
- Who failed to successfully re-phrase the earlier questions (they should write their roles in an open-ended question, while they selected their roles in the earlier questions). None of the participants who passed the above criteria was eliminated by this criterion.

3   Results

3.1   Privacy Awareness

The Importance of Privacy in Transactions. Half of the interviewees (PU1, PU2, PU4, PU7, PU10, PU11) specified that transaction privacy is very important to them. PU1 stated that *"Blockchain transparency creates a guard for some people to accept it as a monetary system. If you ask me to shift all of my traditional transactions to the blockchain, I would have a serious guard against that"*. PU2 and PU4 specified their expectations on being anonymous in blockchain transactions. PU2 said, *"I expect no one realizes my identity although everyone can see the transaction* [on the blockchain]*"*, and PU4 specified *"I don't like anyone knowing my financial transactions either in traditional or crypto. It's completely a private thing"*.

PU11 said, *"anonymity in crypto transactions is useful when you want to be hidden from your government's eyes"*. They stated that it is useful when the law prevents you from using new technologies while you are not working on the darknet or are not pursuing illicit activities.

While PU3, PU6, and PU9 considered the privacy of transactions at an intermediate level of importance. PU6 pointed out that *"on the one hand when I could pay by crypto rather than traditional systems to buy services or transfer money without specifying my identity, it's totally great. On the other hand, this anonymity makes it quite difficult to find a hacker who steals your crypto; you will lose it forever* [and you cannot find him]*, it depends on who can know it. If they are my relatives or friends, it's a matter, but if it is the government, it's OK"*. PU5 and PU12 asserted the privacy of transactions is not important to them. PU5 referred to his low investment in cryptocurrencies stating that *"at the moment my investment is too low, that's why the privacy is not that much important for me; however, I don't want anyone to know it as I'm afraid of future laws on taxing the crypto transactions or if the government bans the crypto transactions"*. In contrast, PU12 stated that privacy is important for those who do money laundering, *"I do not perform anything special or illegal, the privacy does not matter to me.* PU8 specified privacy is not important at all, although their answers to the following questions expressed privacy concerns. When asked about their contradicting answers to the following questions, they replied by *"privacy is not important at all to me as nothing happens if this information is disclosed, however, I prefer it not to be [disclosed]"*.

QNT.[1] Most of the participants said that the anonymity of cryptocurrency transactions is extremely important (46.55%) or very important (24.14%), while a minority considered it less important (Somewhat important: 22.41%, Not so important: 5.17%, Not at all important: 1.72%).

Bitcoin Anonymity. While most of the interviewees categorized Bitcoin as not so anonymous (PU1, PU3, and PU8) or with moderate anonymity (PU4, PU9,

---

[1] We specified quantitative results by starting with **QNT** abbreviation.

PU7, and PU1), four out of twelve stated Bitcoin anonymity is high (PU5) or very high (PU6, PU11, and PU12).

PU1 and PU7 stated that the peer with whom they transacted knew them. PU2 and PU7 stated that it is not at all anonymous outside the network, but its anonymity is great at the Bitcoin network level. PU1 and PU3 mentioned privacy issues as a result of monitoring tools. PU1 explained *"transaction transparency makes it* [Bitcoin] *not so anonymous. There are monitoring tools, e.g. Crystal, that analyzes the network. I would say it is more transparent compared to traditional banking systems"*. PU3 notified monitoring tools such as Cipher Trace and suggested that *"Bitcoin should find a solution for this issue, no idea if it should be handled by wallets! It's better not to use Bitcoin if you want to perform anonymous transactions; I'd suggest Monero or Zcash instead"*. PU8 and PU9 were also aware of the algorithms to find the relationship between accounts and tracing transactions. PU9 elaborated, *"it is possible to trace a specific transaction and recognize how it was funded, for instance in which exchange"*. PU8 also specified the privacy issues regarding wallets where *"the information about your e-mail, your mobile phone, your phone number are recognized"*. PU8 considered the wallets as mobile or web wallets, and their answers applied to the specific wallets that they experienced before. While software wallets on desktop computers neither ask for e-mail nor can connect to mobile SIM cards. They also were unaware that full-node wallets do not suffer from these privacy issues.

Some of the interviewees (PU2, PU4, PU5, PU7, and PU8 mentioned anonymity issues using exchanges or services accepting Bitcoin. PU2 mentioned, *"no anonymity in [using] exchanges"*. However, the privacy issues with exchanges matter when users use centralized exchanges with know-your-customer (KYC). In this question, those interviewees did not mention decentralized exchanges, which do not ask for KYC. PU5 also stated the privacy issues with centralized exchanges where KYC applies; however, they believed *"Bitcoin is still more anonymous than traditional banking"*. PU4 stated that *"although users do not know the entities behind the addresses, the stories where police could find criminals who used Bitcoin indicates the possibility of tracing the transactions"*.

PU10 had a level of uncertainty about Bitcoin anonymity as they said, *"I've just heard Bitcoin anonymity is less than other cryptocurrencies, I'm not sure"*. Among those who considered Bitcoin anonymity very high. PU6 referred to the fact that *"the users don't know to whom the public key belongs, it's an alphanumeric phrase and all the identities are hidden in the network"*. They were confident that no one could find the users who perform Bitcoin transactions as they had heard about the story of the Silk Road [marketplace] developer. They thought the Police had to investigate through sophisticated ways to find him, and the reason was using TOR and Bitcoin payment in designing the system. This caused a misconception that the user was unaware of the possibility of de-anonymization techniques applied in Bitcoin to map the addresses to real identities. PU11 and PU12 wrongly considered Bitcoin is fully anonymous since it uses addresses rather than real identities. PU11 has a misconception about privacy as they thought Bitcoin is based on encryption algorithms which makes it anonymous; they also referred to the fact that *"Bitcoin does not record identities in its blockchain"*. They stated, *"you can transfer coins from a wallet which is not recognized by an identity, you don't know the recipient, and the recipient does not know who the sender is"*.

QNT. The respondents reported Bitcoin anonymity as: Not at all anonymous: 15.52%, Not so anonymous: 27.59%, Somewhat anonymous: 36.21%, Very anonymous: 18.97%, Extremely anonymous:1.72%). One of the users who selected Bitcoin as extremely anonymous jumped into privacy unaware users' question. We asked the unaware users why they believe Bitcoin is fully anonymous. This participant selected "there are no real identities in the transactions (neither names nor personally identifiable information (PII))".

Privacy Risks. The reported risks varied among the interviewees. PU1, PU2, and PU3 specified monitoring tools. PU2, PU5, and PU8 mentioned [Centralized] exchanges and exchange hacks. PU3 and PU8 pointed out address reuse. PU5 reported possession of private keys by web wallets. PU5 and PU8 specified Bitcoin explorers; however, PU8 used that under the name *"crypto scanner"* and according to their explanation, we found that they meant what is known as "explorers". PU4 mentioned tracing transactions by, e.g. police.

PU2 stated, *"exchanges know the history of my transactions, and they are not secure; therefore, they can compromise my privacy. I bought or sold my crypto via the exchanges, [thus,] my identity can be identified, [and] along with tracking systems they can identify my behaviors"*. PU3 mentioned if the address is reused, it could be traced to find the source of other transactions. PU5 pointed out, *"if the exchanges are hacked, the hacker can find to whom these cryptocurrencies belong. [Furthermore] Web wallets such as Blockchain.com have your private key. So, they can access your assets"*, by this, the interviewee meant the corrupted web wallet can spend money on behalf of users, compromising their privacy where it is interpreted that the user got involved in that transaction.

PU8 considered that privacy risks are only related to the wallets and exchanges *"as long as you are not trading and the wallet you are using are not related to you, privacy is OK. Privacy attacks are only implemented in academic papers; I haven't seen any implementation in practice"*. The participant was unaware of current monitoring tools and companies who are working in this context as their businesses. That is why they thought privacy attacks were not implemented in practice and are just proposed in academic papers. Some of the interviewees (PU6, PU9, PU10, PU11, PU12) could not specify any privacy risks associated with Bitcoin. PU12 stated, *"I haven't heard it because the people around me haven't talked about it"*.

QNT. We provided an open-ended question to evaluate user awareness about privacy risks. The majority of participants (68.96%) stated Bitcoin risks they are aware. Among them, three participants misstated "losing money" and "password hack" as privacy risks. "Centralized exchanges (KYC)", "identity identification", "creating transaction graphs", "public and immutable database" were the most reported privacy risks.

Privacy Risk Measures. We present different measures stated by users who answered the previous question. PU2 and PU3 suggested using various platforms and wallets, using Decentralized Finance (DeFi), decentralized exchanges. PU3 also proposed to not directly transfer from personal wallets to other addresses, using mixing, using TOR or VPN, using privacy coins such as Zcash or Monero. PU3 specified that *"monitoring systems are improved every year; thus, I may switch to Monero and Zcash if I want to be anonymous. They developed for this reason and I'm so confident using them for this purpose"*. PU2 proposed to use DeFi, where it is not required to disclose identities. But they mentioned that *"they have higher risks, your wallet or your assets can be easily stolen* [in these non-prominent decentralized exchanges], *therefore, it is better to scatter your assets between different platforms if you have a large amount of money"*.

PU8 mentioned not using exchanges and trying to use wallets that require less identity information; however, as it was mentioned in the previous section, this was due to the unawareness of the participant from decentralized exchanges and desktop/full node wallets. PU5 mentioned that they did not apply any measures to mitigate privacy risks as they have not invested much in the market.

Awareness of De-anonymization Techniques. Three out of twelve (PU1, PU2, and PU3) were aware of how monitoring tools flag the transactions; however, they did not know the algorithms and the techniques that the monitoring tools applied to flag the transactions and find suspicious transactions.

PU1 asserted, *"they* [monitoring tools] *find the suspicious transactions from for example gambling websites. They try to find transactions suspicious of money laundering. They find the suspicious UTXO and trace the UTXO to find the user or the exchange that the UTXO has been sent"*. PU2 specified *"they try to find mixers or ransom by finding different wallets. They can at least find a set of wallets belonging to a criminal group"*. PU3 mentioned, *"if they* [monitoring tools] *collaborate with some explorers they can also tag the transaction with the IP of the user who checked the transaction confirmation"*. They also clarified how the address reuse can be used to relate the transactions to each other"*. PU8 notified the issues with address reuse and the patterns achieved from the transactions with the same amounts. PU5 stated the transaction graphs. However, more than half of the interviewees (PU4, PU6, PU7, PU9, PU10, PU11, and PU12) did not mention any techniques.

QNT. Address reuse 73.68% was the most reported de-anonymization technique that the participants were aware. More than half of the participants (64.91%) said that they are aware of tagging addresses through the information available on the Internet. Transaction graphs with 57.89% and change address detection with 54.39% ranked in the successive positions. In contrast, one-tenth were unaware of any techniques.

Awareness of Correlation Attacks. PU1 and PU2 have heard about the correlation attacks, but they had no information about them. PU3 was aware of IP address mapping to the addresses and finding access patterns as network correlation. They also mentioned, *"it is better to be a full node rather than con-*

necting to third party wallets". PU4 specified the time and amount correlation by services that users pay with Bitcoin, for instance, online shops; therefore, the service is able to provide the information regarding the identity of the users to map to the user's transaction. They also mentioned that *"it highly depends on privacy provided by the service"*. More than half of the interviewees (PU5, PU6, PU7, PU9, PU10, PU11, and PU12) were unaware of the correlation attacks.

QNT. 60% reported that they are aware of network, time, and amount correlation attacks, while 15.79% were unaware of any correlation attacks.

Awareness of Add-on Techniques. While most of the interviewees (PU4, PU5, PU6, PU7, PU8, PU10, PU11, and PU12) were unaware of the add-on techniques. PU1 was aware of mixers, *"I know they collect all the transactions from one side and randomly send them to another side to obfuscate the relationships* [between inputs and outputs]*"*. By collecting transactions from one side, they probably meant the inputs. They also specified that they have heard of CoinJoin and CoinSwap but did not know how they work. They mentioned, *"analyzers can find CoinJoin transactions and flag them... I'm not convinced that CoinJoin can provide better privacy"*. PU3 was aware of mixers and Coin-Join, and they mentioned that *"we can also use exchanges as mixers"*. PU9 has seen CoinJoin and CoinSwap names, but they have not read about them.

QNT. Mixing websites (66.67%) were the popular add-on technique that the participants were aware. The participants' awareness of other techniques was reported as follows: CoinJoin-based techniques (49.12%), threshold signatures (43.86%), off-chain solutions (42.11%), and Fairexchange/Coinswap (31.58%). 17.54% were unaware of any of the techniques. Figure 5 illustrates the awareness of add-on techniques.

Awareness and Usage of Privacy Coins. Except for PU1, PU2, PU3, PU5, and PU8 who were aware of some of the privacy coins, others neither heard of them nor were aware that these coins were developed for privacy reasons. PU1 and PU2 have heard about Monero, but they did not know how it works. PU2 specified *"I just knew that Monero was developed specifically for this* [privacy]*"*. PU1 stated, *"I just wanted to buy one of the privacy coins, just according to the market analysis, however, I didn't"*. PU3 was aware of Zcash and Monero, and they were the only one who owned Monero through the mining. *"I read a paper about Monero and* [I found that] *it could better implement privacy. ...I also tested its mining as its mining was quite easy at that time"*. PU5 was aware of Monero as a privacy coin that provides strong anonymity. They also have heard of Zcash and Decred, but they were unaware that they are developed as privacy coins. PU8 specified that they know Zcash, *"... it uses Zero-knowledge proof to verify transactions, but I don't know how its transactions look like"*.

PU9 has heard there are some privacy coins in the market, but they could not remember their names. PU7, PU10, and PU11 have heard of the name of Zcash or Monero, but they were unaware they are privacy coins. PU4, PU6, and PU12 were unaware of privacy coins.

QNT. Monero (78.95%) and Zcash (70.18%) were the most prominent privacy coins that the participants were aware. Figure 6 outlines the awareness of privacy coins. Monero and Zcash were the top coins that have been owned/bought/mined by the participants. Most of the participants selected, they owned privacy coins both for better anonymity and investment.

3.2   Privacy Preferences

Preference Between Bitcoin Add-on Techniques and Privacy Coins. Most of the interviewees (PU1, PU3, PU4, PU7, PU8, PU10, PU11, PU12) preferred privacy coins rather than Bitcoin to enhance their anonymity in cryptocurrency transactions. The reason for preferring privacy coins rather than Bitcoin add-on techniques varied from the better privacy in built-in techniques to not getting involved in the adversity of using add-on techniques or relying on third-party services. PU1 specified the fear of making the transactions suspicious by using CoinJoin and CoinSwap. They were informed about the possibility of flagging CoinJoin transactions; however, at the time of writing, monitoring tools did not recognize CoinSwap transactions. They are similar to hash-time-locked contracts (HTLC) that are mostly used in payment channel funding transactions. The participant may be afraid of other add-on techniques being flagged by monitoring tools. PU3 specified that *"if privacy is the priority, I'll definitely prefer Monero. I don't like to do a tough task to improve privacy in Bitcoin. Monero has been developed exactly for this* [providing privacy], *its algorithms, its network...... The only situation that forces me to perform a transaction* [where I need privacy] *with Bitcoin is when the destination does not support Monero and I have to pay in Bitcoin"*. They continued that in privacy coins, the developers thought about the privacy concerns, and they can rely on that, *"it does not get me in trouble of using add-on techniques"*.

PU9 preferred to use Bitcoin add-on techniques as they were more familiar with Bitcoin. PU2 and PU5 had different opinions; they preferred neither add-on nor privacy coins. PU2 did not desire to use privacy coins as they thought this anonymity is against the goal of using cryptocurrencies in real life. PU2 clarified their opinion by being against privacy coins with *"they* [privacy coins] *don't have any applications in real life, they are used either for illegal activities or investment, so they don't attract me"*. They preferred to use Bitcoin as *"Bitcoin is the market leader. If it goes up, consequently, other coins go up. It's easily exchanged"*. They also mentioned the problem with changing Monero in the exchanges *"Monero is not listed in most of the authorized exchanges, it may be listed in some unknown exchanges and it's risky to use those exchanges. At the moment, there are lots of risks* [in the crypto market]... *I can't add more risks"*. PU5 preferred using DeFi to provide better privacy rather than add-on techniques in Bitcoin or privacy coins. They noted that *"decentralized exchanges provide privacy in the level of trading, they went one step ahead of privacy coins"*. PU6 also preferred security rather than privacy. They mentioned that if the privacy-enhancing technology endangers security, they preferred not to use them.

QNT. More than half of the participants (63.16%) preferred using privacy coins rather than Bitcoin add-on techniques. Mandatory built-in privacy (91.67%) and stronger anonymity (83.33%) when the technique is considered in design were among the highest reasons for preferring privacy coins. Among those who preferred Bitcoin add-on techniques, Bitcoin's reputation (85.71%) and availability of Bitcoin tools (wallets, explorers, etc.) (71.43%), and Bitcoin market cap (71.43%) were the most selected options.

Preferences Between Bitcoin Built-in and Add-on Privacy Techniques. More than half of the interviewees (PU4, PU7, PU8, PU9, PU10, PU11, and PU12) preferred applying mandatory built-in techniques in Bitcoin protocol, while PU1 and PU3 preferred using add-on techniques whenever they needed better privacy. PU2 preferred not to answer this question as they were not knowledgeable in this context. PU5 suggested not to use Bitcoin for privacy reasons as it still requires improvement in too many other aspects.

PU1 and PU3 pointed out the negative consequence of applying mandatory built-in privacy techniques in Bitcoin. PU1 stated, *"I am afraid of bans by governments or exchanges once built-in techniques apply to the Bitcoin protocol"*. PU3 continued, *"it's a difficult question, as it has personal benefit and public benefit, ... better not to implement mandatory privacy techniques in Bitcoin, there are dark web activities.... and we need some sort of monitoring in Bitcoin since it is the main cryptocurrency"*. For those who preferred using built-in techniques, PU4 referred to the HTTPS story, which became popular after HTTP, and they said, *"in future, we will reach the point that we have to consider privacy aspects in Bitcoin"*. PU9 explained their reason by *"if it* [built-in technique] *introduces a new risk. The risk would be for all the users* [while in add-on techniques it would be for those who use add-ons]*"*. PU10, PU11, and PU12 had better feelings by using built-in techniques rather than add-on techniques.

QNT. While half of the participants preferred applying mandatory built-in privacy techniques in Bitcoin, 29.82% did not know, 12.28% preferred add-on techniques, and 8.77% had other opinions such as being too late to change Bitcoin or doubt about applying built-in privacy in Bitcoin. One of the participants also pointed out that this would cause a "complete crash of that ecosystem, bankruptcy for the grifters".

Preferred Privacy Features in Bitcoin. We asked the interviewees to specify their preferred features of Bitcoin. We also provided them the options (hiding the source, destination, or amount) if they had no statements. Except for one interviewee (PU6) who was unaware of the probability of mapping the addresses to the real identities by stating that *"in my opinion, it is not important that the source and destination addresses are not hidden. They are not related to real identities."*, other interviewees prioritized hiding the source while they preferred hiding the amount, and hiding the destination, for better privacy.

Some of the interviewees added some other features. PU2, PU3, and PU5 mentioned preventing mapping the addresses to the real identities while they knew that it is not related to the Bitcoin protocol. PU9 specified this feature;

however, they did not mention that it is not specifically related to the Bitcoin protocol. PU5 continued *"I also don't like Bitcoin explorers where they trace the transactions, they can find and publicly show from which address to which address the coins have been transferred, and if one of the transactions can be mapped to my real identity other transactions can be revealed"*. PU8 also specified to make it impossible to create transaction graphs. PU2 suggested preventing the wallet from accessing one's mobile data (e-mail, location) in mobile wallets. Not to store IP addresses, and not to get informed which device is connected to the wallet, also suggested by PU2.

QNT. Hiding the source of the transaction (70.18%), hiding the amount (70.18%), and hiding the destination (63.16%) were selected, respectively.

Accepting Extra Fees. Half of the interviewees (PU1, PU3, PU7, PU8, PU10, PU11) accepted paying extra fees for privacy, while the other half were not willing to do so. We asked those who accepted to pay for privacy to specify the fees in a transaction worth $1000, and $31.25 was the acceptable fee on average.

PU1 and PU3 specified that they pay for the technique that they are confident about the level of privacy that can be achieved. PU1 noted that *"if it is, for instance, a special signature,* [which can provide better privacy] *yes, roughly $15–$16, but I never pay to mixers or CoinJoin technique"*. PU3 pointed out the high transaction fees in Bitcoin and its dependency on the size of the transaction. They agreed to pay $50. PU7 and PU10 also said they will pay 5% ($50). PU8 agreed on paying up to 10% of the transaction fee (which relates to the transaction size, therefore, we can not precisely estimate the fees in dollars), and PU11 stated they would pay 2% ($20).

PU4, PU6, and PU9 specified that the current Bitcoin privacy meets their expectations, and they would not pay extra for privacy. Others thought paying for privacy is for famous people, criminals, or those who invested lots of money in the crypto market. PU12 asserted, *"I am not a politician, I am not a big business person who wants to run away from taxes. I have no reason to be anonymous, so I prefer to pay lower fees and be non-anonymous"*. PU5 stated, *"I don't have much money in the crypto market to pay extra fees for its privacy, however, if I had, I wouldn't pay more than a dollar"*.

QNT. While almost half of the participants accepted to pay extra fees for better privacy (53.45%), 32.76% did not accept, and 13.79% did not know. Those who accepted to pay extra fees paid on average $18.13 for a transaction worth $1000 (max. = 200, min. = 0.1, median. = 10). Those who did not accept to pay extra fees selected "current Bitcoin transaction fees are too high", "current level of Bitcoin privacy meets my expectation", "the volume of my investment in the crypto market is too low" as their reasons. Others specified that it would be a paywall for user privacy, or the privacy should be provided by default in a system not asking for more fees to offer it. The others preferred not to use Bitcoin, which is why they did not accept paying extra fees.

Accepting Extra Delays. All of the interviewees (except PU6) accepted waiting longer for better privacy. We asked those who accepted the delays to specify the time they could tolerate. PU1 agreed on less than a day. PU2 referred to the Bitcoin transaction confirmation time, which is too long at the moment. They continued that *"if I know the other party beforehand, let's say 1 to 2 days. If not, I prefer being non-anonymous rather than putting myself at such a risk, the Bitcoin price changes a lot, and waiting for more than a day sounds unreasonable"*. PU4 noted that *"it highly depends on the recipient whether he accepts it or not, it also depends on the importance of that transaction for me, then I would say 4 to 5 h"*. PU3, PU10, and PU12 stated 1 to 3 h, 1 to 2 h, and less than an hour, respectively. PU7 and PU9 could tolerate less than 30 min, while PU5 and PU8 stated less than 10 min, and PU11 could only tolerate it if the delay was less than a minute. PU5 stated that *"nowadays, Bitcoin is considered as an asset rather than a currency for buying or selling* [products or services], *therefore, time is not that much important in Bitcoin... it's not that bad to tolerate extra delays for better privacy; 10 min would be tolerable"*.

PU6 was against extra delays; they noted that *"Bitcoin is a slow network compared to other networks. It's not interesting to make it even slower"*.

QNT. Accepting extra delays varied among the participants (22.41% less than a minute, 29.31% less than an hour, 15.52% less than a day, 5.17% less than a week, and 5.17% less than a month). In total, 77.58% accepted extra delays; Those who did not accept the delays (13.79%) referred to the delays in Bitcoin confirmation or preferring not to use Bitcoin as a privacy option.

3.3 Privacy Wallets

Awareness and Usage of Privacy Wallets. Except for PU3, none of the interviewees were aware of Bitcoin privacy wallets. PU3 has heard of Samourai in a forum; they were also aware of Joinmarket, but they have not used them. They told us, *"it is better to perform ordinary transactions rather than Coin-Join transactions and being flagged by monitoring tools"*. PU8 was unaware of de-anonymization heuristics and add-on techniques such as CoinJoin or mixers; therefore, they thought the privacy wallets are the wallets that create a fresh address for each of the transactions (although this feature is also provided by privacy wallets, they are not the only option), their belief related to their misconception that *"the only way you can have privacy in Bitcoin network is to create a new address for* [each of your] *transactions"*.

QNT. Wasabi and Samourai were the most prominent privacy wallets among the participants. Figure 7 indicates the awareness of the privacy wallets. 43.86% of the participants were unaware of privacy wallets.

Most wallets have not been used. Wasabi with 28.13% and Samourai with 12.50% were among the top ones. 9.38% also reported using JoinMarket wallet. The satisfaction of using the privacy wallet is demonstrated in Table 2. We asked the wallet users to scale their satisfactions on a five Likert scale (*"extremely satisfied"* to *"not at all satisfied"*). 6 out of 9 were very satisfied with Wasabi, 3 out of 4 were very satisfied with Samourai, and 1 out of 3 was very satisfied with Joinmarket. 2 out of 9 and 2 out of 3 were somewhat satisfied with Wasabi and Joinmarket, respectively. While 1 out of 9 and 1 out of 4 reported being not at all satisfied with Wasabi and Samourai.

Trusting Third-Party Wallets. Except for PU8, who did not trust the wallets, other interviewees argued about which wallets they could trust. PU12 had no answer to the question as they were not familiar with the subject of privacy.

PU1, PU2, and PU3 mentioned being open-source as one of the items. PU1 continued that *"if the code is available on Github and can be checked, it gives me a sense of security"*. PU2, PU3, PU4, PU6, and PU7 pointed out being approved by a reliable person. PU3 clarified that *"I can rely on the reviews of reliable experts with a good experience and background in this context"*. PU5 and PU10 pointed to the wallet's reputation and the number of users; however, PU10 did not prefer to use third-party wallets. PU4 added recommendations from trusted websites. PU6 and PU7 also referred to users' reviews about the wallet. PU7 pointed to the number of downloads. PU9 and PU11 specified they should first research to know the wallet. PU11 specified related papers and forums where they could check if the wallet's security and privacy have been approved.

PU8 explained that *"we cannot even trust hardware wallets, how can we trust software wallets. We don't know* [the technology] *behind them. How you can know the code behind them to trust. I cannot trust them, as I don't know the codes and mechanisms behind them"*. The interviewee did not know or did not specify the open-source code where the code can be checked. They exaggerated the untruthfulness of the wallets; they thought there is no way to check the technology and code behind the wallets. We asked them how they perform their transactions while they do not trust any wallets, and they replied, *"I have to do that as I don't have any alternatives. Therefore, I accept its risk"*.

QNT. More than half of the participants (55.17%) asserted they trust the privacy wallet if it is open-source and the code can be checked. In contrast, 22.41% stated that they do not trust third-party services. Trusting information available in forums or provided by friends was selected with the same rate (8.62%). 3.45% did not have any answer to the question. The participant who selected "other" mentioned the importance of *"surviving over a long period"*.

3.4   Discussion

Privacy Awareness. In both quantitative and qualitative results, the majority of the users highlighted the importance of privacy. The numbers show that more people are now aware of Bitcoin anonymity compared to similar previous studies [5,13]. The interviewees who considered Bitcoin is fully anonymous were asked questions about privacy attacks and respective solutions in Bitcoin. Most of them said that they never heard about these privacy issues, but if they knew about them, they would have researched possible solutions to mitigate them. While address reuse and auxiliary information (obtained from exchanges or services) have increased the attention among our participants in the quantitative part, most of the respondents were unaware of the most prominent heuristic in the de-anonymization techniques, namely common input ownership.

We noted that some of the participants in the qualitative study did not know the difference between custodial (e.g., exchanges) and non-custodial wallets. They were either unaware or did not care about the risks of using centralized exchanges to manage their coins. Although some of them were aware of past security hacks to well-renowned exchanges (e.g., Mt. Gox [22], Bitstamp [3], Binance [23]), they continued to use them. Taking this risk is mainly motivated by the ease of using such traditional systems to manage their funds against the complexity of managing the cryptographic keys by themselves. Indeed, recovering lost credentials for accessing exchanges is much easier than recovering cryptographic keys in such a distributed system, especially if no recovery mechanisms or tools are employed. Some participants still use exchanges because they were either actively trading or preferred to be able to react fast when they wanted to trade. Some participants realize the privacy concerns of relying on a custodial wallet (e.g., the exchange may require KYC and is also able to correlate transactions), others did not think about it or were unaware of such privacy issues.

Some participants assumed that blockchain is safe from a privacy perspective as they use addresses rather than real identities. Others considered privacy persevering tools/coins are most likely to be used by criminals or for tax evasion. Both groups refrain from applying privacy-enhancing measures or tools. While privacy misconceptions about encryption of data on blockchain found by [15], our study supports this as there exist participants who had a similar belief that the blockchain uses encryption, the data is safely stored, and there is no way to trace the users on the blockchain. [15] suggested showing a notification to users through their wallets to inform them that the transaction will be publicly available in the network. Wallets are in a good position to educate users regarding privacy by providing notifications or features. One feature that is applied by some wallets [11,19,21] are preventing users from address reuse. The wallets can notify users to prevent reusing the address once the address is created. The wallets can also remove the address and create a new one, once the address gets funded. Indexing the address is another measure to increase users' attention on preventing address reuse.

Most of the participants in the qualitative study were unaware of the add-on techniques (for improving privacy on Bitcoin) or existing privacy-by-design blockchains. In the quantitative study, mixing websites were more popular, while other techniques were selected by less than half of the participants. Even if we consider biased answers among the participants, more than half are still unaware of privacy-enhancing techniques in Bitcoin. A previous study [5] showed that coin mixing services are a popular measure to improve privacy and that more than half of participants were unaware of CoinJoin and ZeroCoin (now called Zcash). Our study considers additional add-on techniques and privacy coins. However, in the quantitative part, more than two-third of participants were aware of Monero and Zcash 78.95% and 70.18%, respectively. Most participants have little to no understanding of privacy-enhancing techniques, neither how to use them nor the mechanism behind them, even if they have heard about them. They did not understand what kind of data these privacy techniques can hide. Some participants think that the privacy-enhancing techniques are too technical for novice users who only use cryptocurrencies for trading and investment purposes. Therefore, a negative understanding of using privacy tools (such as using them for criminal activities or tax evasion) as well as how blockchain can be used for malicious actions needs to be educated either (i) through integration with wallets by providing meaningful notification and privacy features (e.g., generating a fresh address), or (ii) through documentation and social media. Note that a distinction should be made between public privacy and private privacy. While in the former, the information publicly available on the blockchain is visible to everyone. In private privacy, the data is not public but solely available to governments, exchanges, or wallets. For formal research on collaborative deanonymization to achieve private privacy, the reader may refer to [12].

Privacy Preferences. While more than half of the participants preferred to use privacy coins, most of those who chose to use add-on techniques on top of Bitcoin if needed, expected future built-in privacy improvements to Bitcoin. Although this does not seem realistic in the near future, it is instead implemented by wallets or layer two solutions. According to our study, users are willing to accept longer transaction times to achieve better privacy, while half of them dismissed the idea of paying extra fees. Half of the participants were fine with paying extra fees. The interesting aspect here is that most current privacy solutions for Bitcoin (CoinJoin, CoinSwap) require more than one transaction fee, where additional transaction fees should be paid by users. Indeed, multiple CoinJoin rounds may be necessary to achieve adequate privacy. This entails additional transaction fees and consequently higher overall fees. Considering the high Bitcoin transaction fees at the time of writing, using privacy solutions seems relatively expensive. Therefore, privacy solutions should be implemented in a way that requires fewer fees, as it is unlikely that users will pay additional transaction fees for transactions with less amount. Users who were aware of the distinguishability of CoinJoin transactions with the same output amount were not willing to use it. Instead, they favored alternative techniques that preserve indistinguishability, where the transactions cannot be flagged by monitoring tools. PayJoin, Wabisabi [6], threshold signatures, and CoinSwap techniques can provide some level of indistinguishability; however, they have not been widely adopted in practice yet. The possibility of PayJoin transactions being flagged with unnecessary input heuristics has been investigated in [10].

Privacy Wallets. Although their development started around 2015, privacy wallets still struggle to attract more users. Indeed, such wallets are complex and require a minimum understanding of privacy concepts and techniques [9]. On the one hand, current Bitcoin privacy wallets implemented CoinJoin with the same output amount suffer from distinguishability in the blockchain; on the other hand, the newly implemented indistinguishable techniques such as Wabisabi and PayJoin may be banned by governments. This would be a severe problem for the respective wallet developers and users. We found that users prefer to use wallets that support different coins; thus, we can not expect users to install different wallets for different coins and, even worse, install additional wallets for their privacy, as well as having to spend time learning the wallet functions.

4 Conclusion

In this paper, we conducted a study on user perception and preference on Bitcoin privacy. We investigated different add-on privacy techniques in Bitcoin as well as their implementation in practice. We showed the difference between users' preferences and the implementation of privacy techniques in practice. Interestingly, most users preferred privacy coins rather than add-on techniques in Bitcoin. Our results show that participants are more likely to accept delays rather than extra fees to achieve anonymity in Bitcoin. The participants also preferred indistinguishable privacy techniques rather than being flagged by monitoring tools. Therefore, important questions are raised as current privacy wallets offer CoinJoin transactions with equal-sized output that are distinguishable in the blockchain. Overall, we show that users who prefer better privacy are not likely to use Bitcoin, and they favor embedding built-in privacy features in Bitcoin.

Acknowledgments. This research is based upon work partially supported by (1) SBA Research (SBA-K1); SBA Research is a COMET Center within the COMET – Competence Centers for Excellent Technologies Programme and funded by BMK, BMDW, and the federal state of Vienna. The COMET Programme is managed by FFG. (2) the FFG ICT of the Future project 874019 dIdentity & dApps. (3) the European Union's Horizon 2020 research and innovation programme under grant agreement No 826078 (FeatureCloud) (4) OEAD (Austria's agency for education and internationalization) Special Grant.

A   Questionnaire

* 1. Please check the box.
   ☐ I read all the information about objective, the GDPR compliance, and incentives for participants.
  2. How familiar are you with cryptocurrencies?
   ☐ Extremely familiar
   ☐ Very familiar
   ☐ Somewhat familiar
   ☐ Not so familiar
   ☐ Not at all familiar
  3. Where do you get information about cryptocurrencies? (Check all that apply).
   ☐ Word of mouth
   ☐ News
   ☐ Social media
   ☐ Websites
   ☐ Internet search

☐ Forums
☐ Books
☐ White papers
☐ Technical reports
☐ Research papers
☐ Other (please specify)
☐ None of the above

4. Have you ever owned/bought/mined cryptocurrencies?
   ☐ Yes ☐ No

5. Have you ever made a cryptocurrency transaction? Transaction: transferring cryptocurrency from one address to another.
   ☐ Yes ☐ No

6. Which of the following best describes your current role with regards to cryptocurrencies? (Check all that apply).
   ☐ Miner
   ☐ Investor
   ☐ Trader
   ☐ Financial user (using cryptocurrencies for payments)
   ☐ Researcher
   ☐ Curious about the technology (using and following the technology but not technically researching it)
   ☐ Developer
   ☐ Advisor/Consultant
   ☐ Other (please specify)
   ☐ None of the above

7. Which of the following wallets have you used? (Check all that apply).
   ☐ Desktop wallet
   ☐ Mobile wallet
   ☐ Web wallet
   ☐ Hardware wallet
   ☐ Paper wallet
   ☐ Other (please specify)
   ☐ None of the above

8. Have you ever used Bitcoin wallet software?
   ☐ Yes ☐ No

9. Which of the following Bitcoin wallets have you used? (Check all that apply).[2]
   ☐ List of bitcoin.org wallets
   ☐ Other (please specify)

10. Why did you use MyMaps as your Bitcoin wallet? It was shown to whom that selected MyMaps in the previous question.

11. How important is the anonymity of cryptocurrency transactions for you? "The anonymity of a subject means that the subject is not identifiable within a set of subjects, the anonymity set". [Pfitzmann and Hansen, 2010]

---

[2] The list was adopted from https://bitcoin.org/en/choose-your-wallet which contains invalid answer (MyMaps).

☐ Extremely important
☐ Very important
☐ Somewhat important
☐ Not so important
☐ Not at all important

12. How do you define Bitcoin in terms of anonymity?
☐ Extremely anonymous
☐ Very anonymous
☐ Somewhat anonymous
☐ Not so anonymous
☐ Not at all anonymous

13. Are you aware of the anonymity risks associated with Bitcoin?
☐ Yes ☐ No

14. If yes, please list the anonymity risks you are aware of.

15. What measures do you apply to improve your anonymity in Bitcoin?

16. Which of the following de-anonymization techniques in Bitcoin are you aware of? (Check all that apply).
This question contained an invalid answer (Relating the input and output).
☐ Address reuse (reusing the address in different transactions)
☐ Multi-input/common input ownership heuristic (all the inputs of a transaction are controlled by the same entity)
☐ Change address detection (finding the change address and relating it to the owner of the input(s))
☐ Relating the input and output in the transactions with the same output amount (same input index is related to the same output index)
☐ Single-input, single-output (considered as self-payment)
☐ Transaction graphs (analyzing the money flow by creating the transaction graph)
☐ Tagging addresses through the information available on the Internet (finding the owner of the address by searching social networks, forums, etc.)
☐ Cashing out in forks (cash-out in Bitcoin forks (e.g. Bitcoin Cash) which compromise the privacy of the entity in the Bitcoin blockchain)
☐ Other (please specify)
☐ None of the above

17. Which of the following correlation attacks in Bitcoin are you aware of? (Check all that apply).
☐ Network correlation (mapping IP address to Bitcoin address/finding a user's access pattern)
☐ Time correlation (mapping the time of the transaction with the activities in other services such as trading services)
☐ Amount correlation (mapping the amount of the transaction with the activities in other services such as trading services)
☐ Other (please specify)
☐ None of the above

18. Which of the following add-on privacy techniques in Bitcoin are you aware of? (Check all that apply).

☐ Mixing websites/centralized mixers
☐ CoinJoin-based techniques
☐ Fairexchange /CoinSwap
☐ Threshold signatures/Schnorr signatures
☐ Off-chain solutions
☐ Other (please specify)
☐ None of the above

19. Which of the following built-in privacy coins (using techniques such as Zero-knowledge proof, Ring signature, CoinJoin, etc. by design) are you aware of? (Check all that apply).
    ☐ Monero
    ☐ Decred
    ☐ Zcash
    ☐ Horizen
    ☐ Dram
    ☐ Pirate Chain ARRR
    ☐ MobileCoin
    ☐ Dero
    ☐ Verge
    ☐ Other (please specify)
    ☐ None of the above

20. Which features make Dram a privacy coin? (Check all that apply). It was shown to whom selected Dram as a privacy coin.
    ☐ Hiding the amount of the transaction
    ☐ Hiding the source of the transaction
    ☐ Hiding the destination of the transaction
    ☐ Other (please specify)
    ☐ None of the above

21. Which of the following built-in privacy coins have you owned/bought /mined? (Check all that apply).
    Answers from Q.19
    ☐ Other (please specify)
    ☐ None of the above

22. Why did you own/buy/mine privacy coins?
    ☐ For better anonymity
    ☐ For investment
    ☐ Both of the above
    ☐ Other (please specify)

23. Which of the following would you prefer to achieve better anonymity in the cryptocurrencies area?
    ☐ Using add-on techniques implemented by wallets and services in Bitcoin (e.g., mixing techniques such as CoinJoin)
    ☐ Using built-in techniques in privacy coins (Zcash, Monero, etc.)
    ☐ I do not know
    ☐ Other (please specify)

24. Why do you prefer using Bitcoin add-on privacy techniques rather than privacy coins? (Check all that apply).
    ☐ Bitcoin market cap
    ☐ Bitcoin reputation
    ☐ Availability of Bitcoin tools (wallets, explorers, etc.)
    ☐ Bitcoin is listed in most exchanges.
    ☐ Transacting is not as complicated as some privacy coins.
    ☐ Other (please specify)
25. Why do you prefer using privacy coins rather than Bitcoin add-on privacy techniques? (Check all that apply).
    ☐ Privacy-by-design provides stronger anonymity.
    ☐ I prefer using privacy coins that have mandatory built-in privacy which is used by all users and provides better anonymity amongst all users. (using privacy features in some coins is optional)
    ☐ Add-on techniques implemented by third-parties require trust in those tools/services.
    ☐ Other (please specify)
26. Which of the following would you prefer in Bitcoin?
    ☐ Adding mandatory built-in privacy techniques (such as Zero-knowledge proof, Ring signature, Confidential transactions, etc.) to the protocol
    ☐ Using add-on privacy techniques (such as mixing) whenever you need better anonymity
    ☐ I do not know
    ☐ Other (please specify)
27. Please explain in more detail why you chose that option.
28. Which privacy features are you interested in for Bitcoin? (Check all that apply).
    ☐ Hiding the amount of the transaction
    ☐ Hiding the source of the transaction
    ☐ Hiding the destination of the transaction
    ☐ I do not know
    ☐ Other (please specify)
    ☐ None of the above
29. Which of the following Bitcoin privacy wallets are you aware of? (Check all that apply).
    ☐ Dark wallet
    ☐ Sharedcoin
    ☐ Joinmarket wallet
    ☐ Wasabi wallet
    ☐ Samourai wallet
    ☐ Other (please specify)
    ☐ None of the above
30. Which of the following privacy wallets have you used? (Check all that apply).
    ☐ Answers from Q.29
    ☐ Other (please specify)
    ☐ None of the above

31. How satisfied are you with the following privacy wallets?
    ☐ Selected wallets from Q.30.
    ☐ Extremely satisfied
    ☐ Very satisfied
    ☐ Somewhat satisfied
    ☐ Not so satisfied
    ☐ Not at all satisfied
32. Please tell us why you are satisfied/dissatisfied with each of the wallets.
33. Which of the following best describes your opinion to trust third-party privacy wallets to enhance your privacy in Bitcoin?
    ☐ I trust the privacy wallet if it is open-source and the code can be checked.
    ☐ I trust the privacy wallet if it is trusted on forums/websites that I trust.
    ☐ I trust the privacy wallet if it is trusted by my friends.
    ☐ I do not trust third-party services.
    ☐ I do not know.
    ☐ Other (please specify)
34. If you do not trust third-party privacy wallets, why not?
35. Why do you think Bitcoin is extremely anonymous? It was shown to whom selected Bitcoin as fully anonymous.
    ☐ The source address is hidden.
    ☐ The destination address is hidden.
    ☐ The transaction amount is hidden.
    ☐ There are no real identities in the transactions (neither names nor personally identifiable information (PII)).
    ☐ No one can track the transaction flow.
    ☐ I do not know.
    ☐ Other (please specify)

If we say there are some techniques to improve privacy in Bitcoin, how would you answer the fees and delays questions?

36. Would you pay extra fees in Bitcoin transactions to enhance your privacy?
    ☐ Yes (You will choose the preferred fees in the question).
    ☐ No
    ☐ I do not know.
37. How much would you pay for Bitcoin transaction privacy if the transaction's value is $1,000? (Please enter a whole number. Enter the number of dollars you are willing to pay).
38. If you are not likely to pay extra fees for privacy in Bitcoin transactions, why not?
    ☐ Privacy is not important for me.
    ☐ The volume of my investment in the crypto market is too low, therefore it does not seem reasonable to pay more for privacy.
    ☐ The current level of Bitcoin privacy meets my expectations.
    ☐ Current Bitcoin transaction fees are too high and I can not tolerate paying more for privacy.
    ☐ Other (please specify)

39. Would you accept delays in performing Bitcoin transactions to enhance your privacy?
    ☐ No
    ☐ Yes, if it is less than a minute.
    ☐ Yes, if it is less than an hour.
    ☐ Yes, if it is less than a day.
    ☐ Yes, if it is less than a week.
    ☐ Yes, if it is less than a month.
    ☐ I do not know.
40. If you are not likely to accept delays for privacy in Bitcoin transactions, why not?
    ☐ Privacy is not important for me.
    ☐ The current level of Bitcoin privacy meets my expectations.
    ☐ The delays in Bitcoin transaction confirmations are still too long.
    ☐ Other (please specify)
41. Please select "Homophonic substitution cipher".

It is a quality check. If you choose other than Homophonic substitution cipher, we cannot consider your responses, because you are either not paying attention and your answers are not valid, or you are a robot.

☐ Caesar cipher
☐ Monoalphabetic cipher
☐ Homophonic substitution cipher
☐ Polyalphabetic Cipher
☐ Playfair cipher
☐ Rail fence

42. Please tell us your current role(s) with regard to cryptocurrencies.
43. Please provide us with your Monero address; in case you win, we will pay the incentives to this address.
44. Please provide your gender
    ☐ Female ☐ Male ☐ Diverse ☐ Do not want to specify
45. What is your age?
    ☐ 18 to 24 ☐ 25 to 34 ☐ 35 to 44 ☐ 45 to 54 ☐ 55 to 64 ☐ 65 to 74 ☐ 75 or older
46. What is the highest level of education you have completed?
    ☐ Did Not Complete High School
    ☐ High School
    ☐ Did Not Complete College
    ☐ Bachelor's Degree
    ☐ Master's Degree
    ☐ Ph.D.
47. Do you work or study in an IT-related field?
    ☐ Yes ☐ No
48. On what continent do you currently reside?
    ☐ Africa ☐ America ☐ Asia ☐ Australia ☐ Europe ☐ Do not want to specify

B   Related Work

Blockchain security and privacy from a user perspective has been studied in [5, 13,15]. The studies demonstrated the lack of users' knowledge about blockchain privacy issues and showed that most users do not know why privacy techniques are required or how they could mitigate de-anonymization.

Krombholz et al. [13] conducted a user study on Bitcoin security and privacy and identified a large gap between users' understandings on how to remain private and anonymous in Bitcoin. More than a third of their participants thought that Bitcoin is fully anonymous. Fabian and Ermakova [5] found that *almost 18% of users were unaware of the risk of being de-anonymized on blockchain, and half of them knew about the risks and were concerned, while the remainder was aware of the risks but not concerned.* They also investigated whether users are aware of mixing services, and half of the participants were not familiar with the CoinJoin technique. Mai et al. [15] performed a qualitative user study on user mental models of cryptocurrency systems. They found that users assume *that they are anonymous, and blockchain transactions are encrypted, therefore, the data is not publicly readable.* Most of the users pointed out address mapping as a privacy threat. *Identity disclosure through the use of third-party services has also been reported by the users.* In [20], risk management of cryptocurrencies has been studied via interviews with 11 users and 9 non-users. They showed that the misunderstandings of users and non-users can deviate the measures they apply to mitigate the risks.

Most of the previous studies [13,15,20] focused on both security and privacy aspects. With respect to privacy, they mainly investigated Bitcoin anonymity and network privacy aspects. In contrast to network de-anonymization heuristics (such as common input ownership, change address detection, etc.), timing and amount correlation as possible privacy attacks have not been addressed in the previous user studies. Besides, these studies did not investigate privacy wallets and users' preferences on additional fees and delays related to add-on privacy techniques.

C   Methodology

C.1   Qualitative Research

Recruitment. Participants were recruited via social media, universities, and companies with a focus on Blockchain technology. Those who (i) already have little to basic knowledge about blockchain and cryptocurrencies, and (ii) used a cryptocurrency wallet and performed a transaction in the past, and (iii) were at least 18 years old. Were eligible to participate as users. Non-users were recruited with different requirement, (i) not familiar at all with cryptocurrencies, and (ii) not used a cryptocurrency wallet and performed a transaction in the past, and (iii) were at least 18 years old. We did not specify that the interview is about privacy aspects of blockchain and Bitcoin to make sure that the users did not read related materials beforehand. This allowed us to learn about their privacy perception with their actual level of knowledge.

Coding. Grounded Theory [14] was used for coding. Researchers coded the data and grouped statements related to the same concept. In each coding round, we discussed the relations between categories to define higher-level categories. With this method, we were able to revise or add the options to the questions in our quantitative analysis.

Sampling. We selected the participants according to their reported level of knowledge and their usage of cryptocurrencies, ranging from expert to novice users. We interviewed 14 participants, 12 users (age: max. = 45, min. = 26) and 2 non-users (age: max. = 45, min. = 35). 7 out of the 12 users and 1 out of the 2 non-users were working in IT-related fields. Detailed demographics is provided in Table 1. All the user participants have owned /bought /mined cryptocurrencies and have already made a transaction.

Limitations. We asked our participants about their knowledge level regarding cryptocurrencies, field of study/work, previous experience with transactions on blockchain, and gender, if they allowed it. Most participants had university degrees. With regards to age, we unfortunately had no participants in 18–24 and 55–64 age groups, and no participants with high school- or college level of education. However, our sample covers diverse knowledge levels, education/work backgrounds, and genders. Due to the Covid-19 situation, we performed the majority of the interviews online, however, in some cases we had to ask some of the questions several times or request the interviewees to repeat their answers as a result of poor or unstable Internet connections.

C.2   Quantitative Research

Sampling. Our scope was Bitcoin users and UTXO-based privacy coins. Our questionnaire was distributed through different international channels. It was shared in the Bitcoin forums Bitcointalk.org on social media such as Reddit, Telegram, Facebook, Twitter, and LinkedIn. It was also sent to blockchain and cryptography mailing lists, the related international research centers, researchers, university students, and businesses in our country. In total, 101 participants took part in our survey. After applying our exclusion criteria, we reached a final sample of n = 58 for our analysis. Those 58 were eligible based on their self-reported knowledge, completely filled-out questionnaires and passed quality control checks. Detailed demographics and cryptocurrency familiarity are provided in Table 1. The majority of participants (91.38%) reported that they have owned /bought /mined cryptocurrencies. 81.03% made at least one transaction, and 62.96% have used Bitcoin wallet software. Figure 3 demonstrates the self-reported role in cryptocurrency, and Fig. 4 illustrates the wallet types that were used by the participants. The majority of the participants reported themselves as "investors" and "curious about the technology". Desktop wallets and mobile wallets were among the top selected wallet types that were used by participants.

C.3   Ethical Considerations

Our research center is located in (blinded), and is subject to the European General Data Protection Regulation (GDPR). Before the interview in the qualitative part, all participants were asked to sign consent forms in which we specified the goals of the study and the academic context the data will be used for. The consent forms do not include the participants' IDs we assigned for the analysis. To comply with the GDPR, we did not ask any questions that may disclose personally identifiable information (PII); the questions do not allow any inference to the participants' identities. The research objective, the GDPR- and ethical notice regarding the raffle were provided at the beginning of the questionnaire in the quantitative part.

D   Figures and Tables

In this section, the charts and tables are provided. Figure 1 indicates the process of designing our questionnaire. We first prepared a draft of our questionnaire. Then we conducted a Pilot in a Blockchain workshop with 11 participants. We could revise the questionnaire based on the answers and feedback. Next, we performed another Pilot as a think-aloud with 4 blockchain security and privacy experts. We again revise the questionnaire. We then consulted with our legal office to be compliant with GDPR and a usability researcher provided us with her comments on the questionnaire. We then conducted a qualitative interview with 14 participants (12 users and 2 non-users) with open-ended questions. For our quantitative part, we added multi-choice options to some of the questions and asked an editor to Proofread the questionnaire. We Finalized the questionnaire and options Logic and published the questionnaire on survey monkey.

The chart in Fig. 2 illustrates how we defined the questionnaire logic. Interviews with non-users showed that they were not able to answer the questions as answering required basic knowledge of cryptocurrencies; hence we set the logic in a way that if the respondents select "not familiar at all" with the cryptocurrencies, they will jump into the end of the survey. In the following questions, we asked the user privacy awareness, and in the first question, we asked how they consider Bitcoin anonymity. If they selected Bitcoin as extremely anonymous, they jumped into privacy unaware users' question, where we asked them why they believe Bitcoin is extremely anonymous. Privacy-aware users could see the questions regarding De-anonymization attacks and add-ons techniques,

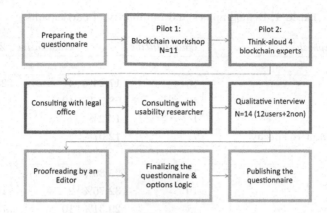

Fig. 1. Designing the Questionnaire

privacy coins, privacy preferences, and privacy wallets. We asked both unaware and aware users about their willingness to pay extra fees or accept delays for better privacy. Before showing this to the unaware users we provided them with the privacy issues in the public blockchain. And finally, we asked them for demographics.

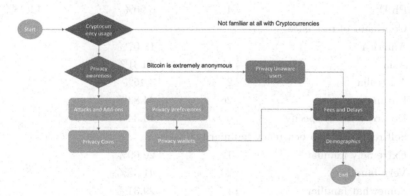

Fig. 2. Questionnaire Overall Logic

Table 1. Demographics and familiarity of participants

Demographichs	Quantitative	%	Qualitative	%
Gender				
Female	10	17.24%	4	28.57%
Male	40	68.97%	10	71.42%
Diverse	1	1.72%		
Do not want to specify	7	12.07%		
Age				
18 to 24	15	25.86%		
25 to 34	19	32.76%	2	14.28%
35 to 44	17	29.31%	10	71.42%
45 to 54	6	10.34%	2	14.28%
55 to 64	1	1.72%		
Highest level of education				
Did Not Complete High School	1	1.72%		
High School	6	10.34%		
Did Not Complete College	3	5.17%		
Bachelor's Degree	23	39.66%	4	28.57%
Master's Degree	21	36.21%	8	57.14%
Ph.D	4	6.90%	2	14.28%
Continent of residence				
America	7	12.07%		
Asia	17	29.31%		
Australia	2	3.45%		
Europe	26	44.83%		
Do not want to specify	6	10.34%		
Self-reported cryptocurrency familiarity				
Extremely familiar	12	20.69%		
Very familiar	24	41.38%		
Somewhat familiar	17	29.31%		
Not so familiar	5	8.62%		

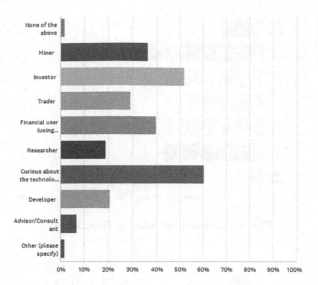

Fig. 3. Current role in cryptrocurrency

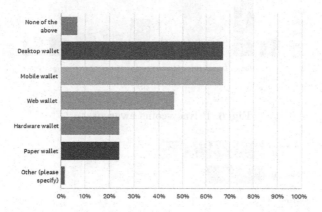

Fig. 4. Wallet type used by participants

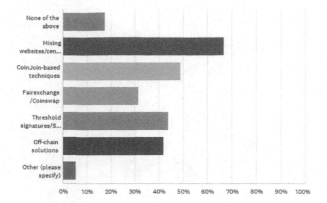

Fig. 5. Awareness of Add-on Techniques

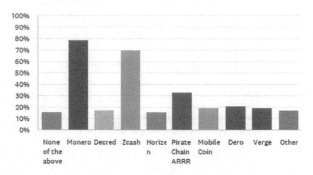

Fig. 6. Privacy coins awareness

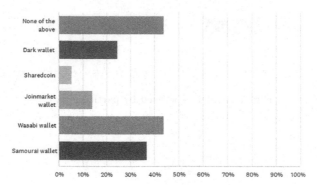

Fig. 7. Privacy wallets awareness

Table 2. Privacy wallets satisfaction

	Very satisfied		Somewhat satisfied		Not at all satisfied		Total
Dark wallet	100.00%	1	0.00%	0	0.00%	0	1
Sharedcoin	100.00%	1	0.00%	0	0.00%	0	1
Joinmarket wallet	33.33%	1	66.67%	2	0.00%	0	3
Wasabi wallet	66.67%	6	22.22%	2	11.11%	1	9
Samourai wallet	75.00%	3	0.00%	0	25.00%	1	4

References

1. Biryukov, A., Tikhomirov, S.: Deanonymization and linkability of cryptocurrency transactions based on network analysis. In: 2019 IEEE European Symposium on Security and Privacy (EuroS&P), pp. 172–184. IEEE (2019)
2. Bonneau, J., Narayanan, A., Miller, A., Clark, J., Kroll, J.A., Felten, E.W.: Mixcoin: anonymity for bitcoin with accountable mixes. In: Christin, N., Safavi-Naini, R. (eds.) FC 2014. LNCS, vol. 8437, pp. 486–504. Springer, Heidelberg (2014). https://doi.org/10.1007/978-3-662-45472-5_31
3. Coindesk: Details of $5 million bitstamp hack revealed. https://www.coindesk.com/markets/2015/07/01/details-of-5-million-bitstamp-hack-revealed/. Accessed 17 Jan 2022
4. English, S.M., Nezhadian, E.: Conditions of full disclosure: the blockchain remuneration model. In: 2017 IEEE European Symposium on Security and Privacy Workshops (EuroS&PW), pp. 64–67. IEEE (2017)
5. Fabian, B., Ermakova, T., Sander, U.: Anonymity in bitcoin?-the users' perspective (2016)
6. Ficsór, Á, Kogman, Y., Seres, I.A.: Wabisabi. https://github.com/zkSNACKs/WabiSabi/releases/download/build-70d01424bbce06389d2f0536ba155776eb1d8344/WabiSabi.pdf. Accessed 3 Feb 2021
7. Ghesmati, S., Fdhila, W., Weippl, E.: Studying bitcoin privacy attacks and their impact on bitcoin-based identity methods. In: González Enríquez, J., Debois, S., Fettke, P., Plebani, P., van de Weerd, I., Weber, I. (eds.) BPM 2021. LNBIP, vol. 428, pp. 85–101. Springer, Cham (2021). https://doi.org/10.1007/978-3-030-85867-4_7
8. Ghesmati, S., Fdhila, W., Weippl, E.: SoK: how private is bitcoin? Classification and evaluation of bitcoin privacy techniques. In: Proceedings of the 17th International Conference on Availability, Reliability and Security, pp. 1–14 (2022)
9. Ghesmati, S., Fdhila, W., Weippl, E.: Usability of cryptocurrency wallets providing coinjoin transactions. Cryptology ePrint Archive (2022)
10. Ghesmati, S., Kern, A., Judmayer, A., Stifter, N., Weippl, E.: Unnecessary input heuristics and PayJoin transactions. In: Stephanidis, C., Antona, M., Ntoa, S. (eds.) HCII 2021. CCIS, vol. 1420, pp. 416–424. Springer, Cham (2021). https://doi.org/10.1007/978-3-030-78642-7_56
11. Joinmarket: Joinmarket. https://github.com/JoinMarket-Org/ joinmarket-clientserver (2015)
12. Keller, P., Florian, M., Böhme, R.: Collaborative deanonymization. arXiv preprint arXiv:2005.03535 (2020)

13. Krombholz, K., Judmayer, A., Gusenbauer, M., Weippl, E.: The other side of the coin: user experiences with bitcoin security and privacy. In: Grossklags, J., Preneel, B. (eds.) FC 2016. LNCS, vol. 9603, pp. 555–580. Springer, Heidelberg (2017). https://doi.org/10.1007/978-3-662-54970-4_33

14. Lazar, J., Feng, J.H., Hochheiser, H.: Research Methods in Human-Computer Interaction. Morgan Kaufmann (2017)

15. Mai, A., Pfeffer, K., Gusenbauer, M., Weippl, E., Krombholz, K.: User mental models of cryptocurrency systems-a grounded theory approach. In: Sixteenth Symposium on Usable Privacy and Security ({SOUPS} 2020), pp. 341–358 (2020)

16. Meiklejohn, S., et al.: A fistful of bitcoins: characterizing payments among men with no names. In: Proceedings of the 2013 Conference on Internet Measurement Conference, pp. 127–140 (2013)

17. Pfeffer, K., et al.: On the usability of authenticity checks for hardware security tokens. In: 30th {USENIX} Security Symposium ({USENIX} Security 2021) (2021)

18. Sabry, F., Labda, W., Erbad, A., Al Jawaheri, H., Malluhi, Q.: Anonymity and privacy in bitcoin escrow trades. In: Proceedings of the 18th ACM Workshop on Privacy in the Electronic Society, pp. 211–220 (2019)

19. Samourai: Samourai wallet. https://samouraiwallet.com/whirlpool (2015)

20. Voskobojnikov, A., Obada-Obieh, B., Huang, Y., Beznosov, K.: Surviving the cryptojungle: perception and management of risk among north American cryptocurrency (non)users. In: Bonneau, J., Heninger, N. (eds.) FC 2020. LNCS, vol. 12059, pp. 595–614. Springer, Cham (2020). https://doi.org/10.1007/978-3-030-51280-4_32

21. Wasabi: Wasabiwallet (2018). https://wasabiwallet.io/

22. Wiki: Mt. gox. https://en.wikipedia.org/wiki/Mt._Gox. Accessed 17 Jan 2022

23. Wired: Hack brief: Hackers stole $40 million from binance cryptocurrency exchange. https://www.wired.com/story/hack-binance-cryptocurrency-exchange/. Accessed 17 Jan 2022

24. Yousaf, H., Kappos, G., Meiklejohn, S.: Tracing transactions across cryptocurrency ledgers. In: 28th {USENIX} Security Symposium ({USENIX} Security 2019), pp. 837–850 (2019)

DeFi22

A Short Survey on Business Models
of Decentralized Finance (DeFi) Protocols

Teng Andrea Xu[1](✉) and Jiahua Xu[1,2,3](✉)

[1] École Polytechnique Fédérale de Lausanne, Lausanne, Switzerland
andrea.xu@epfl.ch
[2] University College London, London, UK
jiahua.xu@ucl.ac.uk
[3] The DLT Science Foundation, London, UK

Abstract. Decentralized Finance (DeFi) services are moving traditional financial operations to the Internet of Value (IOV) by exploiting smart contracts, distributed ledgers, and transactions among different protocols. The exponential increase of the Total Value Locked (TVL) in DeFi foreshadows a bright future for automated money transfers in a plethora of services. In this short survey paper, we describe the business models of various DeFi protocol types—namely, *Protocols for Loanable Funds (PLFs), Decentralized Exchanges (DEXs)*, and *Yield Aggregators*. We then abstract and compare the general business models of those protocol types. Finally, we provide open research challenges that will involve different domains such as economics, finance, and computer science.

Keywords: Decentralized Finance · Value Investing · Blockchain

1 Introduction

Decentralized Finance (DeFi) aims to provide financial services on a blockchain-based infrastructure. A plethora of protocols form the DeFi ecosystem. These protocols are able to replicate classical financial services, such as lending and exchange, without any central institution, via smart contracts and the immutable ledger. In the literature [1,2], DeFi's key features are generally recognized to be *open* to anyone, *transparent*, *non-custodial*, and *composable*, i.e. financial services can be arbitrarily composed to make new financial products. The Total Value Locked (TVL)[1] has seen exponential growth with the so-called "DeFi Summer". TVL grew from \$600m as at the end of March 2020 to \$11bn as at the end of September 2020 [23]. Furthermore, from March 2020 to the time of writing[2], the top-100 DeFi tokens' market cap grew by almost a hundred times—from

---

[1] The TVL is commonly defined as the sum of all assets' value, denominated in USD, deposited in a DeFi protocol, and therefore locked in the underlying set of smart contracts.
[2] 2021-10-31, https://defipulse.com/.

© International Financial Cryptography Association 2023
S. Matsuo et al. (Eds.): FC 2022 Workshops, LNCS 13412, pp. 197–206, 2023.
https://doi.org/10.1007/978-3-031-32415-4_13

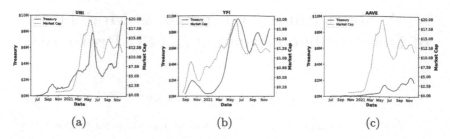

Fig. 1. The figure above shows the top DeFi's protocols daily treasury size, in solid black, and market cap, in dashed red, for each financial service. We select each token according to DeFiPulse TVL. Both measures are smoothed by using a rolling window of 30 days. To date, Uniswap—by default—is not applying any exchange fee but its treasury consists of 43% of the total token supply [4], whereas AAVE and Yearn apply fees for their financial services [5,6]. We can see that market cap drives financial services usage, and thus protocols' revenues. Uniswap and AAVE data are retrieved from CryptoFees API [7], while YFI data is retrieved from YFIstats [8]. The respective correlations between market cap and treasury size are: (a) 0.596, (b) 0.857, and (c) 0.431. (Color figure online)

$1.8bn to $154bn [3]. These recent DeFi milestones foreshadow a bright future for both DeFi's users and investors. We show, in Fig. 1, the top Ethereum DeFi tokens' daily treasury size together with their market cap, smoothed by a rolling window of 30 days. We show a plot for each DeFi financial service, i.e. Uniswap (UNI) for *DEXs*, Yearn Finance (YFI) for *Yield Aggregators*, and AAVE for *PLFs*. To date, there is a lack of literature that offers any clear abstraction on how DeFi protocols generate their revenue stream, a key component for the sustainability of a project. We claim that it is important for both investors and users to understand how DeFi tokens profit. From an investor's perspective, a clear business model with a steady and constant revenue stream are key features before investing in the underlying project. As an end user, DeFi's users look for reliable protocols; hence, a protocol with an efficient and observable business model is likely to be a "secure" protocol. Therefore, the central contribution of this short survey paper is to describe and offer a clean comparison of different DeFi services business models. In this work, we will look into the main DeFi financial services namely: *Protocols for Loanable Funds (PLFs)*, *Decentralized Exchanges* (DEXs), and *Yield Aggregators*. We refrain from analyzing the variety of protocols in technical detail, but rather direct the reader to other resources. The focus of this work is mainly on the protocols' business model. The paper is structured as follows. First, we describe the general PLFs' business model in Sect. 2.1. Subsequently, we explain the dominant cash flows within DEXs and Yield Aggregators in Sect. 2.2 and 2.3. In Sect. 3, we present a first generalized business model in DeFi. Finally, we provide a literature review and conclude the work with Sect. 4 and 5.

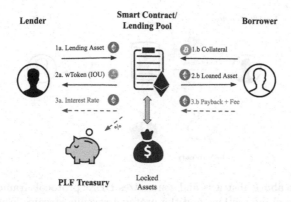

Fig. 2. The figure above abstracts and generalizes the lending protocol framework by showing the main actors and interactions. From left to right, lenders can deposit their crypto-assets to gain additional profits. They receive a PLFs wrapped token or IOU as proof of their deposit. In the center, the smart contract takes care of the deposited assets, loans, and liquidations—if any. On the right, a borrower must deposit collateral before getting the loan. Finally, at the end of the loan, the borrower will have to return the borrowed amount plus an interest; part of this interest will be redistributed pro-rata to all lenders, and the rest will generate revenue for the PLF itself.

2 Major DeFi Protocols

2.1 Protocols for Loanable Funds (PLF)

PLFs let users borrow/lend digital assets in a decentralized fashion. Automated smart contracts behave as middle-men. They lock assets deposited by the lenders and allow borrowers to get liquidity in exchange for collateral [12]. These types of smart contracts are also called Lending Pools [9]. These Lending Pools typically lock a pair of tokens, a loanable token, and a collateral token. By providing liquidity, lenders gain interest revenue depending on the supply and demand. Because there is no guarantee of repayment, borrowers must over-collateralize their position [45]. On top of that, when returning the amount borrowed, the borrowers must pay interest expenses that are redistributed proportionately to the lenders and the governance token holders. When a borrower's loan position becomes liquidated, they will have to pay an additional fee. We show in Fig. 2 a typical generalized PLF use case.

Business Model. PLFs' cash flow depends on the interest rate model, the current underlying demand versus supply, and the total amount borrowed. The interest rate model can be either a linear model, a non-linear model, or a kinked model [11]. The interest rate is driven by the underlying asset demand-supply ratio: the interest rate is higher when the ratio is high, and vice versa. Given the rate of interest, the PLF gets a percentage of it. For example, Compound takes 10% of the interest rate [13]. Besides traditional over-collateralized loans, PLFs

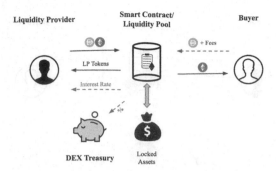

Fig. 3. The figure above abstracts and generalizes DEXs protocols framework by showing the main actors' interactions and the protocol revenue stream. From left to right, LPs deposit a pair of tokens, in this example DAI/ETH, in the Liquidity Pool. In exchange, they receive LP tokens as proof of their deposit. In the middle, a smart contract takes care of locked assets, new deposits, swaps, and fees. The buyer will have to pay a fee for his swap. This fee will be partially distributed pro-rata among all LPs, while the DEX treasury will collect a percentage of it.

offer flash loans[3] that can bring more revenues to the protocol. Flash loans fee rate is usually fixed, e.g. AAVE [14], or even without fees, e.g. dYdX [15].

2.2 Decentralized Exchanges

DEXs operate differently to classical order-book exchanges where traders match market bids and asks. Again, smart contracts are the middle-men and, in this case, are called Liquidity Pools. Investors or, in this scenario, Liquidity Providers (LPs) can deposit, in the case of constant product pools [16], a pair of equal worth tokens—say ETH/DAI as shown in Fig. 3—into these Liquidity Pools. In exchange, they will receive LP tokens as proof of their deposit and earn a percentage of the fee accrued from the buyer when swapping. A price is assigned for each token given the protocol's price function. The buyer that is willing to swap DAI for some ETH will deposit DAI in the Liquidity Pool, plus some fee, and receive ETH. The whole mechanism is called Automatic Market Making (AMM). Further reading on the topic can be found in [17,18]. We show in Fig. 3 a typical generalized DEX use case.

Business Model. When buyers swap, they pay a fee. This fee is split pro-rata between the liquidity providers of the pool as a reward for their contribution to the pool. A percentage of the fee is sent to the protocol's treasury. This share of the fee represents the primary income resource for most AMMs. Balancer, for example, has recently increased its protocol fee[4] from 10% to 50% [19] equaling

---

[3] Flash Loans are a special type of loan where the borrower must return the borrowed amount plus interest in the same transaction without the need for collateral. An in-depth explanation can be found in [10].

[4] Note that the protocol fee is applied on the swap fee.

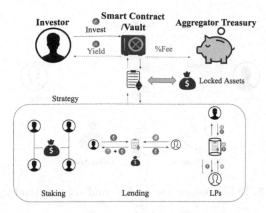

Fig. 4. This figure shows a typical yield aggregator use case. Starting from the top left, the investor chooses his Vault of preference to deposit his savings. The Vault, a smart contract, will run its pre-set strategy; simple staking, lending, or providing liquidity are just examples. More complex strategies combine borrowing and/or leveraging involving multiple steps and protocols—yETH vault is an example of a multiple-step strategy [25]. Usually, Vaults apply a fixed performance fee on the strategy yield.

Bancor's fees [20]. To date, even though it doesn't apply any protocol fee by default [21], Uniswap has the biggest treasury in DeFi with $9bn locked in its treasury [22], which is the value of the 43% of Uniswap total supply [4] locked for the community.

2.3 Yield Aggregators

Yield Aggregators combine different strategies to maximize investors' rate of return. Similar to PLFs and DEXs protocols, smart contracts have a central role. Commonly, smart contracts are referred to as "Vaults" in this domain. In this scenario, shown in Fig. 4, investors deposit their savings into a Vault. Different Vaults run different strategies. These strategies can be straightforward, such as finding the best lending protocol interest rate, or more complex, as borrowing assets and leveraging some other position by exploiting different protocols. For a more in-depth technical insight refer to [23,41].

Business Model. Yield Aggregators cash flow is based on their Vaults' performance. That is, yield aggregators charge a commission on the strategy's profit. Hence, the investor yield will be equivalent to the Vault's total profit minus the protocol's fee. Different tokens apply different fee rates: Yearn Finance v2 applies 20% as performance fee and an additional 2% as management fee [6], Pickle Finance and Idle have 20% and 10% performance fees respectively [26,27]. Harvest is the only yield aggregator that applies 30% of fees but uses the whole reward to buy back FARM—Harvest native tokens—from DEXs and redistribute them to stakers [28].

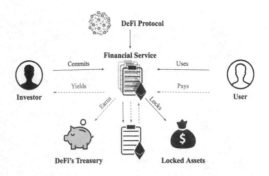

Fig. 5. DeFi common mechanism and revenue strategy.

3   DeFi Business Model

We synthesize the business models reported and give a first general DeFi business model framework (Fig. 5). This framework involves different actors and actions with their naming conventions (Table 1) .

DeFi Protocol A set of smart contracts, with multiple facets—PLFs, AMMs, or Yield Aggregators. They provide open, non-custodial, permissionless, and composable financial services in exchange for a small fee. The fee is applied to any asset movement, for example, borrowing assets or swapping assets.

Investor This actor is willing to hold the underlying protocol risk, such as protocol misbehavior, impermanent loss, or rug-pulls, in exchange for a passive income. Therefore, he mainly deposits his assets and provides liquidity to the financial service.

User The user usually exploits the protocol on the fly, and he never waits for any long-term response—save for the case of Yield Aggregators, where the user is also an investor. This actor requests asset movements, and thus pays interest rates to the protocol.

Financial Service This actor is the core of the whole protocol: Locks assets, satisfies the assets movements requests, and prevents protocol misuse. Furthermore, it can behave as an investor by leveraging other DeFi Protocols. Finally, it delivers yields and earnings to the other actors.

DeFi's services do not come for free. As we have seen, investors can exploit these services to earn passive income. However, this additional interest is somehow "taxed" by the DeFi protocol. On the other side, the users are willing to use the platform in exchange for a fee. Hence, the DeFi protocol has an income from both sides. In classical finance, this market and business model is known as the "Two-Sided Markets", first formalized in [29]. On one side, the investor provides liquidity to the financial service that peer users can use. On the other side, by paying fees, the user provides income to both protocols and investors.

Table 1. An overview of DeFi's naming taxonomy.

DeFi Protocol	Smart Contract	Investor	User	Financial Service
PLFs	Lending Pool	Lender	Borrower	Loan
DEXs	Liquidity Pool	Liquidity Provider	Buyer/Trader	Exchange
Yield Aggregators	Vault	Vault User		Asset Management

4   Literature Review

Our work is strongly related to the canonical empirical asset pricing problem. Evaluating and pricing an asset is perhaps the most renowned problem in classical finance literature. There exist two cardinal analyses to value and price an asset. On the one hand, technical analysis deduces future underlying value from its history of trading, which can involve price changes, trading volume, price moving average, and other historical characteristics [30]. [31] shows how 90% of chief foreign exchange dealers based in London in November 1988 exploited technical analysis for their trades. We observe here a duality between public equity markets and cryptocurrencies trading. On the other hand, fundamental analysis is based on a firm's book value—assets and liabilities—stream of dividends, current earnings, future investment opportunities, etc. [32] studies the role of dividends policies in a firm's share evaluation. The paper shows how firm's value can be explained by its current earnings, the growth rate of earnings, the internal rate of return, and the market rate of return. Remarkable findings in the series of work [33–35], show how firm book value and market equity size are important to explain future company's return. Fundamental analysis is also known as "value investing" [36], or "intrinsic valuation" [37]. Similarly, do high-value tokens perform better than low-value cryptocurrencies as high-value stocks did in the past? Finally, we would like to stress the parallel among firms' share ownership and DAO tokens [42]. Both of them give shareholders voting power on underlying future actions. We will address and expand on these open research challenges in the next Sect. 5.

5   Conclusion

In this short survey paper, we synthesize DeFi's main business models. We claim that it is important for DeFi investors and users to understand which protocol has a reliable cash flow. Moreover, the literature is missing a clear overview of the protocols' business model to date. The main contributions of this short survey paper are as follows. First, we provide a clear understanding and explanation of the most important DeFi's services business model. Furthermore, we establish a novel general framework business model adopted by DeFi protocols. On top of that, the scientific community can address multiple open research challenges:

Value Investing In classical finance, a firm has a high *value* when it has a high book-to-market ratio. In the literature, it is shown that value stock portfolios achieve a higher long-term mean return [36]. Conducting a parallel study on crypto-assets is a straightforward application of Value Investing.

Voting Power DAO tokens grant the holder voting power on the underlying protocol changes, similar to public company shareholders. However, these tokens don't have an initial value, but they acquire it by exchanging and trading. The price discovery of similar DAO tokens is also an open research question.

Regulatory Issues Recently, the cryptocurrency ecosystem has seen significant turbulence. While, China has completely banned all crypto transaction [38], India is working on plans to enforce similar regulations [39]. Finally, the US is willing to regulate the market [40]. We claim that the literature lacks a deep analysis that evaluates DeFi's business models suitability with the current regulatory framework.

DeFi's financial services have seen massive growth since the "DeFi Summer". While some protocols achieved a stable cash flow, many others have been subject to cyber-security breaches [24]. In 2021 only, the whole DeFi world has suffered almost $1bn loss due to hacks [43]. The most recent hack is dated December 1st, 2021. BadgerDAO, a service that allows Bitcoin to be used as collateral over different DeFi protocols, suffered a $120m loss [44]. Albeit the exponential growth in DeFi's users and revenue stream, DeFi is yet a risky infrastructure that has to mature over time. Whether DeFi will replace or co-exist with the classical financial services is yet unclear, leaving us with open research challenges to unveil.

References

1. Werner, S.M., Perez, D., Gudgeon, L., Klages-Mundt, A., Harz, D., Knottenbelt, W.J.: SoK: decentralized finance (DeFi). In: The 4th ACM Conference on Advances in Financial Technologies, pp. 30–46 (2022). https://doi.org/10.1145/3558535.3559780
2. Schär, F.: Decentralized finance: on blockchain-and smart contract-based financial markets. FRB of St. Louis Review (2021)
3. CoinGecko. Coingecko, Top 100 DeFi Coins by Market Capitalization (2021). https://www.coingecko.com/en/categories/decentralized-finance-defi
4. Uniswap: Introducing Uni (2021). https://uniswap.org/blog/uni. Accessed 03 May 2022

5. Wu, J.: OpenFi: AAVE (2021). https://www.johnwu.finance/blog/openfi-aave, Accessed: 2022-05-03
6. Yearn: YIP-51: Set Vault v2 fee structure (2020). https://gov.yearn.finance/t/yip-51-set-vault-v2-fee-structure/7752. Accessed 30 Nov 2021
7. Mihal, D.: CryptoFees (2021). https://cryptofees.info/
8. Finance, Y.: YearnFinance (2022). https://www.yfistats.com/financials/RevProjections.html. Accessed 07 Feb 2022
9. Qin, K., Zhou, L., Gamito, P., Jovanovic, P., Gervais, A.: An empirical study of DeFi liquidations: incentives, risks, and instabilities. In: The 21st ACM Internet Measurement Conference, pp. 336–350 (2021). https://doi.org/10.1145/3487552.3487811
10. Qin, K., Zhou, L., Livshits, B., Gervais, A.: Attacking the DeFi ecosystem with flash loans for fun and profit. In: Borisov, N., Diaz, C. (eds.) FC 2021. LNCS, vol. 12674, pp. 3–32. Springer, Heidelberg (2021). https://doi.org/10.1007/978-3-662-64322-8_1
11. Gudgeon, L., Werner, S., Perez, D., Knottenbelt, W.J.: DeFi protocols for loanable funds: interest rates, liquidity and market efficiency. In: The 2nd ACM Conference on Advances in Financial Technologies, pp. 92–112 (2020). https://doi.org/10.1145/3419614.3423254
12. Perez, D., Werner, S.M., Xu, J., Livshits, B.: Liquidations: DeFi on a knife-edge. In: Borisov, N., Diaz, C. (eds.) FC 2021. LNCS, vol. 12675, pp. 457–476. Springer, Heidelberg (2021). https://doi.org/10.1007/978-3-662-64331-0_24
13. Young, M., Alexandre, A.: DeFi deep dive: yield farm pioneer compound finance (2021). https://beincrypto.com/defi-deep-dive-yield-farm-pioneer-compound/. Accessed 29 Nov 2021
14. AAVE: Flash Loans (2023). https://docs.aave.com/developers/guides/flash-loans#flash-loan-fee. Accessed 2 July 2023
15. Klepatch, J.: Comparison betwen Flashloan providers: Aave vs dYdX vs Uniswap (2020). https://defiprime.com/flahloans-comparison. Accessed 2 July 2023
16. Buterin, V.: Improving front running resistance of x * y = k market makers (2021). https://ethresear.ch/t/improving-front-running-resistance-of-x-y-k-market-makers/1281. Accessed 30 Nov 2021
17. Xu, J., Paruch, K., Cousaert, S., Feng, Y.: SoK: decentralized exchanges (DEX) with automated market maker (AMM) protocols. ACM Comput. Surv. 55(11), 1–50 (2023). https://doi.org/10.1145/3570639
18. Lin, L.X., et al.: Deconstructing decentralized exchanges. Stanford J. Blockchain Law Policy 2, 58–77 (2019)
19. Balancer: Increase the Protocol Fee (2021). https://forum.balancer.fi/t/increase-the-protocol-fee/2533. Accessed 03 May 2022
20. The Serenity Fund: Bancor 2.1 and its impermanent loss insurance (2021). https://medium.com/coinmonks/company-watch-bancor-2-1-and-its-impermanent-loss-insurance-71d87d092e9f. Accessed 30 Nov 2021
21. Uniswap: Uniswap v3 Protocol Whitepaper (2021). https://uniswap.org/whitepaper-v3.pdf. Accessed 30 Nov 2021
22. Mihal, D.: DAOs are the new companies. What's on their balance sheets? (2021). https://openorgs.info/. Accessed 30 Nov 2021
23. Cousaert, S., Xu, J., Matsui, T.: SoK: yield aggregators in DeFi. In: The 4th IEEE International Conference on Blockchain and Cryptocurrency (ICBC) (2022)
24. Cousaert, S., Vadgama, N., Xu, J.: Token-based insurance solutions on blockchain. In: Blockchains and the Token Economy: Theory and Practice (2022). https://doi.org/10.1007/978-3-030-95108-5_9

25. Cronje, A.: yETH vault explained (2020). https://medium.com/iearn/yeth-vault-explained-c29d6b93a371. Accessed 30 Nov 2021
26. Pickle: Fees (2021). https://docs.pickle.finance/fees. Accessed 30 Nov 2021
27. Idle: Fees (2021). https://docs.idle.finance/advanced/fees. Accessed 30 Nov 2021
28. Harvest Finance: Profit Sharing and iFARM (2021). https://harvest-finance.gitbook.io/harvest-finance/general-info/what-do-we-do/profit-sharing-pool-ps. Accessed 30 Nov 2021
29. Rochet, J.C., Tirole, J.: Platform competition in two-sided markets. J. Eur. Econ. Assoc. **1**(4), 990–1029 (2003)
30. Edwards, R.D., Magee, J., Bassetti, W.H.C.: Technical analysis of stock trends. Stock Trend Service, Springfield (1948)
31. Taylor, M.P., Allen, H.: The use of technical analysis in the foreign exchange market. J. Int. Money Financ. **11**(3), 304–314 (1992)
32. Miller, M.H., Modigliani, F.: Dividend policy, growth, and the valuation of shares. J. Bus. **34**(4), 411–433 (1961)
33. Fama, E.F., French, K.R.: Common risk factors in the returns on stocks and bonds. J. Financ. Econ. **33**(1), 3–56 (1993)
34. Fama, E.F., French, K.R.: The cross-section of expected stock returns. J. Financ. **47**, 427–465 (1992)
35. Fama, E.F., French, K.R.: Size and book-to-market factors in earnings and returns. J. Financ. **50**(1), 131–155 (1995)
36. Piotroski, J.D.: Value investing: the use of historical financial statement information to separate winners from losers. J. Account. Res. **38**, 1–41 (2000)
37. Damodaran, A.: Investment Valuation: Tools and Techniques for Determining the Value of Any Asset, vol. 666. Wiley, Hoboken (2012)
38. BBC News: China declares all crypto-currency transactions illegal (2021). https://www.bbc.com/news/technology-58678907. Accessed 03 Dec 2021
39. BBC News: Indian government set to ban cryptocurrencies (2021). https://www.bbc.com/news/technology-59402310. Accessed 03 Dec 2021
40. Haar, R, Time: U.S. officials send mixed messages on crypto regulation. Here's What It All Means for Investors (2021). https://time.com/nextadvisor/investing/cryptocurrency/crypto-regulation-talks-heat-up/. Accessed 03 Dec 2021
41. Xu, J., Feng, Y.: Reap the harvest on blockchain: a survey of yield farming protocols. IEEE Trans. Netw. Serv. Manage. **20**(1), 858–869 (2023). https://doi.org/10.1109/TNSM.2022.3222815
42. Xu, T.A., Xu, J., Lommers, K.: DeFi vs TradFi: Valuation Using Multiples and Discounted Cash Flow, arXiv:2210.16846 (2023)
43. Cointelegraph: Cointelegraph Consulting: Recounting 2021's biggest DeFi hacking incidents (2021). https://cointelegraph.com/news/cointelegraph-consulting-recounting-2021-s-biggest-defi-hacking-incidents. Accessed 03 Dec 2021
44. Thurman, A, CoinDesk: badger DAO protocol suffers $120M exploit (2021). https://www.coindesk.com/business/2021/12/02/badger-dao-protocol-suffers-10m-exploit/. Accessed 03 Dec 2021
45. Xu, J., Vadgama, N.: From banks to DeFi: the evolution of the lending market. In: Vadgama, N., Xu, J., Tasca, P. (eds.) Enabling the Internet of Value. Future of Business and Finance, pp. 53–66. Springer, Cham (2022). https://doi.org/10.1007/978-3-030-78184-2_6

On-Chain Auctions with Deposits

Jan Christoph Schlegel[1]($\boxtimes$) and Akaki Mamageishvili[2]

[1] City, University of London, London, UK
jansc@alumni.ethz.ch
[2] ETH Zurich, Zürich, Switzerland

Abstract. Sealed-bid auctions with deposits are frequently used in blockchain environments. An auction takes place on-chain: bidders deposit an amount that fully covers their bid (but possibly exceeds it) in a smart contract. The deposit is used as insurance against bidders not honoring their bid if they win. The deposit, but not the bid, is publicly observed during the bidding phase of the auction.

The visibility of deposits can fundamentally change the strategic structure of the auction if bidding happens sequentially: Bidding is costly since deposits are costly to make. Thus, deposits can be used as a costly signal for a high valuation. This is the source of multiple inefficiencies: to engage in costly signalling, a bidder who bids first and has a high valuation will generally over-deposit in equilibrium, that is, deposit more than he will bid. If high valuations are likely there can, moreover, be entry deterrence through high deposits: a bidder who bids first can deter subsequent bidders from entering the auction. Partial pooling can happen in equilibrium, where bidders of different valuations deposit the same amount. The auction fails to allocate the item to the bidder with the highest valuation.

1 Introduction

On-chain implementations of auctions often take the following form: bidders deposit an amount that fully covers their bid in a smart contract. The deposit is used as insurance against bidders not honoring their bid if they win. The deposit, but not the bid, is publicly observed during the bidding phase of the auction. In the case of a second-price auction, [14], after bidding is closed the winner is determined by evaluating the non-public bids. The highest bid wins and the winner pays the second highest bid. Leftover deposits are repaid.

Often it is claimed that this auction format is equivalent to a standard second-price auction without depositing. While this is indeed a good approximation if the value of the auctioned item is relatively small for all bidders, the auction has fundamentally different properties if the value of the item is substantial for many bidders. In particular, we claim that this auction format can be vulnerable to entry-deterrence strategies. To illustrate this point consider the instance of the top-level domain (TLD) auction on "https://www.namebase.io/namebase. io" for the TLD "https://www.namebase.io/domains/scholar.scholar" as reproduced in Fig. 1: namebase.io is an example of a marketplace that uses the auction format that we analyze in this paper. Bidders can bid on a TLD such as

© International Financial Cryptography Association 2023
S. Matsuo et al. (Eds.): FC 2022 Workshops, LNCS 13412, pp. 207–224, 2023.
https://doi.org/10.1007/978-3-031-32415-4_14

Bid history

Bid	Date	Bid amount + added blind	Lockup amount
06	Feb 27	101.00 HNS + 601.00 HNS	702.00 HNS
05	Feb 25	100.00 HNS + 0.00 HNS	100.00 HNS
04	Feb 23	75.00 HNS + 0.00 HNS	75.00 HNS
03	Feb 23	50.00 HNS + 0.00 HNS	50.00 HNS
02	Feb 23	0.10 HNS + 1.00 HNS	1.10 HNS
01	Feb 22	1.00 HNS + 0.00 HNS	1.00 HNS

Fig. 1. Bid history and auction details for the top level domain ".scholar" on namebase.io.

".scholar" in the example in Fig. 1. Bidders submit a bid and a blind to the auction. The sum of the two numbers (the "lockup amount"), but not the bid itself, is visible to other bidders during the bidding phase of the auction. At the end of the bidding phase, bids are evaluated according to a second price auction and left-over lockup amounts are repaid. As can be observed in the bid history reproduced in Fig. 1, the sixth bid in the auction involves a substantial lockup amount. Subsequently, no further bid is made. Note that the sixth bid involves substantial over-depositing, i.e. the blind part is much larger than the actual bid. The bidder seems to have successfully engaged in entry deterrence: the large lockup amount likely discouraged further potential bidders to enter the auction and place a bid. In this paper, we want to give a theoretical explanation of this kind of bidding behavior.

The logic of our analysis is as follows: Bidding is costly since depositing is costly. If the deposit has to be staked for a substantial amount of time[1] and can not be used or sold meanwhile, the bidder is, for example, exposed to the volatility of the underlying token price. Other costs of depositing can come from transaction costs when buying the native token that is used to make the deposit, from borrowing costs or from transactions cost for processing the bid on-chain. Even if this cost is relatively small, it can have substantial strategic implications if valuations for an item are expected to be high[2]. A bidder can deter entry

---

[1] For namebase's auction deposits are kept for 10 days after the end of the bidding phase.

[2] Bids can be substantial in these kinds of auctions. For the domain auctions organized by namebase.io, domains have been sold for close to 100000 $: https://newssoso.com/ 2021/02/03/this-nft-web-domain-just-sold-for-record-breaking-84000/. Such auctions can also suffer from speculation, since they allow instant resale, [7].

into the auction by depositing a large amount. This is a costly signal to other bidders that the bidder likely has a high valuation. Another bidder wondering whether to enter the auction infers that this makes it unlikely that he wins the auction, and that he is likely to pay a high price if he wins the auction. Since bidding is costly and the cost of bidding increases in the size of the deposit, he possibly refrains from bidding at all. Since bids are not public, this could be even in the case when he would have had a higher valuation than the first bidder, but the first bidder successfully deters him through over-depositing. Efficiency is lost: with positive probability the item does not go to the bidder with the highest willingness to pay. Moreover, revenue is severely decreased since bidders are deterred from entering the auction. Finally, wasteful over-depositing will take place, bidder 1 will deposit a large amount exceeding his true valuation amount to send a costly signal of his high valuation.

Interestingly the strategy outlined here goes in the opposite direction of other strategies usually observed in online auctions: bidders can have an advantage if they move early because they can scare away other bidders by over-depositing, whereas in other environments bidders want to get late into the auction in order to "snipe" [12].

We flesh out this logic in a stylized model. We study the case of sequential bidding with two bidders. If bidder 1 bids before bidder 2, bidder 1's deposit is visible to bidder 2. This drastically changes the strategic interaction and the equilibrium bidding behavior. Generically, the first bidder will over-deposit if he has a high valuation. This over-depositing is wasteful since it is costly to the bidder and only satisfies the purpose of signalling a high valuation. In addition to the efficiency loss due to over-depositing, there can be additional allocative inefficiencies due to entry deterrence which can come in two forms:

1. Unless there is a very high likelihood of low valuations for the second bidder, the first bidder will refrain from entering the auction if he has a low valuation since he wants to save on the depositing cost when facing a low likelihood of winning the auction.
2. More severely, if high valuations are likely, equilibria exists in which high types of the first bidder are pooled. In the most extreme case, there can exist equilibria with just two deposit levels. The first bidder will choose either not to bid at all or to over-deposit. If the second bidder observes a large deposit he can be deterred from entering the auction since he assigns a substantial likelihood to the first bidder having a high valuation. Thus, he will not bid at all unless his valuation is very high. The equilibrium can be very wasteful. The first bidder can win the auction even though he could have a substantially lower valuation for the item than the second bidder.

As a benchmark, in the appendix, we consider the case of simultaneous depositing or equivalently the case where privacy-preserving depositing is available so that no information is revealed to other bidders. In this case, bidding in equilibrium is approximately truthful. Bids are only shaded by a small amount to incorporate depositing costs. Social welfare is approximately maximised since the item is allocated to the bidder with the highest valuation, and the only loss in welfare is due to depositing cost.

1.1 Empirical Evidence

Among entries in namebase.io's domain database we calculated several summary statistics for the subset of around 5.9 million domains which were resold. Here we take resale as in indicator of relevance. First, we note that the number of bidders for each domain is generically low. Figure 3 shows the skewness of the distribution. While the highest number of bidders for one domain is 28, domains with at most 2 bidders comprise more than 75% and domains with at most 4 bidders comprise more than 96% of all domains. These observations are in line with our assumption on having only 2 bidders. Over-depositing happens in 58% of all bids. In 61% of the sold domains, the winner bidder overdeposits. In 55% of the cases, the winner bidder over-deposits and is also the last bidder. Last two observations can be interpreted as an evidence that overdepositing serves the purpose of deterring other bidders to enter bidding process. On Fig. 4, we plot the ratio between over-deposited quantity over bids, conditional that the bid size is at least 10. That is, we condition on cases where the bids are significantly high. The histogram suggests that depositing incurs at least some opportunity cost, as high ratios diminish. On the other hand, it is still present as a mechanism of signalling.

1.2 Literature

Exploiting auctions through "front running" in the blockchain environment is studied in [5] and [8]. While the entry-deterrence strategies analyzed in our paper can be interpreted as a form of front-running, they are qualitatively very different. Whereas conventional front-running is used to exploit informational advantages, in our setting bidders want to go early to signal information to others. Sequential bidding with constant cost of entry and deterrence is a topic of [3]. With constant cost of entry instead of a constant marginal cost of entry, bidders can only signal through their entry decision but not through deposits. We use standard terminology from signalling games [13] and related solution concepts [6]. Costly signalling in auctions, although in a different environment, has been considered before, e.g. in [10]. Deposit costs in on-chain exchange mechanisms are the topic of [11]. Our paper is remotely related to the literature on all-pay auctions, [1]. In all pay auctions every bidder pays their bid completely, while in our model only some percentage of the bid is paid, because of the opportunity costs of depositing. Sunk costs or, equivalently, money burning can sometimes be useful in optimal mechanism design, [9], in particular, increasing expected surplus.

2   Model and Results

We consider two bidders with independently and identically distributed valuations $v_1, v_2 \in (0, 1)$.

Bidders submit a bid $b(v_i)$ and a deposit $d(v_i)$ such that $0 \le b(v_i) \le d(v_i)$. Note that both are functions of the real valuation v_i. The constant marginal cost of depositing is $c > 0$. The winner of the item is determined through a second price auction. That is, if i makes the winning bid, equivalent to $b_i > b_j$, then his profit is

$$v_i - b(v_j) - cd(v_i),$$

whereas j loses

$$-cd(v_j).$$

Since we have a second price auction, it will generally be the case that in equilibrium a bidder either bids his valuation or his full deposit,

$$b(v_i) = \min\{v_i, d(v_i)\}.$$

In the following we consider sequential bidding. As a benchmark for comparison we consider the case of simultaneous bidding in Appendix A. We assume that bidder 1 moves first and bidder 2 moves second so that bidder 1's deposit (but not his bid) is known to bidder 2 before he chooses his bid. We use the tie-breaking rule that the second bidder wins in case of equal bids. As observed before, bidder 1 bids either his deposit or his valuation so that the strategy of bidder 1 is characterized by a deposit function $d_1 : [0, 1] \to [0, \bar{d}]$ where $\bar{d} \ge 1$ is the maximal deposit a bidder can make.[3] It is always optimal for Bidder 1 to bid $\min\{v_1, d_1(v_1)\}$.

For bidder 2, it is no loss of generality to assume that he does not over-deposit. Otherwise, if $b_2 < d_2$, then the bidder could deposit b_2 instead without changing his bid and become strictly better off by saving on depositing cost. So bidder 2's strategy is characterized by his deposit function $d_2 : [0, 1] \times [0, \bar{d}] \to [0, 1]$ where $d_2(v_2, d_1)$ is his choice of deposit under valuation v_1 if he observes bidder 1 depositing d_1. It is always optimal for Bidder 2 to bid $b_2 = d_2(v_2, d_1)$.

Sequential bidding turns our model into a signalling game. Given that bidders' strategies are fully determined by their depositing functions, we understand a *Perfect Bayesian Equilibrium* to be a triple (d_1, d_2, μ_2) of deposit functions for the two bidders and beliefs $\mu_2 : [0, 1] \times [0, \bar{d}] \to [0, 1]$ for bidder 2[4] where $\mu_2(\cdot, d_1)$ is the cdf for v_1 conditional on observing a deposit d_1 such that

1. Each player's strategy specifies optimal actions, given his beliefs and the strategies of the other player, i.e. $d_1(v_1)$ is a solution to

$$\max_{d_1} Pr_{v_2 \sim F}[b_1 > b_2](v_1 - E_{v_2 \sim F}[b_2 | b_1 > b_2]) - cd_1,$$

where $b_1 = \min\{v_1, d_1\}$, $\quad b_2 = \min\{v_2, d_2(v_2, d_1)\}$,

---

[3] Typically, we think of $\bar{d}$ as a large quantity. It could for example be the number of tokens in the protocol in total.

[4] We do not need to specify bidder 1's beliefs about bidder 2's valuation as they will coincide with the prior F.

and $d_2(v_2, d_1)$ is a solution to

$$\max_{d_2} Pr_{v_1 \sim \mu_2(d_1)}[b_2 \geq b_1](v_2 - E_{v_1 \sim \mu_2(d_1)}[b_1|b_2 \geq b_1]) - cd_2,$$

$$\text{where } b_1 = \min\{v_1, d_1\}, \quad b_2 = \min\{v_2, d_2\}.$$

2. Beliefs are updated according to Bayes' rule whenever applicable, for $0 \leq d_1 \leq \bar{d}$ such that there is a type v_1 with $d_1(v_1) = d_1$ we have

$$\mu_2(v, d_1) = F(v|d_1(v_1) = d_1).$$

All subsequently constructed Perfect Bayesian equilibria will also satisfy standard refinement properties for signalling games like the Cho-Kreps intuitive criterion [4]. Following standard terminology of the signalling literature, we call an equilibrium *separating*, if different types send different messages. In our setting, the type of bidder 1 is the valuation v_1, while a message is the deposit $d_1(v_1)$. Therefore, in a separating equilibrium, the second bidder can exactly determine the valuation of the first bidder from the deposit. We call an equilibrium *separating conditional on entry* if conditional on the first bidder depositing a positive amount, the second bidder can exactly determine the valuation of the first bidder from the deposit. Similarly, we call an equilibrium, *essentially separating (conditional on entry)* if it is separating (conditional on entry) for all types below $\frac{1}{1+c}$. We call an equilibrium *pooling equilibrium* with n deposit levels if bidder 1 uses the same deposit under different valuations and n different deposit levels are observed in equilibrium.

2.1 Separating Equilibria

Suppose there is a separating equilibrium, $d_1(v_1) \neq d_1(v_1')$ for $v_1 \neq v_1'$. In that case, bidder 2 knows bidder 1's valuation when bidding. The equilibrium depositing function will be increasing, $v_1 > v_1' \Rightarrow d_1(v_1) > d_1(v_1')$. Let $d := d_1(1)$. Let $u(d_1)$ be the inverse of the depositing function. For $0 \leq d_1 \leq d$ bidder 2 will bid:

$$d_2(v_2, d_1) = \begin{cases} \min\{d_1, u(d_1)\}, & \text{for } v_2 \geq (1 + c) \min\{d_1, v(d_1)\} \\ 0, & \text{otherwise.} \end{cases} \tag{1}$$

Given the bidding function for bidder 2, the expected utility of bidder 1 when depositing d_1 is

$$v_1 F((1 + c) \min\{d_1, u(d_1)\}) - cd_1. \tag{2}$$

In general, the depositing function d_1 as a function of valuation should satisfy the first order condition:

$$(1 + c)v_1 f((1 + c)d_1) = c, \quad \text{for } d_1(v_1) \leq v_1, \tag{3}$$

$$(1 + c)v_1 f((1 + c)v_1) = cd_1'(v_1), \quad \text{for } d_1(v_1) > v_1. \tag{4}$$

The latter condition is obtained by deriving the expected utility of the first player, (2), with respect to u, and plugging in v_1. Subsequently, we use these first order condition to derive separating equilibria (resp. equilibria that are separating conditional on entry) for different distributions.

Separation for Concave Distributions. The existence of a separating equilibrium where bidder 1 always enters the auction requires that the density function f is strictly decreasing in the beginning, i.e. the cumulative distribution function is concave for low types and hence low valuations are more likely. This is the case, in particular if the entire distribution is concave in which case we obtain:

Proposition 1. *For a strictly concave distribution with $\lim_{x \to 0} x f(x) \le c$, there exists an essentially separating equilibrium for which we have under-depositing for low types.*

Over-Depositing for Convex Distributions. Conversely to the previous result, if the density function is strictly increasing in the beginning, bidder 1 will not enter the auction for low types. More generally, if the entire distribution is convex, conditional on entry we observe over-depositing:

Proposition 2. *For a convex distribution, in equilibrium bidder 1 does not enter the auction for low types. There exists an equilibrium which is essentially separating conditional on entry. In each such equilibrium, conditional on entry, bidder 1 over-deposits.*

Separation Conditional on Entry. While fully seperating equilibria only exist for concave distributions, we can in much more generality obtain equilibria with separation conditional on entry for any unimodal distribution. For the "convex part" of the distribution, we obtain no-entry for low types and over-depositing for higher types. For the "concave part" we can have over- as well as under-depositing.

Proposition 3. *For a unimodal distribution, there exists a maximally efficient equilibrium which is essentially separating conditional on entry.*

2.2 Pooling Equilibrium with Two Deposit Levels

If high valuations are more likely than low valuations we can construct pooling equilibria. We consider the case of only two deposit levels in equilibrium, bidder 1 either deposits 0 or the maximal valuation 1, and show that such an equilibrium can be constructed for the quadratic distribution.

To construct the equilibrium, consider a marginal type of bidder 1, $0 < u < 1$, such that he deposits 0 if his valuation is below u and 1 if his valuation is above u. In that case, if bidder 2 observes a deposit of 0, he will bid 0 himself and win the object for free. If bidder 2 observes a deposit of 1, he knows that the valuation of bidder 1 is between u and 1. We also need to specify what bidder 2 believes off-equilibrium if $d_1 \neq 0, 1$. We assume that in that case bidder 2 believes that bidder 1's type is distributed by:

$$\mu(\cdot, d_1) = \begin{cases} F(\cdot | d_1 \le v_1 \le u), & \text{for } 0 \le d_1 \le u, \\ F(\cdot | u \le v_1 \le \min\{1, d_1\}), & \text{for } u < d_1 \le \bar{d}. \end{cases} \tag{5}$$

Bidder 2 thinks that bidder 1 will bid d_1 for $d_1 \le u$. Therefore, bidder 2, when observing $d_1 \le u$, will bid d_1 in case if this makes him positive profit, $v_2 \ge d_1 + cd_1$, and will not bid in the auction otherwise. Thus, the profit for bidder 1 when depositing and bidding $d_1 \le u$ is as in the previous section:

$$F((1+c)d_1)v_1 - cd_1.$$

This quantity should be non-positive for the marginal type:

$$F(u(1+c)) \le c. \tag{6}$$

The expected profit for bidder 2 of bidding $d_1 \ge d_2 \ge u$, if he observes $d_1 > u$ is:

$$\Pi(v_2, d_1, d_2) := Pr[v_1 \le d_2 | u \le v_1 \le d_1] (v_2 - E[v_1 | u \le v_1 \le d_2]) - cd_2.$$

Let $v(d_1)$ be the smallest valuation of bidder 2 for which he enters the auction if he observes a deposit of $d_1 > u$, i.e.

$$v(d_1) := \min\{0 \le v_2 \le 1 : \max_{u \le d_2 \le d_1} \Pi(v_2, d_1, d_2) \ge 0\},$$

respectively $v(d_1) := 1$ if the min does not exist. We let $v := v(1)$.

At the marginal type $v_1 = u$, bidder 1 must be indifferent between depositing 0 and depositing 1 and bidding his type. Note, moreover, that the marginal type when depositing 1 and bidding his type either gets the object for free or does not get the object (since bidder 2 will either not bid at all in that case, $b_2 = 0$, or bid $b_2 \ge u$, since he believes that bidder 1 has a valuation of u or higher). Thus, his payoff of depositing 1 and bidding his type is

$$F(v)u - c.$$

The marginal type is indifferent between depositing 0 and depositing 1 if

$$F(v)u = c. \tag{7}$$

Quadratic Distribution. For the quadratic distribution

$$(u(1+c))^2 \le c, \tag{8}$$

and

$$uv^2 = c. \tag{9}$$

which can be satisfied in general and pooling equilibria with two deposit levels exist:

Proposition 4. *For large enough c, there exists a pooling equilibrium with two deposit levels.*

The equilibrium exhibits the manifold inefficiencies we have highlighted in the introduction. Bidder 2 is deterred from entry unless his valuation is very high, see the Figure. Bidder 1 may win the auction even if he has a lower valuation. Bidder 1 engages in wasteful over-deposits in equilibrium.

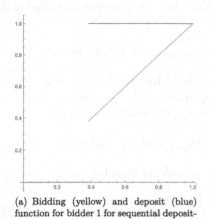
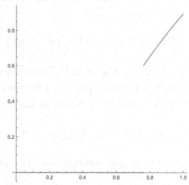

(a) Bidding (yellow) and deposit (blue) function for bidder 1 for sequential depositing.

(b) The bidding and depositing function for bidder 2 for sequential depositing.

3 Conclusion

Given the potentially severe inefficiency of the auction design, it is a natural question how to improve it. Several potential remedies, both cryptographic and economic, can be considered: Encryption of deposit levels is a natural idea. There are several blockchain projects with built-in privacy functionality, e.g. [15], that could be used for this purpose. Privacy preservation in on-chain auction specifically has been analyzed in [2]. Lowering the cost of depositing, for example by shortening the staking time, lowering borrowing costs so that it becomes cheaper to make large deposits or decreasing transaction costs can mitigate the problem. A more radical approach would allow for under-collateralizing of bids where the residual sum has to be paid by the winning bidder only after winning. Finally it is a natural question whether other payment rules than the second price rule would allow for more efficient outcomes in the presence of deposits.

A Simultaneous Depositing

We first consider the benchmark case of simultaneous bidding (and depositing). The following analysis works for any tie-breaking rule to determine the winner in case of equal bids. Since bids are simultaneous it is optimal not to over-deposit, that is $b(v_i) = d(v_i)$ (if $b(v_i) < d(v_i)$, then the bidder could deposit $b(v_i)$ instead, without changing his bid and become strictly better off by saving depositing cost).

Thus the equilibrium bidding function is fully determined by the equilibrium deposit function. We consider symmetric equilibria. Let $d : [0,1] \to \mathbb{R}$ be the equilibrium deposit function for both bidders. The expected profit for bidder i when he deposits and bids an amount $d(w)$ corresponding to type w is given by

$$F(w)(v_i - E[d(v_j)|v_j \leq w]) - cd(w),$$

Taking first order conditions and assuming that d is differentiable, and using the fact that $d(0) = 0$:

$$f(w)(v_i - E[d(v_j)|v_j \leq w]) - F(w)f_{(0,w)}(w)d(w) - cd'(w) = 0$$

where $f_{(0,w)}$ is the density conditional on the valuation being smaller w. By the revelation principle the expression is optimized if he deposits and bids the amount $d(v_i)$ corresponding to his true valuation, i.e. when $w = v_i$, and therefore:

$$f(v_i)(v_i - E[d(v_j)|v_j \leq v_i]) - F(v_i)f_{(0,v_i)}(v_i)d(v_i) - cd'(v_i) = 0.$$

As an example we consider the case of an uniform distribution:

Uniform Distribution. If valuations are uniformly distributed on $(0,1)$ the previous first order condition becomes:

$$v_i - d(v_i) - cd'(v_i) = 0.$$

We can use the boundary condition $d(0) = 0$ and obtain the solution to the differential equation:

$$d(v_i) = v_i - c(1 - e^{-v_i/c}).$$

B   Proofs

Proof (of Proposition 1). By strict concavity and continuity of F, either there is a unique $v > 0$ such that $vf(v) = c$ or $vf(v) < c$ for each $0 < v < 1$. In the first case, define a threshold $\bar{u} := \frac{v}{1+c}$ and in the second case define $\bar{u} := 1$.

First we show that for $0 < v_1 < \bar{u}$, under-depositing and entering is optimal. Let

$$d_1 := \begin{cases} \frac{1}{1+c}f^{-1}(\frac{c}{(1+c)v_1}), & v_1 \leq \frac{1}{1+c}, \\ \frac{1}{1+c}f^{-1}(c), & v_1 \geq \frac{1}{1+c}. \end{cases}$$

By the first order condition (3) this is the optimal depositing strategy, conditional on under-depositing and entering. By the assumption that $0 < v_1 < \bar{u}$, we do have $d_1 < v_1$. First we show that under-depositing in the above way yields strictly positive pay-off and it is therefore optimal to enter. The payoff is positive if

$$v_1 F((1+c)d_1) - cd_1 > 0 \Rightarrow F((1+c)d_1) - \frac{cd_1}{v_1} > 0.$$

Since F is strictly concave with $F(0) = 0$, this follows from the observation that $f(z) > \frac{c}{(1+c)v_1}$ for $0 < z < (1+c)d_1$ by definition of d_1.

Next we derive the optimal deposit function for $v_1 > \bar{u}$. With the first order condition (4) and the boundary condition $d(\bar{u}) = \bar{u}$, we obtain

$$c(d(v_1) - d(\bar{u})) = c(d(v) - \bar{u}) = (1+c)\int_{\bar{u}}^{v_1} vf((1+c)v)dv$$

$$= \frac{F[(1+c)v_1] - F[(1+c)\bar{u}]}{1+c} E[v|\bar{u} \leq \frac{v}{1+c} \leq v_1]$$

$$\Rightarrow d(v_1) = \bar{u} + \frac{F[(1+c)v_1] - F[(1+c)\bar{u}]}{c(1+c)} E[v|\bar{u} \leq \frac{v}{1+c} \leq v_1]$$

We obtain the following equilibrium: Bidder 1 deposits

$$d_1(v_1) = \begin{cases} \bar{u} + \frac{F[(1+c)v_1] - F[(1+c)\bar{u}]}{c(1+c)} E[v|\bar{u} \leq \frac{v}{1+c}] & v_1 \geq \frac{1}{1+c}, \\ \bar{u} + \frac{F[(1+c)v_1] - F[(1+c)\bar{u}]}{c(1+c)} E[v|\bar{u} \leq \frac{v}{1+c} \leq v_1], & \frac{1}{1+c} > v_1 \geq \bar{u}, \\ \frac{1}{1+c} f^{-1}(\frac{c}{(1+c)v_1}), & v_1 < \bar{u}. \end{cases}$$

and bids

$$b_1(v_1) = \begin{cases} \frac{1}{1+c} & v_1 \geq \frac{1}{1+c}, \\ v_1 & \frac{1}{1+c} > v_1 \geq \bar{u}, \\ d_1(v_1), & v_1 < \bar{u}. \end{cases}$$

Note that unless cost is very high ($vf(v) < c$ for each $0 < v < 1$) bidder 1 will over-deposit if his type is high.

Bidder 2 bids his deposit $b_2(v_2, d_1) = d_2(v_2, d_1)$. He bids and deposits

$$d_2(v_2, d_1) = \begin{cases} \frac{1}{1+c}, & v_2 \geq \frac{1}{1+c}, b_1(v(d_1)), \quad \frac{1}{1+c} \geq v_2 \geq (1+c)b_1(v(d_1)), \\ 0, & v_2 < (1+c)b_1(v(d_1)) \end{cases}$$

where $v(d_1)$ is the inverse of bidder 1's deposit function.

His belief if he observes $0 \leq d_1 \leq d_1(\frac{1}{1+c})$ is

$$\mu_2(v, d_1) = \begin{cases} 1, & \text{for } v \geq v(d_1), \\ 0, & \text{for } v < v(d_1), \end{cases}$$

where $v(d_1)$ is the inverse of the depositing function for bidder 1, and his belief when observing $d_1 = d_1(\frac{1}{1+c})$ is

$$\mu_2(\cdot, d_1) = F(\cdot|v_1 \geq \frac{1}{1+c}).$$

Proof (Proof of Proposition 2). In case of under-depositing the profit is

$$v_1 F((1+c)d_1) - cd_1,$$

which is positive only if $v_1 \geq \bar{u} := \frac{F^{-1}(c)}{1+c}$. Thus, types $0 \leq v_1 \leq \bar{u}$ over-deposit or do not enter the auction at all. In case of over-deposits, we get the first order condition:

$$(1+c)v_1 f((1+c)v_1) = cd_1'(v_1).$$

By convexity we have $(1+c)v_1 f((1+c)v_1) \leq F((1+c)v_1)$ and thus for $v_1 \leq \bar{u}$, we have $cd_1'(v_1) \leq F((1+c)\bar{u}) = c$. Therefore $d_1(v_1) \leq v_1$ for $v_1 \leq \bar{u}$ and we don't have over-depositing. Thus, bidder 1 with $v_1 \leq \bar{u}$ never enters the auction.

Next we construct an equilibrium with separation conditional on entry. Suppose all types of bidder 1 above u over-deposit, $d_1(v_1) \geq v_1$ for $v_1 \geq u$. By the same reasoning as before, we have the first order condition

$$(1+c)v_1 f((1+c)v_1) = cd_1'(v_1).$$

and the boundary conditions $d(v_1) \geq v_1$ for $v_1 \geq u$. Choosing $d_1(u) = u$, we have a solution

$$d(v_1) = u + \frac{1}{c} \int_u^{v_1} (1+c)vf((1+c)v)dv = u + \frac{F((1+c)v_1) - c}{c} E[v|(1+c)u \leq v \leq (1+c)v_1].$$

The equilibrium is as follows (see Fig. 2 for a graph of the bidding and depositing functions for bidder 1). Bidder 1 deposits

$$d_1(v_1) = \begin{cases} u + \frac{1-c}{c} E[v|(1+c)u \leq v], & v_1 \geq \frac{1}{1+c}, \\ u + \frac{F((1+c)v_1)-c}{c} E[v|(1+c)u \leq v \leq (1+c)v_1], & \frac{1}{1+c} > v_1 \geq u, \\ 0, & v_1 < \frac{c}{1+c}. \end{cases}$$

and bids

$$b_1(v_1) = \begin{cases} v_1, & v_1 \geq u, \\ 0, & v_1 < u. \end{cases}$$

If bidder 2 observes a high deposit $d_1 > u$ he deposits

$$d_2(v_2, d_1) = \begin{cases} v_1(d_1), & v_2 \geq v_1(d_1), \\ 0, & v_2 < v_1(d_1), \end{cases}$$

where v_1 is the inverse of the deposit function and if he observes a low deposit $0 \leq d_1 \leq \frac{c}{1+c}$ he deposits

$$d_2(v_2, d_1) = \begin{cases} d_1, & v_2 \geq (1+c)d_1, \\ 0, & v_2 < (1+c)d_1. \end{cases}$$

In either case he bids his deposit $b_2(v_2, d_1) = d_2(v_2, d_1)$.

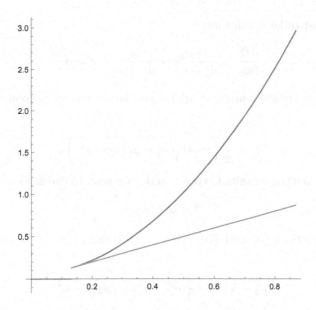

Fig. 2. Bidding (yellow) and deposit (blue) function for bidder 1 for sequential depositing, a uniform value distribution and cost $c = 0.15$. (Color figure online)

We also need to specify beliefs off-equilibrium when bidder 2 observes a deposit between 0 and u. One possibility is to assume that bidder 2 believes that bidder 1 has type u. Thus his beliefs when observing $0 \leq d_1 \leq u$ is

$$\mu_2(v, d_1) = \begin{cases} 1, & \text{for } v \geq u, \\ 0, & \text{for } v < u, \end{cases}$$

his belief when observing $u \leq d_1 \leq \bar{u}$ is

$$\mu_2(v, d_1) = \begin{cases} 1, & \text{for } v \geq v_1(d_1), \\ 0, & \text{for } v < v_1(d_1), \end{cases}$$

and his belief when observing $d_1 \geq \bar{u}$ is given by

$$\mu_2(\cdot, d_1) = F(\cdot | v_1 \geq \frac{1}{1+c}).$$

In conclusion, there is an equilibrium that is essentially (except for the very highest types with valuation above $\frac{1}{1+c}$) separating conditional on entry.

Proof (of Proposition 4). First, we determine the bidding function for bidder 2, if he observes $d_1 > u$ conditional on entering the auction. For $u < d_2 \leq d_1$, we have

$$\Pi(v_2, d_1, d_2) = \frac{d_2^2 - u^2}{d_1^2 - u^2}(v_2 - \int_u^{d_2} v_1 \frac{2v_1}{d_2^2 - u^2} dv_1) - cd_2 = \frac{d_2^2 - u^2}{d_1^2 - u^2} v_2 - \frac{2(d_2^3 - u^3)}{3(d_1^2 - u^2)} - cd_2.$$

Taking first order conditions:

$$\frac{\partial \Pi}{\partial d_2} = \frac{2d_2 v_2}{d_1^2 - u^2} - \frac{2d_2^2}{d_1^2 - u^2} - c = 0.$$

There are two critical points of which the larger one corresponds to a local maximum:

$$d_2 = \frac{1}{2}\left(v_2 + \sqrt{v_2^2 - 2c(d_1^2 - u^2)}\right). \tag{10}$$

To determine the marginal types u and v we need to check whether there are

$$0 < u < v \leq 1$$

such that equations (9) and (10) with $d_1 = 1$ and $v_2 = v$, inequality (8) are satisfied and

$$(d_2^2 - u^2)v - \frac{2}{3}(d_2^3 - u^3) = cd_2(1 - u^2) \tag{11}$$

holds (i.e., the profit for the marginal type of bidder 2 is equal to 0). Similarly, to determine $v(d_1)$, we need to find a $v(d_1)$ that satisfies Eq. (10) with $v_2 = v(d_1)$ and

$$(d_2^2 - u^2)v(d_1) - \frac{2}{3}(d_2^3 - u^3) = cd_2(d_1^2 - u^2). \tag{12}$$

The equilibrium is as follows. Bidder 1 deposits

$$d_1(v_1) = \begin{cases} 1, & v_1 \geq u, \\ 0, & v_1 < u, \end{cases}$$

and bids

$$b_1(v_1) = \begin{cases} v_1, & v_1 \geq u, \\ 0, & v_1 < u, \end{cases}$$

If bidder 2 observes a deposit $d_1 > u$ above the threshold he deposits

$$d_2(v_2, d_1) = \begin{cases} \min\left\{d_1, \frac{1}{2}\left(v_2 + \sqrt{v_2^2 - 2c(d_1^2 - u^2)}\right)\right\}, & v_2 \geq v(d_1), \\ 0, & v_2 < v(d_1), \end{cases}$$

and if he observes a deposit $d_1 \leq u$ below the threshold he deposits

$$d_2(v_2, d_1) = \begin{cases} d_1, & v_2 \geq d_1, \\ 0, & v_2 < d_1. \end{cases}$$

In either case he bids his deposit, $b_2(v_2, d_1) = d_2(v_2, d_1)$. His beliefs are given by Eq. 5. Next, we verify that the deposit functions derived above with the beliefs specified above form a Perfect Bayesian Equilibrium if valuations are quadratically distributed for the case that the marginal cost is $c = 0.22$. In this case the marginal type is $u = 0.382981$ and bidder 2 will enter the auction only if his valuation is above $v = 0.757919$. Note that incentive compatibility for the marginal type of bidder 1 holds as

$$u^2(1+c)^2 = 0.382981^2 \cdot 1.22^2 \approx 0.21831 < c = 0.22.$$

It remains to show that the highest type of bidder 1 and the marginal type of bidder 1 cannot profit by depositing $u < d_1 < 1$ (it is not profitable to deposit more than 1 since depositing becomes more costly but the bidding behaviour of bidder 2 does not change). It is straightforward then to see that also the types $u < v_1 < 1$ cannot profit by depositing $u < v_1 < 1$. The expected profit of bidder 1 when depositing $d_1 < 1$ is

$$Pr[d_1 \geq d_2(d_1, v_2)] - Pr[d_1 \geq d_2(d_1, v_2)]E[d_2(d_1, v_2)|d_1 \geq d_2(d_1, v_2)] - cd_1.$$

Denote by $\bar{v}(d_1)$ the type of bidder 2 with $d_1 = d_2(d_1, \bar{v}(d_1))$. We have:

$$d_1 = \frac{1}{2}(\bar{v}(d_1) + \sqrt{\bar{v}(d_1)^2 - 2c(d_1^2 - u^2)}) \Rightarrow \bar{v}(d_1) = d_1 - \frac{2c(d_1^2 - u^2)}{4d_1},$$

and the profit of bidder 1 when depositing d_1 is

$$\bar{v}(d_1)^2 - \int_{v(d_1)}^{\bar{v}(d_1)} 2v_1 d_2(d_1, v_2)dv_1 - cd_1 \leq \bar{v}(d_1)^2$$

$$- \int_{v}^{\bar{v}(d_1)} 2v_1 d_2(d_1, v_2)dv_1 - cd_1 = \bar{v}(d_1)^2 - \frac{1}{3}$$

$$\left(\bar{v}(d_1)^3 - v^3 + (\bar{v}(d_1)^2 - 2c(d_1^2 - u^2))^{3/2} - (v^2 - 2c(d_1^2 - u^2))^{3/2}\right) - cd_1,$$

where the inequality follows as the marginal type $v(d_1)$ of bidder 2 that enters the auction is decreasing in the deposit. For $c = 0.22$, $u = 0.382981$ and $v = 0.757919$ this is an increasing function in d_1 for $d_1 \geq u$. Thus, it is optimal for bidder 1 to deposit the maximal amount $\bar{d}$ if his type is $v_1 = 1$.

Next, we consider the marginal type $v_1 = u$. Differentiating Eq. (12) with respect to d_1 gives:

$$(2d_2 v(d_1) - 2d_2^2)\frac{\partial d_2}{\partial d_1} + (d_2^2 - u^2)\frac{\partial v(d_1)}{\partial d_1} = 2cd_1 d_2 + c(d_1^2 - u^2)\frac{\partial d_2}{\partial d_1}.$$

Therefore,

$$\frac{\partial v(d_1)}{\partial d_1} = \frac{1}{d_2^2 - u^2}\left(2cd_1 d_2 - (c(d_1^2 - u^2) - 2d_2(v(d_1) - d_2))\frac{\partial d_2}{\partial d_1}\right)$$

$$= \frac{1}{d_2^2 - u^2}\left(2cd_1 d_2 - (c(d_1^2 - u^2) - 2d_2\frac{1}{2}\left(v_2 - \sqrt{v_2^2 - 2c(d_1^2 - u^2)}\right)\frac{\partial d_2}{\partial d_1}\right)$$

$$= \frac{1}{d_2^2 - u^2} \left(2cd_1 d_2 - (c(d_1^2 - u^2) - \frac{1}{2} \left(v_2^2 - (v_2^2 - 2c(d_1^2 - u^2)) \right)) \frac{\partial d_2}{\partial d_1} \right)$$

$$= \frac{2cd_1 d_2}{d_2^2 - u^2} \geq \frac{2cd_1 d_2}{d_1 d_2 - u^2} \geq \frac{2cd_2}{d_2 - u^2/d_1} \geq \frac{2cv(d_1)}{v(d_1) - u^2/d_1},$$

where the first inequality follows as $d_2 \leq d_1$ and the last inequality follows as $d_2 \leq v(d_1)$ and the term $\frac{2cd_2}{d_2 - u^2/d_1}$ is decreasing in d_2. For the marginal type $v_1 = u$, differentiating the profit as function of $d_1 < \bar{d}$ with respect to d_1 yields

$$\frac{\partial}{\partial d_1} (v(d_1)^2 u - cd_1) = 2v(d_1) u \frac{\partial v}{\partial d_1} - c \geq \frac{4cv(d_1)^2 u}{v(d_1) - u^2/d_1} - c \geq \frac{4c(2u^2/d_1)^2 u}{u^2/d_1} - c = 16cu^3/d_1 - c,$$

which is positive for $d_1 \leq 0.89877$. On the other hand, we have

$$\frac{2cd_1 d_2}{d_2^2 - u^2} \geq \frac{2cd_1 d_2}{d_2^2} \geq \frac{2cd_1}{d_2} \geq \frac{2cd_1}{v(d_1)},$$

and, therefore

$$2v(d_1) u \frac{\partial v}{\partial d_1} - c \geq 4cd_1 u - c = 1.531924cd_1 - c$$

which is positive for $d_1 > 0.89877$. Thus, bidder 1's profit is decreasing in d_1 if $v_1 = u$.

C   Empirical Evidence

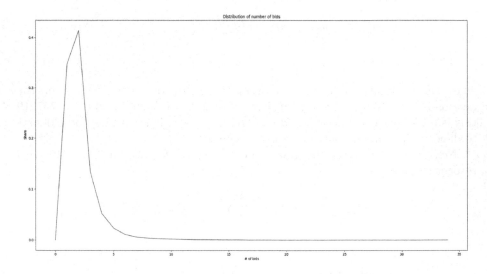

Fig. 3. Distribution of number of bids

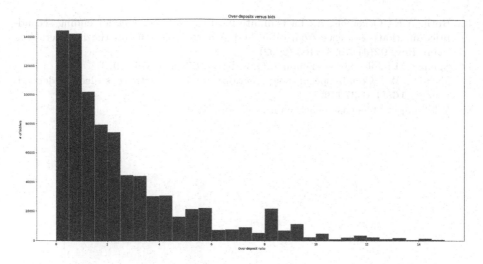

Fig. 4. Overdepositing

References

1. Baye, M.R., Kovenock, D., de Vries, C.G.: The all-pay auction with complete information. Econ. Theor. **8**, 291–305 (1996)
2. Blass, E.-O., Kerschbaum, F.: BOREALIS: building block for sealed bid auctions on blockchains. In: Sun, H.-M., Shieh, S.-P., Gu, G., Ateniese, G. (eds.) ASIA CCS 2020: The 15th ACM Asia Conference on Computer and Communications Security, Taipei, Taiwan, 5–9 October 2020, pp. 558–571. ACM (2020)
3. Che, X., Klumpp, T.: Entry deterrence in dynamic second-price auctions. Am. Econ. J.: Microecon. **8**(2), 168–201 (2016)
4. Cho, I.-K., Kreps, D.M.: Signaling games and stable equilibria. Q. J. Econ. **102**(2), 179–221 (1987)
5. Daian, P., et al.: Flash boys 2.0: frontrunning in decentralized exchanges, miner extractable value, and consensus instability. In: 2020 IEEE Symposium on Security and Privacy, SP 2020, San Francisco, CA, USA, 18–21 May 2020, pp. 910–927. IEEE (2020)
6. Fudenberg, D., Tirole, J.: Game Theory. MIT Press, Cambridge (1991)
7. Garratt, R., Tröger, T.: Speculation in standard auctions with resale. Econometrica **74**(3), 753–769 (2006)
8. Häfner, S., Stewart, A.: Blockchains, front-running, and candle auctions. Front-Running, and Candle Auctions (May 14, 2021) (2021)
9. Hartline, J.D., Roughgarden, T.: Optimal mechanism design and money burning. In: Dwork, C. (ed.) Proceedings of the 40th Annual ACM Symposium on Theory of Computing, Victoria, British Columbia, Canada, 17–20 May 2008, pp. 75–84. ACM (2008)
10. Hörner, J., Sahuguet, N.: Costly signalling in auctions. Rev. Econ. Stud. **74**(1), 173–206 (2007)
11. Mamageishvili, A., Schlegel, J.C.: Optimal smart contracts with costly verification. In: 2020 IEEE International Conference on Blockchain and Cryptocurrency (ICBC), pp. 1–8. IEEE (2020)

12. Roth, A.E., Ockenfels, A.: Last-minute bidding and the rules for ending second-price auctions: evidence from eBay and Amazon auctions on the internet. Am. Econ. Rev. **92**(4), 1093–1103 (2002)
13. Spence, M.: Job market signaling. Q. J. Econ. **87**, 355–374 (1973)
14. Vickrey, W.: Counterspeculation, auctions, and competitive sealed tenders. J. Financ. **16**(1), 8–37 (1961)
15. Whitepaper. The oasis blockchain protocol (2020)

The Case for Variable Fees in Constant Product Markets: An Agent Based Simulation

Marc Sabate-Vidales[1,2] and David Šiška[1,3(✉)]

[1] School of Mathematics, Edinburgh, UK
[2] The Alan Turing Institute, University of Edinburgh, Edinburgh, UK
[3] Vega Protocol, Edinburgh, UK
d.siska@ed.ac.uk

Abstract. We are interested in how the relationship between the fee in a constant product market (CPM) and the volatility of the swapped pair on other liquid exchanges influences the losses/gains of the liquidity providers. We review three classical market making models: Glosten and Milgrom, Kyle and Grossman and Miller and note that these very different models there is always a relationship between volatility and how rational market makers set prices. Motivated by this we set up an agent based model to explore this in the context of CPMs like Uniswap. We conclude that if the fee is too low relative to the volatility of the traded pair then the liquidity providers will end up making a loss over the medium term. From this we go to suggesting that CPM markets need to let liquidity providers set the fee via a governance mechanism especially as volatilities of assets fluctuate. The code for all simulations is available at https://github.com/msabvid/cpm_agent_based_sim.

Keywords: Constant Product Market · Mechanism Design · Agent Based Simulation · Reinforcement Learning

1 Introduction

Automated market makers based on the idea of a constant product market have experienced exponential growth in total value locked and fee income since their introduction to general purpose blockchains [15].

Such constant product markets are a perfect fit for any such general purpose blockchain which provides a virtual machine like Ethereum [8], or Cardano, Polkadot or Solana. The reasons are that the mechanism itself guarantees liquidity (proportional to the amount of assets locked) and they have minimal storage and computational requirements, unlike e.g. limit-order-book-based markets. This makes them ideal for environments where computational power and storage are at a premium. A decentralised market has many advantages over centralised exchanges: pseudonymity, censorship resistance and security, see references in e.g. [15]. CPMs are currently an area of active research, see e.g. [18] and

© International Financial Cryptography Association 2023
S. Matsuo et al. (Eds.): FC 2022 Workshops, LNCS 13412, pp. 225–237, 2023.
https://doi.org/10.1007/978-3-031-32415-4_15

references therein. That said, there a number of issues have been raised around blockchain-based constant product markets, mostly related to miner-extractable-value [12], which has been on the order of $700 million in the 11 months since the beginning of 2020 [16]. For a general introduction to blockchains and general purpose, smart-contract-based blockchains see e.g. [17].

In this article we want to study "impermanent losses" in constant product market from the perspective of optimal market making. There is growing evidence that most liquidity providers on CPMs are losing money see, e.g. [15]. We approach this issue by first recalling the three different models due to Glosten & Milgrom [2], Kyle [3,4] and Grossman & Miller [5]. In all of these models *volatility* of the underlying asset plays an important role in how the market makers set bid-ask spreads. In constant product markets the liquidity providers do not set the price but each such market has a fixed fee which should compensate the liquidity providers for the risk of losses. Even in e.g. Uniswap v3 the trading fee is static "Each pool is initialized with an immutable value, fee, (γ), representing the fee paid by the swappers...", see [19].

Motivated by the insights of the aforementioned models we set up a simple agent-based model (stochastic control problem) to study the relationship between underlying asset volatility, constant product market fee and liquidity provider's losses or gains. Our agent-based simulations show that if the volatility of the asset is high relative to the fee then the liquidity providers always end up making a loss. See Fig. 1. Moreover the losses of LPs increases as the volatility increases and the losses of the LPs decrease as the fee increases.

Related Work

Agent-based simulations on CPMs are not new. Similar agent based model can be found e.g. in [11] where they mainly focused on how the CPM tracks another market price in low-volatility regime. As [11], we see that the CPM price tracks the external asset price, see Fig. 3.

Back to volatility: it is well known that *volatility is not constant*, see e.g. [6]. For this reason, the wisdom of classical market making models and due to the similation study in this paper we argue that CPM protocols should allow LPs set the fee to react to changing volatility. When volatility is low they should set fees lower to attract trading. When volatility is high they should be able to increase fees to compensate for having to often trade at unfavourable price set by the protocol.

In [20] the authors set up a control problem where the LP aims to maintain certain desirable portfolio weight between the two pool assets and the arbitrageur imposes costs on the LP. There the control problem has explicit solution which indicates that small fees are optimal. Note that, however, the objective of the LP is to maintain a certain portfolio weight instead of maximising the portfolio value, which is the objective of the LP in our work. Hence the difference in conclusion about what constitutes optimal.

The work [21] studies how CPM liquidity complements order-book-based liquidity and show that stable general equilibrium exists with endogenous liquidity on both platforms. They further study the impact of adopting CPMs on asset prices and traders' behaviour.

The authors of [22] observe the losses incurred by LPs but attack the problem from a different angle. They set up a model which then allows them to propose a pricing function which maximises the incentive for liquidity provision.

Organisation of the Paper

The paper is organised as follows. In Sect. 2 we review some classical market making models and conclude that all say that market makers need to be compensated more if volatility is higher. In Sect. 3 we describe the model we implement for our experiment and discuss the assumptions. Section 4 recalls classical stochastic control problem setting within which the training of our agent happens while Sect. 5 describes the training algorithm. A full implementation can be found at https://github.com/kGFRqao2/cpm_agent_based_sim. Readers interested only in the implications for mechanism design of CPMs can skip Sects. 4 and 5 and jump straight to Sect. 6 where we present our results. Section 7 contains some concluding remarks and discusses possible future research directions.

2   Review of Classical Market Making Models

We are interested in what the classical market making models in the economics literature have to say about the relation between asset volatility and the fee (or bid-ask spread) a rational market maker would demand.

Glosten and Milgrom Model

This is a one-step (static) model that assumes a binomial evolution of the asset price: from the current level μ it will move to price V_H with probability p or to price V_L with probability $1 - p$ and $V_H > V_L$. Within the model there is a continuum of traders of which proportion α are "informed" in the sense that they know where the price will move and $1 - \alpha$ are "uniformed". The informed ones will only buy if the ask price a set by the MMs satisfies $a < V_H$ or sell if the bid price $b > V_L$. It is assumed that competition between market makers drive their profits to 0 and this assumption is used to calculate what bid and ask they will set. For our analysis here it suffices to note that the ask price will be at a distance from the mid of $c_{p,\alpha,\text{ask}}(V_H - \mu)$ and the bid price will be $c_{p,\alpha,\text{bid}}(\mu - V_L)$. Here $c_{p,\alpha,\text{ask}}$ and $c_{p,\alpha,\text{bid}}$ are constant multipliers that depend on the model parameters.

What is relevant for us is that we see that as the volatility in the model increases (here volatility essentially means $V_H - V_L$), the "fair" bid-ask widens. In other words the market makers want compensation for the asset volatility (which is here expressed via bid-ask but could equally be re-worked as fee). For full details we refer to [2] or [9, Ch. 2].

Kyle Lambda Model

This is another model that assumes a trader with "information advantage". There are also price-insensitive liquidity traders (they need to execute whatever the cost) and a large number of MMs that observe the order flow and compete by setting price. Current price is S, future price is $v \sim N(\mu, \sigma^2)$. The liquidity traders overall place orders $u \sim N(0, \sigma_u^2)$ which is independent of v. The MMs are risk-neutral. When there are no informed traders competition among MMs ensures $S = \mathbb{E}[v]$. The insider is assumed to know[1] the exact value of v. They want to maximize their profit by trading volume x but this trade will shift the prices the MMs rationally offer. The liquidity traders help help him/her by disguising the informed trader's intention to trade x in the overall flow of $x + u$. It is reasonable to assume that the fair price $S = \mu + \lambda(x + u)$. In other words demand to buy (i.e. $x + u > 0$ drives the price up) while demand to sell $x + u < 0$ drives the price down. Careful reasoning, see [3], leads to $\lambda = 2\frac{\sigma}{\sigma_u}$. This is known as Kyle Lambda.[2]

The crucial observation for us here is that, again, the fair price is shifted more if the volatility of the asset is known to be higher.

Grossman and Miller Market Making Model

In this model there are n identival MMs for some fixed asset and there are three dates $t = 1, 2, 3$. At time $t = 1$ a liquidity trader arrives to sell i units of the asset (or purchase if i is negative). At time $t = 2$ there will be another liquidity trader to trade $-i$ units. The market maker is exposed to price moves between the time steps and makes profit/loss accordingly. Thus the focus is on the price changes. At time $t = 3$ the fundamental value will be $S_3 = \mu + \epsilon_2 + \epsilon_3$ where μ is a constant and for $i = 2, 3$, $\epsilon_i \sim N(0, \sigma^2)$ are independent. These are publicly observed such that ϵ_2 becomes known between $t = 1$ and 2 and ϵ_3 becomes known between $t = 2$ and 3. All participants are assumed to be risk averse with $U(x) = -\exp(-\gamma x)$, $\gamma > 0$, describing their utility. Careful analysis in [5] or [9, Ch 2] leads to the conclusion that no market maker will provide liquidity at the efficient price μ. Trading will occur at $S_1 = \mu - \gamma\sigma^2\frac{i}{n+1}$.

Again, as in the previous two models the MMs demand compensation for the risk they take on proportional to the volatility.

Having observed this we proceed to set up a simple agent-based model to explore this in the CPM setting.

3   A Model for Trading on CPM vs. Another Exchange

We will work with two assets α and β (and we'll pretend that α is something like USDT and β is something like ETH). We will assume that:

---

[1] Imagine a takeover bid at price v is coming and the insider knows this.

[2] This model is also covered in [9, Ch.2]. However the authors there swap σ and σ_u. This small typo needs to be taken into account to avoid confusion.

i) There is a liquid centralised spot exchange where at time n asset β can be bought/sold roughly for S_n. The price S_n evolution is given by Geometric Brownian Motion:

$$S_{n+1} = S_n \exp\left((\mu - \tfrac{1}{2}\sigma^2)\tau + \sigma\sqrt{\tau}Z_n \right)$$

where μ is a drift, τ is the length of the time step between n and $n+1$, $\sigma > 0$ is volatility and $Z_n \sim N(0,1)$, $n \in \mathbb{N}$ are independent.

ii) Trading on the centralised exchange happens at price $(S_n + \kappa \times \text{size})$, where $\kappa \geq 0$ covers fees and slippage.

iii) There is a constant product market for exchange between α and β and the parties that committed assets to the pool do not trade on the pool and do not change the allocation. The reserve of α at time n is denoted R_n^{α} and the reserve of β at time n is denoted R_n^{β}. The fee for the constant product market is $1 - \gamma$ and stays constant throughout.

iv) There is an agent that at each time step can decide to either: trade in α or in β or do nothing and moreover the agent refuses to hold inventory (what they buy on the CPM they must sell on the other exchange immediately). The agent maximizes a concave utility function i.e. it is risk-averse.

Let us discuss the assumptions. It is very common that assets that are traded on-chain have (usually more than one) liquid centralised limit-order-book based exchanges and there are agents who, by attempting to arbitrage the price differences, ensure that prices stay roughly in line between various trading venues. Assuming log-normal price moves is naive but fatter tailed distribution will likely only allow the arbitrage trader to make larger gains against the CPM. Thus i) is in our opinion uncontroversial. Note also that it's effectively the same dynamics as considered in [11]. Finally, note that because we Reinforcement Learning approach for our agent our code and algorithm is agnostic to how S_n is generated. We could have run the same simulations with real world data.

Assumption ii) is clearly a massive simplification but it is common in modelling trade execution. There is some evidence of slippage being linear in trade size [9]. Estimating κ is difficult and clearly in reality this isn't constant across time.

Assumption iii) is in our opinion reasonable: due to high gas fees on Ethereum and due to the danger of being front-run by MEV bots most liquidity providers do not attempt to adjust their allocations according to price moves elsewhere and if they do it doesn't lead to profit [15].

Regarding the agent i.e. assumption iv): restricting the agent to holding no inventory is perhaps unrealistic but allowing them to hold inventory will probably only increase their advantage over those holding assets in the liquidity pool and thus it is sufficient to illustrate our point.

The main issue is potentially that the LP in this model only faces "toxic" flow from an "informed" agent. It will be interesting to extend the model to include "price taking" agents who create fee income for the LP without attempting arbitrage but who will only trade if they can execute on the CPM with better price than on the other exchange.

Let us look in detail at the actions the agent can take at each step. Of course if they choose not to trade then there is nothing to consider.

They Choose to Trade in α

1. They choose an amount Δ_{n+1}^α i.e. the USD amount to sell.
2. They trade on the constant product market getting

$$R_n^\beta - \frac{R_n^\alpha R_n^\beta}{R_n^\alpha + \gamma \Delta_{n+1}^\alpha}$$

of β i.e. ETH.
3. They go to the liquid exchange to sell the β (ETH) they got, getting

$$\left(R_n^\beta - \frac{R_n^\alpha R_n^\beta}{R_n^\alpha + \gamma \Delta_{n+1}^\alpha} \right) \left(S_n - \kappa \left(R_n^\beta - \frac{R_n^\alpha R_n^\beta}{R_n^\alpha + \gamma \Delta_{n+1}^\alpha} \right) \right) .$$

4. Their profit or loss, in α (i.e. USD), is

$$P_{n+1}^\alpha = \left(R_n^\beta - \frac{R_n^\alpha R_n^\beta}{R_n^\alpha + \gamma \Delta_{n+1}^\alpha} \right) \left(S_n - \kappa \left(R_n^\beta - \frac{R_n^\alpha R_n^\beta}{R_n^\alpha + \gamma \Delta_{n+1}^\alpha} \right) \right) - \Delta_{n+1}^\alpha .$$

They Choose to Trade in β

1. They choose an amount Δ_{n+1}^β of ETH to sell.
2. They buy Δ_{n+1}^β of asset β (ETH) on the liquid exchange at the cost of

$$\Delta_{n+1}^\beta \left(S_n + \kappa \Delta_{n+1}^\beta \right) .$$

3. They trade on the constant product market, selling Δ_{n+1}^β of β (ETH) getting

$$R_n^\alpha - \frac{R_n^\alpha R_n^\beta}{R_n^\beta + \gamma \Delta_{n+1}^\beta} .$$

of α (USD).
4. Their profit or loss, in α (USD), is

$$P_{n+1}^\alpha = R_n^\alpha - \frac{R_n^\alpha R_n^\beta}{R_n^\beta + \gamma \Delta_{n+1}^\beta} - \Delta_{n+1}^\beta \left(S_n + \kappa \Delta_{n+1}^\beta \right) .$$

Formulation as a Stochastic Control Problem

We will formulate this in the framework of discrete-time continuous state and action space stochastic control. To do this we effectively have to state what the state and action spaces are and formulate the transitions and rewards.

We will work with an exponential utility function $U : \mathbb{R} \to \mathbb{R}$ given by $U(x) = 1 - \exp(-ax)$, $a > 0$ for $x \geq 0$ and $U(x) = x$ for $x < 0$. This is concave and our agent is thus risk-averse.

Our state space is $x = (S, R^\alpha, R^\beta) \in (\mathbb{R}^+)^3$. The initial values should be such that

$$S_0 = \frac{R_0^\alpha}{R_0^\beta}$$

so for example we can have $S_0 = 4700$, $R_0^\alpha = 4700 \cdot 10^4$ and $R^\beta = 10^4$.

There is a parameter $\sigma > 0$ (volatility), $\gamma \in [0,1]$ (with $1 - \gamma$ being "fee") and $\delta \in (0,1)$ a discount factor as before.

The Markov controls are $C = C(S_n, R_n^\alpha, R_n^\beta) \in \{0,1\}$ and $\Delta^\alpha = \Delta^\alpha(S_n, R_n^\alpha, R_n^\beta) \in [0,\infty)$ and $\Delta^\beta = \Delta^\beta(S_n, R_n^\alpha, R_n^\beta) \in [0,\infty)$ The interpretation is that C "chooses" whether to sell α or β. If it's 0 sell α, if it's 1 sell β. Finally Δ^α then determines the amount to trade if we're selling α while Δ^β determines the amount if we're selling β.

The Markov chain updates as:

$$S_{n+1} = S_n \exp\left((\mu - \tfrac{1}{2}\sigma^2)\tau + \sigma\sqrt{\tau}Z_n \right) \tag{1}$$

with $Z_n \sim N(0,1)$.

With $C_{n+1} = C(S_n, R_n^\alpha, R_n^\beta)$ and $\Delta_{n+1} = \Delta(S_n, R_n^\alpha, R_n^\beta) \in [0,\infty)$ the reserves are then updated as

$$
\begin{aligned}
R_{n+1}^\alpha &= \mathbf{1}_{C_{n+1}=0}\left(R_n^\alpha + \Delta_{n+1}^\alpha \right) + \mathbf{1}_{C_{n+1}=1}\left(\frac{R_n^\alpha R_n^\beta}{R_n^\beta + \gamma\Delta_{n+1}^\beta} \right), \\
R_{n+1}^\beta &= \mathbf{1}_{C_{n+1}=0}\left(\frac{R_n^\alpha R_n^\beta}{R_n^\alpha + \gamma\Delta_{n+1}^\alpha} \right) + \mathbf{1}_{C_{n+1}=1}\left(R_n^\beta + \Delta_{n+1}^\beta \right).
\end{aligned}
\tag{2}
$$

The running reward is given in terms of the utility function as follows. Here $\kappa \geq 0$ is a parameter (slippage). Let

$$
\begin{aligned}
P_{n+1}^\alpha := \mathbf{1}_{C_{n+1}=0}&\left[\left(R_n^\beta - \frac{R_n^\alpha R_n^\beta}{R_n^\alpha + \gamma\Delta_{n+1}^\alpha} \right)\left(S_n - \kappa\left(R_n^\beta - \frac{R_n^\alpha R_n^\beta}{R_n^\alpha + \gamma\Delta_{n+1}^\alpha} \right) \right) - \Delta_{n+1}^\alpha \right] \\
+ \mathbf{1}_{C_{n+1}=1}&\left[R_n^\alpha - \frac{R_n^\alpha R_n^\beta}{R_n^\beta + \gamma\Delta_{n+1}^\beta} - \Delta_{n+1}^\beta\left(S_n + \kappa\Delta_{n+1}^\beta \right) \right]
\end{aligned}
\tag{3}
$$

and then

$$f(S_n, R_n^\alpha, R_n^\beta, \Delta_{n+1}^\alpha, \Delta_{n+1}^\beta) = U\left(P_{n+1}^\alpha \right).$$

4   General Discrete Time, Continuous State and Action Space, Relaxed Stochastic Control Problem

We consider a simple discrete-time, infinite-time horizon control problem in continuous space-time with randomized controls on top of continuous convex action space.

Let us first describe the controlled Markov chain: given we're in a state $x \in \mathbb{R}^d$ and our chosen policy is $\pi \in \mathcal{P}(\mathbb{R}^p)$ the system will transition to

$$X_1^{\pi,x} := x + \tau \int b(x,a)\,\pi(da) + (\Delta W)\left(\int \sigma(x,a)\sigma(x,a)^\top \pi(da) \right)^{1/2},$$

where here and elsewhere all integrals without an explicitly stated domain of integration are over $\mathbb{R}^p$. Moreover:

1. $\Delta W \sim \sqrt{\tau} Z$, $Z \sim N(0, I)$ with I a $\mathbb{R}^{d' \times d'}$ identity so d' is the dimension on the driving "noise".
2. $b : \mathbb{R}^d \times \mathbb{R}^p \to \mathbb{R}^d$ is the "drift" of the Markov chain.
3. $\sigma : \mathbb{R}^d \times \mathbb{R}^p \to \mathbb{R}^{d \times d'}$ is the "diffusion" of the Markov chain.
4. for a $d \times d$ positive definite matrix M we define $M^{1/2}$ as the matrix N such that $NN^\top = M$. This is given by the Cholesky decomposition.

We know that without loss of generality it's enough to consider Markov controls $\pi : \mathbb{R}^d \to \mathbb{R}^p$, see [1] or [7]. For a given policy π (Markov control function) the value function is

$$v^\pi(x) := \mathbb{E}\left[\sum_{n=0}^\infty \delta^n \int f(X_n^\pi, a)\, \pi(X_n^\pi, da)\Big| X_0^\pi = x\right],$$

where $\delta \in (0, 1)$ is a discount factor and $f : \mathbb{R}^d \times \mathbb{R}^p$ is the running reward. The value function of the control problem is

$$v(x) = \sup_\pi v^\pi(x)$$

with the supremum taken over all Markov control functions π. The Bellman equation is

$$v(x) = \sup_{\pi \in \mathcal{P}(\mathbb{R}^p)} \left(\int f(x, a)\, \pi(da) + \delta \mathbb{E}[v(X_1^\pi) | X_0^\pi = x]\right), \quad x \in \mathbb{R}^d, \quad (4)$$

again see [1] or [7]. We will use this to derive an approximation and an algorithm based on the classical Policy Iteration Algorithm [1]. From the point of view of Reinforcement Learning this can be seen as an example of an Actor-Critic algorithm [10].

5   Approximation and Algorithm

Let us take some parametric approximations of the Markov policy: $\pi = \pi(x, a; \theta_{\text{pol}})$ and of the value function $v = v(x; \theta_{\text{val}})$. While we do not go into detail of the approximation here, the algorithm that is finally implemented uses neural network approximations for both. See [10, Chapter 9]. One of the reasons for choosing Neural networks is the growing body of work showing that neural networks do not suffer from the curse of dimensionality when approximating solutions to equations like the Bellman equation (4), see e.g. [14] and references therein. Moreover in the case of supervised learning and "sufficiently wide" one hidden layer architectures convergence of gradient descent learning has been proved, see [13] and references therein. Finally, one can show that gradient descent algorithm for entropy regularised reformulation of the control problem introduced in Sect. 4 converges for appropriate conditions on the regularisation, see [23]. For full details of the algorithm not covered here, please see https://github.com/msabvid/cpm_agent_based_sim.

Let us fix N_{MC} to be the number of Monte Carlo samples per batch and N_{batch} the batch size.

Initialise the algorithm with random θ_{pol}.

1. Sample $x_i := \left(S_{0,i}, R_{0,i}^\alpha, R_{0,i}^\beta\right)$, $i = 1, \ldots, N_{batch}$ from some distribution on $\mathbb{R}^d$.

2. For each i generate N_{MC} samples from the density $\pi(x_i, \cdot; \theta_{pol})$ thus obtaining $a_{i,j} := (C_{i,j}, \Delta_{i,j}^\alpha, \Delta_{i,j}^\beta)$, $i = 1, \ldots, N_{batch}$, $j = 1, \ldots, N_{MC}$. We use the so-called re-parametrisation trick to sample from the policy $\pi(x_i, \cdot; \theta_{pol})$. Let $\mathbf{a} : \mathbb{R}^3 \times \mathcal{Z} \times \Theta \to \mathbb{R}^3$ be a generator parametrised by a neural network with weights $\theta_{pol} \in \Theta$ that takes as input the state x_i and a noise vector z sampled from a known distribution supported in $\mathcal{Z} \subseteq \mathbb{R}$ (for example Gaussian). For a fixed x_i, $\pi(x_i, \cdot; \theta_{pol})$ is implicitly defined as the law of $\mathbf{a}(x_i, \cdot; \theta_{pol})$.

3. For each i generate N_{MC} new states of the system starting from x_i with action $a_{i,j}$ and randomness $\Delta W_{i,j}$:

$$X_{1,i,j} := x_i + \tau b(x_i, a_{i,j}) + (\Delta W_{i,j})\sigma(x_i, a_{i,j}).$$

Specifically, $X_{1,i,j} = \left(S_{1,i,j}, R_{1,i,j}^\alpha, R_{1,i,j}^\beta\right)$ where $S_{1,i,j}$ is updated using (1) and the reserves $\left(R_{1,i,j}^\alpha, R_{1,i,j}^\beta\right)$ are updated using (2).

4. Update, using gradient descent step, θ_{val} such that "Bellman error"

$$\sum_{i=1}^{N_{batch}} \left| v(x_i; \theta_{val}) - \frac{1}{N_{MC}} \sum_{j=1}^{N_{MC}} \left[f(x_i, a_{i,j}) + \delta v(X_{1,i,j}; \theta_{val}) \right] \right|^2 \quad (5)$$

is reduced. Notice that this is effectively a Monte-Carlo approximation to (4).

5. Update, using e.g. a gradient ascent step, θ_{pol}, such that

$$\frac{1}{N_{batch}} \sum_{i=1}^{N_{batch}} \frac{1}{N_{MC}} \sum_{j=1}^{N_{MC}} \left[f(x_i, a_{i,j}) + \delta v(X_{1,i,j}; \theta_{val}) \right] \quad (6)$$

is increased.

6. Go back to (1) and repeat until a stopping criteria is reached.

6   Numerical Results

When training the agent we fix the following parameters. The slippage and the fee are set to $\kappa = 0.001, \gamma = 0.99$. The volatility of the price process S_n is fixed to $\sigma = 0.3$, the time step size τ is fixed to 0.1. Once the agent is trained we run the experiment with varying σ and γ and the agent would be using somewhat

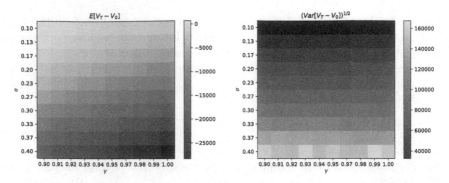

Fig. 1. Approximation of mean and standard deviation of the loss of the liquidity provider for different combinations of σ and γ

sub-optimal responses. The conclusions of the paper are not altered but we could make them more pronounced by re-training the agent to react optimally in each regime.

The soft policy $\mathbf{a}(\cdot, \cdot; \theta_{\mathrm{pol}})$ and the value function $v(\cdot; \theta_{\mathrm{val}})$ are parametrised by feedforward neural networks with two hidden layers with 40 neurons each followed by the activation function $\mathrm{ReLU}(x) := \max(x, 0)$. We ensure that $\Delta^\alpha, \Delta^\beta$ are positive by applying the activation function $\mathrm{Softplus}(x) := \log(1 + e^x)$ to the corresponding output coordinates of $\mathbf{a}(\cdot, \cdot; \theta_{\mathrm{pol}})$. Furthermore, we ensure that $C \in [0, 1]$ by applying the sigmoid activation function to the corresponding output coordinate of $\mathbf{a}(\cdot, \cdot; \theta_{\mathrm{pol}})$. The algorithm is trained for 10 000 iterations of stochastic gradient descent/ascent.

Figure 2 shows the evolution of the Bellman loss (5) and the Bellman approximation of the value function (6) during training.

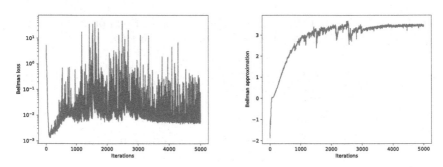

Fig. 2. Left: Evolution of Bellman loss (5) during training iterations. Right: Evolution of Bellman approximation of the value function (6) during training iterations.

Figure 3 shows one simulation of the dynamics of $(S_t, R_t^\alpha, R_t^\beta)$ using the trained policy $\pi(x, \cdot, ; \theta_{\mathrm{pol}})$ for 100 time steps. Following the learned policy, the trader is able to get profit with every trade.

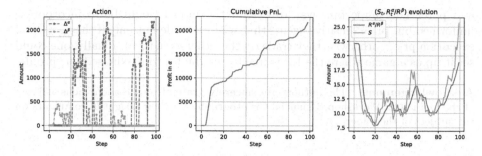

Fig. 3. Simulation of one typical scenario. Left: $(\Delta_n^\alpha, \Delta_n^\beta)$ for each step. Middle: cumulative profit of the trader following the policy. Right: evolution of $S_n, R_n^\alpha / R_n^\beta$.

In Fig. 1 we simulate 100 000 different scenarios and we approximate the mean profit/loss of the pool owner given by $\mathbb{E}[V_T - V_0]$ where $V_t := R_t^\alpha + S_t R_t^\beta$. Our simulations support that if the fee is too low relative to the volatility of the traded pair then the liquidity providers will end up making a loss over the medium term.

7 Conclusion and Future Work

In CPMs the liquidity provider (market maker) doesn't set prices but the fee should compensate them for the fact that they are effectively forced to trade at the price set by the mechanism.

Classical market making models of Glosten and Milgrom, Kyle and Grossman and Miller, while very different, all agree on the fact that if the underlying volatility is large then this should be reflected in the bid/ask spread or the offer price. Translating this to CPMs we get the intuitive feeling that the fee should be set higher if volatility of the underlying is high.

Our agent based simulations confirm this intuition as can be seen in Fig. 1. An actionable conclusion of this study is that CPMs like Uniswap should allow LPs to set the fees via governance especially as asset volatility is well known to be non-constant.

There are several directions in which this can be extended. The first one is to use real world asset price data. This would be relatively straightforward given that the agent trained with reinforcement learning algorithm doesn't need to know the asset price evolution dynamics a priori. The second one would be to extend this to a simulation with several agents who either have to compete on gas fees to access the CPM or after they choose their actions they get randomly ordered to execute their trades. Our intuition is that the agents will learn to be more cautious (they will only trade if the mis-pricing between the CPM and the other exchange is more pronounced) but the relationship between the volatility and the liquidity providers' losses/gains will remain. The third one would allow the arbitrageur to hold inventory over several time steps. The fourth and potentially important way to extend the model would be to incorporate uniformed but price sensitive agents that wish to trade but only if they get good execution price (otherwise they trade on the other exchange). Finally, one could set it up as a game where the LP is free to set the fee to maximise their profits.

Acknowledgements. The authors are sincerely grateful to the anonymous referees of the DeFi 2022 Workshop, Financial Cryptography for their insightful comments on the subject of the paper.

References

1. Bellman, R.: Dynamic Programming. Princeton University Press, Princeton, NJ, USA (1957)
2. Glosten, L.R., Milgrom, P.R.: Bid, ask and transaction prices in a specialist market with heterogeneously informed traders. J. Financ. Econ. **14**(1), 71–100
3. Kyle, A.S.: Continuous auctions and insider trading. Econometrica **53**(6), 1315–1335 (1985)
4. Kyle, A.S.: Informed speculation with imperfect competition. Rev. Econ. Stud. **56**(3), 317–455 (1989)
5. Grossman, S.J., Miller, M.H.: Liquidity and market structure. J. Financ. **43**(3), 617–633 (1988)
6. Gatheral, J.: The Volatility Surface: A Practitioner's Guide. Wiley, Hoboken (2006)
7. Puterman, M.L.: Markov Decision Processes: Discrete Stochastic Dynamic Programming. John Wiley & Sons, Hoboken (2014)
8. Wood, G., et al.: Ethereum: a secure, decentralised generalised transaction ledger. Ethereum Proj. Yellow Pap. **151** (2014)
9. Cartea, A., Jaimungal, S., Penalva, J.: Algorithmic and High-Frequency Trading, Cambridge University Press, Cambridge (2015)
10. Sutton, R.S., Barto, A.G.: Reinforcement Learning. MIT Press, Cambridge (2018)
11. Angeris, G., Kao, H.-T., Chiang, R., Noyes, C., Chitra, T.: An Analysis of Uniswap Markets, arXiv:1911.03380 (2019)
12. Daian, P., et al.: Flash Boys 2.0: Frontrunning, Transaction Reordering, and Consensus Instability in Decentralized Exchanges (2019). arXiv:1904.05234
13. Hu, K., Ren, Z., Šiška, D., Szpruch, L.: Mean-field Langevin dynamics and energy landscape of neural networks. Ann. Inst. H. Poincaré Probab. Stat. **57**(4), 2043–2065 (2021)
14. Gonon, L., Grohs, P., Jentzen, A., Kofler, D., Šiška, D.: Uniform error estimates for artificial neural network approximations for the heat equation. IMA J. Numer. Anal. (2021)
15. Loesch, S., Hindman, N., Richardson, M.B., Welch, N.: Impermanent Loss in Uniswap v3. arXiv:2111.09192 (2021)
16. Flashbots, MEV-Explore v0. https://explore.flashbots.net. Accessed 1 Dec 2021
17. Lipton, A., Treccani, A.: Blockchain and Distributed Ledgers: Mathematics, Technology, and Economics. World Scientific, Singapore (2021)
18. Lipton, A., Sepp, A.: Automated Market-Making for Fiat Currencies (2021). arXiv:2109.12196
19. Adams, H., et al.: Uniswap v3 Core (2021). https://uniswap.org/whitepaper-v3.pdf
20. Evans, A., Angeris, G., Chitra, T.: Optimal Fees for Geometric Mean Market Makers (2021). arXiv:2104.00446

21. Aoyagi, J., Ito, Y.: Coexisting Exchange Platforms: Limit Order Books and Automated Market Makers (2021). http://dx.doi.org/10.2139/ssrn.3805095
22. Capponi, A., Jia, R.: The Adoption of Blockchain-based Decentralized Exchanges (2021). http://dx.doi.org/10.2139/ssrn.3805095
23. Leahy, J.M., Kerimkulov, B., Šiška, D., Szpruch, L.: Convergence of policy gradient for entropy regularized MDPs with neural network approximation in the mean-field regime (2022). arXiv:2201.07296

An Empirical Study of Market Inefficiencies in Uniswap and SushiSwap

Jan Arvid Berg, Robin Fritsch$^{(\boxtimes)}$, Lioba Heimbach$^{(\boxtimes)}$, and Roger Wattenhofer

ETH Zürich, Zürich, Switzerland
{bergar,rfritsch,hlioba,wattenhofer}@ethz.ch

Abstract. Decentralized exchanges are revolutionizing finance. With their ever-growing increase in popularity, a natural question that begs to be asked is: how efficient are these new markets?

We find that nearly 30% of analyzed trades are executed at an unfavorable rate. Additionally, we observe that, especially during the DeFi summer in 2020, price inaccuracies across the market plagued DEXes. Uniswap and SushiSwap, however, quickly adapt to their increased volumes. We see an increase in market efficiency with time during the observation period. Nonetheless, the DEXes still struggle to track the reference market when cryptocurrency prices are highly volatile. During such periods of high volatility, we observe the market becoming less efficient – manifested by an increased prevalence in cyclic arbitrage opportunities.

Keywords: blockchain · automated market maker · market efficiency

1 Introduction

Nakamoto introduced the first fully decentralized cryptocurrency, Bitcoin [13], in 2008. In the following years, several blockchains followed, notably Ethereum [5] which introduced smart contracts. In their initial phase, blockchains only had a few niche applications, and the excitement surrounding them was mainly fueled by the hopes of continuously rising cryptocurrency prices.

However, this changed with the introduction of *decentralized finance (DeFi)*. Suddenly, blockchains had a new purpose: offering financial services without the need of a middleman. *Decentralized exchanges (DEXes)*, which allow users to trade in a fully noncustodial manner, are a main pillar of DeFi. Instead of requiring traders to give up custody of their funds by depositing into a centralized exchange (CEX), traders can now directly swap tokens with a smart contract on the blockchain. The popularity of DEXes is undeniable. The trading volume on all DEXes, which include Uniswap, SushiSwap, Balancer, Bancor, and Curve, exceeded $50 billion in January 2021 and in every month since [9].

Most of these DEXes use a novel market-making mechanism. Rather than matching orders using a limit order book like traditional exchanges, most DEXes use an automated market maker mechanism that executes orders against a *liquidity pool* holding token reserves. The exchange rate in a liquidity pool is determined by a trading function and the amount of funds in the pool. Temporarily,

© International Financial Cryptography Association 2023
S. Matsuo et al. (Eds.): FC 2022 Workshops, LNCS 13412, pp. 238–249, 2023.
https://doi.org/10.1007/978-3-031-32415-4_16

these rates can be inaccurate and vary across different DEXes. Such inaccuracies in the price lead to trades being executed at unfavorable rates if traders are not alert. Further, they can create cyclic arbitrage opportunities. Cyclic arbitrage opportunities indicate erroneous rates and thereby stem from lacking market efficiency, which measures how well the prices reflect all relevant information [12]. As the market is becoming increasingly complex with an ever-growing number of DEXes and liquidity pools, studying the market's efficiency is ever more important.

We investigate the existence and severity of market inefficiencies in two market leading DEXes, Uniswap and SushiSwap, between 12 September 2020 and 23 January 2021. With the optimal routing problem, we find trades that executed with an unfavorable rate – indicating both the presence of price inaccuracies in the market and their effects on traders. Further, we look for past cyclic arbitrage opportunities, which stem from price differences in the market, and use them as a tool to determine how efficient the market as a whole is.

2   Related Work

Numerous studies analyze market efficiency on CEXes [4, 12, 15, 18]. Conversely, we measure the market efficiency on DEXes, by studying the prevalence of price inaccuracies across the market. More precisely, we focus on DEXes using an *automated market maker (AMM)*.

AMMs have been around for quite some time, e.g., the logarithmic market scoring rule used in prediction markets [10]. However, only the recent emergence of DEXes has made AMMs a popular alternative to traditional central limit order book systems. Uniswap and SushiSwap, along with most other DEXes, implement a new type of AMM design called *constant function market maker (CFMM)* [2]. More specifically, Uniswap and SushiSwap use a form of CFMM called *constant product market maker* (CPMM). Angeris et al. [3] formally analyze how closely CPMMs track reference markets and demonstrate the numerical stability of CPMMs under a wide range of market conditions. We, on the other hand, empirically study the efficiency of Uniswap and SushiSwap in tracking the reference market. By looking for optimizable trades and cyclic arbitrage opportunities, both caused by price inaccuracies in the market, we identify moments when some prices on the DEXes do not accurately track the reference markets.

Several works quantify and study *Blockchain Extractable Value (BEV)* in DeFi. BEV measures the extractable profit from the blockchain by including, excluding, and re-ordering the transactions in a block. A broad study on both the amount of extractable and extracted BEV in DeFi is provided by Qin et al. [14]. Daian et al. [6] study front-running in decentralized exchanges and show that these arbitrage opportunities can cause a priority gas auction, which drives up the gas fee for all blockchain users. Through studying back-running on DEXes, Zhou et al. [17] show that this kind of BEV can cause back-run flooding, a denial of service practice on the blockchain. As opposed to focusing on the effects of arbitrage opportunities on DEXes, we empirically study one of their root causes – price inaccuracies in the market.

Danos et al. [8] theoretically study the optimal routing of trades through a network of CFMMs. We apply the special case of independent paths studied by Danos et al. [7] to analyze past trading data. In examining big swaps, we find that a significant fraction executes suboptimally on Uniswap and SushiSwap. Traders are, thus, suffering from price inaccuracies across the market.

Wang et al. [16] focus on cyclic arbitrage trades, a type of BEV, analyzing them theoretically and empirically. In contrast to this work, we study the availability of cyclic arbitrage opportunities in this paper and use it to identify price inaccuracies in the market. We further look for the causes of the inaccuracies and use them as a tool to study the market's efficiency over time.

3 Constant Product Market Makers

CPMMs, which include Uniswap and SushiSwap, are smart contracts running on the Ethereum blockchain. On a CPMM, anyone can create a liquidity pool for an arbitrary token pair. Once created, liquidity providers deposit amounts of equal value of both tokens into the pool. Traders swap tokens with the pool's liquidity and pay a small trading fee, which is distributed pro-rata among all liquidity providers. To execute such a transaction on the blockchain, traders first submit their transaction to the Ethereum *mempool* and wait for a miner to include them in the next block.

The CPMM smart contract determines the output amount the trader receives. The amount returned by the CPMM ensures that the product of the two reserve amounts stays constant. More precisely, consider a pool that holds reserves of a token A and token B. Assume the reserves are R_A token A and R_B token B, and that a trader wants to swap t_A token A. The trader then receives

$$t_B = R_B - \frac{R_A R_B}{R_A + (1-f)t_A} = \frac{R_B(1-f)t_A}{R_A + (1-f)t_A},$$

where f is the transaction fee charged on the input amount (0.3% in Uniswap) [1]. Thus, when swapping an amount of t_A token A, the price per token B is $\frac{R_A + (1-f)t_A}{R_B(1-f)}$. We note that the price per token is increasing in the input amount. The larger the trade gets, the more the trader has to pay per desired token. This effect is a consequence of a trade's *price impact* – the impact of an individual trade on the market price. We also see in the formula above, that a trade's price impact is lower in pools with larger reserves. Thus, it is both the ratio of its assets and the liquidity of the pool that determine the price.

4 Data Description

We analyze data from Uniswap and SushiSwap: Ethereum's two largest DEXes by trading volume. Together they represent the majority of the market, as they account for more than half of Ethereum's DEX trading volume [9]. Further, both use the exact same trading mechanism, making them ideal for analyzing price inaccuracies between markets. More precisely, we collect pool reserve and transaction data between 5 August 2020 and 23 January 2021 for all pools between any of the following five cryptocurrencies: Bitcoin (BTC), Ethereum (ETH), Tether (USDT), USD Coin (USDC), and Dai (DAI). These are some of the most traded tokens and are among those which share the highest number of pools with other cryptocurrencies [11]. Thus, they are well suited for our analysis. The high number of pairwise pools provides a large set of independent paths between cryptocurrency pairs to find optimizable routes and cyclic arbitrage opportunities. For a thorough data description, see Appendix A.

5   Identifying Market Inefficiencies

To find market inefficiencies and study how they evolved over time, we analyze both the optimizability of past transactions and the opportunity for cyclic arbitrage. Price differences, the root cause of suboptimal trades, and cyclic arbitrage opportunities reflect the market's ability to reflect the relevant information.

5.1   Suboptimal Trade Routing

We start with an example of a trade that was executed at an unfavorable rate to illustrate the meaning of suboptimal trade routing (Fig. 1). On 15 November 2020, the original trade exchanged ETH for 16.61 BTC. The trade routed through the ETH-BTC SushiSwap pool, as we show on the left in Fig. 1. We visualize an optimization that executes 99.75% of the trade in the Uniswap pool and only 0.25% of the trade in the SushiSwap pool. By routing the transaction as shown, the trader would have received 18.07 BTC – an 8.79% improvement. We notice that the Uniswap trade offered a better price for this trade. Thus, the market was unsynced at this moment, and thereby prices in at least one pool did not reflect all relevant information – indicative of market inefficiency. As a result of the large trade size, it was optimal to route a small part of the trade through the SushiSwap pool to reduce the trade's price impact.

Fig. 1. Example of original and optimizable swap. The Uniswap pools are represented by solid lines and SushiSwap pools are represented by dashed lines.

We analyze past transactions over $30'000 from 12 September 2020 to 23 January 2021 and check whether they were routed optimally. We focus on large trades since they have a more significant price impact, and the benefit from an optimal routing is greater for these trades compared to smaller ones. These trades are, thus, particularly well suited to study in order to detect inefficiencies in the market. We also note that we exclude swaps that are part of a transaction including multiple swaps. While some of these swaps could be optimizable, others might already be part of optimized routing. Then optimizing one of them without considering the others would overestimate the possibility for optimization.

To identify trades that received unfavorable prices, we apply a special case of the optimal trade routing problem studied by Danos et al. [7]. They provide the solution to the optimal routing problem for trades through a set of independent paths. The solution accounts for the CPMM's transactions fees. We construct the set of independent paths as follows: we include both direct routes (Uniswap and SushiSwap) if they exist. The direct route is the pool containing the input and output tokens. For paths containing multiple pairs, we consider the more liquid Uniswap pool (Fig. 6a). We search for transactions whose output can be increased by more than $30 with optimized routing and consider them optimizable. The threshold accounts for additional gas fees related to potentially routing the trade through several routes. The potential for such optimization indicates either the existence of price inaccuracies or that the market is illiquid.

29'611 out of 108'667 analyzed transactions (Fig. 5) were optimizable – a share of 27%. On average, it is possible to increase the output of an optimizable trade by 0.15% (Table 1) by using an optimized routing. While it might not appear to be a significant proportion, the 0.15% is an invisible tax placed on trades stemming from price inaccuracies present in the market. We further observe that the mean gain is considerably higher than the median gain, suggesting that the tax on the most affected traders is significantly higher. Looking at the top 5% trades, where optimized routing would improve by price most significantly (in percentage terms), we find that the average achievable gain was 0.71% (Table 1). Further, indicating that traders are suffering from these market inefficiencies.

Table 1. Gains achieved by optimized routings.

	All Trades	Top 5% Trades
Mean Gain	0.15%	0.71%

To check whether the market inefficiencies stem from price inaccuracies or the potential lack of liquidity in the market, we analyze how many paths were used by the optimized routings (Fig. 2). We count a path if at least 0.1% of the trade routes through it. 18% of optimizable trades only use a single path with the new routing. Thus, this optimized routing does not include the original path at all. The unfavorable price received, thereby, solely stems from price inaccuracies. We note that the optimized routing for a small proportion of trades consists of at least three paths. There are at most five possible paths in the network (Appendix B, Fig. 6a). These relatively complex routings indicate that the liquidity of the pools also causes unfavorable rates received by large trades.

When we repeat the analysis and include the less liquid SushiSwap pools (Appendix B, Fig. 6b) in the set of independent paths, we find that the optimization potential increases. We perform this adjacent analysis on a smaller

Fig. 2. Proportions of number of paths used by optimized routings.

set of 43'321 swaps, which include all trades originally executed in the following pools: USDC-ETH (Uniswap and SushiSwap) and DAI-ETH (SushiSwap). Here, we find that an even larger proportion of swaps, 33.75% compared to 27% previously, could have been optimized. Further, the average gains are higher in the less liquid pools (Table 2). We find that routing through lower liquidity pools leads to better optimizing possibilities. Thus, it seems to be price inaccuracies across the market driving the unfavorable rates as opposed to the lack of liquidity in parts of the market – indicative of the presence of market inefficiencies in (parts of) the market. The significant number of trades with unfavorable rates shows that traders are experiencing the consequences of these inefficiencies.

Table 2. Gains achieved by optimized routings percent for the two sets of pools.

	More Liquid Pools	Less Liquid Pools
Mean Gain	0.15%	0.16%

5.2 Cyclic Arbitrage Opportunities

Cyclic arbitrage opportunities result from temporary price inaccuracies. By taking advantage of non-equilibrium exchange rates within and between markets, arbitrage traders can profit by trading their funds in a cycle. However, the existence of such opportunities suggests market inefficiency. The exchange rate of at least one pool in such a cycle must not accurately reflect all relevant information. Studying the prevalence and duration of these cycles brings inside new market insights beyond the unfavorable prices experienced by traders.

We identify cyclic arbitrage opportunities retrospectively by searching for directed cycles of pools where a cyclic swap with α tokens A, the returns $\hat{\alpha}$ tokens A where $\hat{\alpha} > \alpha$. In a cycle $c = (e_1, \ldots, e_n)$ each edge e_i present in the cycle represents a pool used in the transactions. For each arbitrage opportunity, we compute the maximum possible profit. The problem's convexity [8] lets us find the optimal, unique solution that maximizes the profit $\hat{\alpha} - \alpha$.

Over six months, from 5 August 2020 to 23 January 2021, we analyze the occurrence of cyclic arbitrage opportunities between ETH, USDC, and USDT on Uniswap. These three cryptocurrencies have the largest pairwise Uniswap pools between them. We plot the daily number of blocks with arbitrage opportunities exceeding 30$ and ETH's daily price movement in Fig. 3. Daily price movement is a volatility measure and given by is $100\% \cdot \frac{p_{high} - p_{low}}{p_{low}}$. Here, p_{high} is the day's highest price and p_{low} is the day's lowest price.

Most arbitrage opportunities are between August and September 2020 (Fig. 3). In this period, Uniswap experienced an incredible increase in daily trading volume. Within six weeks, the volume increased steadily by around 700%,

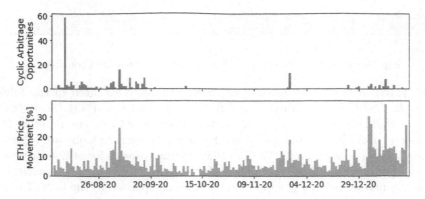

Fig. 3. Daily number of blocks with cyclic arbitrage opportunities and ETH price movement between 5 August 2020 and 23 January 2021.

reaching $500 million at the end of September. Similar daily trading volumes were not consistently reached again until early January 2021. Arbitrage opportunities also experience a sharp decrease starting at the end of September, and we only begin to see a consistent uptake at the end of December. In general, the number of arbitrage opportunities appears to decrease throughout the analyzed period – indicating that the market is becoming more efficient. We observe a second trend when comparing the number of daily arbitrage opportunities to ETH's price movement. With 0.15, the correlation between the two is relatively low. However, after the initial explosion in volume in the summer/autumn of 2020, we find that on days with exceptionally high price movements, we also observe exceptionally many arbitrage opportunities.

To further investigate the influence of external cryptocurrency prices on the number of arbitrage opportunities, we search for cycles in five pools on Uniswap and SushiSwap between ETH, USDC, USDT, DAI, and BTC during the following two periods: (1) 11 September to 3 October 2020, and (2) 23 December 2020 to 23 January 2021. The first period analyzed is characterized by relatively stable cryptocurrency prices – the price of ETH moved by less than 8%. The second period, however, is characterized by highly volatile cryptocurrency prices – the price of ETH more than doubled. By then, the pools containing BTC had accumulated enough liquidity, and we included them in the analysis. The analyzed networks during both periods are shown in Figs. 7a and 7b (Appendix B).

Table 3. Statistics of cyclic arbitrage profits in the two analyzed periods.

	Blocks with Cyclic Arb.	Mean Profit	Avg. Duration
11.09.20–03.10.20	84	0.24%	2.33 blocks
23.12.20–23.01.21	1'061	0.35%	1.43 blocks

We find that 84 out of 140,000 blocks have arbitrage cycles with a mean profit of 0.24% in the first period (Table 3). Stable cryptocurrency prices appear to not allow for many arbitrage opportunities, even in the face of the recent introduction of SushiSwap at the time. The markets' exchange rates are synced. In the second period, we find 1061 blocks with cyclic arbitrage opportunities, and, on average, they present a profit of 0.351% (Table 3).

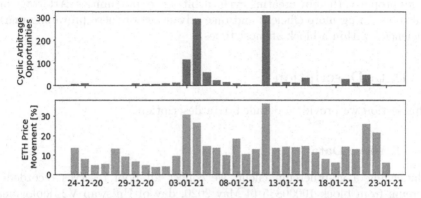

Fig. 4. Daily number of blocks with cyclic arbitrage opportunities and ETH price movement from 23 December 2020 to 23 January 2021.

As suspected, the number of cyclic arbitrage opportunities is significantly higher in the second period, where cryptocurrencies prices are highly volatile. To show the correlation, we plot the distribution of arbitrage opportunities and ETH's price movement in Fig. 4. Two days, 4 January and 11 January 2021, make up for over 50% of all identified opportunities. The price of ETH experienced temporary movements exceeding 20% on both days. Further, the correlation between the number of arbitrage opportunities and the ETH price movement is 0.72. We conclude that, as expected, higher price volatility is more favorable for arbitrage. The floating exchange rates on Uniswap and SushiSwap do not adjust to market price sufficiently fast. For every cyclic arbitrage opportunity, there is at least one pool whose price does not reflect all relevant information. We also observe that arbitrage bots, who profit from the BEV caused by market inefficiencies, become more efficient in the months between the two periods. The arbitrage opportunities are available for 2.33 blocks on average in the first period and only available for 1.43 blocks on average in the second period (Table 3). Since the minimum availability of an arbitrage opportunity we observe is 1, this improvement in the efficiency of arbitrage bots is significant.

6 Conclusion

Traders are actively suffering from market inefficiencies on DEXes: nearly 30% of analyzed trades were executed at an unfavorable price. We show that these erroneous rates stem largely from price inaccuracies across the market's liquidity pools. The market struggled to accurately reflect all relevant price information, especially during the initial volume explosion on DEXes in the late summer of 2020 – evident from the increased number of cyclic arbitrage opportunities. However, the market quickly adapts, and the price inaccuracies largely disappear. Later, we only observe market inefficiencies on days when cryptocurrency prices are highly volatile. Parts of the market do not adjust to external price changes properly, thereby creating cyclic arbitrage opportunities. Arbitrage bots are also becoming more efficient and take advantage of these prevailing market inefficiencies within a block at most times.

A   Data Description

In this section we provide a detailed data description.

A.1   Reserve Data

By launching a go-ethereum client, we collect all pool reserves recorded on Ethereum from block 10000835 (4 May 2020, day of Uniswap V2 deployment) to block 11709847 (23 January 2021) for Uniswap. For SushiSwap, the client exports all pool reserves from block 10750000 (28 August 2020, day of SushiSwap deployment) to block 11709847 (23 January 2021).

A.2   Transaction Data

We collect the transaction data required for the optimal trading analysis from The Graph's Uniswap V2 subgraph[1] and The Graph's SushiSwap subgraph[2] with GraphQL. The Graph is a decentralized protocol for indexing and querying data from blockchains like Ethereum.

For each transaction between block 10000835 and block 11709847, we collect the amounts of tokens swapped, as well as the value of the swap in $. While the subgraphs we use also provide pool reserves, these are updated infrequently and therefore could not be used. For this reason, we collect pool reserves with the go-ethereum client.

We pre-process the transaction data to reflect the reserves at the beginning of each block. These reserves coincide with those at the end of the previous block and are the only information most traders use when submitting their transaction (assuming their transaction is included in the next block). Depending on other transactions executed ahead of the swap in the same block, the pool reserves might shift slightly before trade execution and thus change the exchange rate. We correct this effect by pre-processing the data accordingly such that the transactions reflect the trader's view – based on which we optimize in Sect. 5.1.

---

[1] https://thegraph.com/explorer/subgraph/uniswap/uniswap-v2.
[2] https://thegraph.com/explorer/subgraph/benesjan/sushi-swap.

A.3 Pool Network

Figure 5 visualizes the number of independent swaps exceeding $30'000 in both Uniswap and Suhiswap between 12 September 2020 and 23 January 2021. In Uniswap we have a pool between almost every pair of tokens, while for Suhiswap the liquid pools during the observed time period all included ETH. Nonetheless, even on Uniswap most large trades are executed in pools that include ETH.

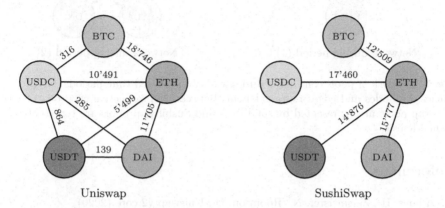

Uniswap   SushiSwap

Fig. 5. The number of independent trades exceeding $30'000 in each existing pool between any pair of the following cryptocurrencies: BTC, ETH, USDC, USDT and DAI, in Uniswap (Fig. 5a) and Suhiswap (Fig. 5b). Data was collected between 12 September 2020 and 23 January 2021.

B Networks

We show the networks used to find optimized routing in Fig. 6 and the networks used to find cyclic arbitrage opportunities in Fig. 7.

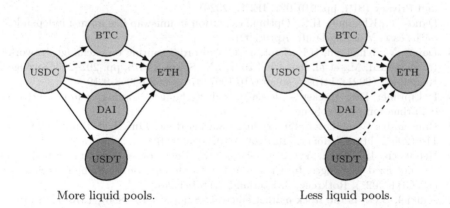

More liquid pools.   Less liquid pools.

Fig. 6. Paths from USDC to ETH for both cases. Uniswap pools are represented by solid lines and SushiSwap pools are represented by dashed lines.

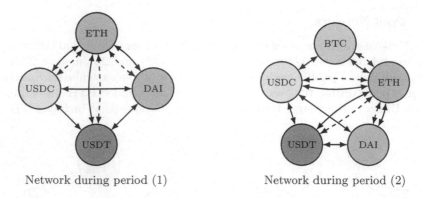

Network during period (1)   Network during period (2)

Fig. 7. Network of pools considered during the two analyzed time periods. Cryptocurrencies are nodes and edges represent pools between the respective cryptocurrencies. Uniswap pools are represented by solid lines and SushiSwap pools are represented by dashed lines.

References

1. Adams, H., Zinsmeister, N., Robinson, D.: Uniswap v2 core (2020)
2. Angeris, G., Chitra, T.: Improved price oracles: constant function market makers. In: Proceedings of the 2nd ACM Conference on Advances in Financial Technologies, pp. 80–91. AFT '20, Association for Computing Machinery, New York, NY, USA (2020)
3. Angeris, G., Kao, H.T., Chiang, R., Noyes, C., Chitra, T.: An analysis of uniswap markets. arXiv preprint arXiv:1911.03380 (2019)
4. Bernard, V., Thomas, J., Wahlen, J.: Accounting-based stock price anomalies: separating market inefficiencies from risk. Contemp. Account. Res. **14**(2), 89–136 (1997)
5. Buterin, V.: Ethereum whitepaper (2013). https://ethereum.org/en/whitepaper/
6. Daian, P., et al.: Flash boys 2.0: frontrunning in decentralized exchanges, miner extractable value, and consensus instability. In: 2020 IEEE Symposium on Security and Privacy (SP), pp. 910–927. IEEE (2020)
7. Danos, V., Khalloufi, H.E.: Optimal execution in uniswap like amms: independent paths case. Working Draft, April 2021
8. Danos, V., Khalloufi, H.E., Prat, J.: Global order routing on exchange networks. In: Bernhard, M., et al. (eds.) FC 2021. LNCS, vol. 12676, pp. 207–226. Springer, Heidelberg (2021). https://doi.org/10.1007/978-3-662-63958-0_19
9. DeFiprime: Dex tracker - decentralized exchanges trading volume. https://defiprime.com/dex-volume
10. Hanson, R.: Combinatorial information market design. Inf. Syst. Front. **5**(1), 107–119 (2003). https://doi.org/10.1023/A:1022058209073
11. Heimbach, L., Wang, Y., Wattenhofer, R.: Behavior of liquidity providers in decentralized exchanges. In: Crypto Valley Conference on Blockchain Technology (CVCBT 2021), Rotkreuz, Switzerland, October 2021
12. Malkiel, B.G.: Is the stock market efficient? Science **243**(4896), 1313–1318 (1989)
13. Nakamoto, S.: Bitcoin whitepaper (2008). https://bitcoin.org/bitcoin.pdf

14. Qin, K., Zhou, L., Gervais, A.: Quantifying blockchain extractable value: how dark is the forest? arXiv preprint arXiv:2101.05511 (2021)
15. Stiglitz, J.E.: The inefficiency of the stock market equilibrium. Rev. Econ. Stud. **49**(2), 241–261 (1982)
16. Wang, Y., Chen, Y., Deng, S., Wattenhofer, R.: Cyclic arbitrage in decentralized exchange markets (2021)
17. Zhou, L., Qin, K., Gervais, A.: A2MM: mitigating frontrunning, transaction reordering and consensus instability in decentralized exchanges. arXiv preprint arXiv:2106.07371 (2021)
18. Zunino, L., Tabak, B.M., Figliola, A., Pérez, D.G., Garavaglia, M., Rosso, O.A.: A multifractal approach for stock market inefficiency. Phys. A **387**(26), 6558–6566 (2008)

SoK: Mitigation of Front-Running in Decentralized Finance

Carsten Baum[1], James Hsin-yu Chiang[2]([✉]), Bernardo David[3],
Tore Kasper Frederiksen[4], and Lorenzo Gentile[3]

[1] Aarhus University, Aarhus, Denmark
cbaum@cs.au.dk
[2] Technical University of Denmark, Lyngby, Denmark
jchi@dtu.dk
[3] IT University of Copenhagen, Copenhagen, Denmark
bernardo@bmdavid.com, lorg@itu.dk
[4] Alexandra Institute, Aarhus, Denmark
tore.frederiksen@alexandra.dk

Abstract. Front-running is the malicious, and often illegal, act of both manipulating the order of pending trades and injecting additional trades to make a profit at the cost of other users. In decentralized finance (DeFi), front-running strategies exploit both public knowledge of user trades from transactions pending on the network and the miner's ability to determine the final transaction order. Given the financial loss and increased transaction load resulting from adversarial front-running in decentralized finance, novel cryptographic protocols have been proposed to mitigate such attacks in the permission-less blockchain setting. We systematize and discuss the state-of-the-art of front-running mitigation in decentralized finance, and illustrate remaining attacks and open challenges.

1 Introduction

Specific instances of front-running in decentralized finance (DeFi) were first quantified by Daian et al. [18] and systematized by Eskandari et al. [23]. Besides imposing a financial penalty on honest users, front-running can also degrade the performance of blockchain networks, as recently observed on the Avalanche blockchain [3]. In order to evaluate the efficacy of front-running mitigation techniques, we first formulate the set of adversarial powers which permit front-running strategies to be exploited: concretely, if users submit their intended

J. Hsin-yu Chiang—This work was supported by the PhD School of DTU Compute.
B. David—This work was supported by the Concordium Foundation and by the Independent Research Fund Denmark (IRFD) grants number 9040-00399B (TrA²C), 9131-00075B (PUMA) and 0165-00079B.
T. K. Frederiksen—This work was supported by "Sikker brug af følsomme data", Performance Contract 2020 and "Digital sikkerhed, tillid og dataetik", Performance Contract 2021–2024, Ministry of Higher Education and Science, Denmark".
L. Gentile—This work was supported by the Concordium Foundation.

© International Financial Cryptography Association 2023
S. Matsuo et al. (Eds.): FC 2022 Workshops, LNCS 13412, pp. 250–271, 2023.
https://doi.org/10.1007/978-3-031-32415-4_17

interaction to a pool of pending transactions, the front-running adversary has
the ability to:

1. Append pending transactions to the blockchain.
2. Infer user intentions from pending transactions and blockchain state.

In this work, we describe common **front-running attacks** (Sect. 2) and assess
three front-running **mitigation categories** (Sect. 3) for their isolated and combined efficacy in neutralizing front-running (Fig. 1). We introduce a speculative
sandwich attack on input batching techniques (Sect. 3.2), which can be mitigated
with private user balances and secret input stores (Sect. 3.3).

Adversarial power	§3 **Mitigation**		
1. Transaction sequencing	§3.1 Fair ordering		
	§3.2 Batching of blinded inputs	Commit & reveal	
2. Inference of user intent		Input aggregation	
	§3.3 Private user balances & secret input store		

Fig. 1. Overview of mitigation techniques

Fair ordering (Sect. 3.1), implemented at the consensus protocol layer, ensures
that the local receipt-order of gossiped transactions seen by a node is consistent with the final transaction ordering in the blockchain. We observe that *fair
ordering* effectively mitigates the miner's ability to freely sequence transactions,
but introduces a front-running adversary which rushes the network.

		User balance & input store	
		Public	Private, secret
Batching of	Commit & reveal	Speculative	Taint of user balances
blinded inputs	**Input aggregation**	Sandwich Attacks	-

Fig. 2. Efficacy: batching of blinded inputs.

Batching of blinded inputs (Sect. 3.2) replaces the *sequential* model of DeFi
interaction with a *round-based* one, where user inputs are blinded in each round
to ensure input independence, thereby thwarting front-running strategies that
rely on prior knowledge of other users' intentions. However, if user balances
are public, the input may still be partially inferred when the valid user's input
space is constrained by its balance: here, we contribute a novel, *speculative* front-
running attack that exploits the *direction* of an automated market maker (AMM)
swap, leaked from the victim's public balance. Furthermore, we highlight differences between *commit & reveal* and *input aggregation* approaches to batching

of blinded inputs (Fig. 2). In commit & reveal schemes, user inputs are revealed *individually*: Although front-running in the specific round is no longer possible, they necessarily leak information about the subsequent balance-update for each participating user, even if the user balances are private. If the taint of private balances is sufficiently strong, this can allow the front-running adversary to infer the users future inputs (e.g. the intended AMM swap direction).

Private user balances (Sect. 3.3) are thus necessary to prevent the leakage of the valid user input space from balances and application state. Although DeFi state must generally remain public to retain its utility [2], we show that it is necessary to shield certain fragments thereof which explicitly reveal future user intent. **Secret input stores** (Sect. 3.3) protect inputs that are evaluated by the application after a time delay [46] or, in the case of order books, whenever a match with other user inputs [7,24] can be found.

2   Front-Running Attacks

AMM Sandwich: We briefly summarize the functionality of constant product AMM's, namely, a liquidity pool holding token balances, r_0 and r_1, of two different token types, τ_0 and τ_1 respectively, s.t. $r_0 \cdot r_1$ is *always* constant when swaps are being carried out between τ_0 and τ_1. A user swaps units of τ_0 for units of τ_1 by authorizing a *left swap* action $\mathsf{SL}(v : \tau_0, w : \tau_1)$. Here, the user is sending $v : \tau_0$ to the AMM in return for at least $w : \tau_1$ (swap limit). For this left swap to be valid, the product of the reserves must be maintained. Thus, the following relation between initial and updated reserves must hold: $r_0 \cdot r_1 = (r_0 + v) \cdot (r_1 - w')$, where $w' \geq w$ and w' represents the units of τ_1 that the user actually gets. We refer w as the swap *limit*. A *right swap* of $\mathsf{SR}(v : \tau_0, w : \tau_1)$ follows similarly: the user sends $w : \tau_1$ for at least $v : \tau_0$ in return such that $r_0 \cdot r_1 = (r_0 - v') \cdot (r_1 + w)$ and $v' \geq v$ where v' represents the units of τ_0 received. Constant product AMM's exhibit *slippage*: subsequent swaps in the same direction exhibit decreasing exchange rates.

User swaps can be "sandwiched", exploiting slippage for the gain of the attacker. Consider a left swap $\mathsf{A} : \mathsf{SL}(v_\mathsf{A} : \tau_0, w_\mathsf{A} : \tau_1)$ submitted by user A. A front-run swap by attacker M in the same direction reduces the exchange rate for the subsequent victim swap: a final back-run swap by M in the opposing direction then profits from an improved exchange rate.

$$\mathsf{M} : \mathsf{SL}(v_\mathsf{M}^\mathsf{f} : \tau_0, w_\mathsf{M}^\mathsf{f} : \tau_1) \quad \mathsf{A} : \mathsf{SL}(v_\mathsf{A} : \tau_0, w_\mathsf{A} : \tau_1) \quad \mathsf{M} : \mathsf{SR}(v_\mathsf{M}^\mathsf{b} : \tau_0, w_\mathsf{M}^\mathsf{b} : \tau_1)$$

Optimal front-run $(v_\mathsf{M}^\mathsf{f}, w_\mathsf{M}^\mathsf{f})$ and back-run $(v_\mathsf{M}^\mathsf{b}, w_\mathsf{M}^\mathsf{b})$ parameters are a function of the victim's swap, inferred from the pending victim transaction gossiped across the network [5].

Scheduled AMM Sandwich: For certain AMM variants, the knowledge of the user's intent to perform a swap can be directly inferred from the blockchain state. Paradigm [46] propose scheduled AMM swaps, or more generally, *scheduled* *inputs.* Let A : SL(15 : τ_0, 10 : τ_1, r) be a swap that is not executed immediately, but scheduled for evaluation together with the first user-AMM interaction *following* blockchain round r, thus requiring no further interaction from A. Since *scheduled* orders are stored in the AMM smart contract and evaluated at the beginning of a known round, the sandwich attack strategy can be exploited, albeit over two block rounds [46]: the front-run is sequenced at the end of round r and the back-run as the first newly submitted swap of round r + 1.

Generalized Front-run Attacks: In decentralized finance, actions exist which are *profitable* for the authorizing user, but which can also be performed by any other agent with a sufficient balance. In the permissionless blockchain setting, *generalized front-runners*, a term coined by Daian [38], are automated agents that identify profitable, pending transactions, which can be authorized by *any* user, and simply replicate these with their own account, thereby depriving the original transaction submitter of it's profit. Since the security of DeFi applications rely on rational agents to solve for profitable arbitrage [21,45,48] and liquidation [41] strategies, the presence of generalized front-running threatens to restrict such opportunities to agents colluding with miners.

3   Mitigation Categories

3.1   Fair Ordering

A recent line of research [30,31,34] has formalized an intuitive notion of γ-*receipt-order-fairness*: given two distinct transactions tx and tx' broadcast by users, receipt-order-fairness of a consensus protocol ensures that tx will be finalized prior to tx' if a γ fraction of network nodes receives tx prior to tx'. However, Kelkar et al. [30] show that even if all nodes agree on the relative order in which any *pair* of transactions were first observed at the gossip stage, a global transaction ordering of all transactions consistent with the local view of pair-wise orderings is not always possible (Condorcet Paradox). Instead, a weaker notion of γ-*batch-order-fairness* is realized in [31], where tx will be sequenced prior to or in the same block as tx' if a γ node fraction receives tx first.

Front-Running Despite Fair Ordering: Although order fairness removes the miner or round leader's privilege to sequence transactions, it assumes that users have secure channels to servers participating in consensus: in practice, however, public blockchains rely on gossip networks to propagate pending transactions. Here, the *rushing* network adversary can control the receipt-order of transactions for each consensus node, thereby rendering the notion of γ-*batch-order-fairness* meaningless. In practice, such a network adversary model may be excessively strong: whereas in the standard setting the miner or round leader incurs no additional cost for front-running victims, a non-trivial communication cost is now imposed on the rushing adversary. Still, since order-fairness clearly cannot *eliminate* front-running attacks in the (realistic) gossip-network setting, the motivation for stronger front-running mitigation properties remains.

3.2   Batching of Blinded Inputs

Batching of blinded inputs is a technique to ensure 1) the independence between user inputs and 2) the prevention of any adversarial sequencing of inputs. Interactions occur in rounds: in each, inputs are committed during the *input-phase*, followed by an *output phase* where the application state is updated after evaluating user inputs with valid parameters. The *collection* of inputs can occur in a smart contract or by a committee executing a cryptographic protocol which authorizes the distribution of funds from a smart contract in the output phase. The update of the application state following each round can result from the evaluation of valid inputs in *randomized* order or an application-specific *aggregation* thereof: for example, a subset of submitted AMM swaps can be aggregated into a single resulting swap. In batching of blinded inputs, we distinguish between **commit & reveal** and **input aggregation** (Fig. 3). Both schemes commit inputs in the input-phase of each round, thereby ensuring input independence. However, while input aggregation keeps the users' input private indefinitely, commit & reveal schemes leak individual user inputs when commitments are opened, thereby offering no *input privacy* by definition. Input privacy is necessary to prevent front-running in *subsequent* interaction rounds: past inputs leak information about updates to private balances (Sect. 3.3), which in turn can be exploited by front-runners, as balances constrain the valid user input space.

		Input independence	Input privacy	Open challenges
Commit & reveal	Hash commitments*	-	-	*Output bias*
	Timed commitments*	●	-	*Delay parameters*
	Threshold encryption**	●	-	*Honest majority*
	Secure multi-party computation**	●	-	*Honest majority*
Input aggregation		●	●	*Abort penalty*
	Homomorphic encryption**	●	●	*Efficiency*

Fig. 3. Batching of blinded inputs sent to a smart contract* or committee**

Past user inputs $\xrightarrow{\text{reveal}}$ Private user balances $\xrightarrow{\text{reveal}}$ Future user inputs

In contrast, input aggregation only outputs the application state update: for aggregated AMM swaps, only reserve updates are revealed, and updates to user balances remain private, if private balances are supported. Naturally, input aggregation can only offer input privacy up to the input batch size.

Commit and Reveal: Although *hash commitments* collected by a smart contract may appear to be an obvious approach to implement the commit & reveal functionality, they suffer from *output bias*, as the adversary can selectively refrain from opening its commitment.

Time-lock puzzles [42] or *timed commitments* [11] generated by users and sent to a smart contract promise to eliminate output bias, since the adversary's commitment can be force-opened after a delay, guaranteeing the inclusion of its input in the output-phase. However, in the worst case, each user time-locked input must be solved separately by a constant number of squaring operations in a randomly sampled group, potentially rendering the approach impractical for larger batches of time-locked inputs [32]. Burdges and De Feo [14] propose a novel *delay encryption* notion and construction, which promises encryption of many inputs to a randomly sampled *session key*. Thus, all delay-encrypted inputs of a given batch can be decrypted after a single extraction process. Delay encryption [14] is constructed from isogeny-based cryptography, a recent and less-well studied class cryptographic assumptions. Finally, it remains an open challenge to match delay cryptography parameters to real-world delays which depend on assumed gate speeds used in practice.

Threshold encryption [22] can realize a commit & reveal scheme with the assumption of an *honest majority* committee holding trapdoor information of the encrypted inputs [44]. In each round, a key pair is produced by the execution of a *distributed key generation* (DKG) protocol and the public is opened, with which users encrypt their inputs in the given round. A subsequent opening of the corresponding secret key by the threshold committee enables the decryption of all inputs of the given round. However, should an encrypted user input fail to be finalized in the block-chain in a given round due to network congestion, the user's intent will be made public after the secret key is revealed for the given round without the user action being executed. Given this leakage, the front-running adversary may now anticipate the re-submission of the same user input in the next round.

Secure multi-party computation [27,47] (MPC) has been proposed [1,36] to realize a commit & reveal functionality with guaranteed input reveal in an anonymous fashion, also formalized as *anonymous committed broadcast* (ACB) in [1]. The anonymization of inputs is achieved by random *shuffling* of user inputs in an efficient manner. Here, *honest majority* MPC protocols [8,19] are favoured, as the output is guaranteed as long as the honest majority assumption holds true. To implement a DeFi application with MPC, an MPC-controlled smart contract is required, to which users send their funds prior to each round.

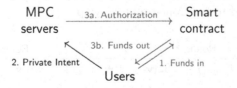

In the output phase of each MPC round, funds in the smart contract are redistributed to users according to the output(s) of the MPC execution. In practice, users can safely delegate the MPC execution to a group of servers [1].

Input Aggregation: Naturally, MPC can realize any aggregation function over private user inputs, and in some instances in an efficient manner. Given the emphasis on the privacy of inputs, *dishonest majority* MPC protocols [10,15,20] are favoured, which ensure that private inputs can never be obtained by the adversary as long as a single participant remains honest. Informal proposals to implement AMM instances in a dishonest majority MPC have been proposed by Li et al. [35]. Although dishonest majority MPC can be aborted by a single dishonest party, a recent line of research [6,7,33] has realized an efficient set of protocols that identify and financially punish the aborting adversary. This achieves a weaker notion of fairness as the rational adversary is incentivized to never abort. Still, the penalty must exceed the financial *option* value of aborting in order to be effective: given that inputs are private, it remains an open research question on how to size financial penalties for identifiable abort in MPC.

Penumbra [40] proposes the use of *homomorpic encryption* to realize the secure aggregation of homomorphically encrypted AMM swap orders. The aggregated swap is then decrypted to reveal the updated AMM reserves. User balances are implemented with private coins (see Sect. 3.3), thus the privacy of the inputs are only dependent on the batch size. We note the non-trivial complexity of aggregating a batch of encrypted AMM swaps with swap limit constraints: *efficient* secure multi-party computation with fully homomorphic encryption schemes remains an open research problem [26]. In [40], consensus validators are proposed to perform the secure computation, consolidating MPC and consensus layers.

Speculative Sandwich w/public User Balances: We illustrate that batching of blinded inputs alone is not sufficient to prevent front-running attacks. Instead, speculative AMM sandwich attacks are possible in blinded input batching schemes as long as the direction of the victim swap is known by the adversary. This can be inferred from *public* user balances, as detailed in the subsequent example. Such speculative sandwich attacks on batched inputs also assume that the adversary in the permissionless setting can "isolate" a single victim's input in a given round, such that only front-run and victim transactions remain: we argue that each batching round has participant limits due to gas constraints or number of clients that MPC servers can support. Thus, the adversary can occupy any arbitrary number of user slots per round and provide invalid inputs[1] on slots not dedicated to the front-running swap.

Round r	Round r+1
$M : SL(v_M^f : \tau_0, w_M^f : \tau_1)$ $A : SL(v_A : \tau_0, w_A : \tau_1)$	$M : SR(v_M^b : \tau_0, w_M^b : \tau_1)$

Fig. 4. Speculative sandwich

---

[1] e.g. AMM swap parameters which cannot be executed in the current AMM state.

In this speculative attack, we assume that private AMM swaps in each blinded input batch are evaluated in a *random* order, as proposed in [1,35]. The front-running M can only speculate on achieving the correct order to execute the sandwich. Since balances are public, M can observe that A's balance of τ_1 is zero: thus, A's submitted swap to the AMM (τ_0, τ_1) must be in the *left* direction. M submits the *front-run* swap in the same direction as the victim in the initial round r. We sketch the attack and refer to Appendix B for a detailed execution.

In the optimistic case shown in Fig. 4, M's front-run swap is evaluated *prior* to the victim swap (in round r), thus enabling M to position the profitable back-run swap in round $r + 1$, where all other users are prevented from submitting inputs. M's front-run parameters can be chosen such that the front-run swap simply does not execute should the front-run *not* be ordered prior to the victim swap in round r, thereby aborting the attack. We refer to Appendix C for the proof that this speculative sandwich is rational for the attacker.

Importantly, if victim A's swap direction were unknown, M would have to guess the direction of the front-running swap. An incorrect guess can result in a loss for M as shown in Appendix D. Thus, we argue that private user balances are necessary for batching of blinded inputs to be effective. Furthermore, for *scheduled* AMM orders introduced in [46], private user balances remain insufficient if scheduled orders are stored in public smart contracts: we sketch a speculative sandwich attack on publicly scheduled swaps in Appendix E. Finally, we note that hash-based commit & reveal schemes permit speculative sandwich attacks even when user balances are private, as the adversary can selectively reveal the appropriate sandwich strategy which matches on the swap first revealed by the victim (Appendix F).

3.3 Private and Secret State

As argued in Sect. 3.2, both the *aggregation* of blinded inputs and use of *private balances and secret input stores* is necessary to mitigate front-running in the current and future rounds. Whilst it may be possible to maintain the *entire* DeFi application state secretly in an MPC instance in order to prevent front-running, this will naturally reduce its utility to users in the permissionless setting. Notably, Angeris et al. [2,16] argue that both *marginal price* and *validity* of a given AMM swap order must be queryable for an AMM interaction to be meaningful. Therefore, we restrict our study of secret state in DeFi applications to *user input stores* [24,46], which maintain submitted inputs until they are evaluated or executed at a later point in time.

Private User Balances: Private block-chain currencies and tokens have been realized with zero-knowledge proof systems: *confidential transactions* [37] shield output amounts with efficient zero-knowledge *range proofs* [13], thereby ensuring that newly created output values do not exceed those spent by the same transaction. Confidential transactions only shield output amounts: a transaction graph connecting outputs can still be inferred from public transactions on the block-chain, permitting coin taint to propagate downstream.

Z-cash [43] style *decentralized anonymous payment* (DAP) schemes break such public links between outputs, as well-formed relations between new and spent outputs are not revealed but publicly verifiable with SNARK [9,25,28, 29,39] zero-knowledge proofs. DAP schemes have also been proposed for DeFi functionality in Manta [17], but here front-running is not mitigated, since the AMM reserve state is public and swap inputs are not batched. Even though swap parameters are blinded in Manta, each individual swap execution results in a *public* update of AMM reserves. Thus, the *affect* of each swap on the current AMM reserves is known, leaking exchanged amounts and permitting sandwich attack strategies.

Importantly, when implementing input batching (Fig. 3) with secure computation *and* block-chains supporting private user balances, zero-knowledge proofs must be generated inside the MPC instance in order to update private user balances. Doing so *efficiently* in MPC or even fully homomorphic encryption remains on open research question.

Finally, Submarine commitments [12] propose that users can rely on k-anonymity alone to privately commit funds during the input-phase without the use of private balances. Here, users commit value to an *k-anonymized* address which can only be withdrawn by a specific smart contract after the address is revealed together with the input by the user.

Secret Input Stores: We note that shielded scheduled AMM swaps [46] or long-running order lists [24] cannot be maintained by encryption alone: encryption of a scheduled swap by a user implies its decryption at a later stage, requiring repeated user interaction, and thus defeating the purpose of scheduled inputs. Alternatively, a decryption by an honest majority committee implies that the round or block-height of the input schedule is known. Instead, we suggest a long-running MPC instance to realize secret input stores in decentralized finance. Here, stored inputs are secret shared across MPC servers: in each round, both newly submitted inputs and secretly stored inputs are secretly evaluated together to update the application state, neither being visible to the front-running adversary.

A   Example: AMM Sandwich

We illustrate a step-wise execution of a sandwich in Fig. 5 and introduce notation for user and AMM state proposed in [4] for this purpose. The wallet of A is modelled as the term $A[v_i : \tau_0, ..., v_n : \tau_n]$, where $v_0, ..., v_n$ are the respective balances of token types $\tau_0, ..., \tau_n$. The state of an AMM holding token types τ_0 and τ_1 is given by its reserve balances $(r_0 : \tau_0, r_1 : \tau_1)$. Thus, we express the system state as a composition of wallets and reserve balances.

$$A[v : \tau] \mid (r_0 : \tau_0, r_1 : \tau_1)$$

Let the initial AMM balance be $(100 : \tau_0, 100 : \tau_1)$. User A wishes to perform the swap $A : \mathsf{SL}(15 : \tau_0, 10 : \tau_1)$. For simplicity, we assume unit values of τ_0

and τ_1 to be equal: given the ratio of AMM reserves is 1, there is no arbitrage opportunity to be exploited [4]. If A's order is executed immediately, A receives $13 : \tau_1$ for the $15 : \tau_0$ it sends to the AMM. Instead, however, if the user swap is sandwiched by attacker M (Fig. 5), A only obtains the minimum amount $10 : \tau_1$, implying a reduction of $3 : \tau_1$. Note that the reserve product is maintained at each execution step and that the sandwich execution preserves the initial reserve ratio: the attack leaves no arbitrage opportunity unexploited. The attacker M's profit of 5 units of τ_0 (or τ_1) is optimal [5]: A receives the minimum amount possible, namely its swap limit.

$$A[15 : \tau_0] \mid M[15 : \tau_0, 10 : \tau_1] \mid (100 : \tau_0, 100 : \tau_1)$$

$$\xrightarrow{M:SL(15:\tau_0,13:\tau_1)} A[15 : \tau_0] \mid M[23 : \tau_1] \mid (115 : \tau_0, 87 : \tau_1)$$

$$\xrightarrow{A:SL(15:\tau_0,10:\tau_1)} A[10 : \tau_1] \mid M[23 : \tau_1] \mid (130 : \tau_0, 77 : \tau_1)$$

$$\xrightarrow{M:SR(30:\tau_0,23:\tau_1)} A[10 : \tau_1] \mid M[30 : \tau_0] \mid (100 : \tau_0, 100 : \tau_1)$$

Fig. 5. Sandwich attack

B   Example: Speculative Sandwich

An execution of a speculative sandwich is shown in Figs. 6 and 7: here, adversary M observes victim A's interaction with an AMM which batches blinded inputs. A has a public balance of $20 : \tau_0$ only, allowing M to infer that A can only perform a *left* swap from τ_0 to τ_1 with an input amount of at most $20 : \tau_0$. The attack strategy is executed over two subsequent rounds beginning in the initial state shown in Fig. 6, where we assume unit values of τ_0 and τ_1 are equal.

$$A[20 : \tau_0] \mid M[7 : \tau_0, 15 : \tau_1] \mid (100 : \tau_0, 100 : \tau_1)$$

Round r

$$\xrightarrow{M:SL(7:\tau_0,6.5:\tau_1)} A[20 : \tau_0] \mid M[21.5 : \tau_1] \mid (107 : \tau_0, 93.5 : \tau_1)$$

$$\xrightarrow{A:SL(15:\tau_0,10:\tau_1)} A[5 : \tau_0, 11.5 : \tau_1] \mid M[21.5 : \tau_1] \mid (122 : \tau_0, 82 : \tau_1)$$

Round r + 1

$$\xrightarrow{M:SR(22:\tau_0,18:\tau_1)} A[5 : \tau_0, 11.5 : \tau_1] \mid M[22 : \tau_0, 3.5 : \tau_1] \mid (100 : \tau_0, 100 : \tau_1)$$

Fig. 6. Successful speculative sandwich

In the first round r, M submits the *front-run* swap in the same direction as the victim's, with *arbitrarily chosen* input amount $7 : \tau_0$. The minimum output amount or swap limit of the front-run is then is chosen to be $6.5 : \tau_1$ such that $(100 + 7) \cdot (100 - 6.5) = 100^2$ holds: thus, if the front-run were executed in the initial state, M would receive *exactly* its swap limit. Since all other user orders (other than the victim swap of A) are suppressed, there is a probability of 0.5 that the front-run is randomly evaluated *before* the victim's swap, as shown in Fig. 6. The *back-run* swap of M in the opposing direction then follows in the subsequent round with probability 1, since M suppresses all user actions other than its own back-run. Assuming equal unit value of both token types, the attack profit for M is 3.5.

Should the front-run ordering fail (Fig. 7), then M's front-run parameters are chosen such that the front-run swap will not execute, resulting in an abort of the speculative sandwich attack. This is due to the chosen front-run parameters: following the execution step of A's swap in Fig. 7, the constant product invariant can only hold if M receives $5 : \tau_1$ for the $7 : \tau_0$ it sends: $(115 + 7) \times (87 - 5) = 100^2$. However, this contradicts M swap limit of $6.5 : \tau_1$, such that the front-run cannot execute in the state following A's swap. M can still perform a back-run in round $r+1$, thereby restoring the initial reserve ratio and extracting an arbitrage profit of 2, which is less than in the successful speculative sandwich execution in Fig. 6. Still, the speculative sandwich attack is always profitable, as shown in Appendix C.

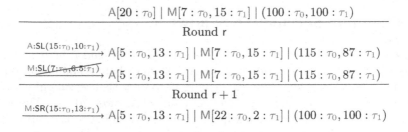

Fig. 7. Aborted speculative sandwich

C   Formalization: Speculative Sandwich

We formalize the example attack trace introduced in Fig. 4 and prove that the attack strategy is either profitable or cost-neutral for the attacker. Again, we assume unit value of τ_0, τ_1 to be equal, and the initial AMM reserve state to be $(r : \tau_0, r : \tau_1)$: in this state, there is no arbitrage opportunity to be exploited, simplifying our analysis. We omit both AMM and transaction fees.

The victim A swap direction is *left*, inferred by M from A's public balance of $v_A^{init} : \tau_0$ (A holds no units of τ_1). The attack strategy is as follows:

1. **Round r**: Front-run victim with $\mathsf{M} : \mathsf{SL}(\mathsf{v}_\mathsf{M}^\mathsf{f} : \tau_0, \mathsf{w}_\mathsf{M}^\mathsf{f} : \tau_1)$ such that

$$(\mathsf{r} + \mathsf{v}_\mathsf{M}^\mathsf{f}) \cdot (\mathsf{r} - \mathsf{w}_\mathsf{M}^\mathsf{f}) = \mathsf{r}^2 \tag{1}$$

2. **Round r + 1**: Back-run victim in opposing direction to reestablish initial AMM reserve ratio, or if attacker balance is insufficient, back-run with largest amount available to attacker M.

We must show that this strategy is always profitable (when the victim swap direction can be inferred by the attacker). We note that there are several variables beyond the attackers control. The ordering of both front-run and victim swap in round r is random. Thus the desired "front-run" ordering of the victim swap in round r may not succeed (the sandwich is unsuccessful if the victim swap precedes attacker front-run swap). Furthermore, the victim swap parameters can be arbitrarily chosen, so that the victim swap may not be *enabled* or execute in a given sequence. Thus, we must exhaustively demonstrate the profitability of the attacker strategy for all possible cases:

1) Successful sandwich & enabled victim swap
2) Successful sandwich & disabled victim swap
3) Unsuccessful sandwich & enabled victim swap
4) Unsuccessful sandwich & disabled victim swap

Case 1: *(successful sandwich & enabled victim swap)*: We illustrate the symbolic execution of the attack trace below in terms of initial balances, chosen swap parameters and exchanged amounts.

⓪ $\mathsf{A}[\mathsf{v}_\mathsf{A}^\mathsf{init} : \tau_0] \mid \mathsf{M}[\mathsf{v}_\mathsf{M}^\mathsf{init} : \tau_0, \mathsf{w}_\mathsf{M}^\mathsf{init} : \tau_1] \mid (\mathsf{r} : \tau_0, \mathsf{r} : \tau_1)$

Round r

$\xrightarrow{\mathsf{M}:\mathsf{SL}(\mathsf{v}_\mathsf{M}^\mathsf{f}:\tau_0,\mathsf{w}_\mathsf{M}^\mathsf{f}:\tau_1)}$ ① $\mathsf{A}[\mathsf{v}_\mathsf{A}^\mathsf{init} : \tau_0] \mid \mathsf{M}[\mathsf{v}_\mathsf{M}^\mathsf{init} - \mathsf{v}_\mathsf{M}^\mathsf{f} : \tau_0, \mathsf{w}_\mathsf{M}^\mathsf{init} + \mathsf{w}_\mathsf{M}^\mathsf{f} : \tau_1] \mid (\mathsf{r} + \mathsf{v}_\mathsf{M}^\mathsf{f} : \tau_0, \mathsf{r} - \mathsf{w}_\mathsf{M}^\mathsf{f} : \tau_1)$

$\xrightarrow{\mathsf{A}:\mathsf{SL}(\mathsf{v}_\mathsf{A}:\tau_0,\mathsf{w}_\mathsf{A}:\tau_1)}$ ② $\mathsf{A}[\mathsf{v}_\mathsf{A}^\mathsf{init} - \mathsf{v}_\mathsf{A} : \tau_0, \mathsf{w}_\mathsf{A}' : \tau_1] \mid \mathsf{M}[\mathsf{v}_\mathsf{M}^\mathsf{init} - \mathsf{v}_\mathsf{M}^\mathsf{f} : \tau_0, \mathsf{w}_\mathsf{M}^\mathsf{init} + \mathsf{w}_\mathsf{M}^\mathsf{f} : \tau_1] \mid$
$(\mathsf{r} + \mathsf{v}_\mathsf{M}^\mathsf{f} + \mathsf{v}_\mathsf{A} : \tau_0, \mathsf{r} - \mathsf{w}_\mathsf{M}^\mathsf{f} - \mathsf{w}_\mathsf{A}' : \tau_1)$

Round $r + 1$

$\xrightarrow{\mathsf{M}:\mathsf{SR}(\mathsf{v}_\mathsf{M}^\mathsf{b}:\tau_0,\mathsf{w}_\mathsf{M}^\mathsf{b}:\tau_1)}$ ③ $\mathsf{A}[\mathsf{v}_\mathsf{A}^\mathsf{init} - \mathsf{v}_\mathsf{A} : \tau_0, \mathsf{w}_\mathsf{A}' : \tau_1] \mid \mathsf{M}[\mathsf{v}_\mathsf{M}^\mathsf{init} - \mathsf{v}_\mathsf{M}^\mathsf{f} + \mathsf{v}_\mathsf{M}^{\mathsf{b}\,\prime} : \tau_0, \mathsf{w}_\mathsf{M}^\mathsf{init} + \mathsf{w}_\mathsf{M}^\mathsf{f} - \mathsf{w}_\mathsf{M}^\mathsf{b} : \tau_1] \mid$
$(\mathsf{r} + \mathsf{v}_\mathsf{M}^\mathsf{f} + \mathsf{v}_\mathsf{A} - \mathsf{v}_\mathsf{M}^{\mathsf{b}\,\prime} : \tau_0, \mathsf{r} - \mathsf{w}_\mathsf{M}^\mathsf{f} - \mathsf{w}_\mathsf{A}' + \mathsf{w}_\mathsf{M}^\mathsf{b} : \tau_1)$

We show that the attack is profitable. For τ_0 and τ_1 of equal unit value, the net change in *value* exchanged by M must be positive. Thus, we must prove

$$\mathsf{profit}_\mathsf{M} = -\mathsf{v}_\mathsf{M}^\mathsf{f} + \mathsf{w}_\mathsf{M}^\mathsf{f} - \mathsf{w}_\mathsf{M}^\mathsf{b} + \mathsf{v}_\mathsf{M}^{\mathsf{b}\,\prime} > 0 \tag{2}$$

Note that the amounts exchanged in the front-run are equal to the front-run parameters $(\mathsf{v}_\mathsf{M}^\mathsf{f}, \mathsf{w}_\mathsf{M}^\mathsf{f})$, as they are chosen such that (1) holds. We consider the **sub-case (a)** in which the attacker M has sufficient balance to perform the back-run swap such that the AMM reserves are restored to the original state and the **sub-case (b)** in which the attacker initially has no balance of τ_1 to perform the back-run: $w_M^{init} = 0$. Here, the funds of τ_1 required to execute the back-run are received entirely in the front-run execution.

For **sub-case (a)**, we rewrite (2) in terms of independently chosen parameters v_M^f, v_A (the attacker only knows the victim swap direction) and initial reserve amounts r. The reserves of the AMM are restored to the initial state in final state ③: summing all step changes to the reserves across the sandwich execution yields

$$r + v_M^f + v_A - v_M^{b\,'} = r \qquad r - w_M^f - w_A' + w_M^b = r$$
$$v_M^f + v_A - v_M^{b\,'} = 0 \qquad -w_M^f - w_A' + w_M^b = 0$$

or

$$v_M^{b\,'} = v_M^f + v_A \qquad w_M^b = w_M^f + w_A'$$

Inserting RHS of equations above into our proof obligation (2) yields

$$\text{profit}_M = -\cancel{v_M^f} + \cancel{v_M^f} + v_A + \cancel{w_M^f} - \cancel{w_M^f} - w_A' >^? 0$$
$$v_A - w_A' >^? 0 \tag{3}$$

To evaluate whether this inequality holds, we must solve for w_A' in terms of v_A and v_M^f chosen independently by the victim and adversary respectively. We exploit the constant reserve product invariant which holds for across the entire execution.

$$(r + v_M^f) \cdot (r - w_M^f) = r^2 \quad \text{(front-run swap)}$$
$$(r + v_M^f + v_A) \cdot (r - w_M^f - w_A') = r^2 \quad \text{(victim swap)}$$

We can derive $r - w_M^f = \frac{r^2}{r+v_M^f}$ from the first equation, and substitute the RHS for $r - w_M^f$ in the second equation to obtain

$$(r + v_M^f + v_A) \cdot \left(\frac{r^2}{r + v_M^f} - w_A'\right) = r^2$$

Solving for w_A' ...

$$\begin{aligned} w_A' &= \frac{r^2}{r + v_M^f} - \frac{r^2}{r + v_M^f + v_A} \\ &= \frac{r^2(r + v_M^f + v_A) - r^2(r + v_M^f)}{(r + v_M^f)(r + v_M^f + v_A)} \\ &= \frac{r^2}{r^2 + (2v_M^f + v_A)r + (v_M^f)^2 + v_A v_M^f} \cdot v_A \end{aligned}$$

and substituting the RHS for w_A' in the proof obligation in (3) finally yields

$$\text{profit}_M = (1 - \frac{r^2}{r^2 + (2v_M^f + v_A)r + (v_M^f)^2 + v_A v_M^f}) \cdot v_A > 0 \qquad (4)$$

The fraction expression above is less than 1 for any choice of positive v_M^f and v_A as the numerator is smaller than the denominator. The attacker profit is thus positive and increases with v_M, justifying the front-run swap by M.

Next, we consider the **sub-case (b)**, where the attacker initially has no balance of τ_1, and restate the profit of attacker for the reader's convenience.

$$\text{profit}_M = -v_M^f + w_M^f - w_M^b + v_M^b{}' >^? 0$$

We assume initial attacker balance in $w_M^{init} : \tau_1$ to be $0 : \tau_1$, so that all the amount of τ_1 available for the back-run in state ② is received in the front-run: thus, substituting $w_M^b = w_M^f$ into the equation above yields

$$\text{profit}_M = -v_M^f + v_M^b{}' >^? 0 \qquad (5)$$

To prove this inequality, we solve for $v_M^b{}'$ in terms of v_M^f and v_A chosen independently by the victim and adversary respectively and initial reserves amounts r. We exploit the constant reserve product invariant which holds throughout the execution.

$$(r + v_M^f) \cdot (r - w_M^f) = r^2 \quad \text{(Front-run)}$$
$$(r + v_M^f + v_A) \cdot (r - w_M^f - w_A') = r^2 \quad \text{(Victim swap)}$$
$$(r + v_M^f + v_A - v_M^b{}') \cdot (r - w_M^f - w_A' + w_M^b) = r^2 \quad \text{(Back-run)}$$

Since $w_M^f = w_M^b$ is assumed in sub-case (b), the 3rd equation (back-run) yields

$$v_M^b{}' = r + v_M^f + v_A - \frac{r^2}{r - w_A'} \qquad (6)$$

From the 2nd equation (victim swap), we solve for w_A' in terms of independent parameters v_M^f, v_A and r

$$w_A' = r - w_M^f - \frac{r^2}{r + v_M^f + v_A}$$

From the 1st equation (front-run) $w_M^f = \frac{r \cdot v_M^f}{r + v_M^f}$, so we can rewrite the above as

$$w_A' = r - \frac{r \cdot v_M^f}{r + v_M^f} - \frac{r^2}{r + v_M^f + v_A} = \frac{r^2}{r + v_M^f} - \frac{r^2}{r + v_M^f + v_A} = \frac{r^2 \cdot v_A}{(r + v_M^f)(r + v_M^f + v_A)}$$

$$r - w_A' = \frac{r(r + v_M^f)(r + v_M^f + v_A) - r^2 \cdot v_A}{(r + v_M^f)(r + v_M^f + v_A)}$$

Substituting the RHS above for $r - w'_A$ in the denominator expression of (6) and then substituting the RHS of (6) for $v_M^{b\,\prime}$ in (5) yields

$$\text{profit}_M = -\cancel{v_M^f} + r + \cancel{v_M^f} + v_A - \frac{r^2(r + v_M^f)(r + v_M^f + v_A)}{r(r + v_M^f)(r + v_M^f + v_A) - r^2 \cdot v_A}$$

$$= v_A - \frac{r^3 v_A}{r(r + v_M^f)(r + v_M^f + v_A) - r^2 \cdot v_A}$$

$$= (1 - \frac{r^2 v_A}{(r + v_M^f)(r + v_M^f + v_A) - r \cdot v_A}) \cdot v_A$$

$$= (1 - \frac{r^2}{r^2 + 2v_M^f r + (v_M^f)^2 + v_A v_M^f}) \cdot v_A \tag{7}$$

The attacker profit is positive but strictly less than the gain (4) obtained in sub-case (a).

Case 2 *(successful sandwich & disabled victim swap)*: Should the victim swap not execute in round r, then M can simply revert the state of the AMM with a back-run in the round $r + 1$ with the same parameter values as in the front-run.

$$\textcircled{0} \quad A[v_A^{init} : \tau_0] \mid M[v_A^{init} : \tau_0, w_A^{init} : \tau_1] \mid (r : \tau_0, r : \tau_1)$$

Round r

$$\xrightarrow{M:SL(v_M^f : \tau_0, w_M^f : \tau_1)} \textcircled{1} \quad A[v_A^{init} : \tau_0] \mid M[v_M^{init} - v_M^f : \tau_0, w_M^{init} + w_M^f : \tau_1] \mid (r + v_M^f : \tau_0, r - w_M^f : \tau_1)$$

$$\xrightarrow{A:SL(v_A : \tau_0, w_A : \tau_1)} \textcircled{2} \quad A[v_A^{init} : \tau_0] \mid M[v_M^{init} - v_M^f : \tau_0, w_M^{init} + w_M^f : \tau_1] \mid (r + v_M^f : \tau_0, r - w_M^f : \tau_1)$$

Round $r + 1$

$$\xrightarrow{M:SR(v_M^f : \tau_0, w_M^f : \tau_1)} \textcircled{3} \quad A[v_A^{init} : \tau_0] \mid M[v_M^{init} : \tau_0, w_M^{init} : \tau_1] \mid (r : \tau_0, r : \tau_1)$$

The attack execution is trivially cost-neutral for M.

Case 3 *(failed sandwich & enabled victim swap)*: We must show that the attacker front-run must be disabled assuming the attacker parameters are chosen as described in the attack strategy. Further, we can demonstrate that the back-run by the attacker is profitable.

$$\textcircled{0} \quad A[v_A^{init} : \tau_0] \mid M[v_M^{init} : \tau_0, w_M^{init} : \tau_1] \mid (r : \tau_0, r : \tau_1)$$

Round r

$$\xrightarrow{A:SL(v_A : \tau_0, w_A : \tau_1)} \textcircled{1} \quad A[v_A^{init} - v_A : \tau_0, w'_A : \tau_1] \mid M[v_M^{init} : \tau_0, w_M^{init} : \tau_1] \mid (r + v_A : \tau_0, r - w'_A : \tau_1)$$

$$\xrightarrow{M:SL(v_M^f : \tau_0, w_M^f : \tau_1)} \textcircled{2} \quad A[v_A^{init} - v_A : \tau_0, w'_A : \tau_1] \mid M[v_M^{init} : \tau_0, w_M^{init} : \tau_1] \mid (r + v_A : \tau_0, r - w'_A : \tau_1)$$

Round $r + 1$

$$\xrightarrow{M:SR(v_M^b : \tau_0, w_M^b : \tau_1)} \textcircled{3} \quad A[v_A^{init} - v_A : \tau_0, w'_A : \tau_1] \mid M[v_M^{init} + v_M^{b\,\prime} : \tau_0, w_M^{init} - w_M^b : \tau_1] \mid (r : \tau_0, r : \tau_1)$$

As described in step (1) of attack strategy, M's front-run parameters are chosen such that

$$(r + v_M^f) \cdot (r - w_M^f) = r^2$$

$$w_M^f = \frac{r \cdot v_M^f}{r + v_M^f} \tag{8}$$

Thus, the front-run swap is only enabled if the received amount is equal or greater to w_M^f shown above. Note, that this doesn't hold if the front-run is executed in state ① of case (3) following the enabled victim swap. We prove this by contradiction: assume that the front-run executes following the victim swap, then the constant reserve product invariant must hold.

$$(r + v_A) \cdot (r - w_A') = r^2 \quad \text{(Victim swap)}$$

$$(r + v_A + v_M^f) \cdot (r - w_A' - w_M^{f\,'}) = r^2 \quad \text{(Front-run)}$$

We solve for $(r - w_A')$ in the first equation and insert into the second equation to obtain

$$(r + v_A + v_M^f) \cdot \left(\frac{r^2}{r + v_A} - w_M^{f\,'} \right) = r^2$$

Further, we solve for $w_M^{f\,'}$ in terms of r, v_A and v_M^f

$$\frac{r^2}{r + v_A} - w_M^{f\,'} = \frac{r^2}{(r + v_A + v_M^f)}$$

$$w_M^{f\,'} = \frac{r^2}{r + v_A} - \frac{r^2}{r + v_A + v_M^f} = \frac{r^2 \cdot v_M^f}{(r + v_A) \cdot (r + v_A + v_M^f)} = \frac{r}{r + v_A} \cdot \frac{r \cdot v_M^f}{(r + v_A + v_M^f)}$$

Comparing with w_M^f in (8), we can infer the following inequality

$$w_M^{f\,'} < w_M^f$$

which cannot hold in a valid execution by definition of swaps: a user cannot receive less than the chosen swap limit. Thus, the front-run cannot be enabled in state ① of case (3).

Next, we prove the profitability of the back-run. Assuming a sufficient balance of the attacker to revert the effect of the victim swap, the swap parameters of the back-run can be chosen to reverse the affects of victim swap on the AMM reserves, which M observes following the output-phase of round r: namely, $v_M^b = v_A$ and $w_M^b = w_A'$. We insert these into the reserve product invariant from the victim swap

$$(r + v_A) \cdot (r - w_A') = r^2 \quad \text{(Victim swap)}$$

to obtain

$$(r + v_M^b) \cdot (r - w_M^b) = r^2$$
$$w_M^b = \frac{r}{r + v_M^b} \cdot v_M^b$$
$$w_M^b < v_M^b$$

For equal unit value of both token types, this is clearly profitable, as M receives more value (v_M^b) as it sends (w_M^b). If attacker has no balance of τ_1 it simply omits the back-run and the attack is aborted, resulting in a cost-neutral execution for the attacker.

Case 4 *(failed sandwich & disabled victim swap)*: As in case (2) - should the victim swap not execute in round r, then M can simply revert the state of the AMM with a back-run in the round $r + 1$

$$
\begin{array}{rl}
& ⓪ \quad A[v_A^{init} : \tau_0] \mid M[v_A^{init} : \tau_0, w_A^{init} : \tau_1] \mid (r : \tau_0, r : \tau_1) \\
\hline
& \text{Round r} \\
\xrightarrow{A:SL(v_A : \tau_0, w_A : \tau_1)} & ① \quad A[v_A^{init} : \tau_0] \mid M[v_M^{init} : \tau_0, w_M^{init} : \tau_1] \mid (r : \tau_0, r : \tau_1) \\
\xrightarrow{M:SL(v_M^f : \tau_0, w_M^f : \tau_1)} & ② \quad A[v_A^{init} : \tau_0] \mid M[v_M^{init} - v_M^f : \tau_0, w_M^{init} + w_M^f : \tau_1] \mid (r + v_M^f : \tau_0, r - w_M^f : \tau_1) \\
\hline
& \text{Round } r + 1 \\
\xrightarrow{M:SR(v_M^f : \tau_0, w_M^f : \tau_1)} & ③ \quad A[v_A^{init} : \tau_0] \mid M[v_M^{init} : \tau_0, w_M^{init} : \tau_1] \mid (r : \tau_0, r : \tau_1)
\end{array}
$$

The attack execution is trivially cost-neutral for M.

D   Speculative Sandwich with Private User Balances

Importantly, when performing the speculative AMM swap attack as shown in C, the direction of the victim swap must be known. If user balances are private, M will have to guess the direction of the front-running swap. However, this is not a profitable strategy: an incorrect guess can result in a loss for M as shown in the trivial example execution below.

$$
\begin{array}{rl}
& A[10 : \tau_0, 10 : \tau_1] \mid M[7 : \tau_0, 15 : \tau_1] \mid (100 : \tau_0, 100 : \tau_1) \\
\hline
& \text{Round r} \\
\xrightarrow{M:SL(7:\tau_0, 6.5:\tau_1)} & A[10 : \tau_0, 10 : \tau_1] \mid M[21.5 : \tau_1] \mid (107 : \tau_0, 93.5 : \tau_1) \\
\xrightarrow{A:SR(17:\tau_0, 6.5:\tau_1)} & A[7 : \tau_0, 3.5 : \tau_1] \mid M[21.5 : \tau_1] \mid (100 : \tau_0, 100 : \tau_1)
\end{array}
$$

Again, assuming equal unit value of τ_0 and τ_1, M realizes a loss of $7 + 15 - 21.5 = 0.5$. No back-run swap is possible that extracts any arbitrage value given that the reserve ratio is already consistent with the assumption that unit values of τ_0 and τ_1 are equal [4]. Thus, speculative sandwich attacks are only rational if the victim swap direction can be inferred, motivating the need for private user balances.

E   Example: Speculative Sandwich of Scheduled Swap

We illustrate an example of a sandwich of a scheduled swap. Such an attack can be exploited despite the batching of blinded user inputs Sect. 3.2, as long as input schedules remain public. Let $A : SL(20 : \tau_0, 15 : \tau_1, r)$ be a swap action that is scheduled to execute as soon as possible *following* block-chain round r, thus requiring no further interaction from the user. Further, let the set of scheduled swap orders be captured in a publicly observable state fragment, i.e. $\Gamma = [\, A : SL(15 : \tau_0, 10 : \tau_1, r) \,]$. In practice, such a scheduled swap order will be *evaluated* prior to the first swap order in round $r + 1$, so that it is not possible for the adversary to place a front-run swap before it in round $r + 1$.

However, the sandwich attack can still be executed by an adversary which prevents honest users from submitting swap. The adversary simply submits the front-run to round r, and the back-run to round $r + 1$, whilst suppressing all other user inputs.

$$A[15 : \tau_0] \mid M[15 : \tau_0, 10 : \tau_1] \mid (100 : \tau_0, 100 : \tau_1) \mid \Gamma$$

Round r

$\xrightarrow{M:SL(15:\tau_0,13:\tau_1)}$ $A[15 : \tau_0] \mid M[23 : \tau_1] \mid (115 : \tau_0, 87 : \tau_1) \mid \Gamma$

Round $r + 1$

$\xrightarrow{A:SL(15:\tau_0,10:\tau_1,r)}$ $A[10 : \tau_1] \mid M[23 : \tau_1] \mid (130 : \tau_0, 77 : \tau_1) \mid$

$\Gamma \setminus [\, A : SL(15 : \tau_0, 10 : \tau_1), r \,]$

$\xrightarrow{M:SR(30:\tau_0,23:\tau_1)}$ $A[10 : \tau_1] \mid M[30 : \tau_0] \mid (100 : \tau_0, 100 : \tau_1) \mid$

$\Gamma \setminus [\, A : SL(15 : \tau_0, 10 : \tau_1, r) \,]$

We emphasize that scheduled swap orders do not require the submitting user A to participate in the round it is scheduled: it is evaluated automatically by the application. Furthermore, since the victim's swap parameters are public, the front-run and back-run parameters can be chosen to optimize M's profit.

F   Speculative Sandwich in Hash-Based Commit and Reveal Schemes

As shown in Appendix C, the speculative sandwich attack is rational as long as the direction of the victim swap is known. Hash-based commit & reveal schemes suffer from selective output by the adversary (Fig. 3), permitting a speculative attack to succeed even if the swap direction cannot be inferred from public user balances. Here the attacker simply commits two front-run swaps of opposing directions in the same round as the victim swap, whilst suppressing other user inputs. In the output-phase, the adversary learns the direction of the victim swap before having to open its own commitments and selectively opens the front-run of the same direction as the victim swap, whilst refraining from opening the other front-run swap. The back-run is then executed as in Appendix C.

References

1. Abraham, I., Pinkas, B., Yanai, A.: Blinder-scalable, robust anonymous committed broadcast. In: Proceedings of the 2020 ACM SIGSAC Conference on Computer and Communications Security, pp. 1233–1252 (2020). https://doi.org/10.1145/3372297.3417261
2. Angeris, G., Evans, A., Chitra, T.: A Note on Privacy in Constant Function Market Makers. arXiv preprint arXiv:2103.01193 (2021). https://arxiv.org/abs/2103.01193
3. Avalanche: Apricot Phase Four: Snowman++ and Reduced C-Chain Transaction Fees. https://medium.com/avalancheavax/apricot-phase-four-snowman-and-reduced-c-chain-transaction-fees-1e1f67b42ecf (2021)
4. Bartoletti, M., Chiang, J.H., Lluch-Lafuente, A.: A theory of automated market makers in DeFi. In: Damiani, F., Dardha, O. (eds.) COORDINATION 2021. LNCS, vol. 12717, pp. 168–187. Springer, Cham (2021). https://doi.org/10.1007/978-3-030-78142-2_11
5. Bartoletti, M., Chiang, J.H.Y., Lluch-Lafuente, A.: Maximizing Extractable Value from Automated Market Makers. arXiv preprint arXiv:2106.01870 (2021). to appear in FC'22. https://arxiv.org/pdf/2106.01870
6. Baum, C., David, B., Dowsley, R.: Insured MPC: efficient secure computation with financial penalties. In: Bonneau, J., Heninger, N. (eds.) FC 2020. LNCS, vol. 12059, pp. 404–420. Springer, Cham (2020). https://doi.org/10.1007/978-3-030-51280-4_22
7. Baum, C., David, B., Frederiksen, T.K.: P2DEX: privacy-preserving decentralized cryptocurrency exchange. In: Sako, K., Tippenhauer, N.O. (eds.) ACNS 2021. LNCS, vol. 12726, pp. 163–194. Springer, Cham (2021). https://doi.org/10.1007/978-3-030-78372-3_7
8. Beerliová-Trubíniová, Z., Hirt, M.: Efficient multi-party computation with dispute control. In: Halevi, S., Rabin, T. (eds.) TCC 2006. LNCS, vol. 3876, pp. 305–328. Springer, Heidelberg (2006). https://doi.org/10.1007/11681878_16
9. Ben-Sasson, E., Chiesa, A., Genkin, D., Tromer, E., Virza, M.: SNARKs for C: verifying program executions succinctly and in zero knowledge. In: Canetti, R., Garay, J.A. (eds.) CRYPTO 2013. LNCS, vol. 8043, pp. 90–108. Springer, Heidelberg (2013). https://doi.org/10.1007/978-3-642-40084-1_6
10. Bendlin, R., Damgård, I., Orlandi, C., Zakarias, S.: Semi-homomorphic encryption and multiparty computation. In: Paterson, K.G. (ed.) EUROCRYPT 2011. LNCS, vol. 6632, pp. 169–188. Springer, Heidelberg (2011). https://doi.org/10.1007/978-3-642-20465-4_11
11. Boneh, D., Naor, M.: Timed commitments. In: Bellare, M. (ed.) CRYPTO 2000. LNCS, vol. 1880, pp. 236–254. Springer, Heidelberg (2000). https://doi.org/10.1007/3-540-44598-6_15

12. Breidenbach, L., Daian, P., Tramèr, F., Juels, A.: Enter the hydra: towards principled bug bounties and exploit-resistant smart contracts. In: 27th USENIX Security Symposium (USENIX Security 18), pp. 1335–1352. USENIX Association, Baltimore, MD, August 2018. https://www.usenix.org/conference/usenixsecurity18/presentation/breindenbach

13. Bünz, B., Bootle, J., Boneh, D., Poelstra, A., Wuille, P., Maxwell, G.: Bulletproofs: short proofs for confidential transactions and more. In: 2018 IEEE Symposium on Security and Privacy (SP), pp. 315–334. IEEE (2018). https://doi.org/10.1109/SP.2018.00020

14. Burdges, J., De Feo, L.: Delay encryption. In: Canteaut, A., Standaert, F.-X. (eds.) EUROCRYPT 2021. LNCS, vol. 12696, pp. 302–326. Springer, Cham (2021). https://doi.org/10.1007/978-3-030-77870-5_11

15. Canetti, R., Lindell, Y., Ostrovsky, R., Sahai, A.: Universally composable two-party and multi-party secure computation. In: 34th ACM STOC, pp. 494–503. ACM Press, Montréal, Québec, Canada, 19–21 May 2002. https://doi.org/10.1145/509907.509980

16. Chitra, T., Angeris, G., Evans, A.: Differential privacy in constant function market makers. Cryptology ePrint Archive (2021). https://eprint.iacr.org/2021/1101

17. Chu, S., Xia, Y., Zhang, Z.: Manta: a plug and play private DeFi stack (2021). https://eprint.iacr.org/2021/743

18. Daian, P., et al.: Flash boys 2.0: frontrunning in decentralized exchanges, miner extractable value, and consensus instability. In: IEEE Symposium on Security and Privacy, pp. 910–927. IEEE (2020). https://doi.org/10.1109/SP40000.2020.00040

19. Damgård, I., Nielsen, J.B.: Scalable and unconditionally secure multiparty computation. In: Menezes, A. (ed.) CRYPTO 2007. LNCS, vol. 4622, pp. 572–590. Springer, Heidelberg (2007). https://doi.org/10.1007/978-3-540-74143-5_32

20. Damgård, I., Pastro, V., Smart, N., Zakarias, S.: Multiparty computation from somewhat homomorphic encryption. In: Safavi-Naini, R., Canetti, R. (eds.) CRYPTO 2012. LNCS, vol. 7417, pp. 643–662. Springer, Heidelberg (2012). https://doi.org/10.1007/978-3-642-32009-5_38

21. Danos, V., Khalloufi, H.E., Prat, J.: Global order routing on exchange networks. In: Bernhard, M., et al. (eds.) FC 2021. LNCS, vol. 12676, pp. 207–226. Springer, Heidelberg (2021). https://doi.org/10.1007/978-3-662-63958-0_19

22. Desmedt, Y., Frankel, Y.: Threshold cryptosystems. In: Brassard, G. (ed.) CRYPTO 1989. LNCS, vol. 435, pp. 307–315. Springer, New York (1990). https://doi.org/10.1007/0-387-34805-0_28

23. Eskandari, S., Moosavi, S., Clark, J.: SoK: transparent dishonesty: front-running attacks on blockchain. In: Bracciali, A., Clark, J., Pintore, F., Rønne, P.B., Sala, M. (eds.) FC 2019. LNCS, vol. 11599, pp. 170–189. Springer, Cham (2020). https://doi.org/10.1007/978-3-030-43725-1_13

24. da Gama, M.B., Cartlidge, J., Polychroniadou, A., Smart, N.P., Alaoui, Y.T.: Kicking-the-bucket: fast privacy-preserving trading using buckets. Cryptology ePrint Archive, Report 2021/1549 (2021). to appear in FC'22, https://ia.cr/2021/1549

25. Gennaro, R., Gentry, C., Parno, B., Raykova, M.: Quadratic span programs and succinct NIZKs without PCPs. In: Johansson, T., Nguyen, P.Q. (eds.) EUROCRYPT 2013. LNCS, vol. 7881, pp. 626–645. Springer, Heidelberg (2013). https://doi.org/10.1007/978-3-642-38348-9_37

26. Gentry, C.: Fully homomorphic encryption using ideal lattices. In: Proceedings of the Forty-First Annual ACM Symposium on Theory of Computing, pp. 169–178.

STOC '09, Association for Computing Machinery, New York, NY, USA (2009). https://doi.org/10.1145/1536414.1536440

27. Goldreich, O., Micali, S., Wigderson, A.: How to play any mental game or a completeness theorem for protocols with honest majority. In: Aho, A. (ed.) 19th ACM STOC, pp. 218–229. ACM Press, New York City, NY, USA, 25–27 May 1987. https://doi.org/10.1145/28395.28420

28. Groth, J.: Short pairing-based non-interactive zero-knowledge arguments. In: Abe, M. (ed.) ASIACRYPT 2010. LNCS, vol. 6477, pp. 321–340. Springer, Heidelberg (2010). https://doi.org/10.1007/978-3-642-17373-8_19

29. Groth, J.: On the size of pairing-based non-interactive arguments. In: Fischlin, M., Coron, J.-S. (eds.) EUROCRYPT 2016. LNCS, vol. 9666, pp. 305–326. Springer, Heidelberg (2016). https://doi.org/10.1007/978-3-662-49896-5_11

30. Kelkar, M., Deb, S., Kannan, S.: Order-fair consensus in the permissionless setting. IACR Cryptology ePrint Archive, vol. 2021, p. 139 (2021). https://eprint.iacr.org/2021/139

31. Kelkar, M., Deb, S., Long, S., Juels, A., Kannan, S.: Themis: fast, strong order-fairness in byzantine consensus. Cryptology ePrint Archive (2021). https://eprint.iacr.org/2021/1465

32. Khalil, R., Gervais, A., Felley, G.: Tex-a securely scalable trustless exchange. Cryptology ePrint Archive (2019). https://eprint.iacr.org/2019/265

33. Kiayias, A., Zhou, H.-S., Zikas, V.: Fair and robust multi-party computation using a global transaction ledger. In: Fischlin, M., Coron, J.-S. (eds.) EUROCRYPT 2016. LNCS, vol. 9666, pp. 705–734. Springer, Heidelberg (2016). https://doi.org/10.1007/978-3-662-49896-5_25

34. Kursawe, K.: Wendy, the good little fairness widget: achieving order fairness for blockchains. In: Proceedings of the 2nd ACM Conference on Advances in Financial Technologies, pp. 25–36 (2020). https://doi.org/10.1145/3419614.3423263

35. Li, Y.: HoneyBadgerSwap: Making MPC as a Sidechain (2021). https://medium.com/initc3org/honeybadgerswap-making-mpc-as-a-sidechain-364bebdb10a5

36. Lu, D., Yurek, T., Kulshreshtha, S., Govind, R., Kate, A., Miller, A.: Honeybadgermpc and asynchromix: practical asynchronous mpc and its application to anonymous communication. In: Proceedings of the 2019 ACM SIGSAC Conference on Computer and Communications Security, pp. 887–903 (2019). https://doi.org/10.1145/3319535.3354238

37. Maxwell, G.: Confidential transactions (2016). https://people.xiph.org/greg/confidential_values.txt

38. Paradigm: Ethereum is a Dark Forest (2020). https://www.paradigm.xyz/2020/08/ethereum-is-a-dark-forest/

39. Parno, B., Howell, J., Gentry, C., Raykova, M.: Pinocchio: nearly practical verifiable computation. In: 2013 IEEE Symposium on Security and Privacy, pp. 238–252. IEEE (2013). https://doi.org/10.1109/SP.2013.47

40. Penumbra: ZSwap documentation (2021). https://protocol.penumbra.zone/main/zswap.html

41. Perez, D., Werner, S.M., Xu, J., Livshits, B.: Liquidations: DeFi on a knife-edge. In: Borisov, N., Diaz, C. (eds.) FC 2021. LNCS, vol. 12675, pp. 457–476. Springer, Heidelberg (2021). https://doi.org/10.1007/978-3-662-64331-0_24

42. Rivest, R.L., Shamir, A., Wagner, D.A.: Time-locked Puzzles and Time-release Crypto (1996). https://people.csail.mit.edu/rivest/pubs/RSW96.pdf

43. Sasson, E.B., et al.: Zerocash: decentralized anonymous payments from bitcoin. In: 2014 IEEE Symposium on Security and Privacy, pp. 459–474. IEEE (2014). https://doi.org/10.1109/SP.2014.36

44. Shutter: Shutter Network (2022). https://shutter.network/
45. Wang, Y., Chen, Y., Deng, S., Wattenhofer, R.: Cyclic arbitrage in decentralized exchange markets. SSRN 3834535 (2021). https://dx.doi.org/10.2139/ssrn.3834535
46. White, D., Robinson, D., Adams, H.: Time-weighted average market maker (TWAMM) (2021). https://www.paradigm.xyz/2021/07/twamm/
47. Yao, A.C.C.: Theory and applications of trapdoor functions (extended abstract). In: 23rd FOCS, pp. 80–91. IEEE Computer Society Press, Chicago, Illinois, 3–5 November 1982. https://doi.org/10.1109/SFCS.1982.45
48. Zhou, L., Qin, K., Cully, A., Livshits, B., Gervais, A.: On the just-in-time discovery of profit-generating transactions in DeFi protocols. arXiv preprint arXiv:2103.02228 (2021). https://arxiv.org/abs/2103.02228

A Systematic Investigation of DeFi Compositions in Ethereum

Stefan Kitzler[1,2], Friedhelm Victor[3], Pietro Saggese[1,2(✉)],
and Bernhard Haslhofer[1]

[1] Complexity Science Hub Vienna, Josefstädter Straße 39, Vienna A-1080, Austria
{kitzler,saggese,haslhofer}@csh.ac.at
[2] AIT Austrian Institute of Technology, Giefinggasse 4, Vienna A-1210, Austria
{stefan.kitzler,pietro.saggese}@ait.ac.at
[3] Technische Universität Berlin, Straße des 17. Juni 135, 10623 Berlin, Germany
friedhelm.victor@tu-berlin.de

The rapid growth of the Ethereum ecosystem since 2020 has been driven by the proliferation of several *DeFi protocols* [10], which are application-layer programs that provide Decentralized Finance (DeFi) services [14,16] such as the exchange of cryptoassets on decentralized exchanges (DEXs) [2,7,15], their lending and borrowing [1,4,8], or the creation and trade of related derivative contracts [11]. DeFi protocols build upon executable software programs, i.e., smart contracts (also known as Code Accounts, or CAs), that can interact by calling each other: their functions can be arbitrarily composed into new financial products and services. Sometimes referred to as *Financial Lego*, DeFi protocols and their smart contracts can build on each other and thereby form compositions. Consider, for instance, the Ethereum transaction depicted in Fig. 1a. To inspect it, we trace its execution. An investor, who controls an externally owned account (EOA), exchanges Ether for the token USDT: she does so by triggering a router contract of a DEX, e.g., Uniswap, which in turn interacts with three other smart contracts: the Uniswap trading pair for the two tokens involved, and the underlying wETH and USDT token contracts. The initial external transaction to the DEX router produces a cascade of internal transactions, shown as ordered arrows in the sequence diagram. Everything occurs within one individual Ethereum transaction. The cascade of internal calls is almost equivalent, and the contracts involved are the same. Thus, the same financial functionality (in this case, a swap) can be triggered by different contracts, e.g., a DEX router or an Aggregation router. In Fig. 1b the same user interacts with the contract of an Aggregation protocol, e.g., 1inch. Intuitively, this structure, consisting of the DEX trading pair, the wETH, and USDT contracts, is reminiscent of Financial Lego that can be incorporated within other protocols.

The notions of composition and composability are often used in the literature [3,5,9,12,13]. However, to the best of our knowledge, a general, technical, or theoretical definition describing such concepts appears to be missing in the academic literature. Therefore, we aim to define DeFi compositions and discuss them systematically by answering the following questions: what is a DeFi composition in the Ethereum ecosystem? How can we identify and measure protocol compositions?

S. Matsuo et al. (Eds.): FC 2022 Workshops, LNCS 13412, pp. 272–279, 2023.
https://doi.org/10.1007/978-3-031-32415-4_18

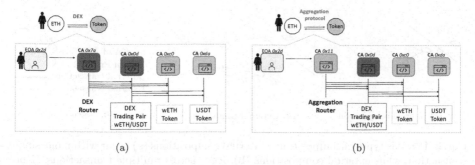

(a)   (b)

Fig. 1. The same financial functionality can be triggered by different contracts, e.g. a DEX router (left) or an Aggregation router (right).

We start by tackling the first question and consider two different possibilities of compositions. The simplest one occurs within one transaction; thus, it is atomic and automated, as the internal calls are triggered automatically. We define it as follows:

Definition 1. *An **internal DeFi composition** is a combination of Code Account (CA) functionalities such that multiple DeFi CAs are called in one execution path, OR at least a common asset links multiple execution paths, each containing at least one DeFi CA.*

We call *DeFi CA* a protocol-specific smart contract that has been implemented as part of a single DeFi protocol. We model an entire transaction as an *execution tree*, that is, we construct an edge-node abstraction so that the external and all the internal transactions are represented as an edge to a new node: the execution tree starts with an EOA-node, is followed by CA-nodes, and the same CA-node appears multiple times if executed more than once. An *execution path* indicates the edge-node path linking the externally called CA to a further internally called CA and all the subsequent originating traces.

The second type of possible composition is instead across multiple transactions. Thus it is not atomic nor automated, as it is sequentially executed by an EOA. We call it an external composition and define it as follows:

Definition 2. *An **external DeFi composition** is a combination of CA functionalities such that multiple DeFi CAs are called in execution paths of different transactions (executed by the same EOA) AND at least a common asset links multiple DeFi execution paths.*

We now illustrate the concept. Figure 2a shows the transaction described in Fig. 1b as a transaction execution tree. A composition takes place as the Aggregation router leverages the liquidity of the DEX trading pair pool to provide a financial service. Figure 2b shows both transactions described in Fig. 1 as transaction execution trees. The composition takes place as two execution paths, one in each transaction, share common assets (represented by the blue and the orange nodes).

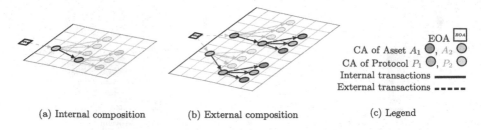

(a) Internal composition   (b) External composition   (c) Legend

Fig. 2. Possible types of compositions. Internal compositions (a) occur within one single transaction, while external compositions (b) occur across multiple transactions. (Note that a composition can take place also indirectly, i.e., the EOA can trigger a CA not associated to a DeFi protocol, which can then call a DeFi CA with a subsequent call to another DeFi CA.)

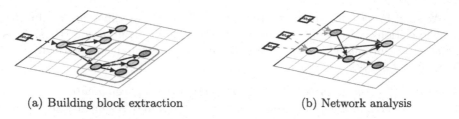

(a) Building block extraction   (b) Network analysis

Fig. 3. Devised approaches to identify compositions. By treating transactions as execution trees (a), we identify nested building blocks, i.e. recurring patterns originating from DeFi CAs which can be exploited by other DeFi CAs. By aggregating multiple transactions as a graph abstraction (b), we look for signs of compositions in the network topology.

The second question is how to identify and measure protocol compositions. We devise two different approaches. The first one is based on modeling transactions as execution trees, i.e., using the edge-node abstraction introduced above. As shown intuitively in Fig. 1, DeFi compositions lead to nested structures of DeFi CAs exploiting other DeFi CAs to provide their financial services. We thus devise a methodology to systematically identify such structures, which we call nested *building blocks*, i.e., recurring patterns originating from internally or externally composed DeFi CAs (Fig. 3a). The second approach aggregates different transactions executed by multiple EOAs, into a graph abstraction. As Fig. 3b shows, each node represents one unique address, and links indicate directed calls from one address to another. In this way, we can investigate whether the network topology reflects the existence of compositions, both statically and by including dynamic aspects, to study the temporal evolution of the DeFi ecosystem (Fig. 4).

Parts of these aspects have already been covered in our previous work [6]: we briefly report here our empirical findings and contributions. We investigated the static aggregated network of DeFi CAs and the internal compositions within single transactions (thus, we disregarded external compositions and did not consider temporal network aspects). We identified the 23 most relevant DeFi protocols

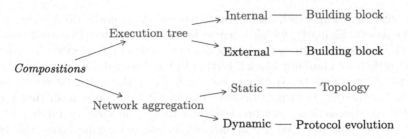

Fig. 4. Taxonomy of the possible approaches to investigate compositions. We highlight in red those that we already covered in [6] (Color figure online).

regarding gas use and total value locked. Then, we manually collected a curated ground-truth dataset of around 1,400 addresses that we labeled as belonging to specific protocols. We also introduced a heuristic to extend it to a more extensive list of 10,663,881 protocol-specific addresses. We gathered all Ethereum transactions from January 2021 to August 2021 and, to distinguish CAs from EOAs, we also gathered all CA *create*-transactions until August 2021. Finally, we selected a subset of transactions whose initial external transactions are directed to a DeFi CA included in our ground-truth dataset.

First, we studied the interactions between protocol-specific CAs, intending to find signs of compositions in the topology. We constructed two network abstractions: the network of smart contracts (DeFi CA network, ~2.5 M nodes) and the Protocol network, in which addresses associated with one protocol are merged into one node (~43,000 nodes). We investigated the degree distribution to identify CAs that implement core functionalities, finding that DEX and lending protocols play a major role. The analysis of the network components showed that interactions mainly occur in the second-largest highly interconnected component. Finally, we measured how effectively community detection algorithms detect protocols. We compared the ground-truth communities of labeled addresses to those identified by the community detection, finding that they do not overlap: we interpreted it as a sign of protocol compositions.

Then, we focused on compositions within individual transactions. When internal compositions occur, DeFi CAs call other DeFi CAs, which in turn can trigger a *building block* (akin to a Financial Lego) of internal calls: one can again think intuitively to the example shown in Fig. 1. We define a building block as follows:

Definition 3. *DeFi building blocks are recurring patterns of internal traces induced by DeFi CAs, which are found as subpatterns of transactions involving at least one DeFi CA.*

We devised an algorithm to decompose calls to DeFi CAs into a nested set of building blocks, potentially induced by DeFi CAs of other DeFi protocols, and extract them. Intuitively, the algorithm works as follows: we model transactions as execution trees, and we generalize the appearing token addresses by relabeling them with the term *Asset*, as we want that building blocks do not depend on specific assets. Similarly, we also generalize all factory deployed contracts. We walk the tree starting from the leaf nodes until a protocol-specific CA is found, and identify it as a building block if further leaf nodes exist, i.e., if it has outgoing calls to other contracts. We compute the hash of the block based on block-specific information in order to collect blocks with the same hash that appear in different transactions. We proceed by walking the tree up further to find other protocol-specific CAs. If it is the case, an internal composition takes place, and we identify a new building block that contains other(s) building block(s) in a nested structure. Thus, internal compositions lead to structures of nested building blocks, and their identification leads to the identification of internal compositions.

Our previous findings [6] show that such nested structures are widespread. We identify building blocks through hashes and label them with the method signature of the DeFi CA that generates them. The "swap" building block of Uniswap is the most common one (it appears more than 21 M times in our dataset), and it is repeatedly found as a substructure of other building blocks. Other frequent building blocks are the Sushiswap "swap" and the 0x "withdraw" building blocks. We have focused on the Uniswap "swap" example because of its simplicity and relevance in terms of occurrences. However, the nested structures and the extracted building blocks are often more complex. In Appendix A we provide a graphic visualization tool that allows investigating the nested structures of various protocols systematically.

We conclude by discussing future work. We plan to devise methods to extend the building block extraction to transactions that form external compositions. Challenges should not be underestimated: is it a sufficient condition to have a common asset linking two transactions executed by the same user? Time could be a constraint. Nonces and timestamps could be exploited to identify sequential transactions. However, even after solving this issue, it might not be straightforward to differentiate between trading strategies that involve the same assets in independent sequential transactions and actual compositions of the same assets. Second, in our analysis, we have so far only considered external transactions directed to DeFi protocol-specific contracts. The next step is to also include transactions that indirectly call DeFi protocols. Finally, a temporal network analysis might help investigate the evolution in time of the protocols, and the network abstraction could be extended to include EOAs and CAs.

A   Visualization Tool

In the main body of the work we focused on the Uniswap "swap" building block to describe the concept of composability in the DeFi Ethereum ecosystem. However, the nested structures and the extracted building blocks are often much more complex. In this Appendix we describe a visualization tool that we implemented to allow a more systematic investigation of the nested structures identified within our dataset. The visualization tool can be found at the following link: https://github.com/PietroSaggese/Visualize_DeFi_compositions.

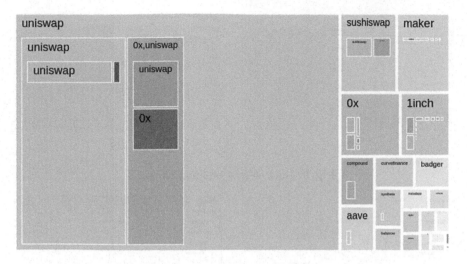

Fig. 5. Main interface of the visualization tool. Transactions are grouped by protocol called in the external transaction.

Figure 5 shows the main interface. Each rectangle corresponds to a protocol, and the size is proportional to the number of external transactions directed to it. Uniswap is by far the largest protocol in terms of external calls directed to protocol-specific CAs. It is possible to browse the rectangles to observe what is the fraction of protocol-specific transactions that contain nested building blocks (i.e., that contain internal compositions) in subsequent levels of depth, and what protocols are further called. This operation is repeated for all levels, until the end of the execution tree of all transactions is reached.

Figure 6a shows 1inch as an example. Each rectangle represents the fraction of transactions that contain further building blocks in the next level of depth. As one can see, a large fraction of calls contains building blocks induced by CAs related to Uniswap and to other DEX protocols. We explore one of the rectangles in Fig. 6b. We investigate the fraction of 1inch transactions that call DeFi CAs of four protocols (curvefinance, sushiswap, synthetix, uniswap) in the next level of depth. The structure is complex, and other building blocks can be found in a repeatedly nested structure. Our second example is the Instadapp protocol. It is reported in Fig. 7 in order to show that nested structures can appear also in deeper levels of the tree structure. We browse the structure up to the fourth level of nestedness (Figs. 7a to 7e) and observe in Fig. 7f that a large fraction of the transactions contain calls to several other protocols (Aave, 1inch, Dydx, Compound, . . .). In summary, these two examples show that building blocks are heavily nested, also in deeper levels of the transaction execution trees, thus being a sign that internal compositions exist, and can be systematically investigated with our visualization tool.

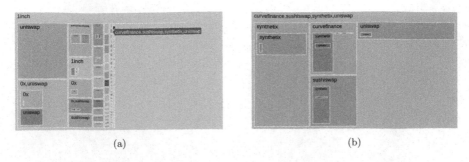

Fig. 6. 1inch nested building blocks.

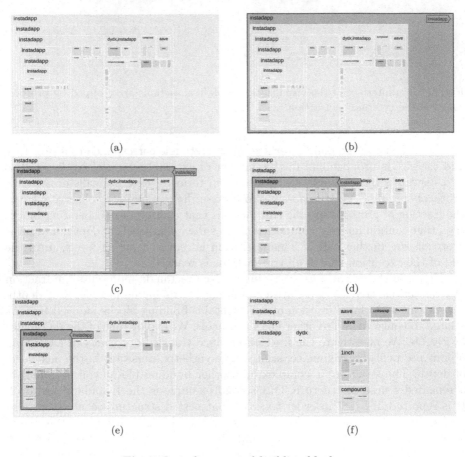

Fig. 7. Instadapp nested building blocks.

References

1. Bartoletti, M., Chiang, J.H.-Y., Lafuente, A.L.: SoK: lending pools in decentralized finance. In: Bernhard, M., et al. (eds.) FC 2021. LNCS, vol. 12676, pp. 553–578. Springer, Heidelberg (2021). https://doi.org/10.1007/978-3-662-63958-0_40

2. Capponi, A., Jia, R.: The adoption of blockchain-based decentralized exchanges. In: Tokenomics '21, arxiv preprint arXiv:2103.08842 (2021)
3. Engel, D., Herlihy, M.: Composing networks of automated market makers. In: Proceedings of the 3rd ACM Conference on Advances in Financial Technologies, pp. 15–28 (2021). https://doi.org/10.1145/3479722.3480987
4. Gudgeon, L., Werner, S., Perez, D., Knottenbelt, W.J.: DeFi protocols for loanable funds: interest rates, liquidity and market efficiency. In: Proceedings of the 2nd ACM Conference on Advances in Financial Technologies, pp. 92–112 (2020). https://doi.org/10.1145/3419614.3423254
5. Harvey, C.R., Ramachandran, A., Santoro, J.: DeFi and the Future of Finance. John Wiley & Sons, Hoboken (2021). ISBN: 978-1119836018
6. Kitzler, S., Victor, F., Saggese, P., Haslhofer, B.: Disentangling decentralized finance (DeFi) compositions. ACM Trans. Web **17**(2), 1–26 (2023). https://doi.org/10.1145/3532857
7. Lehar, A., Parlour, C.A.: Decentralized exchanges. Available at SSRN 3905316 (2021)
8. Qin, K., Zhou, L., Gamito, P., Jovanovic, P., Gervais, A.: An empirical study of DeFi liquidations: incentives, risks, and instabilities. In: Proceedings of the 21st ACM Internet Measurement Conference, pp. 336–350 (2021). https://doi.org/10.1145/3487552.3487811
9. Saengchote, K.: Where do defi stablecoins go? A closer look at what defi composability really means. Technical report, Puey Ungphakorn Institute for Economic Research (2021)
10. Schär, F.: Decentralized finance: on blockchain-and smart contract-based financial markets. FRB of St. Louis Review (2021). https://doi.org/10.1145/3487552.3487811
11. Soska, K., Dong, J.D., Khodaverdian, A., Zetlin-Jones, A., Routledge, B., Christin, N.: Towards understanding cryptocurrency derivatives: a case study of BitMEX. In: Proceedings of the Web Conference 2021 (WWW '21), April 2021. https://doi.org/10.1145/3442381.3450059
12. Tolmach, P., Li, Y., Lin, S.-W., Liu, Y.: Formal analysis of composable DeFi protocols. In: Bernhard, M., et al. (eds.) FC 2021. LNCS, vol. 12676, pp. 149–161. Springer, Heidelberg (2021). https://doi.org/10.1007/978-3-662-63958-0_13
13. von Wachter, V., Jensen, J.R., Ross, O.: Measuring asset composability as a proxy for DeFi integration. In: Bernhard, M., et al. (eds.) Financial Cryptography and Data Security. FC 2021 International Workshops. FC 2021. LNCS, vol. 12676, pp. 109–114. Springer, Berlin, Heidelberg (2021). https://doi.org/10.1007/978-3-662-63958-0_9
14. Werner, S.M., Perez, D., Gudgeon, L., Klages-Mundt, A., Harz, D., Knottenbelt, W.J.: Sok: decentralized finance (DeFi). arXiv preprint arXiv:2101.08778 (2021)
15. Xu, J., Paruch, K., Cousaert, S., Feng, Y.: Sok: Decentralized exchanges (DEX) with automated market maker (AMM) protocols. ACM Comput. Surv. **55**(11), 1–50 (2023). https://doi.org/10.1145/3570639
16. Zetzsche, D.A., Arner, D.W., Buckley, R.P.: Decentralized finance. J. Financ. Regul. **6**(2), 172–203 (2020). https://doi.org/10.1093/jfr/fjaa010

Short Paper: Privacy Preserving Decentralized Netting

Amit Agarwal[1(✉)], Angelo De Caro[2], and Andrew Miller[1]

[1] University of Illinois Urbana-Champaign, Champaign, USA
amita2@illinois.edu
[2] IBM Research, Zurich, Switzerland

Abstract. This paper proposes a secure decentralized protocol that a consortium of local banks can use to complete a netting process in a privacy-preserving fashion without relying on a single central bank. To do so, it makes use of two key ingredients - zero-knowledge proofs and secure multiparty computation (MPC). We use these two primitives to construct a multi-phase protocol and prove its security in the UC framework. We also study the feasibility of using Linear programming based solution to find optimal solution to the netting problem in gridlock scenarios. To do so, we implemented a proof of concept of our proposed protocol using MP-SPDZ [Kel20] (a framework for prototyping MPC applications) and analyzed the costs involved. Compared to prior work [Cao+20], we manage to achieve 40–50% higher percentage settlement of total transaction.

Keywords: Zero-knowledge proofs · Secure multiparty computation · Privacy-preserving Netting

1 Introduction

Nowadays, central banks have multiple responsibilities. They oversee the monetary system for a nation, or a group of them, they oversee monetary policy to implement specific goals such as low inflation, currency stability, and so on. Even though the number of duties of central banks increased over time, they are still responsible to provide the basic means by which large payments are settled electronically. These payments are typically wholesale payments between banks, and central banks are providers of inter-banking payment systems. Essentially, a central bank handles accounts in so-called central bank money for each local bank in its jurisdiction and makes sure that each account maintains a certain level of liquidity i.e. reserve balance. Traditionally, inter-banking payments were not settled immediately but at the end of the day by netting the positions of each bank. As the volume of the value of the transactions increased over time, settling only at the end of the day increased the risk of shortage of liquidity. To avoid dangerous shortage of liquidity, the central banks deployed the so called *real-time gross settlement* systems (RTGS, for short) where payments are settled individually and immediately. The down side of these systems is that they require

© International Financial Cryptography Association 2023
S. Matsuo et al. (Eds.): FC 2022 Workshops, LNCS 13412, pp. 280–298, 2023.
https://doi.org/10.1007/978-3-031-32415-4_19

high liquidity levels . Multiple studies have shown that the liquidity demands in RTGS systems are often reaching substantial fractions of the annual GDP. Shortage of liquidity, also known as *gridlocks* causes halts in the inter-banking payment systems with a detrimental effect on the overall financial system. For this reason, central banks have extended RTGS systems with *liquidity saving mechanisms* (LSM, for short) to increase the total liquidity in the systems. One of the most common LSMs is the familiar netting the central banks used to operate already. In more detail, in order to resolve gridlocks and increase liquidity, central banks operate a *centralized payment queue*. Banks submits their payment instructions to this queue and then the central bank performs a multilateral netting before proceeding with the settlement of the payments in the queue. Central banks are also trusted to preserve the confidentiality of payment instructions coming from each bank. Being a trusted party, or a single point of failure, puts a huge stress on the central banks. Stress that translates to higher operational costs. For the above reasons, central banks are actively searching options to distribute the burden of keeping up and running the system.

Our Contribution. In this paper, we answer the following question:

> *Is it possible to build an inter-banking payment system that supports a distributed and privacy preserving multilateral netting mechanism?*

We answer the above question in the positive by proposing a privacy preserving decentralized netting protocol which obviates the need for the central bank to be actively involved during the various stages of the netting process. We do this by employing Zero-knowledge (ZK) proofs and Secure Multiparty Computation (MPC) techniques. For executing the MPC protocol, we imagine a distributed quorum of server nodes, which could be a consortium among the local banks. Apart from our cryptographic contribution, we also study the feasibility of using Linear Programming based formulation of the netting problem in order to achieve optimal percentage settlement in gridlock scenarios. In more details, we propose a multi-phase protocol:

- *Input phase.* In this phase, banks publish *commitments* and *secret-shares* of their payment instructions (i.e pending transactions) in a confidentiality preserving way.
- *Optimistic phase.* In this phase, each bank publishes a *ZK proof* to show that it maintains enough liquidity to settle all its pending transactions. If a bank does not have enough liquidity to settle all transactions or a bank fails to execute this step for some malicious or non-malicious reason, a more robust, but expensive fallback phase is executed.
- *Fallback phase.* In this phase, an optimization algorithm is executed using fault-tolerant *secure multi-party computation* to compute the optimal set of "partial transaction" values that can be settled. In our experiments, we instantiate the optimization algorithm with Linear programming based *Karmarkar algorithm* to achieve high percentage settlement. At the end of the computation, each bank learns the fraction of each transaction value that got settled.

– *Settlement phase.* In this phase, banks get committed to their final balance which, in turn, will be used as a starting point for future invocations of the protocol.

Related Work. The closest work to what we are proposing in the current paper is due to Cao et al. [Cao+20]. The authors propose a decentralized netting protocol that hides the amount of currency transferred in each given transaction, but not the sender and recipient. This leakage is what allow their protocol to be executed on the ledger. In more detail, each party computes locally her view of the optimal subset of her transactions that can be netted. Then, the party generates a ZK proof to show that: (i) this subset is optimal, (ii) the sums have been performed correctly, and (iii) the current balance after netting is non-negative. A smart contract verifies the ZK proofs and updates its internal state to keep track of the protocol execution. Compared to [Cao+20] i) we manage to achieve a robust fault tolerant solution (which does not get stuck in case some parties abort during protocol) while maximizing the confidentiality of banks, ii) Our distinct focus on "partial settlement" - which allows some fraction of a transaction to be processed (instead of "binary settlement")- enables us to achieve even more efficient handling of gridlock scenarios. This notion of partial settlement has been recommended in [Mar,Mel]. In some settings, our approach yields as much as 50% higher percentage settlement value compared to prior work [Cao+20].

Other two main works are the following: A recent report on the joint venture by the ECB and Bank of Japan [BJ07] describes a decentralized approach for LSM-type bilateral netting in the Stella Project. Their approach makes use of smart contracts that allow banks to conduct payment transfers with LSMs in the distributed ledger environment. Project Ubin [Sin], sponsored by the Monetary Authority of Singapore, explores the use of distributed ledger technology for interbank payment and settlements with LSMs introduced for the purpose of gridlock resolution. The main difference between our work and the solutions proposed in both projects is that we employ advanced cryptographic techniques to find a reasonable compromise between performance and security. We propose a solution based on fault-tolerant multi-party computation (MPC), a direction which has not been explored in the literature.[1].

2   Problem Definition

Based on the netting application described above, we pose a problem definition in terms of a transaction graph. Concretely, we are given a transaction graph representing n banks (as nodes) and n^2 pending transactions (as edges) between each pair of banks. Such a graph can be represented using a matrix $G_{n \times n}$ where $t_{i,j}$ represents the outgoing transaction value from Bank P_i to Bank P_j.

---

[1] A concurrent work on privacy preserving netting using MPC was proposed recently by Atapoor et. al. [ASA21]. However, they work in a model where transactions have a pre-defined priority order of settlement, whereas, we work in a partial settlement model which will be discussed later.

In addition to the pending transactions, each bank P_i has some initial balance b_i. The high-level goal is to settle the pending transactions in the "best" possible way so that the final balance (i.e. balance after the netting process is completed) at each bank remains positive.

The objective is to select a subset of transactions which satisfy the positive balance constraint and at the same time maximizes the total value of the transactions included in the subset. However, finding such an optimal subset of transactions reduces to the Integer Linear Programming problem which is well-known to be NP complete, and thus has no efficient polynomial time algorithm. In prior work [Cao+20, GY20, ASA21], this issue was handled by introducing an additional constraint which requires the subset to satisfy a FIFO-type ordering. The authors also provided a simple efficient algorithm which solves the netting problem under this additional constraint.

In this paper, we take a different approach and aim to improve the settling efficiency of the netting process. To do this, instead of imposing any ordering on the optimal subset, we relax the problem in an orthogonal way. Note that in the original problem formulation, each $t_{i,j}$ is either included or not included in the optimal subset i.e. the decision of whether to include $t_{i,j}$ in the optimal subset is a binary value. We relax this constraint in our problem formulation by allowing any fraction $f_{i,j} \in [0, 1]$ of a transaction to be included in the optimal subset.

Having said that, our objective can be mathematically stated as follows: Find a set of fractional values $\{f_{i,j}\}_{i \in [n], j \in [n]}$, which maximizes the total transaction amount selected i.e. $\sum_{i=1}^{n} \sum_{j=1}^{n} t_{i,j} \times f_{i,j}$, subject to the following **Positive balance constraint**:

$$\forall i \in [n] : \quad b_i + \sum_{j=1}^{n} t_{j,i} - \sum_{j=1}^{n} t_{i,j} \geq 0$$

The above linear programming formulation admits an efficient polynomial time solution using Karmarkar's algorithm [Kar84]. We use the transformation procedure mentioned in [Tom87] to convert the above LP form into a form which is compatible with the Karmarkar's algorithm, implemented it and then did a comparative analysis, based on simulation experiments, with 2 other algorithms: i) FIFO-based solution [Cao+20], ii) Naive algorithm which either selects the entire n^2 set of transactions if the positive balance constraint is satisfied, otherwise returns a null set. Details regarding the comparative analysis can be found in Sect. 5.

In the real world, a new instance of the netting problem will emerge every day. We observe that this real world scenario fits well with the problem relaxation that we have described above wherein we allow "partial transactions" to become part of the final solution. In this way, any left over fractional transactions can be simply carried over to the next day for settlement. Indeed, real-world settlement engines such as T2S [Mar] take such an approach in order to maximize the net percentage settlement value. Therefore, our theoretical relaxation of the problem definition helps achieve an efficient and optimal solution to the netting problem while ensuring that the relaxed definition is still meaningful in the context of real world scenario.

3   High-Level Design

We review the phases of a real-world, central bank operated, netting process where an account of the current balance (i.e. liquidity reserve) of each local bank is maintained by the central bank. Before invoking the netting procedure, each local bank fixes the list of transactions that it desires to settle with other local banks. We call such transactions as attempted/pending transactions. During the netting procedure, some subset $\mathbb{S}$ of the entire set of attempted transactions is selected in a way so that the positive balance constraint is satisfied at each bank. Once the selection is done, all transactions that are part of $\mathbb{S}$ are settled by transferring the required amount and the final balance of each local bank gets updated at the central bank.

We propose a privacy-preserving decentralized protocol, which roughly follows the same flow as above, but obviates the need for the central bank to be actively involved during various stages of the aforementioned netting workflow.

Figure 1 in the appendix shows a high-level flow of our proposed approach for conducting the entire netting process in a privacy-preserving and distributed manner. Before giving an overview of our design, we introduce the following cryptographic tools that underlies our construction:

- **Commitments**: A computationally binding and perfectly hiding commitment scheme , which is additively homomorphic. This can be instantiated using Pedersen commitment scheme [Ped91].
- **ZK proofs**: A non-interactive zero-knowledge argument of knowledge scheme NiZKAoK. This can be instantiated using Schnorr NIZK proofs [Hao17]. For range proofs specifically, one can use Bulletproofs [Bün+18] in Fiat-Shamir mode [FS86].
- **MPC**: A general-purpose secret-sharing based multiparty computation protocol MPC secure against $n/3$ active corruptions. Damgard and Nielsen [DN03] defined an Arithmetic Black Box denoted by $\mathcal{F}_{ABB}$ as an ideal functionality for MPC. Other functionalitlies like $\mathcal{F}_{SFE}$, a functionality for secure function evaluation, behave similarly. In general any MPC functionality providing a reactive interface would suffice for our use. Note that in this setting where we assume atmost $n/3$ active corruptions, MPC protocols also provide guaranteed output delivery [Lu+19] (also known as robustness) in addition to the standard privacy guarantee. This means that as long as the corruption threshold is below $n/3$, malicious parties won't be able to interfere with the correctness of the output. The MPC would be executed by a distributed quorum of server nodes, which could be a consortium among the local banks. For ease of description, we will not discriminate between server nodes and local banks in this paper and assume, without loss of generality, that all banks are part of the MPC consortium.

Now we proceed to give an overview of our design: In our decentralized protocol, the need for central bank in maintaining and updating the balance reserve amounts of each local bank is removed by incorporating commitments and secret shares to each bank's balance which are persistently maintained and updated by all the participating banks. Our proposed protocol then checks for the consistency of commitment values and secret-shares to prevent a malicious bank for modifying its own balance at will. We will now describe how we handle the transaction processing and settlement phase, which forms the core part of a netting process.

At a high level, the transaction processing phase begins with an INPUT phase where banks commit to their pending transactions that are required to be settled. Once the INPUT phase is complete, banks move on to the OPTIMISTIC phase where they send a ZK proof attesting that they maintain enough liquidity to settle all the pending transactions (incoming and outgoing) that they are involved in. If the OPTIMISTIC phase is successful (meaning that all pending transactions can be settled and none of the banks drop out or abort), banks move to the SETTLEMENT phase where they update their own final balance locally and also update the global secret shared state and commitment values representing the final balance of all other banks.

However, if the OPTIMISTIC phase fails, then banks resort to a FALLBACK phase where a fault-tolerant MPC is used to re-conduct the liquidity check step. If the check fails (meaning that all of the pending transactions cannot be settled due to low liquidity), banks use MPC to find the optimal set of transaction values that can be settled as a part of the RESOLUTION step. Finally, the banks move on to the SETTLEMENT phase to update the final balance and global state in accordance with the set of transactions that were computed in the FALLBACK phase. In order to conduct the netting procedure repeatedly over multiple invocations, banks can simply repeat all the steps involved in the protocol starting from the INPUT phase. Also, any unsettled set of transactions from a particular invocation of the netting protocol can be carried over to the next invocation for settlement.

4   Protocol and Security Proof

In Appendix A, we describe the construction of our protocol Π_{netting}, shown in Fig. 3, which materializes the high-level design proposed in Sect. 3. To analyze the security of our construction, we also outline an ideal functionality $\mathcal{F}_{\text{netting}}$ in Appendix B, shown in Fig. 4, which serves as a model of our protocol, and in particular, serves as its formal security specification. Finally, in Appendix C, we provide a proof sketch that our protocol Π_{netting} securely realizes the ideal functionality $\mathcal{F}_{\text{netting}}$.

5   Implementation and Empirical Analysis

We evaluate our proposed approach along 2 axes: i) We compare how much improvement in "Percentage Settlement" do we gain by using Karmarkar based linear programming approach as compared to other approaches, ii) We benchmark the computation and communication costs of the cryptographic steps in our protocol, especially the MPC specific steps. We will now describe our evaluation results in the following subsections.

5.1 Comparison of Different Netting Algorithms

In this section, we compare our Karmarkar based approach for netting optimization with two other approaches - naive algorithm and FIFO based algorithm. The naive algorithm either settles all the pending transactions if the balance constraint is satisfied, otherwise doesn't select any of the pending transactions. The FIFO based algorithm [Cao+20] assigns a priority value to each pending transaction in the outgoing transaction set of each bank, and always tries to settle the highest priority transactions first. We compare these algorithms based on "Percentage Settlement" metric, which is defined as the fraction of total *pending* transaction amount in the input pending transaction graph $G_{n \times n}$ that was settled after the netting process.

In our experiments, we fixed some initial balance, equally allotted to each bank, and randomly sampled transactions for them to attempt from a normal distribution with varying parameters. Specifically, we fix the total number of banks to 10 and generated a random 10×10 size pending transaction graph with the transaction values drawn from a normal distribution with $\mu = 500$ and some fixed σ in the range $[50, 225]$. Then we simulated three algorithms - Karmarkar, naive, FIFO [Cao+20] - and compared them based on "Percentage Settlement". Since the FIFO approach processes the transactions in some user-specified priority order, we fixed an implicit ordering among the outgoing transactions from P_i in the following way: $t_{i,j}$ has higher priority than $t_{i,j'}$ iff $j < j'$. Also, for the Karmarkar algorithm, the maximum number of iterations was fixed to 60.

Figure 2 in the appendix shows the results of our analysis for different parameter values of initial balance and normal distribution. We observe that Karmarkar algorithm performs much better than both the naive and FIFO approach by a significant margin. For e.g. for an initial balance of 160 units and normal distribution parameters fixed as $\mu = 500, \sigma = 75$, Karmarkar had a percentage settlement value of 90% compared to FIFO and naive approach which yielded only 40% and 0% respectively. As expected, the naive algorithm performs the worst with percentage settlement almost close to 0%. In contrast, the percentage settlement by Karmarkar algorithm is *consistently* more than 80%. We also observe that percentage settlement of all 3 algorithms decrease with the increase in standard deviation parameter σ. The FIFO approach performs similar to the naive algorithm for low initial balance (e.g. 40, 80) cases. However, for high initial balance(e.g. 320), FIFO starts providing better percentage settlement values.

5.2 Benchmarking the Cryptographic Cost of Π_{netting}

We implemented the MPC specific steps of our protocol in MP-SPDZ [Kel20] platform which allows rapid prototyping of MPC protocols. We tested our implementation in the malicious shamir mode for different number of banks. In our experiments, the number of MPC nodes was fixed to 4, the program bit length was set to default 64 bit (which determines the cost of comparison operations and the resolution of account balances) and the field size was set to 256 bit prime. We benchmark our implementation in terms of 3 parameters - CPU time (per MPC node), communication cost (per MPC node), and number of MPC rounds. We observe that the total costs are highly sensitive to the number of banks in the system. Also, we noticed that the Karmarkar algorithm is the most expensive step in the entire MPC computation and is responsible more than 99% of the overall cost of MPC specific steps in the protocol. Table 1 in the appendix provides a summary of the combined cost of different MPC steps which includes the expensive Karmarkar step.

Based on the benchmarks from one of the implementations of Bulletproofs protocol [dal], we estimate that the total cost of running the ZK specific steps in our protocol would be on the order of 10–100 milliseconds. This observation, coupled with the fact that the non-Karmarkar steps in the MPC phase only incur less than 1% of the costs presented in Table 1, suggests that our proposed protocol is highly efficient in cases where the liquidity check succeeds. We also note that since the number of MPC rounds in Table 1 is relatively modest, there is much avenue to exploit parallelization between each MPC round to reduce the overall running time. For e.g. if there is enough parallelization to conduct 10 MPC rounds per second, then the total running time for 10 banks (second last row in Table 1) would reduce to around an hour.

6   Conclusion

In this paper, we proposed a distributed privacy-preserving protocol which banks can use to securely conduct the netting process without the need for a central bank to be actively involved. We also provided a sketch of the security proof of our proposed protocol along with empirical analysis of its efficiency and costs.

Note that in the case the honest majority assumption among MPC servers is violated, the MPC nodes might be able to artificially inflate the total liquidity inside the system. A possible future direction of our work is to handle this case using a *publicly auditable MPC* which will guarantee that an external auditor (for example the central bank) can reliably detect in-case such a malicious activity happens.

Appendix

A   Protocol

In this section, we will describe the construction of our protocol Π_{netting}, shown in Fig. 3, which materializes the high-level design proposed in Sect. 3, and also realizes the formal $\mathcal{F}_{\text{netting}}$ functionality described in Appendix B.

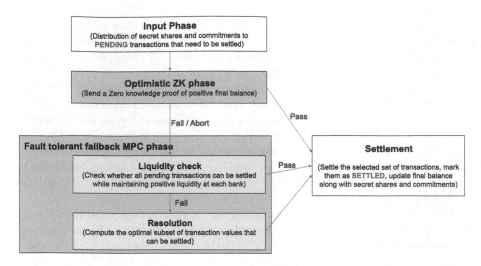

Fig. 1. A schematic of secure and decentralized protocol for the netting process

Table 1. Combined cost of different MPC steps in Π_{netting}, in terms of CPU time, communication and number of sequential rounds, for different number of banks (4, 6, 8, 10, 12) in the system

Number of banks	CPU time (in mins)	Communication cost(in GB)	Number of MPC rounds
4	12	53	9803
6	60	277	18743
8	223	1044	31343
10	686	3152	47543
12	1586	8107	66743

A.1   Protocol Assumptions

Before describing the protocol, we explain the assumptions underlying our construction:

1. Every pair of banks $(\mathsf{P}_i, \mathsf{P}_j)$ should have mutually agreed upon two aggregate transaction values $(t_{i,j}, t_{j,i})$ (i.e. one in each direction) prior to the initiation of the netting protocol.
2. A commitment cmt_{b_i} which encodes the initial balance of each bank P_i is *publicly* available. In addition to this, the value b_i and randomness $r_{b_i}^{\mathsf{cmt}}$ associated with the commitment is *privately* known by each bank P_i.
3. Each bank P_i will have a secret sharing of the global state st which encodes the current balance b_i of each bank P_i at the beginning of each netting day.
4. Each bank P_i has access to a publicly available common reference string crs which has been generated in a secure fashion.

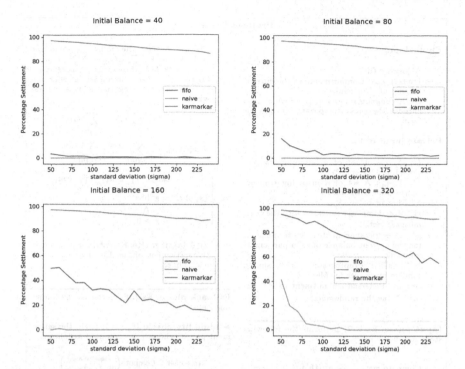

Fig. 2. Comparison of three different netting algorithms (naive, FIFO, Karmarkar) for different values of fixed initial balance (40, 80, 160, 320). The transactions were generated from a normal distribution with $\mu = 500$ and σ varying as per X-axis. The Y-axis shows the percentage of total transaction amount that was settled by applying the netting algorithm

To bootstrap the system, a central bank (acting as a trusted third party) can make commitments and secret shares of initial balances available to all the participating banks along with a crs[2]. Thereafter, the central bank can leave the system and the protocol will ensure that the commitments and secret shares are correctly and securely updated on each invocation of the netting protocol.

We also assume that all parties have access to a public bulletin board which they can use for broadcasting messages. In the real world, this can be instantiated using a blockchain or in general any scheme which implements the authenticated broadcast primitive. For ease of protocol description, we will assume that the MPC protocol is executed in the standard offline-online paradigm. In the offline phase, banks interactively pre-process shared random elements which are used for executing the online phase in an efficient manner. We use the bracket notation $[a]_i$ to denote a secret-share of value a held by P_i.

---

[2] Alternatively, the crs generation can be done in a distributed way by local banks without relying on the central bank as shown in some of the recent works [BGM17, BGG18,KKK20].

Protocol Π_{netting}

Public inputs:

- Algorithm OPT
- $\{\text{cmt}_{b_i}\}_{i\in[n]}$: Commitments to the current balance of all n banks
- crs: A common reference string which also encodes the generator parameters g, h for Com.

Private input of P_i:

- $\{t_{i,j}\}_{j\in[n]}$: A set of n outgoing transactions to each bank P_j
- $\{\widetilde{t_{j,i}}\}_{j\in[n]}$: A set of n incoming transactions from each bank P_j
- b_i: Current balance
- $r^{\text{cmt}}_{b_i}$: Randomness associated with the commitment cmt_{b_i}
- $[\text{st}]_i$: A secret sharing of the state st encoding the current balance of each participating bank
- $[r^{\text{msk}}], [s^{\text{msk}}]$: Preprocessed secret shared random mask bits for MPC
- $\text{cmt}_{r^{\text{msk}}}$: Pedersen commitment to r^{msk} using s^{msk} as the randomness

---

Input phase: Each P_i performs the following steps for all $j \in [n]$:

- Compute $\text{cmt}_{t_{i,j}} \leftarrow g^{t_{i,j}} h^{r^{\text{cmt}}_{i,j}}$, a commitment to $t_{i,j}$ using uniform $r^{\text{cmt}}_{i,j}$
- Send $(t_{i,j}, r^{\text{cmt}}_{i,j})$ to P_j and receive $(t_{j,i}, r^{\text{cmt}}_{j,i})$ from P_j
- If $t_{j,i} = \widetilde{t_{j,i}}$, compute $\overline{\text{cmt}}_{t_{j,i}} \leftarrow g^{t_{j,i}} h^{r^{\text{cmt}}_{j,i}}$ Else set $\overline{\text{cmt}}_{t_{j,i}} := \bot$
- Receive $[r^{\text{msk}}]_k, [s^{\text{msk}}]_k$ from each P_k and reconstruct $r^{\text{msk}}_{i,j}, s^{\text{msk}}_{i,j}$
- Broadcast the following:
  - $\text{cmt}_{t_{i,j}}, \overline{\text{cmt}}_{t_{j,i}}$
  - $\widetilde{t_{i,j}} \leftarrow t_{i,j} + r^{\text{msk}}_{i,j}$, masked transaction inputs for MPC scheme
  - NiZKAoK proof $\pi'_{i,j}$, proving that MPC input $\widetilde{t_{i,j}}$ is consistent with $\text{cmt}_{t_{i,j}}$, using $(t_{i,j}, r^{\text{cmt}}_{i,j}, s^{\text{msk}}_{i,j})$ as witness:

$$\text{ZK} \begin{cases} (x', y', s') : & \text{cmt}_{t_{i,j}} = g^{x'} h^{y'} \\ & \wedge \\ & \text{cmt}_{r^{\text{msk}}} \cdot (g^{\widetilde{t_{i,j}}})^{-1} = h^{s'} \cdot (g^{x'})^{-1} \end{cases}$$

Optimistic phase: Each P_i performs the following steps:

▶ **Input consistency check:** $\forall j, k \in [n] \times [n]$, mark $\text{cmt}_{t_{j,k}}, \widetilde{t_{j,k}}$ as ABORTED and ignore it from any future computation if the following condition holds:

$$\text{NiZKAoK.Verify}(\pi'_{j,k}) = 0 \bigvee \text{cmt}_{t_{j,k}} \neq \overline{\text{cmt}}_{t_{j,k}}$$

▶ **Liquidity check:**

- Check whether the following condition is true: $b_i + \sum_{j=1}^{n} t_{j,i} - \sum_{j=1}^{n} t_{i,j} \geq 0$. If check fails, broadcast "Insufficient liquidity". Else, broadcast a NiZKAoK range proof π_i using (w_1, w_2) as witness where

$$w_1 = b_i + \sum_{j\in[n]} t_{j,i} - \sum_{j\in[n]} t_{i,j}$$

$$w_2 = r^{\text{cmt}}_{b_i} + \sum_{j\in[n]} r^{\text{cmt}}_{j,i} - \sum_{j\in[n]} r^{\text{cmt}}_{i,j}$$

$$\text{ZK} \begin{cases} (x, y) : & \text{cmt}_{b_i} \prod_{j\in[n]} \text{cmt}_{t_{j,i}} \prod_{j\in[n]} \text{cmt}_{t_{i,j}}^{-1} \\ & = g^x h^y \\ & \wedge \\ & x \geq 0 \end{cases}$$

- $\forall j \in [n]$, if NiZKAoK.Verify$(\pi_j) = 1$, begin the settlement phase. Else begin the fallback phase

---

Fallback phase: Each P_i performs the following steps:

▶ **Liquidity check:** If $lc = 1$, begin the settlement phase, where lc is computed as follows:

$$lc \leftarrow \text{MPC.Compute}\left(\genfrac{}{}{0pt}{}{f_{\text{liquidityCheck}}}{\text{st}, \{\widetilde{t_{j,k}}\}_{\forall j,k}}\right)$$

Here $f_{\text{liquidityCheck}}$ is a function that checks whether each bank has sufficient liquidity to net all the pending transactions.

▶ **Resolution:** Compute the optimal fractional transaction values and a secret-shared state $[\text{st}']_i$

$$\{f_{i,j}, f_{j,i}\}_{\forall j}, [\text{st}']_i \leftarrow \text{MPC.Compute}\left(\genfrac{}{}{0pt}{}{\text{OPT}}{\text{st}, \{\widetilde{t_{k,l}}\}_{\forall k,l}}\right)$$

Settlement phase: Each P_i performs the following steps:

▶ If liquidity check was successful:

- Update the secret-share balance of each P_j, stored in st, by adding and subtracting all the shares of incoming and outgoing transactions respectively.
- Update the balance commitment cmt_{b_j} of each P_j by multiplying and dividing the commitments to all incoming and outgoing transactions respectively to obtain $\text{cmt}_{b'_j}$
- Compute own final balance $b'_i \leftarrow w_1$ and the randomness to $\text{cmt}_{b'_i} \leftarrow w_2$ in cleartext.

▶ If liquidity check was not successful, compute secret-shares and commitments to new balance b'_j of each bank P_j by running MPC on the state st′ obtained as the output of Resolution step. Additionally, each P_j obtains b'_j and randomness associated with $\text{cmt}_{b'_j}$ in cleartext as the output of MPC.

Fig. 3. Protocol for Netting procedure

A.2   Protocol description

We will now walk through the various steps in our Π_{netting} protocol. In the Input phase, each bank P_i broadcasts Pedersen commitments $\mathsf{cmt}_{t_{i,j}}$ to all its n set of outgoing transactions. Additionally, it sends the opening to these commitments (i.e. the transaction value along with the randomness) to each of the respective receiving bank P_j of each transaction. The receiving bank then locally checks whether the transaction value $t_{i,j}$ matches with the incoming transaction value $\overline{t_{i,j}}$ that was agreed upon prior to the beginning of netting protocol. If so, the receiving bank P_j also broadcasts a commitment $\overline{\mathsf{cmt}_{t_{i,j}}}$ which acts as an acknowledgement to the fact that P_j has verified and is willing to go ahead with $t_{i,j}$. Aside from the commitments, each bank also provides masked transactions as input to the MPC protocol using preprocessed random values r^{msk} along with a proof π' attesting that each masked transaction input to the MPC protocol is consistent with the transaction value inside the commitment.

The optimistic phase begins with a step where all banks locally check for input consistency of each transaction by verifying the proof and commitment associated with it. Any transaction which fails such a check is ignored from all future computations. Post this, each bank P_i locally checks whether it has enough balance to net all its incident transactions. If so, it broadcasts a noninteractive range proof attesting to this fact. At the same time, it checks the proofs broadcasted by other banks. If all the n proofs verify, then it acts as a signal that each bank in the system has enough liquidity to net the entire transaction graph, and therefore banks can safely begin the settlement phase.

If some of the proofs did not verify, each bank moves to the Fallback phase which is conducted primarily using a $n/3$ fault-tolerant MPC. This phase begins with a liquidity check step where MPC is used to check whether each bank has enough balance to net all incident transactions. If the check passes, each bank moves to the settlement phase. Otherwise a resolution step is executed where banks collectively execute an algorithm OPT, using MPC, to find optimal fractional transaction values that can be netted. In our experiments, we instantiate OPT using the Karmarkar algorithm.

Finally, in the settlement phase, we take two branches depending on whether or not the liquidity check was successful in the earlier phases. If the liquidity check was indeed successful, banks just update the commitments and secret sharing of each bank's balance locally by leveraging the linearity of secret share and homomorphic nature and pedersen commitment respectively. Otherwise, if the liquidity check was unsuccessful in earlier phases, banks use MPC to compute the commitments and secret sharing of each bank's final balance. The use of MPC is needed in this case to account for the fractional transaction values that was computed in the Resolution step. Once the settlement phase is complete, the commitments and secret sharings of final balances serve as the starting point for the future invocation of the Π_{netting} protocol.

B   Ideal functionality

To analyze the security, we begin by describing our ideal functionality $\mathcal{F}_{\text{netting}}$, shown in Fig. 4, which serves as a model of our protocol, and in particular, serves as its formal security specification. The functionality proceeds, like the protocol, according to 4 different phases - Input phase, Optimistic Phase, Fallback phase and the Settlement phase. In each phase, the functionality behaves in a way

---

Functionality $\mathcal{F}_{\text{netting}}$

$\mathcal{F}_{\text{netting}}$ proceeds as follows, running with parties(banks) $P_1, \ldots, P_n$, a internal state st encoding the current balance b_i for each bank P_i, an optimization algorithm OPT, and an adversary $\mathcal{S}$

Input Phase:

- Wait to receive n outgoing transaction values $\{t_{i,j}\}_{j \in [n]}$ and n incoming transaction values $\{\bar{t}_{j,i}\}_{j \in [n]}$ from each bank P_i
- For each outgoing transaction $t_{i,j}$:
  - If $t_{i,j} = \bar{t}_{i,j}$, record $t_{i,j}$ internally
  - If $t_{i,j} \neq \bar{t}_{i,j}$, mark $t_{i,j}$ as ABORTED.
- Send "Transaction $P_i \to P_j$ received" to each bank $\{P_k\}_{k \in [n]}$ and $\mathcal{S}$

Optimistic Phase:
▶ **Liquidity check:**

- If the following constraint is satisfied for all $i \in [n]$, set check ← True else set check ← False
  Positive balance constraint:

$$b_i + \sum_{j=1}^{n} t_{j,i} - \sum_{j=1}^{n} t_{i,j} \geq 0$$

- On receiving ABORT from any bank P_i, set check ← False
- Send check to each bank $\{P_k\}_{k \in [n]}$ and $\mathcal{S}$

If check is False:

- Send "optimistic phase failed" to each bank P_i and $\mathcal{S}$
- Let $\mathbb{F}$ represent the set of banks for which the constraint was not satisfied and $\mathbb{A}$ represent the set of banks from which an ABORT signal was received. Send $\mathbb{F}, \mathbb{A}$ to $\mathcal{S}$
- Initiate the Fallback phase.

If check is True:

- Send "optimistic phase successful" to each bank P_i and $\mathcal{S}$.
- Initiate the Settlement phase

Fallback Phase:
▶ **Liquidity check:**

- Re-execute the *first* step of liquidity check procedure defined in the Optimistic phase.
- If check is False:
  - Send "fallback liquidity check failed" to each bank P_i and $\mathcal{S}$.
  - Initiate the Resolution phase.
- If check is True:
  - Send "fallback liquidity check successful" to each bank P_i and $\mathcal{S}$.
  - Initiate the Settlement phase

▶ **Resolution:**

- $\{f_{i,j}\}_{i \in [n], j \in [n]} \leftarrow \text{OPT}(\text{st}, \{t_{i,j}\}_{i \in [n], j \in [n]})$, compute the optimal fractional transaction values
- Send $\{f_{i,j}\}_{j \in [n]}$ to each sender bank P_i and receiver bank P_j

---

Settlement Phase:

- If liquidity check was successful, compute the final balance b_i' of each bank P_i as follows:

$$b_i' \leftarrow b_i + \sum_{j=1}^{n} t_{j,i} - \sum_{j=1}^{n} t_{i,j}$$

- If liquidity check failed, compute the final balance b_i' of each bank P_i as follows:

$$b_i' \leftarrow b_i + \sum_{j=1}^{n} f_{j,i} \times t_{j,i} - \sum_{j=1}^{n} f_{i,j} \times t_{i,j}$$

- Update internal state st by changing the current balance of each bank P_i to b_i'

Fig. 4. Ideal functionality for Netting procedure

consistent with our desired security properties. In general, these are: Integrity —
only the correct optimization functions are applied to the chosen inputs, and all
balance restrictions are respected; and Confidentiality — each final transaction
is only revealed to the sender and receiver, no one else. We now describe the
functionality in more detail:

Input Phase: In the input phase, the functionality waits to receive a set of n
proposed outgoing and incoming aggregate transactions from each bank P_i. For
each proposed outgoing transaction $t_{i,j}$ received from P_i, it checks whether $t_{i,j}$
matches with the proposed incoming transaction $\overline{t_{i,j}}$ received from P_j. If the
match is successful, it records $t_{i,j}$ internally for further processing. Otherwise
$t_{i,j}$ is marked as ABORTED indicating that it won't be considered for further
processing. This check makes sure that each proposed outgoing transaction is
validated by both the sending and receiving bank before being considered for
further processing.

In either case, $\mathcal{F}_{\text{netting}}$ notifies all banks and the adversary that a transaction
between P_i and P_j has been received. Such a notification captures that the fact
that the occurrence of transaction proposal need not be hidden. This would not
be a problem in the real world because i) Every honest bank P_i is required to
send a padded outgoing transaction $t_{i,j}$ for all n receiving banks (which might
include dummy zero-valued outgoing transactions for receiving banks that P_i
doesn't owe any transaction amount to), ii) The notification does not reveal the
value inside $t_{i,j}$.

Optimistic Phase: Once the input phase is complete, $\mathcal{F}_{\text{netting}}$ starts executing
the Optimistic phase. In this phase, $\mathcal{F}_{\text{netting}}$ optimistically assumes that each
bank P_i has enough liquidity (current balance) b_i to net all the outgoing and
incoming transactions that P_i is involved in. During the check evaluation, it
also listens for an ABORT signal from any bank. This captures the fact that a
malicious bank has the ability to abort the liquidity check procedure(for e.g.
by not participating in the protocol). At the end of liquidity check procedure,
all banks are notified of the result. This captures the fact that $\mathcal{F}_{\text{netting}}$ doesn't
aim to hide from the banks whether optimistic phase was successful or not.
Additionally, in-case the check was unsuccessful, $\mathcal{F}_{\text{netting}}$ leaks the identity of
low liquidity banks to the adversary.[3]

If the check is successful, then $\mathcal{F}_{\text{netting}}$ directly proceeds onto the settlement
phase. However, if the check wasn't successful, then $\mathcal{F}_{\text{netting}}$ proceeds to the
Fallback phase.

Fallback Phase: In the fallback phase, the positive balance constraint is re-
evaluated for each bank and the result is sent to all the banks. Note that in this
phase $\mathcal{F}_{\text{netting}}$ doesn't listen for ABORT signals from any bank. This captures the
fact that the liquidity check in this phase is "fault-tolerant" to aborts. If the

---

[3] This kind of leakage is part of our specification because our proposed protocol doesn't
aim to hide the identity of low liquidity banks at the end of optimistic phase. However, such leakage can be avoided by modifying the protocol to include an MPC step
(alongside ZK proof) in the Optimistic phase.

check passes, $\mathcal{F}_{\mathsf{netting}}$ directly proceeds onto the Settlement phase. Otherwise, it proceeds to the Resolution step.

In the resolution step, $\mathcal{F}_{\mathsf{netting}}$ executes an optimization algorithm OPT by providing the state st (encoding the current balance of each bank) and the set of all pending transactions $\{t_{i,j}\}_{i\in[n],j\in[n]}$ as input. It receives in return a set of fractional values $\{f_{i,j}\}_{i\in[n],j\in[n]}$ where each $f_{i,j}$ is a real value between $[0,1]$ indicating the fraction of transaction $t_{i,j}$ that can be optimally netted. Additionally, the sending bank P_i and receiving bank P_j receives the fractional values pertaining to the transactions they are involved in. This allows the banks to know what fraction of their each incoming/outgoing transaction will be processed in the Settlement phase for balance update.

Settlement Phase: The settlement phase is primarily involved in updating the internal state st to reflect the new balance of each bank P_i. In case the liquidity check was successful in an earlier phase, the final balance b'_i of each bank P_i is calculated by adding the set of all its incoming transaction values to the initial balance and then subtracting the set of all outgoing transaction values. If the liquidity check was not successful during earlier phases, then the fractional values $f_{i,j}$ (which were obtained during the resolution step) are factored in for the final balance calculation.

C   Security analysis

We first offer a very informal explanation of the security properties our construction is designed to provide:

1. **Confidentiality/Privacy**:
   – The hiding property of commitment scheme and the zero knowledge property of ZK proof guarantees that the transaction values remain completely hidden to all participants (except of course the sender and receiver of that transaction who are entitled to learn and attest the value)
   – As long as there is an honest majority of MPC servers, the backup values of each transaction in the form of secret shares do not leak any information about the transaction content (except ofcourse the sender and receiver of that transaction who are entitled to learn and attest the value)

   Note that anonymity of the banks is not a goal here since the banking institutions are public and their identities are already known in the real world. Instead, we think of the balance and transaction amounts which banks want to net as private data. In that sense, our confidentiality property adequately captures the notion of "privacy" and guarantees that privacy of banks is maintained with respect to their balance and transaction amounts.

2. **Integrity**: The soundness of zero knowledge proofs and the correctness of underlying MPC guarantees that a malicious bank would not be able to manipulate its final balance or steal liquidity from other banks.

However since we are using an ideal functionality $\mathcal{F}_{\text{netting}}$ as our security model, our primary validation approach is to show that our protocol Π_{netting} UC realizes [Can01] this functionality. In more detail, we must construct a simulator $\mathcal{S}$ which runs in the ideal world but can simulate the view of any adversary in the real world. The construction of our simulator can be roughly broken down into two aspects: Confidentiality/Simulation: simulation of the protocol messages from honest parties, which guarantees that the protocol does not reveal more information than intended, and Integrity/Extraction: extraction of the inputs of corrupt parties, which guarantees that output must be consistent with the intended function applied to some valid choice of inputs. Henceforth, we'll use $\mathbb{H}$ and $\overline{\mathbb{H}}$ to denote the set of indices corresponding to honest and corrupt parties respectively.

We begin by summarizing the views of the adversary in the Real world, which our simulator must produce:

Real:

▶ Com messages:

- $\{\text{cmt}_{t_{i,j}}\}_{i\in\mathbb{H}, j\in[n]}$, transaction commitments produced by honest parties.
- $\{\text{cmt}_{b_i}\}_{i\in\mathbb{H}}$, initial balance commitments of honest parties.

▶ MPC messages:

- $\{\widetilde{t_{i,j}}\}_{i\in\mathbb{H}, j\in[n]}$, MPC encodings of transaction inputs of honest parties.
- Secret sharings (upto t evaluation points, one for each corrupt party in $\overline{\mathbb{H}}$) of all the intermediate and final MPC computation.
- lc, a cleartext binary value denoting the output of MPC.Compute $(f_{\text{liquidityCheck}}, \cdot)$

▶ NiZKAoK messages:

- crs, common reference string
- $\{\pi\}_{i\in\mathbb{H}}$, zero knowledge proofs for positive balance
- $\{\pi'\}_{i\in\mathbb{H}}$, zero knowledge proofs for input consistency between , and MPC

Next we describe the Ideal world view of our simulator, which it can make use of:

Ideal:

- Result of the liquidity check in the optimistic and fallback phase.
- $\{f_{i,j}\}_{i\in\overline{\mathbb{H}}, j\in[n]}, \{f_{i,j}\}_{i\in[n], j\in\overline{\mathbb{H}}}$, fractional transaction values derived from the optimization algorithm OPT

Having described the views, we will now provide a high-level sketch of how $\mathcal{S}$ will use the ideal world view to simulate the real world view of any adversary in the real world.

$\mathcal{S}$:

- Sample a crs and internally store any trapdoors td_{crs} associated with the crs. Additionally send the crs to the environment.

- Receive inputs $\{\mathsf{inp}_i\}_{i\in\overline{\mathbb{H}}}$, corresponding to each corrupt party, from the environment.
- Run the extractor algorithm on $\{\mathsf{inp}_i\}_{i\in\overline{\mathbb{H}}}$ to extract the plaintext values and then send it to $\mathcal{F}_{\mathsf{netting}}$
- Receive the outputs from $\mathcal{F}_{\mathsf{netting}}$ as described in Ideal.
- Send simulated proofs and commitments, for values described in Real, on behalf of each party in $\mathbb{H}$ generated using $\mathsf{td}_{\mathsf{crs}}$
- Send simulated secret shares for all the MPC messages described in Real on behalf of each party in $\mathbb{H}$

We now turn to the extraction portion of our construction. First we summarize the protocol messages from corrupt parties in the Real world.

Real: The dummy adversary receives the following instructions for each $i \in \overline{\mathbb{H}}$:

- Broadcast the following messages:
  - $\{\mathsf{cmt}_{t_{i,j}}\}_{j\in[n]}$, transaction commitments
  - $\{\widetilde{t_{i,j}}\}_{j\in[n]}$, MPC encodings of transaction.
  - π_i, zero knowledge proof of positive balance
  - π_i', zero knowledge proof for input consistency between commitments to transaction and their MPC encoding.
- For all $j \in \mathbb{H}$, send the plaintext transaction and commitment randomness $(t_{i,j}, r_{i,j})$ to P_j

Next we describe the outputs the simulator must provide to the ideal functionality $\mathcal{F}_{\mathsf{netting}}$:

Ideal: The plaintext values underlying the commitments, MPC encodings and ZK proofs of each party in $\overline{\mathbb{H}}$

We now summarize how $\mathcal{S}$ can construct the Ideal view using Real view.

$\mathcal{S}$:

- Sample a crs and internally store any trapdoors $\mathsf{td}_{\mathsf{crs}}$ associated with the crs. Additionally send the crs to the environment.
- Receive instructions for the dummy adversary, including all the message values, as described in Real.
- Run the MPC extractor to extract the inputs underlying MPC encodings $\{\widetilde{t_{i,j}}\}_{i\in\overline{\mathbb{H}},j\in[n]}$
- For all $i \in \overline{\mathbb{H}}$, if π_i is a valid proof, then output the MPC input which was extracted in the previous step.

Thus, by showing the construction of simulator and extractor, we can ensure that Π_{netting} securely realizes the $\mathcal{F}_{\mathsf{netting}}$ functionality.

D Enhancements

Thanks to generality of the LP formulation, our proposed design is flexible enough to enable different variants of the netting problem to be executed. We summarize 2 such variants below that we executed during our experiments. Details have been omitted due to space constraints.

1. Support for multi-asset transactions: In this variant, each transaction between a pair of banks is associated with more than one assets. For example, a dual-asset transaction between P_i and P_j might have a transaction flow of 100$ from P_i to P_j coupled with a transaction of 80€ from P_j to P_i. Such kind of multi-asset transactions can be easily integrated in our design by accounting for the balance constraints for each of the assets in the Karmarkar LP formulation (along with other phases).
2. Support for priority-based netting: In this variant, each transaction might have a priority value associated with it. Therefore, some transactions might be high priority while others might be medium or low priority. It is necessary to give more preference to high priority transactions during netting. The Karmarkar-based optimization algorithm can be easily adapted to include such priority values by encoding the priorities in the objective function of our LP formulation.

References

[Kar84] Karmarkar, N.: A new polynomial-time algorithm for linear programming. In: Proceedings of the Sixteenth Annual ACM Symposium on Theory of Computing, pp. 302–311 (1984)

[FS86] Fiat, A., Shamir, A.: How to prove yourself: practical solutions to identification and signature problems. In: Odlyzko, A.M. (ed.) CRYPTO 1986. LNCS, vol. 263, pp. 186–194. Springer, Heidelberg (1987). https://doi.org/10.1007/3-540-47721-7_12

[Tom87] Tomlin, J.A.: An experimental approach to karmarkar's projective method for linear programming. In: Computation Mathematical Programming, pp. 175–191. Springer (1987). https://doi.org/10.1007/BFb0121187.pdf

[Ped91] Pedersen, T.P.: Non-interactive and information-theoretic secure verifiable secret sharing. In: Feigenbaum, J. (ed.) CRYPTO 1991. LNCS, vol. 576, pp. 129–140. Springer, Heidelberg (1992). https://doi.org/10.1007/3-540-46766-1_9

[Can01] Canetti, T.: Universally composable security: a new paradigm for cryptographic protocols. In: Proceedings 42nd IEEE Symposium on Foundations of Computer Science, pp. 136–145. IEEE (2001)

[DN03] Damgård, I., Nielsen, J.B.: Universally composable efficient multiparty computation from threshold homomorphic encryption. In: Boneh, D. (ed.) CRYPTO 2003. LNCS, vol. 2729, pp. 247–264. Springer, Heidelberg (2003). https://doi.org/10.1007/978-3-540-45146-4_15

[BGM17] Bowe, S., Gabizon, A., Miers, I.: Scalable multi-party computation for zk-SNARK parameters in the random beacon model. IACR Cryptol. ePrint Arch. **2017**, 1050 (2017)

[Hao17] Hao, F.: Schnorr non-interactive zero-knowledge proof. RFC 8235, RFC Editor (2017)

[BGG18] Bowe, S., Gabizon, A., Green, M.D.: A multi-party protocol for constructing the public parameters of the Pinocchio zk-SNARK. In: Zohar, A., et al. (eds.) FC 2018. LNCS, vol. 10958, pp. 64–77. Springer, Heidelberg (2019). https://doi.org/10.1007/978-3-662-58820-8_5

[Bün+18] Bünz, B., Bootle, J., Boneh, D., Poelstra, A., Wuille, P., Maxwell, G.: Bulletproofs: short proofs for confidential transactions and more. In: 2018 IEEE Symposium on Security and Privacy (SP), pp. 315–334. IEEE (2018)

[Lu+19] Lu, D., Yurek, T., Kulshreshtha, S., Govind, R., Kate, A., Miller, A.: HoneyBadgerMPC and AsynchroMix: practical asynchronous MPC and its application to anonymous communication. In: Proceedings of the 2019 ACM SIGSAC Conference on Computer and Communications Security, pp. 887–903 (2019)

[Cao+20] Cao, S., Yuan, Y., De Caro, A., Nandakumar, K., Elkhiyaoui, K., Hu, Y.: Decentralized privacy-preserving netting protocol on blockchain for payment systems. In: Bonneau, J., Heninger, N. (eds.) FC 2020. LNCS, vol. 12059, pp. 137–155. Springer, Cham (2020). https://doi.org/10.1007/978-3-030-51280-4_9

[GY20] Galal, H.S., Youssef, A.M.: Privacy preserving netting protocol for inter-bank payments. In: Garcia-Alfaro, J., Navarro-Arribas, G., Herrera-Joancomarti, J. (eds.) DPM/CBT -2020. LNCS, vol. 12484, pp. 319–334. Springer, Cham (2020). https://doi.org/10.1007/978-3-030-66172-4_21

[Kel20] Keller, M.: MP-SPDZ: a versatile framework for multi-party computation. Cryptology ePrint Archive, Report 2020/521 (2020). https://eprint.iacr.org/2020/521

[KKK20] Kerber, T., Kiayias, A., Kohlweiss, M.: Mining for privacy: how to bootstrap a snarky blockchain. IACR Cryptol. ePrint Arch. **2020**, 401 (2020)

[ASA21] Atapoor, S., Smart, N.P., Alaoui, Y.T.: Private liquidity matching using MPC. IACR Cryptol. ePrint Arch., 2021:475 (2021)

[BJ07] European Central Bank and Bank of Japan. Payment systems: liquidity saving mechanisms in a distributed ledger environment (2107). https://www.ecb.europa.eu/pub/pdf/other/ecb.stella_project_report_september_2017.pdf

[dal] Dalek cryptography/bulletproofs. A pure-rust implementation of bulletproofs using Ristretto. https://github.com/dalek-cryptography/bulletproofs. Accessed 24 Sept 2020

[Mar] European Central Bank Market Infrastructure Development Division. Insights on partial settlement. https://www.ecb.europa.eu/paym/target/t2s/profuse/shared/pdf/insights_on_partial_settlement.pdf. Accessed 24 Sept 2020

[Mel] BNY Mellon. Partial settlement frequently-asked-questions. https://www.bnymellon.com/emea/en/_locale-assets/pdf/regulatory-information/csdr/partial-settlement-frequently-asked-questions.pdf. Accessed 24 Sept 2020

[Sin] Monetary Authority of Singapore. Project Ubin: Central bank digital money using distributed ledger technology. https://www.mas.gov.sg/schemes-and-initiatives/Project-Ubin

NFT Wash Trading

Quantifying Suspicious Behaviour in NFT Markets

Victor von Wachter[1]([✉]), Johannes Rude Jensen[1,2], Ferdinand Regner[3], and Omri Ross[1,2]

[1] University of Copenhagen, Copenhagen, Denmark
victor.vonwachter@di.ku.dk
[2] eToroX Labs, Copenhagen, Denmark
[3] University of Vienna, Vienna, Austria

Abstract. The smart contract-based markets for non-fungible tokens (NFTs) on the Ethereum blockchain have seen tremendous growth in 2021, with trading volumes peaking at $3.5b in September 2021. This dramatic surge has led to industry observers questioning the authenticity of on-chain volumes, given the absence of identity requirements and the ease with which agents can control multiple addresses. We examine potentially illicit trading patterns in the decentralized NFT markets from January 2018 to mid-November 2021, gathering data from the 52 largest collections by volume. Our findings indicate that within our sample 3.93% of addresses, processing a total of 2.04% of sale transactions, trigger suspicions of market abuse. Flagged transactions contaminate nearly all collections and may have inflated the authentic trading volumes by as much as $149,5 m for the period. Most flagged transaction patterns alternate between a few addresses, indicating a predisposition for manual trading. We submit that the results presented here may serve as a viable lower bound estimate for NFT wash trading on Ethereum. Even so, we argue that wash trading may be less common than what industry observers have previously estimated. We contribute to the emerging discourse on the identification and deterrence of market abuse in the cryptocurrency markets.

Keywords: DeFi · NFT · Blockchain · Wash trading · Graph analysis

1 Introduction

A non-fungible token (NFT) is a unique digital representation of a digital or physical asset. While the NFT standard is used widely to designate ownership of artefacts such as domain name registrations or concentrated liquidity positions in constant function market makers (CFMM) [1], the arguably most recognized use of the NFT standard is within the representation and trade of digital art and collectibles. Here, the NFT is typically used to represent the ownership of a digital image externally stored, either on a server or, more commonly, on censorship resistant distributed file systems such as the Interplanetary File System. A basic NFT standard such as the ERC721 [2] typically denotes an interface implementing the ability to own, transfer and trade the NFT. Standardization led to

© International Financial Cryptography Association 2023
S. Matsuo et al. (Eds.): FC 2022 Workshops, LNCS 13412, pp. 299–311, 2023.
https://doi.org/10.1007/978-3-031-32415-4_20

the emergence of NFT markets, facilitating primary and secondary trading, the presently most dominant of which is OpenSea. Permissionless NFT markets, themselves implemented as smart contracts, enable users to sell and purchase NFTs in two ways: as a fixed-price sale or auction, in which competing bids are locked by the smart contract together with the NFT until a winner is found and the auction is cleared. With the admission of NFTs into popular culture, trade volumes on these markets have seen dramatic growth from a mere \$12 m settled in September 2020, to volumes exceeding \$3.5b in September of the following year, a surge of over 29,060%[1].

Users typically connect to the permissionless markets through public-key cryptography capable of generating an arbitrary number of addresses [3]. As a consequence, user identities remain entirely pseudonymous in NFT markets, making the obfuscation of illicit practices challenging to prevent. As the unique properties of the Ethereum blockchain simplifies adversarial agents to hide in plain sight, we hypothesize that wash trading and strategic bidding amongst multiple addresses controlled by a single or colluding agent, may be a frequent occurrence. As there are no theoretical limits to the number of pseudonymous addresses a single agent can control, we conjecture that adversarial agents likely employ a mixture of manual trading and bots to trade NFTs between clusters of addresses in their control. This behaviour serves the strategic purpose of artificially inflating the trade volume of a given NFT, creating an impression of desirability to uninformed traders [4]. The uninformed traders, looking for a great opportunity to buy a 'hot' NFT will interpret the transaction volume as an authentic expression of interest from other collectors and immediately place a bid or purchase the NFT at an artificially inflated price. Furthermore, novel markets tend to be driven by a volatile search for suitable pricing models [5]. This is undoubtedly the case for the blossoming crypto markets on which the current level of 'irrational exuberance' may result in inefficient markets given the presence of uninformed traders looking to strike gold. Adversarial market participants have been shown to exploit these conditions, primarily by employing strategic wash trading on centralized and decentralized central limit orderbook (CLOB) exchanges [6–9].

Yet, the extent to which these or equivalent practices are being used on NFT markets, remains unclear. To fill the gap, in this paper we study activities between addresses participating in the NFT markets on Ethereum. We pursue the research question: 'To what extent does wash trading occur in smart contract-based NFT markets on Ethereum, and to which extent does this practice distort prices?'. Conceptualizing trading patterns as a graph and proposing two detection algorithms, we identify 2.04% as the lower bound of suspicious sale transactions that closely follow the general definition of wash trading.

2   Literature Review

Wash trading is a well-known phenomenon in traditional financial markets and refers to the activity of repeatedly trading assets for the purpose of feeding mis-

---

[1] https://dune.xyz/sophieqgu/NFT-Marketplaces.

leading information to the market [10]. Typically, one or more colluding agents conduct a set of trades, without taking market risks, that lead to no change of the initial position of the adversarial agents. Most of the early academic publications on wash trading in financial markets focused on colluding investor behaviour (e.g. [11]). Cao et al. [10] were among the first to analyse wash trading by specifying trading patterns. Later, they extended their study using directed graphs on order book data [12]. The literature on the identification of wash trading patterns in the cryptocurrency markets primarily emphasizes CLOB models on decentralized exchanges [9] and centralized exchanges, where wash trading practices have been shown to be especially prevalent [6–8]. Perhaps because the introduction of CFMMs has nearly eliminated the efficacy of wash trading in smart contract-based markets for fungible assets, research on NFTs tends to emphasize either market dynamics and pricing [13,14] or the technical design considerations [15,16]. Thus far, little academic research has examined market abuse in smart contract-based NFT markets [17].

3   Methodology

The Ethereum blockchain is a type of permissionless ledger, in which all transactions and state changes introduced by smart contracts are replicated across all participating nodes in the network [18]. This introduces a high level of integrity to the database, but simultaneously requires the pseudonymization, as anyone with access to the database would otherwise be able to view the balances of users on the network. In Ethereum, this problem is solved with public-key cryptography [18]. Any user on the network can generate a public/private key pair, which can subsequently be used to generate an arbitrary number of addresses. This design presents a fascinating paradox from the perspective of identifying market abuse: Pseudonymous identities are essential in protecting the privacy of benevolent users but, at the same time, they allow adversarial agents to hide in plain sight. Yet, due to the strict ordering of transactions and unique properties of NFT markets, blockchain transaction data presents a powerful and unique opportunity for pattern detection [19] utilizing graph-based algorithms [9,20,21] and address clustering [22,23].

Data Aggregation and Cleaning: We collect transaction data on the 52 leading ERC721 NFT collections on the Ethereum blockchain by trading volume, covering a period between the 1st of January 2018 until 21st November 2021. The dataset contains 21,310,982 transactions of 3,572,483 NFTs conducted by 459,954 addresses. Collectively, the dataset represents $6.9b of the $12.3b total trading volume (49.5%)[2] on all NFT markets since the first block of the Ethereum blockchain[3]. We capture all blockchain transactions related to the selected NFT collections via the OpenSea API. We parse the dataset by 'sale' events emitted by an NFT contract when it is transacted on a smart

---

[2] https://dune.xyz/sophieqgu/NFT-Marketplaces.
[3] The authors will open-source scripts and data upon publication.

contract-based marketplace, indicating that a change of ownership has been recorded on the blockchain, and 'transfer' events indicating that the NFT has been transferred from one address to another. The dataset was subsequently enriched with (I) historic USD prices for settlements in crypto and stablecoins via the Coingecko API and (II) blockchain-specific data via the Etherscan services. (III) To maintain an accurate overview of the NFT markets in the dataset, we collected the deployment date of the four largest NFT on-chain markets manually (Foundation, OpenSea, Rarible, Superrare) and matched the deployment dates with the event emissions. It should be noted that the dataset collected for this analysis pertains only to operations conducted within the Ethereum Virtual Machine (EVM), meaning that we knowingly omit any 'off-chain' transactions or bidding patterns from the analysis. Finally, we pre-processed the dataset with standardized scripts, eliminating a very small fraction of transactions due to obvious technical errors or trades against exotic assets for which the price data tends to be inaccurate.

Building Transaction Graphs: In order to identify suspicious behaviour conforming with wash trading activity, we model the transaction history of each NFT as a directed multigraph $G_{nft} = (N, E)$, where N is the set of addresses and E is the set of ERC721 transactions between addresses. The direction of the edges is given by the transaction flow from sender to receiver, identified by the transaction hash. The weight of the edges represents the USD price at the time of the transaction. This denotation is amenable to the identification of clusters in which a sequence of transactions leads to no apparent position change for any of the addresses involved. Topologically, these patterns form closed cycles. Utilizing Deep-First-Search-Algorithm [24] we identify closed cycles within the data set. We adjust and iterate the algorithm, using the temporal distance between transactions to detect sub-cycles. The proposed algorithm (Appendix) has a linear time complexity of $\mathcal{O}((n + e)(c + 1))$ for **n** nodes (addresses), **e** edges (transactions) and **c** cycles [25]. Figure 1 illustrates a few examples of suspicious cyclic

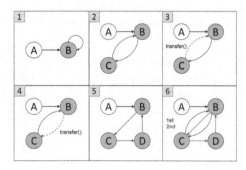

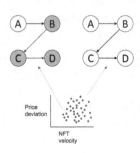

Fig. 1. Detection of suspicious activity through closed cycles. We exclude cycles involving only 'transfer' events. (Color figure online)

Fig. 2. Detection of suspicious activity through a rapid sequence of transactions without taking market risk.

activities. Transactions E belonging to a suspicious cycle are marked in red, and potentially colluding trading addresses N, are highlighted in grey. Example 1 is a self-directed transaction. Examples 2–4 illustrate variations of a cycle with two transactions, where solid lines represent 'sales' and dotted lines represent 'transfers'. Example six depicts a complex graph where edges {B, C} and {B, C, D} form two sub-cycles distinct by time. Further, we analyze path-like transaction patterns, as agents could actively avoid closed cycles. Informed by the definition of wash trading, we consider rapid trade sequences without exposure to market risk as potentially suspicious. Erring on the side of caution, we apply relatively strict thresholds. First, we define the transaction velocity for a sequence as the time elapsed from the initiation to the end. We delimit a rapid trade sequence below 12 h. Second, we delimit the deviation in USD values, a proxy for market risk, in a sequence to a maximum of 5% of the initial price. Combining both threshold flags 0.3% of the sale transactions as mildly suspicious. Figure 2 showcases these path-like trade sets.

The proposed algorithms are highly applicable, in that NFT marketplaces deviate from conventional markets in several ways: First, as NFTs are uniquely identifiable by smart contract address and id, detection does not require volume matching required for fungible tokens (e.g. [9,12]). Second, in contrast to other market designs such as CLOBs the seller can retain certain control over the opposing counterparty, making it potentially easier to conduct cyclical trades. Lastly, due to the transparency of the Ethereum blockchain, we can inspect trading behaviour at the account level without relying on statistical indicators [8].

4   Results

The analysis flags a total of 3.93% of the addresses as suspicious, indicating that these addresses might be controlled by single agents and used to conduct cyclical or sequential wash trading with NFTs. The flagged addresses processed 2.04% of the total sale transactions, inflating the trading volume by \$149.5 m or 2.17% for the period. Of the 36,385 flagged sale transactions, 30,467 were conducted in clusters of cyclical patterns whereas 5,918 were conducted as a rapid sequence. The suspicious activity was executed with just 0.45% of the NFTs in the dataset, indicating a high concentration of illicit activities around a few NFTs (Table 1). While we identify suspicious activities in all NFT collections (Table 2, Appendix), the extent to which a collection is contaminated by flagged transactions ranges from 0.19% to 60.93%, indicating that adversarial agents tend to target specific collections for illicit practices. In general, we observe a predisposition for simple trading patterns. 60.6% of the identified clusters are simple variations with two transactions (equivalent to examples 2–4 in Fig. 1). Complex variations of three (8.7%) or more than three transactions are less common (30.7%). However, we find no signs of self-directed trades. Cyclical patterns are conducted at relatively rapid intervals. Figure 3 illustrates the elapsed time from the first to last transactions, with respect to the number of

Table 1. Overview of the results.

	Dataset	Identified	Percentage
Addresses	459,954	18,117	3.93%
Transactions	1,779,380	36,385 (cyclic: 30,467 sequential: 5,918)	2.04%
Volume in $	6.9 b	149.5 m	2.17%
NFTs	3,572,483	16,289	0.45%

transactions involved. Overall, 48.1% of the identified cycles happen within a single day. 13.2% happen within one to seven days and 13.0% are just below 30 days. Consequently, 74.3% are conducted within 30 days, an important threshold under US regulation[4]. The identified 2-transactions variations have a median execution time of 4.2 h (3-transactions: 54 h), suggesting a preference for simple and fast patterns. We assume this to indicate that adversarial agents are not trading in an automated fashion, which would result in more complex patterns and execution times within a few minutes. Rapid sequential trades, in which a NFT is moved fast between accounts without any market risk, contributed to only 5918 suspicious transactions, equivalent to 0.3% of the transactions across all collections.

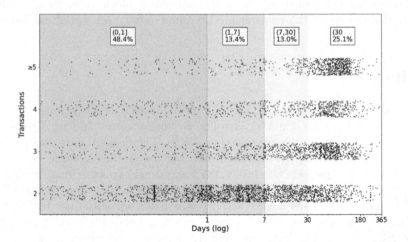

Fig. 3. Elapsed time to close a cycle with respect to the number of transactions involved. 48.1% of the identified cycles happen within a single day.

Further we analyze, at what point within the collections' lifetime suspicious behaviour is most prominent. For each collection, we determine the mean suspicious activity starting with the creation date of the respective collection. Figure 4

---

[4] https://www.cftc.gov/LawRegulation/CommodityExchangeAct/index.htm.

(Appendix) shows a peak of suspicious activity in the first third of a collections' lifetime, possibly in order to raise initial awareness to attract naive buyers. In absolute terms, wash trading is the highest at the beginning of a collections' lifetime, however this is also matched by a high amount of organic traffic. Increasing the price of an asset by faking activity is a central motivation for agents in conducting illicit trading [4]. Analysing if the average price is inflated through wash trading practices, we find that the subsequent sale after a detected wash trade has, on average, an increased price of 30.53%. However, a regression on panel data to measure the impact on the price, led to insignificant results for a majority of collections. Looking into external factors, we found that *age* has a strong positive relationship with the price. While we expected an inverse relationship of the gas price, which impacts the costs per transaction, with the NFT price, we found the effect to be mixed in a majority of cases. We suspect these findings are influenced by the strong bull market, given the current overall positive public sentiment.

Finally, we explore the relationship between executed trades per address and unique trade partners per address. On NFT markets sellers can retain certain control over the opposing counterparty, thus a large number of trades with only few other addresses raises suspicion. Figure 5 (Appendix) visualizes this relationship, whereas addresses which conducted many trades with only a few other addresses would be tilted to the left. Each dot represents an address trading on NFT markets, positioned by the amount of trades and unique trade partners. The size of the dot depicts the number of empirically identified suspicious trades. We find a cluster of suspicious addresses, conducting 25–37 trades with only 12–17 unique trade partners. Furthermore, in contrast to other markets, addresses have relatively few trades, again suggesting a low level of automated trading in this nascent market.

5 Discussion

Given the challenges in interpreting pseudonymous blockchain based data, this study has multiple limitations. First and foremost, it should be made clear that none of the findings presented in this paper present any conclusive evidence of criminal activities or malicious intent. While we delimit a set of behaviours which we find unlikely to be conducted with benevolent intent, we leave it to the reader to assess the likelihood that flagged transactions constitute attempts at wash trading. Any, or all, of the flagged sequences may be erroneous but authentic transactions. Second, the decision of limiting our analysis to a specific subset of cyclical and sequential patterns may result in false negatives as sophisticated attempts at wash trading involving advanced address clusters over longer periods are not flagged by the analysis, at this point. Wash traders may me more careful and evade the analyzed heuristics. Similarly, the analysis pertains exclusively to on-chain transaction events emitted by the NFT contract and does not account for strategic bidding practices, which we suspect may be a popular methodology amongst adversarial agents. Because of these limitations, we hypothesize that the results presented here detect a lower bound for actual extent of adversarial behavior on decentralized NFT markets.

Should wash trading conducted according to the patterns explored in this paper increase over time, smart contract-based NFT platforms may consider the implementation of obligatory or voluntary identification initiatives. Alternatively, trading limitations on trading velocity, price deltas or counterparties can be implemented. In our sample self-directed trades have been non-existent, with indicates successful countermeasures at smart contract or frontend level. Nevertheless, any such attempt at introducing restrictions or limitations may stifle organic market activity and will inevitably create a cat and mouse game, as developers and wash traders race to identify and create increasingly sophisticated patterns. More subtle countermeasures fostering the supervision of NFT markets are the expansion of NFT standards beyond ERC721 and ERC1155, as well as increased data ubiquity. Decentralized NFT markets are transparent, however NFT data is very diverse and difficult to retrieve. Fees potentially play a big role in preventing wash trading, as long as the rewards or incentives are less than the cost-of-attack. Fees on NFT markets are substantial. Fraudulent agents are less likely to perform a wash trade if they are losing several percentages with every transaction. Admittedly, this does neither stop marketplaces itself to perform wash trades nor prevents private offset agreements between the trader and a marketplace.

Even so, with $149.5 m and a median of 2.04% suspicious sale transactions we argue that wash trading may be less common than what industry observers have previously estimated [26,27].

6   Conclusion

We identify what we believe may serve as a lower bound estimation for suspicious trading behaviour on decentralized NFT markets, following the definition of wash trading: sets of trades between collusive addresses, without taking market risk, that lead to no change in the individual position of the participating addresses. Our findings indicate that (I) adversarial agents exhibit a clear preference towards fast and simple cyclical patterns, (II) the level of suspicious activity varies significantly across NFT collections, (III) illicit activity could still be done in a manual fashion, and (IV) the activities do not necessarily produce the intended price impact, as other exogenous factors such as *age* and *sentiment* are more relevant to price discovery.

As a theoretical contribution, we add descriptive knowledge to an emerging field of research where scientific studies are scarce. We contribute to the growing literature on the identification of illicit market behavior in centralized and decentralized crypto markets, by conducting the first in-depth examination of NFT wash trading on the Ethereum blockchain. We contribute empirical statistics of fraudulent behaviour and a set of suspicious transaction graphs to foster the understanding of wash trading in increasingly financialized NFT markets. The valuable insights we generate for practitioners are twofold: First, we provide valuable insights to prevent collectors from buying NFTs that are potentially inflated by wash trading. Second, we discuss practical countermeasures increasing the standards for the wider NFT ecosystem. Further research opportunities are manifold and include studying NFT markets incentivising volume through tokens, the utilization of flash loans for wash trading, as well as researching the correlation between suspicious behaviour and sentiment data.

 This project has received funding from the European Union's Horizon 2020 research and innovation programme under the Marie Skłodowska-Curie grant agreement No 801199

A   Appendix

Algorithm

Algorithm 1. The detection algorithm

1: Input: T timestamped blockchain transactions
2: $L \leftarrow$ empty list of *cycles*
3: **for** $nft \in T$ **do**
4:      $G_{nft} \leftarrow (N, E)$
5:      $G_{nft} \leftarrow$ identifier, weight
6:      label $n \in N$ as discovered
7:      **for** all directed E of n **do**
8:          test for adjacent edges m
9:          **if** m is not labeled as discovered **then**
10:             continue
11:         **else**
12:             $L \leftarrow cycle$
13:             $G_{nft}* \leftarrow G_{nft} - E$
14:             break and recurse
15:         **end if**
16:     **end for**
17: **end for**
18: return L

Table 2. Results for each collection. Column (A) is the share of suspicious addresses, (B) the share of suspicious transactions, (C1) represents the total volume flagged denominated in USD, (C2) the share of the flagged volume and (D) the share of suspicious NFTs

	Collection	Smart contract	Created	Size	(A)	(B)	(C1)	(C2)	(D)
1	0n1-force	0x3bf2...5e9d	Aug-21	7776	4.2	1.6	1732469	1.2	1.7
2	acclimatedmooncats	0xc3f7...5e69	Apr-21	18412	2.8	1.3	357341	0.8	0.5
3	adam-bomb-squad	0x7ab2...78c5	Aug-21	25000	1.3	0.5	206478	0.5	0.2
4	autoglyphs	0xd4e4...7782	Apr-19	512	2	0.7	206032	0.5	0.4
5	axie	0xf5b0...cb8d	Apr-18	243000	1.6	0.3	285055	1.4	0.1
6	bored-ape-kennel-club	0xba30...5623	Jun-21	10000	3.2	1.3	1423011	1.3	0.9
7	boredapeyachtclub	0xbc4c...f13d	Apr-21	10000	4	1.4	11308109	1.4	1.6
8	collectvox	0xad9f...d34c	Aug-21	8888	1.7	0.6	138121	0.4	0.5
9	cool-cats	0x1a92...050c	Jun-21	9933	4	1.3	2299930	1.2	1.4
10	creature-world-collection	0xc92c...aafc	Aug-21	10000	2.6	1	862273	0.9	0.9
11	cryptoadz-by-gremplin	0x1cb1...49c6	Sep-21	7025	5.4	2.1	2964440	1.7	2.2
12	cryptokitties	0x0601...266d	Jan-18	2009725	0.5	2.3	421288	1.6	0
13	cryptopunks	0xb47e...3bbb	Jan-18	10000	10.2	4.3	53892061	2.4	3.7
14	cryptovoxels	0x7998...cf0c	Jun-18	6210	1.5	0.4	54925	0.2	0.4
15	cyberkongz	0x57a2...4f37	Apr-21	4147	3.1	1.6	824246	0.7	1
16	cyberkongz-vx	0x7ea3...7c8b	Aug-21	14334	2.1	0.7	326717	0.5	0.4
17	deadfellaz	0x2aca...a17b	Aug-21	10000	1.4	0.6	175900	0.6	0.5
18	decentraland	0xf87e...5d4d	Apr-18	92598	9.2	9.7	3312118	7.5	0
19	doodles	0x8a90...992e	Oct-21	10000	2.4	1.1	757788	0.8	0.7
20	fluf-world	0xcccc4...a68d	Aug-21	10000	1.8	0.8	434361	0.8	0.7
21	foundation	0x3b3e...5405	Jan-21	103251	9.6	7.8	383853	11.2	0
22	galacticapes	0x12d2...4d14	Sep-21	10000	3	1	540459	1	0.8
23	galaxyeggs	0xa081...7c48	Sep-21	9999	2.8	1.1	577130	1.3	0.9
24	hashmasks	0xc2c7...6928	Jan-21	16384	4.6	2.3	1493358	1.8	1.5
25	jungle-freaks-by-trosley	0x7e6b...4de0	Oct-21	10000	3	1.4	887701	1.3	1.2
26	koala-intelligence-agency	0x3f5f...6360	Aug-21	10000	2.5	1	393869	1	0.8
27	lazy-lions	0x8943...37e0	Aug-21	10080	1.4	0.5	358509	0.6	0.5
28	lootproject	0xff9c...13d7	Aug-21	7779	6.6	2.5	9458899	3.6	1.6
29	lostpoets	0xa720...f466	Sep-21	27515	0.4	0.2	37669	0.1	0
30	meebits	0x7bd2...6bc7	May-21	20000	2.1	0.8	1322740	0.6	0.3
31	mekaverse	0x9a53...ca8f	Oct-21	8888	2.5	1.5	2173946	1.4	0.9
32	mutant-ape-yacht-club	0x60e4...a7c6	Aug-21	30003	3.4	2	7253896	1.7	0.6
33	mutantcats	0xaadb...e46a	Oct-21	10000	1.3	0.4	256031	0.5	0.4
34	pudgypenguins	0xbd35...2cf8	Jul-21	8888	3.2	1.1	1764016	1.3	1.5
35	punks-comic	0x5ab2...c948	May-21	10000	67	56.4	13674620	38.7	19.1
36	rari721	0x60f8...5ee5	May-20	155346	6.4	5.7	2905148	14	0.1
37	rumble-kong-league	0xef01...909a	Jul-21	10000	1.1	0.4	151521	0.5	0.2
38	sadgirlsbar	0x335e...b2d8	Aug-21	10000	1.3	0.6	17836	0.4	0.4
39	sandbox	0x50f5...6d4a	Dec-19	166464	0.9	0.5	200218	0.2	0.1
40	sneaky-vampire-syndicate	0x219b...2539	Sep-21	8888	3.8	1.8	928516	1.4	1.2
41	somnium-space	0x595f...a0fa	Oct-19	5025	1.3	0.5	244005	1.8	0.4
42	sorare	0x629a...6205	Jul-19	329383	13.4	2.3	489009	0.7	0.7
43	supducks	0x3fe1...cbc5	Jul-21	10000	2.8	1.1	544447	1	0.9
44	superrare1	0x41a3...850d	Apr-18	4436	3.9	1.2	92844	0.2	0.6
45	superrare2	0xb932...b9e0	Sep-19	4436	3.2	0.9	419872	0.7	2
46	the-doge-pound	0xf4ee...d043	Jul-21	10000	2	0.8	725137	0.9	0.7
47	the-sevens-official	0xf497...187a	Sep-21	7000	3.4	1.9	878788	2.1	1.3
48	thehumanoids	0x3a50...0edd	Sep-21	10000	1.7	0.7	261715	0.7	0.6
49	tom-sachs-rockets	0x1159...5d26	Aug-21	2000	76.9	60.9	16907477	58.6	54.3
50	veefriends	0xa3ae...beeb	May-21	10255	1.8	1.4	662073	0.7	0.3
51	world-of-women-nft	0xe785...5330	Jul-21	10000	1.6	0.5	539001	0.7	0.5
52	wrapped-mooncats	0x7c40...3572	Mar-21	8903	15	6.1	981392	6.5	3.8

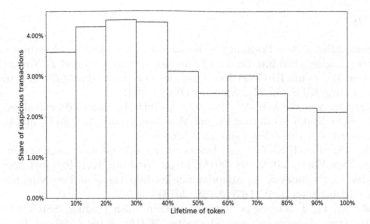

Fig. 4. Wash trading with respect to collections' lifetime. In absolute terms, wash trading is the highest at the beginning of a collections' lifetime, however this is also matched by a high amount of organic traffic.

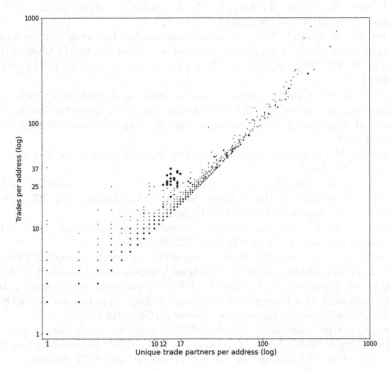

Fig. 5. Trades and unique trade partners. Each dot represents an address trading on NFT markets, positioned by the amount of trades and unique trade partners. The size of the dot depicts the number of empirically identified suspicious trades.

References

1. Uniswap. Mint a New Position | Uniswap V3 (2021). https://docs.uniswap.org//protocol/guides/providing-liquidity/mint-a-position. Accessed 25 Nov 2021
2. Entriken, W., et al.: ERC-721 Non-Fungible Token Standard (2018). https://eips.ethereum.org/EIPS/eip-721. Accessed 09 Oct 2021
3. Jensen, J.R., von Wachter, V., Ross, O.: An introduction to decentralized finance. In: Complex Systems Informatics and Modeling Quarterly (2021). https://csimq-journals.rtu.lv/article/view/csimq.2021-26.03
4. Imisiker, S., Tas, B.K.O.: Wash trades as a stock market manipulation tool. J. Behav. Exp. Finan. **20**, 92–98 (2018). https://doi.org/10.1016/j.jbef.2018.08.00
5. Khuntia, S., Pattanayak, J.: Adaptive market hypothesis and evolving predictability of bitcoin. Econ. Lett. **167**, 26–28 (2018)
6. Aloosh, A., Li, J.: Direct evidence of bitcoin wash trading. SSRN Electron. J. (2019). https://papers.ssrn.com/abstract=3362153. https://doi.org/10.2139/ssrn.3362153
7. Congm, L., et al.: Crypto wash trading. SSRN Electron. J. (2020). https://papers.ssrn.com/sol3/papers.cfm?abstract_id=3530220
8. Le Pennec, G., Fiedler, I., Ante, L.: Wash trading at cryptocurrency exchanges. Finan. Res. Lett. **43**, 101982 (2021)
9. Victor, F., Weintraud, A.M.: Detecting and quantifying wash trading on decentralized cryptocurrency exchanges. In: Proceedings of the World Wide Web Conference, WWW 2021, vol. 2, pp. 23–32 (2021). https://doi.org/10.1145/3442381.3449824
10. Cao, Y., et al.: Detecting wash trade in financial market using digraphs and dynamic programming. In: IEEE Conference on Computational Intelligence for Financial Engineering and Economics (2014). https://doi.org/10.1109/TNNLS.2015.2480959
11. Grinblatt, M., Keloharju, M.: Tax-loss trading and wash sales. J. Finan. Econ. **71**(1), 51–76 (2004)
12. Cao, Y., et al.: Detecting wash trade in financial market using digraphs and dynamic programming. IEEE Trans. Neural Netw. Learn. Syst. **27**, 2351–2363 (2016). https://doi.org/10.1109/TNNLS.2015.2480959
13. Nadini, M., et al.: Mapping the NFT revolution: market trends, trade networks and visual features. Sci. Rep. **11**(1), 20902 (2021)
14. Dowling, M.: Is non-fungible token pricing driven by cryptocurrencies? SSRN Electron. J. (2021). https://papers.ssrn.com/sol3/papers.cfm?abstract_id=3815093
15. Regner, F., Schweizer, A., Urbach, N.: NFTs in practice - non-fungible tokens as core component of a blockchain-based event ticketing application. In: 40th International Conference on Information Systems, ICIS 2019 (2019)
16. Wang, Q., et al.: Non-Fungible Token (NFT): overview, evaluation, opportunities and challenges (2021). http://arxiv.org/abs/2105.07447. Accessed 10 Nov 2021
17. Das, D., et al.: Understanding Security Issues in the NFT Ecosystem (2021). http://arxiv.org/abs/2111.08893. Accessed 25 Nov 2021
18. Antonopoulos, A., Wood, G.: Mastering Ethereum (2018)
19. von Wachter, V., Jensen, J.R., Ross, O.: Measuring asset composability as a proxy for DeFi integration. In: Bernhard, M., et al. (eds.) FC 2021. LNCS, vol. 12676, pp. 109–114. Springer, Heidelberg (2021). https://doi.org/10.1007/978-3-662-63958-0_9

20. Chen, W., et al.: Traveling the TokenWorld: a graph analysis of Ethereum ERC20 token ecosystem, pp. 1411–1421 (2020). https://doi.org/10.1145/3366423.3380215
21. Weber, M., et al.: Anti-money laundering in bitcoin: experimenting with graph convolutional networks for financial forensics. CoRR (2019). http://arxiv.org/abs/1908.02591
22. Victor, F.: Address clustering heuristics for Ethereum. In: Bonneau, J., Heninger, N. (eds.) FC 2020. LNCS, vol. 12059, pp. 617–633. Springer, Cham (2020). https://doi.org/10.1007/978-3-030-51280-4_33
23. Harrigan, M., Fretter, C.: The unreasonable effectiveness of address clustering. In: 2016 International IEEE Conferences (2016)
24. Tarajan, R.E.: Depth first search and linear graph algorithms. SIAM J. Comput. 1(2), 146–160 (1971). https://doi.org/10.1137/0201010
25. Johnson, D.B.: Finding all the elementary circuits of a directed graph. SIAM J. Comput. 4(1), 77–84 (1975). https://doi.org/10.48550/arXiv.1605.06369
26. Coindesk. The fast growing NFT Market is problematic yet promising (2021). https://www.coindesk.com/business/2020/09/21/the-fast-growing-nft-market-is-problematic-yet-promising/. Accessed 27 Nov 2021
27. Bloomberg. Jim Chanos says NFT Market is rife with nefarious Activity (2021). https://www.bloomberg.com/news/articles/2021-09-30/jim-chanos-says-nft-market-is-rife-with-nefarious-activity. Accessed 27 Nov 2021

Voting22

Individual Verifiability and Revoting in the Estonian Internet Voting System

Olivier Pereira[✉]

ICTEAM, Crypto Group, UCLouvain, 1348 Louvain-la-Neuve, Belgium
olivier.pereira@uclouvain.be

Abstract. Individual verifiability remains one of the main practical challenges in e-voting systems and, despite the central importance of this property, countries that sought to offer it to their voters faced repeated security problems.

In this note, we revisit this property in the context of the IVXV version of the Estonian Internet voting system, which has been deployed for the Estonian municipal elections of 2017 and for the Estonian and European parliamentary elections of 2019.

We show that a compromised voter device can defeat the individual verifiability mechanism of the current Estonian voting system. Our attack takes advantage of the revoting option that is available in the Estonian voting system, and only requires to compromise the voting client application: it does not require compromising the mobile device verification app, or any server side component.

This issue, which has been confirmed by the IVXV system designers, adds to an increasingly long list of failures to offer genuine individual verifiability in Internet voting systems deployed for government elections. It prompts for reinforced caution regarding the evidences that are offered regarding the verifiability of voting systems, especially when the verifiability is a property on which is based the decision to deploy a voting system in government elections.

1 Introduction

Estonia remains the only country in the world where Internet voting is used by a large proportion of voters in government elections, with a continuous use since an initial deployment in 2005.

This unique status brought numerous questions regarding the security of the system. In particular, during the 2011 parliamentary election, in which around 24% of the voters submitted their ballot on the Internet [13], Paavo Pihelgas developed and tested malware that would compromise a voting client and modify a vote in a way that would be undetectable by the voter. Pihelgas filed a complaint to the Estonian Supreme Court, asking for the nullification of the votes submitted by Internet, but the complaint was dismissed [9].

Nevertheless, in the 2013 elections, an extension of the Estonian voting system was introduced by Heiberg and Willemson [4], in order to offer *individual*

© International Financial Cryptography Association 2023
S. Matsuo et al. (Eds.): FC 2022 Workshops, LNCS 13412, pp. 315–324, 2023.
https://doi.org/10.1007/978-3-031-32415-4_21

verifiability, that is, a mechanism by which a voter can verify independently that the ballot submitted by her voting device accurately reflects her voting intent, even if that voting device is compromised.

The security of the 2013 Estonian voting system, including the individual verifiability mechanism, was challenged in a detailed analysis by Springall et al. in 2014, who explained how the individual verifiability could be circumvented [11]. The individual verifiability mechanism was also questioned in 2016 by Mus et al. [8], with a focus on its privacy implications, and a variant of that mechanism was proposed. That variant was in turn demonstrated to be flawed by Kubjas et al. in 2017 [7].

In the meantime, an almost complete redesign of the Estonian voting protocol was proposed in 2016 by Heiberg et al. [6]: the new IVXV protocol aims at making the server side operations verifiable by designated auditors, on top of offering a revised individual verifiability mechanism that focuses on the verification of the client-side operations.

Contribution. The present note demonstrates that the IVXV protocol, used for the Estonian municipal elections of 2017 and for the Estonian and European parliamentary election of 2019, does not offer individual verifiability.

The attack that we propose only requires the voting client to be compromised, which is precisely what individual verifiability is supposed to detect. The attack succeeds even if all the server side components and the vote verification app are perfectly honest. It is also independent of any weakness in the voter identification mechanism, and would then still work even if a stronger voter identification mechanism were implemented (e.g., real two-factor). Finally, it can be performed within a short time frame.

These last two features differ from the *Ghost Click* attack on individual verifiability that was proposed by Springall et al. [11] on the 2013 version of the Estonian system: that attack required the adversary to be able to intercept the voter eID PIN code, and the voter to leave his eID card on his computer for a long period of time, or to use the eID card on a regular basis. These differences come thanks to changes introduced in the IVXV protocol.

2   IVXV Individual Verifiability Protocol

The IVXV voting system relies on the following components – we largely use the terminology and notations from the original description [6], and only mention the components that are relevant for our purpose:

Certification Authority. A national certification authority issues, for each voter, a signature key pair $(sk^{id}_{pub}, sk^{id}_{priv})$ that is stored in the smartcard of each citizen's eID card, and can be used to sign documents, provided that the user provides a PIN code. A separate authentication key pair is also provided on the eID, and is used to identify a voter connecting to the vote collection server. Obviously, the reliance on such a public key infrastructure introduces challenges on its own [10] but, for our analysis, we will trust that it is correctly implemented.

Election Organizer. The EO approves the election configuration, and produces an encryption key pair (ek_{pub}, ek_{priv}) that will be used to encrypt the votes.

Voting Application. The $VoteApp$ is a standalone application, available for Windows, macOS and Linux, that the voter can download from the election authority website, and that is signed. It is used by the voters to express their vote intent, prepare the ballot, have it signed by the eID, submit the ballot, and interact with the Vote Verification application. The purpose of individual verifiability is to be able to detect if a corrupted $VoteApp$ tries to modify the vote intent expressed by the voter and cast a ballot supporting a different candidate.

Vote Verification Application. The $VerApp$ is a mobile application available for Android and iOS, that the voter can obtain from the respective App Stores of these environments. It is trusted that the adversary cannot compromise both the $VerApp$ and the $VoteApp$. For our purpose, we will assume that the $VerApp$ is honest, as it is the main use case.

Vote Collector. The VC interacts with the $VoteApp$ and the $VerApp$: it collects the encrypted and signed ballot submitted by the $VoteApp$, and interacts with the $VerApp$ when a voter wants to verify that her ballot captures her vote intent, and was correctly recorded.

Registration Service. The RS interacts with the VC: every ballot received by the VC must also be signed by the RS. This signature will be verified by the $VerApp$.

In terms of security model, it is assumed that that VC and RS are not jointly compromised, and that $VoteApp$ and $VerApp$ are not jointly compromised either.

The IVXV voting process is then as follows (we simplify several internal server side message flows, in order to focus on the relevant aspects of the protocol):

Ballot submission. A voter who would like to submit a vote v installs the $VoteApp$, creates a TLS channel with the VC, identify himself with the eID authentication key and PIN code, picks randomness r from the appropriate group, and produces an ElGamal encryption of his vote as $c = Enc_{ek_{pub}}(v; r)$. The voter then uses his PIN code and eID to produce a signature $\sigma = Sign_{sk_{priv}^{id}}(c)$, and submits the resulting ballot $b = (c, \sigma)$ to VC.

Ballot registration. VC creates an identifier vid for the ballot, verifies the eligibility of the voter and validity of the signature, obtains a time stamp on $H(c)$, and sends a registration request on a signature $\sigma_{VC} = Sign_{sk_{priv}^{VC}}(H(b))$ to RS, who returns a signed confirmation $reg = Sign_{sk_{priv}^{RS}}(H(\sigma_{VC}))$ to VC. This confirmation reg is sent back to the $VoteApp$ together with vid.

Vote verification. When the $VoteApp$ displays the pair (vid, r) to the voter, as a QR code, the voter uses $VerApp$ to capture the (vid, r) pair. The verification app now queries VC in order to obtain the (b, reg) pair associated to vid. The

VerApp verifies the validity of $b = (c, \sigma)$ and *reg*, and displays the identity obtained through σ to the voter. Finally, it performs an exhaustive search on all the candidates until it finds a vote v such that $c = Enc_{ek_{pub}}(v; r)$. The matching v is displayed to the voter, who has to decide whether it is correct.

There are several remarks to be made about this process:

- An important feature of the Estonian Internet voting protocol is that voters have the possibility to submit as many ballots as desired. The last registered ballot will be included in the tally. This offers some level of protection against coercion: if a voter is forced to vote for a given candidate, it may remain possible to submit another ballot that will replace the first one in the tally.
- The Vote verification feature is obviously very sensitive from a privacy point of view: anyone in possession of the verification QR code has the possibility to obtain, in clear, the author and the content of a ballot. For that reason, the individual verifiability process is only authorized during a limited time frame, usually 30 minutes, after ballot submission. Besides, verification can only be performed a limited number of times (usually 3).
- The ballot verification process will not tell the *VerApp* whether a ballot has been overwritten or not. In this way, a voter who was coerced into submitting his QR code to a third party can still submit a new ballot immediately, and the QR code will not inform the coercer of this revote. Furthermore, there is no feedback channel to the voter, that would inform him that a ballot was submitted on his behalf.

3 Revoting and Individual Verifiability in IVXV

The revoting feature of the IVXV Internet voting protocol raises particular difficulties for individual verifiability.

In particular, since there is no way for a voter to know whether a vote that is verified will be tallied, there are a variety of attack scenarios in which a compromised *VoteApp* could fool the verification process. Assuming a compromised *VC* opens for even more attack scenarios, which we do not detail here.

Let us consider a voter who uses a compromised *VoteApp* and intends to express vote v. A compromised *VoteApp* could cast a vote v' on behalf of the voter as follows:

1. When the voter expresses his vote intent v, *VoteApp* runs the ballot submission process honestly, and lets the server-side components run the ballot registration phase. However, as soon as *VoteApp* collects *vid* from *VC*, and before displaying it to the voter, it displays a network connection time-out message, and invites the voter to retry voting. At this point, the voter has no evidence as of whether his vote was actually registered or not, and is led to believe that it was not.
2. As a result, the voter is expected to retry voting. But, this time, the *VoteApp* will prepare a ballot encrypting the vote intent v' (instead of v), which will be

signed with the voter's eID since the voter intends to sign a ballot and has no way of verifying the content of the ballot that he signs. That second ballot is again submitted to VC and registered, returning vid' to the $VoteApp$. From the point of view of the server, this is a normal revote, and that second ballot is the one that will be included in the tally.

3. Now, instead of displaying a QR code with the vid' reference, the $VoteApp$ displays the QR code corresponding to the first ballot, that is, vid and the randomness used to encode the first ciphertext.

4. When the voter scans this QR code, the first vote will be downloaded, and the vote intent v will be displayed to the voter, who will accept the verification steps, even though it is a vote for v' that will be tallied on his behalf.

The visible deviation of the $VoteApp$ from its normal behavior is the network time-out message. However, network connection problems are common, and it would only happen on the first attempt at using the application, which makes it hard to reproduce and unlikely to be reported. Besides, even in that case, network connection problems are something common, and suspicious voter and voting support service would also be comforted by a successful vote verification process after the submission of the second ballot.

There are of course many variations on the network time-out message: for instance, it could be replaced by a crash of the corrupted $VoteApp$, which may happen with a limited probability only, making it harder to observe and reproduce. Network time-outs may also be replaced by the compromised $VoteApp$ intercepting the eID PIN code, and revoting silently on the voter behalf, as in the *Ghost Click* attack [11] on the 2013 version of the voting system. We further discuss this variation and the changes between the 2013 protocol and IVXV protocol in Sect. 5.

4   Mitigations

There are many directions that can be explored in order to mitigate the attack described above, including some of the possible evolutions of the IVXV system that are discussed in the roadmap by Heiberg et al. [5]. However, the directions that may be effective appear to come with relatively important changes in the system and to have a noticeable impact on other properties of the system. As a result, we cannot propose a clean and simple solution to the problem.

Feedback Channel. The addition of an independent vote confirmation channel could possibly help: the voter could be warned every time that a ballot is registered on her behalf, and the vid could be included in the notification. The addition of vid, or of something to the same effect, is crucial in order to give the voter an opportunity to check whether he is verifying his first or second ballot. This feature is absent from previous discussions [5], which focused on a malicious app stealing voter credentials, in which case it is enough to inform the voter than *a* vote was submitted, without requiring the addition of a ballot identifier.

In the security model considered for the IVXV voting system, such a mechanism may however be non trivial to design in a secure way: if the voter uses a compromised voting device, we must be sure that the malware present on the device is unable to delete and/or alter vote confirmations. Besides, since server side compromises are in-scope, we must be sure that the notifications that would alert a voter are actually sent and delivered in the right order. For instance, if the VC is in charge of notifying the voter using a second communication channel, then a corrupted VC could simply choose to delay the notification for the first ballot of our scenario, and to send it when the second ballot arrives.

Verifying the Last Ballot Only. Another approach would be for the server to only answer verification queries for ballots that have not been replaced through a revote: in the scenario described above, a honest VC would refuse the verification of the first ballot after submission of the second.

This protection could however be defeated in several variations of our attack. For instance:

- If the VC is corrupted, then it can decide to participate in the verification of the first ballot only, which would make the voter wrongly believe that no second ballot was submitted. The corrupted VC could also receive the second ballot from the corrupted $VoteApp$ and wait for 30 min until it timestamps it and registers it with RS, so that this ballot would only start to "officially exist" after the end of the verification period of the first ballot.
- If the corrupted $VoteApp$ is able to capture the eID PIN code, and if the eID remains or becomes available on the voter computer more than 30 min after the submission of the initial ballot, then $VoteApp$ can silently submit a second ballot at that time, without the voter's knowledge. This is essentially the Ghost Click attack.

Accepting a Single Ballot. In another approach, the voting protocol could be modified so that VC and RS only accept one single ballot per voter. A new mechanism would then be needed in order to support the verifiability of the submitted ballot even if the $VoteApp$ or the network connection crashes after the ballot submission but before the confirmation message could be sent to the voter.

This would prevent the attack scenarios described above, but would also decrease the coercion resistance of the voting system. Given that the level of coercion resistance offered by an Internet voting system is low anyway, this may not be too damaging regarding that property. Besides, many voters may still be able to go to a voting office in order to vote in person and cancel their Internet ballot.

The possibility to revote also offers usability benefits: a voter who would not feel confident using the system may decide to vote for a first time, for an arbitrary candidate, with the help of someone else, and then vote privately for the candidate of his choice. A system that would accept a single ballot per voter would remove this usability convenience.

An alternate option that would limit the privacy/coercion risk would be to switch to the so-called Benaloh challenge approach [1], in which voters can either verify a ballot produced by the voting client, or cast it as their vote, but not both. Extra care would then be needed in order to make sure that the expected ballot is considered as cast, and is not replaced by a challenged ballot for instance.

Creating a Public Bulletin Board. One more option would be to create a public bulletin board, on which a hash of each registered ballot would be displayed, and the last ballot of each voter clearly marked. This would make it possible for a voter to check at any time whether his ballot has been replaced with another one. This would also offer the possibility for a coercer to observe whether a voter revoted online but, as pointed above, the protection against coercion is low anyway, and may not trump verifiability here. The challenges of properly implementing a secure public bulletin board should also be taken into account.

Heiberg et al. [5] also discuss various directions linked to the use of the eID (e.g., require the signature of two independent devices, promote the use of card readers that have their PIN-pad, increase the control of the use of the eID, . . .). These approaches may help against an attacker who targets voter credentials, but do not help in our case since, in our attack, the voter is actually willing to produce two signed ballots, and would then use then perform all the required authentication steps.

Overall, none of the discussed approaches seems to offer a simple and effective solution, and it seems fairly non trivial to address this individual verifiability issue without affecting the receipt freeness of the protocol at the same time, or creating new usability challenges.

5   Comparison with the 2013 Internet Voting Protocol

The individual verification process that was introduced in the 2013 version of the Internet voting protocol [4] differs in several significant ways from the IVXV protocol that was deployed in 2017.

First, the trust model is different: the 2013 protocol assumes the honesty of the server receiving the ballots and playing the ballot verification protocol, while the IVXV protocol is expected to remain secure as long as only one of VC and RS is honest.

The protocol is also different:

- The $VerApp$ in the 2013 protocol would only receive the ciphertext c from the voting server, and not the voter signature σ (or the RS signature reg), while c, σ (and reg) are sent and verified in IVXV. Keeping the signature off would limit the risks of taking advantage of the verification process in order to prove how a voter voted, since the verification data remain anonymous. This of course introduced the risks of clash attacks: several voters voting in the same way could be pointed to one single ciphertext, while a different ciphertext would be signed by all but one voter. A limit of 3 verifications for each ballot was introduced in order to limit the scale of such an attack.

– The server of the 2013 protocol would only allow the verification of the last vote cast by the voter, that is, the one that will be included in the tally. In contrast, the IVXV protocol allows the verification of any ballot as long as the verification takes places within 30 min after submission. As a result, a voter who submits a first ballot under the watch of a coercer does not need to wait for 30 min before submitting a new ballot: a verification of the first ballot by the coercer would still succeed.

Those two differences only make sense because the voting server is trusted in the 2013 protocol. A corrupted server could indeed send any ciphertext encrypted with the right randomness to the *VerApp*,[1] since it is not bound to send a full ballot signed by the voter, and the voter would have no way to determine whether the ciphertext that is verified is the one that will be included in the tally. Similarly, a corrupted verification server would also have no reason to restrict the verification process to the last submitted ballot.

It turns out that the changes introduced in the IVXV protocol seem to weaken the individual verifiability of the protocol rather than to strengthen it.

The addition of the signature in IVXV does not change anything to our attack, and it does not do anything to prevent the Ghost Click attack [11] either: in both attacks, the ballots that are submitted have a legitimate signature.

The fact that the verification of any submitted ballot is possible for 30 min (and not just of the verification of the last ballot) simplifies the attack process. We take advantage of this by having the voter submitting two ballots within a short time window, and letting the voter verify a vote that has been replaced by a more recent one.

It would be possible to adapt our attack to the 2013 version of the protocol if the voting server is corrupted: the malicious *VoteApp* could obtain two voter signed ballots within a short time frame, and the voting server would just keep the second ballot in memory for 30 min before registering it within the system. (In the presence of a honest voting server, we could not have an attack in which the *VoteApp*, or a third party, would keep the second ballot in memory for 30 min and submit it then: the eID is also needed for the voter authentication to the server in order to submit a ballot. Of course, if the eID is left on the device and if the corrupted *VoteApp* has the PIN code and can silently interact with the eID, then the problem is solved.)

Similarly, the Ghost Click attack would work more easily on the IVXV protocol than on the 2013 version of the protocol: if the eID PIN code can be intercepted, then two signed ballots can be obtained in a matter of seconds, and the corrupted *VoteApp* can first submit the ballot reflecting the voter intent, then show the verification data to the voter, and immediately submit the second signed ballot without letting the voter know that it happened.

---

[1] This is slightly more challenging in the case of the 2013 protocol which uses RSA-OAEP for encryption, compared to the ElGamal encryption used in the IVXV protocol. Indeed, the server would need to obtain the randomness used for encryption in order to produce a different ciphertext encrypted with the same randomness, while ElGamal encryption is just malleable.

Whether or not our attack is easier to deploy than the Ghost Click attack depends on whether the eID PIN code of the voter can be intercepted or not. This may not be particularly challenging when the client is a stand-alone application that is corrupted, or when the voter device is completely under adversarial control. It could make a difference if the voting client were a web application, in which case the introduction of the PIN code would be handled directly by a browser extension interacting with the eID card, and not visible by a corrupted voting application. Besides, many of the mitigations explored by Heiberg et al. [5] would protect against the ghost click attack, but they would be ineffective against the attack proposed here: they seek to inform a voter when ballots are submitted without the voter's knowledge, but this is not the case here.

6   Conclusions

Individual verifiability is a central property that many recent Internet voting systems deployed for government elections tried to offer, and it is no surprise given the high risks of the presence of a malware on the voter's device.

It however showed to be particularly challenging to obtain an effective verification process: the first mechanism proposed for the Estonian voting system, used in the 2013 elections, was shown to be broken by Springall et al. [11]. In 2015, Halderman and Teague [3] showed how to circumvent the verification mechanisms of the iVote system used in New South Wales. In 2019, Haines et al. [2] demonstrated weaknesses in the individual (and universal) verifiability mechanisms of the Swiss Post/Scytl Internet voting system used in Switzerland (for individual verifiability only). The current paper shows that the latest IVXV protocol used in Estonia still fails to offer individual verifiability.

The situation definitely prompts for more caution regarding the security properties that are announced for voting systems, in particular when they are proposed for use in government elections and when the decision of adopting a voting system is based on the trust in its verifiability. Proper security definitions, proofs, and careful reviews seem to remain the best strategy we have. In particular, the pioneer work of Switzerland towards the reliance on rigorous security definitions, proofs and public reviews seems to be the most promising effort towards obtaining a voting system that actually offers the security properties that are announced [12].

Acknowledgement. We would like to thank Sven Heiberg for confirming that the attack scenario described in this paper would succeed on the current implementation of the IVXV protocol and for his helpful and constructive comments. We also would like to thank Vanessa Teague for so many interesting discussions on the security of voting systems and for her review of a previous version of this document. Eventually, we would like to thank the Voting'22 reviewers for their interesting and helpful suggestions. The author was supported by the F.R.S.-FNRS project SeVoTe and by the FEDER-Cryptomedia Project.

References

1. Benaloh, J.: Simple verifiable elections. In: Wallach, D.S., Rivest, R.L. (eds.) 2006 USENIX/ACCURATE Electronic Voting Technology Workshop, EVT 2006. USENIX Association (2006)
2. Haines, T., Lewis, S.J., Pereira, O., Teague, V.: How not to prove your election outcome. In: 2020 IEEE Symposium on Security and Privacy, SP 2020, pp. 644–660. IEEE (2020)
3. Halderman, J.A., Teague, V.: The New South Wales iVote system: security failures and verification flaws in a live online election. In: Haenni, R., Koenig, R.E., Wikström, D. (eds.) VOTELID 2015. LNCS, vol. 9269, pp. 35–53. Springer, Cham (2015). https://doi.org/10.1007/978-3-319-22270-7_3
4. Heiberg, S., Willemson, J.: Verifiable internet voting in Estonia. In: 6th International Conference on Electronic Voting: Verifying the Vote (EVOTE), pp. 1–8 (2014)
5. Heiberg, S., Krips, K., Willemson, J.: Planning the next steps for Estonian Internet voting. In: Proceedings E-Vote-ID 2020, pp. 82–97. TalTech Press (2020)
6. Heiberg, S., Martens, T., Vinkel, P., Willemson, J.: Improving the verifiability of the Estonian Internet voting scheme. In: Krimmer, R., et al. (eds.) E-Vote-ID 2016. LNCS, vol. 10141, pp. 92–107. Springer, Cham (2017). https://doi.org/10.1007/978-3-319-52240-1_6
7. Kubjas, I., Pikma, T., Willemson, J.: Estonian voting verification mechanism revisited again. In: Krimmer, R., Volkamer, M., Braun Binder, N., Kersting, N., Pereira, O., Schürmann, C. (eds.) E-Vote-ID 2017. LNCS, vol. 10615, pp. 306–317. Springer, Cham (2017). https://doi.org/10.1007/978-3-319-68687-5_19
8. Mus, K., Kiraz, M.S., Cenk, M., Sertkaya, I.: Estonian voting verification mechanism revisited. CoRR, abs/1612.00668 (2016)
9. OSCE/ODIHR. Estonia parliamentary elections - 6 March 2011 - OSCE/ODIHR election assessment mission report (2011). https://www.osce.org/files/f/documents/a/9/77557.pdf
10. Parsovs, A.: Estonian electronic identity card: security flaws in key management. In: 29th USENIX Security Symposium, USENIX Security 2020, pp. 1785–1802. USENIX Association (2020)
11. Springall, D., et al.: Security analysis of the Estonian internet voting system. In: Proceedings of the 2014 ACM SIGSAC Conference on Computer and Communications Security, pp. 703–715. ACM (2014)
12. Confédération suisse. Annex to the FCh ordinance of 13 December 2013 on electronic voting (OEV, SR 161.116) (2018). https://www.bk.admin.ch/bk/en/home/politische-rechte/e-voting/versuchsbedingungen.html. Version 2.0
13. Valimised. Statistics about internet voting in Estonia. https://www.valimised.ee/en/archive/statistics-about-internet-voting-estonia

Breaking and Fixing Vote Privacy of the Estonian E-Voting Protocol IVXV

Johannes Müller[✉][iD]

SnT, University of Luxembourg, Esch-sur-Alzette, Luxembourg
johannes.mueller@uni.lu

Abstract. We revisit the e-voting protocol IVXV that is used for legally-binding political elections in Estonia from a privacy perspective. We demonstrate that IVXV is vulnerable to attacks against vote privacy in those threat scenarios that were considered for IVXV originally. We explain how to improve IVXV so that it protects against the privacy issues we discovered.

1 Introduction

More than 15 years ago, Estonia became the first country in the world in which voters could regularly cast their ballots for political elections over the Internet. The initial e-voting system used for political elections in Estonia was a rather naive system whose security relied on trusted voting authorities; in particular, that system did not allow for auditing the correctness of the election result. Not least due to the attacks against the initial e-voting system discovered by Springall et al. [11], Heiberg et al. [4] proposed a new e-voting protocol designed to mitigate trust in the voting authorities and to allow for external auditing. This protocol, which is called IVXV, has been used for legally-binding political elections in Estonia since 2015 until today.

Our Contributions. In this work, we revisit IVXV from a privacy perspective. We discovered that IVXV (described in Sect. 2) does not guarantee vote privacy of all voters, which violates a fundamental right of Estonian voters (Article 1(2) of Riigikogu Election Act). More precisely, in Sect. 3, we present efficient attacks against vote privacy of IVXV that exploit the malleability of the underlying encryption scheme. In Sect. 4.1, we show that the assumptions of our attacks are realistic or within the original threat scenario of IVXV, respectively. In Sect. 4.2, we elaborate on real-world implications of the privacy vulnerabilities. Eventually, in Sect. 4.3, we explain how to fix the privacy issues of IVXV presented in this work.

Responsible Disclosure. We shared our insights with representatives of the Estonian election authorities on August 23, 2021, and discussed our findings with them as well as members from the system provider (Smartmatic-Cybernetica)/a main author of IVXV in an online meeting on September 2, 2021. Following this

© International Financial Cryptography Association 2023
S. Matsuo et al. (Eds.): FC 2022 Workshops, LNCS 13412, pp. 325–334, 2023.
https://doi.org/10.1007/978-3-031-32415-4_22

meeting and a further online meeting, Smartmatic-Cybernetica acknowledged the existence of the privacy issue of the IVXV *protocol* [4] that we present in this paper and declared their intention to fix this issue as proposed in Sect. 4.3. However, they claimed that in the actual *system* used for real-world elections, "there are quite a few physical and organisational safequards implemented" that would already mitigate the risk of these vote privacy issues; we discuss their argument in Sect. 4.1.

2   Protocol Description

In this section, we recall how the IVXV e-voting protocol works on the conceptual level. We restrict our presentation to those phases of IVXV which are relevant for the privacy attacks described in Sect. 3, emphasizing that these attacks also work against the full IVXV protocol, as presented in [4].[1]

2.1   Protocol Participants

The *Election Organizer (EO)* is the administrator of the election who determines the list of candidates/choices, list of voters, etc. EO is also responsible for generating the public/private key material used to encrypt and eventually decrypt the voters' choices.

The *Vote Collector (VC)* is active during the ballot submission phase in which it collects the ballots submitted by the voters. VC checks incoming ballots for eligibility of the respective voter and stores all ballots according to the time at which they have been submitted.

The *I-Ballot Box Processor (IBBP)* is started once the submission phase has closed. IBBP takes as input the ballots collected by VC, verifies its correctness, and removes all data which is no longer needed for the subsequent tallying phase (e.g., voters' signatures).

The role of the *Mixing Service (MS)* is to anonymize votes before they are decrypted by EO. MS takes as input a list of ciphertexts from IBBP, re-encrypts and shuffles this list, and returns the resulting mixed ciphertext list to EO.

Any external party who wants to verify the integrity of the election result (i.e., whether the election result corresponds to the votes submitted by the voters) can run the *Data Auditor* program which takes as input all data published by the election authorities and verifies its correctness.

2.2   Cryptographic Primitives

IVXV employs the following cryptographic primitives:

A *digital signature scheme* $S = (\mathsf{KeyGen}_S, \mathsf{Sign}, \mathsf{Verify})$ for signing ballots and for signing all public data output by the election authorities.

---

[1] To be more precise, in our presentation, we simplified the checks carried out to verify eligibility of voters, and we completely omitted the voters' individual verification procedures.

A *homomorphic public-key encryption scheme* $\mathcal{E} = (\mathsf{KeyGen}_{\mathcal{E}}, \mathsf{Enc}, \mathsf{Dec})$ for encrypting the voters' plain choices. In the IVXV implementation, $\mathcal{E}$ is instantiated with the ElGamal PKE scheme [2].

A *proof of shuffle* π_{Shuffle} which is generated by MS to prove that it shuffled its input ciphertexts correctly. In the IVXV implementation, π_{Shuffle} is instantiated with Verificatum [14].

A *proof of correct decryption* π_{Dec} which is generated by EO to prove that it decrypted the final ciphertexts correctly. In the IVXV implementation, π_{Dec} is instantiated with a Schnorr-based NIZKP [10] to prove knowledge of discrete logarithms.

In the original IVXV paper [4], it had not been specified which security properties these primitives need to provide precisely but the respective instantiations suggest that the signature scheme $\mathcal{S}$, the encryption scheme $\mathcal{E}$, the proof of shuffle π_{Shuffle}, and the proof of correct decryption π_{Dec} are supposed to be EUF-CMA-secure, IND-CPA-secure, and non-interactive zero-knowledge proofs (NIZKPs), respectively.

2.3   Protocol Phases

The IVXV protocol is split into the following phases. In the setup phase, EO creates the key material. In the submission phase, voters can submit their ballots. In the tabulation phase, the ballots submitted by the voters are anonymized and decrypted. In the auditing phase, which can be executed at any point after the election result has been announced, the correctness of the data output by the election authorities can be verified externally.

Setup Phase. The protocol assumes that there exists a public-key infrastructure (PKI) of public verification keys for individual voters. The Election Organizer EO determines the list of eligible voters which are identified by their respective public verification keys. EO also determines the set of valid choices C (i.e., party lists with individual candidates). EO runs the key generation algorithm of the public-key encryption scheme $\mathcal{E}$ to obtain an encryption/decryption key pair $(\mathsf{pk}, \mathsf{sk}) \leftarrow \mathsf{KeyGen}_{\mathsf{Enc}}$. The list of eligible voters, the set of valid choices C, as well as the public key pk are made available to everybody.

Submission Phase. Each voter V_i who wants to vote for some choice $\mathsf{ch} \in \mathsf{C}$ encrypts her choice as $\mathsf{c} \leftarrow \mathsf{Enc}(\mathsf{pk}, \mathsf{ch})$, then signs the ciphertext c with her secret signing key ssk as $\sigma \leftarrow \mathsf{Sign}(\mathsf{ssk}, \mathsf{c})$ and submits the resulting pair $\mathsf{b} \leftarrow (\mathsf{c}, \sigma)$ to the Vote Collector VC.

For each incoming ballot $\mathsf{b} = (\mathsf{c}, \sigma)$, VC verifies whether σ is a valid signature for c w.r.t. a verification key vk of one of the eligible voters. If this is the case, then VC stores b together with the time at which it had been submitted. Voters can re-vote multiple times.

Tabulation Phase. After the submission phase has closed, VC forwards the list of ballots to the I-Ballot Box Processor IBBP who first verifies that all ballots in VC's list were signed by eligible voters only. Afterwards, IBBP removes the ballots of all voters who have also submitted a paper vote. Eventually, IBBP extracts the last submitted ballot of each voter (who did not submit a paper vote), removes the respective signatures, and stores the resulting ciphertexts in a list B_1.

The I-Ballot Box Processor sends the list of ciphertexts B_1 to the mixing service MS which then re-encrypts all ciphertexts in B_1, shuffles the resulting re-encrypted ciphertexts uniformly at random, and computes a proof of correct shuffling π_{Shuffle}.

After that, MS sends the resulting ciphertext vector B_2 to EO which first uses its secret decryption key sk to decrypt all ciphertexts in B_2 to obtain the final result res, and then computes a proof of correct decryption π_{Dec} to prove that it decrypted B_2 correctly.

The tuple $(B_1, B_2, \pi_{\mathsf{Shuffle}}, \pi_{\mathsf{Dec}}, \mathsf{res})$ is the output of the tabulation phase, where the list of plaintexts res determines the raw final election result. Eventually, EO publishes a "sanitized" version of the raw result res from which all invalid choices, if any, were removed.

Auditing Phase. The Data Auditor DA takes as input $(B_1, B_2, \pi_{\mathsf{Shuffle}}, \pi_{\mathsf{Dec}}, \mathsf{res})$ and verifies whether π_{Shuffle} is a valid proof of shuffle w.r.t. the lists of B_1 and B_2, and whether π_{Dec} is a valid proof of correct decryption w.r.t. B_2 and res.

3   Privacy Attacks

We describe two attacks against vote privacy of IVXV [4] which we will call *shifting attacks* and *encoding attacks*, respectively. Both attacks exploit the homomorphic property of the encryption scheme, that is employed in IVXV to encrypt the voters' plain choices (recall Sect. 2), to create maliciously generated ballots that depend on honest voters' ballots [3]. Both attacks slightly differ in terms of the underlying assumptions and their impact: in comparison to the shifting attack, the encoding attack requires qualitatively stronger assumptions but it allows to break privacy of several voters by submitting a single malicious vote. In this section, we focus on the purely technical description of the attacks and refer to Sect. 4 for a discussion of their assumptions and implications.

3.1   Background: Homomorphic Encryption

Recall that a public-key encryption scheme $\mathcal{E} = (\mathsf{KeyGen}_{\mathcal{E}}, \mathsf{Enc}, \mathsf{Dec})$ is *homomorphic* if both the message space $(\mathcal{M}, \cdot)$ and the ciphertext space $(\mathcal{C}, \odot)$ are (algebraic) groups and the encryption algorithm is a homomorphism between these two groups, i.e., $\mathsf{Enc}(\mathsf{pk}, m) \odot \mathsf{Enc}(\mathsf{pk}, m') \in \mathsf{Enc}(\mathsf{pk}, m \cdot m')$ for all $(\mathsf{pk}, \mathsf{sk}) \in \mathsf{KeyGen}_{\mathcal{E}}$ and all $m, m' \in \mathcal{M}$. For example, the ElGamal PKE scheme [2], the one employed in the IVXV system, is homomorphic.

The privacy attacks presented in the remainder of this section are based on the following facts.

Note 1. Let $\mathcal{E}$ be a homomorphic public-key encryption scheme, and let $(\mathsf{pk}, \mathsf{sk}) \in \mathsf{KeyGen}_{\mathcal{E}}$. Then the following statements hold true:

- For all $m_1, m_3 \in \mathcal{M}$, we have that $\mathsf{Enc}(\mathsf{pk}, m_1) \odot \mathsf{Enc}(\mathsf{pk}, m_2) \in \mathsf{Enc}(\mathsf{pk}, m_3)$ holds true for $m_2 = m_3 \cdot m_1^{-1}$.
- For all $m_1, \ldots, m_n \in \mathcal{M}$ and all $\alpha_1, \ldots, \alpha_n \in \mathbb{N}$, we have $\prod_{i=1}^{n} \mathsf{Enc}(\mathsf{pk}, m_i)^{\alpha_i} \in \mathsf{Enc}(\mathsf{pk}, \prod_{i=1}^{n} m_i^{\alpha_i})$.

3.2 Shifting Attacks

The idea of the *shifting attack* is to submit a ballot which contains a vote for ch' if and only if the targeted voter V submitted a vote for ch. If ch' is an unpopular choice, then the adversary learns whether or not V voted for ch by checking whether there exists a vote for ch' in the final election result.

Assumptions. We make the following assumptions:

1. The attacker can learn the ballot of the voter V whose privacy he wants to break.
2. There exists a (valid) choice $\mathsf{ch}' \in C$ which is chosen by none of the (honest) voters with high probability (see 2nd paragraph in Sect. 4.1).
3. The attacker can control one voter.

Impact. The attacker can check whether V voted for ch.

Program. The attacker runs the following program:

1. Submission phase: Learn ballot $b = (c, \sigma)$ of voter V.
2. Submission phase: Submit ballot $b' = (c', \sigma')$, where $c' \leftarrow c \odot \mathsf{Enc}(\mathsf{pk}, \mathsf{ch}^{-1} \cdot \mathsf{ch}')$.
3. After election: Check whether $\mathsf{ch}' \in \mathsf{res}'$.

3.3 Encoding Attacks

The idea of the *encoding attack* is to submit a ballot which encrypts a unique encoding of the choices $\mathsf{ch}_1, \ldots, \mathsf{ch}_k$ submitted by the targeted voters $\mathsf{V}_1, \ldots, \mathsf{V}_k$. The attacker then checks for all possible combinations $\mathsf{ch}'_1, \ldots, \mathsf{ch}'_k$ whether there exists an encoding of these choices in the final result. If the attacker finds such a combination, then he knows that $\mathsf{V}_1, \ldots, \mathsf{V}_k$ voted for $\mathsf{ch}'_1, \ldots, \mathsf{ch}'_k$, respectively.

Originally, the concept of what we call encoding attacks in this paper goes back to Pfitzmann's seminal works [8,9]; here, we use a generalized version of Pfitzmann's attack presented in [6].

Assumptions. We make the following assumptions:

1. The attacker can learn the ballots of the voters $V_1, \ldots, V_k$ whose privacy he wants to break.
2. The attacker can learn the raw election result res.
3. The attacker can control one voter.

Impact. The attacker learns how $V_1, \ldots, V_k$ voted.

Program. The attacker runs the following program:

1. Submission phase: Learn ballots $b_1 = (c_1, \sigma_1), \ldots, b_k = (c_k, \sigma_k)$ of voters $V_1, \ldots, V_k$.
2. Submission phase: Submit ballot $b' = (c', \sigma')$, where $c' \leftarrow c_1^{\alpha_1} \odot \ldots \odot c_k^{\alpha_k}$ and $\alpha_1, \ldots, \alpha_k$ are integers chosen uniformly at random.
3. After election: Let ch $\in$ res be the invalid choice in the raw election result res. Return $ch^1, \ldots, ch^k$ such that $ch = ch_1^{\alpha_1} \cdot \ldots \cdot ch_k^{\alpha_k}$ holds true.

Efficiency. The computational complexity of the encoding attack is $\mathcal{O}(n^k)$, where n is the number of possible choices and k is the number of targeted voters. Hence, in practice, several dozen voters can be targeted efficiently. If the attacker only wants to check whether $V_1, \ldots, V_k$ voted for $ch_1, \ldots, ch_k$, then complexity reduces to $\mathcal{O}(k)$.

4   Discussion

4.1   Assumptions

We show that the assumptions that are sufficient to execute the privacy attacks against IVXV (Sect. 3) are realistic or within the original threat scenario considered for IVXV [4], respectively.

On Learning Targeted Voters' Ballots. The IVXV protocol was explicitly designed in such a way that it "allows to outsource the vote collection task to a third party, as the correct operation of this party is verifiable by voters, third-party auditors and auditors nominated by the election organizer itself" [4]. We argue that the fact that they claimed that *any third party* could perform this task implies that VC should also not be trusted in terms of vote privacy. Since VC receives all incoming messages, an attacker who controls VC can learn all submitted ballots (even if he cannot manipulate them undectably). Hence, the assumption on learning targeted voters' ballots is within the general threat scenario considered for IVXV originally.

In our online meeting, Smartmatic-Cybernetica stated that, unlike in [4], in the system used for real-world elections, the task of VC was not executed by a third party but by a service which they claimed to be protected by physical and organisational safeguards. Even if this is the case, we think that it is undesirable having to trust a party (VC) for vote privacy whose original purpose/role is not to protect vote privacy (but to simply collect votes). Furthermore, since collected votes are not published in IVXV, it is questionable whether all parties (voters, observers, etc.) can have the same view on the data being processed, which is a crucial property for secure e-voting in general (see, e.g., [5]).

On the Existence of Unpopular Choices. For the shifting attack, we assume that there exists at least one unpopular choice (and that the attacker knows a priori that this choice is unpopular). In what follows, we show that this assumption is realistic. The electorate of parliamentary (Riigikogu) elections in Estonia is divided into numerous districts. For each of these districts, there exist party lists which contain several candidates of the respective party. Altogether, each voter can vote for one candidate of one party list in one district, which results into a large number of possible choices in total and a granular public election result. It is therefore not surprising that in the last Riigikogu election [12] in most districts, there existed several candidates that received only one vote in total (most likely, the vote of the respective candidate), or even no votes at all. It is also realistic to assume that an attacker knows a priori for at least one of these candidates that she/he will not receive any votes with high probability (except for her/his own vote).

On Learning the Raw Election Result. For the encoding attack, we assume that the attacker can learn the "raw" election result which also contains invalid plain choices. Unlike in many modern e-voting systems, the Election Organizer EO only publishes a "sanitized" version of the raw result from which all invalid choices have been removed (see [13]), which may contradict our assumption on first sight. However, there exist several parties which learn the raw election result anyway. For example, according to [4], "trusted representatives of political parties, foreign research groups or even local civil activists" may fill the auditor's role. In order to be able to audit a run of the IVXV system end-to-end, an auditor needs to obtain the raw election result; otherwise, it wouldn't be possible to verify the proof of correct decryption employed in IVXV. It can therefore not be ruled out that one of those parties who audit an election has malicious intents. Indeed, the IVXV protocol was explicitly designed in such a way that a possibly corrupted auditor is not able to learn how individual voters voted: "[d]ue to the re-encryption mixnet used, the malicious auditor could not break the ballot secrecy" [4]. This proves that the assumption on learning the raw election result is clearly within the threat scenario considered for IVXV originally.

On Corrupting a Voter. It is realistic to assume that the attacker can control a voter because the attacker can be an eligible voter herself. For the same reason, in case some voters collude, the attacker can execute the privacy attacks multiple times to target even more voters and break their vote privacy.

4.2   Implications

In democratic elections, vote privacy is a *universal* right: the individual vote of *each single* voter must remain secret. All voters, not just the majority of them, must have the right to express their true will without facing personal negative consequences. Indeed, it is particularly important to protect the privacy of those voters who favor less popular parties/candidates because these parties/candidates as well as their supporters are more likely to be threatened than those (who voted for the) ones in power. Additionally, in each election, there exist voters whose individual choices are particularly interesting to single out for non-political reasons. For example, a party of an ongoing trial may want to learn the judge's personal political orientation in order to increase its advantage in the court or to blame the judge being biased.

Furthermore, even if vote privacy of only a fraction of the electorate can be broken, no voter can be sure whether or not she is among the targeted voters. This observation can be exploited to coerce many voters at the same time (not) to vote for a specific party/candidate because each coerced voter will likely follow the coercer's instruction if she knows that the coercer can randomly check whether or not she obeyed.

The mere possibility of these attacks can cause a significant bias in the election result and thus undermine the legitimacy of the government elected.

4.3   Protection

Fortunately, it is straightforward to protect against the privacy attacks presented in Sect. 3, as described next. In the submission phase, each voter computes a NIZKP *of knowledge* π_{Enc} which proves that the voter knows plaintext ch (and randomness r) such that $\mathsf{c} = \mathsf{Enc}(\mathsf{pk}, \mathsf{ch}; r)$. This mechanism is commonly employed in modern secure e-voting systems (e.g., Helios [1]) because, in this way, the ciphertext c is no longer malleable if the correctness of π_{Enc} is verified before further processing (see, e.g., [3]). If IVXV is modified accordingly, the homomorphic privacy attacks presented in this paper are no longer possible.

We note, however, that this modification may not necessarily protect against *all* possible attacks against vote privacy of IVXV. In order to ensure that the IVXV protocol in fact provides vote privacy, a formal reduction proof is necessary. However, the current presentation of IVXV in [4] does not allow for such a proof because the security properties of the underlying cryptographic primitives are not specified precisely (recall Sect. 2) and the overall protocol model is partially underspecified. Furthermore, the threat scenario for vote privacy (as well as the ones for verifiability and coercion-resistance) needs to be stated more explicitly than in the original paper [4] and in the current online documentation.

Recommendations. We recommend to improve IVXV as follows:

1. Voters in IVXV use a NIZKP π_{Enc} as described above.
2. The (fixed) IVXV protocol is presented in full technical details.

3. The threat scenarios for all security properties (verifiability, privacy, coercion-resistance) are described explicitly. Security is formally proven.

We hope that the insights on vote privacy from this paper as well as the ones on verifiability from [7] will make electronic elections in Estonia more secure.

Acknowledgements. I thank Jan Willemson for his open-minded discussions about the vote privacy (issues) of IVXV as well as his critical remarks on a preliminary version of this report. I also thank the anonymous referees for their helpful feedback.

Johannes Müller was supported by the Luxembourg National Research Fund (FNR), under the CORE Junior project FP2 (C20/IS/14698166/FP2/Mueller).

References

1. Adida, B.: Helios: web-based open-audit voting. In: Proceedings of the 17th USENIX Security Symposium, 2008, pp. 335–348. USENIX Association (2008)
2. El Gamal, T.: A public key cryptosystem and a signature scheme based on discrete logarithms. In: Advances in Cryptology, Proceedings of CRYPTO '84, pp. 10–18 (1984)
3. Gennaro, R.: Achieving independence efficiently and securely. In: Anderson, J.H. (ed.), Proceedings of the Fourteenth Annual ACM Symposium on Principles of Distributed Computing, Ottawa, Ontario, Canada, 20–23 August 1995, pp. 130–136. ACM (1995)
4. Heiberg, S., Martens, T., Vinkel, P., Willemson, J.: Improving the verifiability of the Estonian internet voting scheme. In: Krimmer, R., et al. (eds.) E-Vote-ID 2016. LNCS, vol. 10141, pp. 92–107. Springer, Cham (2017). https://doi.org/10.1007/978-3-319-52240-1_6
5. Hirschi, L., Schmid, L., Basin, D.: Fixing the achilles heel of e-voting: the bulletin board. In: 34th IEEE Computer Security Foundations Symposium, CSF 2021, Dubrovnik, Croatia, 21–25 June 2021, pp. 1–17. IEEE (2021)
6. Khazaei, S., Wikström, D.: Randomized partial checking revisited. In: Dawson, E. (ed.) CT-RSA 2013. LNCS, vol. 7779, pp. 115–128. Springer, Heidelberg (2013). https://doi.org/10.1007/978-3-642-36095-4_8
7. Pereira, O.: Individual verifiability and Revoting in the Estonian internet voting system. IACR Cryptology ePrint Archive, p. 1098 (2021)
8. Pfitzmann, B.: Breaking an efficient anonymous channel. In: De Santis, A. (ed.) EUROCRYPT 1994. LNCS, vol. 950, pp. 332–340. Springer, Heidelberg (1995). https://doi.org/10.1007/BFb0053448
9. Pfitzmann, B., Pfitzmann, A.: How to break the direct RSA-implementation of mixes. In: Quisquater, J.-J., Vandewalle, J. (eds.) EUROCRYPT 1989. LNCS, vol. 434, pp. 373–381. Springer, Heidelberg (1990). https://doi.org/10.1007/3-540-46885-4_37
10. Schnorr, C.P.: Efficient identification and signatures for smart cards. In: Quisquater, J.-J., Vandewalle, J. (eds.) EUROCRYPT 1989. LNCS, vol. 434, pp. 688–689. Springer, Heidelberg (1990). https://doi.org/10.1007/3-540-46885-4_68
11. Springall, D., et al.: Security analysis of the Estonian internet voting system. In: Ahn, G.-J., Yung, M., Li, N. (eds.), Proceedings of the 2014 ACM SIGSAC Conference on Computer and Communications Security, Scottsdale, AZ, USA, 3–7 November 2014, pp. 703–715. ACM (2014)

12. Valimised. https://rk2019.valimised.ee/en/voting-result/voting-result-main.html. Accessed 23 Aug 2021
13. Valimised. https://www.valimised.ee/en/internet-voting/documents-about-intern et-voting. Accessed 23 Aug 2021
14. Verificatum Mix Net (VMN). https://www.verificatum.org/html/product_vmn. html

German Voters' Attitudes Towards Voting Online with a Verifiable System

Oksana Kulyk[1], Melanie Volkamer[2]([✉]), Niklas Fuhrberg[2], Benjamin Berens[2], and Robert Krimmer[3] [ID]

[1] IT University of Copenhagen, Copenhagen, Denmark
okku@itu.dk
[2] Karlsruhe Institute of Technology, Karlsruhe, Germany
{melanie.volkamer,niklas.fuhrberg,benjamin.berens}@kit.edu
[3] Johan Skytte Institute of Political Studies, University of Tartu,
Ülikooli 18, 51003 Tartu, Estonia
robert.krimmer@ut.ee

Abstract. A representative study came to the conclusion that more than 63% of German voters would have like to cast their vote for the federal election in 2021 online. In this paper, we aimed to investigate why Germans might be in favour or against online voting, conducting a online survey. We furthermore aimed to study the reactions of people being in favor of online voting if confronted with a verifiable remote voting system, as well as with interventions aimed at communicating that it is important to follow all the steps to verify. Our findings show that the majority of our participants were generally willing to vote online. Convenience emerged as the most popular reason for voting online. The reaction to the verifiable remote voting system was diverse, from our participants being irritated from the complexity, to very positive reactions due to high security level. Nonetheless, the majority of the participants did not change their willingness to vote online after seeing the proposed system. The different interventions had no effect. Furthermore, the majority agreed on the importance of verifiability being in place.

Keywords: user study · verifiable Internet voting · trust

1 Introduction

Internet voting is in the middle of societal discussions again, given the ongoing push towards digitalisation of the society and the COVID-19 pandemic that poses risks with traditional polling-place voting. Especially in Germany, in the context of recent federal elections, internet voting is being widely discussed, with political parties using online voting systems for internal elections[1], and the Federal Office of Information Security issuing guidelines on how to securely conduct

---

[1] https://archiv.cdu.de/artikel/1-digitaler-parteitag-der-cdu-so-funktionierten-die-abstimmungen (Oct 30 2021).

© International Financial Cryptography Association 2023
S. Matsuo et al. (Eds.): FC 2022 Workshops, LNCS 13412, pp. 335–350, 2023.
https://doi.org/10.1007/978-3-031-32415-4_23

elections using online voting for the next so called social elections organized by the health insurance agencies (being the third largest election in Germany)[2]. Some months before the German federal elections in 2021, a nation-wide survey has shown that 63% of Germans would like to cast their vote for the federal elections online[3].

Given that the majority of voters is in favor of e-voting, in this work we aim to gain insights into what exactly are the reasons why people are willing or not willing to vote online. As we expected that most participants have either no experience with online voting or only with black box voting systems (i.e. systems not providing any means to verify that the vote as tallied as cast), we were also interested in their reaction when being confronted with a verifiable voting system. As both the voting procedure and the security guarantees of verifiable voting systems differ from black box voting systems, we aimed to investigate how voters' attitude is affected when gaining some insights into how the voting procedure would look like, and what are the steps they can perform to verify that their vote is not manipulated. We decided to use the idea of return codes as it is implemented in the Swiss voting system for various reasons: e.g. the steps to verify are more integrated in vote casting than it is the case e.g. in Helios [4]; it has been used in Switzerland for actual elections, and past research has improved its usability and has shown that it is usable [17]. Furthermore, we were interested the effect of different interventions explaining in a more or less alarming way that it is important to carefully take all the steps described in the received voting material. This last research question is motivated by the fact that past research has concluded that it is important to motivate voters to verify as well as to explain the importance for the overall security of the system [17]. In particular, we are interested whether such interventions have a negative impact on trust.

To answer all these research questions, we conducted an online survey with 548 participants. Our findings show that the majority (62%) of our participants were generally willing to vote online, which aligns with the nation-wide study, indicating the representativeness of our sample. Convenience emerged as the most popular reason for being in favor of voting online and security concerns and potential for manipulation are the most popular reasons for being against it. 18% changed their attitudes from positive to either neutral or against online voting once confronted with the verifiable voting system. Interestingly, we could not measure a significant difference between different interventions neither wrt. general attitude towards online voting nor trust in the proposed system. We discuss all our findings and deduce future research directions as well as lessons learned for actual elections.

---

[2] https://www.bsi.bund.de/SharedDocs/Downloads/DE/BSI/Publikationen/TechnischeRichtlinien/TR03162/BSI-TR-03162.pdf (Oct 30 2021).

[3] https://www.bitkom.org/Presse/Presseinformation/Zwei-Drittel-sprechen-sich-fuer-Online-Wahlen-aus (Oct 30 2021).

2   Related Work

Studies – e.g. [16, 23–27, 30, 39] – have shown that several human related factors should be considered when developing and introducing a verifiable electronic voting system. Other research has evaluated the usability of verifiable electronic voting systems, e.g. [1–3, 5, 7, 10–14, 17–20, 22, 28, 35, 36]. Several report serious usability issues (incl. that participants have difficulties with detecting manipulations if the adversary manages to tamper with the flow of the verification process) as well as misperceptions. For instance, Distler et al. [10] report that their participants felt less secure after having verified than before. In [7], the authors report a high score of verification efficacy, probably because of the system was developed using a human-cantered security approach. Other base for this work is the research conducted by Marky et al. [21] on the usability of code voting in general. [14] also evaluated the usability and acceptance of code voting and code-based verification. According to this work, a system with the highest security assurance was more accepted by the voters, even if the usability of this system was rated worse compared to less secure systems.

Internet voting as a technology is perceived to be highly disruptive and as such has the potential to change the electoral process as a whole. Studies investigating the take-up of such technologies, have focused on the adoption of the technology in a given context [29], the end-user [9, 34], or the relationship between society and technology. Early adoption of Internet voting has been largely connected to technical competence and experience [33]. Similar patterns were found for the use of verifiability when voting online [32]. Nonetheless, due to their disruptive nature, introducing new technologies in elections can lead to perceived lack of legitimacy which leads to lack of trust and acceptance [6].

3   Background

In this section we describe the approach used in Switzerland to provide voters a mean to verify that their vote as neither manipulated by their own device they use to cast their vote nor by one voting server once received. This approach is one instantiation of so called code-based verifiable voting systems. These approaches issue voters with a unique *polling sheet*, delivered via postal mail. This sheet provides the website address voters can use to cast their votes, instructions, and one or more codes to verify the correct processing of their vote. In this work, we use a variant based on a voting system used in Swiss elections [31], with the polling sheet and user interface modifications developed by Kulyk et al. [17]. While there also exist improvements from [22], we decided to go for the Kulyk et al. [17] because it was evaluated with respect to more attack types than the proposal by Marky et al. [22].

The polling sheet of [17, 22, 31] provides three types of codes: check, confirmation *and* finalization code. In order to cast their vote, the voter first has to identify themselves by entering their password, which is provided on the polling sheet. After selecting the party to vote for and reviewing the choice, the voter is provided on the screen a check code and is asked to check that the displayed check code corresponds to the personalised one on their polling sheet. If the codes match, the voter then has to provide the confirmation code. Otherwise, they are instructed to report the mismatch to the election authorities, using the number on the polling sheet. The voter is informed that once they enter and submit the confirmation code, the vote is considered cast and that they are not allowed to cast a vote via postal or in the polling stations anymore. Once entered the confirmation code, the page with the finalization code is displayed. The purpose of the finalization code is to reassure the voter that the voting system has indeed cast their vote as intended, and giving the voter the possibility to confirm that the code displayed is matching their choice. The corresponding polling sheet is displayed in Fig. 1.

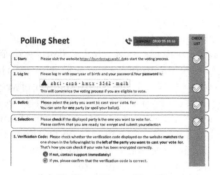

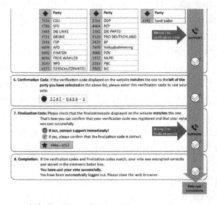

(a) Polling Sheet Top Part   (b) Polling Sheet Bottom Part

Fig. 1. Polling Sheet

4   Methodology

Here we are describing the selected approach for this research.

4.1   Designing the Interventions

Several researchers have noticed a lack of voter's motivation to actually verify as well as misconceptions regarding which information to trust and which not to trust. For the verifiability approach making use of codes it is important (1) that voters only follow all the instructions on their polling sheet, (2) that they call the election organizers in case the instructions on the webpage are different, and (3) that they dial the number provided on the polling sheet (and not a number provided on the webpage). This information was provided in an additional document which we call intervention. We designed three different interventions. These are more or less alarming (see Fig. 2 which also indicates the main differences). The motivation to have three is the following: Being more alarming makes it more likely that voters read and apply it. However, it may cause more distrust in the voting system as warning icons are often recognized as something negative [37].

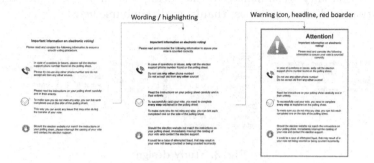

Fig. 2. Interventions: IN-L (low alarming), IN-M, and IN-H (high alarming)

4.2 Research Questions and Hypotheses

We study the topic using both a quantitative and a qualitative approach with two sets of research questions. For the qualitative part, we have posed three research questions.

RQ1: What are reasons for participants being in favour, neutral, or against casting their vote over the Internet for federal elections?

RQ2: What are reasons for participants being in favour, neutral, or against using the introduced system to cast their vote over the Internet for federal elections – while focusing on those who are in general in favor of online voting.

RQ3: What is users feedback on the voting system and the interventions?

Following this qualitative approach, we investigate the effect of being exposed to a particular *verifiable system on people's attitudes towards online voting*, including the effect of three different interventions, using a quantitative approach. We define and test the following hypotheses for those participants who – in general – like to cast their vote online for federal elections:

H1 There is a difference in terms how *willing* participants are to use the proposed system to vote online, depending on the intervention.

H2 There is a difference in terms of overall *trust* in the system, depending on the intervention.

H3 There is a difference in terms of *perceived usefulness of verifiability*, depending on the intervention.

4.3 Study Procedure

The study is structured in the following phases (see also Fig. 3): 'Welcome & Informed content', question on 'Taking part in 2021 federal elections', question on 'Voting online if possible for 2021 federal election', 'introduction of voting system with and without interventions', 'attention check', question on 'Voting wit this system for 2021 federal election', questions on 'general trust, importance of verifiability', 'comments' to the voting system and if applicable to the intervention, and 'demographics, thanks and reimbursement'.

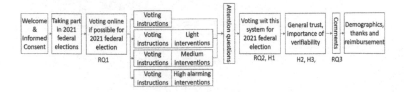

Fig. 3. Study design

For 'general trust, importance of verifiability', we used questions, adapted from a questionnaire introduced in [38][4]. The questions are provided in Fig. 5. The changes that we made included (1) changing the scale from 6-point to 5-point in order to make it more consistent with the rest of our questionnaire, (2) adapting the questions about the voting and the process to verify in order to account for differences between the voting system for which the questionnaire has originally been developed and the system that we evaluate, (3) adapting and expanding the questions about beliefs regarding the possibility of election manipulation to account for different verifiability aspects. Note, items 1–7 are used to evaluate H2 on general trust and items 8 and 9 to evaluate H3 on perceived usefulness of verifiability.

4.4 Recruitment and Ethics

We recruited the participants using the Clickworker platform. We did so one week before the federal election in Germany took place. Participants were paid €1,6 for their participation which was estimated to take 10 min (based on conducted pretests), which corresponds to an hourly fee above the minimal wage in Germany. In order to ensure quality of the collected data, we introduced attention checks in the questionnaire, of which the participants were informed at the beginning of the survey. While there is no mandatory ethical review process at the authors' institutions, we took care to ensure that no harm is being done to the participants, asking for their informed consent and providing them with the information about the purpose of the study, the fact that their participation is anonymous, and that they can decide at any time to stop participating.

---

[4] The original questions were translated to German (using back-&-forward translation).

5   Results

We denote "CG" as the control group, i.e. the participants who did not see an interventions, and we denote "IN-L", "IN-M" and "IN-H" the group with low alarming, medium alarming, and high alarming intervention (see Sect. 4.1) correspondingly. For the analysis of hypotheses H1–H3 we conduct statistical tests (using R package "stats"). For the analysis of research questions RQ1–RQ2 we conduct open coding of participants' open-ended answers using the following procedure: (1) one author developed an initial code book out of 20% of the answers. (2) Afterwards the code book was discussed with a second author and adopted to the code book used for the next step. (3) Two authors coded another 20%. (4) This assignment was discussed while only minor adoptions to the assignment as well as to the code book were necessary. (5) One author coded all answers. Note, the coding was done in German and afterwards translated.

5.1   Demographics

There were 548 participants[5], of them 339 men, 207 women and 2 non-binary persons. The most common age group was 30 to 34 years old with 96 participants, followed by 35 to 39 years old (79 participants); among the rest of the participants, 119 were between 18 and 30 and 254 were above 40 years old. Note, 21 were above 65 years old. Looking at the educational level: 33 finished high-school, 80 completed an apprenticeship, 47 had an entrance qualification for a university of applied sciences, 135 had an university entrance qualification, 253 had an university or university of applied science degree. About their current employment: 1 was a schoolchild, 5 were in a apprenticeship, 60 were students, 295 are employees, 19 were civil servants, 105 were self-employed, 30 were unemployed and 31 answered others mostly retired persons or stayed at home (2 did not answer the question).

5.2   General Attitudes Towards Online Voting (RQ1)

Overall, 62% of participants (343 out of 548) selected either 1 or 2 on a 5-point scale, with 1 indicating "strong agreement" with the statement that they would vote online in the upcoming federal election if it were possible (before seeing the proposed voting system and interventions)[6]. We conduct a qualitative analysis of open-ended answers to the question in which participants were asked to explain their statement whether or not they would vote online if possible. We decided to have two code books. One for the answers of those having stated that they are in favor (i.e. 1 or 2) and one for the answers of those being against online voting (i.e. 4 and 5). Both code books were combined for the answers of those having answered neutrally (i.e. 3 on the scale from 1 to 5). The frequency of codes for

---

[5] Participants who failed attention checks or answered that they have no intention at all to vote in the upcoming election have been excluded.

[6] This percentage matches the Bitkom survey result (see Sect. 1).

both code books is provided on Table 1. The following codes have been identified from answers of participants being *against online voting*:

- Security concerns: Participants either mentioned general security concerns or data protection concerns. Sometimes they just used the term 'security concern' or that they believe that online voting is insecure.
- Manipulation: Participants state that election can be manipulated, individual votes or the entire result can be changed with online voting. Participants talked about manipulations/changes, mentioned hackers or cyber attacks, or about the ease to sell votes as it cannot be checked who cast the vote.
- Lack of trust: Participants stated in general that they do not trust in the government to properly set up such a system or are afraid that such a system is properly implemented, i.e. error free.
- Lack of transparency: Participants stated that they think the process or the system (or even both) would not be transparent, i.e. e.g. it is unclear what happens to their vote, how it works, or whether it is working as expected.
- Vote privacy: Participants mentioned risks in regards to free, secret, and anonymous elections; including mentioning risks on voting while being observed.
- Ritual: Participant stated that it is an important, formal, or well-established act of casting their vote on paper or of going to the polling station on this one Sunday (maybe combining it with a walk or with meeting people). Other stated that they simply prefer to cast their vote on paper.
- Being clearly against online voting: Participants did not see a need for a change or stated that they are against online-voting.
- Being uncertain: Participants were uncertain, i.e. they made a decision in one way or the other but do not have a strong opinion; most likely because they have not yet thought a lot about it or they would need more information in order to decide. Several added this in addition to another statement while two just sad that they are uncertain.
- Others: This code is used for nonsense answers as well as answers that did not appear more than twice: e.g. a statement of one participant that the effort for online voting is much to high.

The following codes have been identified from answers of participants being in *favour of online voting*:

- Timely: Participants stated that it is timely to have online voting or to digitalise elections (as one of the governmental services) or participants stated that they are in favor of having all services and processes being digitized.
- Convenience: Participants mentioned that online voting is more convenient because they save time or effort; or that they can decide when and where they can cast their vote. Furthermore this code covers answers related to statements like: it is (more) easy, (more) convenient, (more) comfortable etc. than the available paper based channels.
- Reliable delivery: Participants stated that compared to postal voting the delivery is much faster; i.e. less issues for people living abroad and no need to cast votes remotely several days/weeks before the actual election day.

- More secure: Participants stated that online voting systems are more difficult to manipulate; or that they can be easier protected against manipulations.
- Environment-friendly: Participants mentioned that this is better for our environment as it safes paper and air pollution (no driving to polling stations).
- Advantages for the state: Participants mentioned one or more reasons related to organizing the election: e.g. less poll workers, costs are reduced, counting is faster. Increasing voter turn out is also one aspect of this code.
- COVID-19 related: Participants mentioned something pandemic related.
- Security concerns: Same as in the previous code book.
- Others: This code is used for nonsense answers as well as answers that did not appear more than twice, e.g. no queues before the polling station.

Table 1. Code frequency for reasons in favor (left) or against (right) online voting – in parantheses indicate the frequency from participants with a neutral attitude.

	# mentions		# mentions
convenience	270 (25)	security concerns	46 (37)
security concerns	73 (37)	manipulation	45 (9)
advantages for the state	37 (0)	ritual	19 (7)
timely	32 (1)	lack of trust	14 (5)
environment-friendly	23 (2)	being uncertain	13 (29)
COVID-19-related	22 (0)	lack of transparency	11 (7)
better security	19 (0)	other	9 (6)
other	14 (6)	being clearly against	4 (0)
reliable delivery	6 (0)	vote privacy	3 (7)

5.3   Attitudes Towards Using the Verifiable Voting (H1–H3, RQ2)

Out of the participants who initially had a positive willingness to vote online, 63% of them (216 out of 343) did not change their willingness after seeing the proposed system. Among the remaining 127 participants, 15 (4%) were more willing to vote online (changing their response from 2 to 1 on a 5-point scale), 40 (12%) were less willing to vote online but still positive (changing their response from 1 to 2), 41 (12%) changed their response to "neutral" (selecting option 3) and 19 (6%) changed their response to "negative" (selecting either option 4 or 5). Figure 4 shows the distribution of responses after seeing the proposed verifiable system. There was no significant difference between the intervention types (ANOVA, $F = 1.697$, $p = 0.167$), hence, *H1 cannot be confirmed*.

For the evaluation of H2, a general trust score was computed from the questionnaire items 1–7. Note, the scores for the last three questions (i.e. questions

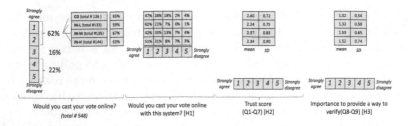

Fig. 4. Descriptive results for Hypotheses H1–H3.

where agreement indicated belief that an undetected manipulation of the election result is possible) were *reversed.* Figure 4 shows the average resulting scores for all groups. There was no significant difference in the trust scores between the intervention types (ANOVA, $F = 0.646$, $p = .586$), hence, *H2 cannot be confirmed.*

For the evaluation of H3, we computed an average score for the answers to questions 8–9 (i.e. the questions that specifically asked about the usefulness of verifiability). Figure 4 shows the average resulting scores for all groups. There was no significant difference between the intervention types (ANOVA, $F = 2.0611$, $p = .105$), hence, *H3 cannot be confirmed.*

Figure 5 shows the average scores for each one of the questions by intervention type and the willingness to vote online after seeing the corresponding intervention. Overall, the usefulness of the verifiability was perceived to be high, regardless of the intervention type or the willingness to vote online after seeing the intervention.

In order to answer *RQ2, that is, to better understand the participants' attitudes towards the proposed system and specific interventions*, we analyzed the statements in which they explain their responses. We derived the following codes while the code frequency is provided in Table 2:

– Only system independent advantages: Participants justified their decision by mentioning general advantages they see for online voting. The mentioned advantages are similar to those coded for RQ1.
– System easy to use: Participants stated that the proposed system seems straight forward or that it is easy to cast a vote or more generally to use it.
– Just too complex: Participants only mentioning that the proposed system is e.g. (too) complex, (too) cumbersome, (too) confusing), and (too) error-prone. This code also contains statements of participants being afraid to make a mistake when casting a vote with this system.
– Just more secure: Participants only mentioning that they would use the system as it seems secure. Some particular saying that this is due to the additional steps to verify their vote.
– Complex but system independent advantages: Participants mentioning that the system is complex but they also state that they still see one ore more advantages of online voting – in general.

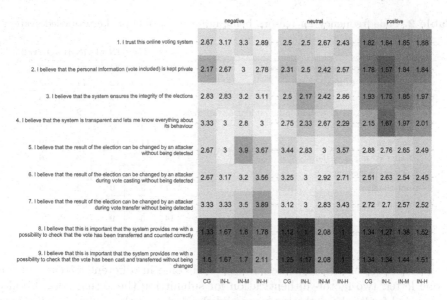

Fig. 5. Average responses after having seen the verifiable system (scale 1 to 5). Lower scores indicate stronger agreement with the statement, except for questions 5–7 where the scores are reversed.

- Complex but secure: Participants mentioning that the system is complex but they also say that this makes it (more) secure.
- Being uncertain: Participants were uncertain, i.e. they made a decision in one way or the other but do not have a strong opinion; most likely because they have not yet though a lot about it or they would need more information in order to decide, e.g. regarding security properties.
- Paper-based is easier: Participants state that they prefer to vote on paper
- Not timely: Participants stated that it does look old-fashion or that the voting system should be all digital, in order to be timely.
- Others: This code is used for nonsense answers as well as answers that did not appear more than twice (overall groups).

5.4   Feedback on the System and the Interventions (RQ3)

We received the following feedback to the verifiable voting system or more precisely to the *polling sheet*: Some participants were requesting more information (e.g. regarding the security features or how to cast an invalid vote). Furthermore, we received the feedback that the amount of codes should be removed to simplify the vote casting process. Related to this aspect, some were recommending to explain why it is so complicated. Interestingly, some recommended to use a different approach to authenticate voters, i.e. using the German federal electronic ID card or 'video-ident' which is used for other sensitive services in Germany. We also received feedback that the process should be more close to what is used

Table 2. Code frequency for reasons being in favor (or not) of the proposed system

	CG	IN-L	IN-M	IN-H	Overall
(+) system-independent advantages	32	36	34	31	133
(+) system easy to use	13	6	12	11	42
(+) more secure	9	13	17	26	65
(+) complex but with system independent advantages	6	6	2	2	16
(+) complex but secure	2	4	2	3	11
(−) too complex	16	11	15	7	49
(−) paper voting is easier	4	5	4	3	16
(−) security concerns	5	2	4	3	14
(−) not timely	1	2	0	2	5
being uncertain	0	1	1	2	4
other	14	5	9	6	34

in the banking context: e.g. the codes should come in different letters and not in one letter, two-factor-authentication for submitting the actual vote. Finally, we received feedback on the language and the design of the polling card, e.g. to simplify the language including concrete proposals such as talking about 'numbers' instead of 'codes' and 'help' instead of 'support' and to improve the design e.g. by putting not all content on one page but using several pages.

Regarding the *interventions*, we received the following general feedback: The design of the intervention should be more aligned with the general voting information and the polling sheet. Several provided feedback to simplify the language (e.g. use the term 'help' instead of 'support'), use a more friendly language, and improve the design (e.g. provide more pictures and highlight important terms). Some were requesting more information (e.g. regarding the security, whom to contact in case of questions, why this is so complicated and why it is important to only trust the paper and not what is displayed on the screen, that it is important to cast the vote unobserved, and what to do in case one loses the Internet connection while voting). Many actually noticed that it would be important to also have the telephone number of the support on the intervention and not just on the polling card. Furthermore, several participants in the IN-H group stated that the intervention is deterrent, too negative, and worrying. Related to this, some stated that they feel like they have done something wrong or must be careful to not make mistakes. Correspondingly, a more subtle design was recommended.

6   Discussion and Conclusion

Overall, convenience was mentioned as the most popular reason for online voting (by 270 of 343 participants). However, even among people who were generally willing to vote online, 73 voiced security concerns. Furthermore, security concerns and manipulations were mentioned as the most popular reason against online voting by the people who were not willing to vote online (in total 91 of

120 participants). For those being neutral regarding online voting, security concerns was also the most mentioned reason. It looks like participants currently value convenience over security (e.g. either implicitly trusting the government to take proper measures against security risks, or considering such risks to be low) – although we talked particularly about German federal elections (and not e.g. some elections or polls in very small groups or local societies). We got the impression, that many consider it as easy as online banking and online shopping – while in particular for online banking they may have forgotten how many steps were necessary to start using it.

Only 6% changed their opinion and stated that they would not want to use the proposed system to cast their vote for the 2021 federal election (12% changed to neutral). Given the open text answers as well as the answers to the seven questions on trust this is kind of surprising as several more complained about the complexity of the vote casting process and/or were not certain how much they can trust the system to detect manipulations. It may be explained as the most prominent reason in favor of still using it were system independent advantages of online voting in general, thus again convenience was rated over security.

Thus, future work should investigate on the one hand why many rate convenience over security as well as on explaining why from a security point of view it needs to be more complicated as voters may expect it to be. The good news from [8] is that it is likely that voters will accept additional steps if they understand why it is necessary. Such additional explanations may also convince some of those being against online voting if they understand which security guarantees the system provides.

Interestingly, several participants compared the (security) mechanisms in place with those they know from other context – in particular from the online banking context. Correspondingly, they e.g. did not like that all codes came with one letter and that authentication happens through a password. As future work it should be investigated whether it is either possible to align verifiable voting systems more with processes voters may know from other contexts or to explain why it is different but still secure when developing information material.

We found that most participants – even being against or neutral to the proposed system and even without having seen any interventions – are clearly in favor of having the possibility to verify their vote. While for federal elections, this is a clear requirement[7], as future work we want to investigate whether people would also see this as an important property for other elections and polls. Note, in Germany so far, we have only seen the use of blackbox voting systems. Thus, if voters would require verifiable voting systems this would help to convince election management boards to change to verifiable systems. Furthermore, the fact that participants see a need for verifiable systems should support the investigations in explaining the need for voting systems being more complex than expected.

---

[7] https://www.bundesverfassungsgericht.de/SharedDocs/Pressemitteilungen/EN/2009/bvg09-019.html (Oct 30 2021).

We found no significant difference between the three intervention groups. The interventions do not seem to change their mind regarding their willingness to use the system, their trust in the system nor their attitude towards the importance of verifiability. Thus, we would recommend to use the high-alarming intervention in a user study to evaluate its effect while evaluating the effectiveness wrt. detecting manipulations as it was studied e.g. in [17,22]. Furthermore, we want to study the trust score further as a measure instrument which ideally can be applied to various systems – also to compare the trust scores between systems. Additional insights on how to design assurances to increase the voters' trust in verifiable systems – e.g. by including explanations on how the verification process works in the proposed system – can be adapted from research on related fields, such as studying assurances in privacy notices [15].

We conclude that the harm of extra interventions – even very alarming ones – is very limited and should be used to increase the likelihood that voters verify. Furthermore, it is important to address voters' expectations – in particular the one that online voting is more convenient than paper based voting channels. This includes to explain that in order to provide verifiability, systems cannot be as easy as they may wanted it to be.

Acknowledgment. This work was supported by funding of the Helmholtz Association (HGF) through the POF subtopic 46.23.01 called 'Methods for Engineering Secure Systems'.

References

1. Acemyan, C.Z., Kortum, P., Byrne, M.D., Wallach, D.S.: Usability of voter verifiable, end-to-end voting systems: baseline data for Helios, Prêt à voter, and scantegrity II. USENIX J. Election Technol. Syst. **2**(3), 26–56 (2014)
2. Acemyan, C.Z., Kortum, P., Byrne, M.D., Wallach, D.S.: From error to error: why voters could not cast a ballot and verify their vote with Helios, Prêt à voter, and scantegrity II. USENIX J. Election Technol. Syst. **3**(2), 1–19 (2015)
3. Acemyan, C.Z., Kortum, P., Byrne, M.D., Wallach, D.S.: Summative Usability Assessments of STAR-Vote: a cryptographically secure e2e voting system that has been empirically proven to be easy to use. Hum. Factors, 1–24 (2018)
4. Adida, B.: Helios: web-based open-audit voting. In: USENIX Security Symposium, vol. 17, pp. 335–348. USENIX Association (2008)
5. Bär, M., Henrich, C., Müller-Quade, J., Röhrich, S., Stüber, C.: Real world experiences with bingo voting and a comparison of usability. In: EVT/WOTE (2008)
6. Blanchard, N.K., Selker, T.: Improving voting technology is hard: the trust-legitimacy-participation loop and related problems. In: Proceedings of the 8th Workshop on Socio-Technical Aspects in Security and Trust, pp. 1–8 (2018)
7. Budurushi, J., Renaud, K., Volkamer, M., Woide, M.: An investigation into the usability of electronic voting systems for complex elections. Ann. Telecommun. **71**(7–8), 309–322 (2016)
8. Budurushi, J., Volkamer, M., Kulyk, O., Neumann, S.: Nothing comes for free: How much usability can you sacrifice for security? IEEE Secur. Priv. Spec. Issue Electron. Voting **15**, 24–29 (2017)

9. Davis, F.D.: A technology acceptance model for empirically testing new end-user information systems: Theory and results. Ph.D. thesis, MIT (1985)
10. Distler, V., Zollinger, M.L., Lallemand, C., Roenne, P., Ryan, P., Koenig, V.: Security-visible, yet unseen? How displaying security mechanisms impacts user experience and perceived security. In: ACM CHI, pp. 605:1–605:13 (2019)
11. Fuglerud, K.S., Røssvoll, T.H.: An evaluation of web-based voting usability and accessibility. Univ. Access Inf. Soc. **11**(4), 359–373 (2012)
12. Gjøsteen, K., Lund, A.S.: An experiment on the security of the Norwegian electronic voting protocol. Ann. Telecommun. **71**(7–8), 299–307 (2016)
13. Karayumak, F., Olembo, M.M., Kauer, M., Volkamer, M.: Usability analysis of helios-an open source verifiable remote electronic voting system. In: EVT/WOTE. USENIX (2011)
14. Kulyk, O., Neumann, S., Budurushi, J., Volkamer, M.: Nothing comes for free: how much usability can you sacrifice for security? IEEE Secur. Priv. **15**(3), 24–29 (2017)
15. Kulyk, O., Renaud, K.: I need to know I'm safe and protected and will check: users want cues to signal data custodians' trustworthiness. In: 2021 Workshop on Human Centric Software Engineering and Cyber Security (2021)
16. Kulyk, O., Volkamer, M.: Usability is not Enough: Lessons Learned from Human Factors in Security - Research for Verifiability. E-Vote-ID, pp. 66–81 (2018)
17. Kulyk, O., Volkamer, M., Müller, M., Renaud, K.: Towards improving the efficacy of code-based verification in internet voting. In: Bernhard, M., et al. (eds.) FC 2020. LNCS, vol. 12063, pp. 291–309. Springer, Cham (2020). https://doi.org/10.1007/978-3-030-54455-3_21
18. MacNamara, D., Gibson, P., Oakley, K.: A preliminary study on a DualVote and Prêt à Voter hybrid system. In: CeDEM, p. 77 (2012)
19. MacNamara, D., Scully, T., Gibson, P.: Dualvote addressing usability and verifiability issues in electronic voting systems (2011)
20. Marky, K., Kulyk, O., Renaud, K., Volkamer, M.: What did I really vote for? In: ACM CHI, p. 176 (2018)
21. Marky, K., Schmitz, M., Lange, F., Mühlhäuser, M.: Usability of code voting modalities. In: Proceedings of CHI Conference on Human Factors in Computing Systems Extended Abstracts (CHI 2019 Extended Abstracts), 4–9 May 2019, Glasgow, Scotland UK, p. 7. ACM, New York (2019). https://doi.org/10.1145/3290607.3312971
22. Marky, K., Zollinger, M.L., Roenne, P., Ryan, P.Y., Grube, T., Kunze, K.: Investigating usability and user experience of individually verifiable internet voting schemes. ACM Trans. Comput.-Hum. Interact **28**(5), 1–36 (2021)
23. Neumann, S., Olembo, M.M., Renaud, K., Volkamer, M.: Helios verification: to alleviate, or to nominate: is that the question, or shall we have both? In: Kő, A., Francesconi, E. (eds.) EGOVIS 2014. LNCS, vol. 8650, pp. 246–260. Springer, Cham (2014). https://doi.org/10.1007/978-3-319-10178-1_20
24. Olembo, M.M., Renaud, K., Bartsch, S., Volkamer, M.: Voter, what message will motivate you to verify your vote. In: USEC. Internet Society (2014)
25. Olembo, M., Volkamer, M.: E-Voting system usability: lessons for interface design, user studies, and usability criteria. In: Information Science Reference, pp. 172–201 (2013). https://doi.org/10.4018/978-1-4666-3640-8.ch011
26. Olembo, M.M., Bartsch, S., Volkamer, M.: Mental models of verifiability in voting. In: Heather, J., Schneider, S., Teague, V. (eds.) Vote-ID 2013. LNCS, vol. 7985, pp. 142–155. Springer, Heidelberg (2013). https://doi.org/10.1007/978-3-642-39185-9_9

27. Olembo, M.M., Volkamer, M.: A study to identify trusted verifying institutes in Germany. Technical report, Technical University Darmstadt (2014)
28. Oostveen, A.M., Van den Besselaar, P.: Users' experiences with e-voting: a comparative case study. J. Electron. Gov. **2**(4), 357–377 (2009)
29. Rogers, E.M.: Diffusion of Innovations. Free Press, NY (2003)
30. Schneider, S., Llewellyn, M., Culnane, C., Heather, J., Srinivasan, S., Xia, Z.: Focus group views on prêt à voter 1.0. In: REVOTE, pp. 56–65. IEEE (2011)
31. Serdult, U., Germann, M., Mendez, F., Portenier, A., Wellig, C.: Fifteen years of internet voting in Switzerland. In: ICEDEG, pp. 126–132. IEEE (2015)
32. Solvak, M.: Does vote verification work: usage and impact of confidence building technology in internet voting. In: Krimmer, R., et al. (eds.) E-Vote-ID 2020. LNCS, vol. 12455, pp. 213–228. Springer, Cham (2020). https://doi.org/10.1007/978-3-030-60347-2_14
33. Vassil, K., Solvak, M., Vinkel, P., Trechsel, A.H., Alvarez, R.M.: The diffusion of internet voting. usage patterns of internet voting in Estonia between 2005 and 2015. Gov. Inf. Q. **33**(3), 453–459 (2016)
34. Venkatesh, V., Morris, M.G., Davis, G.B., Davis, F.D.: User acceptance of information technology: toward a unified view. MIS Q., 425–478 (2003)
35. Weber, J., Hengartner, U.: Usability study of the open audit voting system Helios (2009). http://www.jannaweber.com/wp-content/uploads/2009/09/858Helios.pdf
36. Winckler, M., et al.: Assessing the usability of open verifiable e-voting systems: a trial with the system Prêt à voter. In: ICE-GOV, pp. 281–296 (2009)
37. Wu, M., Miller, R.C., Garfinkel, S.L.: Do security toolbars actually prevent phishing attacks? In: ACM: CHI, pp. 601–610 (2006)
38. Zollinger, M.L.: From Secure to Usable and Verifiable Voting Schemes. Ph.D. thesis, University of Luxembourg, Esch-sur-Alzette, Luxembourg (2020)
39. Zollinger, M.-L., Estaji, E., Ryan, P.Y.A., Marky, K.: Just for the sake of transparency: exploring voter mental models of verifiability. In: Krimmer, R., et al. (eds.) E-Vote-ID 2021. LNCS, vol. 12900, pp. 155–170. Springer, Cham (2021). https://doi.org/10.1007/978-3-030-86942-7_11

Simulations of Ballot Polling
Risk-Limiting Audits

Oliver Broadrick[1], Sarah Morin[1], Grant McClearn[2], Neal McBurnett[5],
Poorvi L. Vora[1], and Filip Zagórski[3,4(✉)]

[1] Department of Computer Science, The George Washington University,
Washington, USA
odbroadrick@gmail.com
[2] Department of Computer Science, Stanford University, California, USA
grantmcc@stanford.edu
[3] Wroclaw University of Science and Technology, Wroclaw, Poland
filip.zagorski@gmail.com
[4] Votifica, Wroclaw, Poland
[5] Boulder, CO, USA

Abstract. In this paper we present simulation results comparing the
risk, stopping probability, and number of ballots required over multiple
rounds of ballot polling risk-limiting audits (RLAs) MINERVA, Selection-
Ordered (SO) BRAVO, and End-of-Round (EoR) BRAVO. BRAVO is the
most commonly used ballot polling RLA and requires the smallest
expected number of ballots when ballots are drawn one at a time and the
(true) underlying election is as announced. In real audits, multiple ballots
are drawn at a time, and BRAVO is implemented as SO BRAVO or EoR
BRAVO. MINERVA is a recently proposed ballot polling RLA that requires
fewer ballots than either implementation of BRAVO in a first round with
stopping probability 0.9 but requires a predetermined round schedule.
It is an open question how these audits compare over multiple rounds
and for lower stopping probabilities. Our simulations use stopping probabilities of 0.9 and 0.25. The results are consistent with predictions of
the R2B2 open-source library for ballot polling audits. We observe that
both BRAVO audits are more conservative than MINERVA, which stops
with fewer ballots, for both first round stopping probabilities. However,
the advantage of using MINERVA decreases considerably for the smaller
first round stopping probability, as one would expect.

Keywords: risk-limiting audit (RLA) · ballot polling audit ·
evidence-based elections · statistical election audit

1   Introduction

The literature contains numerous descriptions of vulnerabilities in deployed voting systems, and it is not possible to be certain that any system, however well-

O. Broadrick, S. Morin, G. McClearn and P. L. Vora—Supported in part by NSF
Award 2015253.
F. Zagórski—Author was partially supported by Polish National Science Centre con-
tract number DEC-2013/09/D/ST6/03927.

© International Financial Cryptography Association 2023
S. Matsuo et al. (Eds.): FC 2022 Workshops, LNCS 13412, pp. 351–365, 2023.
https://doi.org/10.1007/978-3-031-32415-4_24

designed, will perform as expected in all instances. For this reason, *evidence-based elections* [13] aim to produce trustworthy and compelling evidence of the correctness of election outcomes, enabling the detection of problems with high probability. One way to implement an evidence-based election is to use a well-curated voter-verified paper trail, compliance audits, and a rigorous tabulation audit of the election outcome, known as a risk-limiting audit (RLA) [5]. An RLA is an audit which guarantees that the probability of concluding that an election outcome is correct, given that it is not, is below a pre-determined value known as the risk limit of the audit, independent of the true, unknown vote distribution of the underlying election. Over a dozen states in the US have seriously explored the use of RLAs—some have pilot programs, some allow RLAs to satisfy a general audit requirement and some have RLAs in statute.

This paper provides insight into the main approaches to ballot polling RLAs, the BRAVO audit [6], and the newer MINERVA [19] ballot polling RLA, through the presentation of simulation results. While some properties of the two audits may be theoretically derived, for other properties theoretical results are not available. This paper examines the number of ballots drawn over multiple rounds of both audits, for two chosen probabilities of stopping (one high: 90%; the other low: 25%) if the election is as announced.

1.1   Background

This paper focuses on ballot-polling RLAs, which require a large number of ballots relative to comparison RLAs but do not rely on any special features of the election technology. Since comparison RLAs are not always feasible, ballot-polling audits remain an important resource and have been used in a number of US state pilots (California, Georgia, Indiana, Michigan, Ohio, Pennsylvania and elsewhere). In the general ballot-polling RLA, a number of ballots are drawn and tallied in what is termed a *round* of ballots [19]. A statistical measure is then computed to determine whether there is sufficient evidence to declare the election outcome correct within the pre-determined risk limit. Because the decision is made after drawing a round of ballots, the audit is termed a *round-by-round (R2)* audit. The special case when round size is one—that is, stopping decisions are made after each ballot draw—is a *ballot-by-ballot (B2)* audit.

The BRAVO audit is designed for use as a B2 audit: it requires the smallest expected number of ballots when the true tally of the underlying election is as announced and stopping decisions are made after each ballot draw. In practice, election officials draw many ballots at once, and the BRAVO stopping rule needs to be modified for use in an R2 audit that is not B2. There are two obvious approaches. The B2 stopping condition can be applied once at the end of each round: End-of Round (EoR) BRAVO. Alternatively, the order of ballots in the sample can be tracked by election officials and the B2 BRAVO stopping condition can be applied retroactively after each ballot drawn: Selection-Ordered (SO) BRAVO. SO BRAVO requires fewer ballots on average than EoR BRAVO but requires the work of tracking the order of ballots rather than just their tally.

MINERVA was designed for R2 audits and applies its stopping rule once for each round. Thus it does not require the tracking of ballots that SO BRAVO does.

Zagórski *et al.* [19] prove that MINERVA is a risk-limiting audit and requires fewer ballots to be sampled than EoR BRAVO when an audit is performed in rounds, the two audits have the same pre-determined (before any ballots are drawn) round schedule and the underlying election is as announced[1]. They also present first-round simulations which show that MINERVA draws fewer ballots than SO BRAVO in the first round for first round sizes with a large probability of stopping when the (true) underlying election is as announced.

There are no results, either theoretical or based on simulations, regarding the number of ballots drawn over multiple rounds in a MINERVA audit with a pre-determined schedule. Because BRAVO does not need to work on a pre-determined round schedule, it can optimize the size of the next round based on the sample drawn so far. Thus an open question is whether the constraint of a predetermined round schedule limits the efficacy of MINERVA in future rounds, and there is no literature comparing the number of ballots drawn by MINERVA and SO BRAVO over multiple rounds. Note that the Average Sample Number (ASN) computations for BRAVO [6] apply only for B2 audits and are especially misleading as estimates of the number of ballots drawn over multiple rounds when first round sizes are large.

Both BRAVO and MINERVA have been integrated into election audit software *Arlo* [16], and, as such, are available for use in real election audits. Both have been used in real election audits [14,19]. For this reason, it is important to understand their properties over multiple rounds.

1.2 Our Contributions

For a two candidate plurality contest with a risk limit of 10%, we observe the following about the total number of ballots drawn over five rounds:

1. Even when the first round stopping probability is as small as 0.25, the number of ballots required for MINERVA is smaller than that required by SO BRAVO and EoR BRAVO. However, the improvement is considerably smaller than that when the stopping probability is 0.9.
   - The number of ballots required by SO BRAVO for a first round stopping probability of 0.9 is about a third more than that required by MINERVA. On the other hand, for a first round stopping probability of 0.25, it requires only about a tenth more ballots than does MINERVA.

---

[1] Their proof assumes that the number of relevant ballots drawn in each round is know beforehand. In MINERVA, the number of ballots drawn in each round is determined before any ballots are drawn. Because invalid ballots and ballots that are inconsequential for the contest being audited would be drawn in addition to relevant ballots, the assumption used by the proof is not true in general. (We are grateful to Philip Stark for drawing our attention to this.) However, any variation in number of relevant ballots drawn for a fixed round size would be random and not chosen by an adversary; the proof showing the risk-limiting property of MINERVA could hence be extended.

- The number of ballots required by EoR BRAVO for a first round stopping probability of 0.9 is about twice those required by MINERVA. On the other hand, for a first round stopping probability of 0.25, it requires only about a fourth to a half more ballots (depending on margin) than does MINERVA.

2. For a first round stopping probability of 0.9, when consequent MINERVA rounds are the same size (multiplying factor 1), consequent conditional stopping probabilities are about 0.75 and 0.74 respectively for rounds two and three. When the multiplying factor is 1.5, the conditional stopping probabilities for rounds two and three are 0.91 and 0.83 respectively. Both our simulator and the code estimating probabilities and round sizes are flexible enough to enable the study of various predetermined round schedules.

1.3   Organization

Section 2 describes related work. The experiments we performed are described in Sect. 3, and Sects. 4 and 5 present our results. Section 6 has our conclusions.

2   Related Work

The BRAVO audit [6] is a well-known ballot polling audit which has been used in numerous pilot and real audits. When used to audit a two-candidate election, it is an instance of Wald's sequential probability ratio test (SPRT) [17], and inherits the SPRT property of being the most efficient test (requiring the smallest expected number of ballots) if the election is as announced. The model for BRAVO and the SPRT is, however, that of a sequential audit: a sample of size one is drawn, and a decision of whether to stop the audit or not is taken. Real election audits invest in drawing large numbers of ballot, called rounds, before making stopping decisions because sequentially sampling individual ballots has significant overhead (unsealing storage boxes and searching for individual ballots). It is possible to apply BRAVO to the sequence of ballots in a round if the sequential order is retained. This is not, however, the most efficient possible use of the drawn sample because information in consequent ballots is ignored when applying BRAVO to ballots that were drawn earlier in the sample.

We do know a great deal about the properties of BRAVO. The risk limiting property of BRAVO follows from the similar property of the SPRT. Stopping probabilities for BRAVO may be estimated as implemented in [16]; this method is due to Mark Lindeman and uses quadratic approximations. A later method for stopping probability estimates presented by Zagórski et al. [18,19] uses a similar technique for narrow margins and a separate algorithm for wider margins, the results of which match simulation results reported by Lindeman et al. [6, Table 1].

The MINERVA audit [18,19] was developed for large first round sizes which enable election officials to be done in one round with large probability. It uses information from the entire sample, and has been proven to be risk limiting when the round schedule for the audit is determined before the audit begins. That is, information about the actual ballots drawn in the first round cannot inform future round sizes. First-round sizes for a 0.9 stopping probability when the election is as announced have been computed for a wide range of margins and are smaller than those for EoR and SO BRAVO. First round simulations of MINERVA [18] demonstrate that its first-round properties—regarding the probabilities of stopping when the underlying election is tied and when it is as announced—are as predicted for first round sizes with stopping probability 0.9.

Ballot polling audit simulations have been used to familiarize election officials and the public with the approach [12]. McLaughlin and Stark [7,8] compare the workload for the Canvass Audits by Sampling and Testing (CAST) and Kaplan-Markov (KM) audits using simulations. Blom *et al.* demonstrate the efficiency of their ballot polling approach to audit instant runoff voting (IRV) using simulations [2]. Huang *et al.* present a framework generalizing a number of ballot polling audits and compare their performance (round sizes and stopping probabilities) using simulations [4]. This work was prior to the development of MINERVA, and focuses on the comparison between Bayesian audits [11] and BRAVO, essentially studying the impact of the prior of the Bayesian RLA. Some workload measurements have been made [3]. While total ballots sampled can give naive workload estimates [10], Bernhard presents a more complex workload estimation model [1].

3 Experiments

In this section, we motivate and describe the experiments. We consider a two candidate plurality contest, and assume that ballots are sampled with replacement, as is common in the literature. Note that sampling without replacement is more efficient for large sampling fractions, but MINERVA has not been extended for sampling without replacement. We first present relevant definitions.

Definition 1. *An audit A takes a sample of ballots X as input and gives as output either (1) Correct: the audit is complete, or (2) Uncertain: continue the audit.*

All of the audits discussed in this paper are modeled as binary hypothesis tests. Under the alternative hypothesis, H_a, the announced outcome is correct. In particular, the true underlying ballot distribution is given by the announced ballot tallies. Under the null hypothesis, H_0, a tie is the correct outcome[2]. The maximum risk of an audit is the probability that an audit stops, given that the underlying election is a tie [15]. Note that an audit A includes all audit parameters (maximum risk, round sizes, etc.).

Definition 2 (Risk). *The maximum risk R of audit A with sample $X \in \{0,1\}^*$ drawn from the true underlying distribution of ballots is $R(A) = \Pr[A(X) = Correct \mid H_0]$.*

---

[2] or the announced winner lost by one vote, and the number of ballots is large enough that the probability of drawing a ballot for the winner is that of drawing one for the loser.

This leads us to the following definition of an α-RLA.

Definition 3 (Risk Limiting Audit (α-RLA)). *An audit $\mathcal{A}$ is a Risk Limiting Audit with risk limit α iff $R(\mathcal{A}) \leq \alpha$.*

We present measures of stopping probability in the jth round of the audit, given that the underlying election is as announced.

Definition 4 (Stopping Probability). *The stopping probability S_j of an audit $\mathcal{A}$ in round j is*

$$S_j(\mathcal{A}) = \Pr[\mathcal{A}(X) = Correct \ in \ round \ j \ \wedge \mathcal{A}(X) \neq Correct \ previously \mid H_a]$$

Experimentally, using our simulations, S_j would be estimated by the fraction of audits that stop in round j. Note that $\sum_j S_j(\mathcal{A}) = 1$. We can also consider the cumulative stopping probability:

Definition 5 (Cumulative Stopping Probability). *The cumulative stopping probability C_j of an audit $\mathcal{A}$ in round j is $C_j(\mathcal{A}) = \sum_{i=1}^{j} S_j$*

Experimentally, using our simulations, C_j would be estimated by the fraction of audits that stop in or before round j.

Finally, we are also interested in the probability that an audit will stop in round j given that it did not stop earlier:

Definition 6 (Conditional Stopping Probability). *The conditional stopping probability of an audit $\mathcal{A}$ in round j is*

$$\chi_j(\mathcal{A}) = \Pr[\mathcal{A}(X) = Correct \ in \ round \ j \ \mid H_a \wedge \mathcal{A}(X) \neq Correct \ previously]$$

Experimentally, using our simulations, χ_j would be estimated by the ratio of the audits that stop in round j to those that "entered" round j, i.e. those that did not stop before round j.

We simulated audits for a risk limit of 10% (as in [6] and [19]) using margins from the 2020 US Presidential election, limiting ourselves to pairwise margins for the two main candidates of 0.05 or larger. Note that both BRAVO and MINERVA can be extended for multiple-candidate, multiple-winner plurality contests by performing pairwise tests between the winners and the losers [5,18]. Therefore, the two candidate plurality contest is a general case, and these simulations provide insight for multiple-candidate and multiple-winner contests too. Round sizes increase roughly proportional to the inverse square of the margin, so smaller margins are computationally much more expensive to simulate. For each of these states, we simulated $10,000 = 10^4$ audits assuming the underlying election was as announced (H_a), and an additional $10,000 = 10^4$ audits assuming the underlying election was a tie (H_0).

We ran simulations for: (a) 0.9 probability of stopping in the first round, enabling election officials to be done in the first round with very high probability if the election is as announced and (b) .25 probability of stopping in the first round which is more favorable to BRAVO. We ran our simulations for up to five rounds.

For rounds after the first, we chose the round schedule as follows. For both versions of BRAVO, we chose a single round schedule: each round size has the same conditional stopping probability as the first one. As the proof of the risk-limiting property of MINERVA assumes that its round schedule is determined before any ballots are drawn, we could not use this approach for MINERVA round sizes. Instead, we chose to compare two fixed round schedules for MINERVA: one where the additional number of ballots drawn in a round is the same as in the previous round (multiplying factor of 1.0) and the second where the multiplying factor is 1.5. We consider the case of drawing samples of the same size because it may reflect a practical way to continue an audit; if election officials have selected some first round size within reasonable logistical bounds, drawing the same number of ballots in subsequent rounds may be practical. We also consider round sizes with samples increasing by a multiple of 1.5 because this version is integrated into *Arlo*, and the multiplying factor was chosen as it roughly ensures a 0.9 conditional stopping probability in the second round for a first round stopping probability of 0.9.

We used the R2B2 library [9], which provides a framework for the exploration of round-by-round and ballot-by-ballot RLAs. It has implementations of several ballot polling risk-limiting audits as well as a simulator, all written in Python. For each of these audits, the software can compute the stopping condition for a given sample and estimates of the next round size to achieve a desired stopping probability. For a given audit and random seed, the simulator draws random samples, with replacement, using a pseudorandom number generator, given the number of votes for each candidate, and the number of invalid votes, in the underlying election (these need not be chosen to be as announced). When there are more than two candidates, the audit is carried out pairwise for each candidate pair, and votes for all other candidates are considered invalid votes.

After drawing a simulated sample of ballots, the simulator evaluates the given audit's stopping condition for this sample. If the audit stops, the simulation stops, and if the audit continues, the simulation draws another round. The abstract simulator class does not prescribe any one method for choosing round sizes. We implement several classes to support various round size choices: round sizes from an estimate to achieve a desired probability of stopping, predetermined round sizes, and pseudorandomly-generated round sizes.

4 Stopping Probability and Risk

4.1 Stopping Probability as a Function of Round and Margin

For both SO and EoR BRAVO simulations, our software estimated round sizes that would give $\chi_j(\mathcal{A}) = 0.9$ and used those for the simulations. In Fig. 1, we display the proportion of EoR BRAVO audits that stopped in the jth round to all audits which had not stopped before the jth round, for $j = 1, 2, 3$. Though we carried out the simulations for 5 rounds we show only the first three rounds of the simulations because very few audits, $(.1)^{j-1} \cdot (10^4)$ on average, make it to the jth round for $j \geq 4$. In Fig. 2, we display the same proportions for SO BRAVO audits. In both cases, these proportions are estimates of the true value of $\chi_j(\mathcal{A})$ for $j = 1, 2, 3$ as a function of margin. We see that, especially in earlier rounds for which the values are more representative of true audit behavior because fewer simulated audits have stopped, our round size predictions are accurate (the proportions are close to 0.9).

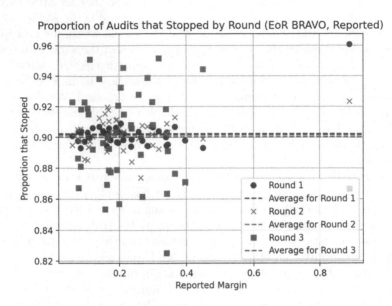

Fig. 1. This plot shows, for each state margin, when the underlying election is as announced, the number of EoR BRAVO audits that stopped in the jth round, as a fraction of all EoR BRAVO audits which had not yet stopped before the jth round for $j = 1, 2, 3$ and $S_1 = 0.9$.

Figure 3 and Fig. 4 show the same proportions for MINERVA round multipliers of 1.0 and 1.5 respectively. We see that the first round size estimates were fairly accurate, with first round stopping probabilities being very close to .9. For subsequent rounds, the multipliers of 1.0 achieved smaller stopping probabilities, as it was not chosen so as to obtain $\chi_j(\mathcal{A}) = 0.9$. The 1.5 multiplier is a good estimate for $j = 2$, but the stopping probability for $j = 3$ is slightly smaller than 0.9. Note that we chose a simple multiplier for future rounds, but one could make more accurate round size estimates before the audit begins.

Finally, we can perform a similar study for $S_1 = 0.25$. See Fig. 5 for an example, MINERVA with round mutiplier 1.5.

4.2 Maximum Risk as a Function of Round and Margin

We also study the proportion of audits that stopped when the underlying election was a tie. This proportion should approach a value less than the risk limit, 10%, as more audits are performed.

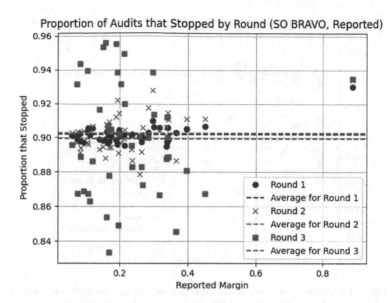

Fig. 2. This plot shows, for each state margin, when the underlying election is as announced, the number of SO BRAVO audits that stopped in the jth round, as a fraction of all SO BRAVO audits which had not yet stopped before the jth round for $j = 1, 2, 3$ and $S_1 = 0.9$.

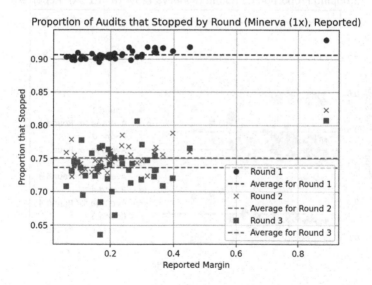

Fig. 3. This plot shows, for each state margin, when the underlying election is as announced, the number of MINERVA audits that stopped in the jth round, as a fraction of all MINERVA audits which had not yet stopped before the jth round for $j = 1, 2, 3$, round size multiple of 1.0 and $S_1 = 0.9$.

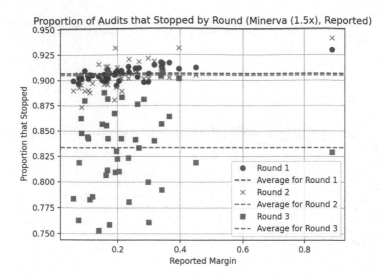

Fig. 4. This plot shows, for each state margin, when the underlying election is as announced, the number of MINERVA audits that stopped in the jth round, as a fraction of all MINERVA audits which had not yet stopped before the jth round for $j = 1, 2, 3$, round size multiple of 1.5 and $S_1 = 0.9$.

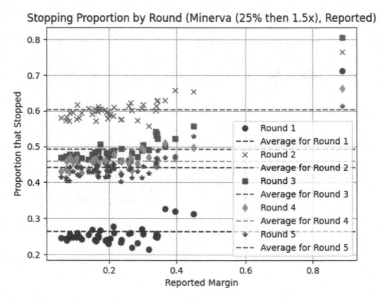

Fig. 5. This plot shows, for each state margin, when the underlying election is as announced, the number of MINERVA audits that stopped in the jth round, as a fraction of all MINERVA audits which had not yet stopped before the jth round for $j = 1, 2, 3$, round size multiple of 1.5 and $S_1 = 0.25$.

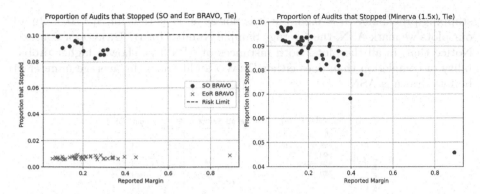

Fig. 6. The left hand plot shows the fraction of EoR BRAVO audits (all states with margins at least 0.05) and SO BRAVO audits (the 13 states for which our simulations are complete so far) that stopped in any of the 5 rounds when the underlying election was a tie. The right hand plot, for each state margin, shows the fraction of MINERVA audits with a round size multiple of 1.5 that stopped in any of the 5 rounds when the underlying election was a tie.

We observe that the risk of EoR BRAVO is roughly an order of magnitude less than the risk limit. These results are as expected, because EoR BRAVO is known to be too conservative [19].

In Fig. 6 we show only the results for the 13 states for which our simulations with an underlying tied election have completed. To estimate the next round size that achieves a desired stopping probability, the SO BRAVO software generates the probability distribution on the number of ballots in the sample ballot by ballot (see [19]) since the stopping condition needs to be evaluated for each individual ballot drawn. Because the underlying tied election causes audits to move on to larger rounds, the simulations are computationally expensive. SO BRAVO is proven to be a Risk-Limiting Audit, and we observe in Fig. 6, that the risk of SO BRAVO is much nearer the risk limit than that of EoR BRAVO, as expected.

Figure 6 shows that fewer than 0.1 of the audits stopped when the underlying election was a tie, for round multiples 1.5, as would be expected for an RLA with risk limit 10%. Unlike EOR BRAVO, the experimental risks here are much closer to the risk limit, showing that MINERVA stops on average with a less conservative risk; MINERVA is sharper. The plot for round multiple 1.0 is very similar.

5   Number of Ballots

In this section we present our data on the expected number of ballots drawn as the number of rounds increases, and on the fraction of audits that stop (an estimate of cumulative stopping probability, C_j) for the states of Texas, Missouri and Massachusetts, with margins of 0.057, 0.157 and 0.342 respectively. Interestingly, we observe that MINERVA has an advantage for a first round size with stopping probability $S_1 = 0.25$, but it is not as large as that for $S_1 = 0.9$. On all our plots we mark ASN, the Average Sample Number for B2 BRAVO for context. Notice that, in all the plots, both instances of MINERVA show a higher probability of completion than does either BRAVO audit when the average number of ballots drawn is ASN.

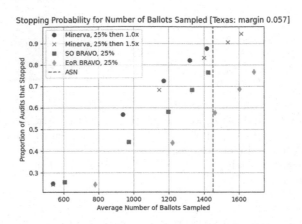

Fig. 7. This plot shows the cumulative fraction of audits that stopped as a function of average number of sampled ballots for all four audits we studied, for the state of Texas, margin 0.057, and first round stopping probability $S_1 = 0.25$.

We observe that the behavior of both MINERVA audits is similar, and that the plot for SO BRAVO is to the right of (more ballots) and below (lower probability of stopping) those for MINERVA, even for a stopping probability as low as 0.25. We observe that the plot for EoR BRAVO shows the worst performance, which is not surprising. We observe similar behavior across margins (see Figs. 7, 8 and 9), though the improvement due to MINERVA reduces as margins get larger. We see also that the improvement due to using MINERVA is not as large as that seen for $S_1 = 0.9$ (see Fig. 10).

For $S_1 = 0.25$, the ratio of first round size of EoR BRAVO to MINERVA is 1.45, 1.37, 1.23 for states Texas, Missouri and Massachusetts, and margins 0.057, 0.157 and 0.342 respectively. This may be compared to 2.03, 1.99 and 1.8 respectively for $S_1 = 0.9$. Similarly, for $S_1 = 0.25$, the ratio of first round size of SO BRAVO to MINERVA is 1.13, 1.08, 1.12 for states Texas, Missouri and Massachusetts, and margins 0.057, 0.157 and 0.342 respectively. This may be compared to 1.38, 1.38 and 1.30 respectively for $S_1 = 0.9$. Note that the effect of such improvements on workload depends greatly on the number of ballots being sampled. For example, a 20% reduction in sample size in Massachusetts might save election officials 10 ballots, whereas the same reduction in Texas could save thousands.

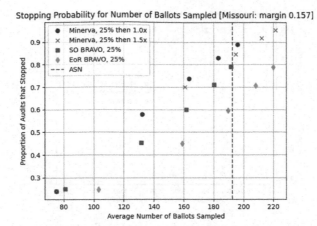

Fig. 8. This plot shows the cumulative fraction of audits that stopped as a function of average number of sampled ballots for all four audits we studied, for the state of Missouri, margin 0.157, and first round stopping probability $S_1 = 0.25$.

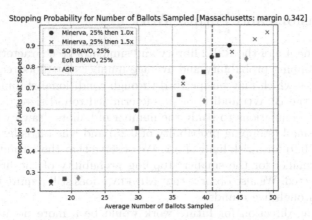

Fig. 9. This plot shows the cumulative fraction of audits that stopped as a function of average number of sampled ballots for all four audits we studied, for the state of Massachusetts, margin 0.342, and first round stopping probability $S_1 = 0.25$.

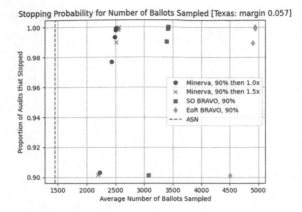

Fig. 10. This plot shows the cumulative fraction of audits that stopped as a function of average number of sampled ballots for all four audits we studied, for the state of Texas, margin 0.057, and first round stopping probability $S_1 = 0.9$.

6   Conclusions and Future Work

We describe the use of the R2B2 library and simulator to characterize the maximum risk, stopping probability and average number of ballots required across round schedules which may be specified through conditional stopping probabilities (as with the BRAVO audits) or pre-determined round sizes (as with MINERVA). We use simulations to study the number of ballots drawn when the first round size is small (stopping probability of 0.25) and when it is large (stopping probability of 0.9) for a risk limit of 0.1. We observe that the advantage of using MINERVA is smaller for the smaller stopping probability of the first round, as would be expected. We also observe that MINERVA does still require fewer ballots all the way through five rounds.

A promising direction for future work would be a more detailed study of the impact of first round stopping probability and different round schedules on overall stopping probability and number of ballots for both MINERVA and BRAVO.

References

1. Bernhard, M.: Election Security Is Harder Than You Think. Ph.D. thesis, University of Michigan (2020)
2. Blom, M., Stuckey, P.J., Teague, V.J.: Ballot-polling risk limiting audits for IRV elections. In: Krimmer, R., et al. (eds.) E-Vote-ID 2018. LNCS, vol. 11143, pp. 17–34. Springer, Cham (2018). https://doi.org/10.1007/978-3-030-00419-4_2
3. Cause, C., VerifiedVoting, Center, B.: Pilot implementation study of risk-limiting audit methods in the state of Rhode Island. https://www.brennancenter.org/sites/default/files/2019-09/Report-RI-Design-FINAL-WEB4.pdf

4. Huang, Z., Rivest, R.L., Stark, P.B., Teague, V.J., Vukcevic, D.: A unified evaluation of two-candidate ballot-polling election auditing methods. In: Krimmer, R., et al. (eds.) E-Vote-ID 2020. LNCS, vol. 12455, pp. 112–128. Springer, Cham (2020). https://doi.org/10.1007/978-3-030-60347-2_8
5. Lindeman, M., Stark, P.B.: A gentle introduction to risk-limiting audits. IEEE Secur. Priv. **10**(5), 42–49 (2012)
6. Lindeman, M., Stark, P.B., Yates, V.S.: BRAVO: ballot-polling risk-limiting audits to verify outcomes. In: EVT/WOTE (2012)
7. McLaughlin, K., Stark, P.B.: Simulations of risk-limiting audit techniques and the effects of reducing batch size on the 2008 California House of Representatives elections (2010). https://www.stat.berkeley.edu/users/vigre/undergrad/reports/McLaughlin_Stark.pdf
8. McLaughlin, K., Stark, P.B.: Workload estimates for risk-limiting audits of large contests (2011). https://www.stat.berkeley.edu/stark/Preprints/workload11.pdf
9. Morin, S., McClearn, G.: The R2B2 (Round-by-Round, Ballot-by-Ballot) library. https://github.com/gwexploratoryaudits/r2b2
10. Ottoboni, K., Bernhard, M., Halderman, J.A., Rivest, R.L., Stark, P.B.: Bernoulli ballot polling: a manifest improvement for risk-limiting audits. In: Bracciali, A., Clark, J., Pintore, F., Rønne, P.B., Sala, M. (eds.) FC 2019. LNCS, vol. 11599, pp. 226–241. Springer, Cham (2020). https://doi.org/10.1007/978-3-030-43725-1_16
11. Rivest, R.L., Shen, E.: A Bayesian method for auditing elections. In: EVT/WOTE (2012)
12. Stark, P.B.: Simulating a ballot-polling audit with cards and dice. In: Multidisciplinary Conference on Election Auditing, MIT (2018). http://electionlab.mit.edu/sites/default/files/2018-12/eas-ballotpollingsimulation.pdf
13. Stark, P.B., Wagner, D.A.: Evidence-based elections. IEEE Secur. Priv. **10**(5), 33–41 (2012). https://doi.org/10.1109/MSP.2012.62
14. Virginia Department of Elections: Results of risk-limiting audit of 3 November 2020 general election in Virginia. https://www.elections.virginia.gov/rla-results-nov-3-2020/
15. Vora, P.L.: Risk-limiting Bayesian polling audits for two candidate elections. CoRR abs/1902.00999 (2019). http://arxiv.org/abs/1902.00999
16. VotingWorks: Arlo. https://voting.works/risk-limiting-audits/
17. Wald, A.: Sequential tests of statistical hypotheses. Ann. Math. Stat. **16**(2), 117–186 (1945)
18. Zagórski, F., McClearn, G., Morin, S., McBurnett, N., Vora, P.L.: The Athena class of risk-limiting ballot polling audits. CoRR abs/2008.02315 (2020). https://arxiv.org/abs/2008.02315
19. Zagórski, F., McClearn, G., Morin, S., McBurnett, N., Vora, P.L.: Minerva– an efficient risk-limiting ballot polling audit. In: 30th USENIX Security Symposium (USENIX Security 21), pp. 3059–3076. USENIX Association (2021). https://www.usenix.org/conference/usenixsecurity21/presentation/zagorski

A First Approach to Risk-Limiting Audits for Single Transferable Vote Elections

Michelle Blom[1]([✉])(iD), Peter J. Stuckey[2](iD), Vanessa Teague[3](iD),
and Damjan Vukcevic[4,5](iD)

[1] School of Computing and Information Systems, University of Melbourne,
Parkville, Australia
michelle.blom@unimelb.edu.au
[2] Department of Data Science and AI, Monash University, Clayton, Australia
[3] Thinking Cybersecurity Pty. Ltd., Melbourne, Australia
[4] School of Mathematics and Statistics, University of Melbourne, Parkville, Australia
[5] Melbourne Integrative Genomics, University of Melbourne, Parkville, Australia

Abstract. Risk-limiting audits (RLAs) are an increasingly important method for checking that the reported outcome of an election is, in fact, correct. Indeed, their use is increasingly being legislated. While effective methods for RLAs have been developed for many forms of election—for example: first-past-the-post, instant-runoff voting, and D'Hondt elections—auditing methods for single transferable vote (STV) elections have yet to be developed. STV elections are notoriously hard to reason about since there is a complex interaction of votes that change their value throughout the process. In this paper we present the first approach to risk-limiting audits for STV elections, restricted to the case of 2-seat STV elections.

1 Introduction

Single transferable vote (STV) elections are a method for selecting candidates to fill a set of seats in a single election, which tries to achieve proportional representation with respect to voters' preferences expressed as a ranked list of candidates. STV elections are used in many places throughout the world including Australian Senate elections, all elections in Malta, provincial elections in Canada, many elections in Ireland, and in more than 20 cities in the USA. STV elections are considered as one of the better multi-seat election methods because they achieve some form of ranked proportional representation, unlike many multi-seat elections, although some consider the complexity for voters of having to rank candidates a drawback.

STV elections are one of the most complex form of election to reason about because the value of ballots can change across the election process. When a candidate achieves a tally of votes large enough to be awarded a seat (a *quota*) then

---

This work was partially supported by the Australian Research Council: Discovery Project DP220101012, OPTIMA ITTC IC200100009.

S. Matsuo et al. (Eds.): FC 2022 Workshops, LNCS 13412, pp. 366–380, 2023.
https://doi.org/10.1007/978-3-031-32415-4_25

each ballot currently in their tally is transferred to the next eligible candidate listed on the ballot, at a reduced value (the *transfer value*). The transfer value is calculated (and there are a number of possibilities here) so the total value of the ballots transferred is no greater than the tally minus the quota, thus enforcing the idea that each vote has a value of 1 which may be used (in parts) in electing multiple candidates.

Risk-limiting audits (RLAs) [4] are a form of auditing of election results to determine with some statistical likelihood that the correct result was determined. They rely on comparing paper ballots, the ground truth of the election, with the electronic recorded information to check the result. The *risk limit* is an upper bound on the probability that an incorrect election outcome will not be corrected by the audit. RLAs are increasingly used around the world, and sometimes their use is mandated by legislation. While RLA methods have been determined for many forms of elections: first-past-the-post [4], any scoring function,[1] instant-runoff voting (IRV) [3], D'Hondt [6] and Hamiltonian elections [2], there are currently no approaches to risk-limiting audits for STV elections. In this paper we make a first step towards this, restricting attention to 2-seat STV elections, which are the simplest form. To do so we generate auditing machinery which should also be useful for larger STV elections, but we leave the exact mechanisms required as future work.

2 Preliminaries

2.1 Single Transferable Vote Elections

STV is a multi-winner preferential voting system. Voters rank candidates (or parties) in order of preference. The S seats are allocated in a way that reflects both *proportionality* (voting blocks should be represented in approximately the proportions that people vote for them) and *preference* (if a voter's favourite candidate cannot win, or receives more than necessary for a seat, that voter's later preferences influence who else gets a seat).

The set of candidates is C. A ballot β is a sequence of candidates π, listed in order of preference (most popular first), without duplicates but without necessarily including all candidates. We use list notation (e.g., $\pi = [c_1, c_2, c_3, c_4]$). The notation $\text{first}(\pi) = \pi(1)$ denotes the first item (candidate) in sequence π. An STV election $\mathcal{L}$ is defined as a multiset[2] of ballots.

Definition 1 (STV Election). *An STV election $\mathcal{L}$ is a tuple $\mathcal{L} = (C, \mathcal{B}, Q, S)$ where C is a set of candidates, $\mathcal{B}$ the multiset of ballots cast, Q the election quota*

---

[1] Any social choice function that is a *scoring rule*—that assigns 'points' to candidates on each ballot, sums the points across ballots, and declares the winner(s) to be the candidate(s) with the most 'points'—can be audited using SHANGRLA (see below).

[2] A multiset allows for the inclusion of duplicate items.

(the number of votes a candidate must attain to win a seat—usually the Droop quota—Eq. 1), and S the number of seats to be filled.

$$Q = \left\lfloor \frac{|\mathcal{B}|}{S+1} \right\rfloor + 1 \tag{1}$$

Definition 2. Projection $\sigma_S(\pi)$ *We define the projection of a sequence π onto a set S as the largest subsequence of π that contains only elements of S. (The elements keep their relative order in π.) For example: $\sigma_{\{c_2,c_3\}}([c_1, c_2, c_4, c_3]) = [c_2, c_3]$ and $\sigma_{\{c_2,c_3,c_4,c_5\}}([c_6, c_4, c_7, c_2, c_1]) = [c_4, c_2]$.*

Each ballot starts with a value of 1, and may change its value as counting progresses. Throughout the count, each eligible candidate has a non-decreasing *tally* of ballots. Ballots can be redistributed between candidates in two ways. If a candidate achieves a quota, their ballots will be redistributed with a reduced value. If a candidate is *eliminated*, their ballots are passed down the preference list at their current value. The following paragraphs describe the algorithm.

Initially, each ballot's value is 1 and each candidate is awarded all ballots on which they are ranked first. A seat is awarded to every candidate whose tally has reached or exceeded Q. When candidate $c \in \mathcal{C}$ achieves a quota, the ballots counting towards their tally are distributed to remaining eligible candidates at a reduced value as follows. (A candidate is eligible if they have not been eliminated, and their tally has not reached a quota's worth of votes.) Let V_c denote the total *value* of ballots counting towards c in the round that c is awarded a seat, and $|\mathcal{B}_c|$ the *number* of those ballots. Each of these ballots is given a new value of τ, and distributed to the next most preferred eligible candidate on the ballot.

One way of computing τ is the *unweighted Gregory method*, given by:

$$\tau = \frac{V_c - Q}{|\mathcal{B}_c|}. \tag{2}$$

This method is used in Australian Senate elections. Note that ballots can increase in value after a second transfer, but never above 1. There are alternative ways to calculate transfer value, but our analysis is agnostic about them, as long as they satisfy some bounds described in Sect. 3.3. Our empirical results use the unweighted Gregory method, but other methods are likely to be very similar. We do not consider randomised methods for distributing votes.

If no candidate has achieved a quota, the candidate c_e with the fewest votes is eliminated. Each ballot currently counting towards c_e is distributed to its next most preferred eligible candidate, at its current value.

Each round of counting thus either awards seats to candidates that have achieved a quota, or eliminates a candidate with the lowest tally. Either way, their ballots are redistributed. This continues until either all seats have been awarded, or the number of eligible candidates equals the number of seats left to be awarded. In the latter case, every remaining candidate is awarded a seat.

Terminology: We will use the term "is seated" to include either way of getting a seat, while "gets a quota" is reserved for getting a seat by obtaining a quota. We say a candidate is "eligible" if it has not been eliminated nor reached a quota.

Table 1. (Example 1) An STV election profile, stating (a) the number of ballots cast with each listed ranking over candidates c_1 to c_4, and (b) the tallies after each round of counting, election, and elimination.

Ranking	Count
$[c_1, c_3]$	8,001
$[c_1]$	1,000
$[c_2, c_3, c_4]$	3,000
$[c_3, c_4]$	5,000
$[c_4, c_1, c_2]$	4,000
Total	21,001

(a)

Seats: 2   Ballots: 21,001   Quota: 7,001

Candidate	Round 1	Round 2	Round 3
	Elect c_1	Eliminate c_2	Elect c_3
	$\tau_1 = 0.2222$		
c_1	9,001	—	—
c_2	3,000	3,000	—
c_3	5,000	6,778	9,778
c_4	4,000	4,000	4,000
Total	21,001	13,778	13,778

(b)

Example 1. Consider a 2-seat STV election with four candidates $C = \{c_1, c_2, c_3, c_4\}$ with ballots B shown in Table 1a. The (Droop) quota for this election is calculated as $Q = \lfloor 21001/3 \rfloor + 1 = 7001$. The election proceeds as shown in Table 1b. Candidate c_1 initially has more than a quota and is elected to a seat.

Using the unweighted Gregory method, the transfer value τ is determined as $2000/9000 = 0.2222$. The 8001 transferable ballots with ranking $[c_1, c_3]$ go to c_3 each with value 0.2222 for a total of 1778. The remaining ballots in c_1's tally have a ranking of $[c_1]$. These ballots have no eligible next preference and are exhausted (not redistributed). Note how some vote value 222 is lost here.

In the next round no candidate has a quota so the candidate c_2 with the least tally is eliminated. The votes in their pile all flow to c_3 as next remaining unelected candidate. Now c_3 has a quota and is elected. □

2.2 Assertion-Based Risk-Limiting Audits

SHANGRLA [5] is a general framework for conducting RLAs. It offers a wide variety of social choice functions, statistical risk functions and audit designs (such as stratified audits or ballot-comparison audits).

This generality is achieved by abstraction: a SHANGRLA audit first reduces the correctness of a reported outcome to the truth of a set $\mathcal{A}$ of quantitative *assertions* about the set of validly cast ballots, which can then be tested using statistical methods. The assertions are either true or false depending on the votes on the ballots. If every assertion in $\mathcal{A}$ is true, the reported outcome is correct. $\mathcal{A}$ generally depends on the social choice function and the reported electoral outcome, and may also depend on the cast vote records (CVRs), vote subtotals, or other data generated by the voting system.

For example, in a first-past-the-post election in which Alice is the apparent winner, $\mathcal{A}$ could include an assertion, for each other candidate c, that there are

Table 2. Summary of definitions.

Quantity/Assertion	Description	Page
Lower and upper bounds		
$L_{\text{basic}}(c)$	First preferences for c	6
$U_{\text{basic}}(c)$	Ballots mentioning c	6
$U_{\text{comp}}(c, c')$	Ballots where c appears before c'	6
$L_{\text{elim}}(w, O)$	Lower bound for w's tally, assuming it is never less than that of each candidate in O	6
$U_{\text{complex}}(c, b, W, \bar{\tau})$	A complex upper bound for c's tally	8
Assertions		
$\text{IQ}(c)$	c gets a quota initially	6
$\text{UT}(c, \bar{\tau})$	c's transfer value is less than $\bar{\tau}$	6
$\text{AG}(w, l)$	w's tally is always greater than l's tally	6
$\text{NL}(w, l, W, \bar{\tau}, G, O)$	w 'never loses' to l, given some assumptions	9

more votes for Alice than c. In this example, $\mathcal{A}$ is both necessary and sufficient: if any assertion $A \in \mathcal{A}$ is false, then Alice did not win (except possibly in a tie). In general, however, the assertions in $\mathcal{A}$ must be *sufficient* to imply that the announced election outcome is correct, but they need not be necessary: the announced electoral result may be correct even if some assertions in $\mathcal{A}$ are false. The assertions we derive for STV in this paper are sufficient but not necessary for supporting the announced election outcome.

SHANGRLA expresses each assertion $A \in \mathcal{A}$ as an *assorter*, which is a function that assigns a nonnegative value to each ballot, depending on the selections the voter made on the ballot and possibly other information (e.g. reported vote totals or CVRs). The assertion is true iff the mean of the assorter (over all ballots) is greater than 1/2. Generally, ballots that support the assertion score higher than 1/2, ballots that weigh against it score less than 1/2, and neutral ballots score exactly 1/2. In the first-past-the-post example above, A might assert that Alice's tally is higher than Bob's. The corresponding assorter would assign 1 to a ballot if it has a vote for Alice, 0 if it has a vote for Bob, and 1/2 if it has a no valid vote for either.

3 Reasoning About STV Elections: Deriving Bounds and Assertions

In order to make verifiable assertions about STV elections we need to examine how we can reason about STV elections. In this section we define testable assertions for reasoning about STV elections (summarised in Table 2).

3.1   Simple Bounds and Assertions

A simple lower bound on the tally of candidate c is the number of first preference votes they receive: $L_{\text{basic}}(c) = |\{\beta : \beta \in \mathcal{B}, \text{first}(\beta) = c\}|$.

Given this bound we can introduce our first type of assertion, that a candidate gets a quota initially: $\mathsf{IQ}(c) \equiv L_{\text{basic}}(c) \geqslant Q$.

Lemma 1. *If $\mathsf{IQ}(c)$ holds then c is seated.* $\square$

The next assertion we introduce is one that upper bounds the transfer value at $\bar{\tau}$ for candidates that have an initial quota: $\mathsf{UT}(c, \bar{\tau}) \equiv L_{\text{basic}}(c) < Q/(1 - \bar{\tau})$. Clearly if the initial tally for c is $T < Q/(1 - \bar{\tau})$ then the transfer value (using the unweighted Gregory method) is $(T - Q)/T < \bar{\tau}$. We use this in Sect. 5.2 to improve upper bounds on tallies.

A simple upper bound on the tally of a candidate c is the number of ballots on which they appear: $U_{\text{basic}}(c) = |\{\beta : \beta \in \mathcal{B}, c \text{ occurs in } \beta\}|$.

We can improve this upper bound when comparing against an alternative candidate c'. The number of ballots where c appears before c' (including the case where c' doesn't appear) is $U_{\text{comp}}(c, c') = |\{\beta : \beta \in \mathcal{B}, \text{first}\left(\sigma_{\{c,c'\}}(\beta)\right) = c\}|$. This is the maximum number of ballots that can appear in the tally of c before c' is eliminated.

We can use this to state a sufficient condition that candidate w's tally is *always greater*[3] than candidate l's: $\mathsf{AG}(w, l) \equiv L_{\text{basic}}(w) > U_{\text{comp}}(l, w)$.

Lemma 2. *If $\mathsf{AG}(w, l)$ holds then candidate w's tally is always greater than l's.*

Proof. Candidate w always has a tally of at least $L_{\text{basic}}(w)$. Candidate l always has a tally of at most $U_{\text{comp}}(l, w)$ while w is not eliminated nor seated. Also, by assumption, $L_{\text{basic}}(w) > U_{\text{comp}}(l, w)$, which means w's tally always exceeds l's tally while w is not eliminated nor seated. $\square$

Corollary 1. *If $\mathsf{AG}(w, l)$ holds then l cannot be seated when w is not.*

Proof. $\mathsf{AG}(w, l)$ implies we cannot eliminate w before l. $\square$

3.2   Improving the Lower Bound

Note that the AG condition is very strong—there are many cases where candidate w does not lose to l but $\mathsf{AG}(w, l)$ does not hold. We can improve this by using the knowledge of easily proven AG conditions to improve lower bounds on the tally of w at any point at which w could be eliminated. At such points, we know that any candidate $o \in O$ for which $\mathsf{AG}(w, o)$ holds must have already been eliminated. Any ballots that would move from o to w on the elimination of o can be counted towards this lower bound. That motivates the following definition for an improved lower bound:

$$L_{\text{elim}}(w, O) = |\{\beta : \beta \in \mathcal{B}, \text{first}(\sigma_{C-O}(\beta)) = w\}|.$$

---

[3] Previous IRV auditing work [3] has used the term *not eliminated before* for this concept, but we reserve it for a more restrictive notion defined below.

This allows us to reason about when w might be eliminated, in particular, and to prove that it cannot be.

Lemma 3. *Given a candidate w and a set of candidates O, suppose $AG(w, o)$ holds for all $o \in O$. Then $L_{elim}(w, O)$ is a lower bound on w's tally at any point at which it could be eliminated.*

Proof. By assumption, w cannot be eliminated before any candidate in O. If any candidate in O is seated, $AG(w, o)$ implies that w must also be seated (Corollary 1). So at any point at which w could be eliminated, all candidates in O are eliminated. Hence all the ballots in $|\{\beta : \beta \in \mathcal{B}, \text{first}(\sigma_{C-O}(\beta)) = w\}|$ contribute to w's tally. Since none of the candidates in O reached a quota, all the ballots still have their full value. $\qquad\square$

3.3   Improving the Upper Bound

The simple AG condition will fail when a candidate appears in many ballots, but the values of these ballots are "used up" by seating earlier candidates. In the following example, $AG(c_4, c_2)$ does not hold, but more careful reasoning allows us to prove that c_4 cannot lose to c_2.

Example 2. Consider a 2-seat election with ballots and multiplicities defined as $[c_1, c_2]$: 30, $[c_4, c_1, c_2]$: 20, $[c_3, c_1, c_2]$: 4, $[c_2, c_4]$: 2, $[c_3]$: 4, where the quota is 21. We cannot show $AG(c_4, c_2)$ since c_2 appears in 30 ballots with c_1. The maximum transfer value in a 2-seat election is $2/3$ (which can only occur if one candidate gets all the ballots initially). If we note that c_1 must be seated, we can see that the maximum value c_2 can derive from these ballots is 20. This still makes it impossible to show c_4 cannot lose to c_2. In fact the actual transfer value is 0.3, and with this c_2 can only gather 9. Using a maximal transfer value of 0.3 we could show that c_4 cannot lose to c_2. We have to be careful to consider the ballots $[c_3, c_1, c_2]$; since these are not in c_1's pile when it obtains a quota, they are not reduced in value. When c_3 is eliminated they are passed to c_2 (since c_1 is already seated) at full value. $\qquad\square$

In order to more effectively upper bound the tally of a candidate, we need to reason about the possible transfer values of ballots that follow this route.

We have the following trivial upper bound on transfer values: the maximum transfer value τ in an S-seat election (using the unweighted Gregory method) is $\tau = S/(S+1)$. This is only possible if one candidate gains all the votes initially.

We now define a complex bound that relies on a number of assumptions. We are trying to find an upper bound on the tally of some candidate c in order to compare them with an alternate winner b.

Assume that all candidates in W are seated (which may happen before, during or after this bound is computed, and may occur by getting a quota or by remaining at the end). The only candidates who may be seated but are not in W are b and c. Let $\bar{\tau}$ be a vector of upper bounds $\bar{\tau}_w, w \in W$, that is the maximum transfer value for any ballot that was in w's pile at the time it was seated (if it was).[4] Candidates in W clearly cannot be eliminated, they are either eligible or seated. Assume also that b is eligible.

Let R be all of the other candidates, $R = \mathcal{C} - W - \{b, c\}$. Let G be candidates for which $\mathsf{AG}(g, c)$ hold for all $g \in G$. Under these assumptions we define an upper bound on the tally of candidate c as follows:

$$U_{\text{complex}}(c, b, W, \overline{\tau}, G) = \sum_{\beta \in \mathcal{B}} U_{\text{complex}}(c, b, W, \overline{\tau}, \beta) \tag{3}$$

where

$$U_{\text{complex}}(c, b, W, \overline{\tau}, G, \beta) = \begin{cases} 0 & \exists g \in G - W \text{ s.t. first}(\sigma_{g,c}(\beta)) = g \\ 0 & c \text{ does not occur in } \beta \\ 0 & \text{first}(\sigma_{b,c}(\beta)) = b \\ mt_w & \text{first}(\beta) \in W \\ 1 & \text{otherwise} \end{cases}$$

where $mt_w = \max\{\overline{\tau}_w : w \in W \text{ precedes } c \text{ in } \beta\}$.

Lemma 4. *Under the assumption that only candidates $W \cup \{b, c\}$ can be seated, and that all candidates in W are seated (though this may happen before, during or after this comparison), with upper bound on the transfer values $\overline{\tau}$, and $b \notin W$ is eligible, and that $AG(g, c)$ holds for all $g \in G$, then $U_{complex}(c, b, W, \overline{\tau}, G)$ is an upper bound on the tally of c.*

Proof. Consider each ballot β, and each case in the definition of U_{complex}.

If there exists, before c, on β, a candidate in $g \in G - W$ then c is preceded on the ballot by a candidate who cannot be eliminated before c and, by assumption, cannot win. Hence β counts 0 towards c's tally.

If c does not occur in β, or b precedes c in β, then clearly the ballot contributes 0 to c's tally (given the assumption that b is eligible).

If the first candidate on the ballot is $w \in W$ then we need to consider whether or not w has been seated. If w is unseated, then the ballot still sits with them and it contributes 0 to c's tally. If w is seated in the last round without a quota, then it contributes 0 to c's tally. If w has obtained a quota, then the ballot has definitely been transferred at least once. If it ends up in c's pile, it can only have been involved with transfers that appear before c. The maximum value it can have is the maximum of the transfer values. This is the overall maximum (since the others are zero.)

The remaining ballots have maximum possible value 1. Note that the case where first$(\sigma_{W \cup R}(\beta)) \in W$ does not imply that a vote has been transferred if it reaches c's pile. It may have been that the winner w was seated before the ballot reached w's pile, in which case it could arrive in c's pile by elimination rather than by transfer.

---

[4] We simply require that an upper bound on a ballot's value is the maximum of the upper bounds on per-candidate transfer values. This is true of transfer values calculated according to the unweighted Gregory method, and weighted methods.

Since each ballot is counted at its maximum possible value given the assumptions, the upper bound is correct. □

We can now define a refined version of the 'always greater' assertion that takes into account this new bound. We define w *never loses* to l, denoted $\mathsf{NL}(w, l, W, \overline{\tau}, G, O)$ as follows. Assume any previous winners are included in the set W with upper bounds on transfer values $\overline{\tau}$. Assume $\mathsf{AG}(w, o)$ holds for $o \in O$ and $\mathsf{AG}(g, l)$ holds for all $g \in G$. Then

$$\mathsf{NL}(w, l, W, \overline{\tau}, G, O) \equiv L_{\mathrm{elim}}(w, O) > U_{\mathrm{complex}}(l, w, W, \overline{\tau}, G).$$

Lemma 5. *Under the assumption that only candidates $W \cup \{w, l\}$ can be seated, and that all candidates in W are seated (though this may happen before, during or after this comparison), with maximal transfer values $\overline{\tau}$, and $\mathsf{AG}(w, o)$ holds for all $o \in O$ then and $\mathsf{AG}(g, l)$ holds for all $g \in G$ then $\mathsf{NL}(w, l, W, \overline{\tau}, G, O)$ implies that w never loses to l.*

Proof. Suppose to the contrary that we are about to eliminate w. By Lemma 3 its tally is at least $L_{\mathrm{elim}}(w, O)$. In order for l to get a seat it cannot already be eliminated. By assumption neither can any of W. By Lemma 4, $U_{\mathrm{complex}}(l, w, W, \overline{\tau}, G)$ is an upper bound on the tally of l, since we have treated all other candidates as eliminated. Before w is eliminated l can never have more tally than this bound. Because the tally of w is greater than the tally of l it cannot be eliminated.

From the above, w can never be eliminated, therefore every candidate who is seated must obtain a quota (otherwise w would be seated at the end). Assume w is not seated. Now none of the ballots in $L_{\mathrm{elim}}(w, O)$ can ever sit with any candidate that is seated, since none of O can be seated if w is not. Then the total tally of the S winners is at least $S \times Q$, and none of the ballots in $L_{\mathrm{elim}}(w, O)$ are included. Suppose to the contrary l is a winner, then its maximum quota when elected is $U_{\mathrm{complex}}(l, w, W, \overline{\tau}, G)$ which is, by the NL assumption, less than $L_{\mathrm{elim}}(w, O)$. Hence $L_{\mathrm{elim}}(w, O) > Q$. But this gives a total tally of votes greater than $(S + 1) \times Q$, more than exist in the entire election. Contradiction. □

4 Deriving Assorters

To use the SHANGRLA framework, we need to determine an assorter for each assertion defined in Sect. 3. It suffices to show how to write each one as a *linear assertion* as per the general framework described by Blom et al. [1].

Assertions AG and NL involve comparing two tallies. These can be straightforwardly written in the standard linear form.

Assertion IQ is of the form $T \geqslant Q$ and assertion UT is of the form $T < a \cdot Q$, for some tally T and positive constant a. These are not immediately in linear form because Q is not a tally nor a simple function of a tally. However, for each of these we can define a linear assertion that is either equivalent or stricter.

To get an assertion of the form $T \geqslant Q$, we instead work with the assertion $T > |\mathcal{B}|/(S + 1)$. This latter assertion can be written in linear form since $|\mathcal{B}|$

is a tally (simply count each valid ballot). To see that this implies our desired assertion, consider that $T > |\mathcal{B}|/(S+1) \geqslant \lfloor|\mathcal{B}|/(S+1)\rfloor$. Since T is an integer strictly greater than the term on the right, which is itself an integer, it must be at least 1 greater than that term. That is, $T \geqslant \lfloor|\mathcal{B}|/(S+1)\rfloor + 1 = Q$.

To get an assertion of the form $T < a \cdot Q$, we instead work with the slightly stricter assertion $T < a \cdot |\mathcal{B}|/(S+1)$, which is clearly expressible in linear form. The floor function has the property that $\lfloor x \rfloor \leqslant x < \lfloor x \rfloor + 1$. Taking the right-hand part of this double inequality and setting $x = |\mathcal{B}|/(S+1)$ gives $|\mathcal{B}|/(S+1) < Q$. Our working assertion therefore implies our desired assertion, $T < a \cdot Q$.

5   RLAs for 2-Seat STV Elections

Given the assertions we have defined in the previous section, we are now ready to define an algorithm to choose a set of assertions that, if validated, will ensure, within the risk limit α, that the election result must be correct. We will try to choose a set of assertions that is expected to be auditable by viewing few ballots. We assume a function $ASN(a, \alpha, \epsilon)$ that returns the *average sample number* for verifying assertion a, that is the expected number of ballots required to verify the assertion a if it indeed holds, given the recorded election data, a risk limit α and expected error rate ϵ.[5] For some assertions there are closed-form formulae for this estimation, but in general we can use sampling to provide accurate estimates. Note that the expected auditing effort is not relevant to proving that the assertions, if verified, certify the election result up to risk limit α. Rather, we use it to suggest a set of assertions that are expected to be easy to audit.

Assume the declared winners of the election $\mathcal{L}$ are $DW = \{w_1, w_2\}$. We need to consider all possible alternative election results $AR = \{\{c_1, c_2\} : \{c_1, c_2\} \subseteq \mathcal{C}, \{c_1, c_2\} \neq DW\}$, and verify assertions that will invalidate all such results.

We first use simple AG assertions to eliminate as many pairs as possible. NonWinners (Fig. 1) finds a set of candidates, denoted NW, that *clearly cannot win*. In NonWinners, we first determine all the *always greater* relationships AG that hold on the basis of the recorded election result (lines 2–4). We then find the candidates c for which there exists at least two other candidates w_1 and w_2 such that $AG(w_1, c)$ and $AG(w_2, c)$ (lines 5–10). For each candidate $c \in NW$, we collect the easiest two AG assertions which verify that c cannot win into NWA. Any alternate winner pair that includes a candidate $c \in NW$ can be immediately ruled out with the chosen AG assertions in NWA.

Once we have a reduced set of alternate winner pairs, we use FindAuditable-Assertions (Fig. 2) to find more complex NL assertions that would rule them out. The initial set of assertions is set to NWA, as produced by NonWinners. The current expected ASN is given by ASN, and this will increase over the course of the algorithm. We then consider every alternate pair of winners, excluding those involving a candidate in NW, and find a set of assertions LA, with an expected audit cost of $LASN$, to eliminate this possibility.

---

[5] The *expected error rate* is the expected proportion of ballots that are counted erroneously when calculating the assorter corresponding to assertion a.

```
NonWinners()
1    AG := NW := NWA := ∅
2    forall w ∈ C, l ∈ C − {w}
3        if AG(w, l)
4            AG := AG ∪ {(w, l)}
5    forall c ∈ C
6        if |{w : (w, c) ∈ AG}| ⩾ 2
7            NW := NW ∪ {c}
8            w1 := argmin_w{ASN(AG(w, c), α, ε) : (w, c) ∈ AG}
9            w2 := argmin_w{ASN(AG(w, c), α, ε) : (w, c) ∈ AG, w ≠ w1}
10           NWA := NWA ∪ {AG(w1, c), AG(w2, c)}
11   return (AG, NW, NWA)
```

Fig. 1. Pseudo-code to calculate definite non-winners c, for which we have at least two candidates where $\mathsf{AG}(w1, c)$ and $\mathsf{AG}(w2, c)$ hold. The function returns the set AG of always greater relations, the set NW of non-winners, and the set of assertions NWA required to verify this.

For a given alternate winner pair $\{c_1, c_2\}$, we can rule out this outcome by finding a candidate $o \in C − \{c_1, c_2\}$ for which we can show that either: o cannot be eliminated before c_2 in the context where c_1 is seated (at some point); or, similarly, o cannot be eliminated before c_1 in the context where c_2 is seated.

We consider each candidate $o \in C − \{c_1, c_2\}$ in turn. We first consider if we can form an NL assertion showing that o cannot be eliminated before c_2 (or c_1) in the context where c_1 (or c_2) is seated. We only need one such NL assertion to rule out the alternate winner pair. As we consider each o, and these two different contexts, we keep track of the easiest of these potential NL assertions. As described earlier, an NL assertion between two candidates w and l will use a number of pre-computed AG assertions to guide which ballots should contribute to a lower bound on the tally of w and an upper bound on the tally of l. When choosing a given NL to rule out the alternate winner pair $\{c_1, c_2\}$, the set LA contains the NL assertion and all AG assertions that it uses (lines 12 and 18).

If we never find a way to eliminate a pair $\{c_1, c_2\}$ then the election is not auditable with this approach; abort. Otherwise, update the global ASN, and add the best assertions for removing $\{c_1, c_2\}$ to $\mathcal{A}$. Finally, return $\mathcal{A}$.

Theorem 1. *The set of assertions $\mathcal{A}$ returned by FindAuditableAssertions (Fig. 2) is sufficient to rule out all alternate election results.*

Proof. Each alternate election result is ruled out by $\mathcal{A}$. For pairs where $\{c_1, c_2\} \cap NW \neq \emptyset$, assume w.l.o.g. $c_1 \in NW$. Then by Corollary 1 there are two other candidates that will be seated if c_1 is seated, which rules out the pair. Otherwise Lemma 5 shows that one of c_1 or c_2 cannot win before another candidate o. □

5.1   Two Initial Quotas Case

The general algorithm described above can be applied to all 2-seat STV elections but there are alternatives for some elections which might be easier to audit.

FindAuditableAssertions()
1 $(AG, NW, NWA) :=$ NonWinners()
2 $\mathcal{A} := NWA$
3 $ASN := \max\{ASN(a, \alpha, \epsilon) : a \in \mathcal{A}\}$
4 **forall** $\{c_1, c_2\} \subset \mathcal{C}, \{c_1, c_2\} \neq \{w_1, w_2\}$
   % for each pair, find the easiest way to eliminate it
5   **if** $(\{c_1, c_2\} \cap NW \neq \emptyset)$ **continue**
6     $LASN := +\infty$
7     $G_1 := \{g : a \in \mathcal{C} - W, (g, c_1) \in AG\}$
8     $G_2 := \{g : a \in \mathcal{C} - W, (g, c_2) \in AG\}$
9   **forall** $o \in \mathcal{C} - \{c_1, c_2\}$
10       $O := \{o' : (o, o') \in AG\}$
         % assume c_1 wins, show c_2 is eliminated
11   **if** NL$(o, c_2, \{c_1\}, \{2/3\}, G_2, O - \{c_1\})$ holds
12          $LA' = \{$NL$(o, c_2, \{c_1\}, \{2/3\}, G_2, O - \{c_1\})\} \cup$
            $\{$AG$(o, o') : o' \in O\} \cup \{AG(g, c_2) : g \in G_2\}$
13          $LASN' := \max\{ASN(a, \alpha, \epsilon) : a \in LA'\}$
14   **if** $LASN' < LASN$
15             $LASN := LASN'$
16             $LA := LA'$
         % assume c_2 wins, show c_1 is eliminated
17   **if** NL$(o, c_1, \{c_2\}, \{2/3\}, G_1, O - \{c_2\})$ holds
18          $LA' = \{$NL$(o, c_1, \{c_2\}, \{2/3\}, G_1, O - \{c_2\})\} \cup$
            $\{$AG$(o, o') : o' \in O\} \cup \{AG(g, c_1) : g \in G_1\}$
19          $LASN' := \max\{ASN(a, \alpha, \epsilon) : a \in LA'\}$
20   **if** $LASN' < LASN$
21             $LASN := LASN'$
22             $LA := LA'$
23   **if** $LASN = +\infty$
24   **abort** % no auditable assertions
25       $ASN := \max(ASN, LASN)$
26       $\mathcal{A} := \mathcal{A} \cup LA$
27 **return** $\mathcal{A}$

Fig. 2. Calculate a set of assertions $\mathcal{A}$ sufficient to verify a 2-seat STV election.

Suppose IQ(w_1) and IQ(w_2) hold. That is, both reported winners achieved a quota initially. We can simply define $\mathcal{A} = \{$IQ$(w_1),$ IQ$(w_2)\}$ with an expected ASN of $\max\{ASN($IQ$(w_1), \alpha, \epsilon), ASN(IQ(w_2), \alpha, \epsilon)\}$.

5.2   One Initial Quota Case

A frequent occurrence in STV elections is that one candidate has a first preference tally that exceeds a quota. We may be able to use this outcome structure
to generate a set of assertions that are easier to audit than those found using
the general algorithm. To generate a set of assertions to audit such a 2-seat STV
election, we start with the assertion IQ(w_1) for the first seated candidate, w_1.

For the second reported winner, w_2, we then assert $\mathsf{NL}(w_2, c, \{w_1\}, \overline{\tau}, G, O)$ for all candidates $c \in \mathcal{C} - \{w_1, w_2\}$ given an assumed upper bound $\overline{\tau}$ on the transfer value of ballots leaving w_1's pile and a set of candidates $o \in O$ for which $\mathsf{AG}(w_2, o)$ holds, and $g \in G$ where $\mathsf{AG}(g, c)$ holds.

For any choice of $\overline{\tau}$, we need to validate that the actual transfer value for ballots leaving w_1's tally is indeed below $\overline{\tau}$. We do this with the assertion $\mathsf{UT}(w_1, \overline{\tau})$.

We could set $\overline{\tau}$ to the reported transfer value, τ_{w_1}, however the UT assertion would then have a zero margin and thus be impossible to audit. The higher we set $\overline{\tau}$, up to a maximum value of $2/3$, the easier it will be to audit. However, as $\overline{\tau}$ increases, the NL assertions formed above (to check that w_2 cannot lose to any reported losing candidate) become harder to audit. This is because the upper bounds (on the tallies of these reported losers) in the context of each NL increase as $\overline{\tau}$ increases. With this increase, the margin of any NL that we can form decreases.

To find an appropriate value of $\overline{\tau}$, we initialise the upper bound to τ_{w_1} and gradually increase it in small increments, δ. For each choice of $\overline{\tau}$, we compute the set of NL assertions required to show that w_2 cannot lose to any remaining candidate, keeping track of the ASN required for that audit configuration. We continue to increase $\overline{\tau}$ while the ASN of the resulting audit decreases. Once $\overline{\tau}$ reaches $2/3$, or the ASN of the audit configuration starts to increase, we stop and accept the least-cost audit configuration found.

6   Experimental Results

We ran the general, one-quota, and two-quota audit generation methods described in Sect. 5, on a range of election instances: four 2-seat STV elections conducted as part of the 2016 and 2019 Australian Senate elections; and several US and Australian IRV elections re-imagined as 2-seat STV elections.[6] We used $\delta = 0.01$ for the one-quota method, and all methods were implemented as ballot-comparison audits. The ASNs for the resulting audits, based on a risk limit of 10% and assumed error rate of 0.2%, are reported in Table 3. A '–' indicates that the given audit generation method was not applicable to the instance, while $+\infty$ indicates that the method could not find an auditable set of assertions. Bold entries are instances where the general method is expected to be more efficient than the one- and two-quota methods.

In general, the one-quota method formed the cheapest audit, where applicable. This is expected to be case as the general approach assumes the highest possible transfer value for ballots leaving the first winner's pile. The one-quota method, in contrast, finds a trade-off between the difficulty of checking that the transfer value for the first winner is less than an assumed upper bound, and the difficulty of NL assertions to check that the second winner cannot lose to any reported loser. The former is easier with a larger upper bound, while the latter are easier with a smaller lower bound.

---

[6] Our code is publicly available at: https://github.com/michelleblom/stv-rla.

Table 3. ASNs for audit configurations generated for four Australian Senate 2-seat STV elections (2016 and 2019), and several US and Australian IRV elections re-imagined as 2-seat STV elections. We report the ASNs of audits generated using the one-quota, two-quota and general methods, where applicable. A risk limit of $\alpha = 10\%$ and error rate of $\epsilon = 0.2\%$ were used.

Election	$|C|$	Valid Ballots	Quota	2-quota ASN	1-quota ASN	General ASN
2016 ACT	22	254,767	84,923	–	66	$+\infty$
2019 ACT	17	270,231	90,078	–	107	$+\infty$
2016 NT	19	102,027	34,010	100	74	569
2019 NT	18	105,027	35,010	100	72	327
IRV elections re-imagined as 2-seat STV elections						
No candidate achieves a quota on first preferences						
NSW'19 Barwon	9	46,174	15,392	–	–	285
2014 Oakland Mayor	17	101,431	33,811	–	–	$+\infty$
2014 Berkeley City Council D8	5	4,497	1,500	–	–	$+\infty$
2009 Aspen City Council	11	2,487	830	–	–	$+\infty$
2008 Pierce CAS	7	262,447	87,483	–	–	$+\infty$
At least one candidate achieves a quota on first preferences						
US elections						
2013 ward 5	5	3,499	1,167	–	114	$+\infty$
OK CC D2 2014	6	13,500	4,501	$+\infty$	100	127
Aspen 2009 Mayor	5	2,528	843	203	51	195
2010 Berkeley CC D1	5	5,700	1,901	–	69	921
2010 Berkeley CC D7	4	4,184	1,395	267	48	89
Oakland 2010 Mayor	11	119,607	39,870	–	1,177	$+\infty$
Oakland 2010 CC D6	4	12,911	4,304	–	$+\infty$	$+\infty$
Pierce 2008 CA	4	153,528	51,177	34	19	23
Pierce 2008 CE	5	299,132	99,711	–	192	$+\infty$
San Leandro 2010 D5 CC	7	22,484	7,495	149	126	230
Australian elections: NSW 2019 Legislative Assembly						
Auburn	5	44,842	14,948	107	25	46
Bathurst	6	50,833	16,945	–	95	125
Blue Mountains	7	49,228	16,410	–	71	$+\infty$
Clarence	6	49,355	16,452	–	116	251
Granville	8	44,191	14,731	67	19	29
Hornsby	9	50,003	16,668	–	123	2,210
Kogarah	**5**	**45,576**	**15,193**	**30**	**30**	**20**
Ku-ring-gai	6	48,730	16,244	–	229	340
Lakemba	6	44,615	14,872	–	60	607
Macquarie Fields	6	52,789	17,597	–	29	39
Murray	**10**	**47,233**	**15,745**	**145**	**50**	**25**
Myall Lakes	6	50,315	16,772	–	28	41
Newcastle	8	50,319	16,774	–	211	$+\infty$
Newtown	7	46,312	15,438	–	49	67
North Shore	9	47,774	15,925	–	509	1200
Northern Tablelands	4	48,678	16,227	–	$+\infty$	$+\infty$
Oatley	5	48,120	16,041	$+\infty$	21	23
Parramatta	7	48,728	16,243	–	26	31
Penrith	**10**	**48,853**	**16,285**	**118**	**40**	**24**
Pittwater	8	49,119	16,374	–	190	223
Port Macquarie	4	52,735	17,579	–	44	57
Riverstone	3	53,510	17,837	41	16	18
Upper Hunter	**8**	**48,525**	**16,176**	**–**	**520**	**145**
Vaucluse	7	46,023	15,342	–	508	$+\infty$

For the instances considered, the two-quota method forms more costly audits than the one-quota and general methods. In instances where there is one dominant candidate that receives significantly more first preference votes than others, the second winner typically has a much smaller surplus. The size of this surplus determines the margin of the assertion used to check that the second winner is seated in the first round.

An advantage of the one-quota method is that we can form more AGs by using the fact that we have a tight upper bound on the transfer value of ballots leaving the first winner, who we know is seated in the first round. We can create more of these AGs than would be possible if we were assuming an upper bound of 2/3 on transfer values. With more available AGs, we can more effectively increase and decrease the bounds on the tallies of candidates within NLs. This allows us to create more NLs, including some that we cannot form under the general method.

7 Conclusion

We have presented the first method we are aware of for risk-limiting audits for STV elections, restricted for the moment to 2-seat STV elections.

We were able to design an efficient audit for all of the *real-world* 2-seat STV elections for which we have data, although the general method is not strong enough for two of them. For other elections—where we re-imagine IRV elections as 2-seat STV elections—we see that if no candidate has a quota initially, we struggle to find an auditable set of assertions. In the case that one or two candidates initially obtain a quota, we are usually able to audit them successfully, with the one-quota method usually requiring less effort, but not always.

The assertions we define in this paper are not specific to 2-seat STV elections. Thus, they provide a starting point for auditing STV elections with more seats. Obviously even the 2-seat case is not easy, so investigating tighter lower and upper bounds on tallies is likely to be valuable.

References

1. Blom, M., et al.: Assertion-based approaches to auditing complex elections, with application to party-list proportional elections. In: Krimmer, R., et al. (eds.) E-Vote-ID 2021. LNCS, vol. 12900, pp. 47–62. Springer, Cham (2021). https://doi.org/10.1007/978-3-030-86942-7_4
2. Blom, M., Stark, P.B., Stuckey, P.J., Teague, V., Vukcevic, D.: Auditing Hamiltonian elections. In: Bernhard, M., et al. (eds.) FC 2021. LNCS, vol. 12676, pp. 235–250. Springer, Heidelberg (2021). https://doi.org/10.1007/978-3-662-63958-0_21
3. Blom, M., Stuckey, P.J., Teague, V.: RAIRE: risk-limiting audits for IRV elections (2019). https://arxiv.org/abs/1903.08804arXiv:1903.08804. Preliminary version appeared in Electronic Voting (E-Vote-ID 2018), Springer LNCS 11143
4. Lindeman, M., Stark, P.B.: A gentle introduction to risk-limiting audits. IEEE Secur. Priv. **10**(5), 42–49 (2012). https://doi.org/10.1109/MSP.2012.56
5. Stark, P.B.: Sets of half-average nulls generate risk-limiting audits: SHANGRLA. In: Bernhard, M., et al. (eds.) FC 2020. LNCS, vol. 12063, pp. 319–336. Springer, Cham (2020). https://doi.org/10.1007/978-3-030-54455-3_23
6. Stark, P.B., Teague, V.: Verifiable European elections: risk-limiting audits for D'Hondt and its relatives. USENIX J. Election Technol. Syst. (JETS) **3**(1), 18–39 (2014). https://www.usenix.org/jets/issues/0301/stark

Short Paper: Verifiable Decryption for BGV

Tjerand Silde[(✉)] [ID]

Department of Mathematical Sciences, Norwegian University of Science
and Technology, Trondheim, Norway
`tjerand.silde@ntnu.no`

Abstract. In this work we present a direct construction for verifiable
decryption for the BGV encryption scheme by combining existing zero-
knowledge proofs for linear relations and bounded values. This is one of
the first constructions of verifiable decryption protocols for lattice-based
cryptography, and we give a protocol that is simpler and at least as
efficient as the state of the art when amortizing over many ciphertexts.

To prove its practicality we provide concrete parameters, resulting in
proof size of less than 44τ KB for τ ciphertexts with message space 2048
bits. Furthermore, we provide an open source implementation showing
that the amortized cost of the verifiable decryption protocol is only 76
ms per message when batching over $\tau = 2048$ ciphertexts.

Keywords: lattice cryptography · verifiable decryption ·
zero-knowledge

1 Introduction

Many privacy preserving applications require one to prove that a ciphertext is
correctly decrypted without revealing the secret key. This is called *verifiable
decryption*, formalized by Camenisch and Shoup [9]. Example use-cases are electronic voting [1], mixing networks [15], DC-networks [10] and fully homomorphic
encryption [16]. These applications usually require decrypting a large number of
ciphertexts.

Unfortunately, the above systems are either not secure against quantum computers or very inefficient. Recent works in lattice-based cryptography are leading
towards voting protocols achieving security even against quantum adversaries,
see, e.g., the shuffles by Aranha *et al.* [4], Costa *et al.* [11] and Farzaliyev *et
al.* [12]. However, few constructions provides verifiable decryption for lattice-
based encryption schemes.

1.1 Contribution

We present a new and efficient verifiable decryption protocol for batches of
ciphertext using the lattice-based encryption scheme by Brakerski, Gentry and

© International Financial Cryptography Association 2023
S. Matsuo et al. (Eds.): FC 2022 Workshops, LNCS 13412, pp. 381–390, 2023.
https://doi.org/10.1007/978-3-031-32415-4_26

Vaikuntanathan [8]. The protocol is direct; the decryption procedure consists of computing a linear equation involving the ciphertext and the key, and then the message is extracted by rounding the result modulo the plaintext moduli. This procedure gives the correct result if the noise-level in the ciphertext is bounded. We use lattice-based commitments to commit to the secret key, and then we prove two relations in zero-knowledge: 1) we prove that the linear equation holds with respect to a fresh commitment to the ciphertext-noise, and 2) prove that the noise is bounded. Together, this leads to an efficient verifiable decryption protocol. We give concrete parameters and estimate the size in Sect. 4.1 and give timings from our proof-of-concept implementation in Sect. 4.2.

1.2   Related Work

We compare to the works on verifiable decryption for lattices by Lyubashevsky et al. [18], Gjøsteen et al. [14] and Boschini et al. [7] in Sect 4.3.

2   Lattice-Based Cryptography

Let N be a power of 2 and $q = 1 \mod 2N$ a prime. We define the ring $R_q = \mathbb{Z}_q[X]/\langle X^N + 1\rangle$. For $f \in R_q$ we choose coefficients as the representatives in $\left[-\frac{q-1}{2}, \frac{q-1}{2}\right]$, and compute inner products $\langle\cdot,\cdot\rangle$ and norms as vectors over $\mathbb{Z}$:

$$\|f\|_1 = \sum |\alpha_i|, \qquad \|f\|_2 = \left(\sum \alpha_i^2\right)^{1/2}, \qquad \|f\|_\infty = \max\{|\alpha_i|\}.$$

We furthermore define the sets $S_{\beta_\infty} = \{x \in R_q \mid \|x\|_\infty \le \beta_\infty\}$ as well as

$$\mathcal{C} = \{c \in R_q \mid \|c\|_\infty = 1, \|c\|_1 = \nu\} \text{ and } \bar{\mathcal{C}} = \{c - c' \mid c \neq c' \in \mathcal{C}\}.$$

2.1   Rejection Sampling

We want to output vectors $z = y + v$ such that z is independent of v, and hence, v is masked by the vector y. If y is sampled according to a Gaussian distribution $\mathcal{N}_\sigma^k$ with standard deviation σ, then we want z to be from the same distribution. $1/M$ is the success probability for rejection sampling, and M is computed as

$$\max \frac{\mathcal{N}_\sigma^k(z)}{\mathcal{N}_{v,\sigma}^k(z)} = \exp\left[\frac{-2\langle z, v\rangle + \|v\|_2^2}{2\sigma^2}\right] \le \exp\left[\frac{24\sigma\|v\|_2 + \|v\|_2^2}{2\sigma^2}\right] = M,$$

so that $|\langle z, v\rangle| < 12\sigma\|v\|_2$ with probability at least $1 - 2^{-100}$. Hence, for $\sigma = 11\|v\|_2$, we get $M \approx 3$. This is the standard way to choose parameters. If the procedure is only done once for the vector v, we can decrease the parameters, to the cost of leaking only one bit of information about v from the given z.

Lyubashevsky et al. [18] suggest to require that $\langle z, v\rangle \ge 0$. Then we can set $M = \exp(\|v\|_2/2\sigma^2)$. For $\sigma = 0.675\|v\|_2$, we get $M \approx 3$, with the effect of rejecting about half of the vectors up front. See [18, Figure 2] for details.

2.2 Hardness Assumptions

We first define the Search Knapsack problem in the ℓ_2 norm, also denoted as SKS^2. The SKS^2 problem is the Ring-SIS problem in its Hermite Normal Form.

Definition 1. *The* $\mathsf{SKS}^2_{N,q,\beta}$ *problem is to find a short vector* $\boldsymbol{x}$ *of* ℓ_2 *norm less than or equal to* β *in* R_q^2 *satisfying* $[\,a \quad 1\,] \cdot \boldsymbol{x} = 0$ *for a given uniformly random* a *in* R_q. *An algorithm* $\mathcal{A}$ *has advantage* ϵ *in solving the* $\mathsf{SKS}^2_{N,q,\beta}$ *problem if*

$$\Pr\left[\begin{matrix}[a \quad 1]\cdot\boldsymbol{x}=0\\ \wedge \quad \|x_i\|_2 \leq \beta\end{matrix}\,\middle|\,\begin{matrix}a \leftarrow_{\$} R_q;\\ \mathbf{0} \neq \boldsymbol{x} \in R_q^2 \leftarrow \mathcal{A}(a)\end{matrix}\right] \geq \epsilon.$$

We also define the Decisional Knapsack problem (DKS^∞) in the ℓ_∞ norm. DKS^∞ is equivalent to the Ring-LWE problem when the number of samples is limited.

Definition 2. *The* $\mathsf{DKS}^\infty_{N,q,\beta_\infty}$ *problem is to distinguish the distribution* $[\,a \quad 1\,] \cdot \boldsymbol{x}$, *for a short* $\boldsymbol{x}$, *from the uniform distribution when given uniformly random* a *in* R_q. *An algorithm* $\mathcal{A}$ *has advantage* ϵ *in solving the* $\mathsf{DKS}^\infty_{N,q,\beta_\infty}$ *problem if*

$$|\Pr[b = 1 \mid a \leftarrow_{\$} R_q; \boldsymbol{x} \leftarrow_{\$} S_{\beta_\infty}; b \leftarrow \mathcal{A}(a, [\,a \quad 1\,] \cdot \boldsymbol{x})]$$
$$- \Pr[b = 1 \mid a \leftarrow_{\$} R_q; u \leftarrow_{\$} R_q; b \leftarrow \mathcal{A}(a, u)]| \geq \epsilon.$$

See [17,19] for more details about knapsack problems over rings.

2.3 BGV Encryption

Let $p \ll q$ be primes, let R_q and R_p be defined as above for a fixed N, let D be a bounded distribution over R_q, let $\beta_\infty \in \mathbb{N}$ be a bound and let λ be the security parameter. The (plain) BGV encryption scheme [8] consists of three algorithms: key generation (KGen), encryption (Enc) and decryption (Dec), where

- KGen samples $a \leftarrow_{\$} R_q$ uniformly at random, samples a short $s \leftarrow_{\$} S_{\beta_\infty}$ and samples noise $e \leftarrow \mathsf{D}$. It outputs keys $\mathsf{pk} = (a, b) = (a, as + pe)$ and $\mathsf{sk} = s$.
- Enc, on input pk and a message m in R_p, samples a short $r \leftarrow_{\$} S_{\beta_\infty}$, samples noise $e', e'' \leftarrow \mathsf{D}$, and outputs ciphertext $c = (u, v) = (ar + pe', br + pe'' + m)$.
- Dec, on input $\mathsf{sk} = s$ and $c = (u, v)$, outputs $m = (v - su \mod q) \mod p$.

The decryption is correct if $\max \|v - su\|_\infty = B_{\mathsf{Dec}} < \lfloor q/2 \rfloor$. The encryption scheme is CPA-secure if the $\mathsf{DKS}^\infty_{N,q,\beta}$ problem is hard for some $\beta = \beta(N, q, p, \beta_\infty)$.

2.4 Lattice-Based Commitments

Let $\mathcal{N}_{\sigma_C}$ be a Gaussian distribution over R_q with standard deviation σ_C. The commitment scheme by Baum *et al.* [6] consists of three algorithms: key generation (KGen), committing (Com) and opening (Open), where

- KGen outputs a public key pk to commit to messages in R_q. We define

$$\boldsymbol{A_1} = \begin{bmatrix} \boldsymbol{I_n} & \boldsymbol{A_1'} \end{bmatrix} \qquad \text{where } \boldsymbol{A_1'} \leftarrow_\$ R_q^{n \times (k-n)}$$
$$\boldsymbol{a_2} = \begin{bmatrix} \boldsymbol{0^n} & 1 & \boldsymbol{a_2'} \end{bmatrix} \qquad \text{where } \boldsymbol{a_2'} \leftarrow_\$ R_q^{(k-n-1)},$$

for height $n + 1$ and width k and let pk be $\boldsymbol{A} = \begin{bmatrix} \boldsymbol{A_1} \\ \boldsymbol{a_2} \end{bmatrix}$.

- Com commits to messages $m \in R_q$ by sampling $\boldsymbol{r_m} \leftarrow_\$ S_{\beta_\infty}$, and computes

$$\mathsf{Com_{pk}}(m; \boldsymbol{r_m}) = \boldsymbol{A} \cdot \boldsymbol{r_m} + \begin{bmatrix} \boldsymbol{0} \\ m \end{bmatrix} = \begin{bmatrix} \boldsymbol{c_1} \\ c_2 \end{bmatrix} = [\![m]\!].$$

Com outputs commitment $[\![m]\!]$ and opening $\boldsymbol{d} = (m, \boldsymbol{r_m}, 1)$.

- Open verifies whether $(m, \boldsymbol{r_m}, f)$, with $f \in \bar{\mathcal{C}}$, is a valid opening of $[\![m]\!]$ with respect to pk by checking that $\|\boldsymbol{r_m}[i]\|_2 \leq 4\sigma_C \sqrt{N}$, for $i \in [k]$, and if

$$f \cdot \begin{bmatrix} \boldsymbol{c_1} \\ c_2 \end{bmatrix} \overset{?}{=} \boldsymbol{A} \cdot \boldsymbol{r_m} + f \cdot \begin{bmatrix} \boldsymbol{0} \\ m \end{bmatrix}.$$

Open outputs 1 if all these conditions holds, and 0 otherwise.

The commitment scheme is hiding if the $\mathsf{DKS}_{N,q,\beta_\infty}^\infty$ problem is hard and it is binding if the $\mathsf{SKS}_{N,q,16\sigma_C\sqrt{\nu N}}^2$ problem is hard, see [6, Section 4].

2.5   Zero-Knowledge Proof of Linear Relations

Let $[\![y]\!], [\![y']\!]$ be commitments such that $y' = \alpha y + \beta$ for some public values $\alpha, \beta \in R_q$. The protocol Π_{LIN} in [4, Figure 1] is a zero-knowledge proof of knowledge, with ℓ_2 bound $B_C = 2\sigma_C\sqrt{N}$ on the responses $\boldsymbol{z_i}$, for the relation:

$$\mathcal{R}_{\mathrm{Lin}} = \left\{ (x, w) \;\middle|\; \begin{matrix} x = (\alpha, \beta, [\![y]\!], [\![y']\!]), w = (y, \boldsymbol{r_y}, \boldsymbol{r_{y'}}, f, f'): \\ \mathsf{Open}([\![y]\!], y, \boldsymbol{r_y}, f) = \mathsf{Open}([\![y']\!], \alpha \cdot y + \beta, \boldsymbol{r_{y'}}, f') = 1 \end{matrix} \right\}$$

When applying the Fiat-Shamir transform [13], we let the challenge $c \in \mathcal{C}$ be the output of a hash function applied to the full transcript. Then, we get the proof $\pi_L = (c, \boldsymbol{z_1}, \boldsymbol{z_2})$, where each $\boldsymbol{z_i}$ is of size $kN \log_2(6\sigma_C)$ bits. We can compress each $\boldsymbol{z_i}$ to get a proof of total size $2(k - n)N \log_2(6\sigma_C)$ bits by checking an approximate equality instead [4, Section 3.2]. We denote by

$$\pi_L \leftarrow \Pi_{\mathrm{LIN}}((y, \boldsymbol{r_y}, \boldsymbol{r_{y'}}, f_y, f_{y'}); (\alpha, \beta, [\![y]\!], [\![y']\!])), \text{ and}$$
$$0 \vee 1 \leftarrow \Pi_{\mathrm{LINV}}((\alpha, \beta, [\![y]\!], [\![y']\!]); \pi_L),$$

the run of the proof and verification protocols, respectively, where the verification protocol Π_{Linv} performs the checks as in the last step in [4, Figure 1] and also verifies that c was computed correctly with respect to the transcript. Π_{Lin} is a sound proof of knowledge in the ROM if the $\mathsf{SKS}_{N,q,2B_C}^2$ problem is hard.

2.6   Amortized Zero-Knowledge Proof of Bounded Openings

Let A be a publicly known $r \times v$-matrix over R_q, let $s_1, s_2, \ldots, s_\tau$ be bounded elements in R_q^v and let $As_i = t_i$ for $i \in [\tau]$. Letting S be the matrix whose columns are s_i and T be the equivalent matrix for t_i, Baum *et al.* [5] give a efficient amortized zero-knowledge proof of knowledge for the relation:

$$\mathcal{R}_A = \left\{ (x, w) \,\middle|\, \begin{array}{c} x = (A, T), w = S: \\ \forall i \in [\tau] : t_i = As_i \wedge \|s_i\|_2 \leq 2 \cdot B_A \end{array} \right\}$$

The protocol Π_A is depicted in [5, Figure 1]. We use a challenge matrix C with entries sampled from $\mathcal{C}_A = \{0, 1\}$. For security parameter λ, we define the number of parallel protocol instances to be $\hat{n} = \lambda + 2$. Denote by

$$\pi_A \leftarrow \Pi_A(S; (A, T)), \text{ and } 0 \vee 1 \leftarrow \Pi_{AV}((A, T); \pi_A),$$

the run of the proof and verification protocols, respectively, where the Π_A-protocol, using Fiat-Shamir, produces a proof of the form $\pi_A = (C, Z)$, where C is the output of a hash-function applied to the full transcript, and the Π_{AV}-protocol consists of the two checks in the last step in [5, Figure 1]. The verification bound on each column of Z is $B_A = \sqrt{2N}\sigma_A$. Note that σ_A, and also B_A, depends on the norm of S (see rejection sampling in Sect. 2.1). Hence, the bound we can prove depends on the number of equations in the statement. Π_A is a sound proof of knowledge in the ROM if $\mathrm{SKS}_{N,q,2B_A}^2$ is hard.

3   The Verifiable Decryption Protocol

The protocol is direct. The prover starts by decrypting the ciphertext (u, v) to obtain the underlying plaintext m as $m = (v - us \bmod q) \bmod p$. Then, he commits to the noise d $(= er + e'' - se')$ in the ciphertexts as $[\![d]\!]$. Finally, he proves two statements in zero-knowledge: 1) the linear relation $p[\![d]\!] = v - m - u[\![s]\!]$ holds modulo q with respect to the noise and a public commitment to the secret key, and 2) the value committed to in $[\![d]\!]$ is shorter than some bound $B < q/2p$.

More precisely, we present a proof protocol for the following relation:

$$R_{\mathrm{DEC}} = \left\{ (x, w) \,\middle|\, \begin{array}{l} x = ((a, b), [\![s]\!], (u_1, v_1), \ldots, (u_\tau, v_\tau), m_1, \ldots, m_\tau), \\ w = (s, r_s, f_s) \text{ such that } \mathrm{Open}([\![s]\!]; s, r_s, f_s) = 1 \\ \wedge \, \forall i \in [\tau] : pd_i = v_i - m_i - u_i s \wedge \|d_i\|_\infty < q/2p. \end{array} \right\}$$

Here, we assume that either a trusted dealer generated the public key and secret key together with a commitment to the secret key, or that the prover already has proved in zero-knowledge that the public key is well formed and that the secret key is committed to in $[\![s]\!]$, using any exact proof from the literature.

The verifiable decryption protocol Π_{DEC}, for prover $\mathcal{P}$, goes as following:

1. $\mathcal{P}$ takes as input a set of ciphertexts $(u_1, v_1), \ldots, (u_\tau, v_\tau)$ and $([\![s]\!], s, r_s, f_s)$.
2. $\mathcal{P}$ runs Dec on input s and (u_i, v_i) for all $i \in [\tau]$ to obtain messages $m_1, \ldots, m_\tau$.

3. $\mathcal{P}$ extracts noise d_i by computing $d_i = (v_i - m_i - u_i s)/p \mod q$ for all $i \in [\tau]$.
4. $\mathcal{P}$ commits to all d_i as $[\![d_i]\!]$, and proves $p[\![d_i]\!] = v_i - m_i - u_i[\![s]\!]$ using Π_{LIN}.
5. $\mathcal{P}$ uses protocol Π_{A} to prove that all $\|d_i\|_2$ are bounded by $B_{\mathrm{A}} \leq \sqrt{2vN}\sigma_{\mathrm{A}}$.
6. $\mathcal{P}$ outputs messages $\{m_i\}_{i=1}^{\tau}$, commitments $\{[\![d_i]\!]\}_{i=1}^{\tau}$ and proofs $\{\pi_{L_i}\}_{i=1}^{\tau}, \pi_{\mathrm{A}}$.

A verifier $\mathcal{V}$ runs the verification protocol Π_{DECV} which checks that all proofs $\{\pi_{L_i}\}_{i=1}^{\tau}$ and π_{A} are valid with respect to (a, b), $\{(u_i, v_i)\}_{i=1}^{\tau}$ and $\{m_i\}_{i=1}^{\tau}$.

Theorem 1. *The verifiable decryption protocol Π_{DEC} is a complete, sound and zero-knowledge proof protocol in the ROM for relation R_{DEC} when $B_{\mathrm{A}} < q/(4p)$.*

Proof. We argue each of the properties as following:

Completeness. It follows directly that Π_{DEC} is complete if the encryption scheme is correct, which is the case when $\|v - su\| < q/2$, and the protocols Π_{LIN} and Π_{A} are complete. Hence, we only need to make sure that $\|v - su\| < q/2$. The protocol Π_{A} guarantees that the noise is bounded as $\|d_i\|_2 \leq 2B_{\mathrm{A}}$. It follows that if $B_{\mathrm{A}} < q/(4p)$ then $\|d_i\|_{\infty} < q/2p$, and the decryption is correct.

Special Soundness. The soundness of the protocol follows directly from the underlying zero-knowledge protocols Π_{LIN} and Π_{A}. With the use of rewinding we can either extract the secret key s or the noise d_i (which reveals the secret key) or some short vectors breaking the SKS^2 problem for the given parameters.

Honest-Verifier Zero-Knowledge. The zero-knowledge property follows directly from the underlying zero-knowledge protocols Π_{LIN} and Π_{A}, which are both honest-verifier zero-knowledge. Hence, with input messages $m_1, \ldots, m_{\tau}$ we can simulate the decryption proof by sampling uniformly random values d_i, committing to them as $[\![d_i]\!]$ and then simulating all the proofs π_{L_i} and π_{A} subsequently.

$\square$

4 Performance

4.1 Parameters and Size

From the verifiable decryption protocol in Sect. 3 we get that the statement consists of τ ciphertexts (u_i, v_i) and messages m_i. Each element u_i and v_i are uniformly elements in R_q of size $N \log_2 q$ bits each. The messages are elements in R_q with coordinates modulo p, and hence, are of size $N \log_2 p$ bits. Each proof π_L are of size $2(k - n)N \log_2(6\sigma_{\mathrm{C}})$ bits, for $\sigma_{\mathrm{C}} = 11\nu\beta_{\infty}\sqrt{kN}$, and the proof π_{A} is of size $(k + 1)\hat{n}N \log_2(6\sigma_{\mathrm{A}})$ bits. However, the norm bound B_{A} depends on the number of equations being proved at once, and hence, if τ is large it is beneficial to prove smaller batches, e.g., of size N, instead of all equations at once (Table 1).

Table 1. Example parameters for the verifiable decryption protocol with more than 128 bits of security against quantum adversaries ensuring correct decryption for honestly generated ciphertexts. Rejection sampling success probability is set to be $\approx 1/3$.

p	q	N	β_∞	M	k	n	$\hat{n}$	ν	σ_C	B_C	σ_A	B_A
2	$\approx 2^{44}$	2048	1	3	3	1	130	36	$\approx 2^{15.9}$	$\approx 2^{22.4}$	$\approx 2^{28}$	$\approx 2^{40.5}$

As a concrete example, we set $p = 2$, $\beta_\infty = 1$ and let D be the ternary distribution over R_q. It then follows that, for honestly generated ciphertexts, $\|v - us\|_\infty \leq p(2N + 1)$. Furthermore, we get the following bound for $\|d_i\|_\infty$:

$$\|d_i\|_\infty \leq 2B_A = \sqrt{8N}\sigma_A \leq \sqrt{8N} \cdot 0.675 \left\|\mathbf{S'C'}\right\|_2 \leq 2\sqrt{N} \cdot \left\|\mathbf{S'}\right\|_1 \left\|\mathbf{C'}\right\|_\infty$$
$$\leq 2\sqrt{N} \cdot (\beta_\infty kN + p(2N + 1)N)\tau.$$

Thus, setting $k = 3, n = 1, \hat{n} = 130, \nu = 36$ and $\tau = N = 2048$ gives us $\|d_i\|_\infty \leq 2^{41.5}$, and we can safely set $q \approx 2^{44}$ to get correctness. We claim more than 128 bits security against a quantum adversary for these parameters using the LWE estimator by Albrecht *et al.* [3] with the **BKZ.qsieve** cost model. A smaller N results in smaller noise, but the size of q would give lower security (Table 2).

Table 2. Sizes for parameters $p = 2, q \approx 2^{44}$ and $N = 2048$ computing proof $\pi_{\text{DEC}} = (\{[\![d_i]\!], \pi_{L_i}\}_{i=1}^\tau, \pi_A)$, where shortness proofs π_A is amortized over batches of size 2048.

Message m_i	Ciphertext (u_i, v_i)	Commitment $[\![d_i]\!]$	Proof π_{L_i}	Proof π_A	Proof π_{DEC}
0.256 KB	22.6 KB	22.6 KB	19 KB	2τ KB	43.6τ KB

4.2 Implementation and Timings

We provide a proof-of-concept implementation of our protocol in C++ using the NTL-library [20]. The implementation was benchmarked on an Intel Core i5 running at 2.3GHz with 16 GB RAM. The timings are given in Table 3. The implementation is very simple, consists of a total of 350 lines of code, and is available online[1]. A comparison of NTL to NFLlib [2] indicates that an optimized implementation could provide speedup by an order of magnitude.

---

[1] github.com/tjesi/verifiable-decryption-BGV.

Table 3. Amortized time per instance over $\tau = 2048$ ciphertexts.

Noise $[\![d_i]\!]$	Proof Π_{LIN}	Verification Π_{LINV}	Proof Π_{A}	Verification Π_{AV}	Proof π_{DEC}
5τ ms	47τ ms	12τ ms	24τ ms	12τ ms	76τ ms

4.3 Comparison

We compare to the verifiable decryption protocols by Lyubashevsky *et al.* [18] and Gjøsteen *et al.* [14]. As noted by [14, Section 8], the protocol by Boschini *et al.* [7] give proof sizes of approximate 90 KB, which is roughly twice the size of π_{DEC}. Furthermore, the run time is several minutes per ciphertext, which would deem it unusable for larger sets of ciphertexts.

Comparison to Lyubashevsky *et al.* (PKC 2021). They give a verifiable decryption protocol for the Kyber encapsulation scheme for a ring of dimension $N = 256$ and modulus $q = 3329$ with secret and noise values bounded by $\beta_\infty = 2$. The proof of correct decryption is of size 43.6 KB. We observe that our proof is of exactly the same size but with a plaintext space of 2048 bits instead of only 256 bits. We expect our proof size to be smaller than theirs for ciphertexts encoding larger messages, but note that they can provide efficient proofs for single ciphertexts for small moduli while our protocol is only efficient in the amortized setting for ciphertext moduli at least 44 bits. Furthermore, our protocol is much simpler, as [18] make use of partially splitting rings and automorphisms by combining proofs of multiplication and range proofs – making the protocol difficult to implement in practice. They do not provide timings.

Comparison to Gjøsteen *et al.* (ACISP 2022). They give a verifiable decryption protocol Π_{ZKPCD} for the BGV encryption scheme. However, because of their noise drowning techniques, they are forced to use a moduli of at least $q \approx 2^{55}$. Their proof size is also depending on the soundness parameter λ, giving a proof of size 14λ KB per ciphertext. For an interactive protocol with $\lambda = 10$ they get a proof of size 3.2× larger than our proof, and for a non-interactive protocol with $\lambda = 128$ their proof size is 41× larger than ours. They have implemented their protocol, and give a cost of at least 4λ ms per ciphertext using NTL, which is similar to our protocol for $\lambda = 19$ and otherwise slower.

They also sketch a protocol Π_{DistDec} [14, Section 8], requiring $q \approx 2^{78}$ and $N = 4096$. This protocol gives a proof of size ≈ 363 KB per ciphertext, a factor 8 larger than our proof. They do not provide timings for this protocol.

References

1. Adida, B.: Helios: web-based open-audit voting. In: van Oorschot, P.C. (ed.) USENIX Security 2008, pp. 335–348. USENIX Association (2008)
2. Aguilar-Melchor, C., Barrier, J., Guelton, S., Guinet, A., Killijian, M.-O., Lepoint, T.: NFLlib: NTT-based fast lattice library. In: Sako, K. (ed.) CT-RSA 2016. LNCS, vol. 9610, pp. 341–356. Springer, Cham (2016). https://doi.org/10.1007/978-3-319-29485-8_20

3. Albrecht, M.R., Player, R., Scott, S.: On the concrete hardness of learning with errors. J. Math. Cryptol. **9**(3), 169–203 (2015)
4. Aranha, D.F., Baum, C., Gjøsteen, K., Silde, T., Tunge, T.: Lattice-based proof of shuffle and applications to electronic voting. In: Paterson, K.G. (ed.) CT-RSA 2021. LNCS, vol. 12704, pp. 227–251. Springer, Cham (2021). https://doi.org/10.1007/978-3-030-75539-3_10
5. Baum, C., Bootle, J., Cerulli, A., del Pino, R., Groth, J., Lyubashevsky, V.: Sublinear lattice-based zero-knowledge arguments for arithmetic circuits. In: Shacham, H., Boldyreva, A. (eds.) CRYPTO 2018. LNCS, vol. 10992, pp. 669–699. Springer, Cham (2018). https://doi.org/10.1007/978-3-319-96881-0_23
6. Baum, C., Damgård, I., Lyubashevsky, V., Oechsner, S., Peikert, C.: More efficient commitments from structured lattice assumptions. In: Catalano, D., De Prisco, R. (eds.) SCN 2018. LNCS, vol. 11035, pp. 368–385. Springer, Cham (2018). https://doi.org/10.1007/978-3-319-98113-0_20
7. Boschini, C., Camenisch, J., Ovsiankin, M., Spooner, N.: Efficient post-quantum SNARKs for RSIS and RLWE and their applications to privacy. In: Ding, J., Tillich, J.-P. (eds.) PQCrypto 2020. LNCS, vol. 12100, pp. 247–267. Springer, Cham (2020). https://doi.org/10.1007/978-3-030-44223-1_14
8. Brakerski, Z., Gentry, C., Vaikuntanathan, V.: (Leveled) fully homomorphic encryption without bootstrapping. In: Goldwasser, S. (ed.) ITCS 2012, pp. 309–325. ACM (2012). https://doi.org/10.1145/2090236.2090262
9. Camenisch, J., Shoup, V.: Practical verifiable encryption and decryption of discrete logarithms. In: Boneh, D. (ed.) CRYPTO 2003. LNCS, vol. 2729, pp. 126–144. Springer, Heidelberg (2003). https://doi.org/10.1007/978-3-540-45146-4_8
10. Corrigan-Gibbs, H., Wolinsky, D.I., Ford, B.: Proactively accountable anonymous messaging in verdict. In: King, S.T. (ed.) USENIX Security 2013, pp. 147–162. USENIX Association (2013)
11. Costa, N., Martínez, R., Morillo, P.: Lattice-based proof of a shuffle. In: Bracciali, A., Clark, J., Pintore, F., Rønne, P.B., Sala, M. (eds.) FC 2019. LNCS, vol. 11599, pp. 330–346. Springer, Cham (2020). https://doi.org/10.1007/978-3-030-43725-1_23
12. Farzaliyev, V., Willemson, J., Kaasik, J.K.: Improved lattice-based mix-nets for electronic voting. Cryptology ePrint Archive, Report 2021/1499 (2021). https://ia.cr/2021/1499
13. Fiat, A., Shamir, A.: How to prove yourself: practical solutions to identification and signature problems. In: Odlyzko, A.M. (ed.) CRYPTO 1986. LNCS, vol. 263, pp. 186–194. Springer, Heidelberg (1987). https://doi.org/10.1007/3-540-47721-7_12
14. Gjøsteen, K., Haines, T., Müller, J., Rønne, P., Silde, T.: Verifiable decryption in the head. In: Nguyen, K., Yang, G., Guo, F., Susilo, W. (eds.) Information Security and Privacy, ACISP 2022, vol. 13494, pp. 355–374. Springer, Cham (2022). https://doi.org/10.1007/978-3-031-22301-3_18, https://eprint.iacr.org/2021/558.pdf
15. Haines, T., Müller, J.: SoK: techniques for verifiable mix nets. In: Jia, L., Küsters, R. (eds.) CSF 2020 Computer Security Foundations Symposium, pp. 49–64. IEEE Computer Society Press (2020). https://doi.org/10.1109/CSF49147.2020.00012
16. Luo, F., Wang, K.: Verifiable decryption for fully homomorphic encryption. In: Chen, L., Manulis, M., Schneider, S. (eds.) ISC 2018. LNCS, vol. 11060, pp. 347–365. Springer, Cham (2018). https://doi.org/10.1007/978-3-319-99136-8_19
17. Lyubashevsky, V., Micciancio, D.: Generalized compact knapsacks are collision resistant. In: Bugliesi, M., Preneel, B., Sassone, V., Wegener, I. (eds.) ICALP 2006. LNCS, vol. 4052, pp. 144–155. Springer, Heidelberg (2006). https://doi.org/10.1007/11787006_13

18. Lyubashevsky, V., Nguyen, N.K., Seiler, G.: Shorter lattice-based zero-knowledge proofs via one-time commitments. In: Garay, J.A. (ed.) PKC 2021. LNCS, vol. 12710, pp. 215–241. Springer, Cham (2021). https://doi.org/10.1007/978-3-030-75245-3_9
19. Lyubashevsky, V., Peikert, C., Regev, O.: On ideal lattices and learning with errors over rings. In: Gilbert, H. (ed.) EUROCRYPT 2010. LNCS, vol. 6110, pp. 1–23. Springer, Heidelberg (2010). https://doi.org/10.1007/978-3-642-13190-5_1
20. Shoup, V.: Ntl: A library for doing number theory (2021). https://libntl.org/index.html

RemoteVote and SAFE Vote: Towards Usable End-to-End Verification for Vote-by-Mail

Braden L. Crimmins[✉], Marshall Rhea, and J. Alex Halderman

University of Michigan, Ann Arbor, USA
bradenlc@umich.edu

Abstract. Postal voting is growing rapidly in the U.S., with 43% of voters casting ballots by mail in 2020, yet until recently there has been little research about extending the protections of end-to-end verifiable (E2E-V) election schemes to vote-by-mail contexts. The first—and to date, only—framework to focus on this setting is STROBE, which has important usability limitations. In this work, we present two approaches, RemoteVote and SAFE Vote, that allow mail-in voters to benefit from E2E-V without changing the voter experience for those who choose not to participate in verification. To evaluate these systems and compare them with STROBE, we consider an expansive set of properties, including novel attributes of usability and verifiability, several of which have applicability beyond vote-by-mail contexts. We hope that our work will help catalyze further progress towards universal applicability of E2E-V for real-world elections.

1 Introduction

In the 2020 U.S. presidential election, 43% of voters cast their ballot by mail, twice as many as four years prior [24]. Although this increase was magnified by the COVID-19 pandemic, it follows on a long-term trend towards greater use of vote by mail [23]. At least 34 states have adopted policies allowing any voter to participate by mail with no excuse, and seven of these states automatically send a mail-in ballot to every voter [19]. These changes make voting by mail a fundamental part of U.S. election administration, and one that is essential to secure. Indeed, corrupting only vote-by-mail ballots would likely have allowed outcome-changing fraud in every U.S. presidential election since the turn of the century.

While end-to-end verifiable voting systems (e.g., [1,10,22,25]) show promise for assuring election integrity, most E2E-V schemes are intended for online or in-person voting and cannot easily be adapted to secure votes cast by mail. In fact, until the recent introduction of STROBE Voting by Benaloh [5], vote by mail (VbM) systems were largely absent from the verifiable voting literature.[1]

---

[1] Remotegrity [25], which is sometimes cited as a vote-by-mail election system, relies on voters casting their ballots over the Internet after receiving them in the mail.

© International Financial Cryptography Association 2023
S. Matsuo et al. (Eds.): FC 2022 Workshops, LNCS 13412, pp. 391–406, 2023.
https://doi.org/10.1007/978-3-031-32415-4_27

We introduce two novel E2E-V systems, RemoteVote and SAFE Vote, that are designed to enable end-to-end verifiable U.S.-style postal voting while improving on aspects of usability and other desirable properties compared to STROBE. To evaluate our schemes and earlier VbM E2E-V proposals, we consider an expansive set of properties, including novel attributes of usability and verifiability. Several of these properties have applicability to systems outside of a VbM context. Lastly, we present a hybrid system that combines ideas from our two schemes and provides more of these properties than any other design known to the authors, although this comes at the expense of reduced practicality. We hope our work will advance the state of knowledge about E2E-V closer to systems that are suitable for deployment in real vote-by-mail elections.

2   Related Work: STROBE

Benaloh's STROBE Voting [5] is a significant step towards achieving verifiable VbM, and identifies the primary difficulty of designing such a system: the unique limitations on communication between the voter and the election authority.

Many verifiable voting systems rely on the Benaloh challenge [3,18], a type of interactive proof that a voter can perform to check the honesty of the encrypting authority. Classically, this mechanism applies to in-person or Internet voting settings, where the voter can perform the interactive step and receive a response immediately. In VbM contexts, however, the only private communication channel between the voter and the election authority is the extremely-high-latency postal system, which imposes a difficult constraint on any kind of interactive challenge.

Nevertheless, STROBE proposes an interactive procedure that is suitable for VbM settings. First, the election authority precomputes multiple encryptions to be sent to the voter and communicates them through the initial ballot delivery. Then, the voter chooses a set of encryptions to use and communicates this choice through the return of their voted ballot. The authority completes the challenge process by posting the decryptions of all spoiled ballots to a public bulletin board.

This design represents a significant advance towards achieving verifiable VbM elections. Even still, as Benaloh acknowledges, there are some important practical drawbacks; in its basic form, for example, STROBE requires that each voter be sent two ballots and only be permitted to cast one. Several concerns are immediately apparent, such as the added printing and mailing costs and the potential for distrust or confusion when voters receive multiple ballots.[2]

Other concerns are more subtle. Suppose, for example, that a cache of ballots are returned but not processed, and the encryptions are spoiled before the mistake is discovered.[3] Those voters lose either their privacy or their ability to validate the election outcome. Alternately, suppose both ballots in a twin set

---

[2] Considerable confusion occurred when voters were merely sent multiple vote-by-mail ballot *applications* in some U.S. jurisdictions during the 2020 election cycle [11,14].

[3] Such incidents are not uncommon, as illustrated by initially uncounted ballots uncovered during Georgia's recount following the 2020 presidential election [8].

are cast. What recourse exists? This might occur due to attempted fraud by the voter, but it could equally well be the result of a misunderstanding of the system. Even if the system isn't misunderstood, it could still be an innocent mistake; for example, two members of a household might accidentally vote both ballots belonging to one of their sets and neither ballot belonging to the other. Counting both ballots would produce false evidence of fraud, because any observer could see that two twin ballots were both returned and counted. Failing to count both ballots disenfranchises one of the two voters. Neither outcome is desirable.

The STROBE paper also proposes an alternative implementation that resolves these concerns by representing two sets of encryptions on a single phys-ical ballot, but this introduces problems of its own. For example, because the ballot is returned before the spoil process occurs, a corrupt election authority would have custody of all evidence of its malfeasance at the time it is revealed. Another concern comes from deciding which set of encryptions should be used; implicit mechanisms for choosing a column to spoil can be easily forged or manip-ulated by a corrupt authority, while explicit mechanisms leak information about who has participated in verification, which could facilitate targeted cheating in subsequent elections.

The ideas underlying STROBE are strong, and indeed a modified version forms the basis of one of our proposals, but further advances will be required for any E2E-V system to be practically usable in real VbM elections. We hope that the two schemes we propose represent progress in that direction.

3 Desirable Properties

To evaluate our proposed schemes and compare them to existing designs, we introduce a set of desirable properties, ranging from attributes of the verification procedures to aspects of usability. Properties that are novel (to our knowledge) are **bolded and italicized** when first introduced.

3.1 End-to-End Verifiability

A common goal of election system design is **end-to-end verifiability**. Systems with this property seek to provide public guarantees that the election result is accurate without relying on trust in the administering authorities. There are three main subproperties that an E2E-V system must have [6]:

Cast as Intended means that a voter can be confident their choices were accurately received by the election authority.

Counted as Cast means any observer can be confident that all choices received by the election authority were tallied correctly in the final result. (This is sometimes split into **collected-as-cast** and **counted-as-collected** [7].)

Eligibility Verifiability means observers can verify that only eligible votes were included in the tally [7], preventing threats like ballot-box stuffing and multiple voting. Many jurisdictions provide this property to some degree through the post-election publication of a list identifying all those who cast a ballot. This allows observers to validate that the number of votes is equal to the number of voters and (at least in principle) that all voters were eligible.[4]

When considering claims of verifiability, it is similarly important to understand who can actually perform the verification for each element of the system:

Universal Verifiability means that any observer can single-handedly verify the property across the entire election [16]. Typically, *counted-as-cast* and *eligibility verifiability* are universally verifiable in E2E-V designs.

Individual Verifiability means that a voter can verify the correct behavior occurred for their own ballot [16]. Typically, *cast-as-intended* is individually verifiable in E2E-V designs. Mechanisms for *universal cast-as-intended* exist [13], but those are beyond the scope of this paper.

Collective Verifiability means that voters can collaborate with each other to verify the system's integrity. Consider a design in which a voter can gain a certain level of confidence (e.g., 50%) that their ballot encryption is honest, but cannot individually increase their confidence beyond that level. Through collaboration with other mutually-trusting voters, each with their own independent partial confidences, these voters can jointly confirm the honesty of the system to asymptotically high degrees of collective confidence.

3.2 Privacy Properties

Another key goal of election system design is to ensure voter privacy. What precisely "privacy" means, however, depends heavily on the threat model, giving rise to a series of properties intended to address different threats:

Ballot Secrecy means that a system does not leak information about voters' choices beyond that which can be deduced from the election result [7].

Receipt Freeness further means a voter cannot prove their choices to a third party after voting and casting their ballot privately[5], even if the voter actively attempts to aid in the construction of such a proof. This has historically been intended as a defense against vote buying [7].

Everlasting Privacy means that a system does not rely on assumptions about cryptographic hardness to provide the two preceding properties. If we do rely on such assumptions, a weakness in the encryption systems used—even if discovered decades later—could reveal voters' choices in previous elections [20].

---

[4] Despite its importance, this property is often ignored in the E2E-V literature, since it is primarily accomplished by existing procedural controls, rather than cryptography.

[5] That the voter must cast their ballot *privately* is implicit in most articulations of receipt freeness, which entertain only supervised voting at the polling place. Failing to articulate it in a VbM context, however, blurs the line with other stronger properties such as coercion resistance. If a voter is compelled to surrender their voted ballot and signed envelope to a coercer, this would "prove their choices to a third party," but substantively this attack is better identified as a failure of coercion resistance.

We further use the more nuanced terms *everlasting ballot secrecy* and *everlasting receipt freeness* to reason about systems that might only provide one of the two traits if cryptographic hardness assumptions fail.

Coercion Resistance means the system ensures no voter can be compelled to exhibit certain voting behavior. Complete definitions entertain not only forcing a voter to choose a favored candidate, but also forcing them to abstain or to randomize their ballot, which would enable targeted disenfranchisement [7].

3.3 Usability Properties

The importance of usability is well recognized in voting system design, and past failures on this front have had enormous consequences.[6] Nevertheless, voting system usability has not been formalized in the same way as other E2E-V properties. Here we attempt to define aspects of usability that can be used to discuss and compare systems (albeit with some room for subjective interpretation):

Ignorability means that a voter can ignore the novel elements of the system and "vote like normal" without compromising the integrity or privacy of their vote; they simply will not be a participant in the verification process.

Harmlessness more strongly means that a voter cannot compromise the integrity or privacy of their vote even if they engage improperly with the system's novel elements. It should not be possible, for example, to inadvertently spoil a ballot by making a mistake involving the verification features.

Selection Consistency means that a voter's selections on their ballot will be directly reflected by the evidence that their vote was *cast-as-intended*, for example in a shortcode receipt that corresponds directly to the markings they made. This property aims to prevent illusory discrepancies, like those that might arise when a ballot is processed before the evidence is generated, which might otherwise create the appearance of fraud where none exists.[7]

3.4 Error Handling Properties

Many election systems are premised, either implicitly or explicitly, on assuming the election was error-free and designing proofs that convince observers of that fact. It is equally important, however, to entertain the possibility that errors might occur and consider how the system might handle them. The following three properties deal with identifying and addressing these errors if they occur.

---

[6] See, for example, the usability failures of "butterfly ballot" punch card systems, which some believe altered the outcome of the 2000 U.S. presidential election [15].

[7] For example, in a jurisdiction which permits straight-ticket voting with contest-specific overrides, the voter may expect to see a commitment to the selections they made, while a homomorphic-tallying election system would instead generate a commitment to the interpreted result of those selections after the straight-ticket rule was applied.

Software Independence means that an undetected error in election software or hardware cannot create an undetectable error in the election's outcome [21]. This means that no malicious software can alter the outcome undetected when there exists a dedicated and trustworthy observer.

Strong Software Independence additionally means that when such an error is discovered, the true result can be recovered without rerunning the election [21], for instance by hand-counting the original paper ballots.

Dispute Resolution means that if a voter accuses an authority of dishonesty, a third party can unambiguously determine whether or not it is true [2]. An important subproperty is **collection accountability**, which means a voter can prove it if the authority misrepresents their choice in the public tally [7].

3.5 Verification Process Properties

Verification processes involve a series of checks that have properties and side effects of their own. We explicitly define these properties here, since they can have substantial implications for the reliability of the system in application:

Advance Verification means that all verification mechanisms can be exercised before the election results are computed. This helps to remove some improper incentives; if an individual must allege fraud before they learn the favorability of the outcome, the political motivation to make false reports is decreased.

Discretionary Verification means that voters are able to choose at will which elements of the system they would like to verify. This eliminates reliance on external decisional systems and allows voters to trust only their own agency. If voters are able to select arbitrary ballots to challenge for a given audit procedure, this is an example of discretionary verification. If instead the ballots are selected by some other process—for example, at random, even through some publicly accountable mechanism—the property is lost.

Independent Verification means that the verification mechanism can be used by an individual voter or observer without participation from the system itself. This forestalls attacks in which a cheating authority feigns inability to cooperate with the challenge process (e.g., by pretending a DDoS attack is preventing voters from logging challenge requests on a public bulletin board). It also reduces the risk due to real logistical problems during the election.

Unobservable Verification means that no adversary can become convinced that a given individual abstained from the verification process. If the adversary is able to learn who abstains, and they monitor this over several elections, they can target later ballot manipulation toward voters who are least likely to detect the fraud. Note that the adversary can learn the identities of *some* of those who engage in the verification process, but not the identities of *everyone* who does, since that would reveal exactly who does not verify.

3.6 Compatibility Properties

E2E-V schemes vary in what modes of voting and what counting methods they support. We consider two aspects of such compatibility:

Vote-by-Mail Compatibility means that a system can provide its intended security properties to voters whose only private communication channel with the election authority is postal mail, although such voters are assumed to also have access to publicly broadcast information.

Complexity Tolerance means that a system enables arbitrary computations on anonymized vote data without compromising security guarantees. Systems with this property can implement any computable tallying system, such as instant-runoff voting. Implementations without this property, including homomorphic systems, are limited in what voting methods they can support.

4   Our Proposed Schemes

Our schemes use a similar approach to STROBE [5]. At a high level, every voter is given a ballot with a unique ID and seemingly random shortcodes beside each candidate. When voting, they can record this ID and the shortcodes corresponding to their choices. The authority posts this same information to a public bulletin board for every ballot they collect, and voters can confirm this "receipt" matches what they recorded to be confident their votes were counted correctly.

There are similarities behind the scenes, too. As with STROBE, we use ElGamal threshold encoding to create a homomorphic encryption for each choice available to the voter.[8] We also generate a shortcode for each candidate that commits to the encryption, such that the mapping between codes and candidates is only known to the voter but observers can use the published shortcode receipt to verify the election tally. Lastly, we generate a single longcode that commits to the encryptions without revealing the candidates they correspond to.

We also introduce a series of departures and enhancements compared to the STROBE framework. First, when we tally votes for a contest, we do it in a two-stage process. We begin by homomorphically tallying each individual voter's choices within the contest to generate a single encryption per ballot cast. We then run these encryptions through a verifiable anonymizing mixnet (e.g., [4,9]) then decrypt and process them in the clear. This means we can represent candidates with a single binary flag each, denoting either that they were selected or were not. Also, there is no need for STROBE's non-interactive zero knowledge proofs that each encryption contains a valid vote; any issues will be recognized when the decryption process occurs, and can affect at most a single voter. The ordinary challenge process suffices to address this risk. A final advantage is that this approach enables *selection consistency* and *complexity tolerance*; because we process the data in the clear, we support arbitrary computation on voters' anonymized

---

[8] Like STROBE, we include abstentions and undervotes within the meaning of "choice." For this reason, in a contest where the voter can select k candidates, we produce k encryptions representing abstentions in addition to the ones representing selected candidates. This way, all choices—including abstentions and undervotes—can be represented as the sum of k encryptions, and are therefore indistinguishable.

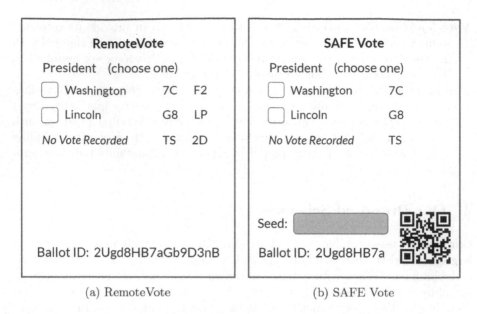

(a) RemoteVote

(b) SAFE Vote

Fig. 1. Ballot designs for our two proposed schemes.

choices and therefore support arbitrary tallying mechanisms. STROBE, by contrast, relies on homomorphism to compute the result, which means it cannot support voting systems that use more complicated tallying methods and cannot always directly represent a voter's selections in the published shortcode receipts.

Second, when we generate our encryptions, we use a random value R to seed a PRNG, and use the output to seed ElGamal for every encryption on a given ballot. This way, revealing R to a voter allows them to reconstruct all the encryptions on their ballot, a property used in SAFE Vote's challenge process.

Third, we do not directly reveal the encryptions involved in our system to the public. Instead, we derive perfectly hiding commitments to these encryptions via the PPATS mechanism introduced in [12] and further elaborated on in [20]. This system is an example of a *commitment consistent encryption* (CCE) scheme, which allows the creation of commitments that can be used as a one-to-one stand-in for encryptions in a homomorphic tally or mixnet, then can be "opened" to the underlying encryption value once they are tallied or anonymized. These commitments offer information theoretic privacy [20], which means the privacy properties remain even if all modern cryptographic assumptions fail. We generate these commitments immediately after generating our encryptions and use them—rather than the encryptions themselves—to derive shortcodes and ballot IDs. After the mixnet step in our tallying, we open the commitments to the underlying encryptions before decrypting. The process is otherwise as previously described.[9] Note that each commitment requires 256 bits of true randomness to generate, which is retained privately by the election authority for use in the tallying process.

Fourth, and lastly, we commit to each encrypted ballot in advance of the election. This means posting the commitments, shortcodes, and ballot ID of each ballot when it is first generated.[10] This is not strictly a difference from STROBE, as this early commitment is still possible in the original design. It is essential for RemoteVote's challenge process, however, and so is important to specify here.

4.1   RemoteVote

RemoteVote ballots (Fig. 1a) look identical to those of single-ballot STROBE, but the challenge process is markedly different. While STROBE attempts to facilitate an interactive challenge through limited communication channels, RemoteVote abandons the idea of interactivity altogether.

This means we sacrifice *discretionary auditing*, but in exchange we gain a number of other valuable properties. Notably, we can perform the challenge process when voters still have custody of their ballots, giving a greater degree of *dispute resolution*. There is also no way for the authority to be confident that any voter abstained from this process, giving *unobservable verifiability*. Recall too that in single-ballot STROBE, the election authority could simply ignore the preference of the voter and spoil whichever column it wanted. In our design, this is no longer the case; compliance with the spoiling procedure is *universally verifiable*.

To implement this scheme, we begin by pairing encrypted ballots.[11] We commit to these pairings by posting them to a public bulletin board and generating a single combined ID from their two longcodes. The paired set is printed on a single physical ballot such that there are two columns of shortcodes beside the candidates' names, one column corresponding to each encrypted ballot. The ballot ID is printed at the bottom of each ballot in human-readable form.

After the ballots are delivered to voters, randomness is generated in a publicly accountable manner (e.g., [17]) and used to deterministically select one column to spoil for each ballot.[12] The secret information for that column's encrypted ballot is posted publicly alongside all the rest of the ballot pair's public information,

---

[9] Using CCEs to implement both a homomorphic and mixnet tallying step is usually infeasible for large-scale elections [12]. However, because the format of possible votes is highly predictable, an exhaustive search of plaintexts is easy, and decryption becomes cheap enough that we can use the PPATS system for both.

[10] Alternately, we can simply post the commitments (which can be used to derive the rest of the information), but posting everything makes the process easier for observers.

[11] Pairs should be constructed such that there is no shortcode collision within a contest.

[12] One effective heuristic would be hashing the randomness with the ballot ID and selecting a column based on the resulting hash's parity.

where it can be accessed at will by third parties. These observers can then validate that the column's encryptions and commitments were all well formed.

With the newly public information, a voter can apply a trusted third-party system to generate a partial image for their ballot based on its ID. This image would display one column of expected shortcodes next to the appropriate candidates, and by validating this against the ballot they were sent, the voter can be sure that the spoiled column of shortcodes represented an accurate set of encryptions. Provided the voter trusts the public randomness, they know that a forged encryption on their ballot would have had a 50% chance of being revealed.[13] This provides *collective verifiability*, because many audits at 50% confidence quickly scale to ensure any large-scale fraud would be detected.

The voter can then vote like normal (*ignorability* and *harmlessness*), return their ballot, and optionally watch that one of the two shortcodes beside each selected candidate appears for the proper contest. Whether that shortcode is from the correct column can be validated by anyone else, because the spoiling of the challenged column is *universally verifiable*.

4.2   SAFE Vote

Scratch Auditing for Fair Elections (SAFE) Vote is an alternate approach that attempts to preserve the interactivity of the challenge process while resolving some of STROBE's other issues. We accomplish this by including a physical challenge mechanism on each ballot. This maintains *discretionary auditing*, but also incorporates *independent auditing* and ensures that the challenge process provides immediate evidence as to whether or not a discrepancy was uncovered. Like RemoteVote, this occurs when the ballot is still in the voter's custody, giving *dispute resolution* through physical evidence of potential fraud.

SAFE Vote ballots (Fig. 1b) contain four special features:

1. Each option has a single corresponding shortcode printed beside it.
2. The longcode is printed as the ballot ID.
3. The value of R is printed on the ballot and concealed by a scratch-off surface.
4. The ballot includes a large QR code, which, when decrypted using R as the key, provides the true randomness used to generate the ballot's commitments.[14]

These modifications can be ignored by voters who do not choose to participate in the verification process, but they enable voters to independently audit the ballot's encryptions if they desire. To do so, voters would remove the scratch-off

---

[13] Even if the voter does not trust the *entire* public randomness, they can still have confidence in this system. Only one in 2^{2^n} possible pairings would be fully resistant to detection, where n is the number of trustworthy bits. Validating that a particular pairing belongs to that set would require computing 2^n hashes if the challenge heuristic uses a secure hash function. This means that an attack on encryption integrity is computationally infeasible for any meaningful number of trustworthy random bits.

[14] Recall that 256 bits of true randomness are necessary per commitment.

surface, revealing R. Trusted third-party software can use this R value along with the QR code to reproduce the ballot's shortcodes and ID in full, and the voter can compare the output against the ballot they were sent. If there are no inconsistencies, voters can be confident that their ballot was correctly encrypted. They can then request a replacement and repeat the challenge as many times as they like, until they are satisfied with the encryptions and cast a ballot.[15]

Ballots received in this system should be processed just as with STROBE, with one exception: in the event that a voter returns a ballot with a removed scratch-off surface, no shortcode receipt should be published. Providing such a receipt when R had been revealed would violate the property of *receipt freeness*, since the two pieces of information combined would reveal the choices of the voter. Instead, the election authority should make a post to the bulletin board identifying that the ballot had its scratch-off removed. The voter's choices should then be transcribed faithfully onto a new encrypted ballot by a multipartisan ballot duplication team, like those currently employed in absent voter counting boards across the country. This new ballot can be cast as normal, so that the voter's selections still appear in the public tally. This ensures that the addition of the system's novel properties cannot introduce new sources of disenfranchising voter error, thereby providing the property of *harmlessness* to our scheme (Fig. 2).[16]

5   Extensions

5.1   Collection Accountability

So far, our schemes lack *collection accountability*, which is vital for *dispute resolution*. It requires that voters be able to prove which commitments they selected, so a corrupt authority cannot misrepresent their choices on the bulletin board.

We can extend our schemes to accomplish this by allowing voters who select a candidate to learn a portion of the corresponding encryption through some mechanism like Remotegrity's scratch-off surfaces [25]. Then, if the election authority posts the wrong shortcodes to the bulletin board, the voter can identify the commitments they actually selected and provide the information about the secret encryptions underlying those commitments as evidence of their choice.

Because no observers are able to verify that the partial encryptions the voter presents are legitimate, this proof must be interactive. After the voter presents the information, the authority can open the commitment to the true underlying encryption—which should be inconsistent with the voter's claim—and present a non-interactive zero-knowledge proof that the opened encryption is a valid vote. If the authority is unable to do so, the challenge is presumably valid.

---

[15] Voters may also simply request multiple ballots up front, if policy permits.

[16] This also introduces the risk that an adversary might change the voter's selections and remove the scratch-off surface to eliminate any direct evidence that the change occurred. A potential solution might be to introduce a grace period where voters who notice their ballots were duplicated in this process can instead spoil them and revote.

Initial Preparation (both schemes):
1. Generate election paramters and vote data
2. For each ballot:
   (a) Roll random R to seed ElGamal
   (b) Encrypt each piece of vote data
   (c) Gen. CCE com'ts to the encryptions
   (d) Gen. shortcodes/longcode from com'ts

RemoteVote Preparation:
1. Pair ballots, avoiding shortcode collisions
2. For each pair:
   (a) Compute ballot ID := Hash(longcodes)
   (b) Publish ID, longcodes, com'ts, shortcodes
   (c) Print ballot (2 shortcode cols., ballot ID)
3. Send ballots to voters

RemoteVote Audit Process:
1. After voters receive ballots,
   R_p := pub. randomness
2. For each ballot, Hash(R_p ‖ ballot ID):
   – If even, publish secret data for col. 1
   – If odd, publish secret data for col. 2
3. Observers can then:
   (a) determine if correct column was spoiled
   (b) associate spoiled shortcodes with cands
4. Voter compares association with their ballot.
   If discrepancy, raise error; else, cast normally

SAFE Vote Preparation:
1. For each ballot:
   (a) Publish longcode, com'ts, shortcodes
   (b) Print ballot (column of shortcodes,
       longcode printed as ballot ID,
       random R beneath scratch-off,
       QR code := Enc(R, commit rand.))
2. Send ballots to voters

SAFE Vote Audit Process:
1. Voter optionally reveals scratch off, then:
   (a) Uses R and QR code to generate full
       ballot image
   (b) Compares with printed shortcodes and
       ballot ID. If okay, encryptions honest
   (c) Requests replacement ballot, repeats
2. Else, voter casts ballot as normal

Ballot Return/Counting (both schemes):
1. Authority receives/validates ballot, then
   publishes ballot ID and selected shortcodes
2. Voter optionally compares w/ their choices
3. Homomorphically tally choices by contest
4. Anonymize aggregated com'ts via mixnet
5. Open com'ts, decrypt, and process in clear
6. Observers validate announced result

Fig. 2. Procedures for initial setup, verification, and counting in our two schemes.

Note that the strength of this proof depends on the integrity of the hiding mechanism. If the encryption for a given candidate became known to an attacker improperly—say by using advanced imaging technology, compromising the printer, or simply by revealing all the information on a ballot and then counterfeiting a new one where the information was still hidden—they could use it to wrongfully implicate the authority for malfeasance. This increases the difficulty of making false allegations, but it may make them more persuasive when well executed.

There are a number of trade-offs associated with this modification. For one, we would lose *everlasting receipt freeness*, because a voter could make a false challenge claiming they selected a commitment they really did not. The election authority would then open this commitment to disprove the claim, revealing the encryption underneath. This allows the voter to produce a receipt that would reveal a candidate they did *not* select once cryptographic assumptions fail.[17]

Additionally, if a voter made a selection and then changed their mind, they would have evidence they could use to falsely implicate an honest authority, but forbidding them from undoing a marking loses *harmlessness*. We can solve this by allowing the authority to post a disclaimer for such ballots, noting that a contrary proof might appear. A corrupt authority could abuse this to evade collection accountability, but it would place a bound on the number of cheated

---

[17] If an attacker can impersonate a voter when making a challenge, they could use a similar strategy to compromise *everlasting ballot secrecy* by making false challenges that reveal other voters' unchosen encryptions.

ballots, and—as with SAFE Vote—we can give a grace period for the voter to spoil and recast their ballot if it has a reported issue.

Note too that collection accountability guarantees only apply to active misrepresentation in the public tally. Ballots could still be susceptible to being excluded from the tally by an attacker who intercepts and discards them, and there is no apparent cryptographic mechanism to guard against this in a VbM context.

5.2 Assigning Voters Private Keys

Another possible extension would be to generate a key pair for each ballot. The public key would be posted to the bulletin board alongside the rest of the ballot's information, and the private key would be printed on the ballot to be disclosed directly to the voter. This would allow the voter to sign their challenge for the collection accountability extension, eliminating the threat to *everlasting ballot secrecy*. This would also allow for procedural controls that keep the authority from learning the mapping between voters and ballots while still allowing voters to exercise the revoting mechanisms discussed previously.[18]

5.3 System Synthesis

RemoteVote and SAFE Vote each have their own advantages and limitations, but by combining them we can get the best of both worlds, albeit in a less practical form. In this hybrid system, we print each ballot with two columns of shortcodes, one of which is spoiled through RemoteVote's public audit process, and the other of which can be spoiled at will by removing a SAFE Vote style scratch-off surface.

This allows for the unification of a number of advantages. Voters can get *discretionary verification* and *individual verification* by choosing to remove the scratch-off and spoil their ballot as they do under SAFE Vote, but a corrupt authority still has no way of reliably identifying safe targets for cheating; voters who do not remove the scratch-off still may have verified the publicly spoiled column, giving *unobservable auditing* as well. We also gain *advance auditing*, because all challenges can be performed before results are published.

The disadvantage is that this system has higher complexity. Between the two columns of shortcodes, two encryptions hidden beside every candidate, two R values concealed under scratch-offs at the bottom, a secret key used to sign challenges, and 512 bits of physically printed randomness per candidate (likely in the form of multiple large QR codes), the ballot would be challenging to use for those wishing to participate in the verification process. They would need to track and make sense of all the novel information presented to them. Perhaps future implementations can maintain these properties while simplifying the mechanism.

---

[18] Note that this breaks *harmlessness*; a voter who leaks their private key and makes a mistake that would allow revoting would compromise the integrity of their ballot.

Table 1. Comparison of properties achieved by our schemes and by STROBE.

	RemoteVote	SAFE Vote	Synthesized	STROBE	Single-ballot STROBE
Individual Cast-as-Intended	○	●	●	○	○
Collective Cast-as-Intended	●	●	●	●	●
Counted-as-Cast	●	●	●	●	●
Eligibility Verification	●	●	●	●	●
Ballot Secrecy	●	●	●	●	●
Receipt Freeness	●	●	●	●	●
Everlasting Ballot Secrecy	●	●	●	◐	◐
Everlasting Receipt Freeness	◐	◐	◐	◐	◐
Coercion Resistance	○	○	○	○	○
Ignorability	●	●	●	○	●
Harmlessness	◐	◐	◐	○	●
Selection Consistency	●	●	●	○	○
Software Independence	●	●	●	●	●
Strong Software Independence	●	●	●	●	●
Collection Accountability	◐	◐	◐	○	○
Dispute Resolution	◐	◐	◐	○	○
Advance Verification	●	●	●	●	●
Discretionary Verification	○	●	●	●	◐
Independent Verification	○	●	●	○	○
Unobservable Verification	●	○	●	●	◐
Vote-by-Mail Compatibility	●	●	●	●	●
Complexity Tolerance	●	●	●	○	○

●=provides property   ○=doesn't provide property
◐=property is implementation dependent

6   Comparisons and Conclusion

Our schemes show that E2E-V can be used to secure VbM with practical usability. They build heavily on STROBE [5], the first VbM-compatible E2E-V framework.

We compare the detailed properties of our schemes to STROBE in Table 1. As shown there, RemoteVote expands on the guarantees provided by single-ballot STROBE, while SAFE Vote trades the property of unobservable verification to gain individual cast-as-intended verification, along with discretionary and independent verification. The synthesized approach we introduced in Sect. 5.3, meanwhile, provides the strongest set of guarantees of any of these systems.

Other mechanisms for comparison exist as well; the formal properties are merely starting points. For example, STROBE fails to resolve disputes where the authority misrepresents the voter's choices in the published shortcode receipts, while single-ballot STROBE *additionally* loses dispute resolution for allegations that a ballot's shortcodes were printed beside the wrong candidates. RemoteVote and SAFE Vote are able to solve these problems with appropriate extensions, but they are still vulnerable to an attack against the processing procedure instead of ballot integrity; e.g., an adversary could unaccountably intercept and discard ballots. All this nuance is lost when dispute resolution is regarded as binary.

Much remains to be done, including producing rigorous proofs of these schemes' properties, creating and field-testing prototypes, and potentially further simplifying the voter experience. Nevertheless, we believe RemoteVote and SAFE Vote are important steps toward usable verifiability for vote-by-mail, which is a necessary precondition for the universal adoption of E2E-V in U.S. elections.

Acknowledgements. We thank Josh Benaloh and Olivier Pereira for insightful discussions and feedback. This work was supported by the Andrew Carnegie Fellowship, the U.S. National Science Foundation under grant no. CNS-1518888, and a gift from Microsoft.

References

1. Adida, B.: Helios: web-based open-audit voting. In: Usenix Security (2008)
2. Basin, D.A., Radomirovic, S., and Schmid, L.: Dispute resolution in voting. In: 33rd Computer Security Foundations Symposium (2020). https://doi.org/10.1109/CSF49147.2020.00009
3. Benaloh, J.: Ballot casting assurance via voter-initiated poll station auditing. In: Electronic Voting Technology. Usenix (2007). https://www.usenix.org/legacy/events/evt07/tech/full_papers/benaloh/benaloh.pdf
4. Benaloh, J.: Simple verifiable elections. In: Electronic Voting Technology. Usenix (2006). https://www.usenix.org/conference/evt-06/simple-verifiable-elections
5. Benaloh, J.: STROBE-voting: send two, receive one ballot encoding. In: Krimmer, R., et al. (eds.) E-Vote-ID 2021. LNCS, vol. 12900, pp. 33–46. Springer, Cham (2021). https://doi.org/10.1007/978-3-030-86942-7_3
6. Benaloh, J., Rivest, R.L., Ryan, P.Y.A., Stark, P.B., Teague, V., Vora, P.L.: End-to-end verifiability (2015). https://arxiv.org/abs/1504.03778
7. Bernhard, M., et al.: Public evidence from secret ballots. In: Krimmer, R., Volkamer, M., Braun Binder, N., Kersting, N., Pereira, O., Schürmann, C. (eds.) E-Vote-ID 2017. LNCS, vol. 10615, pp. 84–109. Springer, Cham (2017). https://doi.org/10.1007/978-3-319-68687-5_6
8. Brumback, K.: Second Georgia county finds previously uncounted votes, Associated Press (2020). https://apnews.com/article/2nd-georgia-county-find-uncounted-votes-018eac6ac24733d63d356ee76f485530
9. Bulens, P., Giry, D., Pereira, O.: Running mixnet-based elections with Helios. In: Electronic Voting Technology. Usenix (2011). https://www.usenix.org/conference/evtwote-11/running-mixnet-based-elections-helios
10. Clarkson, M.R., Chong, S., Myers, A.C.: Civitas: Toward a secure voting system. In: 29th IEEE Symposium on Security and Privacy (2008). https://doi.org/10.1109/sp.2008.32
11. Cunningham, M.: Millions of Americans are receiving absentee ballot applications from outside groups, ABC News (2020). https://abcnews.go.com/Politics/story?id=72821041
12. Cuvelier, É., Pereira, O., Peters, T.: Election verifiability or ballot privacy: do we need to choose? In: Crampton, J., Jajodia, S., Mayes, K. (eds.) ESORICS 2013. LNCS, vol. 8134, pp. 481–498. Springer, Heidelberg (2013). https://doi.org/10.1007/978-3-642-40203-6_27
13. Escala, A., Guasch, S., Herranz, J., Morillo, P.: Universal cast-as-intended verifiability. In: Clark, J., Meiklejohn, S., Ryan, P.Y.A., Wallach, D., Brenner, M., Rohloff, K. (eds.) FC 2016. LNCS, vol. 9604, pp. 233–250. Springer, Heidelberg (2016). https://doi.org/10.1007/978-3-662-53357-4_16

14. Joffe-Block, J.: Four vote-by-mail ballot applications do not mean four votes, Associated Press (2020). https://apnews.com/article/9414462696

15. Kennedy, L.: How the 2000 election came down to a Supreme Court decision, History (2020). https://www.history.com/news/2000-election-bush-gore-votes-supreme-court

16. Langer, L., Schmidt, A., Buchmann, J., Volkamer, M., Stolfik, A.: Towards a framework on the security requirements for electronic voting protocols. In: RE- VOTE. IEEE (2010). https://doi.org/10.1109/RE-VOTE.2009.9

17. Lindeman, M., Stark, P.: A gentle introduction to risk-limiting audits. IEEE Secur. Priv. **10**(5), 42–49 (2012). https://doi.org/10.1109/MSP.2012.56

18. Marky, K., Kulyk, O., Renaud, K., Volkamer, M.: What did I really vote for? On the usability of verifiable e-voting schemes. In: CHI. ACM (2018). https://doi.org/10.1145/3173574.3173750

19. National Conference of State Legislatures: Voting outside the polling place: Absentee, all-mail and other voting at home options, (2020). https://www.ncsl.org/research/elections-and-campaigns/absentee-and-early-voting.aspx

20. Pereira, O.: Verifiable elections with commitment consistent encryption: a primer (2014). http://arxiv.org/abs/1412.7358

21. Rivest, R.L., Virza, M.: Software independence revisited. In: Real-World Electronic Voting: Design, Analysis and Deployment. Ed. by F. Hao P.Y.A. Ryan. CRC Press (2016). https://www.realworldevoting.com/files/Chapter1.pdf

22. Ryan, P.Y.A., Rønne, P.B., Iovino, V.: Selene: voting with transparent verifiability and coercion-Mitigation. In: Clark, J., Meiklejohn, S., Ryan, P.Y.A., Wallach, D., Brenner, M., Rohloff, K. (eds.) FC 2016. LNCS, vol. 9604, pp. 176–192. Springer, Heidelberg (2016). https://doi.org/10.1007/978-3-662-53357-4_12

23. Stewart III, C.: How We Voted in 2020: A first look at the Survey of the performance of American elections. (2020). http://electionlab.mit.edu/sites/default/files/2020-12/How-we-voted-in-2020-v01.pdf

24. U.S. Census Bureau: Voting and registration in the election of November 2020 (2021). https://www.census.gov/data/tables/time-series/demo/voting-and-registration/p20-585.html

25. Zagórski, F., Carback, R.T., Chaum, D., Clark, J., Essex, A., Vora, P.L.: Remotegrity: design and use of an end-to-end verifiable remote voting system. In: Jacobson, M., Locasto, M., Mohassel, P., Safavi-Naini, R. (eds.) ACNS 2013. LNCS, vol. 7954, pp. 441–457. Springer, Heidelberg (2013). https://doi.org/10.1007/978-3-642-38980-1_28

WTSC 2022 Short Summary: WTSC22 - Current and Future Trends

Lelantus Spark: Secure and Flexible Private Transactions

Aram Jivanyan[1,2](✉) and Aaron Feickert[3]

[1] Firo, Yerevan, Armenia
aram@firo.org
[2] Yerevan State University, Yerevan, Armenia
[3] Cypher Stack, Las Cruces, NM, USA
aaron@cypherstack.com

Abstract. We propose a modification to the Lelantus private transaction protocol to provide recipient privacy, improved security, and additional usability features. Our decentralized anonymous payment (DAP) construction, Spark, enables non-interactive one-time addressing to hide recipient addresses in transactions. The modified address format permits flexibility in transaction visibility. Address owners can securely provide third parties with opt-in visibility into incoming transactions or all transactions associated to the address; this functionality allows for offloading chain scanning and balance computation without delegating spend authority. It is also possible to delegate expensive proving operations without compromising spend authority when generating transactions. Further, the design is compatible with straightforward linear multisignature operations to allow mutually non-trusting parties to cooperatively receive and generate transactions associated to a multisignature address. We prove that Spark satisfies formal DAP security properties of balance, non-malleability, and ledger indistinguishability.

1 Introduction

Distributed digital asset protocols have seen a wealth of research since the introduction of the Bitcoin transaction protocol, which enables transactions generating and consuming ledger-based outputs, and provides a limited but useful scripting capability. However, Bitcoin-type protocols have numerous drawbacks relating to privacy: a transaction reveals source addresses and amounts, and subsequent spends reveal destination addresses. Further, data and metadata associated with transactions, like script contents, can provide undesired fingerprinting of transactions.

More recent research has focused on mitigating or removing these limitations, while permitting existing useful functionality like multisignature operations or opt-in third-party transaction viewing. Designs in privacy-focused cryptocurrencies like Beam, Firo, Grin, Monero, and Zcash take different approaches toward this goal, with a variety of different tradeoffs. The RingCT-based protocol currently used in Monero, for example, practically permits limited sender anonymity

S. Matsuo et al. (Eds.): FC 2022 Workshops, LNCS 13412, pp. 409–447, 2023.
https://doi.org/10.1007/978-3-031-32415-4_28

due to the space and time scaling of its underlying signature scheme [13,23]. The Sprout and Sapling protocols supported by Zcash [15] (and their currently-deployed related updates) require trusted parameter generation to bootstrap their circuit-based proving systems, and interact with transparent Bitcoin-style outputs in ways that can leak information [3,5]. The Mimblewimble-based construction used as the basis for Grin can leak graph information prior to a merging operation performed by miners [11]. To mitigate Mimblewimble's linkability issue, Beam has designed and implemented into its system an adaption of Lelantus for use with the Mimblewimble protocol which enables obfuscation of the transaction graph [25]. The Lelantus protocol currently used in Firo does not provide recipient privacy; it supports only mints and signer-ambiguous spends of arbitrary amounts that interact with transparent Bitcoin-style outputs, which can leak information about recipient identity [16]. Seraphis [26] is a transaction protocol framework of similar design being developed concurrently.

Here we introduce Spark, an iteration on the Lelantus protocol enabling trustless private transactions which supports sender, recipient, and transaction amount privacy. Transactions in Spark, like those in Lelantus and Monero, use specified sender anonymity sets composed of previously-generated shielded outputs. A parallel proving system adapted from a construction by Groth and Bootle *et al.* [4,14] (of independent interest and used in other modified forms in Lelantus [16] and Triptych [22]) proves that a consumed output exists in the anonymity set; amounts are encrypted and hidden algebraically in Pedersen commitments, and a tag derived from a verifiable random function [9,18] prevents consuming the same output multiple times, which in the context of a transaction protocol would constitute a double-spend attempt.

Spark transactions support efficient verification in batches, where range and spend proofs can take advantage of common proof elements and parameters to lower the marginal cost of verifying each proof in such a batch; when coupled with suitably-chosen sender anonymity sets, the verification time savings of batch verification can be significant.

Spark enables additional useful functionality. The use of a modified Chaum-Pedersen discrete logarithm proof, which asserts spend authority and correct tag construction, offers an interesting avenue of research toward efficient signing and multisignature operations similar to those of [8,17,19] where computationally-expensive proofs may be offloaded to more capable devices with limited trust requirements; we defer such constructions and analysis to future work. The protocol further adds three levels of opt-in visibility into transactions without delegating spend authority. Incoming view keys allow a designated third party to identify transactions containing outputs destined for an address, as well as the corresponding amounts and encrypted memo data. Full view keys allow a designated third party to additionally identify when received outputs are later spent (but without any recipient data), which enables balance auditing and further enhances accountability in threshold multisignature applications where this property is desired. Payment proofs allow a sender to assert the destination, value, and memo of a coin while proving (in zero knowledge) that it knows the secret data used to produce the coin; this permits more fine-grained disclosure without revealing view keys.

All constructions used in Spark require only public parameter generation, ensuring that no trusted parties are required to bootstrap the protocol or ensure soundness.

1.1 Organization

In Sect. 2, we define standard and novel cryptographic constructions required for the Spark protocol. Section 3 provides an overview of the concepts and algorithms defining the protocol; these include the structure of keys, addresses, coins, and linking tags. We then provide a detailed instantiation of the Spark algorithms in Sect. 4.

Efficiency of our instantiation is analyzed in Appendix A. Proofs of security for two important zero-knowledge proving systems we describe are provided in Appendixes B and C, while overall protocol security proofs are given in Appendix D. Finally, we describe a method for asserting validity of private coin information through payment proofs in Appendix E.

2 Cryptographic Constructions

Throughout this paper, we use additive notation for group operations. Let $\mathbb{N}$ be the set $\{0, 1, 2, \ldots\}$ of non-negative integers.

2.1 Pedersen Commitment Scheme

A homomorphic commitment scheme is a construction producing one-way algebraic representations of input values. The Pedersen commitment scheme is a homomorphic commitment scheme that uses a particularly simple linear combination construction. Let $pp_{\text{com}} = (\mathbb{G}, \mathbb{F}, G, H)$ be the public parameters for a Pedersen commitment scheme, where $\mathbb{G}$ is a prime-order group where the discrete logarithm problem is hard, $\mathbb{F}$ is its scalar field, and $G, H \in \mathbb{G}$ are uniformly-sampled independent generators. The commitment scheme contains an algorithm $\mathsf{Com} : \mathbb{F}^2 \to \mathbb{G}$, where $\mathsf{Com}(v, r) = vG + rH$ that is homomorphic in the sense that

$$\mathsf{Com}(v_1, r_1) + \mathsf{Com}(v_2, r_2) = \mathsf{Com}(v_1 + v_2, r_1 + r_1)$$

for all such input values $v_1, v_2 \in \mathbb{F}$ and masks $r_1, r_2 \in \mathbb{F}$. Further, the construction is perfectly hiding and computationally binding.

This definition extends naturally to a double-masked commitment scheme. Let $pp_{\text{comm}} = (\mathbb{G}, \mathbb{F}, F, G, H)$ be the public parameters for a double-masked Pedersen commitment scheme, where $\mathbb{G}$ is a prime-order group where the discrete logarithm problem is hard, $\mathbb{F}$ is its scalar field, and $F, G, H \in \mathbb{G}$ are uniformly-sampled independent generators. The commitment scheme contains an algorithm

Comm : $\mathbb{F}^3 \to \mathbb{G}$, where $\mathsf{Comm}(v, r, s) = vF + rG + sH$ that is homomorphic in the sense that

$$\mathsf{Comm}(v_1, r_1, s_1) + \mathsf{Comm}(v_2, r_2, s_2) = \mathsf{Comm}(v_1 + v_2, r_1 + r_2, s_1 + s_2)$$

for all such input values $v_1, v_2 \in \mathbb{F}$ and masks $r_1, r_2, s_1, s_2 \in \mathbb{F}$. Further, the construction is perfectly hiding and computationally binding.

2.2 Representation Proving System

A representation proof is used to demonstrate knowledge of a set of discrete logarithms in zero knowledge. Let $pp_{\mathrm{rep}} = (\mathbb{G}, \mathbb{F})$ be the public parameters for such a construction, where $\mathbb{G}$ is a prime-order group where the discrete logarithm problems is hard and $\mathbb{F}$ is its scalar field.

The proving system itself is a tuple of algorithms (RepProve, RepVerify) for the following relation:

$$\{pp_{\mathrm{rep}}, G, \{Y_i\}_{i=0}^{l-1} \subset \mathbb{G}; \{y_i\}_{i=0}^{l-1} \subset \mathbb{F} : \forall i \in [0, l), Y_i = y_i G\}$$

We require that the proving system be complete, special honest-verifier zero knowledge, and special sound; these definitions are standard [14].

An aggregated Schnorr proving system, like that in [12], may be used for this purpose.

As a matter of notational convenience, we drop the set and subscript notation from these algorithms in the case where $l = 1$; this represents the case of a standard (non-aggregated) representation proof.

2.3 Modified Chaum-Pedersen Proving System

A Chaum-Pedersen proof is used to demonstrate discrete logarithm equality in zero knowledge. Here we require a modification to the standard proving system that uses additional group generators and supports multiple assertions within a single proof. Let $pp_{\mathrm{chaum}} = (\mathbb{G}, \mathbb{F}, F, G, H, U)$ be the public parameters for such a construction, where $\mathbb{G}$ is a prime-order group where the discrete logarithm problem is hard, $\mathbb{F}$ is its scalar field, and $F, G, H, U \in \mathbb{G}$ are uniformly-sampled independent generators.

The proving system is a tuple of algorithms (ChaumProve, ChaumVerify) for the following relation:

$$\{pp_{\mathrm{chaum}}, \{S_i, T_i\}_{i=0}^{l-1} \subset \mathbb{G}^2; (\{x_i, y_i, z_i\}_{i=0}^{l-1}) \subset \mathbb{F}^3 :$$
$$\forall i \in [0, l), S_i = x_i F + y_i G + z_i H, U = x_i T_i + y_i G\}$$

We require that the proving system be complete, special honest-verifier zero knowledge, and special sound.

We present an instantiation of such a proving system in Appendix B, along with security proofs.

2.4 Parallel One-out-of-Many Proving System

We require the use of a parallel one-out-of-many proving system that shows knowledge of openings of commitments to zero at the same index among two sets of group elements in zero knowledge. In the context of the Spark protocol, this will be used to mask consumed coin serial number and value commitments for balance, ownership, and double-spend purposes. We show how to produce such a proving system as a straightforward modification of a construction by Groth and Kohlweiss [14] that was generalized by Bootle et $al.$ [4], with a further optimization from Esgin et $al.$ [10].

Let $pp_{par} = (\mathbb{G}, \mathbb{F}, n, m, pp_{com}, pp_{comm})$ be the public parameters for such a construction, where $\mathbb{G}$ is a prime-order group where the discrete logarithm problem is hard, $\mathbb{F}$ is its scalar field, $n > 1$ and $m > 1$ are integer-valued size decomposition parameters, pp_{com} are the public parameters for a Pedersen commitment construction, and pp_{comm} are the public parameters for a double-masked Pedersen commitment construction.

The proving system itself is a tuple of algorithms (ParProve, ParVerify) for the following relation, where we let $N = n^m$:

$$\{pp_{par}, \{S_k, V_k\}_{k=0}^{N-1} \subset \mathbb{G}^2, S', V' \in \mathbb{G}; l \in \mathbb{N}, (s, v) \in \mathbb{F} :$$
$$0 \leq l < N, S_l - S' = \mathsf{Comm}(0, 0, s), V_l - V' = \mathsf{Com}(0, v)\}$$

We require that the proving system be complete, special honest-verifier zero knowledge, and special sound.

We present an instantiation of such a proving system in Appendix C.

2.5 Authenticated Encryption Scheme

We require the use of an authenticated symmetric encryption with associated data (AEAD) scheme. In the context of the Spark protocol, this construction is used to encrypt value, memo, and other data for use by the recipient of a transaction.

Let pp_{aead} be the public parameters for such a construction. The construction itself is a tuple of algorithms (AEADKeyGen, AEADEncrypt, AEADDecrypt). Here AEADKeyGen is a key derivation function that accepts as input an arbitrary string, and produces a key in the appropriate key space. The algorithm AEADEncrypt accepts as input a key, associated data, and arbitrary message string, and produces ciphertext in the appropriate space. The algorithm AEADDecrypt accepts as input a key, associated data, and ciphertext string, and produces a message in the appropriate space if authentication succeeds (and fails otherwise).

Assume that such a construction is indistinguishable against adaptive chosen-ciphertext attacks (IND-CCA2) and key-private under chosen-ciphertext attacks (IK-CCA) in this context [1].

2.6 Symmetric Encryption Scheme

We require the use of a symmetric encryption scheme. In the context of the Spark protocol, this construction is used to encrypt diversifier indices used to produce public addresses.

Let pp_{sym} be the public parameters for such a construction. The construction itself is a tuple of algorithms (SymKeyGen, SymEncrypt, SymDecrypt). Here SymKeyGen is a key derivation function that accepts as input an arbitrary string, and produces a key in the appropriate key space. The algorithm SymEncrypt accepts as input a key and arbitrary message string, and produces ciphertext in the appropriate space. The algorithm SymDecrypt accepts as input a key and ciphertext string, and produces a message in the appropriate space.

Assume that such a construction is indistinguishable against adaptive chosen-ciphertext attacks (IND-CCA2) in this context.

2.7 Range Proving System

We require the use of a zero-knowledge range proving system. A range proving system demonstrates that a commitment binds to a value within a specified range. In the context of the Spark protocol, it avoids overflow that would otherwise fool the balance definition by effectively binding to invalid negative values. Let $pp_{\text{rp}} = (\mathbb{G}, \mathbb{F}, v_{\max}, pp_{\text{com}})$ be the relevant public parameters for such a construction, where pp_{com} are the public parameters for a Pedersen commitment construction.

The proving system itself is a tuple of algorithms (RangeProve, RangeVerify) for the following relation:

$$\{pp_{\text{rp}}, C \in \mathbb{G}; (v, r) \in \mathbb{F} : 0 \leq v \leq v_{\max}, C = \text{Com}(v, r)\}$$

We require that the proving system be complete, special honest-verifier zero knowledge, and special sound.

In practice, an efficient instantiation like Bulletproofs [6] or Bulletproofs+ [7] may be used to satisfy this requirement.

3   Concepts and Algorithms

We now define the main concepts and algorithms used in the Spark transaction protocol.

Keys and Addresses. Users generate keys and addresses that enable transactions. A set of keys consists of a tuple

$$(\text{addr}_{\text{in}}, \text{addr}_{\text{full}}, \text{addr}_{\text{sk}}).$$

In this notation, addr_{in} is an incoming view key used to identify received funds, $\text{addr}_{\text{full}}$ is a full view key used to identify outgoing funds and conduct certain computationally-heavy proving operations, and addr_{sk} is the spend key used to generate transactions. Spark addresses are constructed in such a way that a single set of keys can be used to construct any number of *diversified* public addresses that appear indistinguishable from each other or from public addresses produced from a different set of keys. Diversified addressing allows a recipient to provide distinct public addresses to different senders, but scan transactions on chain only once for identification and recovery of incoming coins destined for any of its diversified public addresses.

Coins. A coin encodes the abstract value which is transferred through the private transactions. Each coin is associated with:

- A secret nonce
- A recipient address
- An integer value
- A memo containing arbitrary recipient data

The recipient address and value are hidden using commitments. The nonce, a part of the recipient address, the value, and the memo are encrypted to the recipient (unless the value is made public as part of a mint operation).

Private Transactions. There are two types of private transactions in Spark:

- Mint transactions. A mint transaction generates new coins of public value destined for a recipient public address in a confidential way, either through a consensus-enforced mining process, or by consuming transparent outputs from a non-Spark base layer. In this transaction type, a representation proof is included to show that the minted coins are of the expected values.
- Spend transactions. A spend transaction consumes existing coins and generates new coins destined for one or more recipient public addresses in a confidential way. In this transaction type, a representation proof is included to show that the hidden input and output values are equal.

Tags. Tags are used to prevent coins from being consumed in multiple transactions. When generating a spend transaction, the sender produces the tag for each consumed coin and includes it on the ledger. When verifying transactions are valid, it suffices to ensure that tags do not appear on the ledger in any previous transactions. Tags are uniquely bound to validly-recoverable coins, but cannot be associated to specific coins without the corresponding full view key.

Algorithms. Spark is a decentralized anonymous payment (DAP) system defined as the following polynomial-time algorithms:

- Setup: This algorithm produces all public parameters used by the protocol and its underlying components. The setup process does not require any trusted parameter generation.
- CreateKeys: This algorithm produces keys that are used when constructing addresses, processing coins, and spending coins.
- CreateAddress: This algorithm produces diversified public addresses used for receiving coins.
- CreateCoin: This algorithm produces a coin of a given value that is destined for a recipient public address.

- Mint: This algorithm produces a transaction transferring public value to recipient public addresses.
- Identify: This algorithm processes a coin to determine if it is destined for a diversified address controlled by a recipient.
- Recover: This algorithm processes a coin to determine if it is destined for a diversified address controlled by a recipient, and produces additional data used for spending the coin or determining if it is already spent.
- Spend: This algorithm produces a transaction consuming existing coins and generating new coins of hidden value to recipient public addresses.
- Verify: This algorithm determines if a given transaction is valid.

We provide detailed descriptions below, and show security of the resulting protocol in Appendix D.

4   Algorithm Constructions

In this section we provide detailed description of the DAP scheme algorithms.

4.1   Setup

This algorithm produces public parameters required for the protocol. The security parameter and resulting public parameters are assumed to be available to all other algorithms, even where not specifically noted.

Inputs: Security parameter λ, size decomposition parameters $n > 1$ and $m > 1$, maximum value parameter $v_{\max}$

Outputs: Public parameters pp

1. Sample a prime-order group $\mathbb{G}$ in which the discrete logarithm, decisional Diffie-Hellman, and computational Diffie-Hellman problems are hard. Let $\mathbb{F}$ be the scalar field of $\mathbb{G}$.
2. Sample $F, G, H, U \in \mathbb{G}$ uniformly at random. In practice, these generators may be chosen using a suitable cryptographic hash function on public input.
3. Sample cryptographic hash functions

$$\mathcal{H}_k, \mathcal{H}_{Q_2}, \mathcal{H}_{\mathrm{ser}}, \mathcal{H}_{\mathrm{val}}, \mathcal{H}_{\mathrm{ser}'}, \mathcal{H}_{\mathrm{val}'}, \mathcal{H}_{\mathrm{bind}} : \{0,1\}^* \to \mathbb{F}$$

and

$$\mathcal{H}_{\mathrm{div}} : \{0,1\}^* \to \mathbb{G}$$

uniformly at random. In practice, these hash functions may be chosen using domain separation of a single suitable cryptographic hash function on public input.
4. Compute the public parameters $pp_{\mathrm{com}} = (\mathbb{G}, \mathbb{F}, G, H)$ of a Pedersen commitment scheme.
5. Compute the public parameters $pp_{\mathrm{comm}} = (\mathbb{G}, \mathbb{F}, F, G, H)$ of a double-masked Pedersen commitment scheme.

6. Compute the public parameters $pp_{rep} = (\mathbb{G}, \mathbb{F})$ of a representation proving system.
7. Compute the public parameters $pp_{chaum} = (\mathbb{G}, \mathbb{F}, F, G, H, U)$ of the modified Chaum-Pedersen proving system.
8. Compute the public parameters $pp_{par} = (\mathbb{G}, \mathbb{F}, n, m, pp_{com}, pp_{comm})$ of the parallel one-out-of-many proving system.
9. Compute the public parameters pp_{aead} of an authenticated symmetric encryption scheme.
10. Compute the public parameters pp_{sym} of a symmetric encryption scheme.
11. Compute the public parameters $pp_{rp} = (\mathbb{G}, \mathbb{F}, v_{max}, pp_{com})$ of a range proving system.
12. Output all generated public parameters and hash functions as pp.

4.2 CreateKeys

We describe the construction of key types used in the protocol.

Inputs: Security parameter λ, public parameters pp

Outputs: Key tuple $(\mathsf{addr}_{in}, \mathsf{addr}_{full}, \mathsf{addr}_{sk})$

1. Sample $s_1, s_2, r \in \mathbb{F}$ uniformly at random, and let $D = \mathsf{Comm}(0, r, 0)$ and $P_2 = \mathsf{Comm}(s_2, r, 0)$.
2. Set $\mathsf{addr}_{in} = (s_1, P_2)$.
3. Set $\mathsf{addr}_{full} = (s_1, s_2, D, P_2)$.
4. Set $\mathsf{addr}_{sk} = (s_1, s_2, r)$.
5. Output the tuple $(\mathsf{addr}_{in}, \mathsf{addr}_{full}, \mathsf{addr}_{sk})$.

4.3 CreateAddress

This algorithm generates a *diversified* public address from an incoming view key. A given public address is privately and deterministically tied to an index called the *diversifier*. Diversified public addresses share the same set of keys for efficiency purposes, but are not linkable without non-public information.

Inputs: Security parameter λ, public parameters pp, incoming view key addr_{in}, diversifier $i \in \mathbb{N}$

Outputs: Diversified address addr_{pk}

1. Parse the incoming view key $\mathsf{addr}_{in} = (s_1, P_2)$.
2. Compute the diversified address components:

$$d = \mathsf{SymEncrypt}(\mathsf{SymKeyGen}(s_1), i)$$
$$Q_{1,i} = s_1 \mathcal{H}_{div}(d)$$
$$Q_{2,i} = \mathsf{Comm}(\mathcal{H}_{Q_2}(s_1, i), 0, 0) + P_2$$

3. Set $\mathsf{addr}_{pk} = (d, Q_{1,i}, Q_{2,i})$ and output this tuple.

Note that we drop the diversifier index i from subsequent notation when referring to addresses in operations performed by entities other than the incoming view key holder, since such users are not provided this index and cannot compute it.

4.4 CreateCoin

This algorithm generates a new coin destined for a given public address. It uses a type bit to determine if the value is intended to be publicly visible.

Inputs: Security parameter λ, public parameters pp, destination public address $\mathsf{addr}_{\mathrm{pk}}$, value $v \in [0, v_{\max})$, memo m, type bit b

Outputs: Coin Coin, nonce k

1. Parse the recipient address $\mathsf{addr}_{\mathrm{pk}} = (d, Q_1, Q_2)$.
2. Sample a nonce $k \in \mathbb{F}$.
3. Compute the recovery key $K = \mathcal{H}_k(k)\mathcal{H}_{\mathrm{div}}(d)$.
4. Compute the serial number commitment

$$S = \mathsf{Comm}(\mathcal{H}_{\mathrm{ser}}(k), 0, 0) + Q_2.$$

5. Generate the value commitment $C = \mathsf{Com}(v, \mathcal{H}_{\mathrm{val}}(k))$.
6. If $b = 0$, generate a range proof

$$\Pi_{\mathrm{rp}} = \mathsf{RangeProve}(pp_{\mathrm{rp}}, C; (v, \mathcal{H}_{\mathrm{val}}(k))).$$

7. If $b = 0$, set the recipient data $r = (v, d, k, m)$; otherwise, set $r = (d, k, m)$.
8. Generate an AEAD encryption key $k_{\mathrm{aead}} = \mathsf{AEADKeyGen}(\mathcal{H}_k(k)Q_1)$; encrypt the recipient data

$$\bar{r} = \mathsf{AEADEncrypt}(k_{\mathrm{aead}}, \mathbf{r}, r).$$

9. If $b = 0$, output the coin Coin $= (S, K, C, \Pi_{\mathrm{rp}}, \bar{r})$ and nonce k; otherwise, output the coin Coin $= (S, K, C, v, \bar{r})$ and nonce k.

The case $b = 0$ represents a coin with hidden value being generated in a spend transaction, while the case $b = 1$ represents a coin with plaintext value being generated in a mint transaction.

The nonce k is returned for use by other algorithms, but is not public.

4.5 Mint

This algorithm generates new coins from either a consensus-determined mining process, or by consuming non-Spark outputs from a base layer with public value. Note that while such implementation-specific auxiliary data may be necessary for generating such a transaction and included, we do not specifically list this here. Notably, the coin value used in this algorithm is assumed to be the sum of all public input values as specified by the implementation.

Inputs:

- Security parameter λ and public parameters pp
- A set of t output coin public addresses, values, and memos:

$$\{\mathsf{addr}_{\mathrm{pk},j}, v_j, m_j\}_{j=0}^{t-1}$$

Outputs: Mint transaction tx_{mint}

1. Generate a set $\text{OutCoins} = \{\text{CreateCoin}(\text{addr}_{\text{pk},j}, v_j, m_j, 1)\}_{j=0}^{t-1}$ of output coins.
2. Parse the output coin value commitments $\{\overline{C}_j\}_{j=0}^{t-1}$ from OutCoins, where each $\overline{C}_j$ contains nonce k_j.
3. Generate a representation proof for value assertion:

$$\Pi_{\text{val}} = \text{RepProve}\left(pp_{\text{rep}}, H, \{\overline{C}_j - \text{Com}(v_j, 0)\}_{j=0}^{t-1}; \{\mathcal{H}_{\text{val}}(k_j)\}_{j=0}^{t-1}\right)$$

4. Output the mint transaction $\text{tx}_{\text{mint}} = (\text{OutCoins}, \Pi_{\text{val}})$.

4.6 Identify

This algorithm allows a recipient (or designated entity) to determine if it controls a coin; if so, it computes the value, memo, and diversifier from the coin (in addition to the coin nonce). It requires the incoming view key used to produce diversified addresses to do so. If the coin is not destined for any diversified address, the algorithm returns failure.

It is assumed that the recipient has run the Verify algorithm on the transaction generating the coin being identified.

Inputs: Security parameter λ, public parameters pp, incoming view key addr_{in}, coin Coin

Outputs: Value v, memo m, diversifier i, nonce k

1. Parse the incoming view key $\text{addr}_{\text{in}} = (s_1, P_2)$.
2. If Coin was generated in a mint transaction, parse $\text{Coin} = (S, K, C, v, \overline{r})$; otherwise, parse $\text{Coin} = (S, K, C, \Pi_{\text{rp}}, \overline{r})$.
3. Generate an AEAD encryption key $k_{\text{aead}} = \text{AEADKeyGen}(s_1 K)$ and decrypt

$$r = \text{AEADDecrypt}(k_{\text{aead}}, \mathbf{r}, \overline{r});$$

if decryption fails, return failure.
4. If Coin was generated in a mint transaction, parse the recipient data $r = (d, k, m)$; otherwise, parse $r = (v, d, k, m)$.
5. Check that $K = \mathcal{H}_k(k)\mathcal{H}_{\text{div}}(d)$, and return failure otherwise.
6. Check that $C = \text{Com}(v, \mathcal{H}_{\text{val}}(k))$, and return failure otherwise.
7. Decrypt the diversifier $i = \text{SymDecrypt}(\text{SymKeyGen}(s_1), d)$.
8. Check that

$$S = \text{Comm}(\mathcal{H}_{\text{ser}}(k), 0, 0) + \text{Comm}(\mathcal{H}_{Q_2}(s_1, i), 0, 0) + P_2,$$

and return failure otherwise.
9. Output (v, m, i, k).

4.7   Recover

This algorithm allows a recipient (or designated entity) to determine if it controls a coin; if so, it computes the serial number, tag, value, memo, and diversifier from the coin (in addition to the coin nonce). It requires the full view key used to produce diversified addresses to do so. If the coin is not destined for any diversified address, the algorithm returns failure.

It is assumed that the recipient has run the Verify algorithm on the transaction generating the coin being recovered.

Inputs: Security parameter λ, public parameters pp, full view key $\mathsf{addr}_{\mathsf{full}}$, coin Coin

Outputs: Serial number s, tag T, value v, memo m, diversifier i, nonce k

1. Parse the full view key $\mathsf{addr}_{\mathsf{full}} = (s_1, s_2, D, P_2)$.
2. Arrange the corresponding incoming view key $\mathsf{addr}_{\mathsf{in}} = (s_1, P_2)$.
3. Run Identify($\mathsf{addr}_{\mathsf{in}}$, Coin) to obtain (v, m, i, k), and return failure if this operation fails.
4. Compute the serial number

$$s = \mathcal{H}_{\mathsf{ser}}(k) + \mathcal{H}_{Q_2}(s_1, i) + s_2$$

and tag

$$T = (1/s)(U - D).$$

5. If T has been constructed in any other valid recovery, return failure.
6. Output (s, T, v, m, i, k).

4.8   Spend

This algorithm allows a recipient to generate a transaction that consumes coins it controls, and generates new coins destined for arbitrary public addresses. The process is designed to be modular; in particular, only the full view key is required to generate the parallel one-out-of-many proof, which may be computationally expensive. The use of spend keys is only required for the final Chaum-Pedersen proof step, which is of lower complexity.

It is assumed that the recipient has run the Recover algorithm on all coins that it wishes to consume in such a transaction.

Inputs:

- Security parameter λ and public parameters pp
- A full view key $\mathsf{addr}_{\mathsf{full}}$
- A spend key $\mathsf{addr}_{\mathsf{sk}}$
- A set of N input coins InCoins as part of a cover set
- For each $u \in [0, w)$ coin to spend, the index in InCoins, serial number, tag, value, and nonce: $(l_u, s_u, T_u, v_u, k_u)$
- An integer fee value $f \in [0, v_{\max})$

– A set of t output coin public addresses, values, and memos:

$$\{\text{addr}_{\text{pk},j}, v_j, m_j\}_{j=0}^{t-1}$$

Outputs: Spend transaction tx_{spend}

1. Parse the required full view key component D from $\text{addr}_{\text{full}}$.
2. Parse the spend key $\text{addr}_{\text{sk}} = (s_1, s_2, r)$.
3. Parse the cover set serial number commitments and value commitments $\{(S_i, C_i)\}_{i=0}^{N-1}$ from InCoins.
4. For each $u \in [0, w)$:
   (a) Compute the serial number commitment offset:

   $$S'_u = \text{Comm}(s_u, 0, -\mathcal{H}_{\text{ser}'}(s_u, D)) + D$$

   (b) Compute the value commitment offset:

   $$C'_u = \text{Com}(v_u, \mathcal{H}_{\text{val}'}(s_u, D))$$

   (c) Generate a parallel one-out-of-many proof:

   $$(\Pi_{\text{par}})_u = \text{ParProve}(pp_{\text{par}}, \{S_i, C_i\}_{i=0}^{N-1}, S'_u, C'_u;$$
   $$(l_u, \mathcal{H}_{\text{ser}'}(s_u, D), \mathcal{H}_{\text{val}}(k) - \mathcal{H}_{\text{val}'}(s_u, D)))$$

5. Generate a set $\text{OutCoins} = \{\text{CreateCoin}(\text{addr}_{\text{pk},j}, v_j, m_j, 0)\}_{j=0}^{t-1}$ of output coins.
6. Parse the output coin value commitments $\{\overline{C}_j\}_{j=0}^{t-1}$ from OutCoins, where each $\overline{C}_j$ contains nonce k_j.
7. Generate a representation proof for balance assertion:

$$\Pi_{\text{bal}} = \text{RepProve}\left(pp_{\text{rep}}, H, \sum_{u=0}^{w-1} C'_u - \sum_{j=0}^{t-1} \overline{C}_j - \text{Com}(f, 0); \right.$$
$$\left. \sum_{u=0}^{w-1} \mathcal{H}_{\text{val}'}(s_u, D) - \sum_{j=0}^{t-1} \mathcal{H}_{\text{val}}(k_j) \right)$$

8. Let $\mu = \mathcal{H}_{\text{bind}}(\text{InCoins}, \text{OutCoins}, f, \{S'_u, C'_u, T_u, (\Pi_{\text{par}})_u, \}_{u=0}^{w-1}, \Pi_{\text{bal}})$.
9. Generate a modified Chaum-Pedersen proof, where we additionally bind μ to the initial transcript:

$$\Pi_{\text{chaum}} = \text{ChaumProve}((pp_{\text{chaum}}, \mu), \{S'_u, T_u\}_{u=0}^{w-1};$$
$$(\{s_u, r, -\mathcal{H}_{\text{ser}'}(s_u, D)\}_{u=0}^{w-1}))$$

10. Output the tuple:

$$\text{tx}_{\text{spend}} = (\text{InCoins}, \text{OutCoins}, f, \{S'_u, C'_u, T_u, (\Pi_{\text{par}})_u, \Pi_{\text{chaum}}\}_{u=0}^{w-1}, \Pi_{\text{bal}})$$

Note that it is possible to modify the balance proof to account for other input or output values not represented by coin value commitments, similarly to the handling of fees. This observation can allow for the transfer of value into new coins without the use of a mint transaction, or a transfer of value to a transparent base layer. Such transfer functionality is likely to introduce practical risk that is not captured by the protocol security model, and warrants thorough analysis.

4.9 Verify

This algorithm assesses the validity of a transaction.

Inputs: either a mint transaction tx_{mint} or a spend transaction tx_{spend}

Outputs: a bit that represents the validity of the transaction
    If the input transaction is a mint transaction:

1. Parse the transaction $\text{tx}_{\text{mint}} = (\text{OutCoins}, \Pi_{\text{val}})$.
2. Parse the output coin values serial number commitments, and value commitments $\{(v_j, \overline{S}_j, \overline{C}_j)\}_{j=0}^{t-1}$ from OutCoins.
3. For each $j \in [0, t)$:
    (a) If $\overline{S}_j$ appears in an output coin in this transaction or in any previously-verified transaction, output 0.
    (b) Check that $v_j \in [0, v_{\text{max}})$, and output 0 if this fails.
4. Check that $\text{RepVerify}\left(pp_{\text{rep}}, \Pi_{\text{val}}, H, \{\overline{C}_j - \text{Com}(v_j, 0)\}_{j=0}^{t-1}\right)$, and output 0 if this fails.
5. Output 1.

    If the input transaction is a spend transaction:

1. Parse the transaction:

$$\text{tx}_{\text{spend}} = (\text{InCoins}, \text{OutCoins}, f, \{S'_u, C'_u, T_u, (\Pi_{\text{par}})_u, \Pi_{\text{chaum}}\}_{u=0}^{w-1}, \Pi_{\text{bal}})$$

2. Parse the cover set serial number commitments and value commitments $\{(S_i, C_i)\}_{i=0}^{N-1}$ from InCoins.
3. Parse the output coin serial commitments, value commitments, and range proofs $\{\overline{S}_j, \overline{C}_j, (\Pi_{\text{rp}})_j\}_{j=0}^{t-1}$ from OutCoins.
4. For each $u \in [0, w)$:
    (a) Check that T_u does not appear again in this transaction or in any previously-verified transaction, and output 0 if it does.
    (b) Check that $\text{ParVerify}(pp_{\text{par}}, (\Pi_{\text{par}})_u, \{S_i, C_i\}_{i=0}^{N-1}, S'_u, C'_u)$, and output 0 if this fails.
5. Compute the binding hash μ as before, check that

$$\text{ChaumVerify}((pp_{\text{chaum}}, \mu), \Pi_{\text{chaum}}, \{S'_u, T_u\}_{u=0}^{w-1}),$$

and output 0 if this fails.

6. For each $j \in [0, t)$:
   (a) If $\overline{S}_j$ appears in an output coin in this transaction or in any previously-verified transaction, output 0.
   (b) Check that $\mathsf{RangeVerify}(pp_{\mathrm{rp}}, (\Pi_{\mathrm{rp}})_j, C)$, and output 0 if this fails.
7. Check that $f \in [0, v_{\max})$, and output 0 if this fails.
8. Check that

$$
\mathsf{RepVerify}\left(pp_{\mathrm{rep}}, \Pi_{\mathrm{bal}}, H, \sum_{u=0}^{w-1} C'_u - \sum_{j=0}^{t-1} \overline{C}_j - \mathsf{Com}(f, 0) \right)
$$

   and output 0 if this fails.
9. Output 1.

5 Key and Proof Structure

The key and proof structures in Spark enable flexible and useful functionality relating to transaction scanning, generation, and disclosure.

The incoming view key is used in Identify operations to determine when a coin is directed to an associated public address, and to determine the coin's value and associated memo data. This permits useful functionality relating to scanning, where a designated device or service can watch for incoming coins without delegating spend authority.

The full view key is used in Recover operations to compute the serial number and tag for coins directed to an associated public address. These tags can be used to identify a transaction spending the coin. Providing this key to a third party permits identification of incoming transactions and detection of outgoing transactions, which additionally allows balance computation, without delegating spend authority. Users like public charities may wish to permit public oversight of funds with this functionality. Other users may wish to provide this functionality to an auditor or accountant for bookkeeping purposes.

Further, the full view key is used in Spend to generate one-out-of-many proofs. Since these proofs can be computationally expensive, they may be unsuitable for generation by a computationally-limited device like a hardware wallet. Providing this key to a more powerful device enables easy preparation of a transaction that can only be authorized by the spend key.

Payment proofs, which we discuss in Appendix E, allow for disclosure of data for individual coins by asserting in zero knowledge that the prover knows the spend key used to authorize the transaction generating a coin to a specific address, in addition to providing the verifier with the value and memo for the coin. Unlike view keys, which provide broad visibility into transactions associated to a public address, a payment proof is limited to a single coin and can be bound to an arbitrary proof context to prevent replay.

Finally, the structure of modified Chaum-Pedersen proofs is linear in the spend key. This means that efficient multisignature constructions, like those introduced in [8,17,19], can likely be modified to this proving system. Such constructions permit the secure construction of a distributed spend key requiring a threshold of signers to authorize transactions. The preprint version of this paper describes one such construction in detail, but leaves a complete security analysis to future work.

Acknowledgments. The authors thank pseudonymous collaborator koe for ongoing discussions during the development of this work. The authors gratefully acknowledge Nikolas Krätzschmar for identifying an earlier protocol flaw relating to tag generation. The authors further thank independent researcher Luke Parker (kayabaNerve) for pointing out the failure of the security model to capture the case of an adversary producing a duplicate serial commitment prior to an honest transaction being added to the ledger.

A   Efficiency

It is instructive to examine the efficiency of spend transactions in size, generation complexity, and verification complexity. In addition to our previous notation for parameters, let $v_{\max} = 2^{64}$, so coin values and fees can be represented by 8-byte unsigned integers. Further, suppose coin memos are fixed at M bytes in length, diversifiers are restricted to I bytes in length, with a 16-byte authentication tag; this is the case for the ChaCha20-Poly1305 authenticated symmetric encryption construction, for example [21]. Additionally, the arguments in [20] imply that Schnorr representation proofs can use truncated hash outputs for reduced proof size. Transaction size data for specific component instantiations is given in Table 1, where we consider the size in terms of group elements, field elements, and other data. Note that we do not include input ambiguity set references in this data, as this depends on implementation-specific selection and representation criteria.

Table 1. Spend transaction size by component

Component	Instantiation	Size ($\mathbb{G}$)	Size ($\mathbb{F}$)	Size (bytes)
f				8
Π_{rp}	Bulletproofs+	$2\lceil \lg(64t)\rceil + 3$	3	
Π_{bal}	Schnorr (short)		1.5	
Π_{chaum}	this paper	$w+1$	$w+2$	
Input data (w coins)				
(S', C')		$2w$		
Π_{par}	this paper	$(2m+2)w$	$[m(n-1)+3]w$	
Output data (t coins)				
(S, K, C)		$3t$		
$\bar{r}$	ChaCha20-Poly1305			$(8+M+I+16)t$

To evaluate the verification complexity of spend transactions using these components, we observe that verification in constructions like the parallel one-out-of-many proving system in this paper, Bulletproof+ range proving system, Schnorr representation proving system, and modified Chaum-Pedersen proving system in this paper all reduce to single linear combination evaluations in $\mathbb{G}$. Because of this, proofs can be evaluated in batches if the verifier first weights each proof by a random value in $\mathbb{F}$, such that distinct group elements need only appear once in the resulting weighted linear combination. Notably, techniques like that of [24] can be used to reduce the complexity of such evaluations by up to a logarithmic factor. Suppose we wish to verify a batch of B transactions, each of which spends w coins and generates t coins. Table 2 shows the verification batch complexity in terms of total distinct elements of $\mathbb{G}$ that must be included in a linear combination evaluation.

Table 2. Spend transaction batch verification complexity for B transactions with w spent coins and t generated coins

Component	Complexity
Parallel one-out-of-many	$B[w(2m+2) + 2n^m] + 2mn + 1$
Bulletproofs+	$B(t + 2\lg(64t) + 3) + 128T + 2$
Modified Chaum-Pedersen	$B(3w+1) + 4$
Schnorr	$B(w+t+1) + 2$

We further comment that the parallel one-out-of-many proving system presented in this paper may be further optimized in verification. Because corresponding elements of the $\{S_i\}$ and $\{V_i\}$ input sets are weighted identically in the protocol verification equations, it may be more efficient (depending on implementation) to combine these elements with a sufficient weight prior to applying the proof-specific weighting identified above for batch verification. Initial tests using a variable-time curve library suggest significant reductions in verification time with this technique.

B Modified Chaum-Pedersen Proving System

The proving system is a tuple of algorithms (ChaumProve, ChaumVerify) for the following relation:

$$\{pp_{\text{chaum}}, \{S_i, T_i\}_{i=0}^{l-1} \subset \mathbb{G}^2; (\{x_i, y_i, z_i\}_{i=0}^{l-1}) \subset \mathbb{F}^3 :$$
$$\forall i \in [0, l), S_i = x_i F + y_i G + z_i H, U = x_i T_i + y_i G\}$$

Our protocol uses a power-of-challenge technique inspired by a method used for aggregating Schnorr signatures [12]. The protocol proceeds as follows:

1. The prover selects random $\{r_i, s_i\}_{i=0}^{l-1}, t \in \mathbb{F}$. It computes the values

$$A_1 = \sum_{i=0}^{l-1} r_i F + \sum_{i=0}^{l-1} s_i G + tH$$

$$\{A_{2,i}\}_{i=0}^{l-1} = \{r_i T_i + s_i G\}_{i=0}^{l-1}$$

and sends these values to the verifier.
2. The verifier selects a random challenge $c \in \mathbb{F}$ and sends it to the prover.
3. The prover computes responses

$$\{t_{1,i}\}_{i=0}^{l-1} = \{r_i + c^{i+1} x_i\}_{i=0}^{l-1}$$

$$t_2 = \sum_{i=0}^{l-1} (s_i + c^{i+1} y_i)$$

$$t_3 = t + \sum_{i=0}^{l-1} c^{i+1} z_i$$

and sends them to the verifier.
4. The verifier accepts the proof if and only if

$$A_1 + \sum_{i=0}^{l-1} c^{i+1} S_i = \sum_{i=0}^{l-1} t_{1,i} F + t_2 G + t_3 H$$

and

$$\sum_{i=0}^{l-1} (A_{2,i} + c^{i+1} U) = \sum_{i=0}^{l-1} t_{1,i} T_i + t_2 G.$$

This interactive protocol can be made non-interactive using the Fiat-Shamir technique, which replaces the verifier challenge c with the output of a cryptographic hash function on transcript inputs. We now prove that the protocol is complete, special sound, and special honest-verifier zero knowledge.

Proof. Completeness of the protocol follows by inspection.

We now show it is $(l+1)$-special sound by building a polynomial-time extractor as follows. Given a statement and initial proof transcript $(A_1, \{A_{2_i}\}_{i=0}^{l-1})$, the verifier sends $l + 1$ distinct challenge values $c_0, c_1, \ldots, c_l$ and receives the corresponding transcript values $(\{t_{1,i}^0\}_{i=0}^{l-1}, t_2^0, t_3^0), \ldots, (\{t_{1,i}^l\}_{i=0}^{l-1}, t_2^l, t_3^l)$ from the prover. From the first verification equation, we build the following linear system:

$$A_1 + \sum_{i=0}^{l-1} c_0^{i+1} S_i = \sum_{i=0}^{l-1} t_{1,i}^0 F + t_2^0 G + t_3^0 H$$

$$A_1 + \sum_{i=0}^{l-1} c_1^{i+1} S_i = \sum_{i=0}^{l-1} t_{1,i}^1 F + t_2^1 G + t_3^1 H$$

$$\vdots$$

$$A_1 + \sum_{i=0}^{l-1} c_l^{i+1} S_i = \sum_{i=0}^{l-1} t_{1,i}^l F + t_2^l G + t_3^l H$$

Subtracting the first equation from the rest, we obtain another linear system:

$$\sum_{i=0}^{l-1}(c_1^{i+1} - c_0^{i+1})S_i = \sum_{i=0}^{l-1}(t_{1,i}^1 - t_{1,i}^0)F + (t_2^1 - t_2^0)G + (t_3^1 - t_3^0)H$$

$$\sum_{i=0}^{l-1}(c_2^{i+1} - c_0^{i+1})S_i = \sum_{i=0}^{l-1}(t_{1,i}^2 - t_{1,i}^0)F + (t_2^2 - t_2^0)G + (t_3^2 - t_3^0)H \qquad (1)$$

$$\vdots$$

$$\sum_{i=0}^{l-1}(c_l^{i+1} - c_0^{i+1})S_i = \sum_{i=0}^{l-1}(t_{1,i}^l - t_{1,i}^0)F + (t_2^l - t_2^0)G + (t_3^l - t_3^0)H$$

Finally, we let the set $\{x_i\}_{i=0}^{l-1} \subset \mathbb{F}$ be defined through the following linear system:

$$\sum_{i=0}^{l-1}(c_1^{i+1} - c_0^{i+1})x_i = \sum_{i=0}^{l-1}(t_{1,i}^1 - t_{1,i}^0)$$

$$\sum_{i=0}^{l-1}(c_2^{i+1} - c_0^{i+1})x_i = \sum_{i=0}^{l-1}(t_{1,i}^2 - t_{1,i}^0)$$

$$\vdots$$

$$\sum_{i=0}^{l-1}(c_l^{i+1} - c_0^{i+1})x_i = \sum_{i=0}^{l-1}(t_{1,i}^l - t_{1,i}^0)$$

Since each challenge is uniformly distributed at random, the square coefficient matrix corresponding to the system has nonzero determinant except with negligible probability, and hence the system is solvable for all $\{x_i\}_{i=0}^{l-1}$. Further, we can form similar linear systems to define corresponding $\{y_i\}_{i=0}^{l-1}$ and $\{z_i\}_{i=0}^{l-1}$ such that we let $S_i = x_i F + y_i G + z_i H$ and the equations in system 1 hold.

It remains to show that these solutions are unique; that is, that no S_i has a different representation with coefficients x_i', y_i', z_i' consistent with successful verification. If this were the case, then we must have the polynomial equation

$\sum_{i=0}^{l-1} c^{i+1}(x_i - x_i') = 0$ in c; however, since c is selected randomly by the verifier, all coefficients of the polynomial must (with overwhelming probability) be zero by the Schwartz-Zippel lemma. Hence each $x_i = x_i'$ (and by the same reasoning, $y_i = y_i'$ and $z_i = z_i'$), and the extracted witness set is unique.

To show the protocol is special honest-verifier zero knowledge, we construct a valid simulator producing transcripts identically distributed to those of valid proofs. The simulator chooses a random challenge $c \in \mathbb{F}$ and random values $\{t_{1,i}\}_{i=0}^{l-1}, t_2, t_3 \in \mathbb{F}$. It also randomly selects $\{A_{2,i}\}_{i=1}^{l-1} \in \mathbb{G}$, and sets

$$A_1 = \sum_{i=0}^{l-1} t_{1,i}F + t_2 G + t_3 H - \sum_{i=0}^{l-1} c^{i+1}S_i$$

and

$$A_{2,0} = \sum_{i=0}^{l-1} t_{1,i}T_i + t_2 G - \sum_{i=1}^{l-1} A_{2,i} - \sum_{i=0}^{l-1} c^{i+1}U.$$

The forms of A_1 and $A_{2,0}$ are defined such that the verification equations hold, and therefore such a transcript will be accepted by an honest verifier. Observe that all transcript elements in a valid proof are independently distributed uniformly at random if the generators F, G, H, U are independent, as are transcript elements produced by the simulator.

This completes the proof.

C   Parallel One-out-of-Many Proving System

The proving system itself is a tuple of algorithms (ParProve, ParVerify) for the following relation, where we let $N = n^m$:

$$\{pp_{\mathrm{par}}, \{S_k, V_k\}_{i=0}^{N-1} \subset \mathbb{G}^2, S', V' \in \mathbb{G}; l \in \mathbb{N}, (s, v) \in \mathbb{F} :$$
$$0 \le l < N, S_l - S' = \mathsf{Comm}(0, 0, s), V_l - V' = \mathsf{Com}(0, v)\}$$

Let $\delta(i, j) : \mathbb{N}^2 \to \mathbb{F}$ be the Kronecker delta function. For any integers k and j such that $0 \le k < N$ and $0 \le j < m$, let k_j denote the j digit of the n-ary decomposition of k. Let $\mathsf{MatrixCom} : \mathbb{F}^{mn} \times \mathbb{F}^{mn} \times \mathbb{F} \to \mathbb{G}$ be an additively-homomorphic matrix commitment construction that commits to the entries of two matrices, and is perfectly hiding and computationally binding.

The protocol proceeds as follows, where we use some of the notation of [16, 22]:

1. The prover selects
$$r_A, r_B, \{a_{j,i}\}_{j=0, i=1}^{m-1, n-1} \in \mathbb{F}$$
uniformly at random, and, for each $j \in [0, m)$, sets
$$a_{j,0} = - \sum_{i=1}^{n-1} a_{j,i}.$$

2. The prover computes the following:

$$A \equiv \mathsf{MatrixCom}\left(\{a_{j,i}\}_{j,i=0}^{m-1,n-1}, \{-a_{j,i}^2\}_{j,i=0}^{m-1,n-1}, r_A\right)$$

$$B \equiv \mathsf{MatrixCom}\left(\{\delta(l_j, i)\}_{j,i=0}^{m-1,n-1}, \{a_{j,i}(1 - 2\delta(l_j, i))\}_{j,i=0}^{m-1,n-1}, r_B\right)$$

3. For each $j \in [0, m)$, the prover selects $\rho_j, \rho_j' \in \mathbb{F}$ uniformly at random, and computes the following:

$$X_j \equiv \sum_{k=0}^{N-1} p_{k,j}(S_k - S') + \mathsf{Comm}(0, 0, \rho_j)$$

$$X_j' \equiv \sum_{k=0}^{N-1} p_{k,j}(V_k - V') + \mathsf{Com}(0, \rho_j')$$

Here each $p_{k,j}$ is defined such that for all $k \in [0, N)$ we have

$$\prod_{j=0}^{m-1} \left(\delta(l_j, k_j)x + a_{j,k_j}\right) = \delta(l, k)x^m + \sum_{j=0}^{m-1} p_{k,j}x^j$$

for indeterminate x.

4. The prover sends $A, B, \{X_j, X_j'\}_{j=0}^{m-1}$ to the verifier.
5. The verifier selects $x \in \mathbb{F}$ uniformly at random and sends it to the prover.
6. For each $j \in [0, m)$ and $i \in [1, n)$, the prover computes $f_{j,i} \equiv \delta(l_j, i)x + a_{j,i}$ and the following values:

$$z \equiv r_A + xr_B$$

$$z_S \equiv sx^m - \sum_{j=0}^{m-1} \rho_j x^j$$

$$z_V \equiv vx^m - \sum_{j=0}^{m-1} \rho_j' x^j$$

7. The prover sends $\{f_{j,i}\}_{j=0,i=1}^{m-1,n-1}, z, z_S, z_V$ to the verifier.
8. For each $j \in [0, m)$, the verifier sets $f_{j,0} \equiv x - \sum_{i=1}^{n-1} f_{j,i}$ and accepts the proof if and only if

$$A + xB = \mathsf{MatrixCom}\left(\{f_{j,i}\}_{j,i=0}^{m-1,n-1}, \{f_{j,i}(x - f_{j,i})\}_{j,i=0}^{m-1,n-1}, z\right)$$

and

$$\sum_{k=0}^{N-1} \left(\prod_{j=0}^{m-1} f_{j,k_j}\right)(S_k - S') - \sum_{j=0}^{m-1} x^j X_j = \mathsf{Comm}(0, 0, z_S)$$

$$\sum_{k=0}^{N-1} \left(\prod_{j=0}^{m-1} f_{j,k_j}\right)(V_k - V') - \sum_{j=0}^{m-1} x^j X_j' = \mathsf{Com}(0, z_V)$$

are true.

This interactive protocol can be made non-interactive using the Fiat-Shamir technique, which replaces the verifier challenge x with the output of a cryptographic hash function on transcript inputs.

We now prove that the above protocol is complete, special sound, and honest-verifier zero knowledge. The proofs proceed similarly to those of [4,16,22].

Proof. Completeness of the protocol follows by straightforward algebra.

To show that the protocol is special honest-verifier zero knowledge, we construct a simulator that, when provided a valid statement and random verifier challenge x, produces a proof transcript identically distributed to that of a real proof.

To produce our simulated transcript on random x, the simulator samples

$$B, \{X_j, X_j'\}_{j=1}^{m-1} \in \mathbb{G}$$

and

$$z, z_S, z_V, \{f_{j,i}\}_{j=0,i=1}^{m-1,n-1} \in \mathbb{F}$$

uniformly at random. It defines

$$f_{j,0} = x - \sum_{i=1}^{n-1} f_{j,i}$$

for each $j \in [0, m)$, and sets

$$A = \mathsf{MatrixCom}\left(\{f_{j,i}\}_{j,i=0}^{m-1,n-1}, \{f_{j,i}(x - f_{j,i})\}_{j,i=0}^{m-1,n-1}, z\right) - xB$$

as well. It uses the final two verification equations to compute X_0 and X_0':

$$X_0 = \sum_{k=0}^{N-1} \left(\prod_{j=0}^{m-1} f_{j,k_j}\right)(S_k - S') - \sum_{j=1}^{m-1} x^j X_j - \mathsf{Comm}(0,0,z_S)$$

$$X_0' = \sum_{k=0}^{N-1} \left(\prod_{j=0}^{m-1} f_{j,k_j}\right)(V_k - V') - \sum_{j=1}^{m-1} x^j X_j' - \mathsf{Com}(0,z_V)$$

Since the challenge x is sampled uniformly at random by construction, the commitment constructions are perfectly hiding, $\{\rho_j, \rho_j'\}_{j=0}^{m-1}$ are sampled uniformly at random in a real proof, and the decisional Diffie-Hellman problem is hard in $\mathbb{G}$, all proof elements in both the simulation and real proofs are either independently uniformly distributed at random or uniquely determined by other transcript elements. Hence the protocol is special honest-verifier zero knowledge.

We now show that the protocol is $(m+1)$-special sound for $m > 1$. That is, we construct an extractor that, when presented with a set of $m+1$ distinct challenges and corresponding responses to the same initial statement, produces a set of extracted witness elements consistent with the statement. Consider a collection of $m+1$ distinct challenges $\{x_\iota\}_{\iota=0}^m$, and corresponding valid responses:

$$\left\{\{f_{j,i}^{(\iota)}\}_{j=0,i=1}^{m-1,n-1}, z^{(\iota)}, z_S^{(\iota)}, z_V^{(\iota)}\right\}_{\iota=0}^m$$

Successful verification on indices $\iota \in \{0, 1\}$ gives the following:

$$(x^{(0)} - x^{(1)})B = \mathsf{MatrixCom}\left(\{f_{j,i}^{(0)} - f_{j,i}^{(1)}\}_{j,i=0}^{m-1,n-1},\right.$$
$$\left.\{f_{j,i}^{(0)}(x^{(0)} - f_{j,i}^{(0)}) - f_{j,i}^{(1)}(x^{(1)} - f_{j,i}^{(1)})\}_{j,i=0}^{m-1,n-1}, z^{(0)} - z^{(1)}\right)$$

For all $j \in [0, m)$ and $i \in [0, n)$, if we let

$$b_{j,i} = \frac{f_{j,i}^{(0)} - f_{j,i}^{(1)}}{x^{(0)} - x^{(1)}}$$

and

$$c_{j,i} = \frac{f_{j,i}^{(0)}(x^{(0)} - f_{j,i}^{(0)}) - f_{j,i}^{(1)}(x^{(1)} - f_{j,i}^{(1)})}{x^{(0)} - x^{(1)}}$$

and

$$r_B = \frac{z^{(0)} - z^{(1)}}{x^{(0)} - x^{(1)}},$$

then we can express

$$B = \mathsf{MatrixCom}\left(\{b_{j,i}\}_{j,i=0}^{m-1,n-1}, \{c_{j,i}\}_{j,i=0}^{m-1,n-1}, r_B\right).$$

If for $j \in [0, m)$ and $i \in [0, n)$ we further define

$$a_{j,i} = f_{j,i}^{(0)} - x^{(0)}b_{i,j}$$

and

$$d_{i,j} = f_{j,i}^{(0)}(x^{(0)} - f_{j,i}^{(0)}) - x^{(0)}c_{j,i}$$

and $r_A = z^{(0)} - x^{(0)}r_B$, then we can express

$$A = \mathsf{MatrixCom}\left(\{a_{j,i}\}_{j,i=0}^{m-1,n-1}, \{d_{j,i}\}_{j,i=0}^{m-1,n-1}, r_A\right)$$

as well. Observe that since the commitment construction is computationally binding, for all $\iota \in [0, m]$ we must have $b_{j,i}x^{(\iota)} + a_{j,i} = f_{j,i}^{(\iota)}$ and $c_{j,i}x^{(\iota)} + d_{i,j} = f_{j,i}^{(\iota)}(x^{(\iota)} - f_{j,i}^{(\iota)})$ for $j \in [0, m)$ and $i \in [0, n)$. This implies in particular that for $\iota \in \{0, 1, 2\}, j \in [0, m), i \in [0, n)$ we have

$$c_{j,i}x^{(\iota)} + d_{j,i} = b_{j,i}(1 - b_{j,i})x^{(\iota)2} + (1 - 2b_{j,i})a_{j,i}x^{(\iota)} - a_{j,i}^2$$

and hence $b_{j,i}(1 - b_{j,i}) = 0$, so each $b_{j,i} \in \{0, 1\}$.

We also have, by construction, that

$$x^{(\iota)} = \sum_{i=0}^{n-1} f_{j,i}^{(\iota)} = x^{(\iota)}\sum_{i=0}^{n-1} b_{j,i} + \sum_{i=0}^{n-1} a_{j,i}$$

for $\iota \in [0, m], j \in [0, m)$, so $\sum_{i=0}^{n-1} b_{j,i} = 1$. This means we can extract $l \in [0, N)$ such that each $b_{j,i} = \delta(l_j, i)$.

Now if we define for each $k \in [0, N)$ the polynomial

$$p_k(x) = \prod_{j=0}^{m-1} [\delta(l_j, k_j)x + a_{j,k_j}]$$

in x, we have $\deg(p_k) = m$ if and only if $k = l$. Verification can therefore be expressed as

$$x^{(\iota)m}(S_l - S') - \sum_{j=0}^{m-1} x^{(\iota)j}\overline{X}_j = \mathsf{Comm}(0, 0, z_S^{(\iota)})$$

$$x^{(\iota)m}(V_l - V') - \sum_{j=0}^{m-1} x^{(\iota)j}\overline{X}'_j = \mathsf{Com}(0, 0, z_V^{(\iota)})$$

for $\iota \in [0, m]$, where the sets $\{\overline{X}_j\}_{j=0}^{m-1}$ and $\{\overline{X}'_j\}_{j=0}^{m-1}$ can be uniquely derived. Consider a Vandermonde matrix V such that the ι row is the vector $(1, x^{(\iota)}, \ldots, x^{(\iota)m})$, and note since each challenge is distinct, we have $\det(V) \neq 0$ with high probability, so the rows of V span $\mathbb{F}^{m+1}$. This means we can find $\{\theta_\iota\}_{\iota=0}^m$ such that the equation

$$\sum_{\iota=0}^m \theta_\iota x^{(\iota)j} = \delta(j, m)$$

holds for $j \in [0, m]$.

We can therefore build a linear combination of each of the two above verification equations, taking advantage of the Vandermonde-derived weights:

$$S_l - S' = \sum_{\iota=0}^m \theta_\iota x^{(\iota)m}(S_l - S') + \sum_{\iota=0}^m \theta_\iota \left(x^{(\iota)j}\overline{X}_j\right) = \mathsf{Comm}\left(0, 0, \sum_{\iota=0}^m \theta_\iota z_S^{(\iota)}\right)$$

$$V_l - V' = \sum_{\iota=0}^m \theta_\iota x^{(\iota)m}(S_l - S') + \sum_{\iota=0}^m \theta_\iota \left(x^{(\iota)j}\overline{X}'_j\right) = \mathsf{Com}\left(0, \sum_{\iota=0}^m \theta_\iota z_V^{(\iota)}\right)$$

These equations provide the remaining extractions

$$s = \sum_{\iota=0}^m \theta_\iota z_S^{(\iota)}$$

and

$$v = \sum_{\iota=0}^m \theta_\iota z_V^{(\iota)}$$

such that $S_l - S' = \mathsf{Comm}(0, 0, s)$ and $V_l - V' = \mathsf{Com}(0, v)$, which completes the proof.

D   Payment System Security

Zerocash [2] established a robust security framework for decentralized anonymous payment (DAP) scheme security that captures a realistic threat model with powerful adversaries who are permitted to add malicious coins into transactions' input ambiguity sets, control the choice of transaction inputs, and produce arbitrary transactions to add to a ledger. Here we formally prove Spark's security within a related (but modified) security model; proofs follow somewhat similarly to that of [2].

The DAP construction is a tuple of algorithms

(Setup, CreateKeys, CreateAddress, CreateCoin,

Mint, Identify, Recover, Spend, Verify)

that is secure if it satisfies properties of completeness, balance, non-malleability, and ledger indistinguishability.

Each security property is formalized as a game between a polynomial-time adversary $\mathcal{A}$ and a challenger $\mathcal{C}$, where in each game the behavior of honest parties is simulated via an oracle $\mathcal{O}^{\mathsf{DAP}}$. The oracle $\mathcal{O}^{\mathsf{DAP}}$ maintains a ledger L of transactions and provides an interface for executing the CreateAddress, Mint, and Spend algorithms. To simulate behavior from honest parties, $\mathcal{A}$ passes a query to $\mathcal{C}$, which makes sanity checks and then proxies the queries to $\mathcal{O}^{\mathsf{DAP}}$, returning the responses to $\mathcal{A}$ as needed. For CreateAddress queries, the oracle first runs the CreateKeys protocol algorithm, then calls CreateAddress using the resulting incoming view key and a randomly-selected diversifier index, and finally returns the public address $\mathsf{addr_{pk}}$. For Mint queries, the adversary specifies the value, memo, and destination public address for the transaction, and the resulting transaction is produced and returned if the inputs are semantically valid. For Spend queries, the adversary specifies the input coins to be consumed, as well as the values, memos, and destination public addresses for the transaction, and the resulting transaction is produced after coin recovery if the inputs are semantically valid, all consumed coins are validly controlled by an address produced by the oracle, and all consumed coins are unspent according to the ledger state. The oracle $\mathcal{O}^{\mathsf{DAP}}$ also provides an Insert query that allows the adversary to insert arbitrary and potentially malicious $\mathsf{tx_{mint}}$ or $\mathsf{tx_{spend}}$ transactions into the ledger L, provided they are semantically valid and pass verification by the oracle.

For each security property, we say the DAP satisfies the property if the adversary can win the corresponding game with only negligible probability.

We now state a lemma that will be useful when examining the security of our construction.

Lemma 1. *Given a ledger, two otherwise valid spend transactions reveal the same tag only if there exist coins with serial commitments S_1, S_2 produced in previous valid transactions and an extractor that produces representations of the following form:*

$$S_1 = \mathsf{Comm}(x, y, \beta_1)$$
$$S_2 = \mathsf{Comm}(x, y, \beta_2)$$

Proof. Let T be the tag common to the two spend transactions. Each transaction has a valid modified Chaum-Pedersen proof. One transaction's valid proof yields statement values $T, S_1' \in \mathbb{G}$ and witness values $x_1, y_1, z_1 \in \mathbb{F}$ such that $U = x_1 T + y_1 G$ and $S_1' = x_1 F + y_1 G + z_1 H$. Similarly, the other transaction's valid proof yields statement values $T, S_2' \in \mathbb{G}$ and witness values $x_2, y_2, z_2 \in \mathbb{F}$ such that $U = x_2 T + y_2 G$ and $S_2' = x_2 F + y_2 G + z_2 H$. Since U and G are independent and Pedersen commitments are computationally binding, we must have (except with negligible probability) that $x_1 = x_2 = x$ and $y_1 = y_2 = y$. Hence $S_1' = xF + yG + z_1 H$ and $S_2' = xF + yG + z_2 H$.

Each transaction further has a valid parallel one-of-many proof. From the first transaction's proof we have (by index extraction referencing an element of its input cover set) a group element $S_1 \in \mathbb{G}$ and scalar $\alpha_1 \in \mathbb{F}$ such that $S_1 - S_1' = \alpha_1 H$. For the second proof, we similarly have $S_2 \in \mathbb{G}$ and $\alpha_2 \in \mathbb{F}$ such that $S_2 - S_2' = \alpha_2 H$.

This means in particular that

$$S_1 = xF + yG + (z_1 + \alpha_1)H$$

and

$$S_2 = xF + yG + (z_2 + \alpha_2)H$$

by combining these results. Since transaction validity requires all input cover set elements to exist as outputs of previous valid transactions, we have extracted representations of the desired form by setting $\beta_1 = z_1 + \alpha_1$ and $\beta_2 = z_2 + \alpha_2$.

Observe that the result also holds for duplicate tags revealed in the same (otherwise valid) transaction, with almost identical reasoning.

D.1   Completeness

Completeness requires that no bounded adversary can prevent an honest user from spending a coin.[1] Specifically, this means that if the user is able to identify a coin using its incoming view key, then it can recover the coin using its full view key and generate a valid spend transaction consuming the coin using its spend key.

---

[1] We note that the security model does not capture the case where an adversary observes a valid transaction prior to its addition to the ledger and generates its own transaction producing a coin with the same serial commitment, possibly rendering the honest transaction invalid. It is possible to mitigate this by allowing duplicate serial commitments on the ledger and requiring either coin identification to account for this by only accepting one such coin, or by binding unique data like linking tags or other additional context into serial commitments to be checked during coin identification.

To see why this property holds, note that by construction, if an honest user is unable to produce a spend transaction for a coin with serial commitment S that it has recovered, the corresponding tag T must appear in a previous valid transaction. The identified coin S must be a commitment of the form $S = \mathsf{Comm}(s, r, 0)$ for serial number s and spend key component r according to the Identify definition. By Lemma 1, any previous transaction revealing T must consume a coin with serial commitment $\overline{S} = \mathsf{Comm}(s, r, z)$ for $z \neq 0$ (since coins must have unique serial commitments). Since the user cannot have identified $\overline{S}$ because z is nonzero, it did not generate the transaction consuming $\overline{S}$, a contradiction since that transaction implies knowledge of the spend key r by extraction.

D.2   Balance

Balance requires that no bounded adversary $\mathcal{A}$ can control more coins than are minted or spent to it. It is formalized by a BAL game. The adversary $\mathcal{A}$ adaptively interacts with $\mathcal{C}$ and the oracle with queries, and at the end of the interaction outputs a set of coins AdvCoins. Letting ADDR be set of all addresses of honest users generated by CreateAddress queries, $\mathcal{A}$ wins the game if

$$v_{\text{unspent}} + v_{\mathcal{A} \to \text{ADDR}} > v_{\text{mint}} + v_{\text{ADDR} \to \mathcal{A}},$$

which implies that the total value the adversary can spend or has spent already is greater than the value it has minted or received. Here:

- v_{unspent} is the total value of unspent coins in AdvCoins;
- v_{mint} is the total value minted by $\mathcal{A}$ to itself through Mint or Insert queries;
- $v_{\text{ADDR} \to \mathcal{A}}$ is the total value of coins received by $\mathcal{A}$ from addresses in ADDR; and
- $v_{\mathcal{A} \to \text{ADDR}}$ is the total value of coins sent by the adversary to the addresses in ADDR.

We say a DAP scheme Π is BAL-secure if the adversary $\mathcal{A}$ wins the game BAL only with negligible probability:

$$\Pr[\mathsf{BAL}(\Pi, \mathcal{A}, \lambda) = 1] \leq \mathsf{negl}(\lambda)$$

Assume the challenger maintains an extra augmented ledger $(L, \boldsymbol{a})$ where each a_i contains secret data from transaction tx_i in L. In that case where tx_i was produced by a query from $\mathcal{A}$ to the challenger $\mathcal{C}$, a_i contains all secret data used by $\mathcal{C}$ to produce the transaction. If instead tx_i was produced by a direct Insert query from $\mathcal{A}$, a_i consists of all extracted witness data from proofs contained in the transaction. The resulting augmented ledger $(L, \boldsymbol{a})$ is balanced if the following conditions are true:

1. Each valid spend transaction $\mathsf{tx}_{\text{spend},k}$ in $(L, \boldsymbol{a})$ consumes distinct coins, and each consumed coin is the output of a valid $\mathsf{tx}_{\text{mint},i}$ or $\mathsf{tx}_{\text{spend},j}$ transaction for some $i < k$ or $j < k$. This requirement implies that all transactions spend only valid coins, and that no coin is spent more than once within the same valid transaction.

2. No two valid spend transactions in (L, a) consume the same coin. This implies no coin is spent through two different transactions. Together with the first requirement, this implies that each coin is spent at most once.

3. For each $(\text{tx}_{\text{spend}}, a)$ in (L, a) consuming input coins with value commitments $\{C_u\}_{u=0}^{w-1}$, for each $u \in [0, w)$:
   - If C_u is the output of a valid mint transaction with augmented ledger witness a', then the value of C_u contained in a' is the same as the corresponding value contained in a for the value commitment offset C'_u.
   - If C_u is the output of a valid spend transaction with augmented ledger witness a', then the value of C_u contained in a' is the same as the corresponding value contained in a for the value commitment offset C'_u.

   This implies that values are maintained between transactions.

4. For each $(\text{tx}_{\text{spend}}, a)$ in (L, a) with fee f that consumes input coins with value commitment offsets $\{C'_u\}_{u=0}^{w-1}$ and generates coins with value commitments $\{\overline{C}_j\}_{j=0}^{t-1}$, a contains values $\{v_u\}_{u=0}^{w-1}$ and $\{\overline{v}_j\}_{j=0}^{t-1}$ corresponding to the commitments such that the balance equation

$$\sum_{u=0}^{w-1} v_u = \sum_{j=0}^{t-1} \overline{v}_j + f$$

   holds. For each $(\text{tx}_{\text{mint}}, a)$ in (L, a) generating coins with value commitments $\{\overline{C}_j\}_{j=0}^{t-1}$ and public values $\{\overline{v}_j\}_{j=0}^{t-1}$, a contains values $\{\overline{v}'_j\}_{j=0}^{t-1}$ corresponding to the commitments such that $\overline{v}_j = \overline{v}'_j$ for all $j \in [0, t)$. This implies that values cannot be created arbitrarily.

5. For each tx_{spend} in (L, a) inserted by $\mathcal{A}$ through an Insert query, each consumed coin in tx_{spend} is not recoverable by any address in ADDR. This implies that the adversary cannot generate a transaction consuming coins it does not control.

If these five conditions hold, then $\mathcal{A}$ did not spend or control more money than was previously minted or spent to it, and the inequality

$$v_{\text{mint}} + v_{\text{ADDR} \to \mathcal{A}} \leq v_{\text{unspent}} + v_{\mathcal{A} \to \text{ADDR}}$$

holds. We now prove that Spark is BAL-secure under this definition.

Proof. By way of contradiction, assume the adversary $\mathcal{A}$ interacts with $\mathcal{C}$ leading to a non-balanced augmented ledger (L, a) with non-negligible probability; then at least one of the five conditions described above is violated with non-negligible probability:

$\mathcal{A}$ **violates Condition 1:** Suppose that the probability $\mathcal{A}$ wins the game violating Condition 1 is non-negligible. Each tx_{spend} generated by a non-Insert oracle query satisfies this condition already, so there must exist a transaction $(\text{tx}_{\text{spend}}, a)$ in (L, a) inserted by $\mathcal{A}$.

Suppose there exist inputs $u_1, u_2 \in [0, w)$ of tx_{spend} that consume the same coin with serial commitment S. Validity of the modified Chaum-Pedersen proof Π_{chaum} gives extracted openings $S'_{u_1} = s_{u_1} F + r_{u_1} G + y_{u_1} H$ and $S'_{u_2} = s_{u_2} F +$

$r_{u_2}G + y_{u_2}H$ and tag representations such that $U = s_{u_1}T_{u_1} + r_{u_1}G$ and $U = s_{u_2}T_{u_2} + r_{u_2}G$. Because transaction validity implies $T_{u_1} \neq T_{u_2}$, we must have $(s_{u_1}, r_{u_1}) \neq (s_{u_2}, r_{u_2})$. Validity of the corresponding parallel one-out-of-many proofs $(\Pi_{\text{par}})_{u_1}$ and $(\Pi_{\text{par}})_{u_2}$ yields indices (corresponding to the same input set group element S) and discrete logarithm extractions such that $S - S'_{u_1} = x_{u_1}H$ and $S - S'_{u_2} = x_{u_2}H$. This means

$$S = \mathsf{Comm}(s_{u_1}, r_{u_1}, x_{u_1} + y_{u_1}) = \mathsf{Comm}(s_{u_2}, r_{u_2}, x_{u_2} + y_{u_2}),$$

a contradiction since the commitment scheme is computationally binding.

The second possibility for violation of the condition is that the transaction tx_{spend} consumes a coin that is not generated in any previous valid transaction. This follows immediately using similar reasoning as above, since transaction validity asserts knowledge of an opening to a commitment contained in the input set, all of which must have been previously generated in valid transactions by definition.

$\mathcal{A}$ **violates Condition 2:** Suppose that the probability $\mathcal{A}$ wins the game violating Condition **2** is non-negligible. This means the augmented ledger $(L, \boldsymbol{a})$ contains two valid spend transactions consuming the same coin but producing distinct tags. Similarly to the previous argument, this implies distinct openings of the coin serial number commitment, which is a contradiction.

$\mathcal{A}$ **violates Condition 3:** Suppose that the probability $\mathcal{A}$ wins the game violating Condition **3** is non-negligible. Let C be the value commitment of the coin consumed by an input of tx_{spend} and generated in a previous transaction (of either type) in $(L, \boldsymbol{a})$. Since the generating transaction is valid, we have an extracted opening $C = vG + aH$ from either the value proof (in a mint transaction) or the range proof (in a spend transaction). Validity of the corresponding parallel one-out-of-many proof in tx_{spend} gives an extracted discrete logarithm $C - C' = xH$, where C' is the input's value commitment offset. But this immediately gives $C' = vG + (a - x)H$, a contradiction since the commitment scheme is binding.

$\mathcal{A}$ **violates Condition 4:** Suppose that the probability $\mathcal{A}$ wins the game violating Condition **4** is non-negligible. If the augmented ledger $(L, \boldsymbol{a})$ contains a spend transaction that violates the balance equation, this immediately implies a break in the commitment binding property since the corresponding balance proof Π_{bal} is valid, which is a contradiction. If instead the augmented ledger $(L, \boldsymbol{a})$ contains a mint transaction that violates the balance requirement, this immediately implies a break in the commitment binding property since the corresponding value proof Π_{val} is valid, again a contradiction.

$\mathcal{A}$ **violates Condition 5:** Suppose that the probability $\mathcal{A}$ wins the game violating Condition **5** is non-negligible. That is, $\mathcal{A}$ produces a spend transaction tx_{spend} by an Insert question that is valid on the augmented ledger $(L, \boldsymbol{a})$ and consumes a coin corresponding to a coin serial number commitment S that can be recovered by a public address $(d, Q_1, Q_2) \in \mathsf{ADDR}$.

Validity of the Chaum-Pedersen proof corresponding to tx_{spend} yields an extracted representation $S' = s'F + r'G + yH$. Validity of the corresponding parallel one-of-many proof gives a serial number commitment S and extraction such that $S - S' = xH$, so $S = s'F + r'G + (x + y)H$.

Now let (s_1, s_2, r) be the spend key corresponding to the address (d, Q_1, Q_2). Since tx_{spend} consumes a coin recoverable by this address, a serial number commitment for the recovered coin is

$$\overline{S} = \mathcal{H}_{\text{ser}}(k)F + Q_2$$
$$= (\mathcal{H}_{\text{ser}}(k) + \mathcal{H}_{Q_2}(s_1, i) + s_2)F + rG$$

for nonce k and some diversifier index i.

Since the commitment scheme is binding, we must therefore have $r' = r$, which is a contradiction since $\mathcal{A}$ cannot extract this discrete logarithm from the public address.

This completes the proof.

D.3 Transaction Non-malleability

This property requires that no bounded adversary can substantively alter a valid transaction. In particular, non-malleability prevents malicious adversaries from modifying honest users' transactions by altering data or redirecting the outputs of a valid transaction before the transaction is added to the ledger. Since non-malleability of mint transactions is offloaded to authorizations relating to consensus rules or base-layer operations, we need only consider the case of spend transactions.

This property is formalized by an experiment TRNM, in which a bounded adversary $\mathcal{A}$ adaptively interacts with the oracle $\mathcal{O}^{\text{DAP}}$, and then outputs a spend transaction tx'. If we let T denote the set of all transactions produced by Spend queries to $\mathcal{O}^{\text{DAP}}$, and L denote the final ledger, $\mathcal{A}$ wins the game if there exists $\text{tx} \in T$ such that:

- $\text{tx}' \neq \text{tx}$;
- tx' reveals a tag also revealed by tx; and
- both tx' and tx are valid transactions with respect to the ledger L' containing all transactions preceding tx on L.

We say a DAP scheme Π is TRNM-secure if the adversary $\mathcal{A}$ wins the game TRNM only with negligible probability:

$$\Pr[\text{TRNM}(\Pi, \mathcal{A}, \lambda) = 1] \leq \text{negl}(\lambda)$$

Let T be the set of all tx_{spend} transactions generated by the $\mathcal{O}^{\text{DAP}}$ in response to Spend queries. Since these transactions are generated by these oracle queries, $\mathcal{A}$ does not learn any secret data used to produce these transactions.

Proof. Assume that the adversary $\mathcal{A}$ wins the game with non-negligible probability. That is, $\mathcal{A}$ produces a transaction tx' revealing a tag T also revealed in a transaction tx. Without loss of generality, assume each transaction consumes a single coin.

Observe that a valid spend binds all transaction elements except for the modified Chaum-Pedersen proof into each such proof via $\mathcal{H}_{\text{bind}}$ and the proof transcripts. Therefore, in order to produce valid tx' $\neq$ tx, we consider two cases:

– the modified Chaum-Pedersen proofs are identical, but tx' and tx differ in another element of the transaction structures; or
– the modified Chaum-Pedersen proof in tx' is distinct from the proof in tx.

In the first case, at least one input to the binding hash $\mathcal{H}_{\text{bind}}$ used to initialize the modified Chaum-Pedersen transcripts must differ between the proofs. Because we model this hash function as a random oracle, the outputs differ except with negligible probability, a contradiction since the resulting proof structures must be identical.

In the second case, because the tag revealed in both tx' and tx is identical, Lemma 1 gives extractions of the form (s, r, y) and $(s, r, 0)$ respectively. Further, the coin $S = \text{Comm}(s, r, 0)$ consumed in tx was generated such that r is a spend key component for an address (d, Q_1, Q_2) not controlled by $\mathcal{A}$. Since $\mathcal{A}$ does not control this address, it cannot produce r without extracting from S or from any set of corresponding diversified address components $\{Q_{2,i}\}_i$ produced from the same spend key. However, each $Q_{2,i}$ is produced linearly against Q_2 and querying $\mathcal{H}_{Q_2}$ with unique (s_1, i) input, a contradiction.

D.4   Ledger Indistinguishability

This property implies that no bounded adversary $\mathcal{A}$ received any information from the ledger except what is already publicly revealed, even if it can influence valid ledger operations by honest users.

Ledger indistinguishability is formalized through an experiment LIND between a bounded adversary $\mathcal{A}$ and a challenger $\mathcal{C}$, which terminates with a binary output b' by $\mathcal{A}$. At the beginning of the experiment, $\mathcal{C}$ samples $\text{Setup}(1^\lambda) \to pp$ and sends the parameters to $\mathcal{A}$; next it samples a random bit $b \in \{0, 1\}$ and initializes two separate DAP oracles $\mathcal{O}_0^{\text{DAP}}$ and $\mathcal{O}_1^{\text{DAP}}$, each with its own separate ledger and internal state. At each consecutive step of the experiment:

1. $\mathcal{C}$ provides $\mathcal{A}$ two ledgers $(L_{\text{left}} = L_b, L_{\text{right}} = L_{1-b})$ where L_b and L_{1-b} are the current ledgers of the oracles $\mathcal{O}_b^{\text{DAP}}$ and $\mathcal{O}_{1-b}^{\text{DAP}}$ respectively.
2. $\mathcal{A}$ sends to $\mathcal{C}$ two queries Q, Q' of the same type (one of CreateAddress, Mint, Spend, or Insert).
   – If the query type is Insert or Mint, $\mathcal{C}$ forwards Q to L_b and Q' to L_{1-b}, permitting $\mathcal{A}$ to insert its own transactions or mint new coins to L_{left} and L_{right}.
   – For all queries of type CreateAddress or Spend, $\mathcal{C}$ first checks if the two queries Q and Q' are publicly consistent, and then forwards Q to $\mathcal{O}_0^{\text{DAP}}$ and Q' to $\mathcal{O}_1^{\text{DAP}}$. It receives the two oracle answers (a_0, a_1), but returns (a_b, a_{1-b}) to $\mathcal{A}$.

As the adversary does not know the bit b and the mapping between $(L_{\text{left}}, L_{\text{right}})$ and (L_0, L_1), it cannot learn whether it affects the behavior of honest parties on (L_0, L_1) or on (L_1, L_0). At the end of the experiment, $\mathcal{A}$ sends $\mathcal{C}$ a bit $b' \in \{0, 1\}$. The challenger outputs 1 if $b = b'$, and 0 otherwise.

We require the queries Q and Q' be publicly consistent as follows If the query type of Q and Q' is CreateAddress, both oracles generate the same address. If the query type of Q and Q' is Mint, then the number of generated coins and the public value of each coin must be equal in both queries. If the query type of Q and Q' is Spend, then:

- Both Q and Q' must be well-formed and valid, so the referenced input coins must have been generated in a previous transaction on the ledger and be unspent. Further, the transaction must balance.
- The number of spent coins and output coins must be the same in Q and Q'.
- If a consumed coin in Q references a coin in L_0 posted by $\mathcal{A}$ through an Insert query, then the corresponding index in Q' must also reference a coin in L_1 posted by $\mathcal{A}$ through an Insert query and the values of these two coins must be equal as well (and vice versa for Q').
- If an output coin referenced by Q does not reference a recipient address in the oracle ADDR list (and therefore is controlled by $\mathcal{A}$), then the corresponding value must equal that of the corresponding coin referenced by Q at the same index (and vice versa for Q').

We say a DAP scheme Π is LIND-secure if $\mathcal{A}$ wins the game LIND only probability at most negligibly better than chance:

$$\Pr[\text{LIND}(\Pi, \mathcal{A}, \lambda) = 1] - \frac{1}{2} \leq \text{negl}(\lambda)$$

Proof. In order to prove that $\mathcal{A}$'s advantage in the LIND experiment is negligible, we first consider a simulation experiment $\mathcal{D}^{\text{sim}}$, in which $\mathcal{A}$ interacts with $\mathcal{C}$ as in the LIND experiment, but with modifications.

The Simulation Experiment $\mathcal{D}^{\text{sim}}$: Since the parallel one-out-of-many, modified Chaum-Pedersen, representation, and range proving systems are all special honest-verifier zero knowledge, we can take advantage of the simulator for each. Given input statements and verifier challenges, each proving system's simulator produces transcripts indistinguishable from honest proofs. Additionally, we now define the behavior of the full simulator.

The Simulation. The simulation $\mathcal{D}^{\text{sim}}$ works as follows. As in the original experiment, $\mathcal{C}$ samples the system parameters $\text{Setup}(1^\lambda) \to pp$ and a random bit b, and initializes DAP oracles $\mathcal{O}_0^{\text{DAP}}$ and $\mathcal{O}_1^{\text{DAP}}$. Then $\mathcal{D}^{\text{sim}}$ proceeds in steps. At each step, it provides $\mathcal{A}$ with ledgers $L_{\text{left}} = L_b$ and $L_{\text{right}} = L_{1-b}$, after which $\mathcal{A}$ sends two publicly-consistent queries (Q, Q') of the same type. Recall that the queries Q and Q' are consistent with respect to public data and information related to the addresses controlled by $\mathcal{A}$. Depending on the query type, the challenger acts as follows:

- Answering Insert queries: The challenger proceeds as in the original LIND experiment.
- Answering CreateAddress queries: In this case the challenger replaces the public address components (d, Q_1, Q_2) with random strings of the appropriate lengths, producing $\mathsf{addr}_{\mathrm{pk}}$ that is returned to $\mathcal{A}$.
- Answering Mint queries: The challenger does the following to answer Q and Q' separately, where t is the number of generated coins specified by $\mathcal{A}$ as part of its queries:
   1. For each $j \in [0, t)$:
      (a) If $\mathcal{A}$ provided a public address $\mathsf{addr}_{\mathrm{pk}}$ not generated by the challenger, it produces a coin using CreateCoin as usual.
      (b) Otherwise, it simulates coin generation:
         i. Samples a recovery key K_j uniformly at random.
         ii. Samples a serial number commitment S_j uniformly at random.
         iii. Samples a value commitment $\overline{C}_j$ uniformly at random.
         iv. Samples a random input used to produce an AEAD encryption key $\mathsf{AEADKeyGen} \to k_{\mathrm{enc}}$.
         v. Simulates the recipient data encryption by selecting random r of the proper length, and encrypting it to produce

$$\mathsf{AEADEncrypt}(k_{\mathrm{enc}}, \mathbf{r}, r) \to \overline{r}.$$

   2. Simulates the value proof Π_{val} on the statement $\{\overline{C}_j - \mathsf{Com}(v_j, 0)\}_{j=0}^{t-1}$.
   3. Assembles the transaction and adds it to the ledger as appropriate.
- Answering Spend queries: The challenger does the following to answer Q and Q' separately, where w is the number of consumed coins and t the number of generated coins specified by $\mathcal{A}$ as part of its queries:
   1. Parse the input cover set serial number commitments and value commitments as $\mathsf{InCoins} = \{(S_i, C_i)\}_{i=0}^{N-1}$.
   2. For each $u \in [0, w)$, where l_u represents the index of the consumed coin in InCoins:
      (a) Samples a tag T_u uniformly at random.
      (b) Samples a serial number commitment offset S'_u and value commitment offset C'_u uniformly at random.
      (c) Simulates a parallel one-out-of-many proof $(\Pi_{\mathrm{par}})_u$ on the statement $(\{S_i, C_i\}_{i=0}^{N-1}, S'_u, C'_u)$.
   3. For each $j \in [0, t)$:
      (a) If $\mathcal{A}$ provided a public address $\mathsf{addr}_{\mathrm{pk}}$ not generated by the challenger, it produces a coin using CreateCoin as usual.
      (b) Otherwise, it simulates coin generation:
         i. Samples a recovery key K_j uniformly at random.
         ii. Samples a serial number commitment S_j uniformly at random.
         iii. Samples a value commitment $\overline{C}_j$ uniformly at random.
         iv. Samples a random input used to produce an AEAD encryption key $\mathsf{AEADKeyGen} \to k_{\mathrm{enc}}$.

v. Simulates the recipient data encryption by selecting random r of the proper length, and encrypting it to produce

$$\mathsf{AEADEncrypt}(k_{\mathrm{enc}}, \mathbf{r}, r) \rightarrow \overline{r}.$$

vi. Simulates a range proof $(\Pi_{\mathrm{rp}})_j$ on the statement $(\overline{C}_j)$.
4. Simulates the balance proof Π_{bal} on the statement

$$\left(\sum_{u=0}^{w-1} C'_u - \sum_{j=0}^{t-1} \overline{C}_j - \mathsf{Com}(f, 0) \right).$$

5. For each $u \in [0, w)$, computes the binding hash μ as defined and simulates the modified Chaum-Pedersen proof Π_{chaum} on the statement $(\{S'_u, T_u\}_{u=0}^{w-1})$.
6. Assembles the transaction and adds it to the ledger as appropriate.

For experiments defined below, we define $\mathsf{Adv}^{\mathcal{D}}$ as the advantage of $\mathcal{A}$ in some experiment $\mathcal{D}$ over the original LIND game. By definition, all answers sent to $\mathcal{A}$ in $\mathcal{D}^{\mathrm{sim}}$ are computed independently of the bit b, so $\mathsf{Adv}^{\mathcal{D}^{\mathrm{sim}}} = 0$. We will prove that $\mathcal{A}$'s advantage in the real experiment $\mathcal{D}^{\mathrm{real}}$ is at most negligibly different than $\mathcal{A}$'s advantage in $\mathcal{D}^{\mathrm{sim}}$. To show this, we construct intermediate experiments in which $\mathcal{C}$ performs a specific modification of $\mathcal{D}^{\mathrm{real}}$ against $\mathcal{A}$.

Experiment $\mathcal{D}_1$: This experiment modifies $\mathcal{D}^{\mathrm{real}}$ by simulating all one-out-of-many proofs, range proofs, representation proofs, and modified Chaum-Pedersen proof. As all these protocols are special honest-verifier zero knowledge, the simulated proofs are indistinguishable from the real proofs generated in $\mathcal{D}^{\mathrm{real}}$. Hence $\mathsf{Adv}^{\mathcal{D}_1} = 0$.

Experiment $\mathcal{D}_2$: This experiment modifies $\mathcal{D}_1$ by replacing all encrypted recipient data in transactions with challenger-generated recipient public addresses with encryptions of random values of appropriate lengths under keys chosen uniformly at random, and by replacing recovery keys with uniformly random values. Since the underlying authenticated symmetric encryption scheme is IND-CCA and IK-CCA secure and we assume the decisional Diffie-Hellman problem is hard, the adversarial advantage in distinguishing ledger output in the $\mathcal{D}_2$ experiment is negligibly different from its advantage in the $\mathcal{D}_1$ experiment. Hence $|\mathsf{Adv}^{\mathcal{D}_2} - \mathsf{Adv}^{\mathcal{D}_1}|$ is negligible.

Experiment $\mathcal{D}^{\mathrm{sim}}$: The $\mathcal{D}^{\mathrm{sim}}$ experiment is formally defined above. In particular, it differs from $\mathcal{D}_2$ by replacing consumed coin tags, serial number commitment offset, and value commitment offsets with uniformly random values; and by replacing output coin serial number and value commitments with random values. In previous experiments (including $\mathcal{D}^{\mathrm{real}}$), tags are generated using a pseudorandom function [9], and the other given values are generated as commitments with masks derived from hash functions modeled as independent random oracles, so the adversarial advantage in distinguishing ledger output in $\mathcal{D}^{\mathrm{sim}}$ is negligibly different from its advantage in the $\mathcal{D}_2$ experiment. Hence $|\mathsf{Adv}^{\mathcal{D}^{\mathrm{sim}}} - \mathsf{Adv}^{\mathcal{D}_2}|$ is negligible.

This shows that the adversary has only negligible advantage in the real LIND game over the simulation, where it can do no better than chance, which completes the proof.

E   Payment Proofs

We describe now the informal security properties required for a payment proving system, describe such a construction, and (informally) prove that our construction meets the requirements.

The security requirements of a payment proving system are as follows:

1. The proof cannot be replayed in a different context.
2. The prover asserts that it knows secret data sufficient to authorize the transaction originally generating a specified coin.
3. The verifier can obtain and confirm the value and memo associated to the coin.
4. The holder of an incoming view key corresponding to a specified public address can successfully identify the coin.
5. A computationally-bound adversary cannot produce valid proofs for the same coin claiming distinct public addresses.

We note that coin identification relies on the assumption that the claimed recipient address was generated using the protocol-specified method from an incoming view key.

E.1   Protocol

A prover wishes to produce a payment proof on a given coin Coin with nonce k to a claimed destination public address (d, Q_1, Q_2). Suppose that tx is the spend transaction on a ledger that produced Coin. The prover does the following:

1. Parses the serial number commitment, value commitment, and recovery key from Coin: (S, C, K)
2. Generates a modified Chaum-Pedersen proof Π_{auth} using the same inputs and proving system as the proof Π_{chaum} from tx, but also binding the tuple (Coin, k, d, Q_1, Q_2), any context relevant to the payment proof instance, and a globally-fixed payment proof domain separator to the proof context.
3. Assembles the payment proof: $\Pi_{\mathrm{pay}} = (\mathsf{Coin}, k, d, Q_1, Q_2, \Pi_{\mathrm{auth}})$

To verify a payment proof on a coin, the verifier does the following:

1. Parses the payment proof: $\Pi_{\mathrm{pay}} = (\mathsf{Coin}, k, d, Q_1, Q_2, \Pi_{\mathrm{auth}})$
2. Parses public data from Coin: $(S, C, K, \bar{r})$
3. Verifies that tx is a valid transaction on its own ledger that originally generated Coin.

4. Verifies the proof Π_{auth} using the data from tx and the additional binding tuple $(\text{Coin}, k, d, Q_1, Q_2)$, and aborts if verification fails.
5. Generates an AEAD key $k_{\text{aead}} = \text{AEADKeyGen}(\mathcal{H}_k(k)Q_1)$ and decrypts the recipient data:

$$(v, d', k', m) = \text{AEADDecrypt}(k_{\text{aead}}, \mathbf{r}, \bar{r})$$

If decryption fails, or if $k' \neq k$, or if $d' \neq d$, aborts.
6. Checks that $K = \mathcal{H}_k(k)\mathcal{H}_{\text{div}}(d)$, and aborts otherwise.
7. Checks that $S = \text{Comm}(\mathcal{H}_{\text{ser}}(k), 0, 0) + Q_2$, and aborts otherwise.
8. Checks that $C = \text{Com}(v, \mathcal{H}_{\text{val}}(k))$, and aborts otherwise.

E.2   Security

We now describe why this construction meets our security requirements.

Requirement 1. To show that a payment proof cannot be replayed in another context, note that since proof context is bound to the transcript of Π_{auth} along with the statement and coin data, the overall payment proof Π_{pay} cannot be successfully replayed against any other context.

Requirement 2. To show that successful verification of a payment proof asserts the prover knows secret data sufficient to authorize the transaction that generated the coin, we simply note that the modified Chaum-Pedersen proof Π_{chaum} from tx uses the same statement input as Π_{auth} (albeit with different proof context).

Requirement 3. To show that the verifier can obtain the correct value and memo for the coin on successful verification of a payment proof, we simply note that successful AEAD decryption provides the unique values for the value and memo originally used to produce the coin, and that the decrypted value uniquely corresponds to the coin's value commitment since the commitment scheme is binding and successful verification implies an opening to this commitment.

Requirement 4. We now show that if the given address (d, Q_1, Q_2) was generated from an incoming view key (s_1, P_2), this key can identify Coin if a payment proof verifies. Successful verification of a payment proof implies in particular that $K = \mathcal{H}_k(k)\mathcal{H}_{\text{div}}(d)$ and that AEAD decryption succeeds on a key generated using $\mathcal{H}_k(k)Q_1$. This implies that the incoming view holder uses the AEAD key

$$s_1 K = s_1 \mathcal{H}_k(k)\mathcal{H}_{\text{div}}(d)$$
$$= \mathcal{H}_k(k)Q_1$$

and hence decryption succeeds. The remaining steps for identification follow from corresponding steps taken during payment proof verification.

Requirement 5. We now show that a computationally-bound adversary cannot produce valid proofs against the same coin for distinct destination addresses. Suppose such an adversary produces for the same coin valid payment proofs

$$\Pi_{\text{pay}} = (\text{Coin}, k, d, Q_1, Q_2, \Pi_{\text{auth}})$$

and
$$\Pi'_{\text{pay}} = (\mathsf{Coin}, k', d', Q'_1, Q'_2, \Pi'_{\text{auth}})$$

on addresses $(d, Q_1, Q_2) \neq (d', Q'_1, Q'_2)$. Note that $\mathsf{Coin} = (S, C, K, \bar{r})$ must be identical in both proofs by definition.

Successful AEAD decryption of $\bar{r}$ on both proofs implies in particular that $d = d'$ and $k = k'$ except with negligible probability. Further, the AEAD keys derived in both proofs must be equal (again except with negligible probability), so $\mathcal{H}_k(k)Q_1 = \mathcal{H}_k(k')Q'_1$ requires $Q_1 = Q'_1$. Finally, since

$$S = \mathsf{Comm}(\mathcal{H}_{\text{ser}}(k), 0, 0) + Q_2$$
$$= \mathsf{Comm}(\mathcal{H}_{\text{ser}}(k'), 0, 0) + Q'_2$$

it also follows that $Q_2 = Q'_2$, a contradiction.

References

1. Bellare, M., Boldyreva, A., Desai, A., Pointcheval, D.: Key-privacy in public-key encryption. In: Boyd, C. (ed.) ASIACRYPT 2001. LNCS, vol. 2248, pp. 566–582. Springer, Heidelberg (2001). https://doi.org/10.1007/3-540-45682-1_33
2. Ben Sasson, E., et al.: Zerocash: decentralized anonymous payments from Bitcoin. In: 2014 IEEE Symposium on Security and Privacy, pp. 459–474 (2014). https://doi.org/10.1109/SP.2014.36
3. Ben-Sasson, E., Chiesa, A., Tromer, E., Virza, M.: Succinct non-interactive zero knowledge for a von Neumann architecture. In: Proceedings of the 23rd USENIX Conference on Security Symposium, SEC 2014, pp. 781–796. USENIX Association, USA (2014)
4. Bootle, J., Cerulli, A., Chaidos, P., Ghadafi, E., Groth, J., Petit, C.: Short accountable ring signatures based on DDH. In: Pernul, G., Ryan, P.Y.A., Weippl, E. (eds.) ESORICS 2015. LNCS, vol. 9326, pp. 243–265. Springer, Cham (2015). https://doi.org/10.1007/978-3-319-24174-6_13
5. Bowe, S., Gabizon, A., Miers, I.: Scalable multi-party computation for zk-SNARK parameters in the random beacon model. Cryptology ePrint Archive, Report 2017/1050 (2017). https://ia.cr/2017/1050
6. Bünz, B., Bootle, J., Boneh, D., Poelstra, A., Wuille, P., Maxwell, G.: Bulletproofs: short proofs for confidential transactions and more. In: 2018 IEEE Symposium on Security and Privacy (SP), pp. 315–334 (2018). https://doi.org/10.1109/SP.2018.00020
7. Chung, H., Han, K., Ju, C., Kim, M., Seo, J.H.: Bulletproofs+: shorter proofs for privacy-enhanced distributed ledger. Cryptology ePrint Archive, Report 2020/735 (2020). https://ia.cr/2020/735
8. Crites, E., Komlo, C., Maller, M.: How to prove Schnorr assuming Schnorr: security of multi- and threshold signatures. Cryptology ePrint Archive, Report 2021/1375 (2021). https://ia.cr/2021/1375
9. Dodis, Y., Yampolskiy, A.: A verifiable random function with short proofs and keys. In: Vaudenay, S. (ed.) PKC 2005. LNCS, vol. 3386, pp. 416–431. Springer, Heidelberg (2005). https://doi.org/10.1007/978-3-540-30580-4_28

10. Esgin, M.F., Zhao, R.K., Steinfeld, R., Liu, J.K., Liu, D.: MatRiCT: efficient, scalable and post-quantum blockchain confidential transactions protocol. In: Proceedings of the 2019 ACM SIGSAC Conference on Computer and Communications Security, CCS 2019, pp. 567–584. Association for Computing Machinery, New York (2019). https://doi.org/10.1145/3319535.3354200

11. Fuchsbauer, G., Orrù, M., Seurin, Y.: Aggregate cash systems: a cryptographic investigation of mimblewimble. In: Ishai, Y., Rijmen, V. (eds.) EUROCRYPT 2019. LNCS, vol. 11476, pp. 657–689. Springer, Cham (2019). https://doi.org/10.1007/978-3-030-17653-2_22

12. Gennaro, R., Leigh, D., Sundaram, R., Yerazunis, W.: Batching Schnorr identification scheme with applications to privacy-preserving authorization and low-bandwidth communication devices. In: Lee, P.J. (ed.) ASIACRYPT 2004. LNCS, vol. 3329, pp. 276–292. Springer, Heidelberg (2004). https://doi.org/10.1007/978-3-540-30539-2_20

13. Goodell, B., Noether, S., RandomRun: concise linkable ring signatures and forgery against adversarial keys. Cryptology ePrint Archive, Report 2019/654 (2019). https://ia.cr/2019/654

14. Groth, J., Kohlweiss, M.: One-out-of-many proofs: or how to leak a secret and spend a coin. In: Oswald, E., Fischlin, M. (eds.) EUROCRYPT 2015. LNCS, vol. 9057, pp. 253–280. Springer, Heidelberg (2015). https://doi.org/10.1007/978-3-662-46803-6_9

15. Hopwood, D., Bowe, S., Hornby, T., Wilcox, N.: Zcash protocol specification (2021). https://github.com/zcash/zips/blob/master/protocol/protocol.pdf

16. Jivanyan, A.: Lelantus: a new design for anonymous and confidential cryptocurrencies. Cryptology ePrint Archive, Report 2019/373 (2019). https://ia.cr/2019/373

17. Komlo, C., Goldberg, I.: FROST: flexible round-optimized Schnorr threshold signatures. Cryptology ePrint Archive, Report 2020/852 (2020). https://ia.cr/2020/852

18. Lai, R.W.F., Ronge, V., Ruffing, T., Schröder, D., Thyagarajan, S.A.K., Wang, J.: Omniring: scaling private payments without trusted setup. In: Proceedings of the 2019 ACM SIGSAC Conference on Computer and Communications Security, CCS 2019, pp. 31–48. Association for Computing Machinery, New York (2019). https://doi.org/10.1145/3319535.3345655

19. Maxwell, G., Poelstra, A., Seurin, Y., Wuille, P.: Simple Schnorr multi-signatures with applications to Bitcoin. Des. Codes Crypt. **87**(9), 2139–2164 (2019). https://doi.org/10.1007/s10623-019-00608-x

20. Neven, G., Smart, N.P., Warinschi, B.: Hash function requirements for Schnorr signatures. J. Math. Cryptol. **3**(1), 69–87 (2009). https://doi.org/10.1515/JMC.2009.004

21. Nir, Y., Langley, A.: ChaCha20 and Poly1305 for IETF protocols. RFC 7539, RFC Editor (2015). http://www.rfc-editor.org/rfc/rfc7539.txt

22. Noether, S., Goodell, B.: Triptych: logarithmic-sized linkable ring signatures with applications. In: Garcia-Alfaro, J., Navarro-Arribas, G., Herrera-Joancomarti, J. (eds.) DPM/CBT 2020. LNCS, vol. 12484, pp. 337–354. Springer, Cham (2020). https://doi.org/10.1007/978-3-030-66172-4_22

23. Noether, S., Mackenzie, A., et al.: Ring confidential transactions. Ledger **1**, 1–18 (2016)

24. Pippenger, N.: On the evaluation of powers and monomials. SIAM J. Comput. **9**(2), 230–250 (1980)

25. Pyrros Chaidos, V.G.: Lelantus-CLA. Cryptology ePrint Archive, Report 2021/1036 (2021). https://ia.cr/2021/1036
26. koe: Seraphis: a privacy-preserving transaction protocol abstraction. GitHub repository release DRAFT-v0.0.11 (2021). https://github.com/UkoeHB/Seraphis/releases/tag/DRAFT-v0.0.11

Fides: A System for Verifiable Computation Using Smart Contracts

Mahmudun Nabi$^{(\boxtimes)}$, Sepideh Avizheh, and Reihaneh Safavi-Naini

University of Calgary, Calgary, AB, Canada
{mahmudun.nabi1,sepideh.avizheh1,rei}@ucalgary.ca

Abstract. Verifiable computation allows a resource-constrained client
to outsource their computation to powerful servers, and efficiently verify their received results. Cryptographic verifiable computation systems,
despite their elegant designs, have limited application in practice because
of the computational cost and difficulty of correct and flexible implementation of complex cryptographic systems. An attractive approach to
verifiably compute general functions is to use more than one server to
compute the same function, and decide the computation result based on
the submitted results of all servers. In this paper, we propose a system
for delegation of computation to two cloud servers using a smart contract
(SC), that guarantees correct computation results as long as at least one
of the two servers is honest. Our work adapts the Refereed Delegation
of Computation (RDoC) model of Canetti, Riva and Rothblum (ACM
CCS'11) to the SC setting. This was first considered by Avizheh et al.
(ACM CCSW'19) who showed that the direct employment of RDoC in
the smart contract setting will be insecure because of the *copy attack*,
where a server copies the result of the other server, and becomes possible due to the transparency of SC. However, the implementation of their
protocol was left as future work. Our work is a new SC-aided RDoC
design with proved security that significantly reduces the computation
of the smart contract. Additionally, it provides security against the mis-
behaviours of the client and an implementation of the design over the
Ethereum blockchain. The proposed system, which is called *Fides*, is the
first implementation of SC-aided RDoC. We discuss the challenges of this
implementation and our design decisions, and present the cost analysis
of the system for an example computation. We also propose extensions
of our work and directions for future research.

Keywords: Refereed delegation of computation · blockchain · smart
contract · verifiable computation · copy attack

1 Introduction

Resource-constrained enterprises and individuals increasingly outsource their
computation and data intensive applications to cloud services such as Amazon's
EC2 and Microsoft's Azure. Outsourcing computation however raises the need
of the outsourcer to be able to efficiently verify the received computation result.

© International Financial Cryptography Association 2023
S. Matsuo et al. (Eds.): FC 2022 Workshops, LNCS 13412, pp. 448–480, 2023.
https://doi.org/10.1007/978-3-031-32415-4_29

Verifying outsourced computation has been studied with two types of adversaries: (i) *rational adversary model* where the adversary has well-defined utility [6,30,33,36], and (ii) *malicious adversary* where the adversary can arbitrarily deviate from the protocol. Verifiable computation (VC) systems with security against malicious adversary have been designed both for general computation [1,10,13,19], and specific computations [16,25,28,46]. These protocols despite their elegant designs have limited use in real applications because of the computation and storage cost, as well as implementation challenges of cryptographic systems [23].

Verifying Outsourced Computation by Replication. A natural approach to verifying computation is to replicate the computation on multiple servers and accept the received results if they all match. Replication of computation for correctness guarantee has been studied in rational [6,30,33,36] and malicious adversary model [7,10,11], where in the former the adversary is assumed to have a known utility they want to maximize while the latter considers an adversary that can deviate arbitrarily from the computation. We consider malicious adversary model.

In [10], Canetti, Rothbulm and Riva (CRR) built on the general *refereed computation model* of Feige and Kilian [17], and proposed Refereed Delegation of Computation (RDoC) that allows an *honest client (referee)* to use only two servers, and obtain guaranteed correct result *if at least* one of the two servers is honest. This is the minimum amount of redundancy. In all these works the client is honest and the goal is to ensure correctness when the servers misbehave.

Smart Contract for Verifiable Computation. A very attractive approach to implementing an outsourcing service with provable guarantee is to implement CRR using a smart contract as the referee. The smart contract will also distribute the funds and ensure correct payments to the honest cloud, and will remove the trust assumption on the client in CRR which could be a significant limitation in practice. Avizheh et al. [4] considered such a system and noted that despite proved security of CRR, its direct application of CRR with a smart contract will be insecure because of a new attack called *copy attack* that arises because of the transparent nature of the smart contract, and allows a malicious server to simply copy the submitted result of the honest server. Copy attack disincentivizes honest behaviour and undermines the underlying principle of replicated computation that is the need for two independent computations. Avizheh et al. also proposed a modification of CRR, called scCRR, that has security against copy attack, and noting the challenges of implementing the scCRR (and CRR) protocol in the smart contract setting, left it as future work.

1.1   Our Work

We design and implement a computation outsourcing service that is managed and run by a smart contract, and is based on the adaptation of CRR to the smart contract setting. We propose a new modified version of CRR, that we call cmCRR, or *committed CRR*, that reduces the computation of the smart contract compared to scCRR, and implement *Fides*, a verifiable computation service, that uses cmCRR as the underlying protocol over Ethereum blockchain.

Two-Server SC-Aided Verifiable Computation Service. We consider three types of parties: a client who wants to outsource their computation, servers who perform the computation, and the smart contract (SC) that is a trusted mediator for transferring funds, and plays the role of the referee in cmCRR.

In cmCRR, the client sends a function $f()$ and the commitment to the input x to the SC, and $f()$ and the opening of the commitment to the two servers (that have been chosen by the client). The servers verify the opening of the committed value, perform the computation, and submit their commitment to the computation result, and the root of a Merkle tree that is constructed on their computation trace and incorporates the server's public key in the last step. Once the SC receives both commitments, the servers open their commitments. If the results match, the computation is complete and correct because at least one server is honest. If they do not match, a *referee protocol* is run by the SC. Our referee protocol is similar to the corresponding protocol in CRR, with an additional Merkle proof that is required to be generated by the servers at each round of binary search and is used to prevent the copy attack. The protocol uses a sequence of challenge-response to determine the first different computation step in the reported computation traces. The SC then performs a single step of the computation to determine the honest server. We prove security against copy attack and correctness of the computation result (i.e. SC's final decision) by effectively reducing them to the collision-resistance property of the hash function that is used in the Merkle tree, and the security of the commitment scheme. To achieve this result however we require the servers to participate in the full protocol, and submit their opening of the commitments. This is realized by requiring collateral from servers who participate in the computation (similar to putting a bid).

Implementation. Fides implements cmCRR over Ethereum blockchain. The main challenge of implementation is efficiently transferring the required information for the single step computation to the SC. The theoretical model of CRR uses a Turing Machine (TM) as the computation model, and defines computation trace as a sequence of *reduced computation state*, consisting TM's current state, current head position and value on that position, and Merkle root constructed on the tape. We use EVM (Ethereum Virtual Machine) to model the computation and Solidity language to express the function $f(x)$. In Sect. 4.1 we describe the EVM configuration equivalent to TM configuration, and define the reduced computation state as EVM machine state consisting the values of stack, memory and storage. The Merkle tree commitment is constructed over the sequence of reduced computation states by each server. The referee protocol determines a single computation step that must be transferred to the SC in case of dispute. We do this by sending the single step data as an executable code (in the form of bytecode) to SC, that is executed as a newly deployed smart contract on Ethereum.

Similar to CRR, cmCRR and Fides require the computation to be deterministic. We note that randomized functions can be made deterministic using a

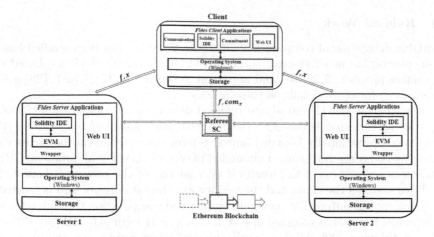

Fig. 1. *Fides.* Client's communication with Server is done through secure channel. SC communications with client and servers happens over public channels. Messages sent and received by SC, and the result of SC functions, are posted on the ledger and are publicly visible. *WebUI* (i.e., a local html file) is developed for each Fides server and the Fides client that runs JavaScript code to load data from its storage and uses *Web3.js* library for interacting with the SC.

pseudorandom generator. We use Ganache framework [18] to simulate a public Ethereum blockchain and Solidity language to write smart contracts.

Fides Implementation and Experiments. Figure 1 shows the overview of *Fides* with two servers, consisting of the following modules.

(i) *Fides client* that processes the function $f()$ for submitting to the SC and sending to the servers, and communicates with the servers and the SC;

(ii) *Fides servers* receive the EVM executable from the client, run it in their EVM *that is not connected to the Ethereum network,* and send the result to the SC. We develop a wrapper program that generates state files for each computation step together with the final result and stores them on the servers. This allows the servers to provide the required information for a single step computation to the SC without the need for any extra processing (see Sect. 4.1 for details).

(iii) *Referee* is a smart contract (SC) that runs on Ethereum blockchain.

As a concrete computation we consider multiplication of two matrices. We measure the execution cost of each server in terms of the *running time*, and the financial cost of executing the referee smart contract on the Ethereum network. Our results are reported in Sect. 4.3. For honest executions, the main cost is the program execution time of the servers, and the financial cost of verifying the results by the SC which is small in our system. For non-matching results, financial cost grows with the size of the computation steps and rounds of binary search stage. This cost can be charged to the malicious server to disincentivize dishonest behaviour.

1.2   Related Work

Verifiable delegation of computation with a single server has been studied based on cryptographic proof systems [12,14,21,35,38–40,42,43] which are based on interactive proofs ([5,22,34]) and argument systems ([8,27,31,32]). Please see Appendix A for more details on these schemes.

Canetti et al. [10,11] introduced refereed delegation of computation (RDoC) with two servers that is based on the *refereed game model of computation* [17] where a computationally bounded honest referee must decide on the honesty of one of the two computationally unbounded players. Canetti et al. protocol, CRR, guarantees correctness of the results if at least one of the provers is honest. In all above systems the client and the verifier are the same entity and is trusted.

Using smart contract for managing outsourced computation through refereed game model has been considered in systems such as TrueBit [41], HB [24], Plasma [37] and Arbitrum [29]. All these works use multiple servers to run the computation off-chain and use a smart contract to work as a referee. Additionally, they consider rational adversary model and do not provide provable correctness guarantee for the outsourced computation. In contrast, in [4] authors adapted CRR to the smart contract setting for malicious adversaries, identified copy attack and proposed scCRR with two servers that uses additional challenge and response in the CRR protocol to achieve correctness and soundness. In cmCRR we reduce interaction with, and computation of, the SC.

Organization. Section 2 reviews preliminaries, Sect. 3 describes our system. Section 3.2 gives security and privacy analysis of our system, and Sect. 4 describes our implementation. Section 5 concludes the paper.

2   Preliminaries

The building blocks of our system are, a family of *collision-resistant hash functions H*, a commitment scheme, and a Merkle tree that is used as a commitment. Detailed definitions of these primitives are in Appendix B. We also give a brief definition of the commitment scheme, and Merkle trees below.

A commitment scheme consists of two algorithms *Commit*() and *Open*(). *Commit*() is a probabilistic algorithm that takes an input value $x \in \{0,1\}^*$ and outputs a public commitment *com* and a private opening d. *Open*() takes the commitment *com*, the private opening value d, and the input value x, and outputs 0 or 1, which indicates an invalid or a valid commitment, respectively. We require that the commitment scheme satisfies two properties, *hiding* and *binding*.

Merkle Tree and Merkle Proof. A Merkle tree is a binary tree that is constructed using a *collision-resistant* hash function where the leaves are the hash values of data elements $d_1, \cdots, d_n$. Every internal node of the tree is the hash of the concatenation of its two child nodes. The root of the Merkle tree is denoted by $r = MH_{root}(D)$, where $D = \{d_1, \cdots, d_n\}$. Given the root r of a Merkle tree, to prove that an element d_i is included in the tree, a *Merkle proof*, $p_i = MH_{proof}(D, d_i)$, is used, which consists of the hash values along the path from

$H(d_i)$ to the root. The $VerifyMHProof(r, i, d_i, p_i) = 0/1$ function verifies whether d_i corresponds to an element in position i of a Merkle tree with root r using the proof p_i.

CRR uses *Turing Machine (TM) representation of computation* and stores the state of computation by a *configuration of TM* which is an ordered triple $(t, s, h) \in \Sigma^* \times \mathcal{K} \times N$ where t denotes the tape content, s denotes the machine's current state, and h denotes the position of the head on the tape, where $0 \leq h < |t|$. Given an initial description of the TM, and a configuration C_i, the next configuration C_i can be easily determined. See Appendix B for details.

CRR [10] uses a *referee protocol* to determine the honest server. The protocol is an interactive challenge-response protocol that determines the first single step computation of the servers that do not match, and is performed by the honest referee to determine the correct server. More details are in Appendix C.1.

Ethereum [9] is a public distributed ledger system that enables users to develop smart contracts and decentralized applications (DApps). A smart contract is a computer program that is executed by each Ethereum node on their EVM. The computation cost of EVM is measured by *gas* which is the unit cost of executing an operation on the Ethereum, and translated into *Ether*, the Ethereum currency.

3   Fides System Design

In this section, we give the security goals, the protocol description and the security analysis of cmCRR system.

Definition 1 [10]. $(S_1, S_2 \cdots S_n, R)$ *is an ϵ-RDoC with n servers and referee R for a function f if the following holds:*

- *For any input x and for any $i \in [1, n]$, if S_i is honest, then for any $(S_1^*, S_2^* \cdots S_{i-1}^*, S_{i+1}^*, \cdots S_n^*)$ the output of R is $f(x)$ with probability at least $1 - \epsilon$.*
- *The complexity of the client is at most quasi-linear in $|x|$ and the complexity of the (honest) servers is polynomial in the complexity of evaluating $f()$ (for example if the complexity of evaluating $f()$ is $O(|x|^2)$ then the complexity of the servers are polynomial in that, e.g. $O(|x|^2)$.)*

We design cmCRR protocol that outputs correct result, or $\perp$ assuming at least one honest server exists (this is done by identifying a deviating server, including the copying server). cmCRR protocol satisfies the following security properties.

- *Correctness.* Client always receives the correct result if the honest server runs the computation (if the malicious server aborts at the initialization stage, $\perp$ is returned to the client).
- *Soundness.* The malicious server will be detected and the correct computation result will not be affected.

Soundness includes copy detection which is important to ensure security of the replicated computation that requires two independent results, as well as incentivizing the honest behaviour.

3.1   cmCRR Protocol

We propose cmCRR, an SC-RDoC scheme that uses an smart contract as a referee which interacts with a client C, two servers S_1 and S_2 and ensures correctness and detection of misbehaviors. We assume, there is a secure channel between each server and the client. We assume servers have reliable computation environments and they publish their results after running the computation. Each entity in the system has a public key Pk_i (or pseudonym which can be obtained by a hash function on Pk_i and taking the first κ bytes where κ is a security parameter) and it is recognized based on that. We do not require a public key infrastructure and the public keys that are used for communicating with the underlying blockchain system suffices.

Details. Algorithm 1 shows the simplified protocol description. We describe each stage below:

Initialization. Client C transforms the function $f()$ to its Turing machine description which we denote by M, $M = TMencode(f())$. C also computes a commitment to the input $x \in \{0, 1\}^\kappa$, denoted by com_x, and sends (com_x, M) to SC, and a message to servers S_1 and S_2 to notifies them to register. Then, servers register by sending their public keys Pk_i to SC which will be stored there. When both servers are registered, C opens its commitment to the input by sending (x, d_x) to both servers through the secure channel. d_x is the opening value for the commitment. Both servers verify that the opening of commitment is correct $(Open(com_x, d_x, x) = 1)$. If any server finds a conflict, then they abort. Otherwise, they accept the computation job by sending an accept message to SC. When SC receives the accept message from both servers it notifies the servers to start the computation.

Computation. Both servers perform the computation and obtain the result y_i. To reveal the computation result, servers follow two steps to prevent copy attack for both computation result and binary search stage. In the first step, they make a commitment to y_i, $(com_{y_i}, d_{y_i}) = Commit(y_i \| Pk_i)$ and construct a Merkle tree on the hashed reduced configuration arrays of their TMs, C_i, and their public key Pk_i. Let's represent the root of this Merkle tree as $MH_{root}(C_i \| Pk_i)$. Each server sends the tuple $(com_{y_i}, N_i, MH_{root}(C_i \| Pk_i))$ to SC, where N_i is the length of the reduced configuration array. Then, SC asks both servers to reveal their commitments. Each server will reveal (y_i, d_{y_i}) which enables SC to check whether its a valid opening under each server's public key. SC checks if y_i received from both servers match with each other or not.
(a) If both $Open(com_{y_i}, d_{y_i}, y_i) = 1$ for $i \in \{1,2\}$ and $y_1 = y_2 = y$, SC sends y to the client as the computation result. (b) If $Open(com_{y_i}, d_{y_i}, y_i)$ is equal to 0 for one server (and 1 for the other server) but $y_1 = y_2 = y$, SC identifies the server who has revealed an incorrect commitment as copying server. SC sends y to the client. (c) If $Open(com_{y_i}, d_{y_i}, y_i)$ is equal to 0 for one server (and 1 for the other server) and $y_1 \neq y_2$, SC identifies the server who has revealed an incorrect commitment as malicious and the other server as honest. Then, it sends the result of the honest server to the client. (d) If $Open(com_{y_i}, d_{y_i}, y_i) = 1$ for $i \in \{1,2\}$ but $y_1 \neq y_2$, they go to the dispute resolution stage which is as follows:

Algorithm 1. *cmCRR Protocol*: Client C has function f and input x, servers S_1 and S_2 receive f and x, and compute $f(x)$ and return output y_1 and y_2 to referee contract SC.

Input: Computation function $f()$ and input x
Output: Computation result y
Initialization: Computation initialization and server registration
1: $C \rightarrow SC$: Initialize (com_x, M) ▷ M: Turing machine description of $f()$
                                                      ▷ com_x: commitment to the input x
2: $S_i \rightarrow SC$: Register (Pk_i) $(\forall\, i \in \{1,\, 2\})$
3: $C \Rightarrow S_i$: Open (com_x, d_x, x), $\forall i \in \{1, 2\}$ ▷ d_x: commitment opening value
                                                               ▷ $\Rightarrow$: secure channel
4: $S_i \rightarrow SC$: $accept$, $\forall i \in \{1, 2\}$
Computation: Execution and result comparison
5: $S_i \rightarrow SC$: receive-Commitments $(com_{y_i},\, N_i,\, MH_{root}(\mathcal{C}_i \| Pk_i))$, $\forall i \in \{1, 2\}$
6: $S_i \rightarrow SC$: receive-Results $(y_i,\, d_{y_i})$, $\forall i \in \{1, 2\}$ ▷ $y_i,\, d_{y_i},\, N_i$: result of computation, opening key, length of $\mathcal{C}_i$
7: SC: compare y_i and verify commitment to y_i
  - If (opening valid) & $(y_1 = y_2)$ $\rightarrow$ no attack
  - Else if (opening invalid) & $(y_1 = y_2)$ $\rightarrow$ copy attack
  - Else if (opening invalid) & $(y_1 \neq y_2)$ $\rightarrow$ incorrect opening
  - Else if (opening valid) & $(y_1 \neq y_2)$ $\rightarrow$ go to Interaction stage
Dispute resolution: Binary search and single-step execution
 – **Binary search:**
8: While $n_b \neq n_g + 1$ do:
    $SC \rightarrow S_i$: get-Reduced-config(j) $\forall i \in \{1, 2\}$
    $S_i \rightarrow SC$: receive-Reduced-config($H^i_{rc_j},\, p^i_{rc_j}$), $\forall i \in \{1, 2\}$ ▷ $H^i_{rc_j},\, p^i_{rc_j}$: Hashed reduced configuration from server i, MProof for $H^i_{rc_j}$
    SC acts as below:
  - If (both hashes match) & (valid MProof) $\rightarrow$ update n_g
  - Else if (both hashes match) & (invalid MProof) $\rightarrow$ copy attack
  - Else if (hashes mismatch) $\rightarrow$ update n_b
 – **Single-step execution:**
9: $S_1 \rightarrow SC$:receive-Single-step-data $(rc_{n_g},\, rc_{n_b})$
    SC performs one step execution and identifies the correct result and the malicious server

---

Dispute Resolution. SC takes the smallest reduced configuration length among N_i, where $i = \{1, 2\}$, as n_b (i.e. the mismatching point), also lets $n_g = 1$ (i.e. the matching point), and specifies the index of the computation step that both parties should reveal their reduced configuration through bisection, $j = n_g + \frac{n_b - n_g}{2}$. Each server S_i will send the reduced configuration $H(rc_j^i)$ for computation step j together with a proof $p^i_{rc_j}$ that shows $H(rc^i_j)$ is in the Merkle tree having root $MH_{root}(\mathcal{C}_i \| Pk_i)$ (this prevents copying during the interaction). SC checks if the hashed reduced configurations, $H(rc^i_j)$, of both servers match or not. (a) If they match it verifies whether the Merkle proof $p^i_{rc_j}$ is valid. If both Merkle proof are valid there is no copy attack, then SC updates n_g (let it be the new matching point) and repeats the bisection again. (b) Else, if one

Merkle proof is invalid the copy attack is identified and SC sends the result of the honest server to the client. (c) Otherwise, if the reduced configurations do not match, SC updates n_b (the new non-matching point) and computes the next computation step j that servers have to reveal their reduced configuration through bisection again.

The bisection procedure and challenge-responses are continued as described above until they reach to $n_b = n_g + 1$. At this stage, SC asks server S_1 to reveal the reduced configurations for computation steps n_g and n_b, i.e. rc_{n_g} and rc_{n_b}, in plain. Then SC runs *VerifyReducedStep* algorithm (please see Appendix C) which identifies the honest server based on the single-step computation.

3.2   Security and Privacy Analysis

In the following we show the that cmCRR protocol ensures the security requirements mentioned in Sect. 3.

Copy Detection. A dishonest server can try to do the copy attack in two situations- (i) *copy the final result in computation stage* and (ii) *copy during the binary search stage* which will be detected by the SC.

Theorem 1. *Let H be a collision resistant hash function that is used to construct the Merkle hash tree on the array of reduced configurations, $\mathcal{C}$, commit() be a hiding and binding commitment scheme and Pk_i be the public key of server i which uniquely identifies Server i. Then cmCRR protocol provides protection against copy attack of honest cloud for (i) the computation stage where the results are published and (ii) the binary search stage where the challenge-response is run.*

Proof. (Sketch) First consider the computation stage, where each server reveals a commitment to their result and their public key, $commit(y_i\|Pk_i)$, in one round and then they open their commitments in the next round. Consider a copy attack where server S_1 has published the $com_1 = commit(y_1\|Pk_1)$ and server S_2 has copied the result. To successfully copy the result, S_2 has to either (i) find y_1 and make a commitment to y_1 using its own public key Pk_2, or (ii) it has to set $com_2 = com_1$ and later opens the commitment com_2 to $y_1\|Pk_2$ where $Pk_2 \neq Pk_1$. Therefore, the success probability of such an attacker is bounded by the maximum probability of breaking either the hiding (case i) or binding (case ii) property of the commitment scheme.

Second consider that server S_2 wants to run a copy attack in the binary search stage. Let's assume server S_1 has revealed $(com_{y_1}, N, root_1)$ after performing the computation and S_2 reveals $(com_{y_2}, N, root_2)$ where $y_1 \neq y_2$ and $root_1 = MH_{root}(\mathcal{C}_1\|Pk_1)$. W.l.o.g we set $N_2 = N_1 = N$. Now consider that S_1 reveals $(H(rc_j^1), p_{rc_j}^1)$ at the computation step j. If S_2 copies $H(rc_j^1)$, then it has to provide a proof $p_{rc_j}^2$ such that it shows $H(rc_j^1)$ is in the Merkle tree with root $root_2$ where $root_2$ includes Pk_2, i.e. $root_2 = MH_{root}(\mathcal{C}_2\|Pk_2)$. Let S_1 generate a proof $p_{rc_j}^1 = (h_1^1, h_2^1, ..., h_{log(N)}^1)$. If $VerifyMHProof(root_1, H(rc_j^1), Pk_1, p_{rc_j}^1) = 1$, S_2 can copy some part of this proof. However it needs to generate a proof, $p_{rc_j}^2 = (h_1^2, h_2^2, \cdots, h_{log(N)}^2)$ that matches with $root_2$. Because for S_2 the Merkle proof is valid if it includes Pk_2, S_2 can copy all the nodes in the path to root $root_1$ except the node before root which is the sibling of Pk_1 (i.e. $h^1_{log(N)}$). If the proof revealed by S_2 is verified without being detected as malicious, then there should be either:

(a) The value $h^2_{log(N)}$ such that it is different from $h^1_{log(N)}$ but $H(h^2_{log(N)}||Pk_2) = H(h^1_{log(N)}||Pk_1) = root_1$, where $root_2 = root_1$ and S_2 has copied $root_1$, or
(b) The value $H(h^2_{log(N)}||Pk_2) = root_2$, where $root_2$ was guessed by S_2 initially.

In case (a), S_2 successfully breaks the collision resistance property of the hash function and in case (b) S_2 breaks the pre-image resistance property of the hash function. Therefore, the success probability of S_2 is bounded by the maximum of the two which is negligible.   □

Using Theorem 1 above and Theorem 1 in [10], we have the following:

Corollary 1. *Assuming the hash function is collision resistant, the commitment scheme is hiding and binding, and Pk_i uniquely identifies server S_i then cmCRR protocol is a computationally sound ϵ-RDoC with two servers for any function computable in polynomial time.*

Discussion. cmCRR scheme also ensures *input privacy* when both parties are honest and *security against malicious client* who may try to send different inputs to different servers (please see Appendix D for the discussion on this and the list of attacks that are prevented in our scheme).

4   Implementation of Fides

We have performed a proof-of-concept implementation of cmCRR system that includes a client who delegates a computation to two servers and uses SC as a referee. We call it *"Fides"* that works directly with EVM instructions following the Ethereum execution model. In the following sections we provide our implementation details of Fides and the obtained evaluation results.

4.1   Challenges and Design Choices

A significant challenge of implementing the cmCRR protocol is specifying a single computation step in an Ethereum Virtual Machine (EVM), and delegating execution of that step to the referee smart contract such that it produces the same result as the honest server's EVM. Details are given below.

(i) Single-step execution on Ethereum network: On Ethereum, each node runs the code inside an Ethereum Virtual Machine (EVM) that understands EVM bytecode only [45]. If the delegated program is written in languages such as C/C++ then to execute the single step of computation, the instruction in C/C++ must be compiled into an equivalent EVM instruction to be

run on the Ethereum blockchain. To achieve this conversion (C/C++ code to EVM bytecode), a software (e.g., a compiler) is required that will work as a bridge between the C/C++ code and the referee contract that is on the blockchain. This requirement makes the single-step execution on Ethereum challenging because an instruction of a C/C++ and its corresponding execution state (e.g., in 8086 architecture) needs to be transformed in to an equivalent EVM execution state. Moreover, it brings another security issue, that is, we need to prove to the referee contract that the transformation is done correctly (which is done off-chain by the servers).

(ii) Deterministic execution of delegated program: CRR [10] and scCRR [4] assume that each execution of the delegated program should be deterministic (i.e., each execution of the program for a fixed input should produce the same result). However, there exists some instructions in the high-level language (e.g., C/C++, Solidity etc.) that are non-deterministic by definition (i.e., they can fetch data from outside). If such instructions are included in the delegated program then execution of the same code can produce different/wrong output having non-identical intermediate step results. Therefore, the presence of non-deterministic instructions will make it challenging for the referee contract to identify the correct result (in case of a dispute).

We have made the following design choices for the implementation of *Fides*:

- Since the referee contract needs to run the single-step computation on Ethereum, we restrict ourselves to *Solidity* language for writing the delegated program whose compiled binaries are equivalent to EVM bytecode. We also require each server to run the computation bytecode inside their private EVM which is not part of the Ethereum network. In this way, the required single step data can be sent directly to SC without the need for any conversion.
- To ensure deterministic program execution, we assume that the input to the delegated program is hard-coded (i.e., input is part of the program itself). Also, if $f()$ is a random function, the client can hard-code an initial random seed in the delegated program and use a pseudorandom number generator within the program to generate the required randomness. This can guarantee that both servers will generate and use the same randomness. Additionally, we note that the program should not use any instructions that requires the program to interact with outside of the current (and local) EVM execution environment. In Appendix E.1 we provide the categories of available EVM instructions in Ethereum and identify the instructions from these categories that are non-deterministic by definition (e.g., EXTCODECOPY, DELEGATECALL, TIMESTAMP etc.) and should not be used in the delegated program.

Adaptation of the Protocol for Ethereum Execution Model. The EVM is a stack-based architecture. Its execution environment consists of a virtual ROM (where the program code is loaded) and three locations to store/access data during execution: *stack*, *memory*, and *storage* [45]. We consider the TM equivalent of an EVM configuration to be as follows:

- The computation is represented as *bytecode* that is the machine code to be executed inside EVM. Each step of the protocol is an execution of a single EVM instruction.
- The EVM machine *state* μ that is equivalent of a TM state includes: (i) current contents of the stack (μ_s) and memory (μ_m), (ii) current values of the program counter (pc), and (iii) the available gas (g).
- Finally, the TM working *tape* is replaced with the contents of the storage of EVM. Before the execution of the program, the storage and the gas values are initialized with the user defined values and others are set to 0.

Suppose, δ is the EVM state-progression function (i.e., transition function). Then $\delta (\mu, I_\mu) = \mu'$ represents that the machine moves from state μ to the next state μ' by executing the instruction I_μ. In other words, the machine state moves from μ to μ' in one step. Here, I_μ is the instruction to be executed in state μ.

We define a *reduced-configuration* (rc) to be the tuple $[pc, (\mu_s, \mu_m), S]$, where S represents the EVM storage contents (i.e., TM tape contents). Our protocol requires that, given a reduced configuration, the referee smart contract should be able get the next reduced configuration by simulating single EVM instruction of the computation on Ethereum. Based on the above discussion, given a reduced-configuration rc_j for state j, the referee contract generates the next reduced-configuration rc_{j+1} by executing a single EVM instruction I_j as follows: $rc_{j+1} = \delta(rc_j, I_j)$.

Therefore, given two consecutive reduced configurations, rc_j and rc_{j+1}, one can efficiently verify this claim by doing the following checks:

(1) Get the next reduced configuration value v' by executing the EVM instruction at step j on the data provided in rc_j (in our implementation we do this by running a new copy of EVM constructed using the instruction I_j and the data of rc_j, by the referee contract. Details of this technique is given in Sect. 4.1).
(2) Verify $v' = v_2$, where v_2 ($= S^{(j+1)}$) is the claimed next state output by the server.
    If the above checks pass, this server is considered as *honest* and its result is accepted as correct. Otherwise, it is considered as *malicious* (and result of the other server is accepted as correct with the assumption that at least one of the servers is honest).

4.2   Fides System Overview

Actors. There are three main actors in the *Fides* system.

(i) The **client** is the outsourcer of the computation who writes the delegated program. To communicate over Ethereum network the client must have an Ethereum address.
(ii) The **server** is the entity that executes the outsourced computation and returns a result. In Fides we require two servers (S_1 and S_2). Each server executes the computation inside an EVM that is isolated from the Ethereum

network. To participate in the protocol each server must have an Ethereum address.

(iii) A **referee** is a *smart contract* on the Ethereum blockchain. This contract enforces the verifiable computation algorithm. It also manages the interactions between the client and the servers.

Details of the functionalities of the Fides actors are described in Sect. 4.2.

Functions in *Fides*. Functionalities in Fides can be divided into three main parts: (1) *FidesClient* (i.e., represents the functionalities of the client), (2) *FidesServer* (i.e., represents the server functionalities) and (3) *FidesReferee*. The steps of the cmCRR protocol is presented in Algorithm 7 in Appendix E.5.

(1) ***FidesClient.*** The client writes the source code of the delegated program, *program.sol*, in Solidity and compiles the program into *bytecode* (also called *EVM code*. We denote this as $B_{f()}$. Then the client generates commitment com_x to the *input* x and initializes the computation process by calling the *initialize()* function of the referee contract with the necessary arguments and sends program to each of the servers (see Sect. 3.1 for details). Algorithm 2 in Appendix E.2 shows the complete pseudo-code of client's functions in cmCRR protocol.

(2) ***FidesServer.*** Each server interested in solving the problem needs to register for the computation by calling the *Register ()* function of the referee smart contract. Once registered, it receives the program from the client, and checks the commitments and inclusion of any non-deterministic EVM instructions to ensure determinism of the execution. If the checks pass, the server executes the computation inside its private EVM and sends its result to the referee contract. In case of inconsistency, during each round of the binary search phase, each server S_i will send the hashed reduced configuration $H_{rc_j} = H(rc_j)$ for a requested index j by the referee together with a proof p_{rc_j}. See Sect. 3.1 for details of computation and dispute resolution process.

After the binary search stage is completed (when $n_b = n_g + 1$), the referee contract simulates single-step of the computation. It asks one of the servers to reveal the reduced configuration rc_{n_g} and rc_{n_b} in plain. To allow the referee to execute the single-step of the computation, the reduced configuration data must be sent as a deployable EVM code. For example to construct the deployable code for step n_g it does the following:

(a) Include additional EVM instructions (as bytecode) that will copy the stack, memory and storage values from rc_{n_g} into the Ethereum's EVM stack, memory, and storage, respectively.

(b) Append the bytecode of the instruction to be executed at step n_g (I_{n_g}) with the bytecode from step (a). We denote this bytecode as B_{n_g}.

(c) Prepend the bytecode (B_{n_g}) with an *initialization* code c_{n_g} that will enable the referee to initialize a new EVM.

The above steps can be performed using the EVM-tool [15]. Finally, the server will send the deployable bytecode ($c_{n_g}B_{n_g}$) to the referee contract for single-step execution. Server's functions in cmCRR protocol are shown in Algorithm 3 in Appendix E.3.

(3) **FidesReferee.** The referee functionalities in our system are written as a smart contract using the Solidity language and deployed on local Ethereum network. Functions of the referee contract are shown in Algorithms 4, 5 and 6 (for lack of space we divided the functions of the referee contract into 3 algorithms. All the functions in these three algorithms reside inside a single contract. See Appendix E.4 for more details). The referee smart contract performs the following functions, (i) registers two servers interested in solving the computation problem, instructs them to perform the computation and receives their returned commitments to the results, (ii) compares the results of the two servers, (iii) verifies the commitments from the servers, and (iv) in case of result mismatch, finds the step of the computation of the two servers' results that do not match by performing a binary search and then identifies the correct result by executing the disputed computation step itself on Ethereum. Single step execution by the referee contract is implemented as below.

Single-Step Execution. In *Fides*, each step of the protocol is an execution of a single EVM instruction. Once the referee contract finds the the step where the servers disagree, it asks S_1 to reveal the values for two consecutive reduced states, rc_{n_g} and rc_{n_b} (s.t. $n_b = n_g + 1$). In response, it receives the deployable bytecode $c_{n_g} B'_{n_g}$ of the reduced configuration rc_{n_g} along with its claimed output v_{n_b} for rc_{n_b}. Upon receiving S_1's response, referee contract will do the following (pseudo-code is given in Algorithm 6):

(i) It will check whether the instruction I_{n_g} at step n_g is a valid instruction or not, by checking it in the published program bytecode ($B_{f()}$).

(ii) If the check passes, then it will deploy the state bytecode $c_{n_g} B_{n_g}$ by calling the *Deploy()* function in the referee contract that takes $c_{n_g} B_{n_g}$ as the function argument, and returns an address for the newly deployed contract. We call this *disp-state contract* (disputed state contract) that holds the runtime bytecode for the configuration rc_{n_g} (provided by the S_1).

(iii) The referee contract then executes the code in the *disp-state contract* by using *(bool status, bytes memory data) = disp_state_address.call ()* and receives the execution result, denoted as v'. If $v' = v_{n_b}$, then the output of S_1 (and so its overall computation) will be accepted as correct. Otherwise, the referee contract identifies S_1 as the "malicious" server, and accepts the results of server S_2 as correct (since at least one server is assumed to be honest).

Note that, execution of *disp-state contract* will fail if it run out-of-gas or an invalid code is provided by the server. If any of these cases happen, it will be considered as a malicious behaviour. In order to prevent execution failure due to out-of-gas problem, we require the client to specify the maximum amount of gas that might be required to perform the single step execution by the referee contract (during the initialization of the computation process). At the end, once the referee contract finds the correct result (as well as the honest server), the honest server will be paid by the client (through the referee contract) based on the amount of gas used for performing the computation.

4.3   Evaluation

To show practicality of our verification protocol, we conducted a number of experiments with *Fides* prototype. The experiments are designed to evaluate the execution complexity (cost) of the server in terms of *running time* and the referee contract in terms of *gas*. We implemented the smart contracts in *Solidity* v.0.5.17. The experiments are performed using *Ganache* [18] - a framework to simulate the EVM on local computer. For development of the smart contracts we used Remix IDE [26]. For our example computation we used matrix multiplication. That is the client writes the delegated program $matrix\_multiplication.sol$ ($= f()$) in Solidity and the input to this program is a $n \times n$ matrix. We evaluated performance of *Fides* client and server programs on Windows 10 with a 3.60 GHz Intel Core i7 CPU and 8 GB RAM.

Cost Analysis. We measured the following costs:

(i) *Program execution cost.* Our goal is to measure the *execution cost (in terms of running time) of the delegated program by a server.* Our matrix multiplication algorithm has run time $\mathcal{O}(n^3)$ for $n \times n$ matrix. The program was executed 3 times for each of the matrix sizes with different inputs and the average time is reported in Table 1.

(ii) *Financial cost of verification.* For verification, *our goal is to measure the financial cost that indicates the actual monetary cost of executing the referee contract on the Ethereum network.* We use *gas* to measure the computation complexity of the smart contract execution and then convert it into the monetary value in US dollar. We considered two scenarios: (i) servers send same results, and (ii) servers send different results.
For the first scenario, the execution cost of the referee contract for verification is limited to comparing the returned results (y_i) and verifying the commitments com_{y_i}. We used *Keccak256* hash function for the commitments. For the second scenario, the referee initiates the *dispute resolution* protocol (called *MCId-malicious cloud identification*). The execution cost in this case will depend on (i) the number of rounds during the binary-search step and (ii) the length of the Merkle proof that is sent along with the hashed reduced configuration in each round. The maximum number of rounds that can be executed is logarithmic in the number of computation steps N and the maximum length of a Merkle proof for reduced configuration is also logarithmic in the size of reduced configuration array $\mathcal{C}$.

In Ethereum, the amount of gas that can be used per block (i.e., the *block capacity*) is bounded by a limit. This limit is called *block gas limit*. The *block gas limit* in Ethereum is set approximately 29.9 million[1] gas by the miners.

---

[1] According to etherscan.io/chart/gaslimit on November,18, 2021.

Table 1. Cost analysis of *Fides*. The left side of the Table shows the program execution cost (in *time*) inside EVM by each server for different matrix sizes. The right side of the Table outlines the transaction execution cost (in *gas*) of calling referee contract's functions for matrix size $n = 10$. The number of rounds in the MCId is $\lceil log_2(N) \rceil = 10$ where the number of computation steps is $N = 780$. The total cost is converted into US$s that represents only the total cost of executing the referee contract on Ethereum and excludes any transaction fee.

Prog. Execution cost		Financial cost of verification		
Matrix Size (n)	Time (sec.)	Phases	Gas Used	
10	5.06	Initialize	115,135	
20	34.40	Register	62,400	
30	111.67	receiveResultCommitments	109,349	
40	317.67	receiveResults	87,275	
50	603	Compare	*Scenario 1* *(results match)*	*Scenario 2* *(results mismatch)*
		verifyCommitments	27,583	27,583
		MCId (dispute resolution)	-	689,556
		Total (Gas)	401,742	1,091,298
		Cost (in ETH)[a]	0.0601	0.1633
		Cost (in USD)[b]	240.29	652.73

[a] According to https://etherscan.io/chart/gasprice on November 18, 2021
[b] According to https://etherscan.io/chart/etherprice on November 18, 2021.

Based on the values in Table 1, the referee contract functions (*Initialize, Register, receiveResultCommitments,* and *receiveResults*) cost around 0.21% to 0.38% of block capacity.

To evaluate the cost of the *MCId* function, we executed this experiment with 3 different disagreement points. For each of these 3 executions we ran the experiment with one honest server and one dishonest server that cheats on one of the three disagreement points. The disagreement points were chosen- one at the beginning (at step $N/4$), one near the middle (at step $N/2$), and one at step $3N/4$ of the computation, where N is the total number of computation steps. For matrix size 10, we had $N = 780$ and for all these 3 executions we had same number of rounds ($\lceil log_2(N) \rceil = 10$) and the same size of the single-step data (≈ 1.2 kB). Note that, in general the size of the single-step data depends on the size of the computation state data at the location of disagreement point, which varies between several hundred bytes to few Kilobytes for this example program. Table 1 shows that the MCId function execution cost is approximately 2.3% of the block capacity. This suggests that the cost increase due to the higher number of rounds will remain acceptable for the current block sizes in Ethereum.

In summary, the results in Table 1 demonstrate that cmCRR requires reasonable program execution time by the servers and the (financial) cost of verification on Ethereum network is minimal. In addition, the client must pay the execution cost for *scenario 1* and the system can penalize a malicious server by asking to pay the cost difference between *scenario 1* and *scenario 2* (that increases with the size of the computation and the number of rounds in binary search phase) in order to disincentivize the malicious behaviour.

Comparison with Other Works. Performance of *Fides* is not comparable to the related works because majority of these works [35, 39, 40, 42] use single server to do the computation and the other work that uses multiple server for computation is [10], which uses a different execution environment compared to Fides. On the other hand, existing works in the smart contract setting such as [24, 29, 37, 41] consider a different model of adversary (e.g., rational adversary) which are not comparable to Fides (that considers malicious adversary) in terms of security they achieve and also lack performance measurements.

5   Concluding Remarks

SC-RDoC offers an attractive model for verifiable computation, that minimizes trust on the client and servers by delegating the referee task to a smart contract. We proposed cmCRR protocol which protects against copy attack and misbehavior of client, and proved its security. We discussed challenges of implementing the single step computation by the referee contract, and showed how our prototype, Fides, addresses these challenges. Our work can be extended to multiple server SC-RDoC. Interesting open questions are to provide a formal security model that can capture copy attack, to hide the single step of the computation from the SC (privacy against an observer), and to allow servers to perform their computation in a commonly used architecture such as X86 while using the smart contract for verifying a single computation step.

A   Related Works: Single Server Outsourcing Computation Schemes

Interactive proof system where a prover proves correctness of a statement to a verifier is a fundamental problem in theoretical computer science [5, 22, 34]. The basic proof systems assume computationally unbounded prover and efficient verifier. *Argument systems* [8, 31, 32] assume computationally bounded provers. Probabilistically checkable proofs (PCPs) [3] assume the prover is unbounded and the proof can be probabilistically verified by a (computationally bounded) verifier by querying a bounded number of bits in the proof. PCPs have been used to construct efficient argument systems [27, 31].

Verifiable delegation of computation (aka verifiable outsourced computation) considers a weak client that delegates the computation of a function f on an input x to a powerful server, and can verify the correctness of the result with significantly less resources than what is required to perform the computation.

Goldwasser, Kalai and Rothblum [21] (GKR) proposed an interactive proof system to prove the correctness of the delegated computations where both the verifier and the prover are efficient. This work was extended by Cormode et al. [14] (CMT). Both GKR and CMT require the computation be represented as a layered arithmetic circuit, and provide security against an unbounded prover. Delegation of general computation using fully homomorphic encryption (FHE) has been proposed in [13,19]. Efficient single server verifiable computation systems have implemented [38–40] using an efficient argument system of Ishai et al. [27]. In these systems, the computation is written as a set of constraints (i.e., a system of equations). Pepper [40] and Ginger [39] use classical linear PCP of Arora et al. [2] and Zaatar [38] uses linear PCP based on quadratic arithmetic programs (QAPs) [20]. Vu et al. [42] proposed Allspice, where a suitable verifiable computation system is chosen among CMT and Zaatar using static analysis. Zaatar uses batching of multiple instances of a single computation to amortize the setup cost. Another concurrent implementation of a verifiable computation system is Pinocchio [35] that uses QAPs [20] for encoding computation. To be practically viable Pinocchio needs key setup whose cost will be amortized over all instances of a computation [12,44].

B   Details of Preliminaries

In this section, we provide an overview of our cryptographic building blocks and the Turing machine model of computation.

Hash Function. We use a family of collision-resistant hash functions H. Roughly speaking, a hash function H is collision-resistant if there is no polynomial time algorithm that can find a collision. That means, it is computationally infeasible to find two distinct inputs m_1 and m_2 such that $H(m_1) = H(m_2)$.

Commitment Schemes. We require that the commitment scheme satisfies two properties, *hiding* and *binding*. Hiding guarantees that for any two messages x_0 and x_1, and $(com_0, d_0) = Commit(x_0)$ and $(com_1, d_1) = Commit(x_1)$, we have that com_0 is computationally indistinguishable from com_1. The binding property requires that it is computationally hard to find a triple (com, d, d') such that for $x \neq x'$, we have $Open(com, d, x) = Open(com, d', x') = 1$.

Turing Machine Representation of Computation. A Turing machine $M = (\Sigma, \mathcal{K}, \delta)$ is an abstract model of computation that is specified by a finite alphabet Σ, a finite set of states $\mathcal{K}$ with a special element I (the starting state), and a transition function $\delta : \mathcal{K} \times \Sigma \rightarrow (\mathcal{K} \cup \{halt, yes, no\}) \times \Sigma \times \{\leftarrow, \rightarrow, -\}$. A configuration of a Turing machine is an ordered triple $(t, s, h) \in \Sigma^* \times \mathcal{K} \times N$ where t denotes the tape content, s denotes the machine's current state, and h denotes the position of the head on the tape, where $0 \leq h < |t|$. For a Turing machine M with configuration (t, s, h) at any point in time, the next configuration (t', s', h') at the following point in time is determined as follows. Let $(s', v', d') = \delta(s, v)$. The string t' is obtained from t by changing v (or t_h) to v'. The new state is s', and the new position h' is equal to $h - 1$, $h + 1$, or h based on whether d' is $\leftarrow$, $\rightarrow$ or $-$, respectively.

C   Function: VerifyReducedStep()

Consider that the two consecutive reduced configurations claimed by server S_1 are: $rc_{n_g} = (s_{n_g}, h_{n_g}, v_{n_g}, p_{n_g})$ and $rc_{n_b} = (s_{n_b}, h_{n_b}, v_{n_b}, p_{n_b})$. First SC checks whether the revealed reduced configurations match the hash values that had received. If one of them does not match it returns the result of S_2 to the client. Otherwise, if both match, then it verifies the single step computation. This approach requires that the SC stores the intermediate hashed reduced configurations. To avoid this storage, one can require that S_1 also reveals the Merkle proof that shows rc_{n_g} and rc_{n_b} are in the Merkle tree constructed on its array of hashed reduced configurations.

To verify the correctness of computation all the following steps should be completed consecutively (every verification should return True). This indicates that S_1 is honest (these steps are checked by $\mathcal{SC}^{\mathcal{L}d, \mathcal{H}}$); if any of the checks return false then the claimed consecutive execution is incorrect and server S_2 is honest:
1) Verify that the Merkle proofs are correct by checking $VerifyMHProof(r_{n_g}, h_{n_g}, v_{n_g}, p_{n_g})$ and $VerifyMHProof(r_{n_b}, h_{n_b}, v_{n_b}, p_{n_b})$. 2) Simulate the Turing machine, starting from rc_{n_g} and obtain the next state s', head position h' and value v' (written as h_{n_g}-th character). 3) Verify that s', h' are equal to s_{n_b}, h_{n_b}. 4) Using p_{n_g} and v', compute
$$r' = MHroot(t_{n_g}|_{[h_{n_g}]=v'} = v')$$
where $t_{n_g}|_{[h_{n_g}]=v'}$ is the tape of configuration rc_{n_g} except for the value v' in its h_{n_g}-th character. For computing r' the property of Merkle hash trees are used. By knowing the Merkle proof for character h_{n_g}, i.e. $MH_{proof}(t_{n_g}, h_{n_g})$, we can compute $MHroot(t')$ where t' equals to t_{n_g} except that the character in h_{n_g} is v'. First, we can compute $d_{h_{n_g}} = H(v')$ which is the data (hash value) stored in position h_{n_g} of the Merkle tree and by then using $MH_{proof}(t_{n_g}, h_{n_g})$ we compute the new hash values along the path to $d_{h_{n_g}}$ (this can be done in logarithmic time in the length of t, without knowing the full tape). 5) Verify that the hash of the root in p_{n_b} equals to r'.

C.1   CRR Protocol

In CRR the *reduced configuration* for a computation step j is given by $rc_j = (s_j, h_j, v_j, r_j)$, where s_j and h_j represent current *state* of TM and the *head* position, respectively, v_j represents the value on the tape at the TM's head position, *tape[head]*, and $r_j = MH_{root}(t_j)$ is the *root* of the Merkle tree on the tape t_j. The reduced configuration rc_j captures the computation state s_j.
The CRR protocol works as follows:

i) The client requests the two servers to execute the function f for the input x. Server $i, i \in \{1, 2\}$ returns its result $y_i = f(x)$ for $i \in \{1, 2\}$ to the client after executing the function along with the number of steps (n) of the execution.

ii) The result is accepted as *correct* if the two results match.

iii) Otherwise, the client initiates a challenge-response protocol to detect the malicious server. The protocol has two functions: (i) *binary-search* and (ii) *verify-reduced-step*.

- The *binary-search* function takes the minimum number of steps, n_b, that is taken by one of the servers to compute $f(x)$, as input, and returns the index n_g of the last reduced configuration matched for the two servers.
- The *verify-reduced-step* function takes two consecutive reduced configurations, $rc_{n_g} = (s_{n_g}, h_{n_g}, v_{n_g}, r_{n_g})$ and $rc_{n_b} = (s_{n_b}, h_{n_b}, v_{n_b}, r_{n_b})$ where $n_b = n_g + 1$, and the proof of consistency $p_{n_g} = MH_{proof}(t_{n_g}, h_{n_g})$ for the tree index h_{n_g} from one of the servers (say S_1), where t_{n_g} is the tape at computation step n_g.

Then it calls $VerifyMHProof(r_{n_g}, h_{n_g}, v_{n_g}, p_{n_g})$ to recompute the Merkel root for the configuration rc_{n_g}, and performs the computation from rc_{n_g} till rc_{n_b} and verifies the Merkel root for rc_{n_b} (invoking $VerifyMHProof(r_{n_b}, h_{n_b}, v_{n_b}, p_{n_b})$).

If both the outcomes (of $VerifyMHProof()$) match, the server (S_1) is considered as honest and its result is accepted. Otherwise, the other server (S_2) is honest and its result is accepted.

CRR protocol provides following guarantees. (1) If any server cheats, the client can successfully detect the cheating assuming collision-resistant hash function used for Merkle tree construction and obtain a publicly verifiable proof of this fact. (2) The client can efficiently determine the correct result as long as there exists a single honest server.

D   Attacks Prevented in cmCRR Protocol

Table 2 shows the summary of some of the important attacks that are considered against cmCRR protocol and how the protocol protect against them.

The cmCRR protocol satisfies the following additional properties:

Input Privacy. Our scheme also provides input privacy with respect to smart contract when the servers are honest. The reason is that the servers receive the input from the client through a secure communication channel and only a commitment to the input is published to SC. As the commitment scheme is hiding the leakage to SC is negligible. Additionally, if both servers are honest they output the same result which is accepted by SC and returned to the client.

Security Against Malicious Client. A malicious client may try to send different inputs to the servers. However, we assume that client has to first commit to the input in the SC and later opens it. If client tries to open the commitment in different ways it will be detected with non-negligible probability.

Table 2. Summary of considered attacks and our proposed solutions.

Attacks	Our Proposed Solutions
(Attacks by the malicious client)	
Sending different/wrong computation/input to the servers	Client should publish the computation and commitment to the input on the Blockchain.
Designing probabilistic computation	Server should check the computation for the set of instructions that are probabilistic.
(Attacks by the server(s))	
Sending wrong result to SC	Using MCId protocol of CRR and executing single-step on Ethereum network.
Copy final result	Using commit and reveal approach for computation result and using a public key to construct the Merkle root $MH_{root}(C_i\|Pk_i)$.
Copy during binary search	By hashing the reduced configuration, and using a Merkle proof for the reduced configuration.
Sending incorrect single-step information (i) incorrect instruction (ii) out-of-gas for bad code	Requires followings: (i) check by the referee contract for the validity of the instruction I_{n_g} in the published program bytecode. (ii) the client specifies in SC the maximum amount of gas that might require for singles-step execution and referee checks whether the gas sent by the server is less or equal to this amount.
False complain against the client's commitments	Abort the computation process and re-outsource.

E Fides

E.1 EVM Instructions

The EVM is a stack-based machine with a predefined set of instructions [45]. Inside an EVM, a smart contract is simply a series of EVM instructions, which are executed sequentially. The execution environment of EVM consists of a virtual ROM (where the program code is loaded) and three locations to store/access data during execution: stack, memory, and storage. In [45] all EVM instructions are divided into the following categories (Table 3):

Table 3. Categories of EVM instructions. (See Appendix H.2 of [45] for the complete list of EVM instructions for each of the above categories.)

Categories	Example Instructions
Arithmetic/comparison/bitwise logic operations	ADD, SUB, MUL, DIV, GT, LT, AND, OR
Stack, Memory, Storage and Flow operations	PUSH, POP, DUP, SWAP, MLOAD, MSTORE, SLOAD, SSTORE, JUMP
Hashing, logging and stop operations	SHA3, LOG, STOP
Environmental information operations	ADDRESS, BALANCE, CALLDATACOPY, CODECOPY, GASPRICE, EXTCODESIZE, EXTCODECOPY
Block information operations	BLOCKHASH, TIMESTAMP, NUMBER, DIFFICULTY, GASLIMIT
System operations	CREATE, CALL, CALLCODE, RETURN, REVERT, DELEGATECALL, SELFDESTRUCT

Based on the above categories we require that the program will not include following instructions (to prevent a malicious client from constructing a probabilistic computation):

- Environmental information operations such as `EXTCODESIZE` and `EXTCODECOPY` that can get an external account's size and code, respectively, during the execution.
- All the block information operations that can get external blockchain related data which can be used to make the program randomized during execution.
- System operations such as `CREATE`, `CALL`, `DELEGATECALL` that are used to create a new smart contract account or message-call to an account with an external account's code.

Since these instructions involve creating/calling codes/data that are outside of the current program execution environment of EVM, therefore, these instructions should not be used in the delegated program. If any such instruction is identified, the server will not execute the delegated program and report it to the smart contract.

E.2   Fides Client Functions

The client functionalities in Fides are shown in Algorithm 2.

E.3   Fides Server Functions

Algorithm 3 shows Fides server functionalities that include: *(i) Registration.* Each participating server will install an Ethereum client (e.g., `geth`) that connects it to the Ethereum network. This client allows the server to work as an Ethereum node having its own EVM. Each server interested in solving the problem will then register for the computation by calling the *Register ()* function of the referee contract and sends its public key Pk (that is used for generating the Ethereum address of the server) as the function argument. Once both servers are registered, the referee contract will update the state of the computation to "Compute" from "Init" and then the servers will receive the computation related information for execution from the client.

(ii) Check commitments and deterministic computation. After registration, each server receives the computation information from the client and checks its validity by verifying the committed values on the blockchain. The servers will verify that the com_x match to what they have received. If any server finds a conflict, then it will aborts. In addition, each server will also check whether the program includes any EVM instructions that produce non-deterministic output.

(iii) EVM execution of computation and send result. After the completion of the above steps, the server will perform the computation inside its EVM. Note that, EVM computation is private and server's EVM is not part of the Ethereum network. The computation bytecode will be sent as the input to the EVM. During the execution, the bytecode is split up into its bytes and each byte is either an EVM instruction or data. Once the execution in EVM is complete, the final computation result (along with the intermediate computation results) will be stored in the storage of EVM. Then the server will obtain the *root* $= (H(MH_{root}(\mathcal{C}_i) \parallel H(Pk_i))$ constructed on hashed reduced configuration array

Algorithm 2. Client functions in cmCRR protocol.

1: **Input:** Solidity program $f()$ and input x
2: **function** MAIN($f()$, x) **returns** ($result$)
3:     /* Step 1: Program compilation and generating commitments */
4:     Compile $f()$ using $solc$ compiler and get the program bytecode $B_{f()}$.
5:     Get (com_x, d_x) = GENERATE-COMMITMENT (x);
6:
7:     /* Step 2: Get Referee contract's address and publish computation data to blockchain. */
8:     referee = web3.eth.contract(address="0x< $referee\_contract\_address$ >");
9:     PUBLISH-TO-BLOCKCHAIN ($B_{f()}$, com_x, $referee$);
10:
11:     /* Step 3: Send computation data to servers */
12:     Connect to servers;
13:     **for server in connections do**
14:         **server.send**(x, $B_{f()}$, d_x);   ▷ d_x: commitment key
15:     /* Step 4: Get computation result from blockchain */
16:     Get $result$ = GET-COMPUTATION-RESULT($referee$);
17:     return $result$;
18:
19: **function** GENERATE-COMMITMENT($message$) **returns** (com,key)
20:     Get key = $getrandbits(256)$;
21:     Set msg = $message$;
22:     Get com = **keccak256** ($key + msg$);   ▷ com: commitment value
23:     return (com,key);
24:
25: **function** PUBLISH-TO-BLOCKCHAIN($program\_bytecode$, com_x, $referee$)
26:                     ▷ Send transaction that invokes referee contract's Initialize() function
27:     referee.functions.Initialize($program\_bytecode$, com_x).transact();
28:
29: **function** GET-COMPUTATION-RESULT($referee$) **returns** ($final\_result$)
30:                     ▷ Get the $final$ $result$ by calling referee contract's getResult() function
31:     Get $final\_result$ = referee.functions.getResult().call();
32:     return $final\_result$;

$C_i = \{H(rc_1), H(rc_2), \ldots, H(rc_{N_i})\}$ and the hash of public key Pk_i of server S_i for $i \in \{1, 2\}$. Here, N_i is the total number of reduced configurations of server S_i. The server will also generate a commitment to its result y_i, $com_{y_i} = Commit(y_i)$ = H $(d_{y_i} \| y_i \| Pk_i)$, where H is a collision-resistant hash function. Finally, the server will send (com_{y_i}, $root$, N_i) to the referee contract. Then, when the server receives the request from the referee for revealing the commitments, it will reveal (y_i, d_{y_i}) pair which enables the referee to check whether its a valid opening.

Note that, at a time an EVM can process a single call with the provided bytecode (i.e., only executing one computation at a time). Therefore, if a server wants to run two computations received from two different clients, the EVM needs to be initialized (i.e., set the stack, memory, and program counter to zero) for each new computation separately depending on the order of the computation request received from the client. However, the storage of the EVM will store the data of all the computations in the address assigned for each computation.

(iv) Send reduced configurations. In case of inconsistency, each server S_i will send the hashed reduced configuration $H_{rc_j} = H(rc_j)$ for a requested index j by the referee together with a proof p_{rc_j} that shows rc_j is in the Merkle tree having root $(H(MH_{root}(C_i) \parallel H(Pk_i))$.

(v) Send single-step data. After the binary search stage is completed (when $n_b = n_g + 1$), the referee contract simulates single-step of the computation. It asks one of the server to reveal the reduced configuration rc_{n_g} and rc_{n_b} in plain. To simulate the single step, the referee contract will create a new EVM and present the received data as a new smart contract that will be run in the new initialized EVM (more details on single-step execution is described in Sect. 4.2). To allow the referee performing this process, the server must send the reduced configuration data as a deployable EVM code. To construct the deployable code the server will do the following to the reduced configuration n_g:

(i) include additional EVM instructions (as bytecode) that will copy the stack, memory and storage values from rc_{n_g} into the Ethereum's EVM stack, memory, and storage, respectively.

(ii) append the bytecode of the instruction to be executed at step n_g (I_{n_g}) with the bytecode from step (i). We denote this bytecode as B_{n_g}.

(iii) Finally, prepend the bytecode (B_{n_g}) with an *initialization* code c_{n_g} that will enable the referee to initialize the new EVM.

The above steps can be performed using the EVM-tool [15]. Finally, the server will send the deployable bytecode ($c_{n_g}B_{n_g}$) to the referee contract for single-step execution.

Algorithm 3 in Appendix E.3 shows the pseudo-code of server's functions in cmCRR protocol.

E.4   Referee Contract Functions

The referee smart contract performs the following functions, (i) compares the results of the two servers, (ii) verifies the commitments from the servers, and (iii) in case of result mismatch, identifies the step of the computation of the two servers' results that do not match by creating and executing a new smart contract account with the single step information (provided by one of the servers). The referee functionalities in our system are written as a smart contract using the Solidity language. The referee contract is published on the Ethereum blockchain and it's execution is performed by the miners in the Ethereum network. Functions of the referee contract are shown in Algorithms 4, 5 and 6 (for lack of space in a single page and discussion purpose we divided the functions of the referee contract into 3 algorithms. All the functions in these three algorithms reside inside a single contract.).

Algorithm 3. Server functions in cmCRR protocol.

1: **Input:** program bytecode $B_{f()}$, input x, commitment keys key_f, key_x
2:
3: **function** MAIN$(x, B_{f()}, key_x)$
4:    /* Step 1: Register for the computation */
5:    referee.functions.Register(Pk_i).transact();   ▷ Transaction to referee contract's Register() function
6:    /* Step 2: Check commitments and program's validity. */
7:    Get com_x from blockchain;
8:    **if** open$(com_x, d_x, x) = 1$ **then** continue; **else** break;
9:    Check $B_{f()}$ for non-deterministic EVM instructions;
10:    /* Step 3: Execute program in EVM and send result to referee contract. */
11:    vm = EVM;   ▷ Initialize VM environment to run the bytecode
12:    (y_i, num_steps) = vm.execute_bytecode $(B_{f()}, x)$;   ▷ y_i: result of computation
13:    Get (com_{y_i}, d_{y_i}) = GENERATE-COMMITMENT (y_i, Pk_i);
14:    **for** j = 1 to num_steps **do**
15:       Get H_{rc_j} = GENERATE-MERKLE-TREE (rc_j);
16:    Get $root$ = GENERATE-MERKLE-TREE $(hashed\_reduced\_configuration\_array)$;
17:    Compute $root_{S_i} = H (root \parallel H(Pk_i))$;   ▷ Pk_i: public key of server S_i
18:    referee.functions.receiveResults$(com_{y_i}, root_{S_i}, num\_steps)$.transact();
19:    Reveal (y_i, d_{y_i}) to referee;   ▷ Referee asks the server to reveal its commitment
20:    /* Step 4: Send hashed reduced configuration during binary-search */
21:    Get rc_{index} = GET-REDUCED-CONFIG $(index)$;
22:    Get $H_{rc_{index}}$ = GENERATE-MERKLE-TREE (rc_{index});
23:    Get $pr_{c_{index}}$ = get_MHproof $(index)$;   ▷ $pr_{c_{index}}$: Merkle Proof for rc_{index}
24:    Send $(H_{rc_{index}}, pr_{c_{index}})$ to referee;
25:    /* Step 5: Send single-step data. */
26:    Get $(deploy\_Code, rc_{n_g}, rc_{n_b})$ = GET-SINGLESTEP-DATA $(index)$;
27:    Send $(deploy\_Code, rc_{n_g}, rc_{n_b})$ to referee;
28: **function** GET-REDUCED-CONFIG$(index)$ **returns** (rc_{index})
29:    Get $v_{index} \leftarrow vm.getStorageAt(index)$;
30:    Get $s_{index} \leftarrow getVMState(index)$;
31:    Set $rc_{index} \leftarrow (s_{index}, v_{index})$
32:    return rc_{index}
33: **function** GET-SINGLESTEP-DATA(n_g) **returns** $(deploy\_code, rc_{n_g}, rc_{n_b})$
34:    Get rc_{n_g} = GET-REDUCED-CONFIG (n_g);
35:    Get I_{n_g};
36:    Create $dc_{rc_{n_g}} = DeployCode (rc_{n_g}, I_{n_g})$;
37:    Get rc_{n_b} = GET-REDUCED-CONFIG (n_b);
38:    return $(dc_{rc_{n_g}}, rc_{n_g}, rc_{n_b})$
39: **function** GENERATE-COMMITMENT$(message, Pk_i)$ **returns** (com, key)
40:    Get $key = getrandbits(256)$;
41:    Set $msg = message$;
42:    Get $com = \mathbf{H} (key \parallel msg \parallel Pk_i)$;   ▷ com: commitment value
43:    return (com, key);
44: **function** GENERATE-MERKLE-TREE$(data\_array)$ **returns** $(Mroot)$
45:    Create MerkleTools Object mt for constructing Merkle tree
46:    $mt.add\_leaf(data\_array)$;   ▷ Adds a value as a leaf
47:    $mt.make\_tree()$;   ▷ Generates the Merkle Tree
48:    Get $Mroot = mt.get\_merkle\_root()$;   ▷ Returns the Merkle root of the tree
49:    return $Mroot$;

Once the computation is initialized by the client,

- The referee contract registers two servers interested in solving the computation problem, instructs them to perform the computation and receives their returned commitments to the results.
- Then it asks both servers to reveal their commitments and checks the validity of the commitments.
- Next (if commitments are valid), it checks whether the y_i received from both servers match with each other or not.
- If true, the referee selects one of the y_i values as the computation result.
- In case of inconsistency, it executes the binary search function to find the steps where the servers disagree. At each round of the binary search, the referee specifies the index j of the computation step for which both parties should respond with their hashed reduced configuration H_{rc_j} together with a proof p_{rc_j}. It then checks whether the hashed reduced configurations of both servers match or not. If they match it verifies whether the Merkle proof p_{rc_j} is valid. If both are valid it updates n_g, else it selects the y_i of the server whose Merkle proof is valid as computation result. Otherwise, if the encrypted reduced configurations do not match, it updates n_b and computes the next computation step that servers have to reveal its reduced configuration.
- Once the binary search stage is complete (i.e., two consecutive reduced states rc_{n_b}, rc_{n_g} are identified such that $n_b = n_g + 1$), the referee contract will simulate the instruction for step n_g to compute the correct output of the reduced configuration for step n_b, compare it to the server's answer and declare the correct result of the computation.

Single-Step Execution. Algorithm 6 shows the functions used by referee contract to perform the single-step execution. Here, the *Deploy()* function uses the CREATE opcode to deploy the bytecode, and obtain the address of the deployed contract. At the end of successful deployment, the runtime bytecode for the configuration rc_{n_g} (provided by the server) will reside alone at its new contract address.

E.5   Steps of cmCRRProtocol

The interactions between different parties involved in the cmCRR protocol are shown in steps in Algorithm 7.

E.6   On-Chain Transactions

As all the communications to and from the smart contract uses the Ethereum network, it introduces delay. We measure the delay in *Fides* when two servers are involved in terms of the number of on-chain transactions that will be sent and received *between the servers and the smart contract* for a given computation. In our implementation, we have four different phases of interactions between the servers and the referee contract, namely - *registration, receive commitments, receive committed results* and the *malicious cloud identification* (MCId). For the first three phases, each server sends a transaction to the referee contract for registration, for sending the commitments to the results, and for revealing the committed results, respectively. So, in each of these three phases there are *two transactions* involved. In the MCId phase, for the binary-search step up to $2log(N)$ rounds are required where at each round the referee sends the index of the next step that both servers should respond. So, in total, up to $4log(N)$ transactions are required for binary-search. Finally, for the single-step case, one of the servers provides necessary data in 1 transaction. So, at most $4log(N) + 1$ *transactions* are required. Based on this delay analysis, we can also estimate the delay for the multi-server case.

Algorithm 4. Functions of the *Referee* smart contract

1: **function** INITIALIZE(com_x, *program_bytecode*) **public**
2:     set $task$ = program_bytecode;
3:     $com\_to\_input = com_x$;
4:     set $index = 0$;
5: **function** REGISTER () **public**
6:     require (index < 2, "Registration complete");
7:     set Cloud[index] = msg.sender;   ▷ Storing cloud's address
8:     update $index+ = 1$;
9:     assert(count < 2);   ▷ Checking whether two clouds registered or not
10:     **emit** *registered* ($Cloud[0]$, $Cloud[1]$);
11:     set state = *Compute*;
12: **function** RECEIVE-RESULT-COMMITMENTS(com_y, MH_{root}, N) **public**
13:     **assert** ($msg.sender == Cloud[0]$ —— $msg.sender == Cloud[1]$);
14:     **if** $msg.sender == Cloud[0]$ **then**
15:         set com_Result[0] = com_y; MRoot[0] = MH_{root}; Tape_length[0] = N;
16:             ▷ (com_Result[], MRoot[], Tape_length[]: array to store commitment to result,
    Merkle root, length of RC array, respectively)
17:     **else**
18:         set Result[1] = com_y; MRoot[1] = MH_{root}; Tape_length[1] = N;
19:     /* if both clouds committed then ask for revealing the result */
20:     **emit** *revealResult* ("Reveal result");
21: **function** RECEIVE-RESULT(y, key_y) **public**
22:     **assert** ($msg.sender == Cloud[0]$ —— $msg.sender == Cloud[1]$);
23:     **if** $msg.sender == Cloud[0]$ **then**
24:         set Result[0] = y; com_key[0] = key_y;
25:             ▷ (Result[], com_key[]: array to store result, and commitment key, respectively)
26:     **else**
27:         set Result[1] = y; com_key[1] = key_y;
28:     /* Once both clouds revealed the results call compare function */
29:     *Compare* ();
30: **function** COMPARE () **internal**
31:     $Open1 = verify\_commitment$(com_Result[0], Result[0], com_key[0]);
32:     $Open2 = verify\_commitment$(com_Result[1], Result[1], com_key[1]);
33:     **if** (Result[0]==Result[1]) && (Tape_length[0]==Tape_length[1]) **then**
34:     $resultMatch$ = true;   ▷ results match
35:         **if** ($Open1$ == true && $Open2$ == true) **then**
36:             $copyDetected$ = false;
37:             $final\_output$ = Result[0]; $resultStatus$ = "Correct result";
38:         **if** ($Open1$ == true && $Open2$ == false) **then**
39:             $copyDetected$ = true;
40:             $final\_output$ = Result[0]; $resultStatus$ = "Correct result";
41:         **if** ($Open1$ == false && $Open2$ == true) **then**
42:             $copyDetected$ = true;
43:             $final\_output$ = Result[1]; $resultStatus$ = "Correct result";
44:     **else**
45:     $resultMatch$ = false;   ▷ results mismatch
46:         **if** ($Open1$ == true && $Open2$ == false) **then**
47:             $IncorrectOpening$ = true; $final\_output$ = Result[0]; $resultStatus$ = "Correct
    result";
48:         **if** ($Open1$ == false && $Open2$ == true) **then**
49:             $IncorrectOpening$ = true; $final\_output$ = Result[1]; $resultStatus$ = "Correct
    result";
50:         **if** ($Open1$ == true && $Open2$ == true) **then**
51:             $IncorrectOpening$ = false;
52:         /* Initiate Malicious Cloud Identification Protocol in Algorithm 5 */;

Algorithm 5. Malicious cloud identification protocol.

1: Set $n_b = min\ (Tape\_length[0], Tape\_length[1])$;
2: Set $n_g = binary - search(n_b)$;   ▷ index of last matched configuration
3: **function** BINARY-SEARCH(n_b) **returns** (int)
4:     Set $idx_s = 0$, $idx_e = n_b$; ▷ idx_s=starting index where clouds agree, idx_e=last index where clouds disagree
5:     Set $mid = \frac{idx_e - idx_s}{2} + idx_s$;
6:     **while** $idx_e > idx_s + 1$ **do**
7:         PG asks for the Hashed reduced-configurations $H(rc_{mid}^i)$ at index mid along with a proof $\rho_{rc_{mid}^i}$ from both server ($i \in \{1, 2\}$);
8:             **if** $(H(rc_j^1) = H(rc_j^2))$ **then**
9:                 Verify proofs $\rho_{rc_{mid}^1}$ and $\rho_{rc_{mid}^2}$
10:                 **if** (both proofs are valid) **then**
11:                                     ▷ mismatch is at the second half $(mid, idx_e]$
12:                     set $idx_s = mid$; update $mid = \frac{idx_e - idx_s}{2} + idx_s$;
13:                 **if** both proofs are invalid **then**
14:                     set $idx_e = mid$; update $mid = \frac{idx_e - idx_s}{2} + idx_s$;
15:                 **if** one of the proofs is invalid **then**
16:                     set $final\_output$ = Result of the honest cloud; return 0;
17:     return idx_s;
18: Client asks *Cloud 1* for configurations rc_{n_g} and rc_{n_b} to perform single step of the computation;   /* $n_b = n_g + 1$ */
19: /* Initiate Single-step execution as shown in Algorithm 6

Algorithm 6. Single-step execution by the referee contract.

1: **function** EXECUTE-SINGLE-STEP($state\_bytecode$, rc_{n_g}, rc_{n_b}) **returns** ($bool$)
2:     Verify B_{n_g} is correct   ▷ check correctness for EVM instruction
3:     ($state\_output$, $status$) = VERIFY-REDUCED-STEP ($state\_bytecode$);
4:     **if** $status = true$ and $state\_output = v_{n_b}$ **then** ▷ v_{n_b}: claimed output for step n_b
5:         return $true$;
6:     **else**
7:         return $false$;
8:
9: **function** VERIFY-REDUCED-STEP($state\_bytecode$) **returns** ($state\_output$, $status$)
10:     Get $desp\_state\_addr$ = Deploy ($state\_bytecode$);   ▷ Address of disp-state contract
11:     Get $(TF, val) = desp\_state\_addr$.call(" ");   ▷ Execute disp-state contract
12:                             ▷ val: Execution result of disp-state contract
13:                             ▷ TF: true/false status of execution
14:     return (val, TF);
15:
16: **function** DEPLOY($state\_bytecode$) **returns** ($desp\_address$)
17:     Get $addr$ = create(0, add($state\_bytecode$, 0x20), mload($state\_bytecode$));
18:     return $addr$;

Algorithm 7. cmCRR Protocol Steps.

1: /* **Step 1: Computation initialization and server registration** */
2: $Client \rightarrow SC$: Initialize $(com_x, B_{f()})$ ▷ $B_{f()}$: compiled bytecode of $f()$
3: $S_i \rightarrow SC$: Register (Pk_i) (for all $i \in \{1, 2\}$)
4: $SC \rightarrow Client$: (registered, S_1, S_2)
5:
6: /* **Step 2: Computation execution by the servers** */
7: $Client \rightarrow S_i$: Compute $(B_{f()}, x, d_x)$ (for all $i \in \{1, 2\}$)
8:
9: /* **Step 3: Send commitments and reveal the result to referee** */
10: $S_i \rightarrow SC$: receive-Commitments $(com_{y_i}, N_i, MH_{root}(C_i \| Pk_i))$ (for all $i \in \{1, 2\}$)
11: $SC \rightarrow S_i$: open commitment (for all $i \in \{1, 2\}$)
12: $S_i \rightarrow SC$: receive-Results (y_i, d_{y_i}) (for all $i \in \{1, 2\}$)   ▷ y_i, d_{y_i}: result of
computation, opening key
13:
14: /* **Step 4: Result verification by the referee contract** */
15: SC: compare y_i and verify commitment to y_i
16:     **if** $(y_1 = y_2)$ and both commitments are *true*: set *result* $= y_1$ (or y_2);
17:     **else** (one of the servers commitment is *false*) "copy detected", set y_i of other
server as "correct result"
18:
19: /* (In case of inconsistency, i.e., $y_1 \neq y_2$) */
20: SC: set $n_g = 1$, $n_b = min(N_1, N_2)$, $j = \frac{n_b - n_g}{2}$
21: $SC \rightarrow S_i$: get-Reduced-config(j)
22: $S_i \rightarrow SC$: receive-Reduced-config($H^1_{rc_j}, p^1_{rc_j}$) (for all $i \in \{1, 2\}$)   ▷ $H^i_{rc_j}$: Hashed
reduced configuration from server i
23: SC: compare $H^i_{rc_j}$ and verify-MHProof $(MH_{root}(C_i \| Pk_i), j, H^i_{rc_j}, p^i_{rc_j})$
24:     **if** *true*: update $n_g = j$, $j = \frac{n_b - n_g}{2}$; **else** "copy detected"
25:     **if** $H^1_{rc_j} \neq H^2_{rc_j}$: update $n_b = j$, $j = \frac{n_b - n_g}{2}$
26: **continue** until $n_b = n_g + 1$
27:
28: /* (Single-step execution, when $n_b = n_g + 1$) */
29: $SC \rightarrow S_1$: get-Single-step-data (n_g)
30: $S_1 \rightarrow SC$: receive-Single-step-data $(stateBytecode_{rc_{n_g}}, rc_{n_g}, rc_{n_b})$
31: SC: execute-Single-step ()
32:     check validity of I_{n_g}
33:     **if** *true*: deploy new EVM in Ethereum: $Deploy\ (stateBytecode_{rc_{n_g}})$
34:     execute new EVM and get value v'
35:     compare value v' with the claimedOutput $v_{rc_{n_b}}$
36:     return true/false
37:     **if** *true*: set *result* $= y_1$; **else** set *result* $= y_2$

References

1. Applebaum, B., Ishai, Y., Kushilevitz, E.: From secrecy to soundness: efficient verification via secure computation. In: Abramsky, S., Gavoille, C., Kirchner, C., Meyer auf der Heide, F., Spirakis, P.G. (eds.) ICALP 2010. LNCS, vol. 6198, pp. 152–163. Springer, Heidelberg (2010). https://doi.org/10.1007/978-3-642-14165-2_14
2. Arora, S., Lund, C., Motwani, R., Sudan, M., Szegedy, M.: Proof verification and the hardness of approximation problems. J. ACM (JACM) 45(3), 501–555 (1998)
3. Arora, S., Safra, S.: Probabilistic checking of proofs: a new characterization of NP. J. ACM (JACM) 45(1), 70–122 (1998)
4. Avizheh, S., Nabi, M., Safavi-Naini, R., Venkateswarlu K, M.: Verifiable computation using smart contracts. In: Proceedings of the 2019 ACM SIGSAC Conference on Cloud Computing Security Workshop, pp. 17–28 (2019)
5. Babai, L.: Trading group theory for randomness. In: Proceedings of the Seventeenth Annual ACM Symposium on Theory of Computing, pp. 421–429. ACM (1985)
6. Belenkiy, M., Chase, M., Erway, C.C., Jannotti, J., Küpçü, A., Lysyanskaya, A.: Incentivizing outsourced computation. In: Proceedings of the 3rd International Workshop on Economics of Networked Systems, pp. 85–90 (2008)
7. Blumberg, A.J., Thaler, J., Vu, V., Walfish, M.: Verifiable computation using multiple provers. IACR Cryptol. ePrint Arch. 2014, 846 (2014)
8. Brassard, G., Chaum, D., Crépeau, C.: Minimum disclosure proofs of knowledge. J. Comput. Syst. Sci. 37(2), 156–189 (1988)
9. Buterin, V., et al.: A next-generation smart contract and decentralized application platform. White Paper 3(37), 21 (2014)
10. Canetti, R., Riva, B., Rothblum, G.N.: Practical delegation of computation using multiple servers. In: Proceedings of the 18th ACM Conference on Computer and Communications Security, pp. 445–454 (2011)
11. Canetti, R., Riva, B., Rothblum, G.N.: Refereed delegation of computation. Inf. Comput. 226, 16–36 (2013)
12. Chen, S., Cheon, J.H., Kim, D., Park, D.: Verifiable computing for approximate computation. Cryptology ePrint Archive, Report 2019/762 (2019). https://eprint.iacr.org/2019/762
13. Chung, K.-M., Kalai, Y., Vadhan, S.: Improved delegation of computation using fully homomorphic encryption. In: Rabin, T. (ed.) CRYPTO 2010. LNCS, vol. 6223, pp. 483–501. Springer, Heidelberg (2010). https://doi.org/10.1007/978-3-642-14623-7_26
14. Cormode, G., Mitzenmacher, M., Thaler, J.: Practical verified computation with streaming interactive proofs. In: Proceedings of the 3rd Innovations in Theoretical Computer Science Conference, pp. 90–112 (2012)
15. Culture, C.: Evm-tools (2019). https://github.com/CoinCulture/evm-tools
16. Duan, J., Zhou, J., Li, Y.: Secure and verifiable outsourcing of nonnegative matrix factorization (NMF). In: Proceedings of the 4th ACM Workshop on Information Hiding and Multimedia Security, pp. 63–68 (2016)
17. Feige, U., Kilian, J.: Making games short. In: Proceedings of the Twenty-Ninth Annual ACM Symposium on Theory of Computing, pp. 506–516 (1997)
18. Ganache: (2019. https://www.trufflesuite.com/ganache
19. Gennaro, R., Gentry, C., Parno, B.: Non-interactive verifiable computing: outsourcing computation to untrusted workers. In: Rabin, T. (ed.) CRYPTO 2010. LNCS, vol. 6223, pp. 465–482. Springer, Heidelberg (2010). https://doi.org/10.1007/978-3-642-14623-7_25

20. Gennaro, R., Gentry, C., Parno, B., Raykova, M.: Quadratic span programs and succinct NIZKs without PCPs. In: Johansson, T., Nguyen, P.Q. (eds.) EURO-CRYPT 2013. LNCS, vol. 7881, pp. 626–645. Springer, Heidelberg (2013). https://doi.org/10.1007/978-3-642-38348-9_37

21. Goldwasser, S., Kalai, Y.T., Rothblum, G.N.: Delegating computation: interactive proofs for muggles. In: Proceedings of the Fortieth Annual ACM Symposium on Theory of Computing, pp. 113–122 (2008)

22. Goldwasser, S., Micali, S., Rackoff, C.: The knowledge complexity of interactive proof systems. SIAM J. Comput. 18(1), 186–208 (1989)

23. Halevi, S.: Advanced cryptography: promise and challenges. In: ACM Conference on Computer and Communications Security, p. 647 (2018)

24. Harz, D., Boman, M.: The scalability of trustless trust. In: Zohar, A., et al. (eds.) FC 2018. LNCS, vol. 10958, pp. 279–293. Springer, Heidelberg (2019). https://doi.org/10.1007/978-3-662-58820-8_19

25. Hu, C., Alhothaily, A., Alrawais, A., Cheng, X., Sturtivant, C., Liu, H.: A secure and verifiable outsourcing scheme for matrix inverse computation. In: IEEE INFO-COM 2017-IEEE Conference on Computer Communications, pp. 1–9. IEEE (2017)

26. solidity IDE, R.: (2019). https://remix.ethereum.org

27. Ishai, Y., Kushilevitz, E., Ostrovsky, R.: Efficient arguments without short PCPs. In: Twenty-Second Annual IEEE Conference on Computational Complexity (CCC 2007), pp. 278–291. IEEE (2007)

28. Jiang, X., Kim, M., Lauter, K., Song, Y.: Secure outsourced matrix computation and application to neural networks. In: Proceedings of the 2018 ACM SIGSAC Conference on Computer and Communications Security, pp. 1209–1222 (2018)

29. Kalodner, H., Goldfeder, S., Chen, X., Weinberg, S.M., Felten, E.W.: Arbitrum: Scalable, private smart contracts. In: 27th {USENIX} Security Symposium ({USENIX} Security 18), pp. 1353–1370 (2018)

30. Khouzani, M., Pham, V., Cid, C.: Incentive engineering for outsourced computation in the face of collusion. In: Proceedings of WEIS (2014)

31. Kilian, J.: A note on efficient zero-knowledge proofs and arguments. In: Proceedings of the Twenty-fourth Annual ACM Symposium on Theory of Computing, pp. 723–732 (1992)

32. Kilian, J.: Improved efficient arguments. In: Coppersmith, D. (ed.) CRYPTO 1995. LNCS, vol. 963, pp. 311–324. Springer, Heidelberg (1995). https://doi.org/10.1007/3-540-44750-4_25

33. Küpçü, A.: Incentivized outsourced computation resistant to malicious contractors. IEEE Trans. Dependable Secure Comput. 14(6), 633–649 (2015)

34. Lund, C., Fortnow, L., Karloff, H., Nisan, N.: Algebraic methods for interactive proof systems. J. ACM (JACM) 39(4), 859–868 (1992)

35. Parno, B., Howell, J., Gentry, C., Raykova, M.: Pinocchio: nearly practical verifiable computation. In: 2013 IEEE Symposium on Security and Privacy, pp. 238–252. IEEE (2013)

36. Pham, V., Khouzani, M.H.R., Cid, C.: Optimal contracts for outsourced computation. In: Poovendran, R., Saad, W. (eds.) GameSec 2014. LNCS, vol. 8840, pp. 79–98. Springer, Cham (2014). https://doi.org/10.1007/978-3-319-12601-2_5

37. Poon, J., Buterin, V.: Plasma: scalable autonomous smart contracts. White paper, pp. 1–47 (2017)

38. Setty, S., Braun, B., Vu, V., Blumberg, A.J., Parno, B., Walfish, M.: Resolving the conflict between generality and plausibility in verified computation. In: Proceedings of the 8th ACM European Conference on Computer Systems, pp. 71–84 (2013)

39. Setty, S., Vu, V., Panpalia, N., Braun, B., Blumberg, A.J., Walfish, M.: Taking proof-based verified computation a few steps closer to practicality. In: Presented as part of the 21st {USENIX} Security Symposium ({USENIX} Security 12), pp. 253–268 (2012)
40. Setty, S.T., McPherson, R., Blumberg, A.J., Walfish, M.: Making argument systems for outsourced computation practical (sometimes). In: NDSS, vol. 1, p. 17 (2012)
41. Teutsch, J., Reitwießner, C.: A scalable verification solution for blockchains. arXiv preprint arXiv:1908.04756 (2019)
42. Vu, V., Setty, S., Blumberg, A.J., Walfish, M.: A hybrid architecture for interactive verifiable computation. In: 2013 IEEE Symposium on Security and Privacy, pp. 223–237. IEEE (2013)
43. Wahby, R.S., et al.: Full accounting for verifiable outsourcing. In: Proceedings of the 2017 ACM SIGSAC Conference on Computer and Communications Security, pp. 2071–2086 (2017)
44. Walfish, M., Blumberg, A.J.: Verifying computations without reexecuting them. Commun. ACM **58**(2), 74–84 (2015)
45. Wood, G., et al.: Ethereum: a secure decentralised generalised transaction ledger. Ethereum Proj. Yellow Paper **151**(2014), 1–32 (2014)
46. Zhang, Y., Blanton, M.: Efficient secure and verifiable outsourcing of matrix multiplications. In: Chow, S.S.M., Camenisch, J., Hui, L.C.K., Yiu, S.M. (eds.) ISC 2014. LNCS, vol. 8783, pp. 158–178. Springer, Cham (2014). https://doi.org/10.1007/978-3-319-13257-0_10

Towards Smart Contract-Based Verification of Anonymous Credentials

Robert Muth[✉], Tarek Galal, Jonathan Heiss, and Florian Tschorsch

Technische Universität, Berlin, Germany
{muth,j.heiss,florian.tschorsch}@tu-berlin.de, tgalal@mail.tu-berlin.de

Abstract. Smart contracts often need to verify identity-related information of their users. However, such information is typically confidential, and its verification requires access to off-chain resources. Given the isolation and privacy limitations of blockchain technologies, this presents a problem for on-chain verification. In this paper, we show how CL-signature-based anonymous credentials can be verified in smart contracts using the example of Hyperledger Indy, a decentralized credential management platform, and Ethereum, a smart contract-enabled blockchain. Therefore, we first outline how smart contract-based verification can be integrated in the Hyperledger Indy credential management routine and, then, provide a technical evaluation based on a proof-of-concept implementation of CL-signature verification on Ethereum. While our results demonstrate technical feasibility of smart contract-based verification of anonymous credentials, they also reveal technical barriers for its real-world usage.

Keywords: blockchain · decentralized apps · anonymous credentials

1 Introduction

Blockchains are increasingly used to host decentralized applications (DApps), which are implemented as smart contracts. In contrast to centralized applications, each blockchain node maintains its own application copy. Local copies are synchronized through a consensus protocol that eventually establishes a globally consistent application state. This equips DApps with novel characteristics, e.g., transparency and censorship-resistance which make DApps interesting in various domains including decentralized finance [1], autonomous organizations [2], and the Internet of Things [3].

Interacting with DApps often requires their users to demonstrate identity-related information. For example, in DApps for crypto-token offerings, where an initial amount of free tokens is released to attract new community members, identity-related information is used to prevent malicious users from exploiting these *airdrops* through Sybil-attacks [4], i.e., repeatedly requesting free tokens using different blockchain accounts. Another example is provided by voting DApps, where voters are required to prove their eligibility through identity-related information, e.g., they need to be over age or live within a certain address range.

© International Financial Cryptography Association 2023
S. Matsuo et al. (Eds.): FC 2022 Workshops, LNCS 13412, pp. 481–498, 2023.
https://doi.org/10.1007/978-3-031-32415-4_30

Unfortunately, in current practices, verification is often realized off-chain using centralized services. For example, during the Stellar airdrop[1], users were required to prove that they have a valid GitHub[2] account with a past registration date to prevent attackers from creating multiple GitHub accounts as their Sybils. The account validity has not been verified on-chain but through an allegedly trusted off-chain verifier. Similarly, in the Open Voting Network implementation for Ethereum [5], the voting initiator approves voters' eligibility off-chain and publishes an acceptance list of eligible voters to the smart contract. In both examples, a dishonest verifier can cheat without being noticed, e.g., by unjustifiably denying access to tokens or the voting.

In order to preserve decentralization and censorship-resistance of such DApps, the verification must be executed on-chain. This, however, introduces two new challenges: runtime isolation of DApps and privacy. Verifying identity-related information typically requires a trusted third party that vouches for the correctness of the information. In the airdrop example, it is not sufficient for the user to claim possession of a GitHub account, but instead GitHub itself must attest to it. Similarly, in the voting example, the required identity information could be attested to by a public institution. However, smart contracts run in an isolated execution environment and can, hence, only access information existent in the same runtime. To access off-chain information, they require an oracle that, however, implies trust [6].

Furthermore, verifying identity-related information typically reveals personal identifiable information to the verifier. This already presents a problem for off-chain usage. However, if the verification happens on-chain, sensitive information becomes accessible to unauthorized blockchain nodes and immutably anchored on-chain for an unknown period of time. Consequently, identity information cannot naively be verified on-chain to protect the users' privacy rights and comply with prevailing privacy regulations.

One approach towards privacy-preserving verification of identity information are *anonymous credentials*. They can be implemented by using zero-knowledge proofs to enable credential verification without revealing sensitive identity attributes to the verifier. While anonymous credentials already existed for long [7], they have increasingly gained attention. For example, they are part of Hyperledger Indy [8] a decentralized credential management system where they are realized based on Camenisch-Lysyanskaya (CL) signatures [7].

Anonymous credentials present a promising solution to overcome the blockchain's privacy limitations and enable non-revealing verification of identity-related information. But anonymous credentials verification happens as part of an interactive procedure among the identity issuer, holder, and verifier. This clashes with a smart contract's limited communication capabilities with off-chain resources. Furthermore, smart contracts are constrained by technical peculiarities that originate from the underlying execution environment, e.g., the

---

[1] https://www.coindesk.com/business/2019/12/13/stellar-tried-to-give-away-2b-xlm-tokens-on-keybase-then-the-spammers-came/.

[2] https://github.com.

Ethereum Virtual Machine [9], and must be considered when implementing the verification of anonymous credentials. To date, no smart contract-based implementation exists for verifying CL signature-based anonymous credentials.

In this paper, we propose a mechanism for smart contract-based verification of anonymous credentials that are issued as part of the Hyperledger Indy credential management routine and, thereby, make the following contributions:

- We propose a procedure for integrating smart contract-based credential verification into Hyperledger Indy. The procedure connects two previously disconnected worlds and, thereby, allows blockchain-enabled DApps to verify anonymous credentials originating from Hyperledger Indy-based systems.
- We present a technical specification that explains the verification of CL-signature-based anonymous credentials in a developer-friendly way. The specification is based on formal descriptions [10] on the one hand, and insights gained from an analysis of the Hyperledger Indy code repository[3] on the other hand.
- We provide a proof-of-concept implementation for verifying CL signatures-based anonymous credentials on Ethereum in Solidity, and we document technical challenges that we encountered during implementation. Our evaluation demonstrates the technical feasibility of smart contract-based verification of anonymous credentials, but it also reveals technical barriers for its real-world usage.

The remainder of this paper is structured as follows: In Sect. 2, we give an overview of anonymous credentials in Hyperledger Indy and show how smart contract-based credential verification can be integrated with the Hyperledger Indy procedure. In Sect. 3, we take a look at the verification of CL signature-based anonymous credentials. Our proof-of-concept implementation is described and evaluated in Sect. 4, and open issues are discussed in Sect. 5. In Sect. 6, we present related work and conclude the paper in Sect. 7.

2   Anonymous Credentials

To set the scene, we first introduce concepts and roles related to anonymous credentials in Hyperledger Indy. Based on this overview, we propose a procedure for integrating smart contract-based verification of anonymous credentials into Hyperledger Indy's standard credential management routine [11].

2.1   Anonymous Credentials in Hyperledger Indy

Credentials can be understood as a set of claims about its holder's identity [12], i.e., statements about specific identity attributes such as the holder's name, address, or date of birth. Hyperledger Indy [8] provides a decentralized system for managing such credentials that is built upon principles of the self-sovereign

---

[3] https://github.com/hyperledger/indy-sdk

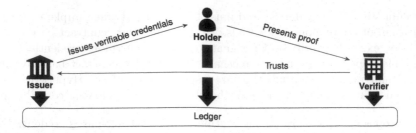

Fig. 1. SSI Model adopted from [12].

identity paradigm [13] where, instead of letting third parties control a holder's identity claims, the holder is in control. To independently verify a credential, additional evidence is required. The evidence is typically attached to the credential by a trusted third party that is able to attest to the holder's attributes, e.g., in form of a cryptographic signature. This makes them *verifiable credentials* [14].

However, a naive verification of signatures constructed on identity attributes could reveal potentially sensitive identity attributes to the verifier which may violate the holder's privacy rights. The concept of *anonymous credentials* [10] addresses this problem by enabling selective disclosure for credential verification, i.e., verifying predicates on sensitive identity attributes without revealing them to the verifier. Therefor, Hyperledger Indy utilizes Camenisch-Lysyanskaya signatures (CL) [15], a signature scheme with zero-knowledge properties.

As depicted in Fig. 1, credential verification requires three roles: the identity *holder* who owns an identity, the *issuer* that issues and attests to identity attributes through verifiable identity claims, and the *verifier* that verifies the identity claims. In Hyperledger Indy, additionally, a public, permissioned blockchain, the *ledger*, is applied as a public and decentralized storage system to make public artifacts accessible to all involved parties. Private credentials of holders are stored in personal wallets that keep them protected from unauthorized access.

2.2 Smart Contract-Based Integration of Anonymous Credentials Verification

In the following, we show how anonymous credentials of Hyperledger Indy can be used for smart contract-based verification, i.e., Ethereum smart contracts. In order to establish compatibility between Hyperledger Indy and Ethereum we define the following requirements:

- No infrastructure modifications: Smart contract developers should be able to draw on existing Hyperledger Indy systems for credential verification. Therefore, on-chain verification should integrate without any modification to the native Hyperledger Indy system.
- No further trust assumption: In Hyperledger Indy, issuers are trusted by the verifier to truthfully attest to a holder's credentials, and no further trust

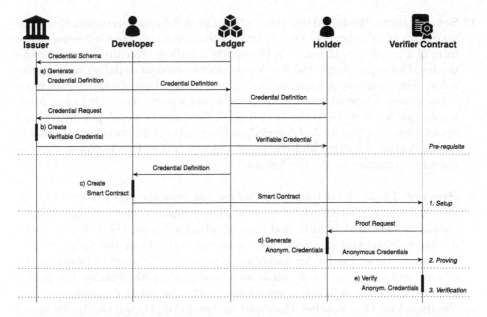

Fig. 2. Adopted proof verification flow of the Hyperledger Indy proof verification procedures with a smart contract verifier.

assumption should be introduced. More precisely, integration should work without trusted oracles [6].

The integration procedure builds upon the native Hyperledger Indy credential verification flow described in [11]. As an extension, we propose a new verifier role, i.e., the *verifier contract*, and introduce the *developer* that is responsible for implementing and deploying the smart contract. As depicted in Fig. 2, the complete proof verification procedure can be divided in three phases: setup, proving, and verification.

Pre-requisite: As a pre-requisite, we assume that a *credential schema* exists that defines a set of identity attributes. From that, the issuer has generated a *credential definition* and registered it on the Hyperledger Indy ledger (Step a). The credential definition is a public artifact that is typically specified by the issuer and accessible on the ledger. Among others, it contains the set of attributes to be verified, the issuer's public key, and a reference to the signature algorithm which, in our case, is the CL-signature scheme.

Furthermore, we assume that the holder is already in possession of the verifiable credential that is required by the smart contract. In Hyperledger Indy, this is done in the form of a *credential request* [11] submitted from the holder to the issuer. On receiving the request, the issuer creates the evidence, here the CL-signature, and returns the verifiable credential to the holder where it is stored in her wallet (Step b).

1. **Setup:** During the initial one-time setup, the developer determines the set of attributes and predicates to be verified on-chain and the attesting issuer in the form of a *proof request*, which in Hyperledger Indy is typically created by the verifier. Correspondingly, the developer selects a credential definition from the ledger. For simplicity, we assume that the determined proof request matches a single credential definition. Based on the issuer's public key, attributes, predicates, and a reference to the credential definition, the developer creates the smart contract (Step c). In Hyperledger Indy, this information is contained in the credential definition and the proof request. Then, the developer deploys the smart contract to the blockchain.

2. **Proving:** The holder obtains the proof request from the smart contract which also includes a reference to the credential definition on the ledger. Based on the credential definition and schema obtained from the ledger as public information, and the verifiable credential taken from the wallet as private information, the holder constructs a zero-knowledge proof based on her CL-signature (Step d) to obtain anonymized credentials. Finally, the holder submits the resulting anonymous credentials to the smart contract.

3. **Verification:** On reception, the smart contract (i.e., DApp) verifies the proof using the on-chain credential definition (Step e).

Successfully verified credentials can then be used as part of the DApp's logic. As shown by the motivating examples, the credential verification can represent a pre-condition for using specific functionality provided by the DApp, e.g., a voting or an airdrop.

3   Proof Verification

Given the high level description of integrating smart contract-based anonymous credential verification into the native Hyperledger Indy credential management routine, we can now focus on the details of proof verification. Therefore, we first introduce the basics of CL-signature verification that, in Hyperledger Indy, are used to construct Zero-Knowledge Proofs (ZKP). Based on this, we describe the actual anonymous credentials proofs, i.e., a primary proof that builds on equality proofs and inequality predicate proofs.

3.1   Signature Proof of Knowledge

Conceptually, ZKPs in anonymous credentials prove knowledge of some discrete logarithms modulo a composite [10], and are referred to as *Signature Proofs of Knowledge*. They enable a credential holder to prove possession of a CL-signature over certain attribute values without revealing other attributes, as well as, to prove that an attribute value lies within a certain range without revealing it. In order to understand how this is accomplished in anonymous credentials, we give an overview of what a CL-signature looks like, and show how a signature proof of knowledge is generated for it. We do this by referencing corresponding steps in the procedure presented in Sect. 2.2.

As part of the pre-requisites, the credential issuer creates the credential definition (Step a). Therefore, she generates a CL-signature key pair based on a credential schema which contains a set of predefined attributes (e.g., attributes of a driver's license). The CL-signature scheme [15] defines the public key in this key pair as the quadruple $(Z, S, \{R_i\}_{i \in A_C}, n)$ where A_C is the set of indices of attributes in the credential schema, n is a Special RSA Modulus [15], and $Z, S, \{R_i\}$ are random quadratic residues modulo n. Then, on receiving a credential request from the holder, the issuer attests to the attribute values $\{m_i\}$, and, for creating a verifiable credential (Step b), generates a CL-signature as explained in [15], such that the following holds:

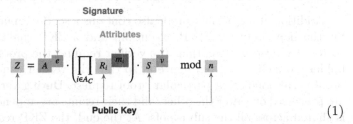

$$Z = A^e \cdot \left(\prod_{i \in A_C} R_i^{m_i}\right) \cdot S^v \quad \text{mod } n \tag{1}$$

While the public key information $Z, \{R_i\}, S$ and n are publicly available on the ledger, the signature (A, e, v) is proven under the strong RSA assumption to be computable only by the issuer [15], who owns the private key, in order to keep the whole equation true. Together with the values of the attributes $\{m_i\}_{i \in A_C}$, the holder is now able to prove possession of the credential. Therefore, she generates a ZKP (Step d) which proves knowledge of the exponents $e, \{m_i\}_{i \in A_C}, v$ but keeps them secret when presenting the proof to a verifier. By doing that, the verifier can still verify that the prover knows those exponents, and thereby, is in possession of a valid signature (Step e).

Additionally, a holder can prove that a credential contains an attribute with a specific value that she reveals. For this, we say $A_C = A_r \cup A_{\overline{r}}$ such that A_r contains revealed attributes and $A_{\overline{r}}$ contains unrevealed attributes which are kept secret. Since A_r and $A_{\overline{r}}$ are mutually exclusive, we can adjust Eq. 1 as follows

$$Z = A^e \left(\prod_{i \in A_r} R_i^{m_i}\right)\left(\prod_{i \in A_{\overline{r}}} R_i^{m_i}\right) S^v \quad \text{mod } n \tag{2}$$

$$\frac{Z}{\left(\prod_{i \in A_r} R_i^{m_i}\right)} = A^e \left(\prod_{i \in A_{\overline{r}}} R_i^{m_i}\right) S^v \quad \text{mod } n \tag{3}$$

This allows us to prove that a credential contains a set of attributes with the revealed values $\{m_i\}_{i \in A_r}$, by proving knowledge of the exponents $(e, \{m_i\}_{i \in A_{\overline{r}}}, v)$ in Eq. 3. We use these insights as a basis for the following proof descriptions.

3.2 Primary Proof Verification

Anonymous credentials, as explained in [16], are based on the previously introduced CL-signature proofs of knowledge. Those proofs are similar to the Schnorr Protocol [17], and are made non-interactive (i.e., only one round instead of commitment, challenge, and response) by implementing the Fiat-Shamir Heuristic [18]. Anonymous credentials structures a proof as a combination of different sub-proofs belonging to a *primary proof* that is used for verifying them altogether. To this end, a primary proof consists of a set of equality sub-proofs $\{\Pr_C\}$ and a set of inequality predicate sub-proofs $\{\Pr_P\}$:

- An *Equality proof* proves that a credential contains expected values
- An *Inequality predicate proof* proves that a credential contains a value that lies within a certain range (e.g., zip code between a given range)

Additionally, a primary proof also contains a set C with necessary information for the non-interactive ZKP execution, and a ZKP challenge c to verify the correct execution. Along that, the verifier requires the proof generator (i.e., the holder) to include a given nonce η, so that the verifier can make sure that the proof corresponds to a particular proof request. During verification, sub-proofs are processed one after the other, and their results are appended to a set $\widehat{T}$ which is shared across all the sub-proofs. At the end, the ZKP responses in each sub-proof are individually processed and the results are aggregated into $\widehat{T}$. Once $\widehat{T}$ is complete, the verifier hashes the final result of $\widehat{T}$, C, and the nonce η. The proof verification succeeds if c equals $H(\widehat{T} \parallel C \parallel \eta)$.

3.3 Equality Proof Verification

In the following, we introduce equality proof verification. We therefore present the cryptographical procedure, as we did for the signature proof of knowledge introduction in Sect. 3.1. In fact, equality proof verification is based on the same technique, but is implemented over a randomized version of the CL-signature [10]. However, we do not intend to recap all proof details, as they are explained in [10].

In a nutshell, an equality proof attests the possession of a CL-signature (i.e., credential) over a set of expected attributes, but without revealing any other information. Still, A_r contains the indices of revealed attributes and $A_{\overline{r}}$ contains the unrevealed attributes. The difference is, a verifier receives $\Pr_C = (\widehat{e}, \widehat{v}, \{\widehat{m_j}\}_{j \in \overline{r}}, A')$ and the revealed attribute values $\{m_j\}_{j \in A_r}$ from a prover, but the original values A, v (cf., Eq. 1) are not directly used. Instead, A' belongs to a randomized CL-Signature (A', e, v') [10] where e, v' are exponents in that signature and $\widehat{e}, \widehat{v}$ belong to ZKPs of knowledge of e and v' respectively. The prover generates this randomized signature based on the original CL-signature she possesses by following the procedure described in [10] to guarantee unlinkability across different proofs.

For completeness, we present the equality proof equation which calculates the sub-proof results $\widehat{T}$. For the sake of simplicity and easy recognition of relevant components, we highlighted the parts in the equality proof equation that belong together:

$$\widehat{T} \leftarrow \left(\frac{Z}{\left(\prod_{j \in A_r} R_j{}^{m_j} \right)\left(A' \right)^{2^{596}}} \right)^{-c} \cdot \left(A' \right)^{\widehat{e}} \cdot \left(\prod_{j \in A_{\overline{r}}} R_j{}^{\widehat{m_j}} \right) \cdot \left(S^{\widehat{v}} \right) \pmod{n}$$

In the end, computing $\widehat{T}$ is a pre-verification step for the given ZKP parameters, and is completed as part of the primary proof verification. At this point, we want to underline that the same c is used for exponentiation as for the final hash comparison in the primary proof.

3.4 Inequality Predicate Proof Verification

An inequality predicate consists of an attribute, one of $>, \geq, <, \leq$ as a comparison operator, and a constant value to compare to. Once again, the credential holder proves that a specified inequality is satisfied without revealing the actual value of the attribute. In order to do that, the prover constructs a zero knowledge proof that the inequality predicate is satisfied. Additionally, the prover attests that the attribute indeed belongs to her, by constructing another zero knowledge proof. This zero knowledge proof is in fact just an equality proof that does not reveal the attribute's value.

Verifying an inequality proof requires processing the associated equality proof first where the index of the attribute in the predicate belongs to $A_{\overline{r}}$ (unrevealed attributes). Afterwards, predicate-specific zero knowledge proofs are processed, each extending $\widehat{T}$ in the primary proof verification. As the computations performed for processing an inequality predicate proof closely resemble those of an equality proof, we leave them out of this section and refer to the anonymous credentials specification [16].

4 Implementation

In this section, we introduce our proof-of-concept implementation for on-chain anonymous credential verification. We therefore present our smart contract implementation and give an overview of its technical design. In reference to Sect. 2, we show how the complex proof verification can be implemented and executed with limited and isolated EVM resources. At the end, we evaluate the transaction costs for proof verification with our implementation.

4.1 Proof-of-Concept

As part of our implementation for anonymous credentials verification, we provide a Truffle Suite project with a single smart contract implementation for the proof verification. In addition to that, we include Mocha (Node.js) test cases for single proof verifications and full proofs with combined equality and predicate proofs. We consider our implementation a proof-of-concept, since we limit it to verification only and focus on the technical feasibility. We also stress, that our implementation should not be considered production ready, yet. The code is available on Github[4].

We use the Hyperledger Ursa cryptography library[5] as a reference implementation and we replicate relevant parts of their test cases to ensure our implementation generates the same results. We also provide additional test cases which are used for our evaluation.

For the smart contract development, we face several challenges regarding the CL-signatures' key size. Firstly, proof verification requires arithmetic operations $(+, -, \cdot)$, exponentiation, and multiplicative inversion modulo a large number. As explained in Sect. 3.3, n is defined by the public key as the modulus. In our case, anonymous credentials and the implemented test cases use n of size 2050 bits[6], which exceeds the size of the EVM's largest data type for numbers (max. 256 bits for unsigned integer). To this end, we integrate a big number library[7] for on-chain computations which ports parts of the OpenSSL big number implementation to Solidity and YAL (inline assembly). The library receives numeric inputs as byte arrays and executes computations in the EVM memory space. With EIP-198 [19] the EVM offers a precompiled contract for computing $a^b \mod n$ where a, b and n can be larger than 256-bit unsigned integers. It is noteworthy that the big number library takes full advantage of this precompiled contract, as it also uses it for efficient multiplication.

Additionally, the big number library and the precompiled contract do not support computing modular multiplicative inverses. However, given a, b, n, it is possible to check if a is the inverse of b modulo n by utilizing the available exponentiation. Our implementation therefore computes the required modular multiplicative inverses off-chain and passes them together with the proof. For this reason, we use another big number library for off-chain computations in JavaScript[8] which pre-computes intermediary results (i.e., modular multiplicative inverses) for a proof verification. As explained above, our implementation verifies that the passed values are correct and aborts the execution otherwise. Thus the values are calculated off-chain, but all passed values are checked on-chain and rejected if necessary.

Lastly, the number of variables necessary for proof calculations leads to capacity shortages for the Solidity compiler. The EVM is designed as a stack machine [9] with a maximum size of 1 024 words (each 256 bits), which is just

---

[4] https://github.com/robmuth/eth-ac-verifier.

[5] https://github.com/hyperledger/ursa/blob/34ef392/libursa/src/cl/prover.rs#L2532.

[6] n is 3074 bits in anonymous credentials [16], but HyperLedger Ursa sets n to 2050 bits.

[7] https://github.com/firoorg/solidity-BigNumber.

[8] https://github.com/indutny/bn.js.

enough to pass a complete proof in a transaction. Unfortunately, the limit of 16 parameters and local variables per function call renders all proof calculations difficult, since our required parameters and calculations (mainly big integer computations) cause stack overflow exceptions during compilation. Therefore, and for better code readability, we utilize pre-defined *struct* data structures to pack multiple parameters, and split computations into multiple functions which allocate and release local variables from the stack for interim calculations.

The Truffle project provides basic migration scripts for the verification contract and the linked big number library. The test cases provide unit tests for the verification procedures, as well as, exemplary credentials. Once passed, they return the corresponding transaction costs for each verification in gas, which we evaluate in the following.

4.2 Evaluation

We evaluate the costs for the deployment of the smart contracts and for transactions created by test cases with exemplary credentials. We therefore compile the smart contracts with Solidity 0.5.16 (enabled optimizer with 200 runs), and analyze the transactions with Ganache 2.5.4. We implement the Hyperledger Ursa cryptography library unit tests into our PoC test cases and additionally generate our own exemplary anonymous credentials, issued with Hyperledger Indy.

Table 1 shows gas costs for the deployment of the smart contracts and function calls of our test cases. While the deployment of a verification contract only puts the compiled byte code on the blockchain storage, executing a proof verification requires passing a full proof to the smart contract and executing the anonymous credentials verification process as explained in Sect. 3.2. In our first test, the credential contains a set of 14 identity-related attributes (e.g., name, date of birth, address, etc.) and reveals the first name with a primary proof and an equality sub-proof. Our second test contains the same attributes and an inequality predicate (i.e., date of birth has to be before a specified date), which is realized as a combination of an equality sub-proof and an inequality predicate sub-proof in the primary proof. By looking at the difference between the gas cost for the first and second test credentials, one can see that the gas costs increase with the number of sub-proofs, especially with inequality predicate proofs. This explains why the gas costs of the third test, which reveals the first name and verifies the date of birth together, is not significantly different from the second test case.

Since gas represents the resource consumption per EVM command [9], proof verification becomes expensive for three reasons: First, the passed arguments (i.e., the proofs) contain large byte arrays, e.g., for each attribute and the corresponding zero-knowledge proof parameters. Second, the complex data structures for handling big numbers require allocation of EVM memory space, which consumes extra gas [9]. Third, calling the precompiled contract for exponentiation and modulo operations [19] allows cheaper computations than an on-chain implementation; but due to the involvement of a large number of these operations in a proof verification, the gas cost add up quickly. We also point out, that the

Table 1. Transaction costs in Gas for smart contract deployments and different proof verification test cases in Ethereum.

Transaction	Gas
Verifier contract deployment	6 711 k
Big number library deployment	77 k
1. Test credential: Primary proof verification with an equality sub-proof	32 001 k
2. Test credential: Primary proof verification with an inequality predicate sub-proof	84 826 k
3. Test credential: Primary proof verification with combined sub-proofs	84 033 k

number of attributes influences the proof size and therefore has an impact on the transaction costs, as well.

In the end, our evaluations show that the gas costs are very high, so the resulting transaction fees (i.e., gas multiplied by the demand-regulated gas price) render it difficult for most DApp use cases. Considering a current exemplary gas price of 100 Gwei, the full proof verification of our test case would cost approx. 8.4 Ether. However, we stress that our proof-of-concept implementation is not optimized for reduced gas costs and there is certainly great potential for optimization (e.g., more efficient memory allocations). Furthermore, gas costs cannot be translated directly to transaction fees in Ethereum, since a transaction sender specifies how much Ether she is willing to pay per gas. This means, the actual transaction costs depend on the blockchain's current transaction load.

5   Discussion

In this section, we discuss remaining open issues that should be considered for practical usages of our proposed solution. To this end, we put the evaluated transaction costs into context and present further options to implement our solution. For completeness, we also take a look at revocability of credentials and explain how it could be integrated into our smart contract implementation. At the end, we briefly discuss our considerations regarding Sybil resistance and unlinkability.

5.1   Transaction Costs

As the evaluation in Sect. 4.2 shows, our proof-of-concept demonstrates the general ability to verify anonymous credentials in a smart contract on Ethereum, and therefore enables compatibility with Hyperledger Indy-based identity platforms. However, the expected transaction costs are too high for current DApp implementations.

Nevertheless, blockchain technologies continue adopting new techniques to address rising transaction costs, scalability limits, and performance issues of execution engines, respectively [20–22]; Especially since hype-driven blockchain applications (e.g., Cryptokitties or ICOs) caused fees to skyrocket [23] multiple times, in the past. The constantly increasing block size limit in Ethereum also suggests that the overall demand will continuously increase. However, since our implementation is EVM-based but not limited to the Ethereum Mainnet, we envisage other blockchains that are compatible with our Solidity implementation (e.g., Polygon/Matic[9] or Polkadot[10]).

In the meantime, we consider two possible ways to implement anonymous credentials verification on-chain: First, the computationally expensive big number operations could be implemented as precompiled contracts into the EVM, i.e., implementing big number data types. Precompiled contracts are natively implemented in the EVM client and can be addressed as external contracts by other smart contracts, but they define their gas costs independently. Doing so, the overall transaction costs of our implementation could significantly decrease in the same way, as EIP-198 [19] decreases costs for big integer modulo operations. Second, in the same manner, the whole verification procedure could be implemented as a precompiled contract. The latter, we at least consider reasonable for instantiating new EVM-based blockchains with anonymous credentials capabilities, since implementing precompiled contracts is common practice for new private networks. Hence, for example, anonymous credentials verification can be implemented as precompiled contract in the official Ethereum client *Geth* which also supports instantiating private and permissioned networks.

5.2 Non-Revocation Proof

Our solution works for credentials that are generally valid, that is, credentials over attributes that neither have an expiry date nor are revocable by their issuer (e.g., date of birth). In contrast, an issuer can create *revocable credentials* for attributes that are subject to change (e.g., address). In this case, it is possible that a revocable credential could have already been revoked by its issuer, by the time a verifier receives a proof based on it. Therefore, a verifier must be able to determine a credential's revocation status in order to accordingly decide whether to accept or reject the given primary proof.

Anonymous credentials in [16] allow a holder to prove that the credentials which were used during the primary proof construction have not been revoked. To this end, tracking of the revocation status utilizes CKS accumulators [24] where a so-called *accumulator value* is regularly published by the credential issuer and it contains information of all non-revoked credentials. When issuing a credential, the issuer additionally provides the holder a *witness* that enables her to prove validity of her credential with respect to the accumulator value. The process of checking the revocation status takes place as part of the proof verification process. In addition to the primary proof, a credential holder also sends a non-revocation proof, which is a zero-knowledge proof constructed over accumulator parameters.

---

[9] https://polygon.technology.
[10] https://polkadot.network.

CKS accumulators make use of weak Boneh and Boyen signatures [25,26], BN-254 curves [27] and type-3 pairing which are all different cryptographic primitives than the ones used by credential attestation proofs. Therefore, verifying those proofs is a subject for future work.

5.3 Sybil Resistance and Unlinkability

In our system, Sybils are re-submissions of already verified anonymous credentials by different holders. Since Sybil attacks can effectively be defeated by a trusted party that guarantees uniqueness [4] we can instrument the only trusted party for that purpose: the issuer. If the issuer provides a unique identifier as an identity attribute, it can be verified on-chain as part of the proof. Thereby, a verifiable one-to-one mapping of proof and holder is established. The unique identifier could be represented as a revealed attribute that is part of the proof construction and verifiable on-chain.

An alternative solution that does not require cooperation from issuers is described in [16]. A verifier can require provers to turn off unlinkability in their proofs. We have shown in Sect. 3.3 that this is possible if a holder does not generate a randomized CL-signature and instead, constructs proofs based on her original CL-signature. Thus, the smart contract keeps track of all proof identifiers and, hence, can identify Sybils.

However, while storing unique identifiers of proof-holder mappings helps to defeat Sybil attacks, it also introduces linkability. Linkability is a privacy-related characteristic and applies in this context if the linkage of anonymous credentials allows unauthorized third parties to derive private information of the holder. In smart contract-based applications, linkability is critical since the history of blockchain transactions is available to all blockchain nodes.

While holders can protect against linkability by using different blockchain accounts each time they interact with the blockchain, this protection becomes ineffective if unique identifiers of holders are stored on-chain. They should, consequently, not naively be used for Sybil resistance but require further considerations to keep holders protected from linkability.

6   Related Work

Smart contract-based verification of anonymous credentials can be regarded as an instantiation of Verifiable Off-chain Computations (VOC) [28], where an on-chain computation, here the credential verifications, is delegated to an off-chain node, here the holder, and only the computational result and a cryptographic proof attesting the computation's correctness are published to the blockchain for verification. In the context of VOCs, the CL-signature-based approach complements other applicable non-interactive zero-knowledge technologies, e.g., zkSNARKs, Bulletproofs, or zkSTARKs [28].

In literature, various papers can be found where zkSNARKs are applied for privacy preserving authentication in DApps, e.g., through ZoKrates [29], a toolkit for zkSNARKs-based VOC. Examples are provided in the context of smart electric vehicle authentication at charging stations [30], patient authentication in health care [31], or consent-based access control [32]. However, these works focus on a particular use case where a particular claim of a particular issuer is verified on-chain. In contrast, our approach enables smart contracts to verify Hyperledger Indy-based credentials and, thereby, to reach multiple issuers.

Hyperledger Indy has become one of the most popular SSI management technologies [33] and is adopted in multiple SSI management projects. IDUnion[11], for example, is a German consortium of public and private organizations that uses Hyperledger Indy to implement a SSI management system. Similarly, the Verifiable Organizations Network[12] is an initiative that leverages Hyperledger Indy to realize SSI and enable digitization of identities in a secure, user-centric manner. With our proposed solution, smart contracts can now verify credentials of any issuer that is part of these projects.

Beyond Hyperledger Indy, other blockchain-based credential management systems exist. In the context of SSI, uPort [34] and Jolocom [35] are two approaches that, instead of building upon a public, *permissioned* blockchain, leverage Ethereum as a public, *permissionless* blockchain. These approaches, however, currently only store non-revealing identity information on-chain but do not provide anonymous credential verification. Given the privacy requirement, this makes them not applicable for smart contract-based credential verification. However, recent improvement proposals (e.g., EIP-725 [36] and EIP-735 [37]) show that there is an interest in establishing Ethereum-based SSI-Systems, which has even yielded the formation of a self-proclaimed SSI alliance[13].

Furthermore, Public Key Infrastructures (PKI) exist as centralized credential management systems, and are traditionally used for managing identity card infrastructures. For example, PKIs are used by universities to manage digital student IDs. On a national scale, the German Identity Cards are managed based on PKIs[14], and on an international scale, the ICAO uses PKIs to manage the global passport infrastructure[15]. However, in contrast to a Hyperledger Indy, in centralized credential management systems identity attributes are limited and can only be attested by a single issuer.

7   Conclusion

Motivated by prevailing limitations observed in different DApp contexts, in this paper, we have made a first step towards verifying identity-related information

---

[11] https://idunion.org.

[12] https://vonx.io.

[13] https://erc725alliance.org.

[14] https://www.bsi.bund.de/EN/Topics/ElectrIDDocuments/securPKI/pki_node. html.

[15] https://www.icao.int/Security/FAL/PKD/Pages/default.aspx.

in DApps in a privacy-preserving and trustless manner. Using the example of Hyperledger Indy as a popular credential management system, we have shown how CL signature-based anonymous credentials can be verified by Ethereum-based smart contracts without introducing further trust assumptions.

With our approach, DApps can verify identity-related information entirely on-chain and, thereby, preserve transparency and censorship resistance as desirable characteristics of DApps. In the airdrop example, account ownership claims issued by GitHub as anonymous credentials could be fully verifiable on-chain and used to mitigate illegitimate token spendings. Similarly, in the voting example, a public authority could issue eligibility claims as anonymous credentials which are on-chain verifiable and, thereby, help voting DApps yield more reliable results.

However, we also revealed aspects that stand between our prototype and a production-ready system. As seen in our technical evaluation, gas costs are currently impractically high due to high verification costs of CL signature-based zero-knowledge proofs. Furthermore, for verifying revocable identity attributes, a revocation system must be integrated into our solution. We also point out that security- and privacy-related aspects as Sybil-resilience and linkability must still be considered for real-world deployments.

The active research and ongoing developments in the field of verifiable credentials and smart contracts, however, let us expect technological advances to emerge from which smart contract-based credential verification may benefit. As one example, a new anonymous credential design, called Anonymous Credentials 2.0, has been proposed in [38] that might be adopted in Hyperledger Indy in the future. However, while it promises more efficient zero-knowledge proofs and, hence, cheaper on-chain verification, we were not able to find public information about the current development state or release dates. In the end, we have shown that CL-signature-based anonymous credentials can be verified in smart contracts and, at the same time, paved the way for the integration of further identity infrastructures and technologies.

References

1. Qin, K., Zhou, L., Afonin, Y., Lazzaretti, L., Gervais, A.: Cefi vs. defi - comparing centralized to decentralized finance. CoRR, abs/2106.08157 (2021)
2. Jentzsch, C.: Decentralized autonomous organization to automate governance. White paper (2016)
3. Ali, M.S., Vecchio, M., Pincheira, M., Dolui, K., Antonelli, F., Rehmani, M.H.: Applications of blockchains in the internet of things: a comprehensive survey. IEEE Commun. Surv. Tutorials 21(2), 1676–1717 (2019)
4. Douceur, J.R.: The Sybil attack. In: Druschel, P., Kaashoek, F., Rowstron, A. (eds.) IPTPS 2002. LNCS, vol. 2429, pp. 251–260. Springer, Heidelberg (2002). https://doi.org/10.1007/3-540-45748-8_24
5. McCorry, P., Shahandashti, S.F., Hao, F.: A smart contract for boardroom voting with maximum voter privacy. In: Kiayias, A. (ed.) FC 2017. LNCS, vol. 10322, pp. 357–375. Springer, Cham (2017). https://doi.org/10.1007/978-3-319-70972-7_20
6. Heiss, J., Eberhardt, J., Tai, S.: From oracles to trustworthy data on-chaining systems. In: IEEE International Conference on Blockchain (2019)

7. Camenisch, J., Lysyanskaya, A.: An efficient system for non-transferable anonymous credentials with optional anonymity revocation. In: Pfitzmann, B. (ed.) EUROCRYPT 2001. LNCS, vol. 2045, pp. 93–118. Springer, Heidelberg (2001). https://doi.org/10.1007/3-540-44987-6_7
8. Hyperledger White Paper Working Group. An introduction to hyperledger (2018). http://www.hyperledger.org/wp-content/uploads/2018/07/HL_Whitepaper_IntroductiontoHyperledger.pdf
9. Wood, G.: Ethereum: a secure decentralised generalised transaction ledger, berlin version fabef25. (2021)
10. Camenisch, J., Gross, T.: Efficient attributes for anonymous credentials. ACM Trans. Inf. Syst. Secur. (TISSEC) 15(1), 1–30 (2008)
11. Hyperledger Indy sdk Repository. Indy walkthrough - a developer guide for building indy clients using libindy (2018). http://github.com/hyperledger/indy-sdk/blob/master/docs/getting-started/indy-walkthrough.md
12. Mühle, A., Grüner, A., Gayvoronskaya, T., Meinel, C.: A survey on essential components of a self-sovereign identity. Comput. Sci. Rev. 30, 80–86 (2018)
13. Allen, C.: The path to self-sovereign identity (2016). http://www.lifewithalacrity.com/2016/04/the-path-to-self-sovereign-identity.html
14. World Wide Web Consortium (W3C). Verifiable credentials data model v1.1 - expressing verifiable information on the web (2021). http://www.w3.org/TR/vc-data-model/
15. Camenisch, J., Lysyanskaya, A.: A signature scheme with efficient protocols. In: Cimato, S., Persiano, G., Galdi, C. (eds.) SCN 2002. LNCS, vol. 2576, pp. 268–289. Springer, Heidelberg (2003). https://doi.org/10.1007/3-540-36413-7_20
16. Khovratovich, D., Lodder, M.: Anonymous credentials with type-3 revocation (2018). http://github.com/hyperledger/ursa-docs/blob/62bc87b/specs/anoncreds1/anoncreds.tex
17. Schnorr, C.P.: Efficient signature generation by smart cards. J. Cryptology 4, 161–174 (1991)
18. Fiat, A., Shamir, A.: How to prove yourself: practical solutions to identification and signature problems. In: Odlyzko, A.M. (ed.) CRYPTO 1986. LNCS, vol. 263, pp. 186–194. Springer, Heidelberg (1987). https://doi.org/10.1007/3-540-47721-7_12
19. Buterin, V.: Big integer modular exponentiation (2017). http://github.com/ethereum/EIPs/blob/master/EIPS/eip-198.md
20. Popov, S.: IOTA: Feeless and free. Blockchain Technical Briefs (2019)
21. Roughgarden, T.: Transaction fee mechanism design for the Ethereum blockchain: an economic analysis of EIP-1559. CoRR, abs/2012.00854 (2020)
22. Busse, A., Eberhardt, J., Tai, S.: EVM-Perf: high-precision EVM performance analysis. In: IEEE International Conference on Blockchain and Cryptocurrency, pp. 1–8 (2021)
23. Spain, M., Foley, S., Gramoli, V.: The impact of ethereum throughput and fees on transaction latency during icos. In: OASIcs, Tokenomics. Schloss Dagstuhl - Leibniz-Zentrum für Informatik (2019)
24. Camenisch, J., Kohlweiss, M., Soriente, C.: An accumulator based on bilinear maps and efficient revocation for anonymous credentials. IACR Cryptology ePrint Arch. 539(01), 2008 (2008)
25. Boneh, D., Boyen, X.: Short signatures without random oracles and the SDH assumption in bilinear groups. J. Cryptology 21, 149–177 (2008)
26. Boneh, D., Boyen, X., Shacham, H.: Short group signatures. In: Franklin, M. (ed.) CRYPTO 2004. LNCS, vol. 3152, pp. 41–55. Springer, Heidelberg (2004). https://doi.org/10.1007/978-3-540-28628-8_3

27. Barreto, P.S.L.M., Naehrig, M.: Pairing-friendly elliptic curves of prime order. In: Preneel, B., Tavares, S. (eds.) SAC 2005. LNCS, vol. 3897, pp. 319–331. Springer, Heidelberg (2006). https://doi.org/10.1007/11693383_22

28. Eberhardt, J., Heiss, J.: Off-chaining models and approaches to off-chain computations. In: Proceedings of the 2Nd Workshop on Scalable and Resilient Infrastructures for Distributed Ledgers, SERIAL 2018. ACM (2018)

29. Eberhardt, J., Tai, S.: Zokrates - scalable privacy-preserving off-chain computations. In: IEEE International Conference on Internet of Things (iThings) and IEEE Green Computing and Communications (GreenCom) and IEEE Cyber, Physical and Social Computing (CPSCom) and IEEE Smart Data (SmartData), pp. 1084–1091 (2018)

30. Gabay, D., Akkaya, K., Cebe, M.: A privacy framework for charging connected electric vehicles using blockchain and zero knowledge proofs. In: IEEE 44th LCN Symposium on Emerging Topics in Networking, pp. 66–73 (2019)

31. Sharma, B., Halder, R., Singh, J.L.: Blockchain-based interoperable healthcare using zero-knowledge proofs and proxy re-encryption. In: 2020 International Conference on COMmunication Systems & NETworkS (COMSNETS), pp. 1–6 (2020)

32. Heiss, J., Ulbricht, M.R., Eberhardt, J.: Put your money where your mouth is - towards blockchain-based consent violation detection. In: IEEE International Conference on Blockchain and Cryptocurrency (ICBC), pp. 1–9 (2020)

33. Soltani, R., Nguyen, U.T., An, A.: A survey of self-sovereign identity ecosystem. CoRR, abs/2111.02003 (2021)

34. Naik, N., Jenkins, P.: uPort open-source identity management system: an assessment of self-sovereign identity and user-centric data platform built on blockchain. In: ISSE (2020)

35. JOLOCOM: A decentralized, open source solution for digital identity and access management (whitepaper) (2019). http://jolocom.io/wp-content/uploads/2019/12/Jolocom-Whitepaper-v2.1-A-Decentralized-Open-Source-Solution-for-Digital-Identity-and-Access-Management.pdf

36. Vogelsteller, F., Yasaka, T.: Erc-725 smart contract based account (2020). http://github.com/ethereum/EIPs/issues/725

37. Vogelsteller, F.: Claim holder (2019). http://github.com/ethereum/EIPs/issues/735

38. Lodder, D.M., Khovratovich, D.: Anonymous credentials 2.0 (2019). http://wiki.hyperledger.org/download/attachments/6426712/Anoncreds2.1.pdf

Dispute-Free Scalable Open Vote Network Using zk-SNARKs

Muhammad ElSheikh[1,2] and Amr M. Youssef[1(✉)]

[1] Concordia Institute for Information Systems Engineering, Concordia University,
Montréal, Québec, Canada
{m_elshei,youssef}@ciise.concordia.ca
[2] National Institute of Standards (NIS), Cairo, Egypt

Abstract. The Open Vote Network is a self-tallying decentralized e-voting protocol suitable for boardroom elections. Currently, it has two Ethereum-based implementations: the first, by McCorry *et al.*, has a scalability issue since all the computations are performed on-chain. The second implementation, by Seifelnasr *et al.*, solves this issue partially by assigning a part of the heavy computations to an off-chain untrusted administrator in a verifiable manner. As a side effect, this second implementation became not dispute-free; there is a need for a tally dispute phase where an observer interrupts the protocol when the administrator cheats, *i.e.*, announces a wrong tally result. In this work, we propose a new smart contract design to tackle the problems in the previous implementations by (i) preforming all the heavy computations off-chain hence achieving higher scalability, and (ii) utilizing zero-knowledge Succinct Non-interactive Argument of Knowledge (zk-SNARK) to verify the correctness of the off-chain computations, hence maintaining the dispute-free property. To demonstrate the effectiveness of our design, we develop prototype implementations on Ethereum and conduct multiple experiments for different implementation options that show a trade-off between the zk-SNARK proof generation time and the smart contract gas cost, including an implementation in which the smart contract consumes a constant amount of gas independent of the number of voters.

Keywords: Open Vote Network · E-voting · Blockchain ·
zk-SNARK · Smart contracts · Ethereum

1 Introduction

E-voting refers to an election system in which voters can cast their vote electronically. The main advantages of e-voting, compared to the traditional paper-based election, include high speed of tallying, cost-effectiveness, and scalability. Using e-voting systems can be crucial in many situations, *e.g.,* the current COVID-19 pandemic renders traditional paper-based voting within organizations a potential health hazard and sometimes not possible because of the work from home setup. Nowadays, there are many e-voting systems that can support a number

© International Financial Cryptography Association 2023
S. Matsuo et al. (Eds.): FC 2022 Workshops, LNCS 13412, pp. 499–515, 2023.
https://doi.org/10.1007/978-3-031-32415-4_31

of voters from a boardroom to a national scale [1,6,16]. However, most of them rely heavily on a trusted central authority, which might lead to violating the voters' privacy. With the emerging of blockchain technology as a decentralized append-only ledger, many researchers have proposed several blockchain-based e-voting protocols (*e.g.,* see [13–15,17,18,21]). Unfortunately, widely deployed blockchains such as Bitcoin and Ethereum suffer from scalability issues. Moreover, they do not inherently provide the privacy required by e-voting protocols. Therefore, a good blockchain-based e-voting system should handle these limitations.

The Open Vote Network is a self-tallying decentralized voting protocol. Self-tallying means that anyone who observes the protocol can tally the result without counting on a trusted authority. The protocol also provides maximum voter privacy; a single vote can only be breached by a full-collusion involving compromising all other votes. McCorry *et al.* [17] presented the first implementation of the Open Vote Network protocol on the Ethereum blockchain. However, their implementation does not provide scalability because all the protocol computations are delegated to the smart contract. This problem is partially solved by Seifelnasr *et al.* [21] by assigning the tallying computations to an off-chain untrusted administrator in a verifiable manner. To address the possibility of a malicious administrator, they added a dispute phase in which an honest voter may interrupt the protocol if the administrator provides an incorrect tallying result. As a result, the protocol lost its dispute-free property.

Contribution. In this work, we provide a new design to deploy the Open Vote Network using Ethereum smart contract. The new design can achieve better scalability without loosing the dispute-free property. Our contribution can be summarized as follows.

1. We develop a smart contract for the Open Vote Network in which all the heavy computations are performed off-chain without loosing dispute-free property.
2. We design three zk-SNARK arithmetic circuits to verify that all the off-chain computations are performed correctly by their responsible parties.
3. We develop a prototype[1] of our design to assess its performance. We also conduct some experiments to estimate the maximum number of voters that can be supported before exceeding the gas limit of the Ethereum block.
4. Finally, we show how to enhance the scalability of our design by modifying the zk-SNARK circuits such that they have statements of a fixed size. Consequently, the smart contract functions which verify the correctness of these zk-SNARK proofs consume fixed gas cost independent of the number of voters. The tradeoff between the zk-SNARK proof generation time and the smart contract gas cost is also experimentally evaluated.

The rest of the paper is organized as follows. In Sect. 2, we briefly revisit some related work on voting protocols implemented on the Ethereum blockchain.

---

[1] https://github.com/mhgharieb/zkSNARK-Open-Vote-Network.

Section 3 recalls the cryptographic primitives utilized in our protocol. In Sect. 4, we provide our design of the zk-SNARK circuits and the smart contracts. In Sect. 5, we evaluate our design and compare it against previous work. In Sect. 6, we provide multiple enhancements to the design in order to achieve better scalability, with different trade-offs between proof generation time and gas cost. Finally, our conclusion is presented in Sect. 7.

2 Related Work

The Open Vote Network is a self-tallying decentralized e-voting protocol. The concept of self-tallying was introduced by Kiayias and Yung [12] for boardroom voting. This work was followed by Groth et al. [7] and Hao et al. [10] who proposed a system that provides better efficiency for each voter. Hao et al.'s protocol has the same security properties and achieves better efficiency in terms of number of rounds. Li et al. [15] presented a new blockchain based self-tallying voting protocol for decentralized IoT. Recently, Li et al. [14] proposed a self-tallying protocol that utilizes homomorphic time-lock puzzles to encrypt the votes for a specified duration of time to maintain the privacy of ballots during the casting phase.

McCorry et al. [17] and Seifelnasr et al. [21] presented two implementations of the system of Hao et al. [10] as smart contracts on Ethereum. As mentioned above, the first implementation suffers from a scalability issue and the second requires a third-party to observe the behavior of the election administrator.

3 Preliminaries

3.1 zk-SNARK

A zk-SNARK refers to a zero-knowledge Succinct Non-interactive Argument of Knowledge scheme which enables a prover to convince a verifier that a statement is true without prior interactions between them [8].

Suppose an arithmetic circuit C with a relation $\mathcal{R}_C$ and a language $\mathcal{L}_C$ takes as input a statement $\vec{s}$ and a witness $\vec{w}$ s.t. $(\vec{s}, \vec{w}) \in \mathcal{R}_C$. A zk-SNARK for this arithmetic circuit satisfiability is defined by the following triple of polynomial-time algorithms [8,9,19]:

- $(\mathsf{pk}, \mathsf{vk}) \leftarrow \mathsf{Setup}(1^\lambda, C)$. Given a security parameter λ and the circuit C, the algorithm generates a common reference string (CRS) that contains a pair of keys; a proving key pk and a verifying key vk. Both keys are considered as public parameters for the circuit C.
- $\pi \leftarrow \mathsf{Prove}(\mathsf{pk}, \vec{s}, \vec{w})$. Given a proving key pk, a statement $\vec{s}$, and a witness $\vec{w}$ s.t. $(\vec{s}, \vec{w}) \in \mathcal{R}_C$, the algorithm generates a zero-knowledge non-interactive proof π for the statement $\vec{s} \in \mathcal{L}_C$ that reflects the relation between $\vec{s}$ and $\vec{w}$.
- $0/1 \leftarrow \mathsf{Verify}(\mathsf{vk}, \vec{s}, \pi)$. Given a verifying key vk, the statement $\vec{s}$, and the proof π, the algorithm outputs 1 if π is a valid proof for the statement $\vec{s} \in \mathcal{L}_C$, and outputs 0 otherwise.

Typically, a zk-SNARK provides the following security properties [9]:

1. **Perfect Completeness:** For each valid statement $\vec{s}$ with a valid witness $\vec{w}$ s.t. $(\vec{s}, \vec{w}) \in \mathcal{R}_C$, an honest prover always convinces an honest verifier, *i.e.*, Verify(vk, $\vec{s}$, π) outputs 1 with a probability equal to 1.
2. **Computational Soundness:** A polynomial-time malicious prover cannot convince the verifier of a false statement, *i.e.*, Verify(vk, $\vec{s}$, π) outputs 1 with a probability ≈ 0 when the statement $\vec{s} \notin \mathcal{L}_C$.
3. **Computational Zero-Knowledge:** A polynomial-time adversary cannot extract any information about the witness from the honestly-generated proof.
4. **Succinctness.** A zk-SNARK is succinct if the honestly-generated proof size is polynomial in λ and Verify(vk, $\vec{s}$, π) runs in polynomial time in $\lambda + |\vec{s}|$.

3.2 Open Vote Network

The Open Vote Network is a decentralized two-round self-tallying e-voting protocol [10]. It is suitable for a boardroom election in which the number of voters is relatively small.

In the beginning, eligible voters $(\mathcal{P}_0, \mathcal{P}_1, \ldots, \mathcal{P}_{n-1})$ agree on a finite cyclic group $\mathbb{G}$ of a prime order q and a generator g in which the Decisional Diffie-Hellman (DDH) problem is intractable. Then, each voter $\mathcal{P}_i$ picks a random value $x_i \in_R \mathbb{Z}_q$ as her private voting key. The Open Vote Network is executed for an election with two options 1 or 0 (implying 'YES' or 'NO') as follows.

Round 1. Each eligible voter $\mathcal{P}_i$ publishes her public voting key g^{x_i} along with a non-interactive zero-knowledge proof of knowledge regarding her private voting key x_i on the public bulletin board. At the end of this round, each voter verifies the validity of other voters' zero-knowledge proof of knowledge, then computes her blinding key Y_i as in Eq. 1.

$$Y_i = \prod_{j=0}^{i-1} g^{x_j} \Big/ \prod_{j=i+1}^{n-1} g^{x_j} \tag{1}$$

By implicitly setting $Y_i = g^{y_i}$, it is easy to prove that $\prod_i Y_i^{x_i} = g^{\sum_i x_i y_i} = g^0 = 1$.

Round 2. Each eligible voter $\mathcal{P}_i$ uses her blinding key Y_i and the private key x_i to encrypt the vote $v_i \in \{0,1\}$ s.t. the encrypted vote $V_i = g^{v_i} Y_i^{x_i}$. Then she publishes the encrypted vote V_i along with a non-interactive zero-knowledge proof of validity to prove that the encrypted vote V_i is well-formed such that $v_i \in \{0,1\}$. At the end of this round and after verifying the non-interactive zero-knowledge proofs of all encrypted votes, anyone who observes the protocol can compute the tally of 'YES' votes by exploiting the homomorphic property in the encrypted votes as follows: $\prod_i V_i = \prod_i g^{x_i y_i} g^{v_i} = g^{\sum_i x_i y_i + v_i} = g^{\sum_i v_i}$. Accordingly, the tally result of 'YES' votes $\sum_i v_i$ can be easily obtained by performing an exhaustive search on the discrete log of $g^{\sum_i v_i}$. This exhaustive search is bounded by the number of voters which is relatively small. For more details, see [10].

4   Protocol Design

In this section, we present our proposed design to deploy the Open Vote Network on the Ethereum blockchain using zk-SNARKs.

4.1   zk-SNARK Arithmetic Circuit

Since validating zk-SNARK proofs on Ethereum are performed over two cyclic groups of prime order p [3], our protocol computations are preformed over a cyclic group $\mathbb{G}$ with a finite field $\mathbb{F}_p$ on the elliptic curve *Baby Jubjub* [2]. $\mathbb{G}$ has a prime order q, a base point (generator) G, and a point at infinity (the neutral element) O. A point $P \in \mathbb{G}$ is presented by its two coordinate values (P^x, P^y).

In our design, we use zk-SNARKs to verify that all off-chain computations are performed correctly by their responsible parties. To this end, we design three zk-SNARK arithmetic circuits: publicKeyGen, encryptedVoteGen, and Tallying corresponding to generating the public key of voters, encrypting the votes, and tallying the result of 'YES' option, respectively.

We design these circuits based on Groth16 zk-SNARK construction [9] because it is a quadratic arithmetic program (QAP) hence it provides a linear-time Setup, quasilinear-time Prove, and linear-time Verify [20]. However, Groth16 enforces some restrictions on the design (*e.g.,* array indices and loop iteration counts must be constant during compiling (Setup) phase).

During the design, we use the following pre-defined arithmetic circuits as building blocks:

- Mux(s, P, Q): Returns P if the selector $s = 0$, and Q if $s = 1$.
- LessThan(a, b): Returns 1 if $a < b$, and 0 otherwise.
- GreaterThan(a, b): Returns 1 if $a > b$, and 0 otherwise.
- CompC(a, c) where c is a constant: Returns 1 if $a > c$, and 0 otherwise.
- Bits2Num($a_0, \ldots, a_{k-1}$): Returns the integer number represented by bits $a_0, \ldots, a_{k-1}$.
- IsPoint(x, y): Returns 1 if the pair (x, y) is a point on the elliptic curve, and 0 otherwise.
- IsEqual(P, Q): Returns 1 if the two points P and Q are equal, and 0 otherwise.
- eADD(P, Q): Point addition $(P + Q)$ on the elliptic curve.
- eSUB(P, Q): point subtraction $(P - Q)$ on the elliptic curve.
- eScalarMUL(a, P): Scalar multiplication (aP) on the elliptic curve.

Let $\kappa = |p| - 1$. Since all operations are preformed over $\mathbb{F}_p$, the number of inputs to Bits2Num must be $\leq \kappa$ bits to avoid overflow when calculating the output value.

publicKeyGen Circuit (C_{PK}). This circuit (see Circuit 1) is intended for the setup of the zk-SNARK to prove that a voter B knows the private key x_B corresponding to the public key $PK_B = x_B G$ in step (1); and the sign of its x-coordinate is 0 (*i.e.,* $pk_B^{x_B} < p/2$), in step (3), to ensure that PK_B follows the compact representation as described in [11] such that x and y coordinates have a one-to-one relation.

encryptedVoteGen Circuit (C_V). This circuit is intended for the setup of the zk-SNARK to prove that a voter B with index i_B forms her encrypted vote V_B correctly s.t. the vote $v_B \in \{0,1\}$ as shown in Circuit 2.

Since the verification time is linearly proportional to the size of the statement $\vec{s}$, we decompose each public key PK_i into its coordinate values (pk_i^x, pk_i^y). Since they have a one-to-one relation, the y-coordinate becomes a part of the statement $\vec{s}$ and the x-coordinate becomes a part of the witness $\vec{w}$ in order to optimize the circuit and reduce the verification time, hence the on-chain computation.

From Eq. 1, the encrypted vote V_B is computed as follows:

$$V_B = v_B G + x_B Y_B \tag{2}$$

$$Y_B = \underbrace{\sum_{i=0}^{i_B-1} PK_i}_{Y_l} - \underbrace{\sum_{i=i_B+1}^{n-1} PK_i}_{Y_g} \tag{3}$$

Accordingly, encryptedVoteGen circuit checks that $v_B \in \{0,1\}$ in step (1); each pair (pk_i^x, pk_i^y) is a point on the elliptic curve in step (5); the sign of the x-coordinate is 0 $(pk_B^{x_B} < p/2)$ in step (6) to verify the one-to-one relation; the correctness of Y_l, Y_g, and Y_B (as in Eq. 3) in steps (8–10), (11–13), and (15), receptively; and the correctness of V_B (as in Eq. 2) in steps (16–18).

Tallying Circuit (C_T). This circuit is intended for the setup of the zk-SNARK to prove the correctness of the tallying result as shown in Circuit 3. Similar to C_V, each encrypted vote V_i is decomposed into its coordinate values (V_i^x, V_i^y), then the y-coordinate becomes a part of the statement $\vec{s}$ and the x-coordinate becomes a part of the witness $\vec{w}$ in order to reduce the on-chain computation. Since we cannot enforce the compact representation for V_i, we instead present the sign of x-coordinate in a single bit S_i then compress every κ sign-bits in one integer number D_j. Hence, we can verify the one-to-one relation between the two coordinates of V_i.

Accordingly, Tallying circuit checks that each pair (V_i^x, V_i^y) is a point on the elliptic curve in step (6). Then, it checks the correctness of $\sum_i V_i$ in step (7); the x-coordinate sign (S_i) of V_i in step (9); the compression of every κ sign-bits into an integer D_j in step (12); the incrementally exhaustive search in steps (17–19); and finally the tallying result (res) s.t. $\sum V_i = (res)G$ in steps (21–22). It should be mentioned that $0 \leq res \leq n$, where $res = 0$ when no voter selects the 'Yes' option and $res = n$ when all voters select the 'Yes' option. Therefore, the exhaustive search counter i in step (16) starts from 0 to n.

Circuit 1: publicKeyGen	Circuit 3: Tallying
Statement $\vec{s}$: PK_B	**Statement** $\vec{s}$: $(res, \{D_j\}, \{V_i^y\})$
Witness $\vec{w}$: x_B	**Witness** $\vec{w}$: $\{V_i^x\}$
1 $PK_B \leftarrow$ eScalarMUL(x_B, G)	1 $l \leftarrow \lceil \frac{n}{\kappa} \rceil$
2 $(pk_B^x, pk_B^y) \leftarrow PK_B$	2 $\{S_i \leftarrow 0, 0 \leq i \leq \kappa l - 1\}$
3 Assert CompC$(pk_B^x, p/2) = 0$	3 $\{D_j, 0 \leq j \leq l - 1\}$

Circuit 2: encryptedVoteGen
Statement $\vec{s}$: $(V_B, i_B, \{pk_i^y\})$
Witness $\vec{w}$: $(v_B, x_B, \{pk_i^x\})$
1 Assert $(1 - v_B) \times v_B = 0$
2 $Y_l \leftarrow O$
3 $Y_g \leftarrow O$
4 for $i \leftarrow 0$ to $n - 1$ do
5 $\quad$ Assert IsPoint(pk_i^x, pk_i^y)
6 $\quad$ Assert CompC$(pk_i^x, p/2) = 0$
7 $\quad$ $PK_i \leftarrow (pk_i^x, pk_i^y)$
8 $\quad$ $e_l \leftarrow$ LessThan(i, i_B)
9 $\quad$ $T_l \leftarrow$ Mux(e_l, O, PK_i)
10 $\quad$ $Y_l \leftarrow$ eADD(Y_l, T_l)
11 $\quad$ $e_g \leftarrow$ GreaterThan(i, i_B)
12 $\quad$ $T_g \leftarrow$ Mux(e_g, O, PK_i)
13 $\quad$ $Y_g \leftarrow$ eADD(Y_g, T_g)
14 end
15 $Y_B \leftarrow$ eSUB(Y_l, Y_g)
16 $T_0 \leftarrow$ eScalarMUL(x_B, Y_B)
17 $T_1 \leftarrow$ Mux(v_B, O, G)
18 $V_B \leftarrow$ eADD(T_0, T_1)

Circuit 3 continued:

4 $sumV \leftarrow O$
5 for $i \leftarrow 0$ to $n - 1$ do
6 $\quad$ Assert IsPoint(V_i^x, V_i^y)
7 $\quad$ $sumV \leftarrow$ eADD$(sumV, V_i)$
8 $\quad$ $V_i \leftarrow (V_i^x, V_i^y)$
9 $\quad$ $S_i \leftarrow$ CompC$(V_i^x, p/2)$
10 end
11 for $j \leftarrow 0$ to $l - 1$ do
12 $\quad$ $D_j \leftarrow$ Bits2Num$(S_{\kappa j}, \ldots, S_{\kappa j + \kappa - 1})$
13 end
14 $t \leftarrow 0$
15 $T \leftarrow O$
16 for $i \leftarrow 0$ to n do
17 $\quad$ $e \leftarrow$ IsEqual$(T, sumV)$
18 $\quad$ $t \leftarrow t + e \times i$
19 $\quad$ $T \leftarrow$ eADD(T, G)
20 end
21 Assert eScalarMUL$(t, G) = sumV$
22 $res \leftarrow t$

4.2 Open Vote Network Smart Contract

Before executing the protocol, an administrator A and a set of n eligible voters run an MPC-based setup ceremony for generating the proving and verifying keys for the arithmetic circuits.

$$(\mathsf{pk}_{C_{PK}}, \mathsf{vk}_{C_{PK}}) \leftarrow \mathsf{Setup}(1^\lambda, C_{PK})$$
$$(\mathsf{pk}_{C_V}, \mathsf{vk}_{C_V}) \leftarrow \mathsf{Setup}(1^\lambda, C_V)$$
$$(\mathsf{pk}_{C_T}, \mathsf{vk}_{C_T}) \leftarrow \mathsf{Setup}(1^\lambda, C_T)$$

After that, similar to [21], the administrator accumulates the list of eligible voters in a Merkle tree $MT_\mathcal{E}$ where the voters' Ethereum account addresses are the tree leaves, and publishes it on IPFS allowing each voter to generate her proof of voting eligibility. Also, the administrator defines the time intervals of the protocol phases, namely, Registering Voters, Casting Encrypted Votes, Tallying the Result, and Refunding.

Smart Contract Deployment. Subsequently, the administrator deploys the smart contract, which initializes the variables used in the subsequent phases, with the following set of parameters and pays a collateral deposit F as shown in Fig. 1.

Deploy: upon receiving $(root_{\mathcal{E}}, \mathsf{vk}_{C_{PK}}, \mathsf{vk}_{C_V}, \mathsf{vk}_{C_T}, T_1, T_2, T_3, T_4, n)$
              from administrator **A**:
              Assert $value = F$
              Set $admin := $ **A**
              Store $root_{\mathcal{E}}, \mathsf{vk}_{C_{PK}}, \mathsf{vk}_{C_V}, \mathsf{vk}_{C_T}, T_1, T_2, T_3, T_4, n$
              Init $voters := \{\}, publicKeys := \{\}, EncryptedVotes := \{\},$
              $Int_Vsigns := \{0,\ldots,0\}, tallyingResult := $ NULL$, index := 0$

Fig. 1. Pseudocode for deployment of the smart contract.

- $root_{\mathcal{E}}$: The root of the Merkle tree $MT_{\mathcal{E}}$.
- $\mathsf{vk}_{C_{PK}}, \mathsf{vk}_{C_V}, \mathsf{vk}_{C_T}$: The verifying keys of the zk-SNARK circuits.
- T_1, T_2, T_3, T_4: The block heights that define the end of the protocol phases.
- n: The number of eligible voters.
- F: A collateral deposit paid by both the administrator and the voters to penalize malicious actors.
- $voters, publicKeys, EncryptedVotes, Int\_Vsigns$: Four arrays of sizes n, n, n, and $l = \lceil \frac{n}{\kappa} \rceil$, used to store the voters' Ethereum account addresses, $\{PK_i\}$, $\{V_i\}$, and $\{D_j\}$, respectively.

Registering Voters. This phase starts immediately after deploying the contract. Each voter B selects her private key x_B and uses publicKeyGen circuit along with $\mathsf{pk}_{C_{PK}}$ to generate the public key PK_B and a zk-SNARK proof π_{x_B}. After that, she invokes Register function in the smart contract with the parameters PK_B and π_{x_B} along with a Merkle proof of voters membership π_B, and pays the collateral deposit F as shown in Fig. 2. On its turn, the function ensures that the voter deposits the correct collateral fee, it is invoked within the allowed interval, and the number of already registered voters does not exceed the total number of eligible voters. After that, it reconstructs the zk-SNARK statement $\vec{s}$ of publicKeyGen circuit. Consequently, Register verifies both the Merkle tree proof of the voter membership and the zk-SNARK proof using $\mathsf{vk}_{C_{PK}}$ key. We utilize the implementation in [4] to verify the Merkle proof. Finally, it stores the public key PK_B and the address of the voter B for the subsequent phases.

```
Register:        upon receiving (PK_B, π_{x_B}, π_B) from voter B:
                 Assert value = F
                 Assert T < T_1
                 Assert index < n
                 Reconstruct s⃗ := PK_B
                 Assert MerkleTree.verify( π_B, B, root_E)
                 Assert zkSNARK.verify(vk_{C_{PK}}, s⃗, π_{x_B})
                 Store publicKeys[index] := PK_B
                 Store voters[index] := B
                 Set index := index + 1
```

Fig. 2. Pseudocode for Register function

Casting Encrypted Votes. After the voters registration phase ends, each voter B, which has index i_B, starts computing her blinding key Y_B to encrypt her vote v_B and generate a zk-SNARK proof π_{v_B} using encryptVoteGen circuit along with the proving key pk_{C_V}. Then, she publishes the encrypted vote V_B publicly by invoking CastVote function in the smart contract. The function verifies that the voter casts the encrypted vote within the allowed time interval, and the voter indeed has the index i_B. After that, it reconstructs the statement $\vec{s}$ of encryptedVoteGen circuit along with vk_{C_V} in order to verify the correctness of the zk-SNARK proof π_{v_B} submitted by the voter. Finally, it stores the encrypted vote V_B and updates Int_Vsigns based on the sign of its x-coordinate, V_B^x, and the voter index i_B as depicted in Fig. 3.

```
CastVote:        upon receiving (V_B, i_B, π_{v_B}) from voter B
                 Assert T_1 < T < T_2
                 Assert B = voters[i_B]
                 Reconstruct s⃗ := (V_B, i_B, publicKeys)
                 Assert zkSNARK.verify(vk_{C_V}, s⃗, π_{v_B})
                 Set EncryptedVotes[i_B] := V_B
                 IF(V_B^x > p/2):
                     Set Int_Vsigns[⌊i_B/κ⌋] := Int_Vsigns[⌊i_B/κ⌋] ⊕ 2^{i_B} mod κ
```

Fig. 3. Pseudocode for CastVote function

Tallying the Result. After the casting phase ends, the administrator obtains all the encrypted votes stored in the smart contract in order to tally the result of 'YES' option. To this end, she uses Tallying circuit along with pk_{C_T} to obtain the result res and its corresponding zk-SNARK proof π_{res}. Then, she invokes

SetTally function to publish this result. The function verifies that the transaction is within the allowed time interval and it is sent by the administrator who deployed the smart contract. Then, the function reconstructs the statement $\vec{s}$ of Tallying circuit to verify the correctness of the tallying result as shown in Fig. 4.

SetTally: upon receiving $(result,\ \pi_{res})$ from administrator A:
                 Assert $admin$ = A
                 Assert $T_2 < T < T_3$
                 Set $\vec{s} := (result,\ Int\_Vsigns,\ EncryptedVotes)$
                 Assert zkSNARK.verify(vk_{C_T}, $\vec{s}$, π_{res})
                 Set $tallyingResult := result$

Fig. 4. Pseudocode for SetTally function

Refunding. Finally, at the end of tallying the result phase, the administrator and voters invoke Refund function to reclaim the collateral fee F that they deposited during deploying the smart contract and registering voters phases, respectively. Before refunding the value, this function verifies that the time to set the tallying result has ended and the transaction sender indeed paid the deposit.

5 Evaluation and Comparison

We developed a prototype of our design to evaluate the gas cost and its scalability. The prototype is available as open-source on Github[2]. We utilize circom (v2.0) library[3] to compile the arithmetic circuits publicKeyGen, encryptedVote-Gen, and Tallying. During the protocol execution, we use snarkjs (v0.4.10) library[4] to handle the MPC-based setup ceremony for generating the proving and verifying keys. Also, we use it to generate the zk-SNARK proofs. We utilize Tuffle framework[5] (v5.4.24) to deploy and test the smart contracts.

The prototype includes three smart contracts: verifierMerkleTreeCon, verifierZKSNARKCon, and eVoteCon. The first two contracts are deployed as generic functions to verify the Merkle tree proof of membership and the zk-SNARKs proofs. Table 1 summarizes the gas units consumed by different functions in the contracts for executing the protocol for 40 voters.

---

[2] https://github.com/mhgharieb/zkSNARK-Open-Vote-Network.

[3] https://docs.circom.io/.

[4] https://github.com/iden3/snarkjs.

[5] https://trufflesuite.com/.

Table 1. The gas cost for functions in the voting contract

Function	Gas units
verifierMerkleTreeCon	192,013
verifierZKSNARKCon	1,346,155
eVoteCon	1,474,818
setVerifyingKey($vk_{C_{PK}}$)	462,309
setVerifyingKey(vk_{C_V})	2,253,285
setVerifyingKey(vk_{C_T})	2,209,576
Register	349,517
CastVote	937,299
SetTally	901,532
Refund	52,253

Scalability Experiments. We also conduct some experiments to estimate the maximum number of voters who can participate in the same election before exceeding the gas limit of the Ethereum block. To this end, we run the prototype with incremental steps starting from 10 voters up to 300 voters. The gas cost of these experiments is shown in Fig. 5. As depicted in Fig. 5a, setting the verifying keys vk_{C_V} and vk_{C_T} consumed an amount of gas units linearly with the number of voters. In contrast, the gas cost for setting the verifying key $vk_{C_{PK}}$ is approximately constant. This behavior is expected since the statement size $|\vec{s}|$ of the circuits publicKeyGen and Tallying is linearly proportional to the number of voters. In contrast, it is constant in the case of encryptedVoteGen circuit. The same behavior is observed for invoking the smart contract functions as shown in Fig. 5b.

It is obvious that setting a verifying key can be made in multiple blocks. In contrast, running the smart contract function must be completed in the same block. Therefore, the gas cost of invoking the functions is the bottleneck against the scalability. With the current gas limit (30M gas units[6] on Jan. 16, 2022), this prototype can be scaled to around 2000 voters.

Comparison with McCorry et al. [17]. The design in [17] and ours provide the same properties specially the dispute-free property. In our design, we delegate the heavy computation to off-chain parties in a verifiable manner. In contrast, in [17] all the computations are performed on-chain. For the sake of fairness, we compare the gas consumption by each voter and the administrator during a 40-voter election in the two designs as summarized in Table 2. In our design, the gas cost per voter and the administrator are around 40% and 70% of the other design, respectively. However, the gas cost increases rabidly with the number of voters in McCorry *et al.* design as deduced from Fig. 4 in [17]. Therefore, our design is more scalable.

---

[6] https://ethstats.net/.

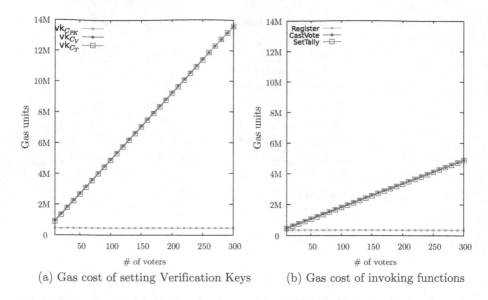

(a) Gas cost of setting Verification Keys   (b) Gas cost of invoking functions

Fig. 5. Gas cost in scalability experiments

Table 2. Gas cost comparison between our implementation and [17]

Sender	Ours	[17]
Voter	1,339,069	3,323,642
Admin	8,719,141	12,436,190

Comparison with Seifelnasr et al. [21]. The implementation in [21] delegates the tallying computation to an off-chain untrusted administrator along with a dispute phase to catch the misbehavior of a malicious administrator. In contrast, we delegate all the computation to off-chain parties without loosing the dispute-free property. Regarding the gas cost, after carefully reviewing the Github code of [21], we found that their estimation does not take into account the 'verifyY' step presented in the pseudocode of cast vote function in which the smart contract should verify that a voter B computes her blinding key Y_B correctly. We argue that this step is the major factor on the gas cost of this function. Moreover, they claimed that their design could be scaled theoretically to support 2^{256} voters because all transactions have constant gas cost except the two functions of registering voters and dispute phase which scales logarithmically with the number of voters since these functions verify the Merkle proof of membership. However, this claim also was based on ignoring the gas cost of the step 'verifyY' which scales linearly with the number of voters.

6 Further Scalability Improvement

Recall that the gas consumption by the functions: $\mathsf{setVerifyingKey(vk}_{C_V})$, $\mathsf{setVerifyingKey(vk}_{C_T})$, CastVote, and SetTally, in the current design, increases linearly with the number of voters because the statement size of the zk-SNARK increases linearly with the number of voters. In this section, we present some modifications to the circuits so that the size of the statement becomes fixed, hence $\mathsf{setVerifyingKey(vk}_{C_V})$ and $\mathsf{setVerifyingKey(vk}_{C_T})$ consume fixed gas units. Regarding the gas consumption associated with invoking the other smart contract functions, we propose some modifications on Register, CastVote, and SetTally functions so that they also consume fixed gas units independent of the number of voters. As a result, the total gas paid by the administrator and each voter is constant, hence achieving very good scalability.

6.1 Fixed Statement Size

Let $commit_{PK} = H(pk_0^y || pk_1^y || \cdots || pk_{n-1}^y)$ denote the hash of the concatenation of the y-coordinates of the voters' public keys. Recall that in encryptedVoteGen circuit, the statement $\vec{s} = (V_B, i_B, \{pk_i^y\})$ and the witness $\vec{w} = (v_B, x_B, \{pk_i^x\})$. By moving $\{pk_i^y\}$ from $\vec{s}$ to $\vec{w}$ and adding $commit_{PK}$ to $\vec{s}$, we can construct a new circuit newEncryptedVoteGen with new $(\vec{s'}, \vec{w'})$ s.t.

$$\vec{s'} = (V_B, commit_{PK}, i_B), \qquad \vec{w'} = (v_B, x_B, \{pk_i^x\}, \{pk_i^y\})$$

The newEncryptedVoteGen circuit is encryptedVoteGen circuit in addition to a new constraint

$$\mathsf{Assert}\ commit_{PK} = H(pk_0^y || pk_1^y || \cdots || pk_{n-1}^y)$$

Therefore, newEncryptedVoteGen has a fixed-size statement and independent of the number of voters, hence setting its verification key will consume fixed gas units. consequently, verifying the zk-SNARK proof will consume fixed gas units. In its turn, the smart contract should check the correctness of $commit_{PK}$ in CastVote function, since the public keys PK_i are known.

Similarly, let $commit_V = H(V_0^y || V_1^y || \cdots || V_{n-1}^y || D_0 || \cdots || D_l)$ denote the hash of the concatenation of the y-coordinates of the encrypted votes in addition to the integer numbers represented the sign-bits of the x-coordinates. Therefore, we can construct a new Tallying circuit with new $(\vec{s'}, \vec{w'})$ s.t. $\vec{s'} = (res, commit_V)$ and $\vec{w'} = (\{V_i^x\}, \{V_i^y\})$. In its turn, the smart contract should check the correctness of $commit_V$ in SetTallying function since the encrypted votes V_i are known.

As a result, the total gas units consumed by $\mathsf{setVerifyingKey(vk}_{C_V})$ and $\mathsf{setVerifyingKey(vk}_{C_T})$ become constant. In contrast, the gas consumption by CastVote and SetTallying functions still increase linearly with the number of voters and depend on how much the used hash function cost. Accordingly, this approach is efficient and can support a high number of voters only if the used hash function is cheap on the Ethereum, *e.g.*, SHA-256.

6.2   Fixed Gas Cost

Due to the structure of $commit_{PK}$ and $commit_V$, they must be calculated after registering all voters and casting all encrypted votes, respectively. Therefore, the voter who casts the first encrypted vote has to pay the linearly increasing gas cost of calculating $commit_{PK}$ on behalf of all the other voters. Similarly, the administrator has to pay the linearly increasing gas cost associated with calculating $commit_V$. To achieve a constant gas paid by the administrator and each voter, we restructure $commit_{PK}$ and $commit_V$ so that they can be calculated in a progressive manner. Hence their gas cost is distributed among all voters. Let the new $commit_{PK}$ be defined as follows:

$$commit_{PK} = H(H(\cdots H(H(0||pk_0^y)||pk_1^y)||\cdots)||pk_{n-1}^y)$$

Accordingly, the smart contract initializes $commit_{PK} := 0$ during its deployment, then during registering the public key PK_i, Register function updates $commit_{PK} := H(commit_{PK}||pk_i^y)$. At the end of the voters registration phase, the new $commit_{PK}$ value is ready to be used by CastVote function to verify the correctness of the encrypted vote sent by each voter.

Similarly, let the new $commit_V$ be defined as follows:

$$commit_V = H(H(\cdots H(H(0||V_0^x||V_0^y)||V_1^x||V_1^y)||\cdots)||V_{n-1}^x||V_{n-1}^y)$$

The smart contract initializes $commit_V := 0$, then during casting the encrypted vote V_i, CastVote function updates $commit_V := H(commit_V||V_i^x||V_i^y)$. By using both the two coordinates of V_i, there is no need of tracking the sign of the x-coordinates. At the end of the casting phase, the new $commit_V$ value is ready to be used by SetTallying function to verify the correctness of the tallying result sent by the administrator.

6.3   Performance Measurements

We evaluate the performance of the two modified designs in terms of the size of the common reference string (CRS) for encryptedVoteGen and SetTallying circuits (*i.e.*, the proving and verification keys sizes); their average proof generation time; and the gas consumption associated with invoking the three functions: Register, CastVote, and SetTally. In particular, we evaluate our implementation using SHA-256 in Sect. 6.1 (referred as *SHA-256*), and SHA-256 and Poseidon [5] in Sect. 6.2 (referred as *progressive SHA-256* and *progressive Poseidon*). As depicted in Fig. 6, the CRS size and the average proof generation time for both circuits increase linearly with the number of voters in our original and modified designs. The highest value corresponds to the *progressive SHA-256* hashing case. As expected, SHA-256 cannot be presented by a friendly arithmetic circuit, *i.e.*, it generates a high number of constraints, hence a large proving key size and high zk-SNARK proof generation time. In contrast, Poseidon hash function is an arithmetic circuit friendly hash function. Regarding the gas cost, Register function consumes fixed gas units in all designs independent of the number of

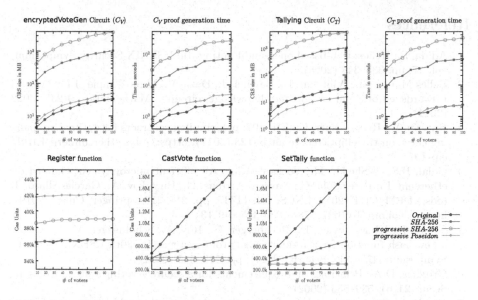

Fig. 6. Performance evaluation of our modified designs. '*Original*', '*SHA-256*', '*progressive SHA-256*', and '*progressive Poseidon*' refer to our original design, the modified designs in Sect. 6.1 using SHA-256, and Sect. 6.2 using the hash functions SHA-256, and Poseidon, respectively.

voters. However, it is the highest in *progressive Poseidon* hashing case. For both CastVote, and SetTally functions, their gas costs for *SHA-256* increase linearly with the number of voters, but *SHA-256* is still more scalable than our original design. In contrast, the two functions consume a fixed gas units in *progressive SHA-256* hashing and *progressive Poseidon* hashing as desired. However, the gas cost of *progressive Poseidon* hashing is slightly higher for CastVote function. The decision of which design to be used should be taken by the administrator and the voters since it presents a trade-off between the proof generation time and the money spent in the form of the gas fees.

7   Conclusion

We presented a dispute-free implementation for the Open Vote Network protocol as smart contracts in which all the heavy computations are performed off-chain. Then, we utilized zk-SNARKs to verify that all off-chain computations are performed correctly by their corresponding parties. Moreover, we developed a prototype of our design to assess its performance. Then, we enhanced its scalability by utilizing progressive hashing to achieve fixed zk-SNARK statement sizes and distribute the gas costs among all voters. As a result, the total gas paid by the administrator and each voter is constant, hence achieving very good scalability.

References

1. Adida, B.: Helios: web-based open-audit voting. In: USENIX Security Symposium, vol. 17, pp. 335–348 (2008)
2. Bellés-Muñoz, M., Whitehat, B., Baylina, J., Daza, V., Muñoz-Tapia, J.L.: Twisted Edwards elliptic curves for zero-knowledge circuits. Mathematics 9(23), 3022 (2021)
3. Buterin, V., Reitwiessner, C.: EIP-197: precompiled contracts for optimal ate pairing check on the elliptic curve alt_bn128 (2017). https://eips.ethereum.org/EIPS/eip-197
4. Galal, H.S., ElSheikh, M., Youssef, A.M.: An efficient micropayment channel on ethereum. In: Pérez-Solà, C., Navarro-Arribas, G., Biryukov, A., Garcia-Alfaro, J. (eds.) DPM/CBT -2019. LNCS, vol. 11737, pp. 211–218. Springer, Cham (2019). https://doi.org/10.1007/978-3-030-31500-9_13
5. Grassi, L., Khovratovich, D., Rechberger, C., Roy, A., Schofnegger, M.: Poseidon: a new hash function for zero-knowledge proof systems. In: 30th USENIX Security Symposium (USENIX Security 2021), pp. 519–535 (2021)
6. Gritzalis, D.A.: Principles and requirements for a secure e-voting system. Comput. Secur. 21(6), 539–556 (2002)
7. Groth, J.: Efficient maximal privacy in boardroom voting and anonymous broadcast. In: Juels, A. (ed.) FC 2004. LNCS, vol. 3110, pp. 90–104. Springer, Heidelberg (2004). https://doi.org/10.1007/978-3-540-27809-2_10
8. Groth, J.: Short pairing-based non-interactive zero-knowledge arguments. In: Abe, M. (ed.) ASIACRYPT 2010. LNCS, vol. 6477, pp. 321–340. Springer, Heidelberg (2010). https://doi.org/10.1007/978-3-642-17373-8_19
9. Groth, J.: On the size of pairing-based non-interactive arguments. In: Fischlin, M., Coron, J.-S. (eds.) EUROCRYPT 2016. LNCS, vol. 9666, pp. 305–326. Springer, Heidelberg (2016). https://doi.org/10.1007/978-3-662-49896-5_11
10. Hao, F., Ryan, P.Y., Zieliński, P.: Anonymous voting by two-round public discussion. IET Inf. Secur. 4(2), 62–67 (2010)
11. Jivsov, A.: Compact representation of an elliptic curve point (2014). https://tools.ietf.org/id/draft-jivsov-ecc-compact-05.html
12. Kiayias, A., Yung, M.: Self-tallying elections and perfect ballot secrecy. In: Naccache, D., Paillier, P. (eds.) PKC 2002. LNCS, vol. 2274, pp. 141–158. Springer, Heidelberg (2002). https://doi.org/10.1007/3-540-45664-3_10
13. Kshetri, N., Voas, J.: Blockchain-enabled E-voting. IEEE Softw. 35(4), 95–99 (2018)
14. Li, H., Li, Y., Yu, Y., Wang, B., Chen, K.: A blockchain-based traceable self-tallying e-voting protocol in AI era. IEEE Trans. Netw. Sci. Eng. 8(2), 1019–1032 (2021)
15. Li, Y., Susilo, W., Yang, G., Yu, Y., Liu, D., Du, X., Guizani, M.: A blockchain-based self-tallying voting protocol in decentralized IoT. IEEE Trans. Dependable Secure Comput. 19(1), 119–130 (2022)
16. Maaten, E.: Towards remote e-voting: Estonian case. In: Prosser, A., Krimmer, R. (eds.) Electronic Voting in Europe - Technology, Law, Politics and Society, Workshop of the ESF TED Programme Together with GI and OCG, pp. 83–90. Gesellschaft für Informatik e.V, Bonn (2004)
17. McCorry, P., Shahandashti, S.F., Hao, F.: A smart contract for boardroom voting with maximum voter privacy. In: Kiayias, A. (ed.) FC 2017. LNCS, vol. 10322, pp. 357–375. Springer, Cham (2017). https://doi.org/10.1007/978-3-319-70972-7_20

18. Murtaza, M.H., Alizai, Z.A., Iqbal, Z.: Blockchain based anonymous voting system using zkSNARKs. In: 2019 International Conference on Applied and Engineering Mathematics (ICAEM), pp. 209–214. IEEE (2019)

19. Parno, B., Howell, J., Gentry, C., Raykova, M.: Pinocchio: nearly practical verifiable computation. In: 2013 IEEE Symposium on Security and Privacy, pp. 238–252. IEEE (2013)

20. Sasson, E.B., et al.: Zerocash: decentralized anonymous payments from bitcoin. In: 2014 IEEE Symposium on Security and Privacy, pp. 459–474. IEEE (2014)

21. Seifelnasr, M., Galal, H.S., Youssef, A.M.: Scalable open-vote network on ethereum. In: Bernhard, M., et al. (eds.) FC 2020. LNCS, vol. 12063, pp. 436–450. Springer, Cham (2020). https://doi.org/10.1007/978-3-030-54455-3_31

Not All Code are Create2 Equal

Michael Fröwis[✉] and Rainer Böhme

Department of Computer Science, Universität Innsbruck, Innsbruck, Austria
`michael.froewis@uibk.ac.at`

Abstract. We describe the impact and measure the adoption of the *CREATE2* instruction introduced to the Ethereum Virtual Machine in the Constantinople upgrade. This change to Ethereum's execution environment is fundamental because it enables to modify the program stored on a given address after deployment, making it much harder to reason about the immutability of smart contracts. We enumerate six use cases and novel attack vectors, and present empirical evidence from all 32 million code accounts created between March 2019 and July 2021. The data shows that the main beneficiaries of the upgrade are wallet contracts, which can now use predictable addresses. But they do not require the more risky feature of mutable smart contracts. So far, the only applications that use the latter are front-running bots and gas tokens.

Keywords: Smart Contracts · Patching · Security · Ethereum Virtual Machine

1 Introduction

The initial design of the Ethereum Virtual Machine (EVM) stipulated that program code associated with the address of a code account cannot be changed. This enabled users to build confidence in the integrity of a smart contract before entrusting it any value. A single exception, the possibility to remove code with the instruction *SELFDESTRUCT*, has caught public attention in 2017, when it caused a \$152 million loss in an incident of a popular wallet [8]. Nonetheless, code removed this way could not be restored or replaced with other code.

The Constantinople upgrade, effective since February 2019,[1] breaks with this convention. It adds *CREATE2*, as defined in EIP-1014, to the EVM's instruction set. The new instruction derives the addresses of code accounts in a more controllable way than the legacy *CREATE* instruction, which is still supported for backward compatibility. Effectively, *CREATE2* enables users to deploy different code to the same address and therefore provides a means to update smart contracts after deployment.

This radical—to some observers unanticipated—change of fundamental functionality has several far-reaching implications. It was motivated by the demand for counterfactual instantiation, i.e., the possibility to commit to program code

---

[1] 2019-02-28 20:52:04 GMT+2.

© International Financial Cryptography Association 2023
S. Matsuo et al. (Eds.): FC 2022 Workshops, LNCS 13412, pp. 516–538, 2023.
https://doi.org/10.1007/978-3-031-32415-4_32

before it is deployed on the chain. This is useful for the efficient establishment of state channels, a nascent off-chain technology [10,13]. Moreover, the upgrade simplifies the maintenance of smart contracts. Previously, rather expensive proxy patterns were necessary to enable patching [14,19]. These become obsolete if code can be updated right away using *CREATE2*.

On the downside, the Constantinople upgrade made it harder to reason about the code that is governing a given address at any future point in time. Many subtleties not only render it virtually impossible for end users to convince themselves about the immutability of any but the most trivial smart contracts. Also developers are prone to run into pitfalls, and automated tools for smart contract verification may require adaptations [1,29]. The mere fact that not all users may be aware of the possibility to update code raises security concerns.

Ethereum is not the only platform affected. The EVM has become the de facto standard runtime environment for smart contract environments including Ethereum Classic,[2] Binance Smart Chain, xDai, POA, and Polygon. At the time of writing, the value administered on these platforms exceeds $100 billion.

The objective of this paper is twofold. First, it offers a comprehensive description of the new possibilities enabled by *CREATE2* and through the interactions between old and new code. This leads us to identify a set of features comprising new threats as well as new opportunities for applications. Second, the paper takes a measurement approach to empirically review the prevalence of these features on the Ethereum blockchain since the Constantinople upgrade in 2019 until shortly before the London upgrade in August 2021. This measurement is based on novel heuristics, which add to the contributions made in this work.

The rest of the paper is organized as follows. Sect. 2 describes how smart contracts could be patched before and after the upgrade. Section 3 discusses the effects of the upgrade and motivates the measurement of six items of interest (IoI). Section 4 presents the data sources, methods and proposed heuristics. Section 5 reports and interprets the measurement results along the IoIs. Section 6 connects to relevant related work. Section 7 concludes.

2   Updating Smart Contracts

This section reviews how smart contracts on Ethereum could be updated before and after the Constantinople upgrade.[3] To do so, we introduce some terminology on how code accounts are referenced on the platform. Before the upgrade, addresses of code accounts were bound to the deployer, i.e., the address which has sent the *CREATE* transaction and a deployer specific nonce. We shall call this approach *legacy addresses*. The upgrade introduced an alternative way to reference code accounts, which replaces the nonce with a commitment to code. We call this approach *code-bound addresses*.

---

[2] Ethereum Classic activated the Constatinople changes in January 2020 [23].

[3] We use *upgrade* to refer to changes of the platform and *update* for the possibility to alter code on the platform.

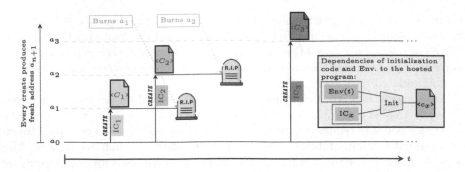

Fig. 1. Pre-Constantinople: addresses are single-use. *Deactivation* "burns" the address, i.e., future reuse is impossible. IC_x stands for initialization code.

2.1 Updating Smart Contracts with Legacy Addresses

For legacy addresses, the address of a new code account is computed as

$$a_{n_d} = \text{createAddr}_{d,n_d}() = (\mathcal{H}(\text{rlp}(d, n_d)))_{0\ldots159}$$

where $\mathcal{H}$ is the 256-bit Keccak hash function, d is the deployer address, n_d is the nonce associated with the deployer address, $\text{rlp}(d, n_d)$ is the Recursive Length Prefix (RLP) encoding of d and n_d, and $(\cdot)_{0\ldots159}$ denotes talking the 160 least significant bits of the value [40]. For externally owned accounts, which are controlled by private keys, n_d is the number of transactions sent. For code accounts, the nonce equals the number of code accounts already created from that address. As nonces increase strictly monotonically, creating the same address twice is unlikely.[4] The Byzantium upgrade[5] introduced a precaution against the residual risk of address collision: account creations fail if either a program or a non-zero nonce is associated with the target address (defined in EIP-684 [9]).

Figure 1 illustrates how new programs are created using legacy addresses. The vertical axis depicts the address space. Every new program is deployed to a new unique address. When a program is *deactivated*, by executing the **SELFDESTRUCT** instruction, the address is burned and cannot be reused. The actual code C hosted at an address a is defined by the output of an *initialization code* IC provided in the **CREATE** transaction. Since the initialization code can access the state of the blockchain, the deployed code can also depend on the environment at the time of creation. In practice, many initialization codes return a constant.

Updating smart contracts created with legacy addresses is complicated. As the code at a given address is fixed, and changing all references to a new address is impractical and risky, developers must prepare their applications for updates by using e. g., the transparent proxy pattern [14,19]. This means splitting a program over multiple code accounts so that the main program is called indirectly from a stub that resides at a permanent address (and thus cannot be updated). The stub

---

[4] The odds are one in 2^{80} accounts, following from the birthday problem.
[5] Effective since 2017-10-16 07:22:11 GMT+2.

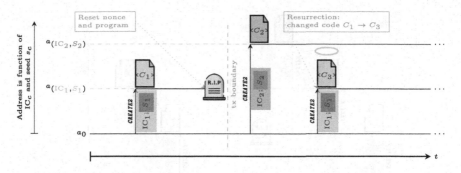

Fig. 2. Post-Constantinople: addresses are reusable. This enables *resurrections*. With the right initialization code, it is possible to change the program code.

stores the address of the current main program in its state, and allows authorized parties to change the value. This way smart contracts become patchable.

Popular libraries, like OpenZeppelin, provide off-the-shelf solutions for this pattern [31]. Several EIPs seek to standardize the proxy pattern [20,25,32,33]. None of the proposals appears to be final and only some of them are used.[6]

2.2 Updating Smart Contracts with Code-Bound Addresses

The *CREATE2* instruction differs from *CREATE* in the way it calculates addresses:

$$a(i, s) = \text{create2Addr}_d(i, s) = (\ \mathcal{H}(\ 255 \parallel d \parallel s \parallel \mathcal{H}(i)\ )\ )_{0...159}$$

where s is a 32-byte seed, i is the initialization code, and $\parallel$ denotes concatenation [10]. Code-bound addresses are tied to the initialization code IC and the deployer address, but not on the nonce. The constant 255 prevents collisions with legacy addresses because RLP encodings starting with 255 would imply petabytes of data. The seed s can be chosen freely to enable factory contracts that create multiple code accounts sharing the same initialization code.

Since *CREATE2* does not bind the address to a nonce, creating collisions is easy: use the same deployer account with the same seed and initialization code IC. However, *CREATE2* fails if the target address already hosts a program [9]; unless the code account is *deactivated*. After deactivation, it is possible to recreate a code account on the same address. We call this *resurrection*.[7]

Figure 2 illustrates a resurrection of an address. Observe that since code-bound addresses commit to the initialization code and not the actual program code, it is indeed possible to deploy a different program after a resurrection. For

---

[6] Using simple heuristics derived from the EIPS we found 223 873 following EIP-897, 0 following EIP-1167, 22 238 following EIP-1822, and 31 432 following EIP-1967.

[7] Deactivation and the resurrection cannot take place in the same transaction because the use of *SELFDESTRUCT* resets the account and its nonce at the very end of the transaction. But it is possible within the same block.

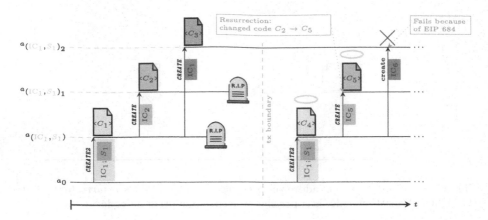

Fig. 3. Post-Constantinople: *cascaded resurrections* of code accounts created with *CREATE* are possible because nonces of code accounts are no longer monotonic.

this the output of the initialization code must depend on the blockchain state. We call this behavior *morphing resurrection*.

```
return address(0xABC...DEF).
    get_code();
```

Example 1.1. Morphing resurrection involving another code account

```
if block.number > 1000000 {
    return "0x123...";
} else {
    return "0x345...";
}
```

Example 1.2. Morphing resurrection with simple condition

Example 1.1, sketches initialization code which fetches the program code to be deployed from the code account at address 0xABC...DEF.[8] Another, less flexible, approach is to include different programs as constants in the initialization code and select the return value based on the state of the environment (e. g., the block height). This is shown in Example 1.2.

2.3   Interaction of *CREATE* and *CREATE2*

Perhaps unexpectedly, the use of *CREATE2* makes it possible to resurrect programs created with the *CREATE* instruction. This requires some indirections. Recall that *CREATE2* can reset the nonce of a code account by resurrecting it. This breaks the monotonicity of nonces which prevented collisions. If the code account we can resurrect with *CREATE2*, has used *CREATE* to generate child code accounts, then these children can be resurrected with *CREATE* [35]. Figure 3 sketches this process, which we call *cascaded resurrection*.

The interaction of *CREATE* and *CREATE2* means that to detect possible resurrections, it is not sufficient to check for the immediate use of *CREATE2*. Instead, the entire deployer chain must be analyzed. Only code accounts deployed with

---

[8] We prefer pseudo-code over Solidity because Solidity does not offer a way to encode explicit returns in constructors without the use of inline EVM assembly.

CREATE before the Constantinople upgrade are safe because it was not possible to have a *CREATE2* transactions in the deployer chain.

More generally, while it was possible to detect the proxy pattern (or the absence thereof) by inspecting the deployed code, the Constantinople update made it much more difficult for users to reason about the immutability of smart contacts. Almost two years after the Constantinople upgrade, we are not aware of any block explorer or open blockchain analytics tool offering a convenient way to see the deployment history of a contract, or simply whether it was created using *CREATE* or *CREATE2*. Etherscan does show if a code account had a resurrection. This is a first step, but users need to know in advance if an account is resurrectable.

3   Measurement Motivation

Updating code accounts by resurrection is a fundamental change to the EVM's security model. Attackers can use (cascaded) morphing resurrections to trick users into depositing value into an account hosting seemingly benign code, and replace it with a malicious version before the victim executes a transaction to claim value back. While community sources suggest that this change might have been introduced unintentionally [28,35,38], the question we ask is how the Constantinople upgrade has affected the ecosystem. To do so, we carry out empirical measurements, including—to the best of our knowledge for the first time—a heuristic to detect potentially resurrectable code accounts.

This section decomposes the effects of the upgrade into six items of interest (IoIs), some offering mainly benefits and others increasing the attack surface. The measurement methods and results in later sections will speak to these IoI.

3.1   IoIs Relating to Feature Expansion

Cheaper Patching (i). *CREATE2* makes updateable smart contracts cheaper. Resurrections avoid the overhead of splitting the smart contracts into multiple code accounts, and the communication overhead required for transparent up-gradable proxies [35]. This way, smart contracts can be patched. Users must be wary if patching is desired and if they trust the party who can patch.

Generalized State Channels (ii). Counterfactual instantiation [13], the possibility to commit to settlement code of a state channel before deployment, was the declared intention for adding *CREATE2* to the EVM's instruction set. Code-bound addresses enable exactly this. However, recall from Sect. 2.2 that the hash is taken over the initialization code that produces the program code. Parties using counterfactual instantiation should check if the counterfactual initialization code is static:

Definition 1. *An initialization code is **static** if its return value does not depend on the environment at execution time.*

If one party could trick the other in agreeing on non-static initialization code, it could appropriate all funds in the state channel independent of the agreement.

Wallet On-Boarding (iii). Using wallet code accounts instead of externally owned accounts has many advantages. Wallets decouple the authentication from the addresses holding funds. This gives users advanced recovery options in the case of lost keys. To create wallet code accounts, users need funds to pay the transaction fee of the creation. Before the upgrade, this meant users had to have a funded externally owned account to claim a new wallet code account. The upgrade made on-boarding easier by using a counterfactual instantiation of the wallet, which can immediately receive funds.

Vanity Addresses (iv). Some users prefer short addresses, found after grinding through hash pre-images. The main rational is to save gas cost. Vanity addresses can (a) be packed more tightly in case of leading zeros; or (b) are cheaper to pass as call parameters, since zero bytes get a discount [40]. In the absence of a common definition of vanity addresses, we define them as follows:

Definition 2. *A **vanity address** is an address with more than four leading zero bytes.*

Vanity addresses for code accounts existed before the Constantinople upgrade. Users had to draw key pairs and then inspect the (legacy) addresses induced by the first few nonces [27]. Code-bound addresses allow to grind though seed space rather than key space. This not only facilitates the process, but also permits to out-source the grinding of vanity addresses for code accounts [3]. Those addresses can then be sold. This makes vanity addresses a commodity on the platform.

3.2   IoIs Relating to an Expansion of the Attack Surface

Honeypots (v). Morphing resurrections simplify the creation of honeypots, i. e., decoy accounts that appear vulnerable but are not. In some way, honeypots are the Ethereum version of advance fee fraud known as "491 scam" in conventional cybercrime [6]. Typically, users must send some funds to a code account (e. g., to pay fees) in order to extract greater values.

Known honeypots use barely known features of the execution environment, popular programming languages, or block explorers to trick users into misinterpreting contracts as vulnerable [39]. Resurrectable code accounts allow an attacker to deploy actually vulnerable code and then front-run the interaction of the victim with a resurrection. Simple countermeasures, which look for *SELFDESTRUCT* instructions, fail if cascaded resurrections and indirections with delegate calls are used to obscure the control flow.

Underpriced Instructions (vi). The gas price of Ethereum instructions is calibrated carefully to render resource exhaustion attacks uneconomical [11,12,34]. Resurrectable accounts offer cheaper permanent storage [5]. The idea is that instead of keeping data in the state of a code account, data can be stored as program code in a new account. Writing data this way costs roughly 2/3 of conventional storage. (Updates are more expensive.) Reading this data can be as cheap as 1/4 of the conventional cost if multiple words are read. While estimating an attacker's break even is beyond our scope, we note that underpriced instructions have enabled DoS attacks in the past [22,24].

4 Data Collection and Method

We parse the Ethereum blockchain until Jul 2021[9]. We extract the set of all deployed code accounts C and build the binary contract–deployer relation $R \subseteq C^2$ by iterating over all internal transactions. Let $(a, b) \in R$ denote that a is deployer of b. Our heuristic to evaluate if a contract is resurrectable is based on the this relation and some heuristics to evaluate the reachability of critical instructions.

Definition 3. *A code account $c \in C$ is **potentially resurrectable** iff this recursively defined function evaluates to true:*

$$
\text{resurr}(c) = \begin{cases} \text{true,} & \textit{if } \text{create2Created}(c) \wedge \overline{\text{sdestrReachable}(c)} \\ \text{false,} & \textit{if } \text{deployer}(c) = \emptyset \vee \overline{\text{sdestrReachable}(c)} \\ \text{resurr}(\text{deployer}(c)), & \textit{otherwise.} \end{cases}
$$

The deployer function is defined as: $\text{deployer}(c) = \{ a \mid (a, c) \in R \}$. It returns either an empty set or a set of cardinality 1 from our deployer relation. The function create2Created is true if c is deployed with $CREATE2$.

The Ethereum node does not distinguish between $CREATE$ and $CREATE2$ in any of their public APIs. Currently, we are aware of two approaches to distinguish between the two: (a) directly instrumenting transaction executions at the level of the runtime environment level or (b) determining that $CREATE2$ was used by ruling out that $CREATE$ was used. We choose the latter since an instrumentation would have to rely on unstable APIs, which makes the method hard to maintain.

To rule out that code was deployed using the legacy method, we compile sets of all legacy addresses with nonces up to n_c, the current nonce of the code account. This is handled by the createAddrs function. If the address in question is not in this set, then it must be a code-bound address:

$$
\text{createAddrs}(c) = \bigcup_{n=0}^{n_c} (\mathcal{H}(\text{rlp}(a_c, n)))_{96\ldots 255}
$$

$$
\text{create2Created}(c) = \overline{\vee_{s \in \text{deployer}(c)} (a_c \in \text{createAddrs}(s))}.
$$

The function sdestrReachable returns true if a $SELFDESTRUCT$ instruction is reachable in the context of c, meaning the account can deactivate itself. Its implementation evaluates the presence of three instructions in the disassembled bytecode of the code account. First, we look for $SELFDESTRUCT$ directly; if present we return true. Second, we look for $DELEGATECALL$ or $CALLCODE$ instructions. Both instructions preserve the context of the caller, thus making it possible that the callee can invoke $SELFDESTRUCT$ in the context of the caller. If we find one of the two we also return true because we cannot rule out that the called code deactivates the account. Otherwise we return false.

To further tell if the code account is able to (a) change its state or (b) change its code upon resurrection, further non-trivial checks are needed. To rule out (a)

---

[9] Block: 12817905 (2021-07-13 11:07:50 GMT+2).

we need to show that the initialization code does not write to storage, or more strictly, that the storage writes do not depend on the system state or user input. To rule out (b) we need to establish that the return value of the initialization code does not depend on system state or user input. Both problems are not decidable for arbitrary program code.

Here we focus on an approximation of (b) to detect morphing resurrections. We run the initialization code of every code account in question in an instrumented runtime environment to find out if it is *static* (Definition 1). Our executions stop as soon as the initialization code accesses the environment to produce its output.[10] If no access to the environment is detected, we verify that the return value corresponds to the program found on-chain.

Static initialization code is only relevant for programs with code-bound addresses. In cascading resurrections, where *CREATE* is used for deployment, the resulting program can change even if the initialization code is static. This is so because legacy addresses are not bound to the initialization code in the first place. Therefore, our complete heuristic to detect potentially morphing resurrections distinguishes between the two cases.

Definition 4. *We call a code account **potentially morphing** if it is potentially resurrectable (Definition 3) and one of the two applies: 1. it was created with* CREATE*; 2. its initialization code is not static (Definition 1).*

Limitations. The heuristic to detect resurrectable code accounts over-estimates the reachability of *SELFDESTRUCT* instructions, i. e., it produces false positives. Conversely, we are not aware of cases in which false negatives could occur. Therefore, from the lens of a security analysis, it always errs on the side of caution.

Our heuristics do not take into account under which circumstances the critical instructions, such as *SELFDESTRUCT*, *CREATE2*, can be reached. For instance, the community has produced examples for counterfactual instantiation without the risk of resurrections [2,4]. This is done by keeping track of already created addresses within the state of the deployer code account. Application code ensures that deployments to addresses on the list fail. Our heuristic is currently blind to such safeguards on the application layer.

Our indicator for static initialization code produces false positives if the value of a transaction is used to decide which program to return at deployment time.

5   Measurement Results

Of the total of 32 634 990 code accounts deployed after the Constantinople upgrade, 15 159 524 (47%) are created with *CREATE2*. We proceed by discussing selected descriptive statistics for actual and then potential resurrections, before turning to the IoIs defined in Sect. 3. Table 2 in the appendix reports all findings with a larger set of indicators.

---

[10] We make an exception for access to the value of a transaction, since popular compilers add checks to avoid accidental value transfer.

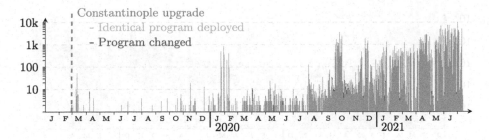

Fig. 4. Number of resurrections per day. Note the log axis.

5.1   Descriptive Analysis of Actual Resurrections

We find 225 032 (0.69%[11]) resurrections since the Constantinople upgrade. They affect 73 583 distinct addresses, with an average of 3.1 resurrections per account (see Table 1). Figure 4 suggest that adoption took off about one year after the upgrade.

Only 41 code accounts have seen *morphing* resurrections (i.e., with code updates), of which 31 use non-static initialization code to modify the program. The remaining 10 are cascaded resurrections deployed with `CREATE`.

To better understand the use of morphing resurrections, we manually investigate the transaction behavior of the associated accounts and searched the Internet for relevant pointers.[12] Information found on Etherscan (tags and comments) and Github (known bots) suggest that 16 of the 41 are likely trading bots. We found that all but 6 of the accounts have interacted with decentralized exchanges (DEXs). Their transaction behavior resembles front-running, such as holding different tokens over time and checking the balances for different tokens regularly. 16 of the 41 accounts are still active at the time of writing (5 Oct 2021). Etherscan tags 11 of them as front-running bots. Furthermore, 25 of the accounts use vanity addresses with up to 7 leading zeros-bytes. This suggests that a tiny group of technically advanced users is responsible for the morphing resurrections in our data.

It is remarkable that a large number of resurrections happened without changing code. Figure 8a in the appendix shows the distribution of unique byte-code instances used in these resurrections. Only four programs make up more than 90% of these resurrections. To better understand the purpose of these non-morphing but resurrecting accounts, we inspect their bytecode. The disassembly reveals that all of the four programs are gas tokens.

Gas tokens are instruments designed to hedge against gas price variations [27]. They make use of Ethereum's feature to refund gas upon freeing storage. The feature's intended purpose is to incentivize storage parsimony. However, it can be exploited to stock up gas when it is cheap by allocating excess storage.

---

[11] of total deployments after Constantinople.

[12] Table 3 lists the accounts that had morphing resurrections along with selected statistics. Table 4 documents our investigations regarding the purpose of these accounts. Both tables are in the appendix.

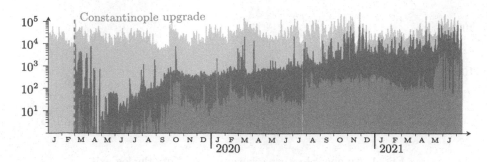

Fig. 5. Number of daily code account-creations since the Constantinople upgrade. All creations (green), code-bound addresses Definition 3 (orange), code-bound addresses without Chi-Gas-Token (blue), potentially resurrectable code-bound addresses Definition 4 (red). Note the log scale. (Color figure online)

To redeem gas tokens when gas prices are high, excess storage is freed within the execution of a consuming transaction. This scheme can be used to subsidize up to 50% of the transaction's gas cost. The use of code-bound addresses for gas tokens has been popularized by 1inch's Chi-Gas-Token [30] to reduce its own gas usage, thus making it slightly more efficient.

The resurrected gas tokens in our data were deployed by only 8 code accounts. Six of them have seen morphing resurrections and are identified as front-running bots on Etherscan (in tags or comments). This and our manual analysis suggest that all of the above mentioned deployers are front-running bots using their own gas tokens to make arbitrage trades even cheaper.

5.2 Descriptive Analysis of Potential Resurrections

Figure 5 shows the creation of code accounts since the Constantinople upgrade. The total number of new code accounts fluctuates roughly between 10^4–10^5 new instances per day.[13] About 45% of all deployments since the upgrade (14 796 170) are potentially resurrectable code accounts, meaning that they satisfy Definition 3. Figure 9 in the appendix shows the degree distribution of the deployer relation used by this heuristic. All accounts that have seen *actual* resurrections (73 583, see Sect. 5.1) are correctly identified as *potentially resurrectable*. This increases our confidence in the validity of the heuristic indicator.

Figure 7a in the appendix shows the number of potentially resurrectable creations relative to the total number of newly created code accounts. Before May 2020, we see very little use of potentially resurrectable programs in relation to the total number of deployments. From May 2020 onwards, the share of potentially resurrectable code accounts rises sharply and stays relatively constant at around 70–80% of all deployments.

We can attribute a large share (~69.25%) to one system, called Chi-Gas-Token. Although its accounts satisfy our resurrection heuristic (Definition 3),

---

[13] 442/12 466/29 865/38 076/279 202 (min/25%/50%/75%/max).

they are not morphing (Definition 4) because their initialization code is always static (Definition 1).

A total of 109 195 resurrectable code accounts do *not* have static initialization code, according to our heuristic. These, plus the accounts with potential for cascaded resurrections (230 of which 159 have static initialization code) add up to 109 354 potentially problematic accounts. Recall that these accounts can potentially update their code at any time. Even worse, this possibility is not apparent even when the source code of the account is inspected. Still, the share of such accounts is small (0.74% of all potentially resurrectable accounts) and it does not seem to increase over time (see Fig. 7b).

5.3   Results on the Items of Interest

Cheaper Patching (IoI i). The very limited number (41) of accounts that had morphing resurrections suggests that only a small group of advanced users are currently aware of this possibility. Front-running bots seem to be the predominant users of morphing resurrection as they can benefit in two ways: a) it allows them to adapt their strategies easily by updating code if needed, and b) it allows them to reuse funds that are already on the account, removing the need to move funds around. Before the upgrade, this would have required a proxy, which adds a layer of indirection and thus increases communication cost. Hence, *CREATE2* mainly improves the transaction efficiency of front-running bots. We have no indication of *CREATE2* being used for cheaper patching elsewhere.

Generalized State Channels (IoI ii). This use case (as well as the next) would imply that we see a value transfer before the first deployment of the code account. To analyze that, we inspect the transaction history and parse the first four transactions of all resurrectable contracts.

For state channels, we would expect at least two participants to pre-fund the account before its creation. In addition, we expect both participants to fund the channel with amounts of the same magnitude, i.e., $\frac{1}{10} < \frac{a}{b} < 10$ where $a, b \in \mathbb{N}$. We find only 360 potentially resurrectable accounts that meet this state channel heuristic. This can mean either a) the heuristic is too restrictive (e.g., state channels use tokens for pre-funding), or b) state channels in practice do not rely on counterfactual instantiation, or c) state channels are barely used. Online information suggests that state channels are not really used on the Ethereum platform. The Github repository of Counterfactual, a project that aims to enable state channels on Ethereum, is archived and has not seen any activity for more than two years.[14] Given that state channels were the main reason for the introduction of *CREATE2* [10], this lack of adoption is surprising.

Wallet On-Boarding (IoI ii). For the purpose of on-boarding, we expect more than one transaction funding the account before it is created. As for state channels, our analysis focuses on ether and does not consider tokens. We find that

---

[14] https://github.com/counterfactual/monorepo, accessed: 15th Oct 21.

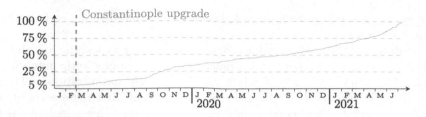

Fig. 6. Adoption of vanity addresses. Almost all of the 351 vanity addresses are created after the Constantinople upgrade. The vanity addresses are deployed by 231 accounts. Only two of them have created more than five vanity addresses. Both are immutable *CREATE2* factories [4].

696 230 of the resurrectable accounts (4.7%) were pre-funded before deployment. This amounts to 95% of the accounts that have been pre-funded after Constantinople.[15] To shed more light into the use of these accounts we analyze their deployers. We find 180 different deployers for all pre-funded addresses. 95% of the accounts where created by 8 deployers only. We could identify 82% of the deployed accounts as either wallets or forwarder accounts. Forwarder accounts are used to create fresh deposit addresses [17,26]. In summary, we observe that wallet on-boarding is indeed a practical use case of *CREATE2* for its predictable addresses, but this use case does not need the feature to update code.

Vanity Addresses (IoI iv). Figure 6 shows that most vanity addresses are deployed after the Constantinople upgrade.

   The upgrade in principle enables the commodification of vanity addresses for code accounts. For this, we would expect a small number of suppliers specialized on grinding vanity addresses and selling them to interested parties by deploying code on their customers' behalf. (Recall that *CREATE2* still binds the derived address to the deployer. Therefore, only the supplier can create a contract at a derived address.) So far, we do not see any indication of trade with vanity addresses. Only one code account deployed a significant share (84 of 351) of vanity addresses.[16] It implements a code account that facilitates deployments using *CREATE2* without the risk of resurrections [4], but it does not include any trading functionality. Moreover, the front-running bot that brings their own version of gas tokens (see Sect. 5.1) also uses vanity addresses. This increases gas efficiency at deployment time because addresses are stored in bytecode without leading zeros.

Honeypots, IoI v. Since we see so few mutating resurrections, it is safe to state that *CREATE2* is not used in honeypots at a large scale.

Underpriced Instructions, IoI vi. It is generally hard to tell if code accounts are repurposed as cheap long-term data storage. Analyzing this would require

---

[15] In total we have seen 731 268 pre-funded accounts after Constantinople. As expected, almost all of them (729 577) were deployed via *CREATE2*.

[16] 0x0000000000ffe8b47b3e2130213b802212439497.

low-level instrumentation of the execution environment to measure the use of EXTCODECOPY and the values derived from it in computations. What we can conclude from our measurement, however, is that resurrections are currently not widely used as a cheap substitute for *updateable* storage, as this would involve morphing resurrections. To evaluate the potential of contracts being used as write-once storage, we make the assumption that such a storage code account would never receive or send any messages. Data is read using the EXTCODECOPY instruction only. We find 697 760 code accounts created using *CREATE2* that match this assumption.[17] Most of them (82%) are Chi-Gas-Tokens, leaving us with an upper bound of 125 692 potential write-once storage accounts.

6   Related Work

This work speaks to how users can verify the immutability of smart contracts, and the tension between immutable code and the ability to correct bugs. It also contributes to the nascent literature measuring the impact of platform upgrades.

Immutability. Fröwis et al. [19] study the immutability of control flow with static program analysis. Using heuristics, they estimate that 40% of the code accounts on Ethereum host program code that could change its control flow by updating dynamic references. Code updates were not on the horizon as the study predates the Constantinople upgrade by several years. Zhou et al. [41] present Erays, an Ethereum reverse engineering tool that lifts EVM bytecode to human-readable pseudo-code. The human-readable representation simplifies manual inspection of smart contracts and thus the identification of mutable code paths. Di Angelo et al. [16] review unintended use-cases of initialization code on Ethereum. They argue that a lack of understanding of the role of initialization code opens opportunities for deception and fraud in scenarios like token harvesting and gambling. In particular, initialization code can be used to circumvent automated checks to tell code accounts and externally owned accounts apart.

Patching. Numerous academic works concern the identification of vulnerabilities in smart contracts [15, 21]. Whereas, only a couple of publications discuss techniques to fix bugs once discovered. We focus on the latter. Rodler et al. [37] present EVMPatch, a tool that uses bytecode rewriting to automate the creation of updateable smart contracts with the transparent proxy pattern. It combines bytecode analysis with regression testing—partly based on the transaction history—to avoid breaks during the update. Azzopardi et al. [7] explore the use of runtime verification to recover from bugs in code accounts. They present ContractLarva, a monitoring framework that allows to encode execution invariants and recovery strategies using a domain specific language. Colombo et al. [14] extend the work of Azzopardi and discuss recovery approaches in the case of

---

[17] To reduce the bias by contracts created towards the end of our observation period, we only considered code account until two month before the end of our measurement period. Without this, cutoff we find 3 158 545 matching code accounts.

violated execution invariants. They describe how invariant-preserving updates could be implemented using the proxy pattern. Dickerson et al. [18] take another approach. They propose proof-carrying code to allow for invariant-preserving updates. Every program deployed comes with a proof that some important invariant is never violated. In the event of a patch, the runtime system ensures that the new code preserves the invariants specified in the original code.

All of the works mentioned above rely on the proxy pattern to enable code updates. The works of Rodler and Dickerson would benefit from the cheaper patch mechanism provided by *CREATE2*. The approach of Azzopardi and Colombo can only partly benefit from *CREATE2*; they reuse the proxy to encode the behavioral invariants the contract must preserve, thus adapting this to *CREATE2* does not immediately avoid expensive indirections.

Platform Upgrades. We are aware of three measurement studies that directly evaluate the effects of platform upgrades. Perez et al. [34] and Chen et al. [12] measure underpriced instructions after the upgrade including EIP-150, which increased gas prices to avoid DoS attacks. Recently, Reijsbergen et al. [36] evaluate the effects of the changes in the calculation of transaction fees introduced by EIP-1559. We deem this under-researched and believe that the governance of platforms such as Ethereum should stand on solid empirical foundations.

7   Conclusion

This work describes the impact and measures the adoption of *CREATE2*, a new EVM instruction that makes address assignment more predictable. Our measurement is motivated by a side effect of *CREATE2* with security implications, namely the ability to patch code accounts in place. We have proposed a novel heuristic indicator to identify *CREATE2*-patchable code accounts, and applied it to the relevant two years of Ethereum blockchain data.

The data shows that *CREATE2* has become the dominant form of deployment since May 2020. But the dominance is largely driven by gas tokens using *CREATE2* to increase their efficiency. As expected, wallet and forwarder contracts have also adopted *CREATE2*. They benefit from the intended use case of *CREATE2*, *counterfactual instantiation*, i.e., contracts that can be funded before they are deployed. Interestingly, we do not find any indication of state channels using *CREATE2*, despite this was the proclaimed reason for the addition of *CREATE2*.

Patching via *CREATE2* has seen very little use since the upgrade. Mainly the infrastructure of front-running seems to take advantage of it. A manual analysis of all relevant accounts lets us conclude that this new and opaque form of code patching is—so far—not used maliciously to defraud users. Still, according to our heuristic there are more than 100k accounts with the potential to change their code in the future. The community is well advised to keep watching this.

In summary, we conjecture that the main reason for the limited use of *CREATE2* for patching is a lack of awareness. Moreover, none of the use cases we discussed, or that were discussed in the proposal of *CREATE2*, use the patching feature. This feature increases the attack surface without need, and offers limited benefit to a few experienced users only.

Acknowledgments. We would like to thank Patrik Keller and Bernhard Haslhofer for their valuable feedback. This work has received funding from the Austrian Research Promotion Agency (FFG) and the Austrian Security Research Programme (KIRAS).

A   Supplemental Figures and Tables

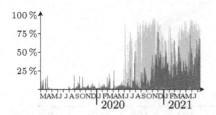

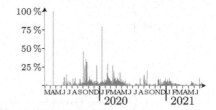

(a) Daily creations of potentially resurrectable code accounts, relative to the total number of creations and the number of creations of code-bound addresses.

(b) Percentage of new potentially resurrectable account creations (red) in relation to total resurrectable code, without Chi-Gas-Token.

Fig. 7. New potentially resurrectable code accounts per day (Color figure online)

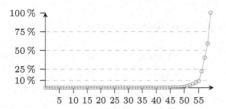

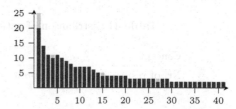

(a) 60 bytecode instances used by 73 554 resurrecting accounts that never changed their code (over a total of 224 830 resurrections). Only four bytecode instances appear in 90 % of the deployments.

(b) 189 bytecode instances used in 202 morphing resurrections on 41 accounts. The light blue parts show the code instances seen more than once. Almost all morphing resurrections deploy fresh code.

Fig. 8. Bytecode instances used in resurrections; redeployment of identical code (left) and morphing resurrections (right). (Color figure online)

Figure 9 shows the cumulative distribution of out-degrees of the deployer-relation.[18] Only 189 919 (0.41%) accounts in our relation have no deployer. These result from deployments from externally owned accounts. Hence, almost all code accounts were created by another code account.

---

[18] The in-degree distribution is binary since every code account has exactly one deployer. Only externally owned accounts have no deployer.

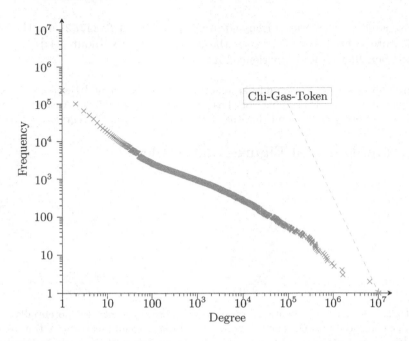

Fig. 9. The Ethereum deployer relation. Only 5 code accounts deployed more than 1 million other code accounts. The biggest contributors are the Chi-Gas-Token ($\approx 10\,\mathrm{m}$), Gas Token.io: GST2 ($\approx 6.4\,\mathrm{m}$), MevBot ($\approx 1.6\,\mathrm{m}$), Bitrex: Controller ($\approx 1.6\,\mathrm{m}$), MMM BSC ($\approx 1\,\mathrm{m}$). MevBot is one of the contracts that have seen morphing resurrections.

Table 1. Distribution of actual resurrections per account

Concept	Statistic		ref
Nr. of resurrections per account	mean	3.1	Sect. 5.1
	min	2.0	–
	25 %	2.0	–
	50 %	2.0	–
	75 %	3.0	–
	max	645.0	–
Nr. of morphing resurrection per account	mean	5.2	–
	min	2.0	–
	25 %	2.0	–
	50 %	3.0	–
	75 %	7.0	–
	max	25.0	–

Table 2. Dataset summary

	Concept	#	Share	of*	Reference
1	Highest block	12 817 905	–	–	Sect. 4
2	Total code accounts created	45 666 538	–	–	–
3	Creations after Constantinople	32 634 990	71.5%	2	Sect. 5
4	Pre-funded before deployment	731 268	2.2%	3	Sect. 5.1, IoI iii
5	State channel pre-funding	7231	–	–	IoI ii
6	Total *CREATE2* creations	15 159 524	46.5%	3	Sect. 5
7	Pre-funded before deployment	729 577	99.69%	4	Sect. 5.1, IoI iii
8	State channel pre-funding	7173	99.2%	5	IoI ii
9	Vanity addresses	351	–	–	IoI iv, Definition 2
	Observed Resurrections				
10	**Total resurrections**	225 032	1.5%	6	Sect. 5.1
11	Accounts with resurrections	73 583	–	–	Sect. 5.1
12	Unique programs	247	–	–	–
13	Unique initialization codes	549	–	–	–
14	Unique deployers	123	–	–	–
15	Vanity addresses	27	7.7%	9	IoI iv, Definition 2
16	Pre-funded before deployment	360	0.05%	4	Sect. 5.1, IoI iii
17	State channel pre-funding	2	0.03%	5	IoI ii
18	**Morphing resurrections**	202	0.1%	10	IoI v
19	Accounts with resurrections	41	0.05%	11	Sect. 5.1, IoI i
20	Unique programs	189	76.5%	12	–
21	Unique initialization codes	18	3.3%	13	–
22	Unique deployers	30	24.4%	14	–
23	Vanity addresses	25	92.6%	15	IoI iv, Definition 2
24	Pre-funded before deployment	1	–	–	Sect. 5.1, IoI iii
25	State channel pre-funding	0	–	–	IoI ii
	Potential for Resurrections				
26	**Potentially resurrectable accounts**	14 796 170	45.3%	3	Sect. 5.2, Definition 3
27	Unique programs	11 024	–	–	–
28	Unique initialization codes	58 295	–	–	–
29	Unique deployers	1218	–	–	–
30	Vanity addresses	66	18.8%	9	Sect. 5.1, IoI iv, Definition 2
31	Pre-funded before deployment	696 230	95.2%	4	Sect. 5.1, IoI iii
32	State channel pre-funding	6323	87.4%	5	Sect. 5.1, IoI ii
33	**Without Chi-Gas-Token**	4 549 820	30.7%	26	–
34	Unique programs	11 023	99.99%	27	–
35	Unique initialization codes	58 294	100%	28	–
36	Unique deployers	1212	99.5%	29	–
37	Vanity addresses	66	100%	30	Sect. 5.1, IoI iv, Definition 2
38	Pre-funded before deployment	696 228	99.99%	31	IoI iii
39	State channel pre-funding	6323	100%	32	IoI ii
40	**Potentially Morphing**	109 354	2.4%	34	Sect. 5.1, Definition 4
41	Unique programs	286	2.6%	35	–
42	Unique initialization codes	29 739	51%	36	–
43	Unique deployers	327	27%	37	–
44	Vanity addresses	46	69.7%	38	IoI iv, Definition 2
45	Pre-funded before deployment	5970	–	–	IoI iii
46	State channel pre-funding	248	–	–	IoI ii

* **of** refers to the row number used as base to calculate the percentage.

Table 3. Accounts with morphing resurrection until mid Jul 2021. USD values based on current ETH Price (Coinbase midpoint price 5th Oct 21).

Address	Deployed	First seen	Last seen	Calls in	Calls out	Nr deploy.	Tsd. USD in	Nr redeploy.	Cascaded	Static	IC
0x45503c34ee615c4ed5fe071fc6ccee06c049b1e3	Apr 03 20	Apr 02 20	Apr 03 20	20	31	0	0.4	9	○	○	○
0x000000000006f65502b7f2bbac6c30a3f67e9a	Jun 21 21	May 01 20	Jul 13 21	1706881	2154591	210025	4511394.6	11	○	○	○
0x000000009b988fbecfd83c55252f78592e609648	Aug 11 20	Aug 11 20	Aug 11 20	3	3	0	0.0	2	○	●	○
0xd1c300000000b961df238f700ef006000097000049	Nov 24 20	Aug 21 20	Nov 24 20	31819	109464	0	0.0	2	○	○	○
0x00f8d52a00f600094ebf903ce0000defb00f20000	Aug 26 20	Aug 26 20	Aug 28 20	50	124	0	18.7	2	○	○	○
0x00000000000740a22fa209cf6806d38f7605385	Sep 29 20	Sep 23 20	Oct 01 20	12083	29775	2729	4592.8	6	○	○	○
0x0000000005af5bf8581e51143248bcf395abb892	Sep 24 20	Sep 24 20	Sep 24 20	19	37	0	0.0	7	○	○	○
0x0000000002bde777710c370e08fc83d61b2b8e1	Oct 26 20	Sep 24 20	Nov 27 20	51592	131551	18412	0.0	11	●	●	○
0x0000000000a32dc5dd625c107898a1c72ad34a	Oct 21 20	Sep 30 20	Jul 13 21	306669	680114	91126	93585.6	7	○	○	○
0x0000000007e35d4ff0153a18de63c4f58f04fd1c	Oct 17 20	Oct 21 20	Nov 27 20	3147	7938	1258	0.0	7	○	○	○
0x00000000000159bc46c8937716994557745ba335c8	Oct 23 20	Oct 17 20	Oct 18 20	74	77	106	11.3	2	○	○	○
0x00000000000f150bd6f54c40a34d7c3d5e9f56	Jun 23 21	Oct 22 20	Oct 23 20	19	120	0	1.1	3	○	●	○
0x0000000000438f975cbde76d5fdd1aa76be46577	May 05 21	Oct 23 20	Jul 13 21	3866901	17286031	1647068	13194058.0	25	●	●	○
0x009eede30408000db000064ab00bd00f1a3000b38	Dec 10 20	Nov 10 20	Jul 13 21	149167	943153	3254	224884.2	3	○	○	○
0x49307d775728daf1d4736ab762de0cefd035e323	Jan 22 21	Nov 22 20	Apr 21 21	14461	183112	0	5555.6	3	○	○	○
0x1d6e8bac6ea3730825bde4b005ed7b2b39a2932d	May 12 21	Nov 26 20	Jun 15 21	798	2774	0	138894.0	2	○	○	○
0x1b3006d57d5d9653a4ecaea6cfb0fd72a1537cc9	Jul 10 21	Dec 06 20	Jul 13 21	93570	218701	29559	13773.4	8	●	●	○
0x577a32aa9c40cf4266e49fc1e44c749c356309bd	Mar 04 21	Dec 06 20	Jul 13 21	281995	659645	79444	49336.1	14	●	●	●
0x0000000000b69ec332f49b7c4d2b101f93c3bed	Apr 24 21	Dec 12 20	Jul 11 21	60693	164671	62131	3316.4	3	●	●	○
0x00000000057367775feb0c8568e7dee77222a26880	May 14 21	Dec 12 20	Apr 24 21	32106	57804	6149	2752.7	4	●	○	○
0x00000000000f095b1b50de78b7a6bc4697b2927	Jun 28 21	Jan 07 21	May 14 21	97	141	141	36.6	3	○	●	○
0x4bd372cd9bedd45e0e23c769bb18f79dd055a32f2	May 04 21	Jan 09 21	Jul 13 21	60853	139957	35553	7050.9	11	●	●	○
0x00000000751edf02c727ea9d0c1c8e64f169e343	Mar 04 21	Jan 15 21	Jul 12 21	1902	6309	579	17.2	7	●	●	○
0x000000000000d736bd9b915d8fe98e9c507df85a	Jan 31 21	Jan 19 21	Jun 01 21	141	1030	500	8.7	2	●	●	○
0xf3c62891b48c51152dca70e0da62f7e1d8c2cc5bb	Jan 21 21	Jan 20 21	Apr 14 21	15843	27097	2951	0.0	4	○	○	○
0xff0cca1818ddc0d66b53a96a9aa8bda9043e1437	Feb 23 21	Jan 21 21	Mar 26 21	5700	20659	1826	8.6	5	○	○	○
0xc79eb641599e51930acd560c9dd60d81ca4fb831	Mar 29 21	Feb 23 21	Feb 26 21	190	139	31	0.0	7	●	●	●
0x0000000b7ca7e12dcc72290d1fe47b2ef14c607	Apr 26 21	Mar 29 21	Apr 08 21	163	6	0	0.0	4	○	○	○
0x0000000003b3cc22af3ae1eac0440bcee416b40	Jun 06 21	Apr 22 21	May 14 21	1240	3546	1178	16.8	2	○	●	○
0x000000099cb7fc48a935bceb9f05bbae54e8987	May 06 21	Apr 23 21	Jul 13 21	665	3771	0	1151.3	10	●	●	○
0x21a3d0b8289de546402fdfff2b1c860975cda090	Jul 02 21	Apr 28 21	Jul 13 21	125222	283691	101796	4991.2	3	●	○	○
0xc654334d2a598c323e04fd1435566b08609af008dc	May 24 21	May 21 21	Jul 13 21	120562	261578	86112	14092.5	4	●	●	○
0x0000000000035b5e5ad9019092c665357240f594e	Jun 07 21	May 24 21	Jul 13 21	68455	153976	42912	5090.3	3	●	●	○
0x55eb586558f2202f8339487886fedba2a1eb7b2d7	Jun 02 21	May 25 21	Jul 13 21	593	1716	117	4.6	4	○	●	○
0x0000000a680073b2eee93abeb4af4d4a096f8	Jun 06 21	Jun 02 21	Jul 13 21	3495	10088	1700	1064.1	3	●	●	○
0x00000000032962b515897668282ad878876299e14	Jul 09 21	Jun 06 21	Jul 13 21	50540	114525	33312	1863.5	3	●	●	○
0x0000000009042b40070c8f83bff12933005dc25257	Feb 28 19	Feb 28 19	Feb 28 19	34	68	0	1470.1	4	○	○	●
0x7f0000006128132800740006000f710002bdbaa9c	May 06 21	Apr 08 19	May 06 21	14	7	0	70.7	5	○	○	○

Table 4. Analysis of morphing accounts; Balances from Etherscan on 5th October 21.

Address	Active	DEX	Known Bot	Bot Comment	Bot tag	Comments	Balance USD
0x0000000000006f65502b7f2bbac8c30a3f67e9a	●	●	●	●	●	by eth	48m
0x00000000000007f1150b46f54c40a34d7c3d5e9f56	●	●	●	●	●	third largest contract deployer	3.8m
0x00000000032962b51588976882d8a8787876299e14	●	●	○	○	●	Miner are top receivers	2.5m
0x5eb58655f8202ff83948786fedba2a1eb7b2d7	●	●	○	○	○	—	833k
0x0000000000eb4ec62758aa93400b3e5f7f18	●	●	○	○	○	comments suggest Nice Hash but transactions look a like	736k
0x0000000999cb7fc48a935bceb9f05bbae54e8987	●	●	●	●	●	Front-running bot	219k
0x00000000035b5e5ad9019092c665357240f594e	●	●	●	●	●			100k
0x0000000006800073b2eee93abeb4af4d4a096f8	●	●	●	●	●			68k
0x493074f75f7284af1d4736ab7f62a0ef035e323	●	●	●	●	●			0
0x1d6e8bacfeea3730825bda4b005ea7b2b39a2932d	●	●	●	●	●			0
0x00000000005f7367f75fcb0c8568e7dee7f222a26880	●	●	●	●	●			0
0x000000000003b3cc22af3aa01eac0440bcse416940	●	●	●	●	●			0
0x00000000b7ca7e12dcc72290d1fe47b2ef14c607	●	●	●	●	●			0
0x00000000004736db9b9915d8fe98e9c507dtf85a	●	●	●	●	●			0
0x455c03c34ee615c4ed5fe071fc6ccee06c049b1e3	○	●	○	○	○			350
0x00000000002bde777710c370ea08fc83d61b2b8e1	○	●	○	○	○			0
0x00000000000a32dc5dd625c107899a1c72ad34a	○	●	●	●	●			0
0x00000000000159bc46c8937f71699455745ba335c8	○	○	○	○	○			0
0x00000000004385f976cde76d5fdd1aa76be46577	○	●	○	○	○			0
0x1b3006d57d5d9653a4ecaea6cfb0fd7a1537fc9	○	●	○	○	○			0
0x577a32aa9c40cf4266ea9f1e44c749c356309bd	○	●	○	○	○			344
0x00000000009f095b1b50da78b7a6bc469f7b2927	○	●	○	●	●			7k
0x000000751edf02c727ea9d0c1c8e64f169e343	○	○	○	○	○	used only USDT	0
0xf3c62891b48c5153dca70e0da62f7e1d8c2cc5bb	○	●	○	○	○	Yearn Link Token see Etherscan Token Tracker, invoked by Ethermine; MEV Sender	0
0xf0cca18184dc0d66b53a96a8bda9043e1437	○	●	●	●	●			0
0x000000003c42172c0bda69d6afeb60bf4b488	○	●	○	○	○			0
0x21a340b8289da5464002f4fff2b1c860975cda090	○	●	○	○	○			0
0xc654334a598c323ae04f41436566b08609af008dc	○	●	○	○	○			0
0x7f0000061281328607400060f710002babha9c	○	○	○	○	○			0
0x0000009b988fbecfd83c55262f78592e609648	○	●	●	●	●	comments suggest Nice Hash but transactions look a like	0
0xd1c300000000b9961df238700ef006009700049	○	●	○	○	○	Front-running bot	0
0x00f8d52a00f600094ebf903ce00000defb00f20000	○	●	○	○	○			0
0x00000000006a5bf8681e51432048bcf396abb892	○	●	○	○	○			0
0x000000000007e35df0153a18de63c4f58f04f41c	○	●	○	○	○			0
0x009eeda30408000db000064ab00b0d00f1a3000b38	○	●	○	○	○			0
0x4b0372cd9bedd45e0e23c769b18f79dd06f5a33f2	○	●	○	○	○			0
0xc79eb641599e51930acd560c9dd60d81ca4fb831	○	●	○	○	○			0
0x0000000009042e40070c8f83bff1293005d2f5257	○	●	○	○	○			0

Active: Account was active in the last 30 days. **DEX:** Account used DEX swap function in a transaction. **Known Bot:** Address can be found in known bot list, https://github.com/flashbots/mev-inspect-rs/blob/master/src/addresses.rs. **Bot Comment:** Etherscan comments suggest front-running, **Bot Tag:** Etherscan tag suggest front-running. Balances are the sum of token an ETH balances.

References

1. EVM - implement EIP 1014: Skinny CREATE2 #1165. https://github.com/trailofbits/manticore/issues/1165. Accessed 28 Oct 2021
2. 0age: Metamorphic. https://github.com/0age/metamorphic. Accessed 07 April 2021
3. 0age: On Efficient Ethereum Addresses (2018). https://medium.com/coinmonks/on-efficient-ethereum-addresses-3fef0596e263. Accessed 20 May 2021
4. 0age: Etherscan CREATE2SafeDeploy (2019). https://etherscan.io/address/0x5df4c8e56fe3a95f98ce3d1935abd1b187525915/. Accessed 07 Apr 2021
5. 0age: On Efficient Ethereum Storage (2019). https://medium.com/coinmonks/on-efficient-ethereum-storage-c76869591add. Accessed 25 May 2021
6. Anderson, R., et al.: Measuring the changing cost of cybercrime. In: Workshop on the Economics of Information Security (WEIS). Harvard University, Cambridge (2019)
7. Azzopardi, S., Ellul, J., Pace, G.J.: Monitoring smart contracts: ContractLarva and open challenges beyond. In: Colombo, C., Leucker, M. (eds.) RV 2018. LNCS, vol. 11237, pp. 113–137. Springer, Cham (2018). https://doi.org/10.1007/978-3-030-03769-7_8
8. Böhme, R., Eckey, L., Moore, T., Narula, N., Ruffing, T., Zohar, A.: Responsible vulnerability disclosure in cryptocurrencies. Commun. ACM **63**(10), 62–71 (2020). https://doi.org/10.1145/3372115
9. Buterin, V.: Prevent overwriting contracts #684 (2017). https://github.com/ethereum/EIPs/issues/684. Accessed 07 Apr 2021
10. Buterin, V.: EIP 1014: Skinny Create2 (2018). https://github.com/ethereum/EIPs/blob/master/EIPS/eip-1014.md. Accessed 07 Apr 2021
11. Chen, T., Li, X., Luo, X., Zhang, X.: Under-optimized smart contracts devour your money. In: 2017 IEEE 24th International Conference on Software Analysis, Evolution and Reengineering (SANER), pp. 442–446. IEEE (2017). https://doi.org/10.1109/SANER.2017.7884650
12. Chen, T., et al.: An adaptive gas cost mechanism for ethereum to defend against under-priced DoS attacks. In: Liu, J.K., Samarati, P. (eds.) ISPEC 2017. LNCS, vol. 10701, pp. 3–24. Springer, Cham (2017). https://doi.org/10.1007/978-3-319-72359-4_1
13. Coleman, J., Horne, L., Xuanji, L.: Counterfactual: Generalized State Channels (2018). https://l4.ventures/papers/statechannels.pdf. Accessed 07 Apr 2021
14. Colombo, C., Ellul, J., Pace, G.J.: Contracts over smart contracts: recovering from violations dynamically. In: Margaria, T., Steffen, B. (eds.) ISoLA 2018. LNCS, vol. 11247, pp. 300–315. Springer, Cham (2018). https://doi.org/10.1007/978-3-030-03427-6_23
15. Di Angelo, M., Salzer, G.: A survey of tools for analyzing ethereum smart contracts. In: 2019 IEEE International Conference on Decentralized Applications and Infrastructures (DAPPCON), pp. 69–78. IEEE (2019). https://doi.org/10.1109/DAPPCON.2019.00018
16. Di Angelo, M., Salzer, G.: Collateral use of deployment code for smart contracts in ethereum. In: 2019 10th IFIP International Conference on New Technologies, Mobility and Security (NTMS), pp. 1–5. IEEE (2019). https://doi.org/10.1109/NTMS.2019.8763828
17. Di Angelo, M., Salzer, G.: Characteristics of wallet contracts on ethereum. In: 2020 2nd Conference on Blockchain Research and Applications for Innovative

Networks and Services (BRAINS), pp. 232–239. IEEE (2020). https://doi.org/10.1109/BRAINS49436.2020.9223287

18. Dickerson, T., Gazzillo, P., Herlihy, M., Saraph, V., Koskinen, E.: Proof-carrying smart contracts. In: Zohar, A., et al. (eds.) Financial Cryptography and Data Security, WTSC Workshop. Lecture Notes in Computer Science, vol. 10958, pp. 325–338. Springer, Heidelberg (2019). https://doi.org/10.1007/978-3-662-58820-8_22

19. Fröwis, M., Böhme, R.: In code we trust? Measuring the control flow immutability of all smart contracts deployed on ethereum. In: Garcia-Alfaro, J., Navarro-Arribas, G., Hartenstein, H., Herrera-Joancomartí, J. (eds.) ESORICS/DPM/CBT -2017. LNCS, vol. 10436, pp. 357–372. Springer, Cham (2017). https://doi.org/10.1007/978-3-319-67816-0_20

20. Barros, G., Gallagher, P.: EIP-1822: Universal Upgradeable Proxy Standard (UUPS) (2019). https://eips.ethereum.org/EIPS/eip-1822. Accessed 07 Apr 2021

21. Grishchenko, I., Maffei, M., Schneidewind, C.: Foundations and tools for the static analysis of ethereum smart contracts. In: Chockler, H., Weissenbacher, G. (eds.) CAV 2018. LNCS, vol. 10981, pp. 51–78. Springer, Cham (2018). https://doi.org/10.1007/978-3-319-96145-3_4

22. Hertig, A.: So, Ethereum's Blockchain is Still Under Attack.... (2016). https://www.coindesk.com/so-ethereums-blockchain-is-still-under-attack/. Accessed 18 June 2017

23. Ardis, I., Tang, W.: ECIP 1056: Agharta EVM and Protocol Upgrades (2020). https://ethereumclassic.org/blog/2020-01-11-agharta-hard-fork-upgrade. Accessed 25 May 2021

24. Jameson, H.: FAQ: Upcoming Ethereum Hard Fork (2016). https://blog.ethereum.org/2016/10/18/faq-upcoming-ethereum-hard-fork/ Accessed 18 June 2017

25. Izquierdo, J., Araoz, M.: EIP-897: ERC DelegateProxy (2018). https://eips.ethereum.org/EIPS/eip-897. Accessed 07 Apr 2021

26. Joveski, B.: USDC payment processing in Coinbase Commerce (2019). https://blog.coinbase.com/usdc-payment-processing-in-coinbase-commerce-b1af1c82fb0. Accessed 18 Nov 2021

27. Breidenbach, L., Daian, P, Tramèr, F.: GasToken.io - Cheaper Ethereum transactions, today. https://gastoken.io/#GST2. Accessed 19 Oct 2021

28. Maurelian: Newsletter 16 - CREATE2 FAQ (2019). https://consensys.net/diligence/blog/2019/02/smart-contract-security-newsletter-16-create2-faq/. Accessed 08 May 2021

29. Mossberg, M., et al.: Manticore: a user-friendly symbolic execution framework for binaries and smart contracts. In: 2019 34th IEEE/ACM International Conference on Automated Software Engineering (ASE), pp. 1186–1189. IEEE (2019). https://doi.org/10.1109/ASE.2019.00133

30. 1inch Network: 1inch introduces Chi Gastoken. https://blog.1inch.io/1inch-introduces-chi-gastoken-d0bd5bb0f92b. Accessed 05 May 2021

31. OpenZeppelin: OpenZeppelin Proxy Contract Implementations. https://docs.openzeppelin.com/contracts/4.x/api/proxy. Accessed 07 Nov 2021

32. Palladino, S.: EIP-1967: Standard Proxy Storage Slots (2019). https://eips.ethereum.org/EIPS/eip-1967. Accessed 07 Apr 2021

33. Murray, P., Welch, N., Messerman, J.: EIP-1167: Minimal Proxy Contract (2018). https://eips.ethereum.org/EIPS/eip-1167. Accessed 07 Apr 2021

34. Pérez, D., Livshits, B.: Broken metre: attacking resource metering in EVM. In: 27th Annual Network and Distributed System Security Symposium, NDSS. The Internet Society (2020)

35. rajeevgopalakrishna: Potential security implications of CREATE2? (EIP-1014) (2019). https://ethereum-magicians.org/t/potential-security-implications-of-create2-eip-1014/2614. Accessed 08 Apr 2021
36. Reijsbergen, D., Sridhar, S., Monnot, B., Leonardos, S., Skoulakis, S., Piliouras, G.: Transaction Fees on a Honeymoon: Ethereum's EIP-1559 One Month Later. arXiv preprint arXiv:2110.04753 (2021)
37. Rodler, M., Li, W., Karame, G.O., Davi, L.: EVMPatch: timely and automated patching of ethereum smart contracts. In: 30th USENIX Security Symposium. USENIX Association (2021)
38. (((Swende))), M.H.: Testing awareness levels here. After Constantinople, can contracts that you interact suddenly change code, in-place? (2019). https://twitter.com/mhswende/status/1093596010545336320. Accessed 06 Oct 2021
39. Torres, C.F., Steichen, M., et al.: The art of the scam: demystifying honeypots in ethereum smart contracts. In: 28th USENIX Security Symposium, pp. 1591–1607. USENIX Association (2019)
40. Wood, G.: Ethereum: A Secure Decentralised Generalised Transaction Ledger (Petersburg revision) (2021). https://ethereum.github.io/yellowpaper/paper.pdf. Accessed 07 Apr 2021
41. Zhou, Y., Kumar, D., Bakshi, S., Mason, J., Miller, A., Bailey, M.: Erays: reverse engineering ethereum's opaque smart contracts. In: 27th USENIX Security Symposium, pp. 1371–1385. USENIX Association (2018)

Not so Immutable: Upgradeability of Smart Contracts on Ethereum

Mehdi Salehi[(✉)], Jeremy Clark, and Mohammad Mannan

Concordia University, Montreal, Canada
salehi.mehdi70@gmail.com

Abstract. A smart contract that is deployed to a blockchain system like Ethereum is, under reasonable circumstances, expected to be immutable and tamper-proof. This is both a feature (promoting integrity and transparency) and a bug (preventing security patches and feature updates). Modern smart contracts use software tricks to enable upgradeability, raising the research questions of *how* upgradeability is achieved and *who* is authorized to make changes. In this paper, we summarize and evaluate six upgradeability patterns. We develop a measurement framework for finding how many upgradeable contracts are on Ethereum that use certain prominent upgrade patters. We find 1.4 million proxy contracts which *8,225* of them are unique upgradeable proxy contracts. We also measure how they implement access control over their upgradeability: about 50% are controlled by a single Externally Owned Address (EOA), and about 14% are controlled by multi-signature wallets in which a limited number of persons can change the whole logic of the contract.

1 Introductory Remarks

The key promise of a smart contract running on Ethereum is that its code will execute exactly as it is written, and the code that is written can never be changed. While Ethereum cannot maintain this promise unconditionally, its assumptions (*e.g.*, cryptographic primitives are secure and well-intentioned participants outweigh malicious ones) provide a realistic level of assurance.

The immutability of a smart contract's code is related to trust. If Alice can validate the code of a contract, she can trust her money to it and not be surprised by its behavior. Unfortunately, disguising malicious behavior in innocuous-looking code is possible ('rug pulls'), and many blockchain users have been victims. On the other hand, if the smart contract is long-standing with lots of attention, and security assessments from third-party professional auditors, the immutability of the code can add confidence.

The flip-side of immutability is that it prevents software updates. Consider the case where a security vulnerability in the code of a smart contract is discovered. Less urgently, some software projects may want to roll out new features, which is also blocked by immutability. There is an intense debate about whether this is a positive or negative, with many claiming that 'upgradeability is a bug.'[1]

---

[1] "Upgradeability Is a Bug", Steve Marx, Medium, Feb 2019.

S. Matsuo et al. (Eds.): FC 2022 Workshops, LNCS 13412, pp. 539–554, 2023.
https://doi.org/10.1007/978-3-031-32415-4_33

We do not take a position on this debate. We note that upgradeability is happening and we seek to study what is already being done and what is possible.

Is there a way to deploy upgradeable smart contracts if all smart contracts are (practically speaking) immutable? Consider two simple ideas. The first is to deploy the upgraded smart contract at a new address. One main drawback to this is that all software and websites need to update their addresses. A second simple idea is to use a proxy contract (call it P) that stores the address of the 'real' contract (call it A). Users consider the system to be deployed at P (and might not even be aware it is proxy). When a function is called on P, it is forwarded to A. When an upgrade is deployed to a new address (call it B), the address in P is changed from A to B. This solution also has drawbacks. For example, if the proxy contract hardcodes the list of functions that might be called on A, new functions cannot be added to B. Another issue is that the data (contract state) is stored in A. For most applications, a snapshot of A's state will need to be copied to B without creating race conditions. Mitigating these issues leads to more elaborate solutions like splitting up a contract logic and state, utilizing Ethereum-specific tricks (fallback functions to capture unexpected function names), and trying to reduce the gas costs of indirection between contracts.

Contributions and Related Work. The state of smart contract upgradeability methods in Ethereum is mainly discussed in non-academic, technical blog posts [2,13]. In Sect. 2, we systemize the different types using these resources, and provide a novel evaluation framework for comparing them.

Fröwis and Böhme [8] conducted a measurement study on the use-cases of the CREATE2 opcode in Ethereum blockchain, which one of them is the Metamorphosis upgradeability pattern discussed in Sect. 2.5. They also find, in a passing footnote, some delegate-call based contracts by assuming compliance with the standards: EIP-897, EIP-1167, EIP-1822, and EIP-1967. In our paper, we contribute a more general pattern-based measurement that is not specific to a standard or a commonly-used implementation. We also are the first, to our knowledge, to study who is authorized for upgrading upgradeable contracts, shedding light on the risks of different admin types.

Recent papers have provided security tools for developers that compose with upgradeablity patterns based on DELEGATECALL [14,18]. Numerous measurement studies have used Ethereum blockchain data but concern aspects other than upgradeability [6,9,15–17,20]. Chen et al. [5] survey use-cases of the *SELFDE-STRUCT* opcode, but they do not cover how it is used in Metamorphosis 2.5.

2   Classification of Upgrade Patterns

Updating vs. Upgrading. Software maintenance is part of software's lifecycle, and the process of changing the product after delivery. Often a distinction is drawn between software *updates* and software *upgrades*. An update modifies isolated portions of the software to fix bugs and vulnerabilities. An upgrade is generally a larger overhaul of the software with significant changes to features and capabilities. We only use the term upgrade and distinguish between retail (parameters and isolated code) and wholesale (entire application) changes to a smart contract. While upgrades to a smart contract's user interface (UI) can significantly change a user experience and expose new features, UIs are governed by traditional software maintenance. Our paper only considers the on-chain smart contract component, which is significantly more challenging to upgrade as it is on-chain and immutable under reasonable circumstances (Fig. 1).

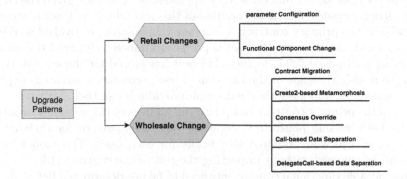

Fig. 1. Classification of upgradeability patterns.

A variety of upgradeability patterns have been proposed for smart contracts. Most leverage Ethereum-specific operations and memory layouts and are not applicable to other blockchain systems.

2.1 Parameter Configuration

We first categorize upgradeability patterns into two main classes: *retail changes* and *wholesale changes*. A pattern for retail change does not enable the replacement of the entire contract. Rather, a component of the contract is predetermined (before the contract is deployed on Ethereum) to allow future upgrades, and the code is adjusted to allow these changes.

The simplest upgrade pattern is to allow a system parameter, that is stored in a state variable, to be changed. This requires a *setter function* to overwrite (or otherwise adjust) the variable, and access control over who can invoke the function. For example, in decentralized finance (DeFi), many services have parameters that control fees, interest rates, liquidation levels, *etc.* Adjustments to these parameters can initiate large changes in how the service is used (its 'tokenomics'). A DeFi provider can retain control over these parameters, democratize control to a set of token holders (*e.g.,* stability fees in the stablecoin project MakerDao), or lock the parameters from anyone's control. In Sect. 4, we dive deeper into the question who can upgrade a contract.

2.2   Functional Component Change

While a parameter change allows an authorized user to overwrite memory, a functional component change addresses modifications to the code of a function (and thus, the logic of the contract). In the EVM, code cannot be modified once written and so new code must be deployed to a new contract, but can be arranged to be called from the original contract.

One way to allow upgradable functions is deploying a helper contract that contains the code for the functions to be upgradeable. Users are given the address of the primary contract, and the address of this secondary contract is stored as a variable in the primary contract. Whenever this function is invoked at the primary contract, the primary contract is pre-programmed to forward the function call, using the opcode `Call`, to the address it has stored for the secondary contract. To modify the logic of the function, a new secondary contract is deployed at a new address, and an authorized set of individuals can then use a parameter change in the primary contract to update the address of the secondary contract.

The DeFi lending platform Compound[2] uses this pattern for their interest rate models[3] which are tailored specifically for each asset. The model for one asset can be changed without impacting the rest of the contract [13].

Upgradeable functional components need to be pre-determined before deploying the primary contract. Once the primary contract is deployed, it is not possible to add upgradeability to existing functions. It also cannot be directly used to add new functions to a contract. Finally, this pattern is most straightforward when the primary contract only uses the return value from the function to modify its own state. Thus, the function is either 'pure' (relies only on the parameters to determine the output) or 'view' (can read state from itself or other contracts, but cannot write state). If the function modifies the state of the primary contract, the primary contract must either expose its state variables to the secondary contract (by implementing setter functions), or it can run the function using `Delgatecall` if the secondary contract has no state of its own.

This upgrade pattern suggests a way forward for wholesale changes to the entire contract: create a generic 'proxy' contract that forwards all functions to a secondary contract. To work seamlessly, this requires some further engineering (Sects. 2.6 and 2.7).

2.3   Consensus Override

The two previous patterns enable portions of a smart contract to be modified. The remaining patterns strive to allow an entire contract to be modified or, more simply, replaced. The first wholesale pattern is not a tenable solution to upgradeability as it as only been used rarely under extraordinary circumstances, but we include it for completeness.

---

[2] https://compound.finance.

[3] https://github.com/compound-finance/compound-protocol/blob/v2.3/contracts/ InterestRateModel.sol.

Immutability is enforced by the consensus of the blockchain network. If participating nodes (*e.g.,* miners) agreed to suspend immutability, they can in theory allow changes to a contract's logic and/or state. If agreement is not unanimous, the blockchain can be forked into two systems—one with the change and one without. In 2016, a significant security breach of a decentralized application called 'the DAO' caused the Ethereum Foundation to propose overriding the immutability of this particular smart contract to reverse the impacts of attack. In the unusual circumstances of this case, it was possible to propose and deploy the fix before the stolen ETH could be extracted from the contract and circulated. Nodes with a philosophical objection to overriding immutability continued operating, without deploying the fix, under the name Ethereum Classic.

2.4   Contract Migration

The simplest wholesale upgrade pattern is to deploy a new version of the contract at a new address, and then inform users to use the new version—called a 'social upgrade.' One example is Uniswap[4], which is on version 3 at the time of writing. Versions 1 and 2 are still operable at their original addresses.

Contract migration does not require developers to instrument their contracts with any new logic to support upgradeability, as in many of the remaining patterns, which can ease auditability and gas costs for using the contract. However for most applications, there will be a need to transfer the data stored in the old contract to the new one. This is generally done in one of two ways. The first is to collect the state of the old contract off-chain and load it into the new contract (*e.g.,* via its constructor). If the old contract was instrumented with an ability to pause it, this can eliminate race-conditions that could otherwise be problematic during the data migration phase. The second method, specific to certain applications like tracking a user's balance of tokens, is to have the user initiate (and pay the gas) for a transfer of their balance to the new contract.

2.5   CREATE2-Based Metamorphosis

Is it possible to do contract migration, but deploy the new contract to the *same* address as the original contract, effectively overwriting it? If so, developers can dispense with the need for a social upgrade (but would still need to accomplish data migration). At first glance, this should not be possible on Ethereum, however a set of opcodes can be "abused" to allow it: specifically, the controversial[5] SELFDESTRUCT opcode and the 2019-deployed CREATE2.

Consider a contract, called Factory, that has the bytecode of another contract, A, that Factory wants to deploy at A's own address. CREATE2, which supplements the original opcode CREATE, provides the ability for Factory to do this and know in advance what address will be assigned to contract A, invariant

---

[4] https://uniswap.org.
[5] "Expectations for backwards-incompatible changes / removal of features that may come soon." V. Buterin, Reddit r/ethereum, Mar 2021.

to when and how many other contracts that Factory might deploy. The address is a structured hash of A's "initialization" bytecode, parameters passed to this code, the factory contract's address, and a salt value chosen by the factory contract.[6] Most often, A's initialization bytecode contains a copy of A's actual code ("runtime" bytecode) to be stored on the EVM, and the initialization code is prepended with a simple routine to copy the runtime code from the transaction data (calldata) into memory and return. Importantly, however, the initialization bytecode might not contain A's runtime bytecode at all, as long as it is able to fetch a copy of it from some location on the blockchain and load it into memory. In order for CREATE2 to complete, the address must be empty, which means either (1) no contract has ever been deployed there, or (2) a contract was deployed but invoked SELFDESTRUCT.

Assume the developer wants to deploy contract A using metamorphosis and later update it to contract B.[7] The developer first deploys a factory contract with a function that accepts A's (runtime) bytecode as a parameter (which includes the ability to self destruct). The factory then deploys A at an arbitrary address and stores the address in a variable called codeLocation. The factory then deploys a simple 'transient' contract using CREATE2 at address T. This contract performs a callback to the factory contract, asks for factory.codeLocation, and copies the code it finds there into its own storage for its runtime bytecode and returns. As a consequence, A's bytecode is now deployed at address T.

To upgrade to contract B, the developer calls SELFDESTRUCT on A. SELFDESTRUCT opcode wipes out the contract's code and storage of the contract account that executes the SELFDESTRUCT opcode. Mechanically, the consequences of SELFDESTRUCT on the EVM are only realized at the end of the transaction. In a followup transaction, the developer calls the factory with contract B's bytecode. The factory executes the same way placing a pointer to B in factory.codeLocation. Importantly, it generates the same address T when it invokes CREATE2 since the 'transient' contract is identical to what it was the first time—this contract does not contain contract A or B's runtime code, it just contains abstract instructions on how to load code. The result is contract B's runtime bytecode being deployed at address T where contract A was.

As it is concerning that a contract's code could completely change, we note that metamorphic upgrades can be ruled out for any contract where either: it was not created with CREATE2, it does not implement SELFDESTRUCT, and/or its constructor is not able to dynamically modify its runtime bytecode.

2.6   CALL-Based Data Separation

To avoid migrating the stored data from an old contract to an upgraded contract, a contract could instead store all of its data in an external "storage" contract. In this pattern, calls are made to a "logic" contract which implements the function (or reverts if the function is not defined). Whenever the logic contract needs

---

[6] Specifically: addr ← $\mathcal{H}$(0xff$\|$factoryAddr$\|$salt$\|\mathcal{H}$(initBytecode$\|$initBytecodeParams)).

[7] "The Promise and the Peril of Metamorphic Contracts." 0age, Medium, Feb 2019.

to read or write data, it will call the storage contract using setter/getter (aka accessor/mutator) functions. An upgrade consists of (1) deploying a new logic contract, (2) pausing the storage contract, (3) granting the new logic contract access to the storage contract, (4) revoking access from the old contract, and (5) unpausing the storage contract.

An important consideration is that the layout of the storage contract cannot be changed after deployment (*e.g.*, we cannot add a new state variable). This can be side-stepped to some extent by implementing a mapping (key-value pair) for each primitive data type. For example, a new uint state variable can be a new entry in the mapping for uints. This is called the Eternal Storage pattern (ERC930). It however requires that every data type be known in advance, and is challenging to use with complex types (*e.g.*, structs and mappings themselves).

A variant of this pattern can introduce a third kind of contract, called a proxy contract, to address the social upgrade problem. In this variant, users permanently use the address of the proxy contract and always make function calls to it. The proxy contract stores a pointer (that can be updated) to the most current logic contract, and asks the logic contract to run the function using CALL. Unlike the functional component pattern (Sect. 2.2), the proxy will catch and forward *any* function (including new functions deployed in updated logic contracts) using its fallback function. With or without proxies, this pattern is very powerful, but instrumenting a contract to use it requires deep-seated changes to the contract code. As our measurements will show, it has fallen out of favour for the cleaner DELEGATECALL-based pattern (Sect. 2.7) that addresses the same issues with simpler instrumentation.

2.7 DELEGATECALL-Based Data Separation

This pattern is a variant on the idea of chaining each function call through a sequence of three contracts: proxy, logic, and storage. The first modification is reversing the sequence of the logic and storage contracts: a function call is handled by the proxy which forwards it to the storage contract (instead of the logic contract). The storage contract then forwards it to the logic contract using DELEGATECALL which fetches the code of the function from the logic contract but (unlike CALL) runs it in the context of the contract making the call—*i.e.*, the storage contract. When upgrading, a new logic contract is deployed, the proxy still points to the same storage contract, and the storage contract points to the new logic contract. Since the proxy and storage contracts interact directly and are both permanent, the functionality of both can be combined into a single contract. It is common for developers to call this the 'proxy contract,' despite it being a combination of a proxy and a storage contract.

This pattern is generally cleaner than using the previous CALL-based pattern because the logic contract does not need any instrumentation added to it. It is an exact copy of what the contract would look like if the upgrade pattern was not being used at all. However this does not mean the pattern in a turn-key solution. Each new logic contract needs to be programmed to respect the existing memory layout of the storage contract, which has evolved over the use of all the previous logic contracts. The logic contract also needs to be aware of any functions implemented by the storage contract itself—if the same function exists in both the storage contract and the logic contract (called a function clash), the storage function will take precedence.

The main issue with function clashes is that the proxy contract needs, at the very least, to provide an admin (or set of authorized parties) the ability to change the address of the logic contract it delegates to. This can be addressed in four main ways:

1. Developers are diligent that no function signature in the logic contract is equal to the signature of the upgrade function in the proxy contract (note that signatures incorporate a truncated hash of the function name, along with the parameters types, so collisions are possible).
2. As found in the *universal upgradeable proxy standard (UUPS)* (EIP-1822): implement the upgrade function in the logic contract, which will run in the context of the proxy contract. Its exact function signature must be hardcoded into the proxy contract. Every logic contract update must include it or further updates are impossible.
3. As found in the *beacon proxy* pattern (EIP-1967): deploy another contract, called the beacon contract, to hold the address of the logic contract and implement the setter function for it. The proxy contract will get the logic contract address from the beacon every time it does a DELEGATECALL. The admin calls the beacon contract to upgrade the logic contract, while normal users call the proxy contract to use the DApp.
4. As found in the *transparent proxy* pattern (EIP-1538): inspect who is calling the proxy contract (using msg.sender())—if it is the admin, the proxy contract catches the function call and if it is anyone else, it is passed to the proxy's fallback function for delegation to the logic contract.

A drawback of the entire DELEGATECALL-based pattern is that logic contracts need to be aware of the storage layout of the proxy contract. In a stand-alone contract, the compiler (*e.g.,* Solidity) will allocate state variables to storage locations, and using DELEGATECALL does not change that, however new logic contracts need to allocate the same variables in the same order as the old contract, even if the variables are not used anymore. This can be made easier with object-oriented patterns: each new logic contract extends the old contract (inheritance-based storage). Other options include mappings for each variable type (eternal storage) or hashing into unique memory slots (unstructured storage). The *Diamond Storage* pattern (EIP-2535) breaks the logic contract into smaller clusters of one or a few functions that can be updated independently, and each can request one or more storage slots in a storage space managed by the proxy contract itself.

2.8   Evaluation Framework

Table 1 summarizes the pros and cons of each upgradeability pattern, omitting consensus override as it is only used in emergencies. Further detail and some take-aways from the evaluation are in the appendix of the full version of this paper [19].

Table 1. An evaluation of upgradeability patterns. • indicates the upgrade method is awarded the benefit in the corresponding column. ○ partially awards the benefit. Empty cells shows that the method does not satisfy the property.

Method	Can replace entire logic	No need to migrate state from old contract	User endpoint address unchanged	No need to instrument source	No need to deploy a new contract to upgrade	No indirection between contracts	No downtime to upgrade	No function selector clashes	No storage clashes
Parameter Configuration		•	•	•	•	•	•	•	•
Component Change		•	•	○		○	•	•	•
Contract Migration	•			•		•	•	•	•
Create2 metamorphosis	•		•	•	•	•		•	•
Call-based	•	•					•	•	•
DelegateCall-based	•	•	•	○			•		

3 Finding Upgradeable Contracts

We now design a series of measurement studies to shed light on the prevalence of the various upgrade patterns. We exclude retail changes from our measurements, because variable changes and external function calls are too commonplace to distinguish. We focus on wholesale patterns, and devote the most effort to finding contracts using the DELEGATECALL-based data separation pattern (Sect. 2.7) as these are the most widely used and there are various sub-types (UUPS, beacon, *etc.*). The other types of wholesale patterns are:

- **Consensus override:** Only 1 occurrence to date (the DAO attack [7]).
- **Contract migration:** Not detectable in code; relies on social communication of the new address.
- **CREATE2-based metamorphosis.** Already measured by Frowis and Bohme [8] in a broader study of all uses of CREATE2. They found 41 contracts between March 2019 and July 2021 that upgraded using this pattern.
- **CALL-based data separation.** We conducted a quick study of 93K contracts with disclosed source code [12]. We identified the Eternal Storage pattern using regular expressions and found 140 instances, the newest having been deployed over 3.5 years ago. We conclude this pattern is too uncommon today to pursue a deeper bytecode-based on-chain measurement (Fig. 2).

3.1 Methodology

Finding Proxies. While not every use of a proxy contract is for upgradeability (*e.g.*, minimal proxies [11], DELEGATECALL forwarders [4], *etc.*), all DELEGATECALL-based upgradeability variants have the functionality of a proxy.

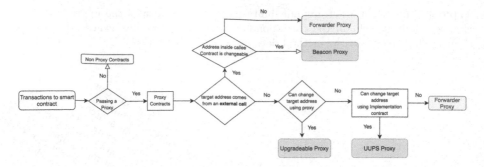

Fig. 2. Flowchart for distinguishing upgradeable contracts (green) from forwarders, and for determining the upgradeability pattern type. (Color figure online)

We therefore start by measuring the number of contracts with a proxy component, and then filter out the *Forwarders* which do not enable upgradeability. To identify proxies, we examine every DELEGATECALL action and see if it was proceeded by a call with an identical function selector to the contract making the DELEGATECALL action, which indicates the contract does not implement this function and instead caught it in its fallback function, and is now forwarding it to another contract at, what we will call, the *target address*. We used an Ethereum full archival node[8] and replayed each transaction in a block to obtain Parity VM transaction traces. DELEGATECALL is one callType of an action within a trace. Specifically, if the data of two consecutive actions of a transaction are equal and a DELEGATECALL is in the second action, it shows that the transaction passes the fallback function (if any other function in the contract is called, other than fallback, then the first four bytes of the data will be changed). The DELEGATECALL indicates the fallback transferred the whole data to the target address without altering it, which means the contract implements a proxy.

Distinguishing Forwarders and Upgradeability Patterns. In an upgradeable contract, the target address for the DELEGATECALL must be modifiable. If it is fixed, we tag it as a forwarder. We define five common patterns for determining the target address cannot be changed:

1. The target address is hardcoded in the contract.
2. The target address is saved in a constant variable type.
3. The target address is saved in an immutable variable type and the deployer sets it in a constructor function.
4. The target address is defined as an unchangeable storage variable.
5. The proxy contract grabs the target address by calling another contract but there is no way the callee contract can change this address.

In the first three situations, the target address will be appeared in the runtime bytecode of the contract. For every proxy-based DELEGATECALL, we obtain the

---

[8] https://archivenode.io/.

target address from the transaction's to address, and we obtain the caller's bytecode by invoking eth_getCode on the full node. If we find the target address in the bytecode, we mark it as a forwarder.

In the fourth case, we find where the target address is stored by the contract by decompiling the contract, with *Panoramix*[9], locating the line of code in the fallback function that makes the DELEGATECALL, and marking the storage slot for the target address. We parse the code and check if an assignment to that slot happens in any function in the contract—this is non-trivial and we refer the interested reader to the appendix of the full version of this paper [19] for the full details. If any assignment is found, we should be sure that the other variable assigned to the target address variable comes from the input of that function. If these conditions are satisfied, there is a function inside the contract that can change the target address and we mark the proxy as an upgradeable proxy contract.

Recall in the Universal Upgradeable Proxy Standard (UUPS) pattern, the logic contract implements a function to update the target address that is run in the proxy contract's context using DELEGATECALL. This is a subcase of the fourth case, where we check the logic contract instead of the proxy contract. If we determine the logic contract can assign values to the logic contract in any function, we tag it as UUPS.

In the fifth case, we rewind the transaction trace from the proxy-based DELEGATECALL and look for the target address being returned to the proxy contract in another action. If we find it being returned by a contract, we apply the methodology from the fourth case to this contract. If the target address is modifiable, we mark it as using the Beacon proxy upgradeability pattern. All contracts that remain after performing all of the checks above are marked as forwarders.

3.2 Results

Our measurements cover block number 10800000 to 12864595, which corresponds to the time-period Sep-05-2020 to Jul-20-2021, and are reported in Table 2. While we found 1.4M unique proxy contracts, many of these share a

Table 2. Results of each DELEGATECALL-based upgrade pattern for the time-period Sep-05-2020 to Jul-20-2021 (2,064,595 blocks).

Proxy Contracts (Total)	1,427,215
Proxy Contracts (Filtered)	13,088
Regular Upgradeable Contracts	7,470
UUPS	403
Beacon	352

---

[9] https://github.com/palkeo/panoramix.

common implementation contract and are part of the same larger upgradable system. As one example, the NFT marketplace OpenSea[10] gives each user a unique proxy contract. After clustering contracts, we find 13K unique systems.

For the 8,225 upgradeable systems (regular, UUPS and beacon), we randomly sampled 150 contracts and manually verified they were upgradeable proxy contracts. We also sampled 150 contracts from the forwarders to verify they are not upgradeable, however we did find 2 false-negatives. Our model did not catch these contracts because a failure happened when decompiling them and our assignment checker detector in turn failed. Note that for UUPS contracts, the implementation contracts are much larger and harder to analyze than the proxy contract itself.

4   Finding the Admin

If a contract is upgradeable, someone must be permissioned to conduct upgrades. We call this agent the admin of the contract. In the simplest case, the admin is a single Ethereum account controlled by a private signing key, called an externally owned account (EOA). A breach of this key could lead to malicious updates, as in the case of the lending and yield farming DeFi service Bent Finance [1]. Bent Finance deployed a *Transparent Upgradeable Proxy* with an EOA admin that was breached (unconfirmed if via an external hack or insider attack). The EOA pushed an updated logic contract[11] which moved tokens valued at \$12M USD into the attacker's account[12] and then upgraded the logic contract to a clean version to cover-up the attack. Based on *The State of DeFi Security 2021* [3] report by Certik,[13] "centralization risk" is the most common attack vector for hacks of DeFi projects.

Control over upgradeability typically falls into one of three categories:

1. **Externally owned Address (EOA):** One private key controls upgrades. It is highly centralized and one malicious admin or compromised private key could be catastrophic. It is also the fastest way to respond to incidents. An EOA may also pledge to delegate their actions to an off-chain consensus taken on any platform, such as verified users on *Discord* or *Snapshot*, however with no guarantee they will abide by it. In our measurements, we cannot distinguish this subtype as these are off-chain, social arrangements.
2. **Multi-Signature Wallet:** Admin privileges are assigned to a multi-signature wallet, requiring transactions signed by at least m of a pre-specified n EOAs. This distributes trust, and tolerates some corruption of EOAs or loss of keys. There is no guarantee different EOAs are operated by different entities and may be security theatre put on by a single controlling entity.

---

[10] https://opensea.io.

[11] https://etherscan.io/address/0xb45d6c0897721bb6ffa9451c2c80f99b24b573b9.

[12] 0xd23cfffa066f81c7640e3f0dc8bb2958f7686d1f.

[13] https://certik.com.

3. **On-Chain Governance Voting:** A system issues a governance token and circulates it amongst its stakeholders. Updates are decided through a decentralized voting scheme where the weight of the vote from an EOA (or contract address) is proportionate to how many tokens it owns. This system is potentially highly decentralized, but the degree depends on the distribution of tokens (*e.g.*, if a single entity controls a majority of tokens, it is effectively centralized). Voting introduces friction: (1) a time delay to every decision—some critical functionality might bypass the vote and use quicker mechanisms (*e.g.*, global shutdown in MakerDAO), and (2) on-chain network fees for each vote cast.

4.1   Methodology

We conduct our measurement on the 7,470 regular upgradeable contracts from Sect. 3. The process can be divided into two main parts: finding the admin account's address and finding the admin type (EOA, multi-sig, or decentralized governance).

Finding the Admin Account's Address. EIP-1967 suggests specific arbitrary slots for upgradeable proxy contracts to store the *admin address*.[14] We first check this specific storage slot using `eth_getStorageAt` on the full node. If it is non-zero, we mark what is stored as the admin address. For non-EIP-1967 proxies, we use a process that is very similar to how we found the storage slot of the target address in Sect. 3. We first find the function in which the admin can change the *target address* (upgrade function). This function is critical and should only be called by the admin. We extract the access control check and mark the address authorized to run this function as the admin address.

Finding the Admin Type. Having the admin address, we can check if the account is an EOA by invoking `eth_getCode` on the address from the full node: if it is empty, it is an EOA. Otherwise, it is a contract address. The most common multisig contract is Gnosis Safe.[15] We automatically mark the admin type as multi-sig if we detect Gnosis safe. We then switch the manual inspection to find other multi-signature wallets (*e.g.*, MultiSignatureWalletWithDailyLimit, *etc.*) and add them to the data set.

In some cases, the admin address is itself a proxy contract—a pattern known as an Admin Proxy. This adds another layer of indirection. We are reusing our methodology for identifying proxy contracts to exact the real admin account, and the proceed as above. Further details of the methodology and implementation are provided in the appendix of the full version of this paper [19].

---

[14] Storage slot 0xb53127684a568b3173ae13b9f8a6016e243e63b6e8ee1178d6a717850b5d 6103.

[15] https://gnosis-safe.io/.

Table 3. Results of each admin type in upgradeable contracts for the time-period Sep-05-2020 to Jul-20-2021 (2,064,595 blocks).

Type	EIP-1967		Non-EIP-1967			
	Regular Admins	Admin Proxy	Regular Admins	Admin Proxy	Arbitrary Slots	Fixed Address
EOA	900	1202	1313	92	2	49
Multisig	255	567	104	16	10	36
Governance/Other	53	462				160

4.2 Results

Of 7470 proxies, 3558 are controlled by an EOA address, 988 are controlled by a known multi-signature wallet, and 2924 addresses are remaining. Table 3 breaks down each sub-category for these. Of the latter 2924 addresses, these are either decentralized governance or another unknown type. After manual inspection, we note some of the unknown contracts use undefined or new patterns for implementing multi-sig contracts; our model has false negatives in detecting multi-signatures. The results demonstrate significant centralization risk in upgradeability: 48% of systems could be upgraded with the breach of a single signing key, and an additional 13% by potentially a small number of signing keys.

5 Concluding Remarks

In our paper, we find that DELEGATECALL-based data separation is the most prominent upgrade pattern in Ethereum in recent years. Our evaluation framework gives some hint as to why this is the case. It avoids the need for a social upgrade, as in contract migration or the CALL-based pattern (without a proxy). CREATE2-based metamorphosis was recently made possible (with the introduction of CREATE2) and its use might grow over time, however it shares one major drawback with contract migration: the need to migrate the whole state from the old contract for each update, even if the update makes minor changes to the logic of the contract. Metamorphic contracts also run the risk of Ethereum removing the SELFDESTRUCT opcode they rely on. A drawback of CALL-based patterns is the heavy instrumentation each new contract needs before it can be deployed, whereas in a DELEGATECALL-based (along with migration and CREATE2-based) upgrade pattern, developers can simply deploy the new logic contract exactly as it is written. Putting these reasons together, DELEGATECALL-based pattern is an attractive option on balance.

The main take-away from studying upgradeability on Ethereum is that immutability, as a core property of blockchain, is oversold. Immutability has already been criticized for being dependent on consensus—both technical and social [21]—however the widespread use of upgradeability patterns further degrades immutability. Finally, as we show, the prominence of contracts that can be upgraded with a single private key (*i.e.*, externally owned account) calls into question how decentralized our DApps (decentralized applications) really are. If the upgrade process is corrupted through a key theft or by a rogue insider, the whole logic of the contract can be changed to the attacker's benefit.

One recent application of our research was finding all contracts that implement the UUPS upgrade pattern, which become important when a vulnerability is discovered in one of the best-known libraries for implementing UUPS. We describe how we can find potentially vulnerable contracts in the appendix of the full version of this paper [19]. While others had found some contracts by looking for specific artifacts left by the UUPS library, we improved the state of the art by looking for the generic pattern of UUPS.

A final discussion point concerns Layer 2 (L2) solutions, such as optimistic rollups and zk-rollups [10]. For the readers that are already familiar with them, their central component is a bridge contract that let computations be performed off of Ethereum (layer 1) and have just the outputs validated on Ethereum. If the bridge contracts is upgradeable, the rules for accepting L2 state are also upgradeable which means every L2 contract is de facto upgradeable even if it does not implement an upgrade pattern. We saw Ethereum override the consensus of the network to revert the DAO hack, which was a rare and contentious event. If a similar attack happened on a L2, reverting would be much simpler and not require a hard fork: the L2 could simply update the bridge contract. For this reason, the consensus override upgrade pattern may be less rare in the future.

Acknowledgements. Our measurements were possible thanks to https://archiven ode.io/. We thank Santiago Palladino (OpenZeppelin) and the reviewers for comments and discussions that helped to improve our paper. J. Clark acknowledges support for this research project from the National Sciences and Engineering Research Council (NSERC), Raymond Chabot Grant Thornton, and Catallaxy Industrial Research Chair in Blockchain Technologies and the AMF (Autorité des Marchés Financiers). J. Clark and M. Mannan acknowledge NSERC through Discovery Grants.

References

1. Bent update. Technical report, Bent Finance. https://bentfi.medium.com/bent-update-12ae69a41dc6
2. Contract upgrade anti-patterns. Technical report, Trail of Bits. https://blog.trailofbits.com/2018/09/05/contract-upgrade-anti-patterns/
3. The state of defi security 2021. Technical report, Certik Company. https://blog.openzeppelin.com/the-state-of-smart-contract-upgrades/
4. Buterin, V.: Delegatecall forwarders: how to save 50–98 contracts with the same code. https://www.reddit.com/r/ethereum/comments/6c1jui/delegatecall_forwarders_how_to_save_5098_on/
5. Chen, J., Xia, X., Lo, D., Grundy, J.: Why do smart contracts self-destruct? investigating the selfdestruct function on ethereum. ACM Trans. Softw. Eng. Methodol. (TOSEM) **31**(2), 1–37 (2021)

6. Chen, T., et al.: An adaptive gas cost mechanism for ethereum to defend against under-priced DoS attacks. In: Liu, J.K., Samarati, P. (eds.) ISPEC 2017. LNCS, vol. 10701, pp. 3–24. Springer, Cham (2017). https://doi.org/10.1007/978-3-319-72359-4_1

7. Dhillon, V., Metcalf, D., Hooper, M.: The DAO hacked. In: Blockchain Enabled Applications, pp. 67–78. Apress, Berkeley, CA (2017). https://doi.org/10.1007/978-1-4842-3081-7_6

8. Fröwis, M., Böhme, R.: Not all code are Create2 equal. https://informationsecurity.uibk.ac.at/pdfs/FB-Ethereum-Create2.pdf

9. He, N., Wu, L., Wang, H., Guo, Y., Jiang, X.: Characterizing code clones in the ethereum smart contract ecosystem. In: Bonneau, J., Heninger, N. (eds.) FC 2020. LNCS, vol. 12059, pp. 654–675. Springer, Cham (2020). https://doi.org/10.1007/978-3-030-51280-4_35

10. McCorry, P., Buckland, C., Yee, B., Song, D.: Sok: Validating bridges as a scaling solution for blockchains. Cryptology ePrint Archive (2021)

11. Murray, P., Welch, N., Messerman, J.: Minimal proxy contract. EIP-1167 (2018)

12. Ortner, M., Eskandari, S.: Smart contract sanctuary. https://github.com/tintinweb/smart-contract-sanctuary

13. PALLADINO, S.: The state of smart contract upgrades. https://blog.openzeppelin.com/the-state-of-smart-contract-upgrades/

14. Perez, D., Gudgeon, L.: Dissimilar redundancy in defi. arXiv preprint arXiv:2201.12563 (2022)

15. Perez, D., Livshits, B.: Broken metre: attacking resource metering in EVM. arXiv preprint arXiv:1909.07220 (2019)

16. Pinna, A., Ibba, S., Baralla, G., Tonelli, R., Marchesi, M.: A massive analysis of Ethereum smart contracts empirical study and code metrics. IEEE Access **7**, 78194–78213 (2019)

17. Reijsbergen, D., Sridhar, S., Monnot, B., Leonardos, S., Skoulakis, S., Piliouras, G.: Transaction fees on a honeymoon: Ethereum's eip-1559 one month later. In: 2021 IEEE International Conference on Blockchain (Blockchain), pp. 196–204. IEEE (2021)

18. Rodler, M., Li, W., Karame, G.O., Davi, L.: {EVMPatch}: timely and automated patching of ethereum smart contracts. In: 30th USENIX Security Symposium (USENIX Security 21), pp. 1289–1306 (2021)

19. Salehi, M., Clark, J., Mannan, M.: Not so immutable: Upgradeability of smart contracts on ethereum. Technical report, arXiv (2022)

20. Victor, F., Lüders, B.K.: Measuring ethereum-based ERC20 token networks. In: Goldberg, I., Moore, T. (eds.) FC 2019. LNCS, vol. 11598, pp. 113–129. Springer, Cham (2019). https://doi.org/10.1007/978-3-030-32101-7_8

21. Walch, A.: The path of the blockchain lexicon (and the law). Rev. Bank. Fin. L. **36**, 713 (2016)

Protocol-Based Smart Contract Generation

Afonso Falcão, Andreia Mordido$^{(\boxtimes)}$ ⓘ, and Vasco T. Vasconcelos ⓘ

LASIGE, Faculty of Sciences, University of Lisbon, Lisbon, Portugal
anfalcao@lasige.di.fc.ul.pt,
{afmordido,vmvasconcelos}@ciencias.ulisboa.pt

Abstract. The popularity of smart contracts is on the rise, yet breaches in reliability and security linger. Among the many facets of smart contract reliability, we concentrate on faults rooted in out-of-order interactions with contract endpoints. We propose SMARTSCRIBBLE, a protocol language to describe valid patterns of interaction between users and endpoints. SMARTSCRIBBLE not only ensures correct interactive behaviour but also simplifies smart contract coding. From a protocol description, our compiler generates a smart contract that can then be completed by the programmer with the relevant business logic. The generated contracts rely on finite state machines to control endpoint invocations. As a proof of concept, we target Plutus, the contract programming language for the Cardano blockchain. Preliminary evaluation points to a 75% decrease in the size of the code that developers must write, coupled with an increase of reliability by enforcing the specified patterns of interaction.

Keywords: Programming language · Smart contract · Protocol specification · State machine

1 Introduction

Smart contracts are a focal point of modern blockchain environments. Such contracts were firstly popularized by Ethereum [19], but soon thereafter other networks developed their own smart contract languages, enabling the implementation of blockchain-based decentralized applications between untrusted parties.

Smart contracts usually operate over user owned assets and, thus, vulnerabilities in programs and in the underlying programming languages can lead to considerable losses. The famous attack on the DAO resulted in a theft of approximately 60 million USD worth of Ether [1,5,7]. Due to recent exploitations of vulnerabilities in smart contracts, blockchain providers turned their attention to the development of robust programming languages, often relying on formal verification, including Liquidity by Tezos [15], Plutus by IOHK [4], Move by Facebook [3], and Rholang by RChain [17]. Such languages aim at offering flexible and complex smart contracts while assuring that developers may fully trust contract behaviour. Unfortunately, for Plutus, the last objective has not been

ⓒ International Financial Cryptography Association 2023
S. Matsuo et al. (Eds.): FC 2022 Workshops, LNCS 13412, pp. 555–582, 2023.
https://doi.org/10.1007/978-3-031-32415-4_34

completely achieved yet. As we show in the next section, in Plutus, assets can be easily lost forever to the ledger with a simple unintended interaction.

To counter unplanned interactions with smart contracts endpoints while automating the development of boilerplate code, we propose SMARTSCRIBBLE, a protocol specification language for smart contracts. Its syntax is adapted from the Scribble protocol language [20] to the smart contract trait and features primitives for sequential composition, choice, recursion, and interrupts. Protocols in SMARTSCRIBBLE specify interactions between participants and the ledger, as well as triggers to interrupt protocol execution. The business logic underlying the contract can be added by the programmer after the automatic generation of the smart contract boilerplate code. The generated code relies on a finite state machine to validate all interactions, precluding unexpected behaviours.

SMARTSCRIBBLE currently targets Plutus, a native smart contract programming language for the Cardano blockchain [14], based on the Extended Unspent Transaction Output model [6], a solution that expands the limited expressiveness of the Unspent Transaction Output model. In UTxO, transactions consist of a list of inputs and outputs. Outputs correspond to the quantity available to be spent by inputs of subsequent transactions. Extended UTxO expands UTxO's expressiveness without switching to an account-based model, that introduces a notion of shared mutable state, ravelling contract semantics [6]. Nevertheless, the framework we propose can be integrated with other smart contract languages and blockchain infrastructures expressive enough to support state machines.

Several works have been adopting state machines to control the interaction of participants with smart contracts. FSolidM [16]—the closest proposal to SMARTSCRIBBLE—introduces a model for smart contracts based on finite state machines. FSolidM relies on the explicit construction of finite state machines for contract specification; instead, we automatically generate all state machine code. On a different fashion, the model checker Cubicle [9] encodes smart contracts and the transactional model of the blockchain as a state machine.

SMARTSCRIBBLE distinguishes itself from other domain-specific languages— BitML, integrated with the Bitcoin blockchain [2], Obsidian [8], a typestate-oriented language, and Nomos [10], a functional (session-typed) language—by abstracting the interactive behaviour and details of the target programming language through a protocol specification, only relying on the smart contract language to implement the business logic and thus flattening the learning curve.

The rest of this paper is organised as follows. Section 2 motivates SMARTSCRIBBLE via an example where assets are lost to the ledger; Sect. 3 presents the protocol language and Sect. 4 focuses on contract generation from SMARTSCRIBBLE protocols. Section 5 summarizes some preliminary results of our evaluation of SMARTSCRIBBLE, and Sect. 6 concludes the paper and points to future work. Appendix A contains the source code for the vulnerable contract we explore in Sect. 2, Appendix B presents input and logs for some simulations, Appendix C provides the source code for the business logic of our running example and Appendix D provides a detailed analysis of the preliminary evaluation results. An implementation is available [11].

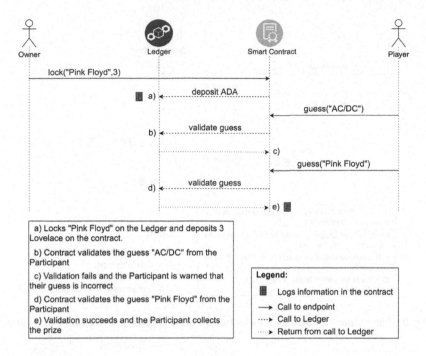

Fig. 1. Diagram of a particular well-behaved flow of operations

2   Smart Contracts Can Go Wrong

This section identifies a weakness of the Plutus smart contract programming language. Although Plutus is developed with a clear focus on reliability, it lacks mechanisms to enforce correct patterns of interactions. As a running example we consider the popular guessing game [4,12], the paradigm for secret-based contracts where participants try to guess a secret and get rewarded if successful; the contract can be found in Appendix A. (An example that falls in this category is a lottery.) Fig. 1 represents a correct sequence of events in the guessing game:

1. The *owner* of the contract locks a secret and deposits a prize in ADA[1] to be retrieved by the first player who correctly guesses the secret.
2. The *player* tries to guess the secret.
3. If the guess matches the secret, the player retrieves the prize and the game ends; otherwise, the player is warned that the guess did not succeed and the game continues.

In Plutus, the parties involved in the protocol are not required to follow valid patterns of interaction. We explore a scenario where one of the parties deviates from the (implicitly) expected flow and show that this leads to a faulty behaviour that is silenced by the blockchain. Figure 2 represents a scenario where the owner

---

[1] ADA is the digital currency of the Cardano blockchain. 1 ADA = 1,000,000 Lovelace.

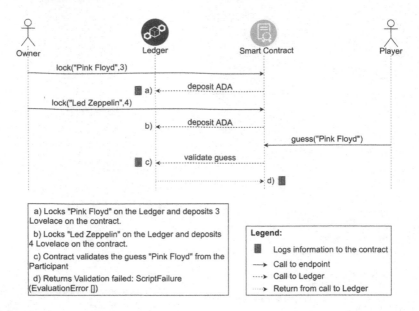

Fig. 2. The owner (incorrectly) locks twice and a correct guess results in a failure

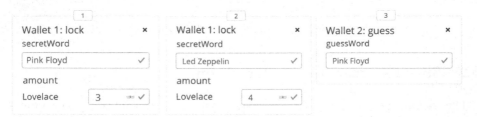

Fig. 3. Playground setup for Fig. 2: the owner makes two consecutive locks, the player guesses the first secret (complete version in Fig. 9, Appendix B)

incorrectly executes two consecutive lock operations and the player provides a correct guess. A simulation of this scenario in the Plutus Playground [12] is illustrated in Fig. 3. Starting with 10 Lovelace in both the owner's and player's wallets, we reach a situation where the log identifies a validation failure for a guess that coincides with that of the first lock (Fig. 4). The final balances in Fig. 5 show that the player did not collect the reward despite having guessed the first secret and the owner lost their money to the contract.

This behaviour is certainly unexpected: rather than overriding the first lock or having the second lock fail, both secrets are stored in the ledger as outputs. When a guess is performed, both stored outputs are compared to the guess and, as a consequence, no guess will ever validate against two different secrets. Furthermore, the prize is irrevocably lost to the contract without any possibility of retrieval. This is an unexpected band of silent behaviour that we want to

```
=== Slot 1 ===
Wallet 1:
ReceiveEndpointCall ("tag":"lock","value":3,"secretWord":"Pink Floyd")
Validating transaction: [..]
=== Slot 2 ===
=== Slot 3 ===
Wallet 1:
ReceiveEndpointCall ("tag":"lock","value":4,"secretWord":"Led Zeppelin")
Validating transaction: [..]
=== Slot 4 ===
=== Slot 5 ===
Wallet 2:
ReceiveEndpointCall ("tag":"guess","guessWord":"Pink Floyd")
Validation failed: [..] (ScriptFailure (EvaluationError []))
```

Fig. 4. Log resulting from the setup in Fig. 3 with a *vanilla* Plutus smart contract; observe that both locks are validated (`Slot 1` and `Slot 3`) and that a correct guess later results in a validation failure (`Slot 5`)

Beneficial Owner	Lovelace
Wallet 1 PubKeyHash 39f713d0a644253f04529421b9f51b9b08979d08295959c4f3990ee6...	3
Wallet 2 PubKeyHash dac073e0123bdea59dd9b3bda9cf6037f63aca82627d7abcd5c4ac29...	10
Script 58d21ee643d76758b95f60fa998190d59c1430a6530f5b0...	7

Fig. 5. Final balances for input in Fig. 3 (Plutus Playground)

prevent. Even in this simple scenario users lose assets to the ledger. Similar situations are very likely to occur in complex contracts, with devastating results.

We propose specifying the interaction behaviour of smart contracts through protocols that describe the valid patterns of interactions between different classes of users and the contract. Our approach prevents unexpected contract behaviours by having contracts automatically validating interactions. The protocol for the guessing game described at the end of next section, detects and avoids further attempts to lock secrets, among other unintended interactions. Note that this type of vulnerability is different from Transaction Ordering Dependence [18] that is related to corrupt miners maliciously changing the order of transactions, and not the order in which the endpoints are called.

3 Specifying Protocols in SMARTSCRIBBLE

Scribble [20] is a language to describe application-level protocols for communicating systems. It comes with tools to generate Java or Python APIs on which developers can base correct-by-construction implementations of protocols.

SMARTSCRIBBLE is based as much as possible on Scribble, even if it covers only a fragment of the language and includes support for smart contract specific features. The base types of SMARTSCRIBBLE include **String**, **HashedString** (strings stored in the ledger), **PubKeyHash** (wallet public key identifiers) and **Value** (an amount in ADA). The protocol constructors are as follows.

Interaction: <EndpointSignature> **from** <Role> {<Trigger>*} describes an interaction between a user playing role Role and the smart contract, by calling a specific endpoint. Endpoint signatures comprise the endpoint name followed by the types of the parameters, e.g., lock (**String, Value**).

Choice: choice at <Role> {Label1: {...} Label2: {...}} denotes a choice made by Role and featuring different alternative branches.

Recursion: rec Label {... Label; } is used to express recurring protocols.

Global escape: do {...} **interrupt** {...} denotes an interaction that can be interrupted by a trigger. The first statement inside the **interrupt** block must be one of the declared triggers; it can be succeeded by any protocol constructor.

In addition, the following declarations can be used in protocols.

Triggers come in two sorts:
- **funds trigger** <TriggerName> introduces a trigger activated based on the amount of funds in the contract.
- **slot trigger** <TriggerName> introduces a time-related trigger (slot is the measure of time in a blockchain).

State: field <Type>*; introduces the fields to be stored in states.

To watch SMARTSCRIBBLE in action we start with a very simple version of the guessing game protocol and gradually make it more robust. Our first version is the straight line guessing game, featuring a sequential composition of three endpoints: lock, guess, closeGame.

```
protocol StraightLineGuessingGame (role Owner, role Player) {
    field HashedString; // save the secret in the contract
    // the owner locks the secret and deposits a prize
    lock (String , Value) from Owner;
    guess (String) from Player;  // the player makes a guess
    // the owner closes the game (no further guesses allowed)
    closeGame () from Owner;
}
```

The StraightLineGuessingGame protocol introduces, in the first line, the roles users are expected to take when interacting with the smart contract: the Owner owns the game; the Player makes guesses. Stateful protocols require state to be kept in the contract. The **field** declaration introduces the types of the fields that are stored within the state machine. In this case, we need a **HashedString** for the secret. Along with the declared fields, SMARTSCRIBBLE creates an extra **Value** field by default, this field is used to manage the funds in the contract, in this instance, we use it to store the prize. The fields are stored in the state machine in the form of tuples, with each element of the tuple corresponding to one of the declared fields. Users may declare repeated types. The tuple with stored contents can be used by the programmer when implementing the business logic. Protocol StraightLineGuessingGame makes use of interaction constructs to describe interactions between a user and the endpoints lock, guess and closeGame. In this protocol, the three endpoints must be exercised once, in the order by which they appear in the protocol, and by users of the appropriate role.

It should be stressed that the guessing nature of the contract is nowhere present in the protocol. Nothing in the protocol associates the **HashedString** in endpoint lock to a secret, or **Value** to the prize. Nowhere it is said that guessing the secret entails the transfer of the prize to the Player's account. Instead, the protocol governs interaction only: which endpoints are available to which roles, at which time. The business logic associated with the contract is programmed later, in the contract language of the blockchain.

Our next version allows the owner to cancel the game after locking the secret (perhaps the secret was too easy or the prize was set too low). The **choice** operator denotes a choice made by a user, featuring different alternative branches.

```
protocol ChoiceGuessingGame (role Owner, role Player) {
  field HashedString;
  lock (String, Value) from Owner;
  choice at Owner {
    proceedWithGame: { // owner wants players to guess
      guess (String) from Player;
    }
    cancelGame: { // the owner chooses to cancel the game
    }
  }
  closeGame () from Owner;
}
```

After locking the secret, the Owner is given two choices: to cancel the game (cancelGame) or to allow a player to make a guess (proceedWithGame). The two branches represent two different endpoints in the contract. The **choice** is in the hands of a single role, Owner in this case. This role should exercise one endpoint or the other (but not both). Protocols for the two branches are distinct. In the case of proceedWithGame, endpoint guess is to be called by Player. The cancelGame branch is empty. In either case, the Owner is supposed to close the game after making the choice.

The third version allows one or more players to continue guessing while the game is kept open by the owner. We make use of **rec**-loops for the effect.

```
protocol RecGuessingGame (role Owner, role Player) {
  field HashedString;
  lock (String, Value) from Owner;
```

```
rec Loop {
  choice at Owner {
  proceedWithGame : { // owner wants players to guess
    guess (String) from Player;
    Loop;
  }
  cancelGame : { // the owner wants to cancel the game
  }
 }
 closeGame () from Owner;
}
```

The **rec** constructor introduces a labelled recursion point. In this case the protocol may continue at the recursion point by means of the Loop label. In any iteration of the loop the owner is called to decide whether the game continues or not (perhaps the secret was found or the owner got tired of playing). If she decides proceedWithGame, a player is given the chance of guessing (by calling endpoint guess) and the owner is called again to decide the faith of the game.

Version three requires a lot of Owner intervention: the continuation of the game depends on her choice—proceedWithGame or cancelGame—after each guess. We want protocols able to terminate automatically, based on guess validation or on the passage of time. Our fourth version takes advantage of the **do−interrupt** constructor and the **trigger** declaration:

```
protocol GuessingGame (role Owner, role Player) {
  field HashedString;
  lock (String, Value) from Owner {
    // triggers for funds and slot
    funds trigger closeGame;
    slot trigger closeGame;
  };
  do {
    rec Loop {
      guess (String) from Player;
      Loop;
    }
  }
  interrupt {
    // close the game when one of the triggers is activated
    closeGame () from Contract;
  }
}
```

In this last version of the protocol, after locking the secret, the Owner has no further involvement. The game ends when one of the triggers is activated. Declarations **slot trigger** closeGame and **funds trigger** closeGame contain the keywords **slot** and **funds**, that instruct the compiler to generate functions in the business logic module where the programmer may define the conditions for these triggers. The primitive role Contract signs the closeGame operation. This is not an endpoint, but an interaction that is executed automatically.

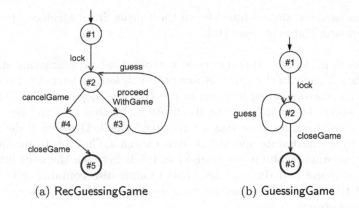

(a) RecGuessingGame   (b) GuessingGame

Fig. 6. Finite state automata for two SMARTSCRIBBLE protocols

Constructors **rec, choice, do−interrupt** and protocol definitions share Scribble's syntax entirely. Interactions are simplified: we remove to <recipient> present in Scribble syntax because in our setting the recipient is always the contract. The declarations **field**, **funds trigger**, **slot trigger** are exclusive to SMARTSCRIBBLE.

4 Smart Contract Generation from SMARTSCRIBBLE

This section details the smart contracts generated from SMARTSCRIBBLE protocols and explain how developers can add custom business logic to complete contract code. To ensure the validation of participants' interactions with the contract we construct a finite state machine from each SMARTSCRIBBLE protocol, whose implementation is automatically generated by our compiler.

Protocols are governed by finite state machines. Figure 6 depicts the automata for the recursive and the **do−interrupt** guessing game in Sect. 3. The correspondence is such that endpoints in the automaton correspond to edges, and pre- and post-interaction points in a protocol correspond to nodes. Sequential composition, **choice** and **rec** generate appropriate wiring. Interrupts call the associated function generating new edges, as in the case of closeGame where an edge links state #2 to the terminal state #3 (Fig. 6b).

The SMARTSCRIBBLE compiler [11] generates code divided in three different modules: *Domain and Library Module*, *Smart Contract Module* and *Business Logic Module*. In this section we give a brief overview of the three modules.

Domain and Library Module includes declaration of errors, the interface for the contract, the definition of state machine inputs, states and the functions to interact with the state machine:

– initialiseSM initialises the state machine; succeeds only if not initialised before.
– runContractStepSM performs a transition, given an input.
– getCurrentStateSM consults the current state.

To implement the state machine we use the Plutus State Machine library, part of the standard Plutus package [13].

Smart Contract Module contains code activated when interacting with endpoints. For example, in the GuessingGame protocol, lock registers the two triggers and calls the corresponding function in the Business Logic Module. The latter function returns either an error or the fields to be stored at the new state. If an error is received, no state transition is performed. Otherwise, the machine advances to the next state and sets its new contents. Changes to the value field stored in the state results in the transfer of funds between the node interacting with the endpoint and the contract. This module also contains code for state transition that is used to define the state machine and boilerplate code specific to Plutus' contracts.

Business Logic Module contains signatures for each of the endpoints in the contract. The actual code is meant to be written by the contract developer. The interaction

lock (**String**, **Value**) **from** Owner;

in the protocol requires a function

lock :: **String** –> Value –> Contract (**Either** StateContents
    Error)

(signature simplified) in the Smart Contract Module that returns either a new StateContents (a tuple composed of the fields stored in the state) or an error. If the value is non-positive, lock returns an error including an error message; otherwise returns a StateContents, that is a pair, composed of the hashed string corresponding to the input and the value. These are the two fields to store in the new state of the state machine (state#2 in Fig. 6b, reached via the guess-labelled edge). The triggers: **funds trigger** and **slot trigger** associated with lock, generate functions with signatures:

lockFundTrigger :: **String** –> Value –> Contract (Value –> **Bool**)
lockSlotTrigger :: **String** –> Value –> Contract Slot

for the respective triggers. In lockFundTrigger, the developer should add an expression with the condition to activate the trigger, e.g., (**funds** –> **funds** 'V.leq'0). In lockSlotTrigger we specify the Slot that activates the trigger.

Corresponding to the

guess (**String**) **from** Player;

in the protocol, a function with the following signature must be written.

guess :: **String** –> Contract (**Either** StateContents Error)

Function guess reads the secret from the machine state (a **HashedString**) and compares it with the hashed version of the input string. If they match, it returns a pair whose second component is zero ADA, otherwise it returns an appropriate error message. The caller to guess (in module Smart Contract Module) detects the difference in the value field of the state and credits the difference in the client's account. Finally, the closeGame () from Contract interaction point needs a function with the same name that, in this case, returns a state with HashedString "Game over" and zero ADA as its fields.

The complete code of the module is in Appendix C; the code for the three functions and two triggers amounts to 13 lines.

5 Evaluation

In this section we demonstrate SMARTSCRIBBLE effectiveness by replicating our running example with SMARTSCRIBBLE's generated code. We also carry out a performance analysis comparing the generated code with expert implementations. (Throughout this section, when referring to expert implementations, we intend to refer to the implementations suggested by the Plutus team).

5.1 SMARTSCRIBBLE in Action

In this section we return to the guessing game. Using the Plutus code generated from the SMARTSCRIBBLE protocol GuessingGame presented in Sect. 3 and the business logic briefly described in Sect. 4, we replicate the scenario in Fig. 2. We use the same conditions that previously resulted in error and the same input as in Fig. 3. The final balances are presented in Fig. 7. In this case, the player can retrieve the prize for guessing correctly; the simulation sees the player terminate with 13 Lovelace. The owner ends with 7 Lovelace as a result of the prize they deposited in the first lock; no funds remain in the script. Thanks to the integration with the state machine, the contract now impedes the second lock from taking effect. As seen in Fig. 10 from Appendix B, the second lock request is labelled as invalid, and no transaction is created:

"Previous lock detected. This lock produces no effect"

This interaction is invalid because for state#2, the state machine only accepts closeGame and guess as inputs (see Fig. 6b). Thus, input lock is considered as invalid and is promptly detected. By doing this, the integration with a state machine guarantees that the game functions as intended by the developer of the protocol. Unlike the implementation proposed by the Plutus providers (that we tested in Sect. 2), this version of the smart contract works as intended.[2]

5.2 Performance Analysis

The discussion for SMARTSCRIBBLE's results follows two different facets: the line of code (LOC) comparison and the evaluation of performance impact on the network.

---

[2] Source code available at https://git.lasige.di.fc.ul.pt/-/snippets/4.

Fig. 7. Final balances for setup in Fig. 3, using SMARTSCRIBBLE (Plutus Playground)

LOC Comparison
To perform the LOC comparison, we use the guessing game together with three other protocols, representative of other smart contract use cases.

Ping Pong A simple protocol that alternates between ping and pong operations, *ad eternum.* No business logic is required for this protocol.

```
protocol PingPongRec (role Client){
    // this protocol stays in the Loop indefinitely
    initialise() from Client;
    rec Loop {
        ping() from Client;
        pong() from Client;
        Loop;
    }
}
```

Crowdfunding A crowdfunding where the owner of the contract starts a campaign with a goal (in ADA), and contributors donate to the campaign. When the owner decides to close the campaign, all the donations stored in the contract are collected.

```
protocol Crowdfunding (role Contributor , role Owner){
    init (Value) from Owner;
    rec Loop {
        choice at Owner{
            continue : {
                contribute (Value) from Contributor;
                Loop;
            }
            closeCrowdfund : {}
        }
    }
}
```

Auction A protocol where a seller starts an auction over some token, setting the time limit. Buyers bid for the token. When the auction is over, the seller collects the funds of the highest bid and the corresponding bidder gets the token.

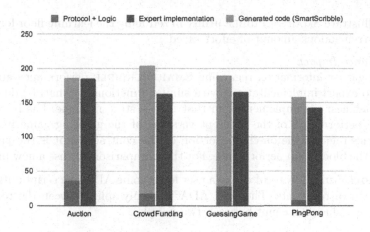

Fig. 8. Comparison of the lines of code (LOC) in SMARTSCRIBBLE against expert implementations, for the four use cases.

```
protocol Auction (role Seller, role Buyer) {
  // The ByteString is supposed to simbolize the Token being
       auctioned, Value is the minimum allowed bid
  field Value, ByteString;
  initialise (Value, ByteString) from Seller{
      trigger slot closeAuctionTrigger;
  };
  do{
    rec Loop {
      bid (Value) from Buyer;
      Loop;
    }
  } interrupt {
    closeAuctionTrigger () from Contract;
  }
  collectFundsAndGiveRewards () from Seller;
}
```

The LOC analysis (detailed in Appendix D.1) is summarized in Fig. 8. We observe that, in all our examples, SMARTSCRIBBLE saves the programmer from manually writing an exorbitant amount of code (most of it boilerplate), supporting our claim that SMARTSCRIBBLE makes Plutus learning process easier, as it generates all standardized boilerplate code automatically, and allows developers to focus only on the logic portion of the contract. In the examples we presented, the business logic is a small portion of the contract's code. We expect this to be the case for the majority of situations, although the weight of the logic section may exceed Auction's 24.67% in complex scenarios. When comparing SMARTSCRIBBLE results with the suggested implementations, we observe a considerable difference between the lines of code written when using SMARTSCRIBBLE and the total length of the contracts proposed by the Plutus team. These results illustrate SMARTSCRIBBLE utility in reducing the learning floor for Plutus and the tremendous amount of effort saved.

Performance Impact

We now gather information regarding SMARTSCRIBBLE performance and compare it to expert implementations with similar functionality that: (i) do not use state machines; (ii) implementation that uses a state machine. Lastly we compare the performance of the different versions of the guessing game in Sect. 3. All metrics refer to the on-chain portion of the contract, as it is the part that impacts the blockchain performance. For this comparison, we use a new protocol:

ShareLockFunds Protocol where a user locks some ADA in a script output and defines two recipients. Then the ADA is evenly split between the recipients (sort of a shared account between two people).

We cannot proceed without introducing the units we use for samples. We collect data for CPU and memory usage. These results were gathered using the budget functionality of Plutus API, as suggested by the Plutus team[3]. The API allows its users to determine the CPU and memory consumption associated with contracts. To measure CPU performance, we use *ExCPU*, a unit with no fixed base, and the output values depend on the types and structures used. For memory we use *ExMemory*: a unit that counts size in machine words, and is proportional. These units allow us to make comparisons between implementations. We stray away from estimating fee costs (in ADA) because fees are very volatile. Moreover, we do not have data about the fee history for smart contracts on Cardano because smart contracts are not deployed yet (as at the time of writing). Moreover, fees depend on the blockchain community, the crypto market, and even the economics of the real world, as a result, such estimations would be unreliable.

The performance analysis is detailed in Appendix D.2 and is summarized in the CPU and memory distribution for the expert versions *without* and *with* state machines, in Figs. 11 and 12 of Appendix D.2, respectively. Performance-wise, the results show that state machines have an inescapable additional overhead when compared to contracts that do not make use of state machines, due to the nature and implementation of the Plutus state machine library. Does this mean we should avoid state machines? The answer is not that simple if we recall the version of the Guessing Game presented in Sect. 2, that does not use any state machine but exposes vulnerabilities that SMARTSCRIBBLE overcomes. SMARTSCRIBBLE adds a substantial overhead, but guarantees that the contract reacts to interactions as expected. Contrarily, in versions that do not employ state machines, behaviour can be unreliable. Additionally, the ratio between CPU usage implementations without state machines and using SMARTSCRIBBLE varies significantly between different use cases: ranging from 49.7% in Guessing Game to 74.8% in Auction. This difference can indicate that, in extreme cases where the on-chain code is very complex the resource consumption may mirror a state machine implementation.

---

[3] https://github.com/input-output-hk/plutus/issues/3489.

SMARTSCRIBBLE and implementations *with* state machines have comparable results as both have identical structures. Using a state machine appears to always carry a significant overhead. The difference between Guessing Game and Auction resource usage is less significant than their counterparts without state machine.

We conclude that using state machines does increase resource consumption of the contracts, thus increasing operation fees. Withstanding this observation, the increase in costs can be interpreted as a *price for security*, a long-term investment for Plutus developers and users, where securer contracts behaviour with costlier fees per interaction can save their assets.

6 Conclusion and Future Work

We present SMARTSCRIBBLE—a protocol language for smart contracts—and a compiler that automatically generates all contract code, except the business logic. The generated code relies on state machines to prevent unexpected interactions with the contract. We claim that SMARTSCRIBBLE improves the reliability of contracts by reducing the likelihood of programmers introducing faults in smart contract code. Our language also flattens the learning curve, allowing developers to focus on the business logic rather than on the boilerplate required to setup a contract, namely in Plutus. Preliminary results point to a $1/4$ ratio between the number of lines of code written by the programmer and those in the final contract.

This paper constitutes an initial report on using protocol descriptions to generate contract code. Much remains to be done. SMARTSCRIBBLE protocols classify participants under different roles, but we currently do not enforce any form of association of participants to roles. We plan to look into different forms of enforcing the association. Business logic is currently manually written in the contract language (Plutus) and added to the code generated from the protocol. We plan to look into ways of adding more business logic to protocols, thus minimising the Plutus code that must be hand written. Some features of SMARTSCRIBBLE are strongly linked with Plutus. The trigger generation is one of those features: it depends on Plutus libraries for the effect. Nevertheless, we believe that SMARTSCRIBBLE can be adapted to target other languages with minimal changes to the syntax and semantics, provided the target programming languages are powerful enough to support state machines. Generating Solidity code might be an interesting option for the future.

Acknowledgements. Support for this research was provided by the FCT through project SafeSessions, ref. PTDC/CCI-COM/6453/2020, by the LASIGE Research Unit, ref. UIDB/00408/2020 and ref. UIDP/00408/2020.

A   Plutus Code for Vulnerable Guessing Game

```
import                 Control.Monad        (void)
import qualified Data.ByteString.Char8 as C
import                 Data.Map             (Map)
import qualified Data.Map                as Map
import                 Data.Maybe           (catMaybes)
import                 Ledger               (Address, Datum (Datum)
     , ScriptContext, Validator, Value)
import qualified Ledger
import qualified Ledger.Ada              as Ada
import qualified Ledger.Constraints     as Constraints
import                 Ledger.Tx            (ChainIndexTxOut (..))
import qualified Ledger.Typed.Scripts   as Scripts
import                 Playground.Contract
import                 Plutus.Contract
import qualified PlutusTx
import                 PlutusTx.Prelude     hiding (pure, (<$>))
import qualified Prelude              as Haskell

newtype HashedString = HashedString BuiltinByteString deriving
    newtype (PlutusTx.ToData, PlutusTx.FromData, PlutusTx.
    UnsafeFromData)

PlutusTx.makeLift ''HashedString

newtype ClearString = ClearString BuiltinByteString deriving
    newtype (PlutusTx.ToData, PlutusTx.FromData, PlutusTx.
    UnsafeFromData)

PlutusTx.makeLift ''ClearString

type GameSchema =
        Endpoint "lock" LockParams
        .\/ Endpoint "guess" GuessParams

data Game
instance Scripts.ValidatorTypes Game where
    type instance RedeemerType Game = ClearString
    type instance DatumType Game = HashedString

gameInstance :: Scripts.TypedValidator Game
gameInstance = Scripts.mkTypedValidator @Game
    $$(PlutusTx.compile [|| validateGuess ||])
    $$(PlutusTx.compile [|| wrap ||]) where
        wrap = Scripts.wrapValidator @HashedString
            @ClearString

hashString :: Haskell.String -> HashedString
```

```haskell
hashString = HashedString . sha2_256 . toBuiltin . C.pack

clearString :: Haskell.String -> ClearString
clearString = ClearString . toBuiltin . C.pack

validateGuess :: HashedString -> ClearString -> ScriptContext
    -> Bool
validateGuess hs cs _ = isGoodGuess hs cs

isGoodGuess :: HashedString -> ClearString -> Bool
isGoodGuess (HashedString actual) (ClearString guess') =
    actual == sha2_256 guess'

gameValidator :: Validator
gameValidator = Scripts.validatorScript gameInstance

gameAddress :: Address
gameAddress = Ledger.scriptAddress gameValidator

data LockParams = LockParams
    { secretWord :: Haskell.String
    , amount     :: Value
    }
    deriving stock (Haskell.Eq, Haskell.Show, Generic)
    deriving anyclass (FromJSON, ToJSON, ToSchema, ToArgument)

newtype GuessParams = GuessParams
    { guessWord :: Haskell.String
    }
    deriving stock (Haskell.Eq, Haskell.Show, Generic)
    deriving anyclass (FromJSON, ToJSON, ToSchema, ToArgument)

lock :: AsContractError e => Promise () GameSchema e ()
lock = endpoint @"lock" @LockParams $ \(LockParams secret amt)
    -> do
    logInfo @Haskell.String $ "Pay " <> Haskell.show amt <> "
        to the script"
    let tx        = Constraints.mustPayToTheScript (
        hashString secret) amt
    void (submitTxConstraints gameInstance tx)

guess :: AsContractError e => Promise () GameSchema e ()
guess = endpoint @"guess" @GuessParams $ \(GuessParams
    theGuess) -> do
    -- Wait for script to have a UTxO of a least 1 lovelace
    logInfo @Haskell.String "Waiting for script to have a UTxO
        of at least 1 lovelace"
    utxos <- fundsAtAddressGeq gameAddress (Ada.
        lovelaceValueOf 1)
```

```
let  redeemer = clearString  theGuess
    tx        = collectFromScript  utxos  redeemer

logInfo  @Haskell . String  "Submitting  transaction  to  guess
    the  secret  word"
void  (submitTxConstraintsSpending  gameInstance  utxos  tx)
```

```
findSecretWordValue  ::  Map  TxOutRef  ChainIndexTxOut  ->  Maybe
    HashedString
findSecretWordValue =
  listToMaybe . catMaybes . Map. elems . Map. map
      secretWordValue
```

```
secretWordValue  ::  ChainIndexTxOut  ->  Maybe  HashedString
secretWordValue  o = do
  Datum  d  <-  either  (const  Nothing)  Just  (_ciTxOutDatum  o)
  PlutusTx . fromBuiltinData  d
```

```
game  ::  AsContractError  e  =>  Contract  ()  GameSchema  e  ()
game = do
    logInfo  @Haskell . String  "Waiting  for  guess  or  lock
        endpoint ... "
    selectList  [lock ,  guess]
```

```
endpoints  ::  AsContractError  e  =>  Contract  ()  GameSchema  e  ()
endpoints = game
```

```
mkSchemaDefinitions  ''GameSchema
```

```
$(mkKnownCurrencies  [])
```

B   Plutus Playground Simulation for the Guessing Game Scenario

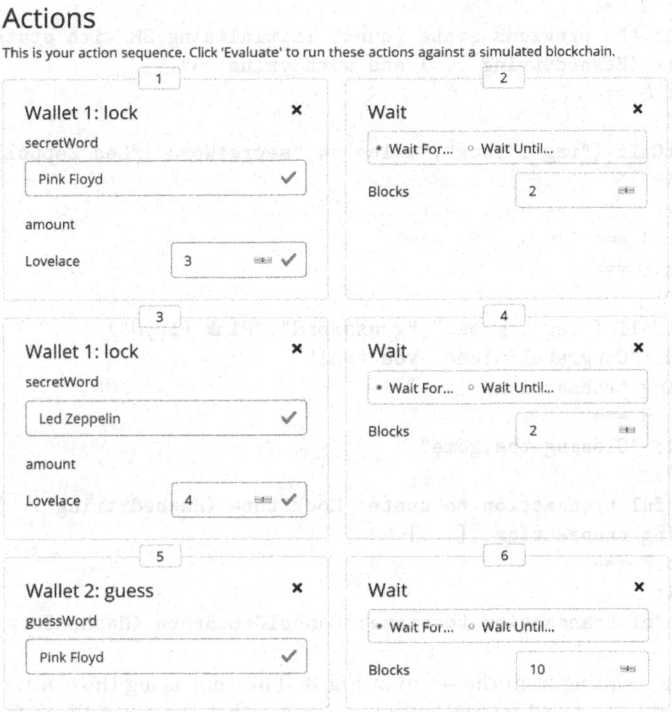

Actions

This is your action sequence. Click 'Evaluate' to run these actions against a simulated blockchain.

Fig. 9. Complete version of Fig. 3. This is the setup to run the scenario illustrated in Fig. 2 in Plutus Playground: the owner (Wallet 1) makes two consecutive locks ("Pink Floyd" and "Led Zeppelin"), the player (Wallet 2) guesses the first secret. Wait in between actions, to let the simulator process the inputs.

```
Validating transaction: [...]
=== Slot 1 ===
Wallet 1:
EndpointCall ("tag":"lock","value":3,"secretWord":"Pink Floyd")
Validating transaction: [...]
=== Slot 2 ===
Wallet 1: "No previous state found, initialising SM with state:
LockState (HashedString ...) and with value: 3"
=== Slot 3 ===
Wallet 1:
EndpointCall ("tag":"lock","value":4,"secretWord":"Led Zeppelin")
Wallet 1: "Previous lock detected.
This lock produces no effect"
=== Slot 4 ===
=== Slot 5 ===
Wallet 2:
EndpointCall ("tag":"guess","guessWord":"Pink Floyd")
Wallet 2: "Congratulations, you won!"
Validating transaction: [...]
=== Slot 6 ===
Wallet 1: "Closing the game"
Wallet 2:
"Successful transaction to state: LockState (HashedString ...)"
Validating transaction: [...]
=== Slot 7 ===
Wallet 1:
"Successful transaction to state: CancelGameState (HashedString ...)"
```

Fig. 10. Log resulting from the setup in Fig. 3. This time using the contract generated from the protocol using SMARTSCRIBBLE; observe that the second lock fails (Slot 3) and therefore the guess from Wallet 2 is successfully validated

C   Plutus Code for Business Logic

Guessing Game Logic Module (SMARTSCRIBBLE)

```
module GuessingGameLogic
  ( lock
  , guess
  , closeGame
  ) where

import              Control.Lens
import              Control.Monad           (void)
import              GHC.Generics            (Generic)
import              Language.PlutusTx.Prelude
import qualified    Ledger.Ada              as Ada
import qualified    Ledger.Value            as V
```

```haskell
import qualified Data.Text              as T
import qualified Data.ByteString.Char8  as C
import qualified GuessGameLibrary        as G
import PlutusTx.Prelude
import qualified Prelude


hashString :: String -> HashedString
hashString = HashedString . sha2_256 . C.pack


zeroLovelace :: Value
zeroLovelace = Ada.lovelaceValueOf 0


lockFundTrigger :: G.AsError e => String -> Value -> Contract
    G.Schema e (Value -> Bool)
lockFundTrigger str val =
    pure $ (\presentVal -> presentVal 'V.leq' zeroLovelace)


lockSlotTrigger :: G.AsError e e => String -> Value ->
    Contract G.Schema e Slot
lockSlotTrigger param1 param2 = pure $ 10


lock :: G.AsError e => String -> Value -> Contract G.Schema e
    (Either G.State G.Error)
lock str val = pure $
  if  val 'V.leq' zeroLovelace
    then Right $ Error $ T.pack $ "The prize must be greater
        than 0; got " <> show val
    else Left (hashString str , val)


guess :: G.AsError e => String -> Contract G.Schema e (Either
    G.State G.Error)
guess str = do
    secret <- mapError (review _GuessingGameSMError) $ G.
        getCurrentStateSM G.client
    if secret == hashString str
      then do
        logInfo @String "Congratulations, you won!"
        pure $ Left (hashString str , zeroLovelace)
      else pure $ Right $ Error "Incorrect guess, try again"


closeGame :: G.AsError e => Contract G.Schema e (Either G.
    State G.Error)
closeGame = do
  logInfo @String "Closing the game"
  pure $ Left (hashString "Game over", zeroLovelace)
```

D   Results

In this appendix, we start by analysing the generated lines of code by SMARTSCRIBBLE and compare it to the amount of code written by the developer and to popular implementations of such protocols in Appendix D.1. In Appendix D.2 we compare the performance of SMARTSCRIBBLE for popular use cases with expert implementations. Section 5 presents a discussion about the evaluation results.

D.1   Lines of Code Analysis

This section compares the amount of lines of code (LOC), written by the developer, of implementations suggested by Plutus' providers, and those generated by our compiler. To carry out the comparison, we use the guessing game together with three other protocols, representative of other smart contract use cases.

Ping Pong A simple protocol that alternates between ping and pong operations, *ad eternum*. No business logic is required for this protocol.

```
protocol PingPongRec (role Client){
  // this protocol stays in the Loop indefinitely
  initialise() from Client;
  rec Loop {
    ping() from Client;
    pong() from Client;
    Loop;
  }
}
```

Crowdfunding A crowdfunding where the owner of the contract starts a campaign with a goal (in ADA), and contributors donate to the campaign. When the owner decides to close the campaign, all the donations stored in the contract are collected.

```
protocol Crowdfunding (role Contributor, role Owner){
  init (Value) from Owner;
  rec Loop {
    choice at Owner{
      continue : {
        contribute (Value) from Contributor;
        Loop;
      }
      closeCrowdfund : {}
    }
  }
}
```

Auction A protocol where a seller starts an auction over some token, setting the time limit. Buyers bid for the token. When the auction is over, the seller collects the funds of the highest bid and the corresponding bidder gets the token.

```
protocol Auction (role Seller, role Buyer) {
  // The ByteString is supposed to simbolize the Token being
      auctioned, Value is the minimum allowed bid
  field Value, ByteString;
  initialise (Value, ByteString) from Seller{
    trigger slot closeAuctionTrigger;
  };
  do{
    rec Loop {
      bid (Value) from Buyer;
      Loop;
    }
  } interrupt {
    closeAuctionTrigger () from Contract;
  }
  collectFundsAndGiveRewards () from Seller;
}
```

Table 1. From left to right: LOC of the SMARTSCRIBBLE protocol, LOC of the generated code, LOC of the business logic, LOC for an implementation suggested by an expert, ratio between LOC of the protocol and the generated code, ratio between LOC written by the programmer (protocol + business logic) and the entire contract, ratio between LOC written by the developer and suggested implementation

Protocol	Protocol (LOC)	Generated (LOC)	Logic (LOC)	Suggested (LOC)	$\frac{Protocol}{Generated}$	$\frac{Protocol+Logic}{Generated}$	$\frac{Protocol+Logic}{Suggested}$
Ping Pong	8	177	0	142	4.52%	4.52%	5.63%
Crowd funding	12	187	6	163	6.42%	9.63%	11.04%
Guessing Game	16	162	13	165	9.88%	17.90%	17.58%
Auction	15	150	22	185	10.00%	24.67%	20.00%

Table 1 summarizes the analysis. Depending on the protocol, the amount of generated code varies from 150 to 187 lines. In all our examples, the generated code is at least 10× larger than the protocol. The business logic greatly varies between contracts; nevertheless, it is important to note that it is extremely likely to be a small portion of the complete contract. We observe that the ratio between all the code written by the programmer (that is, the protocol and the business logic code) and the Plutus code that would otherwise be manually written is less than 1/4 in all analysed contracts. When we compare the suggested implementations[4] with SMARTSCRIBBLE, we conclude that the manually written code with SMARTSCRIBBLE is at most 1/5 of the code in the suggested implementation. Even in implementations developed by experts, the boilerplate portion

---

[4] Implementations available in the Plutus repository.

of the contract is significant. This is represented in Fig. 8 (Sect. 5), where we represent the distribution of the code in SMARTSCRIBBLE against the expert implementations.

D.2   Performance Analysis

In this section, we gather information regarding SMARTSCRIBBLE performance and compare it to expert implementations with similar functionality that: (i) do *not use* state machines; (ii) *use* state machines. Lastly we compare the performance of the different versions of the guessing game in Sect. 3. All metrics refer to the on-chain portion of the contract, as it is the part that impacts the blockchain performance.

In order to increase the sample size for this section, we present the Share-LockFunds, inspired by an example with the same name from the Plutus team[5]:

ShareLockFunds Protocol where a user locks some ADA in a script output and defines two recipients. Then the ADA is evenly split between the recipients (sort of a shared account between two people).

```
protocol ShareLockFunds (role Recipient, role Owner) {
    field PubKeyHash, PubKeyHash; // storing owner and
        recipient public keys
    lock (Value, PubKeyHash, PubKeyHash) from Owner;
    withdrawRecipient () from Recipient;
    withdrawOwner () from Owner;
}
```

Performance Units

Before we "dive" into the data, we explain the units we use for the samples. We collect data for CPU and memory usage. These results were gathered using the budget functionality of Plutus API, as suggested by the Plutus team[6]. The API allows its users to determine the CPU and memory consumption associated with contracts. To measure CPU performance, we use *ExCPU*, a unit with no fixed base, and the output values depend on the types and structures used. For memory we use *ExMemory*: a unit that counts size in machine words, and is proportional. These units allow us to make comparisons between implementations.

We stray away from estimating fee costs (in ADA) because fees are very volatile. Moreover, we do not have data about the fee history for smart contracts on Cardano because smart contracts are not deployed yet (as at the time of writing). Moreover, fees depend on the blockchain community, the crypto market, and even the economics of the real world, as a result, such estimations would be unreliable.

Performance Results

Table 2 contains the results for the performance analysis of contracts without state machine ("Plutus") versus SMARTSCRIBBLE.

---

[5] https://plutus-apps.readthedocs.io/en/latest/plutus/tutorials/basic-apps.html.
[6] https://github.com/input-output-hk/plutus/issues/3489.

Table 2. Performance results for contracts without state machine ("Plutus") and contracts using SMARTSCRIBBLE

Protocol	CPU Plutus	CPU SMARTSCRIB-BLE	$\frac{\text{CPU Plutus}}{\text{CPU SMARTSCRIBBLE}}$	Memory Plutus	Memory SMARTSCRIB-BLE	$\frac{\text{CPU Plutus}}{\text{CPU SMARTSCRIBBLE}}$
Auction	4.25×10^8	5.65×10^8	75.3%	10650	14230	74.8%
Crowd funding	3.80×10^8	5.26×10^8	72.2%	9490	13240	71.7%
Guessing Game	2.65×10^8	5.23×10^8	50.6%	6540	13150	49.7%
Share Lock	3.41×10^8	5.25×10^8	64.9%	8490	13210	64.3%

From left to right: CPU usage for "Plutus" and for SMARTSCRIBBLE; CPU usage ratio between "Plutus" and SMARTSCRIBBLE; memory usage for "Plutus", for SMARTSCRIBBLE and ratio between "Plutus" and SMARTSCRIBBLE. CPU usage measured in ExCPU and memory in ExMemory. Figure 11 contains the visual representation of the data in Table 2. We observe that regardless of the contract, CPU and memory usage for SMARTSCRIBBLE is superior to Plutus contracts without state machine. The ratio of CPU usage between Plutus and SMARTSCRIBBLE ranges from 50.6% in Guessing Game to 75.3% in Auction. When comparing the memory usage, we observe similar results: 49.7% in Guessing Game to 74.8% in Auction. Keep in mind that, in this scenario, we compare performance with contracts that can hide vulnerabilities, as illustrated in Sect. 2. The implementation of state machines ensures the robustness of the contract against out-of-order interactions. With these tests, we conclude that SMARTSCRIBBLE generated contracts impact the performance compared to implementations of the same contract that do not use state machines. Nonetheless, this comparison is unfair, since "Plutus" contracts are more likely to contain vulnerabilities, we expand this rationale in Sect. 5. For this reason, we now focus on the comparison between SMARTSCRIBBLE and specialist implementations of Plutus contracts that rely on state machines.

Table 3 present the comparison results between contracts using state machine and SMARTSCRIBBLE.

Figure 12 contains the visual representation of the results. CPU usage is measured in *ExCPU* and memory in *ExMemory*. From the results, we verify that CPU and memory usage for SMARTSCRIBBLE is similar to suggested implementations with state machine. SMARTSCRIBBLE has a slightly better performance in Guessing Game and Auction, and marginally worst result in PingPong. Once again, when comparing the memory usage, the results are almost identical to CPU. The resource usage differs less between protocols then the data we presented in Table 2.

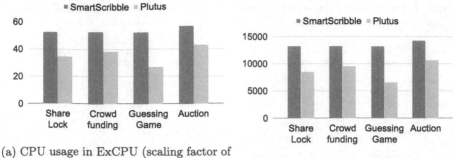

(a) CPU usage in ExCPU (scaling factor of 10^7)

(b) Memory usage in ExMemory

Fig. 11. Performance comparison between solutions without state machine and SMARTSCRIBBLE (using values from Table 2)

Table 3. Results for memory and CPU usage for suggested implementations using state machine and contracts using SMARTSCRIBBLE

Protocol	CPU Plutus	CPU SMARTSCRIBBLE	$\frac{\text{CPU Plutus}}{\text{CPU SMARTSCRIBBLE}}$	Memory Plutus	Memory SMARTSCRIBBLE	$\frac{\text{Plutus Memory}}{\text{SMARTSCRIBBLE Memory}}$
Auction	5.68×10^8	5.65×10^8	100.6%	14310	14230	100.6%
Guessing Game	5.29×10^8	5.23×10^8	108.7%	13300	13150	101.1%
Ping Pong	5.18×10^8	5.22×10^8	99.3%	13030	13120	99.3%

The contracts generated using SMARTSCRIBBLE have structures similar to those implemented by the Plutus team. The slight advantage in performance can be attributed to some verifications experts perform on-chain that are done off-chain with SMARTSCRIBBLE.

In Table 4, we arrive at the data performance that enables us to compare versions of the guessing game presented in Sect. 3.

Table 4. Evolution of memory usage for the each version of the guessing game protocol in Sect. 3 using SMARTSCRIBBLE

Contract	CPU $\times 10^8$	Memory
Straight Line	5.25	13210
Choice	5.34	13450
Rec	5.32	13390
Do-Interrupt	5.23	13150

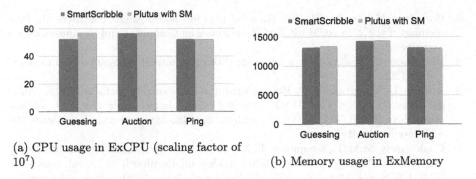

(a) CPU usage in ExCPU (scaling factor of 10^7)

(b) Memory usage in ExMemory

Fig. 12. Performance comparison between solutions that use state machine and SMARTSCRIBBLE (using values from Table 3)

We see that CPU and memory usage is almost identical between different versions of the guessing game. Choice version has the highest resource consumption since it is the protocol that generates the largest amount of states and transactions (recall the state machines in Sect. 3). Do-Interrupt uses fewer resources than the straight-line version because it generates one less state, despite having a more complex protocol. A marginal 2.2% fluctuation separates the lowest and upper bound results in both CPU and memory usages. This analysis is illustrated in Fig. 13.

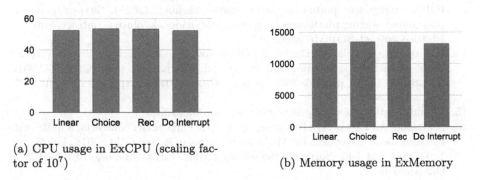

(a) CPU usage in ExCPU (scaling factor of 10^7)

(b) Memory usage in ExMemory

Fig. 13. Performance comparison between iterations of guessing game (using values from Table 4)

References

1. Atzei, N., Bartoletti, M., Cimoli, T.: A survey of attacks on ethereum smart contracts (SoK). In: Maffei, M., Ryan, M. (eds.) POST 2017. LNCS, vol. 10204, pp. 164–186. Springer, Heidelberg (2017). https://doi.org/10.1007/978-3-662-54455-6_8

2. Bartoletti, M., Zunino, R.: BitML: a calculus for bitcoin smart contracts. In: Proceedings of the 2018 ACM SIGSAC Conference on Computer and Communications Security (2018)
3. Blackshear, S., et al.: Move: a language with programmable resources. Libra Association (2019)
4. Brünjes, L., Vinogradova, P.: Plutus: writing reliable smart contracts. IOHK (2020)
5. del Castillo, M.: The DAO attacked code issue leads to $60 million ether theft (2016). https://www.coindesk.com/dao-attacked-code-issue-leads-60-million-ether-theft
6. Chakravarty, M.M.T., Chapman, J., MacKenzie, K., Melkonian, O., Peyton Jones, M., Wadler, P.: The extended UTXO model. In: Bernhard, M., et al. (eds.) FC 2020. LNCS, vol. 12063, pp. 525–539. Springer, Cham (2020). https://doi.org/10.1007/978-3-030-54455-3_37
7. Chen, H., Pendleton, M., Njilla, L., Xu, S.: A survey on ethereum systems security: vulnerabilities, attacks, and defenses. ACM Comput. Surv. **53**(3), 1–43 (2020)
8. Coblenz, M., et al.: Obsidian: typestate and assets for safer blockchain programming. TOPLAS **42**(3), 1–82 (2020)
9. Conchon, S., Korneva, A., Zaïdi, F.: Verifying smart contracts with cubicle. In: Sekerinski, E., et al. (eds.) FM 2019, Part I. LNCS, vol. 12232, pp. 312–324. Springer, Cham (2020). https://doi.org/10.1007/978-3-030-54994-7_23
10. Das, A., Balzer, S., Hoffmann, J., Pfenning, F., Santurkar, I.: Resource-aware session types for digital contracts. In: IEEE 34th Computer Security Foundations Symposium (CSF). IEEE Computer Society (2021)
11. Falcão, A., Mordido, A., Vasconcelos, V.T.: Smartscribble's implementation (2021). https://git.lasige.di.fc.ul.pt/amordido/smartscribble
12. IOHK: Plutus playground (2020). https://prod.playground.plutus.iohkdev.io/
13. IOHK: Language plutus contract state machine (2021). https://marloweplayground-staging.plutus.aws.iohkdev.io/doc/haddock/plutus-contract/html/Plutus-Contract-StateMachine.html
14. Kiayias, A., Russell, A., David, B., Oliynykov, R.: Ouroboros: a provably secure proof-of-stake blockchain protocol. In: Katz, J., Shacham, H. (eds.) CRYPTO 2017. LNCS, vol. 10401, pp. 357–388. Springer, Cham (2017). https://doi.org/10.1007/978-3-319-63688-7_12
15. Liquidity. http://www.liquidity-lang.org/doc/index.html
16. Mavridou, A., Laszka, A.: Designing secure ethereum smart contracts: a finite state machine based approach. In: Meiklejohn, S., Sako, K. (eds.) FC 2018. LNCS, vol. 10957, pp. 523–540. Springer, Heidelberg (2018). https://doi.org/10.1007/978-3-662-58387-6_28
17. Rholang. https://github.com/rchain/rchain/tree/master/rholang-tutorial
18. Sayeed, S., Marco-Gisbert, H., Caira, T.: Smart contract: attacks and protections. IEEE Access **8**, 24416–24427 (2020)
19. Wood, G.: Ethereum: a secure decentralised generalised transaction ledger. Ethereum Proj. Yellow Pap. **151**(2014), 1–32 (2014)
20. Yoshida, N., Hu, R., Neykova, R., Ng, N.: The scribble protocol language. In: Abadi, M., Lluch Lafuente, A. (eds.) TGC 2013. LNCS, vol. 8358, pp. 22–41. Springer, Cham (2014). https://doi.org/10.1007/978-3-319-05119-2_3

Distributed and Adversarial Resistant Workflow Execution on the Algorand Blockchain

Yibin Xu[1(✉)], Tijs Slaats[1], Boris Düdder[1], Søren Debois[2], and Haiqin Wu[1]

[1] University of Copenhagen, Copenhagen, Denmark
{yx,slaats,boris.d,hw}@di.ku.dk
[2] IT University of Copenhagen, Copenhagen, Denmark
debois@itu.dk

Abstract. We provide a practical translation from the Dynamic Condition Response (DCR) process modelling language to the Transaction Execution Approval Language (TEAL) used by the Algorand blockchain. Compared to earlier implementations of business process notations on blockchains, particularly Ethereum, the present implementation is four orders of magnitude cheaper. This translation has the following immediate ramifications: (1) It allows decentralised execution of DCR-specified business processes in the absence of expensive intermediaries (lawyers, brokers) or counterparty risk. (2) It provides a possibly helpful high-level language for implementing business processes on Algorand. (3) It demonstrates that despite the strict limitations on Algorand smart contracts, they are powerful enough to encode models of a modern process notation.

Keywords: Applications of blockchain · Smart contracts · Algorand · Inter-institutional collaboration

1 Introduction

Blockchain technologies rose to prominence by realising decentralised financial systems and instruments [1,5], then branched out into other domains such as supply chain management [16]. The main draw of blockchains is their ability to securely capture and track the ownership of resources [19], e.g., digital cash, real estate, and produce. Smart contracts [1] have added a second dimension to these use cases by allowing blockchains to control the valid movement of resources.

This development has drawn the interest of the Business Process Management (BPM) community [14], to which smart contracts harbor the promise of integrity-protected decentralised automation of process execution. In this community, a process is commonly defined as *a structured, measured set of activities designed to produce a specific output for a particular customer or market* [2]. In practice, e.g., products being traded and shipped in a supply chain and the treatment of a patient in a hospital, or a loan application process within a bank.

© International Financial Cryptography Association 2023
S. Matsuo et al. (Eds.): FC 2022 Workshops, LNCS 13412, pp. 583–597, 2023.
https://doi.org/10.1007/978-3-031-32415-4_35

The latter two of these examples are knowledge-intensive processes. A key approach to formalising knowledge-intensive processes is that of *declarative process notations* [15], which expresses the constraints a process must obey, as opposed to the exact sequencing of admissible activity executions, akin to the difference between an LTL formula and a Büchi automaton. In practice, declarative models tend to be more concise, and for processes subject to rules and regulations, easier to relate to those rules and regulations.

While process notations have been encoded into Solidity [1]), these are plagued by high costs and relatively low performance due to congestion of the Ethereum network and high gas prices [13]. Given the cost of transactions on the Ethereum blockchain in January 2022, creation of a declarative business process contract would cost roughly $350 while the execution of a single event or activity would cost $25.

In the current paper we address this weakness by exploring an encoding from the declarative Dynamic Condition Response (DCR) Graphs process notation to TEAL [5] contracts running on the Algorand blockchain. Transactions on Algorand are cheap, with a current cost, on the 14th of January 2022, of $0.00136, and offer transaction finality in under 5 s. This encoding is not trivial however, as the efficiency and low cost of TEAL contracts carry limitations to the memory space and number of operations as a trade-off.

The contributions of this paper are:

1. We show how DCR Graphs can be efficiently stored in the limited memory space provided by TEAL and through pseudo-code show how their run-time semantics can be encoded without exceeding the operation limit;
2. we analyse the costs of storing and running DCR smart contracts on the Algorand blockchain based on the number of unique activities involved in the process;
3. we provide a prototype implementation of the encoding running on the Algorand testnet;
4. we discuss possible future extensions to the encoding that will allow capturing more complex and rich process descriptions.

In Sect. 2, we proceed to discuss future work. In Sect. 3, we shortly describe the primary attributes of the Algorand network. Section 4 introduces Dynamic Condition Response (DCR) graphs. In Sect. 5, we show how the semantics of DCR Graphs can be encoded as smart contracts on the Algorand blockchain. Section 6 provides a financial analysis, show the maximum cost associated with our approach and how it related to earlier attempts at encoding DCR Graphs in Solidity. Finally Sect. 7 concludes and discusses future work.

2 Related Work

Previous approaches towards process-aware blockchains [8,9,12,18] have focused on providing translations from process models into existing smart contracts languages, particularly, by translating flow-based BPMN diagrams to Solidity. A recent work [10] proposed to reduce the cost of redeployment of the smart contracts when changing the process model by a specially designed interpreter of BPMN process models based on dynamic data structures. [11] presented a model for dynamic binding of actors to roles in collaborative processes and an associated binding policy specification language. We differ from these works by first of all, taking a declarative approach to process modelling and second of all developing a native smart contract language for processes that is directly embedded in the blockchain.

Inspired by institutional grammars, [4] proposed a high-level declarative language that focuses on business contracts, however, no implementation is provided. A high-level vision of the business artifact paradigm towards modelling business processes on a distributed ledger was given in [7]. [17] proposed a lean architecture enabling lightweight and full-featured on-chain implementations of a decentralised process execution system.

3   Algorand Blockchain

Algorand [5] is a late-generation blockchain with a series of features, including high scalability and a fork-free consensus protocol based on Proof-of-Stake. Its smart contract layer (ASC1) aims to reduce the security risk of smart contracts, and adopts a non-Turing complete programming model, which natively supports transactional atomic sets and user-defined assets. These characteristics make it an intriguing smart contract platform to study.

A smart contract language called TEAL [5] is used in Algorand. TEAL is a bytecode-based stack language and is processed by the Algorand Virtual Machine (AVM), with an official programming interface for Python (called PyTeal). In addition to standard arithmetic-logical operators, TEAL also includes operators for calculating and indexing all transactions in the current atomic group, as well as IDs and fields for accessing them. When launching a transaction involving a script, the user can specify a series of parameters. The script includes cryptographic operators that calculate the hash value and verify the signature.

Applications are stateful smart contracts created with Algorand. They are given an Application ID when they are launched. Application Transactions are used to communicate with these contracts. The primary Application Transaction provides additional data that the stateful smart contract's TEAL code can pass and process.

Per transaction call, any application can check the global state of up to two other smart contracts. This is accomplished by including the application IDs of the additional stateful smart contracts in the transaction call to the stateful smart contract. This is known as the Application Array in TEAL. Currently, the developer must know how many additional applications are expected to be sent into the contract call before writing the smart contract code in TEAL.

Figure 1 shows the architecture of the stateful smart contract in Algorand. Each transaction has an Application array, which indicates what smart contract (up to two smart contracts) the transaction will be sent to; an Accounts Array (up to four accounts), which indicates what accounts have opt-in to the smart contract; an Assets Array (up to two assets), which indicates the assets that will be sent to the smart contract; an Arguments Array (up to 255 arguments), which indicates the arguments passed to the smart contract. The maximum length of the stack and scratch space is 1000 and 255 respectively.

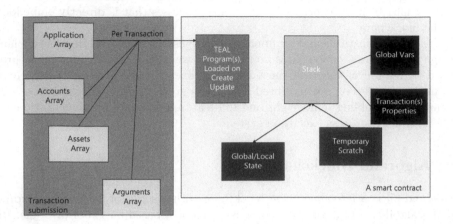

Fig. 1. Stateful Smart Contract Transaction Call Architecture.

3.1 Limitations

For each smart contract, we have the following limitations:

1. 64 Key/Value pairs in the global state.
2. 64 Key/Value pairs in total in the local state of the accounts. There can be four accounts opted in to the smart contract, each of it has 16 pairs.
3. Max key + Value length = 128 bytes
4. A stateless smart contract only returns the result of the execution but will not store states in the blockchain. A stateful smart contract can create and update the states stored in the blockchain.
5. The program (a smart contract consists of an approval program and a clean program) costs no more than 20000 operations in stateless mode. It allows at most 700 operations for each the approval and clear program of a stateful contract. In other words, it allows 700 operations for each execution of the stateful contract. Each operation costs 1, some cryptographic operations are more costly but not used in our prototypical implementation.

Note that the pairs in the local state of the accounts are read-only for other people. People do not need to Opt-in to the smart contract in order to execute the smart contract.

4 DCR Graph

DCR Graphs [6] are a formal declarative notation for describing processes. The base notation focuses on control-flow, i.e., the allowed sequencing of activities. The nodes of a DCR Graph are the executable elements, called events, which can be labelled by a labelling function. The labelling function allows multiple events to share the same label, thereby allowing process activities to occur more than once in a graph, under different constraints depending on their context.

The state of a graph is described by a *marking*, indicating for each event whether it (1) has been previously executed, (2) is currently pending, and (3) is currently included. The evolution of the graph is described by its edges, the relations between events. Through the relations, an event can constrain another event or have an effect on it. There are two possible constraints: the condition ($\rightarrow\bullet$) captures that an event can not be executed unless another event has been executed some time (not necessarily immediately) before it, the milestone ($\rightarrow\diamond$) captures that an event cannot be executed while another event is pending. There are three effect relations: the exclusion ($\rightarrow\%$) removes an event from the process and disables any constraints it may place on other events, the inclusion relation ($\rightarrow+$) includes an event back into the process, re-enabling any constraints it may have had, and the response relation makes another event pending ($\bullet\rightarrow$). Pending events are obligations and must be satisfied by either executing or excluding them before a process can be considered to be in an accepting state.

Definition 1. *A* DCR *Graph is a tuple* $(E, M, L, \ell, \rightarrow\bullet, \bullet\rightarrow, \rightarrow\diamond, \rightarrow+, \rightarrow\%)$, *where*

- *E is the set of events*
- $M = (\mathsf{Ex}, \mathsf{Re}, \mathsf{In}) \in \mathcal{P}(E) \times \mathcal{P}(E) \times \mathcal{P}(E)$ *is the* marking *of the graph*
- *L is the set of* labels
- $\ell : E \rightarrow L$ *is the* labelling function
- $\phi \subseteq E \times E$ *for* $\phi \in \{\rightarrow\bullet, \bullet\rightarrow, \rightarrow\diamond, \rightarrow+, \rightarrow\%\}$ *are respectively the condition, response, milestone, inclusion, and exclusion relations between events*

For DCR Graph G with events E and event $e \in E$, we write ($\rightarrow\bullet e$) for the set $\{e' \in E \mid e' \rightarrow\bullet e\}$, write ($e\bullet\rightarrow$) for the set $\{e' \in E \mid e \bullet\rightarrow e'\}$ and similarly for ($e\rightarrow+$), ($e\rightarrow\%$) and ($\rightarrow\diamond e$).

An event of a DCR graph is *enabled* when (a) it is included, (b) there are no included conditions that have not been executed, and (c) there are no pending and included milestones.

Definition 2 (Enabled events). *Let* $G = (E, M, L, \ell, \rightarrow\bullet, \bullet\rightarrow, \rightarrow\diamond, \rightarrow+, \rightarrow\%)$ *be a DCR Graph, with marking* $M = (\mathsf{Ex}, \mathsf{Re}, \mathsf{In})$. *An event* $e \in E$ *is* enabled, *written* $e \in \mathsf{enabled}(G)$, *iff (a)* $e \in \mathsf{In}$ *and (b)* $\mathsf{In} \cap (\rightarrow\bullet e) \subseteq \mathsf{Ex}$ *and (c)* $(\mathsf{Re} \cap \mathsf{In}) \cap (\rightarrow\diamond e) = \emptyset$.

If an event is enabled then it can be executed. Executing an event e updates the marking of the graph by (a) adding it to the set of executed events, (b) removing it from the set of pending events and adding its responses $(e \bullet \to)$ to the set of pending events, and (c) respectively removing its exclusions $(e \to \%)$ from and adding its inclusions $(e \to +)$ to the set of included events.

Definition 3 (Execution). *Let* $G = (E, M, L, \ell, \to \bullet, \bullet \to, \to \diamond, \to +, \to \%)$ *be a DCR Graph, with marking* $M = (\text{Ex}, \text{Re}, \text{In})$. *When* $e \in \text{enabled}(G)$, *the result of executing* e, *written* $\text{execute}(G, e)$ *is a new DCR Graph* G' *with the same events, labels, labelling function, and relations, but a new marking* $M' = (\text{Ex}', \text{Re}', \text{In}')$, *where (a)* $\text{Ex}' = \text{Ex} \cup \{e\}$ *(b)* $\text{Re}' = (\text{Re} \backslash \{e\}) \cup (e \bullet \to)$, *and (c)* $\text{In}' = (\text{In} \backslash (e \to \%)) \cup (e \to +)$.

We define the language of a DCR Graph as all finite and infinite sequences of such executions, where all pending responses are eventually executed or excluded.

Definition 4 (Language of a DCR Graph). *Let* $G = (E, M, L, \ell, \to \bullet, \bullet \to , \to \diamond, \to +, \to \%)$ *be a DCR Graph. A run of* G *is a finite or infinite sequence of events* $e_0, e_1, \dots$ *such that* $e_i \in \text{enabled}(G_i)$, $\text{execute}(G_i, e_i) = G_{i+1}$, *and* $G_0 = G$. *We call a run accepting iff for each* G_i *with marking* $M_i = (\text{Ex}_i, \text{Re}_i, \text{In}_i)$ *and* $e \in \text{Re}_i \cap \text{In}_i$ *there exists a* $j \geq i$ *such that* $e_j = e$ *or* $e \notin \text{Re}_j \cap \text{In}_j$.

The language $\text{lang}(G) \subseteq L^\infty$ *of* G *is the set of finite and infinite sequences of labels* $l_0 l_1 \cdots$ *such that there is an accepting run* $e_0, e_1, \dots$ *where* $\ell(e_i) = l_i$.

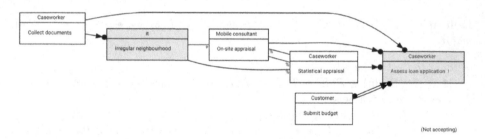

Fig. 2. DCR Graph of a mortgage application process adapted from [3].

As an example, Fig. 2 shows a simplified version of a loan application process encountered in industry [3] modelled as a DCR Graph. The labels of the events contain not only the name of the activity, but also the roles who are allowed to execute them. The loan application should always be assessed by the case worker, shown by the red text and exclamation mark, which denote that the event is an *initial response*. To reach this goal, the case worker must first collect documents and the customer must submit a budget, shown by the condition relations from these two events. In addition, a statistical or on-site appraisal must have been performed. Both are a condition to assess loan application, but they also mutually exclude each other, meaning that if one is executed, the other is excluded and will not block other events from executing. Submit budget also has a response relation towards the assessment, meaning that a loan application must always be assessed (again) after the customer submits a (new) budget. Finally IT may determine that the neighbourhood of the property requires an on-site appraisal. It then excludes the statistical appraisal event and includes the on-site appraisal event, which will re-enable on-site as a condition for the assessment, even if it was previously excluded by a statistical appraisal.

In the initial marking, irregular neighbourhood and assess loan application are blocked as having unsatisfied conditions. Other events are enabled as they are included and have no blocking conditions or milestones. The graph is in a non-accepting state as the assess loan application is included and a pending response.

Executing Collect documents and Submit budget will mark these events as executed. Doing a Statistical appraisal will mark itself as executed and exclude On-site appraisal, meaning that we can execute Assess loan application, which will remove the pending response and bring the graph into an accepting state.

Note that we can still execute Submit budget if new information is provided by the customer, which requires Assess loan application to be executed again.

5 Distributed DCR Graphs as Algorand Smart Contracts

In this section, we transform the DCR Graph into a stateful smart contract in TEAL. We eliminate the labels of the events and only keep the relationships and the IDs of the events. This design is for maintaining the anonymity of the DCR Graphs in the blockchain and saving space for more events.

For each DCR Graph, we maintain three global key/value pairs:

- GC, which records the address of the graph creator as a Byte32 String.
- MK, which indicates the marking of the graph as a Byte16 String;
- TEN, the total event number as an unsigned 64-bit integer.[1]

Each four bits of MK represents the status of an event, with the first bit describing if the event is included or excluded. The structure of the status:

- Excluded: $(xxx0)_2$;
- Included: $(xxx1)_2$;
- Pending: $(xx1x)_2$;
- executed: $(x1xx)_2$.

where x represents either 1 or 0. The number $i, i \in [0, TEN \times 5)$ bit refers to a status of the number $int(i/5)$ event. Only CG can add events or add the relationships between the events.

We maintain two key/value pairs E and E_links for each event E. The key/value pair E indicates the account address which can execute E; E_links indicates the links between E and other events (which event's status needs to be changed after the execution of E and which events are preventing E from execution) as a Byte32 String. Each five bits of the Value represents the links of an event. The structure of the links:

---
[1] Note that integer in TEAL is automatically a uint 64 integer.

- Include: $(xxxx1)_2$;
- Exclude: $(xxx1x)_2$;
- Milestone: $(xx1xx)_2$;
- Condition: $(x1xxx)_2$;
- Response: $(1xxxx)_2$.

Include, Exclude, Response are out-links, meaning that after execution of E, the relevant event will be included, excluded or pended. Milestone and Condition are in-links, meaning E may not be executed if the relevant event is pended or have not executed. For example, given two events A and B with relations $A \rightarrow\bullet B$ and $B \rightarrow\% A$, B_links will indicate both $A \rightarrow\bullet B$ and $B \rightarrow\% A$. $B\_links = (0100000010)_2$ assuming A indexed 1 and B indexed 2.

Given the limitations discussed in Sect. 3.1, our approach can have 61 events in maximum because we have 128 pairs in total and we use two key/value pairs for each event and three pairs for the graph.

We were provided with a breakdown of a database containing 22787 DCR models created by academic and commercial users; we report a summary in Fig. 3. Note that the statistics show that the average number of events within a graph generated in the site is 23 and 92.5% of the graphs have an event number below 61. Therefore, the 61 event limit appears to be a promising start for practical usage.

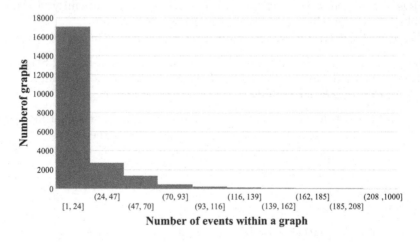

Fig. 3. The statistic from https://www.dcrgraphs.net/.

Figure 4 shows an example of the architecture, and 1_LINK indicates the link K/V pair of event 1.

Algorithms 1, 2, 3, and 4 show the pseudo-code of the operations of adding an event, adding an relationship, executing an event, and updating the status of the events, respectively. In Algorithm 1, we add an event by creating two key/value pairs representing the executor and the links to other events. In Algorithm 2, we add an relationship between two events by updating their links. The executor of an event can execute the event in Algorithm 3, the Algorithm will check in-links of the event to see if it is executable and then update MK via the out-links. In Algorithm 4, CG can update the status of an event.

In the codes, we are not using any operations that require a cost of more than 1. Therefore the four Algorithms are all within 700 operations when there are 61 events in maximum.

An example implementation corresponding to the graph shown in Fig. 2 is in the Algorand testnet, APP-ID:59565714. The link to the Github repository for the source code is https://github.com/XU-YIBIN/DCR-Algorand.

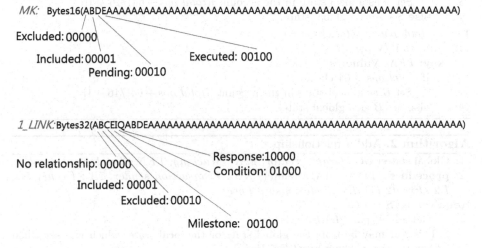

Fig. 4. The structures of the Key/Value pairs.

6 Financial Analysis

When a smart contract is deployed to the Algorand blockchain, it is given an app ID, which is a unique identifier. Furthermore, each smart contract has its own Algorand address, which is created from this unique ID. The address allows the smart contract to function as an escrow account. In order for the smart contract to run, there must be at least $Escrow_{overall}$ amount of microAlgos inside the smart contract, otherwise the transaction fails automatically.

$$Escrow_{global} = 100000 \times (1 + ExtraProgramPages)$$
$$+(25000 + 3500) \times schema.NumUint \qquad (1)$$
$$+(25000 + 25000) \times schema.NumByteSlice.$$

where $Schema.NumUint$ refers to the global integer key-value pairs (the value size is $UInt64bits$); $Schema.NumByteSlice$ refers to the global string key-value

---

Algorithm 1. Add an event

1: Global states: GC : $Graph\ creator$, MK : $Marking$, TEN : $Total\ event\ number$
2: **procedure** ADD AN EVENT(TXS : $Transaction\ sender$, EC : $executor$)
Require: $TXS == GC$ and $TEN < 61$
3:    $TEN \leftarrow TEN + 1$
4:    Set a K/V pair A:
     Key: TEN_links, **Value:** $Byte32(Null)$
5:    Set a Scratch value $total\_ops$, //scratch value is run-time value.
6:      $total\_ops \leftarrow (TEN - 1) \times 2 + 3 + 1$
     // because we have used three key/value pairs at the beginning and we are currently
     adding one more.
7:    **if** $total\_ops > 64$ **then**
8:        Set A as a local state in the account $[(total\_ops - 64)/16 - 1]$
9:    **else** Set A as a global state.
10:     $total\_ops \leftarrow total\_ops + 1$
11:    Set a K/V pair B:
     key: TEN, **Value:**EC
12:    **if** $total\_ops > 64$ **then**
13:        Set B as a local state in the account $[(total\_ops - 64)/16 - 1]$
14:    **else** Set B as a global state.

Algorithm 2. Add a relationship

1: Global states: GC : $Graph\ creator$, MK : $Marking$, TEN : $Total\ event\ number$
2: **procedure** ADD A RELATIONSHIP(TXS : $Transaction\ sender$, $E1$: $Event1\ ID$,
   $E2$: $Event2\ ID$, RT : $Relationship\ Type$)
Require: $TXS == GC$
3:    Get a K/V pair ($E1\_link$,A).
     //This pair may be from the global state or the local state, which was set when
     adding the event (using key:TEN_links).
4:    Get a K/V pair ($E2\_link$,B).
     //This pair may be from the global state or the local state.
5:    Set a scratch value k depanding on RT (include$\rightarrow$ 0, exclude $\rightarrow$ 1 , Milestone
     $\rightarrow$ 2, Condition $\rightarrow$ 3, Response $\rightarrow$ 4).
6:    **if** $k = 2$ or $k = 3$ **then**
7:        Set the $(E1 - 1) \times 5 + k$-bit of B to 1.
8:    **else**
9:        Set the $(E2 - 1) \times 5 + k$-bit of A to 1.
10:    Update K/V pairs ($E1\_link$,A) and ($E2\_link$,B) using updated A and B.

---

pairs. $ExtraProgramPages$ is only needed when the compiled program exceeds $2KB$, which we do not require.

The operation opt-in an account to the smart contract requires:

$$Escrow_{local} = 100000 + (25000 + 3500) \times schema.NumUint$$
$$+(25000 + 25000) \times schema.NumByteSlice. \tag{2}$$

$schema.NumUint$ and $schema.NumByteSlice$ refers to the local states.

Algorithm 3. Execute an event

1: Global states: GC : $Graph\ creator$, MK : $Marking$, TEN : $Total\ event\ number$
2: **procedure** EXECUTE AN EVENT(TXS : $Transaction\ sender$, $E1$: $Event1\ ID$)
3:     Get a K/V pair($E1,A$). //This pair may from the global state or the local state.
Require: $A == TXS$
4:     Get a K/V pair ($E1\_link,B$).
    //This pair may be from the global state or the local state.
5:     **for** i=0 to $TXN \times 5$ **do**
6:         Set a scratch value C_ID, $C\_ID \leftarrow int(i/5) + 1$.
    //$C_I D$ refers to the current event ID.
7:         Set a scratch value k, $k \leftarrow i\ mod\ 5$.
8:         **if** k-st bit of $B.Value$=1 **then**
9:             **if** k=2 **then** // The event C_ID milestone $E1$.
10:                If the $(C\_ID - 1) \times 4 + 1$-st bit of MK is 1, then return false.
11:            **else if** k=3 **then** //The event C_ID condition $E1$.
12:                If the $(C\_ID - 1) \times 4 + 2$-st bit of MK is 0, then return false.
13:    **for** i=0 to $TXN \times 5$ **do**
14:        Set a scratch value C_ID, $C\_ID \leftarrow int(i/5)+1$. //$C_I D$ refers to the current
    event ID.
15:        Set a scratch value k, $k \leftarrow i\ mod\ 5$.
16:        **if** k-st bit of B is 1 **then**
17:            **if** k=0 **then** // The event C_ID should be included.
18:                Set the $C\_ID \times 4 + 0$-bit of MK as 1.
19:            **else if** k=1 **then** //The event C_ID should be excluded.
20:                Set the $C\_ID \times 4 + 0$-bit of MK as 0.
21:            **else if** k=4 **then** //The event C_ID should be pended.
22:                Set the $C\_ID \times 4 + 1$-bit of MK as 1.
23:    Set $(E1 - 1) \times 4 + 1$-bit of MK as 0 //cancel the pending status.
24:    Set $(E1 - 1) \times 4 + 2$-bit of MK as 1 //update the status as executed.

Algorithm 4. Update the status of the event

1: Global states: GC : $Graph\ creator$, MK : $Marking$, TEN : $Total\ event\ number$
2: **procedure** UPDATE STATUS(TXS : $Transaction\ sender$, $E1$: $Event1\ ID$, S : $Status$)
Require: $TXS == GC$
3:     **if** S="include" **then**
4:         Set $(E1 - 1) \times 4$-bit of MK as 1.
5:     **else if** S="exclude" **then**
6:         Set $(E1 - 1) \times 4$-bit of MK as 0.
7:     **else if** S="pend" **then**
8:         Set $((E1 - 1) \times 4 + 1)$-bit of MK as 1.

We use one global integer key-value pair (the number of events), all other key-value pairs are String key-value pairs. $ExtraProgramPages = 0$. Then,

$$Escrow_{global} = 100000 + 28500 + 50000 \times min(TSN \times 2 + 2, 63). \qquad (3)$$

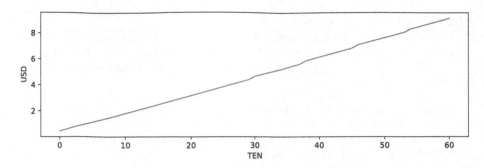

Fig. 5. The relationship between the events and the USD escrowed.

$$Escrow_{local\_i, i \in [0, ceil((TSN \times 2 + 2 - 63)/16))}$$
$$= 100000 + 50000 \times (\min(TSN \times 2 + 2 - 63 - (i - 1) \times 16, 16)). \quad (4)$$

$$Escrow_{overall} = Escrow_{global} + Escrow_{local\_i, i \in [0, ceil((TSN \times 2 + 2 - 63)/16))}. \quad (5)$$

When TSN=61,

$$Escrow_{overall} = Escrow_{global} + Escrow_{local} \times 4 = 3278500 + 3450000 = 6728500. \quad (6)$$

As of January 14th, 2022, 1000000 microAlgos are worth \$1.36. Therefore, the maximum amount of Algo locked for deploying a DCR Graph has a value of \$9.35. Figure 5 show the relationship between the number of events in a contract and the amount of USD locked. Note that the escrow is locked in the account that starts the contract and the remaining of it is released when the smart contract is closed. There is a fee for executing the smart contract.

The fees for executing the smart contract is paid by the escrow account linked to the smart contract or can be set to be paid by the executor. Each execution below 1kB costs a fixed 1,000 microAlgos or 0.001 Algos. Larger transactions use a fee-per-byte ratio. One can also choose to use the fee-per-byte ratio to increase the probability of getting included into a new block, however at the current usage levels of the network this is unnecessary. For our implementation, both contract creation and event execution transactions remain below the 1kB limit. In addition to the locked escrow, the creation fee for a smart contract is the same as a regular transaction, however since the DCR Graph is dynamically constructed through *addEvent*, *addRelation*, and *updateStatus* calls to the smart contract, creating the graph will require $1 + E + R + S$ transactions, where E is the number of events, R is the number of relations, and S is the number of status updates that need to be made to set the marking of the events of the contract to their initial state. A comparison of the costs for contract creation and event execution in Algorand and Ethereum is shown in Table 1. We calculated these numbers based on the example graph used in [13] which contains 5 events, contains 11 relations, and requires 3 status changes to the marking[2]. We

---

[2] [13] does not provide a generalised calculation of gas costs that can be used for a more thorough comparison.

Table 1. Costs and escrow for DCR contract creation and event execution on Algorand and Ethereum based on the example used in [13]. USD prices based on exchange rates on the 14th of January 2022. The calculated dollar cost for Ethereum transactions use a gwei/gas ratio of 150. Event execution cost in Ethereum is given as the mean of the 5 executions reported in [13].

	Algorand	Ethereum	USD Ratio
Contract creation cost (excluding escrow)	0.02 Algo $0.02720	717,709 gas $349.88314	17494
Contract creation cost (including escrow)	0.7485 Algo $1.01796	717,709 gas $349.88314	467
Event execution	0.001 Algo $0.00136	54,496 gas $26.56690	19534

observe a decrease in price by four orders of magnitude for both event execution and contract creation. If one includes the escrow, then contract creation is two orders of magnitude cheaper.

Finally, Algorand provides transaction finality in under 5 s, compared to approximately 3 min for Ethereum. While the latter is acceptable for many practical business processes, this is a notable improvement for more time-critical scenarios.

7   Conclusion

In this paper, we demonstrated how business processes can be executed on the Algorand blockchain through a translation from the declarative DCR process modelling language to TEAL smart contracts. We provided precise calculations of limitations on the size of process models and the cost of their execution. We showed that execution on the Algorand blockchain cuts costs by four orders of magnitude when compared to earlier implementations on Ethereum, bringing the use of public blockchains for business process execution back in the realm of reasonable possibilities. We implemented a prototype that demonstrates the feasibility of our approach and allows for future extensions.

In future work , we intend to extend the prototype, lift current limitations and implement more advanced features of the DCR language. In particular, we will extend the current 61 event limit by creating multiple linked smart contracts that can read each others global states. This operation is supported in TEAL by indicating multiple smart contracts in the Application Array of the transactions.

Currently our implementation describes an event by only using an event ID. This is to preserve privacy and save memory space. When the graph is extended by using multiple smart contracts, we may use space to store more information on the events such as their name and a description.

DCR Graphs support various advanced features such as notions of (logical) time, data-constraints, replication, and more advanced assignments between events, roles, and users [13], we plan to add these to our encoding in the future which will allow for the description and execution of more complex processes.

References

1. Buterin, V., et al.: A next-generation smart contract and decentralized application platform. white paper (2014)
2. Davenport, T.H.: Process Innovation: Reengineering Work Through Information Technology. Harvard Business School Press, Boston, MA, USA (1993)
3. Debois, S., Hildebrandt, T., Slaats, T.: Concurrency and asynchrony in declarative workflows. In: Motahari-Nezhad, H., Recker, J., Weidlich, M. (eds.) Business Process Management. BPM 2016. LNCS, vol. 9253, pp. 72–89. Springer, Cham (2015). https://doi.org/10.1007/978-3-319-23063-4_5
4. Frantz, C.K., Nowostawski, M.: From institutions to code: towards automated generation of smart contracts. In: FAS*W, pp. 210–215. IEEE (2016)
5. Gilad, Y., Hemo, R., Micali, S., Vlachos, G., Zeldovich, N.: Algorand: scaling byzantine agreements for cryptocurrencies. In: SOSP 2017, pp. 51–68 (2017)
6. Hildebrandt, T.T., Mukkamala, R.R.: Declarative event-based workflow as distributed dynamic condition response graphs. In: Honda, K., Mycroft, A. (eds.) PLACES 2010. EPTCS, vol. 69, pp. 59–73 (2010)
7. Hull, R., Batra, V.S., Chen, Y.-M., Deutsch, A., Heath III, F.F.T., Vianu, V.: Towards a shared ledger business collaboration language based on data-aware processes. In: Sheng, Q.Z., Stroulia, E., Tata, S., Bhiri, S. (eds.) ICSOC 2016. LNCS, vol. 9936, pp. 18–36. Springer, Cham (2016). https://doi.org/10.1007/978-3-319-46295-0_2
8. Klinger, P., Bodendorf, F.: Blockchain-based cross-organizational execution framework for dynamic integration of process collaborations. In: WI (2020)
9. Ladleif, J., Weske, M., Weber, I.: Modeling and enforcing blockchain-based choreographies. In: Hildebrandt, T., van Dongen, B.F., Röglinger, M., Mendling, J. (eds.) BPM 2019. LNCS, vol. 11675, pp. 69–85. Springer, Cham (2019). https://doi.org/10.1007/978-3-030-26619-6_7
10. López-Pintado, O., Dumas, M., García-Bañuelos, L., Weber, I.: Interpreted execution of business process models on blockchain. In: EDOC, pp. 206–215. IEEE (2019)
11. López-Pintado, O., Dumas, M., García-Bañuelos, L., Weber, I.: Controlled flexibility in blockchain-based collaborative business processes. Inf. Syst. **104**, 101622 (2022). https://doi.org/10.1016/j.is.2020.101622. https://www.sciencedirect.com/science/article/pii/S0306437920300946. ISSN 0306-4379
12. López-Pintado, O., García-Bañuelos, L., Dumas, M., Weber, I., Ponomarev, A.: Caterpillar: a business process execution engine on the Ethereum blockchain. SPE **49**(7), 1162–1193 (2019)
13. Madsen, M.F., Gaub, M., Høgnason, T., Kirkbro, M.E., Slaats, T., Debois, S.: Collaboration among adversaries: distributed workflow execution on a blockchain. In: SCFAB 2018 (2018)
14. Mendling, J., et al.: Blockchains for business process management-challenges and opportunities. ACM TMIS **9**(1), 1–16 (2018)
15. Pesic, M., Schonenberg, H., van der Aalst, W.M.: DECLARE: full support for loosely-structured processes. In: EDOC 2007, p. 287. IEEE, October 2007

16. Saberi, S., Kouhizadeh, M., Sarkis, J., Shen, L.: Blockchain technology and its relationships to sustainable supply chain management. Int. J. Prod. Res. **57**(7), 2117–2135 (2019)
17. Sturm, C., Szalanczi, J., Schönig, S., Jablonski, S.: A lean architecture for blockchain based decentralized process execution. In: Daniel, F., Sheng, Q.Z., Motahari, H. (eds.) BPM 2018. LNBIP, vol. 342, pp. 361–373. Springer, Cham (2019). https://doi.org/10.1007/978-3-030-11641-5_29
18. Tran, A.B., Lu, Q., Weber, I.: Lorikeet: a model-driven engineering tool for blockchain-based business process execution and asset management. In: BPM, pp. 56–60 (2018)
19. Zakhary, V., Amiri, M.J., Maiyya, S., Agrawal, D., Abbadi, A.E.: Towards global asset management in blockchain systems (2019)

Lissy: Experimenting with On-Chain Order Books

Mahsa Moosavi$^{(\boxtimes)}$ and Jeremy Clark

Concordia University, Montreal, Canada
seyedehmahsa.moosavi@concordia.ca

Abstract. Financial regulators have long-standing concerns about fully decentralized exchanges that run 'on-chain' without any obvious regulatory hooks. The popularity of Uniswap, an automated market makers (AMM), made these concerns a reality. AMMs implement a lightweight dealer-based trading system, but they are unlike anything on Wall Street, require fees intrinsically, and are susceptible to front-running attacks. This leaves the following research questions we address in this paper: (1) are conventional (*i.e.*, order books), secure (*i.e.*, resistant to front-running and price manipulation) and fully decentralized exchanges feasible on a public blockchain like Ethereum, (2) what is the performance profile, and (3) how much do Layer 2 techniques (*e.g.*, Arbitrum) increase performance? To answer these questions, we implement, benchmark, and experiment with an Ethereum-based call market exchange called Lissy. We confirm the functionality is too heavy for Ethereum today (you cannot expect to exceed a few hundred trade executions per block) but show it scales dramatically (99.88% gas cost reduction) on Arbitrum.

1 Introductory Remarks

There are three main approaches to arranging a trade [14]. In a *quote-driven* market, a dealer uses its own inventory to offer a price for buying or selling an asset. In a *brokered exchange*, a broker finds a buyer and seller. In an *order-driven* market, offers to buy (*bids*) and sell (*offers/asks*) from many traders are placed as orders in an order book. Order-driven markets can be *continuous*, with buyers/sellers at any time adding orders to the order book (*makers*) or executing against an existing order (*takers*); or they can be *called*, where all traders submit orders within a window of time and orders are matched in a batch (like an auction).

Conventional financial markets (*e.g.*, NYSE, NASDAQ) use both continuous time trading during open hours, and a call market before and during open hours to establish an opening price and a closing price. After early experiments at implementing continuous time trading on Ethereum (*e.g.*, EtherDelta, OasisDEX), it was generally accepted that conventional trading is infeasible on Ethereum for performance reasons. Centralized exchanges continued their predominance, while slowly some exchanges moved partial functionality on-chain (*e.g.*, custody of assets) while executing trades off-chain.

© International Financial Cryptography Association 2023
S. Matsuo et al. (Eds.): FC 2022 Workshops, LNCS 13412, pp. 598–614, 2023.
https://doi.org/10.1007/978-3-031-32415-4_36

A clever quote-driven alternative, called an automatic market maker (AMM), was developed that only requires data structures and traversals with low gas complexity. This approach has undesirable price dynamics (*e.g.,* market impact of a trade, slippage between the best bid/ask and actual average execution price, *etc.*) which explains why there is no Wall Street equivalent, however, it is efficient on Ethereum and works 'good enough' to attract trading. First generation AMMs provide makers (called liquidity providers) with no ability to act on price information—they are uninformed traders that can only lose (called impermanent loss) on trades but make money on fees. Current generation AMMs (*e.g.,* Uniswap v3) provided informed makers with a limited ability (called concentrated liquidity) to act on proprietary information [24] without breaking Ethereum's performance limitations. Ironically, the logical extension of this is a move back to where it all started—a full-fledged order-driven exchange that allows informed makers the fullest ability to trade strategically.

Contributions. In this paper, we experiment with on-chain markets to understand in detail if they remain infeasible on Ethereum and what the limiting factors are. Some highlights from our research include answering the following questions:

- What type of exchange has the fairest price execution on balance? (A call market.)
- How many orders can be processed on-chain? (Upper-bounded by 152 per block.)
- How much efficiency can be squeezed from diligently choosing the best data structures? (Somewhat limited; turn 38 trades into 152.)
- To what extent can we mitigate front-running attacks? (Almost entirely.)
- Can we stop the exchange's storage footprint on Ethereum from bloating? (Yes, but it is so expensive that it is not worth it.)
- Are on-chain order books feasible on layer 2? (Yes! Optimistic roll-ups reduce gas costs by 99.88%.)
- Which aspects of Ethereum were encountered that required deeper than surface-level knowledge to navigate? (Optimizing gas refunds, Solidity is not truly object-oriented, miner extractable value (MEV) can be leveraged for good, and bridging assets for layer 2.)
- How hard is an on-chain exchange to regulate? (The design leaves almost no regulatory hooks beyond miners (and sequencers on layer 2).)

2   Preliminaries

2.1   Ethereum

We assume the reader is familiar with the following concepts: blockchain technology; smart contracts and decentralized applications (DApps) on Ethereum; how Ethereum transactions are structured, broadcast, and finalized; the gas model including the gas limit (approximately 11M gwei at the time of our experiments) per block. A **gas refund** is a more esoteric subject (not covered thoroughly in

Table 1. Comparison among different trade execution systems.

Type	Description	Advantages	Disadvantages
Centralized Exchanges (CEX)	Order-driven exchange acts as a trusted third party (*e.g.*, Binance, Bitfinex)	Conventional Highest performance Low fees Easy to regulate Low price slippage Verbose trading strategies	Fully trusted custodian Slow withdrawals Server downtime Uncertain fair execution
Partially On-chain Exchange	Order-driven exchange acts as a semi-trusted party (*e.g.*, EtherDelta, 0x, IDEX, Loopring)	High performance Low fees Easy to regulate Low price slippage Verbose trading strategies Semi-custodial	Slow withdrawals Server downtime Front-running attacks Uncertain fair execution
On-Chain Dealers	Quote-driven decentralized exchange trades from inventory with public pricing rule (*e.g.*, Uniswap v3)	Non-custodial Instant trading Moderate performance Fair execution	Unconventional Impermanent loss High price slippage Intrinsic fees Front-running attacks Limited trading strategies Hard to regulate
On-chain Order-Driven Exchanges	Order-driven decentralized exchange executes trades between buyers and sellers (*e.g.*, Lissy)	Conventional Non-custodial Low price slippage Fair execution Verbose trading strategies Front-running is mitigable	Very low performance Hard to regulate

any academic work to our knowledge) that we use heavily in our optimizations. Briefly, certain EVM operations (`SELFDESTRUCT` and `SSTORE 0`) cost negative gas, with the follow caveats: the refund is capped at 50% of the total gas cost of the transaction, and (2) the block gas limit applies to the pre-refunded amount (*i.e.*, a transaction receiving a full refund can cost up to 5.5M gas with an 11M limit). We provide full details of all of these topics in the full version [22].

2.2 Trade Execution Systems

Table 1 illustrates various trade execution systems and summarizes their advantages and disadvantages. A full justification for the table can be found in [22]. Briefly, fully decentralized, on-chain exchanges require the lowest trust, provide instant settlement, and have transparent trading rules that will always execute correctly. Front-running attacks (see Sect. 5 for a very thorough discussion) are weaknesses inherent in blockchains that require specific mitigation.

2.3 Related Work

Call markets are studied widely in finance and provide high integrity prices (*e.g.*, closing prices that are highly referenced and used in derivative products) [11,15,23]. They can also combat high frequency trading [1,5]. An older 2014 paper [8] on the 'Princeton prediction market' [4] show that call markets mitigate most blockchain-based front-running attacks present in an on-chain continuous-trading exchange as well as other limitations: block intervals are slow and not continuous, there is no support for accurate time-stamping, transactions can be dropped or reordered by miners, and fast traders can react to submitted

Table 2. Primary operations of Lissy smart contract.

Operation	Description
depositToken()	Deposits ERC20 tokens in Lissy smart contract
depositEther()	Deposits ETH in Lissy smart contract
openMarket()	Opens the market
closeMarket()	Closes the market and processes the orders
submitBid()	Inserts the upcoming bids inside the priority queue
submitAsk()	Inserts the upcoming asks inside the priority queue
claimTokens()	Transfers tokens to the traders
claimEther()	Transfers ETH to the traders

orders/cancellations when broadcast to network but not in a block and have their orders appear first. The paper does not include an implementation, was envisioned as running on a custom blockchain (Ethereum was still in development in 2014) and market operations are part of the blockchain logic.

The most similar academic work to this paper is the Ethereum-based periodic auction by Galal *et al.* [12] and the continuous-time exchange TEX [18]. As with us, front-running is a main consideration of these works. In a recent SoK on front-running attacks in blockchain [10], three general mitigations are proposed: confidentiality, sequencing, and design. Both of these papers use confidentiality over the content of orders (*cf.* [7,20,27–29]). The main downside is that honest traders cannot submit their orders and leave, they must interact in a second round to reveal their orders. The second mitigation approach is to sequence transactions according to some rule akin to first-in-first-out [17,19]. These are not available for experimentation on Ethereum yet (although Chainlink has announced an intention[1]). The third solution is to design the service in a way that front-running attacks are not profitable—this is the approach with Lissy which uses *no cryptography* and is *submit-and-go* for traders. A detailed comparison of front-running is provided in Sect. 5. Our paper also emphasizes implementation details: Galal *et al.* do not provide a full implementation, and TEX uses both on-chain and off-chain components, and thus does not answer our research question of how feasible an on-chain order book is.

3   Call Market Design

A call market opens for traders to submit bids and asks which are enqueued until the market closes. Trades are executed by matching the best priced bid to the best priced ask until the best bid is less than the best ask, then all remaining trades are discarded. See [22] for a numeric example. If Alice's bid of $100 is executed against Bob's ask of $90, Alice pays $100, Bob receives $90 and the $10 difference (called a price improvement) is given to miners for reasons in explained in the front-running evaluation (Sect. 5).

For our experiments and measurements, we implement a call market from scratch. Lissy will open for a specified period of time during which it will accept

---

[1] A. Juels. blog.chain.link, 11 Sep 2020.

a capped number of orders (*e.g.,* 100 orders—parameterized so that all orders can be processed), and these orders are added to a priority queue (discussed in Sect. 3.1). Our vision is the market would be open for a very short period of time, close, and then reopen immediately (*e.g.,* every other block). Lissy is open source and written in 336 lines (SLOC) of Solidity plus the priority queue (*e.g.,* we implement 5 variants, each around 300 SLOC). We tested it with the Mocha testing framework using Truffle [26] on Ganache-CLI [25] to obtain our performance metrics. Once deployed, the bytecode of Lissy is 10,812 bytes plus the constructor code (6,400 bytes) which is not stored. The Solidity source code for Lissy and Truffle test files are available in a GitHub repository.[2] We have also deployed Lissy on Ethereum's testnet Rinkeby with flattened (single file) source code of just the Lissy base class and priority queue implementations. It is visible and can be interacted with here: [etherscan.io]. We cross-checked for vulnerabilities with *Slither*[3] and *SmartCheck*[4] and it only fails some 'informational' warnings that are intentional design choices (*e.g.,* a costly loop). All measurements assume a block gas limit of 11 741 495 and 1 gas = 56 Gwei.[5] Table 2 summarizes Lissy's primary operations.

3.1 Priority Queues

In designing Lissy within Ethereum's gas model, performance is the main bottleneck. For a call market, closing the market and processing all the orders are the most time-consuming steps. Assessing which data structures will perform best is hard (*e.g.,* gas refunds, a relatively cheap mapping data structure, only partial support for object-oriented programming) without actually deploying and evaluating several variants.

We first observe that orders are executed in order: highest to lowest price for bids, and lowest to highest price for asks. This means random access to the data structure holding the orders is unnecessary (we discuss cancelling orders later in Sect. 6.2). We can use a lightweight *priority queue* (PQ) which has only two functions: Enqueue() inserts an element into the priority queue; and Dequeue() removes and returns the highest priority element. Specifically, we use two PQs—one for bids, where the highest price is the highest priority, and one for asks, where the lowest price is the highest priority.

As closing the market is very expensive with any PQ, we rule out sorting the elements while dequeuing and sort during each enqueue. We then implement the following 5 PQ variants:

1. **Heap with Dynamic Array.** A heap is a binary tree where data is stored in nodes in a specific order where the root always represents the highest priority item (*i.e.,* highest bid price/lowest ask price). Our heap stores its data in a Solidity-provided dynamically sized array. The theoretical time complexity is logarithmic enqueue and logarithmic dequeue.

---

2. **Heap with Static Array.** This variant replaces the dynamic array with a Solidity storage array where the size is statically allocated. This is asymptotically the same and marginally faster in practice.
3. **Heap with Mapping.** In this variant, we store a key for the order in the heap instead of the entire order. Once a key is dequeued, the order struct is drawn from a Solidity mapping (which stores key-value pairs very efficiently). This is asymptotically the same and faster with variable-sized data.
4. **Linked List.** In this variant, elements are stored in a linked list (enabling us to efficiently insert a new element between two existing elements during enqueue). Solidity is described as object-oriented but the Solidity equivalent of an object is an entire smart contract. Therefore, an object-oriented linked list must either (1) create each node in the list as a struct—but this is not possible as Solidity does not support recursive structs—or (2) make every node in the list its own contract. The latter option seems wasteful and unusual, but it surprisingly ends up being the most gas efficient data structure to dequeue. The theoretical time complexity is linear enqueue and constant dequeue.
5. **Linked List with Mapping.** Finally, we try a variant of a linked list using a Solidity mapping. The value of the mapping is a struct with the incoming order's data and the key of the next (and previous) node in the list. The contract stores the key of the first node (head) and last node (tail) in the list. Asymptotically, it is linear enqueue and constant dequeue.

We implemented, deployed, and tested each PQ. A simple test of enqueuing 50 integers chosen at random from a fixed interval is in Fig. 1 and dequeing them all is in Table 3. Dequeuing removes data from the contract's storage resulting in a gas refund. Based on our manual estimates,[6] every variant receives the maximum gas refund possible (*i.e.*, half the total cost of the transaction). In other words, each of them actually consumes twice the `gasUsed` amount in gas before the refund. However, none of them are better or worse based on how much of a refund they generate.

We observe that (1) the linked list variants are materially cheaper than the heap variants at dequeuing; (2) dequeuing in a call market must be done as a batch, whereas enqueuing is paid for one at a time by the trader submitting the order; and (3) Ethereum will not permit more than hundreds of orders so asymptotic behaviour is not significant. For these reasons, we suggest using one of the linked list variants. As it can be seen in Fig. 1, the associated cost for inserting elements into a linked list PQ is significantly greater than the linked list with mapping, as each insertion causes the creation of a new contract. Accordingly, we choose to implement the call market with the linked list with mapping which balances a moderate gas cost for insertion (*i.e.*, order submission) with one for removal (*i.e.*, closing the market and matching the orders). In Sect. 4, we implement Lissy on Layer 2. There, the PQ variant does not change the layer 1 gas costs (as calldata size is the same) and the number of orders can be

---

[6] EVM does not expose the refund counter. We determine how many storage slots are being cleared and how many smart contracts destroyed, then we multiply these numbers by 24,000 or 15,000 respectively.

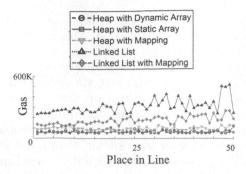

Fig. 1. Gas costs for enqueuing 50 random integers into five priority queue variants. For the x-axis, a value of 9 indicates it is the 9th integer entered in the priority queue. The y-axis is the cost of enqueuing in gas.

Table 3. The gas metrics associated with dequeuing 50 integers from five priority queue variants. Full refund amount is shown but the actual refund that is applied is capped.

	Gas Used	Refund	Full Refund?
Heap with Dynamic Array	2,518,131	750,000	●
Heap with Static Array	1,385,307	750,000	●
Heap with Mapping	2,781,684	1,500,000	●
Linked List	557,085	1,200,000	●
Linked List with Mapping	731,514	3,765,000	●

Table 4. The gas metrics associated with dequeuing 50 integers from four linked list variants. For the refund, (●) indicates the refund was capped at the maximum amount and (◐) means a greater refund would be possible.

	Gas Used	Potential Refund	Full Refund?
Linked List without SELFDESTRUCT	721,370	0	◐
Linked List with SELFDESTRUCT	557,085	1,200,000	●
Linked List with Mapping and without DELETE	334,689	765,000	●
Linked List with Mapping and DELETE	731,514	3,765,000	●

substantially increased. thus, we reconsider asymptotic and choose a heap (with dynamic array) to lower L2 gas costs across both enqueuing and dequeuing.

3.2   Cost/Benefit of Cleaning up After Yourself

One consequence of a linked list is that a new contract is created for every node in the list. Beyond being expensive for adding new nodes (a cost that will be bared by the trader in a call market), it also leaves a large footprint in the active Ethereum state, especially if we leave the nodes on the blockchain in perpetuity (*i.e.*, we just update the head node of the list and leave the previous head 'dangling'). However in a PQ, nodes are only removed from the head of the list; thus the node contracts could be 'destroyed' one by one using an extra operation, SELFDESTRUCT, in the Dequeue() function. As shown in Table 4, the refund from doing this outweighs to the cost of the extra computation: gas costs are reduced from 721K to 557K. This suggests a general principle: cleaning up after yourself will pay for itself in gas refunds. Unfortunately, this is not universally true as shown by applying the same principle to the linked list with mapping.

Dequeuing in a linked list with mapping can be implemented in two ways. The simplest approach is to process a node, update the head pointer, and leave the 'removed' node's data behind in the mapping untouched (where it will never be referenced again). Alternatively, we can call DELETE on each mapping entry

Table 5. Performance of Lissy for each PQ variant. Each consumes just under the block gas limit (~11M gas) with a full refund of half of its gas.

	Max Trades (w.c.)	Gas Used for Max Trades	Gas Used for 1000 Trades	Gas Used for Submission (avg)
Heap with Dynamic Array	38	5,372,679	457,326,935	207,932
Heap with Static Array	42	5,247,636	333,656,805	197,710
Heap with Mapping	46	5,285,275	226,499,722	215,040
Linked List	152	5,495,265	35,823,601	735,243
Linked List with Mapping	86	5,433,259	62,774,170	547,466

once we finish processing a trade. As it can be seen in the last two rows of Table 4, leaving the data on the blockchain is cheaper than cleaning it up.

The lesson here is that gas refunds incentivize developers to clean up storage variables they will not use again, but it is highly contextual as to whether it will pay for itself. Further, the cap on the maximum refund means that refunds are not fully received for large cleanup operations (however removing the cap impacts the miners' incentives to include the transaction). We present a second case study of the cost-benefit of clearing a mapping when it is no longer needed (including our idea to store the mapping in its own contract so it can SELFDESTRUCT with a single function call) in [22]. The unfortunate takeaway is, again, that it is cheapest to leave the mapping in place. Cleaning up EVM state is a complicated and under-explored area of Ethereum in the research literature. For our own work, we strive to be good citizens of Ethereum and clean up to the extent that we can—thus all PQs in Table 3 implement some cleanup.

3.3 Lissy Performance Measurements

The main research question is how many orders can be processed under the Ethereum block gas limit. The choice of PQ implementation is the main influence on performance and the results are shown in Table 5. These numbers are for the *worst-case*—when every submitted bid and ask is marketable (*i.e.,* will require fulfillment). In practice, once closeMarket() hits the first bid or ask that cannot be executed, it can stop processing all remaining orders. Premised on Ethereum becoming more efficient over time, we were interested in how much gas it would cost to execute 1000 pairs of orders, which is given in the third column. The fourth column indicates the cost of submitting a bid or ask — since this cost will vary depending on how many orders are already submitted (recall Fig. 1), we average the cost of 200 order submissions.

The main takeaway is that call markets appear to be limited to processing about a hundred orders per transaction and even that is at the enormous cost of monopolizing an entire Ethereum block just to close the market. Perhaps Lissy can work today in some circumstances like very low liquidity tokens, or markets with high volumes and a small number of traders (*e.g.,* liquidation auctions).

4   Lissy on Arbitrum

Layer 2 (L2) solutions [13] are a group of scaling technologies proposed to address specific drawbacks of executing transactions on Ethereum, which is considered *Layer 1 (L1)*. Among these proposals, *roll-ups* prioritize reducing gas costs (as opposed to other valid concerns like latency and throughput, which are secondary for Lissy). We review two variants, *optimistic roll-ups* and *zk roll-ups*, in [22]. Briefly, in a roll-up, every transaction is stored (but not executed) on Ethereum, then executed off-chain, and the independently verifiable result is pushed back to Ethereum, with some evidence of being executed correctly. We also compare Lissy on Arbitrum to Loopring 3.0 in [22].

We choose to experiment with Lissy on the optimistic rollup Arbitrum.[7] To deploy a DApp on Arbitrum, or to execute a function on an existing Arbitrum DApp, the transaction is sent to an *inbox* on L1. It is not executed on L1, it is only recorded (as calldata) in the inbox. An open network of *validators* watch the inbox for new transactions. Once inbox transactions are finalized in an Ethereum block, validators will execute the transactions and assert the result of the execution to other validators on a sidechain called ArbOS. As the Inbox contract maintains all Arbitrum transactions, anyone can recompute the entire current state of the ArbOS and file a dispute if executions are not correctly reported on ArbOS. Disputes are adjudicated by Ethereum itself and require a small, constant amount of gas, invariant to how expensive the transaction being disputed is. When the dispute challenge period is over, the new state of ArbOS is stored as a checkpoint on Ethereum.

4.1   Lissy Performance Measurements on Arbitrum

Testing Platforms. We implement Lissy using the Arbitrum Rollup chain hosted on the Rinkeby testnet. It is visible and can be interacted with here: [Arbitrum Explorer]. To call functions on Lissy, traders can (1) send transactions directly to the Inbox contract, or (2) use a relay server (called a *Sequencer*) provided by the Arbitrum. The sequencer will group, order, and send all pending transactions together as a single Rinkeby transaction to the Inbox (and pays the gas).

In our Lissy variant on Arbitrum, the validators do all computations (both enqueuing and dequeuing) so we choose to use a heap with dynamic array for our priority queue, which balances the expense of both operations. Heaps are 32% more efficient than linked lists for submitting orders and 29% less efficient for closing. Recall that without a roll-up, such a priority queue can only match 38 pairs at a cost of 5,372,679 gas. Table 6 shows that 38 pairs cost only 6,569 in L1 gas (a 99.88% savings). This is the cost of submitting the `closeMarket()` transaction to the Inbox to be recorded, which is 103 bytes of calldata. Most importantly, recording `closeMarket()` in the Inbox will always cost around 6,569

---

[7] See https://offchainlabs.com for more current details than the 2018 *USENIX Security* paper [16].

Table 6. Gas costs of closing a market on Ethereum and on Arbitrum. ArbGas corresponds to Layer 2 *computation used.*

	Layer1 gasUsed	Layer2 ArbGas
Lissy on Ethereum	5,372,679	N/A
Lissy on Arbitrum	6,569	508,250

even as the number of trades increases from 38 pairs to thousands or millions of pairs. Of course, as the number of trades increase, the work for the validators on L2 increases, as measured in ArbGas. The price of ArbGas in Gwei is not well established but is anticipated to be relatively cheap. Arbitrum also reduces the costs for traders to submit an order: from 207,932 to 6,917 in L1 gas. We illustrate the interaction between the traders and Lissy on Arbitrum including bridges, inboxes, sequencers and validators in [22].

Running Lissy on Arbitrum has one large caveat. If the ERC20 tokens being traded are not issued on ArbOS, which is nearly always the case today, they first need to be *bridged* onto ArbOS, as does the ETH. Traders send ETH or tokens to Arbitrum's bridge contracts which create the equivalent amount at the same address on L2. Withdrawals work the same way in reverse, but are only final on L1 after a dispute challenge period (currently 1 h).[8]

5   Front-Running Evaluation

As we illustrate in Table 7, call markets have a unique profile of resilience against *front-running attacks* [8–10] that differs somewhat from continuous-time markets and automated market makers. Traders are sometimes distinguished as *makers* (adds orders to a market) and *takers* (trades against a pre-existing, unexecuted orders). A continuous market has both. All traders using an automated market maker are takers, while the investors who provide tokens to the AMM (liquidity providers) are makers. Under our definition, a call market only has makers: the only way to have a trade executed is to submit an order. The front-running attacks in Table 7 are subcategorized, using a recent SoK [10], as being *Insertion*, *Displacement*, and *Suppression*. To explain the difference, we will illustrate the first three attacks in the table.

In an *insertion attack*, Mallory learns of a transaction from Alice. Consider Alice submitting a bid order for 100 tokens at any price (market order). Mallory decides to add new ask orders to the book (limit orders) at the maximum price reachable by Alice's order given the rest of the asks in the book. Mallory must arrange for her orders to be added before Alice's transaction and then arrange for Alice's transaction to be the next (relevant) transaction to run (*e.g.,* before competing asks from other traders are added).

In a centralized exchange, Mallory would collude with the *authority* running the exchange to conduct this attack. On-chain, Mallory could be a fast *trader*

---

[8] L1 users might accept assets before they are finalized as they can determine their eventual emergence on L1 is indisputable (*eventual finality*).

Table 7. An evaluation of front-running attacks (rows) for different types of order books (columns). Front-running attacks are in three categories: Insertion, displacement, and suppression. A full dot (●) means the front-running attack is mitigated or not applicable to the order book type, a partial mitigation (◐) is awarded when the front-running attack is possible but expensive, and we give no award (○) if the attack is feasible.

	Who is Mallory? Authority, Trader, Miner, Sequencer		Centralized Continuous Market (Coinbase)	Partially Off-chain Continuous Market (EtherDelta)	Partially Off-chain Continuous Market w/ Roll-up (Loopring)	On-chain Continuous Market (OasisDex)	On-chain Dark Continuous Market (TEX)	On-chain Automated Market Maker (Uniswap)	On-chain Call Market w/ Price Improvement	On-chain Call Market (Lissy)	On-chain Call Market w/ Roll-up (Lissy variant)	On-chain Dark Call Market (Galal et al.)
			A	A,T,M	A,T,M,S	T,M	T,M	T,M	T,M	T,M	T,M,S	T,M
Attack Example	Mallory (*maker*) squeezes in a transaction before Alice's (*taker*) order	Ins.	○	○	○	○	●	○	●	●	●	●
	Mallory (*taker*) squeezes in a transaction before Bob's (*taker 2*)	Disp.	○	○	○	○	●	○	●	●	●	●
	Mallory (*maker 1*) suppresses a better incoming order from Alice (*maker 2*) until Mallory's order is executed	Supp.	○	○	○	●	●	●	◐	◐	◐	◐
	A hybrid attack based on the above (*e.g.,* sandwich attacks, scalping)	I/S/D	○	○	○	○	●	○	○	●	●	●
	Mallory suspends the market for a period of time	Supp.	○	○	○	◐	◐	◐	◐	◐	◐	◐
	Spoofing: Mallory (*maker*) puts an order as bait, sees Alice (*taker*) tries to execute it, and cancels it first	S&D	○	○	○	○	●	○	●	●	●	●
	Cancellation Griefing: Alice (*maker*) cancels an order and Mallory (*taker*) fulfills it first	Disp.	○	○	○	○	●	○	●	●	●	●

who sees Alice's transaction in the mempool and adds her transaction with a higher gas fee to bribe miners to execute hers first (insertion is probabilist and not guaranteed). Finally, Mallory could be the *miner* of the block that includes Alice's transaction allowing her to insert with high fidelity. Roll-ups use *sequencers* discussed in Sect. 5.1.

A *displacement attack* is like an insertion attack, except Mallory does not care what happens to Alice's original transaction—she only cares about being first. If Mallory sees Alice trying to execute a trade at a good price, she could try to beat Alice and execute the trade first. Mallory is indifferent to whether Alice can then execute her trade or not. The analysis of both insertion and suppression attacks are similar. Call markets mitigate these basic insertion and displacement attacks because they do not have any time priority (e.g., if you were to shuffle the order of all orders submitted within the same call, the outcome would be exactly the same). A different way to mitigate these attacks is to seal orders with confidentiality (a *dark* market).

In a *suppression attack*, Mallory floods the network with transactions until a trader executes her order. Such selective denial of service is possible by an off-chain operator. With on-chain continuous markets, it is not possible to suppress Alice's transaction while also letting through a transaction from a taker—suppression applies to all Ethereum transactions or none. A call market is uniquely vulnerable because it eventually times out (which does not require an on-chain transaction) and new orders cannot be added. We still award a call market partial mitigation since suppression attacks are expensive (*cf.* Fomo3D attack [10]). If the aim of suppression is a temporary denial of service (captured by attack 5 in the table), then all on-chain markets are vulnerable to this expensive attack.

Some attacks combine more than one insertion, displacement, and/or suppression attacks. AMMs are vulnerable to a double insertion called a sandwich attack [30] which bookends a victim's trade with the front-runner's trades (plus additional variants). In a traditional call market, a market clearing price is chosen and all trades are executed at this price. All bids made at a higher price will receive the assets for the lower clearing price (and conversely for lower ask prices): this is called a *price improvement* and it allows traders to submit at their best price. A hybrid front-running attack allows Mallory to extract any price improvements. Consider the case where Alice's ask crosses Bob's bid with a material price improvement. Mallory inserts a bid at Alice's price, suppresses Bob's bid until the next call, and places an ask at Bob's price. She buys and then immediately sells the asset and nets the price improvement as arbitrage. To mitigate this in Lissy, all price improvements are given to the miner (using `block.coinbase.transfer()`). This does not actively hurt traders—they always receive the same price that they quote in their orders—and it removes any incentive for miners to front-run these profits.

Other front-running attacks use order cancellations (see Sect. 6.2) which Lissy mitigates by running short-lived markets with no cancellations.

There are two main takeaways from Table 7. Call markets provide strong resilience to front-running only bested slightly by dark markets like TEX [18], however, they do it through design—no cryptography and no two-round protocols. A second observation is that dark call markets, like Galal *et al.* [12], are no more resilient to front-running than a lit market (however confidentiality could provide resilience to predatory trading algorithms that react quickly to trades without actually front-running).

5.1 Front-Running on Arbitrum

In our Lissy variant on the Arbitrum, traders can submit transactions to the Layer 1 Inbox contract instead of directly to the Lissy DApp. This has the same front-running profile as Lissy itself; only the Layer 1 destination address is different. If a sequencer is mandatory, it acts with the same privilege as a Layer 1 Ethereum miner in ordering the transactions it receives. Technically, sequencers are not limited to roll-ups and could be used in the context of normal Layer 1 DApps, but they are more apparent in the context of roll-ups. A sequencer could be trusted to execute transactions in the order it receives them, outsource to a fair ordering service, or (in a tacit acknowledgment of the difficulties of preventing

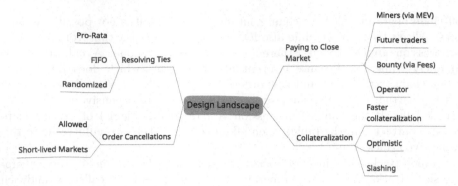

Fig. 2. A design landscape for on-chain call markets.

front-running) auction off permission to order transactions to the highest bidder (called a *MEV auction*). As shown in Table 7, a sequencer is an additional front-running actor but does not otherwise change the kinds of attacks that are possible.

6 Design Landscape

Lissy is a simple base class that implements the core functionality of a call market. To use it in the real world, design decisions need to be made about how it will be used. Figure 2 provides a design landscape for Lissy deployment, with possible extensions and customization.

6.1 Token Divisibility and Ties

A common trading rule is to fill ties in proportion to their volume (*i.e., pro rata* allocation)[9]. This can fail when tokens are not divisible. Consider the following corner case: 3 equally priced bids of 1 non-divisible token and 1 ask at the same price: (1) the bid could be randomly chosen (*cf.* Libra [21]), or (2) the bid could be prioritized based on time. In Lissy, tokens are assumed to be divisible. If the volume of the current best bid does not match the best ask, the larger order is partially filled and the remaining volume is considered against the next best order. We note the conditions under which pro rata allocation fails (*i.e.,* non-divisible assets, an exact tie on price, and part of the final allocation) are improbable. (1) is the fairest solution with one main drawback: on-chain sources of 'randomness' are generally deterministic and manipulatable by miners [3,6], while countermeasures can take a few blocks to select [2]. We implement (2) which means front-running attacks are possible in this one improbable case.

---

[9] If Alice and Bob bid the same price for 100 tokens and 20 tokens respectively, and there are only 60 tokens left in marketable asks, Alice receives 50 and Bob 10.

6.2 Order Cancellations

Support for cancellation opens the market to new front-running issues where other traders (or miners) can displace cancellations until after the market closes. However, one benefit of a call market is that beating a cancellation with a new order has no effect, assuming the cancellation is run any time before the market closes. Also, cancellations have a performance impact. Cancelled orders can be removed from the underlying data structure or accumulated in a list that is cross-checked when closing the market. Removing orders requires a more verbose structure than a priority queue (*e.g.*, a self-balancing binary search tree instead of a heap; or methods to traverse a linked list rather than only pulling from the head). Lissy does not support order cancellations. We intend to open and close markets quickly (on the order of blocks), so orders are relatively short-lived.

6.3 Who Pays to Close/Reopen the Market?

In the Princeton paper [8], the call market is envisioned as an alt-coin, where orders accumulate within a block and a miner closes the market as part of the logic of producing a new block (*i.e.*, within the same portion of code as computing their coinbase transaction in Bitcoin or gasUsed in Ethereum). In Lissy, someone needs to execute closeMarket() at the right time and pay for it, which is probably the most significant design challenge for Lissy.

Since price improvements are paid to the miners, the miner is incentivized to run closeMarket() if it pays for itself. Efficient algorithms for miners to automatically find 'miner extractable value (MEV)' opportunities [9] is an open research problem. Even if someone else pays to close the market, MEV smooths out some market functionality. Assume several orders are submitted and then closeMarket(). A naive miner might order the closeMarket() before the submitted orders, effectively killing those orders and hurting its own potential profit. MEV encourages miners to make sure a profitable closeMarket() in the mempool executes within its current block (to claim the reward for itself) and that it runs after other orders in the mempool to maximize its profit.

Without MEV, markets should open and close on different blocks. In this alternative, the closeMarket() function calls openMarket() as a subroutine and sets two modifiers: orders are only accepted in the block immediately after the current block (*i.e.*, the block that executes the closeMarket()) and closeMarket() cannot be run again until two blocks after the current block.

Another option is to have traders in the next call market pay to incrementally close the current market. For example, each order in the next market needs to pay to execute the next x orders in the current market until the order book is empty. This has two issues: first, amortizing the cost of closing the market amongst the early traders of the new market disincentives trading early in the market; the second issue is if not enough traders submit orders in the new market, the old market never closes (resulting in a backlog of old markets waiting to close).

A closely related option is to levy a carefully computed fee against the traders for every new order they submit. These fees are accumulated by the DApp to use as a bounty. When the time window for the open market elapses, the sender of the first `closeMarket()` function to be confirmed receives the bounty. This is still not perfect: `closeMarket()` cost does not follow a tight linear increase with the number of orders, and gas prices vary over time which could render the bounty insufficient for offsetting the `closeMarket()` cost. If the DApp can pay for its own functions, an interested party can also arrange for a commercial service (*e.g.,* any.sender[10]) to relay the `closeMarket()` function call on Ethereum (an approach called *meta-transactions*). This creates a regulatory hook.

The final option is to rely on an interested third party (such as the token issuer for a given market) to always close the market, or occasionally bailout the market when one of the above mechanisms fails. An external service like Ethereum Alarm Clock[11] (which also creates a regulatory hook) can be used to schedule regular `closeMarket()` calls.

6.4   Collateralization Options

In Lissy, both the tokens and ETH that a trader wants to potentially use are preloaded into the contract. We discuss alternative designs in [22].

7   Concluding Remarks

Imagine you have just launched a token on Ethereum. Now you want to be able to trade it. While the barrier to entry for exchange services is low, it still exists. For a centralized or decentralized exchange, you have to convince the operators to list your token and you will be delayed while they process your request. For an automated market maker, you will have to lock up a large amount of ETH into the DApp, along with your tokens. For roll-ups, you will have to host your own servers. By contrast to all of these, with an on-chain order book, you just deploy the code alongside your token and trading is immediately supported. Even if it is too slow today, there is little reason for developers not to offer it as a fallback solution that accompanies every token. With future improvements to blockchain scalability, it could become the de facto trading method.

Acknowledgements. The authors thank the AMF (Autorité des Marchés Financiers) for supporting this research project. J. Clark also acknowledges partial funding from the National Sciences and Engineering Research Council (NSERC)/Raymond Chabot Grant Thornton/Catallaxy Industrial Research Chair in Blockchain Technologies, as well as NSERC through a Discovery Grant. M. Moosavi acknowledges support from Fonds de Recherche du Québec - Nature et Technologies (FRQNT).

References

1. Aquilina, M., Budish, E.B., O'Neill, P.: Quantifying the high-frequency trading "arms race": a simple new methodology and estimates. Chicago Booth Research Paper (20–16) (2020)

---

[10] https://github.com/PISAresearch/docs.any.sender.
[11] https://ethereum-alarm-clock-service.readthedocs.io/.

2. Boneh, D., Bonneau, J., Bünz, B., Fisch, B.: Verifiable delay functions. In: Shacham, H., Boldyreva, A. (eds.) CRYPTO 2018. LNCS, vol. 10991, pp. 757–788. Springer, Cham (2018). https://doi.org/10.1007/978-3-319-96884-1_25
3. Bonneau, J., Clark, J., Goldfeder, S.: On bitcoin as a public randomness source (2015). https://eprint.iacr.org/2015/1015.pdf. Accessed 25 Oct 2015
4. Brandom, R.: This Princeton professor is building a bitcoin-inspired prediction market (2013). https://www.theverge.com/2013/11/29/5158234/this-princeton-professor-is-building-a-bitcoin-inspired-prediction
5. Budish, E., Cramton, P., Shim, J.: The high-frequency trading arms race: frequent batch auctions as a market design response. Q. J. Econ. **130**(4), 1547–1621 (2015)
6. Bünz, B., Goldfeder, S., Bonneau, J.: Proofs-of-delay and randomness beacons in Ethereum. In: IEEE S&B (2017)
7. Cartlidge, J., Smart, N.P., Talibi Alaoui, Y.: MPC joins the dark side. In: ASIACCS, pp. 148–159 (2019)
8. Clark, J., Bonneau, J., Felten, E.W., Kroll, J.A., Miller, A., Narayanan, A.: On decentralizing prediction markets and order books. In: WEIS (2014)
9. Daian, P., et al.: Flash boys 2.0: frontrunning, transaction reordering, and consensus instability in decentralized exchanges. In: IEEE Symposium on Security and Privacy (2020)
10. Eskandari, S., Moosavi, S., Clark, J.: SoK: transparent dishonesty: front-running attacks on blockchain. In: Bracciali, A., Clark, J., Pintore, F., Rønne, P.B., Sala, M. (eds.) FC 2019. LNCS, vol. 11599, pp. 170–189. Springer, Cham (2020). https://doi.org/10.1007/978-3-030-43725-1_13
11. Félez-Viñas, E., Hagströmer, B.: Do volatility extensions improve the quality of closing call auctions? Financ. Rev. **56**(3), 385–406 (2021)
12. Galal, H.S., Youssef, A.M.: Publicly verifiable and secrecy preserving periodic auctions. In: Bernhard, M., et al. (eds.) FC 2021. LNCS, vol. 12676, pp. 348–363. Springer, Heidelberg (2021). https://doi.org/10.1007/978-3-662-63958-0_29
13. Gudgeon, L., Moreno-Sanchez, P., Roos, S., McCorry, P., Gervais, A.: SoK: layer-two blockchain protocols. In: Bonneau, J., Heninger, N. (eds.) FC 2020. LNCS, vol. 12059, pp. 201–226. Springer, Cham (2020). https://doi.org/10.1007/978-3-030-51280-4_12
14. Harris, L.: Trading and Exchanges: Market Microstructure for Practitioners. Oxford (2003)
15. Hillion, P., Suominen, M.: The manipulation of closing prices. J. Financ. Markets **7**(4), 351–375 (2004)
16. Kalodner, H., Goldfeder, S., Chen, X., Weinberg, S.M., Felten, E.W.: Arbitrum: scalable, private smart contracts. In: USENIX Security Symposium, pp. 1353–1370 (2018)
17. Kelkar, M., Zhang, F., Goldfeder, S., Juels, A.: Order-fairness for byzantine consensus. In: Micciancio, D., Ristenpart, T. (eds.) CRYPTO 2020. LNCS, vol. 12172, pp. 451–480. Springer, Cham (2020). https://doi.org/10.1007/978-3-030-56877-1_16
18. Khalil, R., Gervais, A., Felley, G.: TEX-a securely scalable trustless exchange. IACR Cryptol. ePrint Arch. **2019**, 265 (2019)
19. Kursawe, K.: Wendy, the good little fairness widget: Achieving order fairness for blockchains. In: ACM AFT (2020)
20. Massacci, F., Ngo, C.N., Nie, J., Venturi, D., Williams, J.: FuturesMEX: secure, distributed futures market exchange. In: IEEE Symposium on Security and Privacy, pp. 335–353. IEEE (2018)
21. Mavroudis, V., Melton, H.: Libra: fair order-matching for electronic financial exchanges. In: ACM AFT (2019)

22. Moosavi, M., Clark, J.: Lissy: experimenting with on-chain order books (2021). https://doi.org/10.48550/ARXIV.2101.06291, https://arxiv.org/abs/2101.06291
23. Pagano, M.S., Schwartz, R.A.: A closing call's impact on market quality at Euronext Paris. J. Financ. Econ. **68**(3), 439–484 (2003)
24. Park, A.: The conceptual flaws of constant product automated market making. Available at SSRN 3805750 (2021)
25. Suite, T.: Ganache (2021). https://www.trufflesuite.com/ganache. Accessed 26 May 2021
26. Suite, T.: Truffle (2021). https://www.trufflesuite.com/docs/truffle/overview. Accessed 26 May 2021
27. Thorpe, C., Parkes, D.C.: Cryptographic securities exchanges. In: Dietrich, S., Dhamija, R. (eds.) FC 2007. LNCS, vol. 4886, pp. 163–178. Springer, Heidelberg (2007). https://doi.org/10.1007/978-3-540-77366-5_16
28. Thorpe, C., Willis, S.R.: Cryptographic rule-based trading. In: Keromytis, A.D. (ed.) FC 2012. LNCS, vol. 7397, pp. 65–72. Springer, Heidelberg (2012). https://doi.org/10.1007/978-3-642-32946-3_6
29. Sion, Radu (ed.): FC 2010. LNCS, vol. 6052. Springer, Heidelberg (2010). https://doi.org/10.1007/978-3-642-14577-3
30. Zhou, L., Qin, K., Torres, C.F., Le, D.V., Gervais, A.: High-frequency trading on decentralized on-chain exchanges. In: IEEE Symposium on Security and Privacy (2021)

Hours of Horus:
Keyless Cryptocurrency Wallets

Dionysis Zindros[✉]

Stanford University and Harmony, Stanford, USA
dionyziz@gmail.com

Abstract. We put forth a *keyless wallet*, a cryptocurrency wallet where
money can be spent using a password alone, and no private keys are
required. It requires a smart contract blockchain. We propose a scheme
in which the user uses an OTP authenticator seed to generate a long
series of time-based OTP passwords for the foreseeable future. These
are encrypted and organized in a Merkle tree whose root is stored in a
smart contract. The user can spend funds at any time by simply visually
providing the current OTP password from an air gapped device. These
OTPs can be relatively short: Just 6 alphanumeric characters suffice.
Our OTP scheme can work in proof-of-stake as well as static and variable difficulty proof-of-work blockchains. The low-entropy passwords and
OTPs in our scheme are protected from brute force attacks by requiring that an adversary accompany any attempt by a transaction on the
chain. This quickly incurs enormous economic costs for the adversary.
Thus, we develop the first decentralized *rate limiting* scheme. We use
Witness Encryption (WE) to construct a timelock encryption scheme in
which passwords are encrypted from past into future blocks by leveraging the NP-language having proof-of-work or proof-of-stake performed as
the witness. Witness Encryption is a currently impractical cryptographic
primitive, but our scheme may become practical as these primitives are
further developed.

1 Introduction

The management of cryptocurrency [50] wallet private keys is a hassle. Can we
get rid of them and replace them with a simple short password or a rotating 6-
digit one-time password (OTP) [48, 49]? Users are more familiar with this model,
but this seems, at first sight, impossible to achieve: The blockchain is public
infrastructure, and anyone has access to the public keys and smart contracts [14,
53] governing the conditions under which one can spend. Any short password or
OTP will be easily broken by an offline brute force attack [52].

Perhaps unexpectedly, it *is* possible to build brute force resilient wallets by
leveraging the blockchain infrastructure itself. We build the first *keyless cryptocurrency wallet*. It operates as follows. Alice initially uses her mobile wallet to
generate a high entropy OTP seed. This seed is used to generate a large amount

© International Financial Cryptography Association 2023
S. Matsuo et al. (Eds.): FC 2022 Workshops, LNCS 13412, pp. 615–644, 2023.
https://doi.org/10.1007/978-3-031-32415-4_37

of time-based OTPs (with, say, hourly resolution), which are encrypted and collected into a Merkle tree. The wallet creates a smart contract containing the Merkle tree root on the blockchain and outputs a wallet address to which money can be deposited at any time. The internal nodes of the Merkle tree are posted on a public, high availability location such as IPFS [10] and can also be kept by Alice in any untrusted device, if desired for availability. Alice then disconnects the mobile wallet and keeps it completely air gapped and offline. At any time, Alice can use the offline device to generate a time-based OTP. Without plugging in the offline device via USB or connecting it to the Internet, Alice visually copies the short (perhaps 6 alphanumeric characters long) OTP that appears on the device's screen into her online computer. The wallet on her online computer can then be used to input a target address and amount to be transferred. This second construction allows the user to spend money *at any time*. As the OTPs are very short, this wallet is highly usable. After the initial OTP seed generation, the seed is kept in an air gapped device, ensuring any bugs in the hardware or software cannot be abused to steal it.

Critical to the security of the construction is ensuring that no adversary can brute force the short password or OTPs. Towards that goal, we devise a new cryptographic mechanism to secure cryptocurrency wallet passwords from offline brute forcing attempts. Any adversary who wishes to brute force these passwords *must* do so through the chain itself and record the attempt in a transaction. As such, these attempts are governed by the limitations of the chain: Each transaction costs gas to perform. This gives rise to the first *decentralized rate limiting* mechanism. Through appropriate cryptoeconomic parametrization, we ensure that the adversary will, in expectation, and with any desired probability, lose much more money than they will win out of brute forcing attempts. The parametrization dictates the length of the password based on current transaction gas costs and the capital to be protected.

To achieve this property, we leverage the fact that the network is performing proof-of-work [25] (or proof-of-stake [39]) in a predictable rate in expectation [13]. We use *Witness Encryption* (WE) [31] to encrypt the password in such a way that it can only be decrypted using the *future* proof-of-work/stake that will be performed by the network. As such, the encryption is a *Timelock Encryption* [51] in which the miners function in tandem [41] to decrypt the submitted password. This decryption is a by-product of the proof-of-work/stake they are performing anyway. The miners do not need to know that the passwords have been timelock encrypted. The security of timelock encryption ensures that the passwords will not be decryptable prior to the chain progressing a certain number of blocks. Our security argument stands upon five pillars:

1. a secure *extractable* Witness Encryption scheme,
2. a secure underlying blockchain (with *Common Prefix*),
3. a *preimage/collision* resistant hash function;
4. a secure *pseudorandom* OTP scheme, and
5. a rational adversary.

Our constructions could, in principle, be deployed to any smart-contract–enabled proof-of-work/stake chain such as Ethereum. In particular, we do not require any modifications to the Ethereum consensus mechanism or smart contract virtual machine (EVM). The best known instantiation of the Witness Encryption primitive, which the Timelock Encryption instance makes use of, requires the use of *multilinear maps*. Multilinear maps are (approximately) constructible using ideal lattices. Unfortunately, this construction currently remains impractical. Until such constructions are built, our scheme is of theoretical interest.

Our Contributions. The contributions of this paper are summarized as follows:

- We introduce the first timelock-based *OTP* wallet, with OTP length of just 6 alphanumeric characters. The funds can be spent any time just by providing the OTP password from an air gapped device.
- We put forth the first *decentralized rate limiting* scheme. The scheme protects the user from brute force attacks by an adversary by requiring all attempts to be recorded on the chain.

Secondary contributions include the first instantiation of timelock encryption applied to proof-of-stake blockchains and variable difficulty proof-of-work blockchains, explored in the appendix. Lastly, our security argument, in the appendix, uses a hybrid approach which combines a high-entropy cryptographic parameter—in which classical cryptographic security is ensured with overwhelming probability—with a low-entropy cryptoeconomic parameter whose role is to ensure the attack is uneconomical for a rational adversary. This novel proof methodology may be of independent interest in analyzing blockchain protocols, which often compose cryptography and economics.

Our security assumptions pertain to pseudorandomness, hash security, and lattice-based cryptography. Therefore our wallets are also quantum-resistant.

Related Work. Witness Encryption was introduced by Garg et al. [31] using lattice-based approximate multilinear maps [30]. It was lated improved theoretically [40] and implementation-wise [2], and attacked [1,15,16,18,20,34]. A follow-up lattice-based approach [32] was also attacked [19]. Integer-based multilinear maps were proposed [21,22] and attacked [15,17,47]. Current advancements [42] seem immune to such attacks. Timelock Encryption was introduced by Rivest et al. [51]. Using Witness Encryption and proof-of-work for timelocking was proposed by Liu et al. [41]. Cryptocurrency applications were discussed by Miller [46]. An overview of wallets is given by Karantias [35], and of hardware wallets by Karakostas et al. [3]. The use of OTP [48,49] for wallets was explored in SmartOTP [33]. Password-based wallets appeared as *brain wallets* [52].

2   Preliminaries

Blocks and Chains. The proof-of-work (PoW) [25] blockchain consists of block headers $B = \langle \mathsf{ctr}, \mathsf{tx}, s \rangle$ each of which contains a *nonce* ctr, a short Merkle

Tree [43] root of transaction data tx, and a pointer s to the previous block in the chain [28]. The value $H(B)$, where H is a hash function modelled as a random oracle [8], is used as the s' to include in the next block. Each block satisfies the PoW equation $H(B) \leq T$, where T is the *mining target*. In the *static difficulty model* [27,28], T is assumed to be a constant (we discuss the variable difficulty model in the appendix).

To address blocks within chain C, we use $C[i]$ to mean the ith (zero-based) block from the beginning and $C[-i]$ to mean the ith (one-based) block from the end. $C[0]$ indicates *genesis* and $C[-1]$ the current tip. $|C|$ denotes the chain length. We use $C[i{:}j]$ to denote the subchain starting at the ith block (inclusive) and ending at the jth block (exclusive). Omitting i takes the range to the beginning, while omitting j takes the range to the end. Similarly, we use $C\{A{:}Z\}$ to denote the subchain starting at block A (inclusive) and ending at block Z (exclusive).

Each honest party keeps a local chain C, which may be different from the others. It is known [28] these chains cannot deviate much: The *Common Prefix* property establishes that they share a long common prefix and only deviate with forks of length up to a constant $k \in \mathbb{N}$. Formally, if at any round r_0 an honest party P_0 has adopted chain C_0, then at any round $r_1 > r_0$, any honest party P_1 will have adopted a chain C_1 with $C_0[: -k]$ a prefix of C_1. This gives rise to ledger *safety*: Any transaction that appears prior to $C[-k]$ is *confirmed*, and will eventually appear at the same position in the chains of all honest parties.

The chain of an honest party grows with a certain rate, which is bounded from below and above with overwhelming probability. This is known as the *Chain Growth* property (see [28] for proof for the lower bound; a proof of the upper bound is found in the Appendix). This gives rise to *liveness*: A transaction submitted to the network will eventually appear confirmed to all honest parties after at most $\ell \in \mathbb{N}$ blocks. The two security parameters k and ℓ that govern the evolution of the chain are polynomial in the underlying cryptographic security parameter κ, but constant in the execution time.

Timelock Encryption. Timelock encryption allows us to *timelock* a secret so that it can be unlocked at a prespecified date and time t in the future, but not prior. It consists of a *timelock* algorithm timelock(m, t) that takes message m and timestamp t after which decryption should be possible, and returns ciphertext c encrypted for time t, and a *timeunlock* algorithm timeunlock(c, w) that takes a ciphertext c encrypted using timelock and a witness w illustrating that indeed time t has passed, and returns message m. When the time t has elapsed, it becomes easy to compute a *witness* which is not possible to compute earlier. The timeunlock function can be called with this witness w for time t, and it returns the original message m. Prior to time t, timelock encryption security ensures that ciphertexts corresponding to the encryptions of two plaintexts m_1 and m_2 are indistinguishable.

Witness Encryption. To construct timelock encryption, we use *Witness Encryption* (WE) [41]. In a WE scheme, a plaintext is encrypted into a ciphertext that can be decrypted *only* if a solution to a computational problem is given. More concretely, the Witness Encryption scheme is parametrized by an

NP language $\mathcal{L}$ (a decision problem) and an associated relation $\mathcal{R}$ (which verifies a solution). For each instance $x \in \mathcal{L}$, there exists a witness w such that $x\mathcal{R}w$. For non-instances $x \notin \mathcal{L}$, no such witness exists. The relation $\mathcal{R}$ is polynomially computable. A witness encryption scheme consists of an *encryption* algorithm WE.ENC$_\mathcal{R}(m, x)$ that takes plaintext m and instance x and returns ciphertext c encrypted for this problem instance, and a *decryption* algorithm WE.DEC$_\mathcal{R}(c, w)$ that takes ciphertext c and witness w and returns the decrypted plaintext m as long as $x\mathcal{R}w$. *Correctness* mandates that, whenever $x\mathcal{R}w$, it holds that WE.DEC$_\mathcal{R}($WE.ENC$_\mathcal{R}(m, x), w) = m$. On the other hand, *security* mandates that an adversary given $c =$ WE.ENC$_\mathcal{R}(m, x)$ can extract information about m only if she can also produce (through a helper *extractor* machine) a w such that $x\mathcal{R}w$, except with negligible probability. A correct and secure scheme allows a party to decrypt *if and only if* she can solve the problem instance by providing a witness.

To construct timelock encryption using witness encryption, the problem statement asks for the existence of a series of blockchain work nonces that solve the proof-of-work equation, as illustrated in Fig. 1. The instantiation of timelock encryption using witness encryption begins by identifying the chain tip B. The timelock time t is expressed in chain time: We ask that a certain number of blocks must have been mined on top of B in order for the secret to become decryptable. The witness encryption NP language contains the integers $t \in \mathbb{N}$ indicating that there exists a block with additional block height t descending from the known block B. The witness consists of a series of nonces ctr$_i$ and transaction root hashes tx$_i$ such that $B_0 = B$ and $B_i = \langle$ctr$_i$, tx$_i$, $H(B_{i-1})\rangle$ and $H(B_i) \leq T$, where i ranges from 1 to t. Therefore, the timelock function timelock(m, t) is defined as WE.Enc$_\mathcal{R}(m, x)$ where $\mathcal{R}$ corresponds to the relation checking the validity of the blockchain and x corresponds to the number of blocks t as well as the current chain tip B. The unlock function timeunlock(c, w) is defined as WE.Dec$_\mathcal{R}(c, w)$ under the same relation $\mathcal{R}$ where w consists of the sequence of ctr$_i$ and tx$_i$ (c.f., [41]).

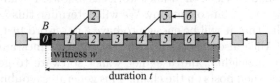

Fig. 1. Timelock implemented using the moderately hard NP language of chain discovery. The problem instance $x = (B, t)$ requests $t = 7$ blocks on top of B. The witness consists of block headers produced sequentially on top of B, irrespective of any temporary forks.

What is the outcome of encrypting secrets in this manner? Whenever a secret is encrypted for block time t following block B, the secret remains hidden until time t has arrived. The secret cannot be decrypted prior to that time, because decrypting it would require the decrypting party to produce (through an extractor) a witness w which is a blockchain of height t extending B. However, due to the *Common Prefix* property of the blockchain, no adversary can do that much sooner than the honest parties converge to that height (even offline!). Furthermore, the *chain growth* rate is bounded both *above* and *below* by a certain *velocity*, and so, while we do not know its exact growth rate, we can give an estimate of how quickly it will grow. With sufficient time elapsed, the miners will produce a witness anyone can use to decrypt the secret. The result is that no one knows the secret prior to the desired block height, but everyone knows it afterwards. Because the adversary can have a chain that is leading by up to k blocks, she has an advantage in decrypting the secret slightly ahead of the honest parties: The secret begins *leaking* to the adversary at block time $t - k$. This will require us to establish certain time bounds in our construction. Our security proof hinges on the *common prefix* property: If an adversary can decrypt the witness encrypted ciphertext *much* earlier than the honest parties, she will need to have produced a chain which significantly deviates from the honest parties' chain, but this is improbable.

Contrary to timelock schemes that require the interested party to devote compute power to decrypt the secret over time, the scheme using blockchain witnesses allows any party (who can remain offline and have limited compute power) to take advantage of the scheme.

3   A Password Wallet

We start by building a password-based wallet without private keys. This construction will be a stepping stone for the next. In this construction, we have a severe limitation: The wallet can only be used to spend *once*, and at a *predetermined time*. Once the wallet has been used, it cannot be reused with the same password. Furthermore, the wallet becomes unusable if the funds have not been spent prior to the maturity date.

From a user point of view, the wallet works as follows. Initially, Alice chooses a secret password with λ bits of entropy. We will determine this λ later, but let us say, with foresight, that it will be enough to have a password just 6 alphanumeric characters long. Alice also chooses a *maturity date*, a timestamp in the future (expressed as chain height), and uses her wallet software to generate a smart contract which she then posts on the chain. This generates a public wallet address for Alice that she can use to receive multiple payments prior to the maturity date. The wallet software can then be discarded and no secret information needs to be kept by Alice, beyond the secret password that she remembers, and the public contract that remains on the chain. No private keys are stored anywhere. A short period before the maturity date arrives, Alice uses the wallet software to connect to the chain network, and enters her password and desired destination. The software issues two transactions to the chain: First, a $\mathsf{tx_{commit}}$ transaction, which lets Alice illustrate prior knowledge of her secret password; and, second, a $\mathsf{tx_{reveal}}$ transaction, in which Alice proves that her previous commitment indeed corresponds to the secret password committed on the chain. The first transaction is posted strictly prior to the maturity date, while the second transaction is posted on or after the maturity date.

Algorithm 1. A password-only wallet with a maturity date.

```
1:  contract PasswordWallet
2:      BLOCK_DELAY ← 2k
3:      c ← ⊥; t₁ ← ⊥
4:      commitments ← ∅
5:      function construct(c̄, t̄₁)
6:          c ← c̄
7:          t₁ ← t̄₁
8:      end function
9:      function commit(z)
10:         require(block.number < t₁ − BLOCK_DELAY)
11:         commitments[z] ← true
12:     end function
13:     function reveal(sk, salt, α_to, w)
14:         z ← H(⟨sk, salt, α_to⟩)
15:         require(commitments[z])
16:         require(WE.Dec_R(c, w) = sk)
17:         α_to.transfer(address(this).balance)
18:     end function
19: end contract
```

The smart contract is illustrated in Algorithm 1. It consists of three methods: a construct method, called when the wallet is initialized; a commit method, called shortly prior to the maturity date; and a reveal method, called after the maturity date. These two last methods are used for spending.

The interaction with the wallet is illustrated in Algorithm 2. When Alice wishes to deploy her wallet, she begins by generating a password $sk \xleftarrow{\$} \{0,1\}^\lambda$. She also chooses a future timestamp at which she will be able to spend her money. She submits this information to her software wallet. The software wallet connects to the blockchain and observes the current stable tip $B = \mathcal{C}[-k]$ and its height t_0. Alice's timestamp choice is translated to a future block height $\Delta \in \mathbb{N}$ which denotes how far in the future, in block height after t_0, she wants to spend her money: If $\Delta = 100$, the money will be spendable when the chain reaches height $t_0 + \Delta$. We set $t_1 = t_0 + \Delta$ to be the height at which spending becomes possible. The software wallet constructs the contract of Algorithm 1 by broadcasting its construction transaction $\mathsf{tx}_{\mathsf{construct}}$ to the network. The constructor accepts two parameters, t_1 and c. The c parameter is a timelock-encrypted ciphertext of her password. Concretely, Alice's software wallet sets $c = \mathsf{timelock}(sk, t)$ by invoking $\mathsf{WE.Enc}_R(sk, x)$. Here, $\mathcal{R}$ denotes the block-validated relation described in the preliminaries. The problem instance $x = (B, t)$ is the tuple consisting of the latest known stable block and the maturity height. Observe now that the ciphertext

c which is published on the smart contract and known to the adversary is a ciphertext which can only be decrypted after t blocks have been mined on top of block B. The transaction returns a wallet address pk at which she can receive money prior to the maturity height.

Algorithm 2. Interacting with the password wallet.

1: BLOCK_DELAY ← $2k$
2: $pk \leftarrow \bot$ ▷ Published so that money can be received
3: $B \leftarrow \bot$ ▷ Published on insecure public storage
4: $t_1 \leftarrow \bot$ ▷ The maturity date
5: **upon** initialize(t) **do**
6:     $sk \xleftarrow{\$} \{0,1\}^\lambda$ ▷ Password is generated with low entropy λ
7:     $B \leftarrow \mathcal{C}[-k]$ ▷ Latest stable block
8:     $x \leftarrow (B, t)$ ▷ NP language problem instance
9:     $c \leftarrow \mathsf{WE.Enc}_\mathcal{R}(sk, x)$
10:     $pk \leftarrow \mathsf{PasswordWallet.construct}(c, t)$
11:     $t_1 \leftarrow t$
12:     **return** sk ▷ The user must remember this
13: **end upon**
14: **upon** spend(sk, α_{to}) **do**
15:     ▷ *At any time prior to* $|\mathcal{C}| < t_1 - \ell - 2k$
16:     salt $\xleftarrow{\$} \{0,1\}^\kappa$ ▷ Generate short-lived high-entropy salt
17:     $z \leftarrow H(\langle sk, \mathsf{salt}, \alpha_{\mathsf{to}} \rangle)$
18:     PasswordWallet.commit(z)
19:     **wait until** $|\mathcal{C}| = t_1$
20:     $w \leftarrow \mathcal{C}\{B:\}$
21:     PasswordWallet.reveal($sk, \mathsf{salt}, \alpha_{\mathsf{to}}, w$)
22: **end upon**

To spend her money, Alice runs the wallet software anew and inputs her public wallet address pk, her password sk, and destination address α_{to}. The wallet software does not have any information beyond this. The software runs an SPV (or full) node which observes a chain $\mathcal{C}$. At any time before its local chain reaches height $t_1 - \ell - 2k$, the wallet generates a new high-entropy salt salt $\xleftarrow{\$} \{0,1\}^\kappa$ (where κ is a security parameter in the order of 128). This salt is short-lived ($\ell - 2k$ blocks) and must survive until the chain reaches height t_1. It then creates transaction $\mathsf{tx}_{\mathsf{commit}}$ which contains a commitment z evaluated as $z = H(\langle sk, \mathsf{salt}, \alpha_{\mathsf{to}} \rangle)$. This transaction is submitted to the smart contract by invoking *commit*. Due to liveness, the transaction is confirmed in a block with height at most $t_1 - 2k$. The contract records the commitment, as the requirement in Line 10 is satisfied, and stores it in the *commitments* set.

After the local chain of the wallet reaches height t_1, the software gathers the block headers $\mathcal{C}[t_0:t_1]$ to construct a timelock witness w. It then creates a transaction $\mathsf{tx}_{\mathsf{reveal}}$ which invokes the reveal method of the smart contract and includes the plaintext password sk, which now becomes public, the plaintext salt, which also becomes public, the target address α_{to}, and the witness w. The reveal method checks that the submitted data corresponds to the previous commitment, and that the stored encrypted password c timelock decrypts to the provided password sk. If so, it sends the money to α_{to}.

The commitments variable is a *set* to avoid denial of service attacks. If the honest party submits a *commit* transaction, the adversary should not be able to overwrite this. Therefore, the wallet stores *all* commit transactions in the set and checks that the correct one is revealed afterwards. The reason why the target address α_{to} is placed in the hash commitment is to avoid front running attacks [23]. The target address is *tied* to the knowledge of the password. If the adversary replays the commitment, she cannot change the target address.

We now give a high-level overview of the correctness and security of this scheme. The *correctness* property of the wallet mandates that the honest wallet user can create a valid spending transaction, i.e., a transaction which executes *reveal* to completion. The *security* property mandates that the adversary cannot create a valid transaction. These properties, together, ensure that the honest user can spend her money, while the adversary cannot.

On the one hand, the scheme is correct, because the honest user can always create the commit and reveal transactions in order, and, due to liveness, these cannot be censored. When time t_1 arrives, the smart contract can verify the veracity of the claims and issue the final transfer. On the other hand, the scheme is secure, because, prior to time t_1 the adversary does not hold a chain of length t_1. Without such a chain, the adversary cannot distinguish a correct from an incorrect guess, due to the security of witness encryption. Any guess the adversary makes is a good as any. However, all of these guesses must be committed to the smart contract sufficiently before time t_1 arrives. And, so, the adversary must choose to blindly submit some guesses and hope that some of them are correct. This very soon becomes uneconomical, even if the password length is quite short. We give more details on the security of the scheme in the Analysis section of the appendix.

One detail to note here is that the time t_1 is given in block time. Because the rate of chain growth can vary, the honest party must monitor the chain and ensure that block height t_1 has not passed. This is one additional limitation of this scheme that makes it unusable. Additionally, the password can only be used once. In the next section, we lift these limitations.

4   An OTP Wallet

The password-based construction has an important limitation: The money can only be spent once at a prespecified date. This makes the wallet unusable. Using the previous construction as a stepping stone, we now move on to describe our *Hours of Horus* scheme. This is an OTP-based scheme in which the OTP is used as the *single factor* for wallet access, without any need of private keys.

The workflow of the OTP wallet is illustrated as a sequence diagram in Fig. 2. At the beginning, Alice initializes a time-based OTP device (such as a mobile

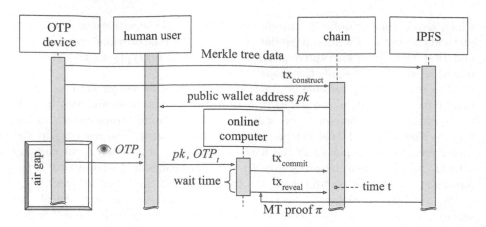

Fig. 2. The sequence diagram of the OTP wallet. After initialization, the OTP device becomes air gapped and the user submits the OTP visually to an online computer at time t.

phone app) which generates and stores an OTP seed (leftmost column). Upon this generation, the device also generates a smart contract, which is constructed and submitted to the chain through a transaction tx$_{construct}$. This transaction generates a wallet address pk to which payers can send money for Alice. The OTP device also constructs a Merkle tree containing a large number of encrypted future OTPs and submits them to IPFS [10] (or other persistent storage service) publicly for availability (rightmost column). Both pk and all internal Merkle tree nodes are public. After this initial phase, the OTP device becomes air gapped.

Whenever Alice wishes to spend, she visually consults her OTP device which displays a time-based OTP key. Using a (newly booted) online computer, she creates a transaction tx$_{commit}$ in which she commits to the OTP, the amount she wishes to spend, and the target address. The wallet waits a short amount of time before submitting the final tx$_{reveal}$ to confirm the spending. This transaction is accompanied by a Merkle tree proof-of-inclusion constructed using the IPFS data. The wallet then releases the payment to the desired address.

The contract deployed as a wallet is illustrated in Algorithm 3. The interaction with the contract by the user is illustrated in Algorithm 4. The constructor accepts a parameter r denoting a Merkle tree root. This is constructed by generating a large number (MAX_TIME) of time-based OTPs for the foreseeable future. For example, to support a wallet with a lifetime of 100 years with an hourly OTP resolution, 876,000 codes need to be generated. Let OTP_t denote the OTP for future time $t \in \mathbb{N}$ (in the example, t ranges from 1 to 876,000). These are generated from the OTP seed in the OTP device by invoking the pseudorandom function $\mathcal{G}(\text{seed}, t)$ whose output has λ bits of entropy. Each such OTP is then timelock encrypted for time t, multiplied by the expected hourly production rate of the blockchain (the *hourly* resolution is an arbitrary choice that can be made differently, giving rise to a tradeoff between how much data must be

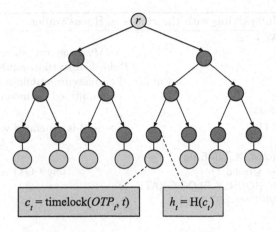

Fig. 3. Each OTP_t is timelocked with time t. All timelock ciphertexts c_t are organized into a Merkle Tree whose root is r.

stored on IPFS versus how often the user can spend her money). Specifically, the software computes $c_t = \text{timelock}(OTP_t, t)$, (setting $c_t = \text{WE.Enc}_{\mathcal{R}}(OTP_t, x)$, where $x = (B, t)$). All of these c_t are then organized into a Merkle tree as illustrated in Fig. 3 using the hash function H whose root is r. This r is submitted to the constructor.

Algorithm 3. Hours of Horus: A short OTP wallet.

```
 1: contract OTPWallet
 2:     BLOCK_DELAY ← 2k
 3:     r ← ⊥
 4:     spent ← ∅
 5:     commitments ← ∅
 6:     function construct(r̄)
 7:         r ← r̄
 8:     end function
 9:     function commit(z, t)
10:         require(t > block.number + BLOCK_DELAY)
11:         commitments[z][t] ← true
12:     end function
13:     function reveal(OTP, salt, α_to, amount, c_t, w, t, π)
14:         z ← H(⟨OTP, salt, α_to, amount⟩)
15:         require(commitments[z][t])
16:         require(¬spent[t])
17:         require(MT.Ver(c_t, t, r, π))
18:         require(WE.Dec_R(c_t, w) = OTP)
19:         spent[t] ← true
20:         α_to.transfer(amount)
21:     end function
22: end contract
```

Algorithm 4. Interacting with the Hours of Horus wallet.

```
 1: BLOCK_DELAY ← 2k
 2: seed ← ⊥                                      ▷ After generation, remains air gapped
 3: pk ← ⊥                                        ▷ Published so that money can be received
 4: c ← []                                        ▷ Published on insecure public storage (e.g., IPFS)
 5: B ← ⊥                                         ▷ Published on insecure public storage
 6: upon initialize do
 7:     seed ←$ {0, 1}^κ                          ▷ Seed is generated with high entropy κ
 8:     B ← C[−k]                                 ▷ Latest stable block
 9:     for t ← 1 to MAX_TIME do
10:         OTP_t ← G(seed, t)                    ▷ Time t OTP with low entropy λ
11:         x ← (B, HOURLY_BLOCK_RATE · t)
12:         c_t ← WE.Enc_R(OTP_t, x)
13:         c ← c ∥ c_t
14:     end for
15:     r ← MT.build(c)
16:     pk ← OTPWallet.construct(r)
17: end upon
18: upon spend(α_to, amount) do
19:     t_1 ← |C| + ℓ + BLOCK_DELAY
20:     salt ← {0, 1}^κ                           ▷ Generate short-lived high-entropy salt
21:     OTP_t ← G(seed, t_1)
22:     z ← H(⟨OTP_t, salt, α_to, amount⟩)
23:     OTPWallet.commit(z, t_1)
24:     wait until |C| = t_1
25:     w ← C{B:}
26:     π ← MT.prove(c_t, c)
27:     OTPWallet.reveal(OTP_t, salt, α_to, amount, c_t, w, t_1, π)
28: end upon
```

When Alice wishes to spend, she calls *commit* by issuing a tx_{commit} transaction. The method takes parameters z and t. Here, z is the commitment $z = H(\langle OTP, salt, \alpha_{to}, amount \rangle)$. For t, Alice looks at her local chain C, obtains its length $|C|$ and evaluates $t = |C| + \ell + 2k$. So, t is a block height at least $\ell + 2k$ blocks in the future. As liveness ensures this transaction will confirm within ℓ blocks, the condition on Line 10 will succeed. The contract records the pair (z, t) in the *commitments* set. Alice waits for her chain to grow to a height of t blocks, at which point she issues the tx_{reveal} transaction calling the *reveal* method. She reveals the OTP (no longer useful to any adversary), the salt, the destination address, and the amount to transfer. These are accompanied by proof-of-inclusion π at position t in the Merkle Tree whose root r is recorded in the contract obtained from the data stored on IPFS (anyone can compute this). Additionally, it is accompanied by a witness that time t has passed by providing the chain portion $C\{B:\}$ (this can also be computed by anyone). The contract verifies the provided data are included in previous commitments, that the Merkle tree proof is valid for the specified position, and that the timelock encryption of the provided OTP corresponds to the given ciphertext.

The honest party will always succeed in creating a valid spending transaction. To see this, note that the party begins creating the commit transaction at time $t - \ell - 2k$. Due to liveness, it becomes confirmed at block $t - 2k$ at most, and so the check in Line 10 will pass. The reveal transaction will be called with the corresponding data and release the funds.

To see why an adversary cannot create a valid spending transaction beyond random guessing, we note that any adversary can either provide a commit transaction prior to block $t - 2k$, or afterwards. If she provides it prior, then the timelock scheme will protect the secret, and so the spending transaction will include a random OTP guess. On the other hand, if she provides it afterwards, it will not be accepted due to the time delay enforced in Line 10. Consult the Analysis section for a more complete argument.

5 Conclusion

We presented the first wallets that work securely without private keys, developing a wallet in which the user spends with an OTP from an air gapped device. We proved our scheme secure through a hybrid cryptographic/cryptoeconomic argument which may be of independent interest (in the appendix). The cryptoeconomic analysis led to a short OTP code: Just 6 alphanumeric characters suffice even for large capital of seven figures and with a conservative economic margin of 90% capital loss for the adversary. Our calculations were also conservative with respect to fees.

We extended our scheme to work in the proof-of-stake model, as well as variable difficulty proof-of-work model (in the appendix). We are the first to extend timelock encryption to proof-of-stake and to effectively use it for the variable proof-of-work case as well (previous considerations [41] considered the variable difficulty case, but did not account for the fact that the decryption time will be varying with the miner population adjustments).

As far as we know, our work is the first to build any useful protocol, and certainly to construct wallets, on top of timelock encryption and blockchains. We believe that timelock encryption and witness encryption is a promising cryptographic direction and, once established, will prove to be cornerstones of future protocol development for blockchains.

Acknowledgements. The author thanks Pyrros Chaidos, Alexander Chepurnoy, and Dimitris Karakostas for reading early versions of this paper and providing useful feedback towards a clearer narrative, and the anonymous reviewers of the Financial Cryptography Workshop on Trusted Smart Contracts conference for their helpful reviews.

Appendix

A Analysis

We now give a more complete analysis of the scheme. First, let us prove that the password-based wallet of Algorithm 1 is correct.

Theorem 1 (Password Wallet Correctness (Informal)). *Let the blockchain have* liveness *and* safety, *and let the witness encryption scheme* WE *be correct. An honest party spending at block height* $t_1 - \ell - 2k$ *or earlier will generate a valid spending transaction for Algorithm 1.*

Proof (Sketch). The contract is created when $B = \mathcal{C}[-k]$ is stable. Due to safety, all the future chains will be extending this block. The contract is initialized with $x = (B, t)$ by issuing the tx$_{\mathsf{construct}}$ transaction. Due to liveness, this transaction is confirmed within ℓ blocks. The honest user then creates a transaction tx$_{\mathsf{commit}}$ when her own chain has length $|\mathcal{C}| = t_1 - \ell - 2k$. Due to liveness, this transaction becomes confirmed for all honest parties after ℓ blocks have elapsed, and is placed in position $\mathcal{C}[t_1 - 2k]$ or earlier. Therefore, Line 10 of the method *commit* succeeds. When $|\mathcal{C}| = t_1$, the honest user calls *reveal*, passing w. Due to the correctness of the witness encryption scheme, the decryption succeeds. The password and salt revealed match the ones committed. Due to liveness, this transaction becomes confirmed.

The correctness of the OTP-based scheme is similar.

Theorem 2 (OTP Wallet Correctness (Informal)). *Let the blockchain have* liveness *and* safety, *and let the witness encryption scheme* WE *be correct. An honest party spending multiple times prior to* MAX_TIME $- \ell - 2k$ *will succeed in creating valid transactions. in Algorithm 3.*

Proof (Sketch). The proof is the same as above, with the difference that the value t is provided at the commit time, not the construct time. The argument that Line 10 will be successful remains the same due to liveness.

Our security analysis is in a hybrid *cryptographic* and *cryptoeconomic* setting. In the system described, we have two security parameters. First, we have the *cryptographic* security parameter κ ($\approx$128 bits), which determines the security of the hash function, the security of the witness encryption scheme, and the security of the blockchain (in terms of liveness, safety, and common prefix). The probability of failure is negligible in this parameter. Any breakage in this parameter can be catastrophic for the system and can potentially provide the adversary with gains without any cost. Secondly, we have the much shorter *cryptoeconomic* security parameter λ ($\approx$35 bits) which denotes the entropy of the chosen user password sk or the length of each OTP OTP$_t$. While this parameter is hopelessly short from a cryptographic point of view (and 2^{-35} is nothing but negligible), we will use it to establish a lower bound in the economic cost of an attack. In particular, we will tweak this parameter so that the return-on-investment of an attack can be made arbitrarily close to -100%. The result will be that the adversary can make the probability of success non-negligible, but at an economic cost which renders such attempts irrational.

We begin by stating our Decentralized Rate Limiting lemma, which establishes that an adversary must necessarily submit transactions to the blockchain in order to have any non-negligible probability of success. The probability of success is determined by the number of transactions submitted by the adversary and made persistent by the system. Based on this result, we will determine the cryptoeconomic parametrization (λ) required to make the system economically infeasible to attack.

Lemma 1 (Decentralized Rate Limiting (Informal)). *Consider a static difficulty proof-of-work blockchain with safety and common prefix. Let the hash function H be collision-resistant and preimage-resistant, and let the witness encryption scheme WE be a secure witness encryption with witness extractability. A PPT adversary who submits fewer than g transactions that are eventually confirmed by all honest parties has a probability of achieving a valid spending transaction in Algorithm 1 upper bounded by $\frac{g}{2^\lambda} + negl(\kappa)$.*

Proof (Sketch). In order for the adversary to have a valid transaction, she must have created a tx_{reveal} in which she passes a password sk, a salt and a α'_{to} address which is different from the honestly provided α_{to} address. This reveal transaction must be confirmed into the chain $\mathcal{C}$ adopted by a verifier honest party P_v and have matching data with a previous tx'_{commit} transaction which was placed earlier in $\mathcal{C}$. Additionally, tx'_{commit} must be in $\mathcal{C}[t_1 - 2k]$ or earlier (due to the check in Line 10). Due to the collision resistance of H, the respective commit transaction must be different from the one (tx_{commit}) provided by the honest party, as $\alpha_{to} \neq \alpha'_{to}$.

Let r_c denote the round during which the spender honest party P_s broadcasts their tx_{commit} transaction to the network, and let r_z denote the last round during which *all* honest parties have chains with length of at most $t_1 - k$.

Let us consider all adversarially generated commit transactions tx^i_{commit} ($i \geq 1$) that are eventually reported as *stable* by P_v (the adversary can also create transactions that do not make it in the chain of P_v, but we will not count these). For these transactions, let us consider the round r_i during which each of these transactions tx^i_{commit} was created.

Case 1: $r_i < r_c$. Since the honest spender has not yet submitted a commitment, the only information that the adversary has is the ciphertext c. If at this round the adversary can distinguish between sk and any other plaintext in $\{0,1\}^\lambda$ with probability non-negligible in κ, then, due to the witness extractability of WE, an extractor can extract a witness w attesting to the existence of a chain of height t_1. But in that case, we can perform a computational reduction to an adversary that breaks the common prefix property of the chain by producing a chain of height t_1 at round r_i when the honest party P_v has adopted a chain of length only $t_1 - \ell - 2k$. This breaks the common prefix assumption.

Case 2: $r_c \leq r_i \leq r_z$. In this case, the honest spender has broadcast a commitment to the network, but there are no chains of length t_1. The adversary now holds both the timelocked ciphertext c and the commitment z. Again the adversary should not be able to distinguish between sk and any other plaintext in $\{0,1\}^\lambda$, except with probability negligible in κ (recall that the salt is kept secret and has κ bits of entropy). Otherwise, we can either perform a reduction to a common-prefix-breaking adversary making use of witness extractability, or we can perform a reduction to a preimage-resistance-breaking adversary.

Case 3: $r_i > r_z$. By the definition of r_z, in round r_i there must exist an honest party with a chain of length at least $t_1 - k$. By the common prefix property, all other honest parties have a chain of length exceeding $t_1 - 2k$.

Let us consider what happens in all of these three cases. In the first two cases, any *single* guess that the adversary places into a transaction can be correct with probability $\frac{1}{2^\lambda} + \mathsf{negl}(\kappa)$. In the third case, while the adversary can potentially guess with better probability (due to the chain reaching its leakage point $t_1 - k$), any such transactions can never make it into the chain eventually adopted by P_v, as the check in Line 10 will fail.

As the transactions that eventually make it into the chain of P_v were all generated prior to r_z, the probability that each of them is a valid spending transaction is upper bounded by $\frac{1}{2^\lambda} + \mathsf{negl}(\kappa)$. If the adversary submits at most g such transactions, and applying a union bound, the overall probability of success is $g(\frac{1}{2^\lambda} + \mathsf{negl}(\kappa)) = \frac{g}{2^\lambda} + \mathsf{negl}(\kappa)$.

The above Lemma is identical for our other construction. We state it for completeness.

Lemma 2 (OTP Decentralized Rate Limiting (Informal)). *Consider a static difficulty proof-of-work blockchain with safety and common prefix. Let the hash function H be collision-resistant and preimage-resistant, and let the witness encryption scheme WE be a secure witness encryption with witness extractability. Let $\mathcal{G}$ be a secure pseudorandom function $\{0,1\}^\kappa \times \mathbb{N} \longrightarrow \{0,1\}^\lambda$. A PPT adversary who submits fewer than g transactions that are eventually confirmed by all honest parties has a probability of achieving a valid spending transaction in Algorithm 3 upper bounded by $\frac{g}{2^\lambda} + \mathsf{negl}(\kappa)$.*

Proof (Sketch). The proof here is identical to Lemma 1, noting that each of the different OTP_t essentially gives rise to independent attack paths to the adversary. Due to the pseudorandom nature of the OTP scheme, any previous OTPs do not reveal any information to our polynomial adversary. An adversary making a spending attempt has a probability of $\frac{1}{2^\lambda}$ of succeeding in each attempt, unless it can be reduced to a collision-resistance-breaking adversary, a common-prefix-breaking adversary, or an adversary breaking the pseudorandomness of the OTP scheme. But all of these events are negligible in κ.

At this point, we have established that the probability of success is negligible in both parameters κ and λ. However, we will keep the parameter λ short, and we will make the κ parameter reasonably long ($\kappa = 128$). Setting $\lambda = \kappa$ would, of course, give sufficient security. The reason for separating these two parameters is that the λ parameter affects the usability of the system: It is the number of characters that must be remembered by the user in the case of a password, or the number of characters that must be visually copied by the user in the case of an OTP.

In the above result, we have expressed the probability as a sum of two terms: $\frac{g}{1^\lambda} + \mathsf{negl}(\kappa)$. This reflects the nature of the two parameters: We opt to calculate the *concrete* probability with respect to λ, but only give an asymptotic probability with respect to κ. This treatment hints at our intentions: Our high-level argument was to condition the system to the overwhelming events that there will be no cryptographic breakage in the hash function, common prefix property, blockchain safety, blockchain liveness, and OTP pseudorandomness. Conditioned under these events, the concrete probability as a function of λ allows us to make an argument of why any attack is uneconomical. This gives rise to our (cryptoeconomic) security theorem.

Theorem 3 (Cryptoeconomic Security (Informal)). *Consider a chain with fee f per transaction. If the wallet of Algorithm 1 or Algorithm 3 is used with a maximum capital of V, then the parametrization $\lambda > \log \frac{V}{f}$ yields a negative expectation of income for the adversary, with overwhelming probability in κ. Additionally, the expected return-on-investment for this adversary is at most $\frac{V}{f2^{\lambda}} - 1$.*

Proof (Sketch). Consider an adversary who submits g transactions that are eventually confirmed by every honest party. This adversary is irrevocably investing a capital of gf for this attack. By Lemma 1, the adversary has a probability of success upper bounded by $\frac{g}{2^{\lambda}}$ (with overwhelming probability in κ). The expected income for this adversary is at most $\mathbb{E}[\text{income}] \leq V\frac{g}{2^{\lambda}} - gf$. Taking $\lambda > \log \frac{V}{f}$, we obtain $\mathbb{E}[\text{income}] < 0$. The expected return-on-investment is $\frac{\mathbb{E}[\text{income}]}{gf} - 1$.

In this scheme, we can set λ big enough to make the return-on-investment as close to -100% as we want. If we want the return-on-investment to be $-1 + \epsilon$ for some $\epsilon \in (0, 1]$, we let $\lambda = \log \frac{V}{f\epsilon}$. In short, we can make the adversary lose an amount arbitrarily close to all their money in expectation.

To consider some concrete parametrization of the scheme, let us assume that we wish to establish a target -90% ($\epsilon = 0.1$) expected return-on-investment for the adversary in a wallet where we want to store up to $V = \$100,000$ in capital at any point in time. Consider a blockchain where the fees per transaction are[1] at least $f = \$1.60$. We obtain $\lambda = \log \frac{V}{f\epsilon} = \log_2 625,000 < 20$ bits. This corresponds to just 6 numerical characters (base 10), or just 4 alphanumeric characters (base 58). A standard OTP authenticator such as Google's Authenticator application is therefore appropriate for such parameters. Increasing the maximum capital that will be stored in the wallet by three orders of magnitude to $\$100,000,000$ requires 5 alphanumeric characters instead.

B   Proof-of-Stake

Contrary to proof-of-work blockchains, a proof-of-stake chain progresses in *slots* (prefixed time durations) during which parties can create blocks or remain silent.

---

[1] This price corresponds to Ethereum–fiat prices and gas fees for simple transfer transactions in May 2021. As smart contract transactions are significantly more expensive, this is a conservative estimation for the fees.

As in proof-of-work, each block header B_i consists of $\langle \mathsf{tx}_i, s_i \rangle$, but now does not include a ctr_i. The blocks created at each slot are accompanied by a signature σ_i created by a designated leader for the slot. A proof π_i illustrating the designated leader is the rightful one is also broadcast together with the block. The probability that a party becomes a leader at a given slot is roughly proportional to the stake they hold within the system. These proofs of leadership are different depending on the system and can be the random outcome of a multiparty computation, as in the *Ouroboros* [39] system, or a verifiable random function [45] evaluated on this randomness, as in the *Ouroboros Praos* [24] construction. In the first system, each slot is allocated to precisely one party, and the production of no blocks, or two competing blocks in the same slot, indicates adversarial behavior. In the second system, it is possible that a slot is allocated to multiple honest parties, or no parties at all. These details do not affect our scheme, as long as the following property is maintained: For any $2k$ consecutive slots, at least $k+1$ slots are allocated to an honest party. Additionally, we will assume that the common prefix property holds here, too.

As in proof-of-work, the chain is split into epochs. At the end of each epoch, a multiparty computation is performed to determine the randomness value for the next epoch based on the stake distribution during the current epoch. Different systems use different MPCs. Our only requirement is that these MPCs provide some evidence u_e that the randomness for epoch e is ρ_e. This evidence must be polynomially checkable in retrospect. This requirement is satisfied in proof-of-stake blockchains, as it is this evidence that allows new nodes to bootstrap correctly [5].

In this section, we adapt our OTP wallet construction to the proof-of-stake setting (the password wallet can also be adapted likewise). For concreteness, we describe a construction for the *Ouroboros* [39] and *Ouroboros Praos* [24] systems, but our results are extensible to other systems as well (such as Snow White [11] and Algorand [44]).

The construction does not change much from the proof-of-work case, so we only provide a sketch of the construction here. The smart contract remains identical, except for the moderately hard NP language describing the existence of a proof-of-work witness. More concretely, the problem instance x is now (ρ, sl, D, t), where ρ denotes the randomness of the current epoch, sl denotes the slot during which block B (the most recently known stable block $\mathcal{C}[-k]$) was generated, D denotes the stake distribution during the current epoch, and t denotes the future time. While the proof-of-stake chains also enjoy the common prefix property, unfortunately, we cannot simply take any blockchain that has length t following B, because the adversary can create blockchains of arbitrary length. The proof-of-stake system ensures that such chains are not taken into account by checking that any blockchain received on the network does not contain blocks that were issued in future slots [39]. However, we cannot incorporate this check in the form of an NP language, as we do not have access to a clock.

Instead, we rely on a critical property of the proof-of-stake system that states that, in any consecutive $2k$ slots, at least $k+1$ will be honestly allocated. Therefore, we reinterpret the parameter t to mean the *number of slots* after block B instead of the *number of blocks*. The witness w consists of two parts: *block* data and *epoch* data. The block data contains a sequence $(\sigma_1, H_1, \pi_1, sl_1), (\sigma_2, H_2, \pi_2, sl_2), \cdots, (\sigma_d, H_d, \pi_d, sl_d)$ of signatures σ_i each with their corresponding slot sl_i, with $sl_i > sl$ and a proof of leadership π_i. As in the proof-of-work case, no transaction data is verified. The epoch data contains a sequence $(\rho_1, u_1), (\rho_2, u_2), \cdots, (\rho_e, u_e)$ spanning all the epochs starting from the epoch of slot sl up until the epoch of slot $sl + t$. For each of these, the randomness ρ_j and evidence u_j of the multiparty computation leading to it (typically a collection of signatures) is included.

The relation $\mathcal{R}$ polynomially verifies that all the signatures σ_i correctly sign their respective plaintext H_i, that the proofs of leadership π_i are correct, and that the evidence u_j for the randomness ρ_j of each epoch is correct. Critically, it also checks that, for every window of length $2k$ slots, at least $k + 1$ blocks have been provided.

This completes the basic scheme. We can improve upon this scheme by noting that blocks and signatures for everything but the most recent epoch are not necessary, as long as the randomness and its evidence for each epoch is given. This evidence can be made quite short using ATMs schemes, in which the evidence consists of aggregate threshold signatures (c.f., [37]). In such an optimization, a constant amount of bits is required per epoch. Blocks only need to be presented for the last epoch in order to have better time granularity. However, here, too, some pruning can occur: It is sufficient that only $k + 1$ blocks and signatures pertaining to the most recent $2k$ slots of the most recent epoch are presented. The relation $\mathcal{R}$ can then simply check the evidence for each epoch randomness, that the $k + 1$ signatures are correct, that they all fall within a $2k$ window, and that the slot during which the last such block was generated is t. Again, the witness encryption can be composed with a zk-SNARK to make the witnesses constant size.

Contrary to proof-of-work where the velocity of the chain is unknown, despite bounded, in the proof-of-stake case we have a much better grasp on how quickly the time t will be reached, as it is a slot number. While the adversary still enjoys some early leakage (k slots early), the timelocked data will be available at the prespecified time. In the proof-of-work case, it is possible that the blockchain growth rate will increase or decrease due to the stochastic nature of block production. As such, the proof-of-stake scheme is naturally fitting to the timelock problem.

C Variable Difficulty Proof-of-Work

In the variable difficulty model, the target T is adjusted based on how the chain evolves. Concretely, the chain is split into *epochs* of constant block length m each. At the end of each epoch, the timestamp at the end of the chain is noted and the mining target is adjusted with the aim of keeping the expected block production rate constant. The way T is adjusted is algorithmically determined, and it is important that it follows certain rules. While we will not articulate the exact rules, we remark that the new value T' must fall within a range $\tau T, \frac{1}{\tau}T$, where $\tau \in (0, 1)$ (for example, Bitcoin sets $\tau = \frac{1}{4}$). This critical condition is necessary to avoid certain attacks [7].

The proof-of-work OTP wallet described in the main body is suitable for the *static difficulty* model in which the mining target T is not adjusted and remains constant. Real blockhchain systems adjust their T parameter dynamically in every epoch [29]. Our construction in this section will work in both models.

The construction for the dynamic difficulty proof-of-work model is similar to the static difficulty proof-of-work construction, with a key difference in the NP language used for witness encryption. The key idea is that, instead of encrypting for a chain descending from B and consisting of t *blocks* in the future, we need to encrypt for a chain descending from B and consisting of blocks that have together accumulated a total of t *difficulty*. More concretely, the witness encryption problem statement $x = (B, t, T_0, r_0, \nu)$ contains B and t as before, but now also contains the term T_0, the difficulty of the chain at the point when timelock encryption took place, the round r_0 during which the first block of the current epoch was generated, as well as ν, the position of block B within its current epoch ($\nu = (|C| - k) \bmod m$, where m denotes the fixed epoch length).

The format of the witness w is now a sequence of block headers in the form $\langle T_i, \mathsf{ctr}_i, \mathsf{tx}_i, H(B_{i-1}), r_i \rangle$, where ctr_i, tx_i and $H(B_{i-1})$ are as before, and, additionally, T_i is the individual block's mining target and r_i is the round during which it was mined (following the notation of Garay et al. [29]). The relation $\mathcal{R}$ checks that the witness provided forms a chain that begins at the last known stable block B, that every block satisfies the dynamic difficulty proof-of-work equation $H(B_i) \leq T_i$, and that difficulty has been adjusted correctly. Specifically, for the difficulty adjustment, it checks that for all $i \geq 2$, if $i - \nu \bmod m \neq 1$, then $T_{i-1} = T_i$ (ensuring difficulty was not improperly adjusted internally within the epoch of B or any subsequent epochs). It also checks that the rounds provided are increasing $r_i < r_{i+1}$, and ensures that the difficulty at the epoch borders $i - 1, i$ with $i - \nu \bmod m \neq 1$ and $i > 1$ has been correctly adjusted by verifying that $T_i = \min(\max(T_i', \frac{1}{\tau}T_i'), \tau T_i')$, where $T_i' = \frac{r_{i-1} - r_{i-m}}{a} T_{i-1}$ is the unclamped target, and the term a indicates the expected block production rate of the system in rounds [29]. To achieve security with overwhelming probability, and not just in expectation, in κ, it is imperative that the τ bounds are also checked by $\mathcal{R}$ (see Bahack [7] for more details on a tail attack). Lastly, the relation checks that the difficulty is sufficient, as required by the t parameter. To do this, the difficulty of each block in the witness is summed up to discover the cummulative difficulty of the fork, checking that $\sum_{\langle T_i, -, -, -, - \rangle \in w} \frac{1}{T_i} \geq t$.

Now that the precise NP language has been established, a couple of things need to be changed in our protocol. First of all, at the time the OTPs are generated, MAX_TIME no longer indicates the maximum lifetime of the wallet (in chunks of HOURLY_BLOCK_RATE blocks), but the maximum total *difficulty* accumulated during the lifetime of the wallet. So we rename it to MAX_DIFFICULTY. This parameter is sensitive in case the difficulty *increases*. Hence, the value must be *increased* sufficiently (at the cost of increased IPFS storage needs) to cover for all foreseeable difficulty adjustments for the expected lifetime of the wallet. One way to do this is to look at past difficulty adjustment trends and extrapolate them to the future for the number of years the wallet is to be usable. In any case, this prediction does not need to be perfect: In the unfortunate case that the OTPs are close to becoming exhausted, which can easily be observed by inspecting the chain as it evolves, the wallet can be sunset by moving the funds to a new wallet with a new lifetime.

Next, the value HOURLY_BLOCK_RATE no longer indicates the number of blocks generated in one hour, but the amount of difficulty that must be accumulated before the next OTP can be utilized. So we rename it to OTP_ROTATION_DIFFICULTY. This parameter is sensitive in case the difficulty *decreases*. Hence, this value must be *decreased* sufficiently (at the cost of increased IPFS storage needs) to allow the user to spend as quickly as desired. As difficulty typically does not decrease, one way to do this is to look at the previous HOURLY_BLOCK_RATE parameter and multiply it by the current difficulty to obtain a lower bound for the future. If one can predict a lower bound for how much future difficulty increases, it is also possible to timelock encrypt with non-uniform difficulty: The difference in the difficulty used to witness encrypt two early consecutive OTPs can be smaller than the difference in difficulty used to witness encrypt two later consecutive OTPs. The precise mechanism to do this effectively depends on the cryptocurrency and empirical measurements.

Lastly, the smart contract must be modified in the security-critical line that ensures that t is sufficiently in the future. In the static difficulty, t counts the number of blocks (or slots in the proof-of-stake case), but here it is counting difficulty. Therefore, it cannot be compared to block.number, and the $2k$ delay (which also counts blocks) cannot be readily applied. Instead, we must use a new variable[2] block.cumdiff, the cummulative difficulty collected by the blockchain if all the difficulty from genesis to the current block is summed up. Additionally, the $2k$ factor must be weighted by the current difficulty $\frac{1}{\text{block.T}}$, where block.T indicates the mining target of the current block.

The algorithms for the variable difficulty OTP wallet appear in Algorithm 5 and 6.

---

[2] This block property is not currently available in Ethereum Solidity, but it is available in web3 as `block.totalDifficulty`. It is an easily implementable solution, but can even be incorporated into a smart contract within the current infrastructure without any forks [36].

Algorithm 5. Hours of Horus in variable difficulty.

```
1:  contract OTPWallet
2:      BLOCK_DELAY ← 2k
3:      r ← ⊥; spent ← ∅; commitments ← ∅
4:      function construct(r̄)
5:          r ← r̄
6:      end function
7:      function commit(z, t)
8:          require(t > block.number + BLOCK_DELAY/block.T)
9:          commitments[z][t] ← true
10:     end function
11:     function reveal(OTP, salt, α_to, amount, c_t, w, t, π)
12:         h ← H(⟨OTP, salt, α_to, amount⟩)
13:         require(commitments[z][t])
14:         require(MT.Ver(c_t, t, r, π))
15:         require(WE.Dec(c_t, w) = OTP)
16:         to.transfer(amount)
17:     end function
18: end contract
```

Algorithm 6. Interacting with variable difficulty Hours of Horus.

```
1:  BLOCK_DELAY ← 2k
2:  seed ← ⊥; pk ← ⊥; c ← [ ]; B ← ⊥
3:  upon initialize do
4:      seed ← {0, 1}^κ                                    ▷ Seed is generated with high entropy κ
5:      B ← C[−k]                                          ▷ Latest stable block
6:      for t ← 1 to MAX_DIFFICULTY do
7:          OTP_t ← G(seed, t)                             ▷ Time t OTP with low entropy λ
8:          x ← (B, OTP_ROTATION_DIFFICULTY · t)
9:          c ← c ‖ WE.Enc(OTP_t, x)
10:     end for
11:     r ← MT.build(c)
12:     pk ← OTPWallet.construct(r)
13: end upon
14: upon spend(α_to, amount) do
15:     t_1 ← ⌈C.cumdiff + (ℓ + BLOCK_DELAY)/C[−1].T⌉
16:     salt ← {0, 1}^κ                                    ▷ Generate short-lived high-entropy salt
17:     OTP_t ← G(seed, t_1)
18:     z ← H(⟨OTP_t, salt, α_to, amount⟩)
19:     OTPWallet.commit(z, t_1)
20:     wait until C.cumdiff = t_1
21:     w ← C{B:}
22:     π ← MT.prove(c_t, c)
23:     OTPWallet.reveal(OTP_t, salt, α_to, amount, c_t, w, t_1, π)
24: end upon
```

The argument for the correctness of the scheme and the security of the scheme remains the same. Some remarks about the security portion are in order. First, recall that any blockchain protocol does not accept blocks with timestamps in the future. In the static difficulty model, this was not important, but in the proof-of-stake and in the variable difficulty model, it is something to consider. In particular, for the variable difficulty case, if the adversary constructs blocks timestamped with future rounds, she can cause the difficulty to drop more than it would be possible in a real-world execution. However, this does not bless the adversary with more mining power. Additionally, such chains will not be mined on by honest parties (because they are considered invalid, as of yet), and so they will only be extended by the adversary. The effect is the contrary of a difficulty raising [7] attack: The total difficulty accumulated as the target difficulty is artificially decreased becomes concentrated to its expected value. Hence, the minority adversary, who does not win in expectation, has an even lower probability of accumulating the difficulty goal described by x in this futuristic chain. Therefore, we shall not be concerned about this behavior.

The Bounded Delay Model. The above high-level analysis, as well as the more detailed analysis of the static case in Sect. A, was in the synchronous setting. However, all the proofs made direct use of high-level chain properties such as the common prefix property, safety, and liveness. The use of the rounds r_c, r_i, and r_z to split time into chunks in the proof of Lemmas 1 and 2 is material to the proof. However, these rounds are defined based on transaction broadcast events and lengths attained by local honest chains. In a setting where the parties incur an unknown bounded delay Δ (which satisfies certain conditions [27]), the properties of the chain still hold, albeit with worse parameters k and ℓ, and the same security proof remains valid.

D   Discussion

Having completed the presentation of our schemes in both static and variable proof-of-work, as well as in proof-of-stake, we now discuss a couple of remarks (and shortcomings) of our scheme.

Large Witnesses. The witnesses to the problem instances of the moderately hard NP language describing chain creation can grow linearly together with the chain. To reduce witness size, a (zero knowledge) proof of knowledge such as a zk-SNARK [9] can be used. In this case, instead of witness encrypting against a decryptor who "knows a witness consisting of a list of chain headers that satisfy the blockchain properties," one can instead witness encrypt against a decryptor who "knows a witness consisting of a zero-knowledge proof of knowledge attesting to the knowledge of chain headers that satisfy the blockchain properties." This composition of witness encryption and zero-knowledge proofs allows the witnesses presented to the blockchain to become constant size. For further details, refer to [41].

Using Standard Time-Based OTP. A standard time-based OTP cannot be used by the user of our protocol, because the chain, as a stochastic process, may have grown faster or slower than expected. The OTP device must know the current height of the blockchain to be able to reveal the correctly indexed OTP (which will reside at OTP index $|\mathcal{C}| + \ell + 2k$). One practical way to achieve this is to have the mobile wallet (or a block explorer) display the current block height, which can then be inputted by the user to the OTP application.

Security of the Online Computer. One critical point of infrastructure is the online computer to which the user inputs their OTP code. If that computer becomes compromised, it can change the target address and amount that the user is inputting and deplete the wallet. One practical mechanism to cut the user's losses is to establish an hourly limit in the amount that can be spent by the wallet. The simplest way is to add an assertion in Algorithm 3 that ensures the amount spent in every *reveal* call is limited. In such a case, the compromised computer can only steal the user's funds *once*, and up to the specified hourly limit, before being detected. More complex schemes can introduce limits for various periods of time, and the contract would have to keep track of how much money has been spent in every period of time.

Two-Factor Wallets. The OTP scheme can be used either as a single-factor (as described in the main body) or as a second factor combined with a private key if desired. It is an effective second factor because, if either, but not both, of the private key or the OTP device become compromised, the wallet remains secure.

A Bounty for the Miners. In our analysis, we have considered a rational adversary who is only allowed to allocate her capital into taking guesses for the user passwords and OTPs and holds a minority of the adversarial power. This worldview is slightly myopic. An adversary with a large capital operating in an open world can also use this money for other purposes such as bribing miners. In fact, let us take a step back and reconsider the *honest majority* assumption of the chain which allowed us to conclude that the properties of common prefix, safety, and liveness hold. What if the miners are not honest, but rational, instead? In this case, the properties do not hold (it is known that the honest protocol is not a Nash equilibrium [26], although it may be close to it [38]). In our case of keyless wallets, the wallet functions as a *bounty* to the miner who creates a long chain fork: If an adversary can violate the common prefix property, then she can, as far as the chain is concerned "go back in time." In such an attack, after the secrets become timelock decryptable, the adversary creates a long chain reorganization and resubmits the correct guess to the wallet. As the reorganization was long, the delay check in the smart contract succeeds and the trial is correctly committed to the chain, granting the adversary the prize. This can be dangerous.

However, It can be argued that such bounties can be created by the adversary herself: If she double spends her money, she creates an incentive for herself to go back in time and reclaim it. But there is a crucial difference: The adversary can only spend her own money in the double spending case. Namely, although in a double spending case, the party receiving the money was harmed by the chargeback, it is the adversary's money that is being double spent, not someone else's. There is another critical difference here: While a single adversary can create such bounties for herself, keyless wallets are *universal* bounties claimable by any miner. We remark, however, that a double spending adversary can twist the double spending attack in a way that makes it a universal bounty: The adversary first creates a legitimate transaction spending some of her own money and receives, say, fiat money in exchange. She then creates a double spending transaction in an alternative fork: That double spending transaction pays 50% of her money to herself, and the rest to the miner who confirms the given block. In this case, all miners are incentivized to confirm this transaction and fork.

Therefore, we argue that the existing blockchain systems are not very different in the way incentives are aligned as compared to our proposed wallet. Nevertheless, as highlighted in the analysis, the proposed wallet does indeed have a different security model from a standard wallet: It is not purely cryptographic, but a cryptographic/cryptoeconomic hybrid. A quantified analysis of the (ir)rationality of conducting a common prefix attack is explored by Bonneau et al. [12].

Temporary Dishonest Majority. Our analysis assumed adversarial minority throughout the execution. However, this may not necessarily be the case. Blockchains have faced situations where the adversarial power has temporary majority spikes, even though the adversary generally controls only a minority [4, 6]. One of the arguments protecting from double spending stems from the ability of the user to set their own local k parameter when they consider which transaction to accept as confirmed. The parameter k is not a global parameter of the system, but it can be set by each user individually at the time of payment. If there are rumours or evidence that the chain may be under attack, the user can delay accepting payments. This is not the case for our protocol. While the user can set the critical $2k$ delay when instantiating the contract, and this is a local choice, this choice cannot be changed later. If an adversary attains majority after the contract has been instantiated, she will be able to roll back the chain sufficiently to steal the user's money. This limitation of the system must be taken into account when deciding about the k parameter of the wallet: The parameter must not only withstand current adversarial bounds, but adversarial bounds through the lifetime of the wallet. One mechanism to deal with this issue is to migrate from a wallet with a small k to a different wallet with a more conservative value when evidence appears that the chain may become attacked in the near future. If the blockchain network cannot be trusted to maintain honest majority, and the adversarial majority spike length is unpredictable, the money cannot be left and forgotten as in a key-based wallet.

Detectability of Brute Force Attacks. One of the advantages of our system is that brute force attacks are not only economically infeasible, but they are also detectable. If an adversary submits a brute force attempt to the wallet, a *commit* transaction will appear on the chain that the honest user will see. As such, the user can decide to move their funds out of their wallet if they observe such behavior. This benefit stems from the fact that the brute forcing of user passwords and OTPs cannot be done offline, but must necessarily be made on the chain. Our rate limiting scheme is therefore not just enabling limiting, but also detection. It is the first scheme of its kind that works in a decentralized manner on-chain.

E   Auxiliary Theorems

The following theorem establishes that chains cannot grow too quickly. It uses the notation adopted from the backbone series [28, 29].

Theorem 4 (Chain Growth Bound). *In a typical execution, consider a round r_0 during which the longest chain that exists on the network has a height of h_0. Then at round $r_1 > r_0$, let h_1 denote the height of the longest chain that exists on the network. The chain cannot grow too quickly:*

$$\Pr[h_1 - h_0 > (1 + \epsilon)(r_1 - r_0)nq\frac{T}{2^\kappa}] \leq \exp(-\Omega(\kappa(r_1 - r_0)))$$

Proof. Let us consider the case where the adversary uses all her queries (if the adversary does not use all her queries, we can force her to do so at the end of her round and ignore the results). Then there will be nq queries per round in total, and $(r_1 - r_0)nq$ queries across all the rounds in $r_1 - r_0$. In typical executions, the longest chain on the network can only grow if a query is successful. The probability of success of a query is $\frac{T}{2^\kappa}$. The random variable $h_1 - h_0$ is hence upper bounded by a Binomial distribution with parameters $\frac{T}{2^\kappa}$ and $(r_1 - r_0)nq$, which has expectation $(r_1 - r_0)nq\frac{T}{2^\kappa}$. Applying a Chernoff bound with error ϵ, we obtain the desired result.

We include the Chernoff bound, referenced at a high level throughout this paper, for completeness.

Theorem 5 (Chernoff bounds). *Let $\{X_i : i \in [n]\}$ are mutually independent Boolean random variables, with $\Pr[X_i = 1] = p$, for all $i \in [n]$. Let $X = \sum_{i=1}^{n} X_i$ and $\mu = pn$. Then, for any $\delta \in (0, 1]$,*

$$\Pr[X \leq (1 - \delta)\mu] \leq e^{-\delta^2\mu/2} \ and \ \Pr[X \geq (1 + \delta)\mu] \leq e^{-\delta^2\mu/3}.$$

References

1. Albrecht, M., Bai, S., Ducas, L.: A subfield lattice attack on overstretched NTRU assumptions. In: Robshaw, M., Katz, J. (eds.) CRYPTO 2016. LNCS, vol. 9814, pp. 153–178. Springer, Heidelberg (2016). https://doi.org/10.1007/978-3-662-53018-4_6

2. Albrecht, M.R., Cocis, C., Laguillaumie, F., Langlois, A.: Implementing candidate graded encoding schemes from ideal lattices. In: Iwata, T., Cheon, J.H. (eds.) ASIACRYPT 2015. LNCS, vol. 9453, pp. 752–775. Springer, Heidelberg (2015). https://doi.org/10.1007/978-3-662-48800-3_31

3. Arapinis, M., Gkaniatsou, A., Karakostas, D., Kiayias, A.: A formal treatment of hardware wallets. In: Goldberg, I., Moore, T. (eds.) FC 2019. LNCS, vol. 11598, pp. 426–445. Springer, Cham (2019). https://doi.org/10.1007/978-3-030-32101-7_26

4. Avarikioti, G., Käppeli, L., Wang, Y., Wattenhofer, R.: Bitcoin security under temporary dishonest majority. In: Goldberg, I., Moore, T. (eds.) FC 2019. LNCS, vol. 11598, pp. 466–483. Springer, Cham (2019). https://doi.org/10.1007/978-3-030-32101-7_28

5. Badertscher, C., Gaži, P., Kiayias, A., Russell, A., Zikas, V.: Ouroboros genesis: composable proof-of-stake blockchains with dynamic availability. In: Proceedings of the 2018 ACM SIGSAC Conference on Computer and Communications Security, pp. 913–930 (2018)

6. Badertscher, C., Gazi, P., Kiayias, A., Russell, A., Zikas, V.: Consensus redux: distributed ledgers in the face of adversarial supremacy. Technical report, Cryptology ePrint Archive, Report 2020/1021 (2020)

7. Bahack, L.: Theoretical Bitcoin attacks with less than half of the computational power (draft). Cryptology ePrint Archive, Report 2013/868 (2013). http://eprint.iacr.org/2013/868

8. Bellare, M., Rogaway, P.: Random oracles are practical: a paradigm for designing efficient protocols. In: Proceedings of the 1st ACM Conference on Computer and Communications Security, pp. 62–73. ACM (1993)

9. Ben-Sasson, E., Chiesa, A., Tromer, E., Virza, M.: Succinct non-interactive arguments for a von Neumann architecture. Cryptology ePrint Archive, Report 2013/879 (2013). http://eprint.iacr.org/2013/879

10. Benet, J.: IPFS: content addressed, versioned, P2P file system. arXiv preprint arXiv:1407.3561 (2014)

11. Bentov, I., Pass, R., Shi, E.: Snow white: provably secure proofs of stake. IACR Cryptology ePrint Archive 2016:919 (2016)

12. Bonneau, J., Clark, J., Goldfeder, S.: On bitcoin as a public randomness source. IACR Cryptology ePrint Archive 2015:1015 (2015)

13. Bonneau, J., Miller, A., Clark, J., Narayanan, A., Kroll, J.A., Felten, E.W.: SoK: research perspectives and challenges for bitcoin and cryptocurrencies. In: 2015 IEEE Symposium on Security and Privacy (SP), pp. 104–121. IEEE (2015)

14. Buterin, V., et al.: A next-generation smart contract and decentralized application platform. White Paper (2014)

15. Cheon, J.H., Han, K., Lee, C., Ryu, H., Stehlé, D.: Cryptanalysis of the multilinear map over the integers. In: Oswald, E., Fischlin, M. (eds.) EUROCRYPT 2015. LNCS, vol. 9056, pp. 3–12. Springer, Heidelberg (2015). https://doi.org/10.1007/978-3-662-46800-5_1

16. Cheon, J.H., Jeong, J., Lee, C.: An algorithm for NTRU problems and cryptanalysis of the GGH multilinear map without a low level encoding of zero. Cryptology ePrint Archive, Report 2016/139 (2016). http://eprint.iacr.org/2016/139

17. Cheon, J.H., Lee, C., Ryu, H.: Cryptanalysis of the new CLT multilinear maps. Cryptology ePrint Archive, Report 2015/934 (2015). http://eprint.iacr.org/2015/934

18. Coron, J.-S., et al.: Zeroizing without low-level zeroes: new MMAP attacks and their limitations. In: Gennaro, R., Robshaw, M. (eds.) CRYPTO 2015. LNCS, vol. 9215, pp. 247–266. Springer, Heidelberg (2015). https://doi.org/10.1007/978-3-662-47989-6_12

19. Coron, J.-S., Lee, M.S., Lepoint, T., Tibouchi, M.: Cryptanalysis of GGH15 multilinear maps. In: Robshaw, M., Katz, J. (eds.) CRYPTO 2016. LNCS, vol. 9815, pp.

607–628. Springer, Heidelberg (2016). https://doi.org/10.1007/978-3-662-53008-5_21

20. Coron, J.-S., Lee, M.S., Lepoint, T., Tibouchi, M.: Zeroizing attacks on indistinguishability obfuscation over CLT13. In: Fehr, S. (ed.) PKC 2017. LNCS, vol. 10174, pp. 41–58. Springer, Heidelberg (2017). https://doi.org/10.1007/978-3-662-54365-8_3

21. Coron, J.-S., Lepoint, T., Tibouchi, M.: Practical multilinear maps over the integers. In: Canetti, R., Garay, J.A. (eds.) CRYPTO 2013. LNCS, vol. 8042, pp. 476–493. Springer, Heidelberg (2013). https://doi.org/10.1007/978-3-642-40041-4_26

22. Coron, J.-S., Lepoint, T., Tibouchi, M.: New multilinear maps over the integers. In: Gennaro, R., Robshaw, M. (eds.) CRYPTO 2015. LNCS, vol. 9215, pp. 267–286. Springer, Heidelberg (2015). https://doi.org/10.1007/978-3-662-47989-6_13

23. Daian, P., et al.: Flash boys 2.0: frontrunning in decentralized exchanges, miner extractable value, and consensus instability. In: 2020 IEEE Symposium on Security and Privacy (SP), pp. 910–927. IEEE (2020)

24. David, B., Gaži, P., Kiayias, A., Russell, A.: Ouroboros praos: an adaptively-secure, semi-synchronous proof-of-stake protocol. Cryptology ePrint Archive, Report 2017/573 (2017). http://eprint.iacr.org/2017/573. To appear at EUROCRYPT 2018

25. Dwork, C., Naor, M.: Pricing via processing or combatting junk mail. In: Brickell, E.F. (ed.) CRYPTO 1992. LNCS, vol. 740, pp. 139–147. Springer, Heidelberg (1993). https://doi.org/10.1007/3-540-48071-4_10

26. Eyal, I., Sirer, E.G.: Majority is not enough: bitcoin mining is vulnerable. In: Christin, N., Safavi-Naini, R. (eds.) FC 2014. LNCS, vol. 8437, pp. 436–454. Springer, Heidelberg (2014). https://doi.org/10.1007/978-3-662-45472-5_28

27. Garay, J., Kiayias, A., Leonardos, N.: The bitcoin backbone protocol: analysis and applications (revised 2019). Cryptology ePrint Archive, Report 2014/765 (2014). https://eprint.iacr.org/2014/765

28. Garay, J., Kiayias, A., Leonardos, N.: The bitcoin backbone protocol: analysis and applications. In: Oswald, E., Fischlin, M. (eds.) EUROCRYPT 2015. LNCS, vol. 9057, pp. 281–310. Springer, Heidelberg (2015). https://doi.org/10.1007/978-3-662-46803-6_10

29. Garay, J., Kiayias, A., Leonardos, N.: The bitcoin backbone protocol with chains of variable difficulty. In: Katz, J., Shacham, H. (eds.) CRYPTO 2017. LNCS, vol. 10401, pp. 291–323. Springer, Cham (2017). https://doi.org/10.1007/978-3-319-63688-7_10

30. Garg, S., Gentry, C., Halevi, S.: Candidate multilinear maps from ideal lattices. In: Johansson, T., Nguyen, P.Q. (eds.) EUROCRYPT 2013. LNCS, vol. 7881, pp. 1–17. Springer, Heidelberg (2013). https://doi.org/10.1007/978-3-642-38348-9_1

31. Garg, S., Gentry, C., Sahai, A., Waters, B.: Witness encryption and its applications, pp. 467–476 (2013)

32. Gentry, C., Gorbunov, S., Halevi, S.: Graph-induced multilinear maps from lattices. In: Dodis, Y., Nielsen, J.B. (eds.) TCC 2015. LNCS, vol. 9015, pp. 498–527. Springer, Heidelberg (2015). https://doi.org/10.1007/978-3-662-46497-7_20

33. Homoliak, I., Breitenbacher, D., Hujnak, O., Hartel, P., Binder, A., Szalachowski, P.: SmartOTPs: an air-gapped 2-factor authentication for smart-contract wallets. In: Proceedings of the 2nd ACM Conference on Advances in Financial Technologies, pp. 145–162 (2020)

34. Hu, Y., Jia, H.: Cryptanalysis of GGH map. In: Fischlin, M., Coron, J.-S. (eds.) EUROCRYPT 2016. LNCS, vol. 9665, pp. 537–565. Springer, Heidelberg (2016). https://doi.org/10.1007/978-3-662-49890-3_21

35. Karantias, K.: SoK: a taxonomy of cryptocurrency wallets. Technical report, IACR Cryptology ePrint Archive 2020:868 (2020)

36. Karantias, K., Kiayias, A., Zindros, D.: Smart contract derivatives. In: Pardalos, P., Kotsireas, I., Guo, Y., Knottenbelt, W. (eds.) Mathematical Research for Blockchain Economy. SPBE, pp. 1–8. Springer, Cham (2020). https://doi.org/10.1007/978-3-030-53356-4_1

37. Kiayias, A., Gaži, P., Zindros, D.: Proof-of-stake sidechains. In: IEEE Symposium on Security and Privacy. IEEE (2019)

38. Kiayias, A., Koutsoupias, E., Kyropoulou, M., Tselekounis, Y.: Blockchain mining games. In: Proceedings of the 2016 ACM Conference on Economics and Computation, pp. 365–382 (2016)

39. Kiayias, A., Russell, A., David, B., Oliynykov, R.: Ouroboros: a provably secure proof-of-stake blockchain protocol. In: Katz, J., Shacham, H. (eds.) CRYPTO 2017. LNCS, vol. 10401, pp. 357–388. Springer, Cham (2017). https://doi.org/10.1007/978-3-319-63688-7_12

40. Langlois, A., Stehlé, D., Steinfeld, R.: GGHLite: more efficient multilinear maps from ideal lattices. In: Nguyen, P.Q., Oswald, E. (eds.) EUROCRYPT 2014. LNCS, vol. 8441, pp. 239–256. Springer, Heidelberg (2014). https://doi.org/10.1007/978-3-642-55220-5_14

41. Liu, J., Jager, T., Kakvi, S.A., Warinschi, B.: How to build time-lock encryption. Des. Codes Crypt. **86**(11), 2549–2586 (2018). https://doi.org/10.1007/s10623-018-0461-x

42. Ma, F., Zhandry, M.: The MMap strikes back: obfuscation and new multilinear maps immune to CLT13 zeroizing attacks. In: Beimel, A., Dziembowski, S. (eds.) TCC 2018. LNCS, vol. 11240, pp. 513–543. Springer, Cham (2018). https://doi.org/10.1007/978-3-030-03810-6_19

43. Merkle, R.C.: A digital signature based on a conventional encryption function. In: Pomerance, C. (ed.) CRYPTO 1987. LNCS, vol. 293, pp. 369–378. Springer, Heidelberg (1988). https://doi.org/10.1007/3-540-48184-2_32

44. Micali, S.: ALGORAND: the efficient and democratic ledger. CoRR, abs/1607.01341 (2016)

45. Micali, S., Rabin, M.O., Vadhan, S.P.: Verifiable random functions, pp. 120–130 (1999)

46. Miller, A.: IRC logs of #bitcoin-wizards on 2015-03-13 on FreeNode (2015). https://download.wpsoftware.net/bitcoin/wizards/2015-03-13.html. Accessed 13 May 2021

47. Minaud, B., Fouque, P.-A.: Cryptanalysis of the new multilinear map over the integers. Cryptology ePrint Archive, Report 2015/941 (2015). http://eprint.iacr.org/2015/941

48. M'Raihi, D., Machani, S., Pei, M., Rydell, J.: TOTP: time-based one-time password algorithm. RFC 6238, RFC Editor (2011)

49. M'Raihi, D., Bellare, M., Hoornaert, F., Naccache, D., Ranen, O.: HOTP: an HMAC-based one-time password algorithm. RFC 4226, RFC Editor (2005)

50. Nakamoto, S.: Bitcoin: a peer-to-peer electronic cash system (2008)

51. Rivest, R.L., Shamir, A., Wagner, D.A.: Time-lock puzzles and timed-release crypto (1996)

52. Vasek, M., Bonneau, J., Castellucci, R., Keith, C., Moore, T.: The Bitcoin brain drain: examining the use and abuse of bitcoin brain wallets. In: Grossklags, J., Preneel, B. (eds.) FC 2016. LNCS, vol. 9603, pp. 609–618. Springer, Heidelberg (2017). https://doi.org/10.1007/978-3-662-54970-4_36
53. Wood, G.: Ethereum: a secure decentralised generalised transaction ledger. Ethereum Project Yellow Pap. 151, 1–32 (2014)

A Scalable Architecture for Electronic Payments

Geoff Goodell[1](✉), D. R. Toliver[2], and Hazem Danny Nakib[1]

[1] University College London, London, UK
g.goodell@ucl.ac.uk
[2] TODAQ Financial, Toronto, Canada

Abstract. We present a scalable architecture for electronic retail payments via central bank digital currency and offer a solution to the perceived conflict between robust regulatory oversight and consumer affordances such as privacy and control. Our architecture combines existing work in payment systems and digital currency with a new approach to digital asset design for managing unforgeable, stateful, and oblivious assets without relying on either a central authority or a monolithic consensus system. Regulated financial institutions have a role in every transaction, and the consumer affordances are achieved through the use of non-custodial wallets that unlink the sender from the recipient in the transaction channel. This approach is fully compatible with the existing two-tiered banking system and can complement and extend the roles of existing money services businesses and asset custodians.

1 Introduction

We consider the problems posed by modern retail payments in the context of the perceived need for compromise between regulatory compliance and consumer protections. Retail payments increasingly rely on digital technology, including both e-commerce transactions via the Internet and in-person electronic payments leveraging payment networks at the point of sale. With cash, customers pass physical objects that are in their possession to merchants. In contrast, electronic payments are generally conducted by proxy: Customers instruct their banks to debit their accounts and remit the funds to the bank accounts of their counterparties. For this reason, non-cash retail payments expose customers to a variety of costs and risks, including profiling, discrimination, and value extraction by the custodians of their assets.

A good central bank digital currency (CBDC) would empower individuals to make payments using digital objects in their possession rather than accounts that are linked to their identities, affording them verifiable privacy and control over their digital payments. However, many existing CBDC proposals require either a centralised system operator or a global ledger. Centralised systems entail risks both for the users of the system as well as for the system operators, and global ledgers present performance bottlenecks as well as an economically inefficient allocation of transaction costs.

© The Author(s) 2023
S. Matsuo et al. (Eds.): FC 2022 Workshops, LNCS 13412, pp. 645–678, 2023.
https://doi.org/10.1007/978-3-031-32415-4_38

We present a system architecture for retail payments that allows transactions to take place within a local context, avoiding the problems associated with performance bottlenecks and centralised system operators. We show how assets that represent obligations of central banks can be created and exchanged, without requiring a central system operator to process and adjudicate all of the transactions, and without undermining the portability of money throughout the system or the ability for regulators to ensure compliance.

Although our proposal takes a decentralised approach to processing transactions, money within our system intrinsically relies upon a trusted *issuer*. This could be the central bank itself, but it could also be a co-regulated federation, such as a national payment network or the operators of a real time gross settlement system. Specifically, the issuer is trusted to oversee the processing of redemptions, wherein CBDC assets are accepted as valid by their recipients.

Our proposal is fully compatible with the function of existing private-sector banks. The architecture provides an effective solution for a variety of different use cases, including those that are sensitive to regulatory compliance requirements, transactional efficiency concerns, or consumer affordances such as privacy and control. We begin with an examination of the properties required to support such use cases.

The remainder of this article is organised as follows. Section 2 identifies the properties that a payment system should have as a foundation for a robust set of technical requirements, Sect. 3 specifies the design of our proposed architecture, Sect. 4 offers a model for how to deploy and manage a central bank digital currency (CBDC) system using our architecture, Appendix F describes several use cases that demonstrate the special capabilities of our proposed design, Appendix G compares our design to other payment systems, and Sect. 5 provides a summary.

2   Payment System Desiderata

To be broadly useful for making payments, and particularly to satisfy the requirements of central bank digital currency, a payment system must have the properties necessary to meet the demands of its use cases. We list the asset-level and system-level desiderata below. In Appendices A and B, we further describe these properties and use cases, and show that they are indeed required.

- Asset-level desiderata
    1. Durability
    2. Self-contained assets
    3. Mechanical control
    4. Delegation
    5. Choice of custodian
    6. Choice to have no custodian
    7. Fungibility
    8. Efficient lifecycle

- System-level desiderata
  9. Privacy by design
  10. Self-determination for asset owners
  11. Local transactions
  12. Time-shifted offline transactions
  13. Accessibility
  14. Monetary sovereignty
  15. Regulatory compliance

Next, we translate the asset-level and system-level desiderata into specific technical and institutional capabilities that are necessary to support a suitable payment system. We begin by identifying the technical requirements for an institutionally supportable digital currency that provides verifiable privacy for consumers, and which does not force consumers to trust additional actors:

- **Blind signatures.** Consumer agents must implement *blinding* and *unblinding* with semantics similar to the blind signatures proposed by Chaum in his original article [3] and further elaborated in his more recent work with the Swiss National Bank [4]. Specifically, it must be possible for users to furnish a block of data to an issuer, ask the issuer to sign it, then transform the response into a valid signature on a new block of data that the issuer has never seen before and cannot link to the original block of data. This allows transactions that do not link the identity of the sender to the identity of the recipient, as a way to achieve privacy by design (9).
- **Distributed ledger.** Participants in a clearing network overseen by a central bank must have access to a suitable distributed ledger technology (DLT) system [5] that enables them to collectively maintain an immutable record that can be updated with sufficient frequency to provide transaction finality that is at least as fast as domestic bank wires. This helps ensure both durability of assets (1) and self-determination for users (10) as described in Section 2.
- **Open architecture.** The system must fully support the semantics for digital currency specified by Goodell, Nakib, and Tasca [2]. Specifically, we assume that retail users of digital currency have access to non-custodial wallets that satisfy certain privacy and accessibility requirements described in Appendix B, specifically requirements (6), (9), (10), and (13).
- **Fungible tokens.** The digital currency tokens themselves must satisfy the fungibility requirement (7) described in Appendix A.
- **Institutional controls.** System operators must possess capabilities that support the policy requirements described in Appendix B, specifically requirements (14) and (15).

Moving to a digital form of currency brings a variety of potential benefits when compared to paper currency, including cryptographic signatures, cryptographic shielding, flexible semantics, reduced management costs, and being able to efficiently transfer units of currency over large distances.

However, it is also important to re-capture some of the benefits of physical currency. In order to have *self-contained assets* with *custodial choice*, we need a representation for our assets that is unforgeable, stateful, and oblivious:

- **Unforgeable.** Every asset must be unique, and it can only be created once. No set of adversarial actors can repeat the process of creating an asset that has already been created. Note that this requirement is different than a "globally unique identifier", which is merely unlikely to be reused by an honest actor, but which any adversarial actor can reuse for any other asset. True unforgeability requires that once an asset is created, it is impossible to reuse its identifier for any another asset. This property is required for durability (1), custodial choice (5), the choice to have no custodian (6), local transactions (11), and time-shifted offline transactions (12).
- **Stateful.** Every asset has its own independent state, and as the state of an asset changes over time, the asset remains unique and unforgeable. No set of adversarial actors, including non-issuer owners, can create a second version of the asset with a different state. Note that this requirement precludes using any kind of "access control token", such as an HMAC, signed attestation, or even a blinded signature scheme asset, which cannot accumulate state over time and must be returned in precisely the same form as created. The requirements of self-contained assets (2), mechanical control (3), and delegation (4) necessitate that assets maintain their own state.
- **Oblivious.** Once finality is achieved following the transfer of an asset to a new owner all of the previous owners, including the issuer, have no obligation to know any aspect of its future state changes and transfers. There is no residual risk to the new owner that the transaction will be undone by either a previous owner or the system itself. Note that encryption does not suffice: there must be no requirement to inform previous owners that state changes have occurred, and previous owners must not be required to do any extra work to accommodate those changes. Otherwise, the self-determination (10) and efficient lifecycle (8) requirements would be compromised.

  Paper bank notes are a good example of obliviousness. No entity knows where every bank note is, or what everyone's billfolds hold. If anyone, including the mint, were guaranteed to know this information, then it would prevent paper money from being useful in many of its required use cases. Although obliviousness and privacy are closely related, obliviousness is really about efficiency: It is acceptable for the mint to know where some bills are and the contents of some billfolds.

These qualities combine together to provide assets, referred to as *USO assets* in this document, that have very similar qualities to paper currency. While assets embodying these qualities are not readily available at this time, this is an area of active study and promising results. Given such assets in combination with the technologies mentioned above, our architecture is able to fulfill the complete list of requirements for a payment system. In particular, CBDC created using our architecture can meet the use case demands of paper currency as well as the demands of electronic payment systems in a single architecture, without requiring trusted hardware or heavyweight consensus systems.

The requirement for a USO asset to be stateful means it must be able to prove its state has finality. The requirement for a USO asset to be oblivious means that the asset must carry a *proof of provenance* (POP) that allows it to demonstrate its validity on its own, as no other part of the system is required to have it. The requirement for a USO asset to be unforgeable means this proof carries the same weight as if it came directly from the issuer itself, so the issuer acts as the *integrity provider* of the POP.

Obliviousness implies there can be other systems between the asset owner and the integrity provider. These systems serve as *relays* in the creation of the POP. Relays are common carriers, like network carriers. In fact a relay knows considerably less than a network carrier: it accepts hashes, and emits hashes of those hashes, and by design is completely oblivious to everything else.

3 An Efficient, General-Purpose Architecture for CBDC

In this section we propose a method for creating a retail central bank digital currency (CBDC) that supports private payments wherein the owner maintains custody of her digital assets. It achieves the necessary properties for a general purpose payment system described in the previous section by extending the approach proposed by Goodell, Nakib, and Tasca [2] with a new asset model that eliminates the need for global consensus with regard to every transaction. While our new approach requires that the central bank must operate some real-time infrastructure, we show that this requirement can be addressed with a lightweight, scalable mechanism that mitigates the risk to resilience and operational security.

Suppose that a user, Alice, wants to withdraw retail CBDC for her general-purpose use in making retail payments. We assume that the recipient of any payment that Alice makes will require one or more valid tokens from a trusted issuer I containing content k that has been signed using signature function $s(k, I)$. We further assume, following the arguments made in earlier proposals for privacy-preserving retail CBDC [2,4], that she will be able to use a *blinding* function b, known only to Alice, to request a blind signature on $b(k)$ to which she can apply an *unblinding* function b^{-1}, also known only to Alice, to reveal the required signature:

$$b^{-1}(s(b(k), I)) = s(k, I) \tag{1}$$

The signature $s(k, I)$ appearing at the beginning of a USO asset's history shows that it was generated correctly by the CBDC's issuer or by one of its delegates, which we shall call *minters*. Minters are subject to a *minting invariant* wherein every time a minter satisfies a request for a set of signatures of a particular value, it must also cancel a corresponding set of CBDC assets of equal value, and vice-versa. The function of a minter, therefore, is to *recycle* CBDC, and not to issue or destroy it.

The proof of provenance of a USO asset allows its recipient to verify that it has the same integrity as if it were in the issuer's database. These proofs of provenance are a powerful enabling feature for a retail CBDC, since assets can be transacted without the need to maintain accounts. Additionally, the expected costs of operating the issuer's infrastructure is much smaller at scale than the costs associated with operating traditional distributed ledger infrastructures in which the record of each transaction is maintained in a global ledger.

However, unlike transferring blinded assets in a classical ledger system, whether distributed [2] or not [4], transferring USO assets from one party to another explicitly leaves behind an audit trail that can be used by the bearers of an asset to recognise the asset when it is inspected, transacted or seen in the future. A USO asset's proof of provenance is permanently updated each time it is transferred to a new recipient. If the same asset were to be associated with multiple transactions, then a single party to any of the transactions would be able to recognise the asset across all of its transactions, which could potentially compromise the privacy of the other parties.

It follows that if Alice wants an asset that she can spend privately, she must create it herself. Alice establishes her own USO asset privately, and subsequently populates it with the signature $s(k, I)$. Having done this she can then safely transfer the asset to Bob without concern. Figure 1 provides a visualisation of the CBDC journey from the perspective of a consumer.

Once Bob receives the asset from Alice, he has a choice. One option is to transfer it to a bank, perhaps to deposit the proceeds into his account with the bank, or to request a freshly minted CBDC asset as Alice had done earlier. If he chooses to deposit the proceeds into his account, then the bank now has a spent CBDC asset that it can exchange for central bank reserves or use to

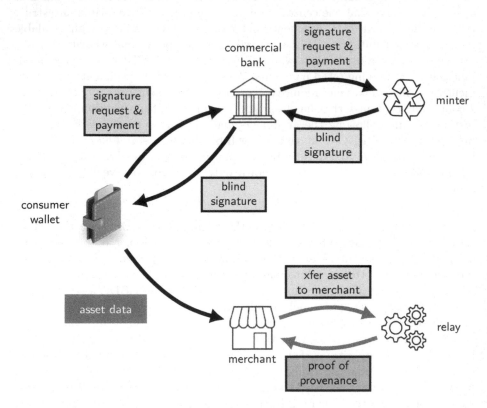

Fig. 1. *Schematic representation of the CBDC journey from the perspective of a consumer.*

satisfy requests for new signed CBDC assets from its other account holders. Alternatively, Bob could transfer the CBDC onward without returning it to the bank, bearing in mind that Bob would not be anonymous when he does; see Appendix F.3 for details.

We organise Alice's engagement lifecycle with the asset in a five-step process, as shown in Fig. 2:

1. First, Alice chooses a service provider that maintains a relay G, and creates a new USO asset that refers to some specific prior commitment G_0 published by the relay. For each CBDC token that Alice wishes to obtain, she generates a new pair of keys using asymmetric cryptography and embeds the public key A and G_0 along with the public key of the proposed digital currency issuer I, the denomination d, and a certificate $s((d, I_d), I)$ containing the key used by the issuer to sign tokens of denomination d into a template for a new, unique

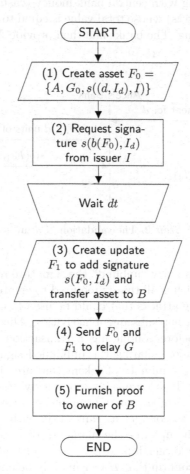

Fig. 2. *Typical consumer engagement lifecycle.* Parallelograms represent USO asset operations.

update $F_0 = \{A, G_0, s((d, I_d), I)\}$ as the foundation for a new asset F. Note that for Alice to ensure that her subsequent spending transactions are not linked to each other, she must repeat this step, creating a new key pair for each asset that she wants to create, and optionally choosing different values for the other parameters as well.

2. Next, Alice creates $b(F_0)$ using blinding function b and sends it to her bank along with a request for a blind signature from a minter using the key for the correct denomination I_d, which in the base case we assume to be the central bank. Alice is effectively requesting permission to validate asset F as legitimate national digital currency (the sovereign legal tender within that jurisdiction), so, presumably, the bank will require Alice to provide corresponding funds, such as by providing physical cash, granting the bank permission to debit her account, or transferring digital currency that she had previously received in the past. See Fig. 3. Alice's bank shall forward her request $b(F_0)$ to the central bank along with central bank money (cash, central bank reserves, or existing CBDC assets) whose total value is equal to the value of the CBDC that Alice is requesting. The bank shall then provide Alice with the signature $s(b(F_0), I_d)$.

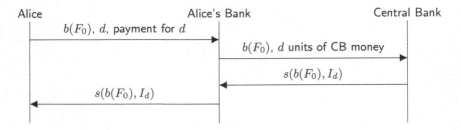

Fig. 3. *Protocol for Step 2.* The validation of d units of digital currency.

3. At this point, Alice can now "unblind" the signature received from the minter to yield $s(F_0, I_d)$, which is all that is required to create valid CBDC. To mitigate the risk of timing attacks that could be used to correlate her request for digital currency with her subsequent activities, Alice should wait for some period of time dt, before conducting a transaction with the valid CBDC received as well as before sharing the unblinded signature $s(F_0, I_d)$. Alice's privacy derives from the number of tokens that are "in-flight" (outstanding) at any given moment. If she transacts too quickly after completing her withdrawal, then her spending transaction might be traced to her withdrawal.

When Alice is ready to conduct a transaction with Bob, she creates a new update F_1 wherein she updates the metadata of F to include the signature $s(F_0, I_d)$ and transfer ownership to Bob using his public key B. Optionally, Alice might want to confirm that B legitimately belongs to Bob's business, in which case Bob could furnish a certificate for his public key. We also imagine that regulators might impose additional requirements that would apply at this stage, which we describe in Appendix C.2. Observe that neither the asset F_0 nor its update F_1 contain any information about Alice, her wallet, or any other assets or transactions.

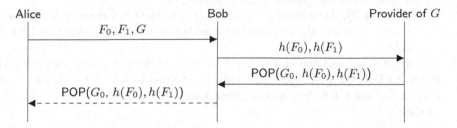

Fig. 4. *Protocol for Step 4, Option 1.* Alice gives Bob possession and control, and Bob registers the update.

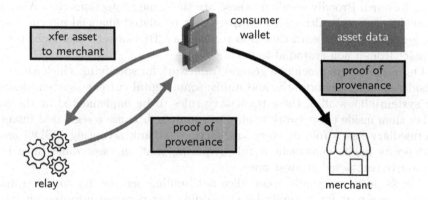

Fig. 5. *Schematic representation of Step 4, Option 2.*

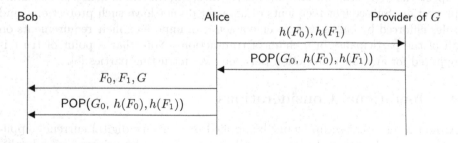

Fig. 6. *Protocol for Step 4, Option 2.* Alice registers the update herself, giving Bob control first and possession later.

4. To consummate the transaction, $h(F_0)$ and $h(F_1)$ must be sent to relay G, wherein h is a selector function that can be used to demonstrate that Alice had committed to creating the asset F_0 and its update F_1, respectively. In particular, h may be a hash function. Alice has two options for how to proceed:

- *(Option 1)*. Alice sends the identity of the relay G along with the asset F_0 and its update F_1 to Bob (see Fig. 4), and Bob sends $h(F_0)$ and $h(F_1)$ to the relay. At this point, Bob may furnish the POP of the transaction to Alice, once he receives it, as a receipt.
- *(Option 2)*. Alice sends $h(F_0)$ and $h(F_1)$ to the relay directly and subsequently furnishes the asset and its proof of provenance to Bob (see Figs. 5 and 6).

5. Finally, if Alice had chosen Option 2 for the previous step, then she should reveal to Bob the POP indicating that the transaction is done. If Alice had chosen Option 1 for the previous step, then Bob will be able to verify this himself.

Note that once Alice has transferred the CBDC asset to Bob, nothing about the asset or its proofs of provenance can be used to link the asset to Alice, her devices, or her other transactions, regardless of what Bob does with the asset going forward. Broadly speaking, these are the same protections that Alice has when she uses cash, although we expect that regulated financial intermediaries will generally always learn that Bob received a CBDC asset when Bob receives an asset from a non-custodial wallet.

Our architecture provides a general framework for specifying which assets are considered valid. Importantly, and unlike some digital currency system designs, our system allows all of these regulatory rules to be implemented at the edge rather than inside the network itself. For example, because a regulated financial intermediary has a role in every transaction, a bank accepting CBDC assets as deposits might implement a rule requiring that an asset must have been previously transacted at most once.

Alice's privacy depends upon Alice not binding her identity to the transaction in some way, for example by embedding her personal information into a transaction or by linking the transaction to a wallet identifier. In all cases, we expect that only the initial consumer, Alice, enjoys the benefits of consumer protection. Subsequent recipients of an asset do not have such protections, and rules enforced by banks that receive assets can impose explicit requirements on all of the participants in a chain of transactions. Note that a point of trust is required for any fair transaction between two untrusting parties [8].

4   Operational Considerations

Although our architecture could be applied to arbitrary digital currency applications, including digital currency and e-money issued by private-sector banks, we assume that this architecture is most useful for the implementation of central bank digital currency (CBDC), wherein central banks would be the issuers of currency for use by the general public to facilitate payments in domestic retail contexts. CBDC would represent part of the monetary base (M0), like cash and central bank reserves.

In this section, we consider operational concerns for the various parties involved in a CBDC distribution, including central banks, private-sector banks, clearinghouses, merchants, and consumers. In particular, we show that the system is able to support lightweight requirements for central banks as well as for end-user devices, including both mobile wallets for consumers and merchant devices at the point-of-sale.

4.1 Operating Model

We present a prescriptive model for how to use our architecture to implement CBDC, explicitly highlighting how CBDC would operate within the context of a modern banking system and institutions. We observe that money constitutes a complex system within an economy, entailing a delicate set of connected relationships among participants. Our proposed architecture avoids undermining this balance of connected relationships by aligning closely to the system architecture implicit to physical cash. In this sense, what we propose is not a radical new system design, but rather a new kind of digital cash that can exist alongside physical cash and other forms of money or money-like instruments used for payments. To support this model, we must consider the processes and institutions that support the circulation of cash and how they would be adapted to support the circulation of CBDC. We also introduce two new systems: an *integrity system* comprising the set of relays, which ensures that digital assets can be safely used to transfer value, and a *monitoring system* comprising the set of minters, for controlling the creation and destruction of currency tokens. Figure 7 illustrates how this would work, and we offer the following narrative description of the lifecycle of a specific CBDC asset:

- **Act I.** A unit of CBDC begins its life as a request from Alice to her commercial bank, which had previously received a set of CBDC vouchers from the central bank in exchange for reserves of equal value. CBDC vouchers are special CBDC assets that can be exchanged for signatures from minters but are not used by retail consumers. Alice's bank debits the value of the request from Alice's bank account and sends the CBDC voucher to the minter along with Alice's request. The minter then signs Alice's request, destroys the voucher, and submits a record of its work to the distributed ledger of the monitoring system, which the central bank and regulators can inspect to understand the aggregate flow of money in the system and verify that the minting invariant is maintained. The minter then sends the signed request back to Alice's bank, which forwards the signed request to Alice.
  Later, Alice uses the signature to create the CBDC asset, which we shall call Bill, and transfers it to Bob. Whenever a CBDC asset changes hands, either the sender or the recipient must send an update to the correct relay to consummate the transaction. Next, Bob transfers Bill to his bank. Importantly, unlike Alice, Bob can execute this transfer immediately if he chooses to do so; there is no particular value in waiting. At the same time, unlike with the system proposed by Chaum, Grothoff, and Möser [4], Bob can wait as long as he likes (subject to optional conditions) before depositing the asset with the bank, since there is no requirement for the issuer or a minter to participate

in the transfers. Finally, Bob's bank credits the value of the transaction to Bob's bank account.

- **Act II.** Soon afterward, Charlie, another customer of Bob's bank, makes a request to withdraw CBDC. The bank sends Bill to the minter to be recycled in exchange for signing Charlie's signature request. The minter destroys Bill, signs Charlie's signature request, and returns the signature to Charlie via the bank.

  Later, Charlie uses the signature to create a new CBDC asset, Bill II, and transfers the asset to Dave. Dave then transfers it to his bank, as Bob had done. Dave's bank decides to bring Bill II back to the central bank in exchange for reserves, instead of recycling it, ending the lifecycle of the unit of CBDC.

Note that Dave's bank could have done what Bob's bank did and save the CBDC to service future requests without vouchers. This recycling process is adiabatic, does not rely upon the active participation of the central bank, and can be repeated an arbitrary number of times in this manner before the ultimate destruction of the unit of CBDC. The minting invariant ensures that the minting system never increases or decreases the total amount of currency in circulation. Instead, it issues a new unit of currency only in response to collecting an old unit of equal value. The central bank is only involved when it engages with banks, specifically by issuing vouchers or accepting CBDC assets in exchange for reserves, and by overseeing the minting operation, passively accepting and analysing reports by minters. The central bank also relies upon the relay system to maintain CBDC integrity, and the DLT system underpins its ability to verify what it must trust.

Note also that Alice's bank could have accepted cash or CBDC assets instead of an equal amount of value from her bank account, although legal or regulatory restrictions applicable to the acceptance of cash or CBDC assets might apply.

Finally, Alice could have transferred money directly to Bob's bank account rather than to Bob. Depending upon Bob's preferences, this might be a better choice. For example, it would reduce the total number of relay requests, correspondingly reducing the operating cost to the relay system and communication overhead for Bob. It would also allow Bob to handle the case in which Alice does not have exact change; Bob could forward Alice's signature request in the amount of her overpayment to his bank along with his deposit, and then return the blind signature for Alice's change directly to Alice.

4.2   Managing CBDC Distribution

The central bank would handle the issuance, expiry, and destruction of its CBDC, as well as managing its value though monetary policy. Meanwhile, one or more clearinghouses or banks would handle all of the real-time processing. As part of the issuance process the central bank may allow one or more clearinghouses or banks to provide signatures on blinded templates, to be used by their customers in the final step of CBDC creation. The central bank would issue a specific

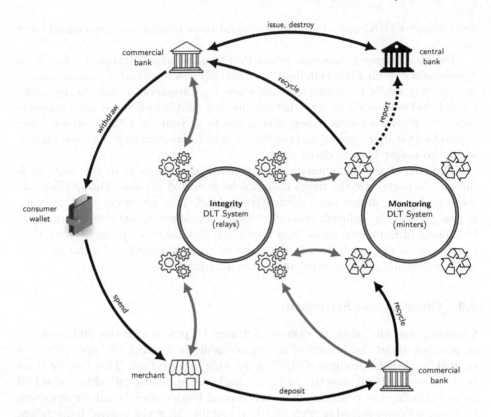

Fig. 7. *Schematic representation of an operating model for a CBDC system.* The diagram depicts the circulation of digital assets, interaction among actors, and supporting functions.

quantity of some currency by explicitly allowing a clearinghouse or bank to create and distribute signatures for making that many units of CBDC.

We introduce the idea of a *minting-plate*, which combines a *minting-key* that can be used to sign blinded templates with a set of rules that govern its use. There is a deep tension between the desire to limit the number of units that can be created with a particular minting-key, and the need to prevent specific units of currency from being connected to particular creation events (i.e. disconnected creation <– fix this with the right name). Because there is no way to connect a particular unit of currency with a particular creation event, there is also no way to tell whether a particular unit of currency was created by a legitimate user of a minting-key, as opposed to a compromised or malicious use of that minting-key.

What can be done is to keep a record of how many units have been reportedly created and how many have been redeemed. Creation is reported primarily by delegated issuers who holds a minting plates, and secondarily by retail banks which channel requests to those delegated issuers. Redemption happens when a bank brings CBDC units back to the central bank in exchange for central bank reserves.

Together, these values can reveal that a particular minting-key has been compromised, which can help limit the damage caused by such a compromise. A minting-key might be associated with a set of parameters to limit, for example, the value of currency signed by that minting-key that is in-flight at any particular moment (issuance minus redemptions), the total value of CBDC cumulatively signed by that minting-key, and the time at which signatures by that minting-key would no longer be considered valid.

The size of the anonymity set, as we shall discuss later in this section, is directly impacted by the limits that can be specified for the minting-plate. As more limits are placed on a particular minting-plate, the amount of currency it can produce is reduced, making it easier for powerful entities to track the behaviour of individual users. It is important to tune those parameters so they provide good risk mitigation in the event of the compromise of a minting-key, while still maintaining a sufficiently large anonymity set.

4.3   Clearing and Settlement

Ensuring that the integrity system continues to produce entries and does not equivocate about the history of is commitments is a major responsibility of a central bank that produces CBDC using this architecture. This can be done by the central bank directly, although such an approach introduces a set of risks, including the possibility that the central bank's operational servers crash or become compromised as well as the possibility that the central bank might change the rules or expectations for the system without warning. Because distributed ledgers are designed to be fault-tolerant and immutable, DLT is a useful tool for systems that require some resilience to crashes and compromise. We suggest that the central bank could take the following approach to using DLT for its integrity system:

1. The central bank enlists several highly trusted but independent institutions to run relays and requires each of them to sign off on each new entry that the central bank produces. This protects against compromise of the central bank: The adversary must also compromise all of the other institutions to cause an equivocation.
2. The institutions employ a crash fault tolerance mechanism, such as Raft [15], to allow a few institutions to be offline without interrupting the operation of the system.
3. The institutions themselves can propose new entries, perhaps via a fixed schedule or round-robin process, instead of requiring the central bank to do it. This avoids issues associated with having the central bank serve as gatekeeper to transactions and allows the central bank to step out of an operational role and focus on oversight and governance.
4. The institutions make a commitment to publish every entry they sign.

This arrangement is sufficient to convert the centralised integrity system into a distributed ledger overseen, but not operated, by the central bank.

The scalability of this architecture can be enhanced by allowing relays to arrange themselves hierarchically. Higher-level relays can aggregate the entries produced by lower-level relays and perform the same process, with the respective lower-level relay operators taking the place of the trusted institutions. Waiting for a higher-level relay to produce an entry might support greater assurance that the proof will be completed, but might be slower than waiting for the lower level relays, which are optimised to minimise latency.

Transactions less than a specified amount might be considered final by transacting parties, and may be covered by appropriate insurance or credit for relay operators, without confirmation from the clearing network. The additional confidence provided by aggregate confirmations, therefore, might be necessary for buying high-value goods, such as a car, but probably not for buying low-value goods, such as a cup of coffee.

A case can also be made for encouraging relay operators to use mechanically external DLT systems as a commitment mechanism, or public bulletin board, for publishing their entries. This practice might also enhance the confidence in those entries, as well as quicker detection of equivocation of compromised relays, because it compels relays to commit to a more unified view of their published entries rather than merely self-reporting them.

5   Discussion

In this article, we have presented an untraceable version of an architecture for a payment system based on proofs of provenance. Our architecture combines three previous lines of work to provide a solution that efficiently provides both consumer protections and regulatory compliance:

- **Distributed ledgers** as a way to create a decentralised, immutable record of commitments, as achieved, for instance, in UTXO systems such as Bitcoin [16].
- **Blind signatures** for untraceable payments, starting with Chaum's early work [3] and continuing through Chaum, Grothoff, and Möser [4].
- **Unforgeable, stateful, oblivious (USO) assets** for transactional efficiency while maintaining integrity, as exemplified in the TODA protocol [9,10].

Each of these individual approaches to digital assets carries a significant set of tradeoffs. By combining all three approaches, we can mitigate the drawbacks without losing the benefits:

- **Enforce accountability and transparency** for authorities and system operators in the manner described by Goodell, Nakib, and Tasca [2], thus requiring authorities or system operators to explicitly and publicly specify changes to the protocol and system rules;

- *Achieve privacy by design* by having users create their own assets and incorporate validation from the issuing authority;
- *Enable transactions without real-time involvement* of the issuing authority, by progressively, and obliviously, building proof structures with logarithmic scaling factors across the relays; and
- *Enable validations without any involvement* of the issuing authority, by incorporating self-validating proofs of provenance as a fundamental part of the digital assets; and
- *Avoid requiring the issuing authority to maintain a database* of individual tokens, balances, or specific transactions, as is done with UTXO-oriented digital currency systems.

Doing this allows the resulting CBDC to be used across a wide variety of use cases, including many of those currently addressed by cash. Our proposal directly addresses the dilemma of maintaining regulatory compliance while preventing abusive profiling that harms consumers. Central banks have an opportunity to repair trust between citizens and the state by sponsoring an architecture that does not force users to trust some third party with data protection, but instead allows users to verify for themselves that their privacy is protected.

Our proposal also addresses the operational and infrastructural overhead that a central bank must incur to manage a payment system through a domestic retail digital currency. It provides an efficient path to the issuance and distribution of a currency as well as the maintenance of its integrity. The distribution and management following issuance can be mediated by existing payment mechanisms and avoiding the costs and risks associated with deploying new infrastructure for that purpose. Our proposal thus encourages working within the current banking system, including commercial banks and payment institutions, rather than undermining them, and provides the capacity to build a deep and resilient governance approach without compromising the efficiency and privacy of individual transactions.

Cash is used in many different situations, as are other payment service solutions. We describe the properties a CBDC must have in order to be efficiently used in those situations, and we show that the technical requirements of our architecture are necessary to deliver a solution with those properties. This allows the CBDC created using our architecture to broadly meet the demands of cash as well as those of electronic payment services, and highlights exactly where other proposals fall short. It is not necessary to make unacceptable compromises between consumer protections and regulatory compliance, and it is not necessary to sacrifice operational efficiency to maintain asset integrity. Indeed, for a currency to be used like cash, it must excel in all three of those aspects. Ours does.

Acknowledgements. The authors are grateful to TODAQ for sponsoring this work. We thank Professor Tomaso Aste for his continued support for our project. We also acknowledge the support of the Centre for Blockchain Technologies at University College London and the Systemic Risk Centre at the London School of Economics, and we acknowledge EPSRC and the PETRAS Research Centre EP/S035362/1 for the FIRE Project.

A   Asset-Level Desiderata

- **Integrity.** We say that an asset has *integrity* if it has a single, verifiable history. Actors in possession of the asset must be able to confirm that the asset is genuine and unique; specifically, any two assets that share any common history must be the same asset. Desired characteristics of integrity include:
    1. **Durability**
        Short of stealing the private key of an issuer or breaking the cryptographic assumptions upon which the system infrastructure depends, it shall not be possible to create a counterfeit token, it shall not be possible for the party in possession of a token to spend it more than once, and it shall not be possible for an issuer to create two identical tokens. In addition, it shall not be possible for any actor to mutate the token, once issued.
    2. **Self-contained assets**
        The asset shall be *self-validating*, which is to say that it shall support a mechanism that allows it to furnish its own proof of integrity, as part of a process of verifying its authenticity to a recipient or other interested party. The purpose of self-validation is to maximise the flexibility of how assets are used and how risks related to asset ownership and state can be managed. In particular, the issuer shall not be required to track the owner or status of the assets that it has created, and payers shall not concern themselves with what happens to an asset once it is spent.
- **Control.** An actor has *control* of an asset if that actor and no other actor possesses the means to specify legitimate changes to the asset, including features that identify its owner. Note that *control* implies the ability to modify the asset in a way that determines the legitimacy of changes made to the asset by its possessor. Desired characteristics of control include:
    3. **Mechanical control**
        The ability to create a valid transaction is vested in the owner. No one but the owner can update the state of a specific asset.
    4. **Delegation**
        The asset owner must be able to retain control of the asset when transferring the responsibility of possession to a custodian. That custodian is then unable to exercise control over that asset, for instance by creating a legitimate update to the asset. The owner chooses who can exercise control, and owners can delegate possession without delegating control.
- **Possession.** An actor has *possession* of an asset if that actor and no other actor can effect changes to the asset or reassign possession of the asset to another actor. *Possession* implies the ability to deny possession to others, including the legitimate owner of the asset, on an incidental or permanent basis (this does not include the possibility for forced legal enforcement to relinquish or return an asset). In principle, the balance among costs and risks

related to the possession of an asset, including the ability to store assets safely, can be independently chosen by various actors in the system. Desired characteristics of possession include:

5. **Choice of custodian**

   Asset owners must be able to choose the custodian entrusted with the possession of their asset. This contrasts with traditional ledger-based approaches in which the ledger is the fixed source of truth about an asset and for which an asset is inextricably bound to that ledger (i.e., moving the asset to another ledger would involve redemption in the first ledger and a new issuance in the next ledger). This property is an essential interoperability feature for any national currency system. To mitigate risks such as custodial compromise or service disruption for sensitive payment systems, asset owners must be able to choose to have the possession of their assets spread across multiple custodians ("multiplexing"), such that they require only some portion of them to respond in order to update the state of their assets. This should be able to occur in a way that is opaque to the custodians ("oblivious multiplexing"), where each is concerned only with its own portion of assets which it is providing custody over and is unaware that other custodians are involved.

6. **Choice to have no custodian**

   The owner of an asset must be able to serve as his or her own custodian. Specialised custodians are good for mitigating risks, but they always introduce costs (transaction fees, account fees, latency, and so on) and risks (for example, intentional or accidental service disruption). To address use cases that are sensitive to those costs and risks it is necessary to allow non-specialised actors to also provide custodianship of assets, and in particular to allow a human owner of an asset to store the asset personally, using his or her own devices.

– *Independence.* Asset owners shall be free to conduct transactions in the future, with confidence that they will be able to use the assets for the use cases they want.

7. **Fungibility**

   Each unit is mutually substitutable for each other unit of same issuer, denomination, and vintage, and can be exchanged for cash or central bank reserves. This is enabled by privacy by design and required for self-determination.

8. **Efficient lifecycle**

   Transactions must be similar in speed to traditional payment systems, capable of having near-instant acceptance. It must be possible for the recipient of an asset to verify that a transaction is valid and final without the need to involve a commercial bank at the time of the transaction, and without forcibly incurring additional costs, risks, or additional technical or institutional requirements. Assets must not expire within an unreasonably short timeframe.

B   System-Level Desiderata

- **Autonomy.** We say that an actor has *autonomy* with respect to an asset if the actor has both possession and control of the asset and can modify the asset without creating metadata that can be used to link the actor to the asset or any specific transaction involving that asset. The term *autonomy* is chosen because it reflects the risk that a data subject might lose the ability to act as an independent moral agent if such records are maintained [1]. Desired characteristics of autonomy include:

  9. **Privacy by design**
     The approach must allow users to withdraw money from a regulated entity, such as a bank or money services business, and then use that money to make payments without revealing information that can be used to identify the user or the source of the money. The assets themselves, and the transactions in which they are involved, must be untraceable both to their owners and to other transactions. The system must be designed to allow all users to have a sufficiently large anonymity set that they would not have reason to fear profiling on the part of powerful actors with access to aggregated data.

  10. **Self-determination for asset owners**
      Asset owners shall be able to control what they do with assets. No recipient can use the system to discriminate against asset owners or impose restrictions on what a particular owner can do. Transactions using an asset shall not be blocked or otherwise flagged by recipients based upon targeting the owner of an asset or targeting a set of assets associated with some particular transaction history.

- **Utility.** The system must be generally useful to the public as a means to conduct most, and perhaps substantially all, retail payments. Desired characteristics of utility include:

  11. **Local transactions**
      It shall be possible to achieve efficient transactions where participants are able to rely upon local custodians to facilitate acceptance of remittances. The system shall not rely upon global consensus to determine or verify the disposition of an asset and shall allow transacting parties to choose an authority or context that they mutually trust, for example to trust a local authority in exchange for faster settlement or when access to a wider network is not possible, without requiring additional trust between counterparties.

  12. **Time-shifted offline transactions**
      It shall be possible for a payer to "time-shift" third-party trust to achieve a form of offline payment by first prospectively paying a recipient and then later, in an offline context, choosing whether to consummate the payment by selectively revealing additional information. Time-shifted offline transactions are akin to purchasing a ticket online and, later, spending it offline.

13. **Accessibility**

The protocol employed by the system must be accessible and open to all users. The system must not impose vendor-specific hardware compatibility requirements and must not require manufacturers of compatible hardware to register with a central database or seek approval from an authority. The functionality of the system must not depend upon trusted computing, secure enclaves, or secure elements that impose restrictions upon what users can do with their devices. The system must not require a user to register before acquiring and using a device, and the possession and use of a physical device must not depend upon a long-term relationship with a trusted authority, registered business, or asset custodian.

– *Policy.* The system must support the establishment of institutional policies to benefit the public and the national economy. Desired characteristics of policy include:

14. **Monetary sovereignty**

Monetary sovereignty entails a central bank and government's ability of controlling the use of the sovereign legal currency within its borders and the mechanisms within which it is used. In support of this end, financial remittances facilitated by the system shall involve direct obligations of the central bank of the applicable jurisdiction.

15. **Regulatory compliance**

The system shall be operated by regulated financial intermediaries that can establish and enforce rules for their customers. The system shall provide a mechanism that would permit financial intermediaries to prove that they have enforced those rules completely and in every case. By extension, the system would allow for the establishment of regulatory requirements for its operators to support reasonable monitoring by tax authorities for the purpose of establishing or verifying the income tax obligations of their clients. Subject to the limitation that both counterparties to a transaction would not generally be known, the system would permit system operators to perform analytics on their customers, for example, by learning the times and size of asset deposits or withdrawals. Ideally, the system would also provide a counter-fraud mechanism by which consumers can verify the validity of merchants.

C   Control Mechanisms

We characterise several control mechanisms that can be used to support our operating model. We suggest that a good CBDC would use these mechanisms, although they do not constitute a strict prerequisite for using our protocol.

C.1   Managing CBDC System Integrity

In addition to managing the lifecycle of the individual CBDC assets, we imagine that the central bank would also take responsibility for establishing the integrity system for those USO assets. This integrity system must continue operating without equivocation, and it is possible to build it in a way so that it would not be impacted by increases in the number of assets, users, or transactions.

As an example, the central bank may declare that only licensed clearinghouses may operate relays that connect directly into its integrity system. Commercial and retail bank relays would connect into those clearinghouses, and relays operated by other money service providers would connect into those, along with third party corporate relays. Because the trust requirements for operating a relay are quite low, similar to those for a network carrier, this provides a rich ecosystem on which consumers can rely with no increase to the operational overhead of the integrity provider system.

Because the scaling concerns are mitigated, there is room to deploy heavyweight solutions for governing this integrity system. While it could be run from a single laptop, it is clearly better to design a system that is as resilient as possible. This means bringing all of the participants in the ecosystem together, such that not only the central bank, but also clearinghouses, commercial banks, retail banks, and so on are participating in a federated or decentralised system, so that only some proportion of them have to be operating correctly for the system to maintain the integrity of its operations.

It is worth explicitly noting that the computational cost of decentralised systems generally stems from two sources: one is the gatekeeping cost of keeping out bad actors, which is the primary reason for the hashing cost of proof of work based systems like Bitcoin and Ethereum; the other is the scaling cost of accommodating transactions, assets, and accounts.

Our proposed architecture eliminates both of these costs. The first is eliminated by only inviting trusted parties to add their efforts to the integrity system. The second by separating the integrity system from maintaining the state of the assets themselves, so that the scaling costs are not borne by the integrity system. Introducing good governance and transparency into the integrity of a system does not necessitate a large increase in energy usage. Our architecture demonstrates this.

C.2   Managing Regulatory Compliance

Ensuring that regulators can perform their duties is clearly an extremely important aspect of a well-functioning economic system, and must be an explicit goal of any realistic CBDC proposal. As we show in this work, regulatory compliance does not have to come at the cost of sacrificing consumer protections. Indeed, not only are regulation and privacy compatible, but our architecture actually allows them both to be achieved more efficiently than current solutions that choose one over the other.

We have two main techniques for ensuring consumer protections. The first is the use of USO assets, which allow the CBDC to be acted upon by its owners unilaterally, regardless of the disposition of the financial apparatus. This means that while the recipient can choose to reject a transaction, no one else in the system, including regulatory bodies, can block it from happening or discriminate against that user.

The second is unlinking the sender from the recipient in the transaction channel. This means that even a powerful entity that knows who withdrew CBDC and knows who deposited CBDC will not be able to match senders to recipients.

How is efficient regulatory compliance possible with strong consumer protections like these? There are four places that regulation applies in our CBDC architecture, and they mirror four cases in which regulation applies to the use of cash. We argue that we can not only satisfy but actually improve upon the established compliance procedures in each case:

1. *When a retail user deposits cash into a bank account.* Banks are often required, for cash deposits greater than a certain size, to request evidence from depositors that the cash to be deposited was obtained legally. From this perspective, CBDC implemented as USO assets is better than cash, because it is possible to automate not just the integrity checks but also the regulatory checks.

2. *When a retail merchant receives cash from a consumer.* When merchants decide to deposit cash that they have received in the course of their business activities into bank accounts, they generally have an interest in knowing that the cash they have collected will be accepted. CBDC implemented as USO assets allows such a merchant to apply the same integrity and regulatory checks that are run by their bank. For example, a regulator might want to associate each recipient of CBDC with a bank account for the purpose of implementing compliance procedures. To satisfy this requirement, we might stipulate that banks must require the recipient of CBDC to furnish a commitment in the form of its bank account details to any sender from which it might receive CBDC, and that the CBDC must include a signature of this commitment from the sender as a prerequisite for the bank to consider the CBDC to be valid.

3. *When a retail merchant spends cash that it has received.* Recipients of CBDC might want to spend it immediately without depositing it first. Because USO assets track their own history, the next recipient is able to know whether the CBDC has travelled around since leaving a bank. Therefore, the asset must carry the burden of proving that its travel satisfies the relevant regulatory requirements, which could be enforced by automated checks run by the bank that ultimately receives it in the form of a deposit.

   In this manner, a regulator might allow CBDC to travel over multiple hops, with multiple recipients of CBDC in succession, without the interactive involvement of a regulated financial institution, provided that the recipient bank account details are included and signed by the respective sender in each successive hop. Note that, although the first sender might be anonymous, the USO asset framework enables it to implicitly demonstrate its possession of the key signed by the issuer of the CBDC. Subsequent senders would be identified by their bank account information as recipient from the previous transaction. Conversely, a regulator might want to enforce a rule that recipients of CBDC can do nothing other than deposit CBDC that they receive directly into the specified bank account. To satisfy this requirement, we would stipulate that banks would enforce a rule that the USO asset must have been transacted no more than once (i.e., only one hop).

The rules are implicitly dynamic. Bob's bank chooses what program to run to conduct the automated regulatory check, and Bob's software uses the same program as Bob's bank, so regulators can change their requirements at any time without needing the issuance of new CBDC. Regulators could do this by asking the banks to update their compliance procedures, and those new requirements would then be applied within the software of consumers and merchants.

4. *Compliance procedures within a financial institution.* A financial institution can prove that in all cases the CBDC it has accepted has met the current regulatory standards. Either the asset passes the automated regulatory checks, or the institution has accepted external evidence to meet the regulatory requirement. We imagine that the latter case would be extremely rare, because consumer and merchant software would automatically reject CBDC that does not meet the regulatory checks that would be carried out by their bank, but it provides an important safety valve.

To achieve the desired regulatory protection, the source and sink of CBDC must be regulated entities. When Alice creates new CBDC, the signature granting it validity must come from a regulated financial entity; this is enforced by the central bank or its delegates such as minters. When Bob brings his CBDC back to a regulated financial entity such as his bank then that entity can return the CBDC to the central bank in exchange for reserves.

Our architecture is compatible with a variety of additional mechanisms for enforcing regulatory requirements, although we recommend careful consideration to verify that such mechanisms are compatible with consumer protection objectives such as privacy and ownership. Note that the first transaction in which a new asset changes hands provides consumer protection, although subsequent transactions do not. In particular, although the initial consumer is protected, the merchant might decide to spend his or her CBDC asset in a second transaction rather than have a bank recycle it, but he or she does this knowing that what the second recipient does with the CBDC asset might expose sensitive information about the second transaction.

Having regulated entities as the source and sink of CBDC is sufficient for a mechanism to ensure full regulatory compliance. More than this, it allows that compliance to be achieved with widespread efficiency gains: for the regulator, for the banks, for merchants, and for consumers.

C.3   Ensuring an Appropriate Anonymity Set

In our formulation, CBDC is generally not held by retail customers in custodial accounts and, for this reason, would not earn interest. Although there are some methods available by which fiscal policy can incentivise or disincentivise spending tokens [11], we expect that retail users would view CBDC primarily as a means of payment rather than a store of value. We stipulate that plausible deniability is essential to privacy [12], and a large anonymity set is a prerequisite to plausible deniability. Inexorably, a trade-off between privacy and flexibility for users lies in the relative timing of withdrawals and remittances, as the strength of the anonymity set is bounded by the number of tokens in-flight between those events.

The template architecture ensures that the consumer chooses the minting-key. We assume that the set of minting-keys signed by the issuer will be available for public perusal on a distributed ledger. The fact that an issuer cannot sign multiple minting-keys without having that fact become observable forces accountability for an issuer that might want to create a covert channel that could reveal information about the consumer. Since retail users would have no particular reason to hold CBDC longer than is necessary to make their payments, just as they would have no particular reason to hold cash, it is important to consider ways to encourage users to hold CBDC long enough to ensure that the anonymity set is large enough to protect their privacy. In service of this objective, we propose some practical mechanisms that can be applied to ensure that the anonymity set is sufficiently large to protect the privacy of everyday users:

- *Encourage consumers to withdraw larger amounts of money.* For example, consumers can withdraw CBDC in fixed-size lots, and then spread out the use of those over a longer time period and blend in with other consumers, thereby making a smaller number of larger-sized withdrawals from the bank. We anticipate that reducing the number of withdrawals will make it harder to link a payment to its corresponding withdrawal, potentially by one or more orders of magnitude. By reducing the number of statistically linkable withdrawal-payment pairs, users can enjoy a larger anonymity set and, as a result, better privacy.
- *Incentivise consumers to use slow relays by default.* We can give users control over the extent to which it might be possible to temporally correlate a withdrawal to the proof data that is created with a payment. This can be accomplished by adjusting the requirements in Step 4 of the user engagement lifecycle (refer to Fig. 2) such that F_1 can only be accepted by relay G if F_0 had previously been published by relay G. Then, relay G can explicitly specify a frequency for its publication of successive updates to ensure a sufficiently large anonymity set, for example, to publish once per minute, hour, or day. The motivation is to increase the cooling off period to increase the number of unspent withdrawals from the same minting-key. The provider of relay G could maintain multiple relays with different frequencies. If we accept privacy as a public good [13] and acknowledge transaction immediacy as a threat to privacy, then the provider could charge more to consumers who demand greater immediacy, as a way of compensating for the negative externalities that would result from shorter time intervals between withdrawals and payments. Since the consumer's message to the relay requires no human interaction, CBDC software could send it after a random delay, or could send it through a remailer network such as Mixmaster [14].

- *Encourage slow transaction settlement when possible.* Not every transaction must be settled immediately; consider the case of online purchases for goods or services to be delivered in the future. For such transactions, if Alice can use Step 4, Option 1 (as shown in Fig. 4) to give Bob direct control and the means to acquire possession of the CBDC, and if Alice trusts Bob not to record the time at which she does so, and if Alice trusts Bob to delay his request for the proof of provenance (and thus settlement) for a sufficiently long time, then Alice can effectively pay Bob immediately. Indeed, Bob's transaction tracking and rate of transactions might influence Alice's calculations about whether this option is safe. Note that this is the same guarantee that payers rely upon to safely use physical cash without being tracked. In the digital context, procuring a strong guarantee about what Bob might do is somewhat harder, and we are pessimistic about the idea that received transactions are not being timestamped, either by Bob or by other observers.

- *Have Alice explicitly give control to Bob during the withdrawal phase.* Alice can give control to Bob in the creation of F_0 during Step 1 of the protocol. Because F_0 is part of the blinded template, neither her bank nor other observers will be able to associate her withdrawal with her payment to Bob. As with the previous approach, this approach requires Alice to trust Bob not to record the time at which he receives the payment from Alice. However, because Bob is able to verify that the CBDC is valid and that he has exclusive control, this approach might be appropriate for immediate delivery of goods or services. Although the size of the transaction might ordinarily reveal information that could link the withdrawal to the payment, this could be obfuscated by having Alice give Bob a larger quantity of CBDC than he requires, and having Bob provide Alice the excess in the form of new CBDC, either immediately or in the future, using the same method.

We also suggest implementing a mechanism to monitor the number of tokens currently in-flight, to support dynamically adjusting parameters that could impact the size of the anonymity set, such as the number of minting-keys, the number of tokens to be issued by each minting-key, and the set of available denominations. Such a mechanism would support not only the management of digital currency issuance and destruction but also public oversight of the entire process.

D   Efficient Settlement

One of the most important features of cash infrastructure is the ability of counterparties to transact in real-time, with minimal involvement of third parties. To the extent that third parties are not involved in transactions, they cannot engage in rent-seeking behaviour and cannot pass the costs they incur along to transaction counterparties in the form of fees. Where third parties are involved, the involvement is generally minimal and highly local, for example to provide cash withdrawal services (e.g. ATM infrastructure) for consumers and cash deposit services to merchants, both of which are used only in aggregate over many transactions. Cash infrastructure also benefits from instant settlement: Once a payer has given cash to a payee, the transaction is settled. There is no way for a payer to unilaterally unwind ("claw back") the transaction.

With modern digital transactions, scalability interferes with the ability to transact in real-time. Transactions take place across a network, which cannot be globally synchronised. Settlement requires pairwise synchronisation between transacting institutions, which must manage risks associated with concurrency. Settlement times for domestic bank wires and direct debits are generally a matter of hours; settlement times for international wires are even longer. Payment networks generally offer short-term credit as a way to support faster settlements.

Our system design provides a mechanism for two transacting parties to enjoy real-time settlements. Recall that, in general, a payer (Alice) must furnish a proof of provenance to a payee (Bob) before a payee will accept payment, and that Alice creates this proof by connecting to the issuer through her chosen relay. If Alice is always assumed to be directly connected to the issuer, then the system will not scale very well: the issuer would have a de facto role in every transaction, and the resulting need to serialise and batch transactions would mean that Alice might be forced to wait.

However, because a payer can choose the relays, Alice has the option to choose one that both she and Bob recognise as trustworthy. Because each of these relays is a checkpoint in building the proof of provenance they can offer guarantees to Bob that Alice's transaction has been incorporated. If Bob trusts a relay that Alice has chosen, then this partial proof of provenance will suffice until Bob has received the full proof of provenance.

Our architecture allows these promises to be made almost instantaneously by these relays, requiring very little computation. Additionally, various mechanisms can be used to reduce the risk that a relay would equivocate by rewriting history to nullify Alice's transaction. These include both traditional institutional and legal guarantees as well as technical mechanisms like distributed ledgers and other means of achieving immutability.

If Alice knows that she is likely to make a purchase within a context in which a particular relay is trusted, then Alice can choose to use that relay for her asset, thus allowing near real-time payments within that context.

We observe that this mechanism offers similar functionality to debit card transaction via a retail payment network, wherein transactions can be accepted in real-time because the retail payment network provides a guarantee to the recipient's financial institution that the transaction will succeed. Our proposed mechanism avoids some of the potential friction intrinsic to this approach by eliminating the need for financial credit, although Bob must trust the relay to fulfill its promise to incorporate the transaction. Additionally, because transactions involve direct obligations of the central bank rather than bank deposits, the requirement for a clearinghouse to resolve counterparty risk among institutions is eliminated.

E   The Fallacy of Anonymous Accounts

There are two chief approaches to mitigating harmful consumer tracing and pro-filing. One approach is anonymous accounts, where the identity of the account holder is decoupled from the account. Anonymous accounts are akin to pre-paid debit cards and have been proposed as a way to protect the rights of con-sumers [6]. The other approach is transactional unlinking, wherein the sender is decoupled from the receiver inside the transaction channel. These two approaches of anonymous accounts and transactional unlinking are actually orthogonal dimensions.

In the absence of transactional unlinking, anonymous accounts don't provide anything useful. Bitcoin is a stark example of this: regular transactions can be trivially de-anonymised, revealing a consumer's entire history, whereas criminals can employ various heavyweight measures to conceal themselves.

In the presence of transactional unlinking, anonymous accounts still don't provide anything useful: the transactional unlinking already stops unwanted trac-ing and profiling, and adding anonymous accounts on top of that only makes enforcing regulatory compliance much more difficult.

Thus, we conclude that anonymous accounts are worse than useless. They do not achieve their stated goals, and they extract a high cost from systems that employ them [7]. We also note that anonymous accounts typically contra-vene AML/KYC recommendations and, because they implicitly link successive transactions done by a consumer to each other, are not actually private for most legitimate retail use.

We assume that the accounts referenced by our system would be subject to AML/KYC data collection and would not be anonymous. The privacy of our approach results from the use of non-custodial wallets to unlink successive transactions involving the same currency. Specifically, a user must "withdraw" funds from a regulated money services business into her non-custodial wallet in one transaction and then "remit" funds into a regulated money services business in the next. Even though the holders of the payer account and the payee account are known, the fact that money has flowed between them is not.

F   Use Cases

In this section, we consider three use cases that demonstrate the power and flexibility of our design and how our proposed architecture can be used to satisfy them. These use cases offer advantages over other electronic payment methods, including modern retail payments via banks or payment platforms as well as unlinkable CBDC proposals such as the one offered by Chaum, Grothoff, and Möser [4]. The users of the system, including consumers and service providers, can choose which of these possibilities to enable and support.

F.1   Disconnected Operation

In some environments, access to the central bank might be slow, delayed, or intermittent rather than real-time, for example where the central bank might be accessible only at certain times. We refer to such environments as "disconnected", and we imagine that this characteristic might apply to some remote or sparsely-populated areas with limited or unreliable connectivity, as well as categorically isolated environments such as certain remote villages, ships in the high seas, aircraft in flight, spacecraft in space, or remote military outposts.

Fair exchange requires the involvement of a mutually trusted third party [8]. However, this does not imply that all transactions must take place with global agreement. In disconnected environments we assume that there exists a local actor who is sufficiently trustworthy to act as a relay for nodes within that environment. This might be a trusted institution, a network operator, or even a distributed system made up of the nodes in that environment.

As long as the recipient trusts that relay to not equivocate, then the recipient can accept a payment that has a proof of provenance that includes that relay, with confidence that it will be possible to complete the proof of provenance to include the integrity provider. Completing that proof is necessary for the payment to be accepted outside of the environment in which the relay is trusted to do its job, but inside of this environment payments can continue to be made without making external network connections. As long as the trusted relay does not equivocate, then nothing that anyone else does, either inside the environment or outside, can adversely impact the payment. Short of equivocating, nothing the trusted relay does, including crashing or denying service, can adversely impact it either.

We note that systems that require global consensus, including all centralised systems and most distributed ledger systems, lack this capability.

F.2   Offline Operation via Time-Shifting

Some environments have no connectivity at all. This might include environments without communication equipment, or environments without a local point of trust. We refer to such environments as truly "offline". Since transactions require a third party [8], it might seem that this means that offline transactions are impossible, but that is not entirely true. The involvement of the third party could take place at a different point in time.

A user can transfer CBDC to an address over which the recipient has control, but without revealing to the recipient the information needed to exercise that control. Then the user can then effectively spend the CBDC offline by revealing information about the transfers to the recipient. In the event that the user decides not to spend all of the CBDC with that recipient, they have the option to use a fair-exchange protocol with the recipient to redeem any CBDC that was transferred but not spent.

In principle, it would be possible to transfer CBDC to a market operator in exchange for tickets (perhaps implemented using blind signatures) and then give the tickets to merchants, and the merchants could use a fair-exchange protocol to redeem value from the market operator. However, this assumes that the merchants are connected to the market operator in real-time so they can verify that such tickets are still available to claim. Similarly, it might be possible to transfer

CBDC to an issuer of cash-like, counterfeit-resistant physical tickets that can be used in a local context to make offline purchases to arbitrary recipients without the need for a real-time network connection.

F.3   Chained Transactions with Embedded Provenance

There are several reasons why a recipient of CBDC might want to move it onward without depositing the CBDC directly into a bank account. We refer to such transactions as *chained transactions*. In such cases the provenance information about successive holders of an asset can be maintained within the CBDC tokens, and chained transactions can carry their own proofs of compliance with the rules of the system. Appropriate use cases might include the following:

- Perhaps a CBDC holder has no access to a bank or access to a bank is difficult as a result of network connectivity or geographic location. Being able to make a series of transactions under such circumstances may provide an important safety net.
- Perhaps a CBDC holder is acting on behalf of a business that seeks to maintain provable records of its internal or external transfers, perhaps to streamline compliance operations, to satisfy auditing requirements, or to move assets without depositing them into a bank account and incurring a delay associated with settlement. For example, a multinational corporation might want to preserve an audit trail of internal transactions, for example to demonstrate compliance with tax regulations concerning the applicable jurisdiction for revenue, in addition to economic efficiency for such internal moves.

G   Analysis

In this section, we compare our architecture to alternative architectures for exchanging value. We begin with a set of mechanical design choices and argue for the choices inherent to the argument that we have proposed. Then, we compare our architecture to other systems for exchanging value in terms of the asset-level requirements and system-level requirements defined in Appendices A and B.

G.1   Design Features

Some of the design features of our proposal distinguish it from alternative proposals available in the current literature on digital currency. We list several of the most important such features here:

- *Regulatory control applies to transactions, not asset ownership.* Our proposed architecture allows regulatory compliance to be automatically enforced by regulated financial institutions that receive CBDC on behalf of their account-holders. This allows comprehensive regulation without introducing a requirement to track the ownership of every token.

- *Non-custodial wallets.* People want custodial accounts because they want strong regulatory controls. Having strong regulatory control at the transaction level allows non-custodial wallets to operate within the regulatory regime, providing efficiencies that make more use cases available to the users of CBDC. This approach allows CBDC to realise the benefit of a token-based approach, while interoperating with traditional custodial accounts as desired, as cash does.
- *Open architecture.* Our approach does not rely upon trusted computing, including trusted software, trusted hardware, or secure elements of any kind. Device manufacturers are third parties, just as other authorities are, and requiring any trusted authority to be part of every transaction compromises the integrity of the system. This is important because we do not wish to require the establishment of a set of trusted hardware vendors, or the assumption that counterparties to a transaction must trust each other's devices. If counterparties do have mutual trust in a third-party, such as an institution, they can use this mutual trust to improve the efficiency of a transaction, as described in Appendix D.
- *Time-shifted transactions.* Because fair exchange always requires a third party to every transaction [8], we observe that there is no way for two counterparties to transact directly without access to a mutually-trusted third party or system. In cases where a mutually trusted system is inaccessible, our architecture allows a time-shifted trust in the form of prepayments, as described in Appendix. F.2.
- *Decentralised transactions.* By allowing transactions to be processed in a decentralised manner, our approach avoids the costs and risks of requiring a ledger or other system component to be under the control of a single actor, who might change the rules without public oversight, discriminate against certain users, equivocate about the history of transactions, or otherwise exercise arbitrary authority.
- *Energy efficiency.* By allowing transactions to be processed locally, our approach avoids the costs and risks of requiring a heavyweight, ledger-based system (distributed or not) to be in the middle of every transaction, allowing the use of the CBDC to be highly energy efficient.
- *No central user database.* Our system avoids introducing centralised identity requirements, leveraging the existing decentralised procedures for identification and compliance that are already widespread among financial market participants. This avoids establishing new mechanisms to track users and aligns with global agreements about compliance requirements.

G.2   A Comparison of Payment System Architectures

Tables 1 and 2 summarise the characteristics of a selection of different payment system architectures, including our proposed architecture. The descriptions of the payment mechanisms are as follows:

- *Cash.* A central bank produces physical bank notes and coins. Retail users circulate them freely, without involving of financial intermediaries. Cash is

Table 1. A comparison of payment system architectures by asset-level considerations.

	Cash	Custodial accounts	Traceable digital currency	Untraceable digital currency	Traceable USO digital currency	Untraceable USO digital currency
Integrity Considerations						
Durability	●	○	○	○	●	●
Self-contained assets	●	○	○	○	●	●
Control Considerations						
Mechanical control	●	○	○	●	●	●
Delegation	○	○	○	○	●	●
Possession Considerations						
Choice of custodian	●	○	○	○	●	●
Choice to have no custodian	●	○	●	●	●	●
Independence Considerations						
Fungibility	●	○	○	●	○	●
Efficient lifecycle	○	○	○	○	●	●

part of the monetary base of an economy; commercial banks can exchange cash for deposits with the central bank. Although bank notes have serial numbers, cash remains fungible because it can be freely exchanged among bearers and because retail users of cash generally do not maintain records that identify individual units of cash.

- *Custodial accounts.* These are retail payments that take the form of transfers between financial institutions. This category covers both the case of private-sector banks offering accounts to retail consumers as well as the case of central banks offering accounts to retail consumers. Such payments might include bank wires, ACH, cheques, direct debit, and third-party transfers via payment networks including but not limited to card payment systems.

- *Traceable digital currency.* Retail consumers hold tokens that are obligations of the central bank. The tokens are bearer instruments and are not held in custodial accounts, although individual tokens can be linked to the identities of their owners. Thus, the consumers are not anonymous and are therefore subject to profiling and discrimination on the basis of their transactions. The issuer must maintain a record of tokens that were spent to prevent double-spending. The record of tokens can be maintained by the issuer directly or by a distributed ledger using a decentralised consensus system.

Table 2. A comparison of payment system architectures by system-level considerations.

	Cash	Custodial accounts	Traceable digital currency	Untraceable digital currency	Traceable USO digital currency	Untraceable USO digital currency
Autonomy Considerations						
Privacy by design	●	○	○	●	○	●
Self-determination for asset owners	●	○	○	●	○	●
Utility Considerations						
Local transactions	●	○	○	○	●	●
Time-shifted offline transactions	●	○	○	○	●	●
Accessibility	●	○	●	●	●	●
Policy Considerations						
Monetary sovereignty	●	○	●	●	●	●
Regulatory compliance	○	●	●	●	●	●

- *Untraceable digital currency.* This approach is similar to traceable digital currency, except that the central bank signs blinded tokens using a blind signature scheme of the sort elaborated by David Chaum [4]. When a user wants to spend a token, the user unblinds the token and returns it to the issuer along with the address of the recipient. Recipients could be anonymous, or not anonymous, depending upon the specifics of the architecture. Chaum's proposal for digital currency implicitly assumes that the sender is anonymous, but the recipient is not anonymous in the usual case [4].
- *Traceable USO digital currency.* This approach to digital currency uses baseline USO assets. The tokens are not blinded, and although tokens can be directly transferred between possessors without the involvement of the issuer, the chain of custody of an asset is transparent and completely traceable to its possessors.
- *Untraceable USO digital currency.* This approach to digital currency is a fusion of USO assets and the Chaumian system. A user approaches an issuer with a request for a blinded token, which the issuer furnishes to the user. When the user wants to spend a token, the user unblinds the token, incorporates it into a specific previously created asset, and transfers the asset to the recipient. It is now up to the recipient to redeem the token with the issuer, or to pass it to another recipient without the benefit of anonymity.

References

1. Shaw, J.: The watchers. Harvard Magazine (2017). https://www.harvardmagazine.com/2017/01/the-watchers. Accessed 01 July 2021
2. Goodell, G., Al-Nakib, H., Tasca, P.: A digital currency architecture for privacy and owner-custodianship. Future Internet **13**(5) (2021). https://doi.org/10.3390/fi13050130

3. Chaum, D.: Blind signatures for untraceable payments. Adv. Cryptol.: Proce. Crypto**82**(3), 199–203 (1983). http://www.hit.bme.hu/~buttyan/courses/BMEVIHIM219/2009/Chaum.BlindSigForPayment.1982.PDF. Accessed 28 Sept 2018

4. Chaum, D., Grothoff, C., Moser, T.: How to issue a central bank digital currency. Swiss National Bank Working Paper 3/2021 (2021). https://www.snb.ch/n/mmr/reference/working_paper_2021_03/source/working_paper_2021_03.n.pdf. Accessed 25 Feb 2021

5. International Organization for Standardization (ISO). Blockchain and distributed ledger technologies - Vocabulary. ISO/22739:2020, 1st edn. (2020). https://www.iso.org/obp/ui/#iso:std:iso:22739:ed-1:v1:en. Accessed 01 Dec 2020

6. Working Group on E-CNY Research and Development of the People's Bank of China. Progress of Research & Development of E-CNY in China (2021). http://www.pbc.gov.cn/en/3688110/3688172/4157443/4293696/2021071614584691871.pdf. Accessed 16 July 2021

7. Goodell, G., Nakib, H.: The development of central bank digital currency in China: an analysis. Opinion Piece, LSE Systemic Risk Centre (2021). https://www.systemicrisk.ac.uk/publications/opinion-pieces/development-central-bank-digital-currency-china-analysis

8. Pagnia, H., Gärtner, F.: On the impossibility of fair exchange without a trusted third party. Technical report, Darmstadt University of Technology (1999). http://citeseerx.ist.psu.edu/viewdoc/download;jsessionid=522B5D1548F0A10C4C18E59C36986F55?doi=10.1.1.44.7863&rep=rep1&type=pdf. Accessed 12 Feb 2021

9. TODAQ Engineering. TODA Proof Structure. https://engineering.todaq.net/todapop.pdf. Accessed 03 June 2020

10. TODAQ Engineering. Security Mechanisms for Protection Against Double-Spending. https://engineering.todaq.net/double_spending.pdf. Accessed 03 June 2020

11. Goodell, G., Al-Nakib, H., Tasca, P.: Digital currency and economic crises: helping states respond. LSE Systemic Risk Centre Special Papers SP 20 (2020). Also presented at 6th Annual Peer-to-Peer Financial Systems Workshop (P2PFISY 2020). https://www.systemicrisk.ac.uk/sites/default/files/2020-09/SP-20_0.pdf

12. Bindschaedler, V., Shokri, R., Gunter, C.: Plausible deniability for privacy-preserving data synthesis. Proc. VLDB Endow. **10**(5), 481–392 (2017) . https://doi.org/10.14778/3055540.3055542. Accessed 20 July 2021

13. Fairfield, J., Engel, C.: Privacy as a public good. Duke Law J. **65**(385) (2015). http://scholarship.law.duke.edu/dlj/vol65/iss3/1. Accessed 20 July 2021

14. Möller, U., Cottrell, L., Palfrader, P., Sassaman, L.: Mixmaster Protocol Version 2. Internet Engineering Task Force Internet-Draft (2004). https://tools.ietf.org/html/draft-sassaman-mixmaster-03. Accessed 03 July 2020

15. Ongaro, D., Ousterhout, J.: In search of an understandable consensus algorithm. In: Proceedings of USENIX ATC 2014, pp. 305–319 (2014). https://www.usenix.org/system/files/conference/atc14/atc14-paper-ongaro.pdf. Accessed 22 Feb 2022

16. Nakamoto, S.: Bitcoin: a peer-to-peer electronic cash system (2009). https://bitcoin.org/bitcoin.pdf. Accessed 04 Oct 2018

UTS: The Universal Token Swapper

Fadi Barbàra[1]([✉]), Alessandro Sanino[2], and Claudio Schifanella[1]

[1] University of Turin, Turin, Italy
{fadi.barbara,claudio.schifanella}@unito.it
[2] Tryvium Travels LTD, London, England
a.sanino@tryvium.io

Abstract. We propose the Universal Token Swapper (UTS), a smart contract acting as a payment processor between buyers and merchants in a multi-token environment for EVM compatible blockchains. UTS gives merchants the ability to accept any token by performing instant conversions. This way, the buyer does not have to convert the tokens before a payment and the merchant is not subject to financial ruins if he does not want bear the risk on speculation on the value of the token received. In addition, UTS can be implemented to follow any regulation by linking the contract to on-chain oracles, bringing regulatory compliance to DeFi and helping merchants take advantage of the new possibilities.

1 Introduction

After the birth of Bitcoin [1], several blockchain-based projects were created, originally with the goal of solving Bitcoin's problems, such as scalability [2]. Subsequently, a new project, Ethereum [3], has extended the "exchange of value" in a "exchange of computation": if the Bitcoin network verifies that an exchange of funds respects the rules of the Bitcoin protocol, in the Ethereum project participants are asked to execute instructions of programs installed on a virtual machine shared by all participants. This is one of the first implementations of a "smart contracts" as defined for the first time in [4].

One of the first problems perceived by the users regarding multiple blockchains was being able to interoperate between them, i.e. exchanging tokens from one blockchain for tokens in the another. Early methods to interoperate were based on centralized methods [5], such as online exchanges. But this comes at a cost. From the users' perspective, the problem with having some funds held in a few addresses controlled by one entity (also called *custodian*) is that you are subject to the power of that entity. In an ecosystem based on pseudo-anonymity, this is dangerous since custodians are not always trustworthy and/or legally traceable. This creates a very strong incentive for custodians to perform malicious human actions on the funds.

To avoid this problem, many types of peer-to-peer fund exchanges have been created in recent years that do not require a centralized party to hold the funds. Examples are atomic swaps [6,7] and what are now called decentralized exchanges (or markets, also called DEX) [8]. Of the latter, various instances

© International Financial Cryptography Association 2023
S. Matsuo et al. (Eds.): FC 2022 Workshops, LNCS 13412, pp. 679–687, 2023.
https://doi.org/10.1007/978-3-031-32415-4_39

have been created, thanks in part to the open source nature of the ecosystem, as in the case of the Uniswap clone Sushiswap [9].

Multiple markets imply different exchange rates between the same token pairs. To take advantage of this situation, new services, called *aggregators*, provide services on exchange protocols and networks. The goal is to give users the ability to exchange their tokens at the most favorable exchange rate [10].

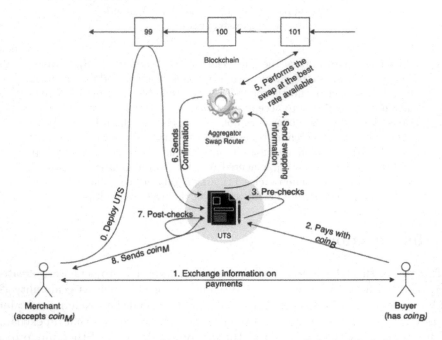

Fig. 1. The DeFi ecosystem lacks a payment processor to link the blockchains to real life commerce and services. UTS solves this problem.

To date, these exchanges are done manually. This is not a problem when the user wants to exchange funds for reasons of financial speculation nature, but it is a problem when a buyer B wants to pay a merchant M who does not accept the tokens owned by B. In this case, B has to manually go to an aggregator or a DEX to exchange the owned tokens for the tokens accepted by M. This, besides being a waste of time and ruining the user experience on the merchant's application, is also an economic problem since it is necessary to spend an additional sum for the exchange fees.

To solve these problems, we introduce the Universal Token Swapper (UTS). UTS is a smart contract that acts as a payment processor currently implemented for EVM compatible blockchains (Fig. 1). An UTS instance can be deployed by any merchant. Through the payment processor the buyer B can pay the merchant M with any token chosen by B. UTS automatically leverages aggregators to operate a swap into a token specified by M. Since UTS is a smart contract for a public blockchain, it is decentralized in nature: any merchant can deploy its version of it. We provide an implementation[1] of the UTS.

The paper is organized as follows. In Sect. 2 we explain the evolution of token exchange from centralized to decentralized methods and explain how a payment processor is the missing piece to connect traditional commerce to the DeFi ecosystem. In Sect. 3 we describe how UTS works and detail the implementation. In Sect. 4 we explain the possible applications of the functions that compose the payment processor and in Sect. 5 we analyze security and costs of the proposed method. We conclude in Sect. 6.

2 DeFi Background and Related Works

In this section we briefly explain what solutions are present to date for exchanging coins and tokens. This is one of the aspects of recent decentralized finance (DeFi). For further details see [11].

The transition from centralized to decentralized markets has not been easy, and it's still not finished. Initially one of the problems was liquidity: decentralized markets did not have access to the same amount of capital as centralized markets [12]. One of the first DEX, EtherDelta [13], used a book of "resting" orders, i.e. signed intents to trade stored off-chain so that each order doesn't waste ethers/gas to be submitted. The EtherDelta smart contract allows the user to deposit or withdraw Ether or any ERC-20 Ethereum token in a decentralized exchange. Another problem of decentralized exchanges was order-confirmation latency and resource-wasting [14]. Bancor [15] was one of the first protocols presented to address this issue using a bonding curve for price setting[2]. In other words, given a token with a total-supply $totSup$, then the supply Sup can be computed as

$$Sup = totSup - outSup$$

where $outSup$ is the outstanding supply. So an increase in Sup means a decrease in $outSup$ and consequently an increase in the rarity of the token supply in the future. The bonding curve has given birth to what are called "continuous tokens", because these tokens that are created in real time and sold according to the formula given by the bonding curve. This way there was no need to waste time and resources in order-posting since a user would automatically use the rate imposed to the market by the bonding curve.

However, Bancor introduced new problems. As informally explained by Buterin [16] and Gün Sirer and Daian [17], Bancor has efficiency problems with respect to on-chain market making. The main problem is that the liquidity of

---

[1] See: https://github.com/tryvium-travels/uts-paper-example.

[2] A bonding curve is a mathematical curve that describes a relationship between price and token supply. Generally the bonding curve formula is such that the price increases as the supply of the token increases. While counter-intuitive, that's obvious once considered that in a bonding curve based token an increase of the supply occurs only as a consequence of an increase in demand [15].

users is managed by a smart contract that by definition cannot keep track nor interpret of events in the real world. This means that in case of a panic in the market generated by a false news, the smart contract generates market prices based on a formula that risks putting in danger the finances of the users. On the contrary, if users could manage their finances by themselves, they could decide not to sell during the panic, and wait for the real news to calm the market. After Bancor, Buterin proposal of a new formula to price a new token $tokenB$ with respect to an old token $tokenA$, the *constant product formula*[3] [16], spawned the new generation of DEXes. Uniswap [8] has been one of the first projects to use the constant product formula and liquidity pools to implement an AMM (automated market maker). Details on AMMs can be found in [18–20].

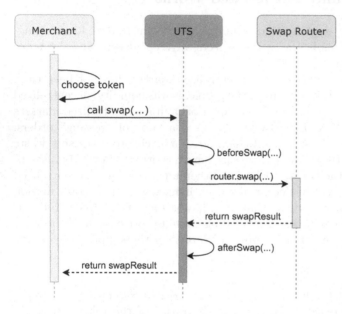

Fig. 2. Design of the UTS payment system.

Multiple markets based on different assumptions have brought arbitrage opportunities and the consequent birth of systems called "aggregators". The aggregator protocol of 1inch [10] was one of the first services able to capture the difference between a quoted price and the executed price where that difference is in favor of the customer. This is called the "spread surplus". Other swap routers like Matcha [21] aggregate the best prices across multiple liquidity sources with the goal of maximizing the value a user receives on each trade.

Despite the possibilities of the DeFi ecosystem, it is not yet possible to automate the token exchange process for non-financial applications[4]. In particular, it is not possible to automate the payment process for services or products. Consequently, today a buyer must keep his cash in many tokens in case a merchant accepts only one of them. This exposes the buyers to financial risks that they may not want to manage. At the same time, merchants also cannot accept mul-

---

[3] Essentially the formula is $price(tokenA) * price(tokenB) = k$ where k is constant, hence the name.

[4] It is possible to practice automated trading strategies, but decisions are made by off-chain algorithms that trigger on-chain trades.

tiple tokens for the same reasons. The goal of UTS is to solve this problem by creating a payment processor with automatic token swapping.

3 Design

We assume that there is a buyer B who buys a service S issued by a merchant M. The other assumption is that the coin $coin_B$ that B wants to use to pay for the service S is different from the coin accepted by M which we denote with $coin_M$. For simplicity we assume that $coin_B$ and $coin_M$ are connected by a rate $alpha$:

$$coin_M = \alpha \cdot coin_B$$

meaning that it is possible to exchange 1 coin $coin_M$ in exchange of α coins $coin_B$. α is variable since there are different DEXs that are able to exchange $coin_B$ for $coin_M$ and vice versa. Specifically, if there are $D_1, D_2, \ldots, D_k$ that are k different DEXs, we denote by α_i the current exchange rate in the DEX D_i. UTS doesn't interact with the DEXs directly. It uses existing services such as aggregators' swap routers like those mentioned in Sect. 2. We denote these services R.

3.1 UTS Design

We now describe the system using Fig. 2 as reference. After the buyer B chooses S, the front end of the merchant site will direct B to a checkout page with the information needed to make the payment. There B can choose the token he wants to use to pay for S. After that and a confirmation from B, the merchant's front end call the `swap` function of the UTS smart contract. The smart contract then starts a sequence of three routines: `beforeSwap`, `routerSwap` and `afterSwap`. In the following we explain them in detail.

`beforeSwap`: In `beforeSwap` the contact performs generic checks on the addresses and coins involved. For example, in the Tether token some addresses are blocked and cannot perform any transaction due to legal reasons, e.g. fraud or theft[5]. If for example B's address is in the list, the `beforeSwap` routine would stop the swap and abort the selling of service S. Of course, the deployer of UTS can perform any other check in this routine: for more details on the possible uses of this function see Sect. 5.

`routerSwap`: The main function `routerSwap` calls the swap router R. The main goal for R is to find the most convenient (for M) exchange rate $\alpha_i, i = 1 \ldots k$ between $coin_B$ and $coin_M$ and consequently perform the swap. The inner working of R is outside the scope of the paper and it follows implementations such in 1inch or Matcha. The function returns the swap-transaction hash in case of success or abort otherwise, e.g. in case of a too high slippage.

`afterSwap`: In case of success, the goal of the `afterSwap` function is to manage the newly received funds. For example, M can automatically stake

---

[5] See for example https://dune.xyz/phabc/usdt---banned-addresses for a list.

the funds or provide liquidity for a loan platform. Otherwise, `afterSwap` can call `beforeSwap` again if `routerSwap` fails and try a new swap again. When `afterSwap` completes the process, it sends the `swapResult` to M's dapp. If successful, B receives a payment confirmation. This ends the work of the payment processor.

Two other functions are need to manage potential problems. We introduce them here for completeness:

`transferFunds`: This function can only be called by the contract owner and works only in case the contract is in a `paused` state (see below). This function transfer all funds in the smart contract to another smart contract chosen by the owner during the function call. This function is used in case of possible security problems and bugs.

`pause`/`unpause`: These two functions secure the contract in case of bugs in the smart contract or in the swap router used. It is critical that these functions be part of this contract in every implementation. In fact in case of bugs, the owner of the contract can call the `pause` function to stop the execution. When the contract is in the pause state, no operation can be performed. This is enforced because all interface functions (the only public ones besides these) check that the contract is not in a `paused` state. If the bug has been solved the owner of the contract can call the `unpause` function to restart the execution.

4   Applications

In the following we explore how these functions, especially `beforeSwap` and `afterSwap`, enable new possibilities for real life commerce.

4.1   Easiness of Commerce

One of the reasons there aren't many merchants accepting tokens in traditional commerce is that merchants don't know which coins to accept. On the one hand, if a merchant M accepts only a subset of tokens then M is effectively losing potential buyers since buyers who don't have the tokens must necessarily exchange them in some market before they can pay for the service which ruins their experience. Consequently buyers will choose other merchants, thus decreasing M's potential profits. On the other hand, accepting all tokens is impossible for M: if the merchant does not exchange the received tokens for a token he trusts immediately after receiving them, then M exposes himself to financial risk; if M does exchange them immediately then it is a time-consuming manual process which necessarily diminishes the benefits of opening up to new payment methods. Moreover, it is also impossible to practically accept all tokens because new tokens are created every day.

UTS can improve this situation. The merchant M can open up to new payment methods even if he does not have any special financial or computer knowledge using the automation properties inherent in the use of smart contracts for payment processing.

4.2   Compliance with Regulations

Another problem of traditional commerce in relation to the new methods of payment through a blockchain is the compliance with regulations. In fact, at the moment regulations are not clear nor shared between to all countries [22–24]. In this sense the functions beforeSwap and afterSwap make the system adaptable to regulation changes and transparent.

The beforeSwap function lets M be sure that there won't be any legal problems in accepting a payment: the function can effectively perform operations such as anti-money laundering (AML) and know-your-customer (KYC) checks before starting any payment. To do that, the function would call other smart contracts or on-chain oracles to abide to any legal framework [25]. This is similar to any payment via a credit-card circuit, but in a decentralized way. This is a clear advantage for M: since the payment rules are on a public blockchain auditable by anybody, it is easy for authorities to check that M is performing a service complying to the financial regulation and it can likely speed up commerce-establishment processes.

The afterSwap function also allows the merchant to treat the revenues in compliance with the law, e.g. by allocating a portion of the funds to pay taxes. This is also transparent for the aforementioned reason.

4.3   Easier (decentralized) Financial Access

Another benefit for M is the possibility to employ the newly received funds instantaneously. In fact thanks to the afterSwap function M can decide how to allocate funds for each sell. For example, M can decide to allocate after-tax funds up to a threshold t_1 in a liquidity pool: this way M earns more money through trading commissions in DEX. Another possibility is to keep funds up to another threshold t_2 in an accrual deposit. Assuming for example a buyer B who decides to buy S in multiple installments, M can request a deposit from B: in this way if B does not pay regularly, M can withdraw the funds he is entitled to from the deposit. The use of a deposit is also an advantage for B. In fact if the deposit is a multisignature shared between B and M, and the deposit is staked, then the deposit value increases while being a secure way for M to receive the installment payments.

In general, then, the afterSwap feature allows both M and B to automatically benefit from all the financial opportunities inherent in the new decentralized finance.

5   Cost Analysis

In Table 1 we reported the gas costs of the contract functions as reported by the Hardhat suite. The function that costs the most is undoubtedly the swap function[6] with an average cost of $143, 285$ gwei. The swap function uses a swap

---

[6] We also evaluated the functions pause and unpause. Both require about $27, 000$ gwei for the gas. The beforeSwap and afterSwap functions were not reported as they depend on the implementation by M.

Table 1. The table lists the costs of the functions as the Hardhat output.

Solc version: 0.8.13		Optimizer enabled: true		Runs: 1000000	Block limit: 30M gas
Contract	Method	Min (Gwei)	Max (Gwei)	Avg (Gwei)	# calls
SimpleOneInchV4TokenSwapper	swap	123,981	181,336	143,099	6
SimpleOneInchV4TokenSwapper	pause	-	-	27,749	4
SimpleOneInchV4TokenSwapper	unpause	-	-	27,702	2

router (the 1Inch one in the tests) to find the best α_i exchange rate for M. In this sense, UTS is comparable to a DEX using a swap router. Therefore, in Table 2 we compared UTS with other DEXs. UTS comes in third, but has not yet been optimized in this respect.

Table 2. Comparison of the `swap` function in different DeFi protocols as seen at https://crypto.com/defi/dashboard/gas-fees. The UTS payment processors is ranking third, but still lacks of gas optimizations.

Protocol	Avg Gas (Gwei)
Curve	112,845
SushiSwap	141,176
UTS	**143,099**
Uniswap V2	149,273
Mooniswap	149,767
DODO	157,185
Crypto.com	180,082
Balancer	206,765

6 Conclusion and Future Works

We have described UTS, a smart contract that aims to link traditional commerce with decentralized finance and we proposed an implementation of its functions. We have shown that the costs of swapping using UTS are comparable to the costs of other DEX. In the futu, we will create templates for the `beforeSwap` and `afterSwap` functions and a platform so as to make the deployment of UTS easier.

References

1. Nakamoto, S.: Bitcoin: a peer-to-peer electronic cash system, p. 9. Whitepaper (2008)
2. Back, A., et al.: Enabling blockchain innovations with pegged sidechains, p. 25. Whitepaper (2014)

3. Wood, G.: Ethereum: a secure decentralised generalised transaction ledger. Yellowpaper **151**, 1–32 (2014)
4. Szabo, N.: Formalizing and securing relationships on public networks. First Monday (1997)
5. Buterin, V.: Chain interoperability. R3 Research Paper (2016)
6. Nolan, T.: Alt chains and atomic transfers. https://bitcointalk.org/index.php?topic=193281.msg2224949#msg2224949
7. Herlihy, M.: Atomic cross-chain swaps. In: Proceedings of the 2018 ACM Symposium on Principles of Distributed Computing, pp. 245–254. ACM, Egham, United Kingdom (2018)
8. Adams, H., Zinsmeister, N., Salem, M., Keefer, R., Robinson, D.: Uniswap v3 core. Whitepaper (2021)
9. Sushi Team. The sushiswap project (2020)
10. 1inch Team. The 1inch API v3.0 (2021)
11. Werner, S.M.: SoK: Decentralized finance (DeFi). CoRR, abs/2101.08778 (2021)
12. Lin, L.X., et al.: Deconstructing decentralized exchanges. Stanford J. Blockchain Law Policy **2**, 58–77 (2019)
13. ethernet. Etherdelta smart contract overview. Githubn (2018)
14. Hsieh, Y.C., Hsueh, C.W., Wu, J.L.: The exchange center: a case study of hybrid decentralized and centralized applications in blockchain. In: 2018 1st IEEE International Conference on Hot Information-Centric Networking (HotICN) (2018)
15. Hertzog, E., Benartzi, G., Benartzi, G.: Bancor protocol. Whitepaper (2017)
16. Buterin, V.: On path independence (2017)
17. Daian, P., Sirer, E.G.: Bancor is flawed (2017)
18. Xu, J., Vavryk, N., Paruch, K., Cousaert, S., et al. Sok: Automated market maker (AMM) based decentralized exchanges (DEXs). Technical report (2021)
19. Wang, Y.: Automated market makers for decentralized finance (DeFi). CoRR, abs/2009.01676 (2020)
20. Bartoletti, M., Chiang, J.H., Lluch-Lafuente, A.: A theory of automated market makers in DeFi. In: Damiani, F., Dardha, O. (eds.) COORDINATION 2021. LNCS, vol. 12717, pp. 168–187. Springer, Cham (2021). https://doi.org/10.1007/978-3-030-78142-2_11
21. Matcha Team. The matcha documentation (2020)
22. Wronka, C.: Financial crime in the decentralized finance ecosystem: new challenges for compliance. J. Finan. Crime **30**, 97–113 (2021)
23. Padilla, R.: DeFi, law and regulation. Technical report, Mimeo (2020)
24. Ushida, R., Angel, J.: Regulatory considerations on centralized aspects of DeFi managed by DAOs. In: Bernhard, M., et al. (eds.) FC 2021. LNCS, vol. 12676, pp. 21–36. Springer, Heidelberg (2021). https://doi.org/10.1007/978-3-662-63958-0_2
25. Breidenbach, L., et al. Chainlink 2.0: Next steps in the evolution of decentralized oracle networks. Whitepaper (2021)

Author Index

© International Financial Cryptography Association 2023
S. Matsuo et al. (Eds.): FC 2022 Workshops, LNCS 13412, pp. 689–690, 2023.
https://doi.org/10.1007/978-3-031-32415-4

Printed in the United States
by Baker & Taylor Publisher Services